# Glendale College
# Library

# THE CAMBRIDGE HISTORY
# OF AFRICA

*General Editors:* J. D. FAGE and ROLAND OLIVER

## Volume I

From the Earliest Times to *c.* 500 BC

# THE CAMBRIDGE HISTORY
# OF AFRICA

# THE CAMBRIDGE HISTORY OF AFRICA

Volume I
From the Earliest Times to *c.* 500 BC

edited by
J. DESMOND CLARK

CAMBRIDGE UNIVERSITY PRESS

CAMBRIDGE

LONDON · NEW YORK · NEW ROCHELLE

MELBOURNE · SYDNEY

Published by the Press Syndicate of the University of Cambridge
The Pitt Building, Trumpington Street, Cambridge CB2 1RP
32 East 57th Street, New York, NY 10022, USA
296 Beaconsfield Parade, Middle Park, Melbourne 3206, Australia

© Cambridge University Press 1982

First published 1982

Printed in Great Britain at the
University Press, Cambridge

*British Library Cataloguing in Publication Data*
The Cambridge history of Africa.
Vol. 1: From the earliest times to c. 500 B.C.
1. Africa – History
I. Clark, John Desmond
960    DT20    79-41599

ISBN 0521 22215 X

# CONTENTS

# FIGURES

# PLATES

# PREFACE

This volume provides the first relatively complete and authoritative overview of African prehistory from the time of the first hominids in the Plio–Pleistocene up to the spread of iron technology after *c.* 500 BC. For this reason it was considered important to amplify the text of each chapter by including a fairly full set of references so that the serious scholar should be able to consult the original sources, not only for supplementary data but also to enable him or her to make a personal assessment by reviewing the interpretations and reconstructions given in the text of the volume. It is certain that interpretations will change and become modified as new discoveries are made, new concepts and strategies are developed and more refined techniques become available. The basic facts as set out here, however, will remain virtually unchanged so that the volume can be expected to continue to form a useful source of reference for a number of years to come, not only for the detailed evidence that it assembles and the bibliography that is cited, but also for the record it constitutes of the ways in which prehistorians and archaeologists look at their material today and the kinds of interpretative models suggested by the theoretical framework in which today's palaeo-anthropologists work. To this end authors have been at pains to distinguish between basic data and interpretations and, where the data are liable to more than one interpretative explanation, to present the alternative possibilities.

For some periods and in some regions, research is proceeding less quickly than in others so that, where new evidence is accumulating more slowly, fewer changes in interpretation are likely to take place. Elsewhere, however, for example in East Africa where research is carried out on the world of the Plio–Pleistocene hominids, or in South Africa where studies are in progress on the palaeoecology of Later Stone Age populations, the speed with which new discoveries are being made and new knowledge produced can be expected quite soon to necessitate some significant revision of the ways in which some of the evidence has been presented in this volume. The data adduced and the views expressed are, therefore, those current at the time of going to press.

xxi

Each chapter is designed to be an entity in itself so that, in some instances, the reader may find reference to or discussion of material presented in greater detail in preceding or succeeding chapters. Where it occurs, this duplication is intentional since material which has a bearing on more than one problem and/or time-period will have different significance for one author than for another and so will be used differently.

Because the date of *c.* 500 BC selected by the General Editors of the *Cambridge History of Africa* as the cut-off point for this volume is, of course, an arbitrary one, though reflecting the time at which urbanism and iron technology began to become important in northern and north-eastern Africa, some minor overlap between volume 2 and the later chapters of volume 1 may well ocur; but this will, in most cases, be insignificant.

Prehistorians normally record radiocarbon dates as being so many years BP (Before the Present) together with the standard deviation (e.g. 12 000 ± 100 BP) indicating that *there is a 68% probability that the true age of the sample falls somewhere within the range given* (i.e. between 12 100 and 11 900 BP). Historians, on the other hand, concerned with calendar years, more commonly record dates as either BC or AD. In a *History* of this kind, covering the time when the written record is replacing prehistory in northern and north-eastern Africa, we have compromised by recording all Pleistocene or earlier results as BP dates, unless there is a specific reason to do otherwise. Holocene radiocarbon dates both uncalibrated and calibrated are given as BC dates and based on the Libby Value (5570 ± 30 years) for the half-life of $^{14}$C. In most cases also, the standard deviation and the laboratory citation have been omitted from the text but may be found either in the footnotes or by reference to the primary source. More recently, the concern to differentiate and emphasize that radiocarbon dates are not calendar dates has led to the adoption by some laboratories and archaeologists of b.p. to denote uncalibrated $^{14}$C dates and BP where the results have been converted into calendar years by calibration against the tree ring chronology established from the bristle cone pine in California and extending back some 8500 years. While emphasizing the need for readers to appreciate this difference, we have thought fit to retain here the more conventional BP form of presenting dates.

The spelling of geographical place names is a continuing problem. We have here tried to follow the usage in the *Times Atlas*. In a number of instances, however, as with many archaeological or palaeontological sites, the names are not in the gazetteer, so that the spellings in general use or in the publications recording the sites have been used. In a very few instances anglicized spellings (e.g. Jebel rather than Gebel) have been adopted.

The volume has not attempted any general explanation of terminology and nomenclature in use by prehistorians north and south of the Sahara. Where expedient for clarification, some explanation of specific terms has been given in the text or footnotes. Those readers who wish to have a more detailed understanding of these terminologies and how they have developed should refer to the volume *Background to evolution in Africa*, edited by W. W. Bishop and J. D. Clark and published by the Chicago University Press in 1967.

It is a pleasure to record here most grateful thanks to my wife, Betty C. Clark, who was not only responsible for translating chapter 8 but whose help with the myriad details of the editing process was a substantial element in my own contribution; and also the staff of the Cambridge University Press, in particular for the painstaking care expended on technical details and on reducing the discrepancies in the volume to a minimum.

*March 1979*                                              J. DESMOND CLARK

CHAPTER 1

# THE PALAEO-ECOLOGY OF THE AFRICAN CONTINENT –

## The Physical Environment of Africa from Earliest Geological to Later Stone Age Times

### THE EVOLUTION OF THE CONTINENT

#### Geological structure and Precambrian history

The continent of Africa, second only to Asia in size, has an unusual combination of features and environments, including many extreme contrasts. It lies astride the Equator but, unlike South America, has northern and southern limits at almost identical latitudes (37° N and 35° S). However, this symmetry does not apply to area, for the northern portion is twice as large as the southern. Much of the interior of Africa, especially in the south, is an elevated plateau, capped in the east by the great piles of volcanic material that form the highlands of Ethiopia and East Africa. Cutting through these highlands are the trenches of the Great Rift Valley, occupied in part by important lakes, both deep and shallow. Volcanic cones form spectacular mountains with peaks rising almost to 6000 m above sea level and snow-clad despite their equatorial situation. In contrast there are areas in Egypt and Ethiopia that are as much as 120 m below sea level – Afar in the Rift system and the wind-scooped Qattara and other depressions in Egypt. In addition to the volcanic cones, there are other mountainous areas, but they are largely uplifted erosional remnants; true mountain chains are confined to the northern extremity (Atlas Mountains) and to the southernmost margin (Cape Ranges). The largest dry, hot desert in the world, the Sahara, stretches from the Atlantic to the Red Sea, forming a significant continent-wide barrier between the narrow Mediterranean littoral belt and the rest of the continent, often conveniently termed 'sub-Saharan Africa'. In contrast to this arid belt are the tropical forests of western equatorial Africa, with rainfall well over 2500 mm per year in Liberia and Cameroun, reaching a top figure four times as high in the mountains of the latter region.

Geologically speaking, almost the whole of the continent has

TABLE 1.1  *The international geological time scale and selected African events*

| Million years BP | Eons | Eras | Periods | Epochs | | |
|---|---|---|---|---|---|---|
| 0 | PHANEROZOIC | CENOZOIC | QUATERNARY | PLEISTOCENE | | |
| 2 | | | | PLIOCENE | (see Fig. 1.7) | |
| 5 | | | | MIOCENE | East African volcanism | |
| 23 | | | TERTIARY | OLIGOCENE | (see Table 1.2) | |
| 38 | | | | EOCENE | | |
| 54 | | | | PALAEOCENE | | |
| 65 | | MESOZOIC | CRETACEOUS | | 'Continental Intercalaire' | Nubian Sandstone |
| 145 | | | JURASSIC | | | |
| 210 | | | TRIASSIC | Numerous epochs | ⎱ KARROO deposition | |
| 255 | | | PERMIAN | | | |
| 280 | | PALAEOZOIC | CARBONIFEROUS | | | |
| 360 | | | DEVONIAN | | ⎱ CAPE deposition | |
| 415 | | | SILURIAN | | | |
| 460 | | | ORDOVICIAN | | *Orogenic/metamorphic episodes* | |
| 520 | | | CAMBRIAN | | *N.W. Africa* | *N.E. and sub-Saharan* |
| 580 | PRECAMBRIAN | | | | 'PAN-AFRICAN' DAHOMEYAN | DAMARAN–KATANGAN |
| 1000 | | | No international subdivision | | PHARUSIAN | KIBARAN–IRUMIAN |
| 2000 | | | | | EBURNIAN | MAYOMBIAN |
| 3000 | | | | | ZAGORIAN | SHAMVAIAN |

*Note:* Figures are estimated ages in millions of years; not to scale.

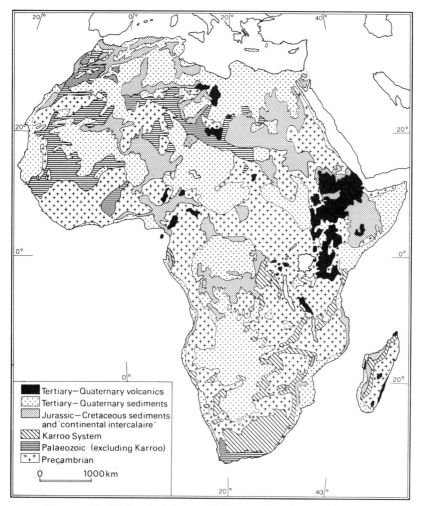

Fig. 1.1 Simplified geological map of Africa, based on the UNESCO (1963)
*Geological map of Africa.*

Legend:

- Tertiary–Quaternary volcanics
- Tertiary–Quaternary sediments
- Jurassic–Cretaceous sediments and 'continental intercalaire'
- Karroo System
- Palaeozoic (excluding Karroo)
- Precambrian

0        1000 km

assumed its present form as a result of progressive uplift, gentle
warping, erosion and deposition during the past 500 million years,
without the strong mountain-building episodes of folding and dislo-
cation that are so familiar in most other continents; the Atlas and Cape
ranges, and part of the Mauritania coast, are the exception. The Atlas
folding is the youngest, being essentially contemporary with the Alpine
orogeny (mountain-building) of the late Mesozoic and early Cenozoic
(see table 1.1), whereas the Cape Ranges and the Mauritania fold belt

3

are middle Palaeozoic to early Mesozoic in age. As these fold belts are marginal and involve so small an area, the greater part of the continent consists of a veneer of Phanerozoic sediments resting on eroded remnants of Precambrian rocks, often collectively grouped as the 'Basement'. Since the end of the Precambrian, most of Africa has behaved as a rather rigid block. Fig. 1.1 is a generalized geological map showing the distribution of the main sedimentary units, some of which will be considered separately below.

The Precambrian basement itself is complex in structure and consists of extensive areas of granitic rocks, gneisses and schists, but also includes thick sequences of sedimentary rocks that have been relatively little altered by metamorphism and often only gently folded. It is startling for American or European geologists to see in Africa rock formations more than 1000 million years old that are still almost horizontal and with little significant alteration despite their antiquity. However, this does not mean that all the Precambrian rocks are little changed or disturbed, for the basement geology is complex and has involved several periods of strong deformation, orogenesis and denu-dation, still recognizable as belts with distinctive trends and with characteristic radiometric ages imprinted on their minerals in the metamorphic process. The UNESCO *International tectonic map of Africa* (1968a) distinguishes Precambrian orogenic belts belonging to six age groups, to some of which names have been attached by various workers (see table 1.1). Stabilization of the basement has been a progressive process and it is possible to recognize certain core areas as having become rigid much earlier than others. The oldest nuclei still preserved contain rocks more than 2500 million years old, some as old as 3600 million. These nuclei are surrounded by younger orogenic belts which, together with the nuclei, build portions of crust that have remained stable for at least the past 900 million years; these stable areas are referred to in the literature as 'cratons' and are shown in fig. 1.2. The remainder of the basement area was widely affected by metamorphic episodes in the very late Precambrian or early Cambrian (600 to 500 million years ago), sometimes called the pan-African orogenesis. The Precambrian basement is the source of most of the mineral wealth of the African continent and the important ore deposits seem to be related genetically to the major cratons and orogenic belts (Clifford 1966, Clifford and Gass 1970). These mineral resources have played an important role in the history of exploration and the development of the continent.

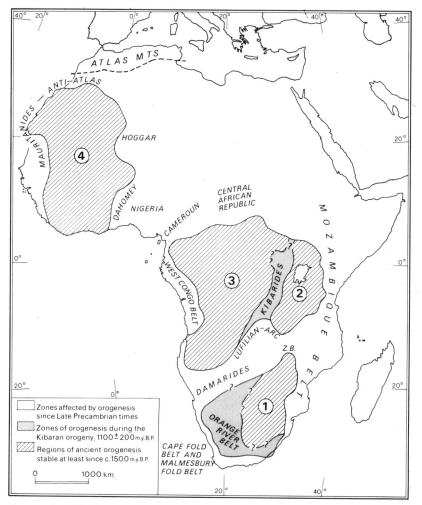

Fig. 1.2    Generalized map of the major orogenic structural units of Africa (excluding the rift valley system). The four older cratons are: (1) the Rhodesia–Transvaal craton, (2) the Tanzania craton, (3) the Angola–Kasia craton, (4) the West African craton. After the Kibaran orogeny, the consolidated Kibarides united (2) and (3) to form the *Congo craton* and the Orange River belt was added to (1) to form the *Kalahari craton*, which were stable during the late Precambrian–early Palaeozoic orogenesis. The Cape folded belt and the Mauritanide-Anti-Atlas belt are mid-Palaeozoic to early Mesozoic in age. The Atlas Mountains represent Alpine (Tertiary) orogenesis. (From Clifford 1966.)

## *Palaeozoic–Mesozoic history*

By the late Precambrian, almost the whole of Africa had become effectively a large stable craton and most of the central area was never invaded by the sea. However, Palaeozoic marine sediments do occur in various parts of North Africa, bounded roughly by a line from Ghana to the Sinai peninsula, and also in the Cape folded belt at the extreme southern end of the continent. Between these two areas the deposits are continental and, in many instances, devoid of fossil material by means of which their age may be fixed exactly. The Lower Palaeozoic marine beds in part of north-west Africa rest on a tillite of considerable lateral extent that marks a major glacial event quite out of keeping with the present environment. The Palaeozoic rocks of this area are mainly limestones and sandstones, with some shales, and the fossils have broad affinities with those of Europe. In the Cape Supergroup[1] at the southern end of the continent, however, the only significant fossils are in Devonian strata and have their closest affinity with the faunas of the Falkland Islands and Brazil. On the other hand, the fossil plants in the upper part of the Cape Supergroup, of Upper Devonian to Lower Carboniferous age, are very similar to the flora from corresponding beds in the Sahara region.

At the end of the cycle of deposition of the Cape Supergroup, southern Africa was affected by an intense glaciation that ushered in the long period of sedimentation of the Karroo Supergroup. This unit has its maximum development in South Africa, where accumulation of upwards of 7000 m of sediment took place in a subsiding basin in the geographical area known as the Karoo. Although it is only in this type area that the succession is complete, the Supergroup is very extensive and reaches as far north as the equator; there are equivalent beds in Madagascar as well (fig. 1.1). The Karroo Supergroup spans the period from later Carboniferous to early Jurassic, ignoring the usual break between the Palaeozoic and Mesozoic eras (see table 1.1). In South Africa, the Karroo is divided into four Groups known from below upwards as the Dwyka, Ecca, Beaufort and Stormberg. The Dwyka is largely glacial tillite and the Ecca mainly dark-coloured shales and grey sandstones, up to 3000 m thick. The Ecca Beds contain fossil plant remains typical of the southern hemisphere *Glossopteris* flora, and some specimens prove that well-protected fleshy fructifications had developed

---

[1] The term Supergroup is now officially replacing System with Group for the subordinate Series, though the well-known, traditional nomenclature may still continue in use for some time.

on the leaves, perhaps suggesting a proto-angiosperm stage of plant evolution (Plumstead 1969). The Ecca Beds also contain extensive and valuable coal deposits, mainly in South Africa and Zimbabwe. The Beaufort Group comprises a thick succession of yellowish sandstones alternating with colourful shales and mudstones indicative of deposition in a swampy environment subject to desiccation and flooding. This unit is remarkable for the abundance of vertebrate fossil remains, including some amphibians but principally reptiles that become increasingly mammal-like in the higher horizons of the Group. It is probable that some of these mammal-like reptiles were already warm-blooded and may even have had hair. Two of the earliest 'true' mammals so far known come from the Stormberg Group in Lesotho and are uppermost Triassic in age (Crompton 1974). The Stormberg Group shows a progressive development of desertic conditions and ends with the outpouring of up to 1000 m of basaltic lavas – the Stormberg or Drakensberg volcanics – now forming a protective cap on the highlands of Lesotho. The Karroo Supergroup thus demonstrates progressive climatic change from glaciation, through warm swamps, to near desert conditions.

In West Africa the continental rocks are commonly grouped under the term used by French geologists, *Continental Intercalaire*, and in the Sudan and Egypt their extension is part of the *Nubian Sandstone*. Although the name Continental Intercalaire should strictly be applied only to rocks of upper Jurassic to mid-Cretaceous age, it has been used broadly to include rocks as old as the late Carboniferous. The same is true of the Nubian Sandstone, which is strictly a unit of unfossiliferous brownish sandstones of Cretaceous age in Egypt, but beds of strikingly similar lithology occur to the south and to the west, some as old as Devonian, and they have been included under the catch-all term of 'Nubian Sandstone'. The Nubian Sandstone and the Continental Intercalaire, both *sensu lato*, thus represent in North Africa the time-equivalent of the southern Karroo Supergroup, but they also include strata that are considerably younger. Jurassic continental deposits are unknown south of the Sahara and those of Cretaceous age are of very limited extent and occur only in localized troughs or basins. It is believed that during most of these two periods erosion was active and there are, indeed, surviving remnants of erosion surfaces ascribed to this interval.

It is notable that during the lengthy period from the Cambrian to the end of the Triassic, marine beds are virtually confined to north-western Africa. There the marine Permian is restricted to a small area in Tunisia, expanding a little into Algeria in the Triassic and also occurring in northern Sinai. These marine beds were laid down on the southern margin of an ancient sea known as the Tethys, of which the present Mediterranean is a shrunken remnant; the faunas have European affinities. The short Devonian marine invasion of the southern tip of the continent has already been mentioned. During the late stages of the Dwyka, a shallow sea also extended over the south-west Cape and southern Namibia but the Devonian and the Permian fossils clearly belong to a southern faunal assemblage and have no link with the Tethys sea. There is thus no sign of any Atlantic or Indian Ocean shorelines in Africa during the Palaeozoic. In Madagascar the Karoo Beds contain occasional marine intercalations of mid-Permian to mid-Jurassic age, but these episodes are followed by well-developed Upper Jurassic marine beds on the west side of Madagascar. There are also two localities in East Africa that have furnished marine fossils – a patch of Lower Triassic near Mombasa and outcrops of Mid-Permian near Kidodi 250 km west of Dar es Salaam. Marine Jurassic beds also occur on the Tanzania coast and extend up through eastern Kenya, Somalia and Ethiopia into Arabia. In north-eastern Zaïre, just south of Kisangani, there is a thin marine limestone of Upper Jurassic age with fossil fish suggestive of a temporary link with the marine area in Ethiopia. There is no marine Jurassic south of Tanzania but such deposits do occur buried on the continental shelf off the southern tip of the continent. On the Atlantic side, mid-Triassic marine deposits occur along the coastal belt of the Spanish Sahara, but not farther south, and Jurassic marine beds just reach Senegal. Early in the Cretaceous the Atlantic coastline was reasonably well defined and by the end of that period the southern Atlantic coast extended along the present shelf area, but offshore, as far north as Walvis Bay. The Upper Cretaceous also saw an extensive marine invasion from the Tethys of a two-branched belt through the western Sahara to the Gulf of Guinea; the West African craton lay as a landmass to the west of it, the Ahaggar massif formed an island in the middle, and the Tibesti massif to the east. From the Gulf of Guinea, marine Cretaceous beds extended down the Atlantic coast, inland of the present shoreline, as far as Moçamedes. Thus by the end of Cretaceous times the African block was established with an approximation of its present shoreline. The extensive Cretaceous seas withdrew from much of the Sahara, leaving a marine embayment in Nigeria during the Palaeocene and Eocene, separated by dry land from the fluctuating Tethys shoreline in the north. Eocene marine beds extend far inland in Algeria, Tunisia, parts of Libya and northern Egypt, but in the Oligocene and Miocene only a limited area of the northern margin of the continent was still inundated. Until the Miocene, Arabia was effectively an integral part of the African continent, from which it became separated by invasion of the sea after faulting had created the Red Sea trough as a major rift system. The Miocene is also the main period for the commencement of volcanicity in East Africa, associated with the massive crustal stresses that formed the Great Rift Valley.

## Continental drift

Ever since the continents were adequately mapped, the parallelism of the opposite shores of the Atlantic has led to comment and speculation. Although Antonio Snider published a reassembly of the continents in 1858 in an endeavour to account for the close similarity between the fossil plants of the Carboniferous in North America and Europe, it was not until the beginning of the present century that serious scientific attention was paid to the matter, largely through almost simultaneous, but independent, publications by Taylor (1910), Baker (1911) and Wegener (1912). Wegener's book of 1915, *Die Entstehung der Kontinente und Ozeane*, established his name as the main protagonist of the hypothesis of continental drift, and his concept of a hypothetical single supercontinent that he called 'Pangaea'. This is now regarded as comprising two major units, 'Laurasia' in the north, made up of North America and Greenland ('Laurentia') plus 'Eurasia', and a southern 'Gondwanaland' embracing South America, Africa, India, Australia and Antarctica. The latter name is derived from the Gondwana Supergroup in India, of Carboniferous to Jurassic age, very similar to the African Karroo Supergroup and to geological units of corresponding age in other parts of the supercontinent. Wegener's ideas were supported strongly by du Toit, who made careful geological comparisons between South America and South Africa, based on his own observations, and demonstrated a host of geological matches. In 1937 du Toit published *Our Wandering Continents*, which stands with Wegener's work as the major pioneer documentation of the hypothesis. However, continental drift was rejected by most geologists until studies of the great mid-oceanic ridges, on the one hand, and of the magnetism preserved in rocks, on the other, produced compelling evidence that drift was a reality. The concept that new oceanic crust is being formed continually

9

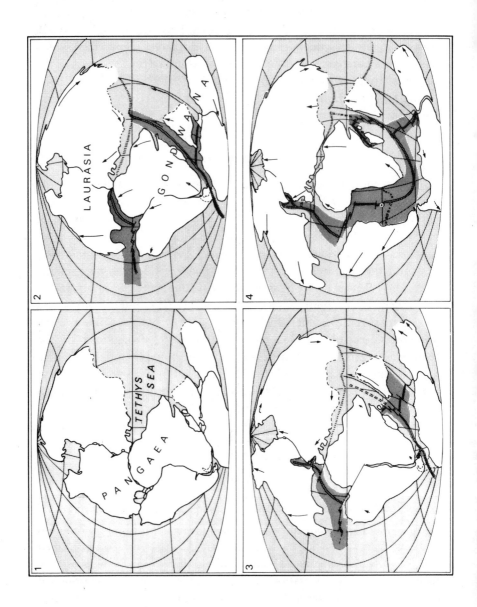

at the crests of the oceanic ridges and eventually consumed again at the deep ocean trenches ('sea-floor spreading'), allied to the concept that the crust of the earth consists of a relatively small number of fairly rigid segments, or 'plates', changed continental drift from a scorned hypothesis to a respectable theory in the 1960s. However, the data at present available leave room for some divergence of opinion in detail and several slightly different reconstructions of Gondwanaland in the Carboniferous–Permian have been produced.

Palaeomagnetic studies have demonstrated that the continental masses have moved in relation to the rotational pole of the earth, with which the magnetic pole coincides approximately. In the Precambrian, Laurentia and Gondwanaland seem to have moved independently, and Laurentia sometimes separately from Eurasia. In the early Palaeozoic they had combined into Wegener's Pangaea, with the south pole situated somewhere in, or near, West Africa (Creer 1970); this explains the glaciation already noted. In the Carboniferous the pole passed through South Africa, accounting for the Dwyka glaciation and also for similar events in South America, India and Australia. By Permian times the pole lay in Antarctica, but relative to present-day Africa was about in the position now occupied by Marion Island. A possible reconstruction, following Dietz and Holden (1970), is given in fig. 1.3.1. The initial rifting of Pangaea in the Triassic is indicated in fig 1.3.2, while 1.3.3 shows the beginning of the split between South America and Africa in the late Jurassic. By the end of the Cretaceous (fig. 1.3.4) South America was well away from contact with Africa, but Africa itself was still almost 15° south of its present position. There is some evidence that Africa had reached its present location by mid-Miocene times, but this is not certain. The meteorological and climatological implications of these changes in the extent of the oceans, as well as in latitudinal position, have not yet been adequately studied and evaluated. The development of the Great Rift Valley is generally regarded as fore-shadowing the creation of a new ocean along its course and the eventual parting of Africa into two separate continental entities.

---

Fig. 1.3   Reconstructions of the continents and of their break-up and separation during the Mesozoic. Black areas indicate apparent overlap in the reconstructions. The double lines represent mid-ocean ridges and the dark stippled areas flanking them show new oceanic crust generated by sea-floor spreading during the period concerned. The arrows are vectors giving the direction and extent of movement during the period. (1) shows the 'universal landmass' of Pangaea at the end of the Permian, about 225 million years ago. (2) gives the situation at the end of the Triassic, 180 million years ago, indicating new crust and movement during the Triassic. (3) shows the position near the end of the Jurassic, 135 million years ago. (4) indicates the situation at the end of the Cretaceous, 65 million years ago. (Modified after Dietz and Holden 1970.)

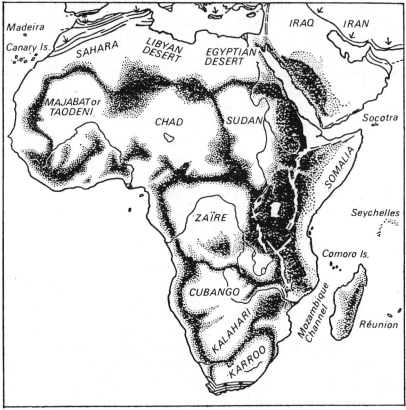

Fig. 1.4   Map showing in a generalized way the tectonic basins of Africa and the intervening swells, plateaux and rift valleys. (From Holmes 1965.)

## Geomorphic evolution

The terrain of Africa is clearly related to its geological history, although the relationships are often complex. For hundreds of millions of years the interior of the continent has resisted crumpling, except at its northern and southern extremities, and has responded by essentially vertical movements of uplift or depression reflected in the development of broad depositional basins bordered by plateaux or ridges. The present structure has been most aptly described as 'basin-and-swell', of which the major elements are shown in fig. 1.4. Some of the basins have long histories, extending well back into the Palaeozoic, sometimes interrupted by uplift and erosion between two or more cycles of depression. Others are not areas of sagging so much as regions that have lagged behind in the positive general uplift that has affected the continent since the disruption of Gondwanaland.

Accompanying this uplift has been marginal downwarping, most strongly marked in the monoclinal flexure of the Lebombo range on the eastern border of Swaziland and its extension southwards into Natal and northwards into Mozambique (Maputo). In southern Africa the zone of maximum uplift is situated roughly 300 km from the coast and headward erosion of streams grading to the new level had produced the magnificent feature of the Great Escarpment, which rims the sub-continent from northern Angola to the Zimbabwe–Mozambique border. The uplift also affected East Africa, but the escarpment is lost in the superimposed effects of rifting and volcanism. The great interior plateau of southern Africa is a reflection of this regional uplift, with the Kalahari–Cubango basin lagging behind and becoming filled with debris from the surrounding rim. The Congo (Zaïre) basin lagged even more but marginal uplift was considerable and the western margin is a weak continuation of the plateau and escarpment as far north as Cameroun. This basin was also in existence in the Mesozoic and the soft sediments were readily dissected to form the great river system that breaches the western rim.

To the north the general uplift has been less marked and the morphology is more influenced by the former presence of the Tethys sea and the Cretaceous inundation of much of the area. The Taodeni basin has a lengthy history going back to the Cambrian or a little earlier, and the same is true of the Sahara–Libya basins, with their important oil resources. The Chad basin, on the other hand, is dominantly Cretaceous and Tertiary. In the Pliocene–Pleistocene, Lake Chad was very extensive but curiously is not in the lowest part of the basin, which lies some 700 km to the north-east. The great Ahaggar massif to the north-west of Chad is an uparched complex of Precambrian igneous and metamorphic rocks surrounded by a rimming plateau of Palaeozoic sediments, with a few mounds of mid-Tertiary to Quaternary volcanics building the peaks to a maximum of 2999 m. The Palaeozoic rocks and underlying basement extend eastwards to the Tibesti massif, where extensive lavas form great volcanic piles covering 60 000 sq. km and with peaks at 3000 to 3400 m. Eocene marine beds lie directly north of Tibesti at elevations of as much as 550 m above sea level, thus indicating the order of magnitude of the uplift in this particular area. The high land to the east of the Chad basin, however, is almost entirely

Precambrian, although Jebel Marra is a volcano, reaching just over 3000 m.

Before the Jurassic, the unknown drainage pattern of Africa must have been controlled by the overall structure of Gondwanaland, but as the coastline developed, new base levels were established and the rejuvenated rivers began the long process of dissection. Uplift of the interior and marginal warping were apparently intermittent and it seems possible to recognize three major periods of planation. King (1967, pp. 241–309) believes that parts of what he has named the 'Gondwana surface' can still be found in Africa as well as in the other parts of the former supercontinent. In Africa such patches lie mainly in the areas of greatest uplift, principally along the top of the Great Escarpment and in non-volcanic highland remnants in East Africa and Ethiopia. Following a phase of uplift, long stability led to the development of the most extensive planation, variously termed the 'African' surface, mid-Tertiary surface, or Miocene 'peneplain'. It is the most widespread surface in sub-Saharan Africa and is typically flat grassland or bushy terrain with unconsumed remnants rising as blocks or inselbergs above it. In East Africa, Miocene lavas and fossiliferous sediments were deposited on an erosion surface, often referred to in this area as the 'sub-Miocene surface'. Uplift in the Miocene led to incision and dissection, to form a number of minor 'post-African' or end-Tertiary surfaces. These are represented by broad flat areas flanking the river systems ('valley-floor pediplains' according to King). Further uplift during the Pliocene has led to incision of the river systems, but headward erosion is the dominant mechanism and the valleys are only widening slowly, while the upper reaches of the streams still flow on the older planation surfaces. The total extent of uplift since the Cretaceous is difficult to assess with certainty and was apparently greater in the south and east than in the west or in North Africa, apart from the crumpled and elevated Atlas mountains. In sub-Saharan Africa, uplift of the order of 900 to 1200 m seems to be demanded, with about half of this amount occurring since the mid Tertiary. However, there has also been some differential warping, which complicates the problem. Although the various erosion surfaces provide a convenient regional frame of reference, they are by no means homogeneous as to age, so correlations between the surfaces in different parts of Africa may be more apparent than real. Nevertheless, they do indicate extensive general uplift which, in itself, must have had a significant effect on the development of the climate.

## *The Volcanic Highlands and Rift Valleys*

The beautiful highlands of East Africa and Ethiopia are in part tectonically elevated domes but owe much of their mass and high peaks to volcanic activity. In East Africa, the bedrock beneath the volcanics consists largely of Precambrian granitic and metamorphic rocks and most of the volcanics lie on the sub-Miocene erosion surface. Some warping and faulting took place, followed by extensive volcanic activity. Although largely fissure eruptions, there were also many central volcanoes that built substantial cones. A number of these Miocene volcanoes now expose thin lenses of fossil-bearing sediment that had been deposited in localized basins or traps on the flanks of the cones and have now been re-exposed as a result of fairly extensive dissection. The deposits can be well dated radiometrically from the associated lavas and most are 18 to 20 million years old, with the earliest at 23 million years and the youngest at about 14 million years (Bishop, Miller and Fitch 1969). The main rift faulting occurred in the mid Miocene in northern Kenya and in the late Miocene or early Pliocene in central Kenya, when the maximum doming lifted the sub-Miocene erosion surface by as much as 1500 m, accompanied by strong down-warping near the coast. This was also the time of the main subsidence of the rift floors, which exposed thousands of metres of lavas in the spectacular rift walls. The troughs were in part occupied by lakes and formed ideal traps for sediment. In the eastern rift the existing lakes are small and relatively shallow and lie in basins of internal drainage. In the western rift the lakes are deeper, with steep shores, so that fossil-bearing sediments are rarely exposed on the flanks except in the Lake Edward–Lake Albert basin. Lake Tanganyika is 1434 m deep, almost half of its depth lying below sea level. Lake Victoria is not part of the rift lake system but occupies a broad and shallow depression between the two arms of the rift.

The Ethiopian dome is separated from the Kenya dome by a zone of lesser uplift represented by the broad depression within which Lake Rudolf lies. The sub-volcanic surface in Ethiopia is formed largely of late Jurassic and early Cretaceous marine sandstones, truncated by an erosion surface on which extensive flood basalts were extruded in the Eocene. These basalts built much of the Ethiopian plateau and were planed off before a second phase of uplift in the Oligocene or early Miocene. The marine beds below the plateau basalts now lie as high as 3000 m, which is a measure of the total uplift of the sub-volcanic surface in the centre of the dome. The major part of the uplift, as in Kenya, was late Pliocene, and the central Ethiopian rift faulting is mainly Miocene or Pliocene. However, the Afar triangle is older and is related to the rifting of the Red Sea, probably in the Eocene, and the massive boundary faults that cut Afar off from the Ethiopian and Somalian blocks are probably Oligocene in age; they had a displacement of at least 1000 m at this time. Depression of the Afar triangle has left part of it below sea level and past marine invasions formed thick salt deposits through evaporation. The depression, fed by the Awash River, also has extensive Pliocene–Pleistocene sediments in which mammalian fossils have been found. On the other side of the Ethiopian dome, the Omo River is flanked by Pliocene–Pleistocene deposits and extensive sediments also occur around Lake Rudolf (now Lake Turkana) in the low-lying belt between the two domed areas. No other parts of the continent exhibit so dramatically the innate forces of the earth as do the volcanic highlands and rift valleys.

### The early to mid Tertiary faunas

Whereas in most parts of the world fossil material can be dated only approximately and by indirect means, it is a fortunate circumstance that in East Africa many sedimentary sequences contain volcanic horizons that can be dated radiometrically to provide 'absolute' ages. Most of the lavas or volcanic ashes contain potassium-bearing minerals that can be assumed to have crystallized at the time of eruption. The radioactive isotope potassium-40 decays at a known rate, producing argon-40 as a daughter product. Provided that the amount of argon-40 originally present was negligible, and that none of the argon-40 produced has escaped during the period since the mineral crystallized, the potassium–argon ratio can be used to calculate the time that has elapsed (a critical account of this and other radiometric dating methods is given in Bishop and Miller (1972)). Potassium–argon (or K/Ar) dating has provided a well-controlled time scale in East Africa, against which the fossil material can be considered, and the inferred faunal succession can then be used to make correlations with fossil-bearing strata lacking radiometric controls. Table 1.2 shows the time distribution inferred for the major fossiliferous deposits of the Tertiary and Quaternary in Africa, and the localities are given in fig. 1.5. The boundaries between the various geological periods follow the ages for subdivisions now generally accepted for the marine sequence and differ from the divisions

TABLE 1.2  *Age distribution of later Cenozoic mammal-bearing deposits in Africa*

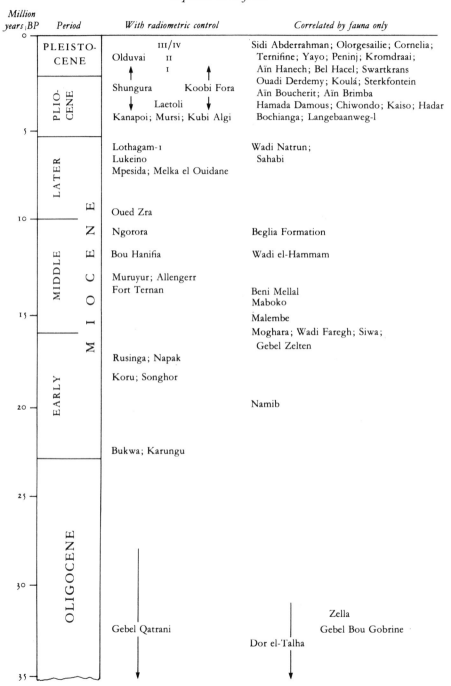

| Million years BP | Period | With radiometric control | Correlated by fauna only |
|---|---|---|---|
| 0 | | | |
| | PLEISTO-CENE | III/IV  Olduvai  II  I | Sidi Abderrahman; Olorgesailie; Cornelia; Ternifine; Yayo; Peninj; Kromdraai; Aïn Hanech; Bel Hacel; Swartkrans |
| | PLIO-CENE | Shungura    Koobi Fora  Laetoli  Kanapoi; Mursi; Kubi Algi | Ouadi Derdemy; Koulá; Sterkfontein Aïn Boucherit; Aïn Brimba Hamada Damous; Chiwondo; Kaiso; Hadar Bochianga; Langebaanweg-l |
| 5 | | | |
| | LATER (MIOCENE) | Lothagam-1 Lukeino Mpesida; Melka el Ouidane | Wadi Natrun; Sahabi |
| 10 | | Oued Zra | |
| | MIDDLE (MIOCENE) | Ngorora | Beglia Formation |
| | | Bou Hanifia | Wadi el-Hammam |
| | | Muruyur; Allengerr Fort Ternan | Beni Mellal Maboko |
| 15 | | | Malembe Moghara; Wadi Faregh; Siwa; Gebel Zelten |
| | EARLY (MIOCENE) | Rusinga; Napak Koru; Songhor | |
| 20 | | | Namib |
| | | Bukwa; Karungu | |
| 25 | | | |
| | OLIGOCENE | | |
| 30 | | | Zella |
| | | Gebel Qatrani | Gebel Bou Gobrine Dor el-Talha |
| 35 | | | |

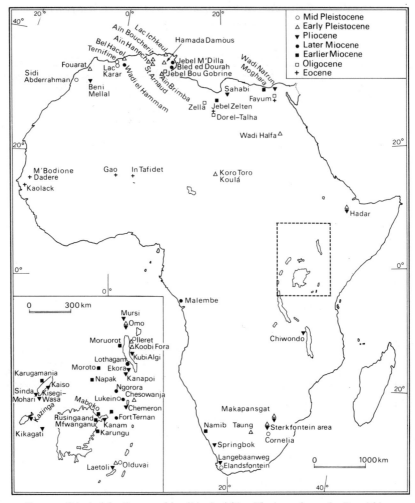

Fig. 1.5  Principal fossil mammal localities in Africa. The inset shows the East African area at an enlarged scale.

used in the past by vertebrate palaeontologists. Thus Fort Ternan, described as late Miocene in the literature, is technically middle Miocene, as also is the 'early Pliocene' site of Ngorora. Lukeino and Lothagam-1 are late Miocene. The Koobi Fora and Shungura formations are best described as Plio–Pleistocene.

The land mammal fauna of the Eocene is very poorly known and consists solely of three genera of proboscideans, one little bigger than a domestic pig and another as large as an elephant. In the Oligocene proboscideans are more varied but still form a major part of the fauna, together with hyracoids that are clearly divided into two different lineages. Proboscideans and hyracoids are manifestly of African origin and indicate a long period of isolated evolution from a pre-Eocene stock. Other Oligocene fossils include insectivores, a bat, rodents and an interesting spectrum of primates, all of which are African at the family and generic level but belong to orders that are known from earlier horizons outside Africa (Cooke 1972, Coryndon and Savage 1973). One carnivore genus is exclusively African, but three others and three artiodactyl genera occur also in Eurasia. The Eocene and Oligocene faunas are known only from North Africa and belong to an estuarine–deltaic environment in a semi-arid setting, but fed by substantial streams with gallery forest. The fauna may thus not be representative of the vast interior of the continent, which is so far unknown at this period. The later Oligocene faunas are completely unknown in Africa.

The early Miocene sites are mainly in East Africa, but there are also occurrences in Namibia and in Egypt and Libya representing several different depositional environments. The faunas are much more varied than in the Oligocene (81 genera compared with 30) and there are many new families, particularly carnivores, rhinoceroses and several artiodactyl groups; three-quarters of the genera are still uniquely African. The first appearance of Proboscidea in Eurasia at this time makes it clear that some faunal interchange took place in the late Oligocene. With the appearance of the varied artiodactyls, the Miocene fauna began to assume the kind of balance between large and small mammals, herbivores and carnivores, that characterizes the African savanna. However, the Bovidae, which now constitute such a prominent part of the fauna, were still very scarce in the early Miocene and show some links with European forms. The later Miocene fauna is enriched in bovids, several tribes having Asiatic affinities, but more than half of the genera were undoubtedly evolved in Africa itself following some early-to-mid-Miocene faunal interchange.

### The later Miocene–Pliocene faunas

Until a decade ago, knowledge of the faunas between the mid Miocene of Fort Ternan and the middle to upper Pliocene of North Africa was scanty, but new discoveries are bridging the gap, especially in East Africa. The most important upper Miocene sites are those of Ngorora, Mpesida, Lukeino and Lothagam, which lie in the area between Lake

Baringo and Lake Rudolf. Ngorora, with an age of about 11 million years, has an assemblage with general resemblances to the Fort Ternan fauna, particularly in respect of the ruminants. However, there are also new elements, such as the earliest hippopotamus and the first appearance of *Hipparion*, inseparable from the characteristic Old World *H. primigenium*. A new rhinoceros, *Brachypotherium lewisi*, occurs, as well as a gomphothere different from the earlier Miocene forms, and a different deinothere also. The Suidae are listriodonts. The late Miocene Mpesida and Lukeino Beds include the first appearance of the proboscidean *Stegotetrabelodon orbus*, regarded by Maglio (1973) as close to the stock from which the true elephants arose. The listriodont suids are displaced by a large and specialized form, *Nyanzachoerus*, that is very characteristic of most of the Pliocene sites in Africa.

The Lothagam Group probably lies astride the Miocene–Pliocene boundary, with the lower unit, Lothagam-1, in the upper Miocene and the top unit, Lothagam-3, in the Pliocene and roughly coeval with the 4-million-year-old Kanapoi Beds. The 'stem' elephant *Primelephas gomphotheroides* occurs, along with a surviving *Stegotetrabelodon*, but by the Kanapoi stage representatives of the three genera *Elephas*, *Loxodonta* and *Mammuthus* are already present. The Kanapoi fauna, and its equivalents elsewhere, includes many other new elements, such as the large suid *Notochoerus*, various hexaprotodont hippopotami, and bovids more like those of the Pleistocene. Although there is obviously a smooth transition between the later Miocene and the Pliocene faunas, the advent of the latter does seem to be marked by a substantial turnover at the generic level, accompanied by a diminution in representation of forms with Asiatic affinities. In addition to the emergence and rapid rise of the true elephants, the most marked changes are in the suids and bovids, which diversify greatly and thereafter tend to dominate the fossil assemblages (Maglio and Cooke 1978).

### Environmental zonation and climatic evolution

Africa today displays the most striking latitudinal zonation of any continent. This can be attributed to the limited extent of high mountain ranges to create vertical ecozonation or impede the free access of maritime air masses to the continental interior. The highland region of East Africa is cooler and drier than the remainder of the equatorial belt and cannot sustain the tropical forest of the lower-lying region to the west, but otherwise the vegetation pattern is remarkably symmetrical in the northern and southern parts of the continent (fig. 1.6). The

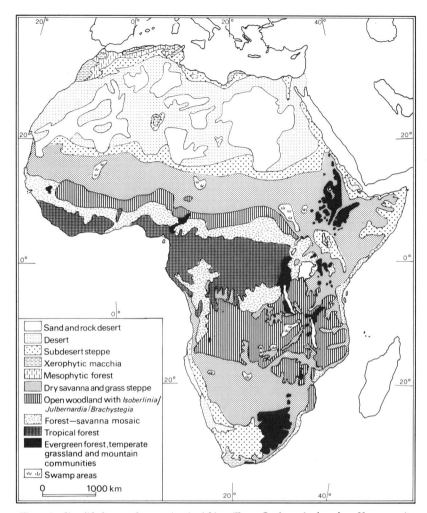

Fig. 1.6  Simplified map of vegetation in Africa. (From Cooke 1963, based on Keay 1959.)

general zonation is clearly related to the vegetation distribution and is shown in fig. 1.7 in terms of arid, semi-arid, humid and perhumid environments, but further recognizing belts of dominantly winter or summer rains, and an equatorial axis with double, equinoctial rainy seasons. Minor enclaves of wetter or drier climates exist but cannot, of course, be distinguished at this general scale.

In effect, the northern and southern peripheries of the continent enjoy Mediterranean-type climates with wet, cool winters or rainy transitional

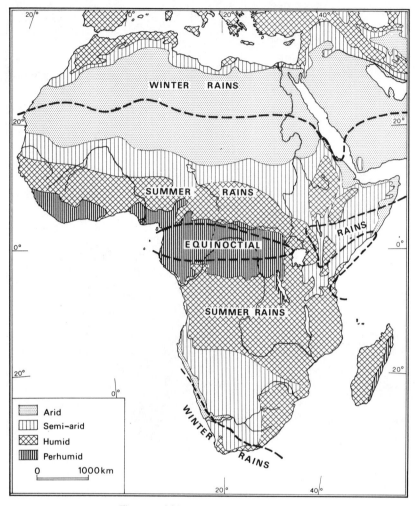

Fig. 1.7   Africa: environmental zonation.

seasons. Snowfall is not uncommon and precipitation is linked to travelling disturbances in the mid-latitude westerly circulation, with upper-level cold air masses occasionally penetrating as far as, or even equatorward of, the tropic circles. Natural vegetation in the humid zones of North Africa and the Cape is open, evergreen woodland, with a small belt of temperate rainforest on the south-eastern Cape coast, and generally grading into a bush steppe or grassland along the semi-arid margins.

Two expanses of desert or semidesert lie athwart the tropic circles, the Sahara in the north, the Namib–Kalahari to the south. Whereas the first of these dry belts spans the width of the continent, extending into Arabia and Somalia, the latter terminates in the high country of eastern South Africa. Vegetative cover ranges from barren, stony or sandy wastes, to semidesert grass and thorn bush or savanna. Rains are scarce and sporadic, with light winter rains most typical of the polar margins, summer thunderstorms on the equatorward fringes, and some overlap in the higher country in between.

A perhumid belt extends along the Gulf of Guinea into the Congo basin, coincident with the major rainforest environments. Short winter dry seasons are typical at the margins but, near the equator, there are conspicuous rainfall maxima in both spring and autumn. Drier conditions prevail at these same latitudes in East Africa, in part due to the stabilizing influence of the cool Somali current offshore, in part due to upper air divergence between the monsoonal air flow from the Atlantic and Indian oceans, and in part related to rainshadow effects in the lower country of the Rift Valley.

The remainder of the innertropical belt is subhumid to humid, with summer rains, and a vegetation cover ranging from deciduous low-tree savanna and dry forest to semideciduous, tall-tree savanna, parkland, or forest–savanna mosaic. The higher plateaux enjoy cool nights, and the major volcanic mountains rise through a perhumid montane zone to alpine meadows or snow-capped summits.

This environmental pattern evolved gradually during the course of the Tertiary. Earlier, in Palaeozoic times, Africa had been somewhere in Antarctic latitudes (fig. 1.3.1). Then, during the Mesozoic, the continental plate drifted towards its present latitudinal position while splitting off from the other Gondwana landmasses (fig. 1.3.2–3). During the early Tertiary, semidesert conditions prevailed in the Congo basin and West Africa as the Kalahari Supergroup accumulated landward of a cold coastal current that swept northwards to what is now the Guinea Coast, along the western margins of a semi-enclosed South Atlantic Ocean (Frakes and Kemp 1972). At the same time, Madagascar and the Indian plate continued to catch much of the moisture from the Indian Ocean monsoon. By the early Miocene, about 20 million years ago, a semblance of modern symmetry had been achieved. However, the westerly circulation was weaker and barely affected the poleward margins of the continent, while the plateaux of the north–south spine of Africa had only begun to arch up, and rift faulting was still localized.

As a result, equatorial forests extended from coast to coast (Andrews and Van Couvering 1975) and the Kalahari probably reached across to the Indian Ocean.

During the late Miocene and Pliocene, mid-latitudes cooled significantly, creating Mediterranean-type environments in northern and southern Africa. The spine of Africa was raised to approximately its present relief, and compartmentalized into mountain blocks and rift valleys, as well as modified by large-scale volcanism.. The forest belt was disrupted, with floras isolated in enclaves or adapted to new montane environments, while many areas were subdivided into increasingly complex mosaics of moist or arid vegetation (Butzer 1977).

It appears that throughout the Tertiary the aridity of the desert belts varied repeatedly, leaving vestiges of humid tropical soils as counterparts to the aeolian sands found under some equatorial rainforests. But no overall trend to late Tertiary aridity can be verified at a sub-continental scale. Instead, the major environmental changes to affect Africa came during the Pleistocene. Cold, glacial climates during the last million years or so repeatedly cooled the ocean surfaces and stabilized the lower atmosphere of the innertropical belt. Evergreen forests in the equatorial belt were reduced to small refuges as semi-arid vegetation expanded over most of the African savanna landscapes. As a consequence, the continent as a whole underwent drastic, pendulum-like changes between relatively wet and dry conditions. However, as the subsequent sections of this chapter will show, the detailed chronology of these large-scale environmental changes has not yet been resolved, and any inter-regional synchronism is complicated by complex variations of atmospheric and oceanic circulation patterns. The net impact is sufficiently unpredictable that deductive approaches must be ruled out in favour of critical regional studies emphasizing empirical data that can be set into tightly-controlled radiometric or stratigraphic frameworks.

## THE AFRICA OF THE EARLIEST TOOL-MAKERS

### Discovery and recognition of australopithecines

The fossil skull of a juvenile individual was recovered in 1924 from limestone workings at Taung, 130 km north of Kimberley, South Africa, and was first described by Professor Raymond A. Dart of Johannesburg in *Nature* on 3 February 1925, under the title '*Australopithecus africanus*: The Man-Ape of South Africa'. Dart's assessment of

the status of the new fossil is well stated in one of the closing paragraphs
of his article:

Unlike Pithecanthropus, it does not represent an ape-like man, a caricature of
precocious hominid failure, but a creature well advanced beyond modern
anthropoids in just those characters, facial and cerebral, which are to be
anticipated in an extinct link between man and his simian ancestor. At the same
time, it is equally evident that a creature with anthropoid brain capacity, and
lacking the distinctive, localised temporal expansions which appear to be
concomitant with and necessary to articulate man, is no true man. It is therefore
logically regarded as a man-like ape. I propose tentatively, then, that a new
family of *Homo-simiadae* be created for the reception of the group of individuals
which it represents, and that the first known species of the group be designated
*Australopithecus africanus*, in commemoration, first, of the extreme southern and
unexpected horizon of its discovery, and secondly, of the continent in which
so many new and important discoveries connected with the early history of
man have recently been made, thus vindicating the Darwinian claim that Africa
would prove to be the cradle of mankind.

Dart's announcement was seized upon with alacrity by the popular
press, which proclaimed in banner headlines the discovery of Darwin's
'Missing Link'. But its reception by the scientific world was largely one
of scepticism and most scientists dismissed it as merely another
anthropoid ape akin to the chimpanzee and gorilla. However, there were
a few supporters, particularly the Scots–South African physician–
palaeontologist Dr Robert Broom who, a decade later, was himself to
make notable discoveries of australopithecines. The principal barrier to
acceptance of the Taung fossil as hominid rather than pongid was the
youth of the individual, about equivalent to a six-year-old modern child,
as young apes are known to be more 'human-looking' than adults. The
lower jaw was also firmly attached to the upper one and the extremely
delicate and difficult task of detaching it was not accomplished until July
1929. With the patterns of the teeth now available for study, their human
characteristics convinced a few scientists that Dart was right, but
scepticism still reigned and the demand for an adult continued (Dart
1959). Taung, alas, produced no further specimens.

In 1934 Broom, a dynamic man of 68, gave up his medical practice
to undertake full-time palaeontological research at the Transvaal
Museum, Pretoria. In 1936, he began to examine caves and lime
workings near Pretoria in the hope of finding more australopithecine
material. Two of Dart's students brought him some baboon fossils from
Sterkfontein, 50 km west of Johannesburg and 65 km south-west of
Pretoria, and Broom visited the site as soon as he could. The quarry

man, Mr G. W. Barlow, had worked at Taung and promised to keep a watch for anything interesting. Eight days later, Barlow produced a beautiful natural brain cast and Broom found the remainder of a somewhat crushed and damaged skull in the quarry face (Broom 1950). It was an adult and Broom named it *Australopithecus transvaalensis*, later making it the type of a new genus *Plesianthropus* (not now considered valid). Associated fossil remains made it clear that the deposit was of considerable antiquity, probably early Pleistocene or Pliocene, and this fact compelled some former sceptics to reconsider their positions; but total acceptance was still a long way off.

During the next two years a lower jaw and a few bones of this creature were found, but in 1938 a schoolboy brought in some teeth from a site some 2 km to the east at Kromdraai. Excavation there yielded much of the skull and lower jaw of a rather different type of australopithecine which Broom named *Paranthropus robustus*. The Second World War interrupted Broom's fieldwork but Dart became interested in a complex of caves in a valley on the farm Makapansgat, near Potgietersrus, 320 km to the north, and this led to the discovery early in 1947 of several fragments of skull and jaw, which Dart named *Australopithecus prometheus*. This was the first discovery of an adult ape-man outside the Sterkfontein–Kromdraai area. In that same year, Broom resumed his excavations at Sterkfontein and a beautiful skull was found, formally designated Sterkfontein No. 5 but soon known to the public as 'Mrs Ples' (short for *Plesianthropus transvaalensis*). A few months later the first pelvis and thigh bone were found, providing strong evidence for a bipedal gait, and the case for recognition of hominid status was greatly strengthened. Although the 'conversion' of Dr William K. Gregory of New York in 1938 had helped to give some credence to the early claims of Dart and Broom for the fossils, the timely visit of Sir Wilfrid Le Gros Clark from Oxford in 1947 and his forthright acceptance of the hominid status of the australopithecines really established the case, although some opposition still continues.

In 1941, Broom was joined in his work by a young assistant, John Robinson, who shared in the new discoveries of 1947. In the following year, Broom and Robinson began work on a new site, Swartkrans, some 2 km west of Sterkfontein, and soon found a lower jaw which Broom named *Paranthropus crassidens*. By 1950 there were several skulls and jaws, as well as more than 200 teeth from Swartkrans, assigned to this robust australopithecine, but two jaws of very different character were found in 1949 and were named *Telanthropus capensis* by Broom and

26

Robinson. *Telanthropus* was compared with the famous Heidelberg jaw and subsequently Robinson reduced it to a synonym of Java man, *Homo erectus*. Broom died in 1951, at the age of 84, by which time the hominid status of the australopithecines was no longer in serious doubt. In addition to the 'true man' from Swartkrans, there were generally considered to be two distinct forms of australopithecine, the gracile *Australopithecus* (with *Plesianthropus* as a synonym) from Taung, Sterkfontein and Makapansgat, and the robust *Paranthropus* from Kromdraai and Swartkrans. Since then, controversy has centred mainly on how many valid species there are and whether *Paranthropus* is a full genus, a subgenus of *Australopithecus*, or a synonym (see chapter 2).

### Geology of the South African cave breccias

The geology of the Taung deposit is essentially different from that of the other sites, which are conveniently grouped as the 'Transvaal cave breccias'. Dolomitic limestones of Precambrian age form a prominent escarpment on the west side of a broad valley within which flows the Harts River, a tributary of the Vaal River. Along the edge of this 30- to 100-m high escarpment, deposits of secondary limestones, or tufa, have been built out in delta-like aprons as a result of evaporation of lime-charged water seeping out of the cliff. Although the fossils are usually referred to as coming from Taung, the village of that name is some distance from the quarry, which is correctly known as Buxton. Peabody (1954) recognized two major and two minor tufas at the Buxton quarries, each of which was sculptured by erosion before the deposition of the next, partly overlapping, lime carapace. Fissures and cavernous openings developed in the tufas at various stages and were filled by firmly cemented sandy material, sometimes containing bone and, in the younger ones, occasional stone implements.

The *Australopithecus* skull came from a cavity filling in the oldest carapace. No other fossils were found in direct association with it but as soon as the discovery was announced, the Northern Lime Company left the important block intact and the site was carefully examined and described by Dr Alěs Hrdlička in August 1925. In 1937 Broom collected material from this face and referred to the deposit as 'Hrdlička's cave', regarding it as an extension of the original 'Dart's cave'. Further excavation was undertaken by Peabody in 1948 and there can be little doubt that all this material came essentially from a single body of deposits. However, the matrix attached to the hominid skull pertains to the younger part of these deposits, which washed into an existing fissure of the oldest tufa carapace only at the time that the next major carapace had begun to develop (Butzer 1974c, Butzer *et al.* 1978). The hominid is therefore somewhat younger than the bulk of the fauna, which comes from sandy deposits washed into the cave by intermittent runoff during an earlier stage of geomorphic development. The total fauna is unfortunately scanty but there are links with the fossil assemblages from the Transvaal cave breccias sufficient to show that they belong to the same broad segment of geological time.

The Transvaal cave breccias comprise sedimentary material laid down in caverns and fissures in Precambrian dolomitic limestones of the Transvaal Supergroup. The limestones dip at fairly low angles and solution along bedding planes and intersecting joint systems results in the formation of subterranean caverns and enlarged fissures. Brain (1958) made a special study of the australopithecine cave deposits and showed that as long as a cavern is cut off from the surface, deposition of dripstone or flowstone occurs, together with insoluble products released from the parent limestone during solution; a grey or banded travertine is the typical result. As soon as an opening to the surface is exposed, external debris enters at a low rate and contaminates the travertine. If bones are introduced at this stage they may form a high proportion of the total deposit. Brain has called this a 'Phase 1' breccia. As the surface opening enlarges, the rate of introduction of external soil increases to a point where the deposit becomes a clastic one with a calcareous cement, or 'Phase 2' breccia (see fig. 1.8). The relative proportion of bone decreases but it is the 'Phase 2' breccias that have been the main source for the many thousands of fossils recovered from these sites. Subsequent to their primary filling, the caverns have been subjected to erosion and new channels, fissures or cavities cut into them so that at several sites breccias of different ages are found in contact. Undermining of the floor may take place, resulting in collapse and the creation of new cavities that can be filled. Because of the antiquity of the australopithecine breccias, erosion has removed most or all of the original roofs, thus exposing the firmly cemented pinkish-brown breccia at the present surface. The exact sequence at each site is thus complicated and correlation must at present rely on faunal data. In an endeavour to deduce the external climate at the time of filling, Brain analysed the cave breccias and compared the clastic material with present-day soils formed from the same parent rock under different climatic conditions. Although the details of his climatic interpretation

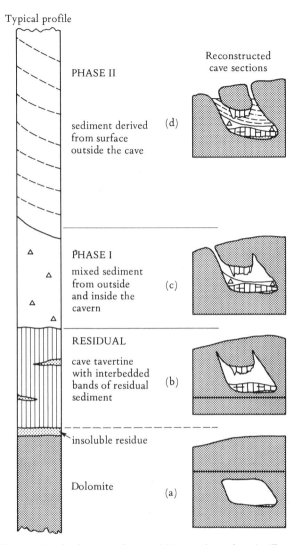

Fig. 1.8  Stages in the development of a typical Transvaal cave breccia. (From Brain 1967.)

have been questioned, it is clear that the environment was broadly like that of the present, with strongly seasonal rainfall and incomplete grass cover. Detailed studies of the clastic fillings of Swartkrans (Brain 1976, Butzer 1976a) and of Sterkfontein and Makapansgat (Partridge 1975) show that despite the overall generic similarity of the breccias, each sedimentary sequence is unique. Depositional breaks, mainly coincident with thickening of the soil outside the caves, alternated repeatedly with episodes of soil attrition at the surface and gradual infilling of the caves below. In other words, the stratigraphy is more complex than was originally thought, the time-spans represented by each cave are considerably longer, and the external climates represented were somewhat more variable.

The faunal material from the australopithecine sites totals about 170 mammalian species, a few reptiles and rare bird remains. Although the larger mammals are the most obvious element, remains of small rodents and insectivores make up more than one-third of the species and are derived almost entirely from the furry pellets regurgitated by owls. Some species are present at most of the sites but others are known only at one. Analyses of the species present at more than one site suggest that the main Sterkfontein and Makapansgat faunal assemblages are the older and the Swartkrans and Kromdraai faunas successively younger (Vrba 1975). The scanty fauna from Taung makes correlation more difficult but its affinities suggest that it may occupy a position intermediate between Makapansgat and Swartkrans. From an ecological viewpoint, the overall picture created by the faunal assemblages is one of dry grassland with rocky areas and scrub, or even localized bush in sheltered locations (Cooke 1978). Taung has more species favouring fairly dry conditions but this is not a strong trend and does not demand an arid environment. The Makapansgat fauna suggests more bush, in keeping with its closed valley setting, and the dominant faunal elements indicate grassland and thorn scrub with water available nearby. Vrba (1975) considers that there was more bush cover at Sterkfontein than was the case later at Swartkrans and Kromdraai.

Stone tools of Oldowan type were discovered at Sterkfontein in 1956 by Brain (1958) on the west side of the original quarry (Sterkfontein Type Site) and this is known as the Sterkfontein Extension Site. The breccias at the extension site are distinctly younger than those of the type site and may be more nearly of the age of the younger deposits at Swartkrans, where stone implements also occur (see p. 48).

### Australopithecines in East Africa

The first australopithecine to be discovered outside South Africa came from Bed I at Olduvai Gorge, Tanzania, where a fine skull was found by Mary Leakey on 17 July 1959. It was described a month later by her husband (L. S. B. Leakey 1959) under the name *Zinjanthropus boisei*, now assigned to *Paranthropus* or to *Australopithecus* by various authorities. Further excavations at this site during the next eighteen months yielded most of a hominid foot and some other bones, as well as the greater part of a mandible and two parietals of a juvenile, about twelve years of age. Volcanic tuffs from Bed I were dated radiometrically at close to 1.75 million years (L. S. B. Leakey, Evernden and Curtis 1961), providing the first real indication of the antiquity of the australo-pithecines. In the next few years two incomplete skulls were discovered in the lower part of Bed II and their morphology was regarded as linking them with the juvenile from Bed I; they were named *Homo habilis*, with the juvenile as the type (L. S. B. Leakey, Tobias and Napier 1964) although some authorities place it in *Australopithecus* as an advanced species. A level high in Bed II also furnished a robust skull cap, now generally regarded as belonging to a form of *Homo erectus*. Thus Olduvai has a robust australopithecine and '*Homo habilis*' as contemporary and *H. erectus* a little younger. No radiometric dates are available for the upper levels in the Gorge, but palaeomagnetic correlation indicates that the lower part of Bed IV has an age close to 700 000 years. The geology has been described in detail by Hay (1976).

Immediately south of Olduvai, on either side of the Vogel River, there are deposits up to 130 m thick known as the Laetolil Beds. They consist largely of fine tuffs and recent work has disclosed the presence of a varied fauna and of important hominid fossils occurring in a zone bracketed by radiometric dates between 3.59 and 3.77 million years ago (M. D. Leakey *et al.* 1976).

Within the past decade, numerous other important discoveries of hominids have been made in the East African region. In the Omo area of south-western Ethiopia, north of Lake Rudolf, there is a thick sequence of fluvio-lacustrine sediments from which mammalian fossils were collected by Professor C. Arambourg, of Paris, in 1932–3. Three decades later, an international expedition resumed work in the Omo Beds (now the Shungura Formation) and Arambourg found the first australopithecine mandible in 1967. During the following six years further mandibular specimens, cranial and postcranial fragments, and numerous isolated teeth of hominids have been found at various horizons. Stone implements also occur. The Shungura Formation is 750 m thick and includes a number of distinctive volcanic tuff horizons that serve as boundaries between members (designated by letters – see fig. 1.9). Some of the tuffs have been dated radiometrically and the dates have been adjusted slightly as a result of detailed palaeomagnetic studies (Shuey, Brown and Croes 1974) to provide an unusually well-controlled

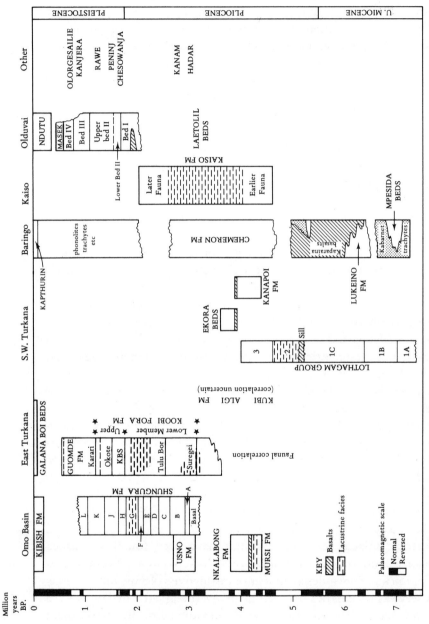

Fig. 1.9 Provisional correlation of major later Miocene to Pleistocene deposits in East Africa. For the Koobi Fora Formation the column represents a 'best fit' correlation with Omo, based on faunas. The horizontal shading indicates predominantly lacustrine facies with few terrestrial fossils.

sequence within which the abundant fossil faunas can be placed. Isolated occurrences to the north of the main Shungura outcrops have been designated the Usno Formation, approximately equivalent to Member B of the main sequence, and have yielded good faunas and many hominid teeth. Also in the northern part of the area is the Mursi Formation, so far without hominids, in which a terminal olivine basalt flow is dated at 4.25 million years. The unfossiliferous Nkalabong Formation overlies faulted and weathered Mursi basalt and approximately fills the time gap between the Mursi and Shungura formations. The sequence is compared with that of Olduvai in fig. 1.9.

In the lower reaches of the Awash River, in the central Afar region of Ethiopia, an extensive area has exposures of clays, sands and gravels which have yielded remarkably well-preserved fossil mammals and hominid remains from the vicinity of Hadar (Taieb *et al.* 1972, Johanson, White and Coppens 1978). A basalt within the succession has been dated radiometrically as close to 3.0 million years, which is consistent with the fossil material as this has a strong resemblance to the fauna from the basal part of the Shungura Formation.

A reconnaissance by Richard Leakey on the east side of Lake Rudolf (now Turkana) in 1968 led to the discovery of extensive fossiliferous fluvio-lacustrine deposits over an area 40 to 50 km in radius around Koobi Fora, which has given its name to the formation represented by these sediments (Bowen and Vondra 1973). The total thickness of the deposits is about 200 m but there are breaks within the sequence and gaps between different areas, so that correlation is rendered difficult. Ashy beds are rarer in the Koobi Fora Formation than at Omo, but certain horizons have been used as reference markers. One of these, known as the 'KBS tuff', has been dated radiometrically by Fitch and Miller (1970) at 2.61 ± 0.26 million years, but other determinations indicate an age of 1.6 million years in part of the area and of 1.82 million years in another area (Curtis *et al.* 1975); there are thus correlation and dating problems still to be resolved. A substantial number of hominid crania, cranial fragments, mandibles, postcranial bones and isolated teeth have been found, mainly in the upper beds, but a number of excellent and important specimens also come from below the KBS marker horizon. Stone tools occur at various levels in the upper part of the sequence, but have also been found below the KBS tuff. Fossil mammals are plentiful and very well preserved (Maglio 1972). Below the Koobi Fora Formation lies a separate unit known as the Kubi Algi Formation, which is poor in fossil remains. Because of the uncertainties in dating, only a tentative correlation is given in fig. 1.9.

To the south-west of Lake Rudolf there are two localities that are older than the Shungura and Koobi Fora formations and have furnished scrappy but important hominid fossils. The younger locality, at Kanapoi, underlies a 4.0-million-year-old basalt and is faunally similar to the Mursi Formation, of closely comparable age. The hominid fragment is the distal end of a humerus attributed to *Australopithecus* sp. The other locality, Lothagam, has an upper unit (Unit 3) with a fauna similar to that of Kanapoi and is older than a basaltic sill dated at 3.71 million years. The underlying Unit 2 consists of some 80 m of lacustrine clays and silts, with no mammalian fossils, and Unit 1 comprises 250 to 500 m of sediments, mainly sandy, with a good mammalian fauna. From this unit comes a fragmental mandible, with only one molar preserved, which is undoubtedly hominid and most probably australopithecine.

Further to the south, in the area west and north of Lake Baringo, there is a remarkable sequence of more than 3000 m of volcanic lavas within which are located seven successive fossil-bearing sedimentary units, and also two isolated occurrences. The oldest sedimentary unit, the Alengerr Formation, has an age somewhere between 14.0 and 12.5 million years, but has a very scanty fauna. The Ngorora Formation is certainly older than 9 million years and younger than 12 million years and has yielded a good deal of fossil material, including a molar that is certainly hominoid. The Mpesida and Lukeino Beds have ages between 6.0 and 7.0 million years and a fauna resembling that of Lothagam-1. The Chemeron Formation, ranging between 2.5 and 4.5 million years in age, has an extensive fauna generally resembling that of the lower Shungura and Kanapoi, and discoveries include a hominid temporal fragment. Two other units, the Aterir Beds and Karmosit Beds, are of roughly similar age, or a little younger, but have yielded few fossils. On the east side of Lake Baringo, an isolated pocket of sediment at Chesowanja has furnished an interesting australopithecine skull associated with a fauna resembling that of Bed II at Olduvai; stone implements also occur. The Baringo sequence is included diagrammatically in fig. 1.9.

### Pliocene–early Pleistocene of North Africa

The area to the north-east of Lake Chad represents a very large basin filled with lacustrine and terrestrial silts, sands and gravels, ranging in age from the Pliocene to the present. Although the stratigraphic relations of the earlier beds are difficult to establish, there are vertebrate fossils exposed in some areas which represent three faunal stages. The earliest of these, the Bochianga group, is found west of Koro Toro, but the assemblage is not very diagnostic and is probably mid Pliocene. The Wadi Derdemy fauna, and that of Koulá, also near Koro Toro, include fossil remains some of which can be matched in the middle and lower part of the Shungura Formation in Ethiopia and are probably late Pliocene in age. At Yayo, to the north of the other sites, a fauna of more advanced character occurs and is probably equivalent in age to upper Bed II at Olduvai. A partial cranium from Yayo was originally described as an advanced australopithecine but this is no longer considered probable.

A number of late Pliocene or early Pleistocene sites occur in western Morocco, northern Algeria and Tunisia – a region sometimes known as the Maghrib. Particularly important from a stratigraphic viewpoint is the Oued Fourarat site, 30 km north-east of Rabat, where marine Pliocene sands and gravels are overlain by Calabrian marine gravels which, in addition to molluscs, contain some well-preserved elephant teeth belonging to two typical North African forms, *Anancus osiris* and *Mammuthus africanavus*. Specimens comparable with the Fourat mammoth occur at the site of Oued Akrech, south of Rabat, also with marine fossils. The occurrence of these species in a marine horizon that can be recognized at many points around the Mediterranean provides one of the very few cases where good correlation is possible between Africa and Europe. *M. africanavus* also occurs at Wadi Derdemy and Koulá in the Lake Chad area, but the form there seems a little more progressive. Closely comparable *M. africanavus* molars occur at Aïn Boucherit (St Arnaud) in Algeria and at Kebili and Aïn Brimba in Tunisia, and there is a poorly preserved skull from Garet et-Tir, Algeria. Slightly more evolved molars are found at Bel Hacel, Algeria, at Lac Ichkeul, Tunisia, and also at Aïn Hanech near St Arnaud. The associated faunas include white rhinoceros, hipparion and some other mammals known south of the Sahara, but there are also a number of species that seem to be restricted to the area north of the main desert belt. True horses make their appearance at Aïn Boucherit and, if the age assessment of the Calabrian is correct, this is earlier than the oldest horses in sub-Saharan Africa, as might perhaps be expected.

*The Plio–Pleistocene faunas*

The Pliocene–Pleistocene boundary is now generally regarded as having an age of approximately 1.8 million years, although this is not formally agreed. Such an age coincides closely with the base of the Olduvai deposits and can be placed as a time line near the top of Member G in the Shungura sequence. It does not correspond to any drastic change in the fauna, for the late Pliocene to early Pleistocene transition is accomplished merely by a progressive decline in the archaic elements and a steady increase in the proportion of living genera and species.

The Pliocene seems to have been a period during which Africa was generally isolated from Eurasia, but in the late Pliocene there was some interchange of faunal material. Furthermore, as a consequence of their increased isolation within sub-Saharan Africa, the genera and species that evolved are no longer represented in the Eurasiatic animal populations. *Equus* makes its appearance close to the Pliocene–Pleistocene boundary, but *Hipparion* persists. Another apparent immigrant is the camel, which occurs in the later Pliocene and in the Pleistocene of North and East Africa. Viverrids become a significant element among the carnivores and the sabre-toothed cats are joined in the late Pliocene by *Felis* and *Panthera*, which have not been recorded earlier. The hippopotami become very diverse, often with several contemporary species in different areas, and the suids radiate rapidly. The archaic bovids decline in the early Pleistocene so that the fauna tends to consist largely of living genera, but extinct species; they are the commonest fossils at all the sites.

In the late Pliocene and early Pleistocene there is a strong general resemblance between the faunas of the north African and central African sites, indicating that the Sahara was not at this time a substantial barrier to movement. However, there are proportionally more differences than in the Miocene, so it may be inferred that the Sahara was playing a role of increasing importance as a barrier. At the end of the Pliocene, faunal interchange between sub-Saharan Africa and Eurasia effectively ceased, although there were still periods during the Pleistocene when elements from central Africa extended their ranges to the north, or even crossed the desertic belt. On the whole, the African faunas appear to have been less sensitive to climatic changes than were those in the harsher glaciated regions of Eurasia and North America. Although the vegetational belts expanded and contracted in response to changes in temperature and precipitation, ecological niches were seldom eliminated and, with rare exceptions, the animals could drift with their shifting environments. Nevertheless, there are many obvious cases at the present day of disjunct distributions that may be attributed to disruption of formerly continuous environments; examples include the montane forest, isolated patches of bird species, and the curious distribution of the oryx, white rhinoceros, giraffe, dik-dik and many small insectivores and rodents.

It is a notable fact that Plio–Pleistocene deposits with significant numbers of fossils are not known in the areas of broadleaf tropical forest, or even in the heavily wooded areas adjoining them. Most of the important sites lie in the savanna areas of relatively dry *Acacia*-wooded grassland or thornveld and this is reflected in the faunas by the abundance of what might be termed a 'game-reserve' spectrum. Typical forest-dwellers are rare and the ones that do occur are usually those that are at home in the bush or gallery forest that so characteristically extends along water courses in Africa, even into astonishingly dry areas. In hilly country the steep-sided ravines often carry quite thick bush, and in the volcanic areas the mature cones have extensive forests on their higher and cooler slopes, despite the fact that their bases may lie in dry steppe. It is thus very difficult to use the fossil assemblages as good indicators of local environment, except to the extent that they may reflect greater or lesser proportions of bush-loving species or those with high water requirements, as compared with forms that favour or demand more open grassland. In a limited geographic area, such as a single site, it is possible to make some inferences regarding changes in the local environment with time but as yet these deductions cannot be employed successfully in deriving a regional or continent-wide picture. Unfortunately, too, pollens are generally not well preserved in the fossiliferous sequences and the vegetational changes are moderately well known only for the later Pleistocene.

### Australopithecine environments

It remains to consider the environmental setting in which the australopithecines lived. This information can best be obtained from analysis of the sediments in which the fossils are found (see Butzer 1971a, chs. 10–14).

In the case of East Rudolf (now East Turkana), the hominid sites and archaeological occurrences come from delta and floodplain deposits, including the silty or sandy channels of intermittent streams or distributary branches, and from extensive delta-fringe marshes and mudflats that probably were seasonally dry (Behrensmeyer 1976). There is, as yet, no clear pattern indicating preferential occurrence of gracile and robust hominids in distinct sedimentary environments. However, in stream beds the frequency of robust australopithecines is significantly greater than that of gracile hominids, whereas the two taxa occur in similar numbers within lake margin deposits. Behrensmeyer (1978) suggests that substantially greater numbers of robust australopithecines inhabited the galeria woodland of riverine habitats than did gracile hominids; both inhabited the more open vegetation of the shorelines and deltaic plains.

In the lower Omo region, the robust and gracile forms not only overlap temporally but may occasionally be found at the same place as part of a single bone assemblage. The bulk of the sites appear to be related to river or distributary channels of the Omo and its former delta (Butzer 1971b, 1976b). Elsewhere in the Rudolf basin, the Kanapoi hominid fragment was found in a sandy lakeshore deposit, while that from Lothagam was related to sandy stream channels, probably within a delta rapidly building up near the margin of the lake.

Further south in the Rift Valley, in the Baringo basin, the Ngorora molar comes from what was once a land surface on a flat, alluvial plain. Another hominid tooth, in the Lukeino Formation, comes from lake beds, while the Chemeron skull fragment comes from grits and sands washed together near a former lakeshore. The Chesowanja hominid and the artifact-bearing beds were laid down in the low-lying fringe of a delta (Bishop 1978).

At Olduvai, the hominid sites of Bed I and lower Bed II were once occupied along the fluctuating shoreline or exposed mudflats of a lake, or adjacent to shallow, intermittent drainage lines derived from high volcanic mountains along the margins of this Rift Valley basin (Hay 1976). The Peninj mandible, from the Natron basin, comes from clayey sands that formed part of a delta accumulation.

In South Africa, Dart (1925) originally believed that the Taung juvenile had inhabited the treeless margins of the Kalahari Desert. However, the fissure filling at Taung included two units, a lower sandy ('dry phase') accumulation and an upper clayey sediment interbedded with tufa ('wet phase'). The associated Taung fauna came primarily from the earlier sands, whereas the hominid was embedded and fossilized in the younger 'wet phase' deposits (Butzer *et al.* 1978). The skull was washed into a deep solution cavity at a time of massive spring discharge along the nearby cliffs, with a thick mat of grass on the adjacent plains and fringing bush near water.

The Transvaal breccias generally represent natural infillings of solution sinkholes once situated on the undulating margins of shallow valleys or just below the adjacent uplands. During accumulation, tree growth was probably limited to such sinkholes and to the valley floors. At Swartkrans, for example, the older, australopithecine breccias include three units. The oldest originally collected on a sinkhole floor that later collapsed into a lower cavern; soil then continued to wash in, as the climate became drier and ground cover was reduced. A moister or less seasonal climate then stabilized the slope soils under a dense mat of vegetation, until increasingly intensive rainfall once again began to remove thin increments of soil that accumulated in the cave below (Butzer 1976a). The hominid fossils in good part represent the prey of leopards using trees around the sinkhole (Brain 1976). The key hominid breccia at Makapansgat is somewhat different, and probably indicates a deep, underground stream. Exactly how the bone concentrations here were transported or collected is unclear.

THE AFRICA OF ACHEULIAN MAN

### Stratigraphy and chronology of the Acheulian

Hand-axes, long held to be the hallmark of the Acheulian techno-complex, have been known from Africa since the late nineteenth century, and have been widely reported on since the 1920s. The majority of occurrences continue to be surface materials that provide little information. Sites where hand-axes were actually recovered from geological deposits have always been few, and the majority of these consist of reworked stone artifacts in stream deposits. Based largely on fieldwork carried out during the 1930s, a number of regional sequences were established that for many years served as a standard for pre-historians as well as for a general stratigraphic framework.

In the Nile Valley, Sandford and Arkell (Sandford 1934, Sandford and Arkell 1933) recognized a suite of high river terraces, apparently linked to successive temporal stages of refinement in hand-axe manu-facture. On the Atlantic coast of Morocco, Neuville and Ruhlmann (1941) identified a series of interdigitated dune sands, beaches and littoral cave deposits that also suggested a progressive development of ancient lithic industries. In East Africa, at Olduvai, Leakey (L. S. B. Leakey 1951) derived an apparently subcontinuous depositional sequence documenting successive industrial phases accompanied by

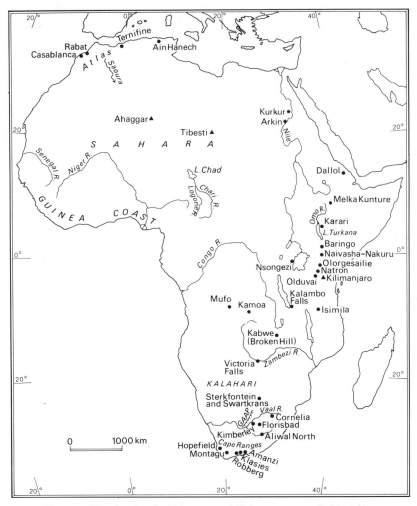

Fig. 1.10   Map showing the Pleistocene and Holocene areas studied in Africa.

changing faunal assemblages. Finally, in South Africa, the Vaal River gravels, as delineated by Söhnge, Visser and Van Riet Lowe (1937), seemed to provide yet another progressive sequence of Acheulian subdivisions. This semblance of scientific order was linked by many, particularly after the 1947 Pan-African Congress of Prehistory, to a stratigraphic scheme of 'pluvials', laboriously constructed in East Africa by Wayland, Leakey and others (L. S. B. Leakey 1952). Since these pluvials were equated with the classical Alpine glacial sequence, it was therefore widely thought, for a time, that a pan-African stratigraphic scheme had been established and that it embraced both cultures and faunas.

As regional studies continued, it became increasingly obvious that the stratigraphic framework had been premature and that the paradigms domin ting prehistoric research had been inadequate. Cooke (1958) and Flint (1959) showed that the lithostratigraphic criteria on which the East African 'pluvial' sequence had been based were unsatisfactory, and their scepticism of the value of the 'pluvial' climatostratigraphic framework for Africa has been confirmed by subsequent research. The classic regional sequences have, in the meanwhile, all been subject to one or more reinvestigations. New areas have been studied, with better implementation of multidisciplinary work methods. Geologically sealed archaeological sites have been increasingly excavated with the proper care, providing a new wealth of information and, in some cases, key fossil material.

Thanks to multiple reinvestigations at Olduvai the true magnitude of chronostratigraphic problems is now apparent (Hay 1976, Isaac 1972, 1975, M. D. Leakey 1975). Dating of this complex sedimentary sequence by potassium–argon and palaeomagnetic reversals and events had emphasized that (1) the Acheulian first appears about 1.5 million years ago, midway in Olduvai Bed II, possibly as much as 750 000 years earlier than in Europe; and that (2) the 'Middle' Pleistocene fauna of middle and upper Bed II is in fact early Pleistocene by European standards. Furthermore, at the younger end of the temporal column, a variety of dating techniques now imply that the Acheulian was replaced by younger industries no later than 175 000 years ago, and that what were once thought to be terminal Pleistocene faunas extend back in time to before 100 000 BP.[1] In effect, these startling realizations would also apply to the faunal horizon represented by most of Bed II and Bed IV at Olduvai, or by the Vaal–Cornelia faunal span in southern Africa. Thus the Acheulian of Africa extended through all of the middle and most of the early Pleistocene.

In view of this revised chronology for the Acheulian in Africa, it is evident that most existing geological sequences are either grossly oversimplified or disturbingly incomplete, when contrasted with the level of local detail available for the later Pleistocene and Holocene. Another realization from recent work is that the continental interior of Africa did not experience the same incisive physical and biological changes that accompanied the waxing and waning of glaciers in high

[1] Before the Present.

latitudes. There have been repeated and significant changes in available moisture during at least the last 30 000 years, but the wavelength of such variability is too short either to give substantial records in the earlier Pleistocene or to provide convenient climatostratigraphic markers. In default of a geological record with conspicuous periodicities or a faunal record with unequivocal environmental sensitivity, stratigraphic correlation is particularly difficult in Africa. There are few long and detailed sequences, and most good archaeological sites or local litho-stratigraphies can only be 'dated' radiometrically or with reference to available palaeomagnetic frameworks. As the following selective survey of key sites or sequences shows, such chronometric dating remains confined to a few locales.

## North Africa and the Sahara

One of the most promising geological contexts in the African mid-Pleistocene is provided by coastal plains. As the glaciers advanced or retreated in high latitudes, so world sea levels changed so that shorelines retreated or advanced. Ideally the impact should be a sequence of littoral dunes and beach deposits, interrupted by palaeosols, and potentially linked with alluvial terraces further inland. This is the case near Casablanca, on the Atlantic margin of Morocco. Neuville and Ruhl-mann's original scheme (1941) was much expanded by Biberson (1961, 1970) at the Sidi Abderrahman quarries. He identified a series of high sea levels, separated by continental deposits, such as regressional dunes and stream alluvia, in part linked with lithic industries or faunas or both. A stratum with a Plio–Pleistocene fauna is followed by a sequence of geomorphic features that can be briefly listed, characterized and identifed by their time–stratigraphic (stage) names.

(1) Thick, weathered, alluvial sands and gravels, with possible frost convolutions towards the top. *Moulouyan*. Possible unifacially worked pebbles.

(2) Erosion of beach platform at +150 m into Moulouyan beds. *Regregian*.

(3) Beach deposits at +90 to 100 m with subtropical mollusca. *Messaoudian*. 'Pebble culture'.

(4) Alluvial gravels, partly ferricrete, with basal traces of frost action, 'cool' continental mollusca, and possibly linked to montane glaciers inland. *Saletian*. 'Evolved pebble culture'.

(5) Erosional beaches with sea caves and fillings at +55 to 60 m; temperate marine mollusca. *Maarifian*. 'Evolved pebble culture'.

(6) Regressional dunes, freshwater limestones, and weathered alluvia. *Amirian*. These beds and most younger units contain significant mammalian faunas; the continental mollusca of the lower Amirian suggest a temperate, humid climate, those of the upper Amirian, cool conditions. Early Acheulian.

(7) Several beaches at $+(16?)25$ to $+34$ m, recorded by erosional forms and deposits, initially with cool mollusca, ultimately including tropical forms. *Anfatian* (and the later, *Harounian*?); uranium series dates in excess of 200 000 BP for the former (Stearns and Thurber 1967). Middle Acheulian.

(8) Alluvial terraces, apparently linked to montane glaciers inland. *Tensiftian*. Middle Acheulian.

(9) Following another beach stage, of uncertain field relations, continental breccias with temperate mollusca. *Presoltanian*. Acheulian.

The subsequent record is of late Pleistocene age and better represented on other Moroccan coastal sectors. The Casablanca sequence remains the most complete in North Africa and allows faunal cross-correlations with other sites in Algeria and Tunisia. However, as presently understood, it is no longer acceptable as a standard sequence. Comparison of the upper half with the littoral stratigraphy of Mallorca suggests that the Casablanca sequence is either locally incomplete or has been oversimplified (Butzer 1975a). Correlations with upland glaciation remain tenuous. Until palaeomagnetic markers have been established, correlations with specific glacial–interglacial cycles must therefore be considered with caution. Most of the archaeological materials in the older half of the Casablanca succession are derived. The 'pebble culture' artifacts were selected from stream or beach gravels and, except for the better choppers and the chopping tools, are often of questionable validity. In fact the earliest Acheulian assemblages of merit come from the Anfatian (Freeman 1975). The younger part of the sequence also provides stratigraphic context for cave or fissure fills that include a number of significant hominid fossils around Casablanca, as well as at Témara, Rabat and Salé, the oldest of which is Anfatian (Jaeger 1975).

Two important Algerian sites are Aïn Hanech and Ternifine. At the former, situated near Constantine, undoubted artifacts (spheroids) in a sandy to gravelly clay were originally believed to be of very early Pleistocene age, on faunal grounds. However, the 'Villafranchian' elements of this fauna were quite probably reworked from an underlying unit (Aïn Boucherit), and the residual fauna is only somewhat older than that of Ternifine (Jaeger 1975). The latter site, near Oran, represents a thick spring accumulation and includes a rich fauna, several specimens of *Homo erectus*, as well as an Acheulian assemblage (Freeman 1975, Jaeger 1975). Ternifine is coeval with or a little older than the Amirian.

Also of interest, in the Algerian Sahara, is the complex of four alluvial terraces of the Saoura, including aeolian and lacustrine components, as well as palaeosols, recognized by Chavaillon (1964) and assigned to the early and mid Pleistocene. Industrial associations comparable to those of Morocco are offered, but there is no fauna and Chavaillon's interpretations of the erosional–depositional cycles, related in large part to a watershed including the Saharan Atlas, are debatable (Butzer and Hansen 1968). The major import of these and other Acheulian occurrences in the Sahara is the apparent restriction of any possible primary sites to proximity of ponded water or small lakes, under hydrological conditions temporarily different from those of today's total aridity (Conrad 1969, Rognon 1967).

The only other long early-to-mid-Pleistocene sequence in northern Africa is that of the Nile Valley in Nubia and Egypt. At least five stages of Nile and wadi gravel accumulation are recorded for this general period, with substantial evidence for increased fluvial activity within the Saharan watersheds (Butzer and Hansen 1968). Acheulian artifacts, all in secondary contexts, occur in at least the three youngest of these terrace complexes, but dating is unavailable. A single good, relatively undisturbed site has been excavated from wadi alluvium at Arkin, Nubia (Chmielewski 1968), probably coeval with the youngest of the Nile gravel terraces.

### Eastern Africa

One of the more interesting Pleistocene sequences in eastern Africa is found on the rim of the Ethiopian plateau, at and upstream of Melka Kunturé, on the upper Awash River. The early-to-mid Pleistocene is represented by four sedimentary cycles that, apart from being rich in volcanic ash or its derivatives, each begin with fluvial detritus and terminate with diatomaceous beds indicative of ponding (Taieb 1974). The oldest, with faunal elements that infer a possible age of 1.5 to 1.2 million BP, includes a relatively undisturbed occupation site without hand-axes, and that may represent a 'Developed Oldowan' (Chavaillon and Chavaillon 1971). This Gomborean cycle has pollen suggesting a relatively open vegetation, much like that of today (Bonnefille 1972). The three younger, Garbian cycles include a number of Acheulian sites that represent winnowed or overlapping channel deposits in some instances, colluvial stone lines (i.e. accumulated by rainwash) in others;

most of these archaeological occurrences are secondary. Pollen spectra indicate a vegetation at least as open as that of today, in part more so. No radiometric dates are available for the Garbian, but an Acheulian cleaver and flake were found in a +90 m upraised coral beach near Dallol, Afar, which was uranium assayed at about 200 000 BP (Roubet 1969).

In the lower Omo basin, south-western Ethiopia, Plio–Pleistocene depositional patterns in a primeval delta persisted until 1.2 million BP, on the basis of potassium–argon dating, or 0.8 million BP on magneto-stratigraphic grounds (Brown and Shuey 1976). There are next to no hominid fossils and no artifacts in the upper third of this sedimentary sequence. The mid Pleistocene was marked by intensive faulting and limited deposition, possibly in response to a generally low level of Lake Rudolf. East of that, lake sedimentation continued until perhaps 1.3 million BP. On the Karari Escarpment, artifactual occurrences that date between 1.57 and 1.32 million BP are found within massive flood silts, related to streams draining into Lake Rudolf (Isaac, Harris and Crader 1976).

Further south, within the Kenya Rift Valley, there are numerous smaller depositional basins with interdigitated fluvial and lacustrine beds that span much of the late Cenozoic. Perhaps the most productive of these has been the Baringo basin work on which, however, remains largely unpublished. Of particular interest is the Kapthurin Formation, which yielded a hominid mandible and Acheulian materials (Margaret Leakey *et al.* 1969). These come from a sandy to gravelly fluvial unit above a tuff with a potassium–argon date of 0.66 million BP (Bishop 1978, and unpublished information). On the margins of the Nakuru–Naivasha basin there is another important Acheulian site at Kariandusi. Here both rolled and unrolled artifacts are found in mixed fluvial and lacustrine deposits, mainly tuff-derived and of sand grade, but including primary volcanic ash and pumice, on top of diatomites (McCall, Baker and Walsh 1967). Potassium–argon dates of 0.93, 0.95, 1.1 and 3.1 million BP are of uncertain reliability, but an age in the vicinity of one million years is not unreasonable.

Further south in the Kenya Rift is the Olorgesailie basin with its cluster of Acheulian sites. These are found within a thick sequence of interdigitated lacustrine and alluvial deposits, both derived over-whelmingly from volcanic material, thrown out by nascent rift floor volcanoes (Isaac 1972a, 1977). The great majority of the sites are linked to sandy or gravelly stream channels, at some distance from contemporaneous lakeshores or swamps. There is also a correlation between channel bars (riffles) and artifact or bone concentrations, implying sorting by water action. Potassium–argon dates of o.425 and o.486 million BP appear to be relevant to these former occupations.

The Natron basin, south of the Tanzania border, includes some of the earliest Acheulian occurrences as well as an isolated australopithecine mandible, the former younger, the latter older than a basalt with normal geomagnetic polarity and six potassium–argon dates ranging from o.96 to 2.27 million BP. This evidence implies an age of between 1.3 and 1.6 million years (Isaac 1972a, b; Isaac and Curtis 1974). The sedimentary matrix is part of a thick sequence of alluvial, lacustrine, and volcanic beds accumulating in a subsiding trough. The sites are associated with sandy alluvial fans or deltaic channels, coeval with a relatively low lake level.

The roster of key Rift Valley locations is completed by the many 'Developed Oldowan' and Acheulian sites from Olduvai Gorge, including upper Bed II, Beds III–IV, and part of the overlying sequence – ranging from about 1.4 to o.2 million years in age (M. D. Leakey 1975). Deposits pertain to the zone of interplay between small lakes or evaporation pans in the basin centre, and an alluvial surface rising to the piedmont (foothills) of nearby volcanoes. The artifact clusters are primarily associated with lake-margin palaeosols and clays that probably represent dried mudflats and marshes, and clayey to gravelly sands that mark stream beds or channel margins (Hay 1976; Kleindienst 1973). The extent to which the alluvial sites (which account for most of the Acheulian concentrations) are undisturbed is not clear, but in at least one case there may be coincidence with a channel bar.

In effect, most of the mid-Pleistocene archaeological occurrences of the Kenya rift come from basin-floor, alluvial contexts, primarily ephemeral or seasonal streams. There is no consistent indication of a regional environment substantially moister than that of today, although discrete, expanded lake episodes can be identified. These relatively low basins also provide no discernible record of the several episodes of glaciation recorded on Mount Kilimanjaro: the second of these glaciations predates a basalt flow of 460 000 BP (Downie 1964, Evernden and Curtis 1965).

In south central Tanzania, the mid-Pleistocene deposits of Isimila include a number of important Acheulian occurrences, related either to a small, closed basin or a tropical dambo, i.e. a valley-floor accumulation with channel sands alternating with clayey units and intergrading with finer-grained lateral rainwash deposits. One such site was situated on the sands of an occasionally active flat, within a braided channel and associated with shrubby vegetation; another was linked to a low interfluve, flanking a channel, and with abundant herbaceous vegetation (Hansen and Keller 1971). Bone from the lower part of the sequence has given a plausible but not unproblematical date of about 260 000 years (Cole and Kleindienst 1974).

From a somewhat comparable environment come the large Acheulian collections from Nsongezi, on the Kagera River of the Tanzania–Uganda border. These occur in secondary contexts, however – in sands, gravels, and rubble lag of complex cut-and-fill beds within an alluvial–lacustrine sequence (Cole 1967).

Perhaps the most informative East African site complex of this period is that of Kalambo Falls, situated on the Zambia–Tanzania border, near Lake Tanganyika, in a small basin just above the fault escarpment. Acheulian concentrations come from 3 m of fine sands interbedded with organic clays and thin lenticles of pebbles (Clark 1969). Good pollen records with preservation of partial tree trunks, branches, leaves, seed pods and fruits indicate repeated vegetation changes contemporaneous with this unit. Pollen spectra from the lowest beds infer swamp and gallery forest at the riverside and a semideciduous dry forest beyond, i.e. a climate warmer and drier than that of today. The intermediate horizons indicate a poorly developed riverine forest, with mixed semideciduous and evergreen dry forest suggestive of a cooler (3 °C?) and wetter (150% of modern rainfall?) environment. The upper beds imply a setting little different from that of today. There is a protein racemization date (on wood) of *at least* 110 000 BP for the five Acheulian living floors that were occupied on sandy to gravelly river banks during the low-water season.

Acheulian sites have also been studied in southern Zaïre, at Kamoa, near Kolwezi (Cahen 1975), in north-eastern Angola at Mufo in the Lunda region (Clark 1963) and near the Victoria Falls in Zambia (Clark 1950, 1975a). Apart from artifacts in one or more alluvial terraces, better sites have been found under or within colluvial deposits, derived from lateritic rubble or aeolian sands, and transported under semi-arid conditions, with an incomplete, grassy vegetation.

The site contexts and sequences reviewed here caution against the assumption that the mid Pleistocene was palaeoclimatically uneventful in East Africa. However, the magnitude and biological impact of the changes implied should not be overemphasized. As Isaac (1975) argues, the complex vertical and horizontal zonation of ecological opportunities in East Africa practically assures the survival of all basic econiches through climatic vicissitudes even of the scale apparent in the late Pleistocene record. However, very significant changes in regional biomass were possible, if not probable, and their ecological significance for early man should not be underestimated. The points to be made here are that environmental changes have occurred throughout the East African Pleistocene, that the details and explanation of these changes are still obscure, but that whatever the scale of any such changes, they were insufficient to eliminate the fundamental ecological mosaic (Butzer 1974a).

## Southern Africa

The Vaal River of South Africa has provided one of the classic sequences of alluvial terraces and industrial successions (Söhnge *et al.* 1937). The Older Gravels, which lack convincing artifacts in undisturbed contexts, represent thin, calcreted conglomerates resting on much older planation surfaces (Butzer *et al.* 1973a, Helgren 1978). Judging by a number of faunal remains of unknown provenance, these Older Gravels span some or all of the Pliocene, possibly extending into the early Pleistocene (Cooke and Maglio 1972, Helgren 1977). Three generations of Younger Gravels have provided a later Middle Pleistocene fauna and a number of secondary Acheulian collections, such as those from Klip River, Pniel (Power's site, in part relatively undisturbed) and Canteen Koppie. Most of these artifactual occurrences suggest channel sites occupied between times when the river was flowing vigorously or when considerable erosion of the slopes was taking place. Another important, if disturbed assemblage (of 'Developed Oldowan' aspect) comes from Cornelia, in a minor Vaal tributary. Here artifacts are found in a basal, gravelly valley fill, succeeded by several units of clayey or silty alluvia, some of which include a rich Middle Pleistocene fauna substantially older than 300 000 years (Butzer, Clark and Cooke 1974, Szabo 1979).

Of particular interest are several cave sites. In the Transvaal, both the Sterkfontein Extension Site and Swartkrans have yielded 'Developed Oldowan' artifacts (M. D. Leakey 1970), and recent faunal studies have further shown the presence of substantial Middle Pleistocene faunas (Vrba 1975). Brain (1976) simultaneously isolated a major, younger sedimentary unit at Swartkrans which includes most of the artifacts as well as the '*Telanthropus*' mandible. These mid-Pleistocene deposits imply a long period with an external environment similar to or slightly moister than that of today (Butzer 1976a). Similar younger units have also been recognized at Sterkfontein (Partridge 1975). Another major cave site of this period is Broken Hill (Kabwe), Zambia, where fissure fills provided an archaic *Homo sapiens* skull, a late Middle Pleistocene fauna and, in overlying or external soil sediments (of uncertain association), a range of late Acheulian to Middle Stone Age artifacts (Clark 1959, 1975b; Klein 1973). A last example is that of Montagu Cave in the Cape, on the margin of the Karroo semidesert. Here a long Acheulian sequence, of presumed late Middle Pleistocene age, is interbedded with lenticles of sand and silt that include oxide-stained silcrete grains of possible aeolian origin (Butzer 1973a).

Lakeshore sites are represented by Doornlaagte and Rooidam, near Kimberley (Butzer 1974b). The former represents a semi-primary Acheulian occupation in an evaporation pan: the location once saw long intervals with standing water, interrupted by repeated desiccation with some aeolian sedimentation and episodic, torrential runoff that swept an influx of crude sediment across the exposed, gently-sloping margins of the pan. Rooidam is a full geomorphic cycle younger and represents a late Acheulian ('Fauresmith'), possibly undisturbed occupation site. It was situated on an aeolian ridge bordering directly on a shallow, periodic lake fed by rainfall and surface runoff. A freshwater limestone 2 m above this occupation level is dated 174 000 ± 20 000 BP by uranium series (Szabo and Butzer 1979). The lithostratigraphic columns at Doornlaagte and Rooidam indicate two long intervals of mixed lacustrine and aeolian accumulation, each terminated by soil formation. A similar pattern with repeated moist intervals is recorded by several cycles of greatly augmented spring discharge on the dolomite Gaap Escarpment (Butzer 1974c). Each of these cycles led to large-scale accumulations of calcareous tufas, in the form of several generations of tufa aprons and carapaces that each rest on a basal rubble of stream, rain- or slope-wash origin that, in part, may have been related to accelerated frost-weathering.

A unique Acheulian spring site is found at Amanzi, near Uitenhage in the south-eastern Cape. Several occupations, in part relatively undisturbed, were located around marshy and well-vegetated spring eyes, at a time of accelerated artesian discharge (Butzer 1973b).

Finally, there are a number of Acheulian sites scattered along much of the Cape and Natal coasts. Some of these were incorporated directly into pebble or cobble beaches, others are linked with lag gravels later eroded from such beaches, and others still are found among former coastal dunes (Butzer and Helgren 1972). Most of these aeolianite sites were apparently related to spring seeps in hollows among stabilized dunes; today they are mainly found in secondary contexts, within rain-wash deposits reworked from various mid-Pleistocene palaeosols (e.g. Brakkloof near Robberg, Geelhoutboom near Klasies River). A significant exception is the Elandsfontein site, near Hopefield, with the Saldanha cranium and a rich Middle Pleistocene mammalian fauna, as well as an assemblage of bones and associated Acheulian artifacts in a relatively undisturbed context. This site was originally located on a stabilized, gently-undulating aeolian surface, at a time when poorly-drained hollows were linked by a number of seasonal streams (Butzer 1973c). Contemporary pollens indicate an open vegetation of bushveld aspect, with some aquatic plants.

The full range of environmental variation in the Cape coast can perhaps be best appreciated on the margins of the perhumid Knysna rainforest, where creation of dune fields repeatedly alternated with formation of deep, semitropical soils of lateritic type (Helgren and Butzer 1977).

Unlike East Africa, where topographic and soil variation is pronounced, southern Africa is rather more uniform, so that any significant environmental changes would necessarily have initiated large-scale rearrangement of the ecological zones. Hints as to magnitude and duration of mid-Pleistocene climatic variation are given by the sequences alluded to above from the Vaal River, the Gaap Escarpment, and the southern Cape coast. These all indicate significant, long-term changes in the volume of water in the rivers or in spring and aeolian activity. So, for example, four or more tufa-accretion cycles of the Gaap are hardly explicable without a rainfall of at least 600–800 mm (compared with 300–400 mm today). Short-term climatic oscillations were superimposed upon these long-term trends, as is illustrated by the mixed lacustrine and weathering products in the sedimentary sequences of Doornlaagte and Rooidam.

At the very least, this South African evidence suggests that mid-Pleistocene environmental patterns were far from stable or predictable. However, there are no useful temporal frameworks, and inter-regional correlations are difficult or impossible. No realistic estimate can be made as to the number of major climatic cycles recorded in southern Africa, and the broad trends suggested here cannot now be correlated with any global events (Butzer et al. 1978a).

*Faunas associated with the Acheulian*

The stone tools found in deposits older than the Pliocene–Pleistocene boundary belong exclusively to the Oldowan industry, which at Olduvai Gorge ranges up through Bed I and the lower part of Bed II, above which is the 'Developed Oldowan'. At Olduvai, the Acheulian industry appears rather abruptly in the middle of Bed II, where an age of 1.4 to 1.5 million years may be regarded as a reliable estimate. The related Karari Industry of East Rudolf has a very similar age, so the appearance of the hand-axe culture may be placed with some confidence at about 1.5 million years BP.

At Casablanca in North Africa and at Rooidam in South Africa, late Acheulian tools occur in deposits estimated to have an age slightly older than 200 000 years, so that this industry ranges through much of the Pleistocene.

Most of the archaeological sites with Acheulian artifacts are isolated deposits covering a very limited part of the record and are difficult to correlate on stratigraphic grounds; fossil material is often scanty and palaeontological correlation difficult. The best stratigraphic sequences with good dating controls are those of Olduvai Gorge, the Omo area and East Rudolf, and these must at present provide the general framework for interpretation. Good faunas from other areas do not suggest any conflict in the evidence.

The mammal fauna of the late Pliocene included a very few forms not separable from the living species, while a number of others are obviously related to living forms, although specifically separable. In addition, however, there were a considerable number of forms that were separable at the generic level but which have not left obvious descendants in the living fauna. There is no evidence for dramatic or sudden changes but rather for progressive extinction of the Plio–Pleistocene taxa and a steady increase in the proportion of now living species. A few extinct species survived into the late Pleistocene or even the Holocene and in some respects the faunas of Acheulian times were a little richer and more varied than those of the present day.

As yet the small mammals, such as the insectivores, rodents, etc., are known from too few sites for any clear picture to emerge, but great interest attaches to these creatures as indicators of local environments and work on them is under way in several areas. The primates are seldom abundant and those that are found are principally the larger forms, especially baboons and colobus monkeys. In South Africa, the extinct genera of baboons and other Old World monkeys (*Parapapio* and *Cercopithecoides*) are important in the australopithecine deposits, together with other extinct species of baboon (*Papio*), but only the latter is also found in Acheulian associations. In East Africa, *Papio* and the gelada baboon (*Theropithecus*) are the most important forms, both in the later Pliocene and in the Pleistocene, but *Cercopithecoides* also occurs in the former. The hominids will be discussed at length in chapter 2.

Carnivores are not common but a fair range of species is represented. The viverrids (mongooses, etc.) belong to living genera, as do the canids and mustelids (weasel family), but the hyaenids and felids are dominated by extinct genera in the pre-Acheulian deposits; few of these extinct genera occur after the early Pleistocene and none after the middle Acheulian. Among the proboscideans (elephants), the gomphotheres do not survive and the most important elephant is *Elephas recki*, represented in the Pliocene by an early stage and in Acheulian associations by an advanced to very advanced stage. In North Africa, *E. recki* is fairly rare and the most important and characteristic species is *Loxodonta atlantica*, which displaces the typical Plio–Pleistocene *Mammuthus africanavus*; *M. meridionalis* is also found, but has not been recorded in deposits with hand-axes. *Loxodonta atlantica* occurs throughout Africa and is succeeded by the living species *L. africana* in the Upper Pleistocene. The curious *Deinotherium bosazi* has a long range, from the later Miocene to the middle of Bed II at Olduvai, but it does not seem to occur with hand-axes. In South Africa, a few archaic elephant fossils have been found in the Younger Gravels of the Vaal River, with typical Acheulian tools and a Middle Pleistocene fauna, but it seems likely that these specimens were derived from older gravel deposits in the valley.

Among the Perissodactyla (odd-toed ungulates, e.g. horse, rhinoceros, etc.), chalicotheres (extinct three-toed ungulates) occur as fairly rare elements in pre-Acheulian associations, but are not recorded from deposits with bifacial tools. The rhinoceroses are reduced to the two living species, which range back well into the Pliocene. The three-toed horse (*Hipparion*) continues throughout the Acheulian, the typical species being *H. libycum*, which possesses very high crowned teeth, commonly with an extra external pillar (ectostylid) in the lowers. *Equus* (true horse) makes its appearance before the Acheulian and both living and extinct species range up to the Holocene.

Artiodactyls (even-toed ungulates such as pigs, hippopotamus, deer, etc.) are the most plentiful fossils in Pleistocene deposits – indeed the only fossils found on many sites. The pigs were a rapidly evolving group and may be useful for broad zonation and correlation. The most widespread genus is *Kolpochoerus* ( = *Mesochoerus*), which appeared in the mid Pliocene, but it does not survive beyond the end of the Acheulian. A characteristic pig in deposits with hand-axes is *Stylochoerus*, but the living wart-hog *Phacochoerus* also seems to range back to the beginning of the Acheulian. Hippopotami are not as varied as in the Pliocene but are found at many sites. The commonest Acheulian form in East Africa is *Hippopotamus gorgops*, which at Olduvai shows progressive evolution up to Bed IV, but has not been noted in later deposits; it also occurs at Cornelia in South Africa. *Hippopotamus amphibius* is present throughout the Middle and Upper Pleistocene.

Among the giraffids, the extinct *Sivatherium* ranges from the Pliocene to the Middle Pleistocene, but does not occur in the Upper Pleistocene. *Giraffa* is represented by two or three extinct species in the Pliocene and early Pleistocene, one of which persists through much of the Acheulian; the scanty material usually makes it difficult to distinguish it from the living *G. camelopardalis*, which certainly existed in the later Acheulian and may be older. Deer do not occur south of the Sahara during the Pleistocene, but in North Africa both *Cervus elaphus* and *Dama dama* are found in deposits containing hand-axes. Camel is found in the later Pliocene and in the Pleistocene both in North and East Africa, but is rare and difficult to identify at the species level.

Bovids are the most plentiful of the artiodactyls and there has been an almost complete turnover from wholly extinct species in the late Pliocene to almost exclusively living species by the Upper Pleistocene.[1] The taxa represented are mainly from the East African record though most also occur in southern Africa. Gazelles are important in North Africa, where, in contrast, the alcelaphines (hartebeest family) are particularly scarce.

Unfortunately, as has been mentioned earlier the assemblages of the larger mammals from open sites are not very sensitive indicators of the environments as they represent a general savanna association. Usually both bush-loving species and inhabitants of the drier open grassland are found together and it is sometimes possible to make broad inferences

---

[1] In East Africa, typical extinct species of pre-Acheulian times include *Taurotragus arkelli*, *Tragelaphus gaudryi*, *T. maryanus*, *T. nakuae*, *Menelikia lyrocera*, *Kobus sigmoidalis*, *K. ancystrocera*, *Redunca darti*, *Simatherium kohl-larseni*, *Connochaetes africanus*, *Beatragus antiquus*, *Parmularius altidens*, an early *Aepyceros*, and several species of gazelles. Typical hand-axe associates include *Taurotragus oryx*, *Tragelaphus grandis*, *Pelorovis oldowayensis*, *Kobus ellipsiprymnus*, the living species of *Redunca*, *Hippotragus gigas*, *Damaliscus niro*, *Rabaticeras arambourgi*, varieties of *Connochaetes gnou* and *C. taurinus*, one or two species of the extinct genus *Megalotragus*, *Aepyceros melampus*, *Antidorcas recki*, and several gazelle species.

from the relative proportions of these elements. However, local circumstances may have strong influences, as also may spells of drought or abnormal rainfall, and the assemblages of fossils probably represent the integrated effects of many years or even decades. It would seem that the assemblages represent the typical 'game park' environment, embracing the characteristic habitats of the larger herbivores and the carnivores that prey upon them.

### Acheulian environment in Africa

Altogether, the mid-Pleistocene record of tropical Africa remains incoherent, despite some promising local sequences. There is no paucity of evidence for environmental change as such, but the nature and patterns of such changes are still problematical. Many more years of fieldwork will be necessary before it can be decided whether or not regional climatostratigraphies can indeed be established, and it is highly doubtful even now that major climatic changes can be simply followed from one climatic province to another. Consequently, the tropical African record does not yet contribute much toward an understanding of the mid Pleistocene. At the same time, it clearly shows that the climatic cycles of higher latitudes are presently of little or no value in analysing mid-Pleistocene records of the tropical continents (Butzer 1974a).

The data presented here illustrate how a good part of recent geo-archaeological research in mid-Pleistocene time-ranges has concentrated on local lithostratigraphic work. Despite initial misgivings by most workers involved, it is increasingly apparent that such 'floating' geological contexts, where there is no opportunity to obtain radiometric dates, are a successful means of approaching stratigraphic problems of the Middle Pleistocene in Africa. Floating stratigraphies also encourage a pragmatic interpretation of site contexts in terms of their environment and regional settings (Butzer 1974a).

At the level of Acheulian man and his settlement patterns, it can be shown that Acheulian occurrences are widely dispersed in Africa, everywhere except in the present rainforest and moist savanna woodland (Clark 1967, 1975b). However, the site contexts reviewed here tend to narrow the apparent range of ecological opportunities exploited. The Acheulian in presently arid settings of the Sahara and the Kalahari borderlands is notably restricted to former alluvial or lakeshore locations, and evidently coincided with periods of wetter climate. Even in the coastal dune environments of the Cape, occupations were related to wet microenvironments and coeval with times of dune stabilization and soil formation under more favourable climatic conditions. Those sites now found in wetter, woodland settings were occupied during intervals of relatively open vegetation or during the drier times of the year. So, for example, the sandy to gravelly stream beds at Isimila, Nsongezi and Kalambo Falls argue for highly periodic runoff and incomplete ground cover within each catchment.

It would seem, therefore, that Acheulian settlement was, at any one time, dispersed through semi-arid to subhumid environments, with open or parkland vegetation. Within this macrosystem, sites were preferentially located near water sources: stream channels, springs, limestone or dolomite caves, lakeshores and coasts. These locales also coincide with the lower elevation range represented within each region, although this may be due in part to the erosion prevalent in upland areas. Extensive and extended use of adjacent uplands (in part with less predictable water supplies) is not precluded, but the persistent paucity of even scattered surface artifacts away from water or raw-material sources does suggest that occupation sites were significantly restricted in their distribution. The basic Acheulian adaptations were, surprisingly, maintained with little obvious change through the course of a million years.

## THE AFRICA OF THE MIDDLE STONE AGE
### AND LATER STONE AGE

*Stratigraphy and chronology of the late Pleistocene and Holocene*

The Middle Stone Age and Later Stone Age are concepts originally devised in southern Africa to describe the range of archaeological materials clearly younger than the Acheulian (or Earlier Stone Age) (Goodwin and Van Riet Lowe 1929). The designations were subsequently extended to eastern Africa. The time span in question, including problematic transition phases such as the First and Second Intermediate periods, was originally thought to be in the order of 25 000 to 40 000 years – extending upwards to the European contact period. Systematic radiocarbon dating and geological examination of key sites have recently shown that the Later Stone Age began no later than 38 000 BP in some parts of South Africa, that many Middle Stone Age sites are older than 50 000 years (Beaumont and Vogel 1972, Butzer 1978a, Butzer, Beaumont and Vogel 1978), and that they are sometimes linked with the high interglacial sea level of about 125 000 BP (Klasies River and Robberg). This view finds additional support in a number of amino-acid dates from Klasies River (Bada and Deems 1975), though these are somewhat problematical, and a terminal date of close to 0.2 million BP for the youngest Acheulian ('Fauresmith') implied by the uranium age for Rooidam. In Ethiopia, potassium–argon dates are believed to place the Middle Stone Age at more than 181 000 BP (Wendorf *et al.* 1974).

As the increased industrial complexity of the Middle Stone Age and Later Stone Age becomes evident, these terms are being reduced to the role of broad concepts that have much the same chronological status as do the Middle and Upper Palaeolithic (plus Neolithic) in Europe and northern Africa. In the present context, Middle and Later Stone Age are informally used, as a matter of convenience, as being approximately coincident with the time-periods of the Upper Pleistocene and early to mid-Holocene, that is from before 130 000 to about 2000 BP.

The record of environmental change over the last 130 000 years in Africa includes a wide range of phenomena. In particular, the continuing paucity of good polliniferous deposits is offset both by the faunal assemblages and by several indicators of past environmental changes provided by soils and geomorphic factors. However, few local sequences record any great time depth, and interpretation is rendered difficult by the inadequate understanding of contemporary processes, by the limited intensity of geomorphologic research in recent decades, and by the nature of the data themselves, which seldom allow precise information as to the amplitude of climatic change. Exceptions to this are situations where the relevant factors can be narrowed down or simplified by reasonable assumptions, e.g. in closed lake basins, where variations in the water supply can sometimes be reconstructed. Less satisfactory but also of some value are the upward or downward movements of vegetation zones or other evidence of specific cold-climate phenomena, including mountain glaciation. Least informative for quantitative reconstructions may be changes of the weathering/erosion balance, stream regimen, or spring discharge. Yet each category of information does ultimately contribute to filling out the qualitative picture and, in conjunction with radiocarbon dating, is now providing an increasingly detailed impression of the directions and extent of environmental changes during at least the last 20 000–30 000 years. The subsequent discussion provides synopses of available information from the basic regions of Africa (for more detailed reviews see Butzer (1971a, ch. 20, 1978b)).

## North Africa and the Sahara

The late Pleistocene of the Maghrib is best represented on low-lying coastal sectors. Here one or more interglacial beaches rise a little above the watermark and occasionally produce warm-loving mollusca with, in Morocco, uranium dates of 75 000–145 000 BP (Stearns and Thurber 1967). Not all these beaches were synchronous, but the youngest set, known as the Ouljian (II), provides a distinct stratigraphic marker in many areas. It is overlain by several sets of rainwash soils (*limons rouges*), often calcreted, followed by cemented coastal dunes (aeolianites) that primarily record falling sea levels accompanying glacial growth in higher latitudes. At the mouths of the streams, this rainwash material and sand dunes may intergrade with locally thick waterborne deposits that extend up into the high country. Elsewhere, they are linked to fossiliferous 'red beds' in a variety of caves. In the mountains, glaciers grew in snow-fed basins, while adjacent slopes were subject to stripping and redeposition of rubble into characteristic 'periglacial' deposits that record deep and effective soil frost. At lower elevations these 'periglacial' rubbles pass into coarse valley fills.

The degree of late Pleistocene cold is impressively recorded by a downward movement of the vegetation belts in Morocco by some 1000–1200 m (Messerli 1967). In general, the environment was sufficiently harsh and seasonally arid so as to be almost treeless, both in the uplands and on the coastal plains (Butzer 1971a, ch. 19; 1975a). Widespread soil and slope denudation speak for an incomplete ground-cover. By contrast, the preceding interglacial was a time of soil stability with limited accumulation of valley deposits. A number of pollen cores in the Mediterranean basin suggest that most of the time-span from 125 000 to 70 000 BP was also characterized by warm–temperate to subtropical woodland vegetation in much of the Maghrib (Butzer 1975a, b). Most of the Holocene was a carbon copy of this interglacial pattern, and there is little substantial evidence of significant Holocene climatic change in the Mediterranean environments of North Africa.

Along the arid to semi-arid littoral of Libya, late Pleistocene and Holocene environmental patterns were of a similar kind, with the onset of glaciation locally marked by accelerated spring activity, and with the glacial maxima cold and accompanied by torrential, periodic runoff and the production of frost-weathered rubble on hillslopes and inside caves.

The Sahara itself was conspicuously less arid during the late interglacial to early glacial time range. Spotty but nonetheless convincing pollen evidence speaks for immigration of Mediterranean or sub-Mediterranean floras along the major river systems and into the moister high country, and open woodlands were probably to be found among the mountains (Van Campo 1975) where the highest peaks (Ahaggar, Tibesti) were subject to local glaciation or frost sculpture during the glacial maximum (Butzer 1973d).

In the Egyptian deserts, it is possible to determine the stratigraphic sequence with reasonable clarity. Beyond the range of radiocarbon dating are several periods of increased stream and spring discharge on the Red Sea coast, in the desert catchment of the Nile and in the Libyan Desert (Kurkur Oasis) (Butzer 1979, Butzer and Hansen 1968). The last of these early wet phases terminated by 25 000 BP and was followed by a climate as dry as that of today. Increased wadi flow is once more apparent from about 17 500 to 8 500 BP (interrupted by several brief but dramatic interludes of reduced stream activity) and again at about 6000–5000 BP, with a period of notable biochemical weathering and soil stability at about 7000 BP. The last phase of accelerated desert runoff dates to the fourth millennium BC, with modern conditions of hyper-aridity established early in Old Kingdom times (Butzer 1976c). These 'late glacial' to mid-Holocene moist intervals were modest, however, and they did not compare with the intensity of earlier wet phases that temporarily produced sub-arid conditions in favoured topographic areas of the Sahara.

A somewhat different climatic sequence has been established for the Saoura Valley, which receives much of its water from the Saharan Atlas (Chavaillon 1964, Conrad 1969). The first of the Saouran fill units (I), dating to more than 40 000 BP, includes organic beds with pollen; but only 6% tree genera are represented, mainly willow, while sedges and reeds are abundant. Unit III (about 34 000–16 000 BP) includes a number of lacustrine beds that appear to correlate with cold-climate deposits in the high Ahaggar and Tibesti as well as with other calcareous lake deposits of the Algerian Sahara that range from more than 35 000 to 17 500 BP. The next, younger cluster of radiocarbon dates, related to marshy soils or lake beds, is at 6600–3000 BP. This 'Neolithic subpluvial' saw a last, temporary improvement of the vegetation, but the frequency of reworked pollen from older beds makes reconstructions from palynological data problematical.

Distinctive patterns are also evident in the monsoonal rainfall belt of the southern Sahara, as exemplified by the Chad basin (Butzer 1978b, Servant, Servant and Délibrias 1969). Two not very well substantiated rises in lake level occurred prior to 21 000 BP; they were followed by a long interval of desiccation and aeolian activity until shortly before 12 000 BP, when the lake began to expand once more. Expansion was interrupted a little before 10 300 BP but then continued, the lake reaching a maximum level with at least intermittent overflows at about 10 000 BP. This high lake stand, with a water surface of 400 000 sq. km, was interrupted by recessions at about 8500, 7500 and again at 6500 BP, terminating at about 4000 BP. The dry interval from somewhat before 21 000 to about 12000 BP saw dune fields invade the savanna across a broad belt from the Atlantic coast to the Nile Valley, suggesting a decline of rainfall from 750 to 150 mm in northern Nigeria (Grove and Warren 1968). The Senegal River dwindled to the extent that dune fields choked off its delta.

## East Africa

With some short breaks, the volume of water in the Nile, also derived from the monsoonal rains of tropical Africa, was greater than today through most of the 'last glacial', until about 4500 BP. In detail, high Nile floods in the period 24 000–18 000 BP can be satisfactorily explained by reduced evaporation over highland Ethiopia, while floods from about 17 500 to 12 000 BP were sufficiently violent to sweep gravel, derived by accelerated local runoff from Sudanese tributaries, right through to Cairo, thereby indicating unusually strong rains in the central Sahara, e.g. in the Tibesti (Butzer 1978b, Butzer *et al.* 1972). A 'wild' Nile, with repeated catastrophic floods of twice the present amplitude, is indicated in the period 12 000–11 500 BP.

This nilotic record is only partly compatible with the lake record (Livingstone 1975), best examplified by Lake Rudolf (Butzer, Brown and Thurber 1969, Butzer *et al.* 1972). One high level of Lake Rudolf involved a rise of 60 to 80 m from shortly before 9500 BP to a little after 7200 BP. A second rise of some 60 to 70 m was accomplished in a few centuries after 6600 BP, terminating at perhaps 4000 BP but followed by a further brief rise of similar extent shortly before 3200 BP. These three rises in level of 60 to 80 m within a 7000-year span had a duration of 1 to 3 millennia each and, with a cumulative thickness of 21 m of related deposits, constitute Member IV of the Kibish Formation. Probably comparable is the record of Member III (45 m thick, before 37 000 BP) with two rises in level, Member II (22.5 m thick, date uncertain) with a single rise, and Member I (over 26 m thick, about 130 000 BP?) with two further rises. Consequently, most of the later Pleistocene experienced a moisture regime comparable to that of the present day, although there have been repeated, relatively brief periods of conspicuous lake expansion at long intervals. These moister intervals each included one or more high-lake events, each lasting a few millennia. It seems increasingly probable that the three ancient phases of deep lakes (Members I–II–III) were contemporaneous with the 'last interglacial', about 130 000–70 000 BP. The 'last glacial', about 70 000–10 000 BP, was in the main part conspicuously dry, with desert varnish and sub-arid soil formation in the Rudolf basin (Butzer 1976b).

Lakes Nakuru and Naivasha were high at some time prior to 20 000 to 30 000 BP, then low until 12 000 BP, reaching maximum levels at about 10 000–7500 and again at about 6600–3000 BP (Butzer *et al.* 1972). A similar history is indicated for Lake Victoria (Livingstone 1975). Computations for the Nakuru–Naivasha basin indicate a 50–65% increase of rainfall for these early Holocene high lakes. It is interesting that the late 'last glacial' dry interval saw a major downward movement of the alpine vegetation belt in Kenya and Ethiopia (Coetzee 1967, E. M. van Zinderen Bakker, personal communication), as well as an advance of the high mountain glaciers. A lowering of the snowline by some 1000–1200 m, coeval with a drier climate, implies a lowering of the temperature of at very least 6.5–8.0 °C. Low lakes at a time of cooler climate emphasize the degree of 'late glacial' aridity.

The Rudolf record underscores a surprising fact, that the full range of moisture fluctuations of the past 5 million years has probably been reproduced within the 10 000 years of Holocene time. Altogether, climatic 'stability' in East Africa is precarious, and difficult to define. So, for example, a non-outlet lake such as Rudolf was 15 m higher than today in 1896 but 5 m lower in 1955, while the range of fluctuation for the past two millennia is greater than 40 m (Butzer, 1971c).

It is fortunate that a number of deep-sea cores, spanning several oceanic circulation segments, have been studied off the coast of East Africa by Olausson *et al.* (1971). Here, each of the two cool interludes (about 110 000 BP and 95 000 BP) (Butzer 1975a) which subdivided the 'last interglacial' saw the trade-wind circulations weakened for some 2000 years with a greater expanse of cold, upwelling waters off the Somali coast. The onset of the 'last glacial' (perhaps 65 000 BP) was almost instantaneous, lasting less than 1000 years, leading to an 8000-year span with increasing upwelling. The second submaximum of the 'last glacial' (about 20 000 BP) was preceded by a 1500-year transition and lasted only 3000 years. Whereas summer temperature deviations were greatest during the first half of the glacial phase, variations in winter cold were greatest during the second half. All but the very last of these cooling trends were surprisingly rapid, evidently in response to sudden, primary changes of the general circulation. The abruptness and brevity of the oceanic circulation shifts documented in these Indian Ocean cores compare well with those of climatic changes in the East African continental record.

## Central and southern Africa

The vicissitudes of the Congo and Guinea rainforests during the late Pleistocene remain poorly understood. The expanded lake filling the Chad basin prior to 21 000 and after 12 000 BP was fed primarily by the Chari and Logone, which derive their waters from the northern fringes of the Congo forest. Similarly, dune activation across northern Nigeria during some ten millennia before about 12 000 BP implies a shrinkage of the Guinea forest belt. There are, indeed, waterborne gravels in many parts of the rainforest that argue for reduced ground cover and longer intervals between flooding. Furthermore, the ancient Kalahari Sands in western Zaïre and Congo were repeatedly subject to wind erosion and reworking during the course of the Quaternary. The problem is one of obtaining a number of well-dated, long and informative sequences in several critical areas. The only two successions currently available come from the southern perimeter of the forest belt, at Kalambo Falls and Mufo.

At Kalambo Falls, gravelly sands with interbedded organic clays are heavily oxidized, as a result of a high but fluctuating watertable, and associated pollen argues for a cooler and moister environment; this unit includes Sangoan occupations with dates of about 46 000–37 500 BP (Clark 1969) that are substantially too young. A new sequence of infilling, with Lupemban (Middle Stone Age) sites, began somewhat before 32 000 and may have continued until as late as 27 500 BP. The pollen spectra suggest a well-developed fringing forest, wet grassy lowlands and a semideciduous dry woodland on higher ground, i.e. conditions both moister and somewhat warmer. In view of revised dating of the Middle Stone Age in southern Africa, there is reason to believe that this warm, moist phase is older than 70 000 BP. A long, presumably dry period with erosion followed until a little before 10 000 BP, when a cool, humid environment was reconstituted for several millennia. The subsequent record at Kalambo Falls is more difficult to interpret, but includes three episodes of renewed deposition by water, the second of which began at about 4000 BP, the last at about 1500 BP.

In the Mufo area, the late Pleistocene apparently begins with the accumulation of a secondary laterite formed by rainwater erosion and deposition; this material was subsequently ferruginized by iron compounds released during the course of intensive weathering on the slopes, and accumulated in the valley subsoil at a time of high watertable (Clark 1963). Subsequently, a long period of drier conditions is indicated by (1) stream deposits that date shortly after 40 000 BP (but may well be older) and include pollen suggestive of a very open vegetation, and (2) thick windblown and runoff sands on slopes and uplands that rest on Sangoan surfaces and include Lupemban artifacts. This early- or mid-'last glacial' record implies aeolian activity on the interfluves and accelerated denudation of poorly vegetated slopes, a pattern apparently widespread in both north-eastern Angola and much of Zaïre. Subsequently, conditions were moister since, in the valleys, the subsoil again became ferruginized, followed by stream deposition of oxidized sands and organic clays that include late Lupemban artifacts and predominantly arboreal pollen. A further phase of wind activity is dated at about 13 000 BP or earlier, and this was followed by renewed stream action and the re-establishment of the open woodland at about 7000–4500 BP and again after 2000 BP, the two phases being separated by a final period of wind action.

These two sequences with their partial but significant differences caution against making generalizations between regions in central as in West Africa.

Distinct patterns can also be recognized in southern Africa, one in the present summer-rainfall province of the interior, the other in the winter-rainfall belt of the Cape coast and the Cape Folded Ranges. Most but not all of the cooler, 'glacial' periods were relatively moist in the interior, with further moist episodes recurring during the Holocene. In the coastal regions, the coldest intervals were very dry, the interstadial-age warming trends apparently being a little more moist, as was the second half of the Holocene (Butzer et al. 1978a). Several categories of evidence can be marshalled to determine rainfall levels in both regions.

On the Gaap Escarpment, increased spring activity is shown by several thick deposits (carapaces) of tufa, dating to well before 32 000 BP; subsequently, minor tufa waterfalls developed at about 21 000–14 000, 9700–7600, 3200–2400 and, on a very local scale only, 1400–400 BP (Butzer et al. 1978a). These relatively brief wet phases were broadly coeval with swampy floodplain aggradations along the Vaal River and its major tributaries (Riverton Formation, Members III–IV–V) well prior to 38 000, 17 000–13 500 and at about 4500–1300 BP (Butzer *et al.* 1973a, 1979; Helgren 1979). The intervening periods were dry, with minimal spring activity on the dolomite escarpment, gullying in the valleys and local wind activity in sandy areas. Earlier alluvial silts of the Vaal River, postdating the Younger Gravels, are known but remain difficult to date.

In the upland 'pans', or closed, shallow basins, as exemplified at Alexandersfontein, deep lakes were created including a 10-m deep, non-outlet lake with an area of about 35 sq. km, during the early Upper Pleistocene (Butzer *et al.* 1973b, 1979). Accelerated spring activity and more intensive soil development in the basin are dated to about 18 000–13 500, 11 500–10 800 and 4500–1300 BP. In the case of the mid-Upper Pleistocene lake – assuming a drop of 6 °C in mean annual temperature, evaporation reduced from 2120 to 1400 mm and a runoff quotient of 9% – it would be necessary to double the present rainfall of 397 mm to maintain the +14 m water level.

Fortunately, the geomorphic evidence is corroborated by fragmentary pollen sequences at Florisbad and Aliwal North (Bakker and Butzer 1973, Coetzee 1967). The Florisbad record requires chronometric revision, since Peat II, formerly dated to 28 450 BP, is older than 42 500 BP (J. C. Vogel, personal communication), and the industry of Peat I (and the broadly contemporary Florisbad cranium) might even be an Acheulian of 'Developed Oldowan' aspect analogous to that of Cornelia (Butzer *et al.* 1974, Clark 1975b) and a dune site at Allanridge Station (Butzer and Volman in preparation). In this perspective, the pollen curve indicates mixed grass and Compositae, with variably drier conditions, prior to 42 500 BP, followed by a wetter and cooler climate and a dense grass vegetation until after 19 000 BP. The sequence is continued at Aliwal North, where the interval 13 200–9500 BP saw repeated oscillations between moist, cool grassland and drier, shrub–grass vegetation; a close chronological correspondence of these moist spells with cool trends in high latitudes is evident. Surprisingly, however, unpublished pollen studies by L. Scott indicate that the basic vegetation mosaic of the Kimberley area has remained relatively unchanged (bush and savanna) during the last 3000 to 8000 years, despite repeated, significant changes of the hydrological pattern.

Evidence of cold Pleistocene environments is limited to the high mountains, with true 'periglacial' forms and deposits at elevations about 1500–1800 m in the eastern Cape and Natal, about 2500 m or so in Lesotho (Butzer 1973e). However, a number of cave sites on the coast (for example Robberg; see Butzer (1973f)) as well as in the submontane zone, show one or more well-developed horizons of frost-shattered roof spall in association with Middle Stone Age levels (Butzer 1973e, f, Butzer *et al.* 1978b). A temperature depression near the coast of at least 10 °C can be inferred for the period of greatest Pleistocene cold.

The environmental sequence of the south-eastern Cape coast can be outlined as follows on geological evidence but also finding a measure of support in the associated faunas (for the geological evidence see Butzer and Helgren (1972); for the fauna see Klein (1974, 1977)): (1) beaches with warm-loving mollusca, intergrading with estuarine and alluvial terraces inland ('early last interglacial'); (2) accelerated denudation, with deposition of slope screes that include frost-shattered detritus; also frost-weathering in caves ('mid-last glacial'); (3) soil development ('late last interglacial'); (4) long interval of limited soil development, with wind activity, accelerating as sea levels rose after 16 000 BP ('last glacial'); (5) alternating soil development and coastal dune reactivation or gullying after 8000 BP, with optimal moisture at about 4200–1000 BP. Parallels as well as some striking differences with the record of the South African interior can be noted.

### Conclusions and overview

Several conclusions can be drawn for the continent on the basis of this overview of late Pleistocene and Holocene environmental changes, as summarized in fig. 1.11.

(1) Unlike the glacial, interglacial or even stadial–interstadial pulsations of high latitudes, African 'pluvial' episodes were all of short duration, some less than 2000 years, few exceeding 5000 years.

(2) There were major contrasts between the several climatic provinces.

(3) The last submaximum of the 'last glacial' (about 20 000–13 000 BP) was relatively dry everywhere except in the interior of southern Africa; the interval from about 17 000 to 12 000 BP was dry or turning drier everywhere except in parts of the Nile basin and the South African interior; all areas, except for the Mediterranean borderlands and Cape coast, experienced one or more moist intervals during the early and middle Holocene.

(4) There was no one-to-one correlation of African climatic changes

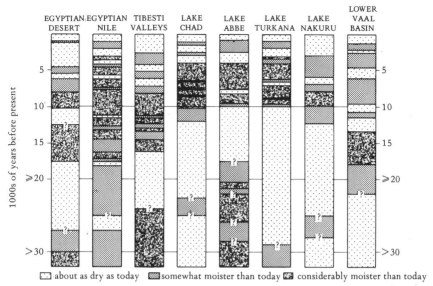

Fig. 1.11   Late Pleistocene and Holocene climatic change. (After Butzer 1978b; the Egyptian columns are after Butzer (1979), the Tibesti column after Jäkel (1978), Chad after Servant (1973) and Maley (1977), Lake Abbé after Gasse (1975), Lake Rudolf after Butzer *et al.* (1969), Lake Nakuru after Butzer *et al.* (1972) and the lower Vaal basin after Butzer *et al.* (1978a, 1979).

with the higher-latitude glacial chronology, and extent, phase, and direction of such changes differed appreciably.

(5) In Africa, climatic changes with a duration of several millennia repeatedly had a greater amplitude than the median difference between 'glacial' and 'interglacial' conditions in high latitudes. The secondary impact of northern hemisphere glaciation was not insignificant, but primary changes of the general circulation appear to have had a direct and far more immediate impact.

As a general rule for tropical Africa, it appears that the glacial maxima were mainly dry, while much of the interglacial time span appears to have been moist. The surprising aridity of the glacial maxima may well have been due in part to reduced evaporation over cooler ocean surface waters, greater atmospheric stability over the tropics and more extensive seasonal or permanent pack-ice in higher mid-latitudes (Butzer 1976d, Kraus 1973). The major exceptions to the rule of glacial aridity were the Kalahari and Vaal–Orange basins. Perhaps the most reasonable explanations for this would be an enhanced anticyclonic circulation with reduced upwelling and cold along the Benguela Current (Williams, Barry and Washington 1974). In this fashion, while a concentration of the monsoonal rains (Kraus 1973) brought West and East Africa into the dry Saharan periphery, the Kalahari experienced greater summer rains (Butzer *et al.* 1978a).

### Late Pleistocene to Holocene faunas

After making allowance for the inadequacy of the fossil record, it seems clear that the proportion of extinct mammalian species declined steadily during the span of time associated with the Acheulian industries and that by the end of that period virtually all the living species of mammals already existed. The later Pleistocene is thus marked by a continuing process of extinction and the present fauna is somewhat impoverished by comparison with that of the final Acheulian and even more so following the further extinctions that occurred near the end of the Pleistocene.

In North Africa, some of the extinct elements of the Acheulian faunas persist in sites with Mousterian and Aterian lithic industries, but the faunas accompanying the Capsian and Neolithic consist almost exclusively of living species. However, the giant buffalo *Pelorovis antiquus* is found well into the Neolithic and *Bos primigenius* may have survived as late as Roman times. The typical African savanna fauna of the Acheulian declined during the later Pleistocene and the gazelles become the most important of the bovids. *Cervus elaphus* died out by Neolithic times, together with the few Eurasiatic immigrants that appeared in the Mousterian, the deer *Megaloceros*, the wild goat *Ammotragus*, the rhinoceros *Dicerorhinus kirchbergensis*, and perhaps the bear *Ursus arctos*.

South of the Sahara, the later Pleistocene fauna also consists predominantly of living species, with a few extinct forms that persist to the beginning of the Holocene. The characteristic elephants of the Acheulian disappear and only *Loxodonta africana* survives. *Hipparion ethiopicum* is no longer present, but a large extinct *Equus* occurs right up to the end of the Pleistocene, together with the living zebrine horses, including fossil remains of *Equus quagga*, which was exterminated in historic times. *Hippopotamus amphibius* is widespread. The pigs all belong to the living species, although there is also material ascribed to the recently extinct Cape wart-hog, *Phacochoerus aethiopicus*, formerly widely distributed in Africa during the Pleistocene. Among the bovids, *Tragelaphus strepsiceros* generally displaces *T. grandis*, but there is a related smaller form occurring in the southernmost part of the continent.

66

*Hippotragus gigas* fades out and only the living species of *Hippotragus* persist. In the south-western Cape, the historically extinct Cape Blue-buck, *Hippotragus leucophaeus*, occurs as a fossil. *Pelorovis oldowayensis* is replaced by *P. antiquus*, but the living buffalo, *Syncerus caffer*, is also present. Among the alcelaphines, *Damaliscus dorcas* and *D. lunatus* are important, but *D. niro* may survive to the end of the Pleistocene. *Rabaticeras* disappears and *Alcelaphus buselaphus* and *A. lichtensteini* are found instead. The wildebeests are represented by living *Connochaetes taurinus*, *C. gnou* and (in the extreme south) by a form that is at least varietally different from the living *C. gnou*. The giant *Megalotragus* is plentiful and differs specifically from the Acheulian form. *Antidorcas recki* disappears and its place is taken by the living *A. marsupialis* or in southern Africa by the extinct species *A. bondi*; in the southern Cape Province it is replaced by another extinct species, *A. australis*. True gazelles no longer occur in southern Africa.

As with the Acheulian fauna, the general assemblages are those of the savannas, but regional differences become more apparent than in earlier times. In the well-documented cave sites in the southern and south-western Cape Province, extinctions involving two genera and six species or subspecies took place between 12 000 and 9000 years ago, in the terminal Pleistocene or earliest Holocene. At this time, there is evidence for diminution of the former areas of open grassland and extension of closed vegetational communities, which must have had an effect on the mammal populations. However, it is suspected that human activity, coupled with the environmental changes, may have contributed to the demise of these late Pleistocene survivors, much as the advent of Europeans sealed the fate of the quagga, bluebuck, and Cape wart-hog in historic times (Klein 1974, 1980).

### Middle Stone Age and Later Stone Age environments

It remains to consider the spatial patterning of Middle Stone Age and Later Stone Age populations within the late Pleistocene and Holocene environmental contexts delineated above.

To begin with, there is evidence not only for an increasing number of industries but also of sites during the late Pleistocene (Clark 1967). These occur throughout the continent, even in what are now forest settings, as well as in a greater range of microtopographic settings than did Acheulian occurrences. However, within the more marginal regional environments (desert and closed forest), sites are both fewer in number and more restricted to favourable microenvironmental opportunities.

It is therefore difficult to provide valid generalizations for a time-range of 130 000 years and a large continent, with considerable environmental diversity through both space and time. A recent study of prehistoric settlement patterning in the semi-arid Kimberley region serves to show a continuing dependency between man and suitable economic opportunities (Butzer in preparation):

(1) There is a close relation of successive occupations (Acheulian, Middle Stone Age, Later Stone Age) throughout the Kimberley area with spring, lakeshore, and riverbank locations.

(2) Except for hillside quarry sites and rare caves, the intervening upland plains show no evidence of artifacts in semi-primary contexts, suggesting that settlement was always strongly circumscribed with respect to suitable micro- or mesohabitats.

(3) The Middle Stone Age occupation is everywhere linked with deposits that imply greater spring activity, expanded lakes, or accelerated fluvial processes during the early Upper Pleistocene. This settlement episode is temporally separated from the latest, local Acheulian by perhaps 100 000 years and from the earliest, local Later Stone Age by at least 30 000 and more probably 50 000 years.

(4) The Kimberley Middle Stone Age industry is regionally circumscribed, and there is nothing technologically similar in this time range among the cave sites of the humid, submontane zone.

(5) This same industry marks a relatively brief (? 10 000-year) occupation of the semi-arid interior, at a time of cooler and substantially moister climate. Even so it may represent an adaptation to a macroenvironment drier than was exploited by Middle Stone Age groups elsewhere. The settlement pattern was highly discontinuous, with springs, lakeshores and permanent streams forming the loci of seasonal occupation, with a periphery of transitory settlement that graded outward into a vast but sporadically utilized economic area.

(6) In view of the striking spatial and temporal disjunctions, the impression obtains that Middle Stone Age groups of the South African interior were few in number, whatever their size.

Similar environmental restrictions on prehistoric hunter–gatherers seem to have applied well into Holocene times, as is borne out by the settlement record in Egypt (Butzer 1976c). Of considerable interest in the Nile Valley example is that the basic exploitation strategy evolved continuously, rather than by quantum jumps, even after the advent of agriculture and well through several stages of implementation of artificial irrigation. This same sensitivity to both the potential and limitations of environmental opportunities seems to have characterized land use in Africa until very recent times.

# CHAPTER 2

# ORIGINS AND EVOLUTION OF AFRICAN HOMINIDAE

## INTRODUCTION

The African continent still preserves, in its equatorial reaches, mankind's closest living relatives, the chimpanzee (*Pan*) and gorilla (*Gorilla*) of the family Pongidae. In favourable parts of the continent there is a substantial fossil record for portions of the past 65 million years of geologic time, the Cenozoic Era. A diversity of primates are documented in the first (Palaeogene) part of that era, but in Africa only towards its end in the Oligocene Epoch. Though primitive still, some species are assigned to the Hominoidea, the primate superfamily which includes Hominidae and Pongidae, living and extinct. Early in the subsequent (Neogene) part of that era, the Miocene affords an abundance of primitive pongids, and in its mid to later parts there is even some suggestive evidence of more hominid-like creatures. Strangely, the fossil record of the African apes is thereafter essentially unknown.

This chapter attempts to set out in a general way the primary evidence for the evolution of Hominidae in Africa since the upper Miocene. The distribution of fossil localities yielding Cenozoic Hominidae on the continent is shown in the map at fig. 2.1. The temporal distributions of the most important fossil hominid occurrences are shown schematically in figs. 2.2 to 2.5. Their relationships are shown, also schematically, in the cladogram at fig. 2.13. The principal taxa of Hominidae most commonly recognized are duly considered but morphological details are generally avoided; the principal known features of each taxon are set out at length elsewhere (Howell 1978). Specimens considered by the author to comprise the hypodigm of a particular hominid taxon are listed in tables 2.1 to 2.8. An effort has been made to avoid an unduly simplistic presentation, for example on the basis of a particular fossil hominid specimen, but to examine the total body of presently available evidence. Inferences and speculations on behavioural aspects of hominid evolution have generally been eschewed.

## STRATIGRAPHIC AND GEOGRAPHIC SETTING

The oldest occurrences of Hominidae are restricted to sub-Saharan Africa. In eastern Africa all known occurrences are related to the Rift Valley System – in Ethiopia, in Kenya and in Tanzania. In southern Africa all known occurrences are related to karstic (solution) fissure and cavern infillings (Brain 1958). The oldest substantiated occurrence is uppermost Miocene. The final Pliocene is well documented. In eastern as well as southern Africa this fossil record continues into the earlier Quaternary.[1] Subsequently the record is best documented in eastern Africa, and only imperfectly in the Maghrib, as it passes up into the mid Quaternary. The late Quaternary has unfortunately a sparse documentation everywhere in the continent (probably largely because of the relative paucity, compared with Eurasia, of occupied caves and rock-shelters). Overall, the most extensive documentation and one still unique to Africa is for the so-called Pliocene–Pleistocene time-range, notably between about 3 and 1 million years ago (see Bishop 1967, 1971, 1972, 1973; Cooke and Maglio 1972; Howell 1972; Maglio 1970).

The temporal relationships of the best-known early hominid successions of eastern Africa are set out in fig. 2.2. These successions, as depicted, are internally and externally consistent on the basis of conventional potassium–argon determinations, magnetostratigraphy, and biostratigraphy.[2]

Leaving aside later mid-Miocene occurrences of *Ramapithecus*,[3] or related taxa, the hominoid nature and distinctiveness of which are fully apparent though the hominid affinities are still a matter of controversy, there is only the scantest of evidence for Hominidae prior to the Pliocene. However, three occurrences in the central Kenya Rift Valley afford suggestive evidence of Hominidae in the upper Miocene time-range: the Ngorora Formation (Bishop and Chapman 1970: Bishop and Pickford 1975, Pickford 1978a), the Lukeino Formation (Pickford 1975, 1978b) and Lothagam Hill (Behrensmeyer 1976a, Patterson, Behrensmeyer and Sill 1970).

[1] The boundary between the Tertiary and the Quaternary is set at about 1.8 million BP (see Berggren 1973) and the boundary between the early and the mid Quaternary at about 700 000 BP (see Butzer 1974a).

[2] For details of the dating see Brock and Isaac (1974), Brown, Howell and Eck (1978), Cerling *et al.* (1979), Curtis *et al.* (1975), Drake *et al.* (1980), Findlater *et al.* (1974), Fitch, Hooker and Miller (1976), Gleadow (1980), Hillhouse *et al.* (1977), Hurford, Gleadow and Naeser (1976) and McDougall (1980).

[3] The hominid status of *Ramapithecus wickeri*, from the mid Miocene of Fort Ternan, Kenya, is still disputed, and it is therefore not considered here (see Simons 1977, Simons and Pilbeam 1978).

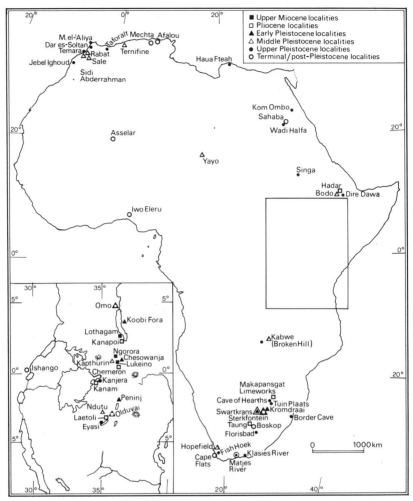

Fig. 2.1  Map showing the principal African localities of late Cenozoic age yielding skeletal remains of Hominidae.

The Lake Baringo area has also yielded isolated occurrences of australopithecines of Plio–Pleistocene age from the Chemeron and Chesowanja localities, and of *Homo* of mid-Pleistocene age from the Kapthurin Formation (Bishop *et al.* 1971). Some 75 km to the south of Lothagam, the Kanapoi Formation outcrops to the west of the Kerio River. It represents some 70 m of fluvial and lacustrine sedimentation overlain by a basalt lava having an age of about 4 million years (Behrensmeyer 1976a). This locality has afforded a very extensive

72

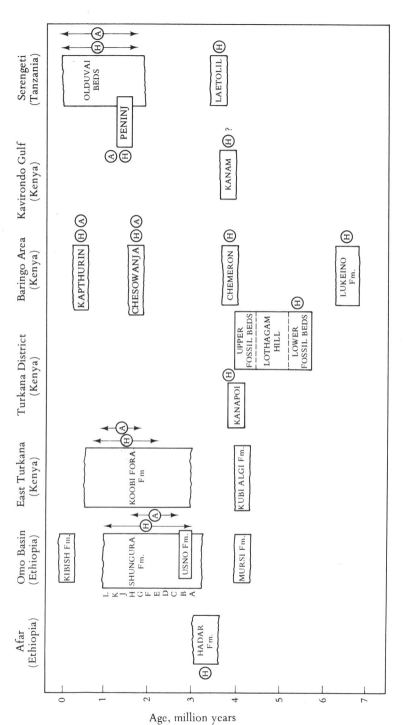

Fig. 2.2    Relative and absolute ages of successions in eastern Africa yielding remains of Hominidae.

73

vertebrate fauna of lower Pliocene age and a single fragment (distal humerus) of a hominid (Patterson 1966).

The Omo succession, extending from more than 4 to about 1 million years ago, yields hominids, usually in fragmentary condition, largely from the 3–1 million years BP time-range. From the East Rudolf (Turkana) succession come hominids, in quantity and often in an excellent state of preservation, for the most part from the ∼ 2–< 1 million years BP time-range, and the Olduvai succession yields hominids from the ∼ 1.8–0.7 million years BP time-range, as well as from the end of the Quaternary. The Peninj occurrence is most probably comparable in age, on the basis of correlative radiometric, magnetostratigraphic and biostratigraphic grounds, with the pre-Lemuta Member portion of the Olduvai succession, broadly correlative with the Olduvai Normal Event (Isaac and Curtis 1974), the next-to-last interval of a normal magnetic field within the protracted span of the Matuyama Reversed Epoch.

The Hadar Formation, in the west central Afar basin, is exposed extensively below the west Ethiopian plateau adjacent to the Awash River. The formation has an aggregate thickness of some 140 m and comprises fluvio-deltaic, lake margin and lacustrine sediments with volcanic tuffs and at least one lava flow (Taieb 1974). Four members are recognized in the formation (Aronson *et al.* 1977, Taieb *et al.* 1976, Taieb and Tiercelin 1979), and rich and diverse assemblages of fossil vertebrates, including Hominidae, are derived from three of these members (Coppens 1978, Johanson *et al.* 1978b, Johanson and Taieb 1976, Roche and Tiercelin 1977, Taieb *et al.* 1972, 1974, 1978b).

The Laetolil Beds, exposed in and adjacent to the Garusi River, outcrop on the eastern Serengeti plateau above the Eyasi Rift escarpment. They have long been known to yield a diverse vertebrate fauna with elements more primitive than the oldest vertebrates from adjacent Olduvai Gorge (Dietrich 1942, 1945, 1950). Remains of Hominidae (a maxilla fragment) were first recovered from this area by Kohl-Larsen in 1939 (Kohl-Larsen 1943, pp. 378–86; Remane 1951a). The initial geological researches there of Kent (1942) afforded a stratigraphic basis recently amplified and extended by Hay in conjunction with palaeoanthropological and related field studies by M. D. Leakey *et al.* (1976). The Laetolil Beds are aeolian tuffs cemented by zeolites representing a single depositional facies and derived from the sodic alkaline volcanic source of Sadimon. The upper fifth of this succession is fossiliferous, including a number of jaws and teeth of Hominidae, bracketed by potassium–argon ages of 3.35 and 3.75 million years.

The several hominid partial crania recovered by Kohl-Larsen in 1935 from sediments between the Mumba Hills and Lake Eyasi, in the floor of the Eyasi trough (Tanzania), have been customarily considered to be of late Quaternary age (L. S. B. Leakey 1936, L. S. B. Leakey and Reeve 1946, Reck and Kohl-Larsen 1936). Amino-acid racemization analysis of hominid bone suggests an age of ~ 34 000 years (Bada and Protsch 1973). Such an approximation is quite in keeping with the essentially modern aspect of the associated mammals (Dietrich 1939).

The *type* specimens of most Pliocene–Pleistocene Hominidae derive from cemented infillings of fissures, sinkholes and caves of the South African Highveld and the Transvaal plateau basin. Initially guesses and subsequently more reasonably founded estimates of their relative and correlative ages were made (Cooke 1963, 1967; Ewer 1956, 1957). However, opinions have been widely divergent over the years. For the moment direct radiometric age calibration, including the use of *fission tracks* (MacDougall and Price 1974), appears to be inapplicable to these occurrences. Geomorphic estimates (McFadden, Brock and Partridge 1979, Partridge 1973, 1978) are generally unreliable, if not ill-founded. Thus, only biostratigraphic methods and palaeo-magnetics would now appear to be productive of consistent results. Such approaches have defined the successive temporal relationships of vertebrate assemblages associated with Hominidae at most of these localities (Cooke 1963, 1967; Ewer 1956, 1957; Hendey 1974). All the occurrences fall within a protracted faunal span sometimes termed Makapanian. Limits to age-spans can be estimated on the basis of the temporal duration (and association) of some mammal taxa (notably proboscideans, suids, bovids, carnivores and cercopithecoids, as well as microvertebrates) in successions in eastern Africa for which there is direct radiometric and magnetostratigraphic control. Employing this approach, and the rate of faunal change in the protracted Omo succession drawn from measures of faunal resemblance (Shuey *et al.* 1978), it is possible to arrive at a set of projected, 'best-fit' age assessments (see fig. 2.3).

Along the Atlantic littoral of Morocco a protracted succession of marine and interrelated continental sediments apparently encompasses much of the late Cenozoic (Biberson 1961, 1963, 1971). The middle and younger units of this important sequence sometimes preserve vertebrate fossils, very often substantial artifact assemblages, and, thus far infrequently, remains of Hominidae. The relevant portions of this succession, and hominid occurrences, are set out in fig. 2.4. Hominids occur in time–stratigraphic units successively designated (older to

| Million years BP | MAKAPANSGAT LIMEWORKS | KRUGERSDORP LOCALITIES STERKFONTEIN | KRUGERSDORP LOCALITIES SWARTKRANS | KRUGERSDORP LOCALITIES KROMDRAAI B | BUXTON-NORLIM |
|---|---|---|---|---|---|
| 0.5 | | | Stratified brown breccia — MB-2 breccia ? 0.5 m.y. | | |
| 1.0 | | | | | |
| 1.5 | | 5:Middle breccia ~ 1.5 m.y. | MB-1 pink to orange breccias ~ 1.7–1.9 m.y. Aggregate thickness ~ 10 m | Fine breccia — Stony breccia ? ~ 1.5 m.y. Aggregate thickness ~ 8 m | |
| 2.0 | | | | | |
| 2.5 | MEMBER V fluvial sandy brown breccia | | | | PHASE 1 flowstones and derived soils — PHASE 2 colluvial redeposited aeolian sands:baboons ~ 2.7–2.9 m.y. |
| 3.0 | MEMBER IV reddish breccia: cercopithecoids ~3.0–3.2 m.y. / MEMBER III grey brown breccia: Bovidae ~3.0–3.2 m.y. | 4: Lower breccia ~ 2.8–3.0 m.y. / 3:Block breccia Aggregate thickness ~17–18 m | | | |
| 3.5 | FLOWSTONE Mbr. II: basal red mud / Mbr. I ; travertine Aggregate thickness ~ 49 m | | | | |
| 4.0 | | | | | |

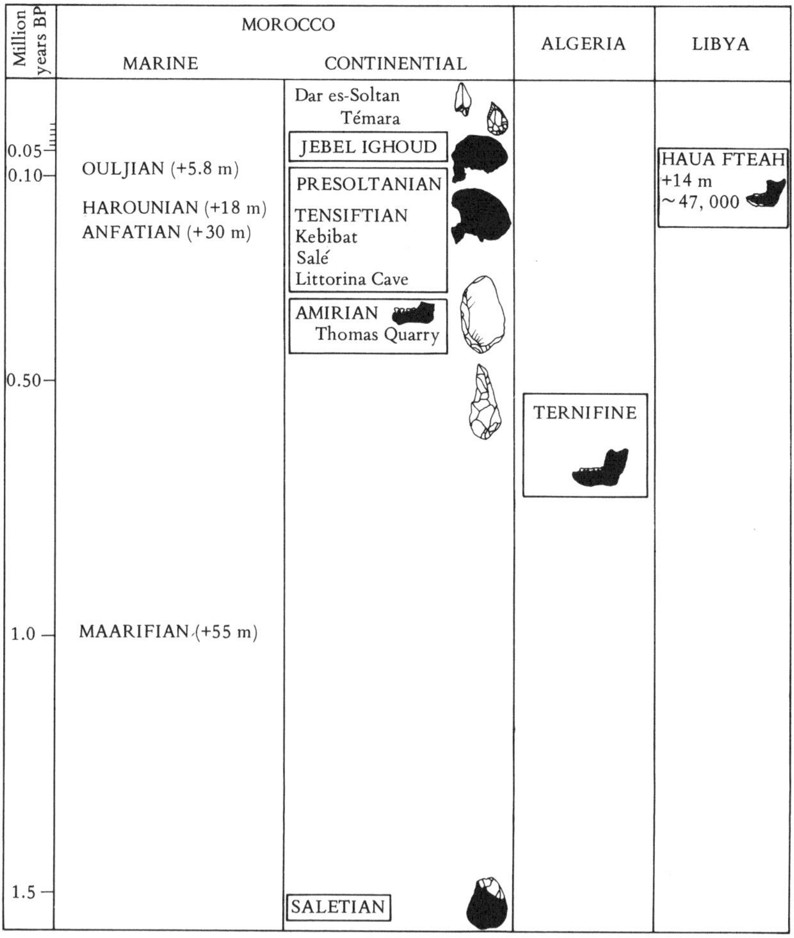

| Million years BP | MOROCCO | | ALGERIA | LIBYA |
|---|---|---|---|---|
| | MARINE | CONTINENTIAL | | |
| 0.05 / 0.10 | OULJIAN (+5.8 m) | Dar es-Soltan / Témara / JEBEL IGHOUD / PRESOLTANIAN | | HAUA FTEAH +14 m ~47,000 |
| | HAROUNIAN (+18 m) ANFATIAN (+30 m) | TENSIFTIAN Kebibat Salé Littorina Cave | | |
| | | AMIRIAN Thomas Quarry | | |
| 0.50 | | | TERNIFINE | |
| 1.0 | MAARIFIAN (+55 m) | | | |
| 1.5 | | SALETIAN | | |

Fig. 2.4 Tentative correlation and suggested age-relationships of localities in North Africa yielding remains of Hominidae.

younger): Amirian, Tensiftian, Presoltanian and Soltanian (Biberson 1964). Whereas the stratigraphic relationships of these formations are quite well defined, there is little or no direct evidence to establish their absolute ages,[1] and there is still scant relevant radiocarbon control on the late Quaternary time-range, except for the long and consistent series of determinations for the Haua Fteah Cave, Cyrenaican Libya (McBurney 1961, 1962, 1967). The very important hominid specimens from Jebel Irhoud, Morocco, are, unfortunately, still of unknown age, although

[1] U-series measurements (see Stearns and Thurber 1965) afford, at best, limiting ages (Kaufman et al. 1971).

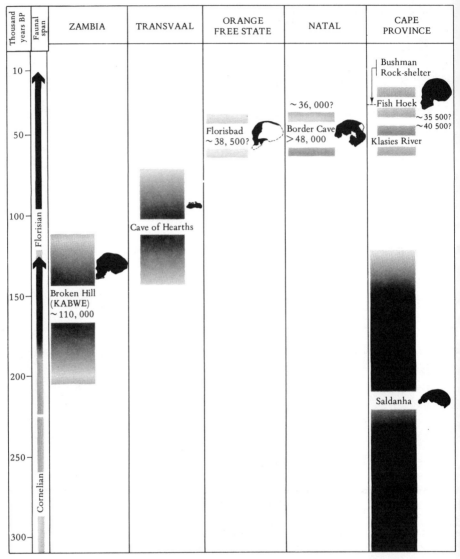

Fig. 2.5  Tentative correlation and suggested age-relationships of localities of later
Quaternary age yielding remains of *Homo sapiens*.

the associated macro- and microvertebrate fauna is of late Quaternary
aspect.

In southern Africa a number of localities have yielded (largely)
incomplete cranial or jaw parts of Hominidae. On the basis of the
associated vertebrate assemblages these can be attributed to older

(Cornelian) or younger (Florisian) faunal spans (Cooke 1963, 1967, Hendey 1974, Wells 1962) which are usually considered as mid to late Quaternary in age. Unfortunately, the actual ages and durations of these 'faunal spans' are largely unknown, although some radiocarbon determinations (Beaumont and Vogel, 1972, Vogel and Beaumont 1972) and amino-acid racemization analyses (Bada *et al.* 1974) afford some limiting values. However, the measure of uncertainty is clearly apparent from fig. 2.5. The oldest occurrences are undoubtedly those from Saldanha (Butzer 1973) and perhaps Kabwe (Howell 1978, Klein 1973) and, maybe, also the Cave of Hearths. All, on faunal grounds, would antedate the late Quaternary (*Florisian*) faunal span (named from the animal associations at the Florisbad site).

The lack of consistent and reliable methods of age assessment for the mid and late Quaternary time-ranges severely inhibits temporal placement of such hominid samples, and thus inferences drawn from comparative morphological studies, and therefore phylogenetic interpretation.

The subsequent portions of this chapter seek to provide a general overview of the documentation in Africa of the fossil record of the family Hominidae, which is not always either straightforward or well defined, so that it is necessary to stress the tentative and even uncertain nature of interpretations and inferences.

CF. *HOMINIDAE* GEN. ET SP. INDET. (A)

Fragments of hominoid fossils of Upper Miocene age from Kenya have been considered by several workers to be attributable to Hominidae. The single upper molar from Ngorora is of Vallesian-equivalent age while the lower molar from Lukeino and the mandible fragment from Lothagam are of Turolian-equivalent age; in terms of the European land-mammal scale their probable ages range from about 10 to 6 million years. These several specimens do deviate in distinctive ways from known near-contemporary apes. They are here referred to Hominidae gen. et sp. indet. (A). Their affinities will remain uncertain until more completely preserved specimens are recovered from sedimentary formations of that time-range.

## *AUSTRALOPITHECUS* R. A. DART, 1925

The extinct genus *Australopithecus* was first announced and described briefly by Dart (1925) but it was not then given formal diagnosis. The provenance and associations of the specimen are well summarized by Peabody (1954) and Butzer (1974b). The type specimen is a partial skull, comprising the fronto-facial region, right cranial base and mandible, and a natural endocranial cast (but missing bones of the cranial vault). It is a juvenile individual with full deciduous dentition and almost fully erupted, still unworn first permanent molars. Much of the initial and protracted controversy over the resemblances and affinities of this specimen were largely a consequence of inadequate appropriate comparative study, its incompleteness and its juvenile age.[1] Thus, Keith concluded that 'in all its essential features *Australopithecus* is an anthropoid ape', and 'the features wherein *Australopithecus* departs from living African anthropoids and makes an approach towards man cannot be permitted to outweigh the predominance of its anthropoid affinities' (Keith 1931).

It is a sad reflection of the then immature state of palaeo-anthropology and of comparative primatology – in respect to data, method and theory – that such dispute and controversy could persist when, within ten to fifteen years after the discovery, the fundamentally hominid features of the dentition had been established by Dart (Adloff 1931, 1932; Bennejeant 1936, 1953; Broom 1929a; Dart 1934; Gregory 1930; Gregory and Hellman 1939a, b, c; Le Gros Clark 1940, 1947, 1952). Moreover, Sollas (1926) clearly established the non-apelike features of the cranio-facial morphology. However, the significance of this distinctive total morphological pattern was largely overlooked by both Keith (1931) and Abel (1931) both of whom employed substantial samples of juvenile apes in their comparative studies. It is necessary to conclude that some influential and respected members of the scientific community were frankly unprepared and unwilling to accept such an unexpected discovery and its attendant phylogenetic implications. Only the subsequent recovery of additional skeletal remains of adult individuals – comprising cranial, jaw and postcranial parts – through

---

[1] Although it has never received thorough morphological description, which it surely still merits, there is a very extensive literature on this specimen. Its salient morphological features have been set out principally by Dart (1929, 1930–1, 1934, 1940a, 1948), by Broom (1925a, b, 1929a; Broom and Schepers 1946), by Hrdlička (1925), by Keith (1931) and by Abel (1931). Robinson (1956) has published details of the dentition, and Holloway (1970) an accurate assessment of endocranial volume (Tobias 1978a, b).

the pioneering efforts of Broom, with the co-operation subsequently of Robinson and again those of Dart, would eventually overwhelmingly convince all but the most dedicated sceptics that *Australopithecus* was a primitive representative of the family Hominidae.

Over a decade was to elapse before skeletal remains of adult hominid individuals comparable to *Australopithecus* were recovered elsewhere, at Sterkfontein, Transvaal, in South Africa. However, initially, comparisons could only be made between a single molar tooth of the permanent dentition in these two samples. It required another decade before the same locality yielded a deciduous dentition and detailed comparisons could then be effected (Broom 1947, Broom, Robinson and Schepers 1950). Within that interval, adult (in 1938) and then juvenile (in 1941) hominid remains, including most of the lower deciduous dentition of a related though in certain respects morphologically distinctive hominid, were recovered at the nearby Kromdraai B locality (Broom 1941, Broom and Schepers 1946). Subsequently, additional evidence of species diversity among such early Hominidae was obtained elsewhere in South Africa (Swartkrans and Makapansgat, Transvaal) and, later, from various localities in Eastern Africa.

## *Species of* Australopithecus

Despite the recovery of hundreds of specimens of Pliocene–Pleistocene Hominidae, and at an ever accelerating rate, there persists substantial disagreement as to their taxonomic status (Corrucini and Ciochon 1979, Howell, Washburn and Ciochon 1978, Oxnard 1975, 1979). Nonetheless, if there is not yet a consensus, progress has been made towards a clearer definition of the problem – through more adequate delineation of temporal relationships of hominid samples, through quantitative assessments of their ranges of variation, and through recognition of lineages (chrono-species) with attendant reduction of synonymy.

By 1950 as many as three genera and five species of early Hominidae were recognized by Broom (1950). Subsequently, and largely through the efforts of Robinson, the (essentially) South African samples were grouped into two genera, two species and four subspecies (Robinson 1954, 1956). Two lineages, one (*Australopithecus*) with affinities to *Homo*, the other (*Paranthropus*) once considered ancestral but ultimately aberrant and extinct without issue, were recognized by Robinson. Robinson finally reclassified *Australopithecus* as *Homo africanus*, considering it as an ancestral species within the *Homo* lineage (Robinson

1962, 1963, 1967). These lineages were presumed to have their bases on inferred ecological differences and dietary adjustments (the so-called dietary hypothesis).

The bases for these alleged differences have not gone unchallenged. Thus Le Gros Clark, personally familiar with or aware of most of the evidence then available, considered that 'such anatomical differences as there may be between the fossil remains..., though they may possibly justify subspecific, or even specific, distinctions, are not sufficient to justify generic distinctions' (Le Gros Clark 1964, p. 167); and, subsequently, 'without doubt a great deal of unnecessary confusion has been introduced into the story of the australopithecines by the failure to recognize their high variability, thereby arbitrarily creating new species and genera that cannot be properly validated' (Le Gros Clark 1967, p. 48).

In due course Tobias (1967a) sought, through thorough comparative studies, to demonstrate the fundamentally similar structure of australopithecines – samples referable to *Australopithecus* – in contrast to the structures exemplified by those samples referable to the genus *Homo*. The differences among australopithecine samples were considered to be at most specific, and three species were recognized and defined; a small gracile form, *Australopithecus africanus*; a succedent more robust species, *A. robustus*; and an extremely robust form (exclusively East African), considered to be nearly contemporary, *A. boisei*.

More recently, and following in part different procedures Campbell (1972) has also sought to recognize the basic generic pattern – biologically and behaviourally/culturally – distinctive of *Australopithecus*. He has suggested two divergent lineages of palaeospecies within the genus: one, *A. boisei*, simple and restricted to eastern Africa; the other, *A. africanus*, complex with four subspecies, represented by two subspecies in southern Africa, one in Eastern Africa and one in insular south-eastern Asia.

Some students of this problem (Brace 1967, 1973; Wolpoff 1971a, 1974) have suggested that differences between samples may largely reflect sexual dimorphism, or at best a subspecies distinction. This attractive, though facile, explanation fails, however, to consider the morphological differences in cranium and dentition which are not merely of size, but of proportions and structure. Thus, it has been shown that analyses of proportions along the tooth row, which reflect in particular proportional differences between postcanine teeth and anterior teeth, 'which, in all cases discriminate well between the living hominid samples used, in every case also discriminate well between *Paranthropus* (= *A. robustus*) and *H. africanus* (= *A. africanus*)' (Robinson and Steudel 1973, p. 520; see also Robinson 1969). Similarly, it has been shown that the dental dimorphism in samples attributed to those two taxa 'as measured by mean differences is greater than expected in either chimpanzee or modern man in both maxillary and mandibular comparisons and it exceeds that of the gorilla in the maxillary. The magnitude of the differences between the two taxa cannot be explained by sexual dimorphism of the sort found in either modern man or chimpanzee' and 'it is also improbable that the differences can be explained in terms of something comparable to gorilla sexual dimorphism' (Greene 1975, p. 86). Bilsborough has reached essentially the same conclusion and considers, as do some other authors (especially Robinson), that there are 'marked differences between gracile and robust australopithecines, with the separation between these two groups often greater than that between *A. africanus* and all members of the genus *Homo*' (Bilsborough 1972).

So far as is known all representatives of the genus *Australopithecus* are basically similar in postcranial morphology. There are, however, usually consistent differences from the total morphological pattern characteristic of the genus *Homo* – in the lower limb, in the axial skeleton and in the forelimb. In these respects differences between lesser taxa of the genus appear largely to be a reflection of body size and robustness. The principal differences between the lesser taxa are in cranial and dental morphology.

Australopithecus afarensis *Johanson, White and Coppens (1978)*

TABLE 2.1   *Remains attributable to* A. afarensis

(* = *same individual*)

|  | Laetoli | Hadar (Afar) |
|---|---|---|
| Partial skeleton | L.H.-21† | 288–1‡ |
| Crania |  | 166–9; 162–28;333–23, 24, 45*, 84, 105; 333–112, 114, 116 |
| Maxillae | Garusi I; L.H.-5 | 199–1; 200–1a; 333–1, 2 |
| Mandibles | L.H.-2; L.H.-4; L.H.-10; L.H.-13 | 128–23; 145–35, 188–1; 198–1; 207–13; 266–1; 277–1; 311–1; 333W-1a-e, 12, 15, 16, 27, 32, 46, 52, 57, 58, 59, 60; 333–10, 43, 59, 74, 86,* 97, 100, 108; 400–1a; 411–1 |

TABLE 2.1 (*contd.*)

| | Laetoli | Hadar (Afar) |
|---|---|---|
| Dentition | M. 18773; Garusi II; L.H.-1; L.H-3(a–t); L.H.-6(a–e);L.H.-7; L.H.-8(a–b); L.H.-11; L.H.-12; L.H.-14(a–k); L.H.-15; -16; -17; -19; -22(a–b); –23; -24;-25; -26 | 161–40; 198–17a, b, 18; 200–1b; 241–14; 249–27; 333W–2, 3, 9a, b, 10, 28, 42, 48; 333–30, 35 44, 52, 66–68, 76, 77, 82, 90, 99, 103, 104; 333–1–4, 17, 20, 25; 366–1; 388–1; 400–1b |
| **Postcranials** | | |
| Clavicle | | 333–94; 333X–6, 9 |
| Scapula | | |
| Humerus | | 137–48a; 322–1; 333W–22, 31; 333–29, 87, 107, 109 |
| Ulna | | 137–48b; 333W–36; 333–11, 12, 38, 119; 333X–5 |
| Radius | | 333W–33; 333–98, 121; 333X–14, 15 |
| Manus | | |
| Carpals | | 33–40, 50, 80, 91 |
| Metacarpals | | 333W–5, 6, 23, 26, 35, 39; 333–14–18, 27, 48, 56, 58, 65, 89 |
| Phalanges | | 333W–4, 7, 11, 20, 21, 29; 333–19–20, 25, 26, 49, 57, 63, 69, 93; 333X–13, 21 |
| Ribs | | 333W–17–19, 30, 41, 45, 47 |
| Vertebral column | | 333W–8, 44; 333–51, 73, 81, 83, 101, 106, 118; 333W–12 |
| Pelvic remains | | 129–52; |
| Femur | | 128–1; 129–1a, 1c; 211–1; 228–1; 333W–40, 56; 333–3, 41, 61, 95, 110, 111, 117 |
| Tibia | | 129–1b; 333W–43; 333–5, 6, 7, 39, 42, 96; 333X–26 |
| Fibula | | 333W–37; 333–9, 85, 120 |
| Pes | | |
| Talus | 75 | |
| Calcaneum | | 333–8, 37, 55 |
| Tarsals | | 333–28, 36, 47, 49 |
| Metatarsals | | 333W–55; 333–13, 21; 333–54, 72, 78 |
| Phalanges | | 333W–25, 51; 333–22, 31, 60, 62, 70, 71 |
| Associated foot elements | | 333–115a–m |
| Manus or pes phalanges, undetermined | | 333W–34, 38, 50, 53, 54; 333–32, 33, 46, 64, 88, 102; 333X–18 |

† L.H. 21(a–z) juvenile skeleton includes partial maxilla, cranial fragments, clavicle, rib, ulna, femur, manus phalanges, and a metacarpal.

‡ AL 288–1 adult (female) partial skeleton comprises 77 bony elements including cranial fragments, mandible, parts of scapula, humeri, ulnae, radii, 4 hand bones, many rib parts, 9 vertebrae, sacrum, left innominate, femur, tibia, fibula, and talus.

*Australopithecus afarensis* is the most recently recognized, morphologically most primitive, and apparently (until now) the oldest known
species of the genus *Australopithecus*. The species has been defined on
the basis of a large, combined sample of skeletal remains from the Hadar
Formation (Afar, Ethiopia) and the Laetolil Beds (Laetoli locality,
northern Tanzania) (Table 2.1) (Johanson, White and Coppens, 1978).

The Laetoli locality has been known to be fossiliferous since its
discovery in the mid 1930s; it yielded its first (recognized) evidence of
hominid presence in 1939. The distinctive nature of that maxilla
fragment was noted some thirty years ago, first by Remane (1951) and
subsequently by Şenyürek (1955). Fragmentary hominid remains –
mostly jaw parts and teeth, but also parts of an infant's skeleton – now
constitute a sample representative of some two dozen individuals. These
fossils, along with the remains of a diversity of other vertebrate species,
derive from various localized exposures of the upper of the two main
sedimentary units – composed of wind-worked and airfall volcanic
ash – which comprise the 130-meter-thick Laetolil Beds. Volcanic tuffs
overlying and underlying the fossil-bearing deposits have ages of 3.6
and 3.8 million years, respectively.

The fossiliferous sediments of the Hadar area, central Afar depression,
were discovered in 1969, and subsequently intensively investigated
between 1972 and 1977 (Johanson and Taieb, 1976; Taieb *et al.*, 1974).
Hominid skeletal remains, comprising varied body parts of some 38
individuals are known from twenty-eight fossil-bearing localities, from
a dozen distinct horizons within the three upper members of the
quadri-partite Hadar Formation. Upwards these are the Sidi Hakoma
Member (17 localities), Denen Dora Member (9 localities), and Kada
Hadar Member (2 localities). A tuff in the upper part of the Kada Hadar
Member, substantially above the uppermost hominid fossil horizon, has
an age of ∼ 2.6 million years; and a basalt in the uppermost part of
the Sidi Hakoma Member has an age of ∼ 3.6 million years. Thus, most
of the Hadar hominid sample appears to have an age broadly equivalent
to the hominid sample from the Laetoli site.

The hominid skeletal parts, which make up this fossil sample,
comprise together nearly all parts of the skeleton, and also represent
various states of maturation. The first-found (1939) specimen(s) from
Laetoli (usually termed Garusi I, II) were attributed once to a distinct
genus (*Praeanthropus*), a choice now known to be both inappropriate and
(in terms of zoological rules) invalid (as no diagnosis was provided).
The question is whether this hominid sample – from two fairly widely

separated localities, but now known to be of broadly comparable age – represents a single taxon, or several taxa; and, in either instance, to which higher taxon/taxa should the sample(s) be assigned? A fundamental resemblance in jaw and tooth morphology, size and proportions – comparable body parts in samples from both localities – affords the basis for attribution to a single taxon, rather than to separate taxa.

The postcranial skeleton of the genus *Australopithecus* is quite distinctive – in comparison with that of genus *Homo*, or with that of extant and extinct Pongidae (apes) – and the Hadar hominid sample affords many such body parts, adult as well as juvenile (the latter sometimes in common with specimens from Laetoli). There are strong resemblances between comparable parts of the post-cranial skeleton relevant to hominid-type locomotion – pelvis and sacrum, hip and knee joints – between the Hadar hominid sample and known examples of *Australopithecus*. The over-all morphology and distinctive structure of these various body parts demonstrate, as in the case of previously known *Australopithecus* species, adaptation to upright posture and effective bipedal gait. Thus, the Hadar/Laetoli hominid sample can only be attributed to genus *Australopithecus* on the basis of these very strong, overlappingly similar, shared character states.

Some body parts, and joint areas, of *Australopithecus* have been very poorly known, or not known at all heretofore. The Hadar sample affords very important, and usually unique evidence of the structure of the shoulder, elbow and wrist joints, hip and knee joints, the ankle/heel region, and most uncommon data on the proportions, morphology and functional structure of the hand and foot. Some of this information derives from body parts of an individual, partial skeleton (AL 288–1), and even much more derives from numerous body parts – sometimes from what are surely portions of the same individual(s) – recovered from the AL 333 site-complex from which body parts of at least 9 adult and 4 juvenile hominid individuals are known.

Overall the Hadar sample confirms and also substantially broadens previous understanding of early hominid stature (generally small, 107–122 cm. for female individuals); upper/lower limb proportions (high humero-femoral indices reflecting quite long forelimbs including forearm length); shoulder joint and elbow joint structure; and hip joint and knee joint structure. Most of these areas were inadequately known previously because of their fragmentary preservation or the lack of associated body parts of the same individual within an *Australopithecus* species.

The foot of any species of *Australopithecus* has been very poorly known previously. Now, almost all elements are known in the Hadar hominid sample – at least 38 specimens – including portions of associated elements of the foot skeleton of several individuals. Overall the foot skeleton is characterized by many fundamentally hominid features, particularly in the heel and ankle, and their respective joints, in the tarsal/metatarsal joints, metatarsals indicative of high longitudinal and transverse arches, and in the development and articulations of the hallux and its extrinsic musculature. However, there are distinct (unique) or primitive (chimp-like) aspects of the ankle joint, the lack of development of the lateral part of the heel, the mid-tarsal articulations which suggest substantial mobility of this region, and in the markedly curved, strongly tendinous-marked toe bones.

The Laetoli locality preserves, in laminated air-fall tuff deposits, an abundance of animal tracks representative of a diversity of species. At one site there is a trail of footprints indicative of at least two, larger and smaller hominid individuals. Estimates of stature (based on footprint length as a percent of body height in modern populations) suggest heights of some 120–130 cm. (smaller individual) to 140–150 cm. (larger individual). The footprints are remarkably human in respect to their spatial relationships, fully adducted great toe, pronounced heel strike, and well-developed medial longitudinal arch. In spite of the primitive features sometimes manifested in the foot bones of this species there is every indication of fully orthograde posture and an efficient striding bipedal gait. (Clarke, 1979; Leakey and Hay, 1979; White, 1980).

The hand skeleton of any other species of *Australopithecus* has been almost totally unknown previously. The Hadar hominid sample includes (minimally) 36 recognized elements of the hand skeleton (some few surely of the same individual); some juvenile finger bones are preserved in a Laetoli individual as well. The hand skeleton shows a mosaic of definitively hominid features (base of the thumb and base of the lateral fingers), some presumably unique features (related especially to musculo-tendinous relationships, both in the palmar area, and in the strongly curved, muscularly marked digits), and primitive characteristics in respect to the relatively short, hardly robust thumb, and the set of the middle finger. The extent to which these, and some other features are generically characteristic of *Australopithecus*, or are species-specific features, remains an open question at this point.

The features which most clearly distinguish, both quantitatively and sometimes qualitatively, the Hadar and Laetoli hominid samples from

other, previously known *Australopithecus* species concern the morphology of the cranio-facial skeleton and the dentition. (This is true, as
well, of differences between other *Australopithecus* species; the postcranial skeleton – so far as it is known, and comparable body parts are
available for comparison – appears to be fundamentally similar in all
known *Australopithecus* species.) There is a substantial, indeed large suite
of characters in this portion of the *A. afarensis* skeleton which is more
primitive overall than any species of *Australopithecus* known heretofore.

Oldest sediments of the Omo Group (southwestern Ethiopia),
represented by the Usno Formation and the lowest members of the
Shungura Formation, have an age broadly comparable with that of the
upper part of the Hadar Formation. These Omo occurrences have
yielded some two dozen hominid teeth (from both the upper and lower
dentition) which are comparable in size and proportions, and show
many of the same morphological features as do their homologues in the
Laetoli and Hadar samples. Thus, there is presumptive evidence of the
presence of *A. afarensis* also early in the Omo succession.

*A. afarensis* has been revealed to be a strongly sexually dimorphic
early hominid species, adapted to an effective bipedal striding gait,
distinctive in a number of aspects of its postcranial anatomy and
demonstrably primitive, in respect to its small brain, massive facial
skeleton and anterior dentition, as well as many features of its cranial
morphology. However, this successful species habituated not only a
mosaic of wooded or more open streamside and lake margin habitats,
but also penetrated very sparsely wooded, open semiarid grassland
situations. Although there is no direct evidence of culturally patterned
behaviour documented for the species, its primitive hominid nature is
clearly established.

These very important discoveries thus afford a hitherto unknown,
indeed unsuspected glimpse into the morphological structure of the
earliest, well-known hominid adaptive grade of organization (Day *et al.*,
1980; Johanson and White, 1979).

The distinctive cranio-facial-dental features pertain to the size and
proportions of the upper incisor teeth; the morphology and distinctive
wear of the canines, premolars, and the functional structure of the
anterior premolar/canine complex, and diastemata, and their interrelationships; the size, proportions, morphology and root structure of
the molar teeth; the morphology of the deciduous molar teeth; the
structure of the face (particularly the palate form, dental arcade shape,
and the circum-nasal and alveolar regions); the form and structure of

the mandibular symphysis, the depth and form of the anterior body, and the orientation of the ascending ramus; relative proportions, form and disposition of the occipital area; the form and proportions of the cranial base, and its elements, including the form and sinus development of the mastoid area, and the mandibular fossa; the expression of masticatory muscular crests on a relatively diminutive neurocranium.

## Australopithecus africanus

The small species (*africanus*) of *Australopithecus* occurs in deposits of Pliocene age in southern and in eastern Africa. It has never been found outside the Afro-Arabian continent and, at least for the moment, its distribution is distinctively sub-Saharan.

In southern Africa it is documented from the cemented infillings (breccias) of two caves in the Transvaal (Sterkfontein, Makapansgat) and the original site (Taung) in the northern Cape Province. The latter site afforded the holotype of this species. In none of those situations is there convincingly sound evidence either for the contemporaneous presence of another hominid species or for direct association of lithic or other materials indicative of recognizably culturally-patterned behaviour.[1]

At Sterkfontein all skeletal remains certainly attributable to *A. africanus* occur in the Lower Breccia (Member B). The overall representation of a diversity of vertebrate species, and their body parts, as well as the preponderance of certain medium- to large-sized bovids, strongly suggests that the accumulation was the consequence of carnivore (perhaps sabre-tooth?) predatory activities (Vrba 1975, 1976).

The distinctive composition and body-part representation of various mammalian taxa, especially Bovidae, from the hominid-bearing infilling at Makapansgat was first noted and stressed by Dart (1957). The species spectrum and the body parts represented indeed suggest, as in the case of Sterkfontein (Lower Breccia), that large carnivores were probably mostly responsible for this richly fossiliferous accumulation.

In eastern Africa *A. africanus* is documented in the Rudolf basin,

[1] Substantial numbers of stone artifacts of Developed Oldowan or even earliest Acheulian type do occur in the Middle Breccia (termed Unit C by Butzer) in the Sterkfontein Extension (or west pit) exposure (Robinson 1961, Robinson and Mason 1962) which is demonstrably *younger* than the australopithecine-bearing Lower Breccia (or Unit B of Butzer). The former has yielded half a dozen hominid teeth of some three individuals of still indeterminate affinity, but which may well prove not to be *Australopithecus*. The various bovids, very fragmented, comprise a variety of species sizes but a low percentage of juveniles, which is perhaps suggestive of scavenging, possibly by hominids (Vrba 1975).

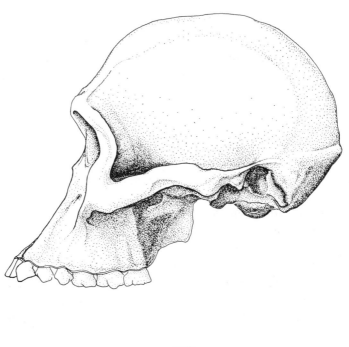

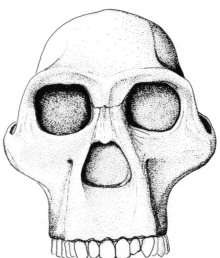

Fig. 2.6   Lateral and facial views of the restored cranium of *Australopithecus africanus* (based on the specimens from Sterkfontein; about one-half natural size).

probably in the Baringo area, and perhaps at Olduvai Gorge. Isolated specimens from Kanapoi (a distal humerus) and from Lothagam (a mandible fragment), Turkana district, northern Kenya, have also been tentatively attributed to the species (Patterson and Howells 1967, Patterson *et al.* 1970). However, the exact affinities of the Kanapoi specimen must remain rather uncertain as there are scant bases for comparison.[1] The Lothagam fragment may indeed represent *Australopithecus* – and if so is the oldest known representative of the genus – but its specific affinities are still undetermined; and it stands quite alone in respect to its very substantial antiquity (probably final Miocene).

The isolated temporal bone from the Chemeron Formation, Baringo area, Kenya, is apparently of very substantial antiquity, perhaps comparable to the Kanapoi occurrence. The specimen is *Australopithecus*-like in overall morphology, but diverges from the morphology found in *A. boisei* (Martyn and Tobias 1967). It most closely resembles *A. africanus* and is here very tentatively referred to that species.

The skeletal remains attributed to this species from various localities are set out in table 2.2. Those specimens only tentatively attributed to the taxon are underlined.

The single most important sample is that from Sterkfontein which represents the remains of probably over forty individuals. The Makapansgat sample is much more fragmentary, and represents only some seven to twelve individuals (Mann 1975). The type specimen from Taung, possessing a full deciduous dentition and erupting first permanent molars, is the best-preserved juvenile individual known of this species. It affords an adequate basis for comparison with subadult individuals from Sterkfontein, but unfortunately, only a single specimen from Makapansgat. Each of the larger samples shows a comparable mean age at death of approximately 22 years, and in each there are few or no infants or 'middle-aged' (over 40 years old) individuals (Mann 1975).

These samples afford a substantial basis for evaluation of basic cranio-facial morphology, dental structure, size and proportions – including variability and (limited) extent of sexual dimorphism – and

[1] Several distal humeri of early Hominidae are in fact known (see tables 2.1–4), but only the specimen from Kromdraai, associated with the type of *A. robustus*, can be precisely identified to species. McHenry (1973) and McHenry and Corruccini (1975) have clearly shown substantial differences between three of the known early hominid humeri, and it is particularly interesting that the oldest, the one from Kanapoi, is the most like that of modern man. Moreover two specimens, either known (Kromdraai 1517) or considered (ER-739) to represent one or another taxon of *Australopithecus*, are the most pongid-like.

TABLE 2.2 Remains attributed to Australopithecus africanus

| | Taung | Sterkfontein | Makapansgat | Omo basin, Ethiopia, Shungura Fm | East Rudolf, Koobi Fora Fm | Chemeron | Olduvai Gorge, Bed I |
|---|---|---|---|---|---|---|---|
| Crania | 1 (+ mand.) | 1511; Sts. 5, 17, 19, 20, 25, 26, 58, 60, 67, 71, 1006; StW-13 | MLD. 1, 3, 10, 37/38 | — | — | 1 (f) | — |
| Maxillae | — | 1512, 1514; Sts. 2, 8, 10, 12, 13, 27, 29, 32, 35, 42, 52, 53, 57, 61, 63, 64, 66, 69, 70; StW-18 | MLD. 6, 9, 11 MLC. 1 | — | — | — | — |
| Mandibles | — | 1515, 1516, 1522; Sts. 7, 18, 24, 36, 38, 41, 52, 62; StW-14 | MLD. 2, 4/18/24, 19/27, 22/34, 29 40 | Omo 18 (C) | — | — | — |
| Dentition | — | 69 | 4 | F = 9 locs. (36) E = 7 locs. (10) D = 8 locs. (10) C = 16 locs. (38) B = 5 locs. (12) | — | — | — |
| Postcranials | | | | | | | |
| Clavicle | — | | | | ER-1500 o; 1504/03 | | H. 48 |
| Scapula/ | — | Sts. 7 | — | Omo 119 (D) | ER-1500 l; 1504/03 | — | — |
| Humerus | — | Sts. 7 | — | | ER-1500 f, j; 1504/03 | | H. 49 |
| Ulna | — | | — | | ER-1500 e, k; 1504/03 | | — |
| Radius | — | Sts. 68 | — | — | | — | — |
| Manus | | | | | | | |
| Carpals | — | Sts. 1526 | — | Omo 18 (C) | | | — |
| Metacarpals | — | | | | | | — |
| Phalanges | — | | | | | | — |

| | Taung | Sterkfontein | Makapansgat | Omo basin, Ethiopia, Shungura Fm | East Rudolf, Koobi Fora Fm | Chemeron | Olduvai Gorge, Bed I |
|---|---|---|---|---|---|---|---|
| Vertebral column | — | Sts. 14 (15 + 3 sac.); StW-8 (4); Sts. 73 (1) | — | — | — | — | — |
| Pelvis | — | Sts. 14, 65 | MLD. 7/8; 25 | — | — | — | — |
| Femur | — | Sts. 14, 34, 1513; StW-25 | — | — | *ER-1500 b, d*; 1503/04 | — | — |
| Tibia | — | — | — | — | *ER-1500 a, c, h, j, r*; 1476 b, c | — | *H. 35* |
| Fibula | — | — | — | — | *ER-1500 g* | — | *H. 35* / *H. 8* |
| Pes | — | — | — | — | — | — | — |
| Talus | — | — | — | — | ER-1476 a | — | — |
| Calcaneum | — | — | — | — | — | — | — |
| Tarsals | — | — | — | — | — | — | — |
| Metatarsals | — | — | — | · | *ER-1500 m* | — | ? *H. 43* (2) |
| Phalanges | — | — | — | — | — | — | — |

*Note*. For the East Rudolf hominids, the following key is employed to differentiate the principal stratigraphic horizons from which they derive:

*Italics* – Sub-Chari, Upper Member, Koobi Fora Formation

**Bold type** – Sub-L/M Tuff Complex, sub-Okote and sub-Koobi Fora Tuff, Upper Member, Koobi Fora Formation

***Bold italics*** – Lower Member, Koobi Fora Formation

93

overall morphology of the axial skeleton and pelvis. However, they afford only partial and very limited insights into the proportions and morphology of the upper and lower limbs. This is a major deficit as it hinders severely comparisons with those body parts known in other Plio-Pleistocene Hominidae from elsewhere in Africa, notably East Rudolf and Olduvai Gorge.

The Omo succession, southern Ethiopia, yields largely fragmentary jaw parts, associated or isolated teeth and a few postcranial parts which have been referred to *A. africanus* (Howell and Coppens 1976). These derive from Members B, C, D, E, F and (lower) G of the Shungura Formation. In the last three members there is evidence for the presence of another species of the genus.

No hominid remains from the Koobi Fora Formation, East Rudolf, Kenya, have as yet been formally attributed to *A. africanus*. However, the author considers that upper and lower postcranial parts (no. ER-1500) from different localities in the Lower Member and probably others (nos. ER-1503/04 and ER-1476) from localities in the earlier part of the Upper Member of that formation may well be assignable to that taxon. They are tentatively so assigned here, with the *caveat* mentioned above that these body parts are either not adequately known or not appreciated among associated paratypes of this species.

A number of hominid postcranial parts from the oldest fossiliferous sediments of Olduvai Gorge have been attributed to the taxon *Homo habilis* (L. S. B. Leakey, Tobias and Napier 1964). However, there is no evidence conveniently sufficient to suggest that only a single taxon is represented by these specimens. In fact, several studies tend to suggest that some or all of these specimens reveal australopithecine and/or pongid features, hence *phenetic* affinities, or a set of similar resemblances (Day and Wood 1968; Lisowski, Albrecht and Oxnard 1974; Oxnard 1972, 1973; Tobias 1978c, Wood 1974a). These arguments, and the author's own observations on the relevant specimens (listed in table 2.2), are sufficiently convincing that the latter are here tentatively attributed to *A. africanus*. However, it should be stressed that these body parts are in fact either poorly known or completely unknown in paratype samples of this taxon, and hence it is more their small size, proportions, and un-*Homo*-like features that suggest this attribution, rather than any appropriately detailed analytical study of comparable body parts.

## Australopithecus boisei *L. S. B. Leakey, 1959*

This exceptionally robust species (*boisei*) of *Australopithecus* (see fig. 2.7) occurs in deposits of final Pliocene and earlier Pleistocene age in eastern Africa. For the moment its distribution is only documented in this portion of the continent and only in sedimentary situations adjacent to the Eastern Rift Valley. In most instances the species is more or less directly associated with another hominid species as well as with lithic materials and sometimes (at Olduvai Gorge and East Rudolf) even occupational situations reflecting culturally-patterned behaviour (which hominid's behaviour is still a subject for debate). The localities and skeletal parts attributed to *A. boisei* are set out in table 2.3.

The holotype of this species of *Australopithecus* is the almost complete cranium with full maxillary dentition of a young adult individual (L. S. B. Leakey 1959, Tobias 1967a). The specimen was recovered at Olduvai Gorge (Tanzania) from site FLK in sediments of Bed I from a land surface (weak palaeosol) formed towards the south-eastern margin of the lake. This surface preserved an ancient hominid occupation site, including patterned distributions of remains of a diversity of vertebrate species and associated artifacts of an Oldowan stone industry (M. D. Leakey 1971). The general and specific stratigraphic situation of the occurrence is exceptionally well documented, and its radiometric age and placement in the geomagnetic polarity scale are extremely well defined (Brock and Hay 1976, Curtis and Hay 1972, Grommé and Hay 1971, Hay 1971).

Additional hominid remains have since been recovered on, or in a surfacial relation to, this same occupation site. They include cranial fragments and upper teeth of one specimen, a molar tooth of a second and a tibia and fibula, largely complete, of a third.[1] The first have at one time or another been considered to represent a hominid other than *A. boisei* and are so considered here. The second has never been assigned to a particular hominid taxon but it too is considered here to represent a hominid different from *A. boisei* (see Wood 1974b). If this interpretation is accepted there is at this particular site evidence for the most direct and immediate temporal, sympatric association of two taxa of early Hominidae.

Hominid remains from some five other localities at Olduvai Gorge very probably represent *A. boisei*. In all, these specimens would seem

---

[1] The three specimens are Hominids 6, 44 and 35 (once attributed to 6); see L. S. B. Leakey (1960). The remains of Hominid 35 have been described by Davis (1964).

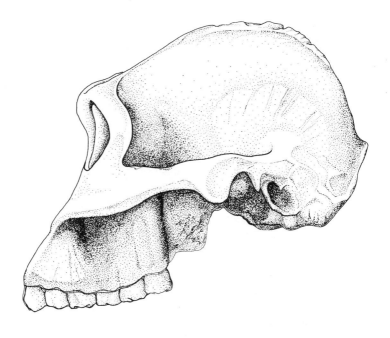

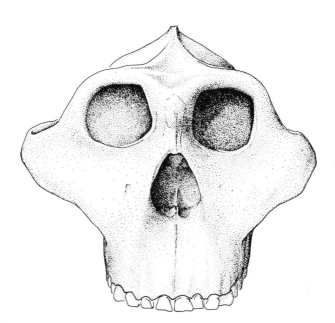

Fig. 2.7   Lateral and facial views of the restored cranium of *Australopithecus boisei* (based on specimens from Olduvai Gorge and Koobi Fora; about one-half natural size).

TABLE 2.3  *Remains attributable to* Australopithecus boisei

| | Olduvai Gorge | Peninj | Cheso-wanja | East Rudolf | Omo basin |
|---|---|---|---|---|---|
| Crania | H. 5 | — | CH-1 | ER-**732, 733,** **406, 407, 417,** **814, 1478, 1170** | L. 338y (E) |
| Maxillae | — | — | — | ER-*405, 1804* | — |
| Mandibles | — | × | — | ER-*404, 725,* *726, 728, 729,* **801, 805,** *818,* **819, 727,** *1468,* **1816, 812, 403,** **810, 1477,** *1469,* *1482, 1803, 1806,* *3230* | Omo 44, 57 (E) L. 7, 74A (G-5) |
| Dentition | H. 3; 26; 30(?); 38; 15 | — | — | ER-**802,** *1467,* **1171, 816, 998,** **1479, 1509** | E = 1 loc. (7) F = 3 locs. (4) G 1–13 = 3 locs. (11) |
| Postcranials | | | | | |
| Clavicle | — | — | — | — | — |
| Scapula | — | — | — | — | — |
| Humerus | — | — | — | ER-*739, 740,* **1504** | — |
| Ulna | — | — | — | — | Omo L. 40 (E) |
| Radius | — | — | — | — | — |
| Manus | — | — | — | — | — |
| Carpals | | | | | |
| Metacarpals | | | | | |
| Phalanges | | | | | |
| Vertebral column | — | — | — | — | — |
| Pelvis | — | — | — | — | — |
| Femur | H. 20 | — | — | ER-**738, 815,** **993,** *1463, 1465,* **1503, 1505, 1592,** *3728* | — |
| Tibia | — | — | — | ER-*741* | — |
| Fibula | — | — | — | — | — |
| Pes | — | — | — | — | — |
| Talus | | | | | |
| Calcaneum | | | | | |
| Tarsals | | | | | |
| Metatarsals | | | | | |
| Phalanges | | | | | |

*Note:* For the East Rudolf hominids, the following key is employed to differentiate the principal stratigraphic horizons from which they derive:

*Italics* – Sub-Chari, Upper Member, Koobi Fora Formation

**Bold** – Sub-L/M Tuff Complex, sub-Okote and sub-Koobi Fora Tuff, Upper Member, Koobi Fora Formation

***Bold italics*** – Lower Member, Koobi Fora Formation

to document the presence of this taxon from near the base of Bed I to close to the top of Bed II, a time-span of almost three-quarters of a million years.[1]

A partial hominid cranium, comprising most of the facial skeleton, the anterior part of the cranial base, and much of the right upper dentition is known from the Chemoigut Beds, Chesowanja, Kenya (Carney *et al.* 1971). Its age has been a subject of concern, but is now considered to be (broadly) earlier Pleistocene, and not particularly late within that time-range (W. W. Bishop, personal communication). It has generally been attributed to *Australopithecus*, although conflicting views have been expressed as to its probable extent of distortion and its presumed endocranial capacity (Szalay 1971, Walker 1972a). It is considered by the author to represent *A. boisei*. Olduvai Gorge has not yet yielded lower jaw parts of this species. The well-preserved adult mandible with complete dentition recovered from the Humbu Formation, at Peninj, Natron basin, Tanzania (Isaac 1965, 1967), was the first such specimen to be attributed to the species (L. S. B. Leakey and M. D. Leakey 1964).

The several members of the Koobi Fora Formation, East Rudolf, Kenya, have yielded numerous and often remarkably well-preserved skeletal remains attributable to this species (see table 2.3). Of these body parts[2] of nearly fifty individuals three derive from the sediments of the Lower Member (below the KBS Tuff), thirty derive from sediments of the lower part of the Upper Member (below the Koobi Fora, BBS, or Lower/Middle Tuff Complexes), and fifteen from sediments of the

---

[1] The specimens include two upper deciduous teeth representing a deciduous canine and upper second molar (Dahlberg 1960). The molar has been variously identified as another deciduous or permanent tooth by L. S. B. Leakey (1958), Robinson (1960) and von Koenigswald (1960). These remains (Hominid 3) come from the upper part of the infilling of a large stream channel, rich in vertebrate fossils and yielding a Developed Oldowan industry (see M. D. Leakey 1971, pp. 197–222) at site BK (uppermost Bed II); an $M_{\overline{2}}$ and two incisors (Hominid 38) at site SC, yielding a Developed Oldowan industry (related to Tuff 11D, upper Bed II); two upper molars and a canine (Hominid 15) associated with a few artifacts at site MNK from a reworked tuff in a former lake-margin context (lower part of upper Bed II); an $M_{\overline{3}}$ (Hominid 26) at site FLK-West (probably derived from lower Bed II); and a proximal femur fragment (Hominid 20) at site HWK (Castle) (probably derived from lower Bed II). The latter specimen has been preliminarily described and attributed to this species of *Australopithecus* (Day 1969).

[2] They include complete and partial crania (8 individuals), maxillae (2 individuals), mandibles (20 individuals), isolated and associated teeth (7 individuals), partial humeri (3 individuals), femora (8 individuals) and tibiae (1 or more individuals) (R. E. F. Leakey and Walker 1973; R. E. F. Leakey, Mungai and Walker 1971, 1972; Walker 1972b) as well as very probably other specimens (especially postcranial) still to be taxonomically assigned. The assignments already made are on the basis of preliminary identifications by Day, R. E. F. Leakey, Walker and Wood, and observations on the original specimens by the author.

upper part of the Upper Member (in or above these tuffs) (R. E. F. Leakey 1970, 1971, 1972, 1973, 1974, Walker and Leakey 1978).

In the Lower Member *A. boisei* is indeed rare, about as infrequent as *A. africanus* appears to have been. A species attributed to *Homo*, on the other hand, is more than five times as common. In the lower part of the Upper Member *A. boisei* is half again as common as a species attributed to *Homo*, whereas in the upper part of that member each taxon is about equally common. This extremely valuable, indeed unique, sample spans about a million years, from 1 million to perhaps 2 million BP, depending upon the posited age of the KBS Tuff (see Findlater *et al.* 1974, Fitch and Miller 1970).

The assignment of postcranial parts to this taxon is not always straightforward as there are several other hominid taxa represented in the East Rudolf succession. Moroever the postcranial skeleton of the genus *Australopithecus* is still incompletely known from the South African paratype samples, so similar body parts are often unavailable for comparative study. However, such attributions can be attempted, first and foremost, on the basis of morphological divergence from the structure characteristic of *Homo*, and secondly the occurrence of several specimens found in close proximity and derived from the same fosssiliferous horizon. There are several instances in which such hominid 'clusters' are known. This is the case in two floodplain palaeo-environments above the Middle Tuff in the Ileret area (Area 1) in which postcrania and mandibles occurred, as well as in another distributary palaeo-environment, just below the Lower Tuff (in Area 6A) in which cranial and jaw parts occurred. It is also the case in the Koobi Fora area (Area 105), in a channel above the KBS Tuff, where cranial and jaw parts and lower-limb bones occurred. Behrensmeyer (1976b) considers that the available evidence favours the close association of *Australopithecus* (*boisei*) with fluvial habitats – including gallery forest and riverine-associated bush – although lake-margin situations were also utilized (where remains attributed to *Homo* appear to predominate).

Skeletal remains attributable to *A. boisei* are not particularly common in the Omo succession, southern Ethiopia (Howell and Coppens 1976). The first firm documentation of this taxon is in Member E, about 2.1 million years ago, of the Shungura Formation, and comprises only a partial mandible (Omo Locality 57) and a series of associated permanent teeth (Locality 338x) as well as a complete ulna (Locality 40). The latter postcranial part is exceptionally poorly known in *Australopithecus*, but the distinctive morphology, size and proportions of this specimen diverge from the *Homo* condition, and are also in accord with other aspects of upper-limb morphology known for *A. boisei* (Howell and Wood 1974).

Only several isolated teeth from three localities represent this taxon in Member F of that formation, and in the lower, fluviatile sediments (Units G-3 and G-5) of Member G isolated or associated teeth from three localities and mandibles from two other localities (Localities 7A and 74A). It has not been surely documented in younger horizons in the Omo succession.

### Australopithecus crassidens *Broom*, *1949*

The robust species (*crassidens*) of *Australopithecus* (see fig. 2.8) is thus far known only from the Swartkrans locality, Krugersdorp area, Transvaal (table 2.4). It might be considered to be a related, sister species of *A. boisei*.

This site has long been recognized to have had a complex history of infilling and related movements of portions of the dolomite in which these cave systems were developed. Recent investigations there have not only confirmed a complex history, but have also revealed a substantially more prolonged period of infilling than was ever previously envisaged (Brain 1976, Butzer 1976, Vrba 1975). These results have important implications for the provenance, associations and relative ages of the numerous hominid remains recovered there.

The Swartkrans cave system comprises an outer cave filled with (a) Pink Breccia, an inner cave filled with (c) Brown (stratified) Breccia and (b) an intermediate Orange Breccia, at the base of the inner cave's infilling. The inner and outer caves are separated by a stone fallen from the roof that forms a floor barrier between them and blocks an underlying lower cave. Australopithecine remains have derived from the infilling (a), or from the intermediate unit (b) below the infilling (c). Recent work at the site has shown that the outer cave infilling (a) is itself complex, as those hominids and certain vertebrate taxa only occur in a localized area. Between a portion of that infilling (termed Member 1) and a younger infilling (termed Member 2) there occurred a prolonged period of erosion and of shaft opening into the site.

The robust australopithecine *A. crassidens*, and a distinctive, more archaic vertebrate fauna is restricted to the initial infilling (Member 1). One hominid specimen, a cranio-facial fragment, SK.847 referred to the genus *Homo*, as well as a few artifacts of Oldowan type, derive from

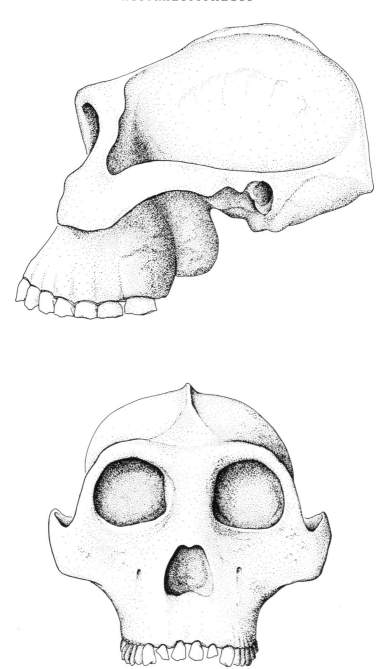

Fig. 2.8   Lateral and facial views of the restored cranium of *Australopithecus crassidens* (based on specimens from Swartkrans; about one-half natural size).

TABLE 2.4   *Remains attributable to* Australopithecus crassidens *and* Australopithecus robustus

|  | Swartkrans | Kromdraai-B |
|---|---|---|
| Crania | SK, 46, 47, 48, 49, 52, 54, 79, 83, 848, 869, 14003; SKW. 11, 29 | 1517 |
| Endocranial cast | SK. 1585 | — |
| Maxillae (with dentition) | SK. 11, 12, 13, 21, 55a, 57, 65, 66, 826, 831a, 838a, 839, 845, 877, 881, 1512, 1590, 1592, 14080, 14129; SKW. 12 | 1602 |
| Mandibles (with dentition) | SK. 6, 10, 12, 23, 25, 34, 55b, 61, 62, 63, 64, 74a, 81, 841a, 843, 844, 852, 858, 861, 862, 869, 876, 1648, 1586, 1514, 1587, 1588, 3978; SKW. 5 | 1517, 1536 |
| Dentition (isolated/associated) | 111 | 1603, 1604, 1600, 1601 (10 teeth) |
| Postcranials |  |  |
| Clavicle | — | — |
| Scapula | — | — |
| Humerus | SK. 860 | 1517 |
| Ulna | — | 1517 |
| Radius | — | — |
| Manus |  |  |
| Carpals | — | — |
| Metacarpals | SK. 84 (1), 14147 | 1517 (1) |
| Phalanges | — | L517 (2) |
| Vertebral column | SK. 853 (L), 854 (Ax), 3981 (T, L), 14002 (T, L) | — |
| Pelvis | SK. 50, 3155b | 1605 |
| Femur | SK. 82, 97 | — |
| Tibia | — | — |
| Fibula | — | — |
| Pes |  |  |
| Talus | — | 1517 |
| Calcaneum | — | — |
| Tarsals | — | — |
| Metatarsals | — | — |
| Phalanges | — | 1517 (2) |

the same infilling (Clarke 1977, Clarke, Howell and Brain 1970). The australopithecine sample comprises over 200 body parts including cranial fragments, mandibles, numerous isolated teeth and postcrania. These represent the remains of over seventy-five individuals, over 40% of which are immature and the remainder mature, but none older than their mid-30s (Mann 1975). Of the total hominid sample isolated or associated teeth are most common, whereas cranial and jaw parts are about half as common. The postcranial skeleton is represented by only a dozen pieces including fragmentary parts of the axial skeleton and upper and lower limbs.

Among the total fossil assemblage (excluding microvertebrates) in this infilling, hominids (14%) and cercopithecoids (13%), represented by some 4 taxa, are about equally common. There are 16 taxa of carnivores which comprise only 10% of the total assemblage. Several other large mammals – including 2 species of pigs, 3 species of equid, a sivathere – and a few porcupines and many specimens of 2 species of hyrax comprise altogether 20% of the assemblage. Nearly half (43%) of the assemblage is represented by bovids from some 16 taxa. These are largely of medium body-size with a high percentage of juvenile individuals. This along with other evidence of the condition of bone and body-part representation in the assemblage strongly supports the conclusion that predators, particularly leopard (*Panthera pardus*) but perhaps also sabre-tooths, were largely responsible for this fossil accumulation (Brain 1970, 1973, 1978; Vrba 1975).

The younger infilling (Member 2) of the Pink Breccia has yielded more advanced Palaeolithic artifacts of an Acheulian-like industry as well as a single hominid specimen referred to the genus *Homo*. This specimen (the SK. 15 mandible) is the type of *Telanthropus capensis* (Robinson 1953b, 1961) and was subsequently transferred by Robinson to the genus *Homo* and correctly referred by him to *Homo erectus*.

The representation of postcranial body parts makes comparison of *A. crassidens* with other *Australopithecus* samples difficult. There are fundamental similarities in proportions and overall structure in the innominate bones and femora of the several samples, here regarded as species, of *A. crassidens*, *A. boisei* and *A. africanus*; and some have argued (Lovejoy 1974, McHenry 1978; McHenry and Corrucini 1978, McHenry and Temerin 1979, Zihlman 1971, Zihlman and Hunter 1972), with good reason, that the postcranial skeleton, except for certain perhaps size-related differences, as well as sample-related differences, does not adequately distinguish these several early hominids. However, Robinson (1972, pp. 245–61) does not share this view, particularly in regard to samples considered (by him) to represent *A. africanus* (Sterkfontein, Makapansgat) and *A. (Paranthropus) robustus* (Kromdraai, Swartkrans), whereas others consider that 'the three australopithecines are, in a number of features, scaled variants of the "same" animal' (Pilbeam and Gould 1974). The various other body parts (hand bones, vertebrae) are too frequently incomparable, or at least as yet unstudied in an analytical, comparative manner. The principal morphological differences between these several samples, which are here considered to be of specific rank, are reflected in certain discernible and often measurable characters of the cranio-facial skeleton and the deciduous and permanent dentition.

## Australopithecus robustus Broom, *1938*

The fortunate recovery (Broom 1938, Broom and Schepers 1946) of hominid remains in 1938 from Kromdraai (Site B), one of several fossiliferous infillings at that locality (Brain 1975), afforded the first association of cranial and postcranial parts of *Australopithecus*. At the time of the discovery, adult cranial and dental parts of the previously known species, *A. africanus*, were just becoming known at nearby Sterkfontein, but were still quite fragmentary. However, morphological differences in comparable body parts – especially the facial skeleton and the morphology and size of permanent teeth – strongly suggested that the Kromdraai individual represented a different hominid taxon. Subsequently, that interpretation was confirmed by the recovery at the same locality of a juvenile hominid mandible with a deciduous dentition morphologically distinct from that of the type of *A. africanus* (Broom 1941). It was not until 1947 that upper deciduous teeth of *A. africanus* became known from the Sterkfontein site (Broom 1947), and still later that lower deciduous teeth were described from the same locality (Broom *et al.* 1950). It was only then, more than a decade after the initial find at Kromdraai, that the polyspecific character of these early Hominidae was clearly demonstrated.

A series of features of the adult cranial base and facial skeleton, as well as certain features and sizes and proportions of the permanent premolar–molar dentition, as well as the inferred size of the incisor–canine dentition (known from sockets and roots only), diverge from the *A. africanus* condition. This difference is further confirmed by the deciduous dentition, particularly the lower molar morphology.

Unfortunately most of the several postcrania associated with the Kromdraai type specimen (TH-1517) lack comparable counterparts in the other South African australopithecine samples. An exception is a partial though well-preserved ilium (TM-1605), which is seemingly of comparable morphology to, but somewhat larger than, *A. africanus* (the former is thought, and the latter is known, to be female), and is overall apparently quite similar to *A. crassidens*, which is probably a male individual (Robinson 1972, pp. 87–99). Unfortunately, there are no counterparts for the upper-limb elements, the two metacarpals of *A crassidens* representing digits different from that known from *A. robustus*. And there are no counterparts at all for the several portions of the latter's foot skeleton.

However, both upper-limb and lower-limb parts of *A. robustus* have some counterparts among some samples of early Hominidae in eastern Africa, including specimens considered to represent *A. boisei* and others attributed to the genus *Homo*. McHenry (1973, 1975a, b) has clearly demonstrated the distinction in (distal) humeral morphology between *A. robustus* and (presumed) *A. boisei*. Comparisons are still lacking for the metacarpal, and for the toe bones. However, the talus is overall broadly similar to a specimen from Olduvai (Hominid 8), and diverges from the structure considered characteristic of *Homo* (Day and Wood 1968).

The Kromdraai B hominid site is one of three infillings, the others being A and C at this locality. The main faunal site (A), lacking hominid remains, is now known to be of different age from the hominid infilling of Kromdraai B (Brain 1975). At least six individuals are represented among the sample from Kromdraai B, including two infants, two older children, and two adolescent to young adult individuals (see table 2.4). All were recovered from the upper part of the infilling. Hominids comprise 7% of the larger mammalian fossils (exclusive of micro-mammals), cercopithecoids (3 species) 43%, carnivores (8 species) 17%, and bovids (3 or more species) 28%, and three other mammals 5%. This site was an elongated solution gallery and the infilling accumulated along its slope. The extremely fragmented condition of the bone accumulation, and the high juvenile bovid percentages with predominantly low-weight species represented, would suggest that hominid hunting practices were at least in part responsible for the accumulation, although carnivores (whose coprolites are present) certainly also occupied the site. However, less than half a dozen possible stone artifacts have been recovered there.

Views of *Australopithecus* have changed markedly in the course of over fifty years since the initial discovery and recognition of the distinctiveness of the genus by Dart. Developments have occurred in many areas relevant to the understanding of such extinct representatives of the Hominidae. Population samples are now known which have afforded insight not only into most of skeletal structure, proportions and body size, but also the nature and extent of sexual dimorphism, and individual growth and development (Mann 1975). *Australopithecus* was not one of a kind, but a well-defined genus with several temporally and spatially distinctive species. The known temporal duration of the genus was of the order of three million years, and during the latter half of that span there is clear-cut evidence for the coexistence of *Australopithecus* species with species of the genus *Homo*. The palaeo-environmental circumstances under which *Australopithecus* species thrived were diverse, in time and in space, and were largely, though not wholly, varieties of open-country habitats (savanna and woodlands, in the broadest sense). Some earlier inferences of habitat differences between the several species of *Australopithecus* have been subsequently shown to be exaggerated or even in error. In-depth study of the microstratigraphic situations in which they occur, and their animal and plant associations, promise to afford a more precise assessment of their palaeo-environmental adjustments. Their animal associations were varied, and characterized by numerous extinct species, and even genera. These small-brained, upright bipedal creatures have sometimes been considered to have been both tool-makers and hunters; but the empirical evidence to support those speculations is either sparse, or ambiguous, or both. Artifacts have *never* been found directly associated with the small species, *A. africanus*, and in practically every instance when found with one or more robust species, a species of the genus *Homo* is also present, often in direct association. Although there is every reason to suppose that these early hominids pursued a predacious–foraging existence there is little to support their reliance upon hunting as a primary subsistence adaptation.

## THE GENUS *HOMO* LINNAEUS, 1758

Few problems in palaeo-anthropology have been more persistently troublesome than the recognition and definition of the genus *Homo*. This has traditionally been a consequence of the fragmentary hominid fossil record, the tendency to oversplit hominid taxa and hence emphasize differences rather than similarities, and the lack of suitable methods to resolve the relative and absolute ages of fossil samples. However, in recent years significant advances have been made toward surmounting these obstacles.

The relative ages of pertinent fossil hominids are now more reasonably and consistently estimated through more precise identification and comparison of associated vertebrate fossils. A variety of chemical tests on specimens of uncertain provenance or with unclear associations frequently enables their relative ages to be more precisely determined.

The refinement and more extensive application of radiometric dating techniques, particularly radiocarbon (and, more recently, amino-acid racemization) for later phases of the Pleistocene, and potassium–argon and palaeomagnetism for earlier phases of the Pleistocene (and the Pliocene), have afforded a generally reliable absolute time-scale for late Cenozoic events, in temperate and tropical latitudes on continents and the sediment-covered floors of major ocean basins.

The abandonment of outmoded typological concepts and the application of principles of the modern synthetic theory of evolution have led to substantial revisions of hominid taxonomy. Such revisions have not only, as we have seen, affected the genus *Australopithecus*, but also particularly extensive synonomy of specimens now assigned to the taxa *Homo erectus* and *Homo sapiens*.

Intensive field investigations, particularly in eastern Africa, have, over the past fifteen years, resulted in the recovery of samples of hominid fossils from situations in which contexts, associations and relative and absolute ages are uncommonly well defined. A number of these finds are of late Lower Pleistocene age[1] and fall within the known range of variation of *Homo erectus*. Among them are associated skeletal parts which add very substantially to an understanding of the overall morphology of that taxon. Other occurrences are of earliest Pleistocene age and demonstrably antedate *Homo erectus*, heretofore the oldest well-defined species of the genus *Homo*. These specimens have an important bearing on the intriguing question of the time and place of origin of the genus *Homo* and, consequently, on the definition of the genus. Interestingly, examination of the literature reveals a paucity of inclusive definitions of *Homo* in spite of the major concern of recent authors to seek to understand the emergence of the genus. Le Gros Clark (1964, p. 86) was among the first to offer a very general definition, later modified and substantially expanded to encompass hominid fossils from Olduvai attributed to a new, early species, *Homo habilis* (L. S. B. Leakey *et al.* 1964, Tobias 1965). Subsequently, Robinson (1968) offered another definition, although his sample was different, and most recently Campbell (1973, 1978) has produced another with again a somewhat different sample.

Each of these several characterizations (for, strictly speaking, they are not diagnoses) of *Homo* are somewhat similar, they stress various

---

[1] That is, antedating the Brunhes Normal Epoch, and falling within the latter part of the Matuyama Reversed Epoch. The base of the Middle Pleistocene is here considered to coincide broadly with the Matuyama–Brunhes boundary (Butzer 1974a).

features of endocranial volume, cranio-facial morphology, and (usually) postcranial structure with regard to posture and gait. However, none really adequately characterizes the fundamental overall structural and adaptive pattern of *Homo* which is only now becoming apparent in the light of the many important new discoveries in Africa. In fact, as most of this fossil material has still to be fully described and compared with other samples, it is surely premature to seek to specify in detail all the features of the genus.[1]

Most (though not all) workers would agree that adaptation for, and dependence upon, culturally patterned behaviour is a diagnostic characteristic of the genus.

## Homo habilis *Leakey, Tobias and Napier, 1964*

Early Hominidae which show trends in cranio-facial, dental and postcranial morphology approximating the genus *Homo*, but which antedate and differ morphologically from *Homo erectus*, are now known from several localities in sub-Saharan Africa. These localities include Swartkrans and Sterkfontein (South Africa), Olduvai Gorge (Tanzania),

[1] The principal features include, at least, the following: stature and body weight greater, often substantially so, than in *Australopithecus*; lower limb more elongated, and upper limb probably relatively shorter than in *Australopithecus*; limb skeleton adapted to fully upright stance and habitual bipedal gait; hand capable of full precision grip, with well-developed opposable thumb; endocranial volume substantially enlarged above that of *Australopithecus* species (though brain to body-size ratios probably similar), and in excess of 600 cc., and ranging to two or three times those values in successive species; substantial changes in cerebral proportions, particularly in regard to expansion of parietal and superior temporal regions, as well as parts of the frontal region; cranial vault expanded as a consequence of increased brain size, with enlarged parietals and temporal squama, and progressively updomed frontal; superior temporal lines rarely approach the mid-sagittal plane, and never form sagittal crest; reduced postorbital constriction; nuchal area smaller than in *Australopithecus*, and progressively reduced along with occipital curvature changes and torus reductions in successive species; occipital condyles set relatively forward on cranial base; supraorbital torus variably developed, but unlike the thin prominent structure in *Australopithecus*, often prominent, thick and continuous with supratoral sulcus in early species, variably reduced and with separate elements in successive species; facial skeleton reduced, only moderately prognathic to orthognathic, and smaller in proportion to neurocranium than in *Australopithecus*; zygomatic arch moderately to lightly built, and temporal fossa of variable size but not as large as in *Australopithecus*; distinct margin between subnasal maxillary surface and floor of piriform aperture; maxillary anterior teeth arranged in parabolic curve, usually without pronounced diastema; mandible generally with U-shaped internal contour, body less deep and robust, due to smaller tooth roots, than in *Australopithecus*, reduced inner symphysial buttressing and planum, with progressive tendency in successive species to develop external incurvature and mental trigone; anterior and posterior dentition harmoniously proportioned; canine teeth moderate- to small-crowned, wearing down from tip, and usually not overlapping after initiation of wear; $P_{\overline{3}}$ bicuspid with tendency to reduce lingual cusp and to formation of single root; $P_{\overline{4}}$ not molarized as in *Australopithecus* species; molars variable in size, with tendency to reduce M3. as well as to reduce some cusps and cingular remnants, and simplify primary groove patterns in successive species; deciduous dentition in which $dm_{\overline{1}}$ incompletely molarized, lingually displaced and frequently open anterior fovea, tuberculum molare, and (in primitive species) paraconid sometimes preserved.

TABLE 2.5  *Remains attributable to* Homo habilis

| | East Rudolf | Omo basin | Olduvai Gorge | Swartkrans | Kanam |
|---|---|---|---|---|---|
| Crania | ER-1470; 1590; 3732 | L. 894-1 (cf.) | H. 7; 13; 16; ?24 | SK. 847, 27 | — |
| Maxillae | — | Omo 75 (G-13) | — | — | — |
| Mandibles | 1483 (?); 1802 | Omo 860 (F-1) Omo 222 (G-5) Omo 427 (G-14) Omo 75 (G-13) | cf. H. 7, 4; 37 | SK. 45 | ?Mandible fragment |
| Dentition | 1590 | G-13, 10 locs. (24) | H. 16; ?21, 27, 39, 41, 44, 45 | SK. 2635 | — |
| Postcranials | | | | | |
| Clavicle | — | — | — | — | — |
| Scapula | — | — | — | — | — |
| Humerus | 1473 (?) | — | — | — | — |
| Ulna | — | — | — | — | — |
| Radius | — | — | — | — | — |
| Manus | — | — | H. 7 | — | — |
| Carpals | | | | | |
| Metacarpals | | | | | |
| Phalanges | | | | | |
| Vertebral column | — | — | — | — | — |
| Pelvis | 3228 | — | — | — | — |
| Femur | 1481; 1475; 1472 | L. 754 (G-4) | — | — | — |
| Tibia | 1481; 1471 | — | — | — | — |
| Fibula | 1481 | — | — | — | — |
| Pes | — | — | — | — | — |
| Talus | | | | | |
| Calcaneum | | | | | |
| Tarsals | | | | | |
| Metatarsals | | | | | |
| Phalanges | | | | | |

*Note:* All the East Rudolf specimens come from the Lower Member of the Koobi Fora Formation.

East Rudolf (Kenya), and the Shungura Formation, lower Omo basin (Ethiopia).

As most of these specimens are still under study by other workers, no attempt is made here to discuss all morphological features of this hominid taxon. The sample is inventoried in table 2.5.

The first assumedly ancient hominid fossil attributed to the genus *Homo* was a portion of a mandible recovered from Kanam West, near Homa mountain, Kenya, and assigned to a new species, *Homo kanamensis*

(L. S. B. Leakey 1935, 1936a). However, doubt was cast on the provenance, and hence the faunal associations and antiquity of the specimen, and this problem has never been finally resolved in spite of efforts to apply radiometric assays to the specimen and to the Kanam vertebrate fauna with which it was thought to be associated (Boswell 1935, Oakley 1960). On morphological grounds Tobias (1960, 1962) concluded that the specimen, which is in any case pathological, had affinities with an advanced species of the genus *Homo*, and was indeed far from really primitive.

The second and again presumably ancient hominid fossil attributed (ultimately) to the genus *Homo* comprised several specimens recovered in association with *A. crassidens* at the Swartkrans locality. The initial and type specimen, which Broom and Robinson (1949) designated *Telanthropus capensis*, was a largely complete mandible with five molar teeth. However, altogether some six specimens have been considered to represent this second hominid at this locality (Robinson 1953b).[1]

The evidence for and against multiple hominid taxa at Swartkrans has been a subject of continuing debate (for arguments *for* see Gutgesell (1970) and Robinson (1953b); for arguments *against* see Wolpoff (1968, 1971a)). However, the evidence now afforded by the new composite cranium convincingly demonstrates a total morphological pattern which approximates to that of a species of genus *Homo* and diverges significantly from *A. crassidens*, the predominant hominid represented at the Swartkrans locality (Clarke and Howell 1972, Wolpoff 1971b). The type specimen of the taxon *Telanthropus capensis* (the mandible SK. 15) is now known to derive from a younger infilling (Member 2) of the Swartkrans cave than that (Member 1) which yields australopithecine remains in such abundance (Brain 1976). The age of this later infilling is still unknown, but an extended episode of erosion preceded it; it yields Acheulian stone artifacts, and its vertebrate fauna is suggestive of the Cornelian Faunal Span (Vrba 1975) and hence of an age sometime in the Middle Pleistocene. In 1961 Robinson had already transferred the remains attributed to *Telanthropus capensis* to *Homo erectus*, and that is the most appropriate attribution for the type mandible, as well as the molar and the proximal radius found closely associated with it. However, it is not the case with the remaining three specimens which

---

[1] The remains comprise: a mandible fragment with two worn molars (SK. 45), an isolated left P$\overline{3}$ (SK. 18a), a proximal radius, the buccal half of a P$\overline{4}$, a maxilla with worn and incomplete I², P² and P⁴, which has now been shown to be part of a cranio-facial fragment previously considered as a robust australopithecine (see Clarke and Howell 1972, Clarke *et al.* 1970).

derive from the earlier, *Australopithecus*-rich infilling and which represent a tiny sample of an ancient species of the genus *Homo*.

At the nearby site of Sterkfontein some half-dozen specimens of hominid teeth and a fragmentary juvenile maxilla were recovered in 1957–8 from excavations in the western or 'Extension' part of the site. The stratigraphic relationships as well as the age of this part of the infilling of the Sterkfontein site and also the affinities of the hominid fragments have been matters of continuing concern (Robinson and Mason 1957). It was originally concluded that this red-brown 'Middle Breccia' overlay the lower, australopithecine-breccia unconformably, and this has since been essentially confirmed by a variety of work at the Sterkfontein locality, and these are now termed Members 4 and 5 respectively. It appears highly probable that a substantial lapse of time intervened between the two accumulations (Butzer 1978, Tobias and Hughes 1969). The faunal assemblages from these successive infillings have still to be fully compared; however, analyses of the Bovidae have clearly demonstrated marked differences in species composition indicative of quite different ages (Vrba 1974). The evidence is still inadequate to provide an accurate estimate of age for the assemblage which might be as little as 0.5 million years or as much as 1.0 million years or so.

Stone artifacts occur in substantial abundance only in this part of the Sterkfontein site and many have been recovered *in situ* from this breccia. A comparison of the artifact sample with other early lithic assemblages, particularly those from Olduvai Gorge, reveals broad similarity in tool types, although proportions vary, with the Developed Oldowan (M. D. Leakey 1970, 1971, pp. 262–9). In the faunal assemblage the bovids are represented by very fragmented remains of a diversity of species of varied weight classes, among which juveniles form only a small percentage. It has been suggested that this occurrence probably represents a hominid occupation site and that such remains may have been scavenged from carnivore kills (Vrba 1975).

These fragmentary remains have been attributed to *A. africanus*, but that attribution has been questioned.[1] Most of a hominid cranium has since been recovered from the younger infilling (Member 5) (Hughes and Tobias 1977) and its cranio-facial and dental morphology diverges

---

[1] These remains comprise: a juvenile maxilla with $M^1$, $dm^2$ and $dm^1$ (SE 255), an $M^2$ (SE 1508), another probable $M^2$ (SE 1579), an incomplete $P^3$ (SE 2396) and a C (SE 1937); for arguments in favour of *A. africanus* see Robinson (1958) and Robinson and Mason (1957, 1962), for arguments in favour of *Homo* see Tobias (1965).

from any *Australopithecus* species, and resembles instead various specimens, including that from Swartkrans, attributed here to *Homo* sp. nov.

Just over a decade ago L. S. B. Leakey, Tobias and Napier (1964) defined a new species, *Homo habilis* (fig. 2.9), and in so doing also redefined the genus *Homo*. The sample of the new taxon was considered to comprise remains of as many as eight individuals, all but one recovered from the pre-Lemuta Member sediments of Beds I and lower II, Olduvai Gorge.[1] These sediments are now known to have an age of 1.6 to 1.8 million years on the basis of radiometric dating and palaeomagnetic studies (Curtis and Hay 1972, Grommé and Hay 1971).

Not all the Olduvai specimens are unambiguously attributable to an ancient species of the genus *Homo*. Thus, a crushed and only partially restored cranium from the base of Bed I considered to represent *Homo habilis* (M. D. Leakey, Clarke and L. S. B. Leakey 1971) has some definite dental resemblances to such an early species of *Homo*, but seemingly a small cranial capacity, perhaps under 600 cc., and some features of the facial skeleton which seem to show resemblances to *A. africanus*. However, the condition of the specimen severely limits its accurate reconstruction. The attribution of other hominid postcranial specimens[2] from Bed I to such a taxon has also been questioned (Day 1976a, b; Wood 1974b). These specimens are all distinguished by their small size, and by certain morphological details which approximate often the condition found in *Australopithecus*, and especially *A. africanus*. They might well represent that taxon, but they are still under study and their affinities are still insufficiently determined.

Soon after the introduction of *Homo habilis*, some interesting and important comparisons were made between specimens attributed to that taxon and some early hominid material from Java (Indonesia) (Tobias

[1] The type of *Homo habilis* comprises cranial fragments (both partial parietals, occipital and other vault fragments, and petrous fragments), mandible with dentition through to $M_2^-$ and a number of hand bones of a juvenile individual (Hom. 7) recovered from or eroded from an occupation site (FLK NNI) in Bed I. An upper molar (left $M_-^1$ germ) was originally considered to belong to this individual, but is manifestly another, still younger individual, now designated Hom. 45. The other individuals considered as paratypes were Hom. 4, Hom. 6, Hom. 8, and possibly Hom. 35; all from Bed I, and Hom. 13 from Bed II, found slightly above the aeolian tuff of the Lemuta Member. Hom. 35 comprises largely complete adult left tibia and fibula, once attributed to Hom. 6, but now considered another individual; they were recovered on the same occupation surface at site FLK I as the type skull of *A. boisei*. Two other specimens were referred to the taxon, Hom. 16, from site FLK II, Maiko Gully, at the base of Bed II, and Hom. 14, cranial fragments of a juvenile individual probably derived from the same horizon as HOM. 13. More recently parts of eight other individuals, three of which (Hom. 27, 37 and 41) derive from lower Bed II and the remainder (Hom. 21, 24, 39, 44 and 46) from Bed I, have been recovered and attributed to this taxon.

[2] These include Hom. 8, 43, 48 and 49 from FLK NNI, Hom. 35 from FLK I and Hom. 10 from FLK NI (level 5).

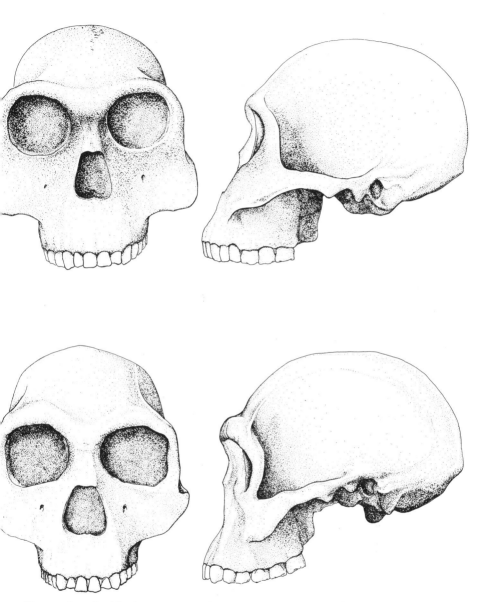

Fig. 2.9  Lateral and facial views of restored crania of (1) presumed male and (2) presumed female individuals of *Homo habilis* (based on specimens ER-1470 and ER-1813 respectively, from Koobi Fora; about two-fifths natural size).

and von Koenigswald 1964). The type mandible (Hom. 7) is extremely similar in morphology and in the size and morphology of its dentition to hominid specimens[1] from the Pucangan and the basal Kabuh Formations, Sangiran, central Java, referred to the taxon *Meganthropus palaeojavanicus* (von Koenigswald 1950) and it was concluded that these hominids represented the same hominid evolutionary grade, and one advanced beyond that represented by *Australopithecus africanus*. Robinson (1953a, 1955) had earlier argued that these Java specimens were most similar to a robust species of *Australopithecus* and von Koenigswald (1973) has since partly concurred with this view.

A paratype specimen (Hom. 13) attributed to *Homo habilis* was shown to have strong resemblances in jaw size and overall morphology and in its dentition to another set of Javanese fossil hominids. These are a series of specimens attributed to *Homo* ('*Pithecanthropus*') *modjokertensis*, the type specimen of which is a juvenile calvaria recovered at Perning, Modjokerto, eastern Java; altogether some six specimens have been attributed to this taxon (von Koenigswald 1936, 1940, 1950).[2] All of these are considered to have derived from the Pucangan Formation, although the exact provenance of some is frankly quite uncertain. This hominid shows some distinct differences in mandibular morphology, in the size of tooth crowns and roots and in the morphology of the permanent dentition from the type (Hom. 7) of *Homo habilis* and specimens attributed to *Meganthropus palaeojavanicus*. It has therefore been suggested that those hominids represented another more advanced evolutionary grade and one which more closely approached *Homo erectus*. Tobias and von Koenigswald (1964) have concluded that 'we think it wisest to keep the Bed II hominines separate from the Bed I habilines'.[3] This is not dissimilar from Robinson's conclusion that 'In

[1] The sample represented by this taxon comprises three principal specimens, all mandible fragments, listed as Sangiran 6 (two specimens of the right and left sides of the same individual '*Meganthropus* A') and Sangiran 8 ('*Meganthropus* B') (Marks 1953) in the inventory of Jacob (1973). Other still unpublished isolated teeth (Sangiran 7a), permanent as well as deciduous, probably also belong to this taxon (von Koenigswald 1950).

[2] It is noted that there is scarcely any morphological basis upon which to make comparisons of the five adult specimens, with the juvenile remains which represent the type. According to the inventory in Jacob (1973), including Perning 1 (type); Sangiran 1b (='Pithecanthropus' B), a hemi-mandible; Sangiran 4 (='Pithecanthropus' 4), partial calvaria and palate; Sangiran 5 (='Pithecanthropus dubius'), a mandible fragment; Sangiran 9 (='Pithecanthropus C'), a right mandible including the symphysis; and Sangiran 22, another mandible fragment (see Sartono 1975). It should be noted that von Koenigswald (1969) considers that Sangiran 5 and Sangiran 9, along with an isolated upper molar, should be attributed to a distinct species, *Homo (Pithecanthropus) dubius*, largely on the basis of lower premolar root structure.

[3] However, Weidenreich (1945) shows that the calvarial morphology of Sangiran 4 certainly appears to diverge in significant ways from the fragmentarily preserved calvaria of Olduvai Hom. 13. It is still unclear to what extent some of these differences may reflect sexual dimorphism; but some surely do not.

terms of the available evidence it would seem that there is more reason for associating the Bed I group of specimens with *Australopithecus* (*africanus*) and the Bed II group with *Homo erectus* than there is for associating the Bed I and II groups with each other.' (Robinson 1965; see also Tobias and Robinson 1966.) Nonetheless it is worth noting that these African hominid specimens are closely similar in age, and the geologically youngest specimens attributed to *Homo habilis* may be substantially older than the oldest remains (at Olduvai Gorge) attributed to *Homo erectus*. In Java, although the contextual evidence leaves much to be desired it would appear that the two grades – *palaeojavanicus* and *modjokertensis* – are at least in part nearly contemporary. If one is to accept the preliminary results from radiometric potassium–argon dating on these formations in Java those hominids *may be* 0.5 to 1.0 million years *older* than *Homo erectus* (Jacob 1972; Jacob and Curtis 1971; also G. H. Curtis, personal communication). However, due to the lack of accurate provenance data the precise temporal relationships and ages of these important hominid specimens are still largely unknown.

An extremely informative hominid fossil sample relevant to the elucidation of the origin of the genus *Homo* derives from the sub-KBS unit of the Koobi Fora Formation, East Rudolf, Kenya. This sedimentary unit probably covers a substantial time-span, to judge from the results of conventional potassium–argon age determination on tuffs capping it (Curtis *et al.* 1975). One specimen (ER-1590) from Area 12 derives from some 15 m below the KBS Tuff; that tuff in nearby Area 10 has an age of 1.54–1.6 million years. Assuming the tuff to have a mean age of 1.57 million years and reasonable sedimentation rates, the specimen should be about 1.8–1.9 million years old. The other specimens, as many as six cranial and jaw parts and postcranial remains including several lower-limb bones of a single individual, derive from Area 131 below the Karari escarpment. Here the overlying KBS Tuff has an age of $1.82 \pm 0.06$ million years. Using that age, and reasonable sedimentation rates, the oldest specimen (ER-1470, a fairly complete cranium), should be between 1.9 and 2.0 million years old. However, the various specimens here attributed to this sample occur at four principal horizons throughout some 40 m of section so the total time-span is probably of the order of 1.8–2.0 million years.

This valuable hominid sample throws important new light on the structure and organization of an ancient species attributable to the genus *Homo*. This includes overall cranial morphology and endocranial capacity (ER-1470, 1590), facial structure (ER-1470), upper (deciduous and permanent) dentition (ER-1590), mandible structure (ER-817, 1483,

1801, 1802) and permanent lower dentition (ER-1801, 1802, 1462) and the size and structure, if not the exact proportions, of the lower limb (ER-1472, 1475, 1481, 1471). In all respects there are significant departures from the structure characteristic of *Australopithecus* species, and on the contrary approximations to a condition resembling genus *Homo*.

Remains of other hominid taxa are also documented in this section. Several fragmentary specimens from low (ER-1474) and higher (ER-1803) in the section are of indeterminate affinities. Two specimens, both mandibles (ER-1482, 1469), from low and higher in the section represent *Australopithecus boisei*. Associated upper and lower postcranial parts of a single individual (ER-1500) from near the top of the section resemble *Australopithecus*, and are tentatively referred by the writer to *A. africanus*.

The uppermost members of the Shungura Formation, lower Omo basin, Ethiopia are generally less richly fossiliferous than the underlying members. Hominid fossils are here very rare. The most important specimen in this regard is a fragmentary hominid cranium with premolar–molar dentition (specimen Loc. 894-1). It derives from uppermost Member G (G-28). The occurrence underlies a tuff dated ∼1.84 million BP, and falls in the lower portion of the Olduvai Event within the Matuyama Reversed Epoch (Brown 1972, Brown and Nash 1976, Brown and Shuey 1976, Shuey, Brown and Croes 1974).

The premolar–molar dentition in size and proportions and preserved morphology resembles that of other specimens attributed to this taxon. Sufficient of the vault bones and parts of the base are preserved to suggest an endocranial capacity substantially larger than in species of *Australopithecus*. The cranial morphology, particularly that of the occipital and inferior temporal areas, also diverges from the *Australopithecus* condition, and in so doing approaches the structure considered to characterize an early species of *Homo* (Boaz and Howell 1977).

Essentially all the hominid skeletal remains attributed to such an ancient species of the genus *Homo* fall within the time-range of about 2.0 to 1.5 million years BP. Campbell believes that 'the boundaries of sequent taxa...should be conventionally agreed upon time-lines, rather than diagnostic morphological features'. He does not believe 'that the morphological distance between the mean of *A. africanus* and *H. erectus* is sufficient to justify creation of another species between them in the lineage' (Campbell 1974; see also Campbell 1963, 1973). Thus he considers that such hominids between 2.0 and 1.3 million years old should be assigned to *A. africanus*, with distinctive chrono- and geographic subspecies, *habilis* (in Africa) and *modjokertensis* (in south-eastern Asia). Campbell defines (arbitrarily) '*Homo* as those hominids leading to modern man and less than 1.3 million years of age', and among which there were elaborated cultural developments in respect to language and to technology which enabled effective occupation and exploitation of Eurasian temperate latitude habitats (Campbell 1972).

This author considers, however, that these early hominids, which are not yet *H. erectus* and which significantly diverge in total morphological pattern of cranio-facial, dental and postcranial morphology from *A. africanus*, represent a distinct taxon. It is a valid species in its own right, although the question of synonymy – different names which may have been applied to what is a single taxon – has not yet been resolved. Moreover there appears to have been considerable phyletic evolution, especially in cranio-facial and dental morphology, within this chrono-species. This is evident both in Indonesia and at Olduvai Gorge, and may also be the case at East Rudolf.

In spite of recent advances toward the documentation of the emergence of the genus *Homo* the gaps that still exist in the fossil record are such as to leave both the locale and the time in question. Recent discoveries in the Hadar Formation, central Afar depression, Ethiopia, tend to suggest that some 3 million years ago hominids with some *Homo*-like features of jaws and permanent dentition may have existed nearly contemporaneously with *Australopithecus africanus* (Taieb *et al.* 1976).

## Homo erectus

The extinct hominid species, *Homo* (ex-Pithecanthropus) *erectus*, was initially established on the basis of a skull cap (see fig. 2.10) recovered in 1891 from fluviatile deposits of the Kabuh Formation (Trinil Beds), exposed along the Solo river, in central Java (Dubois 1895).[1] The species became only really adequately known and its distinctiveness thoroughly established nearly half a century later with the recovery of additional, better preserved calvaria and other skeletal parts from the Sangiran dome and the Ngandong locality, along the Solo river in Java (von Koenigswald 1940, Oppenworth 1932, Weidenreich 1951), and

[1] A fragmentary juvenile mandible attributed to the species, and the first hominid remains found, was recovered from similar deposits south of Trinil at the Kedungbrukus locality in 1890 (Dubois 1891, Tobias 1966). The author considers that the several femora attributed to this taxon by Dubois (1926, 1934) cannot, on morphological grounds, represent this extinct species (see Day and Molleson 1973).

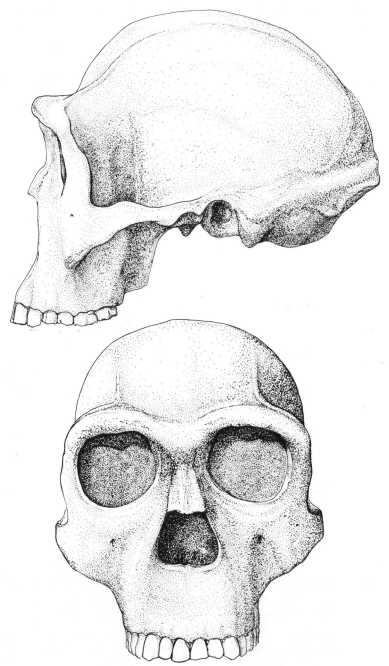

Fig. 2.10  Lateral and facial views of the restored cranium of *Homo erectus* (based on specimen ER-3733 from Koobi Fora; about three-fifths natural size).

from 1923 onwards from excavations of the extensive cavern infilling (Locality 1) at Choukoutien (Hopei), north China, which afforded an unprecedented hominid sample – including calvaria, mandibles, teeth and postcranial bones totalling nearly fifty adult and juvenile individuals – meticulously described by Black and Weidenreich (Black 1931; Black *et al.* 1933; Weidenreich 1936, 1937, 1941a, 1943). The recovery of additional remains from several localities in Java (Jacob 1975, Sartono 1971, 1975) and from renewed excavations at the Choukoutien locality (Woo and Chao 1954a, b, 1973), as well as the Lantian locality, Shensi (Woo 1964a, b, 1966) has further increased the Asian sample of this hominid species and afforded a fuller understanding of its morphology and variability (Woo and Chao 1959).

A diversity of skeletal parts attributable to *Homo erectus* is known from a dozen localities in northern, eastern and southern Africa (table 2.6). In Morocco there are five localities, in Algeria one, in Tchad possibly one, in Ethiopia two, in northern Kenya an extensive area with many localities, in Tanzania one locality and in South Africa two localities. The North African localities have yielded calvaria, jaw parts and teeth, whereas only a mandible and isolated teeth are certainly known from South Africa. Of the several localities in East Africa those of Olduvai Gorge, Tanzania, and East Rudolf, Kenya, have afforded a rich sample of skull and jaw parts, teeth and postcrania, including some associated parts of individuals.

Many designations have at one time been applied to specimens now reasonably assigned to this species, and by a decade ago the assignment of the species *erectus* to the genus *Homo* was quite commonly accepted, as the morphology did not justify distinction at the generic level (Campbell 1963, 1965). The first hominid remains in Africa to show *Homo erectus* features were recovered in 1933 from a quarry in the consolidated dune of Kébibat, south of Rabat, Morocco (Marçais 1934). It is now at least clear that this formation represents a continental littoral accumulation during the (middle) Tensiftian stage, or at latest in the subsequent Presoltanian stage, which are generally considered to correspond to the Penultimate Glacial stage of Europe (Biberson 1961, 1964). The relative age of the specimens has been discussed on various occasions and thorium–uranium measurements on mollusca from an overlying horizon suggest an age of $\sim 200\,000$ years (Biberson 1963, 1964; Choubert and Marçais 1947; Lecointre 1960; Neuville and Ruhlmann 1942; Stearns and Thurber 1965). Study of the remains revealed their general resemblance in mandibular morphology and

TABLE 2.6  *Remains attributed to Homo erectus*

| | North Africa | | Eastern Africa | | | South Africa |
|---|---|---|---|---|---|---|
| | Morocco | Algeria | Ethiopia | East Rudolf | Olduvai | |
| Crania | Salé Sidi Abderrahman - Thomas Quarry | Ternifine (par.) Yayo (Chad)? | L. 996 (ff)-Omo, Gombore II, Melka Kunturé (ff) | 1466 (f), 1805, 1821 (f), 3733 | H. 2, 9, 12, ?25 | — |
| Maxillae | Mifsud-Giudice | — | | 807, **1814** | H. 11 | SK. 15; (+18, 43 teeth) |
| Mandibles | Mifsud-Giudice Sidi Abderrahman (a) Thomas Quarry (b) Littorina Cave | Ternifine (3) | — | 731, 820, 992, 1811, 1801, 1730, **1501, 1502+ 1812, 1507** | H. 22, 23, 51 | |
| Dentition | — | Ternifine (7) | — | 732 (6), 808 (8), 809 (3), 803 (2) | | STE (7) |
| Postcranials | | | | | | |
| Clavicle | — | — | — | — | — | — |
| Scapula | — | — | — | — | — | — |
| Humerus | — | — | — | — | H. 36 | — |
| Ulna | — | — | — | 1591? | — | |
| Radius | — | — | — | — | — | ?SK. 18 |
| Manus | | | | | | |
| Carpals | | | | | | |
| Metacarpals | | | | | | |
| Phalanges | | | | | | |
| Vertebral column | — | — | — | — | — | — |

TABLE 2.6 (cont.)

| | North Africa | | Eastern Africa | | | South Africa |
|---|---|---|---|---|---|---|
| | Morocco | Algeria | Ethiopia | East Rudolf | Olduvai | |
| Pelvis | — | — | — | — | | — |
| Associated postcranials | — | — | — | 803 (upper and lower) 164 (manus phalanges) | H. 28 | — |
| Femur | — | — | — | **737, 1809** | H. 28; ?34 | — |
| Tibia | — | — | — | ?**1810**; 813B | ?H. 34 | — |
| Ribula | — | — | — | — | — | — |
| Pes | — | — | — | | | — |
| Talus | | | | 813A | | |
| Calcaneum | | | | | | |
| Tarsals | | | | | | |
| Metatarsals | | | | | | |
| Phalanges | | | | | | |

*Note*: For the East Rudolf hominids, the following key is employed to differentiate the principal stratigraphic horizons from which they derive:
*Italic figures* – Sub-Chari, Upper Member, Koobi Fora Formation
**Bold figures** – Sub-L/M Tuff Complex, sub-Okote and sub-Koobi Fora Tuff, Upper Member, Koobi Fora Formation

proportions, and in the size and morphology of the upper and lower dentition to *Homo erectus* (Arambourg 1963; Vallois 1945, 1960). Another partial hominid mandible, of (earlier) Tensiftian age (Arambourg and Biberson 1955, 1956; Biberson 1956) and with *H. erectus* features was subsequently recovered (in 1955) from Littorina cave, in the Schneider pit, at the huge Sidi Abderrahman quarry system, south-west of Casablanca (Biberson 1956, 1971). Also of younger Tensiftian age is a hominid skull cap and part of the upper jaw with several teeth. It was recovered from a quarry just north of Salé in Atlantic Morocco and the morphology is distinctively *Homo erectus* (Jaeger 1973, 1975a).

A left mandible, preserving several teeth and showing *H. erectus* morphology, particularly in the dentition, has also been recently recovered from still older continental deposits, probably of the final Amirian stage or later, in the Thomas Quarry 1, south-east of Sidi Abderrahman (Sausse 1975).[1] These remains, along with the specimens from artesian lake sediments at Ternifine, near Palikao, Algeria, are the oldest known hominids and the earliest documented occurrence of *Homo erectus* in northern Africa. The Ternifine specimens include three mandibles (with dentition), a parietal, and two mandibular and seven maxillary teeth, three of the latter deciduous molars (Arambourg 1963). The richly fossiliferous deposits yielding these specimens have been considered to be correlative with the Amirian stage of Atlantic Morocco (Biberson 1963). However, there is scarcely any appropriate biostratigraphic basis for a really precise assessment of the relative and absolute age of this locality and its important fossils.[2]

All the ocurrences of *H. erectus* in the Maghrib are associated with an Acheulian stone industry.

Although the ill-preserved fragment of a hominid frontal and face from Yayo in northern Tchad has been considered to be australopithecine (Coppens 1961, 1962, 1965, 1966) its facial morphology diverges in important aspects from *Australopithecus* and in so doing approaches more closely the structure characteristic of *Homo*. The relative age of the occurrence is based solely on a few associated and essentially undiagnostic mammal species, including a loxodont elephant

---

[1] Some cranial parts and eleven upper permanent teeth reported by Ennouchi (1972) from a nearby locality (Thomas Quarry 2) were recovered from a solution cavity in the Amirian-age dunes and hence must be of more recent geological age, perhaps Tensiftian (see Jaeger 1975a, b).

[2] The Ternifine macro- and micromammals are overall more primitive than those of other 'Middle' Pleistocene fossiliferous localities in the Maghrib, and still have certain important resemblances to faunal assemblages attributed to the provincial 'upper Villafranchian' (Arambourg 1962, Jaeger 1969, 1975a, b). However, on the evidence of the micromammals it is possible that a substantial time gap, perhaps as much as 0.3 million years, might exist between the latter and

which is inseparable from *L. africana* (Coppens 1965, Maglio 1973), a species of Middle to Late Pleistocene and, of course, more recent age.

An extensive sample of *Homo erectus* remains is now known from eastern Africa. The largest collections are from the post-Lemuta portion of the fluvio-lacustrine deposits at Olduvai Gorge (Tanzania) and from the upper part of the Koobi Fora Formation of East Rudolf (Kenya).

Remains of ten individuals attributable to *Homo erectus* have been recovered from Olduvai, of which two derive from Bed II, and seven from Bed IV.[1] Apparently all or most of these hominid remains occur within the later part of the Matuyama Reversed Epoch, and hence are older than 700 000 years (Hay 1976, p. 119; A. Cox, personal communication). The remains are thus probably very broadly contemporaneous with typical *Homo erectus* from Java (Jacob 1973; G. H. Curtis, personal communication). Most, if not all, of the *H. erectus* specimens from Olduvai appear to be associated with an Acheulian stone industry.

This species is very well documented in the upper Koobi Fora Formation, East Rudolf. The sample comprises body parts of over 20 individuals, including cranial parts of 5 individuals, mandibles of 9, associated teeth of 4, upper-limb parts of 3, and lower-limb parts of 6 individuals (R. E. F. Leakey 1976a). These specimens are about equally divided in provenance between the lower or Koobi Fora Unit, and the upper or Chari Unit of the upper part of the formation. They range in age from < 1.6 million years (the age of the type KBS tuff in Area 105) to ~ 1.2 million years (the age of the Chari tuff from Area 1) (Curtis *et al.* 1975, Fitch and Miller 1976). Hence the sample broadly spans the same time-range as is the case at Olduvai Gorge, except that some still younger occurrences are present at the latter locality. The Olduvai and East Rudolf samples afford a wealth of new data on African populations of *Homo erectus*. They also afford important new evidence on the structure and variation of body parts hitherto unknown in this species.

Extremely fragmentary remains attributable to *Homo erectus* are known from two localities in Ethiopia. Member K of the Shungura

the Ternifine locality. There is some macro-and microfaunal evidence, admittedly indirect and inferential, to suggest that Ternifine may well be younger than the Ubeidiya locality (Israel) the fossiliferous horizons of which probably antedate the Brunhes Normal Epoch on the basis of potassium–argon and palaeomagnetic measurements (Horowitz, Siedner and Bar-Yosef 1973, Siedner and Horowitz 1974). However, there is still unfortunately no direct evidence which would permit the Ternifine locality to be placed either before or after the Brunhes–Matuyama epoch boundary, at just under 0.2 million years BP.

[1] Bed IV was formerly subdivided into units IVa and IVb, but the latter, upper part is now given separate formational status and termed the Masek Beds. Hom. 23 derives from these beds. Hom. 34, the affinities of which are unclear as the remains are pathological, derives from Bed III or the base of Bed IV (Hay 1971).

Formation, lower Omo basin, has afforded parietal and temporal fragments with the characteristic morphology of this species. The remains date from toward the close of the Matuyama Reversed Epoch, in that portion preceding the Jaramillo Normal Event, and hence have an age of between about 1.0 and 1.2 million years (Shuey *et al.* 1974). One of the Acheulian occupation places (Gombore II) at Melka Kunturé, in the Ethiopian highlands south of Addis Ababa, has also yielded a partial parietal bone which is suggestive of this species. The age of this occurrence is unknown, but generally considered to fall within the (later) Middle Pleistocene (Chavaillon 1973; Chavaillon, Brahimi and Coppens 1974). Substantial parts of a hominid cranium with *Homo erectus* affinities have also been recovered from the Bodo locality in the middle Awash valley (Conroy *et al.* 1978).

Two localities in South Africa have afforded hominid remains attributable to *Homo erectus*. It is now known that a mandible, two lower premolars and an associated proximal radius, all considered to represent the same individual, derive from a post-australopithecine infilling at the Swartkrans locality (Brain 1978, Butzer 1978). The associated fauna suggests a substantially more recent age, presumably later Middle Pleistocene, than the initial, australopithcine-rich infilling. The faunal assemblage of this infilling is distinctive in the predominance of smaller, low-weight bovid species and the high percentage of juvenile individuals. Vrba (1975) considers this pattern is indicative of predation, with a specialization on smaller prey, and to result from hominid hunting activities. This infilling has yielded a number of stone artifacts which seemingly resemble the Developed Oldowan Industry of eastern Africa (M. D. Leakey 1970).

Descriptive, comparative and analytical studies are still insufficient to permit any full explication of the structural transformations which occurred between the earliest species of *Homo* and *Homo erectus*. However, it is now clear that the total morphological pattern and the adaptive grade of the latter can only be evaluated through reference to the structure characteristic of the former species. The fundamental distinctions between *Homo erectus* and *Australopithecus* have long been recognized and are now well established.[1]

---

[1] Useful summaries are to be found in Brace (1967, pp. 71–81), Howells (1966), Le Gros Clark (1964, pp. 88–122) and Tobias (1974). Other useful general discussions are: Coon (1962, pp. 371–481), Ferembach (1965), Gieseler (1974), Howells (1973, pp. 63–82) and Pilbeam (1975). For discussion of changes in the dentition see Petit-Maire and Charon (1972), Pilbeam (1972, pp. 157–70) and Robinson (1956). For changes in cranial morphology see Bilsborough (1973), Heintz

The locomotor skeleton of *Homo erectus* has been sometimes considered to be morphologically and functionally indistinguishable from that of *Homo sapiens*. Certain evidence suggestive of that conclusion is faulty, and substantially expanded knowledge of the postcranial skeleton of this species now confirms a number of distinctive morphological features, particularly of the lower limb. Nonetheless, the functional locomotor capabilities would appear to have been similar overall to *Homo sapiens* with respect to adaptation for habitual erect posture and efficient striding bipedal gait. These adaptations include an alternating pelvic tilt mechanism, a powerful hip extensor mechanism for erecting or raising the trunk, a pelvic rest mechanism, posterior displacement of the centre of gravity behind the hip joints, transferral of body-weight to the pelvis by way of the sacral suspensory mechanism, powerful hip flexion, and powerful knee extension (Day 1971). Other portions of the lower limb are less well known, in particular the foot skeleton. Nonetheless, the tibia has strong soleus muscle attachments; the talus shows the form and joint morphology of a propulsive, arched foot and the form, buttressing and torsion of the third metatarsal is also in keeping with the full development of a transverse arch and adaptations to withstand propulsive forces (Day 1973a).

The axial skeleton and the forelimb are still imperfectly known in this species, although the latter (except the hand) is now more fully documented in the fossil record than before. Although much of the relevant skeletal material is not yet fully published or even analysed, it would appear that the forelimb morphology also diverged in some distinctive ways from the *Homo sapiens* pattern. However, the functional significance of these divergences is still unclear. The overall close approximation to the *Homo sapiens* condition is noteworthy by comparison with the many divergences from the structure characteristic of *Australopithecus*.

The most obtrusive distinctions between *Homo erectus* and *Homo sapiens* are those of cranio-facial and dental morphology. The differences are many and complex, and their interrelationships are ill-understood. It is generally considered that transformation in the form and proportions of the cranial vault are, in complex ways, related to the growth, proportional alteration and probable reorganization of the

(1967) and Weidenreich (1941b, 1947). For changes in brain size and certain proportions (largely on the basis of endocranial casts) see Holloway (1972, 1974, 1975) and Tobias (1971a), and for changes in the postcranial skeleton see McHenry (1975a, b). Some of the cultural aspects of the problem are discussed by Campbell (1972), Freeman (1975a), Howell (1972) and Isaac (1972a, b).

cerebral cortex and underlying structures. However, the remarkable reduction in thickness of vault bones, and the modification of cranial superstructures in size, extent, and form is another, as yet ill-understood, matter. The reduction of the facial skeleton and mandible is in part associated with changes in the absolute and relative size of teeth, particularly roots and their supporting bone and associated areas of stress absorption and transmission. However, other changes in facial structure, and, particularly, in dental morphology are largely uninvestigated.

*Homo erectus* was a successful, widely distributed early human species having a temporal duration of the order of a million years. However, population samples of the species are still smaller than those of *Australopithecus* species, and the skeletal biology is still incompletely known. It is now established that the species diverged not only in cranial and dental morphology, but also in postcranial morphology from the condition characteristic of *Homo sapiens*. Racial or subspecific differences have been suggested for the several East Asian and African population samples. In recent years the origins of *erectus* have been recognized to lie earlier than had previously been supposed, and are now considered to be in an antecedent species of the genus *Homo* present some two million years ago. Robust species of *Australopithecus* persisted into the temporal span of *Homo erectus* in Africa and are known even from the same immediate locales. Perhaps the latter species played some role in the extinction there of the last species of *Australopithecus* about a million years ago. The enhanced evidence of cultural capacities, expressed in residues on occupational sites, in elements of material culture, hunting practices, use of fire (in northern latitudes), and overall intensified manipulation of the environment and its products, affords this species a distinctively more familiar human aspect in comparison with *Australopithecus* species.

## Homo sapiens *Linnaeus, 1758*

The origin of *Homo sapiens* is still largely unknown. The source, the time and the place of the differentiation of the species, and the circumstances under which that transformation occurred are each matters in need of further investigation. Nevertheless, the fossil record in Africa does afford examples of a number of Pleistocene hominids which are relevant to the understanding of the earlier history of *H. sapiens*, and should deservedly be attributed to that species.

Surprisingly there appears to be no inclusive definition of our own polytypic species. Perusal of an extensive relevant literature reveals an unexpected lack of concern with the biological distinctiveness of a now dominant mammalian species. Most characterizations, including those of philosophers and theologians, and even a number of biologists, are based on a single or but few traits. For the most part those of the former employ behavioural attrib⁻ ،es to establish a 'difference in kind' between human and non-human animals which may well be relevant at the familial and generic level. Many, and probably most, such attributes are impossible to infer from the prehistoric record, although some might well be relevant to the delineation of the species *sapiens*.

Other definitions are largely or wholly biological and suffer from various deficiencies. First, and foremost, is the emphasis on single traits – particularly brain size (hence cranial capacity) – rather than an appreciation of a total morphological pattern. Le Gros Clark (1964, pp. 50–1) afforded such a definition, portions of which remain useful. However, he excluded from the sample those antecedent human populations of mid and earlier Upper Pleistocene age which nonetheless have some features indicative of the species. The temporal duration of the species, and data relevant to its origins, are thus avoided by this restricted definition.

No attempt is made here to seek to provide an inclusive definition of the species *sapiens*. However, certain evolutionary trends and derived features – behavioural as well as morphological – are apparent when comparisons are made between late Pleistocene/Recent populations of *Homo sapiens sapiens* and the antecedent human species, *Homo erectus*. Ultimately a more complete knowledge of these trends and of the more important derived features will afford a basis for assessing the temporal duration of the species *sapiens*.

A scattered, diverse and unfortunately still quite scant set of evidence now tends to suggest that the origin of *Homo sapiens* is to be sought among human populations of Middle Pleistocene age. These populations, by definition, would thus have been in existence already during some part of the Brunhes Normal Epoch, less than 700 000 years ago. Unfortunately the temporal relationships between (late) *Homo erectus* populations and (earliest) representatives of *Homo sapiens* are still very ill-defined. Nonetheless most (if not all) students of the problem consider it likely that the former gave rise to the latter.

The most useful fossil record relevant to this issue is that afforded by hominid occurrences in western Europe and in north-western Africa (Morocco).

In western Europe emergent *Homo sapiens* (subsp. indet.) fossils are documented from fluviatile sites attributed to the (late) Holsteinian Interglacial stage (Swanscombe, Steinheim), and from various cave infillings generally attributed to several successive phases of the Penultimate Glacial Complex (Montmaurin, Orgnac, La Chaise, Lazaret). Not only do these hominid remains reveal features which diverge from the distinctive *Homo erectus* morphology, but there are still certainly (or possibly) older specimens, associated with Biharian-type mammal faunas and dating from the earlier part of the Brunhes Normal Epoch, somewhat after 700 000 years ago, which similarly show some such divergent features. These specimens include Mauer (Germany), Vertésszöllös (Hungary), and Petralona (Macedonia), and perhaps even Vergranne (Doubs, France). Consequently the *erectus–sapiens* transition may ultimately prove to fall within the earlier part of the Middle Pleistocene.

In the Maghrib a number of isolated hominid finds from the Moroccan littoral derive from sedimentary formations considered to represent the upper part of the Middle Pleistocene (there is, however, no palaeomagnetic control against which their age may be judged). These are specimens attributed to the marine Anfatian stage (Salé), the lower and middle continental Tensiftian stage (Littorina cave, Sidi Abderrahman; Kébibat, and Thomas Quarry 2, Casablanca, respectively). The Thomas Quarry 1 mandible is perhaps mid-Tensiftian in age.[1] The time-span encompassed by these finds is still uncertain; but, on the basis of thorium–uranium measurements it may be estimated to extend from 0.3 to 0.1 million years.

The incomplete Salé cranium shows features which are overall broadly within the known range of *Homo erectus* morphology. However, the occipital and parietals reveal features divergent towards the *sapiens* condition.[2] The partial mandibles from Littorina Cave, Sidi Abderrahman (Arambourg and Biberson 1955), and from Thomas Quarry 1, Casablanca, (Sausse 1975), so far as they are preserved, show features of both teeth and jaw structure which fall broadly within the range of *Homo erectus*.

The second hominid individual recovered from the Thomas Quarry

[1] Both individuals '1' and '2' from the Thomas Quarry, Casablanca, derive from a solution cavity in Amirian-age aeolianite, the infilling of which is surely of Tensiftian age, and perhaps the middle to later part of that stage (Jaeger 1975a).

[2] These are: in the occipital, increased curvature between upper and lower scales, reduced occipital torus and associated supratoral depression, inferior displacement of inion relative to opisthocranium; and in regard to the parietals, lack of a sylvian crest, and reduced temporal portion of the middle meningeal vascular system.

is also a subadult individual, and has still to be described. It preserves much of the frontal, including the orbital and nasal area, much of the upper dentition, and part of the parietal (Ennouchi 1972). It is the first such specimen to preserve the upper facial region and the dentition and hence has a particular usefulness in revealing cranio-facial as well as dental morphology, and thereby affording a basis for comparison with the Kébibat specimen. The brow-ridges are strongly developed, and the dentition reveals in most of its elements a number of still non-modern *sapiens* features, although morphological details are not yet available.

The hominid specimen from Kébibat (Mifsud-Giudice Quarry), near Rabat, comprises portions of the fragmented vault, left maxilla and much of the mandible of a mid-adolescent individual. It reveals a mosaic of more primitive, *erectus*-like and more advanced *sapiens*-like features (Saban 1975, Vallois 1945, 1960).

The Kapthurin Beds, Baringo, Kenya, may well prove to afford evidence of such an early representative of *Homo sapiens* in eastern Africa. The remains derive from the middle (Middle Torrent Wash) of five members of this 100-m thick fluviatile and tuffaceous formation. The remains occurred in association with a limited mammal fauna, and an Acheulian industry distinguished by the use of raw material (lava), worked with a proto-Levallois (Victoria West) technique of flake production.[1] There is still doubt as to the age of this occurrence. An underlying lava has afforded a seemingly reliable age of ∼ 230 000 years (W. W. Bishop, personal communication); however, overlying tuffs have afforded a preliminary age more than twice that value. At any rate, an age within the upper part of the Middle Pleistocene is probably a reasonable estimate of its relative antiquity.

The human remains, a nearly complete mandible of a young adult individual and several postcrania are briefly described by Tobias (in M. Leakey *et al.* 1969). This specimen appears to have a less evolved morphology than the Kébibat specimen, and hence perhaps approaches rather more closely that of the specimen from Littorina Cave, Sidi Abderrahman. In any case, it reveals some important divergences from *Homo erectus*.

In the upper and lower facial skeleton, in the dentition, with respect to size, robustness, proportions and a number of morphological characters, it is apparent that these various hominid remains diverge from the usual *Homo erectus* morphological pattern. Unfortunately there are no cranial or postcranial remains as yet known, or of which

---

[1] See ch. 3 for a discussion of these stone-tool-making techniques.

published accounts are available,[1] which would afford additional and much needed evidence of the morphology of other portions of the skeleton.

A partial hominid cranium recovered from deposits exposed about the seasonal Lake Ndutu, Serengeti plains, Tanzania is also relevant to the emergence of *Homo sapiens* (Clarke 1976, Mturi 1976). It occurred in sediments yielding quantities of bovids, and stone artifacts of uncertain industrial affinities, perhaps a facies of Acheulian. These sediments appear to be correlative with the upper part of the Masek Beds of Olduvai Gorge nearby, where amino-acid racemization ages of 0.5 million years have been obtained. The hominid specimen reveals a broadly *erectus*-like form of the cranial vault, but in the vault, cranial base and the upper facial region there are features which diverge from that condition and hence approach *Homo sapiens*.

Stringer (1974) has recently projected a set of cranial features for an early (initial?) form of *Homo sapiens*. His inference of that morphological structure is largely derived from multivariate morphometric analyses of still primitive ( = non-modern) *sapiens* crania from geological horizons (mostly) younger than those in question here. It is a reasonable though still indirect characterization of the principal cranial features to be expected in an early *Homo sapiens* population, and to that characterization should be added aspects of jaw and tooth morphology. However, with the absence of well-preserved specimens, including associated skull parts, and the almost total lack of postcrania from well-defined stratigraphic contexts the delineation of the origin of *Homo sapiens* must remain one of the major problems in human palaeontology.

Human populations demonstrably of early Upper Pleistocene age, or even uppermost Middle Pleistocene age, are still very poorly known throughout the African continent. Moreover relative ages are quite uncertain, as are often stratigraphic contexts and cultural associations. Absolute ages of various species are and continue to be the subject of intensified research efforts. No well-defined or acceptable palaeoclimatic scheme exists for the later Pleistocene in these subtropical and tropical latitudes. A vertebrate biostratigraphy is still at best approximate, 'gross' rather than 'fine' in resolution, in southern Africa comprising ill-defined 'faunal spans' or 'mammal ages' of still undetermined duration. So long as this situation prevails the elucidation of the

---

[1] There is a nearly complete right ulna, a metatarsal and several possibly hominid (manus) phalanges associated with the Kapthurin mandible from Baringo, Kenya, which are as yet undescribed.

TABLE 2.7  *Remains attributed to* Homo sapiens neanderthalensis
*and* rhodesiensis

|  | Northern Africa | Eastern Africa | Southern Africa |
|---|---|---|---|
| Crania | Jebel Irhoud, Mor. (1; 2) Témara, Mor. Taforalt, Mor. (ff?) | Eyasi, Tanzania (1; 2) | Hopefield, Cape (1) Broken Hill (Kabwe), Zambia (1; 3) |
| Maxillae | Mughalet el-'Aliya, Mor. (1) |  | Broken Hill (2) |
| Mandibles | Haua Fteah, Libya (2) Hebel Irhoud 3 (1) Témara | Kapthurin, Baringo | Cave of Hearths, Transvaal Hopefield (ff) |
| Dentition | Témara Mughalet el-'Aliya (1) |  |  |
| Postcranials |  | East Rudolf – ER-999 (femur) Kapthurin (ulna) | Broken Hill (10 postcranial bones of some 3 individuals) |

later Pleistocene evolution of African Hominidae must remain problematical.

On morphological grounds at least two extinct subspecies of *Homo sapiens*, within different geographic areas, are now usually recognized. *H. sapiens rhodesiensis* was seemingly restricted to southern Africa, and the type skull was the first non-modern human fossil recovered on the African continent. *H. sapiens neanderthalensis* is still known only from the south Mediterranean littoral and the Atlantic littoral of Morocco, although there is no reason to exclude the distribution of such populations substantially southward, particularly when the Saharan area represented much less of a barrier. Moreover some recent evidence now suggests the presence of another distinctive subspecies in the eastern African area perhaps about the time of, or subsequent to, the transition from Middle to Upper Pleistocene. The known specimens are inventoried in table 2.7.

## Homo sapiens rhodesiensis (*fig. 2.11*)

The age and temporal duration of this extinct subspecies are poorly known. At the moment the temporal position and relationships of specimens comprising the sample of the subspecies are based largely, if not wholly, on comparative vertebrate biostratigraphy. Conventional radiometric dating procedures have proven ineffective or inappropriate to the problem, but recent developments in the amino-acid racemization

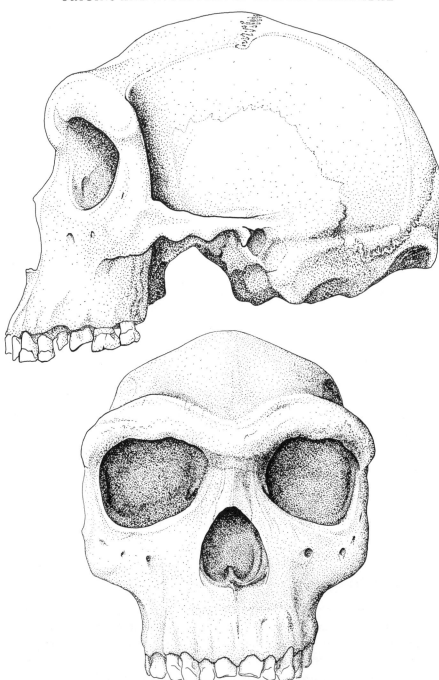

Fig. 2.11  Lateral and facial views of the restored cranium of *Homo sapiens rhodesiensis* (based on a specimen from Kabwe, Zambia; about two-thirds natural size).

method are sufficiently promising to afford at least approximations of age relevant to the temporal placement of some representatives of the sample.

Only three, or possibly four, hominid finds from sub-Saharan Africa are customarily attributed to this subspecies. These are specimens from Kabwe (formerly Broken Hill), Zambia, representing the type; from Elandsfontein, Saldanha Bay, and the Cave of Hearths, Transvaal, South Africa; and from Lake Eyasi, Tanzania.

Since the Kabwe (Broken Hill) human remains (representing at least three and probably four individuals) were recovered in 1921 from a deep cave in a limestone hill, in the course of open-cast mining, their geological age has been a periodic concern of palaeo-anthropology. Over the past quarter-century some progress has been made towards resolution of this problem, although considerable uncertainty still remains and perhaps always will, due to the mode of occurrence and the circumstances of the find. The ore body was composed of lead (below) and zinc (above), but as the cranium (four times as rich in zinc as lead) has been documented as having been recovered in the *lowest* level under pure lead, it must have been incorporated in a zinc 'pocket' within the lead carbonate (Clark *et al.* 1950). The association of the various other skeletal parts, including another maxilla and postcranials, with the type cranium has been disputed (Hrdlička 1930); but for the most part these either have high lead contents, or about equal contents of lead and zinc, and hence must derive from the same stratigraphic source. This appears also to be true of the non-human vertebrates and the lithic and bone artifact assemblage (Clark 1960, Oakley 1957). The identity of the latter is still in dispute, although it was at one time considered to be of 'Middle Stone Age' character, and hence suggestive of an Upper Pleistocene age – perhaps some 40–50 000 years ago – for the occurrence. The vertebrate assemblage is usually attributed to the Florisbad–Vlakkraal faunal span (Cooke 1967). Nearly 30 vertebrate taxa have been identified at one time or another; but the assemblage still requires restudy. However, of 24 larger species a minimum of 6 (25%) are surely extinct. At any rate it tends to suggest that the occurrence may well antedate the Upper Pleistocene 'Gamblian' (Klein 1973), as has often been assumed. Recently a preliminary age of ~110 000 years has been suggested on the basis of amino-acid racemization of hominid bone from the site (Bada *et al.* 1974). If confirmed, this would indicate an initial Upper Pleistocene age for the occurrence.

The other southern African locality yielding cranial remains of this subspecies is Elandsfontein (or Hopefield), near Saldanha Bay, Republic of South Africa. The stratigraphic occurrence of the hominid remains, artifact assemblage and rich vertebrate fauna has posed a problem since the discovery of the locality. However, controlled excavations and critical geological studies appear to have resolved most of the problems (Butzer 1973, Mabbutt 1956, Singer and Wymer 1968). A local stratigraphy is definable, but any correlation with external events is unfortunately minimal. The vertebrate fossil and artifactual occurrences accumulated on a calcareous Lower Duricrust ('hardpan') horizon subsequently enriched in iron which was part of shallow pans and associated streams behind an extensive cemented coastal dune forming a barrier to the sea. It apparently represented 'a fairly smooth sand slope traversed by braiding channels connecting shallow pans which might dry out seasonally' (Mabbutt 1956). The environment appears to have been moderately dry overall, predominantly fluvial, with little or no aeolian activity; palynological analyses suggest an open, bushveld-type vegetation, with little macchia, but with aquatic plants. A subsequent history of sand accumulations, ferruginization, land-surface formation and deflation is recognizable. Although wetter and drier climatic oscillations have been recognized their significance and external correlation are still unknown.

Radiocarbon determinations (on bone) only afford a minimal age ($> 35\,000$ years) for the fossil assemblage. Hence any age assessment can only be made on the basis of comparative biostratigraphy. The vertebrate assemblage is diverse, a total of 48 mammal species having been recognized. There are 36 species of larger mammals of which 20 (55%) are extinct. This is very substantially higher than either the Kabwe assemblage or any faunal assemblage of demonstrably Upper Pleistocene age in southern Africa.

The Elandsfontein fauna is frequently compared with faunal assemblages recovered from the Younger Gravels Complex, lower Vaal River basin (Wells 1964) and that from the Cornelia area of the upper Vaal drainage (Butzer, Clark and Cooke 1974). Altogether there are 22 extinct species in the combined assemblages[1] of which about 65% are

---

[1] The assemblage from the Vaal Younger Gravels, excluding obviously older Plio–Pleistocene elements, comprises 30 species of large mammals of which at least 14 (47%) are extinct. The latter assemblage comprises 24 species of large mammals of which 16 (66%) are extinct. They share 15 species of which 11 are extinct. Although it is impossible to effect correlation between the fossiliferous alluvia of the upper and lower Vaal valley (Butzer *et al.* 1973), in each instance there is sufficient geomorphical and stratigraphic evidence to indicate a pre-Upper Pleistocene age. However, which portion(s) and how much of the Middle Pleistocene record is represented is difficult to ascertain. Elandsfontein shares 16 species overall, of which 12 are extinct, with the Vaal

known elsewhere in Africa, both north and south of the Sahara, in Middle Pleistocene contexts. Thus, there is almost overwhelming palaeobiological evidence to indicate a substantial and Middle Pleistocene age for these occurrences. The resemblance (45 %) of the Kabwe fauna to that of Elandsfontein is about the same as that of Elandsfontein to Cornelia. This would tend to support an older, rather than younger (Upper Pleistocene) age for the former occurrence, although presumably the resemblance is such that an age younger than Elandsfontein is to be expected. Thus, the duration of this subspecies might well span several hundred thousand years, from the (later) Middle to (earlier) Upper Pleistocene.

The absolute and relative ages of the partial hominid mandible, associated with an evolved Acheulian industry at the Cave of Hearths, Transvaal, are also unknown. The associated fauna comprises only 18 species, of which only 5 are definitely extinct. All of the species represented are found in one or other of the larger mammal assemblages already discussed; but the available evidence and the fragmentary nature of the fossils which severely limits accurate identification to species, make it impossible to assess the relative age of the occurrences on biostratigraphic grounds.

The several partial hominid cranial parts recovered from sediments exposed along the shores of Lake Eyasi, Tanzania, are frequently considered to represent the same, or a related human subspecies. An age has recently been suggested of as young as $\sim$ 34 000 BP for these human remains on the basis of a $^{14}$C determination (Protsch 1975). If this date is confirmed, and if these fragmented remains indeed represent the *rhodesiensis* subspecies, its duration would be extended well into the later part of the Upper Pleistocene. At least 35 mammal taxa are recorded from this occurrence (Cooke 1963, Dietrich 1939) of which 29 are larger species and only 2 extinct (*Theropithecus* cf. *oswaldi*, *Pelorovis* cf. *bainii/nilssoni*), and the fauna is essentially modern in aspect, which would be in keeping with a late Upper Pleistocene age.

The type specimen of *H. rhodesiensis* from Kabwe represents the most completely preserved cranial remains known of this subspecies, and also includes various parts of the postcranial skeleton, including portions

Younger Gravels assemblage. It shares 11 species overall, of which 8 are extinct, with the Cornelia assemblage. Of all the represented species, the number of extinct ones shared by each of these pairs of assemblages is almost identical (72–75 %). In relation to the size of the smaller of any two assemblages compared, the order of sharing (Simpson's coefficient of similarity) is: Younger Gravels:Cornelia = 62.5 %, Elandsfontein:Younger Gravels = 53 %, Elandsfontein: Cornelia = 46 %, indicating a rather closer (and not unexpected) resemblance between the former pair, and rather similar resemblances between the latter two pairs.

of upper limb of the same individual.[1] Some postcranial parts and a maxilla exhibit the same fundamental morphological pattern (see Wells in Clark *et al.* 1950), but are less robust and surely, or probably, represent females.[2]

The recovery of the hominid cranium at Elandsfontein (Saldanha Bay) clearly demonstrated that the Kabwe specimen was not unique, and affords evidence of the variability within the subspecies. There is a 'striking resemblance' between these specimens, in terms of overall size, contours and most features of morphology (Singer 1954).[3]

The juvenile right partial mandible from the Cave of Hearths (Bed 3) has been tentatively referred to this subspecies, and this is a reasonable attribution (Tobias 1971b). It represents a pre-teenage individual, with only slight wear on the molars and premolars, of which three only are preserved, and with the broken roots of the anterior teeth. (A proximal radius, may or may not derive from the same horizon.)

Several authors (particularly Wells 1957) have noted some resemblances of the several Eyasi human cranial remains to the *rhodesiensis* subspecies. Originally these had been attributed to an *erectus*-like form, even though some similarities to Kabwe man were also appreciated (Weinert 1939). The Eyasi specimens represent parts of at least two and probably three individuals, very badly broken and heavily mineralized. Parts of one cranium have been reconstructed, and include a fair amount of the vault, some of the base, and several upper teeth; it has been considered to be a female of this subspecies.[4] Other specimens are largely fragments, including half an occipital.[5] Though fragmentary

[1] The type is BM(NH)E.686 and the postcranial remains comprise: partial humerus (E.898), sacrum (E.699), ilium (E.689), femora (E.720) and tibia (E.691).

[2] Thus a partial maxilla (E.687), though large, has a shorter subnasal region, shallower palate, rather more transverse orientation of zygomatic process, and inferiorly inclined and slightly hollowed infraorbital surface. Unfortunately the extreme wear and extensive caries have obliterated the morphological details and even the individual sizes of the upper teeth.

[3] The differences are quite trivial, and include in the former specimen: a distinct ophyryonic groove; less broad supraorbital torus, with its anterior edge evenly curved outwards; prominent, more angular shape of median frontal ridge; smaller superior scale of occipital; and reduced angular torus.

[4] An age of 34 000 years (by isoleucine racemization determination) has recently been suggested for these remains by Protsch (1975).

[5] Cranium no. 1: a low, flat frontal with postorbital constriction, and sharp-margined supraorbital torus and expanded glabella; lack of marked occipital angulation, and some occipital torus development; relatively small mastoid process; reduced angulation of the petrous axis; high maxilla, with subnasal guttering, and probably high palate; $\underline{C}$ large crowned, with strong mesio-buccal curvature, strong mesio-lingual swelling, and lingual grooves. The partial occipital (no. 2), more robust than the other individual, is also more openly curved, preserves the supramastoid crest, and an occipital torus passing towards it via an expanded angular region, and an external inion-like development of the central segment of the torus.

these specimens do exhibit some *rhodesiensis* characteristics. They also very much merit further description and comparative study.

## Homo sapiens neanderthalensis (*fig. 2.12*)

Skeletal remains attributed to Neanderthal peoples are uncommon in Mediterranean Africa, and like the Mousterian industry with which they are associated, are unknown into or south of the Sahara (Balout 1965a, b). Three localities, all cave infillings, have thus far yielded skull parts attributed to this subspecies: Haua Fteah, in Cyrenaican Libya, the Mugharet el-'Aliya, near Tangier, northern Morocco, and the Jebel Irhoud, south-east of Safi, southern Morocco. Recently human remains have been recovered from another littoral cave complex, Dar es-Soltan, close to Rabat, but their affinities have not been specified.

The specimens from the Haua Fteah, two left mandible fragments of young adult and adolescent individuals, were recovered from an interface between levels 32 and 33 in association with a Mousterian industry of Levallois facies.[1] Radiocarbon determinations suggest an age of 47 000 years BP.

Although the specimens are admittedly very fragmentary there appear to be similarities in particular with south-west Asian Neanderthals from the Tabun and Mud sites (Israel) and Shanidar (Iraq).

Two calvaria and a juvenile mandible representative of this subspecies have been recovered from the lower infilling of a solution cave in a Mesozoic limestone hill at Jebel Irhoud, Morocco. They were found in the course of the exploitation of the site for barite, and hence precise contextual and associational details are largely lacking (Ennouchi 1962a, 1963, 1965). However, a substantial and diverse vertebrate assemblage of Upper Pleistocene (Presoltanian/Soltanian), aspect, with several now extinct species, was also present, along with traces of fire (burnt bones and artifacts), and a substantial, finely fashioned Mousterian industry of Levallois facies (Balout 1970).[2]

These remains differ from most European and some south-west Asian Neanderthal populations, and like those from es-Skhul and from Jebel

---

[1] See McBurney (1967). For descriptions of the industries see ch. 5, this volume. The overall morphology and special features of the specimens suggest Neanderthal affinities (see Tobias 1967c, Trevor and Wells 1967). These include: reduced height and accentuated breadth of the ramus, shallow sigmoid notch, substantial angulation between intraramal crests related to enlarged ramal breadth, enlarged ramal recess; and some characteristics of the dentition, especially +5 molar pattern, enlarged anterior fovea, and enhanced trigonid/talonid breadth ratio.

[2] The principal morphological features of the three specimens have been summarized by Ennouchi (1962b, 1968, 1969), and the endocranial casts have been examined by Anthony (1966).

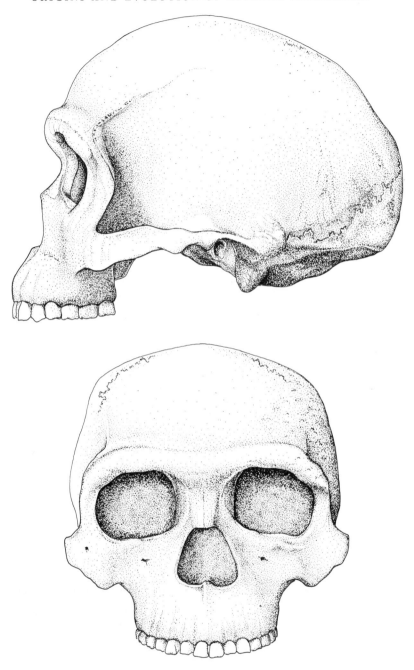

Fig. 2.12  Lateral and facial views of the restored cranium of *Homo sapiens neanderthalensis* (based on a specimen from Jebel Irhoud, Morocco; about one-half natural size).

Qafzeh, Israel, exhibit anatomically modern features particularly in respect to the facial skeleton. It has even been suggested (Ferembach 1972) that the total morphological pattern suggests affinity with later human populations associated with the Iberomaurusian Industry of the Maghrib.

The skeletal morphology of the peoples responsible for the Mousterian-related Aterian Industry, widespread across northern Africa and the Sahara in later Pleistocene times (see chapters 4 and 5), has remained almost unknown. Exceptions have been a small and uninformative parietal fragment from Pigeon Cave (level D), Taforalt, Beni-Snassen mountains, and a facial fragment and teeth of two individuals from Mugharet el-'Aliya (High Cave, layer 5), near Cape Spartel, Tangier, Morocco (Howe 1967, Roche 1953), in each instance with final Aterian associations. The Tangier specimen at least reveals some facial and dental features which are anatomically non-modern and most closely resemble Neanderthal morphology.

Most recently human remains, in some quantity, have been recovered from the infilling of one of the solution caves in the dunar sandstones of the Dar es-Soltan, near Rabat, an area previously known, from the researches of Ruhlmann (1951), to preserve a cultural succession from the Aterian to the Neolithic of Capsian tradition. The former industry was previously shown by [14]C determination to have an age of about 30 000 years for its earlier phase.[1] The remains, including maxillary, mandible and vault parts of at least two adolescent and adult individuals, derive from the lower levels of the infilling associated with an Aterian assemblage (Débenath 1972, 1975; Ferembach 1976a). Although morphological details have still to be published there is some indication that these human remains are of Neanderthal affinities.

The Témara mandible was recovered from Contrebandiers Cave, south-west of Rabat. It was first considered to derive from remnants of an older, brecciated infilling of a cave cut in what was thought to be a cliff of the Harounian transgressive stage (Biberson 1964, Vallois and Roche 1958) and this older infilling was presumed to date from the preceding continental Presoltanian stage, of upper Middle Pleistocene age. Further researches at the Contrebandiers site (Ferembach 1976b, Roche and Texier 1976) have revealed the nature of the successive infillings and human occupations there. Sixteen horizons are represented

---

[1] The available radiocarbon determinations relevant to the age of the Mousterian industry, of which the 'middle' phase is very probably older than 40 000 years, have been discussed by Camps (1968, 1974).

which postdate the Ouljian transgression of early Late Quaternary age. The initial human mandible, as well as other fragmentary human remains and the parieto-occipital portion of the cranium, all derive from an Upper Aterian occupation in level 9.

In general present knowledge of Pleistocene subspecies of *Homo sapiens* is substantially less extensive than that for extinct species of genus *Homo* or even for *Australopithecus*. In Africa the hominid fossil record for the (later) Middle Pleistocene and the earlier portion of the Upper Pleistocene is unexpectedly scant. This is perhaps a consequence of the general rarity of cave and rock-shelter occupation sites in many parts of the continent prior to late and post-Pleistocene times. For the most part elements of the postcranial skeleton are unknown, but the scant parts available indicate a total morphological pattern approximating closely to the modern human condition. Cranial morphology is also imperfectly known, but there is definite evidence of transformations in the vault and cranial base toward the modern human condition; however, the facial skeleton is still unreduced and its distinctive morphology is particularly characteristic of the *neanderthalensis* and *rhodesiensis* subspecies.[1]

## Homo sapiens afer

The late Pleistocene evolution of Hominidae in sub-Saharan Africa is still largely a matter of speculation. Although a fair number of human remains attributed on one basis or another to that time-range have been recovered over the past half-century, their primary contexts and varied associations are often poorly, if at all, established. The absence of any well-established stratigraphic framework for the Upper Pleistocene in sub-Saharan Africa has been a major obstacle. The literature on the subject is large, frequently typological, and unduly speculative considering the limited facts available. The concept of a Boskop race (*H. sapiens capensis*) has a long and complex history dating back to a first attempt to define the parameters of such a prehistoric population in 1937. The state of the problem was thoughtfully evaluated by Singer (1958) who was among the first to appreciate how really fragile was the basis upon which the concept had been established. In recent years some progress has been made towards the establishment of a stratigraphic

---

[1] The subject has been most recently and critically reviewed by Rightmire (1974, 1975); earlier considerations of the available evidence and its varied interpretation are those of Galloway (1937), Dart (1940b), Wells (1952, 1959), Tobias (1961) and Brothwell (1963).

succession for the Upper Pleistocene of southern Africa, most notably in the southern Cape and in the Orange–Vaal drainages (Butzer and Helgren 1972, Butzer *et al.* 1973), towards elucidation of palaeoenvironments and palaeoclimates (Bakker and Butzer 1973), towards the clarification of the faunal and cultural associations of human fossils, and towards the assessment of their 'absolute ages' by radiometric and other methods (Bada and Deems 1975, Protsch 1975, Vogel and Beaumont 1972). In spite of some progress many uncertainties and unresolved problems remain.

Wells (1969, 1972) has suggested that all (or most?) southern African human remains of later Pleistocene age should be attributed to the subspecies *H. sapiens afer* Linnaeus, 1758, a taxon to include the ancestral stock of which African Bushmen and Negroes are a 'divergent specialization'. Protsch (1975) has most recently followed essentially the same procedure; but he has, unfortunately in the author's view, chosen to retain *H. sapiens capensis* as a category to include an arbitrary aggregate of supposedly older but anatomically modern human remains considered to be 'Boskop' or 'Boskopoid'. Not only does he consider such a group as ancestral to subsequent African populations (cf *H. s. afer*), but also proposes 'the world-wide evolution of all earliest anatomically modern fossil hominids from *Homo sapiens capensis* of Africa'. As there is scarcely any morphological justification for this procedure (or that conclusion, either) it is not followed here.

The antiquity of this subspecies is still in doubt. It may have been as much as 50–60 000 years if all specimens attributed to it are accepted as of that subspecies, and if their age assessments are at all close to being correct. Human remains of latest Pleistocene age attributed to this population include specimens from Bushman Rock Shelter, Transvaal ($\sim$ 29 000 BP), Mumbwa, Zambia ($\sim$ 29 000 BP), Lukenya Hill, Kenya ($\sim$ 18 000 BP) and Matjes River, Cape, South Africa ($\sim$ 10 000 BP). Older representatives are considered to include specimens from Border Cave, Natal[1] ($\sim$ 45 000 BP, and perhaps $\sim$ 60 000 BP), Fish Hoek, Cape, South Africa ($\sim$ 35 000 BP), Florisbad, Orange Free State ($\sim$ 39 000 BP), Klasies River Mouth Cave 1, Cape, South Africa (estimated $\sim$ 70–80 000 BP by aspartic-acid racemization). The mammal assemblages from the latter two sites correspond to the Florisbad–Vlakkraal Faunal Span in which as many as perhaps nine (Florisbad) to four (Klasies 1) large

[1] The partial skeleton from Tuinplaats, Springbok Flats, Transvaal (Broom 1929b, Schepers 1941, Toerien and Hughes 1955) is sometimes considered as similar to the Border Cave adult individual. Unfortunately scant evidence of any sort exists which would permit an accurate assessment of either its relative or absolute age (Protsch 1975, Wells 1959).

TABLE 2.8  *Remains attributed to* Homo sapiens afer/sapiens

| | North-west Africa | North-east Africa | | Eastern Africa | | Southern Africa | |
| --- | --- | --- | --- | --- | --- | --- | --- |
| | | Egypt | Sudan | Ethiopia | Kenya | Zambia | South Africa |
| Crania | Taforalt (ff) | Kom Ombo: 2 (ff) | Singa | Kibish Formation, Member 1: 3+ | Kanjera: 40 parts of 4 crania Lukenya Hill: 1 | Mumbwa: 4, 2 with associated postcranials | Border Cave, Boskop: postcranials Fish Hoek Klasies River (ff) Florisbad |
| Maxillae | — | — | | — | — | — | |
| Mandibles | — | — | Wadi Halfa: 1 | Dire Dawa | — | — | Klasies River: 2 |
| Dentition | — | — | | — | | | |
| Postcranials | — | — | | Kibish: partial vertebral column, upper and lower limbs | Kanjera: post-cranial fragments, innominate | Mumbwa | Border Cave Fish Hoek: some postcranials |

mammals represent extinct species. The author also assigns the several human specimens from the (lower) Kibish Formation, lower Omo basin, southern Ethiopia, to this same subspecies. The ages, relative or absolute, of the Tuinplaats (or Springbok Flats) and Cape Flats specimens remain unresolved and, hence, are not considered here.

All human remains attributed to this subspecies show a total morphological pattern which is overall of anatomically modern aspect. In most instances there is, as has been noted in the literature referred to, substantial overlap with the range of variability found among later prehistoric or extant indigenous human populations of sub-Saharan Africa. The skeletal remains attributed to this subspecies are listed in table 2.8.

Very probably the demonstrably oldest documented human specimens referable to this subspecies are those fragmentary remains which derive from several (earlier) Upper Pleistocene occupation horizons overlying a 6–8-m raised beach, at the Klasies River Mouth 1 cave (Bada and Deems 1975). It has been suggested that two distinct populations may be represented in the sample (Singer and Smith 1969, Wells 1972).

On the basis of radiocarbon age determinations indicative of minimum age and the results of amino-acid racemization studies, the Border Cave human remains clearly have a substantial Upper Pleistocene antiquity (Beaumont 1973, Beaumont and Boshier 1972, Protsch 1975). The several specimens are associated either with a 'Final Middle Stone Age' (Pietersburg) assemblage (infant) or a pre-'Early Late Stone Age' assemblage (adults), but not recovered, unfortunately, in the most optimum circumstances to guarantee contextual and associational details (Cooke *et al.* 1945). A description of the salient features of these several individuals is given by Wells (1950) and de Villiers (1973, 1976).

The provenance and associations of the Fish Hoek or Skildergat (Cape) skull are still in doubt although Protsch (1975) has recently suggested it has a very substantial antiquity ($> 35\,000$ years BP), probably was associated with a fully developed 'Middle Stone Age' (Stillbay) industry, and should be considered a representative of the same human group as the Border Cave (adult) individual. Keith (1931) affords a quite full description of the specimen.

The partial cranium from Florisbad, Orange Free State, has been the subject of continued interest and discussion since its discovery in 1932. Its context, in relation to the eye of a thermal spring, and the question of its association with other vertebrate fossils and distinctive 'Middle

Stone Age' industry (Hagenstad variant) have been largely resolved through chemical assays and radiometric age determination (Bada *et al.* 1973, Oakley 1954, Protsch 1974). All appear to have been associated and are of similar age, well over 40 000 years. However, the affinities of the hominid cranium are still in question; some authors consider the specimen to have resemblances to *H. s. rhodesiensis*, while others consider it to be more anatomically modern, and hence another (and more recent) subspecies. The latter interpretation appears more reasonable, although admittedly the specimen requires further reconstruction and restudy (its salient features are referred to in Drennan (1937), Dreyer (1935, 1936, 1938, 1945) and Galloway (1937)).

The Bushman Rock-shelter, Transvaal affords a long 'Middle Stone Age'(Pietersburg) succession (layers 43–8) overlain by sparse 'Later Stone Age' occupations (layers 27–30) (Protsch and de Villiers 1974). An infant partial mandible was recovered in association with early 'Late Stone Age' (between layers 14 and 18). The specimen differs from the Border Cave infant in respect to its overall contour, form of the mental protuberance, and the morphology of the genial area, and appears to show some specific Negro affinities.

In eastern and north-eastern Africa the hominid fossil record of the later Pleistocene is extremely scanty. The partial cranium from Singa, lower Blue Nile, and a badly preserved mandible, lacking tooth crowns, from Wadi Halfa, Sudan, are generally considered to be of late Pleistocene age, $\sim$ 17 000 and $\sim$ 15 000 years BP respectively; both are associated with industries considered to be of 'Middle Stone Age' affinity. Of broadly comparable age, $\sim$ 17 600 years, are fragments of a cranial vault from the Lukenya Hill rock-shelter (south-central Kenya) associated with a 'Later Stone Age' industry. The partial mandible from Porc Epic Cave near Dire Dawa, Ethiopia, is presumably also of later Pleistocene age, but without any firm dating. It was obtained from a breccia which incorporated only 'Middle Stone Age' occupation residue.

The several human remains from the Kibish Formation, lower Omo basin, Ethiopia, are considered to be substantially older. Human cranial remains, and some associated postcrania, were recovered (in 1967) from a situation considered to represent the lower part (Member 1) of the Kibish Formation, lower Omo basin, south-western Ethiopia (Butzer and Thurber 1969, R. E. F. Leakey, Butzer and Day 1969). The unit of the Kibish Formation was accumulated when Lake Rudolf stood some 60 m higher than its present ($+375$ m) level, and flooded the whole of the lower Omo valley (Butzer *et al.* 1972). At least two (of three) specimens are thought to derive from different localities related to the upper sedimentary units (5 and/or 6, or 7 units) of that member. As they have comparable nitrogen and uranium values they are considered to be broadly contemporaneous. An age as old as ∼ 130 000 years has been suggested for the specimens on the basis of thorium–uranium measurements. However, the reliability of this method has still to be adequately demonstrated, and even if this determination appears reasonable, it is nonetheless unconfirmed. The radiocarbon determinations (on shell) from overlying members, with a minimum age > 37 000 years, have also been questioned. The mammal fauna associated with one (no. 1) of the specimens, with few species represented and none of them extinct, is frankly unhelpful and also unconvincing of any very remote antiquity (Day 1973b).

Day (1971) considered the Kibish Formation human remains to be closely contemporaneous, and as 'representatives of the African segment of evolving Upper Middle Pleistocene *Homo sapiens* that show a diversity of skull form at least as wide as that known for Upper Pleistocene sapiens from other parts of the world'. Subsequently, as a result of multivariate analyses he concluded that specimens 1 and 2 were different from one another, as well as distinct from several modern *Homo sapiens* populations (Day 1973b). Although he suggested an 'intermediate group' to include these specimens and various other Middle Pleistocene hominids of Asia (Ngandong) and sub-Saharan Africa (Kabwe, Elandsfontein) there is little to support such a conclusion. In almost every comparable morphological feature there is divergence not only from the evolved *H. erectus solensis* condition, but also from that presumably characteristic of *H. sapiens rhodesiensis*. Stringer's (1974) analysis (in which $D^2$ distances were employed) has subsequently demonstrated that these specimens (nos. 1 and 2) are not only morphologically dissimilar, and hence may well *not* represent the same population, but also that their closest morphological resemblances are with *sapiens* cranial remains of late Pleistocene age. With that conclusion the author is in complete agreement.

The Kibish 1 specimen (from the KHS site) includes a partial cranial vault, half mandible and some postcranial elements. The latter fall wholly within the modern *sapiens* range of variation. The Kibish 2 specimen comprises much of a cranial vault. These specimens from the Kibish Formation unquestionably represent a subspecies of *Homo sapiens*, but a subspecies morphologically different from and very probably more recent than *H. sapiens rhodesiensis*. The specimens appear to be not only morphologically dissimilar, and hence may well not represent the same human population, but their closest morphological resemblances are with *sapiens* cranial remains of late Pleistocene age. Their temporal position is still insecurely established and merits further investigation. The lack of this important datum severely inhibits assessment of their affinities with African human populations of later Pleistocene age.

The Lukenya Hill human remains comprise only a partial frontal and parietal of an adult individual. Its resemblances to African Negro specimens have been noted (Gramly and Rightmire 1973). The partial (right) mandible from Porc Epic Cave, Dire Dawa, is unfortunately poorly preserved as are its five teeth, which lack crowns and any enamel (Vallois 1951). The mandible from Wadi Halfa (site 6B28) is a badly eroded specimen without tooth crowns, and without useful morphological details.

The Singa cranium is the most complete hominid specimen from the later Pleistocene of north-eastern Africa. The specimen is a nearly complete brain case, lacking the facial skeleton and the cranial base. At least one extinct species, *Pelorovis antiquus*, may be associated with the level from which the artifacts and human cranium derived. Attention has been directed to its overall Bushman-like character (Wells 1951, Woodward 1938).

No effort is made here to deal with the vexatious questions of the origins and affinities of modern human populations of Africa. However, a few points are worth making in this regard. In north-western Africa (the Maghrib) dissimilar human populations appear to be associated with the geographically-exclusive 'Epi-Palaeolithic' Iberomaurusian (or Mouillian) and Capsian industries – the former characterized by Cro-Magnon-like Mechta–Afalou peoples (also known from Sahaba in lower Nubia), and the latter by probably intrusive proto-Mediterranean peoples. The origin of African Negro peoples still remains largely unknown, and is usually attributed to the absence of archaeological and human skeletal documentation from the forested and wooded areas of the equatorial reaches of the continent. However, such peoples were apparently present in West Africa at least some 11 000 years ago (Iwo Eleru, Nigeria), about the lakes of the Western Rift Valley several thousand years later (Ishango), and not long thereafter in portions of the southern Sahara (Asselar). Most human skeletal remains from various Later Stone Age and related occurrences in the Eastern Rift

Valley in Kenya, of late and post-Pleistocene age, show definite Negro cranial features, although their 'caucasoid' affinities were once stressed. The origin of the Khoisan (Bush-Hottentot) peoples also remains enigmatic, although such peoples appear to have been present in southernmost Africa in the latest Pleistocene (Matjes River).

### COEXISTENCE OF HOMINID TAXA

Fossil evidence of the coexistence of several hominid taxa has been treated by some authors as inconsequential if not utterly dismissed. The competitive-exclusion principle has been invoked as a basis for the impossibility of multiple, coexistent hominid taxa, and the single-species hypothesis – which maintains that 'because of cultural adaptation, all hominid species occupy the same, extremely broad, adaptive niche' (Wolpoff 1971a) – proposed to account for the existence and 'continued survival of only one hominid lineage'. However, as a consequence of continued recovery of hominid skeletal parts in Africa, coexistence of several hominid taxa is now well documented at least for the Plio–Pleistocene time-range. In most instances it is a matter of species of *Australopithecus* coexistent with one or another pre-*sapiens* species of genus *Homo*; several such instances are listed below.

(1) At Swartkrans, Transvaal, in the Member 1 infilling, a single individual attributed to *Homo* sp. occurs in association with nearly 90 individuals of a robust australopithecine, *A. crassidens* (Clarke and Howell 1972).

(2) At Olduvai Gorge, Tanzania, several hominid taxa, including *Homo* sp. ('*habilis*') and *Homo erectus* (which appears first in the uppermost reaches of Bed II) and *Australopithecus boisei* occur within the Bed I–II portion of that succession (see M. D. Leakey 1978). At several well-defined geological horizons at least two hominid taxa are recorded in circumstances which suggest not only contemporaneity, but *sympatry*. In relation to Tuff I$^B$ at least four *Homo* sp. individuals occur with at least three *A. boisei* individuals; below Tuff I$^C$ at least two *Homo* sp. individuals occur with an *A. boisei* individual, and (possibly) with an individual representing *A. africanus*. In lower Bed II, above Tuff I$^F$, three individuals of *A. boisei* occur in a horizon yielding a *Homo* sp. individual; between Tuff II$^A$ and II$^B$ remains of an *A. boisei* individual occur in sediments yielding at least five *Homo* sp. individuals. *A. boisei* last occurs in uppermost Bed II, above Tuff II$^D$, in sediments yielding two *Homo erectus* individuals.

(3) At East Rudolf (Kenya) the Lower and Upper members of the Koobi Fora Formation afford sufficient evidence of the association of species of the genus *Homo* with at least one species of *Australopithecus*, *A. boisei*, and perhaps *A. africanus* as well. In the Lower Member (sub-KBS unit) *Homo* sp. is some four times as common as *A. boisei* and at several localities these taxa have been found in comparable geological horizons. In the sub-Koobi Fora unit of the Upper Member *Homo* sp. and *A. boisei* occur initially in about equal frequency and these taxa are found in comparable geological horizons. In the upper part of that unit *Homo erectus* occurs, in about equal frequency as *A. boisei*; in at least two localities (in areas 105 and 130) these taxa have been found in immediate proximity. *Homo erectus* is demonstrably near contemporaneous with *A. boisei* in this sedimentary formation (R. E. F. Leakey and Walker 1976). In the upper, sub-Chari unit of the Upper Member *A. boisei* is more than twice as common as *H. erectus*; these taxa have been found in the same general collecting localities in comparable geological horizons.

(4) In the Shungura Formation, lower Omo basin, Ethiopia, *A. africanus* appears to overlap *A. boisei* (Members E to lower G), and it is not unlikely that a *Homo* sp. coexisted with *A. boisei* in the uppermost part (Members upper G to H) of that succession.

(5) There is a strong probability that a (morphologically) non-australopithecine species with *Homo* affinities overlaps in time, though may not necessarily have been living in the same environment, as *A. africanus* in the Hadar Formation, central Afar, Ethiopia.

The geological occurrence of early hominid fossils in Africa and their morphological features now leave no doubt that there was coexistence temporally, and even spatially, of at least two hominid taxa, and very probably through a substantial span of Pliocene and earlier Quaternary time. Evidently Hominidae experienced a substantial adaptive radiation at least as early as Pliocene times, if not earlier. For probable relationships of Hominidae during the Plio–Pleistocene see cladogram, fig. 2.13.

## EXTINCTIONS

At various times extinctions have been proposed or inferred to account for the evolutionary history of Hominidae. However, with the previously very incomplete nature of that fossil record, and the probable existence within it of important gaps, such inferences have been necessarily largely speculative.

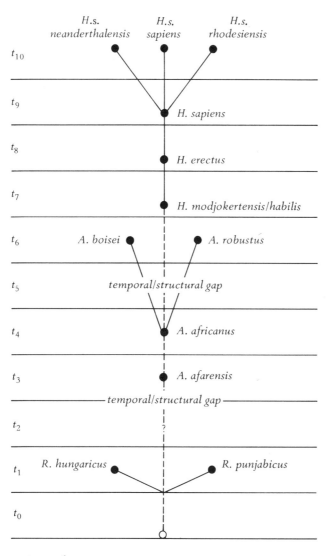

● Known forms

○ Hypothetical morphotypes

Fig. 2.13  Cladogram of relationships of Hominidae taking time $(t_1-t_8)$ into consideration.

Within the species *Homo sapiens* there is scarcely any direct evidence of the extinction of particular subspecies or populations within Africa. However, various workers have questioned the temporal and phylogenetic affinities of specimens which would now commonly be attributed to several populations, of mid to late Quaternary age, of *Homo sapiens*. The extinction of particular populations has been at least implied if not explicitly suggested. Thus, most recently, Protsch (1975) has favoured the origin of the subspecies *rhodesiensis* from an antecedent subspecies *capensis*, and the ultimate extinction of the former during the time of *H. sapiens afer*. However, the temporal relationships of particular fossil specimens attributed to these several subspecies are still far from resolved. It is thus at least as likely, if not more so, that the *rhodesiensis* subspecies was ancestral rather than descendant.

Similarly, *Homo erectus* has sometimes been presumed to have been a descendant, ultimately extinct, species derived from a more *sapiens*-like ancestral stock. However, there is scant evidence to support that interpretation, and the known temporal span of *Homo erectus* largely and probably wholly antedates that of *Homo sapiens*.

The most convincing evidence for extinction within Hominidae is of one or more species of *Australopithecus*. The disappearance from the fossil record of *A. boisei* and of *A. robustus/crassidens*, at a time when *Homo erectus* was already present and a well-established species, is now recognized at several localities in sub-Saharan Africa. Various speculations have been offered as to the basis for the disappearance of the former, largely framed in terms of diet, behaviour and competition. It is also worth noting that this disappearance is also part of a larger pattern of (mammalian) faunal turnover and replacement within the continent, of the order of a million or so years ago.

### CULTURAL ASSOCIATIONS

Cultural associations and occupational residues, in their natural contexts, afford the only direct evidences of hominid behaviour and adaptation in the later Cenozoic (see also chapter 3). Inferences and speculations on cultural capabilities, on object use and tool-making, on predatory behaviour and subsistence activities, and on habitat utilization ultimately derive only from such basic data. It is thus worthwhile to indicate briefly the nature and extent of those associations in relation to fossil hominid occurrences.

There has been no dearth of speculation as to the behavioural capabilities and adaptive adjustments of emerging Hominidae. However, the first substantial, widespread and incontrovertible evidence for the utilization of stone as a medium in which to produce tools, and for the accumulation of occupational residues at circumscribed locations dates to about 2 million years ago. In almost all instances known there is direct or indirect evidence of the presence of at least two (and possibly three) hominid species more or less closely related to these occurrences. These occurrences are not all of the same sort, and it is most probable that their differences reflect overall some, if not the total, of earlier hominid culturally patterned behaviours and adaptations.

Numerous artifact occurrences are recorded from the lowest units of Member F of the Shungura Formation, Omo basin, in or above Tuff F, having an age of 2.04 million years (Chavaillon 1976, Merrick, 1976, Merrick and Merrick 1976). These occur largely in relation to stream-channel situations, including a braided river system, and under substantially drier conditions than are recorded earlier in the Omo succession. Both *A. africanus* and *A. boisei* are represented in this sedimentary unit, but no hominid remains are directly associated with any of the artifact localities. The artifact occurrences are often of very low density, but spatially widely distributed; several high-density occurrences (comparable to those at Olduvai Gorge) are also known, however, and one or two appear to be undisturbed occupation residues. Artifacts are almost always small, made in a limited number of raw materials, and both large and small shaped tools are either infrequent or wholly absent. Other artifact occurrences are also known, always in derived condition, the channel gravels in the lower units of Member G, having an age of 1.9 million years.

Some half-dozen artifactual occurrences are documented in the Lower Member of the Koobi Fora Formation, East Rudolf, in channel situations within the KBS Tuff, or in one instance below that tuff (Isaac 1976, Isaac, Harris and Crader 1976). These occurrences range in age from 1.8 to 1.6 million years (Curtis *et al.* 1975). Although hominids (both *A. boisei* and *Homo* sp., and very probably, but rarely, *A. africanus*) occur in the same horizons, and broadly the same general areas as the artifact concentrations, none have been found in direct association. Several distinct forms of occurrence have been recognized, apparently always close to stream channels. These include several, usually low-density artifact scatters of limited extent; an artifact and fragmented bone concentration (including parts of upwards of ten ungulate species) of substantial size suggestive of an occupation site or camp; and a smaller occurrence of much of a single hippopotamus with a few tools and other artifacts suggestive of a butchery site. All the occurrences are distinguished by the generally low density of artifacts, high frequency of flakes and flaking debris, rarity of larger shaped (core) tools, absence, or near absence, of small (or larger) flake tools, and limited variety of raw material employed which must have been brought from at least a short distance away as it was not locally available. The lithic industry represented is overall quite comparable to the Oldowan of Olduvai Gorge. See Chapter 3 for a discussion of the implications of this evidence.

The most numerous sites, richest in artifactual and cultural remains that are asociated with early Hominidae, are those of Olduvai Gorge, Beds I and II. In all eighteen hominid occupation situations are documented within Bed I sediments, and a total of sixty-three for Bed II sediments – encompassing a total time-span of approximately a million years (Hay 1976, M. D. Leakey 1971, 1977). From this restricted and persistent small sedimentary basin derives the most complete history, as yet, of an earlier Pleistocene record of hominid adaptation and cultural capabilities ever recovered anywhere. In the earlier portion of this succession at least two and probably three hominid taxa are represented and are specifically associated with occupational residues (M. D. Leakey 1977). In direct association with two Oldowan industry sites is the robust australopithecine, *A. boisei*; in one instance that species occurs associated with postcranial parts considered to be *A. africanus*. The former species is also associated in at least one occurrence with a Developed Oldowan industry in the uppermost reaches of Bed II, some three-quarters of a million years later. An early species of the genus *Homo*, *Homo* sp. indet. ('*habilis*'), occurs at 11 occupational situations, from lowermost Bed I (6 occurrences), through middle Bed I (2), lower Bed II (1) and middle Bed II (2) – a time-span of 0.2 million years. In at least two occurrences in Beds I and mid-II there are direct associations of this taxon with *A. boisei*, and in other situations there is demonstrable temporal contemporaneity on strati-graphic grounds.

The hominid occupation occurrences and their associated residues afford unique testimony to the cultural capabilities, habitat adjustments and overall adaptation of early hominids within this time-span. Un-fortunately these occurrences *do not* afford a basis for the direct assessment of such capabilities and differential adjustments between the several hominid taxa represented through this time-range; the differences in their behaviours are not readily discernible from these varied occupational situations. Within occurrences of the Oldowan industry, with which all *Homo* sp. indet. and/or almost all *A. boisei* individuals are associated, there are substantial differences, at least in degree, in respect to the spatial distribution of occurrences and their form and extent, which is suggestive of spatial segregation of activities. There are also considerable differences in the density of artifactual and/or food-debris residues, including transported (distal) or more immediate (proximal) elements and the occurrence, frequency, and body-part representation of vertebrate taxa. Also noteworthy is the overall diversity in composition and character of the artifactual element. Limited sorts of lithic raw materials were selected, transported some-times, and utilized for the fashioning of particular categories and forms of implements. Very probably home bases (of several activity types), workshop sites, butchery sites and even other occurrences of undeci-pherable activities are represented within this unique spectrum. It has been suggested that probably the bulk of these and later occurrences (in Bed II) at Olduvai represent dry-season occupation sites (Speth and Davis 1976).

The Developed Oldowan Industry succeeds the Oldowan in lower Bed II and occurs thereafter through even Beds III and IV. From middle Bed II (above the Lemuta Member) onwards it occurs in parallel with an Acheulian industry. As already mentioned there is a single hominid occurrence, that of *A. boisei*, directly associated with a Developed Oldowan assemblage. That industry shows some shifts in the exploi-tation and transport of raw material, an increase in tool types, the appearance of new sorts of shaped tools, overall greater artifact diversification, perhaps related to functional specialization, and greater variation in assemblage composition from one occurrence to another. Occupation sites show an increase in the proportion of artifacts to bone refuse, increased bone breakage and fracture, and differences in prey species represented.

In the Upper Member of the Koobi Fora Formation, East Rudolf, there are several artifact occurrences (Karari Industry) below the Okote Tuff Complex (1.56–1.50 million years), and a large number of such occurrences between that tuff complex and the overlying Karari–Chari Tuffs (1.3–1.2 million years) (Harris and Isaac 1976). Hominid skeletal parts are abundant within this portion of the succession but direct associations of hominid remains with artifact occurrences are infrequent. In one instance there is a direct, proximal occurrence of *A. boisei* and

*Homo erectus* remains with the distinctive Karari Industry; in another instance the former occurs with a scatter of such artifacts, above a more substantial occupation occurrence. The Karari Industry, which shows some similarities to, but other features distinctive from the Developed Oldowan, shows very substantial assemblage diversity and differences in tool types. It is known from at least fifty sites, a number of which preserve a variety of bone debris and evidently represent either home bases or butchery sites.

The upper levels of the Chemoigut Formation, Baringo area, attest to another situation where, in a marginal saline lake setting associated with inflow channels, robust australopithecine cranial parts occur in two of some five horizons yielding an Oldowan or Developed Oldowan industry (Bishop, Hill and Pickford 1975, Harris and Bishop 1976).

Artifacts of a Developed Oldowan type also occur in the Member 1 infilling of the Swartkrans locality (M. D. Leakey 1970). The associated hominids there are robust australopithecines, in abundance, and several individuals of *Homo* sp. indet. The context of the artifact/hominid association is still unclear, but, as has been said, a variety of evidence suggests strongly that carnivore activity, and particularly leopard predation, may have been largely responsible for the vertebrate accumulation (Brain 1968, 1970, 1978; Vrba 1975). A few artifacts of undetermined industrial affinity are known from the Kromdraai B locality, the type occurrence of *A. robustus*. Both Brain (1975) and Vrba (1975) have suggested that the vertebrate accumulation here and its condition is suggestive of predation, and believe that hominid hunters were at least in part, if not largely responsible.

It is too often assumed that *Homo erectus* is predominantly associated with occurrences of the Acheulian Industry, at least in Africa (and Europe). However, the relationships are really not that firmly and widely established at least as yet; and the cultural associations are surely different in eastern Asia. It is now known that the earliest manifestation of the Acheulian, at least in Eastern Africa, is of earlier Quaternary age. At Olduvai and in the adjacent westerly reaches of the Natron basin the industry appears only slightly less than 1.5 million years ago, about 1.2–1.3 million years BP (Isaac and Curtis 1974, M. D. Leakey 1975). In the Koobi Fora area of East Rudolf *Homo erectus* skeletal parts are known from this and the subsequent range of time, up to about 1.2 million years BP or so, but there is little evidence of typical Acheulian associations (R. E. F. Leakey 1976b, R. E. F. Leakey and Walker 1976).

At Olduvai an Acheulian industry is present throughout the upper reaches of Bed II and is represented in Beds III, IV and the Masek Beds. The distinctive Developed Oldowan Industry is, however, also present throughout this same time-range (M. D. Leakey 1975). Direct associations of *Homo erectus* are unknown in Bed II – although the species is demonstrably present by Tuff II$^D$ times – and only two occurrences in lower and upper Bed IV and probably one occurrence in the Masek Beds afford such associations. In the last respect a recently reported hominid cranium with some *Homo erectus* features occurs in the Lake Ndutu area, probably in the upper (Norkilili Member) of the Masek Beds, in association with a presumed Acheulian industry (Clarke 1976, Mturi 1976). The only other direct association known for the moment in eastern Africa is that from the Gombore II locality, at Melka Kunturé, upper Awash valley, Ethiopia (Chavaillon *et al.* 1974).

In southern Africa direct associations of *Homo erectus* and the Acheulian are still unknown, unless it should indeed prove to be that the *Homo* aff. *erectus* mandible (Swartkans 15) from the Member 2 infilling occurs in an artifactual context which is demonstrably representative of that industry (C. K. Brain, personal communication).

Although a diversity of Acheulian occurrences of varying ages are recorded in the Maghrib (Freeman 1975b), only three afford confirmation of the presence of *Homo erectus*. Thus, 'older' Acheulian bifaces and spheroids, as well as some half-dozen mammal species, were recovered with the Thomas Quarry 2 hominid cranium (Ennouchi 1972). However, the nature of this association remains unknown. The fragmentary hominid mandible from Littorina Cave, Sidi Abderrahman, occurred in a lens-like filling, along with a small variety of mammal remains, mostly ungulates, all suggestive of hyena accumulation (Biberson 1956, 1961, 1964). A very substantial evolved Acheulian industry (stage VI of Biberson) occurred in a partially contiguous infilling, and was hence essentially contemporaneous, though presumably not directly associated with, or a part of, the bone accumulation. The artifact assemblage is not large, only about 250 pieces, but is quite diversified in implement types and often sophisticated in the refinement of some tool classes and the elaborateness of retouch.

Ternifine is usually considered to afford the most direct evidence for a *Homo erectus* Acheulian industry association in the Maghrib. The site was a small, spring-fed lake and the substantial vertebrate fauna, hominid cranial remains and Acheulian artifacts were all recovered from basal clays and overlying sands. However, there are no available details on these occurrences nor on their spatial or vertical relationships and associations one with another. The industry includes a substantial diversity of large shaped tools and heavy-duty tools, as well as some small flakes and flake tools (Balout, Biberson and Tixier 1967). The industry is most like an early phase (stage III of Biberson) of the Moroccan Acheulian; comparisons with assemblages from eastern Africa, particularly Olduvai, have still to be made.

There are, for the moment, no direct cultural associations known anywhere on the African continent with those hominids here considered to represent early representatives of *Homo sapiens*.

## PALAEO-ENVIRONMENTAL SETTINGS

Only in recent years have palaeo-environmental settings and adjustments of Cenozoic Hominidae been sought to be established on an empirical basis. The evidence is still relatively scant, and incomplete, but at least a beginning has been made, as set out in the second part of chapter 1 of this volume.

## CONCLUSION

From a few portions of the African continent pioneering and ever-intensified palaeo-anthropological researches have revealed the most protracted fossil record of hominid evolution known anywhere. There are tantalizing suggestions of hominid-like primates in the later Miocene, between 10 and 5 million years ago, with the proto-hominid source earlier still. Indeed the continent may prove ultimately to have been the setting for the origin of the family of mankind.

The adaptive success of the hominid experiment is well documented in the Pliocene, and into the earlier Quaternary, by the several successive and/or allopatric species of the genus *Australopithecus*. From some species representative of that genus, probably related closely to *A. afarensis*, the genus *Homo* arose. The sequential phyletic evolution of several species of *Homo* is increasingly illuminated by new discoveries within the continent. The origins and biological nature of earlier representatives of *Homo sapiens* are still scantily revealed; but the evolution and differentiation of more modern human subspecies remain almost wholly unknown.

# CHAPTER 3

# THE EARLIEST ARCHAEOLOGICAL TRACES

## AN INTRODUCTION TO THE EVIDENCE

This chapter is concerned with archaeological studies of developing technology and culture from the earliest traces to the end of the Middle Pleistocene – that is to say, over a time-span from about two million years ago to about one hundred thousand years ago. The African record of this vast time-span illustrates better than any other the dictum that history, through prehistory, is joined to natural history (Childe 1941, p. 4). In interpreting the evidence, we have continually to bear in mind the fact that we are dealing not with a mere extension of history or ethnography, but with human behaviour patterns in the making. We need to think in terms of changing adaptive systems that involved simultaneous growth in the capacity for culture and in culture itself.[1]

In chapter 2, Howell treats aspects of the anatomical and physiological transformation which brought human cultural capability to its modern level of complexity. The changes involve amongst other things modification of the hind limbs for bipedal locomotion, shortening of the arms and modification of the hands for increased dexterity. Most important of all has been the reorganization and enlargement of the brain and it is to this that we can attribute those qualities of humanity that set our species apart from all other mammals: skill, 'insight', cunning, aesthetic sense and above, all, linguistic communication and social co-ordination.

We know that in the last few million years of human evolution these abilities arose or were greatly expanded, but yet fossil human bones provide scant documentation of the pathway by which the transformation came about. To complement that record we must turn to palaeolithic archaeology for information. The evidence is of course

---

[1] The word 'culture' is used by anthropological archaeologists to denote all those aspects of thought and behaviour that are learned through participation in society – including traditions of craft and technology, which may be termed 'material culture'. The same word may also be used as a designation for a distinctive body of traditions and practices representing *the* specific culture of a particular time span in a particular area (e.g. the Natchikufan Culture of the Central African Later Stone Age). For this latter usage in Stone Age archaeology, the word 'Culture' has largely been replaced by the term 'Industry' or 'Industrial Complex' which makes explicit the fact that the entities are recognized only from the characteristics of craft products.

fragmentary and based on material objects, but yet it does appear that significant aspects of the process of cultural development can be discerned. The African sequence of archaeological documents with which this chapter is concerned is at present the longest known Pleistocene record and in some aspects also the most intensively studied.

### The nature of the record

Many accounts of prehistory are cast as narratives in which so-called 'cultures' defined from artifact design features are represented as undergoing episodic change through space and time. For the purposes of this kind of prehistory the recognition of valid cultures is the first prerequisite, to be followed by operations designed to map their distribution and to trace their origins and fate.

Until the last two decades, this approach was commonly adopted by scientists concerned with the Lower Palaeolithic,[1] and much of the now somewhat obsolete earlier literature treats the subject in this way. However, it is now widely, but not universally, believed that early Pleistocene cultures defined on the basis of comparatively simple stone artifacts are not on the same scale or even of the same nature as the cultures with which, for instance, a student of the Iron Age works. This revision of approach to early prehistory has been connected with a surge of interest in the stages whereby human economic and social systems developed over the vast span of the Pleistocene. The new research movement owes its origins and momentum to the demonstration by L. S. B. Leakey, M. D. Leakey, J. D. Clark, F. C. Howell and others that it was possible to excavate and interpret living-sites dating even from the very early phases of cultural development.

The energies of Palaeolithic archaeologists were formerly devoted primarily to the detailed study of stone artifacts but, as indicated, emphasis is steadily changing. However, artifacts remain central ingredients of the evidence. Firstly, it is through the presence of artifacts that one recognizes the places where early humans were particularly active and it is through the presence of artifacts that archaeologists can

---

[1] Stone Age remains from the Pleistocene geological epoch are conventionally assigned to the 'Old Stone Age' or Palaeolithic. In Europe and North Africa, three divisions are commonly recognized: the Upper Palaeolithic period, which extends from 10 000 BP back to about 35 000 BP; the Middle Palaeolithic (Mousterian) period, which extends back to about 100 000 BP; and the Lower Palaeolithic which extends back to the beginning of the archaeological record. In sub-Saharan Africa the equivalents of these same periods tend to be called Later, Middle and Earlier Stone Ages, though the Later Stone Age also includes what would be called Mesolithic in Europe.

distinguish prehistoric food-refuse from natural materials. Secondly, in addition to this, artifacts preserve in their form evidence regarding their practical function and regarding the culturally determined habits and preferences of their makers.

In summary, then, this chapter will reflect contemporary endeavour in African Palaeolithic prehistory by being more concerned with what is known of long-term developments in human ecology, technology and social grouping than with such versions of culture history as those expounded in the classics of African Palaeolithic literature.[1]

As already indicated, the excavation of undisturbed archaeological sites provides the crucial evidence for attempts to understand early prehistory in socio-economic and ecological terms. Of these there are of the order of one hundred only, scattered through more than two million years of time and through the 30 million sq. km of the continent. Ideally each horizon at a locality yields an assemblage of stone artifacts the form and composition of which presumably reflects the combined effects of technological capabilities, craft traditions, available materials, and the discarder's immediate needs for stone equipment. Archaeologial interpretation involves making implicit or explicit judgements about the relative importance of these interacting influences, and this is often problematic. At some sites bone food-refuse is also preserved and provides the basis for assessments of hunting methods, and of aspects of diet. In very rare instances only, remains of plant foods and materials are preserved.

Reconstruction does not only depend on the inventories of artifacts and food-refuse. In addition, observations on context and arrangement can be of critical importance. Thus the arrangement of materials and features within a site or the size of the site itself may give information on activities, community size and organization. On a different scale, the spatial relations of sites to each other or to features in the surrounding country, can be informative of the microenvironments which were ecologically attractive to early human groups. Finally, on a very large scale, the distribution of sites in relation to the gross environmental zonation of Africa and the Old World (see chapter 1) may be indicative of major features of developing human adaptation.

---

[1] Classic works on the earlier Stone Age of Africa include the writings of Alimen, Balout, Goodwin and van Riet Lowe, L. S. B. Leakey, and Vaufrey. For a guide to these, and for references, see the bibliographical essay relating to this chapter.

## The basis of society and culture: economic organization

Several fundamental differences between human behaviour and that of other primates are associated with the way in which food is obtained and consumed. In Africa, prehistoric archaeology has provided an important opportunity for investigating the long-term record of the stages by which the contrast arose.

Amongst mammals in general, including all non-human primates, the acquisition of food is an individual pursuit of each adult even if the animals feed in social groups. However, all known human societies engage in the sharing of some food amongst adults and in some degree of collective social responsibility for its acquisition. In large-scale societies supported by farming, extension of the web of interdependence has led to a situation which otherwise has behavioural parallels only amongst the social insects. The beginnings of this contrast appear to lie before the oldest known archaeological occurrences. Excavations at the early sites of Koobi Fora and Olduvai Gorge[1] have revealed patches of old ground surfaces on which there accumulated localized concentrations of discarded stone artifacts, artificially introduced stones and broken-up mammal bones. These range from six or seven metres to twenty metres in diameter, and in one instance at Olduvai there may also be a simple stone footing for a shelter made of branches (fig. 3.1). In their general features these patches of artifacts and bone refuse resemble the majority of pre-agricultural camp sites and it is hard to explain them without invoking in some degree certain fundamental facets of human behaviour, namely: relatively extensive meat-eating, and hunting; recurrent transport of food to a particular place, presumably for sharing; organization of behaviour and movements around a spatial focus which can be termed a camp or home-base.

The Plio–Pleistocene concentrations of material at Olduvai and Koobi Fora are marked as being of proto-human causation by the presence of the artifacts, and it will be difficult to find and study proto-human sites, if such there be, that are older than those used for the practice of stone-tool-making.

Table 3.1 shows lists of species of animals represented amongst the broken-up bone at these sites. It can be seen that the full size-range of the African Fauna is represented, from large pachyderms to small creatures such as rodents and tortoises. At one stage it was widely

---

[1] References for these and other sites are given in the bibliographical essay under the appropriate region.

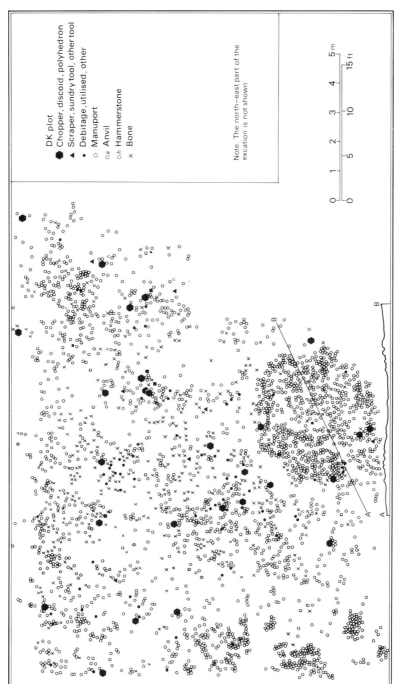

Fig. 3.1 Plan of the occupation surface as exposed by excavation at the site of DK, level 3, Bed I, Olduvai Gorge. The plane shows the pattern of natural stones that seems to represent the footing of a hut or shelter. (After M. D. Leakey 1971.)

DK plot
⬣ Chopper, discoid, polyhedron
▲ Scraper, sundry tool, other tool
• Debitage, utilised, other
○ Manuport
○a Anvil
○h Hammerstone
× Bone

Note: The north–east part of the excavation is not shown

0    1    2    3    4    5 m
0    5    10    15 ft

TABLE 3.1  *Types of animal represented among the bones associated with artifacts in the Early Stone Age Sites of East Africa*

| | DK | FLK NN-3 | FLK Zinj. | FLK N-6 | FLK N-1+2 | MNK Main | SHK | BK | Koobi Fora KBS | Koobi Fora HAS |
|---|---|---|---|---|---|---|---|---|---|---|
| **Primates** | | | | | | | | | | |
| Hominids | · | × | × | · | × | · | · | × | · | · |
| Galagos | × | · | · | · | · | · | · | · | · | · |
| Baboons | × | × | · | · | · | · | · | × | · | · |
| **Carnivores** | | | | | | | | | | |
| Mongooses | × | × | × | · | × | × | · | · | · | · |
| Dogs, jackals, foxes | × | × | × | · | · | × | · | · | · | · |
| Hyenas | × | · | × | · | · | · | · | · | · | · |
| Large cats | · | · | · | · | · | · | · | × | × | × |
| Sabre-tooth tigers | × | · | · | · | · | · | · | · | · | · |
| **Antelopes and bovines** | | | | | | | | | | |
| Waterbuck and relatives | × | × | × | · | · | × | × | × | × | × |
| Kudu and relatives | × | × | × | × | × | × | × | × | × | · |
| Sable and relatives | · | · | · | × | × | × | · | · | · | · |
| Wildebeest, Hartebeest, etc. | × | × | × | × | × | × | × | × | × | × |
| Gazelles | × | · | × | × | × | × | × | × | × | × |
| Pelorovis and 'buffaloes' | × | · | × | × | × | × | × | · | × | · |
| Duikers | · | · | · | × | · | · | · | · | × | · |
| **Giraffes** | | | | | | | | | | |
| Lybitherium | × | · | · | · | × | × | × | × | · | · |
| Giraffa | × | · | · | × | × | × | · | × | × | · |
| **Suids** | | | | | | | | | | |
| Mesochoerus | × | · | × | × | × | × | × | × | × | · |
| Metridiochoerus | × | · | × | · | · | × | × | × | × | · |
| Other pigs | × | × | × | · | × | · | · | · | · | · |

TABLE 3.1 (*cont.*)

| | DK | FLK Nn-3 | FLK Zinj. | FLK N-6 | FLK N-1+2 | MNK Main | SHK | BK | Koobi Fora KBS | Koobi Fora HAS |
|---|---|---|---|---|---|---|---|---|---|---|
| Hippopotami | | | | | | | | | | |
|   *Hippopotamus* spp. | × | · | · | × | × | × | × | × | × | **B** |
| Proboscidea | | | | | | | | | | |
|   *Deinotherium* | × | · | · | · | · | · | · | · | · | · |
|   *Elephas recki* | × | · | · | **B** | · | × | × | × | · | · |
| Rhinoceros | | | | | | | | | | |
|   *Ceratotherium* (white rhino) | × | · | · | · | × | × | × | × | · | · |
| Equines | | | | | | | | | | |
|   *Equus* | × | × | × | × | × | × | × | × | · | · |
|   *Hipparion* (three-toed) | · | · | × | × | × | × | × | × | · | · |
| Hares, etc | × | × | × | × | × | · | · | · | · | · |
| Porcupines | × | × | × | × | × | · | · | · | × | · |
| Other rodents | × | × | × | × | × | × | · | × | · | · |
| Birds | × | · | × | · | · | × | × | × | · | · |
| Tortoises and turtles | × | × | × | × | × | × | · | × | · | · |
| Lizards and snakes | × | × | × | × | × | × | · | × | · | · |
| Amphibia | × | × | × | · | · | · | × | × | · | · |
| Fish | × | × | × | × | · | · | × | × | ? | ? |
| Mollusca | × | · | × | · | · | · | × | · | · | · |

*Note*: The entries are given common names to facilitate intelligibility for non-technical readers, but in fact most of the species are extinct. For details see M. D. Leakey (1971) and Isaac, Harris and Crader (1976). It can be seen that the animal remains best represented on the sites are those of medium to medium-large ungulates including antelope, equines and pigs. **B** denotes a form which dominates a bone assemblage.

163

reported that there had been a small-game hunting phase in the development of human socio-economic capabilities. The archaeological evidence now available shows clearly that if, as seems likely, there was such a phase then it must have preceded the known archaeological record. Intensification of the importance of meat-eating for subsistence is widely regarded as having been a critical ingredient in the evolutionary reorganization of behaviour that led to modern man. Meat is more readily carried about and shared than are plant foods, so it may have been hunting and scavenging that led to the critical adaptive shift towards forms of social organization that involved some co-operative economic effort and partial division of labour. However, the gathering of plant foods would immediately have become an equally important part of the pattern. It is interesting that amongst mammals the main faint parallels to human food-sharing occur amongst social carnivores. Chimpanzees have also been observed to practise incipient sharing when they kill and eat a small animal as they occasionally do, but their behaviour is more aptly termed 'tolerated scrounging' than true sharing.

Hunting, food-sharing, division of labour, organization around a home-base and tool-making can be viewed as a set of behaviours fundamental to human differentiation. The evidence from African sites suggests that by two to three million years ago these behaviours had been intensified and integrated to form a novel kind of adaptive mechanism that one might term proto-human. This behavioural level in part coincides with the Oldowan classificatory group of artifact assemblages (see p. 168), though the two conceptual categories are not coincident or synonymous.

In addition to expanding the subsistence base of hominoid existence, involvement in hunting and food-sharing probably placed crucial selection pressures on insight, social co-operation and ability to transmit and receive information. Presumably these selection pressures acted on the genetic basis for the proto-human adaptive complex and led to the progressive enlargement of hominoid capacity for technology, language and culture – developments that are in part reflected in enlarged brain volumes, expanded ecological range and more elaborate artifact assemblages.

In spite of the probable formative influence of hunting on human evolution, it seems that exclusive dependence on hunted protein has been the exception rather than the norm in the prehistoric past. Ethnographic information on non-agricultural peoples suggests that there was a plant-food subsistence gradient between warm, low- and middle-latitude regions and cold, high-latitude regions. In the former, foraged fruits, cereals, roots, etc. form half or more of the diet, while in the arctic extremes plant foods are only seasonally available and have much less importance. Because plant foods are as yet so poorly represented in archaeological evidence for the diet of early man, it is hard to document their importance relative to the animal food to which the bone-refuse bears witness. Most archaeologists suspect that throughout prehistory including the early phases under discussion, vegetable foods were of crucial importance as staples or as major complements of meat.

As indicated in the commentaries on the regional sequence of southern Africa, the australopithecine sites of Makapansgat, and Sterkfontein may represent a state of behavioural adaptation that preceded the proto-human level documented at Olduvai and Koobi Fora. Such a stage may well have involved predation and tool use without stone-tool manufacture. However, it is not yet clear to what extent the accumulation of broken and damaged bones at these sites was due to hominid activity as opposed to carnivore activity and other natural agencies. Until the context and accumulation mechanisms are better known, these sites cannot be included as firm documents in a history of human subsistence and economy in Africa.

The archaeological record in Africa does not indicate any drastic changes in subsistence patterns during the time-range of the Acheulian, that is, from one and a half million years ago to one hundred thousand years ago. Sites vary in the quantity of broken-up bone that they contain, but given very unequal conditions of bone-refuse preservation it is hard to assess the extent to which this variation is due to differences from site to site in the quantities of meat consumed. It seems likely that this was one important factor in determining the quantity of bones, and if this is so, then it can fairly be said that the archaeological record is consistent with the view that throughout this time-range, human subsistence involved an opportunistic combination of hunted and scavenged meat and foraged plant foods. Table 3.2 shows a selected list of sites classified into varying grades of density of discarded artifacts and bone refuse.

Lower and Middle Pleistocene men seem to have been eclectic hunters and scavengers, but as yet we have very little specific information on the techniques they used. Progressive trends, if there were any, are hard to detect. M. D. Leakey (1971) reports that, at Olduvai, there is

TABLE 3.2. *A selected list of important sites classified according to the relative density of stone artifacts and bone refuse found on them*

SITES OF TYPE A   Abundant stone artifacts and few or no bones

> Olduvai MNK Chert factory site
> Peninj RHS
> Olduvai ER-HR
>    FC West
> Melka Kunturé (various)
>
> Sidi Abderrahman Levels LMO
> Kharga Oasis*
> Kalambo Falls*
> Montagu Cave*
> Wonderboompoort*

(In those cases marked with an asterisk, the lack of bone could well be due to conditions inimical to its preservation; at other sites the absence of bone may reflect the fact that it never was present.)

SITES OF TYPE B   The remains of the carcass of a single large
   animal plus a modest number of associated artifacts

> Koobi Fora HAS (hippopotamus)
> Olduvai FLK N level 6 (elephant)
>    FLK II Deinotherium level (deinothere)
> Isimila, Sands 4 (hippopotamus)
> Olorgesailie (HBS) (hippopotamus)
> Melka Kunturé, Simburro III (*Pelorovis* buffalo)

SITES OF TYPE C   Coincident, fairly high concentrations
   of bones and artifacts

> Olduvai FLK-*Zinjanthropus* level
>    FLK NN level 3
>    SHK annexe
> Koobi Fora KBS
> Melka Kunturé Garba IVD
> Olorgesailie I3
>    DE/89B
> Cornelia
> Hopefield (Saldanha)
> Sidi Abderrahman STIC
> Ternifine (a spring eye)
> Sidi Zin

a slight rise in the incidence of very large animals in sites that are younger than one and a half million years by comparison with those dating to between one and a half, and two million years, but the differences are minor. Also the oldest examples of sites showing extensive predation on many individual members of a single gregarious species are associated with the period after one and a half million years ago. For example, at Olduvai, the site of SHK II provides evidence of the slaughter of springbok-like gazelle (*Antidorcas recki*) while at

BK II one or more herds of buffalo-like *Pelorovis* seems to have been successfully bogged and butchered. Half a million years ago at the site of Olorgesailie, gelada-like baboons (*Simopithecus*) were the prey, and so successful were the hunters that the remains of more than fifty of these animals lie strewn amongst several hundred hand-axes at one site. In these instances, the archaeological evidence bears eloquent witness of the hunting prowess of early men, and it seems likely that in these cases, social co-operation was involved. However, in general it seems that during their long tenure of the African continent, men have not been the ravening carnivores that are depicted in some literature – rather, human subsistence has depended on opportunistic and varied foraging and hunting strategies that have promoted flexibility and ingenuity.

### The classification of Early Stone Age artifact assemblages and their terminology

Virtually all the artifacts that have come down to us from the Lower and Middle Pleistocene of Africa are stone artifacts made by percussion. The archaeological record does demonstrate development in their degree of complexity, but we now recognize that the process of change in lithic technology did not involve universal or irreversible trends. Observations and measurements suggest the following interrelated progressive changes.

(1) A rise in the number of tool designs represented amongst the shaped tools.

(2) A rise in the maximum number of technical acts involved in making the most elaborate pieces.

(3) A rise in the degree of standardization and refinement of the most elaborate artifacts.

Stages can be recognized in the history of African Stone Age industries on the basis of these trends; however, it is a rise in the maximum elaboration observable amongst a variety of assemblages, that distinguishes the stages, not a universal or general rise in elaboration (fig. 3.2). Under these circumstances only a very limited number of stage subdivisions are useful. For many individual assemblages a minimum age only can be determined from the morphology rather than the exact kind of stage–age classification that was formerly fashionable amongst prehistorians.

The current classification of stone industries is the end-product of a long history of changing concepts and usages. A more detailed

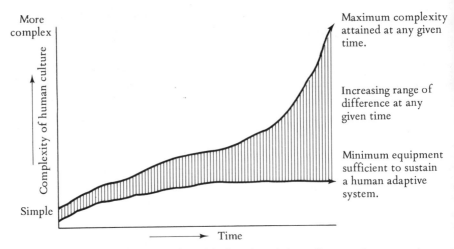

Fig. 3.2    Change in the complexity of material culture through time: a diagrammatic representation showing how the maximum level of complexity may have risen progressively while the minimum level reached a stable level and then remained more or less constant.

account is given at the end of the chapter but since the following terms will be used from the outset, they need brief explanation: The tool forms referred to are best defined by reference to fig. 3.3.

(1) *Oldowan (Industrial Complex)*. This is used to refer to a set of end-Pliocene and Lower Pleistocene assemblages in which choppers, polyhedrons, discoids and various rather informal scrapers are the most characteristic shaped tools. True bifaces are not present, and spheroids, scrapers, etc. are less important than in the Developed Oldowan. Industries of this level and aspect have been referred to as 'mode 1' by J. G. D. Clark (1969).

(2) *Developed Oldowan (Industrial Complex)*. This is a set of late Lower Pleistocene industries in which Oldowan forms such as choppers etc. continue to be important but to which rare badly-made bifaces are added. Spheroids and scrapers are relatively more numerous and the small 'flake' tools may be more diversified than in the Oldowan industries.

(3) *Acheulian (Industrial Complex)*.[1] This is a set of late Lower and

---

[1] The term 'Acheulian' is used as a label for an apparently related set of Lower and Middle Pleistocene artifact occurrences that are distributed over Africa, south-west Eurasia and parts of southern Asia. The name itself derives from St Acheul, in France, where the distinctive features of the Industrial Complex were initially recognized during the mid nineteenth century. The name 'Oldowan' is taken from Oldoway, the original German spelling of Olduvai; the Oldowan has in the past also been known as the 'pebble-tool culture' or the 'pre-Acheulian'.

Middle Pleistocene industries in which bifaces (hand-axes and cleavers) form a well-developed and conspicuous part of the assemblage. Small scrapers, awls and Oldowan tool forms are also commonly part of these assemblages. Opinion is divided over whether the term should be restricted to assemblages showing 40% or more of bifaces or used to cover a wide range of contemporary, sympatric assemblages of which only *some* are dominated by bifaces. The debate turns on whether one thinks that this distinction is due to differences between tool-kits discarded by the same people at different times and places (see p. 241), or by members of distinct, coexisting 'cultures'. The Acheulian is ranked as a 'mode 2' pattern of technology by J. G. D. Clark.

Table 3.3 shows these terms in relation to other partially synonymous terms which will be encountered in the literature but which are not used here. The similarities of tools and techniques that bind each of these sets of assemblages as broad classificatory entities are in fact rather generalized and many prehistorians are now sceptical that the common patterns of stone-working are really indicative of sufficient overall tradition to justify the use of terms such as 'Acheulian culture' etc. The label 'Industrial Complex' is preferable since it makes explicit the fact that it refers primarily to basic features of stone craft. Clarke's (1968) term 'techno-complex' may be even clearer.

---

Fig. 3.3   Drawings illustrating some of the more important forms of early stone implement and sketches suggesting ways in which they can be used. Archaeologists do not yet know very much about the specific functions of early tools so that the sketches are speculative. Many of the forms illustrated may well have been used in a much wider variety of ways than is shown here. Items 1 to 3 are cores as well as tools and the flakes struck in shaping them would be useful knives, as shown in 8.

1   A *bifacial chopper* shown in front and side view and in use for cutting a branch which could then be made into a digging-stick or spear.

2   A *hand-axe* or *biface* such as characterizes Acheulian industries. One possible use is in skinning and cutting up animal carcasses. They could also be used in cutting bark and wood.

3   A *pick* – here shown in use for hacking off a piece of bark which could be used as a tray container for gathered food.

4   A *spheroid* formed of a battered rounded stone, shown in use for breaking a bone so as to extract marrow.

5   A *scraper* made by the trimming of a concave working edge on a stone flake, here shown in use for sharpening a stick.

6   An *awl* or *borer* formed on a flake by two converging lines of retouch scars that define a stout point such as could be used for piercing hide or for grooving wood.

7   A *scraper* with convex working edges trimmed along two margins of a flake. Here shown in use for scraping hide so as to prepare leather, but equally suitable for whittling and shaping wood.

8   An unretouched *flake* being used as a knife for cutting through the skin of an animal carcass. Flakes such as this are the commonest objects on almost all early archaeological sites. They have usually been treated by archaeologists simply as by-products from the making of core tools, but they make very effective knives and were almost certainly extensively used as such.

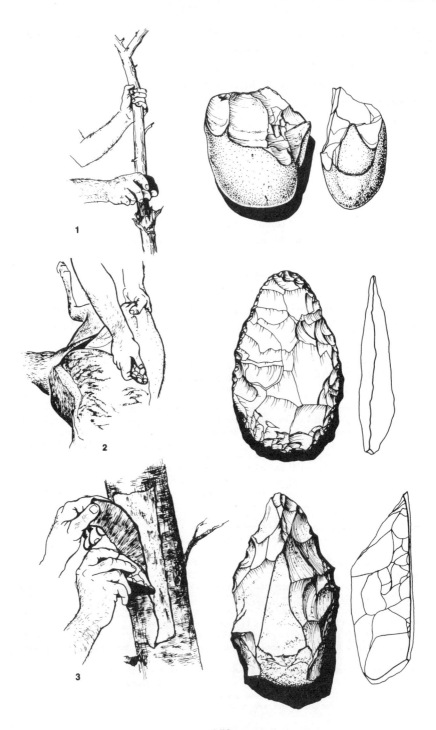

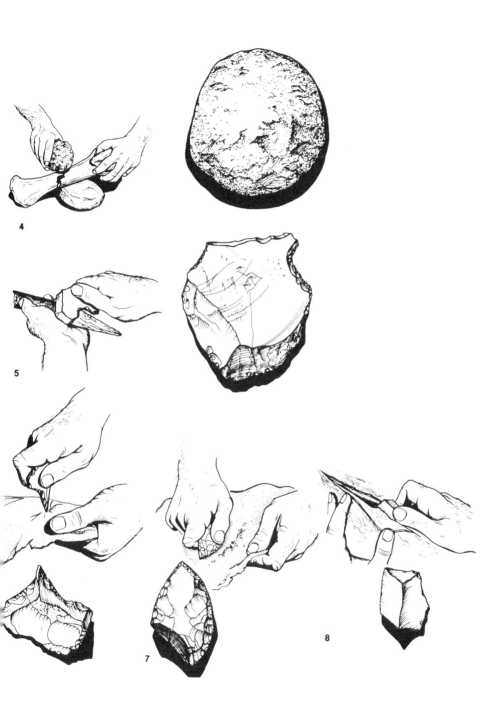

**4**

**5**

**7**

**8**

TABLE 3.3   *A simplified summary of usages for the designation of earlier Stone Age industries and industrial complexes*

| | Terms used in this chapter[a] | Partially equivalent earlier usages |
|---|---|---|
| Acheulian industrial complex | Late (Upper) Acheulian industries | Acheulio-Levallois; Fauresmith |
| | { Middle Acheulian industries | 'Stellenbosch culture' (South Africa) or Chelles–Acheul culture (East Africa) |
| | Lower (Early) Acheulian industries | Chellean, Abbevillian, Clacto-Abbevillian |
| | Developed Oldowan[b] | Hope Fountain; African Tayacian; Acheulian type B |
| | Oldowan | 'Pebble(-tool) culture'; pre-Acheulian; Kafuan[c]; *Civilization du galet aménagé* |

[a] Follows as far as possible the resolution on terminology reported in Bishop and Clark (1967).

[b] Many scholars believe that Developed Oldowan industries are for the most part a distinct facies of the Acheulian rather than a distinct 'culture' (see text).

[c] The Kafuan was at one time believed to be a pre-Oldowan stage of technology, but it has been shown that the type series from the Kafu valley is indistinguishable from naturally broken stones. Wayland proposed the term 'Kafuan' in a paper entitled 'A possible age correlation of the Kafu Gravels' (Wayland 1926). This was more widely publicized in Wayland (1934), and in van Riet Lowe (1952b). Later Bishop (1959) showed that the breaking of pebbles assigned to the Kafuan should be considered as natural.

### Chronology

Our understanding of the true scale of time-intervals in human evolution and prehistory has been revolutionized by the application of geophysical dating techniques. Data gathered mainly in the last decade demonstrate that the archaeological evidence is spread out through a period of two to two and a half million years, a time span of four or five times longer than that allowed for in most estimates published before 1960. Table 3.4 lists the geophysical dates relevant to this chapter and the left-hand part of fig. 3.4 shows their configuration, while the right-hand sector indicates estimated age-relationships amongst important sites for which no direct dates have yet been obtained. These estimates depend upon faunistic correlations and general geological considerations. They are highly uncertain. From this diagram it can be seen that assemblages classified as Oldowan date from about two million to one and a half million years. Assemblages classifiable as Acheulian began to be made about one and a half million years ago (Isaac and Curtis 1974, M. D. Leakey 1971) and they continued to be made

TABLE 3.4  *A summary of geophysical and geochemical dates for Earlier Stone Age occurrences in Africa*[a]

| Age estimate, years BP | Degree of uncertainty | Method[b] | Region | Industry | Site and stratigraphy | Reference |
|---|---|---|---|---|---|---|
| < 60 000 | | | | | [14]C determinations for 'Earlier Stone Age' and Lower Palaeolithic sites have been obtained for sites such as Kalambo, Amanzi, the Cave of Hearths, etc. Some of these give 'infinite' ages, others give apparently finite ages of 60 000 years or less. We now realize that the 'Earlier Stone Age' probably lies outside the range of [14]C dating and that the apparent results should be set aside. They are thus not itemized here. | |
| 50 000–95 000 | — | Th/U | North-west Africa | Late Acheulian | Morocco – deposits of the Ouljian high sea level (post-Acheulian, pre-Aterian) | — |
| 115 000 | Probably a minimum age | Th/U | South Africa | Late Acheulian ('Fauresmith') | Rooidam | Butzer (1974a) |
| 130 000 | Probably a minimum age | Th/U | East Africa | Undetermined | Member 1 of the Kibish Formation, Omo | Butzer (1976) |
| 145 000 | — | Th/U | North-west Africa | Late Acheulian | Morocco – deposits associated with the Harounian high sea level | — |
| 190 000 | — | Amino-acid racemization | East and South Africa | Late Acheulian | Kalambo Falls Mkamba Member | — |
| 200 000 | Range from 180 000 to 210 000 | Th/U | East Africa | Acheulian | Dallol, Afar | — |
| 200 000 | — | Th/U | North-west Africa | Acheulian | Morocco – Anfatian high sea level | — |
| 230 000 | — | K/Ar | East Africa | Acheulian | Lava believed to underlie the Kapthurin Formation | — |

173

TABLE 3.4 (*cont.*)

| Age estimate years BP | Degree of uncertainty | Method[b] | Region | Industry | Site and stratigraphy | Reference |
|---|---|---|---|---|---|---|
| 260 000 | +70 000? −40 000 | Th/U | — | Acheulian | Isimila – bone from Sands 4 | Howell et al. (1972) |
| 425 000 | ±9 000 | K/Ar | East Africa | Acheulian | Olorgesailie Member 10 | — |
| 486 000 | — | K/Ar | East Africa | Acheulian | Olorgesailie Member 4 | — |
| 660 000 | ? | K/Ar | East Africa | Acheulian | Tuff in the Kapthurin Formation | Bishop (1972) |
| ≥ 700 000 | — | Palaeomag. | East Africa | Acheulian | Kilombe | Bishop 1978: 329–36 |
| > 700 000 | Minimum only | Palaeomag. K/Ar | East Africa | Acheulian and Developed Oldowan | Gadeb | Clark and Kurashiua (1979) |
| > 700 000– 1 600 000 | Minimum only | Palaeomag. | East Africa | Developed Oldowan | Chemoigut Formation, Chesowanja | Bishop et al. (1975) |
| 700 000– 1 600 000 | — | Palaeomag. | East Africa | Acheulian and Developed Oldowan | Olduvai Bed, II, III and Lower IV | — |
| 928 000– 1 100 000 | A range of dates | K/Ar | East Africa | Acheulian | Kariandusi Beds, beneath the site | — |
| 1 300 000– 1 470 000 | Secure | K/Ar for tuffs above and below | East Africa | Karari Industry and Acheulian elements | Koobi Fora Formation, Upper Member | — |
| 1 300 000– 1 600 000 | — | K/Ar and palaeomag. | East Africa | Lower Acheulian | Humbu Formation of the Peninj Beds | — |
| 1 400 000 | ? | K/Ar and palaeomag. | East Africa | Lower Acheulian | Olduvai EF-HR | — |
| 1 600 000– 1 800 000 | — | K/Ar | East Africa | KBS Industry (= Oldowan) | Koobi Fora | Curtis et al.[c] (1975) |
| 1 600 000– 1 900 000 | 35 dates, very secure | K/Ar and palaeomag. | East Africa | Oldowan and Developed Oldowan A | Olduvai Bed I and Lower Bed II | — |

TABLE 3.4 (*cont.*)

| Age estimate years BP | Degree of uncertainty | Method[b] | Region | Industry | Site and stratigraphy | Reference |
|---|---|---|---|---|---|---|
| 2 060 000– 1 930 000 | — | K/Ar and palaeomag. | East Africa | Shungura Industry | Members E and F of the Shungura Formation, Omo | — |
| 2 630 000 | ±50 000 | K/Ar | East Africa | (? = Oldowan) (? = Oldowan) | Hadar[d] | |

[a] Most of these dates have been listed with source information in Isaac (1972b). Only references not given there are listed on the table.

[b] Th/U = thorium/uranium; K/Ar = potassium/argon; Palaeomag. = palaeomagnetic reversal chronology; $^{39}$Ar/$^{40}$Ar = a special refinement of K/Ar. For a general account of these methods see Michels (1973) and Bishop and Miller (1972).

[c] Recent work has shown conclusively that the age of the KBS industry is 1.8–1.9 million years. This supersedes previously published dates of 2.4–2.6 million years (Hay 1980).

[d] Artifacts have been reported from the Hadar Formation, Ethiopia, by Roche and Tiercelin (1977) and a date of 2.6 million years by Aronson *et al.* (1977). Confirmation is awaited of the stratigraphic relations between the artifacts and the date.

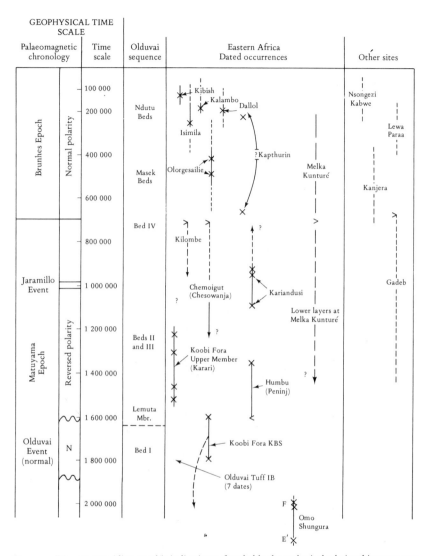

Fig. 3.4 Diagram providing graphic indications of probable chronological relationships amongst some of the most important Early Stone Age sites discussed in the text. Chronometric determinations (dates) are shown with an ×, plus a line indicating graphically something of the

until about one-tenth of a million years ago, that is 100 000 years ago. During this vast time-span some rise in the maximum degree of tool refinement allows us, in most regions, to distinguish between Lower (early) and Upper (late) Acheulian assemblages. Sometimes a three-fold division is possible. During the entire duration of Acheulian craft practices various assemblages not dominated by bifaces, including Developed Oldowan assemblages, were also manufactured in the same parts of Africa.

Around the beginning of the Upper Pleistocene, that is to say perhaps between 70 000 and 120 000 years ago, techniques and design features characteristic of the 'Middle Stone Age' began to be at least locally prominent in stone-craft (see p. 245 and chapter 4). Unfortunately chronometric resolution is poor in this time-range and information of all kinds on the changeover is scant so that ideas about its nature are correspondingly uncertain and controversial.

Radiocarbon determination on wood associated with the late Acheulian assemblages of Kalambo Falls have been widely used as the basis for statements regarding the date of the 'end of the Acheulian'; the relevant age estimate being between 42 000 and 60 300 years. However, careful scrutiny of the reports shows that these values should be treated only as *minimum* ages. Recent measurements of the degree of amino-acid racemization in the wood may indicate a much greater age for the Kalambo Acheulian assemblages (see p. 202 and chapter 4).

Whatever the nature and duration of the transition, it seems certain that by 50 000 years ago, assemblages classifiable as 'Acheulian' were no longer being made.

### *Geographic patterns*

The fact that the African continent contains the longest *known* record of the biological and cultural relics of early man raises a variety of important questions with regard to the geography of early man. Were the earliest tool-makers confined to Africa? Was Africa, in that sense, the cradle of human origins? Then, too, one should go on to ask whether or not it is known that within Africa certain regions and/or environments were occupied rather than others. The paragraphs that follow deal first with broad aspects of intra-African distribution patterns and then with wider inter-continental relationships. More detailed treatment is postponed until after the regional summaries which follow this section of the chapter.

Fig. 3.5 shows the distribution of sites assigned to the Oldowan

Industrial Complex or pebble-tool culture. The map shows that a substantial number of occurrences have been claimed at localities ranging over large parts of the continent. However, the majority of these claims are based on isolated finds of small assemblages of simple artifact forms. Such finds are no longer acceptable to most archaeologists as valid records, and in fact only a very limited number of occurrences of stone artifacts are known for which there is good independent evidence of Oldowan classificatory status. All such sites are marked by name on the map and discussed at least briefly in the appropriate section of the regional summaries.

Although the confirmed sites are few in number, they are scattered about between eastern Africa, southern Africa and northern Africa, and this suggests that even during the earliest known archaeological phase, tool-making hominids were spread out over a very large part of the African continent. The ecological conditions prevailing at these sites are very varied, but it might be remarked that none of the confirmed very early sites was situated in an extreme environment such as a desert or a rainforest. Put another way, all of these sites appear to be associated with environmental conditions that involved open country with scattered or patchy tree vegetation. One is therefore inclined to think of the hominids responsible for the earliest detectable traces of proto-human culture as having been creatures that lived mainly in the broad belt of savanna and open country that forms an irregular arc between the Sahara and the denser forested vegetation of the Congo basin and the West African coastal belt. The existing information is consistent with this view but the stock of data is so meagre that it cannot really be said to prove it.

Fig. 3.6–7 shows the recorded distribution of archaeological occurrences classified as Acheulian. In practice this means the distribution of sites at which hand-axes and cleavers were prominent finds. It can be seen that these are scattered over most of the continent. Again, sites are common in the vast arc formed by southern Africa, East Africa and the Sahel. The gaps within this configuration are in most cases associated with poorly explored terrain rather than with interpretable breaks in the distribution of the tool-makers. However, this is not entirely true of parts of the Congo basin and West Africa: work has been done in these areas leading to records of many Stone Age sites and yet there appears to be a lack of what might be called typical Acheulian. Such sites as do occur are commonly characterized by thick, heavy, boldly flaked tools with a Sangoan aspect. With these indications

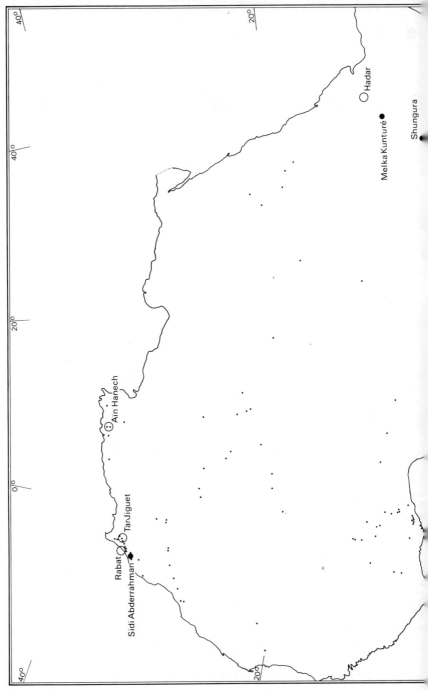

Fig. 3.5    The distribution of sites known or believed to be older than 1.5 million years
(i.e. Oldowan). (Modified from J. D. Clark 1967.)

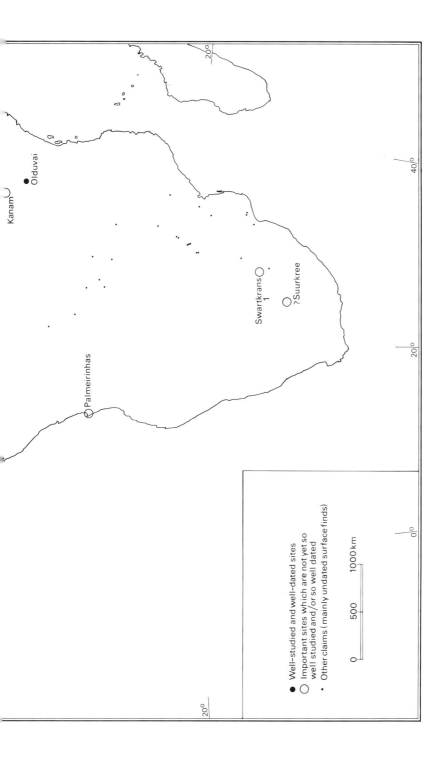

- ● Well-studied and well-dated sites
- ○ Important sites which are not yet so well studied and/or so well dated
- · Other claims (mainly undated surface finds)

Olduvai

Kanam

Swartkrans
1

○ ?Suurkree

Palmeirinhas

0    500    1000 km

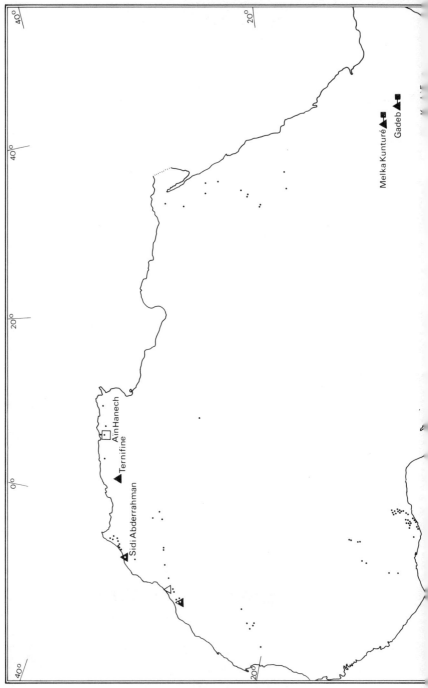

Fig. 3.6   The distribution of sites known or believed to be between 1.5 and 0.7 million years
(i.e. Early Acheulian and Developed Oldowan).

182

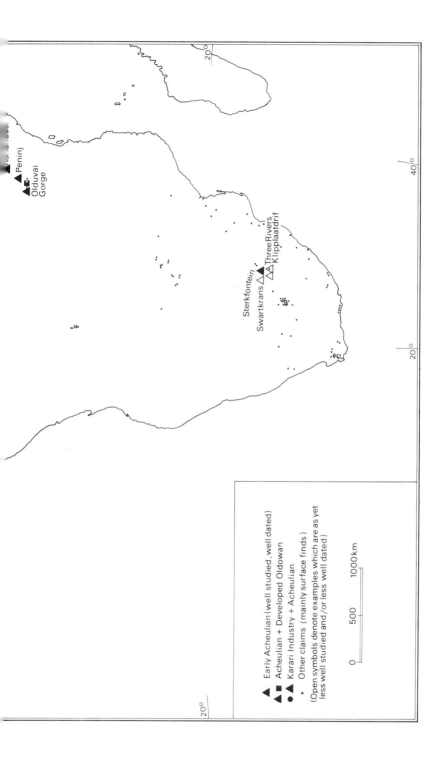

Peninj

Olduvai
Gorge

Sterkfontein
Swartkrans ▲ △ Three Rivers
△ ▲ Klipplaatdrif

20°

40°

20°

20°

20°

▲ Early Acheulian (well studied, well dated)
▲ ■ Acheulian + Developed Oldowan
▲ ▲ Karari Industry + Acheulian
• Other claims (mainly surface finds)

(Open symbols denote examples which are as yet
less well studied and/or less well dated)

0        500       1000km

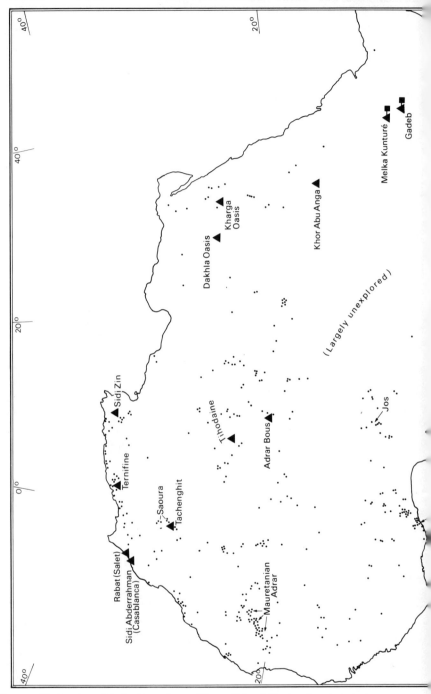

Fig. 3.7 The location of Earlier Stone Age and Lower Palaeolithic sites thought to be between 0.7 and 0.1 million years old (i.e. Acheulian plus Developed Oldowan/Hope Fountain).

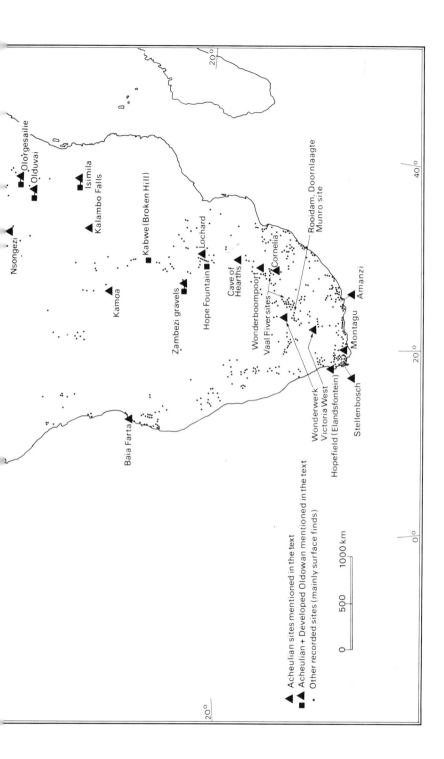

Olorgesailie
Olduvai
Nsongezi
Isimila
Kalambo Falls
Kabwe (Broken Hill)
Kamoa
Lochard
Zambezi gravels
Hope Fountain
Cave of
Hearths
Cornelia
Wonderboompoort
Rooidam, Doornlaagte
Munro site
Vaal River sites
Amanzi
Montagu
Baia Farta
Wonderwerk
Victoria West
Stellenbosch
Hopefield (Elandsfontein)

▲ Acheulian sites mentioned in the text
▲
■ Acheulian + Developed Oldowan mentioned in the text
• Other recorded sites (mainly surface finds)

0     500    1000 km

20°
20°
0°
20°
40°

in mind, J. D. Clark has suggested that early men may not have made extensive use of the relatively humid equatorial forest zone until very late Acheulian times or later, in Sangoan–Lupemban times. This is a valuable and plausible hypothesis, but it should be realized that dating evidence is so meagre that it cannot be regarded as proven.

Many parts of what is now the Sahara Desert contain an abundance of Acheulian artifacts, especially the southern parts. This seems to be a clear indication that conditions in these areas were not always as harsh as they now are, but it is unlikely that the environment was ever more favourable than that of a semi-arid steppe or dry savanna. It should be remembered that the Achuelian forms of artifacts were made during a time-span of more than a million years, so that the observed distribution pattern may be compounded of sites belonging to a great many oscillations that periodically turned what is now desert into less harsh steppic environments.

Artifact assemblages that are classified as Acheulian also occur in the Mediterranean basin and in Eurasia as far north as a line that runs roughly along the Rhine, the Alps, the Caucasus, the Zagros and the Himalayas. Only rare and rather atypical specimens of hand-axes and cleavers occur beyond this line in continental Eurasia (fig. 3.8).

The sub-Saharan hand-axe distribution merges with that of the Mediterranean, through sites along the Atlantic seaboard of Morocco and Mauritania, and through sites in Ethiopia and along the Nile. Presumably we are justified in regarding the distribution of the habit of making hand-axes as one that was geographically continuous over most of Africa and the adjoining warm, temperate and tropical Eurasia. It is debated whether the continuity of this technological habit was due primarily to idiosyncratic, historic community of tradition, or was due to economic and functional practices conditioned by the features of this major zone.

A question arises as to when the distribution of stone-tool-making became so broad that it spanned Africa and the adjoining parts of Europe and Asia. We will need more reliable dating information from other regions besides East Africa before this question can be settled. Suffice it to say that almost all artifact occurrences in the temperate zone are younger than the last geomagnetic reversal at about 700 000 years ago. That is, they occupy only the second half of the time-span of the East African Acheulian. In western Asia, the site of Ubeidiya, which is in the Jordan Rift, very close to Africa, is the oldest known, and can be dated at between 0.7 and about 1.0 million years BP. Turning to the

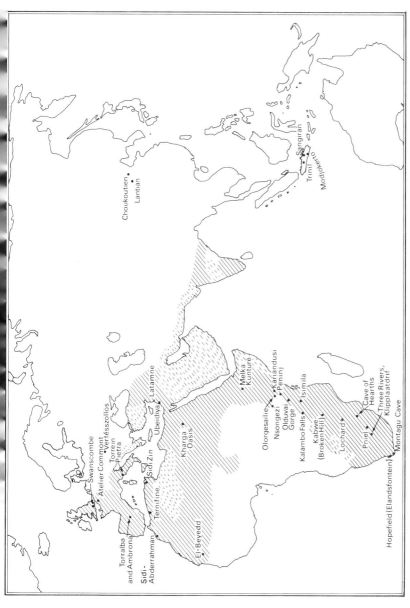

Fig. 3.8  The African Acheulian in relation to the overall distribution of sites of this period (~ 1.5–0.1 million years). The main area in which the Acheulian is found is hatched. Selected important archaeological sites outside Africa are marked. Important sites with human skeletal remains are marked both in Africa and elsewhere.

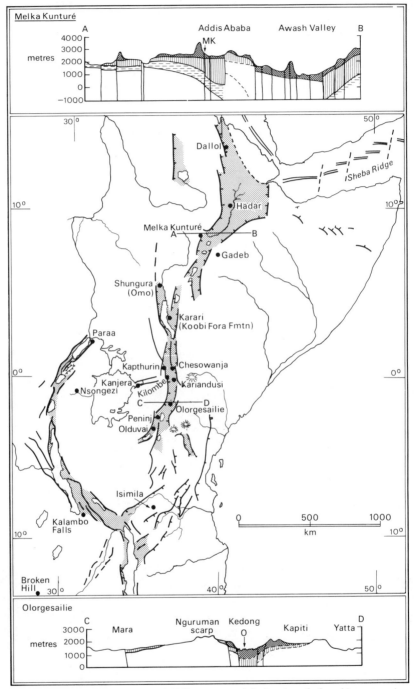

Fig. 3.9  East Africa showing the Rift Valley system and the location of selected important sites. Above and below are cross-sections of the Rift Valley taken at line A–B in Ethiopia and line C–D in Kenya.

Asian tropics, we simply do not know how old the oldest Indian Acheulian material is, but in Indonesia the record of hominid fossils seems to go back to a time between 1 and 2 million years ago, so it may be that the entire archaeological record discussed in this chapter must be seen as that of a segment of a larger web of hominid population that was spread over most of the Old World tropics and the warm temperate zone. Until fairly recently, lions, leopards and cheetahs had distribution patterns of this kind, and in the same way early humans may have been dispersed through a range of habitats that differed in detail but which were not extreme in terms of cold or humidity. Fig. 3.8 provides a graphic summary of information on the relationships between African evidence and evidence from other parts of the world.

The sections which follow provide, for reference purposes, a brief commentary on the Earlier Stone Age evidence from each region of Africa, with particular attention being given to brief description of the most important sites in each region. The subsequent sections of the chapter resume general interpretative discussion.

### EAST AFRICA

This region is traversed by the Rift Valley system which has created particularly favourable conditions for the preservation of traces of early man (fig. 3.9). Furthermore the volcanism associated with the Rift allows fossils and archaeological sites to be dated by the potassium–argon technique. This combination of circumstances gives the eastern sub-continent an Early Stone Age record of unique importance, which begins with sites that are at present the world's oldest known dated archaeological occurrences. Moreover, the practice of careful excavations at well-preserved early sites was initiated in this region through the work of L. S. B. and M. D. Leakey at Olorgesailie in 1943, and it has been continued by the Leakeys, J. D. Clark, Howell, Chavaillon and many others. Thus in eastern Africa, our knowledge of Lower and Middle Pleistocene archaeology can be based to a greater extent on excavation data than is usually the case (table 3.5).

*Olduvai Gorge* in northern Tanzania preserves a record of human evolution that is a standard of reference not only for Africa but for world prehistory. L. S. B. Leakey began working there in the 1930s, and he was soon joined by M. D. Leakey who has been in charge of the archaeological research since the 1960s and who still continues to work there.

TABLE 3.5 *A chronological list of important sites in eastern Africa*

| Geological time period | Time-scale, million years | Substantial excavated assemblages dated by geophysics | Excavated assemblages lacking direct geophysical dating | Sites with known stratigraphy but not yet studied by excavation | Selected important surface sites |
|---|---|---|---|---|---|
| Early Upper Pleistocene | 0.05 | | ?Nsongezi MN (A) | Somali Acheulio-Levallois | |
| | 0.1 | Kalambo Falls (A) | Broken Hill (DO) | | |
| | 0.2 | Dallol (A) | Kapthurin (A) | | Mega |
| | | Isimila Sands 4 (A+DO) | | | |
| | 0.3 | Olorgesailie (A+DO) | | Paraa | Lewa |
| | | | | Kanjera | |
| Middle Pleistocene | 0.4 | Olduvai Masek Beds (A+DO) | Melka Kunturé (middle levels) | | |
| | 0.5 | | | | |
| | 0.6 | | | | |
| Lower Pleistocene | 0.7 | Kilombe (A) | | | |
| | 0.8 | Olduvai Bed IV (A+DO) | | | |
| | 0.9 | Gadeb (A+DO) | Melka Kunturé (lower levels) | | |
| | 1.0 | ?Kariandusi (A) | Kanyatsi (O?) | | |
| | | Olduvai Upper Bed II (A+DO) | | | |
| | 1.2 | Peninj (A) | | Chesowanja, Chemoigut Formation | |
| | | | | Kanam | |
| | 1.4 | | | | |
| | 1.6 | KBS (O) | | | |
| | | Olduvai Bed I (O) | | | |
| | 1.8 | | | | |
| Pliocene | 2.0 | Shungura F | | | |

*Note*: The dating information is relatively precise for sites in the column on the left, while the ages of sites in the other columns may have uncertainties

190

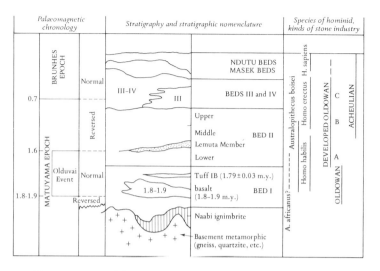

Fig. 3.10   The components of the stratigraphy of Olduvai Gorge, Tanzania. The columns on the left show the palaeomagnetic zones which have been determined and their relationship to the named segments of global reversal chronology, and also to its time-scale. The centre columns show the sequence of layers and their labels. The two best-dated horizons are individually marked. On the right are shown the forms of hominids and the varieties of stone-tool assemblage as identified by M. D. Leakey.

Olduvai Gorge provides the world's longest quasi-continuous cultural sequence: fig. 3.10 provides a simplified diagram of the stratigraphy and dating as it is now understood. Intensive geological research at Olduvai by Hay has produced a well-defined stratigraphy and chronology, and also detailed reconstructions of changing palaeoenvironments. In 1951, L. S. B. Leakey set out a scheme involving the 'Oldowan Culture' and eleven stages of the 'Chelles–Acheul Culture'. Subsequent research by the Leakeys has led them to make extensive revisions to their initial system of classification and nomenclature. Sites from Bed I and the lowermost part of Bed II yield stone tool-kits that generally have choppers, polyhedrons and discoids as their most prominent shaped tools (fig. 3.11). In 1951, the name 'Oldowan' was introduced as a classificatory term for these and it is still retained. A detailed scheme of subdivision and development does not now turn out to be justified. From Middle Bed II times onwards, that is to say from about 1.5 million years ago, the situation became more complex. Artifact assemblages of essentially Oldowan aspect continued to be made though with subtle changes such as an extension of the repertoire

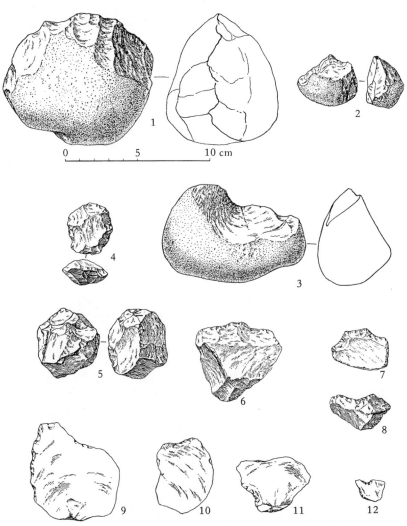

Fig. 3.11   Examples of artifact forms found at one of the Oldowan sites in Bed I, Olduvai Gorge (DK). Specimens 4 and 8–12 are made of quartz, the others are of lava. 1–3, Choppers; 4, discoid; 5, polyhedron; 6–8, scrapers; 9–12, utilized flakes. (After M. D. Leakey 1971.)

to include various additional tool types and, at least initially, a great increase in the number of spheroids (battered round stones). This later series of Oldowan-like assemblages has been grouped by M. D. Leakey under the term 'Developed Oldowan' (fig. 3.12). Some trends can be recognized within the series, notably a rise in the proportional representation of small scrapers and related small tools. Division into

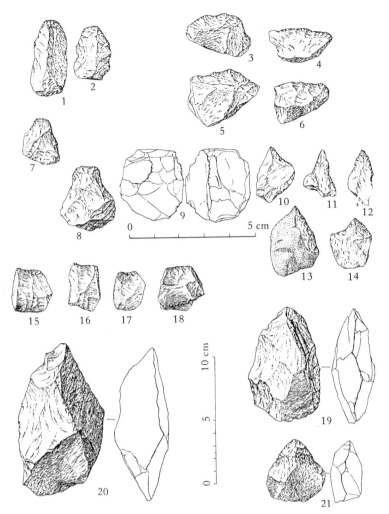

Fig. 3.12   A Developed Oldowan assemblage. Selected artifacts from site BK, Bed II, Olduvai Gorge. All are of quartz and quartzite except 19 and 20 which are of lava. The polyhedron is shown at half the scale used for the other pieces. Spheroids, another form characteristic of Developed Oldowan, are like more battered, rounded polyhedrons. 1–2, End scrapers; 3–6, side scrapers; 7–8, nosed scrapers; 9, polyhedron; 10–14, awls; 15–18, *outils écaillés*; 19, biface; 20, trihedral form on a lava flake; 21, diminutive biface. (After M. D. Leakey 1971.)

phases A, B and C reflects contrasts of this kind within the sequence. The sites belonging to phase A of the Developed Oldowan include one at the place where the chert for making stone tools was obtained (Stiles, Hay and O'Neil 1974).

After about 1.5 million years, the Developed Oldowan stone-tool

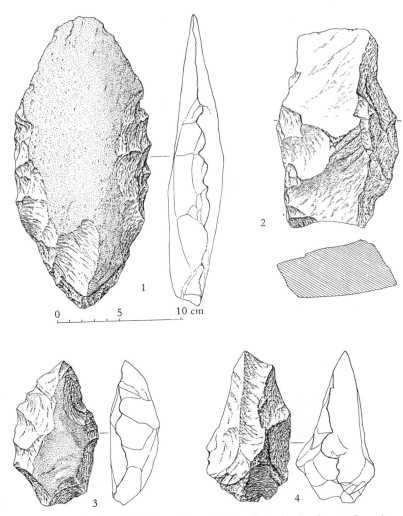

Fig. 3.13 Early Acheulian artifact forms: three specimens of large, lava hand-axes and one cleaver from the site of ER-HR, upper Middle Bed II, Olduvai Gorge. 1, Biface on a flake from a boulder; 2, cleaver on a flake; 3–4, bifaces. (After M. D. Leakey 1971.)

assemblages were not the only variety to be made and discarded at Olduvai. There are others which include a contrasting, prominent series of large, sharp-edged bifacial tools, namely hand-axes and cleavers. These assemblages are classified as 'Acheulian' (fig. 3.13). Recent researches show that they do not display steady, progressive change through time at Olduvai and division into phases or stages is thus not justified. The biface series from each site tends to show its own peculiar technical habit and style, and the degree of refinement of tools fluctuates through time.

Small numbers of bifaces are also found in Developed Oldowan tool-kits, but they are very rare and in general smaller and less effectively made. Opinion is currently divided over the meaning to be attached to the existence of contrasting sets of assemblages (see p. 241).

Hominid fossils occur at all levels in the Olduvai sequence. In Bed I there are at least two contrasting forms that have been generally put into the taxa *Australopithecus (Zinjanthropus) boisei* and *Homo habilis*. Some authorities now argue that the latter material should be split between an advanced form which can be termed *H. habilis* and less advanced or relict forms which are classifiable as *A.* cf. *africanus* (R. E. F. Leakey 1974). The robust, big-toothed form (*A. boisei*) seems to have persisted through Bed II times before it became extinct. Advanced forms of *H. habilis* have been recovered from mid and upper Bed II, but in addition the fossil remains of larger, more muscular forms have also been found and are attributed to African varieties of *Homo erectus*. Of the fragmentary material available from Bed IV, all the identifiable specimens have been tentatively classified as *H. erectus*. An early example of *H. sapiens* is now known from the Ndutu Beds (see chapter 2).

Both *A. (Zinjanthropus) boisei* and *H. habilis* specimens have been recovered in direct association with Oldowan and Developed Oldowan assemblages. At WK, in Bed IV, part of a *H. erectus* pelvis and femur were found with an Acheulian industry. However, for the most part, all that can be said is that the hominid and the archaeological materials are interdigitated with each other and no firm conclusions can yet be reached regarding relationships between specific biological entities and particular cultural manifestations.

In addition to its importance as a key record of changing technological ability and habits, Olduvai provides crucial evidence on broader aspects of the ecology and behaviour of early hominids. These are taken up in the appropriate sections that follow.

For many years the Olduvai Bed I sites were the oldest known archaeological occurrences, but somewhat earlier examples have since been discovered in the *Shungura Formation* of the Lower Omo Valley in southern Ethiopia. Merrick and Chavaillon have excavated several sites in Member F, which are securely dated to 2.0 ± 0.1 million years. The artifacts consist largely of small, sharp flakes and fragments manufactured by the deliberate smashing of quartz pebbles. The series includes numerous very useful-looking sharp edges and points, but it lacks any very clear design principles and does not specifically resemble the Oldowan of Olduvai, although both are fairly simple, generalized applications of an empirical knowledge of stone fracture to the task of getting useful edges and points. None of the Shungura Member F sites that have been so far excavated have been suitable for the study of bone food-refuse. However the sites occupy a variety of situations within the regional palaeo-environmental mosaic and research is in progress on the land-use patterns that they represent.

Most recently, Chavaillon has announced the recovery by excavation of material from Member E. For these finds an age of between 2.0 and 2.2 million years is indicated on a combination of potassium–argon and palaeomagnetic evidence.

Very early archaeological traces of hominid activities have also been found in the *Koobi Fora Formation*, to the east of Lake Rudolf (now Turkana). In 1969 R. E. F. Leakey's expedition discovered artifacts at the site KBS that appeared to be 2.6 ± 0.26 million years old. An extensive excavation programme directed by Isaac has shown that one site, HAS, represents an association of artifacts with a hippopotamus skeleton, and is assumed to represent a butchery episode, though whether the animal was killed by the hominids or merely found dead cannot be ascertained. The other site, KBS, consists of a scatter of discarded artifacts and bone fragments from the carcasses of several animals. Presumably this, like the Olduvai Bed I sites, was the camp-site of hominids who were becoming involved in a distinctively human set of behaviours: tool-making, meat-eating and food-sharing.

The dating of the KBS and HAS sites has been subjected to further study and a series of conventional potassium–argon measurements made by Curtis and co-workers require that the dating be reconsidered. His results imply an age of 1.8 ± 0.01 million years for the sites. Further tests have resolved the controversy in favour of the 1.8 m. yr. date. The stone artifact assemblages from these sites fall within the technological and morphological range of the Oldowan of Bed I at Olduvai, except that small secondarily retouched scrapers have not yet been found among the KBS and HAS samples.

The Upper Member of the Koobi Fora Formation spans a time-range equivalent to that of Middle and Upper Bed II at Olduvai, that is to say 1.6–1.2 million years BP. This has yielded a wealth of distinctive artifact assemblages for which the name Karari Industry has recently been proposed (Harris and Isaac 1976). The assemblages resemble the Developed Oldowan by including numerous choppers, polyhedrons and discoids, but differ in a lack of spheroids and, most important, in the presence of a highly characteristic series of fairly elaborate core-scraper forms. As at Olduvai, bifaces form a component of the total tool-form repertoire though they are rare and have not as yet been recovered from the excavation of an occupation site. Sites of the Karari Industry occur in a variety of contexts within the riverine floodplains and the lake-margin flats that flanked the shores of the proto-Lake Rudolf (now Turkana). Some of the sites preserve small quantities of bone refuse, others do not, presumably largely through failure of preservation mechanisms. Detailed studies by Harris and Isaac are in progress to examine possible relationships between variations in assemblage characteristics and other indicators of activity patterns.

The Koobi Fora Formation has yielded a particularly great wealth of hominid fossils, including numbers of relatively complete specimens and a more than usually extensive representation of postcranial elements. As at Olduvai, at least two and probably three taxa are represented: namely a robust, big-toothed and small-brained *Australopithecus* cf. *boisei*; a small-toothed and small-brained form that may be *A.* cf. *africanus*; and a comparatively large-brained form with a medium-sized dentition. The best-known specimen of this last variety of hominid is the 1470 skull which has been classified as a member of the genus *Homo* without being assigned to a species. These three varieties of hominid coexisted through the time that the KBS and the Karari artifacts were being made, with two of the lineages later becoming extinct, leaving the descendants of 1470 to go on and evolve into mankind. There is no conclusive evidence regarding the relationships between the species and the technical traditions, but we tend to assume that the *Homo* populations at least were tool-makers.

On the north-west flanks of the *Lake Natron basin*, the Peninj Group of formations has yielded assemblages of artifacts that underlie a lava flow dated at 1.3 million years and overlie a flow dated to sometime in the Olduvai event, i.e. 1.8–1.6 million years BP. A well-preserved mandible of *A.* cf. *boisei* comes from a horizon just below this. The assemblages, excavated by Isaac, have as their most conspicuous elements hand-axes and cleavers, made on large flakes by a minimum of secondary trimming. They clearly resemble the Olduvai Bed II material from the site EF–HR and are definitely to be classified as early Acheulian.

These four localities – Shungura, Koobi Fora, Peninj and Olduvai – are the only ones yet studied in detail that are certainly of Lower

Pleistocene age, that is to say older than 700 000 years when the last geomagnetic reversal took place. There are other sites which very probably belong with this set, such as Kanam, near Lake Victoria (Nyanza) and Kanyatsi in the Western Rift Valley, but up-to-date detailed information is not available on these. The site complex east of Lake Baringo at Chesowanja is also probably of Lower Pleistocene or late Pliocene age and seems to contain an abundance of artifacts comparable to the Oldowan or Developed Oldowan. Preliminary reports on palaeomagnetic determinations for Kariandusi and the newly discovered site at Kilombe suggest that both these two Acheulian sites in the high central sector of the Kenya Rift may be older than 700 000 years. The bifaces from these two sites are well made and would previously have been classified as Middle and Upper Acheulian. If their early date is confirmed then this is evidence of yet another breakdown in the notion that early Pleistocene prehistory was characterized by an orderly sequence of progressive changes.

Having detected this early distinct set of Oldowan, Developed Oldowan and early Acheulian sites, we are left with a residue of occurrences which derive from a period between about 700 000 years and about 100 000 years BP. This vast span of time is one for which our ability to make reliable chronological distinctions and to discern historical patterns is at a minimum. Several important groups of sites come from this interval and continuing research is constantly adding to the stock. For the time being it is wisest to treat the evidences that we have as belonging to a single set that one can designate as Middle Pleistocene and as 'Acheulian' *sensu lato*.

The first Middle Pleistocene site complex to be investigated by modern methods was that of *Olorgesailie*. This is a small sedimentary basin in the floor of the Gregory Rift Valley, about 65 km from Nairobi (fig. 3.14). Studies were begun by M. D. and L. S. B. Leakey and subsequently extended by Isaac and others. The results show that prehistoric populations made continual use of the area during the time that it took for some 60 to 70 m of fine-grained sediments to accumulate, perhaps in the order of 100 000 years. Potassium–argon dates indicate an age of about 0.5 million years for the sediments. Some sixteen significant artifact assemblages have been recovered and these show great variation both if the percentage composition of their shaped tools is compared and if the morphological norms of specimens of the same category in different sites are compared. Most of the differences are not patterned in a way that shows clear sequential change through time, so

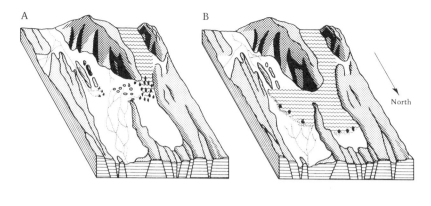

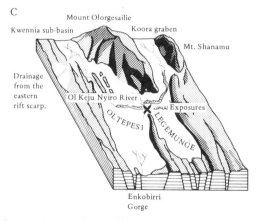

Fig. 3.14 Block diagram showing the palaeogeographic context of the Olorgesailie Acheulian sites and showing how conditions changed over time. At Olorgesailie a lake basin formed on the floor of the Rift due to faulting and earth movement. The size of the area covered by lake waters varied. At times of lower water Stone Age camps were established on the flood plains around the lake (A); at other times these areas would be inundated and covered with silt (B). Further earth movements have tilted the whole basin to the south causing the Olkeju Nyiro River to flow on southward and to erode the deposits which had previously formed (C).

that in dealing with them culture–historic and evolutionary lines of explanation, which had been conventional, broke down. The Olorgesailie data helped to focus the attention of prehistorians on the problem of whether diversity implies a multiplicity of cultural systems or whether a single cultural system can generate diversity through activity differentiation or other causes. In addition, the Olorgesailie sites provide valuable information on food-refuse and land-use patterns (see p. 229).

At *Isimila*, in central Tanzania, a local sediment trap was formed through an impediment in the drainage of a small tributary valley. The strata that accumulated and which are now being eroded contain vast accumulations of artifacts. It was formerly customary to date these to the very end of the Middle Pleistocene, that is to say to a period around about 100 000 BP. However, a thorium–uranium determination has raised the possibility that the site complex may cover a time-span extending back to about 260 000 years ago (Howell *et al.* 1972). Geochemical determinations of this kind cannot be treated as reliable dates, but this measurement does at least encourage a realization that we do *not* know how old Isimila is, and that it may be as old as the value indicated.

A team comprising Howell, Kleindienst and Cole worked at Isimila in 1957 and 1958; work was resumed by Keller and Hansen in 1970. As at Olorgesailie, an unexpected variety of assemblages was recovered with important differences even between occurrences at the same horizon. Comparative study of the Olorgesailie and Isimila materials led Kleindienst in 1961 to offer the first comprehensive typological classification and to formulate the first clear overall statement of the problems of explaining variation amongst these early samples of material culture. Bone is not preserved at Isimila except in the poorly-exposed lowermost levels.

In 1963 at *Melka Kunturé* in Ethiopia, Dekker discovered a site complex spanning a considerable segment of Middle and Late Pleistocene time. An extensive programme of research and excavation has been directed by Chavaillon since 1965 and is still continuing. Melka Kunturé (formerly spelled Kontoure) is some 50 km south of Addis Ababa on the western shoulder of the Rift Valley. Earth movements have formed a barrier across the headwaters of the Awash River so that fluviatile and swamp sediments have intermittently accumulated in the valley. Where these layered deposits are eroding they have been found to contain a wealth of archaeological sites. The lowest levels have yielded assemblages that Chavaillon compares with the Oldowan and Developed Oldowan, and to which an age of over 700 000 years can be assigned on the basis of palaeomagnetic evidence. The middle levels of the sequence contain an abundance of Acheulian material. As in the other site complexes mentioned, there are great differences between each individual occurrence. The uppermost beds which are attributed to the Upper Pleistocene and Holocene contain at their base material which combined normal Acheulian cleavers and diminutive bifaces with elements that might be considered as characteristic of the Middle Stone

TABLE 3.6    *The sequence of industries at Kalambo Falls*

| Stage–age classification | Industrial complex | Industry | Dates BP |
|---|---|---|---|
| Iron Age | — | Kalambo Falls Industry | 930–1905 |
| Later Stone Age | — | Kaposwa Industry[a] | 3900 |
| Second Intermediate | — | Polungu Industry[b] | 9500 |
| Middle Stone Age | Lupemban | Siszya Industry | 27000–30500 |
|  |  | Nakisasa Industry | 31700 |
| First Intermediate | Sangoan | Chipeta Industry | 38000–46000 |
| Earlier Stone Age | Acheulian | Bwalya Industry | 60000 (> 110000 on the basis of racemization measurements) |

[a] This was formerly designated 'Wilton'.
[b] This was formerly designated 'Magosian'.

Age, namely *racloirs* and other flake tools often made by means of the Levallois method. Overlying this are occurrences of Middle Stone Age and Late Stone Age industries with bifacial, 'Stillbay', projectile points and backed microliths respectively.

The importance of Melka Kunturé is enhanced by the fact that this is one of the few African Acheulian sites for which information on associated vegetation has been obtained by means of pollen analysis. There is evidence in all the pollen spectra for the prevalence of grasslands around all the archaeological sites, but there are also significant stands of riverine forest nearby in some instances, and in others a greater incidence of mountain forest and alpine vegetation than is the case today. Details of relationships between the archaeological record and the pollen record have not yet been worked out.

Other studies are being initiated in Ethiopia and valuable new information is currently becoming available (Wendorf and Schild 1974). J. D. Clark has discovered a sedimentary basin at Gadeb on the eastern side of the Rift Valley (J. D. Clark and Kurashina 1976). This contains both classic biface-dominated Acheulian material and assemblages that are effectively devoid of bifaces (cf. Developed Oldowan). The Afar Depression has also yielded one of the few Middle Pleistocene artifacts from Africa to be geophysically dated: a hand-axe associated with a strandline dated at 180000–200000 years BP by the thorium–uranium technique (Roubet 1969).

One of the most important Early Stone Age sites yet discovered in

Africa is that at *Kalambo Falls* in north-eastern Zambia. Here in 1954 J. D. Clark found deposits which contain an abundance of Acheulian artifacts at their base, while successively younger layers contain Sangoan, Lupemban, Later Stone Age and early Iron Age assemblages. Each distinctive stratified set of material culture has been given a formal name as a prehistoric industry. The scheme of nomenclature proposed by J. D. Clark and Kleindienst is shown in table 3.6; this also serves to illustrate the recent trend for scholars to establish more exactly-defined nomenclature using local names to designate each distinctive group of assemblages as an industry. The column on the left contains the stage or age classification, while the adjacent column contains those broad palaeocultural classificatory names that are being retained as labels for industrial-complex divisions. All dates over 30 000 BP should be treated as minimum ages rather than definite dates.

The particular importance of the Kalambo Falls site complex for our understanding of the Lower Palaeolithic is two-fold: firstly, the sequence spans the changeover from patterns of stone-craft that are purely Acheulian to subsequent ones which are non-Acheulian. It therefore has high potential for advancing our understanding of the nature and implications of this transformation in material culture. Secondly, the lower levels were waterlogged and have yielded the best preserved series of wood specimens and plant remains that have yet been found associated with the Acheulian in Africa. Indeed such material is so rare anywhere in the world that the site has global importance. Pollen is also preserved. The wood specimens consist mainly of logs and branches that had been washed in by the river, but some specimens appear to have been shaped into clubs and digging implements. Some of the logs are charred and one patch of ash and fire-reddened ground has been identified. A rough arc of stone may mark the footing of a simple branch shelter. Edible fruits represented include *Syzygium*, *Xylopia*, *Diospyros*, *Parinari* and *Borassus*. No doubt these were eaten, although the evidence is only circumstantial.

The Acheulian levels at the base of the sequence have yielded assemblages that include both large cutting tools (hand-axes, cleavers and knives), heavy-duty tools (picks, choppers and core-scrapers) and various small tools such as scrapers and awls. In composition the assemblages overlap extensively with those from Isimila, and to a lesser extent with Olorgesailie. However, both the large tools and the small tools at Kalambo Falls look better made and more refined (cf. fig. 3.15). The customary assumption that such greater refinement was necessarily connected with a younger age is not now a foregone conclusion.

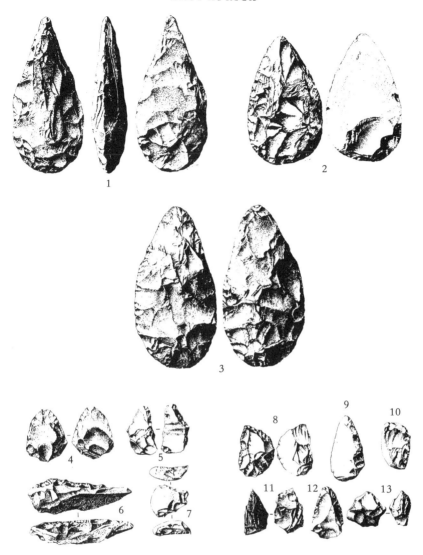

Fig. 3.15    Later Acheulian artifacts from the various levels at the site of Sidi Zin, Tunisia.

*Bifaces*

1  Hand-axe with bifacial trimming
2  Hand-axe made on a large flake and
   with one face only partly trimmed
3  Bifacial hand-axe

*Small tools*

4  Small tool with bifacial trimming
5  Double alternate side-scraper
6  Double side-scraper

7  Denticulate nosed scraper on a pebble
8  Irregular partly bifacial scraper
9–10  Side-scrapers
11  Irregular thick scraper
12  Nosed scraper
13  Micro-chopper

(After Gobert 1950.)

203

It was previously suggested that the Acheulian levels proper at Kalambo Falls were separated from the Sangoan levels by a series of three transitional horizons (J. D. Clark 1964). Now that the extent of variation amongst Acheulian occurrences is better understood it is generally agreed that all of these levels must be treated simply as Upper Acheulian (J. D. Clark 1974a, Sampson 1974). Nonetheless, it may be significant that artifacts that seem to be prototypic to the Sangoan–Lupemban core-axes do seem to occur in small numbers in these uppermost Acheulian layers.

The Acheulian-bearing deposits at Kalambo Falls are truncated by a disconformity above which is material that appears to have been carried in by slope processes and then covered with sediments. This is the material of Sangoan aspect. Although it differs from the underlying Acheulian in having a much higher proportion of small scrapers, it must be pointed out that the observed proportion of small tools in the Kalambo Falls Sangoan does not fall outside the range of values known to occur in such Middle Pleistocene site complexes as Olorgesailie, Isimila and Olduvai Bed IV. Of greater significance is the increase in the number and degree of distinctness of the core-axes, which now reach some 9% of the shaped tools. This trend is further developed in the assemblages that comprise the local Siszya Industry within the Lupemban Industrial Complex (see chapter 4).

There is a series of radiocarbon dates for the Kalambo Falls archaeological horizons. If these are taken at their face value then the transition from Acheulian to Sangoan at this locality can be said to have occurred between 60 000 and 45 000 years ago. However, $^{14}$C samples from the range are all but devoid of radioactivity and it is probably safer to regard all these determinations as minimum ages. In other words, the transition was not younger than about 50 000 years BP, but may have taken place appreciably earlier. Preliminary reports of amino-acid racemization determinations on the fossil wood suggest ages that are two or three times greater than the $^{14}$C minimum age (Lee, Bada and Patterson 1976).

In Angola (see p. 215) it has been shown that the assemblages of Sangoan aspect are contemporary with typical Lupemban artifacts. This possibility cannot be ruled out for north-east Zambia.

The most important site complex in the western part of East Africa is that at *Nsongezi* in the Kagera Valley, Uganda. This has been the subject of a succession of investigations that began with the pioneer Wayland, who invited van Riet Lowe to carry out archaeological

researches there. Subsequent work has been done by O'Brien, Posnansky, Bishop and finally by Cole (see bibliographical essay, p. 946).

The Nsongezi sector of the Kagera Valley lies some 100 km to the
west of the present shores of Lake Victoria, but there is clear geological
evidence that the lake basin as we now know it was only formed during
Pleistocene times. It occupies a down-warped depression in the earth's
crust between the two uplifted zones that are associated with the eastern
and western Rift Valleys. The direction of drainage in the Kagera and
many other valleys has been reversed from a westward flow to an
eastward flow. Sedimentation in the valley thus has been controlled by
complex interaction between local tectonics and the level of water in
the Victoria basin. Earlier workers were not fully aware of the
complexity of the system and their interpretations both of the basic
stratigraphy and their climatic inferences have been superseded.

Excavations by Cole demonstrated the existence of an Acheulian
assemblage from the M–N Horizon Rubble Tongue, and of a Sangoan
assemblage from the Upper Rubble horizon which disconformably
overlies the former. The succession can also be traced in the Orichinga
tributary valley where still younger deposits contain assemblages that
resemble in some respects the Lupemban and Tshitolian of the Congo
basin (see p. 215). Nsongezi thus constitutes one of the stratified
sequences in which Acheulian and post-Acheulian assemblages can be
seen together in stratigraphic succession. Unfortunately, in spite of the
wealth of technical artifact data and of geological data amassed by Cole,
the site cannot be dated with any certainty, and it has also yielded only
a minimum of palaeo-ecological evidence. Near Nsongezi, along the
shores of Lake Victoria, in Sango Bay, selected surface collections from
hilltops in the general vicinity produced the aggregate of heavy picks,
core-scrapers and other distinctive heavy-duty tools that led Wayland
to suggest that there had formerly existed a Sangoan 'culture'. It is not
presently clear whether these items represent a cultural episode of
limited duration or whether they represent a facies of material culture
that was intermittently part of the repertoire of Stone Age men during
both Acheulian and post-Acheulian times.

The preceding summary demonstrates that East Africa has yielded
a comparatively large stock of excavated archaeological samples from
the time-range between 1.0 million and 100000 years BP and it has
been shown that we cannot at present recognize significant culture-
historical or culture-geographic patterns amongst these. The series of
assemblages seem for the most part to show extensive permutation

amongst a limited set of fairly simple technological and typological components. Put figuratively, it can be said that the ingredients of the material-culture recipe remained very much the same while the proportion of admixture varied extensively and erratically. The section on material culture provides additional information on the technical elements and some possible lines of interpretation are discussed under the heading of 'Variation' (pp. 241–5).

There is one newly discovered site complex that has been shown to include significant technical elements that are otherwise unknown in eastern Africa. This lies to the west of Lake Baringo, in the Kapthurin Formation. It was explored and studied by Margaret and R. E. F. Leakey and its contents show that some assemblages that are classified within the Acheulian of eastern Africa, included large-scale applications of the Levallois method, such as are already known in the Acheulian of southern Africa (see p. 239) and also the manufacture of refined blades. A mandible has been found in the same beds and is said to show features reminiscent of *Homo erectus*.

SOUTHERN AFRICA

The southern sub-continent can be taken as the area limited to the north-west by the Zambezi–Congo watershed and to the north-east by the intersection of the Rift Valley system with the lower Zambezi. It is a vast region that projects southward from fully tropical latitudes to a termination in the temperate zone of the southern oceans. Most of the land surface is made up of huge plateaux with comparatively slight relief. In the north these are extensively wooded while further south they tend to be grasslands, as in the Transvaal high veld, or to be dry scrub-covered plains, as in the great Karroo. The plateaux are interrupted by the broad valleys of the Zambezi and Limpopo, which carry bushveld and riverine forests. The valley of the Vaal–Orange drainage system also traverses most of the width of the sub-continent, but does not act as a major interruption in the regional vegetation pattern.

Round the southern and eastern margin runs a rim of highlands, sometimes in the form of folded mountains, sometimes as a cuesta with an east-facing escarpment. Between the highlands and the Indian Ocean is a coastal plain of variable width. Characteristically this carries denser vegetation than that of the plateau at the corresponding latitude.

This sub-continent, like East Africa, contains a complex mosaic of environments that include a full range from arid lands such as the Namib, the Kalahari and the Karroo, to tracts of moist lowland forest in the lower Zambezi and Limpopo valleys and on parts of the eastern coastal plain. The mosaic is less fragmented than that of East Africa, and large tracts show considerable homogeneity. Clearly the region as a whole offered a wide range of opportunities to early hominids and the hundreds of early sites discovered show that the sub-continent has been widely, and presumably continuously, occupied for the past 2 or 3 million years. The environmental diversity would certainly have buffered the hominid population as a whole against any too drastic effects of climatic fluctuation.

For the earliest part of its prehistory Southern Africa shares with East Africa the distinctive importance of furnishing both an osteological and an artifact record of hominid ways of life. The combined record comes from a series of ancient caves and fissures formed in the dolomitic limestone area of the Transvaal and northern Cape Province. The only drawback is that the southern African sites cannot yet be securely dated by geophysical chronometric techniques.

Five of the Transvaal cave sites have yielded significant fossil remains of early hominids: one set, Taung, Makapansgat Limeworks and Sterkfontein Type Site, has yielded material attributed to the comparatively gracile species *Australopithecus africanus*. The second set, Kromdraai Site B and Swartkrans (Phase A) has yielded the robust hominid *Australopithecus (Paranthropus) crassidens* and *A. robustus*. However, Swartkrans has also produced traces of a second, more advanced hominid that is assigned to the genus *Homo*. Stone artifacts have not been recovered in definite association with *A. africanus* fossils, although claims have been made that they occur in the upper strata at Makapan.

The Swartkrans Phase B breccia contained artifacts which have been classified by M. D. Leakey as Developed Oldowan. Recent researches by Brain have shown that deposits of three distinct ages are present at Swartkrans as a complex interpenetrating series of breccias and solution cavity infillings. Most, but perhaps not all, artifacts come from Phases B and C. At Sterkfontein, in addition to Member 3 (Type Site) with its *A. africanus* fossils, a second, younger set of deposits termed Member 5 have been excavated at the 'Extension Site'. Until recently the latter had yielded only fragmentary and more or less unidentifiable hominid remains, but in 1976 a relatively complete cranium was found which is assigned to the genus *Homo*. The site also contains a good sample of a stone industry. The material, which includes rough biface forms, some of which are on large flakes, has been classified by M. D. Leakey as Developed Oldowan, and as Acheulian by Mason. Associated with the stone implements in this instance is an assemblage of broken-up antelope bones, which are apparently food-refuse. Because the proportion of juveniles represented is exceptionally low, Vrba (1975) has suggested that the tool-makers may have been scavengers rather than hunters.

On the basis of palaeontologial evidence Vrba has recently suggested that the Swartkrans A archaeological occurrence is older than that of Sterkfontein Extension. She suggests a date of 1.0–1.5 million years for Swartkrans and 0.5–1.0 million for Sterkfontein. These are only tentative chronological guesses but it is clear that these two artifact occurrences are amongst the oldest known in southern Africa.

Dart has made important claims that the Makapansgat deposits provide evidence of the behaviour patterns of hominids before the invention of flaked stone implements. Specifically he suggested that *A. africanus* selected and used particular parts of mammal skeletons as tools: for instance humeri as clubs, ulnae as daggers and antelope tooth-rows as scrapers. He referred to the practice of using bone, teeth and horns for tools as the 'Osteodontokeratic culture'. The impressive volume of bone associated with the *A. africanus* fossils at Makapansgat led Dart to argue that it resulted from the intensive activity of the australopithecines as predators. These views of Dart's, which have been amplified and disseminated in Ardrey's (1961) book *African genesis*, have aroused much interest and controversy. The debate has at least shown very clearly that what we believe about the nature of our early ancestors affects what we choose to believe about human nature today.

At the time of Dart's original researches on the Makapansgat evidence it seemed reasonable to suppose that bone assemblages would be unbiased samples of all the elements of the skeletons that had contributed to them. The study of many diverse bone assemblages from different parts of the world now shows that this is not so, and that most natural bone accumulations are biased in the sort of way that led Dart to assert that there had been selection for tool usage. At Swartkrans, Brain has shown that the remains of the robust australopithecine *A. robustus* probably accumulated at the bottom of a sinkhole shaft because leopards had hunted these hominids and hung their corpses in trees that sprouted out of the cavern system. Additionally, Vrba has suggested that the faunal assemblage with *A. africanus* at Sterkfontein Type Site has characteristics suggesting that the cave was the lair of large felines, perhaps sabre-tooth cats, which hunted australopithecines amongst other creatures. It thus becomes clear that in the absence of more specific evidence from Makapansgat, we cannot assume that *A. africanus* was the principal predator responsible for killing and accumulating large quantities of bone.

The broad trends of hominid evolution make it seem likely that upright bipeds such as the australopithecines would have been tool-users to a greater extent than chimpanzees and that very probably they would have been more carnivorous than other living primates. Specific evidence, however, is still lacking for either aspect of the behaviour of these extinct forms.

In addition to the cave and fissure sites that date from the Lower Pleistocene and perhaps the later Pliocene, traces of Acheulian and other Earlier Stone Age remains have been found at literally hundreds of localities scattered over most parts of the sub-continent (fig. 3.6). Of course, many of these are records only of surface finds for which information on dating and context is lacking. Equally, in most instances, comprehensive collections have not been made and full technical characteristics of the assemblages cannot be determined. Table 3.7 provides a list of some of the most important sites, differentiating between those where samples have been recovered by excavation and those for which the geological context has been well determined but where the samples were obtained largely by means other than formal excavation. In addition the names of a few surface and superficial sites are included on the grounds of their historical importance for the development of interpretation and terminology.

The chart is segmented chronologically in as far as it is possible. However, even less precision is attainable than in the case of East Africa. As can be seen, by far the largest group of sites must be assigned simply to the Middle Pleistocene. Another set can be tentatively put into the early part of the Upper Pleistocene, which is roughly the time-span from about 120 000 to 60 000 or 70 000 years BP. For the Cave of Hearths, Montagu Cave and Wonderwerk, the age estimate is based on the fact that in each case the Acheulian cultural levels immediately underlie Middle Stone Age levels. Radiocarbon dates are available from a number of the sites: for example, Montagu Cave, Cave of Hearths, Amanzi, Broken Hill (Kabwe), Hopefield; but it is becoming increasingly clear that, as in the case of Kalambo Falls, the age determinations cannot be taken at face value. It seems probable that all the Acheulian occurrences in question are outside the time-range of $^{14}$C dating, and

TABLE 3.7  *A chronological list of important sites in southern Africa*

| Age/geological period | Major excavated occurrences | Stratified but not excavated | Historically important surface sites |
|---|---|---|---|
| ∼ 60 000<br><br>Early Upper Pleistocene and Late Middle Pleistocene? | Montagu Cave<br>Wonderwerk Cave<br>Cave of Hearths<br>Rooidam (0.11 million years?)<br>Doornlaagte<br>Munro Site<br>Mairton<br>Amanzi | Hangklip? | Lochard<br>Fauresmith |
| ∼ 125 000<br>Middle Pleistocene | Cornelia<br>Swartkrans B<br>Elandsfontein | Vaal River Younger Gravels<br>Zambezi Older Gravels | Victoria West<br>Stellenbosch |
| ∼ 700 000<br><br>Lower Pleistocene | Klipplaatdrif<br>Three Rivers<br>Suurkree<br>Sterkfontein Member 5<br>Swartkrans Member 1 | | |
| ∼ 1.8 million<br><br>Pliocene | [fossils but no artifacts:]<br>Sterkfontein Member 4<br>Taung?<br>Makapansgat | | |

*Note:* It is now known that the $^{14}$C ages for Kalambo Falls and Amanzi should be disregarded and the only chronometric determination is that for Rooidam (see text). Sites are grouped into sets which are tentatively assigned to geological time divisions on the basis of fauna when present, or a general geological reckoning. No great precision or certainty attaches to any of these assignments.

that the apparent ages obtained may be due to small amounts of organic contaminants. Only for the site of Rooidam in the Vaal Valley has an alternative geochemical dating method been successfully applied. Thorium–uranium results from Rooidam suggest an age of between 110 000 and 170 000 years for the calcium carbonate associated with the assemblage (Butzer 1974a). This is a very plausible result, but the reservations of many scientists about the method nonetheless requires that it be treated with caution.

At the outset, archaeological investigations of the Pleistocene in southern Africa followed the standard European pattern with the greatest amount of research effort being devoted to the recovery of materials from river gravels or from raised marine beaches. The classic studies were those of van Riet Lowe in the valley of the Vaal River, and of J. D. Clark in the Victoria Falls area of the Zambezi valley. These studies served to document the existence in Africa of a prehistoric and Quaternary-geological record fully as extensive as that of Europe. They also led to the formulation of palaeolithic prehistory in terms of orderly stages of development in stone technology. As we have seen, the results of subsequent work at sites such as Isimila, Olorgesailie, Olduvai and Kalambo Falls have cast doubt on the historical validity of stages such as are implied by the numbered subdivisions of the Acheulian set up to classify river-gravel materials.

Just as earlier models of Palaeolithic prehistory presupposed that there had been a readily discernible succession of technological stages within such major entities as the Acheulian, so it tended to be assumed that the Earlier Stone Age and the Middle Stone Age would have been linked by transitional technical traditions that combined the elements of both major epochs. In southern Africa two categories of intermediate industry came to be recognized: the Fauresmith and the Sangoan. The former had its type area in the open country of the central plateau of South Africa, especially the western Orange Free State; while the latter was believed to be centred in the Congo basin with extensions into the more heavily vegetated sectors of southern Africa, such as the Zambezi valley, parts of Zimbabwe and perhaps also parts of the Transvaal and Natal.

Mason was the first to point out that there was no secure basis for subdividing the hand-axe industries into Chellean, Acheulian and Fauresmith stages. Subsequently, Humphreys has shown that the Fauresmith occurrences of the type area are contemporary with non-Fauresmith Acheulian assemblages in adjoining or even overlapping areas. The peculiarities of the type-Fauresmith can be shown to be specifically associated with the use of lydianite (indurated shale) as a raw material for the artifacts. The term Fauresmith can still be used to cover the distinctive industries of the type area, but it is clearly no longer appropriate as a general label for relatively late hand-axe-containing industries. Equally it is true to say that virtually no examples have been found of assemblages that are transitional between the Acheulian and the Middle Stone Age, so that the term cannot be used in that sense either. In considering Nsongezi and the East African evidence we have already seen that there are legitimate grounds for similar doubts with regard to the meaning of the term Sangoan (see also p. 205). There is some evidence that towards the end of the vast period during which hand-axes were made, they became smaller in size. Although this can be seen in a few stratified sequences and regional successions, there is no guarantee that it was in fact a universal trend.

There are no absolutely certain known examples of Oldowan industries in southern Africa in the sense of assemblages of core tools and flakes that can be shown geochronologically to antedate the practice of making Acheulian artifact forms such as hand-axes. Mason (1962a) has tentatively identified the possible existence of one such occurrence at Suurkree in deposits of the 200-ft (65-m) terrace of the Vaal (Butzer *et al.* 1973). The Swartkrans and Sterkfontein Extension Site assemblages, as currently known, contain hand-axes, but now that it has been discovered that the Swartkrans site contains interpenetrating deposits of very different age, it may well prove that the Developed Oldowan assemblage described by M. D. Leakey is a mixed one and that a non-biface Oldowan-like assemblage does exist in the Phase A breccias.

Two sites which were investigated by Mason appear on stratigraphic and typological grounds to belong to an early stage of the Acheulian.[1] These are Three Rivers and Klipplaatdrif, in the Vaal valley. The majority of other sites simply have to be treated as an undifferentiated set which are more constructively studied for the information that they give on socio-economic systems than for conventional culture–historic purposes.

Several cave sites in Southern Africa have yielded Acheulian assemblages stratified beneath Middle and Later Stone Age layers. Most important amongst these are the Cave of Hearths in the Makapan valley of the Transvaal and Montagu Cave in the mountains near Cape Town.

Amongst the well studied and reported southern African sites, Sterkfontein, Cave of Hearths, Hopefield, Cornelia and Munro have yielded particularly useful associations of Acheulian artifacts and bone food-refuse. Amanzi has also preserved plant remains, but these were not specifically modified or concentrated by the Stone Age occupants.

There has been less opportunity in southern Africa than in East Africa for systematic investigation of the nature and meaning of variability among Middle Pleistocene occurrences. However, sufficient unselected

---

[1] The Acheulian Industrial Complex was formerly known as the 'Stellenbosch Culture' in South Africa.

excavated samples are beginning to be available to make such studies possible. Of particular interest in this connection are the several stratified sequences of Acheulian levels such as those of Montagu Cave and the Cave of Hearths. These should permit a study of short-term variation through time.

Broken Hill (Kabwe) in Zambia has provided two important sets of evidences. First, during mining operations in 1923 there was discovered an underground cave system that contained fossils and artifacts. The fossils included the remains of at least two human skeletons, including an almost complete cranium (see chapter 2). The artifacts consisted of various flakes and flake tools, bolas stones, etc. Since the assemblage lacked such characteristic Acheulian artifact forms as hand-axes and cleavers, and since it also lacked the specific tool forms and techniques characteristic of the full Middle Stone Age, it was classified as a proto-Stillbay assemblage. The whole series of finds was assigned to an Upper Pleistocene age. Klein (1973) has re-examined the faunal evidence and points out that it is more like a Middle Pleistocene fauna. Now that we know that assemblages of flake tools without bifaces are often found interdigitated with Acheulian occurrences it seems better to regard the Kabwe artifacts and the Rhodesian Man skeletal remains as belonging to the complex of Middle Pleistocene evidence.

The second contribution of Kabwe is an occurrence outside the cave which was excavated by J. D. Clark (1959b) and which yielded a presumably Middle Pleistocene tool assemblage dominated by small scrapers and other small tools.

In addition to Kabwe, hominid fossils of known or probable Acheulian age have been recovered from the Cave of Hearths and from Saldanha (Hopefield, Elandsfontein). At Wonderboompoort, a spectacular accumulation of Acheulian material has been found in association with what appears to have been a natural game-trap – a narrow defile connecting two valleys which are separated by a very steep rocky ridge.

## THE CONGO BASIN AND ADJOINING AREAS

This region has yielded an abundance of relatively heavy, boldly flaked stone artifacts such as choppers, picks, rough hand-axes, etc. (table 3.8). The majority of these specimens probably date from the Upper Pleistocene and form parts of assemblages that can be classified as Sangoan–Lupemban. Very few sites have yet furnished the kind of

TABLE 3.8    *Chronological list of sites in the Congo basin and immediately adjoining areas*

|  | Excavated assemblages | Collections of known stratigraphic provenance |
|---|---|---|
| Sites possibly of early Upper Pleistocene or late Middle Pleistocene age | Katentania Pupa River Kamoa | ? Chiumbe River Gravels Luembe River Gravels (Mufo, Cauma, Chingufo mines) |
| Sites of unknown age – presumably in part Middle Pleistocene | | Baia Farta (Acheulian) Luembe and other 10 m terrace artifacts from Angola |
| Sites of possibly Lower Pleistocene age | | ? Palmeirinhas (Developed Oldowan?) ? Calumbo (Developed Oldowan?) Kanyatsi (L. Albert basin) (Oldowan?) |

*Note:* All these sites probably lie beyond the range of ${}^{14}$C dating. In the absence of either fauna or other radiometric dates no precision or certainty is possible.

geological evidence that is required before they can meaningfully be classified as Oldowan or early Acheulian. Over most of the area the earliest confirmed archaeological traces seem to belong in the Sangoan–Lupemban Industrial Complex.

Pioneer and reconnaissance work in Zaïre and Angola was done by Bequaert, Mortelmans, Breuil, Janmart, van Moorsel, L. S. B. Leakey and others. The most complete studies of regional stratigraphy and archaeology are those of J. D. Clark in the Lunda area of north-east Angola, and the work of Anciaux de Faveaux in the Katanga, followed by Cahen and by Schokkenbroek. Other detailed studies in the Plain of *Kinshasa* have been achieved by Colette, Van Moorsel, and De Ploey, but most of the material recovered belongs to the Sangoan–Lupemban (see chapter 4).

Exploratory work has been undertaken in recent years north of the Congo River in Gabon and the Central African Republic by Blankoff and by de Bayle des Hermens. Most of the limited number of sites so far discovered are probably Sangoan–Lupemban or later, but there does seem on typological grounds to be some Acheulian material. The records of pebble-culture localities require dating evidence before their significance can be accepted.

In Angola, J. D. Clark has investigated sites, especially that of

*Palmeirinhas*, where simple artifacts without Acheulian elements are associated with beach deposits 100 m above sea level. These may well be samples of Oldowan or Developed Oldowan industries.

Excellent stratigraphy has been exposed as a result of diamond mining in the Lunda region of north-east Angola. The 10-m gravels have yielded rolled specimens that on typological grounds could be Oldowan and early Acheulian. It seems safe to guess that they are of at least late Middle Pleistocene age, more than 100 000 years old, but beyond this their dating is a matter of conjecture. Scattered specimens of apparently later Acheulian aspect have been recovered from the 3–4-m terrace at various mines and from the land surface underneath the redistributed Kalahari Sands II (see chapter 4). These sands contain relatively abundant material of Sangoan aspect, together with scarcer specimens of refined Lupemban lanceolates. This makes it clear that the end of the Acheulian did not amount to a degeneration in stone-craft as has often been supposed. Demonstration of the interrelationship between heavy-duty tools and refined delicate forms has led J. D. Clark to introduce the compound term Sangoan–Lupemban for the industries succeeding the Acheulian (see chapter 4).

J. D. Clark has also investigated an Acheulian site on the + 100-m beach conglomerates at Baia Farta near the coast, and scattered localities with Acheulian bifaces and cleavers have been discovered in various parts of south-west Angola and in the Kasai. The central part of the basin and the lower Congo seem only to have yielded very few rather doubtful Acheulian specimens.

The Western Rift Valley forms a watershed between the Congo basin and East Africa, and its archaeology could equally well be discussed in connection with either region. However, it seems to contrast with the rest of East Africa and with the Gregory Rift in the paucity of occurrences of early artifact assemblages. The fossiliferous Kaiso Beds have not so far yielded any traces of hominid bones or of stone artifacts. Sediments of very early Pleistocene age at Kanyatsi in the Lake Albert basin seem to contain small quantities of a simple flaked-stone industry.

## TROPICAL WEST AFRICA

The part of Africa that lies to the west of the Cameroun and north of the great Gulf of Guinea can be treated for our purposes as a natural subsector of the continent. Along the coastal belt, and for several hundred kilometres inland, humid tropical conditions tend to prevail and natural vegetation climax is commonly lowland forest. North of about the 8° N parallel there is a transition to savanna. At about latitude 12° N the savanna gives way to the arid fringes of the Sahara. A corridor of more open vegetation reaches the coast at about 2° of longitude. The area, like the adjoining Congo basin, is subject to high rainfall and supports numerous large perennial rivers such as the Benue, Niger, Volta, Bandama, Sassandra, Gambia and Senegal rivers. Most of the terrain lies well below the 600-m contour and only a few areas are subject to upland or montane conditions – notably the Jos plateau (northern Nigeria), Mount Nimba (Liberia) and the Fouta Djallon (Guinea).

By comparison with the drier parts of sub-Saharan Africa, this area, like the Congo basin, has yielded comparatively little good evidence of Lower or Middle Pleistocene Stone Age occupation. Andah, Davies, Descamps, B. Fagg, Mauny, Shaw, Soper and various others have carried out reconnaissance in many parts, but yet finds of early material have been sparse and often from contexts where reliable estimation of age is difficult. Three possible explanations can be offered: (1) that this region was uninhabited or was very sparsely and sporadically occupied during the Earlier Stone Age, (2) that the stone tools made here during this time-range were so roughly made that they are hard to detect and (3) that deep weathering and persistent erosion has destroyed most of the earlier artifacts. These possible explanations are not mutually exclusive.

Crude-looking stone artifacts can be found associated with gravel deposits, and raised beaches in many places. Some of these may be of early date, but many are probably of late Quaternary age. Many may be representatives of some kind of West African equivalent of the 'Sangoan', though this is by no means a well-proven and well-understood entity (Ogusu 1973) (see also chapter 4).

Possible examples of pre-Acheulian 'pebble-tool' occurrences have been reported (e.g. Davies 1964, 1967) but as yet none involve either satisfactory assemblages or good dating evidence. They are best regarded as unproven.

Sporadic finds of hand-axes and other bifaces have been made in many parts of the region. Most are of rather coarse pick-like aspect, and these may pertain to a 'Sangoan' facies rather than to a normal Acheulian.

The best examples of fully characteristic Acheulian *assemblages* from tropical West Africa, have been recovered on the Jos plateau. Tin-mining operations cut into fluviatile deposits that fill in a series of abandoned river channels. Several hundred hand-axes and cleavers have been

GEOLOGICAL TIME
DIVISIONS

| Southern Africa | Central Africa | West Africa | North-west Africa | Nile Valley and Eastern Sahara | |
|---|---|---|---|---|---|
| Vaal River gravels · Rooidam ✕ · Amanzi · Hangklip · Cave of Hearths · Montagu · Cornelia · Elandsfontein | ? Kamoa Pupa Mufo etc. · Baia Farta | >✕ ? Jos plateau sites ? | Ouljian ✕ Harounian ✕ Anfatian >✕ · Ternifine ? Saoura ? Adrar ? | Kharga · Dakhla Arkin Khor Abu Anga · Tihodaine · Nile terraces ? | UPPER PLEISTOCENE |
| Sterkfontein M5 · M2? · Klipplaatdrif and Three Rivers · Swartkrans M1 | Kanyatsi ?Palmeirinhas ? | STIC | Sidi Abderrahman LMN · Ain Hanech | | MIDDLE PLEISTOCENE |
| | | | | | LOWER PLEISTOCENE |
| | | | | | PLIOCENE |

range of uncertainty about the age of the archaeological site in question. For sites represented
by dotted lines these indicate the range of time within which the age probably falls (the lines do
not indicate duration).

recovered from various mining sites such as Maiidon Toro, Pingell and Nok. The two latter yielded assemblages in which hand-axes predominate, as is usual in Acheulian occurrences, but Maiidon Toro is unusual in having cleavers predominant, followed by picks, with hand-axes in the minority. The morphology of the bifaces is of Middle or Late Acheulian character, but they cannot be dated at all precisely. Previously published correlations with pluvial chronology should almost certainly be disregarded. Radiocarbon measurements have been made on associated organic materials in waterlogged deposits, but it seems clear that the material is beyond the range of the method. No undisturbed, stratified patch of artifacts has yet been recognized and excavated, but this should surely be possible one day.

Surface scatters of normal Acheulian assemblages are also known from the Sahel and the fringes of the desert, but as yet there have been no excavations or intensive studies.

At Asochrachona near the coast of Ghana, Davies has reported Acheulian artifacts associated with beach deposits. Overlying this level there is said to be a 'Sangoan' industry and Middle Stone Age material in non-marine strata. Further work at this site has been done by Andah and reports are awaited (see also chapter 4).

On balance it seems probable that intensive and effective occupation of the heavily vegetated parts of West Africa did not take place until the Upper Pleistocene, and that the oldest widespread industries are some kind of regional equivalent of the Sangoan.

## NORTH-WEST AFRICA AND THE SAHARA

This region, though mainly arid today, comprises a wide range of environments. Clearly, in the past, many parts were less dry and the diversity may well have been less. Along the northern and north-western margin, Mediterranean conditions prevail. Inland from this fringe the ridges and valleys of the Atlas range provide another distinctive set of conditions. South and east of the mountains lie the millions of square kilometres of *erg*, *reg* and *hamada* that constitute the Sahara. Then in the belt extending from Mauritania to Khartoum there are outliers of the great African *Acacia* savannas. Lower Palaeolithic material occurs in profusion in all these zones, except the high Atlas. It appears to range from Lower Pleistocene ('Villafranchian') to early Upper Pleistocene in age. Excellent stratified sites have been discovered and studied geologically, but none has yet been excavated by modern methods (table 3.9).

TABLE 3.9 *Chronological list of some selected, important and well-known sites in north-western Africa and the Sahara*

| Estimated geological time divisions | Excavated assemblages | Stratified sites collected but not excavated | Famous surface sites |
|---|---|---|---|
| Early Upper Pleistocene or late Middle Pleistocene | Sidi Zin<br>Sidi Abderrahman: Cape Chatelier | E.g.<br>El-Ma el-Abiod<br>Tit Mel'il<br>Oued el-Khemis<br>Jebel d'Ougarta | |
| Middle Pleistocene<br>(0.1–0.7 million years?) | Sidi Abderrahman: Grotte des Littorines, Grotte des Ours [Yielding hominid remains]<br>Casablanca: Thomas Quarry<br>Rabat: Témara, Salé | Tihodaine<br>Mauritanian Adrar:<br>Aderg, Aroui,<br>Tazamout, El-Beyyed<br>Adrar Bous<br>Lac Karar<br>Saoura: various | Tabelbalat:<br>Tachenghit |
| Early Middle or late Lower Pleistocene<br>(0.7–1.5 million years?) | Ternifine<br>Sidi Abderrahman: STIC, Horizon MNO | ?Saoura: various | |
| Lower Pleistocene<br>(> 1.5 million years?) | Aïn Hanech | Tardiguet er-Rahla<br>Casablanca and Rabat: various<br>Arbaoua<br>Saoura: various | |

The regional sequence appears to begin with stone industries of pre-Acheulian age which are presumably equivalent to the Oldowan of East Africa, though they have usually been termed pebble-culture or *civilization du galet aménagé*. It has been common practice to set up numbered, serial divisions of the industries, e.g. Acheulian stages I, II, III etc. The best-known stratified sequence is that from the Atlantic seaboard of Morocco, where detailed studies have been made by Biberson. Here, the gently inclined continental margin has preserved a superb stratified record of numerous alternating transgressions and regressions of the sea. At famous quarries such as that of *Sidi Abderrahman*, near Casablanca, several layers of shoreline deposits are each overlain by consolidated dunes which thus separate the series of transgressive deposits. Artifacts are locally abundant in the sequence. Assemblages have been recovered from very diverse situations: in beach deposits, in karstic caves cut into consolidated dunes and later covered up, and in the deposits of small streams that traversed the marshy coastal plains, as in the case of the famous *STIC site* where an early Acheulian industry was found associated with fauna. Several fragmentary fossils of early men have been found in the same suite of deposits, notably the Rabat, Sidi Abderrahman, Témara and Salé specimens (see chapter 2). All of these can be attributed to *Homo erectus*, or to early *H. sapiens*.

The stone industries are believed to show continuous technological and cultural development in the area over the whole span of the Pleistocene. Comparison with other areas is made difficult by the paucity of excavated sites and assemblages.

Thorium–uranium measurements offer some geophysical basis for estimates of the age of the last three marine transgressions and associated industries (Stearns and Thurber 1965). These results must be regarded with caution since the method is fraught with difficulties (Broeker and Bender 1972, Thurber 1972).

| | | |
|---|---|---|
| Ouljian transgression | Aterian Industry | 75 000 (50 000–95 000) years BP |
| Presoltanian regression ⎫ Harounian transgression ⎭ | Acheulian Stage VIII | 145 000 years BP |
| Tensiftian regression | Acheulian Stage VII | |
| Anfatian transgression | Acheulian Stages IV–VI | ⩾ 200 000 years BP |
| Amirian regression | Acheulian Stages I–III | |
| Maarifian transgression | Pebble-culture Stage IV | |
| Saletian regression | Pebble-culture Stage III | |
| Messauoudian transgression | Pebble-culture Stage II | |
| Moulouyan regression | Pebble-culture Stage I | |

Important though this sequence is, more recent developments in Quaternary studies imply that resolution is probably very much less complete than is implied by the table, since we now have reason to believe that during the time represented there have been some fifteen or sixteen interglacials and their associated transgressions.

As the map in fig. 3.6 shows, very numerous 'Lower Palaeolithic' finds have been made all over north-west Africa. Most of the information stemming from these finds is technical data relating to the morphology of selected artifacts recovered from eroded surfaces, and it is beyond the scope of this review to summarize these. However, the following important stratified sites deserve individual mention.

At *Aïn Hanech* in Algeria, outcrops of a major sedimentary formation have yielded fossil animal bones and an interesting but unusual sequence of artifact assemblages. The character of the fauna implies a late 'Villafranchian' age for the deposits, which thus probably date to some time between 1 and 2 million years ago. Three archaeological horizons have been recognized. The lower two, which can in effect be treated as a single occurrence, have yielded an assemblage dominated by faceted, battered spheroids. Some core-choppers and flake forms are also present. The fauna is associated with these levels. From conglomeratic deposits, which overlie these beds, an industry with rough bifaces has been recovered, though very little attention has been devoted to this level in the literature. The spheroid assemblage is in some respects reminiscent of the Developed Oldowan at Olduvai, which is also interstratified with hand-axe-bearing assemblages.

At *Ternifine* in Algeria, sands which accumulated in a small, spring-fed pool were quarried by Arambourg and others. The deposits have yielded a rich Middle Pleistocene fauna together with well-preserved *Homo erectus* fossils and an excellent sample of an early Acheulian industry, which included hand-axes, cleavers, choppers and also small tools. There are no geophysical age determinations and the date of the site can only be estimated. It is probably at least 0.5 million years old and seems unlikely to be much more than 1 million years old.

*Sidi Zin*, in Tunisia, is a site where rich 'Upper' Acheulian assemblages and fossil faunal remains were recovered by Gobert from deposits laid down in and around the pool of a spring at the confluence of two ravines. There are three Acheulian horizons plus a Mousterioid horizon in the capping tufa. The Acheulian assemblages differ from each other in a manner that seems to involve both style and perhaps activity and function. The faunal remains, which seem to be food-refuse, include elephant, rhinoceros, an equine (*Equus mauritanicus*), aurochs, gnu, *Bubalis*, gazelle and barbary sheep. The site is generally considered to be of early Upper Pleistocene age, but there is no precise dating evidence.

At the southern fringes of the area, comprehensive systematic collections of Acheulian material have recently been made at *Adrar Bous* in Niger, and are in course of analysis by J. D. Clark and co-workers. Other major sites have been located by Biberson all along the foot of the *Mauritanian Adrar*. Further east are other famous sites, such as those of the *Fezzan* (Libya) and of *Tihodaine* (Algeria), but as yet researches have largely been of a reconnaissance nature.

### THE NILE VALLEY AND ADJOINING DESERT OASES

The Nile Valley forms a corridor of lush vegetation and water resources that cuts across the eastern end of the Saharan arid zone. On either side lies desert country, but to the east of the river valley there is a series of vast topographic hollows that dip down below the regional watertable thereby establishing oases. The most famous of these are the Fayoum, Kharga, Dakhla and Bir Sahara. Both the Nile and the oases have yielded evidence of early Stone Age occupation.

The Nile Valley, like most other major river valleys, contains a series of fluviatile deposits at elevations above the reach of the modern river and pioneer studies such as those of Sandford and Arkell concentrated on these. In Middle and Lower Egypt 'terraces' were recognized at altitudes of 90 m, 65 m, 48 m, 30 m, 15 m and 3 m above the modern floodplain. The three highest terraces appeared devoid of all traces of stone tools, while the next three were reported to contain several evolving stages of hand-axe industry. The lowest terrace was reported to contain only 'Levalloisian' and 'Mousterian' artifacts. Studies of the heights and the gradients of the terraces led earlier workers to attempt elaborate interpretations of relations to changing climate and fluctuating sea level. However, as in the case of many other river-terrace systems, it is now recognized that the known geological and archaeological records are very fragmentary relative to the length and complexity of the Pleistocene, so that many of the earlier interpretations must be put aside pending studies involving modern methods and a fresh approach; the earlier work has been well summarized by Alimen and by McBurney (see bibliographical essay, p. 947).

The only excavated earlier Stone Age sites yet reported from the Nile

Valley are those in the Arkin area of Nubia which were investigated by Chmielewski. At *Arkin 8*, concentrated patches of discarded artifacts were found in a thin lens of residual fluvial or colluvial deposits that lie within the shallow bed of a wadi tributary of the Nile. It has been suggested that each concentration represents a camping place, and that some of these show arrangements of stones that may have been the footings of wind-breaks. In one case a hollow is reported as a possible example of a scooped-out hut floor. Cairn-like heaps of material are also mentioned. All these suggestions of possible structures are important in view of the rarity of such traces from the earlier Stone Age; however, until more details are available the published reports of them are difficult to evaluate. The shallow depth of the deposits encasing the occurrences makes the recognition of structures a particularly difficult matter.

Some 2500 artifacts were recovered from the Arkin 8 site. These are partly made on medium-sized quartz cobbles and pebbles from gravel deposits in the area and partly on slabs of ferruginized sandstone. Smallish hand-axes of varied form are fairly numerous. There is a distinctive series of bifacial ovates – which appear to be simply oval cobbles which have been sharpened all round by the removal of flakes from both faces. There are neat polyhedral and discoid cores plus numerous flakes. The Levallois technique (see p. 239) is scarcely in evidence and flake scrapers, while present, are uncommon.

At the site of Arkin 5 other assemblages were recovered by a combination of excavation and surface collection. It is suggested that this was a quarry site and that certain hollows in the surface of the Nubian sandstone were quarry pits, later used as stone-working places. Again, the shallow depth of the deposits that mantle the occurrences is an obstacle to secure, detailed interpretation. The Arkin 5 assemblage is notable for its strong Levallois component and for a number of bifacial foliate forms that resemble 'Lupemban lances' (see chapter 4).

Although it was not recovered by excavation, mention must be made of a very large collection of a hand-axe-dominated series of stone tools from further south, namely at *Khor Abu Anga*, near Omdurman. A small wadi or gully has cut deeply into fluvial deposits. As erosion and small-scale quarrying proceeded during several years prior to 1949, Arkell collected more than a thousand artifacts most of which come from gravel layers exposed near the base of the section. Of these, 185 items were definitely *in situ*. Neatly made almond-shaped, pointed and heart-shaped forms predominate, but as at Arkin 5 there are thin foliate, 'Lupemban'-like pieces.

Wendorf (1968) grouped the Arkin occurrences, Arkell's material and various surface finds as the 'Acheulian of Khor Abu Anga type'. Apart from strong indications that the material is appreciably older than the late Pleistocene industries of Nubia, there are no data to indicate the age-span of these occurrences.

Earlier Stone Age material has been found in and around the various oasis depressions to the east of the Nile. Much of this has been recovered as surface collections and is of uncertain value for modern archaeology, but there have also been a number of important excavations.

The classic study was that carried out at Kharga Oasis by Caton-Thompson and Gardner in the years 1930–2. They recovered late Acheulian artifacts from a mound that represented the deposits of an ancient spring and from sheets of gravels interstratified with limestone tufas found along the scarps surrounding the oasis depression. The older assemblage from the spring mound contains a varied series of 370 well-made hand-axes. Cleavers were present but very rare. Other elements include a few cores and choppers and very rare flake tools. Only half as many flakes as hand-axes were found, implying either that the large tools were made elsewhere or that the water currents from the spring have swept most of the flakes away. Levallois elements are present but very rare.

The material from the gravels of the Refuf pass appears to document an Acheulian industry broadly comparable to that of the spring mound, overlain by a later industry of which the Levallois technique was a conspicuous part. Subsequent Pleistocene industries in the area were classified in the monograph as Levalloisian, Khargan, and Aterian (see chapter 4).

In recent years an international research group that includes Wendorf, Said and Schild has continued the exploration of oases and has located and excavated important additional 'late Acheulian' sites in spring mounds at Dakhla Oasis which is reported to have yielded hand-axe-dominated assemblages that are comparable to that of the Kharga springs. A 'final Acheulian' assemblage has also been excavated from a fossil spring at the edge of the Bir Sahara depression.

None of the oasis sites can be dated with any precision. They can be shown to be older than Aterian, Mousterian and so-called Levallois occurrences, the earlier stages of which can be shown to have been well beyond the range of the $^{14}$C technique (i.e. > 50 000 years BP). Most workers suspect that these sites are of late Middle or early Upper Pleistocene age (i.e. 200 000–100 000 years BP), but even this is uncertain.

They clearly document at least the periodic existence of times when desert conditions were much less extreme than now, but correlation with particular palaeoclimatic episodes would be purely conjectural. It is not even known whether they correspond consistently to glacial or to interglacial times.

In prehistoric times, the Nile Valley constituted a strip of typically African plant and animal communities which reached northwards into the Mediterranean basin. It may well be that the valley was an important link in the web of Middle Pleistocene cultural interconnections; however at present the number of well-documented, well-dated archaeological assemblages is too small for one to make any direct assessment of cultural continuities. The presence in the Sudan of forms reminiscent of the Lupemban industries of equatorial Africa is a possible indicator of interconnection.

SOME GENERALIZATIONS AND INTERPRETATIONS

*Site characteristics and site location*

We may hope to learn something about land use and camping habits from comparative study of the settings in which sites occur. Table 3.10 provides lists of selected important African Early Stone Age sites classified according to their topographic contexts. The categories are only rather vaguely defined and, since some sites could be classified into more than one division, this has been indicated.

The predominance of sites associated with lake basins and with river-valley sedimentation is presumably largely a consequence of the fact that these topographic situations provide optimum conditions for the preservation of very ancient material. However, research has shown that even within a lake basin, the early archaeological sites often tend to be associated with stream courses. It seems very likely that there were often various advantages that encouraged early social groups to camp in the bed of a seasonal stream or on its banks: for instance, water courses are often tree-lined and provide better than usual shade as well as a range of fruiting trees; then, too, the sandy substratum of a stream bed is more comfortable for sitting and resting than most other parts of the terrain. Finally, for early humans, proximity to pools of water or to places where water-holes could be dug may well have been an important attraction. Acheulian materials also accumulated in quantity around springs such as Ternifine, Kharga Oasis, Sidi Zin and Amanzi.

*and context found amongst early sites in Africa*

| Time divisions | Lake basins and pans (alluvial and lake margin situations) | River valleys, including swamps and dambos | Springs | Marine coast and coastal plain | Hills and plateaux[b] | Caves[b] |
|---|---|---|---|---|---|---|
| Mainly Middle and early Upper Pleistocene (< 1.5 million years) | Olduvai Beds II–IV[a]<br>Olduvai Masek Beds[a]<br>Koobi Fora (Karari)[a]<br>Peninj[a]<br>Chesowanja[a]<br>Olorgesailie<br>Kapthurin[a]<br>Kariandusi<br>Doornlaagte<br>Rooidam<br>Tihodaine<br>Gadeb | Melka Kunture[a]<br>Isimila<br>Kalambo Falls<br>Lochard<br>Cornelia<br>Kilombe<br>Jos tin mines<br>Arkin<br>Pupa<br>Kamoa<br>(plus many sites in the valleys of the Vaal, Zambezi, Nile, etc.) | Ternifine[a]<br>Sidi Zin<br>Amanzi<br>Kharga Oasis<br>Dakhla Oasis | Casablanca–Rabat sites[a]<br>Dallol<br>Baia Farta<br>Hangklip<br>Cape Point<br>Mossel Bay, etc.<br>Hopefield | Kharga passes<br>Dury's Site (Kenya)<br>Nanyuki<br>Tachenghit and many other Saharan sites<br>Wonderboom-poort[c] | Grotte des Ours<br>Kabwe (Broken Hill)[a]<br>Montagu Cave<br>Cave of Hearths[a]<br>Wonderwerk Cave |
| Lower Pleistocene (> 1.5 million years) | Olduvai Bed I[a]<br>Olduvai Lower Bed II[a]<br>Koobi Fora KBS[a] | Omo G (Shungura)[a]<br>?Tardiguet<br>?Aïn Hanech | | Palmeirinhas<br>Casablanca: e.g. Deprez Quarry<br>Sidi Abderrahman | | Sterkfontein Member 5<br>Swartkrans A[a] |
| Pliocene (> 1.9 million years) (All except Omo F lack artifacts) | Hadar (Afar)[a],[d] | Omo F (Shungura)[a] | | | | Sterkfontein Member 4[a]<br>Makapansgat[a]<br>Taung[a] |

[a] With hominid fossils.

[b] All the caves listed are in 'Hills and plateaux' terrain except the Grotte des Ours (Casablanca) which was a marine coast site as well as being a cave.

[c] Wonderboompoort is a narrow defile through a range of hills.

[d] Artifacts have been reported from a horizon that may be about 2.5 million years old at Hadar (see table 3.4). If confirmed, this will be the oldest known occurrence.

There are sites in many different parts of Africa that are associated with former marine strandlines or are situated on coastal plains. We lack any clear evidence as to whether the food resources of the shore were used or whether the occupation of coastal areas was simply an extension of normal terrestrial land use. In Atlantic Morocco, where dunefields buried and preserved whole areas of former coast, no buried shell-middens of Acheulian age have been reported, but shellfish may easily have been eaten, with individuals feeding on the shore without accumulating any middens.

At an earlier stage in the development of Palaeolithic studies it was common to devote a great deal of attention to efforts to relate archaeological sequences to raised-beach sequences. This was partly done in the hope that it would allow of correlations with a simple global sequence of eustatic sea-level changes induced by glacials and interglacials. It transpires that the history of changes in the ocean, and in relations between continents and oceans, was much more complex than had been supposed, and these studies have lost much of their original cogency. Coastal relics of the earlier Stone Age, like any others, only deserve careful study when, as in Morocco, sites and assemblages are well preserved.

Rock-shelters and caves form a far less important source of archaeological evidence for the Earlier Stone Age than they do for later periods. It has sometimes been argued that this is because the practice of using rock-shelters only developed rather late in prehistory. This may be so, but it cannot be deduced with safety from the present evidence. Caves and rock-shelters are in general unstable features of the landscape. As cliff faces weather and erode, shelters at their base are normally destroyed, and only a few such sites could be expected to survive more than 100 000 years. Of the few cave sites that do contain Earlier Stone Age material, two are large, comparatively indestructible caverns that seem to belong to the very end of the period under consideration: Montagu Cave and the Cave of Hearths. Others, such as La Grotte des Ours at Casablanca, have survived because the whole cliff, cave and all, was buried by sand dunes which became consolidated. The cave site was rediscovered only as a result of quarrying operations. In any case, La Grotte des Ours appears to have contained a spring and, very likely, water rather than shelter was its attraction.

The Transvaal australopithecine sites represent early Plio–Pleistocene associations of hominid fossils and, in some cases, artifacts with caverns and fissures. However, recent work by Brain (1970) at Swartkrans and by Vrba (1975) at Sterkfontein Type Site suggests that the former notion that the early hominids used these sites as habitations may have to be revised. As explained in the regional summary section, the hominid bones at Swartkrans may well have been concentrated by leopards and the Sterkfontein Type Site may well have been the lair of sabre-tooth felines, who carried in hominid corpses and other carcases. These Transvaal sites have survived millions of years of erosion largely because they were relatively deep caverns and because their sedimentary infillings were consolidated to form resistant breccia.

There are comparatively few well-preserved stratified sites that have been preserved on hilltops and uplands, though presumably early Stone Age men camped in these situations as frequently as did their successors. Erosion and weathering has long since destroyed most such accumulations and the record available for study will always be biased in favour of sites in topographic depressions. The table lists a few exceptions that are known to me.

There are a few sites known in distinctive topographic situations that strongly suggest particular usage patterns. For instance, the Acheulian site of Wonderboompoort in the Transvaal is on the flank of a narrow defile that traverses a mountain ridge. The locale provided a natural game-trap, which was used and reused so that truly prodigious quantities of artifacts accumulated there.

## The structure and patterning of sites

Very few completely undisturbed early Stone Age camp sites have yet been discovered and excavated in their entirety, so that one can see their size and layout, and make inferences regarding the scale of social groups and perhaps gain clues to aspects of the conduct of daily life. One example that comes close to this ideal is the *Zinjanthropus* floor, FLK I, at Olduvai. As fig. 3.16 shows, this site consists of an irregular patch of discarded stone tools and stone chippings which is coincident with a scatter of fragmentary animal bone. In the centre of the site there is a subsidiary patch characterized by anomalously high densities of broken-up bone and quartz flakes. This central area gives the appearance of having been the focus of those activities that led to the discard of small flakes, and that caused the smashing of bone. Perhaps this was a focus both for stone-knapping and for feeding on meat and bone marrow. Perhaps a particularly good shade tree grew here. On the outer fringe of the site was the cranium of *Zinjanthropus* while fragmentary remains attributable to *Homo habilis* were also found eroding from the edges of the site.

Many palaeo-anthropologists believe that the big-toothed australo-pithecines of the *Zinjanthropus* and *Paranthropus* variety were not makers of stone tools. If this is so, then the individual whose skull came to rest on the edge of the camp site may have been either a victim of the hunting skill of the tool-making hominids or maybe a fortuitous earlier or later visitor attracted to the site by the same features as had attracted the tool-makers.

The patch of material at the FLK site is approximately 18 m in diameter. The refuse scatters of individual, short-term sites, where they can be distinguished, tend to have approximately this scale from the oldest archaeological sites right down to the inception of agriculture. Some other early sites are much bigger than this, as for instance, the sites at Kalombo Falls, but in these instances there are often reasons to believe that the large occupation area formed as a palimpsest of numerous imperfectly superimposed smaller ones. If this tentative generalization about site size is sustained by future research, it may have the implication that the sizes of social aggregates retained a similar order of magnitude through this time range, perhaps with a normal maximum of some thirty to fifty individuals. Many of the sites are consistent with the notion that they were occupied by even smaller groups, perhaps comprising only a few adults and infants. It is entirely possible that these early Stone Age societies consisted of variable aggregations of hominids which coalesced and dispersed in response to seasonal changes in subsistence opportunities. Amongst recent non-agricultural peoples, the units modulated by fission and coalescence are commonly some kind of family unit that involves mated males and females and dependent children. There is no way to tell when in prehistory pair-bonding began to be a feature of human life. This whole question of group size in prehistory requires much more deliberate research and the foregoing remarks are speculative.

At a number of excavated sites, traces have been discovered that are tentatively interpreted as the remains of structures. The oldest of these is at the site of DK I in Bed I Olduvai. Here, M. D. Leakey found a concentration of stones that formed an open-sided ring: see fig. 3.1. She has argued that this could well have been the footing that stabilized the bases of a series of branches that were leant up against each other to form a conical shelter. An arc of stones suspected of being part of a wind-break has also been detected at Kalombo Falls. At Melka

Kunturé, in part of their Developed Oldowan horizon, J. and N. Chavaillon have found what appears to them to be traces of diggings that delimit some kind of platform. Similarly at Arkin in Nubia, it has been suggested that there may be traces of a scooped-out occupation floor.

Many earlier Stone Age sites contain large quantities of unshaped stones or angular rubble that appears to have been carried to the camp place. The tentative suggestion has at times been offered that these constituted paving. This seems uncomfortable and unlikely; it is much more probable that the stone was introduced either for use in the pounding of plant foods, or for throwing as missiles, which is surely an ancient human skill of crucial importance.

In general, then, the traces of structures on very early sites are slight, and sometimes of debatable significance. In the main it would seem that early hominids lived in the open or used the natural cover of shady trees and bushes. However, there is nothing improbable about the notion that when occasion demanded simple temporary shelters were constructed from branches stabilized if necessary by stones. Caves were used at least from time to time.

### Early stone tools: technology, function and fashion

Because of the relative durability of stone, artifacts formed by the deliberate fracture of this material are by far the commonest archaeological relics from the earliest phases of prehistory. Their importance is two-fold: firstly, they serve as markers of former human activity, so that our very ability to recognize early sites depends on the presence of stone artifacts. Thus, even though the foregoing sections on early hominid patterns of life were not based directly on the study of stone tools, they were made possible by the propensity of artifacts to indicate places where tool-makers were active. However, artifacts also serve as sources of information in their own right, and the detailed interpretation of their morphology has been one of the principle preoccupations of Palaeolithic scholars. The study has developed over more than a century, during which time emphasis and objectives have changed and diversified in subtle ways. Until recently there was very little explicit attempt to examine and discuss the assumptions and the logic behind the studies, so that scholars have often talked at cross-purposes without realizing it. This situation still exists to some degree, but it is being improved as a result of modern trends towards offering careful

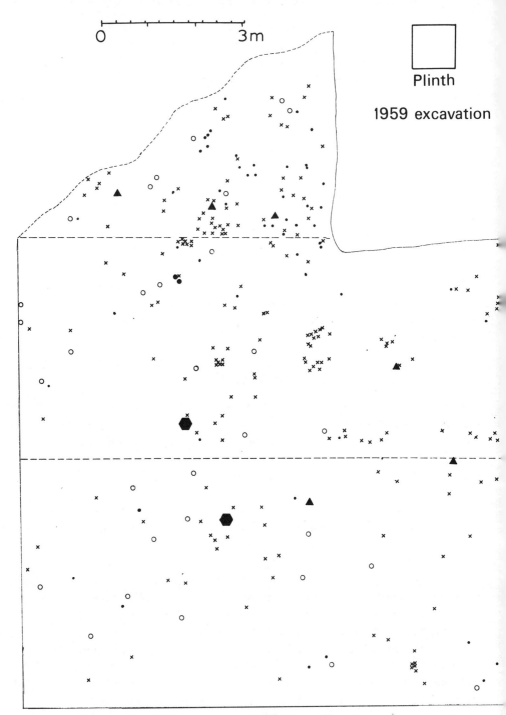

Fig. 3.16 The 'Zinjanthropus' site at FLK, Bed I, Olduvai Gorge. A plan showing the distribution of an old ground-surface which was uncovered by excavation. A dense patch of discarded artifacts and introduced stones (manuports) coincides with a dense patch of broken-up animal bones. (After M. D. Leakey 1971.)

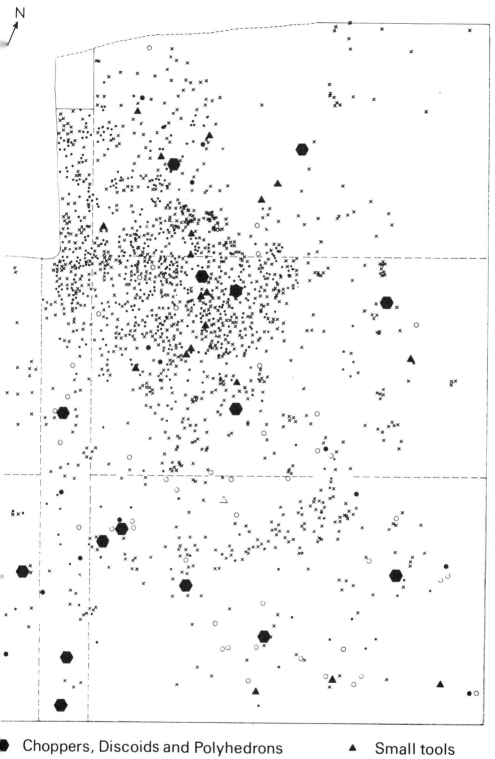

N

Choppers, Discoids and Polyhedrons ▲ Small tools

Hammerstone ∘ Manuport

Debitage and utilized debitage ✕ Bone

definition of terms and towards formulating deliberate statements of theoretical stance. The full technical details of research on artifacts fall outside the scope of this essay, but an outline of the main issues is essential.

All early stone artifacts depended on an empirical appreciation by prehistoric men of the principles of conchoidal fracture of stone. In simplified terms this amounts to the fact that if a block of homogeneous stone is struck hard enough, near an edge, a thin sliver of stone is detached. The detached piece has a number of characteristic features and is given the technical label of *flake*. The parent block of stone, which of course now shows a scar where the flake was detached, is known as a *core*. Since both flake and core owe their existence to the activities of an artisan, they can both be fairly included in the category of *artifact*.[1]

The process of flaking can be used to achieve two main purposes. Firstly, the artisan can detach flakes in order to use them directly for the purposes that we use knives, planes, chisels, spokeshaves, etc. Any series of flakes knocked from a block of stone will include a variety of very sharp edges and points, so that if one is not fussy about the exact shape of the utensil, items suitable for many functions can be picked out from a set of flakes. Secondly, the process of flaking can be used to adjust the shape of a piece of stone in a manner analogous to that in which a sculptor imposes form by removing chips. Where flaking is undertaken in order to determine the shape of the piece from which the flakes were removed, the process is referred to as *trimming*, or in the case of the removal of very small, closely spaced flakelets, it is called *retouch*.

The distinction between the series of objects termed flakes, and the cores from which they were struck, is straightforward; it has its basis directly in the physics of fracture. However, there is another distinction that is regarded as important by prehistorians which is rather more arbitrary. It has been customary to distinguish so-called *tools* from other artifacts. Because this involves the use of an everyday word which has nonetheless been given a special restricted meaning, confusion often results. For Palaeolithic prehistorians, the distinction between tools and non-tools usually does not depend on whether an object was used as an implement; it depends on whether the shape of the object is judged to have been deliberately determined by a recognizable sequence of

[1] Good illustrated accounts of the main processes involved in making and using stone tools are to be found in Howell (1965, pp. 110–15) and in various of the general works referred to in the bibliographical essay.

technical acts. Only pieces showing such purposive shaping qualify as tools in the technical sense. Tools, *sensu stricto*, are recognized through the fact that their forms have been altered by trimming or retouch so as to produce potentially useful edges or points.

Throughout the Pleistocene, ordinary flakes were probably used extensively without any retouch or trimming. They may well have been functionally the most important utensils of daily life, but by convention, because they cannot consistently be distinguished from mere by-products, they are separated from the tools and put in a category that is designated as *waste*, or as *debitage*. Do not be misled into believing that these categories contain only unwanted and unused items. Where flakes and other non-tools show clear signs that are interpreted as damage due to use, they are often classified into the category *utilized*; while objects that show trimming or retouch for which no clear organizational principle is distinguished are often put in the category *modified*.

We have seen that the two main binary distinctions made amongst stone artifacts are between cores and flakes, and between tools and non-tools. These distinctions in combination provide the following conceptual scheme:

|  | Purposive shaping for use = tools | Not purposely shaped = non-tools or debitage |
|---|---|---|
| Comparatively large blocks from which flakes have been struck = cores | Core-tools | Cores |
| Flakes and flake fragments | Flake-tools | Waste flakes |

Notice that when flakes are trimmed or retouched by the removal of very small flakes, they become in a sense miniature cores, but the craftsman's intention to shape them for a particular use is usually clear and they are generally non-controversial examples of tools. In contrast, it is often difficult to decide whether some relatively large block of stone has had flakes removed primarily on account of a need for sharp flakes, or whether it was flaked largely in order to give the block itself a form that would be suitable for use. In the first case, the object should be classified as a core, in the second as a core-tool. Clearly the two possibilities are not mutually exclusive and the distinction is often a false one. Many of the larger flaked stone objects in Early Stone Age assemblages were probably both cores and tools. A final complication to this scheme arises from the fact that in Africa there are many instances of tools such as the hand-axe and the cleaver being made from extremely large flakes in spite of the fact that these tool categories are conventionally regarded as varieties of core-tools.

Having provided this very brief introduction to the fundamental grammar of early stone industries, we should be in a position to examine the contribution that a study of the artifacts makes to our overall understanding of Pleistocene prehistory. However, there are such widespread misunderstandings about the nature of artifact studies that it seems wise to offer also a brief preliminary comment on the objectives of stone-tool analysis. I would currently recognize three kinds of information that prehistorians seek to gain from Pleistocene artifacts.

(1) Artifacts can be used as indicators of the level of technological sophistication and skill of prehistoric peoples at different times in the past. At the outset of Palaeolithic researches artifacts were perhaps envisaged primarily as markers of the progressive evolution of technology. However, judgements of what constituted advanced and what primitive technology were, and indeed still are, in large measure subjective.

(2) The detailed form of artifacts can be considered as expressions of conventions that are determined by the specifics of the culture of the makers. Close resemblance between artifact assemblages has often been taken as indicative that their makers shared a common tradition which was often designated as a particular prehistoric 'culture', e.g. Fauresmith Culture. The converse argument is also often applied, namely that if artifact assemblages differ markedly then they cannot have been made by members of the same 'culture'.

(3) Artifacts are also agents of adaptation: they played important functions in the economic and social lives of their makers, and they can be studied for the light that they throw on the practical aspects of Stone Age activities.

Clearly the form of every stone assemblage is determined by the interaction of complex factors and each of the foregoing lines of interpretation is only an aspect of what is needed for a holistic understanding. However, much confusion has been engendered in earlier literature owing to a common failure to make sufficiently explicit distinctions amongst these several aspects.

The first step in the development of the technology of stone artifacts must have been the empirical discovery already mentioned of the fact that hitting two stones together in the right way produced two useful results: a sharp-edged flake and a jagged-edged core. It seems very likely that long before that discovery, earlier generations of hominids had been making more and more use of sticks, branches and of sharp-edged natural fragments of stone and bone. We do not as yet have satisfactory direct evidence of this hypothetical pre-stone-tool phase. The main claimant for this status has been Dart's osteodontokeratic culture at Makapansgat, but for reasons already explained, many prehistorians regard this as a dubious and unproven case. In any event, recent researches have shown that the magnitude of the gap between man the tool-maker and the apes is less wide than was formerly believed. We now know that chimpanzees make and use various simple tools in the wild (Goodall 1968, 1972) and also that it has proved possible for humans to teach apes to make stone tools and use them (Wright 1972). It is thus no longer unduly fanciful to hypothesize a sub-human phase of evolution that involved the use of more and more objects as aids.

Stone artifacts are almost all that survives from the tool-kits of the early hominids, but it is important to remember that they were almost certainly not the only tools that were in use. From ethnography we can see that only a small amount of rather basic equipment is required for non-agricultural peoples to live a fully human life in the tropics. The apparatus consists of only four or five categories: sticks with a sharpened end suitable for digging; one or more weapons such as a club or a staff with a pointed end, suitable for use as a spear; some kind of bag, basket or tray; stones for pounding and nut-cracking; and finally some kind of knife or other cutting tool. It is this last function that was normally fulfilled by stone artifacts though under some circumstances bamboo, tusks, animal teeth and hard woods may have replaced or complemented stone. Another human tool-using capability that has probably had decisive importance is the ability to throw stones with devastating force and accuracy, a skill which gives humans enjoyment and which is readily learned. The knowledge of how to make and use all of these basic items was universal by the beginning of historic times. Stone-tool manufacture is the only one of the set for which we have anything approaching a complete record, but many anthropologists suspect that all of these simple tool forms are likely to have had more or less equally ancient beginnings. Fig. 3.17 shows a conjectural timetable for basic components of human equipment. The oldest known example of each category is shown, whether it is an African document or not. Conjectural earlier existence is suggested by dotted lines.

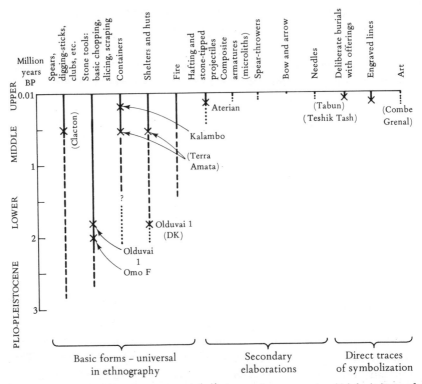

Fig. 3.17  A diagram illustrating current information on the sequence in which basic items of equipment and aspects of material culture became incorporated during the development of mankind. The oldest known archaeological instance is indicated where appropriate (in parentheses if it is not an African instance). Dotted lines denote uncertainty.

The functional importance of stone tools in the lives of the hominids once they had discovered how to fracture stone at will, probably had two aspects. Firstly, being in possession of sharp-edged flakes and jagged-edged chunks facilitates the acquisition of digging-sticks, clubs and spears, and allows their functional parts to be shaped so as to improve their efficiency. Secondly, on occasions when meat from large mammals was an item of diet, the ability to penetrate the hide and to break up the carcass was crucially facilitated by even the smallest and simplest of stone flakes.

Much of the earlier literature on stone tools tended to imply that the initial stages of development comprised a long, gradual sequence of progressive technological changes. However, I consider it equally possible that the discovery of conchoidal fracture was a threshold that immediately put all the hominids to whom the knowledge spread in possession of a fair range of useful artifact forms. I consider it likely that all the stone industries known to be more than 1.5 million years old represent very much the kind of material that one would expect to find being made by hominids who had mastered the basic methods of fracture by percussion. It is mainly material which lacked very definite, arbitrary design rules. As we have seen, very few well-excavated assemblages have been recovered that are firmly dated to this age range. All are from Africa. They contain the following components:

| | Age, million years BP | Flakes | Cores | Core-tools | Flake-tools | Raw material |
|---|---|---|---|---|---|---|
| Omo, Shungura F | 2.0 | × | × | — | — | Quartz |
| Koobi Fora KBS | 1.8 | × | × | × | — | Lava |
| Olduvai Bed I | 1.6–1.8 | × | ? | × | × | Quartz and lava |

The largest samples of this set come from Bed I Olduvai where they constitute the basis for the definition of the Oldowan Industry. For present purposes, the other very early industries are being classified within the Oldowan Industrial Complex, although they differ amongst themselves. It seems probable that the main differences amongst these are as likely to be due to differences in the properties of the available raw materials as anything else. These assemblages are grouped by J. G. D. Clark as mode 1. They are all dominated numerically by numerous thin, sharp-edged flakes and flake fragments. In some cases there are also heavier jagged-edged scrapers, discoids and polyhedrons. Simple though the assemblages are, they are all fully adequate to enable the performance of the basic tasks enumerated above. Figs. 3.3 and 3.11 illustrate some of the forms represented in the Oldowan and allied industries.

Around 1.5 million years ago, new varieties of tools began to appear. The most conspicuous of these were hand-axes and cleavers (fig. 3.13). These forms are much larger than the normal range of Oldowan artifacts, and they seem to me to show more explicit arbitrary aspects in their design. As they develop, they involve increasingly active imposition of form on the stone in which they are made. By contrast, the Oldowan forms are seen to represent more opportunistic fabrication of edges on the margins of such lumps of stone as were accessible. At the outset, hand-axes and cleavers are commonly but not invariably associated with another novelty, namely the practice of striking large flakes of between 10 and 25 cm in maximum dimension. These often have shapes that fall within the shape range of hand-axes and cleavers. The earliest known examples of these tool forms consist of big flakes that have had their shape adjusted by a minimum of trimming. It seems possible that the primary innovation was the discovery of how to strike the big flake, with the form of hand-axes and cleavers being later fixed because these shapes proved to be particularly useful.

However this may be, the hand-axe and the cleaver became established as common artifact forms over a very large part of the Old World and, as we have seen, constitute the hallmark of the so-called Acheulian industries. In spite of a great deal of variation in their size, shape and technology, these tools clearly constitute a related series that is often known by the generic French term *biface*.

Other novel ingredients that became conspicuous in some assemblages that are younger than 1.5 million years are heavy pick forms, especially at Peninj, and large core-scrapers, especially in the Karari Industry from the Upper Member of the Koobi Fora Formation. In north-west Africa, bifaces with narrow, concave-sided points are common in the early stages. At Olduvai, spheroids became much more common, apparently replacing hammer-stones in some degree. Also at Olduvai this period witnessed the start of a trend towards an increase in the number and variety of flake tools such as scrapers and awls.

So we see evidence that in the time-range between 1.0 and 1.5 million years ago, the overall repertoire of shaped tool forms increased in number. This certainly seems likely to be a reflection of a rise in the level of cultural competence of the tool-making hominids. There are also other indications of increased complexity in cultural systems. From now on through the remainder of the Stone Age, there is an increasing tendency for different assemblages to contrast with each other even when they are of essentially the same age. Put in technical terms, there was increasing intra-assemblage differentiation, and, as a concomitant, increasing inter-assemblage variation.

At Olduvai this finds expression in the existence of more than one distinct kind of assemblage. From middle Bed II times onwards, some assemblages contain prominent series of hand-axes and cleavers, and fall readily into the category Acheulian; other assemblages involve subtle changes of the pattern that prevailed in Bed I times. These latter are assigned to a sequential series of phases of the Developed Oldowan. As we have seen in the region-by-region reviews, this pattern of marked variation amongst essentially synchronous assemblages from the same sedimentary basin, is manifest in all East African Middle Pleistocene site complexes for which we have appropriate data. East Africa has proved to be a testing-ground for ideas regarding the historical and anthropological meaning of this variation, and I will return to the question.

After the appearance about 1.5 million years ago of the innovations that ushered in the first assemblages that can be called Acheulian, there was no comparable overall change in the character of artifacts until the very end of the period with which this chapter is concerned, namely at about 0.1 million years ago. There were, to be sure, some weak trends of change, but no dramatic universal developments or innovations.

A hand-axe can be said to be more or less refined depending on the degree to which a thin, regular shape is achieved, with evenly curved faces and regular edges. The record seems to show that there was some tendency to a rise in the maximum degree of refinement. There are no Lower or early Middle Pleistocene counterparts for such extremely well-made series of bifaces as the late Acheulian specimens from Kalambo Falls. However, some hand-axe assemblages that are probably essentially the same age as Kalambo Falls are not noticeably more refined than assemblages that are much older. We have therefore come to the realization that hand-axe assemblages cannot be reliably dated by their degree of refinement.

There is one novel technique which locally made its appearance during the time-span covered by the Acheulian assemblages: this is the Levallois method of flake production. It certainly shows a comparatively advanced level of mental and technical competence, though, of course, its absence in other areas does not prove that the inhabitants were incapable of executing it. Full accounts of the Levallois method can be found in standard texts on stone tools, so suffice it to say here that it is a label given to a series of highly organized procedures in the working of a core that yields to the artisan a single regular flake, the shape of which has been deliberately and consciously predetermined by the preparatory steps. Depending on the design adopted by the stone-knapper, the technique can produce more or less circular, oval, triangular or rectangular flakes. The Levallois method became a distinctive technical ingredient in several parts of Africa that are thousands of kilometres apart: notably in the Vaal River valley where it is known as the *Victoria West technique*; in Morocco and in parts of the western Sahara. In general it is not much in evidence in the East African Acheulian assemblages, but a fully developed instance has recently been discovered in the Kapthurin site complex in Kenya. We do not know whether it developed entirely independently in each of these instances, whether knowledge of the technique diffused, or whether it was a technical concept that was vaguely familiar over a far wider area than those in which it was conspicuously applied.

In the earlier Stone Age of some parts of Africa, the Levallois method was characteristically applied so as to produce flakes large enough to serve as blanks from which hand-axes and cleavers could be made. Because the cores and flakes differ from those commonly found in Europe by being larger and very probably older, a label 'proto-Levallois' is sometimes used for the African instances. However, the distinction implied by the prefix 'proto-' now seems superfluous.

In Morocco, the results of Biberson's studies suggest a sequence of development in which the size of Levallois cores and flakes diminished through time as also did the size of the bifaces. Latterly the Levallois method was being used to produce flakes of very modest sizes and the whole industry began to have a Middle Palaeolithic, or so-called *Mousterian*, aspect. Similar changes may well have occurred in other parts of Africa. The Fauresmith variant of the late Acheulian in South Africa involves elaborate Levallois forms that are of smaller size than in the normal Acheulian in the adjoining Vaal valley. Equally the main occurrences of hand-axes in Somalia are associated with Levallois technology and have always been assumed to be comparatively late. The use of the Levallois method became more widespread, but not universal, in the Middle Stone Age which followed after the period with which this chapter is concerned.

The application of the Levallois method is best understood as one possible response to the problem of breaking up lumps of raw material. It seems to have been a solution particularly favoured where boulders about the size of a football and large cobbles were being exploited as in the Vaal, Kapthurin and Morocco. Elsewhere large, generally side-struck flakes were struck from blocks and boulders which were given only simple preparation: this technique is sometimes referred to as the *Tachenghit technique*.

Much of the previous literature dealing with the Earlier Stone Age in Africa concerned itself almost exclusively with core-tool forms such as hand-axes, cleavers, picks and choppers. However, as we have seen even back in the Oldowan industries of Plio–Pleistocene times, flake-tools can be an important and conspicuous element. Almost all undisturbed, excavated assemblages contain a fair proportion of small scrapers, nosed tools and beak-shaped implements (*becs*) made on flakes, flake fragments or other small pieces of angular, broken-up stone.

In many instances these small tools far outnumber the core-tools which may even be absent entirely. At Olduvai M. D. Leakey has termed the industries in which bifaces are atypical and subordinate or absent, as the *Developed Oldowan*. Similar assemblages had previously been recognized elsewhere and were grouped under the label 'Hope Fountain' which term has now largely fallen into disuse. Kleindienst (1961) suggested the designation Acheulian Type B, which reflects her belief that these small scraper-dominated assemblages were really the products of the same culture-technological system that produced the biface-dominated classic Acheulian assemblages.

### Variation

In the regional review sections of this chapter, we have seen that for many areas only very coarse chronological sets can be distinguished at present amongst the Earlier Stone Age occurrences. The groupings may in some cases span 0.5 million years or more. We have also seen that within these groupings the characteristics of the stone artifact assemblages may differ extensively, and that even within the confines of a single site-complex such as that of Olduvai, Olorgesailie or Isimila far more variation has been found than was expected. It is now necessary to specify more exactly the nature of this variation and to report briefly on current discussions on its anthropological and historical meaning.

For convenience we may recognize two important components of variability in African Middle Pleistocene industries: (1) differences in the percentage frequency of all major classes of artifacts; of special note are variations in the ratios of bifaces:small tools:heavy-duty tools; (2) differences in norms for the shapes of such widespread and stylistically sensitive tool categories as the bifaces.

Fig. 3.18 displays aspects of variation as it has been observed in East Africa which is the segment of the continent for which we have the most extensive comparable data. It can be seen that the proportion of bifaces and of small tools can both vary from 0 to almost 100%. It is also true that sets of tools belonging to the same 'type' may differ very noticeably from each other in shape. Initially it was assumed that the variations would be found to conform to some historical and geographic pattern; that is to say, that certain variants would be found to belong to specific past cultural episodes or to particular regional expressions of culture.

241

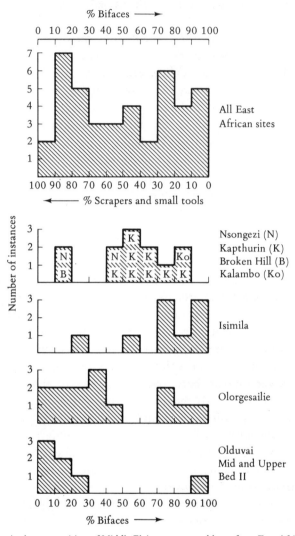

Fig. 3.18  Variation in the composition of Middle Pleistocene assemblages from East Africa. The histograms show that some assemblages are dominated by scrapers and small tools, and are termed Developed Oldowan or Acheulian type B, others are dominated by bifaces and are designated as 'classic' Acheulian.

This is normal archaeological expectation, and of course, some aspects of the differentiation are so patterned. However, a very large proportion of the total variation does not seem to show regular patterns in relation to either time or space. Recognition of this fact has confronted archaeologists with a puzzle.

At present, there are three main contending lines of explanation for the observed variation that cannot be related to resolvable divisions of space and time. Hypothesis 1 recognizes that a major component of the variation is due to the difference between biface-dominated assemblages or classic Acheulian, and non-biface-dominated assemblages, or Developed Oldowan. The hypothesis suggests that each of these assemblage-types was made by the members of one of two separate cultural systems which existed side by side in the manner of two distinct 'tribes', over a very long time. It is sometimes considered possible that a separate species of hominid was responsible for each (see, for example, M. D. Leakey (1971)), that is to say, that there were coexistent but not interbreeding populations. One line of evidence which has been advanced in support of this view, is that at Olduvai, when bifaces occur in the Developed Oldowan assemblages, they are irregular and atypical as though they had been made by craftsmen who were only vaguely aware of the form and the technique. This kind of hypothesis has also been advanced and debated in connection with analogous variability among European Pleistocene assemblages. One can designate these kinds of explanation as *parallel-phylum* models.

Hypothesis 2 contends that Stone Age people were liable to need different kinds of tools in connection with different tasks or activities that were carried out in different places. If each tool-kit is discarded in whole or in part at these different centres of activity, then, it is argued, a complex jigsaw of variation will result, in which the variants are not related to time or macrogeography. This kind of viewpoint was first advanced by J. D. Clark (1959b) and has subsequently been espoused by Kleindienst (1961) and by Binford (1972) who has also advocated its applicability to the European Palaeolithic. This explanatory model for dealing with variability is generally known as the *activity variant* model, and the supposed varieties have often been termed *activity facies*.

Hypothesis 3 involves the contention that there is a great deal of latitude in the exact form of a stone tool-kit that would have enabled early hominid gatherer–hunters to thrive (Isaac 1972a), that is to say, that tool-kits with many different detailed characteristics may all have been equally effective. If this was so, it might be expected that tool-making habits would drift about restlessly as a result of fortuitous changes and temporary local quirks of habit and fashion. Different social groupings within a region might even be expected under such circumstances to show idiosyncrasies in their craft practices due to varying skill and shifting whims. Then imagine that this restlessly changing cultural scene is observed from a far distance, so that the details of chronological sequence and the fine mosaic of idiosyncrasy became blurred. It might then be expected that the variation would appear as unpatterned. This view can be termed the *random-walk* model.

Clearly these three rival hypotheses are not mutually exclusive. In particular hypotheses 2 and 3 can be combined so that variation could be regarded as due to a combination of activity differentiation and of drift. Most prehistorians are somewhat sceptical of the prolonged coexistence of entirely separate cultures, but it must be admitted that if there were in fact separate species of tool-making hominids, then the explanation is a possible one.

Perhaps because the activity-facies model appeals to our modern sense of orderliness and efficiency, it has often been assumed that it must be correct. However, while we can be reasonably sure that it is part of the story, there are as yet remarkably few cases where evidence of special activities has been offered that is independent of the artifact characteristics. One of the best-established activity facies of assemblage variants is associated with sites where the carcasses of large animals have been butchered (J. D. Clark 1972). In these cases we commonly find assemblages dominated by flakes, small informal tools and core-choppers.

Above and beyond the restless and puzzling variation there are only very weak overall trends discernible in material culture: as we have seen there is some rise in the maximum level of craft refinement, and in the maximum level of intra-assemblage complexity. However, the minimum level of artifact assemblage complexity certainly did not rise much after about 1 million years ago, and we do not have the data even to guess at what happened to the average level, though one might expect that it did rise. Presumably the explanation for the persistence of stone-tool-making habits that were simpler and more casual than the best level known to have been possible lies in the fact that even the simpler assemblages provided their makers with a perfectly adequate basis for making the digging-sticks, spears and bags on which the real quality of life depended. A much more difficult problem then faces one in offering an explanation of why some stone tool-kits become more refined and varied. Perhaps during this time-span, the kind of web of cultural rules and norms that now govern the lives of all living peoples was becoming more elaborate. The overall qualities of these webs of rules might be adaptive even if many of the individual strands were not. The occasional elaboration of stone tools may thus be explicable not so much as related to the improved efficiency of the tools themselves as related to much more far-reaching changes in social and cultural systems as a whole.

## Fire

The oldest definite traces of fire on an African archaeological site are those on the Acheulian floors at Kalambo Falls. They are between 60 000 and 200 000 years old. In Eurasia, traces at sites such as Choukoutien, Vertésszöllös, Terra Amata and Torralba Ambrona show that the use of fire goes back as far as 0.5 million years ago, when the cold temperate zone was first colonized.[1] It has sometimes been deduced from this that the use of fire became current in Africa only rather late in prehistory. However, this is not a legitimate conclusion, since we now know that under tropical conditions of weathering, traces of fire would not survive at sites such as Olduvai, Olorgesailie and Isimila. We have to admit that we simply do not know when fire began to be used regularly. It seems unlikely that it would have been appreciably later than the inception of use elsewhere, and fire may perfectly well have been tamed long before mankind spread outwards from the tropics.

## The end of the Acheulian

For more than a million years of Lower and Middle Pleistocene time, prehistoric man in Africa made, used and discarded hand-axes, cleavers, and the other tools that are distinctive of the Acheulian. Then during the early part of the Upper Pleistocene the practice effectively ceased and patterns of stone technology came into being for which we can use the term Middle Stone Age as a label. As is explained in chapter 4 these post-Acheulian industries tend to show that the manufacture of elaborate, standardized large cutting tools and core-tools became much less frequent, although the making of them did persist with modifications, especially in the Sangoan–Lupemban industries of the Congo basin and adjoining areas. In some instances Middle Stone Age assemblages show extensive use of the Levallois method and sometimes of blade-producing techniques but neither is universal. Sometimes Middle Stone Age small tools seem to have been more carefully made than Acheulian, in other instances they are indistinguishably informal and irregular. There is only one widespread trait of Middle Stone Age

[1] For a good review of the use of fire see Oakley (1956). The dating for the early evidence of fire in Eurasia is discussed in Isaac (1972b) and in various papers in Butzer and Isaac (1975).

industries that sets them apart from Early Stone Age industries. The former very commonly contain carefully-made pieces which show clear signs of having been designed to be set on the end of a shaft in the manner of a spear-point. However, such are effectively unknown in assemblages of Acheulian age. Perhaps the change in technological mode and the decline in the importance in most areas of large formal tools was related to the spread of the practice of hafting. This is at present a purely speculative notion which has been borrowed from Australian prehistory. Clearly we should be in a better position to understand the disappearance of hand-axes if we knew what they had been used for in the first place.

We have very few satisfactory stratified sequences that give us a chronicle of the changeover from Acheulian to post-Acheulian technical modes. In South Africa at the Cave of Hearths and at Montagu Cave, layers of perfectly characteristic Acheulian material culture are overlain directly by Middle Stone Age assemblages without any signs of a transition. The Kalambo Falls sequence at one point seemed to provide clues, but it now appears that the so-called transitional Acheulian–Sangoan assemblages fall fully within the range of variation of normal Acheulian industries. Nsongezi may provide a stratified record of the changeover but the dating and the details are as yet far from clear. As already mentioned, Biberson interprets the sequence in Morocco as showing gradual reduction in the size of bifaces and an increasing importance and refinement for the Levallois method until the industry became in effect a Mousterian of Acheulian tradition. This is an attractive orderly model but we do not know how widely applicable it is.

It was formerly fashionable to think in terms of various industries as transitional between the Early and the Middle Stone Age: the Third Pan-African Congress of Prehistory gave formal status to this notion by setting up the division of 'First Intermediate Period' between the two. Entities such as the Fauresmith, the Sangoan and the Acheulo-Levalloisian were classified under this rubric. However, most pre-historians are now uneasy about the arrangement. As we have seen in the regional reviews, the Fauresmith Industry emerges as a local facies of late Acheulian, the character of which was primarily determined by the form and mechanical properties of the indurated shale used.

We have also seen that, in the Congo basin, the Sangoan has proved to be a facies of the Sangoan-Lupemban rather than an independent transitional culture.

Conventional ideas about the time at which the changeover occurred have also had to undergo fairly drastic revision in recent years. We know now that fully characteristic Middle Stone Age industries extend back as far as the effective range of the radiocarbon method, that is to at least 50 000 years BP. Some signs have been found that Middle Stone Age craft patterns extend at least locally to the time of the high sea level associated with the last interglacial, i.e. about 70 000 years BP. In the Mediterranean fringes of Africa the pre-Aurignacian and early Mousterian industries seem to belong to the same span of time. Potassium–argon dates for Middle Stone Age industries in Ethiopia, would, if accepted, imply an age of more than 150 000 years (Wendorf *et al.* 1975).

Various finite radiocarbon dates have been published for Acheulian industries, but all of these should now be treated with great scepticism, since the small amount of radio-activity detected could equally well be due to contamination. The youngest dates obtained for Acheulian industries by methods other than $^{14}$C are thorium–uranium dates of 145 000 BP from the Harounian transgression in Morocco and of 110 000 BP from Rooidam in South Africa. These are unconfirmed data but they are entirely credible and in combination with other information lead to the tentative conclusion that the Acheulian mode of stone-craft went out of use during the interval before about 70 000 to 100 000 years ago. For the moment we have to admit that we know very little about the manner in which the change occurred or about the causes of it. There is no reason to believe that there was any particularly dramatic disruption in the flow of development of the economic and social lives of the Stone Age people living in Africa during this phase of change in artifact forms.

## CHAPTER 4

# THE CULTURES OF THE MIDDLE
# PALAEOLITHIC/MIDDLE STONE AGE

### INTRODUCTION

The 'Middle Palaeolithic', to use the term current in North Africa and the Sahara, or the 'Middle Stone Age', as it is known to archaeologists working south of the desert, is that part of the prehistoric cultural record that follows the Lower Palaeolithic or Earlier Stone Age, and precedes the Upper Palaeolithic or Later Stone Age. This might seem so obvious as to be hardly worth mentioning but it is at least a statement that few archaeologists would dispute whereas attempts to define these 'Ages' more specifically – in terms of time, artifact assemblages, technological and socio-economic levels or on the basis of the associated human physical types – all result in considerable divergence of views.

In Eurasia and northern Africa, there has been a tendency to use the term 'Middle Palaeolithic' synonymously with that of the most characteristic industrial or techno-complex of the early and middle stages of the Last Glaciation, namely the Mousterian, a complex exhibiting several distinct traditions both in time and space.[1] But there are also other industrial entities that are closely related through technique and/or chronological affinities which can less easily be accommodated under the term Middle Palaeolithic. In addition, it can also now be demonstrated that the essential characteristics that constitute the Mousterian Complex began well before the early Würm Glaciation and not only extend back into the preceding interglacial episode (Eemian) but have technical origins (i.e. proto-Levallois method (see p. 255)) which are closely rooted in the Acheulian in the Middle Pleistocene. Again, it is no longer possible to identify all makers of the Mousterian Complex as Neanderthalers since Mousterian assemblages are now known to be associated with skeletal remains that are not always

[1] Several recurrent traditions of the Mousterian that make very variable use of the Levallois method are present in Europe, North Africa and the Middle East. These are known as the *Mousterian of Acheulian Tradition*, characterized by the presence of hand-axes; the *Quina–Ferrassie Mousterian* sometimes subdivided into a non-Levallois facies with a large number of side-scrapers (Quina) and a Levallois form of this facies; the *Denticulate Mousterian* with many notched and denticulated tools; and the *Typical Mousterian* which appears to combine in varying proportions most of the characteristic artifact forms (except hand-axes) of the other three traditions.

Neanderthal (*Homo sapiens neanderthalensis*) but in some cases belong to modern man (*Homo sapiens sapiens*). Bordes has demonstrated that the wide variability in the composition and technology of assemblages that have been termed Mousterian makes it impossible to define with any precision the spatial and chronological levels of the complex. More successful, he believes, would be an attempt to define a Mousterian *stage of evolution* and, when the post-Acheulian but 'non-Mousterian' traditions are also taken into account, it becomes very clear that the term 'Middle Palaeolithic' has meaning only if it is applied in the sense of a general level of cultural evolution, which may develop earlier in some regions or persist later in others. In Eurasia and northern Africa, this evolutionary stage is distinguished by certain specialized flaking techniques for the production of particular kinds of flakes and blades that were then retouched into various forms of 'light-duty' equipment. Stone artifact assemblages with individual but regularly recurring characteristics are identified as facies/variants or traditions and some believe these to be the products of genetically discrete human populations (Bordes 1961). Others hold that they represent equipment associated with certain sets of economic activities and that changing environmental factors played an important part in determining what activities were carried out, and so what tool-kits were manufactured, at any one locality (Binford and Binford 1966). Again, there are others who believe that temporal patterning does exist in some of these traditions (Mellars 1970), but evidence for evolutionary development of one variant out of another still remains to be determined.

The situation is generally similar in regard to the term 'Middle Stone Age' in sub-Saharan Africa, although considerably less is known about the complexes of this period there than about those of the Middle Palaeolithic in Eurasia. A 'Middle Stone Age', falling between the 'Earlier' and the 'Later Stone Ages' was first identified by Goodwin (1928) and was defined primarily from the use of certain techniques that were already foreshadowed by their sporadic but prior appearance in the Earlier Stone Age. Clearly, a time factor was also implied and each new 'Age' is defined as *the time when 'the new technique became dominant and replaced previous modes'* (Goodwin 1946). Assemblages were, thus, assigned to 'Ages' on the basis of certain dominant techniques and end-products[1] and within each Age, archaeological units, classified as

[1] Those of the Middle Stone Age were an accentuation of the use of the Levallois technique (see fig. 4.1) and the production of retouched sub-triangular shaped flakes and bifacial, foliate forms of tool.

*industries*, were recognized. In some cases, the industry might show more than one stage of temporal development and spatial or regional differentiation was also made on the basis of variability in tool typology and stylistic composition; Goodwin also noted that this variability was often connected with the use of different kinds of raw materials. Later, greater emphasis came to be placed on the chronological connotations of the term 'Middle Stone Age' and, when first relative and then radiometric methods of dating became more generally available, it became apparent that, within the time-range ascribed to the Middle Stone Age, there were sometimes other archaeological entities which, on morphological grounds, could be more easily classified as belonging to either the Earlier or the Later Stone Age. In an attempt to circumvent this problem a 'First' and 'Second Intermediate Period' were interpolated into the sequence before and after the Middle Stone Age respectively (J. D. Clark and Cole 1957, p. xxxiii). This, however, did nothing to clarify definitions and in 1967 (Bishop and Clark 1967, pp. 896–7) it was recommended that all of these terms should be abandoned since they were indicative neither of industrial content nor of time-stratigraphy. The 'Intermediates' have now largely disappeared but the others have tended to remain as informal terms (outside the formal nomenclature of graded units) as they still carry connotations that remain useful, but, when the chronological units of the different industrial entities and their interrelationships are better known, it may be that some closer measure of definition will become desirable and possible. Goodwin's original concept of the criteria for assemblage classification is closely comparable to Bordes' concept of a Mousterian level of evolution and it is in this sense, therefore, that these terms 'Middle Palaeolithic' and 'Middle Stone Age' still have some meaning and are used here.

The earliest appearances of both these levels of cultural patterning occur at much the same time throughout the African continent as in Eurasia. The basic techniques employed in each are the same, though there is a considerable variability, both quantitatively and stylistically, in the preferences shown for certain types of stone tools over others and in the development of special regional forms of tool. Whether Upper Palaeolithic/Later Stone Age technology supervened at much the same time in both zones remains to be determined, although it now seems increasingly probable that this was so. Within this general technological mode or level of cultural evolution[1] a number of discrete

[1] The Middle Palaeolithic/Middle Stone Age compares to 'mode 3' in the evolutionary sequence of cultural modes proposed by J. G. D. Clark (1969).

*complexes* have been recognized each of which can be subdivided into *industries* and smaller units (*phases* or *facies*) defined in accordance with the more rigid procedures for nomenclature that are receiving wider application today (Bishop and Clark 1967, pp. 890–4). Archaeologists and geomorphologists are concerned with establishing local regional sequences based on detailed studies of a few key sites that can provide the chronological and cultural framework. Sometimes these also yield evidence of socio-economic patterning and indications of a closer identification between the human populations and their exploitation of the resources of the environment, as these can be seen through the individuality of the tool-kits. Some of these regional sequences are better known than others and there are still some areas where the only available evidence comes largely from surface collections. In spite of this incompleteness, however, understanding of the antiquity of the Middle Palaeolithic/Middle Stone Age on the African continent is growing and it will eventually be possible to perceive how the local sequences correlate to produce a more precise understanding of the highly significant level of cultural evolution represented by this Age which was a time when regional patterns began to emerge and when neanderthaloid and other palaeo-anthropic populations were replaced by modern man.

## ORIGINS AND CHRONOLOGY

For clarification, let us accept the concept of *the dominant technological mode* as the basis for defining the Middle Palaeolithic/Middle Stone Age. Let us also accept that observed changes in technique and tool form are not necessarily always the result of population movements but may be a reflection of the adoption of innovative methods of tool production, on the one hand, or of the degree to which preferences or inherited methods of exploitative behaviour require to be modified to meet changes in resource availability, on the other. It may then be expected that, in some cases, artifact forms of an earlier mode (e.g. hand-axes or choppers of the Acheulian or Developed Oldowan) might continue in use in some Middle Palaeolithic/Middle Stone Age contexts while, at the other end of the range, it can be anticipated that an increasing number of Upper Palaeolithic/Later Stone Age forms will begin to make their appearance. Indeed, such trends *are* apparent in the Middle Palaeolithic/Middle Stone Age but, when it comes to establishing continuity or transitional stages either out of the Lower Palaeolithic/ Earlier Stone Age or into the Epi-Palaeolithic/Later Stone Age, this is rarely, if ever, possible. The reason for this is that the radiometric chronology is still very incomplete so that there is no means of accurate correlation between sequences at different localities and often, indeed, no way of determining the age differences between stratified assemblages at the same site. A very small number of well stratified and dated assemblages exist but in most cases the hiatus separating these assemblages from those of the succeeding mode can be seen to be considerable. When industrial innovations are adopted that represent better, more efficient ways of doing old things or the introduction of new activities, the artifact assemblages can be seen to exhibit what amounts to a sudden or dramatic change in composition over what had gone before. If, however, the number of dates were large enough and the dating techniques sufficiently precise, it would probably be found that such a seemingly 'sudden' change would, in fact, cover one or two thousand years, especially if it had been climatically induced. Moreover, it is probably unrealistic to expect that technologically transitional industries between one Age and another will ever be found since any primary context assemblage represents the range of tools and the method of working them needed for a particular set of activities during a single moment in time. When the obvious break with tradition makes it perfectly clear that innovative techniques have been adopted this carries, of course, as has already been said, no built-in implication that the population responsible for the assemblage has necessarily changed its composition.

The Middle Palaeolithic/Middle Stone Age makes its first appearance more than 100 000 years ago during the Last Interglacial (Eemian), in Africa a time of somewhat increased rainfall, warmer climate, and transgressive sea level, and the possibility exists that the beginnings of Middle Stone Age technology may be nearly 200 000 years old (see n. 1, p. 280). The most reliable dating evidence is derived from deep sea core records correlated against the thorium–uranium ($^{230}$Th/$^{234}$U) radiometric method of dating,[1] and, so far as the upper limits are concerned, from radiocarbon and by extrapolation. These show that the extremes of the Last Interglacial fall between about 125 000 and 75 000 BP (Shackleton and Kennett 1975, Shackleton and Opdyke 1973). The evidence comes both from northern Africa – the Mediterranean and Atlantic coast of Morocco – and from southern Africa, particularly from localities along the south coast. The latest assemblages that are essentially Acheulian in character, having, that is to say, a significant

---

[1] For descriptions of the various radiometric and chronometric methods of dating, the reader is referred to Bishop and Miller (1972) and to Michels (1973, pt. III, pp. 115–219).

proportion of hand-axes and/or cleavers of Acheulian type, appear to date from between 200 000 and 100 000 years ago and, although admittedly the dating evidence is very inadequate, the indications are that by 100 000 years ago the Acheulian Industrial Complex had everywhere been replaced by specialized flake industries of Middle Palaeolithic/Middle Stone Age type that sometimes used also various new forms of 'heavy-duty' equipment.[1]

At one time, before radiometric dating techniques became available, the Middle Stone Age, notably in South Africa, was believed to be younger than 10 000 years and to date to the post-Pleistocene (Söhnge, Visser and van Riet Lowe 1937). Further stratigraphic sequences and, after 1950, the advent of radiocarbon dating, suggested that the Middle Stone Age was appreciably older and broadly contemporary with the industries of the Upper Palaeolithic in Europe, having an age of about 40 000 to 13 000 BP (J. D. Clark 1962). Since 1972, however, an increasing number of older radiocarbon dates (Vogel and Beaumont 1972) and several significant studies of stratified sequences, particularly in South Africa, have pushed back the beginning of the Middle Stone Age still further, and show that its more characteristic industries had already ceased to be made by about 35 000 BP though, on the evidence of the available dates, the more evolved complex forms appear to have persisted for a further 10 000 to 15 000 years in some localities. The Middle Palaeolithic/Middle Stone Age of Africa is, therefore, now shown to be in large part the contemporary of the Middle Palaeolithic industries of Eurasia, a dating that is fully confirmed by the technology of the lithic industries.

[1] On the Moroccan coast, terrestrial sediments (Presoltanian) which are less than 200 000 years old (Butzer 1975) contain the latest Acheulian (Stage VIII) recognized on this coast. The small triangular and cordiform bifaces, cleaver flakes, scrapers and other attributes suggest, however, that this assemblage might equally well be classified as a 'Mousterian of Acheulian Tradition' and it shows, besides, considerable continuity with the earlier Acheulian assemblages at Casablanca (Freeman 1975). Comparable final or evolved Acheulian assemblages are also known from the Algerian and Tunisian plateau (El-Ma el-Abiod, Sidi Zin); the Saharan slopes of the Atlas in Morocco (Aïn Fritissa) and in the eastern desert at Bir Sahara (Schild and Wendorf 1975), but their dating is uncertain. Mousterian industries with bifaces occur in Nubia though they are, as yet, unsatisfactorily dated there; and small cordiform bifaces are also sometimes present with Aterian industries. Typologically evolved Acheulian assemblages in Africa south of the Sahara also remain largely undated. The Acheulian horizons at the Kalambo Falls are certainly older than 110 000 BP, probably more than twice that age (Lee, Bada and Peterson 1976) and contain a number of scraper forms that closely resemble those of the Middle Stone Age. On the high veld in the eastern Cape, specialized Acheulian (Fauresmith) from Rooidam dates to between 100 000 and 200 000 BP (see chapter 1) and, similarly, contains tool forms that become dominant in the succeeding Middle Stone Age.

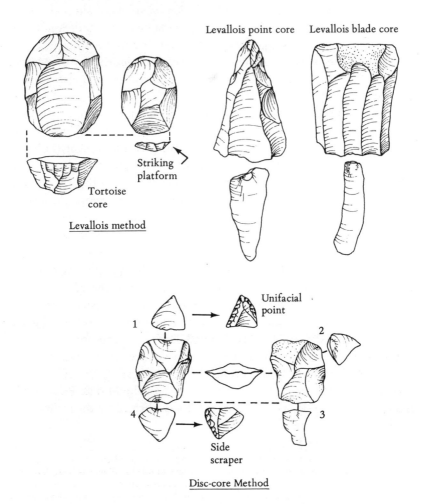

Fig. 4.1 Specialized core techniques of the Middle Pleistocene/Middle Stone Age to show flake forms obtained from three different kinds of core prepared by the Levallois method and those resulting from the use of the disc-core method. (After J. D. Clark 1970, fig. 29.)

## TECHNOLOGY

The industrial traditions that fall within the time-range with which we are dealing are characterized, in particular, by two specialized methods of flake production known as the *Levallois* and the *disc core* techniques. Both are designed to minimize wastage of raw material, especially where this had to be carried from 'quarry sites' to occupation camps several kilometres distant and conservation of material was important (McBurney and Hey 1955, pp. 168–9). The Levallois method used during the Middle Palaeolithic/Middle Stone Age is a refinement on the 'proto-Levallois' technique that is found with certain Acheulian industries. The raw material is often more carefully selected and the cores are generally smaller and better prepared, the flakes removed being light and often thin, allowing them to be retouched to form a range of scraping, sawing and cutting edges and pointed tools. Most of these Levallois cores show some form of radial preparation of the surface from which the flake will be removed; striking platforms are usually prepared and exhibit a varying number of preparation facets. One characteristic type of core is ellipsoid in plan form, another sub-triangular, another more rectangular, and the purpose of each was to remove a single large flake, the shape of which was predetermined by the shape and flaking direction on the release face of the core. Thus, oval/ellipsoid Levallois flakes were removed from the classic 'tortoise cores'; triangular, Levallois points are the product of the sub-triangular cores and parallel-sided blades and triangular flake forms come from the sub-rectangular Levallois blade cores. After the removal of each flake, it was necessary to re-prepare the flaking surface before a new flake could be struck and, clearly, some wastage of material ensued. With the disc or Mousterian core technique, wastage was further reduced in that the core was radially flaked by alternately removing flakes from first one and then the other face round the circumference of the core. The flakes removed are often short and triangular in plan form, sometimes simulating Levallois forms (pseudo-Levallois), and they were similarly retouched into side-scrapers, points, etc. In certain regions, notably Ethiopia and Malawi, there is evidence to suggest that when they became too small to continue to be used by this method, cores that began as Levallois were sometimes further reduced to disc cores by flaking of this kind. It is occasionally possible to demonstrate this on a workshop floor by reassembling the flakes onto the core.

Regional variations on these basic core forms are often distinguishable (Crew 1975). In Nubia and in Ethiopia, a special form of sub-triangular Mousterian core, known as a *Nubian core* (Nubian core type II) (see figs. 4.3.15 and 4.6.8) was used, in which the preparation is characterized by the removal from the apex, or distal end, of two flakes, one down each converging side edge of the core, prior to the removal of the main flake at the proximal end. In Nubia also a kind of Levallois core with the platform on a side rather than end (para-Levallois) is common. In the Orange River basin in South Africa, both single- and double-ended Levallois cores for blades are general forms. Again, sub-triangular cores with fine radial flaking yielding thin ellipsoid and triangular flakes are characteristic of the Tshangulan Industry in Rhodesia and of the final Lupemban in the Zaïre basin.

As well as the specialized Levallois and disc-core methods, flakes and blades were also produced from non-Levallois cores, as in the Orange River basin, for example. Such cores may show one or two platforms which may be in the same plane or opposed and some of them approach the prismatic core of Upper Palaeolithic type (fig. 4.10.6). There is similar variability in the flakes and blades, in the nature of retouch and in the preferred tool forms which makes it possible to recognize regional traditions. As will be seen, these traditions show that there is a greater degree of continuity between stratified assemblages at a single site or within a limited locality through time than can be observed between contemporary assemblages from different geographical regions. The differing properties of the predominant raw materials used for manufacturing stone tools in the various localities is likely to have played an important part in establishing modes in tool forms in these regional expressions. It seems likely, therefore, that the Middle Palaeolithic/ Middle Stone Age populations in the continent may have consisted of a number of independent groups – all with similar life-styles and possessing a common knowledge and level of technology but each, by virtue of the low population density and the semi-isolation in which they lived due to geographical and other factors, developing its own particular preferences in equipment forms and ways of exploiting the selected resources of the environment. This can best be seen by examining more closely the cultural sequences in the main regions of the continent.

## NORTH AFRICA

### The Maghrib and the Sahara (figs. 4.2–4)

The winter rainfall climate of north-west Africa supports a Mediterranean pattern of vegetation. On the coastal plains and parts of lower elevation is found open and dense maquis vegetation alternating with cork-oak forest and open steppe. This is replaced on the Mediterranean slopes of the plateau and in the Atlas by montane scrub forest and on the plateau proper by high grassland with patches of forest and maquis surviving as relics on the higher ridges and ranges. Proceeding

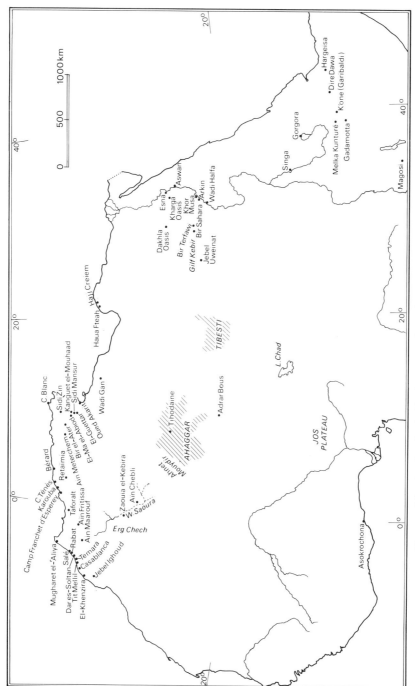

Fig. 4.2   Map showing the sites in the northern half of the continent referred to in the text.

Camp Francher d'Esperey
C Ténès
Karouba
Bérard
C Blanc
Sidi Zin
Kanguet el-Mouhaad
Sidi Mansur
Retaïmia
Ain Meterchem
Bir el-Ater
Bir el-Abiod
El-Guettar
El-Ma el-Guetar
Oued Akrit
Wadi Gan
Haua Fteah
Hajj Creiem

Mugharet el-'Aliya
Dar es-Soltan
Salé
Tit Mellil
Temara
El-Khenzira
Casablanca
Rabat
Jebel Ighoud
Taforalt
Ain Fritissa
Ain Maarouf
Zaoua el-Kebira
Ain Chebli
W Saoura
Erg Chech

Afnet
Mouydir
AHAGGAR
Tihodaine
Adrar Bous
TIBESTI
L. Chad
JOS
PLATEAU
Asokrochona

Dakhla
Oasis
Esna
Aswan
Kharga
Oasis
Khor
Musa
Bir Sahara
Arkin
Wadi Halfa
Bir Terfawi
Gilf Kebir
Jebel
Uwenat

Singa
Gorgora
Magosi
Melka Kunturé
Gadamotta
K'one (Garibaldi)
Hargeisa
Dire Dawa

1000 km
500
0

20°
40°
20°
0°
20°
40°
0°
20°
40°
0°
20°

257

southward, on the Saharan side of the plateau the grassland is replaced by desert steppe giving place to true desert in the south. During the warm, temperate Eemian Interglacial, the Mediterranean forest most probably expanded considerably onto the plateau. The pollen record for this time in the Maghrib is not as well known as is that in the Sahara, but the pollen diagram from the spring site of El-Guettar in southern Tunisia, associated with several Middle Palaeolithic levels, clearly shows that the Mediterranean vegetation was able to spread into southern Tunisia during Mousterian times whereas the site today is on the border between plateau and desert steppe.[1] Pollen counts from the Oued el-Akarit site, east of El-Guettar and on the coast, similarly show the presence of Mediterranean-type forest.[2] With the onset of the last (Würm) Glaciation, after 75 000 BP, the Atlas Mountains became glaciated and the vegetation belts were lowered by more than a thousand metres. Grassland replaced forest and maquis on the plateau and coastal plain, and there was much dune formation on the coast and in the northern Sahara. Southern Tunisia experienced a semi-arid climate with cold winters (Van Campo and Coque 1960) and evidence for seasonal frost activity is to be seen in the development of screes and exfoliated pieces of rock in the deposits of caves and rock-shelters. The Maghrib, during the early Würm, would have been cold and windy, but, because of the lowered evaporation rate, there was no lack of surface water (Butzer 1971, ch. 19, and chapter 1 of this volume).

The fauna associated with Middle Palaeolithic occupation sites in the Maghrib is predominantly one of Ethiopian species with elephant, rhinoceros, zebra, wart-hog, large antelopes, such as wildebeest, hartebeest, eland, reedbuck, the extinct giant buffalo, and even hippopotamus on the Moroccan coast, as well as other species of northern African and/or Levantine origin of which the most important were pig (*Sus scrofa*), aurochs (*Bos primigenius*), a giant deer (*Cervus algericus*), the barbary sheep (*Ammotragus lervia*), several species of gazelle and the wild ass. The presence of Eurasiatic immigrants into the fauna of north-west Africa is seen as being due to the existence of a corridor for migration along the south-east Mediterranean coastlands by which species were able to pass from the Levant into northern Africa and *vice versa* (Jaeger 1975).

[1] The ratio of arboreal to non-arboreal pollens fluctuated between 4.4% and about 35% with grasses and compositae predominant and with cedar, live and deciduous oaks and cypress (Leroi-Gourhan 1958).

[2] The arboreal pollens amount to 2% with pine well represented (Van Campo and Coque 1960).

In the Sahara during the Eemian Interglacial and Würm Glaciation, the vegetation patterns are known from a number of pollen studies carried out mostly in the north-east, central and south-western parts. These all show evidence of a less arid climate and, contemporary with the glaciation, lowered temperatures and lower evaporation rates that allowed the dry Mediterranean vegetation to establish itself on the higher massifs (Ahaggar, Tibesti, etc.) and lakes and swamps to form in the depressions, round which Middle Palaeolithic groups were able to settle. This more favourable climatic regimen persisted, no doubt with fluctuations, until about 20 000 years ago when a period of severe aridity set in that lasted for about 10 000 years. Since no assemblages are with certainty dated to this time, the aridity must have rendered large parts of the desert and the marginal grasslands of the Sahel to the north and south untenable as places for human occupation, so that some population movement can be expected to have taken place at this time.

The Middle Palaeolithic of the Maghrib and Sahara is usually divided into two broad complexes, the *Mousterian* and the *Aterian*, though at many sites it is not always possible to be certain which of the two is represented. There is some stratigraphic evidence to support the belief that the Aterian is a direct derivative of the Maghrib Mousterian but the evidence for the antiquity of the Aterian is growing and it is probable that the two tool-kits may have been manufactured simultaneously for a time, the differences being activity-orientated.

The Mousterian of the Maghrib (fig. 4.3.1–8) is based on the use of the Levallois and disc-core techniques but the assemblages show varying degrees of Levallois debitage, and a preponderance of several forms of side-scraper (*racloirs*) together with a lesser number of Mousterian points, denticulates, end-scrapers, truncated and naturally backed pieces and rare burins. It compares, therefore, with the Typical Mousterian tradition of Western Europe. The distribution of the Mousterian in the Maghrib is comparatively limited[1] suggesting that some overall reduction in the human populations may have taken place there at this time, though why this should have been so is not clear since many Mousterian sites of this period are known from Spain and other southern European countries. Most of the Mousterian sites are situated on the plateau or inland and only two are known from the coast.

[1] It is known from only a small number of sites, only ten of which are stratigraphically controlled – six in Tunisia, three in Morocco and one in Algeria – although there are some twenty more surface assemblages that are typologically Mousterian. From the same area there are 180 pre-Mousterian and 198 post-Mousterian (Aterian) sites.

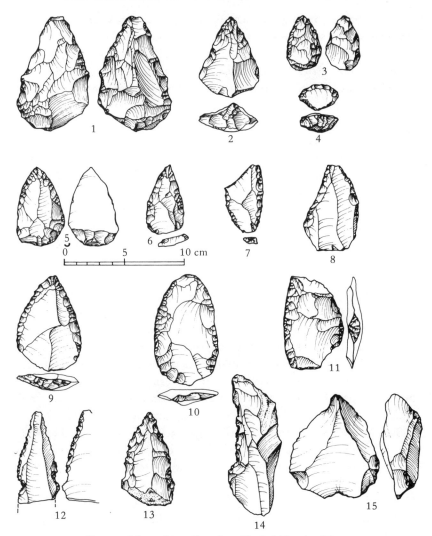

Fig. 4.3   Mousterian artifacts from North African localities.

*Sidi Zin*
1, 3  Diminutive bifaces
2  Mousterian point
4  Side-scraper

*Jebel Irhoud*
5  Mousterian point with basal retouch to
   remove bulb and platform
6  Mousterian point
7  Double side-scraper on Levallois flake
8  Convergent scraper

*Hajj Creiem*
9  Mousterian point on Levallois flake
10  Double side-scraper on Levallois flake
11  Transverse scraper on Levallois flake

*Denticulate Mousterian from the Nile Valley*
12–14  Denticulates from Site N2, Dongola
   Reach, Sudanese Nubia

*Wadi Halfa*
15  Nubian core of the Nubian Mousterian,
   Type A, from Site 1038 Wadi Halfa area

(Nos. 1–4 after McBurney (1960), 5–8 after Balout (1965b), 9–11 after McBurney and Hey (1955),
12–14 after Wendorf and Schild (1975) and 15 after Marks (1968).)

At Casablanca, on the Moroccan coast, an assemblage classified as 'Mousterian of Acheulian Tradition' has been found (Freeman 1975; see also n. 1 on p. 253) and again at Tit Mellil, on the inland side of Casablanca, a 'Mousterian of Acheulian Tradition' underlies Aterian layers in fossil spring sediments associated with remains of elephant, rhinoceros and hippopotamus (Antoine 1939). At the High Cave (Mughwret el-'Aliya) at Tangier, the industry from the lowest cultural layer (Layer 9) under the Aterian can probably be assigned to a Mousterian, since it contained no tanged artifacts though two small bifacially flaked points are present.

The most important Mousterian site in the Maghrib is at Jebel Irhoud (or Ighoud) between Safi and Marrakech, where mining operations for barium exposed a cave occupation with a typical Mousterian industry associated with a fauna of grassland species, two Neanderthal crania and some hearths. The industry comprises predominantly side-scrapers and Mousterian points with a much smaller number of end-scrapers and other forms (Balout 1955, 1965a, b) (fig. 4.3.5–8). No typical tanged Aterian points were present but the way in which some of the faceted striking platforms tend to curve over on the proximal ends of the side edges of the Mousterian flakes might have given rise to the idea of the tang, which is a specialized Aterian invention. Jebel Irhoud has produced the only radiocarbon date for a Mousterian industry, namely, > 32 000 BP (Ennouchi 1962).

In eastern Morocco the large cave at Taforalt provides the best evidence for the Mousterian which is there stratified below four Aterian layers. The lowest archaeological horizon (Layer G) yielded an assemblage of Levallois flakes, side-scrapers, some denticulated and notched pieces and a crude (Tayacian) point is silicified sandstone which contrasts with the Aterian assemblages with tanged and bifaced points made mostly in flint that are found in the levels immediately overlying. The Taforalt evidence also makes it likely that some of the industries in quartz from sites on the Algerian coast, particularly the assemblage from Cape Ténès (Lorcin 1961–2), where they overlie Tyrrhenian beach deposits and are overlain in turn by Iberomaurusian assemblages, may also belong to a pre-Aterian/Mousterian stage, though this is, as yet, unproven (Balout 1965a, b). The cave site of Retaimia in the hill country south of Oran contained an assemblage of 'typical Mousterian' form and is the most representative site of this stage yet known from Algeria, the most common retouched pieces being side-scrapers and Mousterian points.

In northern Tunisia, Acheulian horizons at the fossil spring site of Sidi Zin are capped by a tufa containing a small numer of rather crudely made artifacts ascribed to the Mousterian; these include side-scrapers, thick points, three small bifaces and several abruptly retouched pieces of flint (fig. 4.3.1–4). At Cap Blanc a raised beach yielded flakes and a disc in quartzite and in red sands, overlying this horizon, Aterian artifacts are found (Vaufrey 1955, pp. 102–3). At another coastal site, but in southern Tunisia (Oued el-Akarit) and again situated close to fossil springs, the Mousterian, without any tanged pieces, is contained within clays sealed by more than four metres of silt (*limon*). Inland, in southern Tunisia, are several more sites where a Mousterian assemblage can be recognized in circumstances that sometimes suggest it is older than the local Aterian, notably at Sidi Mansur.[1] If there is continuity and perhaps contemporaneity between the Mousterian and the Aterian, as is generally believed, then it is to be expected that the earlier stages of this Middle Palaeolithic continuum will exhibit a mode of Mousterian form whereas the later stages will emphasize the Aterian aspects. Thus, while the Mousterian forms predominate in the earlier assemblages, a variable blade element is present with the Levallois and disc-core techniques in the Aterian, and Upper Palaeolithic elements of the tool-kit increase in importance in the later stages. The Aterian is, therefore, characterized by varying proportions of tanged and bifacially retouched tools (Group I); by Mousterian forms – side-scrapers, points, etc. – (Group II); and by tools more typical of the Upper Palaeolithic – end-scrapers, burins, borers and backed forms (Group III). If the Aterian can no longer be considered as an extended Mousterian contemporary with the European Upper Palaeolithic (Vaufrey 1955, p. 405) neither is it simply a Mousterian with the addition of tanged tools though the Aterian is characterized in particular by the presence of tanged or pedunculate flakes worked into points and other specialized tool forms.

The tang is an invention of great significance, for it is the earliest indisputable evidence for the intentional hafting of tools. Although Mousterian sites in Eurasia and Middle Stone Age assemblages south of the Sahara have yielded flakes with their striking platforms removed, presumably to facilitate hafting, the most convincing evidence of

---

[1] Sometimes also designated Mousterian are the sites of Aïn Metherchem and El-Guettar in southern Tunisia, but, if the presence of only one tanged point of Aterian type is sufficient cause to assign the assemblage to the Aterian, then these industries would more correctly be assigned to that complex.

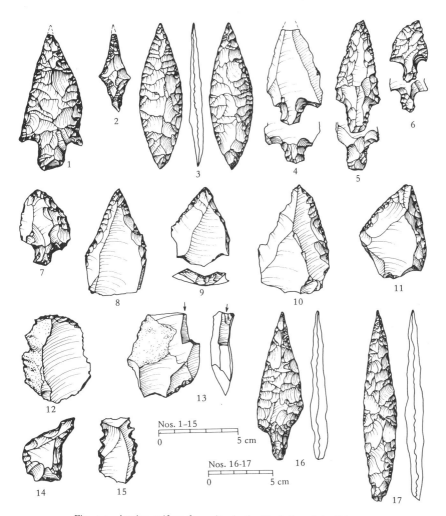

Fig. 4.4 Aterian artifacts from sites in the Maghrib and the Sahara.

*Mugharet el-'Aliya, Tangier*
1 *Pointe marocaine*

*Tit Mellil, Morocco, Zone A*
2 *Pointe pseudo-saharienne*

*Aïn Fritissa*
3 Bifacial foliate point

*Zaouia el-Kebira, Saoura Valley, north-west Sahara*
4 Levallois flake with tang
5–6 Tanged, triangular points with invasive retouch

7 End-scraper on a tanged Levallois flake
8 Mousterian point on a Levallois point
9 Retouched Levallois point
10 Convex side-scraper
11 Double side-scraper
12 End-scraper
13 Angle burin on a snapped flake
14 Canted borer
15 Denticulate on a Levallois flake

*Adrar Bous, Niger, Central Sahara*
16 Tanged bifacial point
17 Lanceolate bifacial point

(No. 1 after Howe (1967), 2 after Antoine (1939), 3 after Tixier (1960), 4–15 after N. Chavaillon (1971) and 16–17 after J. D. Clark (1975).)

hafting is the Aterian tang, a north-west African invention that is found spread throughout the whole of that region of the continent and a very large part of the Sahara. It also confirms that the various forms of proximal reduction and retouch found on artifacts from other regions are indeed indications that stone tools have now begun to be mounted in various ways in those areas, thus considerably improving their efficiency. One direct result of the widespread adoption of hafting techniques throughout the Old World from this time is the general reduction in the overall dimensions of the stone implements of Middle Palaeolithic tool-kits since the flaked stone artifacts now formed only the working (cutting, scraping, etc.) parts of the tool and could be made correspondingly lighter and smaller. A tang may either imply a socket – a broken bone or a reed, for example – into which the stem is fitted and which forms a handle and perhaps a collar to join the stone working end to a wooden handle or shaft, or, again, a split wooden haft may be used; but, in all cases, the stone is held securely by the aid of mastic and/or binding. The most characteristic tanged tools of the Aterian are points, but several other forms of tool also exhibit tangs (scrapers, burins, etc.) so that the tang must be considered as a general hafting device and not simply as one for mounting points, with the inference that they may have been the heads of projectile weapons.

If typology is an acceptable indication of the chronological position of an assemblage within an industrial continuum, then one of the earliest known assemblages to contain an Aterian tanged piece is at the site of El-Guettar[1] where, under 7 m of deposits and in the middle of an artificial pile of limestone balls near the bottom of the sequence, was found one typical Aterian tanged point, and a second tanged piece (a canted scraper) came from a slightly higher level. This unique find of a pile of stone spheroids, some artificial, some natural, is 1.30 m in diameter at the base and 0.75 m high. Mixed in with it were a large

[1] Here several assemblages of Mousterian aspect are found stratified within *chott* (salt lake) deposits, partly cut through by spring activity and intercalated with the sandy deposits within the eye. They show characteristics of both the Typical Mousterian (of La Ferrassie type) from France and the Levallois–Mousterian of Palestine (Gruet 1954). Similar to the El-Guettar Mousterian/Aterian is that from Aïn Metherchem on the plateau to the north where two localities are known with a single tanged, canted scraper. In the Maghrib, the Aterian proper is best known from Algeria, in particular from the plateau around Tebessa, close to the Tunisian border, and at many coastal sites. The type-site is Bir el-Ater in the Oued Djebanna in eastern Algeria where *Helix* shells associated with a 'Middle Aterian' have been dated to > 35 000 BP. The 'Djebannian' form of the 'typical Aterian' (based on values from Khanguet el-Mouhaad), while generally preserving its Mousterian flavour, is characterized also by a greater number of points with Aterian tangs, end-scrapers and burins which comprise nearly one-fifth of the total number of tools (Tixier 1967, p. 795).

4.1 1 The pile of sixty spheroids, retouched flake tools, *débitage* and broken bones found resting on a narrow ledge in the lower levels of the fossil spring at El-Guettar. (After Gruet 1955, p. 460.)

2 The thirty spheroids found together in a fossil spring at Windhoek, Namibia, and two flaked tools in quartz from the same site. (After Gruet and Zelle 1955, p. 459.)

*facing p.* 264

number of retouched flint tools and manufacturing waste together with many teeth, splinters and pounded fragments of bone. The circumference at the base appeared to have been ringed by a number of larger stones. This cairn was resting on a natural step adjacent to the central eye of the spring (plate 4.1.1). A magical significance, a kind of cairn of offerings to the spirit of the spring (since some of the finest retouched tools lay on or near the top of the pile) has been suggested as the purpose behind this feature. Less appealingly, but not impossibly, it could be an accumulation of occupation waste that had either fallen into the eye from an adjacent living-floor, or been intentionally piled in the spring since, if this lay within a fissure well below the surface, it might have been necessary to have a place to stand to collect the water. It is still surprising, however, that so many spheroids (precise number not stated) should have been found together, since, although spheroids are known from a number of other Middle Palaeolithic/Middle Stone Age assemblages, there is only one other site where they are found in similar numbers (see p. 340).

Partly on stratigraphic, partly on typological evidence, several stages of Aterian have been recognized by earlier workers but, if stratigraphic evidence remains the most convincing proof, there is justification only for two, or, if the somewhat controversial assemblages from El-Guettar and other sites are considered to be early Aterian, then a three-fold subdivision would appear justified, the earliest being in part contemporary with the Mousterian (Ferring 1975).

On the Mediterranean coast, the Aterian is now known from several sites to be more than 30 000 years old.[1] The late Aterian in the coastal region, and elsewhere for that matter, is inadequately dated. The assemblages of this stage (fig. 4.4.1–2) comprise relatively large numbers of tanged forms, often small, and bifacially worked points and there are significant numbers of Levallois blades; end-scrapers often predominate over side-scrapers. At Taforalt, in eastern Morocco, two lower Aterian assemblages (Layers H and F) are less developed than is the uppermost (Layer D) which, by reason of the number of bifacial points, the greater frequency of end-scrapers and tanged pieces, might be considered late.

---

[1] At Berard, on the Algerian coast, the complex occurs in a red sandy silt (*limon rouge*) together with burned limpet (*Patella*) shells dated to 31 800 ± 1900 BP within a stratified sequence of consolidated dune sands and *limons rouges*. In a still lower *limon rouge* beneath two regressional consolidated dunes, further artifacts occur immediately overlying and in contact with the 6–8 m (neo-Tyrrhenian) beach, suggesting that the earliest Aterian is likely to date well before the thirtieth millennium BP. Further west on the Oran coast, Aterian is again found (Camp Franchet d'Esperey; Karouba) resting on the beach and in the immediately overlying *limon rouge* suggesting an age in the early stages of the Last Glaciation.

From this level two radiocarbon dates of about 32 400 BP and about 34 600 BP suggest that the Aterian tradition may have come to an end in the Maghrib shortly after this time (Roche 1972). In the Atlantic coastal areas of Morocco the Aterian occurs again in caves[1] and on open sites, including fossil springs. This Moroccan Aterian shows some regional differences from that in Algeria, namely, in the increased percentages of tanged forms and the low frequencies of foliate points and end-scrapers. At Dar es-Soltan the lower industry is dated to > 30 000 BP and the upper horizon to > 27 000 BP.[2] Inland, in central Morocco, a 'typical Aterian' assemblage from Aïn Maarouf has been dated to 32 000 ± 600 BP and another spring site, Aïn Fritissa (fig. 4.4.3), perhaps shows best the earliest phase of the regional Aterian here.

Throughout the Sahara desert the Aterian is spread generally north of latitude 15° N, westward into Mauritania and eastward into the oases of the eastern desert, though this tradition is not yet recorded convincingly from the Nile Valley itself. This distribution has been the cause of the Aterian's being described as a desert-orientated development. It is found here almost entirely on open sites adjacent to lacustrine or swamp sediments in the depressions and valleys of the main water courses.[3] In the Ahaggar itself, the Aterian belongs somewhere in this 'wetter' interval after the post-Acheulian arid period (Rognon 1967).

It is of interest that, as yet, no convincing Mousterian sites have been reported from the central or western Sahara. And, since there is a stratigraphic break between the Upper Acheulian and the Aterian (e.g. in the Saoura and Erg Tihodaine) it seems probable that the appearance of the Aterian can be interpreted as evidence of repopulation of the desert. Unfortunately, the majority of the assemblages there are surface collections and they are mostly undated. The few dated assemblages

[1] In each of the caves of El-Khenzira and Dar es-Soltan, stratified over deposits of the 6–8-m (Ouljian = Tyrrhenian II) beach, were two horizons of Aterian occupation; at the former these are what have been termed 'typical Aterian' and, at the latter, the upper assemblage is typologically evolved and late.

[2] The evolved form of the Aterian in this level is comparable to that from the High Cave at Tangier (Layers 5 and 6) and is characterized by finely-made bifacial foliate and tanged forms of point (*pointe marocaine; pointe pseudo-saharienne*) as well as the more usual range of artifacts. Its age is in general agreement with that indicated by the dates for the late Aterian from Taforalt. At the Tit Mellil fossil spring, again, two stratified Aterian levels occur, in the upper of which these evolved point forms are also found.

[3] Caution needs to be exercised in correlating Aterian assemblages with laterally contiguous lacustrine sediments, unless direct stratigraphic association can be proved. Thus, there is no proof of the association of Aterian with the often-quoted date from Fachi in the Chad drainage of 21 350 ± 350 BP. Dates from the north-west (Erg Chech and Ahnet–Mouydir basin) show that the lakes were already in existence by 35 000 years ago (Conrad 1969).

show, however, that the Aterian in the desert belongs to a similar time-range to that found in the Maghrib, namely, from somewhere earlier than 45 000 years ago to more than 30 000 years ago.

In the north-western Sahara, the most important localities are situated in the Saoura valley where they consist of habitation sites stratigraphically located in the sedimentary cycle correlated with the Würm Glaciation in Europe (Saouran units 1 and 2: see J. Chavaillon (1964)). Dates from the later part of the sequence give minimal ages of > 38 000 and > 39 000 BP (Alimen, Beucher and Conrad 1966). The assemblage from Zaouria el-Kebira (fig. 4.4.4–15) has relatively high values of tanged forms and denticulate pieces; end-scrapers are relatively more common and the bifacial foliate is absent. This increased percentage of tanged forms and of end- as opposed to side-scrapers appears to be a characteristic of the Aterian in the north-western parts of the Sahara (N. Chavaillon 1971).

Sites north and west of the Ahaggar massif show characteristics similar to those of the 'Djebanna facies' (see n. 1, p. 264) in the type area of Algeria but with increased numbers of tanged points and other implements and, in particular, large foliate point forms. One such site is at Aïn Chebli in the foothills west of the depression into which the Saoura formerly drained (Mery and Tixier 1972); here choppers are also an important tool type. Similar assemblages are again found further to the east and north around former lakes such as at Erg Tihodaine (Arambourg and Balout 1955) and at Meniet (Hugot 1963). The numbers of bifacial and tanged points and the end-scraper values suggest that these are later rather than earlier Aterian assemblages and may be termed an Upper Aterian of Saharan tradition.

Further south and east, in the central Sahara, a number of sites are known, perhaps the most important being at Adrar Bous where camp and workshop sites are situated around the edges of a large swampy depression and lake (J. D. Clark, Williams and Smith 1975). Here the Aterian is stratified within about 2 m of silts associated with an old soil horizon and overlain by old dune deposits. The upper part of the silts has been deflated and the artifacts show a high degree of abrasion and polishing by wind, indicating that the Aterian occupation was terminated and followed by a period of severe aridity that can tentatively be equated with that recorded in the Chad basin between 22 000 and 12 000 years ago. The Adrar Bous Aterian (fig. 4.4.16–17) shares regional traits in common with the Aterian sites in the south central Sahara and in northern Tchad, in particular, in the presence of large bifacial foliate, even lanceolate, points and bifacial forms with tangs. The preferred material is a fine, chert-like silicified vitric tuff which, so far as is known, does not occur locally but had to be imported from more than 60 km away. The Levallois technique for flakes, points and blades predominates, but there are also blades from non-Levallois cores. Side-scrapers are the commonest scraper forms and characteristic is a double side-scraper, often strangulated, on a blade. Denticulate values are low, end-scrapers are rare as also are burins and spheroids. The only recognizable 'feature' at the Aterian sites at Adrar Bous was what appeared to be a game lookout situated on a hill-top overlooking one of the main sites and the swamp to the south. It consisted of a circular area about 2 m in diameter, cleared of rocks, in which were a number of artifacts, while others lay close by among the adjacent rocks. The use of game-viewing vantage points on the hills at this time receives some confirmation also from the excavation of a fine Aterian lanceolate on the top of another hill at the northern side of the massif (cf. fig. 4.17).

Adrar Bous has, in addition, produced one stratified site overlying an Acheulian which may be older than the Aterian assemblages described above. It is made in rhyolite and vitric tuff, and most of the tools are side-scrapers, together with denticulate and notched forms; only one tanged and one bifacially flaked piece are doubtfully associated. The usual Levallois debitage contains a number of both large flakes and blades. Whether this Adrar Bous 'Mousterioid' assemblage can be classified within the Mousterian must await further excavation, but its pre-Aterian age is fairly well established on stratigraphic grounds and the Mousterian is met with again in the western desert of Egypt where it has been known for some time from surface collections from the Gilf el-Kebir, Jebel Uweinat and other localities. Only recently, however, have excavations provided evidence of its age and associations and its relationship to the Aterian.

The Mousterian occurs in the lacustrine and shore deposits in depressions fed by springs at Bir Sahara and Bir Terfawi, now one of the most desolate areas of the western desert. Its appearance follows a period of aridity during which the springs that attracted Acheulian man dried up, and the oldest Mousterian tools occur in the topmost levels of this old dune deposit. Five successive Mousterian horizons were recognized and the sites are all large, homogeneous occupation areas with considerable numbers of artifacts, though no special working or other activity areas could be distinguished. The assemblages show a heavy preponderance of denticulate and notched forms which place them clearly in the Denticulate Mousterian tradition, though at one site the addition of a component of Typical Mousterian tradition may have functional implications. This emphasis on denticulate forms associated with the western desert prehistoric population exists even into the Neolithic. In offshore deposits, collections of bone waste from a supposedly adjacent occupation floor showed that Mousterian man shared the area with the white rhinoceros, an extinct camel, the wild ass and the giant buffalo. Two dates are available, $> 41\,500$ BP and $40\,750 \pm 3270$ BP (Schild and Wendorf 1975).

There is evidence that the Aterian is separated from the Mousterian at these sites by a further period of aeolian activity and dunes, dune sands and salt marsh sediments separate the two lacustrine episodes at Bir Sahara where the whole sequence probably lies beyond the limits of the radiocarbon dating method.[1] At Bir Terfawi, the correlated upper lacustrine sediments contain three horizons with Aterian tools. One of these is associated with clustered concentrations of animal bones, covering an overall area of about 6000 sq. m, and suggesting that Aterian man killed and butchered these animals in the shallow waters of the lake; many retouched tools, mostly large denticulates, are associated with these bone concentrations. Among the animals represented, besides those referred to with the Mousterian, are large and small gazelles, wart-hog, jackal and ostrich. The same stratigraphic unit gave a date of $44\,190 \pm 1380$ BP (Wendorf and Schild 1979), which again is probably beyond the limits of the method. Two of the assemblages have many denticulate pieces, while another had a greater number of Typical Mousterian forms, with which also there are the characteristic bifacial foliates and rare tanged pieces.

Nearer the Nile, the oases of Dakhla and Kharga have yielded both Mousterian and Aterian assemblages, but they can be stratigraphically distinguished only at the latter site where they are associated with mound springs in the floors of the oasis and with the tufas on the scarp. The Mousterian is strongly dependent on the Levallois method but has produced very few retouched tools. Typologically the Aterian is a late form characterized by Levallois flakes and points, bifacial foliates, rare tanged pieces and end-scrapers but no side-scrapers (Caton Thompson 1952, pp. 81–9 and 128–32). It is the furthest east that an Aterian assemblage has been certainly recorded. At all these western desert sites

---

[1] The upper freshwater lacustrine series at Bir Sahara gave a date of $30\,870 \pm 1000$ BP but was possibly contaminated by younger carbonates since the top of the unit gave a date of $> 44\,700$ BP.

the evidence indicates some local rainfall (as at Kharga Oasis), suggesting a dry steppe environment with shallow lakes and swamps fed by springs in the depressions which supported abundant plant and animal life.

## Northern Libya

To the north in Cyrenaica, the long and important cultural sequence found differs in several important respects from that which we have been considering. The industries of the Eemian Interglacial and of the Last Glaciation are best seen from the excavations in the cave of Haua Fteah near the coast, west of Derna. This site has provided the longest stratified and radiometrically dated sequence in the whole of North Africa (McBurney 1967, pp. 75–105). The occupation deposits in the cave were tested to a depth of over 13 m of which all below the 5.5-m level is assigned to the Middle Palaeolithic. Below the level (Layer 33) of radiocarbon-dated horizons, the time-scale is based on isotopic calibration between the marine shells representing food waste in the cave deposits and deep sea core records from the central and eastern Mediterranean, correlated also with cores from the Atlantic, and checked against climatic indications provided by the deep sea cores, mammalian faunas and the sedimentology of the cave deposits.

The climatic record at Haua Fteah shows that, prior to the Mousterian, (or Levallois–Mousterian, which is the term that has been used to describe this Cyrenaican tradition of the Middle Palaeolithic), there was a long period of warmer climate, the contemporary industry being known as Pre-Aurignacian. The earliest Levallois–Mousterian first appears at the end of this time when the climate was still temperate, continues through a time when the climate was appreciably colder than today and gives way to the first appearance of the Upper Palaeolithic (Dabban) in a short temperate episode about 40 000 years ago. These climatic fluctuations are well seen at other localities in the Middle East and Europe and can be correlated respectively with the Eemian Interglacial, the early Würm Glaciation and the warmer episode between the early and main Würm. The early Levallois–Mousterian can be seen to make its appearance, therefore, about 75 000 to 80 000 years ago. This industry is characterized by many discoidal cores and a high percentage of faceting and Levallois flakes coming also from small radially-prepared Levallois cores; blade forms are, by contrast, rare. The finished tools are mostly side-scrapers and Mousterian points with some notched forms. The early assemblage (Layer 34) with high values for end-scrapers and burins also has a significant but rare bifacial foliate point constituent. In general, therefore, the Cyrenaican Mousterian shows a number of broad similarities with those of Palestine and the Zagros Mountains. A characteristic also are the pebbles with evidence of pitting and cutting (*compresseurs*) that may have served as anvils on which tools were retouched by indirect percussion or, perhaps, as the anvil/hammer used with the bipolar flaking method. A series of hearths are present throughout the Levallois–Mousterian levels and the artifacts appear to be grouped around them, as in settlement sites. There were also found two Neanderthal jaw fragments, one of which dates to 45 050 ± 3200 BP.

In contrast, the industry below the Levallois–Mousterian is strikingly different. It belongs within the Interglacial and therefore probably dates from between about 125 000 and 80 000 years ago. It consists almost entirely of blades struck by direct percussion, many of which have been utilized while some have been further retouched to form burins and backed knives. There is also a little evidence for bifacial hand-axe technique; the Levallois method is very rare indeed. One particularly interesting bone piece is believed to be part of a flute associated with this Pre-Aurignacian industry which, in northern Africa, is known only from the Haua Fteah. However, similar assemblages occur on the Levantine coast and it is known also in inland Syria where it is succeeded by an industry (Jabrudian) with many side-scrapers and diminutive hand-axe forms struck by direct percussion, with minimal traces of the Levallois method. The appearance and subsequent disappearance of this predominantly blade industry at this early time is hard to interpret and whether it has an ecological/functional base, or whether it implies ethnic movements, cannot be determined at this time. At Haua Fteah, besides the remains of terrestrial animals, the food waste with the Pre-Aurignacian is characterized by numbers of seashells which thus represent some of the oldest evidence for the use of marine resources yet known.

The Pre-Aurignacian and the Levallois–Mousterian together lasted for some 60 000 years.[1] One particularly interesting site in the wadi tufa is at Hajj Creiem in Wadi Derna. This is a hunter's camp situated close to a small pool and dating to the early part of Levallois–Mousterian

---

[1] Confirmation for this long time-period is provided by the coastal sequence, where a series of tufas followed by alluvial deposits overlie the 8-m beach at the mouths of the wadis and, in turn, are covered by scree deposits with the earliest Upper Palaeolithic (Dabban). The Levallois–Mousterian occurs in the tufas and in the alluvium.

times. The occupation covered an area of approximately 1800 sq. m and contained an estimated 2000 flint artifacts, the raw material for which had been carried from the seashore some 8 km distant to the north, and worked into side-scrapers, and Mousterian points on thin Levallois flakes (fig. 4.3.9–11). The site is believed to represent a temporary camp of a few days' duration only and to have existed for the butchering and processing of meat from the animals, the remains of which were discovered lying on the floor. Analogy with the space requirements of San Bushman in the Kalahari today suggests that there might have been about thirteen people at the site and the amount of meat available to them was prodigious for estimates suggest that some 5–10 Barbary sheep, 3–4 zebra, 2–3 buffalo and a gazelle, providing between 2800 and 4075 kg of usable meat, were butchered and eaten by the group.

Significantly, therefore, the Aterian appears to be absent from most of northern Libya and Egypt. It is certainly less common in Tunisia than in Morocco and Algeria and only one site of Maghrib tradition in the Wadi Gan, all Upper Aterian, is recorded from western Tripolitania. In northern Cyrenaica the Aterian influence is recognized at three sites. In two of the early horizons of Levallois–Mousterian at Haua Fteah (Layers 30–1), and in the lowest Levallois–Mousterian level (Layer 34), the high incidence of end-scrapers and burins as against side-scrapers and points is also seen as an Aterian trait; further evidence of the contemporaneity of some Mousterian and Aterian industries is thus proven. In the desert to the south, in the Libyan sand sea, other Aterian sites are recorded and at one, Aterian artifacts have been found manufactured from a rare natural glass. In general, however, in northern Libya, the place of the Aterian is taken by the Mousterian which appears to continue up to about 40000 years ago when it is abruptly replaced by an Upper Palaeolithic complex (the Dabban).

### The Nile Valley

Along the lower reaches of the Nile, no living-sites of this time have yet been investigated but, on the upper Nile, particularly from the now flooded area upstream from the Aswan High Dam in Nubia, the Middle Palaeolithic is known. On geomorphological and some radiometric dating it is divided into three complexes – a Mousterian, an Aterian-related Middle Palaeolithic and, finally, a Khormusan complex (Wendorf 1968, Wendorf and Schild 1975). These can be seen as three modes in a continuing tradition of long duration. The earliest, the Mousterian,

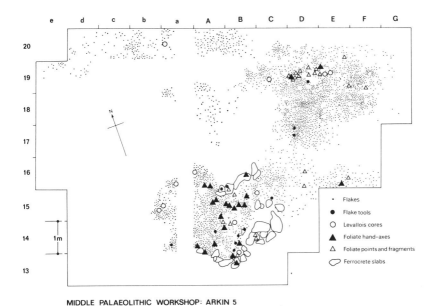

MIDDLE PALAEOLITHIC WORKSHOP: ARKIN 5

Fig. 4.5   Aterian-related Middle Palaeolithic workshop floor at Arkin 5, Nubian Nile Valley, showing concentrations and walling. (After Chmielewski 1968.)

is generally found on the tops and pediment slopes of inselbergs lying back from the river and belongs mostly to a time of intermittent soil formation before the deposition of the main Nile Valley sediment. It is made up of three variants – a Denticulate Mousterian (fig. 4.3.12–14), generally similar to that from the eastern desert; a Nubian Mousterian A (fig. 4.3.15), in which important constituents are side-scrapers and points of typical Mousterian form, as well as Upper Palaeolithic elements (end-scrapers and burins); and a Nubian Mousterian B, which is the same as the last except for the addition of rare Acheulian hand-axes. These assemblages show no recognizable time trends and it is possible that the Denticulate and Typical Mousterian emphasis they exhibit has a functional origin.

The next complex is one that is believed to be contemporary with the Aterian in the Sahara; it is characterized by the presence of bifacial foliates and very rare tanged pieces and has, therefore, been classified as an Aterian-related Middle Palaeolithic. Levallois technology and typology predominate. Some of these sites are workshops (Arkin 5 (fig. 4.5) and Arkin 6A) where foliates were made and all stages of manufacture are present from the finished tools, through numerous broken pieces, to the crude 'Sangoan-like' (see pp. 288–9) roughouts.

273

Also associated with this complex is the upper of two occupation assemblages (at Khor Musa, site 440) near Wadi Halfa stratified within the upper part of a fossil dune and covered by riverine silts that are now recognized as belonging to the oldest yet recorded period of alluvial aggradation within this stretch of the Nile sedimentary sequence. The Mousterian sites in the lower horizon in the dune belong to an arid period when the Nile was low. While the assemblages from both horizons are similar, with many denticulate forms and a bifacial foliate from the upper one, this last is associated with a large number of fish bones and few mammal bones, while with the lower occupation, the food waste is almost entirely from wild cattle (*Bos primigenius*).

The latest expression of the Middle Palaeolithic in the Nile Valley is that named the Khormusan which was previously thought, on radiometric dates, to have been the equivalent in age of the Upper Palaeolithic (20 000 to 15 000 BP). More recent determinations, however,[1] have shown that the age of the Khormusan is most probably beyond the lower limit of the radiocarbon method. The complex is based on Levallois technology and has a large number of denticulate and Upper Palaeolithic forms, in particular burins. The makers again specialized in the hunting of the aurochs. Settlements were large with several hearths, and recognizable clustering of artifacts and fauna suggest either repeated reoccupations, or camps occupied contemporaneously by several family or activity-orientated groups. Assemblages comparable to the Khormusan and a Denticulate Mousterian with foliates are known also from further south in the Dongola reach in the Sudan. It is of particular interest that nothing approaching the Khormusan Complex has yet been found in the western desert and it appears to be confined to the Nile Valley itself and its stratigraphically later age makes it likely that it may also in fact be contemporary with the arid episode that brought the Aterian occupation in the desert to an end (see also chapter 5).

ETHIOPIA AND THE HORN (fig. 4.6.1–9)

The cool Ethiopian high plateau lands, often over 2500 m, contrast markedly with the hot, arid regions of the Afar rift and the more easterly parts of the Horn in Somalia, but Middle Stone Age populations were

---

[1] New determinations for the Khormusan give dates of > 41 480 and > 36 000 BP which point to the probability that it is contemporary with the high-level silts overlying the Aterian-related horizons in the dune at Khor Musa.

able to occupy both with evident success. Habitats range from cave and spring sites to pans, streams and river-bank occurrences, though the distribution is still very inadequately known (J. D. Clark 1954, pp. 170, 192). The small number of excavated sites shows that the Middle Stone Age covered a considerable period of time and exhibited characteristics of both the Nile Valley and a number of sub-Saharan Middle Stone Age traditions. The Levallois technique, that first made its appearance with the Upper Acheulian, is the underlying method of production for the flakes and blades and the latter, in particular, became especially important at the younger localities where the main tool forms are unifacial and bifacial leaf shaped and sub-triangular points and side- and end-scrapers, together with some backed forms, denticulates and utilized blades. An earlier stage is also recognizable in which the Levallois debitage is more variable and where there are fewer retouched tools. The Middle Stone Age in Ethiopia and the Horn resembles in general, therefore, the typical Mousterian of Levallois facies of Europe though there are, in addition to the Levallois cores, an important percentage of core forms for the production of non-Levallois flakes.

In Ethiopia, the more interesting localities are an open site on the plateau (Melka Kunturé) with a series of stratified Middle Stone Age horizons, two quarry and workshop sites using obsidian, and two cave occupations. The Middle Stone Age occurs stratified in alluvial sediments (ferruginized sands and gravels) and tuffs of Upper Pleistocene age overlying the formation with the Acheulian Complex at Melka Kunturé in the upper valley of the Awash on the Ethiopian plateau at an altitude of about 2440 m. At one of the sites, Garba III, a particularly interesting sequence of seven stratified levels is found, the lowest of which is a living-floor with fauna associated. Full details of these horizons have not yet been published, but the sequence shows some evolutionary development. In the lowest horizon are rare choppers, small pointed, cordiform and sub-triangular hand-axes and a cleaver. The next horizon above has small bifaces and side-scrapers, together with Mousterian points, some points with parti-bifacial retouch and rare burins and end-scrapers; in the later horizons these Upper Palaeolithic elements are accentuated. The light-duty tools are made predominantly from obsidian but it is interesting that the debitage is mostly non-Levallois (Hours 1973). This sequence is undated, but it is of considerable importance since it could, in part, be representative of the assemblages belonging to the interval between the Acheulian and the advent of the

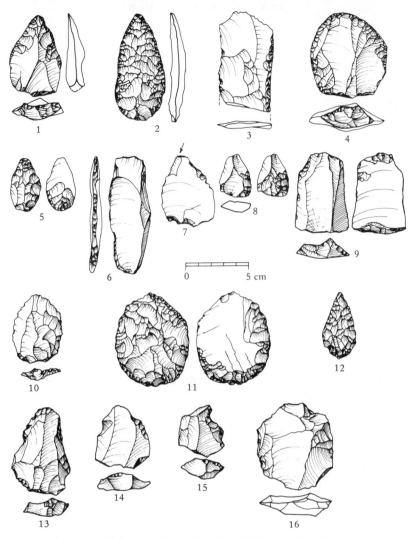

Fig. 4.6   Middle Stone Age artifacts from Ethiopia and East Africa.

*Gadamotta, Lake Zwai, Ethiopia*
1 Unifacially retouched point on a *pointe Levalloise* (ETH-72-85)
2 Bifacial point (ETH-72-85)
3 Side-scraper (ETH-72-1)
4 End-scraper on Levallois flake (ETH-72-1)

*K'one, Middle Loam, South-west Afar Rift, Ethiopia*
5 Parti-bifacial point
6 Trimming flake from a Levallois core having the appearance of a backed blade

7 Single-blow burin
8 Nubian core
9 'Sinew-frayer' type of double-ended flake core

*'Middle Stone Age' from the Melawa Gorge, Nakuru, Kenya*
10 Levallois flake
11 Parti-bifacially retouched discoid
12 Unifacial point

*Ndutu Beds, Olduvai Gorge*
13–15 Flakes with facetted striking platform and modification
16 Disc core

(Nos. 1–4 after Wendorf and Schild (1974), 5, 8–9 after Kurashina (1978), 6–7 after J. D. Clark (1975), 10–12 after L. S. B. Leakey (1931) and 13–16 after M. D. Leakey (1972).)

main Middle Stone Age complex, best seen at the quarry and cave sites described below.

The Middle Stone Age populations resorted over a longish period of time to obsidian outcrops on the rim of an ancient caldera at Gadamotta overlooking Lake Zwai in the Galla Lakes area of the Ethiopian rift, in order to replenish their supplies of raw material. Seven occupation floors at two localities are known here, occurring in old soil horizons interstratified with a thick series of volcanic sediments, including ashes, that may be more than 180 000 years old. These occupations are mostly extensive spreads of factory waste within which are much smaller concentrations, or piles, of flaking waste. One site, however, is a shallow saucer-shaped depression, possibly artificially excavated, about 30 cm deep and about 7.5 m in diameter which may be the floor of a communal living or workshop camp. A considerable number of finished tools and resharpening flakes as well as small worked-down Levallois cores were found in this concentration. The assemblages at the Gadamotta sites (fig. 4.6.1–4) show few developmental trends though bifacial points and side-scrapers are more common in the lower horizons, while end-scrapers and blades struck from non-Levallois cores increased considerably toward the top of the sequence (Wendorf and Schild 1974).

A second quarry/workshop locality is situated at the K'one (Garibaldi) caldera complex at the south-west corner of the Afar rift. Here outcrops of obsidian occur on the caldera rim where large flakes and nodules were roughly dressed and then carried down to the floor of the caldera where shade and possibly water were available. Here the pieces were trimmed into Levallois and discoid cores for the production of flakes and blades and many were then further worked into side- and end-scrapers, rare burins and backed flakes as well as foliate and sub-triangular points that were unifacially and bifacially retouched (fig. 4.6.5–9). Again, within the spreads of workshop debris occur restricted, dense concentrations of flaking waste, similar to those found at Gadamotta. Among them, points and scrapers occur in all stages of manufacture together with the sections of points broken in the course of production. The dense concentrations presumably represent the debris from a single flaking either lying as they fell, when they were removed by the workmen, or, perhaps, dumped from a receptacle, such as a basket, into which the flaking was done so as to minimize the risk of injuries which might occur if the very sharp obsidian were to remain scattered across the site.

Some of the Levallois cores are of diminutive proportions and sometimes the final flakes or points removed from them are still present and can be fitted back onto the cores. One particularly interesting and not uncommon artifact at K'one is a core resharpening flake or blade, designed to remove the steep retouched side edge of a Levallois point core. The abrupt retouch has a superficial resemblance to backing while the sharp edge of the core sometimes also showed signs of utilization. Indeed, a few have been deliberately retouched by bipolar flaking further to modify the edge of what must now be classified as a backed knife. Another most interesting form is a core for blades and triangular flakes made on a thick, flaked fragment and having a striking platform set at an angle to the main release face and formed by a number of flaking facets. These cores were first termed 'sinew frayers' and are a characteristic form in the Kenyan and Ethiopian rift with Later Stone Age industries based upon the use of obsidian. Their presence with the Middle Stone Age is, therefore, strongly suggestive of some continuity in flaking traditions between the Middle and Later Stone Age complexes.

These quarry sites are probably the outcome of seasonal visits for the replenishment of stocks of raw material repeated over a long period of time. They represent temporary camps and workshops from which most of the completed tools and many of the Levallois cores were removed to be further reduced on the home sites situated most probably by the shore of Lake Zwai or along the Awash River. Associated old soil features, together with remains of hippopotamus, alcelaphine antelopes and zebra at Gadamotta and of a mole rat (*Tachyoryctes* cf. *splendens*) at K'one, suggest a reasonably well-distributed rainfall supporting an open savanna habitat.

The living-sites are at present not so well known. One at Gorgora near the northern shore of Lake Tana in northern Ethiopia is a cave with some 4 m of ashy deposit containing three stages of a well-developed Middle Stone Age characterized by unifacial and bifacial points of sub-triangular plan form and side-scrapers made in chert. In the latest stage, end-scrapers, backed blades and burins are also said to be present (L. S. B. Leakey 1943). Near Dire Dawa is the cave of Porc Epic which opens out of a cliff face and commands a view of one of the main valleys into the escarpment giving access between the plains to the north and the high plateau to the south. The Middle Stone Age occupation is contained within a breccia believed to have been formed during a period of higher rainfall and probably lowered temperatures.

The increased amount of water coming from the back of the cave probably brought the occupation to an end and sealed the deposit under an intermittent layer of dripstone. The large numbers of foliate points made in chert and obsidian, the latter carried in from sources at least 40 km distant, the lesser importance of scrapers and the selection of blades and long flakes for use as knives suggest that this may have been a seasonal hunting camp. The site is important also for the Neanderthal jaw fragment found in the Middle Stone Age breccia (J. D. Clark and Williams 1978).

To the north of Dire Dawa lies the Afar rift, the central and northern parts of which, though they have not yet produced *in situ* Middle Stone Age assemblages, preserve important evidence of climates very different from the desertic conditions of the present day. Between 80 000 and 200 000 years ago, an advance (transgressive phase) of the sea turned the northern part into a gulf of the Red Sea, while further to the south, in the plains of the lower Awash, there existed, at the same time, an extensive freshwater lake. A further episode of deep-water lake development is dated to between about 34 000 and about 24 000 BP.[1] The Acheulian was still present 200 000 years ago (Roubet 1969) but the Middle Stone Age can be expected to have replaced it before the close of the earlier lacustrine episode.

In Somalia, the Middle Stone Age can be divided on stratigraphic grounds into three stages. The earlier two are found in successive valley-fill sediments and, in the scarcity of retouched pieces, the assemblages resemble those of the earlier Middle Palaeolithic from Kharga Oasis. The Levallois and disc-core methods predominate and the most characteristic retouched forms are rare, bifacial, foliate points. The latest stage was described as 'Somaliland Stillbay' because of the resemblance between the point and other forms found there with those of the so-called 'Stillbay Industry' from South Africa. This phase is specially well developed in red alluvial sediments on the upper slopes of the river valleys of northern Somalia, in particular, near Hargeisa, where numbers of finely-made point forms are found, together with scatters of flaking waste on sites that appear to represent short-term living-camps. The characteristic tools, made from chert, are bifacial and unifacial, foliate and triangular points, end- and side-scrapers, backed flakes, rare burins and denticulate pieces. Some assemblages, from pans in the north and cave sites in the south, contain typologically advanced and often diminutive forms that might be even later. The Middle Stone

---

[1] 34 000 $\pm^{2100}_{2900}$ and 23 560 $\pm$ 740 BP (Gasse 1974, Gasse and Rognon 1973).

Age in the Horn is associated, therefore, with renewed stream and spring activity suggesting that it was, in part, contemporary with a period of increased rainfall and probably lowered temperatures which must certainly antedate the time of the main Würm Glaciation in Europe. How early the Middle Stone Age makes its first appearance in the Horn is still uncertain. The Acheulian was contemporary, as we have seen, with the marine incursion from the Red Sea into the northern Afar about 200 000 years ago, but if potassium–argon dates associated with the Middle Stone Age from Gadamotta[1] are substantiated, then the beginning of this mode must be extended back even beyond the Eemian Interglacial, on correlated dates and climatic events from other parts of the world (Stearns 1975).

EAST AFRICA (fig. 4.6.10–16)

Just as the eastern Rift Valley forms a boundary between two major culture areas to the east and west today, so in prehistoric times the complexes to the west associated with thicker vegetation, and heavier rainfall patterns, in particular those parts lying within the Lake Victoria basin, formed part of a prehistoric culture area that embraces the whole of the Congo drainage basin and extends northwards to the Nile/Congo divide in the Central African Republic. Within and east of the Rift the topography is one of high plains and undulating plateaux, supporting grasslands and acacia parkland with evergreen forest on the high ridges and mountains and fresh- and saltwater lakes contained within some of the depressions. Although several recent studies have been completed and detailed investigations of occupation sites of this time have been carried out or are under way, very little published information exists on the Middle Stone Age from the savanna regions of East Africa. Very little is known also about the contemporary and preferred food animals with Middle Stone Age assemblages from eastern Africa – either bone waste is not preserved or the remains have not yet been reported. Mostly, it would seem that the animals favoured were large to medium-sized antelopes, zebra and pig, together with the extinct giant buffalo, the almost complete skeleton of one coming from sediments in the Naivasha rift.

[1] At Gadamotta, ages of 181 000 ± 6000 and about 149 000 years have been obtained from interstratified ashes (Wendorf et al. 1974). The first date is not greatly different from that of about 240 000 BP for a 'Stillbay' from alluvial sediments in the Melawa Gorge in the Naivasha rift in Kenya though it is harder to reconcile with the age of about 400 000 years for the so-called 'pseudo-Stillbay' from the Kinangop plateau overlooking the Rift (Evernden and Curtis 1965).

The first Middle Stone Age artifacts from East Africa were reported from the Naivasha–Nakuru section of the Kenya Rift Valley in the 1930s (L. S. B. Leakey 1931). Several Middle Stone Age localities, where the assemblages were originally described as 'Kenya Stillbay' are now known from within this section of the Rift Valley and from northern and central Tanzania, notably from Olduvai Gorge. They are characterized by a comparatively low incidence of Levallois/discoid-core technology, together with unspecialized cores having one, two or more platforms, and in some cases (Enderit Drift) by the presence again of the 'sinew frayer' core. Blades, or elongated flakes, are not common (maximum 12%) and sometimes non-existent, and of the flakes there is a persistent number of 'Levallois-type' with radial preparation and faceted striking platforms. Many of these flakes show only minimal modification due to use and this is especially so with the earlier assemblages. The most common retouched pieces are simple side- and convergent scrapers, together with points of various forms, simple piercing or grooving tools (becs), truncated pieces, end-scrapers and burins (fig. 4.6.10–12). The sites are situated in a wide range of environments from forest ecotone to the arid and semi-arid short grass plains and thornbush.

The oldest assemblage is probably that coming from the Ndutu Beds at Olduvai Gorge (M. D. Leakey et al. 1972), which were laid down within the gorge after erosion had cut deeply into the older Plio–Pleistocene Formation. They are contemporary with intermittent faulting, erosion and fluvial deposition within the gorge, terminating with an accumulation of windblown tuffs. The age of the upper part of the Ndutu Beds is estimated at about 50 000 years and bone from a lower level has been dated by amino-acid racemization to about 56 000 BP. The artifacts are made from lava, and discoid and unspecialized cores and flakes obtained by the Levallois method – some minimally retouched – are found (fig. 4.6.13–16). Formal tools are rare but include scrapers, a discoid and two choppers. Remains of the giant extinct gelada baboon (*Simopithecus*) have been identified from the basal unit and suggest that the lower part of the Ndutu Beds may belong in the Middle Pleistocene and be as much as 200 000 years old. The 'unspecialized' Middle Stone Age from the Ndutu Beds had been compared with that associated with three fragmentary human crania from Lake Eyasi basin that are considered to represent a 'rhodesioid' stock. An amino-acid racemization age of about 34 000 years has been obtained on one of these cranial fragments (Bada and Protsch 1973), though they might be expected to be appreciably older (see n. 1, p. 295).

In the ecotone between the forest and grassland in the eastern Rift, at an altitude of about 2135 m, on the slopes of Mount Eburu, is the site of Prospect Farm. Here are a series of occupation and workshop floors in the open, interstratified between old soil horizons and thick layers of pumiceous sediments from the volcano. The artifacts are made from obsidian and lava, and the Levallois and discoid-core methods, as well as unspecialized core preparation, provided the flakes for retouch into scrapers, points and a lesser number of other tools. Between 30 and 70% of the flakes are minimally modified by use. In the three earlier occurrences the dominant forms were simple side- and convergent scrapers. In the middle horizon, the convergent scraper is replaced by a greater number of points. In the top Middle Stone Age level this trend is continued and there are also a number of flat discoid scrapers, perhaps used as knives. The points are generally partly or fully retouched bifacially, though the standard of finish is not high. The predominant forms of point in all these Middle Stone Age assemblages from the eastern Rift range between ovate through foliate to short triangular examples. There is also a tendency for the retouch to become more invasive and flatter through time (Anthony 1972, Merrick 1975).

In the Nakuru–Elmenteita lake basin to the north, another Middle Stone Age occupation locality has been excavated at Enderit Drift. This occurs in a channel fill cut, when the lake level was low, into older sediments of a high level Upper Pleistocene lake. Several separate occurrences were found in the sandy fill of the channel and, because of the special nature of the stone-tool equipment, are considered to represent temporary camps used for hunting and butchery. These occurrences sometimes take the form of heavy concentrations of obsidian artifacts (100 to 500 per sq. m) together with many bone fragments; the raw material for the tools must have been carried at least 10 km to the site. These are mostly scrapers, points and bifacial pieces together with some blunted (truncated) forms and *becs*. No doubt because the material had to be carried in, the flaking waste is all small and includes very few cores. The assemblage from this site resembles that from the upper horizon at Prospect Farm (Merrick 1975). East of Nairobi, in the ecotone between the highlands and the Athi Plains, is Lukenya Hill where several rock-shelters were occupied during Middle Stone Age times. The evidence from one excavated shelter here (Shelter Gv Jm 16 (see Merrick 1975)) shows that the Middle Stone Age occupation terminated well before 17 000 years ago, as sufficient time had elapsed for the deposit to become brecciated and extensively eroded, and for a large part of the shelter roof to have collapsed onto the top of it before the Later Stone Age made its appearance. The site appears to have been only sporadically occupied, since the artifact density is low, but a wide variety of tools are represented. These comprise convergent and simple side-scrapers, points and miscellaneous bifacial pieces (about 18%), various blunted flakes, borers and technical burins. Again, unspecialized cores outnumber the discoid and Levallois-like forms. The occupants used quartz, chert or chalcedony and obsidian, obtaining the quartz locally; the chalcedony must have been carried in from more distant sources. A greater degree of selectivity through time is reflected in the increased use of the finer-grained rocks in the later occupational stages.

It is not clear where in the East African high grassland tradition the occurrence known as 'pseudo-Stillbay' from old swamp deposits on the Kinangop plateau at about 2440 m belongs. Most of the tools are short, stubby points and side-scrapers worked generally only on one side, but there are also rare, diminutive hand-axes. Since the retouch is of the scalar kind found on the earlier occurrences at Prospect Farm and bifacial points are rare, this 'pseudo-Stillbay' probably belongs in the earlier part of the sequence, though whether it can be accepted as being as old as 400000 years ago as potassium–argon dating suggests (see n. 1, p. 280) must await further detailed investigation of the site.

Mention must be made here also of the site of Magosi in semi-arid north-eastern Uganda where, in 1926, an excavation in a silted-up rock cistern produced what was then believed to be an occurrence combining Middle Stone Age and Later Stone Age artifacts and technology which was thus considered to be transitional between the Middle and the Later Stone Ages (Wayland and Burkitt 1932). Industries with similar composition from other parts of sub-Saharan Africa (see p. 313) led to their being designated as 'Magosian' and grouped together to form a 'Second Intermediate' period dating, it was believed, to the closing stages of the Upper Pleistocene (J. D. Clark 1957). Subsequent re-excavation of the Magosi site (G. H. Cole 1967a) showed that not only was the original assemblage highly selected but that artifacts from two separate occurrences had been mixed together. The new excavation showed that the cistern had been dug out by a Later Stone Age population into older deposits, which were incompletely cemented by carbonates, and yielded a Middle Stone Age assemblage. Within the top of this deposit, there were found a small number of lunates and backed bladelets but it seems most probable that these belong with the 'upper occurrence' since none were found in the lower part of the deposit. The assemblage, made in quartz and chert, is not large, comprising about a dozen small scrapers, twenty bifacial points and point fragments, and a few burins; small radially-prepared Levallois cores are also present. The age of this 'lower occurrence' remains unknown but it clearly belongs in the Middle Stone Age, most probably in the later part.

The concept of a 'Magosian' was based on the belief that, in a long cultural continuum, 'transitional' industries would be found, but Magosi now demonstrates what has subsequently been found to be the case also at a number of other 'Second Intermediate' occurrences, namely, that these are culturally mixed assemblages in secondary context and can in no way be considered as transitional. From north-east Uganda to the coast at Mombasa, surface finds show that the predominantly light-duty Middle Stone Age, known at one time as 'Kenya Stillbay', was widely spread throughout the more open savanna (thornbush and grasslands) of East Africa during the early Upper Pleistocene but the existence of a late and evolved form of Middle Stone Age still has to be convincingly demonstrated. Among localities in East Africa where a 'Magosian' stage was recognized are the Gorgora rock-shelter in Ethiopia and Nasera (Apis Rock) Shelter in northern Tanzania (L. S. B. Leakey 1936) which contains a long cultural sequence through the Middle Stone Age into the Later Stone Age. Recent excavation (Mehlman 1977) shows that the supposed 'Magosian' assemblages are a composite of Middle and Later Stone Age artifacts. The deposits of the Later follow those of the Middle Stone Age without any hiatus and a local industry, the Naseran (dated *c.* 22000 B.P.), predominantly microlithic and characterized by unifacial points and scrapers, appears to be transitional between the Middle and Later Stone Age as it has elements of both. Kisese II rock-shelter in central Tanzania is another site that appears to span the time of this change-over (J. Deacon 1966, Inskeep 1962), for the earlier occurrences which have been ascribed to the 'Second Intermediate' are dated to between about 31500 and 18000 years ago. The dominant forms are convex and concave scrapers, splintered pieces (*outils écaillés*), 'sinew frayers', together with small numbers of burins, small circular scrapers, and rare small backed forms. This can hardly be considered an industry in the Middle Stone Age tradition, but neither is it a fully microlithic, Later Stone Age form. The terms 'Magosian' and 'Second Intermediate' have now been abandoned, but the process of change and the concept of cultural transition, from one technological/typological mode to another, will be further considered below.

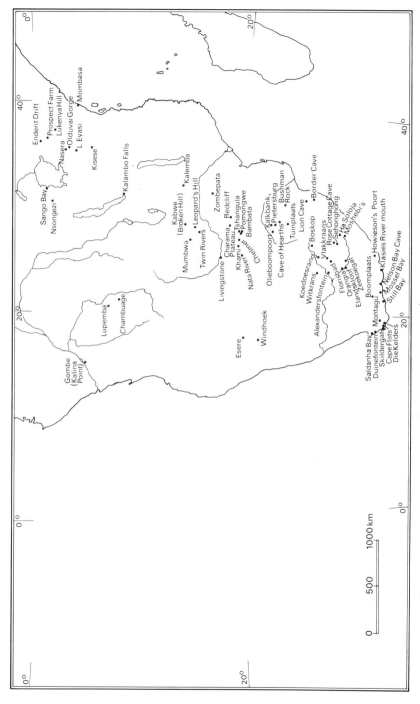

Fig. 4.7   Map of the southern part of the continent to show the archaeological sites and localities referred to in the text.

## WEST AFRICA AND THE FOREST/SAVANNA REGIONS OF EQUATORIA (figs. 4.7–8)

West of the eastern arm of the Rift Valley some Middle Stone Age occurrences comparable to the light-duty specialized flake and core complex of the East African open savanna and steppe environment are found. In the huge region lying further to the west, however, there occurs a very different techno-complex. This region includes the Lake Victoria basin, the western arm of the Rift and the whole of the Congo (Zaïre) basin up to and over the divide with the Nile drainage in the north, as well as the Zambezi drainage in the south, together with the savanna and forest country of West Africa. This vast region, much of it low lying (610–150 m) is today characterized by a more closed vegetation pattern – woodland savannas with tall grass – giving place to a mosaic forest and savanna and, in the areas of high, monsoonal rainfall (1000–2000 mm a year), into moist, evergreen forest.[1] During much of the Upper Pleistocene, however, a large part of this region was subjected to considerable drying and cooling which brought about important readjustment of the vegetation belts.[2] This drying may have first made itself felt during the late Acheulian since it is from this time that human populations became permanently established in these equatorial high-rainfall regions.

Both the Victoria basin and that of the Congo preserve a long record of cultural activity and the several industrial stages that can be recognized there help to emphasize the length of time during which the 'Middle Stone Age' tradition was being practised. In the Victoria basin, at Nsongezi, the old lake sediments exposed by the Kagera River in what was once an arm of the lake show that the late Acheulian there coincided with a time when the lake receded and rubble and scree were able to

[1] Today plant foods are plentiful in the region and also the larger mammals that served as food. Some favoured grassland localities, for example the Western or Albertine rift, supported until recently, a huge biomass of elephant, hippopotamus and buffalo (see Bourlière 1963). Game is, of course, much less gregarious in the forest but lesser concentrations of these large mammals were previously to be found in the savanna woodlands.

[2] Those western parts of the continent that came under the increased influence of the south Atlantic wind systems and the northward extension of the cold Benguela Current into the Gulf of Guinea, resulting from the expansion of the Antarctic ice sheet coincident with the Würm Glaciation in Europe, experienced significant climatic change during the Upper Pleistocene. The effects these events brought about sometimes extended many hundreds of kilometres into the interior of the continent causing the moist lowland forests to retreat and the semi-arid bush and grassland that replaced them were insufficient cover to prevent the redistribution of sands by wind on the uplands, erosion of the valley slopes and redeposition of these sands and other sediments at lower elevations in the valley bottoms.

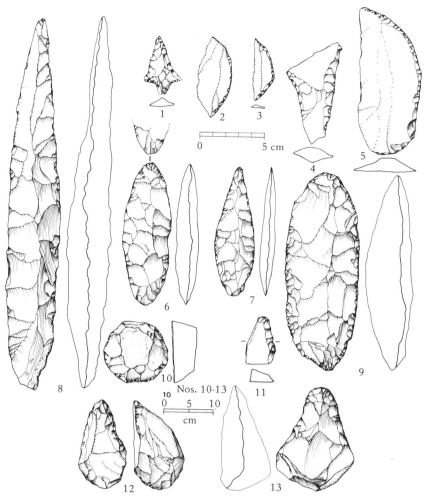

Fig. 4.8  Middle Stone Age artifacts of the Lupemban Industrial Complex
from the Congo (Zaïre) basin.

*Lupembo-Tshitolian Industry, from*
*Mbalambala, Dundo, north-east Angola*
1  Bifacial winged and tanged point
2-3  Backed blades
4  *Tranchet* with bifacial retouch
5  Backed flake
6  Bifacial core-axe
7  Bifacial point
(In quartzite or chalcedony)

*Upper Lupemban (Djokocian) Industry, from*
*Gombe (Kalina Point), Kinshasa*
8  Bifacial lanceolate
9  Double-ended core-axe
(In quartzite)

(After J. D. Clark 1970.)

*Lower Lupemban/Sangoan Industry, from*
*Redeposited Kalahari Sands II north-east*
*Angola, and Ochreous Sands Member, Site*
*B2/59, Kalambo Falls, Zambia*
10  Core-scraper, from Camafufo, north-east
    Angola
11  Denticulate end- and side-scraper, from
    Kalambo Falls
12  Pick, from Mussolegi, north-east
    Angola
13  Core-axe, from Kalambo Falls
(In quartz, quartzite or silicified mudstone)

287

form on the exposed land surfaces (M–N horizon) during a period of drier climate which has been correlated with the time when windblown tuffs accumulated on the surface at the Olduvai Gorge. Two further transgressions of the lake followed when silts and old swamp sediments were laid down, each being terminated by one or more drier episodes when new rubble was able to form on exposed surfaces (G. H. Cole 1967b). The artifact assemblages from the post-M–N horizon sediments preserve a record of an evolving techno-complex that has been chiefly noted for the heavy-duty element of the tool kit. These artifacts are picks and core-axe forms, often crudely made in the earlier stages but becoming more refined and smaller through time. With these tools are found heavy core-scrapers or push-planes, polyhedral stones and choppers, together with a variable light-duty component. Another most characteristic tool is a finely-made lanceolate point, between 15 and 30 cm long (fig. 4.8.8). In the later stages, wedge or trapeze-shaped cutting tools (*tranchets*) and bifacial, tanged points occur in some regions. The techno-complex has been divided on stylistic and typological grounds into three, sometimes four, stages and regional facies or variants are clearly distinguishable.

These pick and core-axe forms were first reported from the hills overlying Sango Bay on the west side of Lake Victoria (Wayland 1923), and subsequently have been found in many parts of Equatoria, as well as in the savannas of the Zambezi drainage and even as far south as the high rainfall areas on the south-east side of the continent in Natal and Mozambique. They were believed to be representative of a 'Sangoan Industry' and were placed in an intermediate ('First Intermediate') stage between the Acheulian and the Middle Stone Age. They are generally associated with the basal sediments of the Upper Pleistocene sequence in the stream courses or found on the hillslopes and ridges, as well as on the islands of Lake Victoria which would have been hills when the water level was lower. A characteristic of these assemblages was the almost complete absence of any light-duty component. However, subsequent excavations in open and cave sites have shown that at the all-purpose camps the light-duty element predominates over the heavy-duty forms. It now becomes apparent, therefore, that the latter are, in fact, only one part of the flaked stone equipment and, more probably, relate to some special activity associated with the localities where they occur. It has been suggested that they are equipment used for working wood and its by-products, and if this is so, then they are comparable to the heavy 'arapia blocks' and core-scraper forms used by the

Australian aborigines for primary wood-working which, similarly, are found only at special-activity localities.

It is also apparent that such heavy-duty equipment is not confined to a single period of time but can now be seen to make its appearance through a wide range of space and time, wherever the circumstances so required it. Since, therefore, the 'Sangoan', as originally defined, is representative of only one component of the stone-tool equipment of the early Upper Pleistocene, and the assemblages from the general-purpose occurrences have already been given separate industrial status, the term might now be used more specifically in the sense of a special-activity 'Sangoan facies' which may transgress both time and space.

Excavations in Bas Zaïre (lower Congo) from 1926 (Colette 1931), in the south-western parts of the basin in Shaba (Breuil, Cabu and van Riet Lowe 1944) and Angola (J. D. Clark 1963) as well as on both sides of Lake Victoria (G. H. Cole 1967b, L. S. B. Leakey and Owen 1945), reveal an evolving tradition, often based on the use of fine-grained quartzite and chalcedony, and known as the *Lupemban Industrial Complex* after the site of Lupemba in Shaba where several developmental stages were first recognized.[1] The Sangoan pick and core-axe forms are characteristic only of the Lower Lupemban stage (fig. 4.8.12, 13), which is dated to a probably minimum age of some 40000 years since the main part of this stage must lie beyond the radiocarbon method.[2] Associated with this stage are pollens which indicate that the environment was an open one and probably also colder, evidence of the tropical forest being no longer present (J. D. Clark and Bakker 1962). The artifact assemblage comprises, besides the heavy-duty equipment (including some more shapely core-axes), rare, long, bifacial, foliate forms and a small-tool element best seen from

[1] See J. D. Clark (1963). The two most-studied regions in the Congo basin are the Stanley Pool area on the lower Congo (van Moorsel 1968, de Ploey 1965) and Lunda in north-east Angola (J. D. Clark 1963, 1968). Both of these regions are characterized by thick mantles of old Kalahari Sands that often bury very deeply the solid geology which is exposed only in the valley bottoms. During the later Pleistocene the semi-arid conditions resulted in much erosion of these sands and several stages of redeposition under colluvial and fluvial agencies in the valleys. It is within these redeposited, reddened, clayey sands and within the alluvial gravels and fine-grained sediments in the valley bottoms that the Later Pleistocene sequence belongs in both primary and secondary contexts.

[2] In Zaïre and the Victoria basin, the Lupemban Complex follows and is in part contemporary with a period of low stream levels and laterite formation on the valley sides, sealing gravels and rubbles with Acheulian hand-axes. In the Lunda rivers (e.g. at Mufo), the Lower Lupemban occurs in gravels mostly below present stream level, associated with wood. Dates of $38\,000 \pm 2\,500$ BP from north-east Angola (J. D. Clark 1963, p. 19) and of $> 42\,000$ BP from Kalina (Bas Zaïre) (D. Cahen 1976) have been obtained for earlier Lupemban horizons.

dispersed concentrations of flaking waste in the sands of the valley sides.

The next stage (Upper Lupemban) (fig. 4.8.8, 9) is found in the later accumulations of gravels and sands in the valleys. The rougher, 'Sangoan-type', picks and core-axes have now been largely replaced by numbers of shapely, ellipsoidal core-axes and a proportionately smaller increase in the numbers of lanceolates. It is at this time that regional differences are now easily recognizable.[1] The latest stage (termed *Lupembo-Tshitolian* in Zaïre) (fig. 4.8.1–7) now combines Lupemban technology and tool forms with that of a new and succeeding industrial complex known as the Tshitolian (see also chapter 5). In this stage there is an overall reduction in the size-ranges of the tools; points and core-axes undergo still further refinement; and there is greater variability in shape including carefully denticulated pieces. Also new forms of *tranchets* made from snapped sections of flakes are now found, together with side-scrapers and backed and truncated flakes. The Levallois method of core preparation is now more consistently met with for flake and blade production, though the lanceolates and core-axe forms continue to be made from thick fragments by bifacial trimming. This Lupembo-Tshitolian is the latest Middle Stone Age phase in the Congo and Victoria basins. It remains to be satisfactorily dated there, though an age of about 30 000 years would not be unexpected; younger ages have been recorded.[2]

Kalambo Falls has produced the only open-air living-site yet excavated that is ascribed to a 'Sangoan' industrial stage, here named the *Chipeta Industry* (J. D. Clark 1974, pp. 78–9) (fig. 4.8.11, 13). The site appears to be a briefly-occupied, general-purpose camp covering a limited area within a sandy channel and, although the dating is still not absolutely certain,[3] it would seem that the first appearance of 'Sangoan'

[1] For example, between Zaïre and the Victoria basin. In the latter, large forms of *tranchets* make their appearance, and the Levallois and discoid-core technology appear to be well established. On the other hand, in Zaïre, there is a greater specialization in the point forms and the specialized core technology is still either rare or absent at this time.

[2] A date of 14 840 ± 80 BP is recorded for an assemblage of this stage from Kalina Point (Bas Zaïre) and this is consistent with the date of 27 500 ± 2300 BP for a horizon with a similarly evolved stage at the Kalambo Falls on the Zambia–Tanzania border (D. Cahen 1976, J. D. Clark 1969, p. 79).

[3] The sediments that contain the Chipeta Industry are fluvially-deposited ochreous sands and overbank deposits that have been laid down in a channel cut deeply into the fine gravels of the earlier cycle with the Acheulian. Light-duty scrapers and small pointed and denticulate pieces form some 75% as against the ±12% of heavy-duty picks and core-axes and some 6% or less of Acheulian forms. The Chipeta Industry ('Sangoan') at Kalambo Falls dates to between >46 000 and about 38 000 BP and associated pollens and macro-plant remains indicate a climate and environment similar to or perhaps warmer than the present day. However, the time taken to lay

forms at the site may have taken place nearer 100 000 than 50 000 years ago as originally thought. There follow at the Kalambo Falls, two more stages of the Lupemban Industrial Complex (Nakisasa and Siszya Industries) in which the core-axe and pick forms become more refined as do also the lanceolates. The raw material used for tools has been more carefully selected and there is a range of scraper and unifacial point forms comparable to those of the Middle Stone Age industries in the east and southern African savannas. Again, dating is uncertain but it can be expected that the latest expression of the Middle Stone Age at the Kalambo Falls is at least 30 000 years old.

Middle Stone Age technology makes its final appearance in the Polungu Industry which probably dates to the close of the Pleistocene. The point forms are now small and finely finished. Levallois and disc-core technology is, similarly, of an evolved form and the implements are often of diminutive proportions; a bored stone fragment is also associated.[1] This long Lupemban Industrial Complex of Equatoria evolved within what had been previously, during the Middle Pleistocene, a forest-covered and generally unfavourable region. It expanded rapidly into this hitherto 'empty zone' under the generally drier climatic conditions that now pertained and developed over some 70 000 years a characteristic tool-kit with emphasis on the axe and adze forms and long blade-like points that best demonstrate the manner in which these populations chose to exploit certain resources of their environment.

In West Africa, there is widespread evidence that between 23 000 and about 12 000 years ago the southern Sudan and much of Senegal/Ghana was dry; Lake Chad almost dried up (Servant 1973) and the Niger flowed only as far as the inland delta.[2] This arid period is contem-

down the upper part of the depositional unit containing the Acheulian and the following erosional episode, prior to the channel filling with the Chipeta Industry, appears to have lasted at least 50 000 years on the evidence of the amino-acid racemization age of > 110 000 years for wood associated with the Acheulian (Lee et al. 1976).

[1] The Polungu Industry appears to belong in the time-period 10 000–20 000 BP but, here again, dating is unsatisfactory since, at a site (Kalemba) in eastern Zambia, the change from Middle Stone Age technology to an emphasis on the earliest small flake/blade traditions of the Later Stone Age was already taking place about 30 000 years ago (D. W. Phillipson 1973).

[2] Extensive parallel dune fields (now fixed) spread southwards into the southern Sudan (Grove and Warren 1968), into Hausaland (Burke, Durotype and Whiteman 1971), into Niger (Faure 1962) and Upper Volta (Boulet 1972) far beyond the present area of active dune formation, reaching latitude 13°N and beyond. The mouth of the lower Senegal river was blocked by large dunes accumulated during a regressive marine episode when the sea level may have been − 100 m (Elouard and Faure 1972). Pollen evidence from near Abidjan on the Guinea coast shows a grassland, more open environment about 23 000 years ago and it is clear that the Guinea coast experienced a much drier climate than today with extension of the savanna at the expense of the forest (Van Campo 1975); indeed, relicts of the desertic flora persist today up to about 9°N (Aubréville 1962).

poraneous with the main and later Würm Glaciation in Eurasia. Prior to this time there is evidence for a period of high sea level divided into two stages on the Senegal and Mauritanian coasts (Inchirian) (Elouard and Faure 1972). The later of these 'stages' ended sometime well before 40 000 years ago and it seems likely that it may correlate with the Eemian. Lake Chad and other south Saharan lakes, as we have seen, were also high around this time and contemporary with the Mousterian/Aterian occupation of the desert. The archaeology of this time period in western Africa south of the Sahara is still very imperfectly known. Late Acheulian artifacts occur on the Jos plateau and sparsely at various surface sites in Ghana and other West African countries in the savanna/forest zones. A succeeding 'Sangoan' phase is recognized on the basis of the characteristic picks, core-axes, choppers and heavy-duty scrapers. Quartz is almost universally the raw material used for making these and the later Middle Stone Age tools. The 'Sangoan' is found mostly concentrated in the river valleys and, although a small amount of flaking waste is sometimes associated, these appear to be special-purpose occurrences (Soper 1965). The most important site is Asokrochona in Ghana (Davies 1967) where an occurrence with heavy-duty equipment and much flaking waste appears to be a workshop. It overlies a transgressive beach level with Acheulian tools and presumably dates to sometime during the equivalent of the early Würm Glaciation or before. The Middle Stone Age is stratified above the 'Sangoan' at Asokrochona. Here and elsewhere it is marked by the general reduction in the heavy-duty equipment and an increase in the number of small flake tools. Except in parts of Nigeria, however, these occurrences contain a relatively low percentage of formal tools. Some rare Lupemban-like lanceolates occur in Ghana and characteristic savanna types of foliate point and both end- and side-scrapers sometimes occur at the sites in northern Nigeria but, in general, these are rare and informality appears to be the chief characteristic of all these low-latitude occurrences in West Africa. They are found in small concentrations in stone lines, red loams and aeolian sands which pass below sea level and inland clearly relate to a time when the streams were still actively eroding and to the drier period of aggradation that followed. The West African Middle Stone Age presents, therefore, a considerable contrast, both with the desert-orientated Aterian complex to the north and that of the Lupemban in the higher rainfall regions of Equatoria – a contrast that cannot be based solely on the use of quartz in place of finer-grained rocks so that regional preferences and traditions are clearly discernible here.

## THE WOODLANDS AND GRASSLANDS OF SOUTH CENTRAL AFRICA (fig. 4.9)

Much of this region consists of undulating plateau lands covered with deciduous woodlands of *Brachystegia–Julbernardia* type and is drained by the Zambezi system in the south and that of the Congo in the north. Between them are a number of large, shallow swamps and lakes and, on the eastern side, the extension of the Rift Valley contains the deep lake basins of Tanganyika and Malawi (Nyasa). While regional forms of the Lupemban Complex are present in the north in the Congo system and Lake Malawi, in the main part of the Zambezi basin the heavy-duty equipment of 'Sangoan' facies, though present at the beginning of the post-Acheulian sequence, is mostly absent from the Middle Stone Age occurrences that resemble more those of the open savanna and steppe of southern Africa.

Probably the oldest and certainly the most important site in the woodland savanna is that of Kabwe (Broken Hill) which produced from a deep cave the nearly complete skull and some postcranial remains of *Homo rhodesiensis*. Although these were found in mining operations and there remains some uncertainty as to the fauna and stone artifacts believed to have been associated, there is now every reason to suppose that 'Broken Hill Man' is representative of the early *Homo sapiens* stock present more generally in southern Africa at the end of the Middle and beginning of the Upper Pleistocene.[1] Excavations adjacent to the site of the cave at Kabwe showed four successive horizons with artifacts – the lower two with Acheulian occurrences, the next with 'Sangoan' forms and the top one with light Middle Stone Age artifacts. Light-duty artifacts from the cave were formerly referred to a 'proto-Stillbay' industrial stage but it can now be seen that they would not be out of place with a late Acheulian or, more probably, an early Middle Stone Age ('Sangoan') industrial phase. The artifacts (fig. 4.9.1–6) are mostly in quartz and comprise convergent and simple side-scrapers, notched flakes and flakes with faceted platforms, a core scraper and spheroids together with four simple bone tools (J. D. Clark 1959a). An amino-acid

[1] The associated cave fauna comprises 23 large mammal species of which 5 are extinct forms of savanna animals and the closest comparisons are with the fauna from Elandsfontein at the Cape which has produced another *H. rhodesiensis* skull-cap and an industry of late Acheulian type (Bada *et al.* 1974; Klein 1973; see also p. 320).

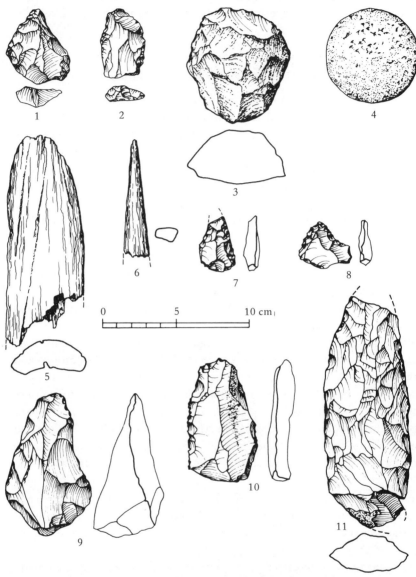

Fig. 4.9   Middle Stone Age artifacts from Zambia.

*Kabwe (Broken Hill), from cave deposits that yielded the fossil remains of* Homo sapiens rhodesiensis

  1 Convergent scraper
  2 Bifacially retouched tool
  3 Core-scraper
  4 Spheroid
  5 Spatulate tool made on a section of ivory split from an elephant tusk
  6 Distal end of a pointed bone tool
(In quartz, limonite, ivory or bone)

*Twin Rivers Kopje, from bone-bearing breccias*

  7 Unifacial point (distal end missing)
  8 Convergent scraper
  9 Diminutive hand-axe
 10 Denticulate side-scraper on Levallois flake
 11 Bifacial lanceolate
(In quartz or chert)

(Nos. 1–6 after J. D. Clark *et al.* (1950) and 7–11 after J. D. Clark (1970).)

racemization date of about 110 000 BP was obtained from some of the hominid and faunal fossils.[1]

Clearly later in age, are the occurrences in the cave sites at Mumbwa and Kalemba and in the fissures on the top of Twin Rivers Kopje (fig. 4.9.7–11), at each of which local quartz is the predominant raw material. The assemblage from the lowest level at Kalemba is characterized by the use of the Levallois/disc-core method for the production of a number of parallel-sided flake/blades. Retouched tools comprise single side- and convergent scrapers, denticulated forms and unifacial points. It is dated to > 34 000 BP (D. W. Phillipson 1973). The Mumbwa Industry is similar but includes rare, sub-triangular and foliate bifacial points, burins and backed forms together with pigment. Both these sites were probably general-purpose camps and that at the top of Twin Rivers Kopje on the edge of the hill country overlooking the grasslands of the Kafue Flats, dated to about the same period as Kalemba,[2] is likely to have served a similar purpose and, situated as it was, it also commanded an extensive view of game movements on the plain below. The occupation was clearly contemporary, as was that at Mumbwa, with wetter climatic conditions during which dripstone was able to form in fissures. Artifacts are similar to those from Mumbwa and Kalemba with the addition of some larger, Lupemban-like, foliate forms and small 'Sangoan-type' core-axes and choppers. A number of surface assemblages from the upper Zambezi valley round Livingstone and elsewhere confirm the evidence of the excavated sites that the main Middle Stone Age in Zambia and southern Malawi has relatively few finely-finished point and scraper forms, and a diminished number of heavy-duty tools; denticulates are significant, as also spheroids.

The time when the Middle Stone Age gave place to the earliest Later Stone Age mode appears to be fairly well established, if the dates are not in error. At some sites (Kalemba, Leopard's Hill, Kalambo Falls) there are occurrences in which the Levallois/disc-core technology, now associated with some quite small cores, is found together with single-platform and bipolar cores for the production of small blades, an increase in the number of small backed and truncated flake and blade

[1] It is likely, therefore, that the Kabwe type-site and its contents may fall within the same age-range as that of the early Middle Stone Age assemblage from the Ndutu Beds and, probably, also as that of the fragmentary crania ascribed to the 'rhodesioid' stock, with artifacts, from Lake Eyasi referred to on p. 281 and, if so, the racemization data of 34 000 BP on these crania is too recent.
[2] The radiocarbon dates for this Twin Rivers assemblage are 22 800 ± 1000 BP and > 33 000 BP. See also J. D. Clark (1971).

forms and a number of crude, irregular scrapers. Some of these 'intermediate' assemblages, while in part they perpetuate the basic Middle Stone Age method of flake production, yet in their tool forms have more in common with the Later than with the Middle Stone Age mode. The interface between the Middle Stone Age and an industry of this type at Kalemba is dated between about 24 500 and about 21 500[1] and at Leopard's Hill between 25 000 and 21 000 BP. In Zambia again, therefore, it appears that the Middle Stone Age mode, both tool-kit and technology, was probably replaced sometime around 30 000 years ago. However, there are other occurrences at Mumbwa dated to about 10 000 BP (K. Savage, personal communication) and at Kalambo Falls probably dating between 10 000 and 20 000 BP where the greater emphasis appears to be either on the Middle Stone Age mode and tool forms or to be more equally divided. Discoid-core technology is also believed to have persisted into late times in the upper reaches of the Zambezi (L. Phillipson 1975). However, it is unclear at present whether any or all of these occurrences should be included within the Middle Stone Age. In the light of the evidence from Zimbabwe (p. 313) an evolved Middle Stone Age technology and tool-kits were still present there up to 15 000 years ago so that a similar persistence in other parts of the tropical savanna north of the Zambezi would not be altogether unexpected. The human remains from Mumbwa (with radiocarbon dates of 18 000 ± 370 and 20 450 ± 340 BP), which are believed to be burials, can probably, therefore, be associated with the final Middle Stone Age at that site.

## SOUTHERN AFRICA (figs. 4.10–14)

South of the Zambezi, Middle Stone Age industries occur in almost all parts of the sub-continent except for the eastern (Natal) side of the Drakensberg Mountains above 1500 m where, due, it is thought, to the lowered temperatures of the earlier Würm Glaciation, dense *Podocarpus* forest covered these slopes down to as much as 1000 m below the present forest line (Willcox 1974). The forests of the Cape winter-rainfall belt – just as the dense montane forests in tropical Africa – may also have proved uninviting to human populations until the introduction of food-producing economies. Other habitats – ranging from the Namib and Kalahari Deserts of the west and centre, the Karroo and grasslands of the central high plateau to woodland savannas and coastal

---

[1] The radiocarbon date for Kalemba is 22 650 ± $\frac{2000}{1000}$ BP.

thicket vegetation of the northern, eastern and southern parts of the continent – provide numerous examples of Middle Stone Age occupation sites in the open and in caves and rock-shelters.

These Middle Stone Age industries exhibit no highly distinctive or specialized forms such as the tanged artifacts that identify the Aterian Complex in north Africa. It is, however, possible to recognize several technological traditions or *complexes* each of which shows in varying ways the general characteristics of the Middle Stone Age as originally defined by Goodwin. Each is also distinguished from the others by varying proportions of the characteristic tool forms and technological or stylistic preferences and further distinguished by regional expressions – known formerly as *variants* but now in some cases more precisely defined as *industries*. Technically and typologically related industries have recently been grouped into three *complexes* named after the key sites – Pietersburg, Bambata and Howieson's Poort (Sampson 1974).[1] The simplest explanation of such relationship is that the *complexes* represent successive stages of technological development, each region exhibiting its own degree of variability. In this case, observed similarities would be part of the general developmental trend of Middle Stone Age stone technology, so that grouping into complexes might be taken to imply the existence of more esoteric relationships between the industries than, in fact, pertain. Nevertheless, there is now evidence to suggest that these complexes may, indeed, be something more than simply three successive technological stages within the Middle Stone Age mode.

In some regions a long developmental Middle Stone Age sequence can be recognized, e.g., at the Cave of Hearths in the northern Transvaal, but in many cases the sites occur in the open and were occupied on a single occasion only and probably for a relatively brief period of time; in such cases geomorphological and radiometric dating provide the only reliable means of arranging these assemblages in a cultural sequence. Unfortunately, many of the earlier radiocarbon dates for Middle Stone Age assemblages must be considered unreliable since either they were obtained in the early stages of the method, before it

[1] In the *Pietersburg Complex* are grouped those stratified and unselected assemblages which are characterized by the use of utilized and discontinuously retouched blade and blade fragments and a few marginally retouched convergent flakes and scrapers. The *Bambatan Complex* comprises assemblages that are distinguished by a significant number of retouched tools, especially points and scrapers, together with the presence of end-scrapers, burins and some backed forms. The *Howieson's Poort Complex* and related assemblages contain, in addition to some of the Bambatan forms, a significant increase in bladelets and also true lunates and backed blades; dimensions are generally appreciably smaller.

had been refined, or the material dated (e.g. calcite or bone) was unsatisfactory. Moreover, the main part of the Middle Stone Age in southern Africa can also now be seen to lie well beyond the lower limit of the radiocarbon method, i.e. > 40 000 BP. The upper limit may, as we have seen, be regionally variable if the available dates are reliable. In most areas the mode had disappeared by 35 000 years ago, in others the technology does not seem to have been replaced until about 20 000 BP while in others again (e.g. north-western Zambia and possibly Zimbabwe) Middle Stone Age technology may have lingered on even later.

Another major problem still remaining is whether the main modes/complexes and their respective industries are sequential, the one giving place to the other through time, or whether they are contemporaneous or overlapping, or whether, again, they may be transgressive of time and space appearing early at one locality, for example, and at a much later date at another. At present it appears that each of these possibilities may exist. The evidence for sequential or stochastic replacement of one complex by another will not be determined satisfactorily, however, until a number more well stratified and dated sequences become available and until many of the reliably dated assemblages are properly described and illustrated. At present, names have been attached to undefined assemblages which, after proper analysis, may well be found to have no more than superficial resemblance to the industry with which they are currently identified (for instance, those ascribed to the Howieson's Poort Complex from the Rose Cottage Cave, Ladybrand).

Developmental trends from assemblages with comparatively simple forms to those with more evolved retouch and a greater range of tool types appear to be stratigraphically demonstrated at a number of sites in South Africa and Zimbabwe (e.g. the Cave of Hearths, Transvaal; Pomongwe and Zombepata Caves, Zimbabwe). In other regions – the South African south coast or Border Cave, for instance – no such directional development can be demonstrated and instead the change through time is stylistic. Thus, at Nelson Bay for example, the earliest Middle Stone Age is characterized by well-made, uni- and bifacial, leaf-shaped points. Above this occurs a Howieson's Poort assemblage distinguished by backed blades and crescents. The latest Middle Stone Age, not present at Nelson Bay Cave, shows a number of essentially local variants or *facies*.

In southern Africa the Middle Stone Age certainly lasted for about 70 000 years or, if the correlation of climatic events and strata at Border

Cave is confirmed, for as much as 140 000 years (Butzer 1978) and the radiometric/isometric dates associated with assemblages belonging to each of the complexes show that each apparently covers a wide range of time as well as of space. Thus, if the dating and the industrial ascription are not at fault, the Middle Stone Age succession is not solely one of progressively evolving technology and refinement through time, and some other interpretation of its variations must be sought. One explanation might be the same as that advanced to explain the various Mousterian traditions, namely, that they represent the stone tool-kits of culturally and genetically distinct populations that persisted for long periods of time in relatively unaltered form, their appearance, disappearance and reappearance being related to migratory movements. Another interpretation might be that the differing complexes were evolved independently and in semi-isolation by more than one of the scattered Middle Stone Age populations, in response to a need for exploiting particular kinds of resources – large game, small game, marine resources, etc. – so that differences in the tool-kits would reflect differences in the resource base without any necessity to invoke population movement. A third explanation might be a combination of the other two in that, while the stone equipment is related to the resources exploited, it is at the same time also related to changing ecological and geographical conditions, in particular to changes in the game population of the exploitation area, as these became readjusted to alterations in the local habitat – from more open to more closed vegetation and vice versa, for example. Thus, where a choice of tool-kit existed, the one adopted would have been that which best fulfilled at the time the requirements of the group making use of that particular site. At the same time, readjustment of the animal and plant communities can also be expected to have had an effect on regional densities among the human population. This third alternative is that which is preferred here.

Environmental changes during the earlier part of the Upper Pleistocene have been well demonstrated from the southern coastal caves and parts of the South African high veld, and it now becomes clearer that the human populations which were dependant on the game animals were equally mobile and/or adaptive within the general limits of their technological ability. Thus, inhospitable environmental conditions on the plateau – stronger winds and lowered temperature during the early Last Glacial – appear to have restricted the occupation sites to favoured river valleys and other sheltered localities, while the sea-level regression of the main Würm Glaciation opened up considerable areas of the continental shelf off the south coast for occupation by animals and man. Attempts to provide a general review of the Middle Stone Age in southern Africa are still hindered, however, by many geographical gaps where little or no research has been carried out and by the uncertainties in the dating and assemblage identifications referred to above.

The antiquity of the earlier Middle Stone Age is best demonstrated by the evidence from several cave sites on the South African south coast where the raw material used was predominantly hard quartzite obtained in unlimited quantity from the local Table Mountain Sandstones. At the Klasies River Mouth Caves, where the chronostratigraphic record is the most informative in southern Africa, the Middle Stone Age occupation spans the period of the Last Interglacial and the earlier part of the Last Glacial, i.e. from > 125 000 to 70 000 BP.[1] The complete occupation sequence at these caves, some 22 m thick, consists of sand, shells and silt containing the Middle Stone Age, resting immediately above and intercalated with the upper part of the 6–8-m beach of the Last Interglacial high sea level (Wymer and Singer 1972).

Throughout the whole of the main Middle Stone Age sequence, the occupants made use of marine as well as terrestrial foods, indicating that the shore was never far away. These marine resources decline only with the youngest Middle Stone Age occupation levels and the cave was abandoned shortly thereafter and not reoccupied until about 6000 years ago with the return of the sea to near its present level. The abandonment of the site appears, therefore, to coincide with the beginning of the regression and low sea level about 60 000–70 000 years ago during the early and main stages of the Last Glacial.

The Middle Stone Age sequence consists of three main industrial stages. The earliest (MSA industries I and II) in a sand and shell midden > 12 m thick, show overall size reduction of artifact through time; long blades and blade cores are very abundant while the Levallois and disc-core technologies appear to be rare or absent. There are few formal tools except for points and the artifacts mostly show discontinuous marginal retouch and utilization. This tool-kit is overlain by 1.5 m of alternating dark grey and light silty sand containing an Howieson's Poort

---

[1] Based on the evidence of stratigraphy (Butzer 1978), high temperature values from oxygen-isotope analysis of marine shells from the base of Klasies River Mouth Cave (R. G. Klein and N. Shackleton, personal communication, Butzer 1978) and amino-acid racemization dates (Bada and Deems 1975). Racemization dates of 110000 BP for the lowest occupation, 89000 and 90000 BP for the middle occupation levels and 65000 BP for a Howieson's Poort horizon (for which there are conflicting radiocarbon dates, the oldest being > 38000 BP) have been obtained.

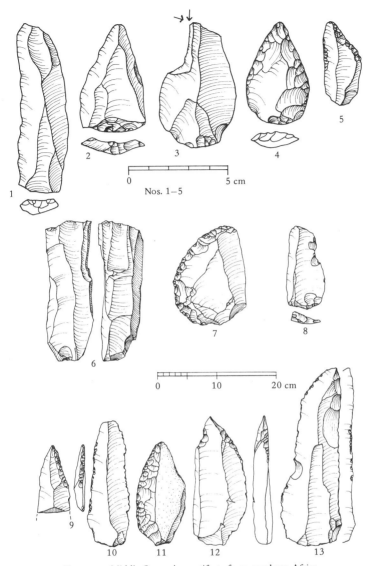

Fig. 4.10   Middle Stone Age artifacts from southern Africa.

*Mossel Bay Industry, from Mossel Bay Cave*
 1  Levallois blade
 2  Levallois point
 3  Canted dihedral burin
 4  Unifacially retouched point
 5  Blade with blunted back
(In quartzite)

*Earlier Orangian Industry, from Elandskloof,*
*Orange Free State*
 6  Prismatic blade core
 7  Side-scraper
 8  Utilized blade fragment
(In indurated shale)

*Earlier Pietersburg Industry, from Bed 4, Cave*
*of Hearths, Transvaal*
 9  Retouched blade fragment
 10–12  Discontinuously retouched and
     edge-damaged blades
 13  Side-scraper
(In quartzite)

(Nos. 1–5 after Keller (1969) and 6–13 after Sampson (1974).)

industry with backed blade forms which is so different from the preceding that it probably is an indicator of very different exploitation techniques. The blade industry is contemporaneous with a marked cool oscillation within the Last Interglacial at about 95 000 BP (Butzer 1978). Above this again there is apparently a return to the earlier, more informal tradition (MSA III and IV). Small unifacial points, denticulates and scrapers, common at first, are replaced by pointed flake-blades and smaller blades. Occupation at the end was sporadic extending into the regression at the onset of the Last Glacial *c.* 70000 BP (J. Deacon 1979, Sampson 1974, Wymer and Singer 1972).

At Nelson Bay Cave on the Robberg Peninsula (Butzer 1973), the sequence is similar but acid groundwaters have destroyed the bone with the Middle Stone Age assemblages, which are located in a pale brown loam, partly aeolian, partly organic in origin, which contains several discrete Middle Stone Age occupation levels associated with hearths.[1] Dating is conflicting and unsatisfactory but these Middle Stone Age assemblages have been correlated with the Klasies River sequence and would appear to belong in the earlier part of the tradition coincident with the Last Interglacial and early Last Glacial and to be more than 50 000 years old. The later part of the Middle Stone Age sequence is missing at Nelson Bay Cave for the overlying post-Middle Stone Age industry dates to 18 100 ± 550 BP.

At Die Kelders Cave I (Klein 1975a, Tankard and Schweitzer 1974) further west on the south coast, a similar sequence is contained within the lower part of an occupation deposit some 7 m thick with four Middle Stone Age layers belonging in time to the early Last Glacial and sealed by a rock fall that is probably younger than 45 000 and older than 33 000 years. Again, marine animals occur in the food waste and again during the major marine regression to > 90 m within the main Würm Glaciation, the cave was abandoned by man and not reoccupied until < 3000 years ago. The earlier Middle Stone Age industries, in quartzite

---

[1] The climate at this time was wet and the lower part of the loam appears to be contemporary with deposits of the Last Interglacial beach at the back of the cave. The artifacts from these levels have not yet been described though it might be expected that they will show affinities with the Mossel Bay Industry. Above are black loams with much organic material and rock spalls from the roof, indicating significant frost-weathering induced by a probable drop of about 10 °C in winter temperatures (Klein 1974). Artifacts are abundant in these levels and comprise flakes and blades, mostly unretouched though sometimes with discontinuous trimming. The most significant artifacts, however, are a series of large backed lunates and blade/flakes characteristic of the third complex – the Howieson's Poort Industry (Klein 1972). The termination of this industry coincided with wetter and warmer, and then drier conditions and a rock fall.

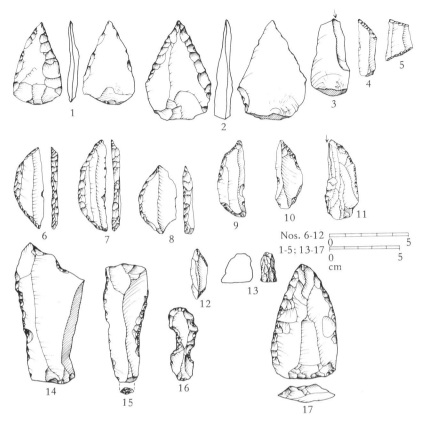

Fig. 4.11   Middle Stone Age artifacts from Howieson's Poort Occurrences in southern Africa.

*Howieson's Poort type site*
1–2  Unifacial points
3   Burin on a break
4   Truncated bladelet
5   Trapeze
(In quartzite)

*Nelson Bay cave*
6–8  Backed blades
(In quartzite)

*Montagu Cave, Layer 2*
9–10  Backed blades
11   Burin on a truncation
12   Trapezium
13   Microblade core or carinated scraper
14–15  Blades showing retouch and
      edge-damage
16   Notched and strangulated scraper
17   Unifacial point
(In chert or quartzite)

(Nos 1–5 after J. D. Clark (1970), 6–8 after Klein (1972) and 9–17 after Keller (1973).)

and with little retouch, from these south coast sites resemble one of the regional Middle Stone Age forms named the Mossel Bay Industry from the assemblages at the Cape St Blaise Cave at Mossel Bay where the same assemblage of blade and snapped blade fragments together with some utilized and convergent flake forms was first found (Goodwin and Malan 1935, Keller 1969) (fig. 4.10.1–5).[1] The Die Kelders Middle Stone Age is believed to postdate the Howieson's Poort Industry as seen at Klasies River.

Inland but still south of the main escarpment in an outlier of the 'Little Karroo' is the important cave site of Montagu (Keller 1973) in the Table Mountain Sandstones. Here the Middle Stone Age occurs unconformably between an Acheulian and the Later Stone Age. No fauna is preserved, but seven Middle Stone Age occupation surfaces, which may be up to 0.8 m thick, were found with concentrations of artifacts and several fire-places and other features, and below these again were other diffuse scatters of Middle Stone Age artifacts. The age-range is from about 19000 to > 50000 years and if this represents a single industrial tradition, it covers nearly 30000 years. But the possibility is suggested by the dates that there is, in fact, an unconformity and a period of non-occupation between the upper and lower levels. From the quartzite used as raw material were produced many long blade and flake forms, sometimes retouched and utilized, coming from Levallois, discoid and non-Levallois cores (fig. 4.11.9–17). But the occupants also made use of small pebbles of quartz and chalcedony to produce artifacts which were often of microlithic proportions. These assemblages have all been described as comparable to that from Howieson's Poort and besides blades and convergent flake forms (sometimes trimmed into end-, convergent and notched side-scrapers), there are also backed and truncated blades and flakes, together with lunates and burins made from quartz and chalcedony. Another characteristic artifact in chalcedony is what could be variously described as a single-platformed microblade core, a keeled scraper or a *busqué* burin (fig. 4.11.13).

While between about 40000 and about 15000 years ago there was a long hiatus in the occupation of the caves in the south coast cliffs and in several of the more interior sites in the Cape Folded Mountain Belt, some of the caves in this mountain zone continued to be favourable for occupation, and an important sequence is currently being excavated at

[1] Similar assemblages occur again in the basal industry in the Skildergat Cave, Fish Hoek, at the Cape, where the sequence is generally similar to that at the caves of Klasies River Mouth and Nelson Bay, with the relatively unmodified Middle Stone Age, which has been termed the Mossel Bay Industry (Sampson 1974), overlain by layers with a Howieson's Poort Industry and, again, by levels with an assemblage resembling that from the lower levels. This cave is also important for the human burial which was found in the upper part of the deposit with the Mossel Bay Industry. Dating of associated animal bone suggests that this burial probably belongs within the layer in which it was found but the possibility cannot be excluded that it might have been buried *into* these deposits from the overlying Howieson's Poort horizon.

Boomplaas Cave on the south side of the Swartberg within the Cape biotic zone and near the ecotone with the arid Karroo to the north (H. J. Deacon and Brooker 1976). This site was almost continuously occupied from about 80 000 years ago and, therefore, covers the period missing from the coastal sites. The lower part of the sequence prior to about 40 000 BP contains a Howieson's Poort industry with backed blades, interstratified in a series of oxidized, ashy and dark carbonized loams. Above, a late phase of the Middle Stone Age terminated about 32 000 BP. Significant environmental changes are demonstrated by the remains of game animals represented in the food waste. During the first half of the Middle Stone Age occupation, browsing animals, in particular the small grysbok, predominated, indicating the presence of much closed bush, but during the second half of the occupation wildebeest and other grazing animals dominated the food waste, indicative of a grassland environment (J. Deacon 1979).

Equally important sequences, a few of them impressively dated, come from cave sites on the high interior plateau and escarpment country. One of the most significant is found in the Cave of Hearths in the northern Transvaal (Mason 1962) uncomformably overlying a rock fall which occurred during climatic conditions comparable to those of today and which sealed the Acheulian deposits. The dating is unsatisfactory but the successive occupation layers show a developing sequence of three stratified assemblages of what the excavator (Mason 1962, pp. 244–5) has described as the Pietersburg Industry. It is based on the predominant use of quartzite with later additions of finer-grained rocks and it existed during a time when the climate was wetter than that of the present. The two earlier assemblages or occurrences (Earlier and Middle Pietersburg) are characterized by minimally retouched or quite unretouched but 'utilized' flakes and blades from specialized and unspecialized cores; trimmed scrapers and point forms are rare and the Earlier Pietersburg contains a number of very long blades and large Levallois flakes (fig. 4.10.9–13). The third occurrence (Later Pietersburg) has many retouched points and scrapers as well as some backed blade forms.

An alternative interpretation of the assemblages from this stratified sequence has been proposed by Sampson (1974, pp. 157–62). Only the lower two assemblages are included by him in the Pietersburg Industry, as he defines it, and with it he associates two other Industries (the Mossel Bay and the Orangean) in a Pietersburg Complex (see also n. 1, p. 297). Mason's Later Pietersburg in Beds 6–9 is divided into an earlier occurrence that represents a regional industry (Mwulu Industry) included within a Bambata Complex and a later occurrence containing backed blades and lunates and showing also a significant decrease in the overall dimensions of the artifacts. According to Sampson, the affinities of this last occurrence lie with the Howieson's Poort assemblages. These two interpretations can be correlated as follows:

| | Mason | Stratigraphy | Sampson |
|---|---|---|---|
| Pietersburg Industry | Later Pietersburg | Beds 6–9 | { Howieson's Poort Assemblage<br>Mwulu Industry |
| | Middle Pietersburg | Bed 5 } | Pietersburg Industry |
| | Earlier Pietersburg | Bed 4 } | |

Whichever interpretation is accepted, the taxonomic sequence from the Cave of Hearths serves as a yardstick against which single component open sites and shorter cave sequences in the Transvaal can be correlated. For example, an open site at Koedoesrand had, because of its large blades and other artifacts in indurated shale, been recognized as one of the very few Earlier Pietersburg assemblages known up to now (Mason 1962, pp. 248–78); at Mwulu's Cave, the sequence of three occupation levels of ash and sand separated by two layers of sterile red sands thought to be indicative of dry conditions contain Pietersburg assemblages comparable to those from Beds 5 and 6–9 at the Cave of Hearths (Sampson 1974, pp. 198–202; Tobias 1949) (fig. 4.12.1, 3, 4, 6–9, 11–13); and an open-air butchery site at Kalkbank, associated with broken and piled bones from animal kills, contains artifacts that show it to belong to the time of the industry in Beds 6–9 of the Cave of Hearths sequence and it has, amongst other tools, some small hand grindstones (fig. 4.13.1–2) and two lower grindstones.

Some indication of the age of this Pietersburg sequence comes from Olieboompoort Cave, the cave sequence at Bushman Rock Shelter in the eastern Transvaal and Border Cave, Ingwavuma, on the borders of Zululand and Swaziland. At Olieboompoort, there is a date of > 33 000 BP for a Later Pietersburg and at Bushman Rock Shelter the industry, made in indurated shale, is a fairly developed form of the Later Pietersburg (Louw 1969). From the middle level comes a radiocarbon date of > 51 000 BP and there is a hiatus of some 12 000 years between the end of the Middle Stone Age and the earliest Later Stone Age assemblage. Older horizons below the base of the excavation presumably

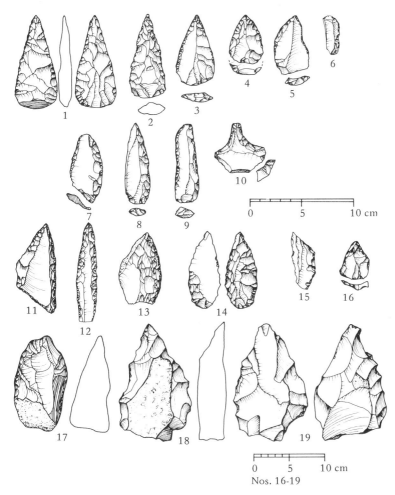

Fig. 4.12   Middle Stone Age artifacts from south central Africa.

*Later Middle Stone Age Mwulu Industry, from Mwulu's Cave, Transvaal*
1  Bifacial point (in felsite)

*Later Middle Stone Age Bambata Industry, from Bambata Cave, Zimbabwe*
2  Bifacial point
5  Backed flake with concave edge-damage on cutting edge
10  Borer
(In quartz, chalcedony and felsite)

*Later Middle Stone Age Mwulu Industry, from Beds 6–9, Cave of Hearths, Transvaal*
3, 4, 12  Unifacial points
6  Retouched bladelet
7, 9  Double side-scrapers
8, 13  Single side-scrapers

11  Angled side-scraper
(In quartzite, felsite, indurated shale and quartz)

*Later Middle Stone Age 'Stillbay Industry', from sites in the south-western Cape*
14  Parti-bifacial point
15  Backed blade
(In quartzite

*Earlier Middle Stone Age Charaman Industry (formerly 'Proto-Stillbay'), from Zimbabwe*
16  Small triangular flake with marginal retouch and facetted striking platform
17  Small unifacial core-axe or pick
18–19  Diminutive hand-axes
(In chalcedony or quartzite)

(Nos 1–10 after J. D. Clark (1970), 11–15 after Sampson (1974) and 16–19 after C. K. Cooke (1966).)

307

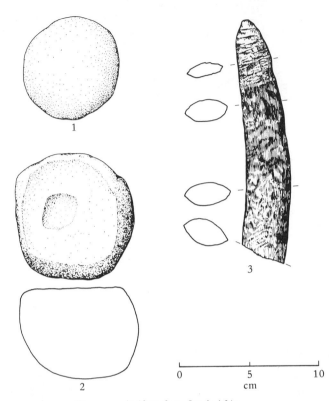

Fig. 4.13    Artifacts from South Africa.

*Later Middle Stone Age (Upper Pietersburg) butchery site at Kalkbank, Transvaal*
1  Spheroid
2  Combination pestle and upper grindstone with dimple scarring

*Earlier Middle Stone Age, from Peat I, Florisbad, Orange Free State*
3  Part of a curved wooden throwing-stick, the proximal end with cut marks that help to give
  a firmer grip when throwing; associated with the skull of *Homo helmei*

(Nos 1–2 after Mason (1958) and 3 after J. D. Clark (1951).)


contain even earlier stages of the Middle Stone Age and a single long
blade recovered in a deep sounding made subsequently may be evidence
of an Earlier Pietersburg assemblage such as exists at the Cave of
Hearths. At the Border Cave, Ingwavuma, the Middle Stone Age
associated with bone waste from meals is divided into three stages –
Pietersburg, 'Epi-Pietersburg' (=Howieson's Poort) and 'post-
Howieson's Poort' (Beaumont *et al.* 1978) – and occurs in sandy and
ashy occupation sediments with much rock spalling from the roof,
especially after the second of the stages (the 'Epi-Pietersburg'). Also

a feature of the occupation associated with this stage are two 'white ash' layers, of which the significance is to be discussed. Two human burials – of an adult and an infant – are believed to belong to the Pietersburg or 'Epi-Pietersburg' occupation of this site and of especial interest is part of a conus shell of marine origin found with the infant skeleton in a shallow grave. The artifact assemblages from these sites still have to be described but the radiocarbon dates and extrapolated chronology indicate an antiquity comparable with or greater than that of the coastal sequences (Beaumont *et al.* 1978, Butzer *et al.* 1978).

In the lower levels at the Border Cave, some developmental trends are recognizable in the Pietersburg Industry, possibly to be equated with the Lower and Middle Pietersburg of the Cave of Hearths, and made in rhyolite, quartz and chalcedony. The occupational sequence shows similarities to that from the south coast. The Pietersburg component is succeeded by Howieson's Poort assemblages with many narrow, ribbon-like blades and lunates made on fragments of Levallois blades, the backing being mostly on the ends of the arcs. With these are also small, sub-triangular, pressure-flaked points but apparently no burins (Sampson 1974, p. 202). Above these assemblages are those named 'post-Howieson's Poort' in which formal blade tools are rare but include trapezes and forms with proximal reduction for hafting. Radiocarbon dates for this terminal assemblage at Border Cave have values of > 49 100 BP. The oldest radiocarbon date for the Howieson's Poort is > 48 700 BP and an aspartic-acid racemization result on bone from this layer, in which the human remains may have been located, gives an age of about 60 000 years (Beaumont 1973, Protsch 1975).

In the foothills west of the Basutoland massif, the Rose Cottage Cave, Ladybrand, contains another important stratigraphic sequence though, as yet, only the briefest description of the assemblages is available. The sequence begins with an unspecialized Middle Stone Age (Sampson 1974, pp. 248–9) at the base, followed by two levels with what have been described as Howieson's Poort assemblages. These are technically and typologically evolved, often of very small dimensions, and contain a proportion of backed flakes, blades and lunates. A date for the upper of these two horizons indicates that it is > 50 000 years old. An overlying deposit of allegedly sterile sands, the result of spring activity at the back of the cave, dated to about 26 000 BP again points to a long hiatus between the Middle Stone Age and succeeding Later Stone Age occupations.

What is probably a related, sophisticated, blade industry of Middle Stone Age tradition has been found at three sites at about 2500 m altitude in the mountains of eastern Lesotho. At each of these sites – Ha Soloja, Sehonghong and Moshebi's – the industry contains lunates, other backed blade pieces, borers and burins and dates to between 30 900 and > 40 000 years BP (Carter and Vogel 1974). It is probably the equivalent of the Howieson's Poort Industry from Ingwavuma and the south coast caves.

In the high grasslands of the semi-arid upper middle reaches of the Orange River basin, the raw material used was almost exclusively indurated shale. The quarries are situated at the outcrops on the plateau edge from where the material was carried down to the occupation sites in the main valley and tributary streams. These occupations almost all consist of a single horizon in the open and three Phases have been recognized with the first two grouped to form an Orangian Industry, as yet undated (Sampson 1974, pp. 162–70). The emphasis here is on the production of blades and, more rarely, of triangular flakes struck from Levallois and non-Levallois cores, with a preponderance of cutting tools or knives. The overall dimensions of the artifacts diminish through time and, not unnaturally, with distance from the quarry sites. At Elandskloof the earlier Orangian stage (fig. 4.10.6–8), stratified unconformably above an Acheulian with a high proportion of flake/blades, is characterized by discontinuously trimmed and retouched, longish blades and blade fragments. In the second stage/Phase, smaller examples of the same forms occur, together with some burins and unifacially trimmed points. One of these Orangian Industry occupation sites preserves a number of hunting blinds and sleeping-hollows (p. 335). The Phase 3 assemblages are characterized by numbers of utilized blades, blade fragments and flakes struck from prismatic and cylindrical blade cores; formal tools and the Levallois technique are not found.

In the north-west, near Kimberley, the Alexandersfontein Pan area in what is now the arid to semi-arid Karroo vegetation zone enjoyed more rain and lowered temperatures during most of Middle Stone Age times. Two stages of Middle Stone Age occupation are recognized – an earlier group of assemblages in which retouch is characteristic and a later group comprising many blades with little or no retouch, comparable to the Phase 3 assemblages from the Orange River basin (Butzer 1973). This emphasis on blades is repeated in the many surface sites known from

Namibia (South West Africa) though retouched points and scrapers are not uncommon here.[1]

On the high plateau at sites such as Florisbad, Vlakkraal and others in the 'zuurveld' grasslands and at the hunting camp-site of Witkrans on the scarp of the Harts River valley, dated about 32 000 radiocarbon years ago, springs were active. Florisbad is particularly important for the stratified sequence of three peat levels representing times of spring quiescence separating sands deposited during periods of activity. The lowest peat is probably more than 100 000 years old and is beyond the range of the radiocarbon method. It has produced an important fauna with several extinct forms of giant antelope besides the incomplete cranium of *Homo helmei* associated with a pollen spectrum indicative of a drier-loving vegetation. The artifact assemblage comprises choppers, polyhedrons, pounding stones and perhaps long blades such as occur with the earliest Middle Stone Age in the Transvaal. This peat has also produced what may be the grip-end of a wooden throwing-stick (fig. 4.13.3). Peat II has now been dated to $> 42\,600$ years BP and just below this is an artifact assemblage made on long narrow blades of indurated shale but with several unifacially retouched points and scrapers. The assemblage from Vlakkraal is similar and is associated with a fauna with several extinct species (e.g. horse, giant buffalo, alcelaphines and gazelle). The increased importance of retouch at these sites is reminiscent of the later Middle Stone Age assemblages from Zimbabwe and also of certain inadequately known and mostly surface collections from the western Cape and Natal where silcrete and other fine-grained rocks were used and which belong to what has been called the 'Stillbay Industry' after a site in the western Cape (fig. 4.12.14–15). Although they have never been adequately described, it seems probable that the assemblages stratified between the basal (? Mossel Bay) industry and the 'Howieson's Poort' layers in the Skildergat Cave may belong to this 'Stillbay' tradition. Bone from these layers and that from which the human remains are presumed to have come has given a date of some 36 000 BP, but this is clearly a minimal age (Protsch 1973).

The small rock-shelter, set below the top of a steep scarp in the eastern Cape, from which the assemblage named after Howieson's Poort was recovered, is more likely to have been a seasonal hunting-camp than

---

[1] In Namibia also assemblages with Lupemban-like forms of unifacial foliate point and core-axe are known to occur (MacCalman and Viereck 1967). Two such assemblages are also recorded from the central Transvaal (Mason 1962) and one from the northern Cape (Humphreys 1974).

a base-camp because of the limited area for occupation and the shallowness of the deposit. The assemblage combines Middle Stone Age flaking methods with a dominant non-Levallois blade technology and the characteristic tools are backed and truncated blades and flakes, burins and unifacial points (fig. 4.11.1–5). A date of c. 18700 BP was obtained for this occupation but, in view of the considerably greater ages ascribed to the Howieson's Poort assemblages from Klasies River Mouth, Nelson Bay Cave, Boomplaas, Border Cave and other sites, it seems likely that the dated sample from the type-site was contaminated due to the shallowness of the deposit and is, therefore, too young. The probable age of the Howieson's Poort Complex is, therefore, between about 95 000 and 80 000 years BP.

The Middle Stone Age sequence on the central plateau between the Zambezi and Limpopo valleys appears to be much less variable than does that in South Africa. At the same time it can be seen to combine characteristics of the traditions found in the woodlands north of the Zambezi with those of the high grasslands and bushveld south of the Limpopo. A 'Sangoan' stage succeeding the Acheulian has been recognized from the valley of the Zambezi and from the Limpopo tributaries but it now seems more probable (see p. 289) that this heavy-duty equipment is an integral part of the earlier Middle Stone Age tradition, here called the *Charaman Industry* which takes its name from surface assemblages on the Charama plateau at 1220 m elevation in open woodland. Assemblages of the Charaman Industry (C. K. Cooke 1966) have been found in the lower part of two cave sequences in the Matopo Hills (Bambata and Pomongwe caves) and at the base of an open-site sequence at Khami near Bulawayo (C. K. Cooke 1957). At the open sites the heavy-duty equipment is prominent while many more light-duty tools and waste pieces are associated with the cave occupation sites. The Charaman comprises picks, core-axes and small bifaces together with many utilized flakes and flake blades, some struck from Levallois and discoid cores (fig. 4.12.16–19). Retouch is characterized by denticulation and notching forming simple sub-triangular points and various scraper forms. This light-duty equipment is invariably made in quartz or other fine siliceous rock, whereas the larger tools are usually made in coarser-grained rocks. The only date available is > 42 000 BP from Pomongwe Cave. On the evidence of the associated fauna, the Charaman

Industry is younger than the human fossils from Kabwe (Broken Hill) and is probably the equivalent of the earlier Lupemban industries of the humid tropics.

The succeeding industry appears to be a logical development out of the earlier Middle Stone Age and is known as the Bambata Industry after the first excavated cave sample from the Matopo Hills. The assemblages contain numbers of unifacially and bifacially retouched points, end- and side-scrapers, burins, borers, backed and truncated flakes and blade fragments as well as grindstones (fig. 4.12.2, 5, 10). Another feature of these sites, as of the Charaman, are the crayons or pencils of pigment that are associated. More than one hundred sites of the Bambata Industry are known from the escarpment mountains in the east as far as north-western Botswana and, as already stated, assemblages with a comparable degree of retouch and similar tool forms occur in the Transvaal, Free State and the Cape. In Zimbabwe the Bambatan assemblages show no significant developmental trends and the industry is generally considered to be contemporary with a long period of increased rainfall. At Zombepata, Redcliff and Tshangula the Bambata occupations are sealed by rock falls from the roof which appear to date to between 21 000 and 25 000 years ago (C. K. Cooke 1971).[1] There is every reason to suppose that the Bambata Industry was of the same general antiquity as the Pietersburg Industry assemblages from the Border Cave but in Zimbabwe there follows an evolved form, that preserves the Middle Stone Age technological tradition, which is named the *Tshangulan* (formerly Umgusan) *Industry*. This is what used to be called 'Rhodesian Magosian' and it shows an overall decrease in artifact dimensions. Diminutive forms of triangular points, showing evolved retouch, occur together with an increased number of blades struck from non-Levallois cores and sometimes retouched to form lunates and small backed blades (fig. 4.14.1–4). Burins and circular scrapers (fig. 4.14.11) occur as well as flat, thin discs which may have been adze blades. At some sites bored stones are present. This Tshangulan Industry is widespread on the watershed stretching into the main river valleys to the north and south but is not the same as the Howieson's Poort assemblages from the Cape. Radiocarbon-dated samples indicate that its time range lies between about 25 000 and 13 000 BP and, if these dates are reliable, it clearly represents one of the latest expressions of Middle Stone Age technology in southern Africa,

---

[1] Radiocarbon date for the Bambatan Industry at Zombepata is > 39 900 and at Pomongwe about 40 720 BP (C. K. Cooke 1967, 1978).

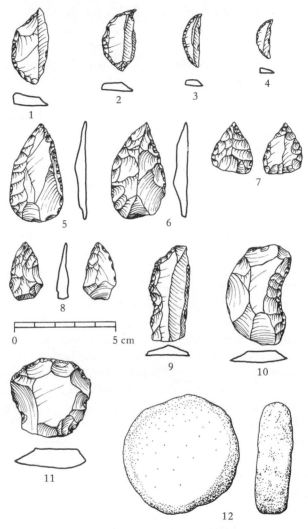

Fig. 4.14   Artifacts of the Tshangula Industry
from Pomongwe Cave, Zimbabwe.

1–4  Backed lunates
5, 6  Unifacial points
7, 8  Bifacial points
9, 10  Side-scrapers

11  Circular scraper
12  Combination pestle and grinding stone
(In chalcedony or quartz)

(After Sampson 1974.)

contemporary, in fact, with the earliest Later Stone Age industries in the Cape winter-rainfall region.

Although the Tshangulan has some elements in common with the 'Epi-Pietersburg' levels at the Border Cave and the Howieson's Poort levels at Rose Cottage Cave, they are separated in time by some 50000 years or more. It is of considerable interest, therefore, that at Zombepata, as also at Bambata, there are two levels in the middle of the Bambatan occupation that show a significant increase in the number of small blades. These levels must be more than 40000 years old and another such layer has been recognized at Redcliff in the same age-range (Cooke 1978). It seems probable, therefore, that these intercalated layers with blades may be the equivalent in Zimbabwe of the Howieson's Poort Complex in South Africa. The Tshangulan, if it is correctly dated, cannot now be considered as belonging with the Middle Stone Age proper but as a local tropical complex that has continued to use a prepared core technology.

## MIDDLE STONE AGE TRADITIONS

In the Middle Stone Age of Africa, therefore, there is a significant trend in each region towards tools of smaller dimensions and an increasing variety of tool forms. Retouch is a more variable trait and seems to be independent of space and time, being related more directly, it would seem, to behavioural patterning and to the raw material available. Fig. 4.15 shows the chronological relationships between the various traditions in the main regions of the continent. In North Africa, the only cultural assemblage that can with confidence be ascribed to the Last Interglacial is the Pre-Aurignacian blade industry from the Haua Fteah, but it seems probable that the earliest Mousterian in the Maghrib, Cyrenaica and on the Moroccan coast makes its appearance towards the end of that time and, in some instances, common elements shared with the Acheulian are evidence for some as yet undemonstrated continuity. Although it is still inadequately dated, there is reason to believe that the contemporary form in Equatoria and the south-central African savannas is represented by the earlier part of the Lupemban Complex with heavy-duty ('Sangoan') equipment and large bifacial foliates. In South Africa the earliest Middle Stone Age industries of the south coast and interior plateau are also characterised by high proportions of minimally modified blades, though the Levallois technique is also already present.

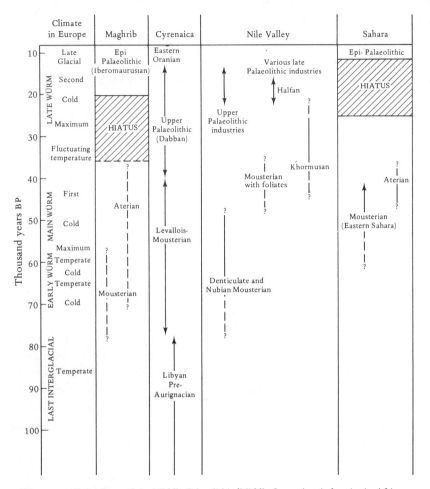

Fig. 4.15    Chronology of the Middle Palaeolithic/Middle Stone Age industries in Africa.

With the onset of the early part of the Last Glacial (from 75 000 to about 35 000 BP) these regional traditions become more varied and a greater degree of local differentiation is evident; the specialized core techniques (Levallois and disc) are everywhere apparent. In north-west Africa, the Aterian Complex, specializing in the use of tangs, is in part contemporary with, and later replaces, a Typical Mousterian tradition. In Cyrenaica, the Mousterian shares a number of traits in common with assemblages of the Levallois–Mousterian from the Levant. In the Nile Valley, there are at least two regional Mousterian forms (Denticulate

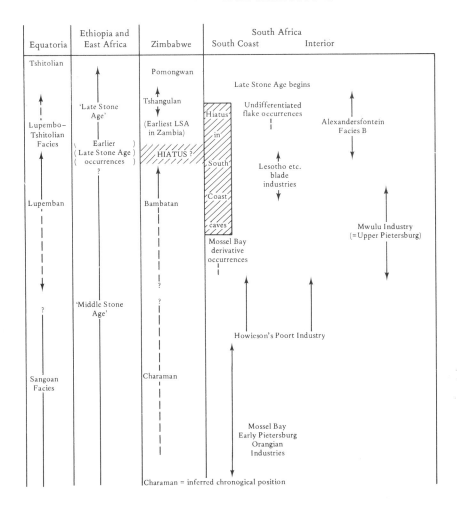

and Nubian). The Aterian was widely distributed in the western and central Sahara and it is doubtful whether an earlier Mousterian tradition was ever present there. Throughout most of the eastern Sahara, however, the Aterian appears to have replaced the Mousterian, though the latter continued on in the Nile Valley adopting a few Aterian traits – but not the tang – and a late form (Khormusan) gave place to a diminutive or micro-Levallois tradition (Halfan) about 20 000 years ago. The Aterian was wholly or in part contemporary with the later stages of the Lupemban Complex of Equatoria and the presence of tanged forms in the late Lupemban (Lupembo-Tshitolian) and of long foliates in the Aterian of the central Sahara, suggests that the Sahel/Sudan zone of West Africa south of the desert was a region of interaction between these two major exploitation patterns, the one making use of the resources provided by the semi-arid to arid desert habitats and the other of those of the more closed vegetation zones of the high-rainfall belts. While the desert populations adopted mostly light equipment – projectile points, scrapers and knives – those of the savannas made greater use of adze- and axe-like stone tools probably for working wood for several purposes including the making of other tools and utensils. They also used long projectile points or knives probably designed for the specialized hunting of large game. In East Africa, the emphasis is more on stubby, sub-triangular points and convex and circular scraper forms but, as in the Aterian and on the Nile, the later stages contain a significant Upper Palaeolithic element.

The South African evidence for a Middle Stone Age developmental trend is less easy to interpret as it is complicated by facies changes resulting partly from different raw materials and the varied regional adaptations these and local preferences produced. The new dates make a three stage framework of 'Complexes' (Pietersburg, Bambata and Howieson's Poort) unacceptable – or unproven – until regional sequences are more firmly dated and better described. There is more evidence for relationships between succeeding assemblages from any one geographical area than for contemporary assemblages from different regions, probably for the reasons stated; this is well seen when comparing the sequences in Zambia, Zimbabwe and the Congo Basin. But in South Africa the Howieson's Poort Complex seems to cut across this geographical continuity, occurring in widely separated, different ecological regions. The significance of this 'interpolation' of radically different tool forms is not yet known. Is it the outcome of environmentally induced new exploitation strategies, of an improved technology or of a new ethnic element in the gene pool? There are too many gaps and uncontrolled variables to be able to offer any convincing hypothesis as yet. Why also, as seems to be the case, was this relatively short lived complex replaced by a return to the technology of the earlier part of the Middle Stone Age? By about 40 000 years ago the Middle Stone Age mode was replaced in most of the continent though in some parts, such as Zimbabwe (Tshangulan) and the northern Cape and Free State (Alexandersfontein Pan; Orange River Phase 3) Middle Stone Age technology lingered on for another 20 000 years or more.

In view of the time-depth now established for the Middle Stone Age in the continent it appears unlikely that these discrete assemblage traditions could be the tool-kits of culturally and genetically different but contemporary human populations and they may more realistically be viewed as cultural adaptations to changing exploitation patterns which in turn reflect the modifications in the availability of plant and animal resources that changing climate and sea level etc. brought about. Improvements in equipment and exploitation strategies through time can be expected to have made the populations that adopted them more efficient and to have led to a closer relationship between themselves and the resources they were using. While two tool-kits may not show any significant differences, though it can be demonstrated that their makers occupied different macroenvironments, important differences might be expected in the manner in which this equipment was used. It is also likely that any such specialization will be reflected not so much in the gross morphological differences between the types of stone tools but rather in the relative proportions in which these artifacts occur and in the wear patterns on the edges that result from the different ways of using the tools. The differences between the various contemporary forms of the Middle Palaeolithic/Middle Stone Age in the Maghrib, Cyrenaica, the Nile Valley, Equatoria and in southern Africa must reflect regional preferences and adaptations based on long traditional usage, the adjustments being more those of style, interacting with raw material and technique. On the other hand, more fundamental changes, such as those from blade to Levallois flake technology in Cyrenaica or in southern Africa, might be related to population changes or to the adoption of significantly different exploitation patterns by the same population, or, again, to a combination of both.

## HUMAN REMAINS

As has been shown in chapter 2, it was during the time of the Middle Palaeolithic/Middle Stone Age that modern man first made his appearance in the continent, replacing the neanderthaloid and all other forms of early man. From north Africa there are no human fossils that can be securely dated to the time of the Last Interglacial but, so far as the Maghrib is concerned, it may be expected that the human population would not have been greatly different from the *Homo* sp. groups represented by the fossils from Thomas Quarry 1 (Casablanca) and Rabat and the cranium from the Plateau de Salé. Indeed, the first two, associated with a 'Presoltanian' fauna, could be of early Last Interglacial age and the contemporary industries, though Acheulian, show many Mousterian forms. Some of these fossils have been described as 'pre-Neanderthal' and the retention of some *Homo erectus* (*Atlanthropus*) characteristics has suggested a locally-evolving lineage (Howell 1960, Jaeger 1975) but, as yet, the origin of these late Middle/early Upper Pleistocene hominids remains unknown.

In sub-Saharan Africa the *Homo rhodesiensis* lineage appears to have been widespread and must, in fact, be contemporary with the Maghrib fossils, on the new racemization dating from related faunal assemblages. At Kabwe (Broken Hill), the associated artifact assemblages are probably of late Acheulian or early Middle Stone Age ('Sangoan') date and, at latest, might fall within the beginning of the Last Interglacial. The artifacts thought to be associated with the fragmentary Lake Eyasi crania are Middle Stone Age flakes from Levallois and disc cores and some Sangoan-like core-axes while those with the Saldanha cranium are Upper Acheulian and the fauna is a Middle Pleistocene one. It seems probable, therefore, that the rhodesioid lineage may have been present over a very long period of time in sub-Saharan Africa from the later Middle to the beginning of the Upper Pleistocene.

With the onset of the Last Glacial it is certain that a Neanderthal population was present in north Africa (Jebel Irhoud; Haua Fteah) but the extent to which this has its roots in the older 'pre-Neanderthal' population, or might be intrusive from the Levant, has yet to be determined, and there is evidence to suggest that both these sources may have contributed to the gene pool. The Neanderthal fossils from Jebel Irhoud and Haua Fteah are associated with Mousterian industries, as might be expected, but the recent discovery of a partial cranium and postcranial bones associated with an early Aterian industry at Dar es-Soltan, as well as an occipital bone and jaw fragment from an upper Aterian level at Témara, is the first indication of what the makers of this complex may have been like. These belong to our own species – modern man – and are described as early representatives of the Mechta–Afalou race (Ferembach 1976a, b) that is associated with the earlier Epi-Palaeolithic in the Maghrib. It would seem, therefore, that modern man may already have replaced the neanderthaloid populations in north-west Africa by 40 000 years ago.

The population of north-eastern Africa during the early part of the Upper Pleistocene appears to show both neanderthaloid and non-neanderthaloid (modern) characteristics since two fossils associated with

Middle Palaeolithic/Middle Stone Age assemblages from the Upper Nile and Ethiopia are said to exhibit traits of both. It is, however, unknown whether this is an indication of hybridization or an emergent modern form from the neanderthal.[1]

Some of the earliest examples of modern man known from the continent may be the crania from Kanjera and Omo (Kibish Formation) in East Africa. Although the industry associated with the Omo fossils is unknown, those from Kanjera, at one time thought to be of Acheulian age, can more probably be associated with the Middle Stone Age assemblage there.[2]

In southern Africa, the base of the stratigraphic and cultural sequence preserved in Border Cave (Ingwavuma) may date to about 195 000 BP (Butzer et al. 1978) and the human fossils (adult jaw and cranial bones and a child's skeleton) said to come from the base of the Howieson's Poort or the top of the Pietersburg layers, would, therefore be at least ~ 95 000 years old. Other equally early mandible and cranial fragments from the Middle Stone Age II levels at Klasies River show both modern and robust features. The fossils from Mumbwa, Bushman Rock Shelter and Skildergat Cave are associated with ages ranging between about 18 000 and 36 000 years BP but these again must be considered minimal. The Boskop and Cape Flats fossils were not found in association with artifacts but Tuinplaats, which resembles Border Cave, is said to have been found with a late stage of the Pietersburg Industry. These are all fairly robust forms, of normal stature, wherever this can be determined, and it is claimed for some (Skildergat, Boskop) that they exhibit features suggesting that they represent an ancestral Khoisan stock. Others again (Tuinplaats; Cape Flats) show none of these 'paedomorphic' (Bushman) features. The infant jaw from Bushman Rock Shelter may represent an early 'negroid' form of modern man and is believed to have an age of 29 500 years and to have been associated with an assemblage transitional between the terminal Middle and Later Stone Ages (Protsch and de Villiers 1974). The latest interpretation of the Border Cave and

[1] The earlier of the two is probably that from Singa on the Blue Nile south of Khartoum, associated with an 'unspecialized' Middle Stone Age assemblage and two extinct faunal species. The associated calcretes are dated, from another site, to about 17 000 BP but this must be considered a minimal age. The association of the neanderthaloid mandibular fragment from the Porc Epic Cave, Dire Dawa (Vallois 1951), with a fully developed Middle Stone Age industry is now confirmed but it is, as yet, undated (J. D. Clark and Williams 1978).

[2] The thorium–uranium age of ~ 130 000 years that has been quoted for the Omo fossils should be treated with considerable caution but, even so, it is most probable that they belong within the earlier part of the Upper Pleistocene.

Tuinplaats fossils is that they represent an early, unspecialized form of modern man (*Homo sapiens sapiens*) from which the Khoisan and negroid lineages could have evolved (Rightmire 1979).

There are two older human fossils from South Africa that belong within the late Middle/earlier Upper Pleistocene time-range. The juvenile mandibular fragment (and proximal part of a right radius) associated with a late Acheulian industry and a terminal Middle to Upper Pleistocene fauna in the Cave of Hearths suggests a robust individual and the jaw is said to show characteristics in common with the Rabat and Témara fossils from the Maghrib (Tobias 1968). Probably somewhat later in age is the partial cranium and face from Florisbad ascribed to an early, relatively robust form of *Homo sapiens*. The associated industry and fauna suggest a very early Upper Pleistocene or older age while the dating for Peat II of > 42 600 BP seems to confirm an appreciably earlier dating for the human fossil and artifacts from the lower peat. Since the mandible and cranial fragments associated with the Middle Stone Age II levels in the Klasies River Mouth Cave are > 95 000 years old and show some comparable robust features, they suggest that the Florisbad fossil has an even greater antiquity (Rightmire 1976a, b).

It is as yet unknown whether modern man evolved via a Neanderthal stage from the late *Homo erectus*/rhodesioid gene pool. Another possibility is that some essentially modern but seemingly early fossils such as the crania from Omo and the Border Cave fossils, may have derived directly from a more archaic *sapiens* form, of which the Florisbad skull is representative, thus bypassing Neanderthal. Both are possible, but only further stratified, well-dated fossils and associated cultural remains can determine which was the more probable course. If the first was the correct one, then it presupposes that modern man evolved contemporaneously in each of the main geographical regions of the continent. If the second hypothesis is shown to be more likely, then a relatively rapid diffusion of 'modern' genes from some as yet unidentified source area must be supposed. If the Border Cave fossils are as old as they appear to be, then it could be claimed that southern Africa lay within this source area (Beaumont *et al.* 1978, Rightmire 1979), and these South African fossils can be seen as relatively unspecialized representatives of the ancestral form from which the later Khoisan and negroid races evolved (Beaumont *et al.* 1978, Rightmire 1979).

However this came about, there seems good reason to suppose that, before the end of the Middle Palaeolithic/Middle Stone Age, the African populations were all of anatomically modern form. If, as this author believes, the unique advantage modern man possessed over all other forms was the ability to communicate by means of a fully developed language system, then the rapidity with which the modern lineage appeared in all parts of the occupied Old World might be seen as the outcome of increased gene flow and natural and social selection processes operating between semi-isolated but open communities and so eliminating the outmoded, archaic characteristics. Such changes could probably have come about without any major population movements, through the kind of communication that exists among all open-system hunting–gathering groups.

Only further research and more complete material will elucidate the relationships these various fossils bear to each other but, nonetheless, it appears to be very evident that the Middle Palaeolithic/Middle Stone Age spans the time of two major genetic changes in the human populations of the continent. The first was at the end of the Middle and the beginning of the Upper Pleistocene when the pre-neanderthaloid/rhodesioid populations were replaced by early *Homo sapiens* stock and the second during the Last Interglacial and the early part of the Last Glacial when modern man (*H. sapiens sapiens*) successfully established himself over all the other, more archaic, forms, and the genetic changes leading to differentiation of the Khoisan and negroid populations may have already begun. The north African neanderthaloids and the sub-Saharan early *H. sapiens* forms reflect separate populations which most probably derive their distinctiveness from long isolation and adaptation to prevailing ecological conditions in the continent's major ecosystems. Such adaptation is also demonstrated by the behavioural patterning and economies of the Middle Stone Age populations of these same regions.

## MIDDLE STONE AGE REGIONAL PATTERNING, BEHAVIOUR AND ECONOMY

The Middle Palaeolithic/Middle Stone Age is spread generally throughout the continent, except in some mountain regions, and, relatively speaking, the number of known sites is greater than in the Lower Pleistocene. However, the poulations can never have been large and occupation appears to have been confined essentially to certain especially favourable microhabitats such as stream courses, lake and swamp sides, sea-shores, springs and caves and rock-shelters. Often, moreover, these sites are located in the ecotone between two or more major environmental zones where a range of resources was available – for example, El-Guettar where, from the spring, the resources of the plateau and the desert were equally accessible; Twin Rivers at the boundary between the floodplain grasslands and the open woodland of the plateau; Witkrans where the valley, escarpment, and Kalahari Desert could all be exploited; and Klasies River Mouth where resources of closed bush, grassland and the sea-shore were available. The range of habitats is very extensive and the thick stratified sequences in some cave sites show that, for many Middle Stone Age populations, the pattern was one of transhumance between a small number of base-camps which would be seasonally reoccupied with regularity over a long period of time. At some localities few or no major unconformities are found in the Middle Stone Age occupation deposits (e.g. Cave of Hearths, Bambata, Pomongwe) but at others (Rose Cottage Cave, Moshebi's Shelter) sterile sediments indicate periods of non-occupation which may correlate with relatively unfavourable cold and dry times during the Last Glacial when the mountains may have been abandoned and occupation concentrated in a few favourable places on the interior plateau. Clearly, some population movement coincided with game movements and during such times other ecological readjustments can also be expected. The tropics appear to have offered generally favourable conditions and the occupation sequence there is often continuous. In contrast, on the southern Cape coast the later part of the Middle Stone Age sequence is missing. On faunal and sedimentological evidence, there can be no doubt that, with the general lowering of sea level during the main Würm Glaciation, the shoreline in places where the continental shelf was gently sloping was removed some 60 km to the south of the caves on the Robberg Peninsula and the animal and human populations moved to new localities that are now once again beneath the sea. A similar explanation might be invoked to explain the hiatus between the Aterian and the Epi-Palaeolithic in the Maghrib. Although here the extent of newly-exposed shelf and coastal plains would not have been so great because the shore line slopes more steeply especially in the Mediterranean, now buried sea-coasts can be expected to have provided a more favourable area for settlement than the less sheltered parts of the plateau, especially if the game population had become redispersed and the human groups had begun to make more systematic use of marine sources of food. In the same way, in the Sahara, the generally unfavourable arid conditions appear to have been responsible for bringing the Middle Stone Age occupation there to an end and the depopulation of the desert may have led to increased numbers entering, for example, the valley of the Nile where more evolved industries (Khormusan, Halfan) are evidence of a continuing Middle Stone Age tradition. The drier environment pertaining in the Congo basin during much of the Upper Pleistocene encouraged settlement in this previously forest-covered region.

The tool-kits themselves can provide little convincing evidence of precisely how the different kinds of implements may have been used and, as yet, no wear-pattern studies have been carried out. Cutting equipment is one of the most important in all of these industries. Scrapers are always the most significant part of the retouched stone equipment. They were probably used for preparing hides, for scraping and adzing the wood for spear-points and clubs (both present in the Middle Pleistocene) and for making other artifacts. Boring tools – for making holes in skin, wood products, bone, horn or shell; the development of tangs; the reduction of the proximal ends of points; the long lanceolate forms from Equatoria; the well-shaped stone balls and, at the end, the bored stone – all suggest increasingly more elaborate and efficient equipment in which at least two different materials (e.g. stone and wood) were combined by the use of mastic, greenhide or other binding material to produce more efficient knives, spears with improved cutting potential and two-piece clubs.

The use of bone for tools is still likely to have been mainly fortuitous (as handles for Aterian tools or selected limb-bone parts for use in butchering a carcase as at Kalkbank (pp. 329–30)). There is, however, occasional evidence for some intentional shaping of bone as of the 'flute' fragment from Haua Fteah (see plate 5.1) and the awl-like point fragment from Kabwe (fig. 4.9.6). While, therefore, the properties of bone as a suitable material for tools appear to have been recognized at this time, it may be expected that the availability of the many hard woods, especially in the tropics, and the greater ease with which they could be worked, precluded any significant use of shaped bone tools before the Later Stone Age.

In the more humid tropics the many and evolving core-axe forms are interpreted as evidence for the increased importance of wood and wood products – inner and outer bark, resins, latex, soft and hard woods – as well as of the increased use that was made of the food resources of the woodlands and forest ecotone and of the equipment needed to climb up to hives and to extract honey. What is probably a portion of a broken wooden implement, perhaps a digging- or throwing-stick, comes from a late Middle Stone Age open-air workshop at Chambuage Mine, north-east Angola (J. D. Clark 1968, pp. 109–21) and from Peat I at Florisbad comes what may be a portion of a curved throwing-stick with cut marks at one end resembling the grip cuts on an Australian throwing-stick (J. D. Clark 1955) (fig. 4.13.3).

In the savanna also the presence of hand grindstones – a combination pounder and grinder (fig. 4.14.12) – and nut-cracking stones is also an indication of the increasing importance of collected grains and hard seeds in particular at the Transvaal, Zimbabwe and Zambian sites. Although such foods must have been of major importance in the savanna, there do not appear to have been any grindstones in the caves of the southern coastal zone but, instead, the exploitation of sea-foods there, as also at the Haua Fteah, Cyrenaica, is now the best-documented and oldest evidence for the use of marine resources known anywhere in the world. Indeed, this evidence is not confined only to the caves but open-air shell-middens dating to early in the Last Interglacial are now reported from 'Sea Harvest', Saldanha Bay (Klein 1975a; also personal communication). However, the Middle Stone Age groups appear to have been only incompletely adapted to coastal environments as, while the bones of seals and penguins (i.e. flightless birds) are common in the food waste, those of fish and flying sea-birds are either absent or very rare and become important only with the beginning of the Later Stone Age. It can be inferred, therefore, that Middle Stone Age man at the coast had not yet developed efficient methods of fowling or of securing fish. Changes in the proportions of the different kinds of molluscs collected are probably not indications of dietary preferences but rather of environmental changes in the seawater temperature and levels that affected natural distributions.[1] At the same time that marine resources began to be exploited, there is evidence that freshwater sources were similarly being used on the Nile and perhaps generally in the large river and lake systems. The later Mousterian occupants of the Wadi Halfa area of the Nile Valley also had begun to exploit the fish resources of the river as abundant remains of catfish, Nile perch, *Tilapia*, etc. are found at one site (Site 440 at Khor Musa). The Mousterian hunters, like the makers of the later Khormusan Industry on the Nubian Nile (40 000–30 000 BP) also concentrated on the hunting of wild cattle

[1] Thus, at the Klasies River Mouth Cave, molluscs were collected from intertidal pools and rock ledges from the zones exposed at low tide. At the beginning (Middle Stone Age I) limpets and *Turbo* were the main species. Later (Middle Stone Age II), preferences alternated between these two forms. In the 'Howieson's Poort' layers chitons, *Turbo* and mussels were the most important at first while in later times the emphasis was again on limpet collection (Voigt 1973).

(*Bos primigenius*) together with gazelle, wild ass and hippopotamus (Wendorf and Schild in press).

Some of the best evidence for changing ecological conditions and hunting practices during the Middle Palaeolithic/Middle Stone Age is provided by the associated faunal remains at the sites. In north Africa, several extinct forms, as well as genera and species that now exist only in the Ethiopian fauna of tropical Africa, are present at Mousterian and/or Aterian occupation sites. Elephant and rhinoceros, a giant deer, an immigrant of the Palaearctic fauna, hippopotamus, giant buffalo, wild cattle, a large zebra, the wild ass, pigs, Barbary sheep and a range of large to medium-sized antelopes and gazelles are represented in the food waste in proportions that can be taken as showing the frequency of their local availability.[1] The main Middle Stone Age occurrences in sub-Saharan Africa, on the other hand, are associated predominantly with medium-sized species but with certain giant forms – horse (*Equus capensis*), an alcelaphine (*Megalotragus* sp. = ? *Alcelaphus helmei*), wildebeest (*Connochaetes grandis* = ? *C. gnou* sub-sp.), buffalo (*Pelorovis antiquus*) an extinct springbok (*Antidorcas bondi*) and a giant wart-hog (? = *Stylochoerus* sp.) being the most important. The buffalo and *Megalotragus* persisted until about 12 000 years ago and the latest known occurrence of *A. bondi* is about 38 000 BP at the Border Cave. While in some cases (e.g. that of the giant buffalo) man may have hastened their extinction, it is evident that the major factor in their disappearance was environmental.[2]

While, however, the Middle Stone Age populations were essentially hunters of large game wherever it was to be found, they also sometimes made use of small animals in certain microhabitats where the large game was scarce or absent. At Die Kelders Cave, for example, while remains of eland, pig and other large land animals are present, they are rare and

---

[1] Thus, for example, at Kabwe (Broken Hill) five out of the twenty-three large mammal species are now extinct; the composition of the Duinefontein 2 fauna suggests a similar age and a relationship to the earlier fauna from Elandsfontein. At Chelmer (H. B. S. Cooke and Wells 1951) on the Zambezi/Limpopo watershed, a fauna dating to pre-Bambata Industry times has about 50% of extinct forms. In the fauna from Florisbad, some of these extinct forms still persist suggesting a comparable but somewhat later age. The fauna from the horizon that produced the Singa skull in the Sudan may also belong to this time-range.

[2] For example, five extant grassland species and subspecies present in the Cape biotic-zone faunas up to the end of the Pleistocene do not occur there after that time due to the expansion of bush and forest communities in the early Holocene, but they are found today in the grasslands north of the Great Escarpment. Similar shifts in vegetation and animal communities are also recorded for the South African sites and at Klasies River Mouth Caves, the fauna of the early part of the Last Interglacial shows a big percentage of alcelaphines (hartebeest, wildebeest, etc.) and a much lower percentage of closed-vegetation species (bushbuck, grysbok). During the middle part of the Last Interglacial, the browsing species increased and the grazers (alcelaphines) declined. In early Last Glacial times, this trend is reversed and the grassland species increase significantly; at the same time there is a reduction in the number of seal remains (Klein 1975a, b; 1978b).

the inhabitants mostly made use of such small animals as tortoises, mole rats, hares and the small grysbok antelope (Klein 1975a). A high proportion of the food waste at Pomongwe also is from small mammals – hyrax, duiker and steenbok – which were presumably the most abundant meat available at the season the cave was occupied. In fact, the resource-potential appears to have remained remarkably constant throughout the later part of the Middle Stone Age. The composition of the faunas with the Bambatan and Tshangulan occupations at this cave are remarkably similar except for the absence of the extinct zebra and some of the larger antelopes from the later occupation layers (Sampson 1974, p. 245). The faunal sequence at the Border Cave and, probably, also that from Redcliff in Zimbabwe, also reflect the environmental changes of the later Pleistocene though they are, perhaps, not so pronounced here as in the winter-rainfall belt (Klein 1977).[1]

Until more studies have been undertaken on the regional behaviour of the various game animals, little can be said as to the season at which sites were occupied. At the Border Cave the fact that no young of the wildebeest or hartebeest are found in the food waste may indicate that neither the animals nor man were present at the site when the young were born (Klein 1977). Again, isotopic study of marine shells from the Wilton layers at Nelson Bay Cave (Klein 1975b) shows that the shellfish were collected during the winter and it might be postulated that the same may also have been the case throughout the Middle Stone Age.

Features of some of the faunas found with the southern African Middle Stone Age probably reflect hunting strategies and practices connected with butchery and processing of meat. For example, the Border Cave faunas yielded a high percentage of very young buffalo, but this is not reflected in the remains of other antelope species at the site which suggests that the aggressive nature and herd structure of the buffalo may have dictated special hunting methods for this species. Again at Klasies River Mouth and Nelson Bay Caves there are many buffalo and large antelopes but the commonest is the eland. It is suggested that the reason for this is that the eland is both favoured meat

[1] The present-day lowveld mosaic of thicket, grassland and savanna is probably not significantly different from what it was around the Border Cave about 70 000 years ago. Moreover, certain trends are present, as also in the south. During the main and evolved Pietersburg (Full/Final Middle Stone Age) occupation in the early Last Glacial, the percentage of species represented in the food waste (e.g. buffalo and bushpig) suggested a more closed bush habitat. In the later ('Post-Final Middle Stone Age') stage, coinciding with the amelioration of the climate in the succeeding interstadial, grassland forms (zebra and wart-hog), as at the Cape, are more evident.

and also relatively easy to hunt. At the same time the scarcity of bushpig and wart-hog is put down to their general aggressiveness when cornered. The same may have been the case with the extinct giant buffalo which is, nonetheless, however, well represented at these sites where their remains consist either of very young/newly born or fully adult animals and it is suggested that the Middle Stone Age hunters may have sought out gravid females or killed them in the process of calving (Klein 1975a).

There is a distinct difference in the pattern and part-survival of food bones, as also of artifacts, on kill or butchery sites as compared with base-camps. At base-camps the remains of small animals are generally more complete than are those of large animals showing that the whole carcase was carried back to the camp in the case of a small animal whereas only selected parts of the larger mammals (usually limbs and head) were transported from the kill-site (Klein 1977). Only a few kill-sites are known but several other sites can be possibly identified as seasonal hunting camps. It is large animals that are usually found and the kill-sites generally seem to be located close to some natural hazard such as a swamp or lake, a cliff or a sinkhole into which game was driven in the manner well documented for historic times. Reference has already been made to the Mousterian/Aterian kill-sites at Hajj Creiem on the Cyrenaican coast and at Bir Terfawi in the eastern Sahara; both are adjacent to water and at both an appreciable amount of meat must have been secured. The bones of white rhinceros, camel, giant buffalo, wild ass and gazelle were found in discrete concentrations at Bir Terfawi, together with the tools used in butchery. This concentration – even piling – of bones is a distinctive feature of Middle Palaeolithic/Middle Stone Age hunting-camps. The quantity of bone fragments with the pile of spheroids at El-Guettar (plate 4.1.1) may, in part, demonstrate this practice and it is clearly present in the intentional piling of butchered animal remains at the lake- or dambo-side Kalkbank site (fig. 4.16). Here a small number of artifacts (50), mostly light- and heavy-duty scrapers, utilized flakes and bone fragments, together with two spheroids and two hand grindstones were found associated in an area of about 1.8 sq. m with a concentration of broken bones that appeared to have been intentionally stacked in a pile some 30 cm high on a sandbank by the edge of the lake or swamp. These remains represent some thirteen species, mostly bovids, equids and suids, including three extinct forms, and come from at least forty individual animals. Broken distal ends of humeri and tibiae are the commonest fracture bones in the pile and

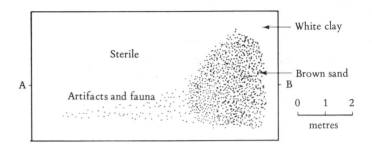

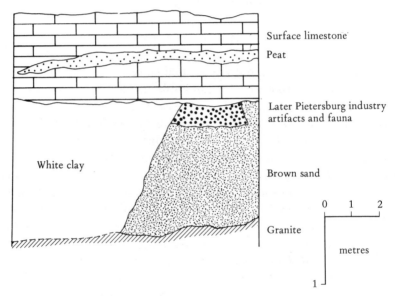

Fig. 4.16 Plan and section of the Middle Stone Age (Upper Pietersburg) butchery site by the edge of the former lake or pan at Kalkbank, Transvaal, South Africa. (After Mason 1958.)

it is possible these may have been used in the butchery process and then discarded just as selected bison bones were used at New World bison kill-sites.

Individual butchery concentrations are demonstrated at the elephant kill-site of Mwanganda's in northern Malawi (fig. 4.17) where three groups butchered different parts of the animal; and again at the early Last Interglacial site of Duinefontein 2, 50 km north of Cape Town

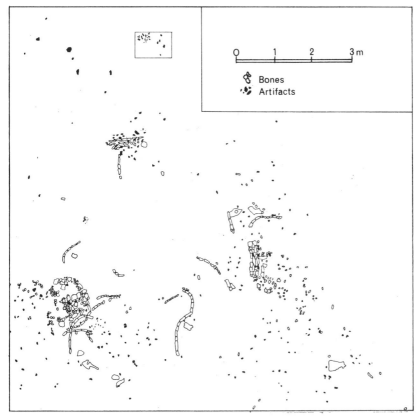

Fig. 4.17  Plan of the elephant butchery site of earliest Middle Stone Age date, at Mwanganda, Karonga, Malawi. The artifacts in the inset rectangle are those found beneath the femur at the upper left. (After Clark and Haynes 1970.)

(fig. 4.18), where two successive vlei-side occupation horizons indicate that the site was used for a long time. Twenty-four species are represented, including elephant, rhinoceros, hippopotamus, kudu and eland, zebra ('giant Cape horse'), a very large species of the existing buffalo (*Syncerus*), alcelaphines, blue antelope and springbok. The bone scatter was concentrated and, while the upper horizon is, perhaps, more specifically a butchery site with many unretouched Middle Stone Age flakes, most of the animals' limb bones are missing. The lower occurrence may represent a base-camp because the stone artifact/bone ratio is much higher and more retouched tools are present (Klein 1976). Certain other sites, by reason of the specialized nature of the tool-kit, its dispersal and manner of occurrence and the features of the bone

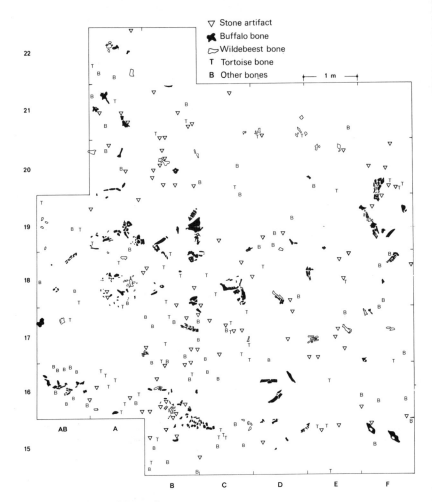

Plan of Duinefontein 2, horizon 2

Fig. 4.18   The Middle Stone Age butchery site at Duinefontein 2, south-western Cape, showing the distribution of bones and artifacts. (After Klein 1976.)

waste, are considered possibly to have been hunting-camps occupied sporadically and seasonally over a long period of time. For hunters, localities permitting observation of game movements would always have importance, such as the overlook at Adrar Bous and the Porc Epic Cave, Dire Dawa, strategically situated to observe the game migrations between the plateau and the Afar lowland plains via the escarpment wadis at the beginning and end of the winter season. This cave may have been occupied once or twice a year. The site is difficult of access and the bone waste is comparatively scarce and much of it very broken up and often burned which suggests that the game may have been butchered elsewhere and, in general, only the meat carried into the cave. In the tool forms there is a concentration on points and knives. Witkrans is another such escarpment cave, this time overlooking the Harts River valley and adjacent to what was probably a migration route between the Kalahari and the valley bottom. Here the artifacts – mostly points and various scraper forms, burins and utilized blades – are found in dispersed concentrations. Some 57% of the fauna represent small to medium-sized non-migratory animals while 42% are migratory and of medium to large size. These last are predominantly grassland species indicating that the site may have been of particular importance in the spring (October/November) when the animals dispersed westwards into the Kalahari and/or when they returned to the valley in the winter (July–September) (J. D. Clark 1971).[1]

Of especial interest are the layers of dispersed ash and carbonized material associated in particular with the early blade Howieson's Poort tradition and comparable occurrences in southern Africa. Relatively thick layers of this kind could be areas of burned bedding but, because of their similarity to such features in Later Stone Age contexts and at the present day in Malawi, they may more probably be seen as evidence of meat-drying operations carried out during the rains or other inclement seasonal conditions. This process has been fully recorded in the field from Malawi where meat is dried using a structure formed of two lines of wooden stakes supporting a grid of green sticks on which the meat is laid to dry over a fire that is kept burning until the process is complete. A considerable amount of ash accumulates in an extended hearth from this process which, during the rainy season, has to be carried out under shelter. This season is also usually the time when the migratory animals are on the move and more dispersed hunting in larger groups becomes possible. Another feature of this drying process is the jugging of the meat on the bone, the butchered limbs and other portions of the carcase being pounded or chopped to break the bone into very small pieces making it easier to divide the meat into strips for drying as well as for transport and consumption; not a little of the

[1] Evidence of another possible open-air hunting-camp may be seen in the small number (28) of artifacts distributed over a very limited area in what was then the delta of the Nata River draining into the Makarikari Lake in northern Botswana. The specialized nature of the artifacts – points, knives and utilized pieces with scraping edges – possibly indicates a hunting-camp though no bone was present (Bond and Summers 1954).

Fig. 4.19  Surface VII (Howieson's Poort Industry) at Montagu Cave, western Cape, showing circular feature and dense scatter of artifacts. (After Keller 1973.)

bone becomes burnt in the drying process. Similar comminuted bone waste is a feature reported also from the Border Cave and Klasies River Mouth. Drying of meat not only means that it can be kept more conveniently and used over several weeks to form a reserve of protein but also that it can serve as a medium of exchange between groups. It now seems very probable that the drying of meat was one of the major developments in resource-processing to take place during the Middle Stone Age.

Few features showing the layout of camps are known. Many of the investigated sites are caves and rock-shelters where distinguishing of individual occupation floors is difficult or more often impossible due to compaction of the deposits. However, at Montagu Cave (Keller 1973, pp. 38–42 and pls. III–XVII) seven such surfaces in the 'Howieson's Poort' layer were successfully isolated and it was found that the occupation debris was concentrated towards the back of the cave. Three fire-places were identified on one of these surfaces and on others arrangements of large stones and some empty areas may be evidence of some kind of simple structure and of sleeping places (fig. 4.19). In the Orange River Scheme area, however, was discovered a most interesting, relatively undisturbed camp-site belonging to the second stage of the Orangian Industry (Sampson 1974, p. 169) (fig. 4.20). The camp, of which half still remained intact, was situated on the bank of a small tributary stream close to the entrance to a narrow gorge which may well have been used as a game trap of some kind. Seven semicircular structures delineated by large stones were preserved and these partly enclosed dense artifact scatters, among them heaps of cores and collections of utilized blades, on the protected, leeward side of the semi-circles. These are interpreted as the foundations of thornbush blinds for night hunting. They are associated with five other structures comprising stone walls enclosing shallow, artificially excavated hollows and, since these contained no artifacts, they are thought to have been sleeping hollows for a group of perhaps six adults. The total size of the group occupying the camp is conservatively estimated at about twelve individuals, a figure that may be compared with the estimate of about thirteen individuals at the Hajj Creiem butchery site. Also in the Orange River Scheme area at Zeekoegat 27 but associated with a Phase 3 assemblage is another kind of feature (Sampson 1974, pp. 249–50) (fig. 4.21). Here the distribution scatter suggests a temporary encampment with an area about 10 m in diameter within a wall of thornbush anchored with dolerite boulders. Within the enclosure are

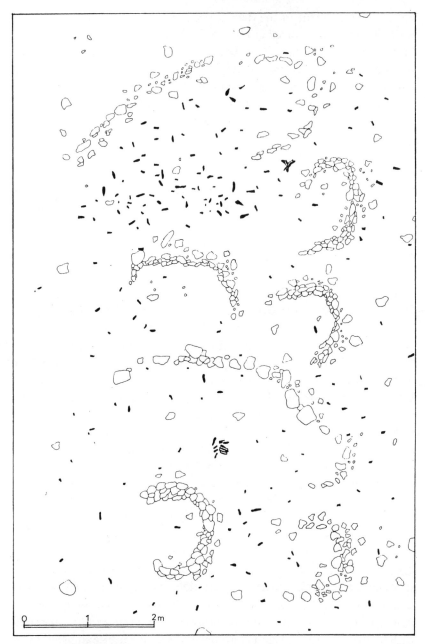

Fig. 4.20   Orangian Industry stone structures interpreted on analogy with !Kung San as blinds for night hunting (larger structures with artifact scatters) and sleeping hollows (smaller structures). (C. G. Sampson, personal communication.)

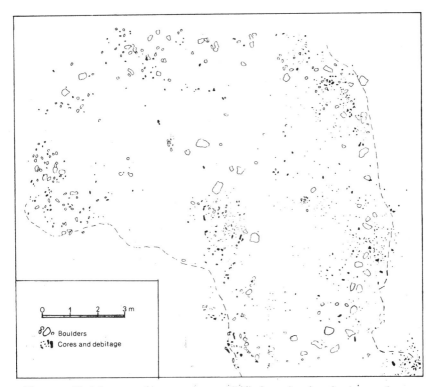

Fig. 4.21  Workshop area of late to early post-Middle Stone Age date, for the manufacture of blades; at Zeekoegat 27, Orange River, Orange Free State. (After Sampson 1974.)

four flaking areas with dense concentrations of non-Levallois flaking waste, cores and hammerstones together with 'handfuls' of blades. All these artifacts are concentrated close to where the perimeter 'wall' would have been.

Other specialized workshop areas associated with quarry sites have already been referred to from Nubia (Arkin) (fig. 4.5) and Ethiopia (Gadamotta, K'one) (fig. 4.22). Here again, what seems to have been individual working waste can be easily recognized from the distribution scatters. One special kind of quarry site is found at Lion Cavern in Swaziland where Middle Stone Age occurrences dating to about 44 000 BP (Dart and Beaumont 1968) overlie an area of the floor of the cave which had been mined for the extraction of iron ore to be used as pigment. Many of the Middle Stone Age cave sequences in what are considered to be the base-camps contain 'pencils' or crayons of rubbed haematite, limonite, manganese, ochres and other pigment-yielding

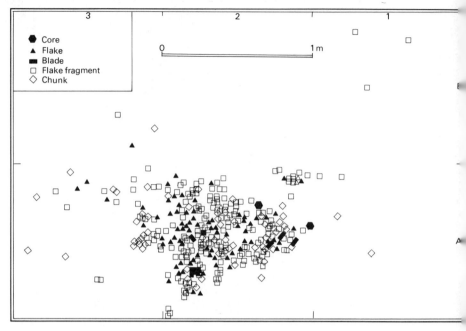

Fig. 4.22   Middle Stone Age workshop concentration in the Lower Loam, K'one, Ethiopia.
(After Kurashina 1978.)

mineral material and it is clear that the use of paint was a common feature of Middle Palaeolithic/Middle Stone Age society; ochre-stained scrapers are found at El-Guettar, and from Olieboompoort Cave has come a grindstone with haematite staining (Mason 1962, p. 259 and fig. 142); and six pieces of ground haematite have been found in Nubia at one of the Khormusan sites together with two modified bone tools (Marks 1968b). Pigment might be used for a variety of purposes – painting the body, weapons and utensils – but, as yet, there is no indication that it was employed to paint on the walls of the rock-shelters. However, the earliest rock paintings in southern Africa – on portable pieces of stone – occur in the 'Apollo 11' shelter in Namibia (South West Africa) and are now reported to be about 28 000 years old.[1] Manifestations of symbolic expression are now known from several Mousterian and one even earlier context in Europe (Marshack 1976) and lend support to this earliest date for rock painting in southern

[1]  The painted slabs come from a layer beneath that containing the early Later Stone Age (about 19 000–20 000 BP) and three results from associated charcoal indicate unquestionably a date between 27 500 and 25 000 BP (Wendt 1975, 1976).

Africa. The conus shell ornament buried with the infant at Border Cave, besides being further evidence for aesthetic interests at this time, is also an indication of contacts with the coast some 90 km to the east. Again, the bone 'flute', if such it is, from Haua Fteah attests some preoccupation with musical expression.

It may also be mentioned in passing that one of the things that attracted man to the Border Cave may have been the presence of salt earth, the value of which can be readily appreciated when it is considered that available sources of usable salt must have been just as limited then as they are today. Another possible use for salt may also have been for the preservation of dried meat.

It would seem likely that some of the more readily discernible features on a camp floor would be cooking hearths but, perhaps because they can so easily be dispersed, very few have, in fact, been recognized. Unlike the extended and thick ash 'hearths' resulting perhaps from the meat-drying process, cooking hearths are usually of restricted diameter and identified by two or three stones set fairly close together, sometimes associated with charcoal. These represent the oldest 'fire-places' yet known from Africa and are recorded from Haua Fteah in Cyrenaica, from Montagu, Boomplaas and Klasies River Mouth caves in the Cape biotic zone and from Border Cave in the lowveld. Possibly also the small stone circles on one of the rubble horizons with an Upper Lupemban industry at Kalambo Falls may be fire-places (J. D. Clark 1969, p. 103) as may be others from Mumbwa Cave 2 where one, in particular, was associated with an 'ashy stratum'. There is no doubt that, by now, cooking was a regular feature of human society and fire must surely have been used for other purposes as well, in particular for warmth and for the shaping of weapons and utensils by a process of controlled charring and scraping as artifacts with fire crackle are not uncommon at many sites (e.g. El-Guettar; Porc Epic Cave, Dire Dawa).

Other features at Mumbwa were interpreted as denoting graves (Dart and del Grande 1931). Certainly during the Middle Stone Age there is evidence for intentional burial of the dead which can be presumed by then to have been a general practice. Besides the Mumbwa burials, those at Skildergat and Border Cave, the latter including both adults and infants, may be cited and it is clear that, by this time, there must have been a universal belief in some kind of afterlife.

The last feature that must be mentioned concerns two, perhaps three, concentrations of, often well-rounded, stone balls associated with spring sites (plate 4.1). The best documented is the pile of about sixty spheroids varying in diameter between 4.5 and 18.0 cm from El-Guettar (pp. 264–5). At Windhoek, however, another collection of 36 balls (plate 4.1.2) was found in a spring tufa (Fock 1954) together with two flaked artifacts – a unifaced point and a fragmentary quartz tool. It is not known how these balls were arranged but the association of so many, again with a spring, is significant. They weighed between 600 and 1200 g and many of them bear a small groove or depression 1.5 cm in diameter pecked into the stone. A third find of many balls, made during well-digging, is reported from Esere in northern Namibia. Spheroids are commonly associated with Mousterian sites in the Maghrib and with Middle Stone Age sites in south central Africa and it seems likely that they served a dual purpose as hunting weapons and as pounders for processing plant foods and for smashing the bones of kills brought back to the spring-side camp. While the size and form and the wear on some of these spheroids suggest continued use for pounding (preparing meat or tough plant foods, breaking bones to extract marrow, etc.) the smaller, more perfect spheres are likely to have had some secondary use. Perhaps they constitute evidence of a stone-headed throwing club, the ball being mounted in a greenhide sleeve, or perhaps they were even hafted in pairs or threes to form an entangling weapon like the South American bolas.

## CONCLUSION

Clearly, there remains much to be learned regarding the evolution of human society during Middle Palaeolithic/Middle Stone Age times. However, due to a number of recent discoveries and investigations, we are now better able to understand and assess the development which took place during the more than 70 000 years covered by this period. During the earlier part of the Middle Palaeolithic/Middle Stone Age, approximately 125 000 BP, when the pre-Neanderthal and Neanderthal populations of big-game hunters occupied northern Africa and the rhodesioid and related stock was widespread in sub-Saharan Africa, it is clear that individual local traditions were already developing in the various regions. Although these earliest Middle Stone Age groups may have been only imperfectly adapted to exploiting local resources, their descendants, by the time this technological mode came to be more generally replaced, more than 30 000 years ago, had evolved a number of innovative strategies for resource exploitation and improved social organization and had established, in particular, a habitual pattern of transhumance between one or more base-camps, each with several temporary foraging-camps, including a regular use of marine and freshwater food sources. These improvements were made possible by the great intellectual stimulus derived from the coming of modern man more than 40 000 and perhaps more than 90 000 years ago, and a pattern of behaviour was established which, although it underwent many refinements over the millennia, remained essentially the same until the introduction of domestic plants and animals.

# CHAPTER 5

# THE LATE PALAEOLITHIC
# AND EPI-PALAEOLITHIC OF
# NORTHERN AFRICA

## INTRODUCTION

Most of the geographical area considered in this chapter falls into what
is sometimes called 'white Africa', where much of the modern
population is more closely related, culturally and biologically, to the
south-west Asian and circum-Mediterranean peoples than to those
south of the Sahara. There are obvious geographical and historical
reasons for these physical, religious and linguistic similarities in recent
times. It is probable that an analogous situation existed during the
period of prehistory discussed here, but it is difficult to measure the
extent of the relationships. Although never sealed off from the regions
south of the deserts and at times even enjoying considerable cultural
and genetic exchanges with them, northern Africa nevertheless remained
a sub-region of Africa that was marked by its ties with the lands to the
east, and perhaps to the north, of the Mediterranean. The cultural
features during the Late Palaeolithic and Epi-Palaeolithic were therefore
the products, on the one hand, of influences from outside the area and,
on the other, of prolonged selection and sorting of various elements
by human adaptive strategies suitable to the physical features and the
resources peculiar to the local environments within North Africa.

The area involved is very large and extends from the Atlantic to the
Red Sea and from the Mediterranean to the southern part of the Sahara
(fig. 5.1). This southern boundary is difficult to fix with precision, but
it can be considered to correspond approximately to latitude 16° N and
thus to run from about Dakar to Khartoum and eastward to the Red
Sea, cutting across the republics of Senegal, Mauritania, Mali, Niger,
Tchad and Sudan. This coincides today more or less closely with a
climatological and vegetational boundary (the grass steppe immediately
south of the subdesert steppe), although the boundary was not
necessarily the same in prehistoric times. The area of about 10 million
sq. km includes a number of broad environmental zones. These vary
considerably in temperature, vegetation and topography, but the

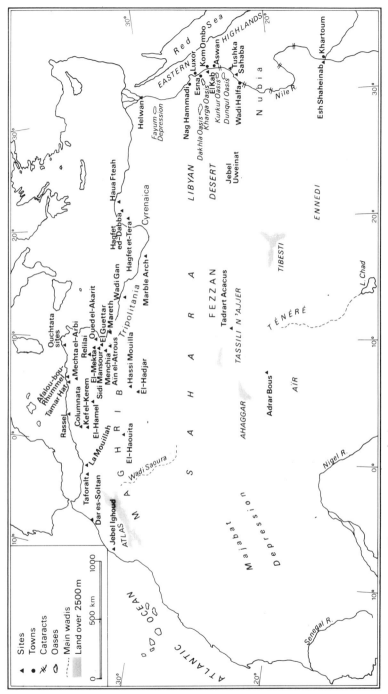

Fig. 5.1   Northern Africa and the principal Late Palaeolithic and Epi-Palaeolithic sites.

343

dominating presence of the Sahara Desert imposes on all of them a greater or lesser degree of aridity, even on those bordering the Mediterranean. Precipitation is very light and sporadic in the Sahara and the Nile Valley but winter rainfall is important in the Maghrib and in north-eastern Libya. Throughout northern Africa vegetation is unevenly distributed in quantity and type, ranging from coniferous and evergreen forest and shrub in the mountains of the Maghrib and Cyrenaican Libya to dispersed desert shrubs and patches of brush grass in the Sahara, with a zone of subdesert steppe in the far south. The Saharan highland zones such as Tibesti and Ahaggar with altitudes of up to 3400 m, and the Nile Valley with its own peculiar riverine character, might be considered today as anomalous islands of vegetation surrounded by desert.

Within this vast territory there was considerable cultural diversity in late Pleistocene and early Holocene times, even before the beginnings of recognizable food-producing, if we are to judge by the archaeological remains. Much of this archaeological diversity is still poorly understood in terms of causative factors and local adaptive processes. It is particularly difficult to construct an evolutionary or developmental framework that would be suitable for all sub-regions of North Africa, since links between them are usually hard to demonstrate with any certainty. The emphasis in this chapter, therefore, is on local adaptation and differentiation by sub-region, with some attempt as well to indicate how the various sub-regions may at times have been linked by common rhythms of change or innovation. It is notoriously difficult to make macroevolutionary reconstructions over large areas until the micro-evolutionary processes within sub-regions have been worked out; in North Africa we are still some distance from this goal for the period in question.

An explanation is necessary for the terminology used here to denote cultural periods or stages. Even today, after more than a century of archaeological research, there is no common terminology applied throughout the region. Chronologically, and to some extent morphologically, the cultural manifestations included under the terms Late Palaeolithic and Epi-Palaeolithic correspond to what are usually called Upper Palaeolithic and Mesolithic in Europe.

The criteria for the Upper Palaeolithic of Europe have never been clearly or unambiguously defined, and some authors have preferred the terms Advanced Palaeolithic and Leptolithic. Generally speaking it refers to the period from the end of the Middle Palaeolithic (the various

Mousterian variants) until the close of the Pleistocene geological epoch, that is, from approximately 35 000 BC to about 8300 BC; technologically it is often seen as characterized by an increased use of blades, particularly those removed from the nucleus by the indirect-percussion or punch technique (see fig. 5.3.1), by more specialized tool-kits including greater use of tools made of bone, ivory and antler; it is marked by the proliferation of sculpture, painting and engraving; and it seems everywhere in Europe to be the unquestioned product of biologically modern man, *Homo sapiens sapiens*. By and large this bundle of criteria is suitable for Europe since the characteristics tend to cluster fairly tightly there. In North Africa, however, the degree of fit is considerably less, and some of the usual European characteristics are missing or very unevenly represented. Although in at least one part of the region (Cyrenaica) an industry based on blades removed by the punch technique appeared about as early as similar industries in Europe, the situation seems to be different in other parts of North Africa where such industries appeared considerably later. Artifacts of bone are far less common than in Europe, and are generally simpler. No trace of art is known until long after specialized industries based on blades had developed, indeed perhaps not until the very close of the Pleistocene or the beginning of the Holocene. Thus it seems best in northern Africa to avoid the expression Upper Palaeolithic with its connotations of criteria that may be missing in this region or, if present, may be distributed in time and in space in different ways than in Europe.

It is difficult to devise a classificatory system that is acceptable for each of the sub-regions. For example, recent radiocarbon dates have convinced most prehistorians that the whole of the Aterian belongs within the Middle Palaeolithic, as many aspects of its stone-working technique and its typology suggest. Since, however, the terminal phase has not yet been dated, some think it possible that this may be partly contemporary with the Upper Palaeolithic. The position taken in this chapter is to regard as 'Late Palaeolithic' those Pleistocene industries that succeed the Mousterian in each sub-region, and as 'Epi-Palaeolithic' those industries produced by hunting–gathering–fishing groups in Holocene times up to the establishment of observable food production. Obviously this is not a clear-cut division, and at least one industry (the Iberomaurusian in the Maghrib) straddles the two epochs. The two terms are roughly equivalent, at least chronologically, to the Upper Palaeolithic and the Mesolithic of Europe. The terminology is rather unsatisfactory since it refers in part to finite chronological periods and

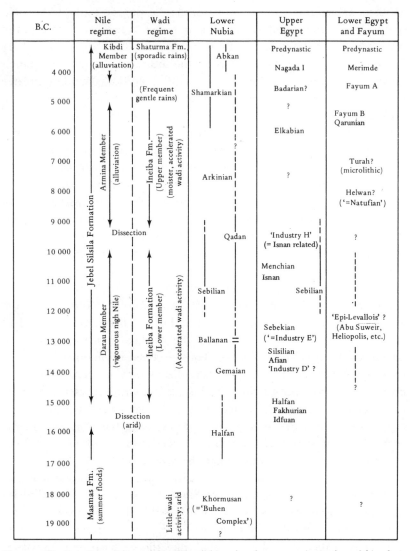

| B.C. | Nile regime | Wadi regime | Lower Nubia | Upper Egypt | Lower Egypt and Fayum |
|---|---|---|---|---|---|
| 4 000 | Kibdi Member (alluviation) | Shaturma Fm. (sporadic rains) | Abkan | Predynastic | Predynastic |
| | | | | Nagada I | Merimde |
| 5 000 | | (Frequent gentle rains) | Shamarkian | Badarian? | Fayum A |
| 6 000 | | | | ? | Fayum B Qarunian |
| 7 000 | Armina Member (alluviation) | Ineiba Fm. (Upper member) (moister, accelerated wadi activity) | ? | Elkabian | Turah? (microlithic) |
| 8 000 | | | Arkinian | ? | Helwan? ('=Natufian') |
| 9 000 | Jebel Silsila Formation | Dissection | | | |
| 10 000 | | | Qadan | 'Industry H' (= Isnan related) | ? |
| 11 000 | Darau Member (vigourous nigh Nile) | Ineiba Formation (Lower member) | Sebilian | Menchian Isnan | |
| 12 000 | | (Accelerated wadi activity) | | Sebilian | 'Epi-Levallois' ? (Abu Suweir, Heliopolis, etc.) |
| 13 000 | | | Ballanan | Sebekian ('=Industry E') | |
| 14 000 | | | Gemaian | Silsilian Afian 'Industry D' ? | ? |
| 15 000 | | Dissection (arid) | | Halfan Fakhurian Idfuan | |
| 16 000 | | | Halfan | | |
| 17 000 | Masmas Fm. (summer floods) | Little wadi activity; arid | | | |
| 18 000 | | | Khormusan (='Buhen Complex') | ? | ? |
| 19 000 | | | ? | | |

Fig. 5.2 The Late Palaeolithic and Epi-Palaeolithic cultural sequences in northern Africa from 20 000 BC, and the principal riverine, wadi and climatic fluctuations in the lower Nile Valley. N.C.T. = Neolithic of Capsian Tradition; N.S.T. = Neolithic of Sudanese Tradition.

in part to technological stages; nevertheless it serves the purpose of organizing the discussion presented here and of being consistent with the traditional terminology used in North Africa (fig. 5.2).

Prehistoric research in North Africa began in the nineteenth century, but most of our knowledge of the Late Palaeolithic and Epi-Palaeolithic

| Libyan Desert | Cyrenaican Libya | Maghrib | | Sahara North | Centre and South | Saharan art |
|---|---|---|---|---|---|---|
| (Hiatus?) | | | N.C.T. | | Ténéréan | Bovidian Pastoral style |
| | Neolithic | Neolithic | | N.C.T. | N.S.T. | |
| Libyan Culture | | | Upper Capsian | | Microlithic fishermen | Round Head style |
| | Libyco-Capsian | 'Elasso-lithic' | | | | |
| (Hiatus?) | | Typical Capsian | Keremian ? | Mellalian | | Bubalus style |
| | | ? | | Ounanian? | | ? |
| | | | | Macroblade Industry | | ? |
| | | ? | Collignon ? | | | |
| | Eastern Oranian | Ibero-maurusian | | ? | | |
| Khargan? | | | | | | |
| Aterian? | | | Horizon | | | |
| | Late Dabban | ? | | | | |
| ? | | | | | | |
| | | | | Aterian? | | |

has been accumulated in the present century. Work in the Maghrib has been fairly continuous, but in Libya and the Sahara most of the research has been done since the Second World War. In Egypt and the northern Sudan information has expanded enormously under the stimulus provided by the construction of the new Aswan Dam. However, some areas are still relatively unknown, particularly the Atlantic coast, the zone between the Nile and the Red Sea, and many parts of the Sahara.

In addition to the unevenness of sampling throughout the region, there are other weaknesses which impede the construction of a satisfactory synthesis for the Late Palaeolithic and Epi-Palaeolithic of North Africa. Few sites except surface concentrations have been investigated extensively so as to reveal the distribution patterns of the remains within the occupation area. Generally speaking the environmental aspects of prehistoric occupations, and in particular the subsistence patterns, have been neglected until recent years. Most of the emphasis in the past has been on establishing cultural chronologies and on demonstrating the affinities between successive or contemporaneous groups of lithic assemblages. A common assumption has been that similarities in morphology, style and frequency of tool types reflect groups belonging to the same ethnic populations and occupying the same cultural level; alternative explanations (for example, that the variability between two or more assemblages might simply reflect differences in behaviour required by different subsistence or other activities by the same group of people) have been nearly ignored. It is very likely that many of the industries or assemblages discussed in this chapter do not represent 'cultures' or separate social groups in the anthropological sense, but instead are units of complex adaptive systems which can only be understood through study of the economic, demographic and technological variables involved. Some attempts are now being made to examine the new Nilotic data in this light, but over most of North Africa the traditional approach is still the accepted one; in addition, changes through time or across space have usually been explained in the past in terms of rather simple reactions to climatic and environmental changes, to migrations of people and other poorly defined diffusionary influences, or even in some cases to a kind of inherent technological or stylistic trend in a given direction such as the microlithicism or geometricism of lithic artifacts.

A broad definition of the Late Palaeolithic/Epi-Palaeolithic of North Africa is that it represents a period during which the lithic assemblages are increasingly characterized by tools made on blades produced by the indirect-percussion or punch technique of removal from the nucleus (see fig. 5.3.1); and there is increasing popularity of such tools as burins, end-of-blade scrapers and backed knives, and often of complex tools which combined several discrete types on a single piece, e.g. a burin and a scraper. Around 15 000 BC small tools approaching microlithic proportions became frequent, and many were probably used as composite tools or weapons where a number of small stone pieces including geometric forms were mounted with gum or mastic in wooden or bone

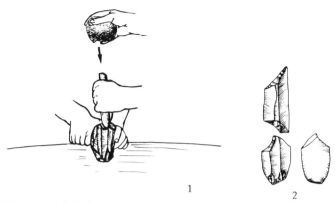

Fig. 5.3   1 The indirect-percussion or 'punch' method of blade production.
2 The microburin method, as used to fashion a geometric microlith. The basal section, snapped across the retouched notch, is the microburin.

hafts as superior cutting or piercing implements. There are exceptions to this definition, but in broad terms it is useful. There may have been other characteristics as well setting this period off from preceding and succeeding periods, especially in the economy, the settlement types, the symbolic and social systems and the human physical type, but these are less well documented or identifiable. However, one of the features of northern Africa is that older traditions of stone-working continued until rather late, contemporaneous with the more 'advanced' techniques and types. This is especially true of the 'prepared-core' or Levallois method of detachment of blades and flakes which lasted in the Maghrib and Sahara until possibly after 18 000 BC and in the Nile Valley until around 10 000 BC; it had essentially disappeared long before this in Europe, south-western Asia and Cyrenaica. The close of the Late Palaeolithic/ Epi-Palaeolithic is marked, in principle, by the introduction of food production, but in practice this change of status is often difficult to establish archaeologically. Frequently, therefore, the presence of pottery is regarded as a useful marker for the end of the Palaeolithic and the beginning of the 'Neolithic', since this feature is often associated with food-producing people; and the pressure-flaking of stone tools, especially of arrow-heads and leaf-shaped blades, whereby part or all of the surfaces are formed by pressing off flattish chips, is often taken as another characteristic of the beginning of the Neolithic in this region.[1]

[1] It hardly requires emphasizing that if Palaeolithic is taken to mean a hunting–gathering economy and Neolithic a food-producing one, then the presence of pottery or pressure-flaking is not a universal proof of a 'Neolithic' stage; there are a number of prehistoric and recent instances

Because of the considerable geographical and cultural variability found in this enormous region, it is most convenient to discuss the prehistoric materials on the Late Palaeolithic and Epi-Palaeolithic time-ranges according to four sub-regions: (1) Libya and especially the province of Cyrenaica, (2) the lower Nile Valley of Egypt and northern Sudan, along with the oases of the western desert, (3) the Maghrib, (4) the Sahara. Although this division on geographical grounds is to some degree arbitrary, it does serve as a means of describing cultural differentiations which probably reflect, in part at least, environmental differences. The procedure adopted in the presentation is to discuss first the sub-regions where the earliest Late Palaeolithic occurs (Cyrenaican Libya and the Nile Valley), and then proceed to those areas where it seems to appear more recently. In our present state of knowledge this strategy is more useful than one that would attempt to trace the prehistoric sequence as a single unit across the whole region; or than one that would discuss specific themes such as techniques and technology, subsistence and economic adaptations, settlement types, etc., without regard for sub-regions or sequential stages. A chronological table of the principal archaeological events in each of the sub-regions discussed after 20 000 BC is given in fig. 5.2.

## CYRENAICA AND NORTHERN LIBYA

The most important Palaeolithic discoveries from Libya have been made in the north-eastern province of Cyrenaica, but a few finds have also been made further west along the coast in Sirtica and Tripolitania. In Cyrenaica there is a very informative concentration of sites not far from the present coastline in the Jebel el-Akhdar or 'Green Mountain', which is one of the two zones of Libya that today enjoys favourable climatic conditions. It catches some of the winter rains from the west and also receives some precipitation from the north. Consequently along several hundred kilometres of coastline and for about 50 km inland the annual rainfall is considerably higher than in adjoining parts of Libya and Egypt. About 40 km south of the coast the Mediterranean-type vegetation changes to bushy steppe, and further inland this becomes stony desert. The physical environment in Late Palaeolithic times was probably not very different from that of today, allowing for overgrazing

where both these elements are associated with hunters, gatherers and fishermen and are absent among agriculturalists. These criteria are most useful where technological rather than economic aspects are taken to distinguish between the Palaeolithic and the Neolithic, as is usually the case for the francophone prehistorians working in North Africa.

and poor land management for the past few millennia. Although these environmental zones fluctuated somewhat during Pleistocene times, the Jebel el-Akhdar range was from at least Middle Palaeolithic times onward the scene of important occupations in caves formed in the limestone hills. By far the most important of these sites is the Haua Fteah, excavated by McBurney between 1951 and 1955, but others are the nearby caves of Hagfet ed-Dabba and Hagfet et-Tera.

The Haua Fteah is undoubtedly the most important single Palaeolithic and Epi-Palaeolithic site between the Levant region of south-western Asia and the Maghrib, and in terms of stratigraphic value is probably the most significant site in North Africa. The deposits contain assemblages extending from some 70 000 or so years ago to the Neolithic and historic periods, and within this context important climatic and environmental reconstructions have been attempted. Although only a relatively small proportion of the total deposits have been sampled, which requires some prudence in interpreting the evidence, the results have had considerable impact on earlier views of the Late Palaeolithic of northern Africa. Perhaps the most important has been the demonstration that industries of 'Upper Palaeolithic' type were established in North Africa much earlier than was thought; indeed, this fact presents one of the great puzzles in the prehistory of the region, as will be discussed later.

One of the most intriguing discoveries at the Haua Fteah was of a rough industry made on blades which underlies the Middle Palaeolithic of Mousterian type, and thus precedes by many thousands of years the more orthodox Late Palaeolithic industry mentioned in the preceding paragraph. This very early blade industry below the Mousterian has been called 'Libyan Pre-Aurignacian' and has a parallel in the Levant region where another early blade industry, the Amudian (sometimes also called Pre-Aurignacian), is reported in a Middle Palaeolithic context in several sites in Syria and Israel. At Haua Fteah it seems to occur during a warm interval whose exact age is uncertain; although a Last Interglacial date of about 80 000–65 000 years ago has been suggested, it may be somewhat younger in the early Last Glacial period. It has been described as an archaic industry with an emphasis on tools fabricated on heavy blades removed from the coarse prismatic nuclei without use of the punch technique. Burins (chisel-shaped tools) of various types, especially large ones made on flakes, form an important part of the industry; there are also rough flake-scrapers of various kinds, and many utilized flakes and blades (fig. 5.4.1–4). There may also be a musical

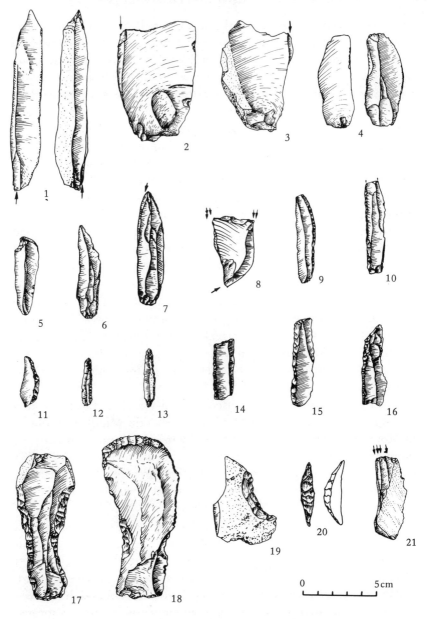

Fig. 5.4  Artifacts from Haua Fteah, Cyrenaica, Libya.

*Libyan Pre-Aurignacian Industry*
  1  Awl-burin
  2–3  Burins
  4  Utilized blade

*Dabban Industry*
  5  Chamfered blade
  6  Backed blade
  7–8  Burins
  9–10  Backed blades

*Eastern Oranian Industry*
  11–13  Backed bladelets
  14–16  Backed blades

*Libyco-Capsian Industry*
  17  Bilaterally retouched blade
  18  End-scraper
  19  Notched piece
  20  Lunate microlith
  21  Burin

instrument, perhaps a whistle or flute, the oldest of its kind yet known anywhere (plate 5.1). No bone tools occur, however. The people responsible for this industry were hunters of wild cattle, gazelle, zebra and Barbary sheep, collected land snails and, since the cave was then near the sea-shore, exploited marine molluscs; this indicates a considerable versatility in utilizing local food resources.

Just what this enigmatic Libyan Pre-Aurignacian represents or reflects is very difficult to say. No skeletal remains have been found, so it is unknown whether the people were neanderthaloid (as were the succeeding Mousterian population at Haua Fteah, apparently), or a more modern physical type. It has some resemblances to the Amudian of the Levant in its typology and technology of lithic artifacts, and occupies a similar stratigraphic position, but it is apparently not identical. One plausible suggestion is that it represents a direct intrusion into North Africa of human groups from south-west Asia perhaps following the diffusion of Palaearctic game animals westward along the Mediterranean littoral. These groups were closely adapted to a Mediterranean-type environment and had little success in expanding to other parts of the continent. So far it has been found only in the Haua Fteah where its duration was at least 5000 years. Whatever its real nature, its impact on other zones of North Africa or on the succeeding industries seems to have been negligible, and it apparently was submerged by the predominant Mousterian traditions in the Jebel el-Akhdar.

The Mousterian at Haua Fteah (sometimes also called the 'Levalloiso-Mousterian') lasted for perhaps 30 000 years after the Pre-Aurignacian had disappeared; the climate was for the most part cooler and moister but it is uncertain whether this change was in any way connected with the cultural replacement. Sometime after 40 000 years ago, probably in the interval between 38 000 and 32 000 BC, there was a fairly abrupt replacement of the Mousterian industrial tradition in the Jebel el-Akhdar by one which marks the real beginning of the Late Palaeolithic in this area and, indeed, in northern Africa: the Dabban. This typical 'Upper Palaeolithic'-type industry apparently did not evolve out of the preceding Mousterian locally, nor can its origins be traced back to the long-vanished Libyan Pre-Aurignacian. It may represent a true diffusion from outside the Jebel el-Akhdar, perhaps from south-western Asia since nothing as old is yet known in Africa, and possibly (though this is speculative until Dabban human remains are known) by men of modern *sapiens* type. Whatever its origins or the associated human type, the Dabban represents one of the oldest known variants of post-

Mousterian blade industries, being approximately contemporary with others then emerging in Europe and south-west Asia (Lower Perigordian, early Aurignacian, Baradostian).

The Dabban Industry is characterized by stone tools made on well-made blades that were apparently detached from prismatic nuclei by the 'punch' or indirect-percussion method (fig. 5.4.5–10). A few discoidal cores resembling Mousterian ones are found but the Levallois method seems absent. The artifacts include burins, small backed blades and some backed bladelets that were probably mounted in perishable handles, and rather peculiar 'chamfered blades'.[1] There may be a developmental trend through the long lifetime of the Dabban (at least 20 000 years) towards simplification and coarser quality of tools, particularly near the end when some Mousterian-like features are present. The climate at the beginning seems to have been dry and perhaps warm, while after 30 000 BC it became colder and perhaps even drier. The principal game animal was the Barbary sheep (*Ammotragus*), but wild cattle or buffalo, zebra, gazelle and to a lesser extent antelope and rhinoceros were also hunted. Birds, tortoises and snails were also consumed.

It is curious that there is no certain case of Dabban occupation known in any other part of North Africa. In view of its very long persistence in the Jebel el-Akhdar one might expect such an apparently successful adaptation to spread to other regions. Yet this does not seem to have occurred, although there may have been some contacts with the perhaps partially contemporaneous(?) latest Aterian groups. Possibly the peoples responsible for the Dabban Industry, in spite of their long occupation of the coastal uplands of Cyrenaica, had a narrow adaptive range that hindered their expansion into other territories with different environments (although this lack of adaptability hardly fits the traditional notion of the expansive potential of 'Upper Palaeolithic' groups). One also wonders if some Dabban sites on the former coastal plain are not now under water.

The long Dabban occupation came to an end sometime between 15 000 and 13 000 BC. Whether there was an actual break in habitation of the area is not certain, but at approximately 12 000 BC a new industry, apparently unrelated to the Dabban, replaces it at Haua Fteah and

[1] These chamfered blades, from which a spall has been removed transversely to the long axis (see fig. 5.4.5) have sometimes, probably erroneously, been called burins. Their real function seems unknown. They also occur in the early Upper Palaeolithic of Lebanon and Palestine and perhaps indicate some connection between North Africa and the Levant, but just what kind of connection is difficult to define at present.

Hagfet et-Tera sites. This has been called Eastern Oranian, because of its resemblances to the Iberomaurusian (sometimes called Oranian) of the Maghrib. There are some typological and technological parallels between the two, especially in the great emphasis placed on small backed blades which sometimes attain microlithic size and represent, in one level at Haua Fteah, about 98% of the total worked pieces (fig. 5.4.11–16). In both regions the nuclei are usually small, and bone tools are rare. The time-range is also comparable, with the Eastern Oranian lasting from about 12 000 BC to around 8500 BC or slightly later. However, the exact nature of the relationship, if any, between the Maghrib and Cyrenaica at this time remains unclear, and the recent discovery of comparable industries in the Nile Valley of Upper Egypt further complicates the situation; the direction from which the Eastern Oranian arrived in the Jebel el-Akhdar, if an indigenous development is excluded, is also uncertain. Cool, dry climatic conditions seem to have reigned at the beginning, with probably a shift to warmer conditions around 10 000 BC. The Eastern Oranians living near the coast, at Haua Fteah, seem to have hunted Barbary sheep as the main game, while at Hagfet et-Tera, on the edge of the desert, gazelle was the principal animal hunted; in addition, both groups consumed varying proportions of equids, bovids, rabbits and snails. These differences in subsistence patterns may be related to the location of each site as it permitted the exploitation of several microenvironments simultaneously, to seasonal factors of relative abundance and to the kinds of occupancy and activity at each site. Finally, two fragmentary mandibles attest to the presence of fully modern *sapiens* man in Cyrenaica by this time.

A sudden technological change at perhaps around 8000 BC saw the replacement of the Eastern Oranian by another industry, the Libyco-Capsian. This industry, although not identical with its contemporary, the Typical Capsian of the Maghrib, does show some resemblances: although large backed blades are absent in Cyrenaica and there are fewer geometric microliths and microburins, nevertheless various scraper and burin types and large notched and denticulated flakes and blades do recall some aspects of the Maghrib Capsian (fig. 5.4.17–21). In addition there are now some grinding stones, more bone tools, polished bone artifacts, decorated ostrich eggshell, some shell beads and possibly a bird engraving on a pebble. The Libyco-Capsian is believed to coincide with a climatic change towards local higher temperatures after about 8000 BC; indeed, one explanation for its abrupt appearance here is that it represents desert-oriented groups of hunters and collectors who were already adapted to arid environments and so found it easy to expand into the Jebel el-Akhdar when warmer, drier conditions transformed the scrub–woodland environment into a more desert-like one. It is not yet known whether some degree of human control over animals and plants was being achieved at this time in Cyrenaica, analogous to events occurring even earlier in south-western Asia and, possibly, the Nile Valley. Barbary sheep and large bovids were the main game animals, while large quantities of snails and perhaps ostrich eggs were eaten; the role of plant foods in the subsistence is unclear. The Libyco-Capsian is fairly typical of a number of industries found in North Africa between the close of Pleistocene times (conventionally placed at about 8300 BC in northern Europe) and the development of recognizable food-producing societies. These industries are transitional in a chronological and perhaps in an economic sense, and further study of them should yield much valuable information on human adaptation to various environmental zones and in particular on the degree to which they reflect societies that were technologically and economically 'pre-adapted' to formal food producing.

Just as with the preceding industries, the origins of the Libyco-Capsian remain unknown. The sharp contrast in artifact types and styles with the Eastern Oranian probably shows that there was no outgrowth of one from the other, and indeed there may have been a hiatus between the two occupations. While an ultimate origin in the Maghrib or in south-western Asia has been suggested, another possible source lies in the Nile Valley of Egypt where a profusion of pre-Neolithic industries has been revealed in recent years. Nor can anything be said about the physical type represented by the Libyco-Capsian, or the degree if any of biological continuity with the Eastern Oranian, in the absence of satisfactory skeletal material.

Sometime around 5000 BC appear the first demonstrable signs of food production in Cyrenaica in the form of domesticated sheep or goats (the precise identification is uncertain), associated with such features as pressure-flaking on stone tools, and pottery. Again the direction of stimulation is not clear and it is not sure whether the Nile Valley or the Fayum Depression of Egypt, where food production was possibly present also by this time, played any important role in the diffusion of these new elements to the Jebel el-Akhdar; south-western Asia, the Maghrib or even the Sahara may have been as significant. The absence of any important changes in the stone tools between the Libyco-Capsian and the Neolithic may indicate a basic continuity of population rather than any sudden replacement by new people; possibly it involved a gradual infiltration of new 'Neolithic' elements into a culture that was already to some extent pre-adapted economically and technologically. At any rate societies based on herding of cattle, sheep and goats persisted in the Jebel el-Akhdar throughout the local Neolithic period, and in fact into historic times.

Little can be related with confidence about the other two provinces of northern Libya (Sirtica and Tripolitania) during the period under consideration here. This region is mainly desert steppe and has yielded virtually no traces of occupation in spite of the possibility that there were linkages of some kind between the Maghrib and Cyrenaica during Eastern Oranian and Libyco-Capsian times. A few microlithic sites without pottery have been reported, but almost nothing more is known.[1]

## THE LOWER NILE VALLEY AND ADJACENT OASES

This sub-region extends from the Mediterranean to Khartoum, but so far virtually all our information comes from a much more restricted area between the Second Cataract in northern Sudan to about the latitude of Luxor in Upper Egypt. Lower Egypt, the central Sudan and the areas away from the valley are little explored and poorly known; inevitably this creates a bias in evaluating the archaeological material. In addition, virtually all finds come from open-air sites (sometimes sealed, but often surface collections exposed by erosion and deflation of deposits) rather than from cave or rock-shelter sites as is often the case in Libya, the Maghrib and south-western Asia. This last factor may itself involve a distorting variable when comparisons are made with regions where enclosed types of sites are the rule, since we may not be comparing at all times the same kinds of human activities.

Knowledge of the Late Palaeolithic and 'pre-Neolithic' archaeology in this general area has greatly expanded in recent years. As a consequence of this increase in information and understanding, the interpretation of events has been considerably modified. Following the pioneer research carried out in Egypt between the two world wars and

[1] A microlithic industry found at Marble Arch near Sirte, and termed the 'Sirtican', may be a contemporary of the Capsian and Libyco-Capsian. In Tripolitania another microlithic industry at Wadi Gan, although poorly known, may provide a tenuous link with the anomalous Epi-Palaeolithic bladelet industries in southern Tunisia. Between the Jebel el-Akhdar and the Nile Delta virtually nothing is known, although a narrow zone of somewhat less arid conditions encourages the belief that sites linking the two areas may eventually be found.

somewhat too readily accepted by many prehistorians, there developed a belief that the sub-region was highly conservative, even stagnant culturally in comparison with Europe, western Asia or even other parts of North Africa. Emphasis was placed on the isolation of Egypt from other areas, and on the peculiarly self-sufficient continuity of tool-making for a very long period of time. It was thought that the equivalent of the Upper Palaeolithic elsewhere was represented in Egypt and adjoining areas by industries continuing the Levallois tradition of flake-removal, and these industries were often lumped under the term 'Epi-Levalloisian'. Industries based on blades and bladelets did not arrive, it was generally thought, until the close of the Pleistocene, long after they had appeared elsewhere.[1]

This picture has been altered in many respects since about 1960 when the construction of the new High Dam at Aswan in Upper Egypt and the flooding of Egyptian and Sudanese Nubia provoked a new burst of archaeological activity in the two countries. It now appears that, although the older interpretative model still holds for the period before about 20 000 BC, for the later part of the Pleistocene and the early Holocene (especially from about 16 000 to 9000 BC) a very different situation existed that renders the area much less anomalous than hitherto thought. Although many gaps still remain in knowledge, it is apparent that for this period at least there was much less continuity and much more variability than usually believed, and very likely the degree of isolation from other areas was less marked than supposed. Having stated this, however, it must be stressed that not all of the former viewpoint has been invalidated. Egypt and the northern Sudan were relatively unchanging and 'conservative' until a surprisingly late date if we compare them with Cyrenaica or south-western Asia, and in this respect they resemble the Maghrib. This argument is of course based on present evidence, which may be changed by future discoveries. Another necessary proviso is that the lithic assemblages or industries found (which are nearly all we have to go on in this area) need not reflect with absolute fidelity either the cultural level attained or distinct, identity-conscious socio-cultural groups of people; the apparent lack of innovation in some aspects of the stone tools may in fact disguise other

---

[1] This model in reality has several variants, and some authors insisted more than others on the isolation, self-sufficiency and 'retardation' of Egypt. Nevertheless, until the 1960s virtually all writers emphasized the high degree of technical (and hence cultural) continuity and, with few exceptions, observed no elements or trends resembling those known at this time in more 'advanced' regions. See particularly the works of Vignard, Sandford and Arkell, Caton Thompson and Huzayyin, to mention only those writers who have carried out fieldwork in Egypt and the Sudan.

developments in subsistence and adaptive behaviour which, although less well preserved in the archaeological record, were on a par with those in other regions where 'Upper Palaeolithic'-type industries had been established long before.

Nevertheless, if one compares only the industries, it is apparent that the rate and the kind of change through time in this sub-region were different from those known elsewhere. We may eventually have to accept this phenomenon as a genuine reflection of slow evolutionary tempo. Just what factors might have been responsible for this – whether geographical isolation that hindered diffusion of ideas or people from outside, or the weakness of pressures that might have promoted significant independent modifications among the local groups – is not certain. Perhaps both factors were operative. It is doubtful that it can be attributed to survival of physically more archaic types of man in this area, although the complete absence of human skeletons until around 15 000 BC makes it impossible to demonstrate this point. Whatever were the causes, Egypt and the northern Sudan, and particularly the Nile Valley, offer an interesting amalgam of continuity and innovation whose study should eventually be valuable in terms of extracting significant generalizations about human behaviour and adaptation in a peculiar natural environment under the stresses of changes in climate, weather, resource availability and other factors.

In late Pleistocene times, as today, the Nile was the central fact of human occupation in Egypt and the northern Sudan. The river in this region, sometimes called the Saharan Nile, was flanked on both sides by lands that even in the late Palaeolithic were never better than semi-arid. Thus even during the most arid periods a permanent source of water passed from an intertropical zone south of the Sahara toward the mid-latitude Mediterranean basin, and permitted some human occupation in a severe desert. In this unusual environmental situation conditions apparently were such that a considerable amount of cultural variability could develop and some significant economic innovations take hold (Wendorf and Schild 1976, pp. 229–319).

The Nile was probably always a stabilizing factor in the human ecology of Egypt and the Sudan. In spite of periodic fluctuations in volume it could be relied on even in less favourable episodes as a source of fish, molluscs, hippopotamus and waterfowl – that is, it complemented the terrestrial resources and acted as a factor of predictability for the hunters and gatherers of the region. Thus the areas of greatest resource potential and of human settlement would be those zones where the riverine and terrestrial resources intersected, as where valleys leading into the inland hills and plains debouched into the great river valley. Presumably these would be the areas of most intense cultural development, though not necessarily of greatest cultural continuity. The populations of the less stable environmental zones, such as the stretches of river with narrow floodplains and little access to abundant hinterland resources, or the inland zones away from the Nile, would presumably be more delicately balanced in their subsistence logistics; consequently groups living in such 'marginal' zones would be more easily affected by environmental changes than would those living in richer zones. Thus we might expect that in times of deteriorating conditions, groups from less stable areas would tend to flow into those zones where ecological collapses would be less pronounced, leading at times to the displacement, coexistence and even merging of populations with different technological and other traditions. This phenomenon is probably one, though certainly not the only, factor to consider in examining the very great, almost anarchic, cultural diversity found in the Nile Valley in late Palaeolithic times. In addition, there were undoubtedly considerable seasonal fluctuations in available food resources which required various technological and social adaptations on the part of the valley-dwellers. Probably certain of the subsistence activities – hunting large game animals in and away from the floodplain, plant-collecting, fishing, fowling, shellfish-gathering and others – were more important in some months of the year than at other times, so the accommodation to spatial and temporal resource zonation would require a complex pattern of planning of these activities and occupation of the appropriate sites.

Recent geological research in the Nile Valley and in the adjoining wadis has shown that the sequence of events during the past 50 000 or so years was far more complex than was thought previously. Former assumptions concerning the relationships of the river terraces with Mediterranean sea levels and with world-wide climatic changes have had to be very drastically modified, while a new sequence based on studies of sediments, both riverine and wadi, and dated by radiocarbon determinations has been set up.[1] Generally speaking, a close corre-

[1] Unfortunately the two principal studies of the geological and climatic events in the lower Nile Valley during the Upper Pleistocene and early Holocene that have been published in recent years are not always in agreement on details of correlation or on the processes involved; and even when they do agree the unnecessary duplication of terminologies for essentially the same phenomena causes some confusion in correlating the geological contexts for the archaeological data. In this chapter the system proposed by Butzer and Hansen (1968) is used, since only here have the criteria for definition of the various geological formations been clearly put forth and consistently applied; in addition their interpretations are based on studies of wadi activities (always

(a)

(b)

5.1    Worked bone tube with perforations, possibly the mouthpiece of a flute or whistle.
Libyan Pre-Aurignacian; from Haua Fteah, Cyrenaica, Libya. (Enlarged $3\frac{1}{2}$ times.)

spondence is seen between the East African pluvial conditions and the amounts of Nile discharge, while the pluvials also corresponded in most cases with the periods of increased precipitation in Egypt and Nubia that were responsible for stream activity in the local wadis.

The modern flood regime of the Nile goes back to at least 50 000 years ago, with the summer flood sedimentation pattern being established by this time. Before this, winter alluviation was the rule. Down to about 3000 BC the river was higher and had much greater velocity. Deposits of silt and other sediments of southern origin were laid down at heights up to 34 m above present flood level. These periods of aggradation were interrupted a number of times by periods of downcutting and erosion, when the river's discharge was reduced following lessened pluvial conditions in the monsoonal area of East Africa. Local climates in Egypt and Nubia were usually arid during these intervals of dissection, when wadi activity was also reduced; undoubtedly the vegetation cover, and dependent animal life, were also affected by these changes. However, measuring the intensity of change from 'wetter' to 'arid' conditions in Egypt and Nubia is not easy, particularly in the absence of good palynological data from the lower Nile Valley. Very likely during the period from about 50 000 years ago the local climatic conditions were never better than semi-arid, and the changes involved may have been no more than a shift from conditions resembling those of today (with a few millimetres of rain annually) to semi-arid conditions with enough annual rainfall (between 50 and 100 mm) to permit some grassland and trees even some distance from the river banks.

Generally speaking, the cooler and less arid conditions tended to correspond with the periods of high Nile level and aggradation, but this is a highly complex situation, not yet fully understood, and there may have been at times arid conditions while the river was high. In any case, the vegetation and fauna, and thus ultimately human activities, were affected as profoundly by the alluviation and downcutting alternations of the Nile as by the relatively minor changes in local temperature and precipitation, at least as far as the riverine or floodplain zones were concerned. When the Nile flowed high and strong there would be ample grazing and water for game animals, while during periods of downcutting these zones would be considerably restricted for animals and men. Many of the cultural shifts discussed in this chapter should be seen against this changing background of land availability and use.

a better indicator of local climates) as well as of Nilotic behaviour, whereas the interpretations offered in Wendorf (1968) depend too narrowly on Nilotic phenomena.

In the north of Egypt around the Delta conditions would not be the same, however, and probably a more typically Mediterranean climate was the rule.

The general picture of the Nile Valley in Late Palaeolithic times would thus show a much higher and more powerful stream than exists there today, in spite of short intervals when it shrank considerably. Streams from the wadis leading to the Eastern Highlands (the 'Red Sea Hills'), which today are inactive except for brief spates, were also contributing to the Nile and watering the terrain east of the river. A desert steppe interrupted by occasional oases fed by underground springs or by uplands with slightly greater precipitation extended away from the valley and presumably supported some game. Vegetation nearer the floodplain perhaps consisted of acacia, tamarisk and sycamore; there were also probably rich grazing lands in the floodplain and up the seasonally inundated wadis, and these pastures merged gradually into semidesert scrub or bush and finally into desert wasteland. There were no such wadis on the west bank. Channels and lagoons of the Nile harboured fish, while clams, oysters and edible plants grew in the waters. Seasonal ponds created by seepage from the Nile existed between consolidated sand dunes. These conditions would be especially present in sections of the valley where large embayments at the mouths of important wadis permitted unusually rich concentrations of resources, as on the Kom Ombo Plain in Upper Egypt. While on the whole the Pleistocene fauna of Egypt and Nubia is not well known, animal remains dating to between about 15 000 to 10 000 BC recently collected in Upper Egypt illustrate the kinds of food available: wild cattle, hippopotamus, hartebeest, gazelle, Nubian ass, hare; many species of migratory birds especially ducks, geese and herons; and Nile catfish, perch and turtle. The typical 'Ethiopian' fauna of elephant, giraffe and rhinoceros was not present at this time (Churcher 1972).

It should of course be remembered that the Nile Valley was not a homogeneous zone during Late Palaeolithic times, either ecologically or culturally. Industries found in Nubia are usually absent in Upper Egypt (although there are some exceptions), while there seem to be strong differences between those in Upper and Lower Egypt. Apparently regional specialization was already well developed even within the valley, and at times there may have been a number of fairly distinct culture-areas along the river. Possibly Nubia was more isolated than was the area north of Aswan, and was less subject to cultural influences from the Mediterranean basin.

A somewhat schematic version of the main archaeological events in

Egypt and Nubia is shown in fig. 5.2 against the background of Nilotic and wadi stream activities and the putative changes in temperatures and humidity since about 20 000 BC.

The cultures of the period before 20 000 BC are not well known and the immediate background to those industries that are termed Late Palaeolithic in this chapter is poorly understood. In Nubia the Middle Palaeolithic is better known than it is in Egypt proper (where most of the late Pleistocene sediments before 30 000 BC are missing, at least in Upper Egypt), and the 'Nubian Mousterian' is said to resemble typologically the Typical Mousterian of Europe and south-west Asia. Several other Middle Palaeolithic variants have also been described from Nubia (a 'Nubian Middle Palaeolithic' apparently different from the Mousterian, and a 'Nubian Denticulate Mousterian'), but none are precisely dated and little information is available concerning the types of adaptation they represent. They may have lasted until around 33 000 BC. An eastern outlier of the Aterian Industry of the Sahara penetrated into the Libyan Desert and may have reached the Nile in northern Sudan. These events presumably corresponded to a period (the Korosko Formation of the Nile Valley) when the river was declining in velocity and the local climatic regime was more arid with less wadi activity. The ultimate developments of these various Middle Palaeolithic industries are not known, nor is it clear whether there was any significant gap in the human occupation of the valley before the appearance of the Late Palaeolithic industries.

Possibly the earliest known industry of the Late Palaeolithic in the lower Nile valley (the Khormusan, or, as it has also been called, the Buhen Complex) has an archaic look. It continues the Levellois method of Middle Palaeolithic industries, and may in most respects be considered a late version of the latter group. Light-duty flake tools are the rule, denticulate pieces are frequent, and burins are important (fig. 5.5.1–6). All known sites are very close to the Nile in Sudanese Nubia near Wadi Halfa. The people hunted large savanna and Nilotic animals, and also did some fishing. Although the Nile was high at this time (the Masmas Formation), the local climate was arid and wadi streams nearly inactive; this may explain the concentration of sites on the river bank. Radiocarbon dates at first suggested that this industry might have begun as late as 20 000 BC and disappeared around 16 000 BC but two new dates of more than about 39 490 BC and more than about 34 000 BC suggest that it is essentially earlier than, and not contemporary with, the industry (Halfan) described below.

Another industry in the Levallois tradition (the Halfan) has a wider

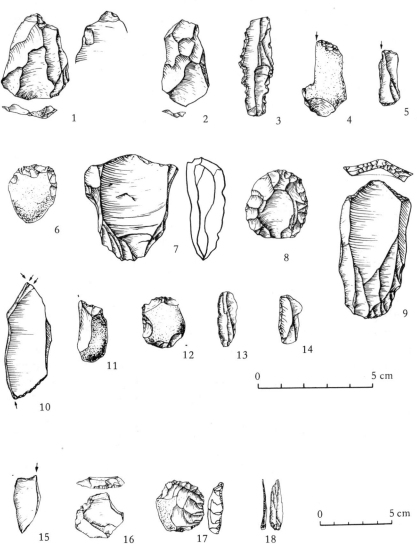

Fig. 5.5   Artifacts from the lower Nile Valley (Nubia and Upper Egypt).

*Khormusan Industry*
  1–2 Levallois flakes
  3 Denticulate
  4–5 Burins
  6 Scraper

*Halfan Industry*
  7 Levallois nucleus
  8 Scraper
  9 Halfan flake

  10–11 Burins
  12 Denticulate
  13 Backed microblade
  14 Truncated microblade

*Idfuan Industry*
  15 Burin
  16 Denticulate
  17 Scraper
  18 Ouchtata-backed bladelet

distribution along the Nile in both Nubia and Upper Egypt. Its time-range is not certain but a duration of several thousand years, between about 17 000 and 15 000 BC seems reasonably certain. The people were mainly hunters of savanna animals, including wild cattle and hartebeest, but they also consumed Nile fish and perhaps, judging from the possible presence of grinding stones, used plant foods as well. Many of the stone tools are quite small and have been termed microblades and microflakes; they are often removed from small unprepared nuclei and have one edge blunted or 'backed' by what is often called Ouchtata-like retouch.[1] In addition there are small quantities of burins and scrapers (fig. 5.5.7–14), a few bone tools, and perhaps microburins.[2] It is interesting to find this simple microblade technique in the Nile Valley at this early date, apparently some millennia before it appears in the Sahara or the Maghrib; it is not yet clear if it represents an indigenous evolution from a highly specialized Levallois flake technology or if it should be seen in terms of stimulus diffusion from some other region.

The archaeological developments from around 15 000 BC onward are extremely complex and not yet well understood. Not only were there often differing traditions in the three main regions of the lower Nile Valley, as shown in fig. 5.2 (Lower Nubia, Upper Egypt and Lower Egypt), but the economic emphasis seems at times to have been different. On the whole Lower Nubia appears to have persisted in several versions of the Levallois tradition (the Gemaian around Wadi Halfa, with much the same subsistence base as the Halfan, and the Qadan who hunted, fished and probably exploited wild grains), but the Ballanan around 13 000 BC represents a non-Levallois industry based on microliths and may be intrusive from Upper Egypt; these people hunted large savanna animals and also fished. But in Upper Egypt there begin to appear about 16 000 BC a confusing variety of industries, and one has

---

[1] The Ouchtata retouch (named after a group of Epi-Palaeolithic sites in northern Tunisia) refers to a light, usually semi-abrupt blunting on the edges of blades and bladelets. It is also found in several later industries of the Nile Valley, including the Sebekian (see figs. 5.6.16–20, 5.10.10–12). It is not yet clear whether or not its wide distribution in northern Africa denotes the diffusion of a specific technique, or whether it was developed independently in a number of regions.

[2] The microburin method (or technique) is a specialized way of working small blades and sometimes flakes which appears in the Late Palaeolithic in Europe, North Africa and the Near East. The microburin is not a true burin but a by-product of the technique and was probably not itself used as a tool. The technique involves notching the blade so as to fracture it at a designated place, as shown in fig. 5.3.2. It is often associated with the manufacture of geometric microliths such as triangles or trapezes (as in the Capsian Industry), but it can also be employed to make very pointed backed blades or bladelets as in the Iberomaurusian of the Maghrib and in the Silsilian of Upper Egypt (see figs. 5.9, 5.6).

the impression that it is in this zone that the greatest variability and the most rapid cultural changes occurred after 15 000 BC. The local forerunners of these Upper Egyptian industries are unknown, since there is little evidence of human occupation here just before this time. There is no good explanation for this apparent hiatus after the (still undated) 'Middle Palaeolithic' of Upper Egypt. It is difficult to accept that in spite of the prevailing arid climate the entire valley in this zone was abandoned for many thousands of years, including the rich and relatively well-explored Kom Ombo Plain; one possible explanation is that most sites falling in this period have, in contrast to those in Nubia, been destroyed or deeply buried by later geological events.

Between 16 000 BC and 10 000 BC Upper Egypt sees a very complex series of swiftly shifting 'cultures' based on several stone-working techniques and subsistence strategies. Then after about 10 000 BC there is another apparent hiatus in the archaeological record lasting for three or four thousand years. These Upper Egyptian industries seem to have been much shorter lived than those in Nubia, although this may only reflect inadequate archaeological data. Apparently beginning at the very close of the Masmas (= Dibeira-Jer) Formation (about 20 000–14 000 BC), perhaps during an arid interval of Nilotic downcutting, these industries appear and disappear during the succeeding Jebel Silsila Formation (or the Sahaba Formation as other authors term part of this phase of Nile behaviour). Generally speaking the Jebel Silsila Formation corresponds to the period between about 15 000 and 3000 BC and represents a number of fluctuations in river velocity, wadi activity and local precipitation, but the period between about 15 000 and 10 000 BC saw high flood levels, heavy alluviation, accelerated wadi activity and a somewhat moister climate with more frequent rains. These seem to have provided optimal conditions for human life in this part of the Nile Valley and for the profusion of different industrial traditions, although it is by no means certain that each of the 'industries' defined reflects a single social or cultural group in the usual ethnographic sense.

The archaeological sites of this period are at times fairly large, which may indicate some permanency of settlement, or repeated occupations of the same localities, or both. This seems to contrast with the preceding Halfan sites, which are small, and may reflect some important demographic shifts after about 16 000 BC in the Nile Valley. The subsistence activities carried out also seem to reflect a good deal of variability or even specialization. Thus two apparently contemporary industries in Upper Egypt, probably dating to between 16 000 and 15 000 BC, show

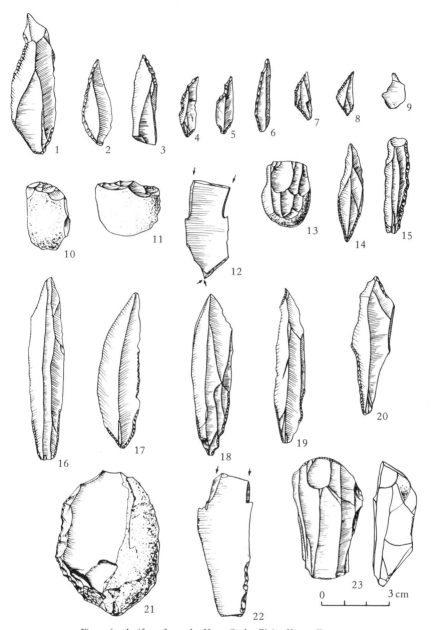

Fig. 5.6 Artifacts from the Kom Ombo Plain, Upper Egypt.

*Silsilian Industry*
1 Partially backed blade with tip removed
  by microburin method
2–6 Backed bladelets
7–8 Geometric microliths
9 Microburin
10–11 Scrapers
12 Burin
13 Bladelet nucleus

*Sebekian Industry*
14–15 Laterally retouched bladelets
16–18, 20 Blades with Ouchtata retouch
19 Perforator
21 Scraper
22 Burin
23 Blade nucleus

very different emphases: the Idfuan, which is in the Levallois tradition and has many burins and end-scrapers (fig. 5.5.15–18) was apparently based on big-game hunting, while the Fakhurian, with many microlithic tools but no use of the Levallois method, seems to have been based on fishing and shellfish-collecting. On the other hand, the subsistence base of a somewhat later microlithic industry, the Silsilian, found on the Kom Ombo Plain around 13 000 BC (fig. 5.6.1–13) seems to have been wild cattle, hartebeest and gazelle, while an immediately succeeding industry (the Sebekian – see fig. 5.6.14–23) in the same area with many long retouched blades but, like the Silsilian, no use of the Levallois method, was apparently rather generalized in its economy: not only large terrestrial mammals including wild cattle, gazelle and hartebeest but also hippopotamus, many species of waterfowl and several species of Nile fish were consumed. There would seem to be no one-to-one correlation between the type of lithic industry used by a group and the species of food exploited, and the explanation of the observed differences in tools might be sought in factors other than subsistence needs alone.

Special mention should be made of another Nilotic industry, the Sebilian, which occurs in both Upper Egypt and Nubia. For many years after its recognition by Vignard in 1919 on the Kom Ombo Plain it was considered the principal, if not the sole, representative of the Upper Palaeolithic in Egypt.[1] Many prehistorians accepted Vignard's hypothesis that the Sebilian was very long-lived, having evolved locally from the Egyptian Mousterian, developed through three stages and finally disappeared under the stress of arid conditions at the beginning of the Holocene when it had attained a highly specialized microlithic level. Today, after the recent fieldwork, it is apparent that a different interpretation is necessary. It seems to have been a very short-lived industry centring probably around 11 000 BC and probably no more than a few millennia older and younger than that. Its evolutionary pattern is not yet well known, nor its origins, but a development from a simple flake industry using the Levallois method of stone-working to a microlithic one with rather large geometric forms and microburin technique is quite likely (fig. 5.7.1–11). The association of the Levallois and the microburin methods in a single industry is probably unique. Its unusually great geographical distribution along several hundred kilometres of the Nile Valley means that there is a good deal of variation

[1] The formerly current stereotype of Egypt as a culture-area that was isolated, conservative and even stagnant during the equivalent of the Upper Palaeolithic had its origins largely in this view of the Sebilian, which in turn was mainly due to an inadequate understanding of Sebilian chronology. See especially Vignard (1923) and Caton Thompson (1946).

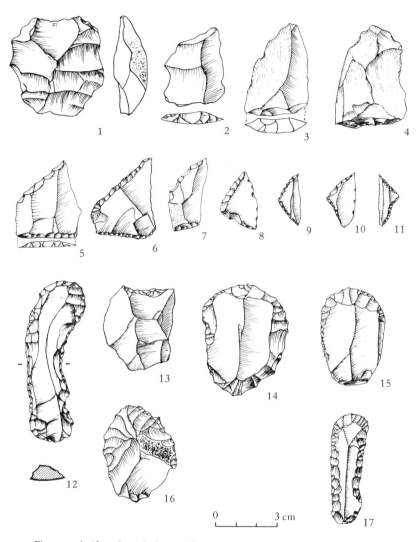

Fig. 5.7 Artifacts from the lower Nile Valley, Upper Egypt (Kom Ombo Plain).

*Sebilian Industry*
1 Levallois nucleus
2–4 Basally truncated flakes
5–7 Trapezoidal or bitruncated flakes

8–10 Triangles
11 Irregular triangle

*Menchian Industry*
12–17 Scrapers on thick blades and flakes

369

in tool types from one area to another. The people responsible for the Sebilian assemblages also seem to have exploited a broad range of food resources: large game animals, fish, shellfish, birds and (judging by the presence of simple grinding stones) some wild plants. It may have originated somewhere outside the Nile Valley, possibly in the Libyan Desert, although at present this is only speculative.

At about this time in both Upper Egypt and Nubia there are some indications of a trend among some populations towards an apparently new subsistence feature, the use of wild plant foods in considerable quantities. An industry, the Menchian, found on the Kom Ombo Plain at roughly 10 000 BC (that is, possibly contemporary with the Sebilian) may reflect this. In addition to a heavy emphasis on large blades, flake scrapers and notched tools (fig. 5.7.12–17), it possesses many upper and lower grinding stones made of sandstone slabs. Although some of these slabs show stains of red ochre, they seem too numerous to have been intended for producing pigments alone. A somewhat similar assemblage (the Isnan) found further north near Esna contains not only grinding stones but also flint blades with glossy edges which suggest use for cutting or reaping plants. It is possible, as some palynological data indicate, that some still unidentified wild grains or cereals were being fairly intensively exploited as a food resource (Wendorf, Said and Schild 1970, and unpublished information). Something of this kind has also been reported for another industry, the early Qadan of Nubia around 12 500 BC, while the possible grinding stone already mentioned in the Halfan industry on the Kom Ombo Plain may carry this activity even further back to around 15 000 BC. Whether this kind of subsistence can be described as incipient cultivation remains to be seen, but it does not seem to have culminated in true plant domestication in Egypt. One reasonable explanation for this trend towards plant use may be found in the recent evidence for increasing population growth and even demographic pressure on food resources in the Nile Valley from 15 000 BC onward. This may have been partly instrumental in inducing some groups to resort to a greater use of wild plant foods, especially of wild grasses, to supplement the traditional animal proteins; the slightly moister climatic conditions of the time may have encouraged more abundant growth of these plants. However, there seems to have been no permanent occupation of sites at this time, although some of them were fairly large, and no traces of solid or permanent architecture have been found. It is possible that it was this absence of sedentary life that was in part responsible for the failure of the populations in Upper Egypt and Nubia to develop a more intensive form of plant cultivation when the hyper-arid climatic conditions of about 10 000 BC may have seriously reduced the extent of the stands of wild grasses; instead of adapting to plant cultivation in order to maintain the traditional kinds of settlement in the face of reduced plant and terrestrial game resources, the response of some if not most groups in the Nile Valley (like some of the slightly later groups in the Sahara and in Europe) was to develop economies with, it seems, a heavy emphasis on fishing.

After 10 000 BC Nubia continued to be inhabited by groups (as expressed by the Qadan, Arkinian and other industries) who were both hunters of land mammals and fishermen, and this situation essentially continued until the introduction of food production, pottery and other 'Neolithic' features in the area after 5000 BC. In Upper Egypt, however, there is a gap in the archaeological record although, as already suggested, probably no real hiatus in habitation. Groups like those responsible for the 'Industry H' may have continued the putative cereal-grinding briefly, but probably most groups reverted to hunting and fishing economies. In spite of several climatic fluctuations toward hyper-arid conditions after 10 000 BC there was (contrary to older speculations) no catastrophic deterioration of living conditions in Holocene times. A site that probably illustrates this occurs at El-Kab around 6000 BC. It seems to represent a special-purpose encampment of hunters and fishermen, occupied for a short period by people employing a highly microlithic industry (the Elkabian) containing many backed bladelets of various types (fig. 5.8.1–6). No trace of food production is evident in this site although by this time village-based cultivation and animal husbandry was already well established in south-west Asia. It is of course possible that any larger, more permanent settlements in Upper Egypt at this time would be located away from the river and are not yet identified archaeologically. Presumably other hunting and fishing groups continued to occupy the valley in Upper Egypt until Badarian times, and it has recently been suggested that some of these people may have been keeping certain game animals such as wild cattle, gazelle and perhaps others in captivity; that is, these groups were in a sense pre-adapted to the true animal husbandry based on goats and sheep that was later introduced from south-west Asia sometime after 5000 BC when, perhaps simultaneously, domesticated strains of wheat and barley developed elsewhere were also transmitted to Egypt.[1] Whether this quite plausible hypothesis is confirmed depends on future

---

[1] J. D. Clark (1971a). The Dynastic Egyptians' celebrated custom of taming certain animals (hyenas, gazelles, etc.) which at a later period were dropped from their repertory of food animals may thus be a tradition extending into Neolithic and even Epi-Palaeolithic times.

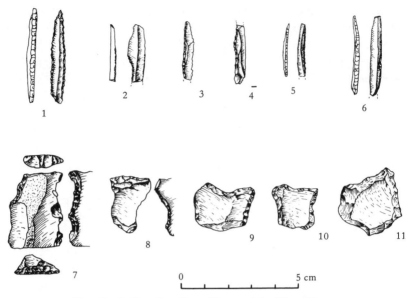

Fig. 5.8   Artifacts from Upper Egypt and the Libyan Desert.

*Elkabian Industry*
1–6 Backed bladelets

*Khargan Industry*
7–11 Truncated and notched flakes

research in this part of North Africa; however one might interpret in this light the rock drawings of groups of seemingly wild cattle, as well as of gazelles, recently found engraved on the cliffs at Jebel Silsila near Kom Ombo and which may be older than 5000 BC. These engravings are located high on the sandstone cliffs at the mouth of a wadi and overlooking a former floodplain although the modern Nile is now several kilometres distant. It is difficult to suggest a precise age for this art since it is not directly associated with any archaeological sites in the area, and is executed in a style not yet identified elsewhere in Egypt. No animals are clearly domesticated, including the herds of cattle, suggesting a hunting art. The technique of engraving and some stylistic traits most closely resemble those in some rock drawings from Cyrenaica which may be Libyco-Capsian (Smith 1968a).

North of Luxor, and particularly in Lower Egypt, far less is known about the Late Palaeolithic and the immediately pre-Neolithic cultures. Some sites are known, especially around Cairo and the Delta, but they are poorly dated and their economic bases are enigmatic. Probably a tradition emphasizing small stone tools and a reduced form of the Levallois method of stone-working (sometimes called 'Diminutive

Levalloisian') was prevalent in this part of the valley, but it would be surprising if other industries with different techniques and typologies, especially those based on blade and bladelet tools, were not also present. Unfortunately, not until food-producing sites appear is there a reasonably sound basis for the prehistory of Lower Egypt. There may have been earlier traces of contacts with south-west Asia (as, for example, the resemblances between industries from the now-destroyed sites at Helwan near Cairo and the Natufian of ninth-millennium Palestine suggest), but insufficient reliable data are available to demonstrate this satisfactorily.

Virtually nothing is known of the Egyptian Palaeolithic in the desert and highlands east of the Nile, although the former existence there of streams and better-watered uplands makes it possible that human occupation may have been important at times. The area west of the Nile (where, paradoxically, the environment was probably less favourable for habitation) is much better known. In the otherwise forbidding Libyan Desert the presence of a number of oases with permanent water derived in some cases (Kharga, Dunqul and Kurkur Oases) from the underlying watertable permitted Late Palaeolithic and Epi-Palaeolithic groups to survive. The situation before around 20 000 BC is poorly known, but apparently some Middle Palaeolithic groups frequented the oases and parts of the desert itself. Somewhat later, perhaps as early as 20 000 BC, the Khargan Industry occurred in several of the oases. Although it is in some ways reminiscent of the Sebilian, it seems to be a desert or at least a non-Nilotic specialization with a heavy reliance on tools on short, thick flakes made by the Levallois method (fig. 5.8.7–11). As in the Sebilian, many of the flakes are truncated or abruptly backed on their edges; it is possible that both industries are derived from a common ancestral tradition. Little is known of Khargan subsistence patterns although presumably hunting was the main activity. Some round and oval stone rings at Dunqul Oasis may represent the bases of habitations or structures of some kind, and are among the earliest yet known in Egypt. How long the Khargan lasted is still unclear, but it may have continued until as late as 9000 BC.

At one time it was considered that the Aterian at Kharga Oasis, with its typical stemmed and foliate points, might have been in part contemporary with the Khargan in the western desert. This now appears much less likely in view of the new, earlier dating for the Aterian which has already been dealt with in chapter 4. Apparently none of the more typical blade or bladelet industries of Upper Egypt ever penetrated into the Libyan Desert, while there is little evidence for the Khargan or Aterian in the Nile Valley. The lack of interaction between the two environments may reflect a high degree of specialized adaptation of the various groups to their particular milieus. It also suggests that increasing aridity in the Libyan Desert in the late Pleistocene may have had the effect of concentrating the inhabitants around those oases with better sources of water rather than promoting migrations towards the Nile Valley, and simultaneously of limiting the movements of the people using blade and bladelet industries to the vicinity of the river.

At several of these oases there may have been, between 6000 and 5000 BC or even earlier, an occupation by groups designated the Libyan Culture. During the somewhat moister conditions then prevailing these people may have supplemented their hunting economy with a kind of incipient cultivation of wild grasses, or even animal-herding. Direct evidence of this is lacking, but the presence on the sites of many grinding stones suggests considerable use of plant foods, such as was perhaps present in the Nile Valley even earlier. However, the practice seems to have endured for only a short time in the oases; it was perhaps aborted by increasing desiccation and probably genuine food production was only introduced during Dynastic times as herders from the Nile Valley periodically visited the desert springs.

It is not certain to what extent the Fayum Depression in Lower Egypt experienced habitations parallel to those in the oases further south. Possibly a Late Palaeolithic industry, or several, belonging to the 'Epi-Levalloisian' tradition existed here but it is poorly known; just as in the Libyan Desert oases, none of the industries characteristic of the Nile Valley based on blade and bladelet tools seem to have penetrated to the Fayum during the late Pleistocene. However, between 6000 and 5000 BC an Epi-Palaeolithic group of fishermen and hunters utilizing microlithic tools and bone harpoons lived around the edges of a lake that was much larger than the shrunken one that now exists. Possibly this fishing and hunting (and plant-collecting?) tradition goes back further than this in the Fayum, but we do not know if it stemmed from groups in the Nile Valley or from contemporaneous lakeside-dwelling people in the Sahara. They seemed to have survived in the Fayum until about the time of the settlement there of food-producing groups of the Fayum A Culture, around 4000 BC;[1] but here, as in the Nile Valley, the

---

[1] However, if the normal radiocarbon determinations are corrected for fluctuations against the bristlecone-pine correlations, it is possible that the Fayum A sites may be nearly a thousand years older than this, around 5000 BC. The Neolithic site of Merimda near the Delta may be nearly as old (see chapter 7).

It might also be mentioned that the Fayum Epi-Palaeolithic described above seems to include

exact nature of the interactions between the indigenous hunters–gatherers–fishermen and the people responsible for introducing the animal and plant domesticates of south-west Asian origin remains poorly understood. Presumably, through processes of acculturation and economic displacement, the food-producers had succeeded in eliminating any surviving hunters and gatherers from the valley and the richer oases by the beginning of Dynastic times at least.

In summary, our views on the human occupations of the lower Nile Valley have undergone considerable modification in the past decade. It is clear that the valley itself, and some of the adjacent hinterland, was not a marginal region in the economic sense but was a zone of high energy concentration which was actively exploited by a number of groups in different ways. Nor, probably, was the population of the valley as isolated or cut off from contacts with contemporaneous groups elsewhere in North Africa as was usually thought. Nevertheless, in spite of the great increase in archaeological data for the Late Palaeolithic and Epi-Palaeolithic, much remains to be explained. The seemingly anarchic industrial diversity seen in Nubia and Upper Egypt between about 16 000 and 10 000 BC raises several important theoretical issues. We are not yet sure of the extent to which the diversity in lithic assemblages reflects different economic postures, or distinct groups of people, or intrusions of new concepts (through idea-diffusion or actual migrations) from outside the area. In some cases, as already suggested, it is possible that a single social or cultural grouping may have been responsible for more than one assemblage as it pursued different subsistence activities, e.g. seasonally; conversely, quite different cultural groups may have utilized very similar stone tools. One possibility to consider is that there was a small number of broad technological traditions – perhaps only two, based on the Levallois and the non-Levallois lithic techniques, with each of these traditions reflecting to some extent a cultural dichotomy that persisted through time for five or six thousand years; and that the individual industries within each of these traditions might be mirrors in some cases of definable social groupings, in other cases of functional adaptations to various subsistence needs. The role of periodic ecological collapses, with the subsequent population shuffles and recombinations, must also be considered in viewing this diversity in the Nile Valley, particularly in Upper Egypt. It is possible, for instance, that periodic fluctuations in the level of the Nile could strongly influence the

part of what was formerly called Fayum B and which was erroneously believed to represent a reversion to hunting and fishing *after* the introduction of food-producing by the Fayum A culture (Caton-Thompson and Gardner 1934; Wendorf *et al.* 1970, p. 1168).

well-being and opportunities of the valley inhabitants. Groups living in areas where the floodplain was narrow and constricted between high cliffs or terraces (as is the case immediately north and south of Kom Ombo between Aswan and Edfu) might be constrained during cycles of abnormally high or low Nile levels to migrate, in whole or in part, to larger zones with richer and more stable ecosystems where river fluctuations mattered less. This might in fact account for some of the rapid appearances and disappearances of industries mentioned above for the Kom Ombo Plain.

Another important problem revolves around possible changes in demographic and settlement patterns between roughly 20 000 and 5 000 BC, both in local zones such as the Kom Ombo Plain (where one estimate suggests that several hundred persons might have lived at a time as hunter–gatherers) and in the Nile Valley as a whole. It is difficult to speak with certainty about population pressures as agents of cultural change until more is known about the available resources and the carrying capacities of the different zones; but certainly some of the outstanding problems of the valley and adjoining oases may be clarified when this is better investigated. Possibly the Nile Valley between about 20 000 and 5 000 BC is an illustration of an environmentally circumscribed zone in which the surrounding deserts offered little real possibility for absorption of any excessive population growth. This situation might well have encouraged economic specialization and technological innovations among some groups, with subsequent cultural differentiation. Social fission and geographical expansion under the same pressures would further intensify the cultural diversity and the archaeological variability.

It has been suggested that the large cemeteries believed to be associated with the Qadan Industry in Nubia (which allegedly lasted from 12 000 to 9000 BC, although a longer duration of from 13 000 to 4000 BC had once been claimed) reflect the existence of larger communities and closer identification with a particular territory than before; while the presence on some of the skeletons of signs of violent death (severe fractures, stone points embedded in the bones) might indicate conflict and competition under conditions of population stress (J. D. Clark 1971, p. 50). This argument is persuasive, although the problem of accurately dating these burials makes it difficult to establish that this demographic growth and pressure coincides with the development of intensive use of plant foods between 12 000 and 10 000 BC. It may be that some of the cemeteries reflect a later stress period during the Qadan, when the alleged emphasis on plant foods had already dwindled in importance.

## THE MAGHRIB

The Jeziret el-Maghrib or 'Island of the West' extends for about 3000 km from the Atlantic to the Gulf of Gabès, and includes the northern parts of the states of Morocco, Algeria and Tunisia. The topography is complex but can be grouped in three main zones: the coastal plain with the mountainous *tell*; the high plains, an arid and windy steppe zone inland; and the northern Sahara including the mountains of the Saharan Atlas and the Anti-Atlas to the west. Climatic conditions vary considerably from north to south today, as they undoubtedly did in prehistoric times. The *tell* and coastal plain with a Mediterranean climate is the richest in terms of vegetation and archaeological sites. Probably the climate in the Maghrib was cool and relatively dry during the late Pleistocene and there are no indications of true pluvial conditions during the time of the Last or Würm Glaciation of Europe. There undoubtedly were some fluctuations in both temperature and moisture, but these are not yet well documented and a precise correlation with the archaeological sequence remains to be worked out. While there was a good deal of variation in food resources from one zone to another, especially in quantity, the fauna was composed of both African and Palaearctic elements and most of these species lasted into at least early Holocene times. The Late Palaeolithic groups hunted wild cattle, antelopes, zebras, Barbary sheep, gazelles, pigs, a giant deer, a giant buffalo and a rhinoceros; the elephant, hippopotamus and giraffe had, however, probably disappeared after Aterian times, by 20 000 BC or so.

Just as in Egypt, industries which belong to the 'typical' Upper Palaeolithic pattern seem to appear later in the Maghrib. The early part of the period corresponding to the Upper Palaeolithic in Europe, south-western Asia and Cyrenaican Libya might have been filled by a late survival of the Aterian. Its chronology is uncertain in the absence of many radiocarbon determinations, but it was probably still in existence by 30 000 BC and possibly could have lasted until at least 20 000 BC in the Maghrib. There seems to be no evidence of contemporaneity with, or development toward, the Iberomaurusian, Capsian and other industries that followed the Aterian in this region.[1]

---

[1] It is of course true that the apparent contrasts in lithic artifacts between the Aterian and its successors may be deceptive, and that these differences may mask more fundamental similarities

How long the Aterian survived is not known. It may have lasted longer in the Sahara than in the Maghrib, though prehistorians are divided on whether it survived late enough to contribute its bifacial flaking tradition and its stemmed points to the Neolithic there; on the whole this seems improbable. Since it is never found stratigraphically above an Epi-Palaeolithic industry in the Maghrib, the usual inference is that it had vanished there well before 13 000 BC. Whether or not there was a hiatus in the occupation of the Maghrib after the Aterian, it remains true that the first of the late Palaeolithic industries seems to appear considerably later than in Cyrenaica though earlier than, apparently, in Egypt or the Sahara. The earliest known date is about 20 000 BC for the Iberomaurusian of Algeria, at Tamar Hat. These late Palaeolithic industries possess no stemmed points, no flat or invasive retouch, practically never use the Levallois method of stone-working, have very few side-scrapers, and are almost always based on blades and bladelets. Two features appear in the Maghrib for the first time: the microburin technique and Ouchtata retouch, although both were known even earlier in the Nile Valley of Egypt. Thus there seems to have been a sharp break in the lithic techniques and artifact forms, with no good evidence for continuity from the local Mousterian or Aterian.

The two principal Epi-Palaeolithic industries of the Maghrib are the Iberomaurusian and the Capsian. For a number of years from the first decade of this century these were believed to be contemporaneous with the Upper Palaeolithic of western Europe and one popular hypothesis maintained that the 'Lower Aurignacian' of France developed from a Capsian invasion of Europe. The research carried out after 1930, particularly by Vaufrey, conclusively showed that both Iberomaurusian and Capsian were much younger than supposed, with no ancestral relationship to the Upper Palaeolithic of Spain or France; indeed, radiocarbon determinations reveal that the Capsian is wholly post-Pleistocene, and most of the Iberomaurusian is probably of terminal Pleistocene age.

These two industries have very different geographical distributions. The Iberomaurusian is mainly found on or near the littoral from Morocco to Tunisia, though some sites are also known inland. The

in methods of resource exploitation and adaptation. Unfortunately past archaeological research has not been especially oriented to approaches that might resolve this important problem. In the meantime some authors group the Mousterian and Aterian together as 'Recent Palaeolithic' and use the term Epi-Palaeolithic for those industries in the Maghrib occurring between around 12 000 BC and the local Neolithic. I use the term Epi-Palaeolithic in this sense in treating the Maghrib.

Capsian, on the other hand, is an exclusively inland phenomenon which barely reaches the *tell* and is almost wholly concentrated on the high steppe-like plains of Tunisia and eastern Algeria. There are in addition a number of other industries that seem to be rather localized, especially those known as the Keremian, the 'Horizon Collignon', and some microlithic assemblages of central Algeria and southern Tunisia.

The term Iberomaurusian was given early in this century when it was thought that this group of North African assemblages was related to microlithic assemblages in Spain. This relationship has never been satisfactorily demonstrated, but the term nonetheless has nomenclatural precedence over such other suggested terms as Mouillian (after the site of La Mouillah in Algeria where it was first identified) and Oranian.[1] Essentially but not completely littoral in their distribution, the Iberomaurusian sites are generally found on or near the present coastline, particularly in sand dunes. However, it is probable that many Iberomaurusian sites, including perhaps the earlier ones, were drowned as the late Pleistocene shorelines were inundated by the rising waters of the Mediterranean in Holocene times. Thus many of the present coastal sites may have been located further inland originally, and need not reflect a purely coastal mode of subsistence. Cave and rock-shelter sites are also known, on the littoral and in the *tell*. Several sites often classed as Iberomaurusian (El-Hamel and Columnata) are found several hundred kilometres south of the coast near the edge of the desert, and this occurrence presents some interesting problems.

Radiocarbon datings indicate that the Iberomaurusian had appeared by about 20 000 BC and that it lasted, in Algeria, until around 7500 BC. This is a considerably longer time-range than that of the Eastern Oranian of Cyrenaican Libya, which it resembles in some ways. In Morocco the Iberomaurusian may have lasted even later, perhaps until the arrival of the Neolithic. Thus the Iberomaurusian is for the most part a final Pleistocene industry which lasted for at least ten millennia; it preceded the Capsian although the two may have overlapped slightly around 8000 BC. The Iberomaurusian also yields the first certain evidence of the presence of *Homo sapiens sapiens* in the Maghrib.

There is a great deal of variation in stone tools lumped under the single rubric Iberomaurusian, and possibly the concept should be redefined in the future. Basically the assemblages are composed of tools

---

[1] Breuil had suggested the name Oranian after the former Algerian province of Oran where many of the sites are located. This term is still used by many prehistorians although the original expression, Iberomaurusian, was never officially abandoned; and a somewhat similar industry in Cyrenaica has been named Eastern Oranian (Gobert and Vaufrey 1932, pp. 487–90).

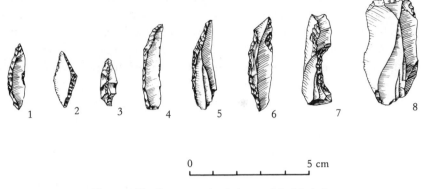

0            5 cm

Fig. 5.9    The Iberomaurusian Industry of the Maghrib.

1–6 Backed bladelets                  8 Scraper
7 Notched bladelet

made on small blades and microliths which, in some cases, may be as much as half the total collection. There are few burins or end-scrapers, and the small numbers of geometric microliths are restricted to little triangles, segments of circles and occasional trapezes; the microburin technique was used to produce pointed backed bladelets called La Mouillah points (fig. 5.9.1–8). However, some large heavy implements are also present including scrapers, choppers and rubbing stones. Bone implements are few and simple, limited to awls, smoothers, 'knives' and points. At the site of Taforalt in Morocco there is an interesting fragment of what may be a barbed bone harpoon, reminiscent of those of comparable age in the European Upper Magdalenian (Roche 1963, fig. 34, 2). Personal ornaments are also rare and simple, the archaeological indications being restricted to perforated sea shells and stones; red and yellow ochre may have been used for pigments or body painting. Ostrich eggshell was apparently not engraved as in later industries.

Although traditionally the Iberomaurusian has been considered an impoverished and monotonous industry (that is, when compared to the more spectacular Capsian), the bladelet tools are very variable and often ingenious in form. They probably reflect highly complex and intricate functions as barbed, cutting or piercing portions of composite implements of which the organic (wooden?) sections have disappeared. However, there have not been enough studies made to determine the functions of the various tools, nor how the variability in assemblages may be related to different activities and social groups. Similarly, little is known in detail of how the broad mass of Iberomaurusian assemblages developed through time. It undoubtedly changed over the many millennia of its existence, and some authors have attempted to divide it into three evolutionary phases – a Proto-Iberomaurusian, a 'classical' phase and an 'evolved' phase – but this is probably an oversimplification based on insufficient stratigraphic data and radiocarbon determinations.

This problem of diversity within the Iberomaurusian through time and space might be better studied when more is known about the subsistence strategies of the various groups. There may well have been movements of people for seasonal and other purposes to and from the littoral, along the shoreline and from one zone to another in the inland environmental zones, even to the borders of what is now desert–steppe. The vegetation, and probably the climate, were not essentially different from those of today although there were probably some fluctuations in temperature and moisture throughout the Iberomaurusian. Juniper, oak, Aleppo pine, pistachio and various shrubs and grasses have been recorded. The people, although primarily hunters of mammals in the coastal valleys and adjoining mountains, also exploited a wide range of other resources, both marine and terrestrial. Some quantities of land snails and sea molluscs were consumed, birds and perhaps rodents were eaten at times, and some freshwater (and possibly sea) fishing is also suggested. No evidence for boats is known, but net and line fishing might have been carried out from the shore. Flat 'grinding stones' and perforated stone balls hint at plant processing and digging-sticks. Thus the Iberomaurusians obtained their food from a wide range of sources, but it is unlikely that each of these foods was concentrated in a single zone or available at all times of the year, and fairly regular movements within the territory of each local group to take advantage of optimum conditions may have been the rule. It is logical to suppose that the occupied sites and the tools in them should to some extent reflect these varying activities.

A considerable amount is known of the Iberomaurusian peoples from study of the several hundred skeletons known, which often are found in large cemeteries within caves. The physical type is usually called the Mechta–Afalou (after two famous sites), and represents a robust population often compared to the Cro-Magnons of Upper Palaeolithic Europe. The group interments perhaps indicate that a developing sense of territoriality was already in existence; and in addition the skeletons provide a good deal of information about the demography, health and behaviour of the people. Much of this comes from the cave of Taforalt in Morocco. Here the population of two hundred people (spread over a period of perhaps several millennia) shows few fractures or signs of traumatic death, but there is a high rate of infant mortality and some gene-related traits that suggest considerable inbreeding during, possibly, some seventy-five generations at this site. Dental abscesses and caries, arthritis, rheumatism and many other miseries show that their health was often poor. Probably as a response, there were attempts at healing, and indeed the oldest known case of trepanation occurs here: the operation on the skull was apparently successful since there are traces of cicatrization, and this suggests considerable skill and knowledge of anatomy.

The second major subdivision of the Epi-Palaeolithic, the Capsian, was for many years considered the industry *par excellence* of the Maghribian Upper Palaeolithic. Its splendid stone tools attracted much attention from prehistorians and the Iberomaurusian was often reduced to a poor offshoot. Today, as already mentioned, the Capsian has been considerably deflated in both time and space. It is seen as a rather localized and wholly Holocene manifestation, restricted geographically to Tunisia and northern Algeria and lasting from roughly 8000 to 4500 BC. Nevertheless the Capsian is one of the most interesting industries in North Africa, and after – or in spite of – many years of research still has much to offer to prehistorians interested in understanding the cultural processes of post-Pleistocene hunters and gatherers. In a sense it is a transitional industry, since it extends from the end of the (basically Pleistocene) Iberomaurusian to the beginning of cultures with some of the accoutrements of the 'Neolithic' including pottery and, probably, food production. It is likely that some of the Capsian groups who were already adapted to more sedentary lives and to intensive gathering strategies served as mechanisms by which new exploitative techniques and devices originating outside the Maghrib were adopted and widely diffused in the sixth and fifth millennia BC.

Judging from the distribution of sites, the Capsian groups were adapted to life in the rather arid hinterland of the Maghrib, on the high plains of Tunisia and eastern Algeria for the most part with some expansion in the Upper Capsian into central and even western Algeria. The Capsian never reached Morocco, but there may be traces on the northern fringes of the Sahara. Its makers occupied rock-shelters and caves at times, but they are best known from the open-air mounds or middens composed of earth, stones, ashes and culinary refuse variously called *escargotières* or (more correctly) *ramadiyas* (in Arabic, ash heaps).

A very large number of Capsian sites exist and the site density is often considerable. While it is difficult to arrive at absolute or even relative demographic estimates, it seems that population densities were often high, particularly in the Tebessa area of eastern Algeria. A fair amount is known about Capsian subsistence patterns, though not enough to build a reliable model of their economic and settlement systems. They were hunters and particularly gatherers of the high plains rather than of the mountains or coastline. Their mammalian game included antelope, wild cattle, Barbary sheep, gazelle, zebra, hare and tortoise, but usually bones do not occur in large quantities. Ostrich eggs were probably consumed but, interestingly enough, not the birds themselves. There are some suggestions that antelopes may have been very selectively slaughtered or even kept under some form of control at times. One source of proteins, though not necessarily a major one, were the land snails which are found in immense quantities in some sites. These may have been collected throughout the year but particularly in the spring and summer. Many of the Capsian sites may have been only seasonally occupied, but this point is not yet determined. Wild-plant-collecting was possibly even more important in the total subsistence pattern than hunting and snail-gathering. No actual plant remains are preserved or identified, but they may have included fruits, bulbs, roots, herbs and various wild grasses, perhaps with some wild cereals as well. A number of artifacts seem to point to plant-collecting and preparation: perforated stones that may have been digging-stick weights for procuring bulbs and roots, flint blades with lustre on the cutting edges, several bone 'sickles' or reaping knives with flint bladelets inset, and many grinding stones showing traces of wear. Food was apparently cooked with the aid of hot stones, perhaps boiled in wooden, hide or basketry containers or roasted in earth ovens. It is uncertain whether domesticated dogs were present.

Traditionally the Capsian has been divided into two phases: the Typical Capsian and the Upper Capsian. These were thought to be successive stages in development, though the evolutionary linkages between them have never been clear. More recently the situation has become more complex as radiocarbon determinations indicate that the Typical Capsian, which probably began around 8000 BC, had lasted considerably longer than was thought, to 5000 BC or even a few centuries later; while the Upper Capsian had begun by at least 6500 BC. Thus there was considerable overlap in time of these two 'phases', and

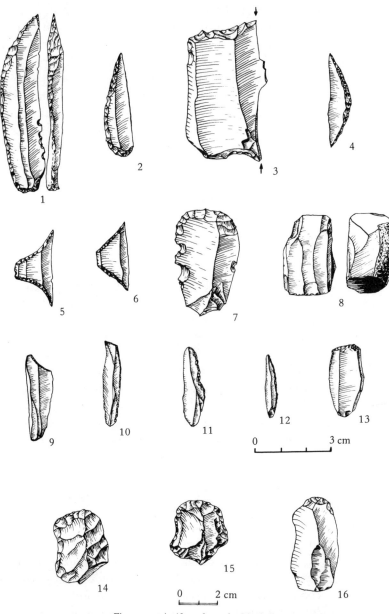

Fig. 5.10   Artifacts from the Maghrib.

*Capsian Industry*
1  Backed blade
2  Backed bladelet
3  Burin
4  Lunate microlith
5–6  Trapezoidal microliths
7  Scraper

*Horizon Collignon*
8  Bladelet nucleus
9  Truncated bladelet
10–12  Retouched bladelets
13  Scraper

*Keremian Industry*
14–16  Scrapers

obviously a revision of previous thinking about not simply Capsian chronology but also the significance of the typological and technological variability among the tools is required.

In general the Capsian lithic artifacts are considerably larger than those of the Iberomaurusian, particularly those classed as Typical Capsian. Very large backed blades and burins are common, as well as heavy end-scrapers on blades and flakes, and notched and strangulated blades. But there are also microlithic implements, even in the Typical Capsian, and the microburin technique is present. Many backed bladelets also occur. The Upper Capsian is characterized by much smaller tools with many more microliths which are now more diversified among many styles of scalene triangles, crescents, trapezes and backed bladelets (fig. 5.10.1–7). Many of the smaller blades were removed from the nuclei by pressure flaking rather than direct or indirect percussion. Just what this tendency towards microlithicization means in terms of functional shifts or style changes related to distinct social groups is unknown at present. Bone artifacts are more common in the Upper Capsian, particularly polished awls (for leather-working?), and at times human long bones were fashioned into artifacts. Decorated ostrich eggshells were apparently used as water bottles, as among the modern Bushmen.

The evidence for art in the Iberomaurusian is ambiguous, being largely represented by several engraved and carved stones reported from the Moroccan site of Taforalt. However, there is now a fragment of a baked clay figurine of an animal, apparently a Barbary sheep, from Tamar Hat dating to about 10 000 BC which would thus be the first unequivocally associated evidence of art in the Maghrib and possibly in North Africa. With the Capsian portable art objects are frequent and take the form of sculpted stones (masks or human faces, animal heads, possibly phalli and vulvas), engraved stone plaques with figurative and geometrical designs, and many fragments of ostrich eggshell with incised geometric or figurative designs (fig. 5.11.1–6). Some of the eggshells were perhaps painted as well. In addition to this portable art, some of the rock drawings in the Maghrib may belong to the Capsian rather than to the Neolithic, though there is much debate on this point. Shell beads are abundant and probably served for personal ornamentation or even for exchange.

One of the peculiarities of the Maghribian Epi-Palaeolithic populations was their emphasis on body mutilation, before and after death. Among both Iberomaurusians and Capsians tooth evulsion was practised

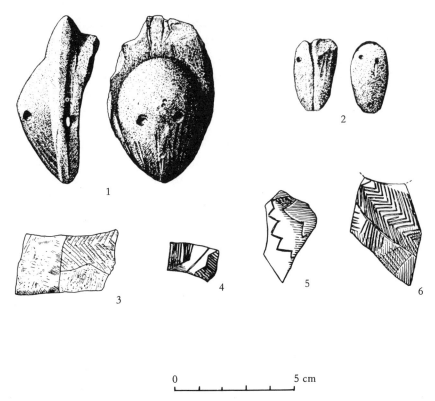

Fig. 5.11   Capsian art of the Maghrib.

1–2 'Masks' in carved limestone
3–6 Engraved ostrich-eggshell fragments

on the living; but whereas among the former the two upper central incisors, and occasionally the two lower ones also, were removed from all adults after puberty, among the Capsians there seems to have been more emphasis on the lower incisors, particularly in females.[1] The purpose of these practices or rituals is not known, although conceivably they may have been mechanisms for demonstrating local group identities. The Capsian skeletons were often modified after death as well, and the skulls in particular were often sawn, cut or drilled. One very

[1] It should be mentioned that the distinction between the Capsian and Iberomaurusian in this respect is less clear-cut than was formerly thought. Some Capsian adults suffered no tooth removal; in some cases they were removed from men as well; and among some Capsian females it was the upper incisors that were removed. In any case the small sample of Capsian skeletons known (23, all from the Upper Capsian) makes it dangerous to generalize. Similarly, the contrast between the 'robust' Iberomaurusian physical type and the 'gracile' Capsian type has probably been exaggerated in the past. See Vallois (1971, p. 399).

unusual 'trophy skull' from Algeria recently studied has most of the back cut away to reduce the face to a kind of mask; further (a unique feature in prehistory and ethnography, apparently) a false tooth made of bone had been skilfully carved and inserted in the jaw after death to replace a missing molar (Vallois 1971). The physical type of the Capsian population tends to be more gracile than the usual Ibero-maurusian individual (although there is some overlapping); faces are long and narrow with smaller mandibles and less facial–cranial dysharmony. They are sometimes called proto-Mediterranean, implying some ancestry to living peoples like the Berbers, but they are more robust than modern Mediterranean populations.

The existence of these two contrasting Epi-Palaeolithic manifestations in the Maghrib raises important questions concerning the nature of each. At one time, before the proper chronology was established, the Iberomaurusian was said to be simply a 'lateral facies' of the Capsian, while at least one claim has been made that the Iberomaurusian and Capsian industries were made by the same groups of people during their winter sojourns on the coast and their summer occupations of the high plains respectively (Leakey 1953). This is unlikely, if only because of the differences in age, for the Iberomaurusian preceded the Capsian by some thousands of years. The differences in art and, to some extent, in physical type also argue against this ecological and subsistence explanation. We seem to be dealing with two broadly differing classes of local groupings, but we do not yet know what the differences mean in functional or cultural terms. Similarly, it is not clear why there is so little sympatry in their geographical distributions: why did the people using Iberomaurusian tools make so little use of the steppe zones inland, and why did the groups with Capsian assemblages fail to exploit the coastlines of Tunisia and eastern Algeria even after the Iberomaurusian had disappeared there? Is it likely, for instance, that until around 8000 BC the high plains with their cool, arid conditions were too inhospitable for Epi-Palaeolithic peoples? These are problems that cannot be solved with the available data.

There is a need for much more research on such topics as the subsistence activities in individual sites and zones, the carrying capacities of the zones, the degrees of sedentarism as reflected by the settlement remains, and any changes in population density through time. Information of this kind could throw light on the nature of at least some of the changes in artifact forms and frequencies observable within both the Iberomaurusian and the Capsian. For instance, it is possible that the alleged 'stagnation' or 'conservatism' of the Iberomaurusian, in contrast to the apparently more rapid changes in the Capsian assemblages through time, might be better investigated in this light. Most Ibero-maurusian sites are located at no great distance from the Mediterranean, and evidence for considerable exploitation of marine and littoral foods is found. If it is accepted as a postulate that marine ecological conditions often tend to be more stable than terrestrial ones (since the food chains are less subject to periodic collapse), then one might see the stability of the Iberomaurusian industrial equipment over a long period as reflecting this environmental predictability. Although the Ibero-maurusian groups were by no means totally committed to use of marine resources, nevertheless the sea was a stabilizing factor that was relatively insensitive to minor climatic–environmental changes that might affect the marginal inland zones more severely, with subsequent repercussions on the fauna and flora on which the Capsian groups depended. On the coast changes in water level, temperature and currents would take place only slowly, and any adjustments required in the subsistence strategies could be made more gradually. In this respect the Mediterranean probably functioned in much the same way as the Nile did in Egypt and Nubia. It is thus conceivable, although difficult to demonstrate at present, that the coastal Iberomaurusian people exploiting marine resources were considerably more sedentary than were the Ibero-maurusian groups occupying the inland sites that have survived, and that their settlements were larger and more complex. Similarly, one can speculate that one effect of a rise in sea level at the close of the Pleistocene was to reduce some areas exploited by these groups along the littoral and to pressure some of them towards other adaptive forms of life. These might include (1) less specialized patterns of exploitation of the littoral zone, involving greater mobility and concomitant changes in technology and settlement type, and (2) expansion by some Ibero-maurusian groups into the far interior, with increasing reliance on the inland food resources and eventually a complete divorce from the traditional pattern of full-time or part-time coastal frequentation. There are some archaeological data that may support this hypothesis, but none, however, that suggest the Iberomaurusian was transformed in this way into the earliest Capsian.

But the Iberomaurusian and Capsian do not reflect the entire Epi-Palaeolithic occupation of the Maghrib. A number of other variants are now recognized. In most cases they are not well dated, and little is known about them apart from their stone tools. The sampling of known sites is also small, and in some cases there may be mixtures of artifacts from several different periods. Nevertheless these variants do suggest that human occupation of the Maghrib was more complex than a simple bipartite division. This situation is analogous to that in the Nile Valley, where a far more complex picture with many different and often short-lived industries has emerged in recent years.

Perhaps the most interesting of the variants is that known as the *Horizon Collignon*. Discovered by a Dr Collignon in 1887 at Sidi Mansour near Gafsa, central Tunisia, it is also found at Lalla East nearby, and possibly at Ouchtata in northern Tunisia. It is sometimes argued that it may be the earliest blade industry in the Maghrib, or even the earliest stage of the Iberomaurusian. This is not impossible, but unfortunately up to now this industry has not been precisely dated either stratigraphically or by isotopic means. It seems to be earlier than the Typical Capsian, but now much further back it extends is not established. The industry is mainly composed of small blades with backing or Ouchtata retouch on the right margin and with unretouched, often splayed tips (fig. 5.10.8–13). There are no large backed blades, no burins or microburins, and no typical geometric microliths. In some ways, especially in its technology, it is reminiscent of the Iberomaurusian (although, interestingly enough, it resembles even more closely the Sebekian industry of Upper Egypt dated to 12 000 BC or earlier); hence a number of prehistorians have suggested that it is a good candidate for the hypothetical ancestral Iberomaurusian and have termed it Proto-Iberomaurusian or Iberomaurusian I. This implies that the Horizon Collignon is older than 13 000 BC, which would agree with the Nile Valley dating for the Sebekian. However, the issue cannot be decided until the age of the Horizon Collignon Industry is determined, for, if as other prehistorians suggest, it is no older than about 9000 BC, then the picture changes considerably. Virtually nothing is known of the subsistence or other activities of the people responsible for the Horizon Collignon artifacts and it is not possible to say whether it represents a very localized and highly specialized group of assemblages designed for certain specific functions.

There is another enigmatic and heterogeneous collection of assemblages found at various localities in central and southern Tunisia, sometimes near the brackish lakes or *chotts* but also near the northern fringe of the Sahara. They occur at such sites as Oued el-Akarit, Menchia, Mareth and Aïn el-Atrous, and all contain a very high percentage of sharply pointed backed bladelets, little or no evidence of microburin technique, and few or no geometric microliths. Some authors have considered them variants of the Iberomaurusian, but it may be that they are more closely affiliated with certain early Holocene industries of the northern Sahara. Research in the area of the *chotts* of Tunisia and eastern Algeria, which apparently existed as important lakes during the Pleistocene, might throw some light on these industries and particularly on the modes of adaptation they represent.

Another poorly known variant, this time from the high plains of western Algeria, is known as the Keremian (after the site of Kef el-Kerem). Its age is uncertain since it is known only from a few surface or unstratified midden sites. It probably belongs to Holocene times and is perhaps a contemporary of the Capsian. Its most striking characteristic is the abundance of end-scrapers (about half of the tool-kit) made on thick blades and heavy flakes (fig. 5.10.14–16); there are also backed blades and bladelets and very small triangles and lunates. The microburin technique is present. Generally the tools are simply, even crudely made. In some ways it resembles an industry of Nubia known as the Arkinian which perhaps began about 7500 BC, while there are also some parallels with the Libyco-Capsian of Cyrenaica. Just what these parallels mean is uncertain; they do not necessarily reflect historic relationships and they may simply indicate convergences due to common needs to use large numbers of scrapers. Unfortunately little is known about the subsistence patterns of the Keremian, although some grinding stones are found; hence its significance in the Maghribian Epi-Palaeolithic remains to be determined.

Finally, another group of assemblages in several localities in central Algeria, near the boundary of the *tell* and the northern Sahara, is characterized by its extremely small tools. The term 'Elassolithic' (ultra-microlithic) has been applied to these assemblages at such sites as Columnata and El-Hamel, where they date to the seventh millennium BC, contemporary with the Typical and perhaps Upper Capsian. Again, their real significance is not clear. They have variously been considered a local variant of the Upper Capsian, or even a derivative of the Iberomaurusian with an emphasis on tools made on very small bladelets. Some authors have used the term Columnatian for the industry found about 6300 BC at Columnata site. Interestingly, the human skeletal remains from this site are basically of the Mechta–Afalou type found in the Iberomaurusian, but are less robust and have patterns of tooth evulsion more typical of the Upper Capsian people. This may reflect the survival here in the former Oran province of the Mechta–Afalou type, perhaps now evolving locally into a more gracile form independently, or it may indicate biological (and presumably social) contacts with Capsian groups. One possible interpretation of the physical and archaeological data is that in this area of the Maghrib survivors or descendants of the Iberomaurusian peoples were now receiving considerable stimulus, both genetic and cultural, from the expanding Capsian groups who under conditions of demographic instability were moving westward from their traditional centres in Tunisia and eastern Algeria. This trend towards microlithicization of stone tools is apparent in a number of areas of the Maghrib, the Sahara and Egypt (cf. the Elkabian) in the seventh millennium; it may represent both the movements of people and the diffusion of new subsistence adaptations and technological shifts, but the details are not yet grasped.

It remains to attempt some explanation of the origins or sources of these various Epi-Palaeolithic industries of the Maghrib. Unfortunately little can be said with much confidence. The earliest stages of any Palaeolithic industry are difficult to trace, particularly in the absence of a fine chronological framework. In the case of the Maghribian Epi-Palaeolithic there has been much speculation and, generally speaking, a tendency to search for origins outside the region, often outside Africa itself.

As already mentioned, there is little evidence for indigeneous development of the earliest known Epi-Palaeolithic industry, the Iberomaurusian, from the only known immediate predecessor in the Maghrib, the Aterian. It seems likely that the first Epi-Palaeolithic occupants came from outside, perhaps from the east. The manner and the moment of their arrival are unknown, but we can imagine small bands of hunters and gatherers gradually enlarging their territories through fission, population expansion and exploration into new areas over many centuries or even millennia. Nor is it known whether a few or many infiltrating groups were responsible for this early peopling of the Maghrib, or if they found themselves competing with earlier occupants such as the ones who made the Aterian tools. It is conceivable that an assemblage like the Horizon Collignon might represent this stage of settlement, but this too remains unclear at the present time.[1]

Today there is a tendency to look eastward for Iberomaurusian origins – first to the Eastern Oranian of Cyrenaican Libya, and more

---

[1] A 'terminal Mousterian' with Upper Palaeolithic-type blade tools has been reported from the site of El-Guettar in central Tunisia but its significance is unknown; it seems to be earlier than the local Epi-Palaeolithic but how much older is not certain (Gruet 1954, p. 56).

recently to the Nile Valley. In Egypt such industries as the Sebekian and the Silsilian, dating to around 13 000 BC or somewhat earlier, do present interesting parallels to the Horizon Collignon and the classic Iberomaurusian respectively.[1] However, the time differences between these industries in the Nile Valley and in the Maghrib are not great and, if a diffusionary model is adopted to explain the resemblances, one could almost as easily argue for movement from west to east. It is probably premature to accept, without further evidence, a hypothesis of simple migration from the Nile Valley to the Maghrib passing, perhaps, through Cyrenaica. Reality was undoubtedly far more complex than this, even if diffusion was involved rather than convergences, and the roles of south-western Asia or of the Sahara in the establishment of the Epi-Palaeolithic of the Maghrib remain to be defined. Finally, it may also be premature to rule out all possibility of contact between the late Upper Palaeolithic of Spain and the Iberomaurusian. This hypothesis was favoured by the creators of the term early in this century but has not been regarded with much enthusiasm in recent years and it has been asserted that there were no such contacts between the two regions until the Neolithic.[2]

There is no greater unanimity about the origins of the Capsian. Various hypotheses have been suggested – movement of peoples from south-western Asia or from Cyrenaica; indigeneous development in North Africa from some predecessor like the Dabban or the Horizon Collignon; settlement from Sicily by way of boat-using people blown across the Gulf of Gabès in a storm. None of these are very convincing, and no good candidate has yet appeared in the Nile Valley. The Keremian does have a parallel in Nubia, but as already mentioned the significance of this is not clear. In other words, we still know very little about the origins of any of the Epi-Palaeolithic industries of the Maghrib, or the circumstances in which they implanted themselves or

---

[1] The Sebekian and the Horizon Collignon industries have in common the emphasis on blades and bladelets with Ouchtata retouch usually near the bases and plain, often splayed tips; and the absence of typical geometric microliths, large backed blades and (for the Sebekian at least) microburins. The Silsilian and the Iberomaurusian share an emphasis on bladelets, often backed, and the removal of microburins from the tips; together with a small number of geometric microliths and a low proportion of burins and scrapers (Smith 1966, pp. 343–4).

[2] Recent, and still largely unpublished, discoveries in Greece indicate that by 6000 BC some Mesolithic groups of hunters, gatherers and fishermen were transporting the volcanic stone obsidian from the island of Melos in the Cyclades to the Greek mainland at Franchti Cave; the minimum distance of open sea travel was about 50 km. In view of this we should not discount similar voyages in the western Mediterranean in pre-Neolithic times, perhaps across the Straits of Gibraltar in spite of its strong currents. After all, Palaeolithic men had long before this crossed a fairly wide stretch of water to colonize Australia.

developed. Indeed, in one sense the question of ultimate origins represents a false problem whose importance has often been exaggerated by prehistorians. Had more effort been devoted, in the Maghrib and elsewhere in North Africa, to an understanding of just what each of these industries represents in functional and adaptive terms, we might now be closer to knowing something concrete about their origins.

At the other end of the Epi-Palaeolithic sequence is the problem of the eventual transformation of the hunters and gatherers by Neolithic peoples or Neolithic influences. There seems to have been a fair amount of continuity between the last Capsian groups and those people, usually called Neolithic of Capsian Tradition, who had incorporated in their assemblages such new traits as polished stone, bifacially worked stone points and even some pottery. However, it is not certain that most of these 'Neolithic' peoples were food-producers in spite of the name given them. The problem of the arrival or indigenous development of food-producing in North Africa still requires much study. Domesticated cereals from south-west Asia had probably reached Egypt around 5000 BC, and domesticated goats or sheep were in Cyrenaica about the same time. The coasts of Morocco and western Algeria were probably frequented by seafaring food-producers about this time also, and some of the domesticates and technological traits may have reached the late Capsian people in this way: possibly, as already suggested here, some of these groups were already very intensive collectors and thus, in a sense, pre-adapted to a life based on food production. They may even have exploited some indigenous plants to a degree that approached cultivation before the foreign cereals were introduced and supplanted them.

It is possible that food production was established for some time on the coast and even in the central Sahara before any substantial change came about in the lives of the groups living between these two zones. In the eastern Maghrib the descendants of the Capsians seem to have survived from about 4000 BC to 2500 BC as scattered, semi-nomadic populations with economies based on hunting and collecting; in spite of their occasional use of pottery and a few other 'Neolithic' items added to their microlithic tools, they lived essentially Epi-Palaeolithic lives in wooded and mountainous zones. Possibly survivors of the Ibero-maurusian tradition continued in much the same way in some parts of the western Maghrib, until by the second millennium BC they were absorbed by, or converted into, food-producers of one kind or another.

## THE SAHARA

There is not one Sahara but many. This immense area of almost 9 million sq. km shows much diversity in geography, climate and human occupation. Differences in altitude and shifts in the subtropical anti-cyclonic belt account for part of the considerable variation in vegetation, fauna and human carrying capacities. The area can be roughly subdivided into a northern, a central and a southern zone, all of which seem to have seen essentially cool, relatively dry conditions during the last part of the Pleistocene from about 18 000 BC to 10 000 BC. Climatic evidence recently obtained from the Lake Chad area in the southern zone indicates that for some 20 000 years before 20 000 BC conditions were generally humid and favourable, and possibly the Aterian may have persisted during this time in the Sahara, though there is every indication that it had disappeared by the onset of the major arid period after 20 000 BC.

The Aterian peoples seem to have been more successful in their adaptation than were those other groups like the Dabban and early Iberomaurusian, and not until about 8000 BC, apparently, are industries based on blades and bladelets found in the Sahara. There was clearly a hiatus in human occupation between the Aterian and the Epi-Palaeolithic at Adrar Bous in Niger, and there is no good evidence of contacts anywhere between the Aterian and the earliest Epi-Palaeolithic.

In the northern Sahara of Algeria a number of sites (e.g. Hassi Mouillah, El-Hadjar) have been found around the *chotts*. They have yielded bladelet industries that are sometimes called the Saharan Epi-Palaeolithic (or more recently 'Mellalian'), and they were present by at least 6500 BC. Their economic bases are virtually unknown but some may have been fishing communities, at least seasonally. The climate was sub-arid if not arid and the lakes were shrinking under increasing desiccation. The lithic tools include many backed bladelets, few or no geometric microliths, some grinding stones and worked pieces of ostrich eggshell (fig. 5.12.1–5). A few other bladelet industries have been reported in the northern Sahara, most of them poorly documented or dated, and in some cases there are claims of Capsian affinities. These seem to have persisted until the fifth or fourth millennium BC when, under somewhat more favourable conditions of temporary moister climate perhaps, various 'Neolithic' traits like pottery and bifacially flaked points appear. However, just as in the analogous Neolithic of Capsian Tradition of the Maghrib, the economy was essentially based on hunting and gathering with no good evidence

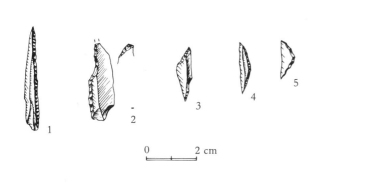

Fig. 5.12    Artifacts from the Sahara.

Epi-Palaeolithic of the northern Sahara        Ounanian Industry, central Sahara
1–3  Backed bladelets                          6  Tanged point or perforator
4–5  Geometric microliths

of food-producing, and this may have continued in some zones of the northern Sahara as late as 1000 BC.

In the central and southern Sahara other blade and bladelet industries have recently been reported and some may go back to at least 8000 BC. Their origins are obscure but colonization from the Maghrib and northern Sahara is a possibility. At Aïr and Adrar Bous, in Niger, a series of industries have been found and they indicate at least periodic occupations by hunters, gatherers and sometimes fishermen until the appearance of Neolithic herdsmen. Perhaps the earliest of the Holocene industries is one based on macroblades. Another, the Ounanian, is non-microlithic and is characterized by a kind of stemmed point or perforator (fig. 5.12.6). Although these are not microlithic industries, there is no evidence to suggest an evolution from the local Aterian. Around the sixth millennium they seem to be replaced by groups using true microlithic tools. These communities apparently were composed of hunters and fishermen who occupied the areas around the temporarily replenished lakes and swamps and exploited fish, hippopotamus and land mammals. They used bone harpoons and leisters for fishing, and various kinds of stone arrowheads. They also had coarse impressed pottery. Possibly these people at Adrar Bous were contemporaries of the groups with somewhat similar subsistence patterns at Early Khartoum in the Sudan, and they may have persisted until the appearance around 4000 BC of the Ténéréan, a Neolithic culture based probably on herding and seasonal nomadism.

Not much is known of the Epi-Palaeolithic occupants of the central Sahara apart from a number of surface collections and a few site studies. Further explorations will undoubtedly increase our knowledge of human occupation, but at the present it seems that most of the Sahara was lightly settled between 18 000 BC and the arrival of the food-producers. Although cattle-herders were present by the fifth millennium, it is difficult to say when plant cultivation began; indeed, there is no direct evidence of this until around 1100 BC when carbonized grains are found in Mauritania. Whether some of the groups generally included under the rubric 'Neolithic of Sudanese Tradition' actually cultivated plants as early as the seventh millennium BC is a burning question. This has been suggested for a few sites in the Ahaggar and Tibesti highlands, perhaps based on indigenous African grasses, and it has been proposed that here (as in the Libyan Culture of Egypt) there may be a case of local independent evolution toward food-producing, based on grains such as millet and sorghum. This is by no means unlikely, but better evidence is needed to support it.

Whatever may have been the indigenous trend, it seems that eventually in the central Sahara the last of the hunters and gatherers were incorporated into or displaced by the nomadic herdsmen and particularly by the cattle-keepers. Cattle may have been locally domesticated in the Sahara, and herding may have been a means of land use ideally suited to increasingly arid conditions as lakeside fishing and, perhaps, cultivation became increasingly difficult. In situations of competition for scarce resources herding was probably one way of maintaining an equilibrium between human population and reduced resources and of utilizing marginal lands unsuited for cultivation. How late the various groups of hunters, gatherers and fishermen – essentially Epi-Palaeolithic in spite of their adoption of pottery and other 'Neolithic' elements – survived as such in each zone remains to be established. We might imagine that for many centuries, even millennia, there was some kind of symbiotic relationship between them and the pastoralists like that between the Bushmen and Herero of the Kalahari Desert today, with the former providing local goods and even services in exchange for milk, meat and other products.

THE EARLY ART OF NORTH AFRICA

There is no single style of prehistoric art in North Africa but a number of styles that differ according to period, to geographical area and no doubt to culture. How much of this art can be attributed to the Late Palaeolithic and Epi-Palaeolithic peoples described in this chapter?

For at least three-quarters of a century there has been controversy over the age and cultural context of the art, and especially of the rock art engraved and painted on cliffs, outcrops and boulders, in North Africa. It is found from the Atlantic to the Red Sea Hills and from the Maghrib steppes and mountains to the southern Sahara. At the beginning of this century many of the rock paintings and engravings were thought to be of Upper Palaeolithic age like those in Western Europe, just as the Capsian was believed to be related to the European Aurignacian. This belief gradually disintegrated until by the 1940s there was a strong swing in the opposite direction; this view, particularly as propounded by Vaufrey, held that the rock art belonged entirely to the Neolithic of Capsian Tradition (which had been powerfully influenced by the Predynastic and Dynastic cultures in Egypt) and that nothing was older than the fifth millennium BC.

More recently there has been a relaxation of this rigid chronological framework and a willingness to accept older ages for the beginning of the art. There seems no question that some of it is the work of pre-agricultural hunters and gatherers, as some radiocarbon determinations and stratigraphic evidence show. Some writers are prepared to see it as beginning with the final Palaeolithic and early Mesolithic of Europe, and to be derived from such styles as those of the Spanish Levant or of southern Italy; others champion a purely African derivation.

As already mentioned, the evidence for art of any kind in the Iberomaurusian is ambiguous. A clay animal figurine occurs at Tamar Hat c. 10000 BC and several carved and incised stones are reported from Taforalt c. 9000 BC. No such art occurs in any other known Iberomaurusian site, although of course it may have been expressed in perishable materials such as wood or bark. There are no engraved ostrich eggshells, and no wall art at all is found along the littoral of the Maghrib.

However, the reality of art in the Capsian, and especially in the Upper Capsian, is unquestioned. It was present by about 6500 BC and perhaps earlier in the form of incised ostrich eggshell, engraved stone plaques with both figurative and geometric drawings, and sculpted stones (fig. 5.11.1–6). In addition it is possible that some of the rock drawings in the Maghrib are of Capsian age and even of Capsian manufacture, while some of the rock engravings in the old Sud-Oranais district of Algeria usually attributed to the Neolithic may be descended from this Capsian tradition. These Neolithic drawings may represent a continuation of the trend in Capsian engraving and sculpting towards figurative and naturalistic representations of animals and other objects, perhaps influenced to some degree by the food-producing colonists now established on the coast of the Maghrib.

So there seems little doubt that portable art objects, at least, were being produced by some of the Epi-Palaeolithic hunters and gatherers of the Maghrib. Similar evidence is rare in other parts of North Africa, apart from some decorated ostrich eggshell fragments from the northern Sahara Epi-Palaeolithic sites, and the bird drawing incised on a pebble ascribed to the Libyco-Capsian of Haua Fteah between 8000 and 5000 BC. No such portable art is known with certainty from the Nile Valley. On the other hand, there are some indications that part of the rock art of the central Sahara, of Cyrenaica and even of the Nile Valley may be the work of various groups who, whether one labels them Epi-Palaeolithic or Neolithic, were basically hunters, gatherers and fishermen.

The earliest recognized rock art in North Africa (with the possible exception of some simple Capsian engravings at El-Mekta in Tunisia) is found in what has come to be known variously as the Large Wild Fauna, or Hunter, or *Bubalis*, period or style. This art is represented by engravings only, and is found in the southern Maghrib and the central Sahara particularly. The most characteristic element is the extinct giant buffalo *Bubalis* (or *Homoïoceras*) *antiquus*, but there are also large naturalistic drawings of cattle, rhinoceros, hippopotamus, giraffes, equids and rams. Sometimes the animals, especially the rams, bear discs between their horns or show collars, pendants and perhaps lassos. The deep grooves are sometimes polished, and inside the figures there may be polishing or pecking as well. Humans are also shown, in hunting scenes and occasionally in coitus positions. The age of this art is not certain but some radiocarbon and archaeological data suggest it goes back well beyond 6000 BC and is the product of people who, although virtually unknown in detail, were basically hunters of large mammals. Indeed, recently one student of Saharan art, Mori (1974), has argued on the basis of superpositions of drawings observed in the Tadrart

Acacus area of south-western Libya not far from the Tassili that the earliest of these engravings may go back to the close of the Pleistocene, between 9000 and 8000 BC presumably. In the central Sahara there may have been a variant of this hunters' art in which the giant buffalo rarely figured, and no representation of this animal is found east of the Fezzan in Libya.

In some parts of the Sahara this Large Wild Fauna or *Bubalis* phase is followed by what has been termed the Round Head style of art. This features some engravings but, more particularly, many paintings, probably the earliest in North Africa. These paintings feature the enigmatic 'white Martians' – human figures, often gigantic, with round and usually faceless heads which are sometimes horned and masked. There are also depictions of such wild animals as giraffes, elephants, rhinoceros, ostriches and even the giant buffalo. This art style is not found east of the Ennedi, in Tchad. It began long before 6000 BC apparently, and may have ended during the sixth millennium when it seems to have been replaced by the more famous paintings and engravings of the Bovidian Pastoral phase which lasted until the third millennium. The Bovidian Pastoral art was the production, judging from the artistic and some archaeological evidence, of food-producing nomadic (or at least transhumant) herdsmen who kept large herds of fully domesticated cattle and were probably organized in powerful tribal groups. The Round Head phase or style, on the other hand, is less well known. There are some indications that it may have been associated with some of the groups that archaeologists assign to the so-called Neolithic of Sudanese Tradition; that is, the artists were pottery-using hunters and fishermen who herded some goats and perhaps even cattle, and may have practised a kind of incipient plant cultivation to supplement their diet. It is worth considering that some of the earlier Saharan and Maghribian rock art may document the still-hypothetical stage of animal husbandry suggested by some zoologists and prehistorians: a long phase of animal-herding without formal domestication in the zoological sense but with a policy of protection and killing that was ultimately selective for certain desired characteristics. It is not inconceivable that cattle were on the way to indigenous domestication from local wild stock in the Sahara as well as in the Nile Valley.

In the eastern part of the desert, including the Nile Valley, most of the rock art belongs to the Bovidian Pastoral phase or later and is the work of food-producers. However, it would be curious if there were no traces at all of art attributable to the Epi-Palaeolithic groups who were present in the Nile Valley and in the deserts. One indication of such behaviour has already been mentioned, the engravings of cattle and other animals (antelopes or gazelles, hippopotamus) on the cliffs at Jebel Silsila near Kom Ombo in Upper Egypt (see p. 372 above). Engravings of cattle and Barbary sheep, apparently wild, are known also in Cyrenaican Libya and may date to the Libyco-Capsian between 8000 and 5000 BC.

In summary, it now seems likely that the earliest art in North Africa goes back to very early Holocene, if not to final Pleistocene times. None of it can be assigned to the Aterian and it was apparently the product of peoples who were basically Epi-Palaeolithic hunters, gatherers and, perhaps, fishermen. The ultimate sources of this art remains to be established; for the 'northern' art in the Maghrib and perhaps in coastal Libya some stimulus from outside Africa is not unlikely although connections with Europe are difficult to demonstrate. The Round Head style and the succeeding styles of the Sahara are probably local developments spread widely by groups exploiting an environment that fluctuated considerably in humidity and vegetation but was a good deal more hospitable than is the modern Sahara. The mechanisms of diffusion of both the Epi-Palaeolithic and the food-producers' art are not well understood, however, nor are the means by which some of this art may have been transmitted to the hunters, gatherers and herdsmen south of the Sahara.

It is tempting to suggest that the early art of North Africa appeared in the context of some industrial or technological innovation such as microlithicism in stone tools, which itself was perhaps related to more successful methods of exploiting natural resources and especially animal life. This may have required ritualistic behaviour that was on occasion marked in concrete form by engravings and, later, by paintings. While this remains an interesting hypothesis, we are unfortunately unable up to now to establish any firm correlations between artistic and industrial innovations, or to see any causal links. Virtually nothing can be said with assurance about the purposes or meanings of the art, which was probably rooted in multiple functions: as sympathetic magic to improve the chances for success in hunting, as representations to commemorate events in social life, and as ritual to instruct individuals or mark passages from one status to another. Perhaps at times the art was the work of highly competent 'specialists', while other examples may be the products of individuals for reasons of personal satisfaction or pleasure.

PHYSICAL TYPES AND RACES IN NORTH AFRICA

Mention has already been made of the skeletal materials found with the Late Palaeolithic and Epi-Palaeolithic industries throughout North Africa. Without exception they belong to the modern physical type, *Homo sapiens sapiens*. Virtually nothing is known of the Aterian populations. Some Mousterian remains from Jebel Irhoud in Morocco suggest that features more typical of modern man than of classic Neanderthals were already present, and it is possible that the presumably later Aterians (or at any rate some of them) may have been even more *sapiens*-like. One would expect, too, that the people who were responsible for the Dabban Industry of Cyrenaica would have been fully modern physically. At the moment, however, this is an argument with no supporting evidence from bones. The earliest post-Mousterian remains in Cyrenaica date to the Eastern Oranian about 10 000 BC, in Egypt and Nubia there are no known fossils until around 15 000 BC, while in the Sahara nothing occurs until well into the Holocene when a number of 'Neolithic' skeletons are found.

Not only are human skeletons of the Late Palaeolithic very rare until after about 12 000 BC; but when they do become numerous after that date they are very unevenly distributed in space. They cluster in the central and western Maghrib on the one hand, and in Nubia on the other. While the hundreds of skeletons now known permit very valuable studies in palaeopathology, palaeodemography and microevolution, they still leave unanswered many important questions about the origins of the Late Palaeolithic/Epi-Palaeolithic populations of North Africa.

As already mentioned, most of the many Iberomaurusian skeletons belong to the Mechta–Afalou type, characterized by robust skulls with thick walls, pronounced brow-ridges, high and prominent noses, large mandibles with pronounced chins, and tall, well-muscled bodies. The cranial capacity was also large. Apparently the two Eastern Oranian mandibles from Cyrenaica belong to this type also. The Capsian physical form tended to be more gracile, a 'primitive Mediterranean' type, but there seems to have been some overlapping at times with the Mechta–Afalou type (see n. 1 on p. 386).

There have been a number of hypotheses to explain the origins of these first *Homo sapiens sapiens* of the Maghrib, the Mechta–Afalou population. Although comparable physically to Cro-Magnon man of Europe who had appeared much earlier, there is no real evidence for direct movements of people across the Mediterranean; but, as already suggested, it cannot be entirely ruled out. Movement of peoples from south-western Asia into North Africa is another possibility, but the scarcity of well-documented skeletons in the Upper Palaeolithic of the latter region is a handicap in seeking fossil candidates there. In recent years there has been a noticeable tendency to look for an indigenous evolution in North Africa itself for the Late Palaeolithic/Epi-Palaeolithic people and especially for the robust Mechta–Afalou type.[1] It is suggested that from a Neanderthal or neanderthaloid stock somewhere in North Africa there was an independent evolution towards a more modern but still somewhat 'archaic' form as represented by the Mechta–Afalou type, with the unknown Aterian people perhaps constituting the intermediate stage.

This hypothesis is constructed on both skeletal and industrial evidence. Several cemeteries in the Nile Valley of Nubia contain over a hundred skeletons which are said to resemble the Mechta–Afalou type and to date to final Pleistocene times. It is suggested that this population is the result of biological evolution from the local Neanderthals (who admittedly are still unknown), just as somewhat later the Halfan Industry, basically in the old Levallois tradition, increasingly developed Epi-Palaeolithic features such as microblades and Ouchtata-like retouch. From this industrial context, and from the somewhat later blade and bladelet industries like the Silsilian and Sebekian, there developed the sources for the Iberomaurusian-type industries of Cyrenaica and the Maghrib. The 'evolving Neanderthals' of the Nile Valley may have migrated westward and in time, via the Aterians, developed into the Mechta–Afalou type, while a similar physical type developed in the Nile Valley itself as illustrated by the cemeteries mentioned above (Ferembach 1972, Tixier 1972).

The great weakness of this hypothesis is that no human skeletal remains at all are yet known in Egypt and Nubia from the Mousterian, Aterian, Khormusan or Halfan industries. In addition a fragmentary skeleton apparently dating to about 15 000 BC recently reported from Upper Egypt is actually less robust than those from the later cemeteries in Nubia. There is thus little direct evidence to suggest either an indigenous development within the Nile Valley or (even if there were such a development) a simple unidirectional trend in physical evolution or a homogeneous population. The absence of reliably dated skeletal

[1] This trend in North Africa is part of an increasingly popular acceptance by physical anthropologists and prehistorians that both *Homo sapiens sapiens* and Upper Palaeolithic-type industries might well have developed in independent fashion in a number of regions of the Old World rather than diffusing from a single centre; see various articles in Bordes (1972).

remains between *c.* 15 000 and 30 000 BC in this sub-region is one of the greatest lacunae in our present knowledge. In these circumstances it is difficult to know which region has priority, for the robust population of the Nile Valley might well be intrusive from elsewhere in Africa or Asia rather than the products of an indigenous evolution from hypothetical Nubian Neanderthals. In any case, it seems simplistic to consider human evolution in North Africa as if it were a sealed environment without reference to other regions. Since archaic forms of *Homo sapiens* were already present in the lower Omo basin of Ethiopia and the Kavirondo area of Lake Victoria (Kenya) considerably earlier than any reported hitherto from North Africa, it seems unreasonable to neglect contributions from other parts of Africa; while south-western Asia may also have contributed to some extent.

Another unresolved problem concerns the apparent trend towards less rugged physical types throughout the Epi-Palaeolithic of the Maghrib, the Neolithic of the Sahara, and perhaps other areas as well. In the Maghrib the Iberomaurusian and Capsian populations seem to demonstrate this process of gracilization in the Epi-Palaeolithic; in the Saharan 'Neolithic' (where, it must be recalled, much of the population were basically hunters, gatherers and fishermen) there was a considerable range from robust to gracile types but through time the trend was apparently in the direction of progressive gracilization. The causes of this trend are still unknown, but among the factors to be considered in this microevolution are local differentiation by mutation, genetic drift and selection in favour of weight reduction and slenderness in dry, hot environments, especially in the Sahara; genetic changes resulting from shifts in rules governing marriage and residence as communities became more sedentary, larger and perhaps more endogamous internally; and migrations of new people of less robust 'Mediterranean' type from south-western Asia.

It is difficult to be precise about the racial groups represented among the Epi-Palaeolithic and 'Neolithic' skeletons. A common assumption is that the Epi-Palaeolithic populations of the Maghrib and of the northern Sahara were caucasoid like those of south-western Asia and Europe at this time. This may be so, but the present evidence seems inconclusive on this point. The Saharan 'Neolithic' populations may have included non-negroid Mediterranean types resembling the Capsian people to the north, and negroids in the central and southern Sahara. The rock art may supplement the skeletal evidence to some degree, though only rarely; it is likely that both 'Afro-Mediterranean' (basically caucasoid) and 'negroid' individuals can be distinguished in the art of the Bovidian Pastoral phase in the Sahara, but it is doubtful that any such racial identifications can be made for the earlier phases during the *Bubalis* and Round Head periods, or during the Capsian of the Maghrib.

## CONCLUSIONS AND INTERPRETATIONS

A number of general points emerge from this examination of the Late Palaeolithic and Epi-Palaeolithic of northern Africa.

First, there is no good evidence of any blade-tool industry's developing directly out of a Middle Palaeolithic or Mousterian-type industry in North Africa itself. Rather, it seems that the Dabban Industry, present in Libya sometime before 30 000 BC, was (like the much earlier Libyan Pre-Aurignacian) an intrusion into Cyrenaica from outside that zone and probably from outside the African continent. Nor is there unequivocal evidence that any of the later blade and bladelet industries of North Africa which appeared after 20 000 BC were derived from indigenous sources. The same holds for the origins of the earliest known specimens of *Homo sapiens sapiens* in this region; no local ancestor can be designated with any degree of confidence. The implication of this at the present time (and of course it may have to be modified by future discoveries) is that the early blade-tool industries and the earliest modern men in North Africa owed more to the diffusion from outside of styles, techniques and people than to purely local developments. Furthermore, until about 15 000 BC changes occurred only slowly if we are to judge by the stone tools. Even the Dabban Industry is remarkably stable throughout its long lifetime. It is not until around 15 000 BC in the Nile Valley, and apparently slightly later in Cyrenaica and the Maghrib, that many new elements appear and change becomes far more rapid and continuous.

Second, North Africa in the Late Palaeolithic, especially after 20 000 BC, fits into the general pattern discernible in other parts of Africa and Eurasia of showing considerably greater *regional* diversity in artifact assemblages. This may be the corollary of higher population densities and more specifically differentiated patterns of ecological adaptation than in earlier times. Whatever the causes, the consequence was a series of industrial mosaics within regions and sub-regions, in contrast to the more uniform and widespread styles of preceding periods.

Third, there is some evidence of technological specializations at this time that may reflect more successful means of resource exploitation.

Among the artifacts perhaps increased efficiency in manufacture and function is shown by the use of the punched-blade technique of stone-working, by the greater emphasis on blades and bladelets, and by the wider use of bone for tools in some areas. It is often suggested that composite implements uniting stone and organic materials (e.g. flint blades arranged in a bone or wooden haft) represent a technological advance over earlier devices for purposes of hunting, processing of foodstuffs and manufacture of other artifacts, and very possibly this is true. It is still unknown, however, if any significant new techniques of energy capture, such as bows, spear-throwers, nets or boats were devised as aids in the expansion of subsistence in North Africa at this time. There is also very little evidence for permanently settled sites or for architectural features expected to last for more than a brief period. Nevertheless there is some reason to believe that, just as in several other regions of the Old World in final Pleistocene and early Holocene times, there was increasingly intensive exploitation of local food resources, especially plant foods, and a corresponding development of more elaborate techniques for procuring and processing these foods; there may also have been closer relations between some human groups and certain animal species. In parts of the Sahara and the Nile Valley in the early Holocene there seems to have been much greater emphasis placed on fishing in the economies, perhaps in the face of local environmental deterioration; at times this may have resulted in greater sedentarism and larger communities near the rivers and lakes. Thus there may have been throughout northern Africa during the period considered here an intensification of certain aspects of the so-called 'broad-spectrum revolution' in subsistence strategies.[1] The increased population densities

[1] Some prehistorians believe that there occurred in south-western Asia about 20 000 BC a shift in emphasis in food-procuring from a narrow reliance on larger hoofed animals to a more eclectic exploitation; hoofed animals remained dominant in the diet but the wider range of foods now included fish, migratory birds, invertebrates (land snails, crabs, molluscs), and especially plant foods like nuts and grains. If this broad-spectrum revolution did in fact occur in Asia on the scale and at the time postulated, then one might suggest that it was related in some way to the rather sudden appearance of industries emphasizing blades and bladelets in the Nile Valley by at least 15 000 BC and in Cyrenaica and the Maghrib slightly later. The mechanisms responsible for the putative diffusion into Africa may have been varied: possibly the pressures of growing population in the Palestinian region was a factor, while the greater ease with which large parts of North Africa could now be occupied and exploited more intensively by these less specialized hunter–gatherers may have been another. In the long run such groups might have had greater expansive potential than had the indigenous, more specialized hunters and so may have absorbed or eliminated them as competitors. Nevertheless, it should be recalled that some of the preceding groups in Cyrenaica at least (the Libyan Pre-Aurignacian and the Dabban) also seem to have exploited a wide range of animal foods, both terrestrial and marine, although it is not clear how significant small game, molluscs, etc. were in the total subsistence. It is a pity we know so little in detail of the economies in the Maghrib and the Nile Valley before about 15 000 BC.

in certain regions (if one can interpret in this way the larger number of archaeological sites known) might have been both cause and effect of this shift in economic emphasis.

Finally, it is still difficult to explain satisfactorily the similarities and differences in the distribution of various elements throughout North Africa. The resemblances between various industries of the Nile Valley and some of those in Cyrenaica and the Maghrib have been mentioned here. Do they reflect population movements and contacts, or are there less obvious explanations tied to gradual transformations and adaptations across several broad environmental zones? Or, what explanation other than 'innate conservatism' can be offered to account for the very late survival of the Levallois method of stone-working in the Nile Valley to the end of the Pleistocene? We do not know. Similarly, it is not clear why rituals and practices associated with the dead and the living (tooth evulsion, skeletal mutilation, deposition of grave-goods and use of ochres in burials) should be so common in the Maghrib and nearly or completely absent in the Nile Valley and (perhaps) Cyrenaica. Again, although figurative or decorative art seems late everywhere in North Africa as compared with Europe, the emphasis on art and personal decoration seems much stronger in the Epi-Palaeolithic of the Maghrib and the Sahara than elsewhere in the region. These behavioural differences between sub-regions are probably related in some way to differences in belief systems, ideologies and methods of expressing symbolically attitudes towards the human and natural universes, and they may eventually be linked both with developments in the technological–economic systems and with the concomitant shifts in structure of the human aggregates involved in the adaptive changes mentioned above.

It is clear that archaeological opinion about general cultural developments in the late Pleistocene and early Holocene of northern Africa has changed considerably since a few decades ago, when the emphasis was placed on the conservatism and even the cultural retardation of this region in the context of world prehistory. As already indicated here, this perspective, and the old view of North Africa as a 'refuge area', have had to be modified following recent research, although not totally discarded. Seen from adjacent continents, the succession of Late Palaeolithic events in North Africa seems different from those known in Europe and south-west Asia. In these two regions industries termed Upper Palaeolithic succeeded the several Mousterian variants before 30 000 BC and quickly became the dominant archaeological manifestations. Older or 'transitional' traditions were quickly eliminated or very drastically modified, and while the succeeding industries show considerable variation in each region this variability was nevertheless expressed within fairly closely defined limits. But this kind of succession was apparently not the pattern in North Africa. Not only was the total transformation to blade-type industries much more gradual and delayed, but one industry (the Dabban), although possibly installed in northern Africa as early as its Upper Palaeolithic equivalents in other continents, seems to have coexisted as an enclave for a very long time with industries basically in the older Middle Palaeolithic tradition of Levallois-method stone-working and more traditionally standardized tools. There is in North Africa no horizontal or even gently sloping line of demarcation between the older and the newer traditions; rather, because of the existence of the Dabban, the line is jagged and uneven, and some 'conservative' features such as the use of the Levallois method flourished in the Nile Valley long after it had virtually disappeared in Europe, western Asia and even other parts of North Africa.

The significance of this uneven pattern of change is not clear, nor the causes. Geographical isolation and the difficulty of diffusion or migration to North Africa from other continents have been offered as explanations in the past, yet they are by themselves inadequate. Similarly, it is hazardous to suggest that differences in neurophysiological capacity were responsible, particularly since so few human remains are known in northern Africa.

In Europe and western Asia it is sometimes argued that the rapid displacement of the older traditions of stone-working which utilized a rather restricted range of tool types made largely on flakes and non-punched blades was due to some technical superiority of the newer methods and associated tools. If this is universally true, then it is difficult to account for the apparent failure of these innovations to spread rapidly and widely throughout North Africa after their early installation in Cyrenaica before 30 000 BC. Here the prehistorian faces a familiar problem: how much of the apparently static, unchanging nature of his purely archaeological remains in certain periods and places masks considerable change of other kinds, and how much of the archaeological change in material culture is an illusion hiding a static reality beneath? One possible explanation of the phenomenon of North African 'retardation' places less emphasis on the innate technical superiority of the techniques and artifacts *per se*, and more on the social and cultural qualities of the makers; that is, the real factors in the rapid acceptance of the typically Upper Palaeolithic elements in Europe and western Asia were the development of superior forms of social organization (including more efficient types of division of labour and of collaboration in group activities connected with subsistence) and of superior means of communication between the humans who served as the vectors for the new procedures. Another possible argument is that some peculiarities in many of the North African environments, or in the human adjustments to them, made the newer artifacts of much less value than elsewhere until quite late, after 20 000 BC or so when they may have been associated with some direct advantageous features including superior methods of obtaining and processing larger quantities of foodstuffs. One might also wonder if the relative stability of climate and physical environment in North Africa in the late Pleistocene, as contrasted with the more drastic shifts in European temperatures, vegetation and fauna, is not part of the explanation.

These problems invite research strategies based on intimate studies of human adaptation and techniques of food appropriation in the various zones of North Africa. If the productive potential of the areas in which each site or group of sites is located can be estimated even roughly, then this may be a means of evaluating the significance of changes in technology observed in the archaeological record, particularly as these changes may be correlated with observable shifts in prehistoric demography. We might expect that in zones of high and expandable food resources, the rate and kind of technological invention and change would be different from those in areas where the productive potential for hunters and gatherers was more limited. With perseverance it may eventually be feasible to define more precisely the processes responsible for the cultural diversity and discontinuities in this part of the continent. It might convincingly be argued, for instance, that a consequence of more varied and more efficient exploitation of food resources would be a decrease in the size of the geographical range over which a given human group roamed, and that this in turn would often lead to the development of somewhat more contrasting patterns of artifacts and styles peculiar to a given area – in part related to the particular needs for exploitation of specific local resources, and in part as mechanisms of social isolation for group self-identification and differentiation from competing groups in the same area. This might help explain, for instance, some of the geographical facies archaeologists have tried to define within the Capsian of the Maghrib, and some of the rather highly localized industrial variants found in the final Pleistocene in Upper Egypt and Nubia.

These analyses of internal features within North Africa as a whole – including the thorny problem of the nature of any diffusion and exchanges between the several sub-regions – cannot be divorced from the need for a better understanding of the degree to which northern Africa was articulated culturally with adjacent regions. It is necessary to know much more about the reciprocal relationships between North Africa and the savanna and forested zones further south if we are to evaluate the alleged role of North Africa as a 'screening zone' through which certain techniques and styles (and even genes) filtered into southern and eastern Africa. Recent discoveries in Africa south of the Sahara suggest that this role may have been exaggerated by prehistorians in the past; the use of blades made by the punch technique, for instance, seems about as ancient in the 'Middle Stone Age' industries of some parts of southern Africa as it is in North Africa, although admittedly they were proportionately less important in the assemblages. Similarly, the role of south-western Asia at the beginning of and throughout the Late Palaeolithic and Epi-Palaeolithic of North Africa has yet to be properly defined. Influence from the east was probably far more significant than contacts across the Mediterranean, but we cannot yet identify with much assurance those elements in North Africa that were of external rather than of indigenous origin. Traditionally most prehistorians have tended to look to the Levant area of western Asia for the source of the blade-tool tradition and of *Homo sapiens sapiens* in North Africa. This seems logical enough where the Libyan Pre-Aurignacian and the Dabban are concerned, but evidence of close relations after the Dabban is scarce. Possibly the blade and microlithic industries of the Nile Valley after 15 000 BC owed something to what is generally called Upper Palaeolithic III to VI (or Antelian to Kebaran) in Palestine, but the detailed archaeological sequence in the Levant is still too inadequately known and dated to permit any degree of certainty about this. One might with nearly as much persuasion argue that at times movements of people or of techniques were in the opposite direction. Future investigations in the Sinai and Negev deserts may help to resolve this question.

# CHAPTER 6

# THE LATER STONE AGE
# IN SUB-SAHARAN AFRICA

Throughout the greater part of sub-Saharan Africa, as in many other
parts of the world, the majority of the most recent lithic industries show
a marked degree of typological similarity, being dominated by the
microlithic components of composite artifacts. It is now known that
industries of this type were established throughout most regions of the
sub-continent between about the sixteenth and the seventh millennia
BC, although in some places their typological antecedents may be traced
back into far earlier times. The broad geographical continuity of the
stone industries of this time, together with their correspondence in
many basic features with those of the stone-tool-using societies encountered by early European settlers and travellers in southern Africa,
lead to the recognition of a loosely defined *Later Stone Age*. Although of
some utility in the general or semi-popular presentation of archaeological
material, such broad cultural–stratigraphic terms as 'Middle Stone
Age', 'Later Stone Age', etc. are now seen to be of limited value in
the detailed ordering and synthesis of the steadily growing body of
primary data.

In much of sub-Saharan Africa, more especially in the eastern and
central areas, the study of Stone Age archaeology was largely inspired
by pioneer researchers in South Africa. It is to South African work that
may also be traced the cultural–stratigraphic nomenclature which has
been somewhat acritically applied to industries far removed from the
inadequately described sites and industries for which it was originally
propounded, as well as many of the models, concepts and misconceptions
which have for long been an integral part of African archaeological
thought.

South Africa was the first, and only major, part of the sub-continent
where European colonizers and settlers came into contact with indigenous people who regularly used stone tools. Encounters with such
peoples are described in the writings of several travellers who journeyed
inland from the Cape of Good Hope during the second half of the
eighteenth century. During the century that followed, the stone-
tool-using societies were to a large extent exterminated; and digging

410

for stone implements and 'Bushman skeletons' became a popular pastime, particularly in coastal regions. The first paper to give a detailed account of contemporary stone-tool using was the work of Kannemeyer in 1890, the result of his observations in the Orange Free State. By the end of the century a great deal of artifactual material, most of it poorly documented, had been amassed in museum and private collections. Peringuey of the South African Museum published a pioneer classificatory system in the early 1900s; his primary division was between 'Palaeolithic' artifacts and 'Bushman relics'. The latter class comprised most of those artifacts which were later attributed to the Middle Stone Age or to the Later Stone Age. Peringuey's classification of South African Stone Age industries, which clearly showed the influence of recent local ethnographic observations, formed the basis of research for the next three decades, until the appearance of Goodwin and van Riet Lowe's *The Stone Age Cultures of South Africa* (1929). Here, the Later Stone Age was recognized as a separate entity, but was still intimately connected with the recently observed stone-tool-using societies:

With the dawn of the Later Stone Age we arrive at a wider and better known field. We are in a position to give not only the lists of implements made and used, but also the foods, clothing, industries, arts and physical characteristics of its people. We recognise a Neo-anthropic group, and, definitely belonging to it, those 'Bushmen' our immediate forebears so sanctimoniously annihilated in a fit of righteous indignation that lasted well over a century (p. 147).

The link with recent 'Bushmen' appears to be an integral part of Goodwin and van Riet Lowe's somewhat inexplicit definition of their Later Stone Age. Archaeologically, this was stated to include the 'Wilton' and 'Smithfield' industries, neither of which were at that time adequately defined, although their family resemblance was recognized. 'Most typical of these Later Stone Age industries – Smithfield and Wilton – is the flat striking platform, the fine longitudinal parallel flaking, and the even, steep secondary trimming' (p. 150). It was the classification of Goodwin and van Riet Lowe, with subsequent modifications, which until recently formed the basis for the classification of African Stone Age industries far beyond its original area, through the loosely formulated extension of concepts never adequately defined.

The link of the Later Stone Age industries *en bloc* with the recently surviving stone-tool-using people of southern Africa, shown above to be of long standing, has been responsible for many misconceptions and erroneous generalizations. It was responsible, first of all, for the belief, only recently dispelled by steadily increasing numbers of radiocarbon dates, that all the typologically Later Stone Age industries were of comparatively recent date. Even with the much longer chronology now indicated by radiocarbon dating, which extends in some areas through the last 18 000 years or more, the application of recent ethnographic parallels to the Later Stone Age as a whole is a practice which dies hard. In the absence of detailed evidence for their relevance, such practices involve numerous unwarranted assumptions, as does the commonly held view that the Later Stone Age industries as a whole are necessarily to be attributed to a people of the same physical stock as the remnant stone-tool-using populations in South Africa in the eighteenth and nineteenth centuries. In many areas Later Stone Age industries continued to be made until the last few centuries; and many disciplines, such as ethnography, traditional history and historical linguistics, can undoubtedly play their part in describing the societies responsible for these industries. Great caution must, however, be exercised in projecting this non-archaeological evidence back into more remote periods.

In West Africa and the Congo basin the study of Stone Age archaeology is a more recent phenomenon, and one which has developed without a terminological strait-jacket such as was imposed on corresponding work in South Africa by the work of Goodwin and van Riet Lowe. Here, the presence of ground stone artifacts led to the early definition of 'neolithic' industries, although the detailed study of the associations of such artifacts is still, after seventy years, an urgent need in many areas. In West Africa it has only comparatively recently been demonstrated that microlithic aggregates may long antedate the appearance of the ground stone 'neolithic' artifacts. Nomenclature of the chipped stone industries was largely established on a local basis; and the diversity of the usages of individual investigators in different areas for long resulted in a certain confusion and lack of precision comparable with that prevailing in eastern and southern Africa, but without the misleading semblance of order which the application of Goodwin and van Riet Lowe's terminology imparted to the Stone Age archaeology of the latter region.

It will be apparent from the foregoing that the concept of the Later Stone Age in sub-Saharan Africa is not based on any clear and unambiguous definition. The criteria for its recognition are essentially technological, being based on the general similarity of the prehistoric chipped stone industries to those of the final stone-tool-using societies, the emphasis being on small blades and the use of steep backing-retouch

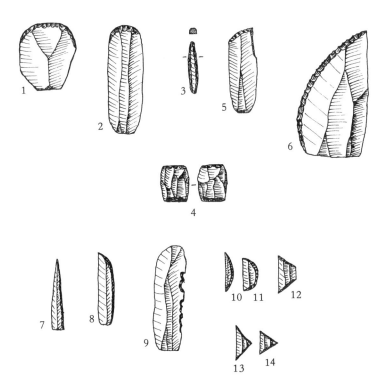

Fig. 6.1   A selection of standard Later Stone Age tool types.

1  Convex flake scraper
2  Blade-end scraper
3  Drill
4  *Outil écaillé*
5  Angle burin
6, 8  Curved backed blades

7  Straight backed blade
9  Denticulate
10–11  Crescents
12  Trapezoidal microlith
13–14  Triangular microliths

(After Tixier 1967.)

to produce microlithic implements and other tool types.[1] It is now clear that such industries do not belong to any single finite period of time, but that they developed in some parts of the sub-continent many millennia before comparable industries became prevalent elsewhere. Furthermore, in many areas, artifacts previously regarded as being of Later Stone Age type are now known to form integral parts of far earlier

[1] Fig. 6.1 shows a selection of the Later Stone Age tool types most commonly encountered in sub-Saharan Africa, and is reproduced here in place of definitions of the terms used in the following descriptions of individual industries.

413

aggregates, being contemporary and intimately associated with artifacts which cannot meaningfully be subsumed within a practicable definition of the Later Stone Age. In South Africa, blade-based industries, some of which contained a strong microlithic element, became prevalent at an extremely early date, probably well in excess of 40 000 years ago, but they have conventionally been regarded as belonging to the Middle Stone Age.[1] One result of recent research, facilitated by the rapidly increased use of radiometric dating techniques, has been to demonstrate the inadequacy and unworkability of the conventional popular sub-divisions such as Middle Stone Age and Later Stone Age, but no satisfactory and generally accepted scheme has yet been proposed in their place. A desirable outcome, but one which is still unattained, would be the use of a hierarchy of typologically-based cultural–stratigraphic terms which will permit generalizations up to the level of Industrial Complex. At high levels of generalization, it is likely that the increased availability of absolute age determinations, at least for the period of time covered by the subject matter of this chapter, will eventually enable time–geographical designations to take the place of the present unsatisfactory terms of broader cultural abstraction.

J. G. D. Clark's recognition of five modes of lithic technology broadly concordant with the conventional divisions of the Stone Age, although based primarily on the European and Levantine cultural successions, is of general applicability in sub-Saharan Africa and eliminates many of the pitfalls inherent to the conventional 'Age' system. It avoids both the correlation of industrial phases with finite time-periods and, to a lesser extent, the artificial compartmentalization of processes of industrial and cultural development (J. G. D. Clark 1969). Three modes are relevant to that part of the African succession discussed in this chapter. These, with their dominant lithic technologies, are mode 3 (flake tools produced from prepared cores), mode 4 (punch-struck blades with steep retouch) and mode 5 (microlithic components of composite artifacts). Of these, mode 3 corresponds broadly with the Middle Stone Age of the conventional nomenclature. True mode 4 industries are found only rarely in sub-Saharan Africa, being restricted, so far as is at present known, to the Horn and adjacent regions of East Africa, although they have recently also been recognized in the southern Sahara. Mode 5 industries are, however, widespread; and most industries of the conventional Later Stone Age are of this type.

---

[1] These and other industries, notably those named 'Magosian' and formerly attributed to a 'Second Intermediate' period, are discussed in chapter 4.

Although these modes, as defined by J. G. D. Clark, form a homotaxial sequence, apparently of world-wide applicability, it is inherent to the system that they do not form watertight compartments, but that elements of the technologies of earlier times are seen to continue alongside more recent innovations. The degree to which earlier technologies were adapted to uninterrupted economic functions obviously had a bearing on the degree of this continuity, which may thus be expected to show significant variation between adjacent regions and environments. While recognition of these phenomena provides the framework for a more comprehensive reconstruction of human industrial development, it also presents initial difficulties in subdivision and in the establishment of an adequately defined cultural–stratigraphic nomenclature. Clark's taxis does, however, provide a useful form of reference to the dominant technology of an industry, without the outmoded chronological implications of the conventional nomenclature.

### ARCHAEOLOGICAL EVIDENCE FOR THE LATER STONE AGE OF SUB-SAHARAN AFRICA

In the regional survey which follows, reference is frequently made to the conventional cultural designations of the various industries encountered; such usage, in inverted commas, is a matter of convenience and does not necessarily suggest that any affinities and correlations thereby implied have demonstrable validity. An attempt is made to summarize the evidence for the inception and progress of the Later Stone Age cultures in each region of the sub-continent up to the time of the first appearance of techniques of food production. The subsequent development of these cultures is discussed in chapter 11.

### WEST AFRICA (fig. 6.2)

Attempts at an overall survey of the mode 5 industries of West Africa are hampered by the scarcity of stratified and dated sites and by a plethora of small aggregates, often poorly documented, from surface or unstratified contexts. Until recently, the evidence for the early establishment of microlithic industries in the region rested on the dated succession from a single site, the rock-shelter of Iwo Eleru in western Nigeria. As in parts of central Africa, there is evidence that in some areas industries of essentially mode 3 technology continued until

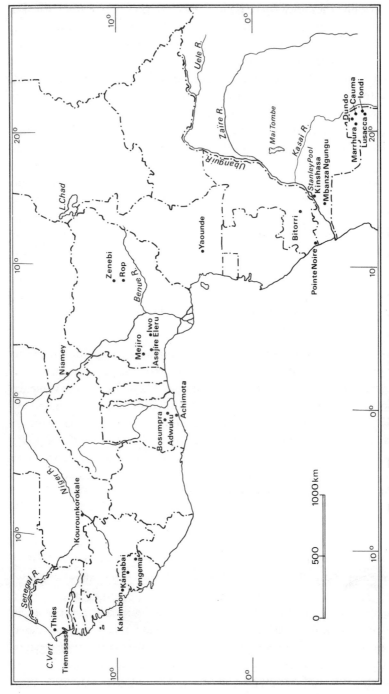

Fig. 6.2   Western sub-Saharan Africa, showing sites mentioned in the text.

416

comparatively recent times. However, the characteristic Later Stone Age industries of West Africa are dominated by essentially microlithic chipped stone artifacts, which are frequently found associated with ground stone tools and with pottery. It is now known, as had long been suspected, that in most parts of West Africa comparable microlithic material is found without ground stone artifacts in aceramic, pre-Neolithic, industries; but it is rarely possible to distinguish these two phases on the basis of the microlithic material alone. Indeed, it now appears that there is a considerable degree of similarity between the microlithic industries of the aceramic Later Stone Age and those later phases which are associated with pottery and ground stone tools. Arguments from the presence or absence of the latter artifacts are hampered by their frequent removal and use for magical purposes by many recent West African societies. Detailed elucidation of the local successions of mode 5 industries must therefore await the investigation of many more datable stratified sequences. All that may safely be offered at this stage is an outline account of the few and widely scattered well-documented preceramic occurrences.

In Senegal, although large numbers of mode 5 occurrences have been described, there is relatively little stratigraphical and dating evidence. The immediately preceding industry has been variously termed 'Mousterioid' and 'ultimate Middle Stone Age' (Davies 1967, p. 141; Hugot 1967). It is characterized by generally diminutive flakes struck from prepared, predominantly discoidal cores, and by a dearth of formalized finished tools. The date at which it was superseded is not known. The earliest phase of the Senegal Later Stone Age is best exemplified at Tiemassas, 80 km south of Dakar, where an extensive lagoon-side site has yielded rich exposures of stone industries extending over several kilometres. The possibility cannot be ruled out that more than one phase of occupation was represented, although it has not yet proved possible to separate these stratigraphically. The occurrence of a mode 5 industry and the absence both of pottery and of ground stone artifacts indicate that a pre-Neolithic, microlithic horizon is present at the site. Artifacts attributed to this phase include large backed blades and crude crescents, together with bifacially flaked foliate projectile points (fig. 6.3.1) some of which have finely denticulated edges reminiscent of certain Tshitolian examples from lower Zaïre. A single concave-based point and a tanged example are more reminiscent of Saharan styles; indeed, an Aterian ancestry has been suggested for the Tiemassas industry (Dagan 1956, 1972). Farther to the north, around

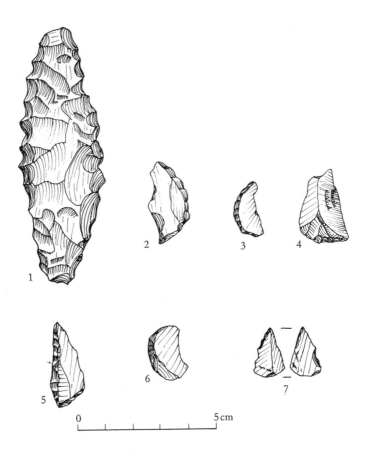

Fig. 6.3  Later Stone Age artifacts from West Africa.

1 Bifacial point from Tiemassas      3–4 Microliths from Mejiro
2 Microlith from Adwuku      5–7 Microliths from Rop

(Nos. 1, 2 after Davies (1967), 3, 4 after Willett (1962) and 5–7 after Rosenfeld *in* Fagg *et al.* (1972).)

Dakar, sand dunes which are tentatively correlated with those overlying the artifact-bearing levels at Tiemassas contain smaller and more regular microliths. From these, presumably later, industries the bifacial projectile points of Tiemassas are virtually absent. It is not clear whether any of the Cap Vert microlithic aggregates predate the introduction of ground stone artifacts and of pottery; certainly in the majority of cases such Neolithic traits appear to be associated, and at Thiès they are dated to around the eleventh century BC. This mode 5 industry is generally held to be of northern origin, '*de tradition capsienne*'; the extent to which this apparently strong similarity is due to the remarkable flint-like raw material available in the Dakar region has not yet been demonstrated (Corbeil, Mauny and Charbonnier 1951; Vaufrey 1946).

Sparse finds from the virtually unexplored region of the upper Senegal suggest that the local sequence there may broadly parallel that of the coast. In Mali, bifacial points resembling those of Tiemassas but of cruder workmanship (due largely, one suspects, to the inferior raw material) are found in the lower levels of Kourounkorokale rock-shelter, south of Bamako. Here, two main horizons were recognized, of which the lower one appears to contain a pre-Neolithic mode 5 industry comprising crude choppers and chipped, unground axes of shale and dolerite, together with quartz crescents, trapeziform microliths, backed blades and side-scrapers. These quartz forms are basically identical to those from Ghanaian and Nigerian sites but have the addition, unknown further south, of the Tiemassas points noted above. There was no pottery. Also from the lower level at Kourounkorokale came a series of bone tools including simple points and a number of uniserially barbed bone harpoon-heads, perforated for the attachment of the line (Szumowski 1956). Comparable harpoon-heads from the southern Sahara are dated as early as the sixth millennium BC which, in the absence of absolute dating evidence from Kourounkorokale itself, would appear not unreasonable as a tentative estimate for the age of the initial phase of that site's occupation.

In Guinea, many aggregates of a markedly distinct type have been described, but all are undated. These clearly belong to the general milieu of the Later Stone Age but their detailed stratigraphy and associations are inadequately recorded (Davies 1967, Delcroix and Vaufrey 1939). Both open sites and caves have yielded crude bifacial core-axes, which appear to continue throughout the sequence into comparatively recent times; and these have led to the suggestion that the industries of this region may be related to those of the Congo basin. Associated with them are convex and strangulated scrapers, backed blades and trapezoidal microliths such as are sometimes referred to as transverse arrowheads or *tranchets*, together with, in many cases, ground stone celts and pottery. In the present state of our knowledge it is impossible to say whether or not there are mode 5 industries in this area which antedate the introduction of the latter artifacts. Such a phase may be present in the cave of Kakimbon near Conakry; its affinities with Tiemassas appear to be at least as strong as those with regions to the east.

Further to the east, in Sierra Leone, some of the presumably contemporary industries are of non-microlithic type, as at Yengema Cave (Coon 1968). Here, the basic stone industry, which continues throughout the sequence, is mainly of coarse quartz and dolerite made into crude choppers and various flake-scrapers; there are also many scaled pieces. In the middle phase of the Yengema succession bifacially flaked picks and 'hoes' are added to the aggregate, and in a final, Neolithic, phase ground stone tools and pottery make their appearance. Thermoluminescence dates for this pottery indicate an age between the mid third and the late second millennium BC, but the rest of the sequence is undated. Microlithic implements were introduced into the area at about this time; they occur in association with pottery and ground stone artifacts in Kamabai rock-shelter around the middle of the third millennium (Atherton 1972). There is thus at present no evidence for truly microlithic pre-pottery industries in Sierra Leone.

In Ghana, a large number of surface occurrences, mainly undated, have been attributed to a Neolithic phase (Davies 1967, pp. 180–90). There are indications for a certain degree of continuity with the final Middle Stone Age industries, but there are as yet no stratified sequences to illustrate the interrelationship between the two phases. The Mesolithic is distinguished by the introduction of conical cores alongside diminutive discoid types, and by the appearance of geometric microliths which are often made on blades. A large and characteristic Mesolithic aggregate comes from an open site at Adwuku, north-east of Accra (fig. 6.3.2). The collection, predominantly of quartz, includes trapeziform microliths and backed blades; end-scrapers are also frequent. No ground stone artifacts were noted and the few potsherds appeared to be of recent deposition. A very comparable chipped stone industry at Achimota Cricket Pitch is associated with ground stone artifacts and is considered to be somewhat later than the Adwuku material, although pottery was not preserved. The distribution of microlithic industries of this type extends northwards into the Niamey region of Niger and into Upper Volta. In the latter country, at Rim, a pre-pottery Later Stone Age industry appears to predate 3000 BC.

Recently intensified archaeological research in Nigeria has put the later prehistoric sequence there on a firmer footing than that at present available in neighbouring countries. The longest dated succession of microlithic industries in West Africa, as well as the oldest demonstrated local occurrence of such an aggregate, comes from the rock-shelter of Iwo Eleru, situated deep in the high forest of western Nigeria. Excavations there have revealed accumulated deposits, 2 to 3 m deep, which contained a microlithic stone industry throughout. The initial occupation of the site has been dated to the tenth millennium BC. The inception of the microlithic industry in the area must thus predate that time by an as yet unknown period. The significance of a human burial described as showing negroid physical features, which was recovered from this early horizon, is discussed in greater detail below. The stone industry, for which a quantified description is not yet available, has a very low proportion of intentionally retouched tools, among which crescents are the most frequent type together with triangular microliths and *tranchets*. Awls, scrapers and chisel-like forms also occur. No discontinuities were observed either in the stratigraphy or in the typology of the chipped stone industry which continued, on the evidence of the radiocarbon dates, until at least the second half of the second millennium BC. Pottery and ground stone artifacts both make their appearance by the middle of the fourth millennium. Iwo Eleru is interpreted by Shaw as indicating that 'in West Africa, a microlithic industry has a long and continuous existence; into its later stages come pottery and ground stone axes'. He notes the general similarity of the Iwo Eleru material with other West African microlithic aggregates, such as those from Bosumpra, Mejiro, Rop and Kourounkorokale (Shaw 1969a, 1972).

The Iwo Eleru discovery lends support to the view that the apparent rarity of microlithic industries in the deepest forest may be largely due to lack of archaeological exploration in those areas. Other undated Nigerian occurrences of microlithic aggregates, which appear to ante-date the introduction of pottery and ground stone artifacts, are those of Mejiro rock-shelter near Old Oyo, and Rop rock-shelter, some 50 km south of Jos (fig. 6.3.3–7) (Fagg *et al.* 1972, Willett 1962).

As we have seen, however, the West African stone industries of the last 10 000 years BC were not exclusively microlithic. At Asejire, less than 150 km west of Iwo Eleru, there is evidence which appears to indicate the local survival of mode 3 (Middle Stone Age) technology into the fourth millennium BC. There is also a single radiocarbon date in the same millennium for comparable material from the outwash of Zenebi Falls in northern Nigeria. At the Ukpa rock-shelter near Afikpo in eastern Nigeria, a pottery-associated non-microlithic industry spans the whole of the last three millennia BC (Shaw 1969b).

Available information on the Later Stone Age of West Africa is, as we have seen, virtually restricted to descriptions of the stone artifact aggregates. There is an almost total lack, from sites of this period, of published evidence concerning the economic activities and settlement patterns. The application of radiometric dating techniques to Stone Age sites in this region is a comparatively recent development, but sufficient analyses have now been conducted to provide an outline chronology. It is clear that mode 5 industries were of widespread occurrence, being present in some areas by the tenth millennium BC, although mode 3 technology continued to prevail in some areas such as Sierra Leone and parts of Nigeria until the third millennium or even later – perhaps until the inception of the Iron Age in some places. The processes of development of the West African mode 5 industries remain largely unknown. Those of the more northerly Sudanic regions may owe their origin to influence or diffusion from the southern Sahara; and it is possible that such industries, modified through encounter with drastically changed environmental conditions, inspired the development of microlithic technology in the savanna and forest regions further south. Within much of the latter zones there are signs of greater continuity from mode 3 technologies than is observed further north. In places, mode 3 industries survived virtually unmodified for many millennia despite the adoption of fully microlithic techniques in adjacent areas. While the forest must have severely restricted inter-group contact, many forest-dwellers probably maintained closer relationships with their contemporaries to the north. It was doubtless from the latter direction that such Neolithic elements as pottery and ground stone artifacts were introduced, generally during the fourth and third millennia BC, but perhaps somewhat later in the far west. These later developments are discussed in detail in chapter 11.

## THE CENTRAL SUDAN AND THE CONGO BASIN

West Africa is separated from the rest of sub-Saharan Africa on the one side by the densely forested Congo basin and on the other by the vast northern area – stretching between Cameroun and the southern part of the Sudan Republic – where the forest thins out northward to savanna, then to sahel and eventually to the southern Sahara Desert. The whole of this northern area is very inadequately known archaeologically. As in much of the southern Sahara, dated stratified sequences are virtually absent; for the greater part such evidence as we do possess is based on chance finds and the collections of non-archaeologists. The associations of such finds, among which it is hardly surprising that large ground stone artifacts of Neolithic type predominate, remain almost completely unknown. In the Central African Republic, more data are becoming available, but the relevant stratified sites are not yet excavated that would enable us to determine whether any mode 5 industries predate those which are associated with pottery and with ground stone artifacts (de Bayle des Hermens 1975). Since in both the Nile Valley and the western savanna early microlithic aggregates are now known which substantially predate the introduction of such artifacts, and since later industries widely distributed through the savanna show a marked degree of similarity, it is reasonable to suppose that a comparable sequence will eventually be demonstrated in this central region also.

Similarly, evidence for the chipped stone artifacts of any pre-pottery mode 5 industries in the northern part of the Congo basin has not yet been recovered. As in the case of the Nigerian and Ghanaian forests, only when specific and detailed searches are made in the forests of northern Congo and Zaïre will such industries, if they occur there, be brought to light.

It is thus due primarily to the uneven distribution of research that a survey of the Later Stone Age in the Congo basin is best based on the sequence elucidated by relatively intensive investigations in northern Angola and in south-western Zaïre. While a comparable sequence may have prevailed in some areas north of the Congo River, there are no good reasons for assuming that it is valid for the whole region.

In north-eastern Angola, around Dundo, extensive exposures made by mining the alluvial deposits of the Tshikapa, Kasai and intervening rivers for diamonds have produced a relatively detailed prehistoric succession linked to a series of climatic fluctuations, for which a number of radiocarbon dates are available (J. D. Clark 1963, 1968). The earlier stages of this succession have been described in chapter 4. As in most other regions where the relevant parts of the archaeological sequence have been investigated in detail, a considerable degree of continuity is apparent between the mode 5 industries and their predecessor. The earlier phase of the Dundo Later Stone Age, known as the Lower Tshitolian, is differentiated from the preceding Lupembo–Tshitolian by a general diminution in the size of its artifacts, by a decrease in the dependence on prepared discoid cores and a corresponding increase in the frequency of pyramidal and biconical types, and by a marked proliferation of backed microlithic forms (notably *petits tranchets*) at the expense of the core-axes.

Later Stone Age sites show a concentration of settlement in the valley bottoms, away from the scarps which had been favoured in earlier times.

This shift may be connected with the break-up of the evergreen forest galleries perhaps brought about by fire and human activity as well as by climatic deterioration. The characteristic artifact of the later aggregates, the *petit tranchet*, is thought to have served as a transverse arrow, well suited to hunting small creatures under dense forest conditions.

The Lower Tshitolian from the Dundo region was first described in detail from workshop–living-sites at Iondi and Lusacca Mines, where the aggregates comprised small discoid prepared cores as well as flake-blade cores, together with backed blades, crescents, trapezes and *petits tranchets*, rough core-axes resembling miniature picks, and occasional foliate points and hand-axe choppers. The evolution of these industries appears to have been a gradual process which began around the twelfth to the tenth millennia BC (fig. 6.4.1–6).

The later development of the Tshitolian industrial tradition in the Dundo region is not well known, but it is clear that it survived in evolved form until long after the inception of pot-making, an event which is perhaps best attributed to the earliest Iron Age inhabitants of the area around the beginning of the Christian era. The most informative of these late sites in the Dundo area is at Marrhura on the Tshikapa River. The site is seasonally inundated and is best interpreted as a combined factory and fishing camp rather than a place of permanent settlement. Upper Tshitolian stone artifacts were here associated with a substantial quantity of undiagnostic potsherds. Bored stones, found at a number of northern Angolan sites, are thought to belong to the Upper Tshitolian but the absence of other ground stone artifacts from this region is noteworthy.

Further to the north, in the Kwango and Kasai Provinces of Zaïre, the Tshitolian has been shown to occur in two facies, one of which is found in plateau environments, generally around pans; the other in the river valleys. They are distinguished by the dominance of core-axes and points in the plateau sites and of *petits tranchets* in the valleys. In the absence of dating evidence, it is possible that the two facies are chronologically distinct, but it seems at least as reasonable to regard them as activity-variants dependent on the distinct environments of the open plateaux and the more densely wooded valleys. The possibility that the same population, seasonally migrating, was responsible for both variants must also be borne in mind.

To the north-west, in lower Zaïre, the Tshitolian is characterized by diminutive core-axes and small bifacial foliate and lozenge-shaped

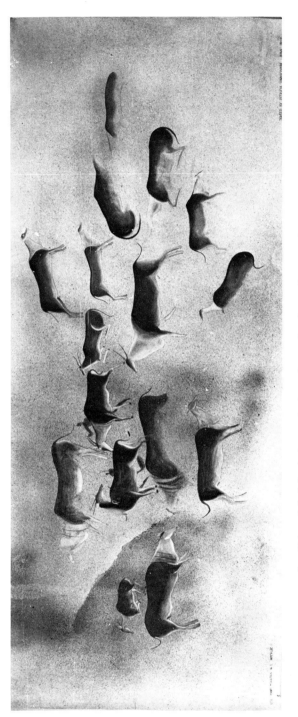

6.1 Frieze of shaded polychrome eland superimposed on hunter figures, at Ikanti Mountain, Himeville, Natal. (Facsimile tracing by Patricia Vinnicombe.)

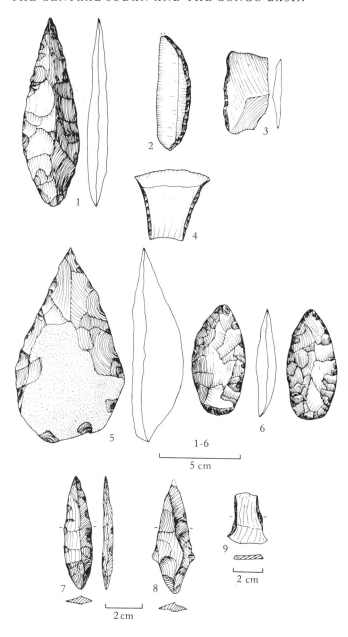

Fig. 6.4   Tshitolian artifacts.

1–6 From the Dundo region, north-eastern Angola (after J. D. Clark 1963)
7–9 From the Kinshasa area (after van Moorsel 1968)

points, as well as by *petits tranchets* made on flakes. Sites around Mbanza Ngungu (the former Thysville) are particularly rich in the latter type (Mortelmans 1962). In the later stages of the Tshitolian, aggregates of this region also include ground stone axe-like implements which are discussed at greater detail in chapter 11.

On the Plain of Kinshasa, as in the Dundo region, the local Tshitolian may be regarded as showing much continuity from the late Lupemban industries, which are here characterized by finely made elongated core-axes, slender bifacial foliate points including diminutive forms interpreted as arrow-points, some of which have finely serrated edges, and occasional *tranchets*, including bifacial types (van Moorsel 1968). These aggregates (fig. 6.4.7–9) are broadly contemporary with, or slightly later than, the Lupembo-Tshitolian of the Dundo region to which they closely correspond typologically. Tshitolian industries appear in the Kinshasa area around the eighth millennium BC: these sites are concentrated along the shores of the Stanley (Malebo) Pool and on the offshore islands, occurrences of this phase being sparse on the plain itself. There is a general diminution of all artifact types; large bifacial points no longer occur, but the small arrow-points increase in frequency, being now less regular in shape and no longer serrated. *Tranchets* are more common and smaller in size, invariably unifacial, but crude and irregular in comparison with those from Dundo. A later phase of the Tshitolian is found on the plain away from the Stanley Pool. The trends noticed earlier continue, with further reductions in artifact size and increased dominance of small *tranchets* and points, which now include a number of tanged and winged forms. Very occasional ground stone artifacts make their appearance in this local late Tshitolian. True geometric microliths and crescents are not found in the Kinshasa area, although they do occur in apparently contemporary industries on the Kwango Plateau and near Lake Leopold II (Mai Ndombe). On the Plain of Kinshasa there are radiocarbon dates for the late Tshitolian in the late fifth and early fourth millennia BC; similar industries apear to have continued well into the Christian era and to have overlapped chronologically with the first ceramic cultures of the area.

Further to the north, in Congo–Brazzaville, *tranchet* forms are still less frequent. An aggregate described as 'late Tshitolian' from Bitorri Cave is dated to around 2000 BC. Large core-axes continued in use until a late period; near Pointe Noire these are associated with many small bifacial points and with pottery (Droux and Kelley 1939). In Gabon, surface occurrences of artifacts described as Tshitolian, among which predominate core-axes and projectile points comparable to those from Yaounde in Cameroun, presumably provide a tenuous geographical link with the West African material described above.

Elsewhere in Zaïre true mode 5 industries are known only from the far east, in Kivu and Shaba, where the Stone Age succession, as in Rwanda and Burundi, is best considered in the context of contemporary developments in East Africa. In the intervening regions only occasional out-of-context finds of chipped stone artifacts have been recorded; these are generally crude bifacial types and it may well prove that in much of this area a mode 3 technology survived until the advent of the ground stone Neolithic industries discussed in chapter 11.

Knowledge of the Later Stone Age of this central African region is virtually restricted to the area of northern Angola and lower Zaïre, where the appearance of mode 5 technology would seem to have been a gradual process which took place between about the twelfth and the tenth millennia BC. There is a marked degree of continuity from the mode 3 Lupemban industries, whose influence continued throughout the development of the partly microlithic Tshitolian. Considerable inter-site variation is apparent within restricted areas and the significance of this is imperfectly understood. The geographical extent of the Tshitolian Industrial Complex also remains unknown. Conditions in this region are not conducive to the preservation of organic material; thus neither human skeletal remains nor tangible evidence for subsistence activities have so far been recovered. Tshitolian industries continued until the advent of the Iron Age around the beginning of the Christian era; at an unknown date before that various Neolithic elements were added to its aggregates in the lower Congo area, but these do not appear to have penetrated into north-eastern Angola.

## EASTERN AFRICA (fig. 6.5)

The great variability in the geology, resulting in a diversity of the materials available for stone implement manufacture, and climate of eastern Africa have been at least partly responsible for the wide range of distinctive Later Stone Age industries. Several incomplete regional sequences are available but many of these were investigated before the advent of radiocarbon dating. It is only in recent years that absolute age determinations have been obtained for the Later Stone Age in this part of the continent. Full reports on many of the dated sites are not yet available; and their relationship to those previously investigated is

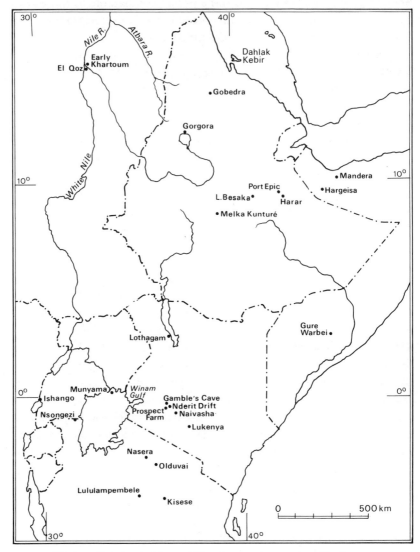

Fig. 6.5 Eastern sub-Saharan Africa, showing sites mentioned in the text.

not always clear. Early work, largely by L. S. B. Leakey between 1926 and 1939, established a succession of industries linked to a pluvial sequence primarily on the basis of their correlation with ancient high lake levels in the Gregory Rift or of the pedology of the deposits from which the various aggregates were recovered. As a result of these correlations, a very high antiquity was postulated for the establishment of mode 5 industries in this region. Subsequent work has tended to cast doubt on the correlations used, and the age of the earliest East African Later Stone Age has become once again an open question. Radiocarbon dates now indicate that in some areas at least these industries have an antiquity of up to eighteen millennia but, since dated sequences showing their antecedents are not yet available, it is not unreasonable to suppose that still earlier dates may be forthcoming, akin to those recently announced from Maputi in eastern Zaïre.

One of the earliest East African occurrences of a truly microlithic Later Stone Age industry comes from Munyama Cave on Buvuma Island, Lake Victoria, where the lower half of the deposit is dated between the thirteenth and the eighth millennia BC. The associated industry (fig. 6.6.1–4) was made almost exclusively of quartz and was dominated by tiny well-made backed bladelets, mainly of pointed type but including a few which could be described as crescents or triangles, acompanied by minimally retouched scrapers on flakes and cores; there were no bored stones or ground axes. This material bears a marked resemblance to the 'Nachikufan I' industry of Zambia (see below), with which it is broadly contemporary. A possibly equivalent aggregate from the Kondoa region of northern Tanzania occurs in the middle levels of Kisese II rock-shelter. It seems that the microlithic Later Stone Age first appeared there around the seventeenth millennium BC, in a sequence which was previously dominated by large flake scrapers. The earliest microlithic aggregates at Kisese were characterized by backed bladelets; only later did crescents become a frequent feature. Microlithic industries of this same general type are also recorded from sixteenth-millennium BC contexts at Lukenya Hill in southern Kenya, and in the Naisiusiu Beds at Olduvai Gorge in northern Tanzania (Gramly and Rightmire 1973, Inskeep 1962, M. D. Leakey et al. 1972, van Noten 1972).

One of the most problematical industries of the East African Later Stone Age is that generally known as the 'Kenya Capsian',[1] which occurs in its most developed form in the Lake Nakuru basin of the Gregory Rift. Almost the only raw material used was obsidian, and it is doubtless to this that the outstanding quality and unusual size of some of the artifacts are to a large extent due. The very high antiquity originally postulated for the earliest phases of the 'Kenya Capsian' is not now credited, based as it was on the concurrence of backed blades

[1] Prior to 1948 this industry was known as the 'Kenya Aurignacian'. Both terms presuppose affinities with far-distant industries with which no satisfactory link can, in fact, be demonstrated.

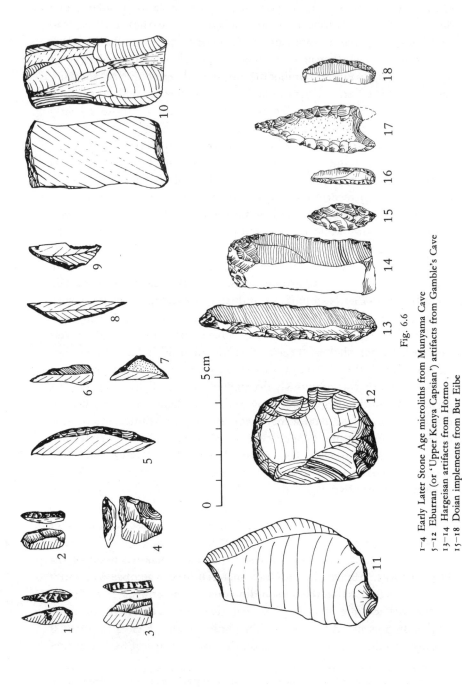

Fig. 6.6

1–4 Early Later Stone Age microliths from Munyama Cave
5–12 Eburran (or 'Upper Kenya Capsian') artifacts from Gamble's Cave
13–14 Hargeisan artifacts from Hormo.
15–18 Doian implements from Bur Eibe

(Nos. 1–4 after van Noten (1971), 5–12 after L. S. B. Leakey (1931) and 13–18 after J. D. Clark (1954).)

with mode 3 Middle Stone Age material in deposits which had been correlated with high lake levels attributed to the Gamblian pluvial. The correlation of these deposits and their supposed dating are now open to serious doubt. Occurrences such as those in the Malewa River valley near Naivasha, where backed blades of 'Lower Kenya Capsian' type were found in association with Middle Stone Age artifacts, do no more than demonstrate that, as in many other areas, the first local occurrences of backed blades are in the context of predominantly mode 3 industries of as yet unknown age (mode 3 industries are known to have continued in the Gregory Rift until at least the eighteenth millennium BC (Isaac, Merrick and Nelson (1972)). Material akin to Leakey's 'Lower Kenya Capsian' has, however, recently been reported from Nderit Drift near Elmenteita, where an obsidian aggregate comprising delicate awls, backed blades and burins, but apparently lacking crescents, is securely dated to the late eleventh millennium BC. Dates in the ninth millennium have been recorded for a 'Kenya Capsian' occurrence at Prospect Farm, Nakuru, but it is not clear to which phase of the industry this occurrence belongs. At Prospect Farm the 'Kenya Capsian' overlay an aggregate dominated by small oval scrapers, which in turn covered mode 3 material of the Middle Stone Age (Anthony 1967, Isaac *et al.* 1972, L. S. B. Leakey 1931).

The 'Upper Kenya Capsian' (recently renamed Eburran), in aggregates of which crescents form a dominant part (fig. 6.6.5–12), was initially defined on the basis of the sequence at Gamble's Cave south of Nakuru (L. S. B. Leakey 1931, 90–171). Three successive phases, A–C, were reported; A being the earliest industry present at the site. Radiocarbon dates in the seventh millennium BC have recently been obtained for the initial occupation of Gamble's Cave. Phase B coincides with the peak of workmanship in the knapping of obsidian. From near the interface between phases B and C comes a fragment of a uniserially barbed bone harpoon-head, as well as a single sherd of pottery, to a discussion of which we shall later return. Phase C, which may be of considerably later date than B, is marked by a decline in the standard of stone workmanship. All three phases have aggregates containing backed blades, crescents, burins and end-scrapers, associated with ostrich-eggshell beads and bone points. Above the 'Upper Kenya Capsian C' at Gamble's Cave was a thick layer of rock debris with a few hearths around which were scattered artifacts of so-called Middle Stone Age type. This material, which has never been illustrated or described in any detail, may perhaps indicate the late survival of mode 3 technology in some nearby areas.

The final phase in the occupation of Gamble's Cave is represented by an aggregate described as Elmenteitan. This differs from the 'Upper Kenya Capsian' through the presence of double-edged blades from which the bulbs of percussion have often been removed, as if to facilitate hafting. Such blades largely replace the backed blades of the earlier industry. Some Elmenteitan occurrences have yielded evidence for food production and are discussed further in chapter 11.

The distinction between the Eburran or 'Upper Kenya Capsian' and the various industries attributed to the East African 'Wilton' is not a clear one. The latter term has been used to designate a spectrum of more generalized mode 5 technological traits in which many occurrences attributed to the Eburran or 'Upper Kenya Capsian' could readily be subsumed. The quality and availability of fine raw material, together with the specialized environment of the Gregory Rift, where Lake Nakuru, then far larger than at present, was rich in fish, which presumably encouraged a more sedentary existence than was practicable elsewhere in the region at this time, would doubtless have combined to encourage the development of the specialized industry known in the archaeological literature as the Eburran or 'Upper Kenya Capsian'. A recent comparative study of the East African Later Stone Age aggregates has failed to indicate any other well defined groupings within the available material. Neither does the available evidence permit the isolation within the East African 'Wilton', of clearly defined phases.[1] Many of these aggregates are of late date, such as those in rock-shelters near the Winam (Kavirondo) Gulf shore of Lake Victoria, and that at Nsongezi rock-shelter on the Kagera River (Gabel 1969, Pearce and Posnansky 1963).

The Later Stone Age of central and southern Tanzania remains little known. In the Iramba area the rock-shelter of Lululampembele contains a crescent-dominated microlithic aggregate overlying a level in which scrapers and *outils écaillés* (splintered pieces) were accompanied by very few microliths. A radiocarbon date in the first half of the second millennium BC is associated with the upper level; pottery is restricted to the very top of the sequence and is, presumably, of Iron Age date.

---

[1] Leakey's original subdivision recognized a 'Wilton A' (from open sites) which was distinguished from 'B' (found in caves and rock-shelters as at Nasera ('Apis rock') and at sites near Nairobi) by its lack of the small points which were thought to link the latter aggregates with their predecessors. Leakey's 'Wilton C' occurs in lake-shore shell-mounds, notably beside Lake Victoria; on these sites stone tools of any sort are very rare, scrapers particularly so. Leakey regarded pottery as being an integral part of all three 'Wilton' industries, that from 'Wilton C' sites being exceptionally coarse. For a recent examination of the variation between East African 'Late Stone Age' industries see Nelson (1976).

The lower aggregate is undated, but comparison with Kisese suggests that it may be very considerably older (see also pp. 429, 463) (Odner 1971).

ETHIOPIA AND THE HORN

It is now necessary to retrace our steps northwards and briefly to consider the very inadequate state of our knowledge of the Later Stone Age succession on the Ethiopian plateau and in the Horn of Africa. Few absolute age determinations are yet available; and only the most tentative estimates – based on long-range correlations such as have frequently been disproved by radiocarbon dating in other parts of the continent – can be made as to the ages of the majority of the industries here discussed. It is considered that the earliest Later Stone Age industry in this region was that named Hargeisan, the distribution of which is centred on the northern part of the Somali plateau and the rift of the Gulf of Aden on the Red Sea coast to the north (J. D. Clark 1954). This mode 4 industry (fig. 6.6.13–14) is characterized by backed blades, burins, end-scrapers, small unifacial points reminiscent of those of the final phases of the local Middle Stone Age and occasional convex-based arrow-heads. Various writers have compared the Hargeisan both with the earlier phases of the 'Kenya Capsian' and also with industries from the Ethiopian plateau to the west. The Hargeisan was followed by an industry described as 'Wilton', best known from a rock-shelter at Mandera in northern Somalia. Here crescents, short end-scrapers and small convex scrapers predominate; there are also occasional burins and sherds of undecorated pottery. This Somalia 'Wilton' is one of a number of basically similar regional industries which are widely distributed through the Horn. Knowledge of the relative and absolute dating of these variants, as of their cultural interrelationships, is virtually non-existent.

In southern Somalia and adjacent parts of north-eastern Kenya, there are indications of a late continuation of essentially mode 3 industries in which there can be discerned a decrease with time in the use of the prepared-core technique and an increasing emphasis on blade production. This industry, which has been named 'Magosio-Doian', is replaced in turn by a 'Doian' industry (fig. 6.6.15–18). At Gure Warbei two 'Doian' phases were distinguished; the first was characterized by backed blades and unifacial *limaces*, the second by pressure-flaked bifacial and unifacial points and by pottery. A coastal variant of the 'Doian' has also been recognized in middens some 300 km south of Cape

Guardafui, as have forms described as Neolithic, aggregates of which include large pressure-flaked foliate points. No clear evidence for food production has, however, yet been found in association with such aggregates in this area. Associated iron slag suggests a late continuation of occupation at some 'Doian' sites.

Further inland an outline sequence has recently been established in east central Ethiopia (J. D. Clark, personal communication). A backed blade industry, predating the eleventh millennium BC, has been recovered near Lake Besaka in the southern Afar Rift; the tool types, which include microlithic forms, appear to resemble those of the Eburran. In a subsequent phase the makers of this industry may be shown to have been in contact with the Red Sea coastal regions. Rare pottery may be evidence of trade with the inhabitants of the neighbouring plateau. Human burials, some showing signs of burning, were interred below small stone mounds. The final phase of the southern Afar Stone Age succession is dated to the second millennium BC and is marked by a proliferation of scrapers and by abundant pottery. It seems probable that this development may be linked with the introduction into the region of domestic animals. To the east, around Dire Dawa and Harar, the cave of Porc Epic has been shown to contain a pottery-associated mode 5 industry overlying one of Middle Stone Age type. Comparable material occurs in rock-shelters to the south of Harar.

Elsewhere in highland Ethiopia, evidence for mode 5 industries is very sparse. Only isolated undated finds have been described and no coherent synthesis can yet be attempted. In Shoa, stratified occurrences which have been investigated at Melka Kunturé remain undated, as does the sequence at the Gorgora rock-shelter on the northern side of Lake Tana. Here, the upper levels contained a 'local non-Wilton microlithic industry' containing rough lunates, small backed blades and scrapers, as well as undecorated pottery. This overlay a 'Magosian' industry which retained many mode 3 features (L. S. B. Leakey 1943, Moysey 1943); the published account gives only a general description of the aggregates, which were derived from large, arbitrarily excavated levels. The Gorgora data cannot therefore be regarded as indicating any more than general trends of industrial development.

Further north the only sequence is at Gobedra rock-shelter near Aksum in Tigre. Here, on the plateau of northern Ethiopia, the earliest industry is one of large backed blades which bear only minimal retouch. It was replaced around the ninth millennium BC by a microlithic industry in which two phases are recognized, only the second of which is associated with pottery. The most recent inhabitants of Gobedra, produced an industry dominated by scrapers comparable to those which have been found on protohistoric Aksumite sites. Elsewhere in northern Ethiopia, such late industries are almost the only ones known; they are discussed in chapter 11. An exception is a fine microlithic industry from Dahlak Kebir, off the Red Sea coast of Eritrea. Obsidian, which does not occur on the islands, and which must therefore have been imported over a 20-km sea route (unless, as seems improbable, this occurrence predates the eustatic rise in sea level which took place around the eighth millennium BC), was used for the production of crescents, backed blades and small convex scrapers comparable to those of some Somalian 'Wilton' industries described above (Blanc 1955, D. W. Phillipson 1977a).

Finally, it is necessary to discuss a group of sites which, although widely separated geographically, appear closely linked in their material culture and in their economic basis. The specialized fishing settlements of the Lake Nakuru basin have already been discussed and considered to be an idiosyncratic but integral part of the general spread of East African Later Stone Age communities. They are, however, also seen as representative of a widespread series of settlements whose scattered distribution is mirrored in the diversity of their lithic industries.

In addition to Lake Nakuru, settlements of this type are indicated from the shores of Lakes Edward and Rudolf and from the banks of the White Nile. The Ishango site is situated near the affluence of the Semliki River on the north-eastern shore of Lake Edward (de Heinzelin de Braucourt 1957). Three Later Stone Age levels lay on an old beach some 10 m above the modern lake level (fig. 6.7). The stone industry was of quartz and, like that of many other lake-shore sites, of remarkably crude appearance. Mode 3 techniques appear to have continued alongside the production of crude backed microliths. Mullers and grinders were also frequent. In all three levels, numbers of barbed bone points or harpoon-heads were found. These show a typological time-dependent progression from small biserial examples in the lowest level, through larger biserial forms, to uniserial specimens in the uppermost Later Stone Age layer. It has been suggested that the small biserial points served as arrow-heads for shooting fish and that the larger ones, which replaced them and which often show notches at the base as if for the attachment of a line, were true harpoons used for the same purpose. Simple bone points, awls and needles were also found. The mammal remains represented include forest species which no longer occur in the

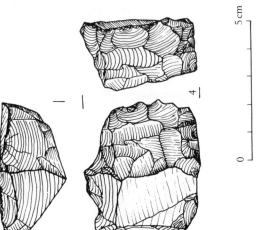

5 cm

0

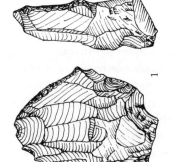

Fig. 6.7  Artifacts from Ishango. (After de Heinzelin 1957.)

1 Side scraper      2 End scraper
3 Uniserial harpoon  4 Core scraper
5, 6 Biserial harpoons

vicinity and which presumably indicate a somewhat moister climate than that prevailing today. The fish and mollusc remains include species which no longer occur in Lake Edward. A date somewhere between the ninth and the fifth millennia BC is generally regarded as probable for the Ishango settlement.

Uniserial harpoons comparable to those from the upper level at Ishango have recently been reported from several sites near former strandlines of Lake Rudolf in both Kenya and Ethiopia. In the Omo valley, deposits which represent a large northward extension of the lake during the late Pleistocene and early Holocene have yielded several such harpoons from contexts dated to around the eighth or seventh millennia BC. Near the southern end of Lake Rudolf uniserial harpoons have been recovered from several sites, notably Lowasera and Lothagam, dated to around 6000 BC. In this area, pottery, which did not occur at Ishango or in the Omo valley sites, appears to be contemporary with the bone harpoons, sherds bearing stamped decoration and incised wavy lines having been recovered. These settlements are associated with a high beach laid down when the waters of Lake Rudolf reached 80 m above their present level (Barthelme 1977; Brown 1975; Butzer, Brown and Thurber 1969; D. W. Phillipson 1977b; Robbins 1974).

There are clear connections between the harpoons and pottery from Lake Rudolf and those from the broadly contemporary site of Early Khartoum, over 1500 km to the north-north-west. This latter site (fig. 6.8) produced a microlithic aggregate dominated by quartz crescents, triangles and trapeziforms, together with larger crescent-adzes, long narrow backed blades, borers and crude scrapers (Arkell 1949). There were also rectangular backed blades neatly trimmed at each end as if for hafting in line, as were the sickle blades from the Neolithic Fayum. Ground stone artifacts include grooved pebbles, which were presumably used as net-sinkers, bored stones and rubbers, some of which were used for the grinding of ochre and others probably in the manufacture of bone tools. Among the latter, the most characteristic were the harpoons, almost all of which were uniserial and had multiple grooves cut transversely around the base for the attachment of the line; occasional specimens were perforated instead. Pottery was abundant and included conical-based forms; some sherds bore cord-impressions but the characteristic ware from Early Khartoum was decorated with multiple horizontal wavy lines. In the later horizons this wavy-line pottery is elaborated by the addition of multiple punctate designs. None of this pottery is burnished, in contrast to later wares from the same

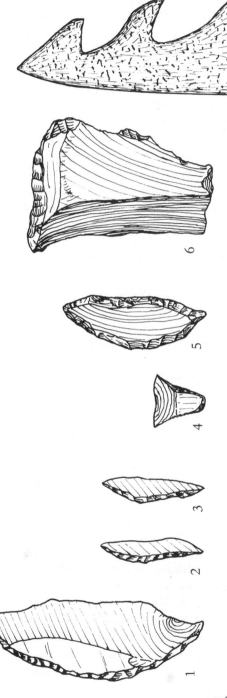
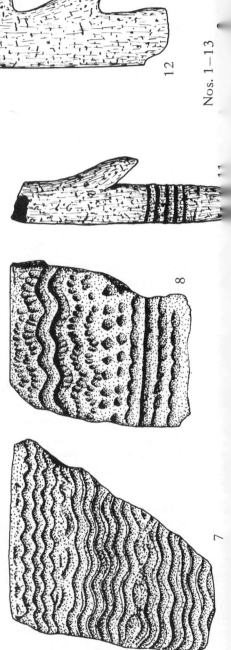

Nos. 1–13

438

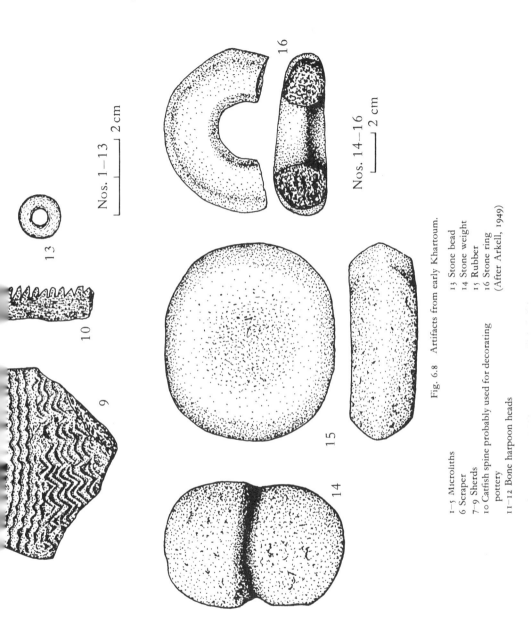

Nos. 1–13 |—————| 2 cm

Nos. 14–16 |—————| 2 cm

Fig. 6.8  Artifacts from early Khartoum.

1–5 Microliths
6 Scraper
7–9 Sherds
10 Catfish spine probably used for decorating pottery
11–12 Bone harpoon heads

13 Stone bead
14 Stone weight
15 Rubber
16 Stone ring
(After Arkell, 1949)

439

region. The inhabitants of Early Khartoum were buried within the site in tightly contracted positions; one skull has been reconstructed and is said to display possible negroid affinities. There are indications that the Early Khartoum site was occupied for a prolonged period and on at least a semi-permanent basis; walls of wattle and sun-dried daub are reported and the degree of typological evolution of the pottery styles which took place during the occupation lends support to this hypothesis. As at Ishango, fishing formed the economic basis for the settlement. This is attested by the presence of harpoons, net weights and fish bones, while shells of a type still used as bait by Sudanese fishermen also occurred in the archaeological deposits. There is no evidence for cultivation at the site; the animal bones recovered are exclusively of wild types. These include swamp species indicative of a climate wetter than the present one, with the Nile flowing at an appreciably higher level than it does today.

There has been considerable doubt as to the date of the Early Khartoum settlement. In the absence of directly related radiocarbon determinations one must rely on uncertain correlations with other dated sites. Technologically, typologically and, at El-Qoz, stratigraphically, it predates the 'Khartoum Neolithic' sites such as Esh-Shaheinab (discussed in chapter 11) for which a radiocarbon age in the second half of the fourth millennium BC is regarded by some as unacceptably recent. Barbed bone points directly comparable with those from Early Khartoum have recently been recovered from three sites further upstream along the White Nile. One of these occurrences is dated to the end of the seventh millennium BC and is apparently contemporary with a high Nile level which may correlate with that indicated at Early Khartoum (Adamson, Clark and Williams 1974).

Unburnished dotted wavy-line pottery comparable to that of the later part of the occupation of Early Khartoum has an enormously extended distribution west of the Nile valley through the southern Sahara. It has been found, for instance, in the lowest level of Delebo cave in Ennedi, where a later continuation of the same style is dated to the second half of the sixth millennium BC. Even further afield, comparable sherds at Amekni in the Ahaggar are dated to the end of the seventh millennium. Such far-ranging correlations may be open to charges of 'trait-chasing', but they do seem to indicate the archaeological acceptability of an early date, perhaps in the order of 7000 BC, for the initial settlement of Early Khartoum. However, there is no *a priori* reason why the site should not be regarded as a late representative of what was obviously a prolonged and widespread economic adaptation. It is significant that these settlements belong to a time when high levels are attested for all the East African lakes as well as for Lake Chad and other, now extinct, water sources in the southern Sahara. The distribution of the settlements is closely correlated with that of the contemporary lakes and rivers. The characteristic artifact, the bone harpoon, was almost certainly employed in the exploitation of the rich fish resources which this environment afforded.

Despite the uneven distribution and comprehensiveness of research, an overall picture of the East African Later Stone Age is now beginning to emerge. In Tanzania and in southern Kenya, mode 5 microlithic technologies appear to have become established between the eighteenth and fifteenth millennia BC. In at least one site, their predecessor was a scraper-dominated industry distinct from the classic Middle Stone Age aggregates of the region. In the Rift Valley area of Kenya and further north in northern Somalia, there are mode 4 blade industries, dated in the former area to the eleventh millennium; there is no indication that these were preceded by microlithic industries which were thus locally of considerably later inception than they were further to the south. Survival of mode 3 elements also appears to have been stronger in the more northerly areas. Considerable typological differentiation may be discerned between the microlithic aggregates in various areas, but it is difficult to separate the effects of raw material on this phenomenon from those of cultural distinctions. It is within the range of these heterogeneous mode 5 industries that, from the seventh millennium onwards, widely dispersed fishing communities may be recognized. These depended on the relatively intensive exploitation of richly concentrated aquatic resources, which permitted the establishment of semi-permanent settlements, some, at least, of which may have been occupied on a seasonal basis. Although these early sites have yielded no evidence for food production, it appears that they subsequently provided the human context for the acceptance of food-production techniques, as will be discussed in chapter 11.

SOUTH CENTRAL AFRICA (fig. 6.9)

As members of one of the longest and best-known mode 5 sequences in sub-Saharan Africa, the Zambian industries form a convenient reference point for a discussion of Later Stone Age societies over a much wider area. On the northern and eastern plateaux, separated by the Luangwa valley, microlithic industries are now known to have prevailed through the last seventeen millennia; and there are strong indications

Fig. 6.9   Southern sub-Saharan Africa, showing sites mentioned in the text.

that these may have been locally derived from their mode 3 Middle Stone Age predecessors through a process which began some 7000 years earlier. Mode 3 industries, however, probably continued in the more southern and western parts of the country until comparatively recent times, being replaced between the fifth and second millennia BC by microlithic industries whose origin may probably be traced to the later

442

stages of the sequence now established in the more northerly plateau regions.

Two sites in Zambia have yielded evidence for an industry putatively ancestral to those of the fully microlithic Later Stone Age. Both are situated in undulating *Brachystegia*-covered plateau country, at approximately 1000 m above sea level, near the lip of the northern slope of the middle Zambezi valley. At Kalemba rock-shelter in the extreme south-east of Zambia, the ancestors of that transitional industry may be traced back to a developed mode 3 occurrence before 35 000 BC. Both here and at Leopard's Hill Cave, 50 km south-east of Lusaka, the period between the twenty-third and the twentieth millennia BC is marked by an industry which retains many typological features of its predecessors but is evidently ancestral in many important and basic respects to its microlithic successor. A steady diminution in artifact size is accompanied by a trend towards increased bladelet production. Bladelets and flake-blades were rarely retouched, except by use, although a few crude backed forms mark the first local appearance of this technique (Miller 1969, D. W. Phillipson 1973). At both Kalemba and Leopard's Hill this transitional industry (fig. 6.10.1–2) was succeeded, around the fifteenth millennium BC, by true microlithic mode 5 aggregates of the type referred to in the literature as 'Nachikufan I' (fig. 6.10.3–5).

The faunal remains associated with the 'Nachikufan I' Industry at Kalemba indicate a change from the earlier hunting pattern which was based upon the exploitation of herds of zebra and the larger gregarious antelope. In their place, the makers of the microlithic tools relied increasingly upon smaller, more solitary, creatures, such as are found in the wooded environs of the site today. This altered hunting emphasis could indicate change either in cultural factors (food preferences) or in the climatic conditions prevailing within the territory exploited by the site's inhabitants. A shift to wetter conditions is in fact indicated by the pedology of the deposits which contain the earliest microlithic industries at Kalemba and it may reasonably be concluded that open plains, where the earlier inhabitants had hunted large gregarious creatures, were no longer present within easy reach of the site. 'Nachikufan I' was the industry of hunters who exploited a wooded environment closely approximating to that which prevails at the present time.

'Nachikufan I' aggregates have a wider distribution than those of the succeeding 'Nachikufan' stages (J. D. Clark 1950a, Miller 1972). First recognized in the Muchinga Mountains to the west of the Luangwa valley, they are now known from the eastern plateau, from the Lusaka

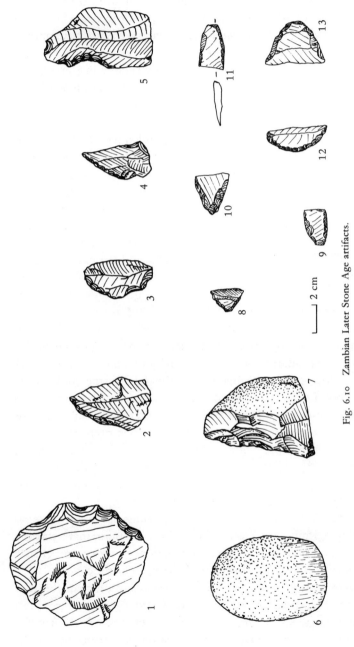

Fig. 6.10   Zambian Later Stone Age artifacts.

1–2   From 'transitional' levels at Kalemba
3–5   From 'Nachikufan I' levels at Kalemba
6–8   From Nachikufu
9–13   Makwe Industry from Makwe

(Nos. 1–8 after J. D. Clark (1950a) and 9–13 after D. W. Phillipson (1973).)

444

area and, to the west, from a site near Solwezi on the Zambezi–Congo watershed. Their distribution is effectively restricted to the *Brachystegia*-covered plateau areas; in particular, they have not been recorded from the Kalahari Sand regions of the south and west, nor from the Zambezi valley. Radiocarbon dates indicate a duration of some 6000 years from the fifteenth to the ninth or tenth millennia. 'Nachikufan I' industries have a fully fledged mode 5 typology, characterized by pointed backed bladelets which outnumber crescents. Among the latter, deep forms and geometrics are characteristically rare. Various scraper forms occur, but are outnumbered by the microliths. Bored stones are frequently encountered, being particularly numerous at Nachikufu itself.[1] Ground stone axes may also occur. Occasional bone points are the only non-lithic artifacts so far recorded.

The next industrial phase, 'Nachikufan IIA', is dated between the eighth and the sixth millennia BC, while phase IIB is placed in the fourth and early third millennia. In phase IIA pointed backed bladelets are largely replaced by backed and truncated flakes, which in turn yield pride of place in phase IIB to deep crescents and geometric microliths. Bored stones and ground axes are attested in both phases (fig. 6.10.6–8). Both phases have a more restricted distribution than did 'Nachikufan I'; and are best seen as parts of a series of contemporaneous regionally-differentiated industries. Their counterparts in other areas are described below.

· The Later Stone Age industries east of the Luangwa follow a distinct development parallel to that discussed above. Events immediately following the local 'Nachikufan I' phase are not yet clearly understood, but by 5000 BC the Makwe Industry was well established, characterized by a variety of microlithic tools which greatly and increasingly outnumber the scrapers (fig. 6.10.9–13). Over the next two millennia backed flakes and bladelets were gradually replaced by crescents and geometrics, among which idiosyncratic, very deep triangular forms enjoyed a brief vogue. Ground axes were frequent, but bored stones – present in underlying 'Nachikufan I' horizons – do not occur in the Makwe Industry, except in its earliest phase. Bone points in a variety of types form an important part of the aggregates. Tubular bone beads are replaced by disc beads, first of bone and latterly of shell, which material was also fashioned into a variety of pendants. The final stages of the Later Stone Age sequence of eastern Zambia are characterized

---

[1] A single bored stone occurs in the lowest, pre-'Nachikufan I' level at Leopard's Hill cave (J. D. Clark 1970: 241).

by a predominance of crescents to the virtual exclusion of all other implement types. This industry, best known from Thandwe, continued well into the present millennium, long after the arrival of Iron Age immigrants (D. W. Phillipson 1973).

In Malawi, there is further evidence for the early establishment of mode 5 industries; the lowest relevant aggregate at Hora Mountain dates to the fifteenth millennium BC. It seems probable that subsequent developments there closely paralleled those in eastern Zambia, but no detailed succession has yet been worked out. At the Fingira rock-shelter site in central Malawi, the microlithic aggregates of the last 2000 years BC included deep crescents and trapezoidal forms which may be related to those of the somewhat earlier Makwe Industry.

The last four millennia BC in northern Zambia are represented in the archaeological record by a variety of microlithic industries, the relationships of which are as yet imperfectly understood. At Kalambo Falls, mode 5 aggregates attributed to the Kaposwa Industry (fig. 6.11) are made on mudstone and other fine-grained materials which differ markedly in fracture patterns from the quartz generally used elsewhere (J. D. Clark 1974: 107–52). The final stage of the Later Stone Age sequence in this area shows a high degree of inter-site variation. There was a general diminution in size of microliths; and the types of these and of scrapers recognized in the earlier phases continued, but with no particular forms in overall dominance. Grindstones, bored stones and ground axes continued at most sites. The heterogeneous aggregates classed as 'Nachikufan III' have yielded dates ranging from the middle of the second millennium BC to the nineteenth century AD.

It will be seen from the above outline that the industries classed as 'Nachikufan' cover a time-span of more than sixteen millennia. A consistent series of sequential phases has been recognized but the nature of the changes involved is not yet clear. In particular, we do not know to what extent the sequence is an illusory compartmentalization of a continuous typological evolution; for a contrary view see Sampson and Southard (1973). It is now clear that 'Nachikufan I' is a representative of an early microlithic industry, characterized by a dominance of pointed backed bladelets, which was widely distributed in the plateau areas of east-central Africa and which was derived, at least in substantial part, from the mode 3 industries of that region. Later 'Nachikufan' phases were progressively localized and show increased inter-site variation. They may represent differential local developments from a 'Nachikufan I' common ancestor.

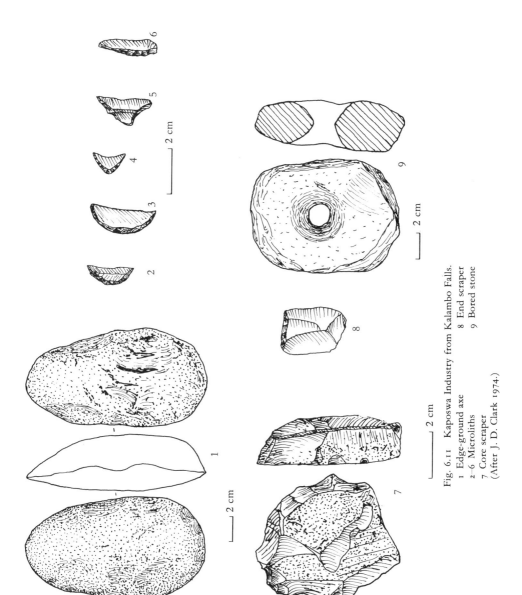

Fig. 6.11 Kaposwa Industry from Kalambo Falls.

1 Edge-ground axe
2–6 Microliths
7 Core scraper
8 End scraper
9 Bored stone

(After J. D. Clark 1974.)

447

Until recently, the microlithic industries of Zambia were held to be subdivisible into 'Nachikufan' on the northern and central plateaux and 'Wilton' in the south and west. The higher proportion of microliths, particularly crescents, in the 'Zambian Wilton' was held to represent a response to the more open country of the south, which favoured hunting with the bow and crescent-tipped arrow, while the denser woodland of the northern regions resulted in the greater use of the concave scrapers and other putative woodworking tools of the 'Nachikufan' industries. Recent research has provided some degree of support, but not conclusive proof, for these usages. It is possible that the above describes a generally valid distinction between the mode 5 aggregates in the two areas. However, we now know that 'Nachikufan I' and 'IIA' predate the demonstrable presence of microlithic 'Wilton' industries in the south, which are probably contemporary only with phases IIB and III in the north. Furthermore, these two latter phases share at least as great a typological similarity with the 'Wilton' industries as they do with the earlier 'Nachikufan' phases. What was once seen as a largely geographical and environmental distinction may thus be regarded as based at least as firmly on chronological factors. It is plausible to regard the 'Wilton' industries of Zambia as further examples of regionally differentiated derivatives of the earlier 'Nachikufan' phases, marking a spread of mode 5 industries into new territories in which mode 3 had previously held sway long after its replacement on the northern plateaux.

The clearest and most detailed picture of the 'Zambian Wilton' is obtained from excavations at Gwisho Hotsprings on the southern edge of the Kafue Flats (Fagan and van Noten 1971, Gabel 1965). The area supports enormous herds of game, in a rich environment which was evidently exploited to the full by the Later Stone Age inhabitants of the area during a period of some one and a half millennia, commencing shortly after 3000 BC. Conditions in the largely waterlogged spring deposits secured the preservation of vegetable and other organic remains, enabling a uniquely detailed picture of the economy and material culture of a Later Stone Age settlement to be reconstructed (fig. 6.12). Grass-lined hollows, probably used for sleeping, were discovered, as were settings of posts interpreted as the remains of wind-breaks. Unfortunately the excavations did not succeed in isolating individual occupation phases so, despite the richness of the deposits, little information was recovered concerning settlement plans or processes of technological development. The microlithic industry is attri-

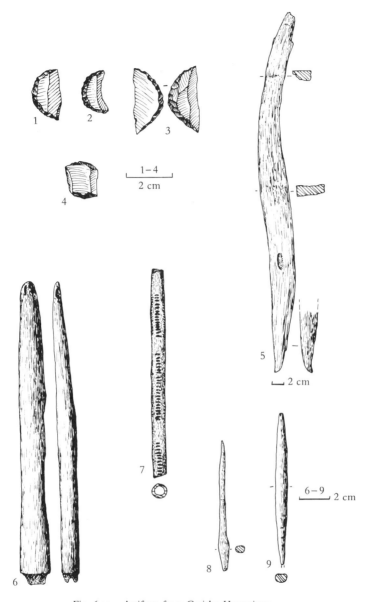

Fig. 6.12    Artifacts from Gwisho Hotsprings.

1–4 Microliths                    7 Carved bone tube
5 Wooden digging-stick            8 Wooden arrow-head
6 End of wooden bow (?)           9 Wooden link shaft

(After Fagan and van Noten 1971.)

449

buted to the 'Zambian Wilton': crescents, backed flakes and backed bladelets were the dominant types, geometric microliths being uncommon. Scrapers, generally small and convex, were few, with concave forms virtually absent. Bored stones and ground axes are extremely rare. There was a variety of grinding and pounding stones which were presumably used in the preparation of vegetable foods. Wooden and bone artifacts occurred in considerable variety. Clear preference was exercised in the selection of hardwoods, particularly *Baikiaea plurijuga* which was used for the production of digging-sticks, bows, arrow-heads and fire drills. Digging-sticks were also made of softer wood, as were link-shafts. Bone was utilized principally for the production of points and bodkins comparable to those found in broadly contemporary rock-shelter sites over a wide area, and for finely decorated bone tubes the significance of which is unknown. Beads were of shell and exclusively of the disc type. Over thirty human skeletons have been recovered. These, with one or two loosely contracted exceptions, were buried in an extended position in shallow scooped-out graves within the main settlement areas and had no grave-goods other than shell beads. Further occurrences attributed to the 'Zambian Wilton' have been described from Mumbwa Cave and from the Victoria Falls region (J. D. Clark 1942, 1950b; Inskeep 1959).

Upstream of the Victoria Falls the Zambezi flows through the extensive Kalahari Sand plains of Zambia's Western (formerly Barotse) and Northwestern Provinces. Here, stone of any sort is extremely rare and, although finds of isolated stone artifacts have been reported far from the natural occurrences of the raw material, the distribution of Stone Age sites closely follows that of outcrops of suitable stone. This does not mean that Stone Age occupation was limited to these areas, for the absence of stone may have encouraged the utilization of other materials which have not survived in the archaeological record. That the severely restricted sources of raw material probably served a wide area is indicated by the substantial accumulations of mode 3 factory debris which surround them as, for instance, at Cholwezi. In view of these large quantities of mode 3 material, the comparative overall scarcity of microlithic aggregates in this upper Zambezi region is remarkable. They generally occur as a thin scatter in superficial deposits along the river bank, as in the dunes beside Chavuma Pool. Although any conclusions from such observations are subjective and necessarily tentative, a strong impression is gained that the microlithic mode 5 technology here is exclusively of late date and that the mode 3 industries continued into comparatively recent millennia. Radiometric dating, available only in the south of the region, at Kandanda in Sesheke District, confirms a late date for the inception of the microlithic industries. Throughout this upper Zambezi region the Stone Age industries show stronger affinity to those of northern Angola and adjacent parts of the Congo basin than they do to those from elsewhere in Zambia (L. Phillipson 1975).

Climatological factors allow the tentative proposition of an explanation for the late inception of mode 5 technology in this south-western region of Zambia. The area is one where low rainfall and leached sandy soils combine to produce arid conditions, and an open plains vegetation, with its characteristic fauna, would have continued there long after the onset of more densely wooded vegetation further to the north and east. It is not until the third millennium BC that conditions warmer and moister than those of the present are indicated in neighbouring western Ngamiland and it is tempting to suggest that here, as in eastern and northern Zambia over 10 000 years earlier, such conditions provided the stimulus for the adoption of a microlithic technology.

It is uncertain to what extent the Zambian evidence for the late inception of mode 5 industries in this region holds good for adjacent parts of the Kalahari Sand country. That in some places such industries were of significantly earlier date is demonstrated at the Mungo rock-shelter near Nova Lisboa in west-central Angola, where an industry described as 'Wilton' is dated to between the ninth and the sixth millennia BC (H. J. Cooke 1975, Vogel and Marais 1971).

Although regional clustering is apparent in the Zambian microlithic industries of the last three millennia BC, we are not yet in a position to define discrete groups, or indeed to state whether or not such groups actually existed. The 'Zambian Wilton', 'Nachikufan IIB' and 'III', together with the Makwe Industry in the east, take their places as parallel developments from a common ancestral tradition, presumably represented by 'Nachikufan I'. A similar status is possible for the Kaposwa Industry from Kalambo Falls. The 'Wilton' industries probably represent the first extension of the microlithic tradition south and west from the plateau zone to which its earlier manifestations were restricted (D. W. Phillipson 1976).

SOUTHERN AFRICA (fig. 6.9)

When we turn our attention to the Later Stone Age industries of southern Africa, we find a veritable mass of published data, although these are of very uneven geographical distribution. Despite this large quantity of material, it is still difficult to attempt more than a very tentative overall synthesis. There are few dated and fully analysed regional sequences; and several key sites with long multicomponent successions are still awaiting adequate publication.

Following the pioneer work of Goodwin and van Riet Lowe, published in 1929, it became accepted practice to classify most southern African Later Stone Age aggregates as either 'Smithfield' or 'Wilton'. Until recently, neither of these groups was fully defined on the basis of complete stratified aggregates from dated contexts; and consequently the attribution of further occurrences to these rather nebulous entities gave rise to much confusion. 'Wilton' industries, characterized by small convex scrapers and microlithic backed crescents, were known primarily from coastal regions, although scattered occurrences of closely related variants gradually became known from several inland areas. In general, 'Smithfield' industries were regarded as macrolithic and (with the exception of the nebulous 'Smithfield C') lacking the backed implements characteristic of the 'Wilton'. The 'Smithfield' was said to be concentrated in inland areas, notably the Transvaal, Orange Free State and northern Cape, with related occurrences on the Natal and south Cape coasts (J. D. Clark 1959).

Detailed descriptions have recently been published of two dated sequences which enable a complete revision of the older interpretation to be proposed. After presenting summaries of these sequences, we shall here discuss the latest evidence for contemporary successions in adjacent areas, and finally the general trends which may be observed in the inception and development of the Later Stone Age of southern Africa as a whole.

In the middle Orange region, the earliest phase of the Later Stone Age may be shown to postdate a blade industry of Middle Stone Age type. It appears to represent a complete break with the earlier material and is characterized by convex scrapers on large flakes. This phase (fig. 6.13.1–4) is not well documented since it occurs only on open sites which have not yet been dated, although markedly similar aggregates elsewhere have been dated to before the seventh millennium BC. This industry was apparently followed by a prolonged hiatus in the middle

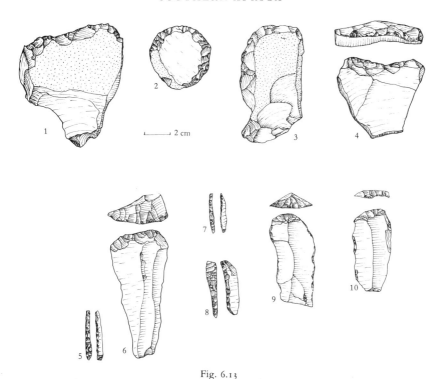

Fig. 6.13
1–4 'Oakhurst Complex' scrapers from Zeekoegat 13 (after Sampson 1967a)
5–10 Artifacts from Glen Elliot shelter, northern Cape (after Sampson 1967b)

Orange sequence. Its successor (fig. 6.13.5–10), attributed only to the third millennium BC, is marked by the introduction of backed microlithic elements. It is noteworthy that the first mode 5 industry attested from this region, like that from the upper Zambezi area which is only slightly less arid, dates from the time of the onset of milder, moister conditions which are attested in western Ngamiland after about 2400 BC. Subsequently, in a phase which covers most of the last two millennia BC, microliths – notably crescents – dominate the aggregate although the old scraper tradition did continue, represented by implements of markedly reduced size. Early in the present millennium, the dominance of microliths continued, although the crescents gradually gave way to increased numbers of backed blades and the small scrapers yielded to larger blade-end examples, which, in contrast to their earlier counterparts, appear to have been used unhafted. The final phases are differentiated by the presence of pottery, glass beads and occasional metal objects which presumably indicate contact, whether direct or indirect, with an incoming Iron Age population. The backed microlith element is finally replaced by a proliferation of blade-end scrapers and bone points (Sampson 1972). The Later Stone Age sequence of the middle Orange area is thus seen as one in which two scraper-based industries are separated by several phases of an apparently quite distinct tradition in which backed microliths form an important element. There appear to be no valid reasons for separating these inland mode 5 industries from the general continuum commonly known as the 'Wilton' Industrial Complex.

It is to this 'Wilton' tradition that we must now turn. In South Africa, it is characterized by the predominance in its component industries of small convex scrapers and backed microliths. It was named from an aggregate recovered in 1921 from a cave and rock-shelter on the farm Wilton not far from Alicedale in the eastern Cape. The site is some 50 km from the sea. No detailed, quantified description of the material then excavated has ever appeared, but it has nevertheless given its name to an enormous number of generally similar industries from as far afield as Angola and Ethiopia; a 'Nigerian Wilton' has even been proposed. In 1967 the Wilton site was reinvestigated and several phases of occupation recognized; it is believed that all except the earliest belong to a single tradition (J. Deacon 1972). The earliest aggregate, mainly in quartzite and other local materials, is dominated by large scrapers, backed microliths being rare. A similar industry has been recovered from the basal deposits of several other rock-shelters in the eastern Cape, notably Melkhoutboom, where it is dated to the eighth millennium BC. The overlying layer at Wilton is subdivided into several levels and detailed analysis shows the developmental trends clearly (fig. 6.14.1–6). The appearance of many chalcedony artifacts suggests that the inhabitants' range of territory now extended into the Bushman River valley. Round scrapers, smaller than those of the previous layer, continue to dominate the industry. Backed microliths steadily increase in frequency, reaching a maximum of 40% of the retouched implements during the third millennium BC. Crescents likewise reach their peak at this level, yielding ground thereafter to various backed blade forms. The later stages are marked by a greater variety of tool types, while a decrease in the frequency of sea shells suggests that the inhabitants now relied more on inland areas for their food supplies than had their predecessors. This late phase is dated to the second half of the first millennium BC. Subsequently pottery makes its appearance in association with a stone industry from which backed microliths have virtually disappeared. It

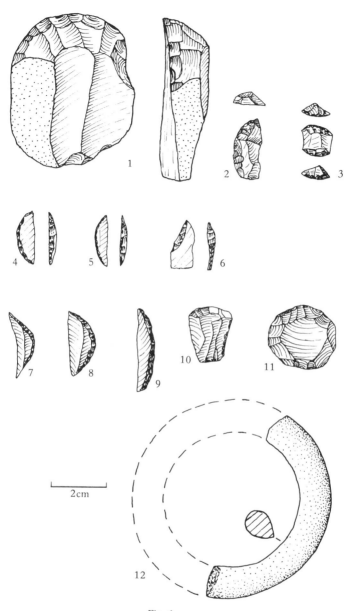

Fig. 6.14
1–6 Artifacts from Wilton rock-shelter (after Deacon 1972)
7–12 Matopan artifacts from Nswatugi, Matopo Hills (after Sampson 1974)

has been suggested that 'the increased variance in the norms of scraper manufacture and the apparent disintegration of the cohesive factors governing artefact manufacture would seem to typify a cultural system in decline' (J. Deacon 1972, p. 37). A comparable aggregate at Scott's Cave in the Gamtoos valley rather over 100 km west of Wilton also has associated pottery at a level dated to around the eighth century AD (H. J. Deacon 1966, H. J. Deacon and J. Deacon 1963).

There are clear parallels between the Wilton succession, which appears to be representative of those from further west along the south Cape coast, and that described above from the middle Orange region. Taken together, the two sequences permit the reconstruction of a framework to which may be fitted many other Later Stone Age occurrences from a wide area of southern Africa. A succession of scraper-based industries, provisionally named after the Oakhurst site near George, falls generally between the twelfth and the eighth millennia BC, but its antecedents may be traced into still earlier times, as at the Nelson Bay Cave at Plettenberg Bay. At the latter site the beginning of the microlithic succession is dated to early in the seventh millennium BC. These data provide confirmation for the problematical sequence at Matjes River rock-shelter where a scraper-based industry overlain by a microlithic one has been known for some years. At all these sites, as through the greater part of the southern Cape Province, the microlithic industries of the Wilton Complex appear to have been succeeded, during the first millennium BC or slightly before, by aggregates in which varied scraper forms again progressively replaced the microliths (J. Deacon 1974, Klein 1974).

In the coastal and mountain regions of the Cape, economic changes may be shown to have paralleled the typological developments now recognized. The practitioners of the early scraper-based industries hunted mainly the larger gregarious antelope such as may be assumed to have been common on the coastal plains, exposed by the lowered sea levels of the final Pleistocene. The later Wilton folk subsisted on vegetable foods, notably bulbs and corms, and hunted smaller non-gregarious antelope. These resources would have been less readily available in winter and it is at this season that coastal sites appear mainly to have been occupied (J. Deacon 1974, Klein 1974, Parkington 1972).

In most parts of the Cape Province we thus see evidence for two macrolithic phases, any interrelationship between which remains poorly understood, separated by a prolonged period when the dominant industries were microlithic. During this period, the population of the inland plateau, if indeed the region was then occupied, appears to have been extremely sparse (J. Deacon 1974). The concept of the central plateau's being a separate culture-area throughout the Later Stone Age thus falls away.

The evidence from Namibia is in keeping with that described from the Cape Province. Microlithic industries are underlain by aggregates, such as that found on a ninth-millennium BC elephant-kill site near Windhoek, in which large flake scrapers are the dominant type. Similar material comes from the 'Apollo 11 Cave' near the confluence of the Orange and Fish rivers. Ostrich-eggshell beads and a marine shell pendant were associated, and the occurrence is securely attributed to the 5000-year period preceding the eighth millennium BC. This horizon of the 'Apollo 11 Cave' is also of considerable importance as having yielded dated examples of rock paintings such as rarely occur in stratified contexts: stone slabs, one of which bears a representation of a human figure, and another an indeterminable animal. In the eighth millennium or shortly thereafter, microlithic aggregates make their appearance; and from this time until recent centuries all Namibian Later Stone Age aggregates appear to be of this type (Wendt 1972). In the Brandberg, the microlithic tradition appears to have continued until late in the first millennium AD, by which time pottery and copper artifacts had been added to the artifact assemblages. Its successor, an industry of irregular steep scrapers and end-scrapers associated with bone artifacts and pottery, has been referred to the 'Brandberg Culture', but related material is widespread in the territory (Rudner 1957).

In Zimbabwe, a broadly similar sequence is indicated, although comparatively little detailed research has been devoted to the Later Stone Age sequence in contrast to the preceding and succeeding periods and to the rock art. Dated successions are available only from the Matopo Hills near Bulawayo.

Pomongwe Cave provides the framework for the Matopo Hills sequence (C. K. Cooke 1963). The earliest level to concern us here consists of consolidated white ash, overlies a horizon which yielded a Tshangulan ('Magosian') aggregate of the final Middle Stone Age, and is dated to the eighth millennium BC. The industry represented in the ash layer, the Pomongwan, is dominated by large circular scrapers which account for over nine-tenths of the retouched implements from this level, most of the remainder being made up of related scraper forms. Backed microliths, which occur in both the underlying and the overlying layers, are completely absent. Associated with the scrapers are bone points, needles and ostrich-eggshell beads comparable to those found with the succeeding Matopan microlithic aggregates. With the exception of the nearby Tshangula Cave, no other Zimbabwe sites have yielded Pomongwan material although, as has been shown, contemporary scraper-dominated industries have a wide distribution south of the Limpopo. Despite this convincing correlation, the possibility that the Pomongwan may represent a specialized activity-variant is suggested by its exclusive occurrence in ash deposits – at Pomongwe the scrapers were concentrated around traces of a large central fire – and its idiosyncratic typology. (In this context it is relevant to note that a strikingly differential distribution of the various artifact types was observed in the Tshangula levels at Pomongwe, in parts of which were concentrations of scrapers to the virtual exclusion of other types.)

Overlying the Pomongwan at both Tshangula and Pomongwe is a deposit containing a microlithic mode 5 aggregate. This represents the industry, originally known as 'Wilton', to which the local term Matopan is now applied so as not to presuppose a long-distance correlation with what was, until recently, an inadequately described industry in the eastern Cape. The Matopan (fig 6.14.7–12) appears to have lasted from the sixth millennium BC until after the arrival of Iron Age peoples in the area during the first millennium AD. Unfortunately, no detailed analysis of this aggregate has yet appeared, and so we are able neither to evaluate the degree to which it developed through this 6000-year period, nor to compare it effectively with contemporary industries elsewhere. At Amadzimba Cave in the Matopo Hills, this aggregate is dominated by small convex scrapers; backed microliths are markedly less frequent and among them the backed blades easily outnumber the crescents. Amadzimba also yielded a remarkable and varied collection of bone tools including points (perhaps for arrows), bodkins, link-shafts and eyed needles. Ostrich-eggshell beads were accompanied by a few tubular bone examples (C. K. Cooke and Robinson 1954). In the Matopo Hills, at sites such as Bambata and Madiliyangwa, characteristic Early Iron Age potsherds are associated with the upper levels of the Matopan, indicating that the microlithic industries survived until long after the beginning of the Christian era. At these and other sites there are also found sherds of Bambata ware. The affinities of this material, which has so far only been found in Later Stone Age contexts, remain problematical but will be discussed further in chapter 11.

Only isolated occurrences of mode 5 industries have so far been reported from other areas of Zimbabwe and, while it is clear that several regional variant industries are present, no overall sequence can yet be discerned. In the north-west, the aggregate from Bumbusi rock-shelter near Wankie is said to share many features with the 'Zambian Wilton' of the Victoria Falls region. Material excavated from the post-Middle Stone Age layers of Pfupi and other rock-shelters near Marandellas includes bored stones, ground axes, and a variety of large scraper types, including concave forms which do not generally occur in the Matopan but are rightly considered to be reminiscent of the 'Nachikufan' industries from further north (Robinson 1952). Similar aggregates seem to be widespread in Mashonaland, but the available typological descriptions are not sufficiently detailed for us to ascertain whether they bear a special resemblance to any particular 'Nachikufan' phase (fig. 6.15.4–6). This doubt, together with the absence of any absolute dates for the Pfupian sites, prevents a discussion as to whether these industries represent an earlier establishment of mode 5 technology than was the case in Matabeleland.

Two sites in the Limpopo valley in the extreme south of Zimbabwe have yielded late occurrences of scraper-dominated Later Stone Age industries, dated to within the last one thousand years, in which microliths are either very scarce or absent. This material has been designated the Dombozanga Industry and is clearly related to contemporary occurrences in the Transvaal, which will be discussed below. It has not been found elsewhere in Zimbabwe (C. K. Cooke and Simons 1969, Robinson 1964).

It is not easy to correlate the Zimbabwe Later Stone Age sequence, or that from more southerly regions of South Africa, with that which is indicated in the Transvaal. A rock-shelter at Heuningneskrans in the Lydenburg district contains, below three strata of 'Smithfield' material, an 'early Late Stone Age' aggregate in association with a radiocarbon date in the twenty-third millennium BC. When further details of this material have been published, it may be expected to throw further light on the antecedents of the Transvaal Later Stone Age which at present remain poorly known. An 'early Smithfield' occurrence from an open site at Zevenfontein, north of Johannesburg, appears to bear a marked resemblance to the 'middle Smithfield' from nearby Uitkomst and other cave and rock-shelter sites (fig. 6.15.7). At Uitkomst a radiocarbon date in the eighth millennium BC is believed to be associated with this phase of the occupation. The 'Smithfield' occupation of Heuningneskrans dates between the late twelfth and the late sixth millennia, while at

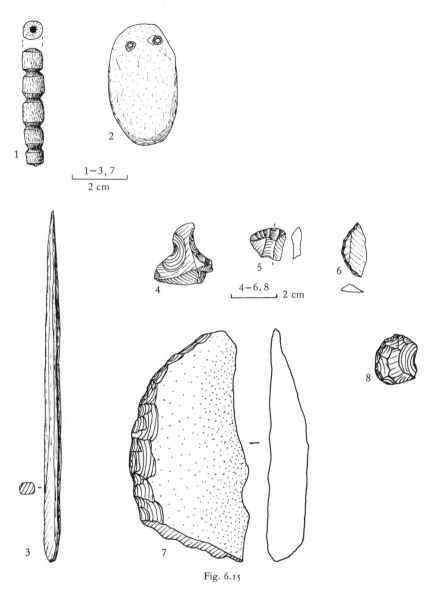

Fig. 6.15

1–3 Bone heads in process of manufacture, shell pendant and bone point: from Amadzimba
4–6 Artifacts from Pfupi
7 'Middle Smithfield' scraper from Uitkomst
8 'Later Smithfield' scraper from Olieboompoort

(Nos. 1–3 after Cooke and Robinson (1954), 4–6 after Robinson (1952) and 7–8 after Mason (1962).)

Bushman rock-shelter a Later Stone Age industry described as 'poor and consisting largely of trimmed quartz chips' is securely dated to the eleventh millennium BC (Beaumont and Vogel 1972, Louw *et al.* 1969, Mason 1962: 303–10).

There follows a gap in the known and dated Transvaal sequence until the appearance of 'later Smithfield' industries (fig. 6.15.8) which are marked by a proliferation of cylindrical wooden and bone arrow-points and which are dated to the ninth to eleventh centuries AD, being thus contemporary with Iron Age settlement in this region. A similar macrolithic aggregate from Pietkloof is associated with pottery. Whether the last six millennia in the Transvaal were marked by microlithic industries, as was the case in the middle Orange area, is not known, but it is remarkable that very few microlithic aggregates have so far been reported from the province. The indications are that most, if not all, of these aggregates are of late date. For example, 'Wilton'-like material from Northcliff, Johannesburg, includes artifacts made of imported glass; while microliths from a rock-shelter at North Brabant in the Waterberg of the north-western Transvaal are associated with pottery compared with that from nearby Bambandyanalo (Mason 1951, Schoonraad and Beaumont 1968). These occurrences are presumably to be correlated with those already discussed from the Zimbabwe side of the Limpopo. It is thus possible that future research in the Transvaal will demonstrate some degree of continuity of the macrolithic 'Smithfield' tradition from the eighth millennium BC until after the coming of the first Iron Age immigrants.

As noted above, any attempt at an overall synthesis of the southern African Later Stone Age industries must be provisional and tentative, as well as being restricted to general trends in the major regions. Considerable difficulty is experienced in recognizing or defining the first appearance of these industries in the archaeological record. Aggregates of small blades which, although they include backed microliths, are not predominantly of mode 5 type, have a far greater antiquity in this area than has been attested in any other part of sub-Saharan Africa. However, no satisfactory demonstration has yet been made of continuity between these early blade aggregates and the classic mode 5 'Wilton' industries of the last seven millennia BC. In fact, in many areas, a markedly contrasting industry appears to precede the 'Wilton' and effectively to separate it from the earlier blade industries. These intervening industries are dominated by large flake scrapers, and backed microliths are either completely absent or very poorly represented. They have been collectively attributed to an 'Oakhurst Industrial Complex' by Sampson (1974).[1] In southern Africa the widespread industries of the 'Oakhurst Complex' are dated from the twelfth to the eighth millennia BC. They were replaced in many areas by the microlithic Wilton Complex, the earliest dates for which fall in the seventh millennium. River valleys and coastal areas seem to have become increasingly preferred as foci of settlement at this time; and fish seems to have formed the basis of the diet in many areas. These changes may confidently be linked with the eustatic rise in sea level which took place at this time, flooding the extensive plains beyond the present south coast on which earlier populations had hunted herds of large gregarious antelope. With the inundation of this hunting territory, the Wilton people turned their attention to other sources of food, notably the smaller more solitary creatures which favoured a more densely wooded habitat. In the central plateau regions, the appearance of the Wilton Complex seems to have been considerably later than it was in the south; and broadly contemporary with the corresponding event in the upper Zambezi valley: in the Transvaal it is possible that the technological tradition of the 'Oakhurst Complex' continued throughout the time-span covered by the Wilton Complex in the Cape. In Lesotho and adjacent regions of the Drakensberg, microlithic industries of 'Wilton' affinities seem to have continued until the annihilation of the last stone-tool-using societies only a century ago. In most other areas south of the Transvaal the Wilton Complex was in turn again replaced by a scraper-dominated, non-microlithic series of industries. These appeared in the coastal areas of the south-western Cape as early as the late first millennium BC, but spread slowly not reaching the middle Orange area until the present millennium. Pottery, previously unknown in southern Africa, is found in many of these aggregates from around the beginning of the Christian era. The significance of these late industries is discussed in greater detail in chapter 11.

[1] The term 'Oakhurst Complex' has not met with the acceptance of all archaeologists working in southern Africa (e.g. Klein 1974). The term 'early Late Stone Age' proposed by Beaumont and Vogel (1972) subsumes Sampson's 'Oakhurst Complex' with a number of pre-'Wilton' blade occurrences, and has not been adequately defined.

THE INDUSTRIAL SUCCESSIONS

Having surveyed the very incomplete evidence for regional sequences in the Later Stone Age of sub-Saharan Africa, it is now necessary to re-examine these sequences in an attempt to provide a tentative outline of industrial development in the sub-continent as a whole. The great geographical and temporal lacunae in our knowledge, taken with the inadequacies of much of the available data, restrict such an attempt to the construction of working hypotheses only.

The earliest true microlithic mode 5 industry so far known in the sub-continent occurs in the highlands of eastern and central Africa, in a broad belt stretching from Lake Victoria and southern Kenya, through Tanzania and northern Zambia to the Zambezi. These industries are dominated by small pointed backed bladelets acompanied by true crescents and varied scraper forms; bored stones are found in the south of the area but the presence of ground stone axes, while probable, is not yet certain. In Zambia, this industry has been referred to as 'Nachikufan I'; no general term has been applied to the clearly closely related aggregates from East African sites, such as those from Munyama and Kisese. These industries were widespread by the fifteenth millennium BC. Their typological antecedents may be traced back at least a further seven millennia at sites such as Kalemba rock-shelter in eastern Zambia, where the emergence of mode 5 technology from a mode 3 predecessor is clearly illustrated. There is no reason to attribute this development to any other process than indigenous technological innovation. Indeed, granted the primogeniture of these mode 5 industries, it is difficult to see how any other origin could be postulated. There is now an increasing body of evidence which links the development of these mode 5 industries with the onset of warmer, moister conditions and the denser vegetation cover which significantly reduced the availability of the herds of zebra and large gregarious antelope which had formed a large part of the hunters' prey in earlier times.

Meanwhile other mode 3 industries were being continued, probably by distinct communities, virtually unmodified by these developments. That diverse industrial traditions could coexist in relatively close proximity is demonstrated by the discoveries, at Leopard's Hill Cave and Twin Rivers Kopje (J. D. Clark 1971; see also ch. 4 of this volume) situated within 80 km of each other on the Lusaka plateau, of backed bladelet and mode 3 aggregates respectively, both dated to around the twenty-first millennium BC. Significantly, Twin Rivers is located on the edge of the open Kafue Flats, while Leopard's Hill is in more densely wooded hill country.

Regional differentiation in mode 3 industries led to the development in some areas of techniques of blade-production and backing; these later gave rise to the manufacture of microliths. The start of these processes may be traced far back in the archaeological record of the Middle Stone Age; by the thirty-fifth millennium BC the mode 3 industry at Kalemba was clearly distinguished from its contemporaries in most other parts of the central African plateau by its emphasis on the production of flake-blades. The type of demographic situation here postulated would explain the periodic intrusions of aggregates with high blade-frequencies observed in the mode 3 Bambata successions at Zombepata and Redcliff in Mashonaland, at a time between 35 000 and 40 000 BC (C. K. Cooke 1971); a comparable situation in the Cape Province of South Africa is best illustrated at Klasies River Mouth (Sampson 1972, pp. 112–13). It is interesting to note that a bored stone was apparently recovered from one of the blade-rich horizons at Zombepata.

Parallel developments in the Middle Stone Age of South Africa have been discussed above in chapter 4. Development of blade-production techniques took place earlier and with greater refinement there than in the central African region described above; by 40 000 BC blade industries were established in the Drakensberg area and on the south coast. The Tshangula Industry of Zimbabwe, established by the twenty-fourth millennium BC, occupies a comparable position. These blade industries, however, do not seem to have proved directly ancestral to fully mode 5 Later Stone Age industries. At some sites they were displaced by classic mode 3 aggregates; at others, aggregates attributed to the 'Oakhurst Complex' intervened between them and the microlithic 'Wilton'; elsewhere there are long hiatuses in the occupation sequences, across which no industrial continuity can be demonstrated.

The industries of the 'Oakhurst Complex', found from the Matopo Hills of Zimbabwe southwards to the south Cape coast and westwards to Namibia, are as yet imperfectly understood. They contain numerous large flake scrapers, to the virtual exclusion of other tool types, and are dated to between the twelfth and the eighth millennia BC. The status of the possibly ancestral 'Robberg Industry' of the south Cape coast remains problematical (Klein 1974).

Industries broadly comparable with those of the 'Oakhurst Complex', but at least twelve millennia older, are known from further north. These also occupy a stratigraphical position preceding the first local microlithic industry; and appear to antedate or accompany, rather than to postdate, the development of blade-production techniques within the local Middle Stone Age milieu. In central and eastern Zambia there was a typological progression from the scraper-dominated aggregates of that region to the microlithic 'Nachikufan I'; south of the Zambezi no such industrial continuity is yet securely demonstrated between industries of the 'Oakhurst Complex' and their microlithic successors. These factors, considered in conjunction with the unspecialized nature of the relevant technology, indicate that it would be unwise in the present state of our knowledge to attempt to derive the 'Oakhurst Complex' from these northern counterparts.

Throughout the area of its distribution, the 'Oakhurst Complex' was replaced by microlithic mode 5 industries attributed to the Wilton Industrial Complex.[1] Here again, the beginning of mode 5 technology may be linked with a reduction in the availability of hunting grounds on the open plains, caused this time by a eustatic rise in sea level. These microlithic industries show parallel developmental stages over a considerable area, but their ancestry remains uncertain. Their contrast with earlier industries is marked, and no continuity can be demonstrated with the blade industries of the evolved Middle Stone Age. North of the Zambezi, microlithic industries were present for more than seven millennia prior to the start of the Wilton Complex in South Africa; however, there is no sign of a genetic link between them either in Zimbabwe (where mode 5 industries appear to have been introduced, perhaps from the north, at about the same time as the corresponding event in the Cape) or in the Transvaal (where an industrial tradition allied to the 'Oakhurst Complex' may have continued for several millennia after its displacement elsewhere, and where microlithic aggregates are not recorded until very recent times). Future research may disclose an early southwards spread of microlithic technology into the currently unexplored areas of Mozambique or southern Angola/ Namibia, but for the present the Wilton Complex is probably best regarded as an autochthonous South African development. In parts of South Africa and Lesotho the Wilton Complex appears to have

---

[1] The term 'Wilton' has in the past been applied somewhat injudiciously to microlithic aggregates in many parts of sub-Saharan Africa. Now that the sequence from the type-site has been fully described it will be appropriate to restrict the use of the term to aggregates from the Cape Province and neighbouring areas which have a close and demonstrable affinity to those from Wilton itself: otherwise the term will become once again a meaningless abstraction.

continued into the second millennium AD; elsewhere it was superseded by a series of non-microlithic scraper industries which will be discussed in chapter 11.

In Zimbabwe and Zambia, as in other parts of eastern Africa, microlithic industries continued until the close of the Stone Age. They were descended from an initial mode 5 industry of 'Nachikufan I' type but show increasing inter-regional differentiation from about the ninth millennium BC onwards; the crescents and geometric microliths, which became dominant in these industries in place of the pointed backed bladelets of 'Nachikufan I', are here far more numerous than in the broadly contemporary 'Wilton' aggregates of South Africa. Ground stone axes are clearly evidenced in northern and central Zambia from at least the eighth millennium. Such artifacts are extremely rare in southern Africa, East Africa and the Congo basin at this time; their appearance in Zambia was very likely an independent development. Mode 5 industries do not appear to have spread into the upper Zambezi area until the last two millennia BC, when they replaced a local late continuance of essentially mode 3 technology. Here, as in the Cape interior thirstlands, warmer, moister conditions at this time are attested in the climatological record.

In the more northerly parts of eastern Africa, several regional mode 3 industries developed techniques of blade production. It is probable that the development of these evolved Middle Stone Age industries, including those known in the literature as 'Magosian', was regionally differentiated and proceeded at different times and paces in the various areas. At the same time, other mode 3 industries continued their traditional technologies without these modifications. Variation in raw materials doubtless influenced the nature and extent of these techno-logical developments in the various aggregates.

Parts of eastern Africa were the scene of true mode 4 industries based on fine punch-struck obsidian blades, including many backed forms but lacking true microliths. These industries have been found in northern Somalia and in eleventh-millennium-BC contexts in the Gregory Rift of Kenya. Both to some extent probably owe their striking typology to the raw material employed. Comparable industries were probably of widespread occurrence in Ethiopia at broadly the same time-period. Nowhere in this region is there convincing evidence for their develop-ment from the preceding evolved mode 3 industries. Their origin, whether intrusive (and, if so, whence) or authochthonous, must for the present remain an open question pending further research.

Later developments in eastern Africa involve the spread of microlithic mode 5 technology in which numerous regional variations may be recognized. A developed microlithic technology was practised in the Lake Victoria area and in southern Kenya from the thirteenth millennium BC, and probably as early as the sixteenth. Inception of this technology in the more northerly parts of eastern Africa was almost certainly of later date, and may have been at least partly inspired from the south. In the Nile Valley of Nubia, mode 5 industries such as the Silsilian extend back to about the fourteenth millennium BC, but their contribution to the Later Stone Age development of Ethiopia and the Horn remains unknown.

Semi-permanent settlements developed beside Lakes Rudolf and Edward and on the banks of the White Nile from about the seventh millennium BC. Their economy was based on the exploitation of the rich fishing and fowling environments which these areas afforded. The lithic industries practised at these settlements were diverse and apparently rooted in the respective local traditions; other aspects of the material culture, however, notably the bone harpoon-heads and the pottery, form a typological link between these eastern African sites and a number of broadly contemporary settlements spread over an enormous area of the Sahara and sahel, as far north as Ahaggar and westwards to Mali.[1] These are seen as providing the setting for the spread of incipient food production, and are discussed further in chapter 11.

While a certain degree of continuity may be discerned in the Later Stone Age successions of the southern and eastern half of Africa, that of the western Congo basin stands in sharp contrast. However, the general model for the gradual emergence of the Later Stone Age industries from their predominantly mode 3 Middle Stone Age predecessors holds good for the Congo basin also; the cultural differentiation of this area can be traced back to the establishment of the Lupemban Middle Stone Age industry and probably to the area's initial settlement. In both the Dundo area of northern Angola and the environs of the Stanley Pool on the Congo River, the typology of the Later Stone Age Tshitolian industries shows clear continuity from that of their Lupemban predecessors. The gradual process of diminution of general artifact size, the increase in emphasis on blade production and the proliferation of microliths, notably *petits tranchets*, took place mainly between the twelfth and the eighth millennia BC. It appears to have proceeded

---

[1] Sutton (1974) has referred this material to an 'aquatic civilization' and has tentatively suggested that it may be the work of people speaking Nilo-Saharan languages.

somewhat earlier and more rapidly in the Dundo area than around the Stanley Pool. We are here concerned with the wider correlations of these sequences; and these are not easy to ascertain because of the broad expanse of archaeologically unexplored (and perhaps prehistorically sparsely inhabited) territory which surrounds the investigated areas. In the absence of any indications for contact or interaction in these intervening areas between the makers of the Tshitolian industries and those of the eastern microlithic industries which predated them, it may be tentatively assumed that the development of the former owed no significant debt to the broadly contemporary parallel developments elsewhere on the sub-continent.

In West Africa, in contrast to the other regions of the sub-continent, there are few indications for the local origins of the Later Stone Age industries. The evolution of the local mode 3 Middle Stone Age technology does not seem to have led in the direction of blade production; and in several areas such as Sierra Leone and parts of Nigeria the mode 3 technology may have continued at least until the third millennium BC. To the north of the forest, microlithic industries – possibly derived from the southern Sahara – seem to have been general, but the chronology of their appearance remains unknown. The makers of microlithic industries had penetrated parts of the Nigerian forest by the tenth millennium BC. The extent to which these possibly northern-derived West African microlithic industries share an ultimate common ancestry with their counterparts far to the east, in Ethiopia and the Nile Valley, remains unknown.

It may be concluded that most of the regional Later Stone Age industries are best regarded as indigenous developments from their Middle Stone Age predecessors. Such developments took place at different times in the various regions following broadly parallel directions, but reflecting the diversity of their ancestral industries. At least four largely independent inventions or developments of mode 5 technology may be discerned in sub-Saharan Africa. The earliest of these took place in southern Africa, where the development of small-blade aggregates took place within the milieu of the local Middle Stone Age between about 40 000 and 15 000 BC. Although backed forms, including large crescents, were present in some of these southern aggregates, there is no indication that this branch ever evolved to produce fully microlithic mode 5 industries. Parallel development further north on the plateau of eastern and central Africa proceeded more slowly but by the sixteenth millennium BC had led to the appearance of true microlithic industries of 'Nachikufan I' type. These are presumed to have been generally ancestral to subsequent central African microlithic traditions; whether it is also from them that the Wilton Complex of South Africa is to be derived must for the present remain uncertain. A comparable development of the technology of microlith production may be discerned within the later mode 3 industries in northern parts of East Africa and in the Horn. The age of these is unknown; and their influence on the local development of the subsequent microlithic industries cannot yet be ascertained. Largely independent parallel development in the western Congo basin gave rise to the Tshitolian industries between the twelfth and the eighth millennia BC. The appearance of mode 5 technology in West Africa is attested from the tenth millennium BC.

This enquiry has highlighted the broadly parallel development of indigenous technologies at different times, which sometimes resulted in the contemporaneous occurrence of industries at markedly contrasting stages of development within a single region. Processes of industrial or technical development did not occur without contact, inspiration and mutual influence from adjacent cultures; on the other hand, the idiosyncracies and independence of many of the local successions are such that we can safely preclude the possibility of a single common ancestor for all the microlithic industries of sub-Saharan Africa. Furthermore, we may state with some confidence that migration, or even substantial population movement, on other than a regional scale, probably played a comparatively minor part in the dissemination of the microlithic technology.

## PHYSICAL ANTHROPOLOGY

In most areas where human skeletal remains have been preserved in Later Stone Age contexts, there are indications of careful and stan-dardized burial customs (limitations of space unfortunately preclude their description here). In addition to their intrinsic interest and the tentative inferences concerning religious beliefs which may be drawn from them, the burial customs frequently show marked regional differentiation, while within individual regions prolonged continuity is apparent. Our primary concern here is briefly to summarize the physical anthropology of the Later Stone Age human remains.

All human skeletal remains associated with Later Stone Age industries in sub-Saharan Africa are attributed to *Homo sapiens sapiens*. The modern population of the sub-continent is physically heterogeneous, comprising a number of not very clearly differentiated racial types. A similar heterogeneity is apparent in the prehistoric populations and it is clearly of considerable interest to attempt to trace the ancestry of the recognized modern races in the palaeo-anthropological record. Since such an attempt must be based almost exclusively on osteological evidence and since statistically there is considerable overlap in the variability of the skeletal characteristics of the various modern groups, it is clear that conclusions based on single or incomplete individuals must be regarded as extremely tentative. These considerations render several of the earlier attributions of Later Stone Age human remains highly dubious; and the following survey is restricted to more general attributions and conclusions.

Three major prehistoric groups may be recognized: a Khoisian group apparently ancestral to the physical stock of the San and Khoikhoi populations of southern Africa, a group showing negroid physical characteristics, and a third group which may be related to the caucasoid population of north-eastern Africa. Descendents of these three groups form the major part of the population of sub-Saharan Africa today. Anthropologists are aware that among the modern population the three groups are not always clearly defined: there are some indications that the earlier populations may have been even less clearly differentiated than are the more recent ones. Unfortunately, there are at present no adequately described finds of human skeletal material definitely attributed to the evolved mode 3 industries. It is therefore impracticable to attempt a correlation between physical and industrial evolution prior to the Later Stone Age. The remains discussed below frequently come from disparate time-depths; and in very few areas are series of stratified finds available for the formulation of a detailed sequence.

A considerable degree of confusion has arisen from the human skeletal remains recovered from East African Later Stone Age sites, particularly those said to display characteristics, such as dolichocephaly and prominent chins and nasal bones, which were at one time regarded as representing an essentially non-African physical type (Cole 1963, L. S. B. Leakey 1935). Skulls showing these features were recovered from the 'Upper Kenya Capsian C' horizon at Gamble's Cave as well as from later 'neolithic' contexts. At any rate during the later phases of the local Later Stone Age contrasting brachycephalic folk were apparently also present in the region. Skeletons of the latter group are said to have much in common with the generalized Khoisan type known

470

to have been widespread in central and southern Africa at this time. The early dolichocephalic population could be interpreted as indicating the early establishment in eastern Africa of the general caucasoid physical stock which is still widespread in northern Kenya, Somalia and parts of Ethiopia. These modern populations are not invariably fully distinguishable from their negroid neighbours – a situation reflected in the archaeological record by certain negroid features which have been noted in some East African Later Stone Age remains (Rightmire 1975). Widely dispersed finds from Later Stone Age sites in central and southern Africa have been stated to show similar dolichocephalic characteristics; and it is perhaps also possible that the East African remains could be regarded as representing something less distinctive than a separate race within the generally heterogeneous, predominantly Khoisan, population of eastern and southern Africa.

From Later Stone Age sites in central and southern Africa many predominantly Khoisan skeletal remains have been recovered (Gabel 1966, Wells 1957); unfortunately in the majority of cases the archaeological contexts are inadequately documented or the skeletal material itself has been incompletely studied (for a summary of the South African material see Sampson (1972)). A major exception is the group of thirty-three skeletons from Gwisho Hotsprings in southern Zambia. In all respects the Gwisho skeletons fall within the known range of anatomical variation for prehistoric Khoisan populations (Brothwell 1971, Gabel 1965). There was considerable sexual dimorphism, particularly in stature; and both sexes were significantly larger than their recent San counterparts. Those skulls sufficiently well preserved for measurement showed a tendency towards dolichocephaly, but this was not so extreme as in the East African individuals described above. Other Later Stone Age human skeletal material from central Africa is fragmentary or not well dated: where conclusions can be drawn as to the physical affinities of the individuals concerned, these have pointed to connections with large Khoisan physical types. A comparable picture is indicated for southern Africa, but very few adequate skeletal descriptions are available, and these mainly relate to comparatively recent periods.

In West Africa and the sudanic belt, conditions for the preservation of skeletal material are generally poor. What evidence we have suggests that the Later Stone Age population here was significantly different from that of eastern and southern Africa, and that it should be regarded as generally ancestral to the present negroid population. Human remains described as 'negroid' have been recovered in the sudanic belt at Asselar in Mali (dated to the fifth millennium BC) and at Temaya Mellet in Niger, while the single reconstructible skull from Early Khartoum, also stated to be negroid type, suggests a considerably wider distribution. The distribution of this type has recently been extended southwards into the Nigerian forest, as well as backwards in time to near the beginning of the West African Later Stone Age, by the discovery of a human skeleton in the basal horizon of the Iwo Eleru rock-shelter, dated to the tenth millennium BC (Brothwell and Shaw 1971). This specimen has been described as physically ancestral to the West African negroid type, while retaining certain earlier features.

No human remains have been recovered from the territory of the Lupemban and Tshitolian industries of the western Congo basin, so the physical type responsible for these industries remains unknown; it is often assumed that the Later Stone Age population of this area may have been more akin to the negroids of West Africa than to the Khoisan peoples of the east and south. Perhaps in due course the two groups will be seen as less sharply differentiated than was formerly believed. The modern pygmies have been regarded as related to both the negroid and the Khoisan groups, while the fragmentary prehistoric human remains from Ishango are similarly related, though apparently not pygmoid.

The Later Stone Age distributions of the three physical types thus appear to be broadly distinct. The Khoisan population was dominant in southern and eastern Africa; particularly in the latter region there may have been some overlap with a dolichocephalic, possibly caucasoid, type. In West Africa and, perhaps, in the Zaïre forests the contemporary population appears to have been of a type more directly ancestral to the present negroids. The finds at present available for study are insufficient to indicate whether or not there were significant changes in these distributions during the period here under study.

ECONOMIC SUMMARY

There is a broad similarity in the material culture of the Later Stone Age folk throughout the sub-continent. It is therefore pertinent to attempt an overall synthesis of the archaeological and other evidence concerning the economies and general ways of life to which the material culture relates. Much of the detailed evidence on which this discussion is based has been noted above: it is widely scattered through time and space, and a synthesis of the type here attempted necessarily involves the bringing together of diverse elements to produce a composite picture which may not represent in detail the prevailing conditions at individual sites.

Thin surface scatters of artifacts, which are all that remains of many open-air settlement sites which lacked a natural focus such as a spring, cave or rock-shelter, indicate that such settlements were usually transitory. As in earlier times, many doubtless represent encampments established for a single task such as butchering a kill. It is probable that many rock-shelters and other sites which show signs of long occupation were repeatedly inhabited for short periods, rather than used for prolonged periods of continuous settlement. Sites which provided some form of natural shelter were clearly favoured. Elsewhere, the only artificial shelters which are indicated are simple semicircular wind-breaks of branches, perhaps strengthened around the base with settings of stones; comparable structures are known from far earlier times also. Evidence is beginning to accumulate for the seasonal habitation and exploitation of individual sites and environments, a factor which would frequently be mirrored in the activities conducted and, consequently, in the typology of the artifacts deposited.

The mean sizes of these Later Stone Age settlements are considerably smaller than those of the later food-producing societies, and are held to indicate site populations of some eight to twenty-five persons. Calculations based on rock-painting representations have given comparable results (J. D. Clark 1972, Maggs 1967). These population figures are within the size-range of bands of recent hunter–gatherer societies in sub-Saharan Africa. Investigations conducted throughout the postulated territorial range of a prehistoric group may be expected eventually to provide a somewhat clearer understanding of prehistoric patterns of exploitation than can be obtained by the study of individual sites: such research, pioneered elsewhere, has but recently been applied to the Later Stone Age of sub-Saharan Africa (Carter 1970, Parkington 1972).

The material culture of the various Later Stone Age societies has been described and discussed in detail above, and little recapitulation is necessary. The primary information which can be derived from artifact studies is technological; we have remarkably little reliable data on the actual purposes to which many Later Stone Age artifact types were put, although logical inferences can often be made, and these may sometimes be supported by ethnographic observations. It is clear that many types of microlith were hafted, and study of hafting methods may throw considerable light on the uses to which the tools were put. Observation of edge damage and utilization patterns on artifacts provides another line of information (D. W. Phillipson 1976, L. Phillipson and D. W. Phillipson 1970). It is clear from such research, from ethnographic observations and from certain rock paintings that some microliths were used as arrow-points and barbs; various bow types are depicted in the paintings and a fragment of a wooden bow was recovered from a third millennium BC context at Gwisho Hotsprings in southern Zambia. Osteological evidence confirms that of rock paintings in demonstrating that even the largest mammals were on occasion successfully killed. Poison was doubtless applied to the arrows, as is done by most recent hunting societies; pods of one plant (*Swartzia*) used for the production of such a poison were preserved in the Gwisho deposits (Fagan and van Noten 1971). Other stone-tool types were clearly designed for cutting or scraping purposes such as skinning and butchering, for working skin, and for shaping objects of wood or bone. Other subsistence activities (such as fishing) have less often left a distinguisable imprint on the stone-tool aggregates. Microliths used as barbs for fish-spears are not readily differentiated from those used for arrows. Perishable materials used for nets and traps have not survived in the archaeological record. It is only when specialized bone artifacts, such as barbed harpoon-heads, were developed that fishing equipment is reflected in the archaeological aggregates with the prominence which it must frequently have held. The gathering of vegetable foods would require little specialist equipment, although digging-sticks which might have been used for excavating roots and tubers (as well as for digging water-pits) have occasionally been preserved. Some of the bored stones which are widely distributed on Later Stone Age sites were almost certainly used as weights for digging-sticks – a practice which is not infrequently depicted in rock paintings as well as being recorded ethnographically both in southern Africa and in Ethiopia. The scarcity of imperishable specialized equipment for food-gathering and the infrequent preservation of traces of actual vegetable foods in the archaeological record have probably resulted in a tendency to underestimate the importance of such foods in the Later Stone Age diet.

After lithic tools and the by-products of their manufacture, the artifacts most frequently encountered on Later Stone Age sites are items of personal adornment. Bone and shell beads and pendants have a wide distribution and in some areas, notably eastern Zambia, changing fashion led to an evolution of their styles which was considerably more rapid than the contemporary changes in stone tool typology. Beads and pendants were not only worn on the body and in the hair but they were also sewn onto skins and other clothing; such is the practice of people who make similar artifacts today and it is also frequently represented in the rock paintings, particularly those of southern Africa. The occurrence of ochre and other colouring matter is noted in many areas from the earliest phases of the Later Stone Age, and has sometimes been recorded in even earlier contexts. This material could have been used for the decoration of clothing or for direct adornment of the body; it does not necessarily indicate such a very high antiquity for the practice of rock painting in all areas.

## ROCK ART

Most regions of sub-Saharan Africa where suitably protected rock surfaces occur have produced evidence for rock paintings and, to a lesser extent, engravings. Their distribution is shown in fig. 6.16. Both techniques were used for the execution of naturalistic and schematic representations: the majority of the latter appear to be of relatively recent date. Local stylistic sequences in the rock art have been recognized in many areas, but evidence for the absolute date of the art or for its correlation with the practitioners of particular prehistoric industries is extremely rare. It is clear, however, that the art is, as far as sub-Saharan Africa is concerned, essentially a local development, and that links once claimed between it and superficially similar representations in the western Mediterranean area, or with other alien cultures, cannot be regarded as securely demonstrated. Only in southern Africa can the execution of rock art be shown to predate the last few millennia. The 'Apollo 11 cave' in Namibia has yielded examples of painting securely stratified in 'Oakhurst Complex' and earlier horizons; while on the south Cape coast comparable material occurs in association with Wilton Complex deposits, dated between the sixth and the fourth millennia BC at Matjes River and Klasies River Mouth. It seems probable, however, that the great majority of the surviving rock paintings in all areas probably belong to relatively recent periods; and the same may well prove to be true in the case of the engravings also (Fosbrooke et al. 1950, Summers 1959, Willcox 1963).

Despite elaborate hypotheses which are sometimes attempted regarding the mystic or religious significance of the rock art, it seems

Fig. 6.16 Distribution of rock paintings in sub-Saharan Africa. (After J. D. Clark 1967.)

probable that much of the earlier naturalistic representations were primarily decorative in intent. Human beings are the most frequently occurring subject matter in most areas, followed by animals. Illustrations of inanimate objects are relatively rare. The high artistic quality of much of the surviving art, particularly that of southern Africa, places it among the finest ever produced in these media. The peak of achievement was probably reached in the shaded polychrome paintings of Natal and Lesotho which were executed by the final Later Stone Age folk around the middle of the present millennium (plate 6.1). As has been shown, the subject matter of the rock art throws considerable light on many aspects of the life and economy of the sub-Saharan African Later Stone Age; but its greatest contribution is to the study of the early food-producing societies, as will be discussed in chapter 11.

CONCLUSION

Such, in outline, is the present state of our knowledge of the Later Stone Age societies of sub-Saharan Africa. The survey has indicated the gradual evolution of the Later Stone Age industries from their local predecessors, there being clear evidence that, in at least some parts of the sub-continent, this was an essentially autochthonous development which was largely independent of external stimulus. In this respect, as previously, sub-Saharan Africa followed the homotaxial process of the development of stone implement technology which has been demonstrated to apply to most major regions of the world. An unusual feature of the sub-Saharan African succession is that the microlithic Later Stone Age industries frequently developed directly from a Middle Stone Age predecessor, whose technology was based on the production of flakes from prepared cores, without the intervening invention or adoption of punch-struck blade industries of Upper Palaeolithic mode 4 type. This distinction from the European and west Asian sequences has sometimes given rise to the view that sub-Saharan Africa at this time was a cultural backwater, isolated from the mainstream of human development. However, as we have seen, parts of the sub-continent saw the first inception of a stone-working technology basically identical to that prevailing in Europe during Mesolithic times. In fact, this mode 5 technology was locally developed in central Africa at a date significantly earlier than that of the introduction of its counterpart into Europe. Both the conservatism of the earlier industries and their success in developing this new technology are presumably indications of their functional suitability to the economic needs of their time, and thus of their makers' fitting adaptations to their environment.

# CHAPTER 7

# THE RISE OF CIVILIZATION IN EGYPT

## ORIENTATION

Through Pharaonic Egypt, Africa lays claim to being the cradle of one of the earliest and most spectacular civilizations of antiquity. The aim of this chapter is to trace the development of this civilization from the introduction of a south-west Asian-style subsistence economy into the Nile Valley to its florescence at the beginning of the Old Kingdom, conventionally dated about 2700 BC. Egyptologists conventionally divide this span into a Predynastic Period, prior to the traditional First Dynasty of the Egyptian chronicler Manetho, and a subsequent Early Dynastic Period, which corresponds with Manetho's first two dynasties. This division has been justified by assuming that the beginning of the First Dynasty corresponded with the political unification of Egypt and marked a critical break in Egyptian history. While it is evident that political unification played a major long-term role in shaping the cultural patterns of ancient Egypt, this achievement was part of a continuum of social and cultural change that was well advanced in late Predynastic times and reached its culmination in the Old Kingdom. Because of this, it is profitable to view the entire formative period of Egyptian civilization as a single unit.

Although the Egyptian script was developed during the Early Dynastic Period, written sources for this period are extremely limited and present numerous epigraphic difficulties. Even the succession of kings and the identifications of the royal Horus-names appearing on the monuments of this period with the *nebty-* or *insibya*-names given in the later king-lists are far from certain in many cases (see appendix, p. 547).[1] For both the Predynastic and Early Dynastic periods the archaeological evidence tends to be largely restricted to cemeteries in Upper (southern) Egypt, while in the north the Predynastic Period is mainly represented by habitation sites that have been found in marginal locations and are often poorly reported. Few stratified sites have been carefully excavated and there is a dearth of reliable palaeobotanical or palaeozoological data.

[1] For an outline of what is known about the dynastic history of the first two dynasties, see Edwards (1971, pp. 1–35).

These shortcomings of the archaeological data have recently been discussed in detail by a number of scholars, so that there is no need to repeat their strictures here (see Arkell and Ucko 1965). Because of this, I have chosen to focus on the positive, rather than the negative, aspects of the work that has been accomplished to date.

This synthesis differs from many earlier ones in two important respects. Firstly, all inferences about Egyptian prehistory that are based principally on myths, religious texts and the distribution of religious cults at a later period have been rejected. By treating this material as an accurate reflection of political events in prehistoric times, Sethe (1930) was able to postulate the existence of a Deltaic kingdom the power of which spread over the whole of Egypt long prior to the First Dynasty; however, many alternative and mutually exclusive historical interpretations of the myths he used have been offered (Griffiths 1960, pp. 119–48), while other scholars, notably Frankfort, have rejected the proposition that there is any historical basis to these myths (Frankfort 1948, pp. 15–23). Whatever historical events may have influenced Egyptian religious traditions, they can only be interpreted in the light of what we know about the development of Egyptian culture from other sources. The present study therefore limits itself to archaeological and contemporary epigraphic data.

Secondly, those once-fashionable interpretations that automatically assumed that in antiquity all cultural changes resulted from the intrusion of new groups of settlers into an area have been eschewed. Petrie argued that the Fayum A culture represented a 'Solutrean migration from the Caucasus', which he stated was also the homeland of the Badarian people. The Amratian white-lined pottery was introduced into Egypt by 'Libyan invasions', while the Gerzean culture was brought there by the 'Eastern Desert Folk', who overran and dominated Egypt. Finally, Egypt was unified by the 'Falcon Tribe' or 'Dynastic Race', that 'certainly had originated in Elam' and came to Egypt by way of Ethiopia and the Red Sea (Petrie 1939, pp. 3, 7, 77). In each case, Petrie's arguments were based on alleged connections between a limited number of traits found in Egypt and elsewhere, while the continuities in the Egyptian cultural pattern as a whole were ignored.

Ideas of this sort have continued to exert a strong influence on interpretations of early Egyptian development. On the basis of limited similarities between the Badarian culture and the Khartoum Neolithic, Arkell (Arkell and Ucko 1965) and Baumgartel (1970, p. 471) have proposed a southern origin for the former. Vandier has suggested that an invasion is necessary to account for the development of the Gerzean culture (Vandier 1952, pp. 330–2) and Emery (1961, pp. 38–42) has recently maintained that the Early Dynastic culture was introduced by a 'master race' coming from the east. Each of these suggestions has been specifically denied by other Egyptologists (see Arkell and Ucko 1965). Today, however, a growing number of Egyptologists follow the lead of Frankfort and Kantor in emphasizing the continuities rather than the discontinuities in Egyptian prehistory (see again Arkell and Ucko 1965). While foreign cultural traits can be shown to have diffused into Egypt and become part of the Egyptian cultural pattern during the period we are considering, there is no convincing archaeological or physical-anthropological evidence of large-scale migrations into Egypt at this time. It also now is recognized that cultural diffusion did not necessarily involve large-scale migrations and that in order to understand why traits were accepted at any particular period a thorough knowledge of the recipient culture is essential. The latter point justifies concentrating on the developmental continuities in Egyptian culture in the absence of any clear-cut breaks in the archaeological record.

Prior to the last decade of the nineteenth century, no archaeological finds were known that dated prior to the Third Dynasty. It was in 1894, after a season at Koptos, that Petrie and Quibell began clearing the large cemeteries at Naqada and El-Ballas (Petrie and Quibell 1895). These produced the first clear evidence of the Amratian (or Naqada I) and Gerzean (or Naqada II) cultures. Further excavations revealed these cultures to be widely distributed in Upper Egypt. It was not, however, until Brunton and Caton Thompson had worked in the vicinity of El-Qāw, between 1922 and 1925, that the still earlier Badarian culture was identified (Brunton and Caton Thompson 1928). The village sites of the Northern Egyptian Predynastic Sequence were discovered still later. The Fayum A sites, the only ones for which final reports are available, were excavated by Caton-Thompson and Gardner between 1924 and 1926 (Caton Thompson and Gardner 1934): Merimda, in the western Delta, by Junker between 1928 and 1939; Ma'adi by Menghin and Amer after 1930; and El-Omari by Debono between 1943 and 1952 (for references to this literature see Hayes (1965, pp. 139–46)). The conviction that Egypt was not an important centre of plant and animal domestication and a consequent shift of interest to south-western Asia are, in part, responsible for the dearth of fieldwork on Predynastic sites in recent years. Since 1952, the most important work on this period has been restudies of earlier data by Baumgartel (1955, 1960), Kaiser (1956, 1957) and Kantor (1965).

Studies of Early Dynastic Egypt began with Amélineau's rough-shod excavations of the royal cemetery of the First and Second Dynasties at Abydos, which began in 1895 (Amélineau 1889–1905). This was followed by the systematic re-excavation and publishing of this site by Petrie between 1899 and 1901 (Petrie 1900, 1901a). In 1896–7, de Morgan excavated a large First Dynasty tomb at Naqada and, in 1897–8, Quibell and Green carried out excavations at Hierakonpolis which yielded, among other treasures, the famous slate palette of King Narmer (B. Adams 1974, Quibell 1900, Quibell and Green 1902). Further discoveries were made by Petrie at Tarkhan and other sites and, in 1912, Quibell found traces of large Early Dynastic tombs near the Step Pyramid at Saqqara. Firth began to excavate these tombs in 1932 and, after his death, this work was carried on by Emery between 1936 and 1956 (Emery 1949–58). From 1942 to 1954, Saad cleared a vast Early Dynastic cemetery, containing many graves of less important officials, at Helwan, on the east bank of the Nile opposite Saqqara (Saad 1969).

## Chronology

Unlike in south-western Asia, few stratified sites have been discovered in the Nile Valley that could serve as a basis for working out a cultural chronology for Predynastic Egypt. Merimda appears to have been such a site, but, for the most part, its stratigraphy has gone unrecorded. This leaves the tiny site at El-Hammamiya, which was inhabited intermittently from Badarian into Gerzean times, as the only stratified Predynastic site with any chronological significance.

In an effort to work out a chronology for the graves of the Amratian and Gerzean cultures, Petrie developed his system of 'Sequence Dating', which constituted the first substantial application of the principles of seriation in archaeology (Petrie 1901b, pp. 4–8: for recent appreciations of Petrie's seriation see Kendall 1969, 1971). This system was based on fluctuations in the popularity of different types of pottery from some 900 graves, each containing not less than five different types. On the basis of these fluctuations, Petrie assigned each grave to one of fifty successive temporal divisions, numbered 30 to 80. The time-scale is uncertain, so that it can only be said, for example, that S.D. (Sequence Date) 40 is theoretically earlier than S.D. 41; further, there is no reason to believe that the interval between S.D. 49 and 50 is necessarily the same as between S.D. 60 and 61. It appears that the nearer Petrie's divisions are to the historic period, the shorter periods of time they represent. Petrie placed the transition between the Amratian and

Gerzean cultures at about S.D. 40 and saw the transition between the Gerzean and Early Dynastic Period (his Semainean Period) starting about S.D. 65. The beginning of the Early Dynastic Period is now placed at about this stage. In terms of cultural development, the most important feature of Petrie's system is its assumption of enough stylistic continuity and uninterrupted change to permit the construction of a single developmental sequence from Amratian through into Early Dynastic times. This continuity harmonizes very poorly with the importance that Petrie attached to migrations as a principal source of cultural change.

Continuities in varied categories of artifacts suggest that the Badarian culture is earlier than the Amratian one and ancestral to it. The site at El-Hammamiya provides stratigraphic evidence that the Badarian culture came to an end before the end of the Amratian. Kaiser suggests, however, that, since certain types of Amratian pottery are found in some Badarian sites, the two are likely to have been contemporary with each other and represent parallel cultures, or ethnic groups, inhabiting different parts of Upper Egypt (Kaiser 1956, pp. 96–7; see also Hays 1976). Arkell and Ucko (1965) have pointed out that the mixture of pottery could have come about as a result of the contamination of an early site with later sherds and Kantor has argued that the similarities between the two cultures can better be interpreted as evidence that Badarian developed into Amratian (Kantor 1965, pp. 3–4). Brunton also defined a Tasian culture which he claimed represented an earlier phase of the Badarian. It is now generally agreed that the graves which are assigned to this culture, and which have never been found in isolation from Badarian and Old Kingdom ones, do not constitute a valid assemblage (Arkell and Ucko 1965, Kantor 1965, p. 4). This leaves the Badarian as the earliest known Predynastic culture in Upper Egypt.

Petrie's pottery classification has been described as 'the paraphernalia of the Dark Ages' and the cultural chronology derived from his system of Sequence Dating is now highly suspect in some of its details (Lucas and Harris 1962, p. 385, n. 3; Ucko 1967). On the basis of a re-analysis of the Predynastic cemetery at Armant, Kaiser (1957) has worked out an alternative system which differs in many small respects from that of Petrie and in which the Amratian–Gerzean sequence is divided into three stages and eleven sub-stages. On the whole, however, the general cultural sequence that Petrie worked out has stood the test of time remarkably well (Vandier 1952, p. 233).

Not enough material has been published so far to permit a seriation

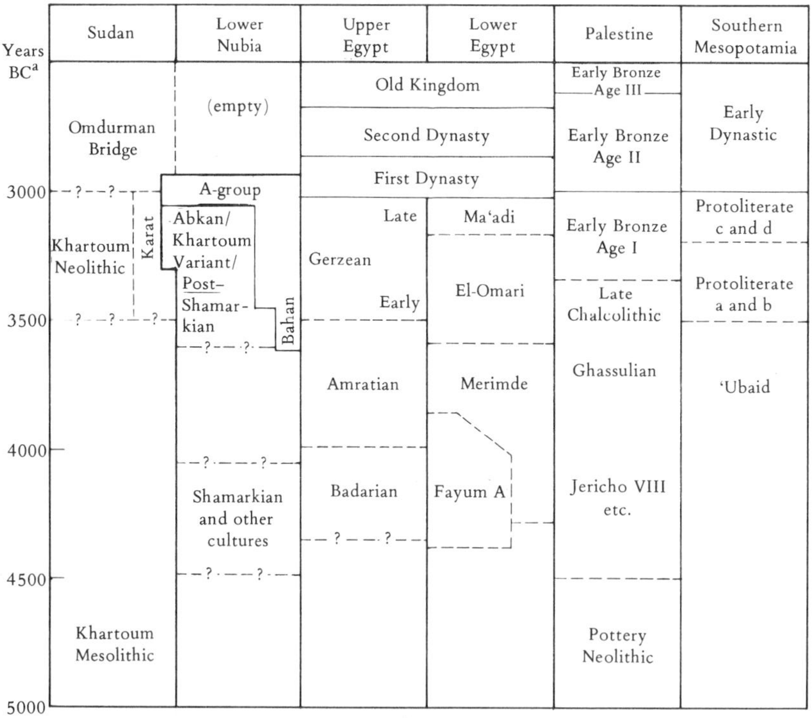

| Years BC[a] | Sudan | Lower Nubia | Upper Egypt | Lower Egypt | Palestine | Southern Mesopotamia |
|---|---|---|---|---|---|---|
| | | (empty) | Old Kingdom | | Early Bronze Age III | Early Dynastic |
| | Omdurman Bridge | | Second Dynasty | | Early Bronze Age II | |
| 3000 | – ? – – ? – | A-group | First Dynasty | | | |
| | Khartoum Neolithic | Karat  Abkan/ Khartoum Variant/ Post–Shamar-kian | Late  Gerzean | Ma'adi | Early Bronze Age I | Protoliterate c and d |
| 3500 | ? – – ? – –?– | Bahan  – –? – – ?· | Early | El-Omari | Late Chalcolithic | Protoliterate a and b |
| | | | Amratian | Merimde | Ghassulian | 'Ubaid |
| 4000 | | – ? · – – – ? – | | | | |
| | | Shamarkian and other cultures | Badarian | Fayum A | Jericho VIII etc. | |
| 4500 | | – ? · – – ? · – | – ? – –· ? – – | | | |
| | Khartoum Mesolithic | | | | Pottery Neolithic | |
| 5000 | | | | | | |

[a]Dates before 3000 BC based on [14]C dates using 5568-year half-life

Fig. 7.1  Relative chronology of Egypt and neighbouring regions.

of artifacts from the habitation sites which belong to the distinctive Northern Egyptian Predynastic Sequence. On the basis of similarities in specific types of artifacts, the Fayum A culture has been roughly correlated with the Badarian, the apparently long-inhabited site of Merimda with the Amratian, and El-Omari and Ma'adi with successive stages of the Gerzean (Kantor 1965, pp. 4–6). The main reason for suggesting that Fayum A was earlier than Badarian was the total absence of metal in Fayum A. Metal is also lacking at Merimde and El-Omari, however, which clearly are coeval with the Upper Egyptian Sequence. Although Baumgartel has argued that the Northern Sequence is culturally retarded and that hence all of these sites date much later, radiocarbon datings support the generally-accepted sequence and pro-posed correlations with the south (Baumgartel 1955, pp. 14–17, 120–2). These dates also provide possible support for the priority of Fayum within the Northern Sequence, since the dates for Fayum A overlap only with the earlier ones from Merimda. The later Merimda dates correlate with the two available for Amratian, while the one date for El-Omari correlates with those for the Gerzean culture (fig. 7.1).

Since the first radiocarbon dates became available, it has been observed that dates for earlier Egyptian historic material are consistently younger than the calendar dates established on the basis of dynastic chronologies. This led some Egyptologists to doubt the applicability of this dating technique to their region or to use it only as a means of establishing relative dates, while others became concerned that the historical chronology might be too long (Hayes 1970, pp. 192–3; H. S. Smith 1964; Trigger 1968, p. 64). Recent calibrations of dated tree-rings of bristlecone pine with the radiocarbon dates that these tree-rings have yielded have indicated major fluctuations in the formation of $^{14}$C, which have now been studied as far back as 5200 BC. These studies indicate that radiocarbon dates are approximately 200 years too recent by the end of the mid second millennium BC and some 800 or 900 years too recent by the beginning of the sixth millennium. While these calibrations remain at the experimental stage, they would place the majority of radiocarbon dates for the Early Dynastic Period between the calendar dates 3400 and 2650 BC. Traditionally, Egyptologists have dated the beginning of this period between 3100 and 2900 BC and the end of the Second Dynasty about 2686 BC (Derricourt 1971, Suess 1970).

If the calibrations that have been suggested for dates prior to 3000 BC are accepted, they would extend the duration of the known Predynastic sequences over a much longer period. Known radiocarbon dates for Fayum A would fall roughly between the calendar years 4700 and 5200 BC; Merimda between 3500 and 5200 BC (and, rejecting one date, between 4600 and 5200 BC); and the single date for El-Omari between 4000 and 4200 BC. Only two dates are available for the Amratian culture, but these fall about 4500 to 4700 BC, while the three Gerzean dates range between 3500 and 4600 BC. Two potsherds from the lowest Badarian level (below the breccia) at El-Hammamiya recently have yielded thermoluminescent dates of $5580 \pm 420$ and $5495 \pm 405$ BC. Five other presumably Badarian sherds from higher levels in the site date, according to depth in the deposit, to between $4360 \pm 355$ and $4690 \pm 365$ BC; while a Gerzean sherd from the still higher 2.5-foot level is dated $3775 \pm 330$ BC.[1] More thermoluminescent dates must be obtained before their implications can be considered.

[1] For details of these determinations see Derricourt (1971). For correct attributions of dates to the Amratian and Gerzean cultures see Arkell and Ucko (1965) and Kantor (1965, p. 5). For

The radiocarbon dates suggest a longer duration for the Gerzean culture than the archaeological evidence indicates is at all likely. The radiocarbon calibrations prior to 3000 BC may be too early. Alternatively, the Gerzean sample is small and the dates were obtained early in the development of the radiocarbon method, using specimens whose radiocarbon content may have been altered by contamination with fossil fuels during long periods of unprotected storage in museums. It may be significant in this respect that the date for a sample collected recently from the Fayum Kom K site is several hundred years more recent than for two samples collected by Caton-Thompson. More determinations will be needed from Egypt, and the proposed calibrations carefully tested, before an acceptable radiocarbon chronology is worked out prior to 3000 BC.

### Environment

The Nile floodplain was formerly believed to have been a vast swampland, unfit for permanent settlements. It was believed that, at first, human beings lived only along the edges of the valley, locating their camp-sites at the foot of cliffs or on rocky promontories. Only as the highlands turned into desert was man forced to settle in the jungle-like valley bottom and to begin the arduous process of clearing it. Passarge and Butzer have come to the conclusion that the topography of the valley is such that swamps were always a minor feature of the landscape, except in the northern Delta. Most of the plain consisted of seasonally flooded natural basins which supported various grasses and brush vegetation during the dry season. The higher levees along the river were covered with trees, such as acacia, tamarisk and sycamore, and the ones that remained permanently out of the water were ideal sites for year-round habitation. Butzer has also obtained evidence which indicates that the Delta has not extended seaward in recent millennia and that physical conditions there in Predynastic times were little different from what they are today. Raised sand deposits would have provided ideal loci for settlement within the inner Delta, immediately adjacent to the rich soils of this area (Butzer 1959, Passarge 1940). These observations run completely counter to Baumgartel's argument that the Delta was

the thermoluminescent datings see Caton-Thompson and Whittle (1975) and Whittle (1975). It should also be noted that the currently accepted, but admittedly somewhat speculative, chronology of early Egyptian history has recently been called into question by Mellaart (1979). On the basis of radiocarbon determinations, Mellaart proposes to date the beginning of the First Dynasty at about 3400 BC and the end of the Second Dynasty at about 2950 BC. Mesopotamian periods are moved correspondingly back in time.

unfit for human settlement much before the Early Dynastic Period (Baumgartel 1955, p. 3).

Instead of there being unremitting desiccation in north-eastern Africa at the end of the last Ice Age, there is evidence of increased rainfall and runoff on the steppes adjacent to Egypt at several intervals thereafter. The first appears to have lasted from about 9200 to 6000 BC, while another began about 5000 BC and, after a dry interval, continued after 4000 BC. Fairly abundant vegetation persisted in the wadis of northern and eastern Egypt until as late as 2350 BC, by which time a level of aridity comparable to the present was established (Butzer 1971, p. 584). At the maxima of precipitation, the northern Red Sea Hills supported tree cover and grazing land, while trees and wild grasses also grew in the wadis on both sides of the Nile and fish lived in the pondings along these wadis (Murray 1951; W. A. Fairservis, personal communication). During such periods, these upland areas and wadi systems, as well as the Nile Valley itself, supported considerable numbers of elephant, giraffe, rhinoceros, ostrich, wild ass and cattle, as well as antelope, gazelle, ibex and deer. That the adjacent deserts had become far more habitable than they are today during the period that saw the rise of Egyptian civilization vitiates the suggestion that an increase in population, resulting from climatic deterioration on the neighbouring steppes, played a major role in encouraging the development of civilization in the Nile Valley (Butzer 1971, p. 594). The moister climate appears to have facilitated the movement of human populations into and through the desert and this, in turn, may have encouraged more communication and more rapid cultural change in the Sahara.

There is considerable evidence that both the river bed and floodplain of the Nile in Egypt have slowly aggraded throughout historic times, as the result of the annual deposit of a thin layer of silt. Although an average rise of 10 cm per century is frequently quoted, Butzer has shown that the rate of deposition has varied considerably from one period to another. Between about 4000 and 3000 BC, the Nile floodplain in Lower Nubia appears to have been six to seven metres higher than at present (Butzer 1959, Butzer and Hansen 1968, pp. 276–8). A review of annual flood heights recorded on the Palermo Stone later in the Old Kingdom indicates a decrease in the average height and volume of the Nile flood during the First Dynasty. Bell (1970) has estimated that the difference between the average flood height of the First Dynasty and that of the Second to Fifth Dynasties is not less than a decline of 0.7 m.

It appears that throughout Egyptian history most settlements have been built on the floodplain, while, in Upper Egypt at least, cemeteries are frequently located in the desert, just beyond the edge of the cultivation. As a result, most living-sites, except those located on high ground or built, like the town of Kom Ombo, on tells formed by the debris of earlier villages, have either been buried under more recent deposits of silt or washed away by changes in the course of the river. This explains the low ratio of Predynastic, and later, living-sites to cemeteries that has been recovered in Upper Egypt (Butzer 1966). It also appears that between 8000 and 5000 BC the Egyptian floodplain was lower than it is today and the valley narrower; hence in most places even the cemeteries that were located along the margins of the flooded land at that time are now buried under more recent deposits of alluvium (Butzer 1971, p. 587; Wendorf, Said and Schild 1970). Butzer has shown that in Middle Egypt, which was hitherto often believed to be uninhabited in Predynastic times, cemeteries of this period are likely to have been either destroyed by shifts in the channel of the river or buried under substantial later deposits of sand and alluvium. Dunes have been particularly active on the west bank of the Nile in this part of Egypt, while, on the east bank, few landforms which would have been close to the edge of the valley in Predynastic times yet which remain unburied by later silts can be found north of Deir el-Gabrawi (Butzer 1961). The Predynastic habitation sites that have survived are all on scarps or embankments several metres above the present alluvium. According to Butzer, their preservation is fortuitous, since it was only sites at this height that have escaped the inundations and lateral expansion of irrigation in recent years.

This suggests that known distributions of Predynastic cultures may be determined more by geological than by cultural factors. For example, it is possible that both the Badarian and Amratian cultures extended almost as far north as did the Gerzean. Moreover, while all the people of Upper Egypt are assumed to have buried their dead on the margins of the Valley, it seems likely that most of the richest and culturally most advanced settlements were built on now-buried levees along the banks of the river and hence have never been discovered by archaeologists. This raises the possibility that the small Badarian settlements studied by Brunton, or the El-Hammamiya site, may be the encampments of simple pastoral groups, living both geographically and culturally on the fringes of a more advanced society. There is good evidence that an important part of the Predynastic settlement at Hierakonpolis extended onto the floodplain, where the settlement was located in historic times (Butzer 1966, Vandier 1952, p. 519).

## Language

Numerous similarities have long been apparent in the grammar, lexicon and phonology of ancient Egyptian and the Semitic languages. Because of this, it is often stated that Egyptian is either a Semitic language obscured by change or a creole language resulting from the mixing, in Predynastic times, of an 'African' and a Semitic language. This African language is sometimes identified as a Hamitic language (which some-times is, and sometimes is not, believed to be distantly related to Semitic) and sometimes as a 'Negro' language (Lambdin 1961, Vergote 1970). Such speculation has been closely related to theories that there were various migrations into Egypt from south-western Asia in prehistoric times and that these have resulted in ethnic and cultural changes.

Borrowings from some Semitic language or languages are well attested in historic times and Kees and others are probably correct in concluding that these languages exerted a strong influence over Egyptian in late Predynastic times, when there is also evidence of south-west Asian influence in the realms of art and material culture generally (Kees 1961, p. 42). There is, however, no evidence of an 'African substratum' in ancient Egyptian, in the sense that it can be proved that all of the similarities with the Semitic languages found in Egyptian are borrowings superimposed on an identifiable, specifically African language. On the contrary, Greenberg (1955, pp. 43–61) has shown that many of these similarities are not borrowings at all, but indicate that both Egyptian and the Semitic languages are derived from a common ancestor. He has also demonstrated that Semitic, ancient Egyptian and Cushitic, found to the east of the Nile (principally in Ethiopia), and Berber and Chadic, found in the western Sudan, constitute five co-ordinate branches of the Afroasiatic (or Hamito-Semitic) language family. It now seems likely that the Cushitic languages constitute not one, but two, major branches of Afroasiatic (Cushitic proper and Omotic) alongside Berber, Egyptian, Chadic and Semitic (Fleming 1969). Greenberg has the impression that Old Kingdom Egyptian and Akkadian are slightly more differentiated than Romanian and Portuguese, which would suggest 5500 to 6000 BC as the time when the branches of Afroasiatic became separate from one another (Trigger

7.1 Gerzean painted pottery vessel. This fine red-on-buff Gerzean jar found near Akhmīm is decorated with aardvarks. Today these animals range from South Africa to as far north as Ethiopia. Height 32 cm. (Courtesy of the Brooklyn Museum.)

*facing p.* 488

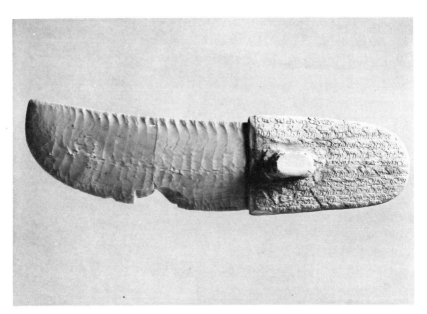

7.2 Flint knife with ivory handle found near Edfu. The handle is decorated with rows of animals and birds, while the boss is pierced lengthwise for a thong to secure the knife. This knife, found in a controlled excavation, is a fine example of late Predynastic flint-work and ivory carving. Length 23.2 cm. (Courtesy of the Brooklyn Museum.)

1968, p. 74, based on J. H. Greenberg, personal communication). While no studies of the lexical aspects of proto-Afroasiatic have been undertaken in order to shed light on the geographical point of origin of these languages, the 'principle of least moves' would suggest the eastern Sudan, or perhaps Egypt, as likely areas (Fleming 1969). Alternatively, while western Africa seems an unlikely point of origin, it is possible that, if special economic conditions, or population pressures, existed in south-western Asia, the language family might have been carried westward into Africa from that region. Although it is as yet impossible to trace the spread of Afroasiatic in the archaeological record, it does not seem impossible that Chadic and Berber were carried into the western Sahara during the 'wet phase' that began about 5000 BC.

In any case, it appears quite likely that the Predynastic cultures of Egypt were associated with a people who already spoke Egyptian and that later, specifically Semitic, borrowings were made from a closely related group of languages. These borrowings are, however, much less spectacular than was formerly believed and cannot be construed as evidence of creolization or massive population mergers. Of the hypothesized non-Afroasiatic 'African substratum' no trace exists.

### Physical Anthropology

Just as some linguists have tried to discern an 'African substratum' in the Egyptian language, so some Egyptologists have assumed that the earliest Predynastic population was negroid, and see in any caucasoid element evidence of the later migration of 'Hamito-Semitic' types into the country. Too often there has been a tendency to attribute the cultural development of Egypt to the repeated incursions of people of the latter type. Batrawi, on the other hand, has shown from the careful study of osteological evidence that there was very little change in physical type in Upper Egypt from Predynastic times into the historic period (Batrawi 1945, 1946). Although there was some variation within the population, the Upper Egyptian people were mostly small in stature and had long narrow skulls, dark wavy hair and brown skin. This continuity in physical type does not provide evidence of migration or gene flow, although it cannot rule out the possibility that new groups of similar physical type entered Upper Egypt from time to time.

Skeletons found at Merimda, El-Omari and Ma'adi suggest that the Predynastic inhabitants of the Delta were taller and more sturdily built than the Upper Egyptians and that their skulls were broader. Morant

(1925) saw in such skeletons evidence for the early existence of a 'Lower Egyptian type', which persisted in the north into the Hellenistic period and gradually modified the physical type present in Upper Egypt. The most recent use of physical anthropological findings to advance culture–historical arguments has been Emery's acceptance of Derry's theory of a 'Dynastic Race' as proof that the Early Dynastic civilization was brought into Egypt by a 'civilized aristocracy or master race'. Emery claims that this group may have originated along the Indian Ocean and also may have laid the foundations of the Sumerian civilization (Emery 1961, pp. 39–40). Edwards has suggested more cautiously that 'the fresh knowledge they may have brought with them' accounts for the 'acceleration in cultural progress observable at this time' (Edwards 1971, pp. 40–1). According to Derry (1956), a massively built, mesocephalic people entered Egypt about the start of the First Dynasty; probably from Asia, since they can be identified with the armenoid physical type found in that region. By the end of the First Dynasty, they had penetrated as far south as Abydos and gradually were merging with the indigenous population. It would appear that, in fact, the Predynastic population of Lower Egypt was ancestral to Derry's 'Dynastic Race' and that he was interpreting a basically geographical difference as an irruption of new settlers into the Nile Valley (Berry, Berry and Ucko 1967, Hayes 1965, p. 135). The population of the Delta was probably in contact with south-western Asia in prehistoric times, and settlers may have entered the region and mingled with the local population throughout this period, as they did in later times. This process may explain some of the similarities that Derry noted between these people and the armenoid type, common in Syria and Lebanon. It is prudent, however, to assume that whatever gene flow went on in northern Egypt, at least in later Predynastic times, was incidental to cultural development. To go further and attribute the Early Dynastic culture, or any earlier one, to the appearance of an intrusive ethnic group is to transgress permissible limits of inference.

PREDYNASTIC EGYPT

*Predynastic Subsistence Patterns*

The lower reaches of the Nile and the Tigris–Euphrates valleys are both extensive, but circumscribed, areas of rich, easily cultivated alluvium. As such, they shared the potential of becoming centres of high population density and of early civilizations. In spite of this, the differences between the two areas were very great. The natural floodplain of the Nile Valley was wider and richer than the Mesopotamian one and the annual floodwaters more predictable and less difficult to control. Moreover, salination did not pose a serious problem to the Egyptian farmer as it did in Mesopotamia. Merely by modifying natural basins to retain the floodwaters for longer periods, it was possible to convert the edges of the Nile floodplain into highly productive agricultural land. This was particularly easy to do from Abydos southwards, where these basins were smaller and more easily managed than in Middle Egypt or the Delta. Grain was one of ancient Egypt's principal exports and Herodotus, who travelled widely, stated that the Delta was the easiest land to work in the known world (Butzer 1976, pp. 18–22; Frankfort *et al.* 1949, pp. 39–51, 138–9). Throughout Predynastic times periodic rainfall over the catchments of wadis draining towards the Nile seems to have facilitated a limited amount of agriculture along the margins of the Nile Valley. Farming of this type may have been of no small importance in the early phases of the development of an agricultural economy in this area.

The general settings of Egypt and Mesopotamia were even more different than their river valleys. Mesopotamia was flanked by a series of highly diversified local environments embracing a variety of different altitudes, rainfall patterns and distributions of vegetation. Particularly in the north and west, these included areas that had witnessed the earliest development of sedentary agricultural life. Such diversity was conducive to trade, communication and, under pressure from expanding populations, innovations in subsistence patterns. The relative ecological uniformity of the Sahara and its limited potential for sustaining more than a meagre population even under the most favourable conditions provide a striking contrast with the Mesopotamian hinterland and explain the rudimentary cultural development of this region into later times. While the political, economic and cultural relationship between the Nile Valley and its Saharan hinterland is a subject that deserves careful study, it seems clear that the peoples of the Sahara played a far less important role in the rise of Egyptian civilization than the peoples bordering on Mesopotamia did in that area.

With the development of intensive agriculture in the Nile Valley, its inhabitants became increasingly isolated from their Saharan neighbours by a distinctive and internally highly differentiated way of life; the Egyptians had little motivation, of an economic or any other sort, for much reciprocal interaction with them. To no small degree, the power of the Egyptian state must have rested on the scorn and distrust that the Egyptian peasant felt towards the desert-dwellers and on his inability to adapt to life outside the Nile Valley. Ancient Egyptian civilization reflected in many ways this economic and cultural independence from the cultures of its desert hinterland, which contributed in no small degree to the self-sufficiency and ethnocentrism that, more than for most other early civilizations, were its special hallmarks (Frankfort *et al.* 1949, p. 45).

The lack of geological deposits in the Nile Valley north of Aswan which can be dated to between 8000 and 5000 BC hinders an understanding of the beginnings of a food-producing economy in this area. Moreover, the study of the Predynastic cultures to date has been such that even more recent food-producing sites which lacked or contained only very simple pottery are likely to have been overlooked. It has been pointed out, quite correctly, that there is no reason to believe that the Fayum A and Badarian cultures are necessarily the oldest food-producing cultures in this part of the Nile Valley (Arkell and Ucko 1965). In a recent paper, Clark has reviewed the evidence for the independent origin of food production in the Nile Valley. He stresses the rich faunal resources of the region in early Holocene times and draws attention to the wide range of edible and potentially domesticable trees and plants there (possibly including wild barley). He queries whether this rich environment provided the basis for a population increase that encouraged the subsequent manipulation of these resources or whether, as in parts of sub-Saharan Africa, this very richness of natural resources inhibited rather than stimulated innovation. He also suggests that the rapid adoption of an agricultural complex that was largely of external derivation might have taken place more easily if earlier local experimentation had made the Egyptians aware of the advantages to be gained by doing this (Clark 1971).

In spite of this, direct evidence for what was happening prior to 5000 BC is available only from south and west of the Egyptian Nile Valley. As P. E. L. Smith has explained in chapter 5, Wendorf has postulated a reliance on wild grains among some late Pleistocene groups in Nubia and Upper Egypt, beginning well before 10000 BC. While putative evidence, in the form of grinding stones, persists into Terminal Palaeolithic times (about 6000–5000 BC), there is no clear evidence of increasing sedentariness or group size. Wendorf has therefore suggested that a trend towards incipient cultivation was reversed when increasing desiccation made wild grains less abundant before the populations of Egypt and Nubia had become fully dependent on them (Wendorf 1968, vol. II, p. 1059; Wendorf *et al.* 1970). Hobler and Hester (1969) have suggested the specialized collecting or incipient cultivation by floodwater farming of unknown grains (perhaps millet, *Panicum turgidum*) at the Dunqul Oasis, west of the Nile, at about 6000 BC. They also suggest that it may have been from this area that ideas of food production were introduced up and down the Nile Valley. Possible cultivation in the Ahaggar has been suggested by pollen grains of *Pennisetum* from Amekni, dated to between 6100 and 4800 BC and by a 'type of cultivated grass' at Meniet from the first half of the fourth millennium BC (Camps 1969, p. 188, also this vol., ch. 8, pp. 566–9; Hugot 1968). Whatever the status of this evidence, collecting wild grass or incipient food production did not lead to the development of sedentary communities in the Sahara; instead the pattern appears to have given way to nomadic pastoralism as domestic animals became available and as the climate of the Sahara deteriorated (P. E. L. Smith 1972).

The best evidence of increasing sedentariness in Holocene times in the Nile Valley is the presumably pre-agricultural 'Khartoum Mesolithic' culture, whose type-site appears to have been inhabited, at least seasonally, for a considerable period of time. At this site, a wide variety of animal bones were found, bone harpoons indicate that fishing was important and grinding stones are reported, although Arkell believes that these were used only for grinding ochre. The apparently negroid population that inhabited this site also gathered the fruit of wild trees, such as *Celtis integrifolia*. Shelters were constructed of reeds covered with clay, and brown pottery bowls were decorated with wavy lines and later also with dots (Arkell 1949). Related pottery has been found as far north as Dongola and from Kassala, in the east, west to the Ennedi, Ténéré and Ahaggar; some of the latter has been radiocarbon dated to between 6000 and 5000 BC (Arkell and Ucko 1965, Clark 1971, Marks 1968). This pottery is, however, associated with different lithic industries and therefore seems to have diffused among established local groupings. Its wide distribution may bear witness to the growing sedentariness made possible by a highly successful collecting economy which flourished along the southern fringes of the Sahara during a period of increased rainfall, in the fourth millennium or earlier. It must be remembered, however, that the rich resources of the Nile Valley seem to have given rise to at least some permanently occupied settlements in Egypt already in Upper Palaeolithic times (Clark 1971).

The domesticated plants and animals that were of major economic importance in Predynastic Egypt generally seem to have been utilized in south-western Asia at a still earlier period (Wright 1971). The important plant domesticates were wheat, barley and flax (all efficient winter-rainfall crops) and the domesticated animals were sheep, goats, dogs, cattle and pigs. The only obviously locally domesticated animal was the donkey (*Equus asinus*), which is convincingly represented as tame in the art of the late Predynastic period (Zeuner 1963, pp. 375–6). The herding of gazelles has also been suggested for the Gerzean period on the basis of kill patterns, although the true significance of this evidence is far from certain (Reed 1966). There is no evidence of either *Panicum* or *Pennisetum* species in Egypt in early times, despite the alleged use of millet farther west; however, grains of *Echinochloa colonum*, a *Panicum*-type grass, have been found in the intestines of corpses from the Predynastic cemetery at Naga ed-Deir and it has been suggested that this plant was being cultivated as a cereal at that time (Clark 1971, Dixon 1969). It has also been conjectured that the Ethiopian domesticate enset (*Ensete edule*) might have been an important food crop in Egypt before it was displaced by wheat; however, the alleged representations of enset on Gerzean pottery are generally believed to be aloes (Simoons 1965). Whatever steps towards plant and animal domestication may have been taken locally, these domesticates appear to have given way before the superior types of domesticates that had been developed in south-western Asia.

On the basis of evidence from the Fayum, Wendorf is of the opinion that the technological and typological differences between the local Terminal Palaeolithic industry and Fayum A, which is only about 1000 radiocarbon years later, are so great that Fayum A is unlikely to have developed from a local Palaeolithic culture. He therefore suggests that the early Predynastic cultures record the arrival of a new population in Egypt, who brought with them the cultural base from which Egyptian civilization was to develop (Wendorf *et al.* 1970). If, in fact, the Afroasiatic language family originated elsewhere than in Egypt, the appearance of this 'new population' might correspond with the arrival of the first ancient Egyptian-speakers in their historic homeland. Unfortunately, the Fayum is somewhat peripheral to the Nile Valley, so that the transition between the Terminal Palaeolithic and Predynastic cultures may have been somewhat later than it was along the River Nile. In view of the variety of Palaeolithic industries in the Nile Valley at any one time and the long gap that remains in the archaeological record, it seems best to leave open the possibility that, in some fashion, the lithic traditions of Predynastic times evolved from a Palaeolithic culture native to the Nile Valley. It has been suggested that the bifacial technique of stone-working may have spread north from a nuclear area in the Congo and western Sudan during a period of climatic amelioration in the Sahara (Clark 1962). It is also possible that the movement of domesticates across the Sinai peninsula was aided by the wet phase that began about 5000 BC, although an unconfirmed relationship between the microlithic industry found near Helwan and that of the Natufian culture (about 9500–7500 BC) may suggest possible ties between Egypt and Palestine while the latter area was passing through a stage of incipient agriculture and animal domestication. While the Natufian corresponded with a period of climatic amelioration, no evidence of domesticates has been forthcoming, although pig bones occur in refuse heaps (Reed 1966).

Wheat, barley and flax are already present in the Fayum A culture. The only species of wheat prevalent in early times was emmer (*Triticum dicoccum*). A small amount of club wheat (*T. compactum*) has been found at Merimda and El-Omari, but Helbaek is of the opinion that it was a stray, accompanying other crops, which did not establish itself in Egypt (Dixon 1969). Wild emmer (*T. dicoccoides*) occurs in the upper part of the Jordan Valley, while einkorn (*T. monococcum*) seems to have been domesticated in west central Turkey about 6000 BC. Although both emmer and einkorn have been identified as grown at Jericho as early as 6500 BC, only the former made its way into Egypt (J. M. Renfrew 1969). Barley was an important crop in Egypt from early times and occurs in the abdominal contents of a large number of human bodies of Pre-dynastic date from Naga ed-Deir in Upper Egypt (Dixon 1969). The wild ancestor of barley (*Hordeum spontaneum*) is widely dispersed around the fringes of the fertile crescent. Reports of naked barley in ancient Egypt have not been substantiated and four- and six-rowed hulled types appear to be most common. Six-rowed hulled barley requires large amounts of water and thus was suited for cultivation in the Nile Valley. It is reported from Ali Kosh, in Iran, about 6000 BC, but became an established food crop in south-western Asia only after the appearance of irrigation about 5500 BC (Wright 1971). The wild ancestor of flax (*Linum bienne*) occurs in the Kurdish foothills and may have been domesticated there (J. M. Renfrew 1969). Although current evidence favours an Asian origin for all the principal Egyptian cultigens, Vavilov and Sauer have maintained that wheat and barley were first domesticated in Ethiopia (Simoons 1965, Wright 1971). While this now seems highly unlikely, the possibility must be left open that rainfall regimes resulted in distributions of wild plants in early Holocene times different from those postulated on the basis of modern distributions. Some surprises may therefore be in order.

The full complement of domestic animals, except for the donkey, is generally assumed to have been present in Egypt throughout the Predynastic period; however, osteological studies are lacking for most sites. According to Reed, bones of domestic goats are attested with certainty no earlier than the Amratian period, while domesticated sheep and dogs are attested in the Gerzean, and probably domesticated cattle and pigs also. Goat skins have been reported, however, from Badarian sites; dogs, resembling the greyhound or saluki type, are represented on leads on an Amratian pottery vessel; and what seem to be models of domesticated cattle have been found in graves of the same period (Reed 1966, Zeuner 1963, pp. 138, 222).

There is no evidence that the wild ancestor of the goat (*Capra hircus aegagras*) lived in Africa or that wild sheep (*Ovis orientalis*) were ever found south of Syria. Likewise, there is no support for Arkell's suggestion (in Wright 1971) that the dwarf goat, found at the Gerzean site of Tukh and at Esh-Shaheinab, is descended from the so-called 'native dwarf goat' found in Algeria and Zaïre (Reed 1966, Wright 1971). Sheep and goats were both domesticated in south-western Asia considerably earlier than the first known Predynastic cultures and the earliest dated occurrence of one or both these animals in north-eastern Africa is in the Neolithic levels at Haua Fteah (radiocarbon-dated about 4800 BC), while the earliest occurrence to the south of Egypt is at the 'Khartoum Neolithic' site of Esh-Shaheinab (radiocarbon-dated about 3100 to 3500 BC) (Arkell 1953, pp. 15–18; Higgs 1967). While it is possible that these domesticates reached Haua Fteah by way of the Mediterranean and north-west Africa, it is equally possible, and perhaps more likely, that they spread south and west after reaching northern Egypt across the Sinai peninsula. The absence of other domesticates at both Haua Fteah and Esh-Shaheinab further suggests that sheep and goats may have reached north-eastern Africa ahead of other domesticates. Prior to the Middle Kingdom, Egyptian sheep were a screw-horn, hair variety, also known in Mesopotamia. Goats display a range of horn types similar to those found in Neolithic and Bronze Age sites in Palestine (Zeuner 1963, pp. 138, 178).

Zeuner is of the opinion that both long- and short-horned breeds of domestic cattle in Egypt were descended from the native long-horned wild cattle of North Africa (*Bos primigenius*), although Gaillard has argued that a separate subspecies of wild short-horned cattle lived in Upper Egypt during the late Pleistocene (Zeuner 1963, p. 222).[1] Wild pigs also seem to have been abundant in the Delta and Reed believes it likely that these were domesticated by the Egyptians rather than domesticated pigs being driven across the Sinai Desert. It would appear, however, that, even if Egyptian domesticated pigs and cattle were bred from North African wild ancestors, the idea of their domestication must have come from south-western Asia, where there is a definite priority for domesticated pigs and a highly likely priority for domesticated cattle. Although cattle are not milked in parts of West Africa at the present time, there is definite evidence that they were milked in Egypt at least as early as the Old Kingdom.

While the late Neolithic economy of Egypt appears to be an extension of that found in the Near East, an older indigenous pattern of hunting, fishing and utilizing wild plants appears to have played an important role in the subsistence economy of Egypt until the late Predynastic Period. As the population increased and the onset of desiccation began to affect the adjacent deserts, natural plant resources diminished and many species of animals began to die out or were drastically curtailed in numbers. Elephants, giraffes and ostriches seem to have disappeared from both the desert and the floodplain in late Predynastic times, while the remaining savanna-type species, including antelope, ibex and gazelle, were decimated before the start of the Middle Kingdom (Butzer 1958, p. 114). On the other hand, large swamp- and river-dwelling animals, hippopotami and crocodiles, managed to survive throughout the Pharaonic period, although their habitats continued to diminish as a result of land clearance. The disappearance of animals from the floodplain probably resulted, in large part, from the pre-empting of their natural habitats by human beings for fields and for grazing land for their animals. This trend would have been intensified after the First Dynasty by lower flood levels, which resulted in a narrower floodplain. It is uncertain from the archaeological record when an increasing population made it necessary to supplement simple floodplain and runoff cultivation by increasingly modifying natural basins. While the drainage works that Herodotus later claimed were carried out at the beginning of the First Dynasty suggest a long-standing familiarity with the problems connected with large-scale irrigation projects (Baumgartel 1970, p. 482),

---

[1] These are almost certainly female *Bos primigenius* (Reed 1966).

additional proof of this is lacking. Basin agriculture and flash flood cultivation can be practised on a small scale and it seems likely that, as in Mesopotamia, large-scale undertakings were a result of centralized control rather than an important factor in the development of this control (Frankfort 1956, p. 33; Nims 1965, p. 34).

### The Northern Predynastic Sequence

Knowledge of Predynastic sites in northern Egypt is extremely limited. No sites of this period have been discovered as yet in the inner Delta, which was almost certainly the key area of settlement in northern Egypt in Predynastic as it was in later times (Wilson 1955). Most of these sites now either lie below the watertable or are covered by more recent settlements. A small number of sites found at the apex of the Delta and around its margins indicate that in Predynastic times the cultural pattern of this region was different from that of Upper Egypt. The principal sites are, however, few in number and located some distance apart, hence it is not always possible to distinguish clearly between temporal and geographical variations in culture. All of these sites appear to be characterized by undecorated, or simply incised, monochrome red or black pottery. Throughout all of Egypt, early Predynastic pottery tends to lack handles, spouts or fancy lips and to take the form of open bowls, cups and dishes. Later, closed and fancy forms of vessels become more common. There is, however, a total absence in the Northern Predynastic Sequence of the fancy decorated pottery found in Upper Egypt (Baumgartel 1955, pp. 17–18).

The oldest known components of the Northern Predynastic Sequence seem to be the habitation sites of the Fayum A culture.[1] These were located along the northern and north-eastern shores of an old lake level in the Fayum Depression. The encampments seem to have consisted of mat or reed huts erected in the lee of buttes or mounds near the fertile soil along the edge of the lake. Possibly to avoid ground moisture, the communal underground granaries associated with these settlements were located on higher ground some distance from the settlements. Bones of sheep, goats and possibly of domesticated cattle were reported, although none were examined by specialists. The granaries yielded the remains of emmer wheat and six-rowed barley.

[1] For a summary of the archaeological data related to Predynastic northern Egypt see Hayes (1965, pp. 91–146); for Upper Egypt see Baumgartel (1955, 1960) and Vandier (1952, pp. 167–466, 497–609).

While the Fayum A people were clearly agriculturalists and may have kept domesticated animals, they appear to have remained dependent on hunting and fishing to a considerable degree. Large mammals, including elephants, crocodiles and hippopotami, were hunted, and fish and mussels were taken from the lake. Small harpoons and bevelled points made of bone were preserved, but no fish-hooks. The harpoons are said to resemble those from Palestine rather than the kinds found in the Republic of the Sudan and East Africa. Shells, which were used for ornaments, were obtained from both the Mediterranean and the Red Sea. A few amazonite beads do not necessarily indicate contact with the Tibesti region to the west, since this mineral also occurs in the Nile basin (Lucas and Harris 1962, pp. 393–4).

Many of the stone tools are large, thick flakes with notches and denticulates. Sickle flints were set in wooden handles; stemmed and winged arrow-heads and leaf-shaped pieces were bifacially chipped, and celts were chipped and provided with polished cutting edges. Baskets were common and used to line granaries, and rough linen cloth was being manufactured. Pottery was made from coarse, straw-tempered clay and consisted mainly of bag-shaped vessels and flat-bottomed dishes. Some vessels had a burnished red slip, others a plain rough surface. McBurney suggests that the pottery, as well as other aspects of the culture, show connections with the coastal areas of the Levant (McBurney 1960, pp. 233–8). Although the most substantial site (Kom W) was 600 m long, the lack of house structures does not suggest a strongly sedentary settlement pattern. It has been speculated that these sites were probably seasonal ones. To what degree the Fayum settlements were representative of life in the Nile Valley at that time remains problematical. Communal granaries occur in many (but not all) Pre-dynastic sites in Egypt and suggest that village or local groups played an important corporate role in the allocation of resources. Even if few villages were larger than extended kin groups, these corporate activities must have enhanced the status of local headmen (Baumgartel 1970, pp. 482–3).

The earliest evidence of fully sedentary village life in the Nile Valley is the site of Merimda, on the western margin of the Delta. It has been estimated to cover about 180000 sq. m with cultural debris up to 2 m deep (Butzer 1966, Kemp 1968a). Although the site was dug in arbitrary levels and its stratigraphy not properly recorded, radiocarbon dates suggest that it may have been inhabited for 600 years. In general, the pottery and stone artifacts resemble those of Fayum A, although the shapes and decoration of the pottery are more varied and elaborate. Polished black pottery is found only in the upper layers of the site. The pear-shaped stone mace-heads found at Merimda may be derived from Asian models and are likely prototypes for the later Gerzean ones. A special type of vessel supported by four modelled human feet is also found in the Amratian culture (Kantor 1965, p. 5).

In the early stages, the inhabitants of Merimda appear to have lived in sparsely scattered wind-breaks or pole-framed huts. These dispersed 'farmsteads' frequently became engulfed in sand and, at one point, there is evidence of extensive sheet-flooding resulting from rainfall (Butzer 1966). In the higher levels of the site, the occupation is denser and there is evidence of semi-subterranean adobe huts, whose walls rose several feet above the ground and probably were covered by a pitched roof. Not one of these houses was over three metres in diameter and most were so small they could only have been lived in by one adult or a woman and her children. Clusters of single-adult dwellings, usually occupied by groups of patrilineal, polygamous kinsmen are found in various parts of modern sub-Saharan Africa and analogous settlements appear in the archaeological record of the Natufian and pre-pottery Neolithic cultures in Palestine (about 9000 to 6500 BC). Flannery has queried whether the African compounds may not be surviving examples of a settlement type that once stretched from Palestine into north-eastern Africa (Flannery 1972, Trigger 1965, p. 60). At Merimda a number of these huts were found laid out in ragged rows on either side of what was believed to be a street; but the plan suggests that alternatively they might have been part of a double ring of huts (Vandier 1952, pp. 117–19). Granaries, consisting either of baskets or clay jars buried up to their necks in the ground, were scattered throughout the village and seem to have been associated with individual dwellings. What appear to have been circular clay-lined threshing floors are also reported. Butzer has tentatively estimated that Merimda had a population of 16000, although it is far from certain that the entire site was occupied at any one time or that the occupation was sufficiently dense to support this estimate. Kemp considers it likely that Merimda was a relatively small community. He also demonstrates that the evidence is insufficient to prove that, at Merimda, the custom was to bury the dead within the village in such a position that they faced the hearth of their former home. Kemp (1968a) suggests that a small number of adults may have been buried in the empty spaces that existed between the houses at any one period. Similar practices are attested in Upper Egypt in spite of the importance apparently placed on cemeteries and grave-goods there in Predynastic times. The graves found within the limits of Merimda contained almost no grave-goods.

Approximately contemporary with the final occupation at Merimda is a group of settlements and cemeteries collectively known as El-Omari. These are clustered in and around the mouth of the Wadi Hof, between Cairo and Helwan. In Predynastic times this wadi was probably suitable for growing crops. The pottery is predominantly red or black and almost devoid of decoration, although vasiform and lipped vessels are more common than at Merimda. Most of the stone tool types found at Merimda also occur at El-Omari, although there is a greater emphasis on flake and blade tools, that appears to foreshadow the predominance of blade tools in the still later settlement of Ma'adi. Unfortunately, El-Omari has been less completely explored than either the Fayum sites or Merimda, and only cursory accounts of the excavations have been published. The main settlement, which like Merimda appears to have been lived in for a lengthy period, occupies a gravel terrace sloping down to the estuary of the Wadi Hof. Traces of many oval shelters made of poles and basketwork were found on the surface of the site, as well as various sized pits lined with matting or baskets. These were all probably granaries, although the excavators believed the larger ones to be semi-subterranean huts (Vandier 1952, p. 156). Still larger areas enclosed with reed fences were probably pens for domestic animals. Evidence of an area given over to flint-knapping was found on the outskirts of the settlement. A smaller site, apparently contemporary with this one, was found near two natural rain catchments on one of the highest terraces of the Jebel Hof. Many cores and hammerstones suggest considerable amounts of flint-working, but numerous burials in and around the site, as well as millstones, indicate that it too was a settlement. The relationship between the upper and lower settlements is unclear, although it does not seem impossible that the former was established as a naturally-defended outpost of the latter. Another small, and possibly later, village was discovered in a branch of the estuary of the Wadi Hof.

Bodies were interred within both of the older settlements. In the larger settlement, these burials were made over a long time; some were disturbed by later building on the site, while later ones were placed in granaries of an earlier period. Bodies were generally laid on their left side, head south, as they were in Upper Egypt, but not at Merimda. One skeleton was found holding a staff about 35 cm long and similar to the *ames* sceptre associated with kings and deities in historic times. It has been suggested that he may have been a local headman. Grave-goods were generally sparse, as they were at Merimda. Two cemeteries containing dispersed graves covered with stone tumuli appear to have been associated with the later village.

Ma'adi is located 10 km north-west of El-Omari. Here a sprawling site up to 2 m thick and covering some 18 hectares flourished from late Predynastic into Early Dynastic times. The dwellings at Ma'adi are concentrated in the central part of the site. For the most part, they consist of oval huts or horseshoe-shaped wind-breaks constructed of posts driven deep into the ground to support walls of wattle or reeds covered with mud. Grindstones and storage jars or storage pits were sometimes found inside, or closely associated with, these houses, which continued to be built throughout the history of the site. Two rectangular structures were also noted; one with walls of reeds and straw, the other built of logs laid horizontally. A number of spacious subterranean chambers were dug to a depth of over 2 m into the sandy soil. These were circular to rectangular in plan, were entered by stairways and evidently were dwellings, since they contained hearths, as well as traces of roof-poles. Special storage areas existed on the periphery of the settlement, which recall the segregated granary areas associated with the Fayum A settlements. Pottery storage jars, about 1 m high and buried up to their necks in the sandy soil, occupied the northern outskirts of the settlement. On the south side were numerous storage pits, with vertical or sloping sides and sometimes lined with mud or basketwork. Many of these storage pits contained carbonized grain, but basalt vases, carnelian beads and other valuable items were also found inside them. It has been suggested that the settlement was protected by palisades and ditches. Burials within the settlement were limited, with few exceptions, to the bodies of unborn children and three cemeteries have been found in the vicinity of the town. The grave-goods in the Wadi Digla cemetery are richer than in the other two. A number of dogs and gazelles were buried in graves of their own in these cemeteries.

Hunting and gathering seem to have been less important at Ma'adi than they had been in the earlier sites of northern Egypt. The remains of wild animals are sparse and limited to ibex and to riverine species, such as hippopotami, turtles, fish and molluscs. On the other hand, at Ma'adi there is evidence not only of agriculture and herding but also of advanced craft specialization. A copper axe-head spoiled in casting and masses of copper ore indicate that copper was being processed at

Ma'adi. Ma'adi is the oldest site in northern Egypt in which copper artifacts have been found. Although copper tools and weapons have not survived in large numbers, traces of disintegrated copper artifacts occurred with some frequency in the site. Ma'adi is located at the mouth of the principal wadi leading eastward to the copper deposits of Jebel 'Ataqa and the Sinai and Baumgartel has suggested that a copper industry connected with the first exploitation of the Sinai mines might have been the reason for Ma'adi's existence; however, no evidence has been adduced that indicates that the Egyptians were mining copper in the Sinai peninsula at this period, or to any significant degree in Pharaonic times (Baumgartel 1955, p. 122; Hayes 1965, p. 129; Rothenberg 1970). More likely Ma'adi was an important entrepôt handling trade between the Nile Valley, the Sinai peninsula and Palestine. Gerzean pottery and stone artifacts occur at Ma'adi and have been interpreted as evidence of increasing cultural influence from the south, which can already be noted at El-Omari. On the other hand, in historic times the main road from Egypt to Palestine passed by Ma'adi, before crossing the eastern Delta. Kantor (1965, p. 9) has established the existence at Ma'adi of a 'considerable body' of imported pottery from the Early Bronze Age I culture of Palestine, which is coeval with the late Predynastic Period. It is therefore possible that copper was being imported from the east at this time, rather than that the Egyptians were going to the Sinai peninsula to mine it themselves. While these alternative explanations must be considered further, it is possible that the Upper Egyptian influences in the north came about as a result of long-distance trade in which, at least during early Gerzean times, the people of Ma'adi and other sites in north-eastern Egypt were playing a key role.

Although the Predynastic cultural sequence in northern Egypt remains poorly defined, the sites in this area are distinguished from those of Upper Egypt by their monochrome, mainly undecorated, pottery and by a greater scarcity of jewellery, sculpture and decoration. On the other hand, the suggestions that pigs, either wild or tame, were eaten in northern Egypt but not in the south; that in the north people were buried inside their settlements rather than in cemeteries; and that settlements in northern Egypt are substantially larger than in Upper Egypt are all dubious distinctions between the two areas. The sequence of sites known at present suggests that, as the Early Dynastic Period was approached, there was progressively less reliance on hunting and an increasing emphasis on crops and herding. It is possible, however, that because of the rich natural resources of the Delta, the transition there was slower than it was in Upper Egypt. While communities such as Ma'adi appear to have played an important role as entrepôts through which goods and ideas from south-western Asia filtered into the Nile Valley in late prehistoric times, the main cultural and political tradition that gave rise to the cultural pattern of Early Dynastic Egypt is to be found not in the north but in the south. To understand why this was so, we must examine the cultural development of Upper Egypt.

### The Upper Egyptian Predynastic Sequence

Cemeteries of the Badarian culture have been excavated along the eastern flank of the Nile Valley between El-Matmar and El-Etmanieh. In addition, Badarian habitation sites have been found in the stratified site at El-Hammamiya, at El-Matmar, at El-Mostagedda and at the foot of the cliffs at El-Badari. Few of these sites are more than a few centimetres thick. Although Kaiser believes that the Badarian culture was confined to this area, typical Badarian artifacts have been found at Armant, Hierakonpolis, and in the Wadi Hammamat (Kantor 1965, p. 4; Hayes 1965, p. 147; for Hierakonpolis, W. A. Fairservis, personal communication). It therefore seems likely that more Badarian sites will eventually be found elsewhere in Upper Egypt (fig. 7.2).

The remains of the Badarian culture appear to reflect a simple, semi-sedentary way of life. No certain evidence of house structures has been noted in any of the Badarian settlements, whose inhabitants presumably lived in skin tents or huts made of mats hung on poles. The site at El-Mostagedda consisted of a circle of grain pits, some lined with baskets or matting, which outlined an area of ash and sand. Cemeteries were located in the desert behind the settlements. The typical Badarian grave was an oval or rectangular pit roofed over with sticks or matting. Graves contained one or more bodies, loosely contracted on their left side, head south. The body was covered with mats or hides, and food and other offerings were placed in the graves. The offerings included rectangular stone palettes, ivory spoons, and small ivory or stone vases; all of which appear to have been associated with the grinding and use of green face-paint. These items were to remain a part of the Predynastic burial kit. Fancy ivory combs and ivory and clay human figurines were also placed in graves. Although graves were of different sizes, the absence of obvious distinctions of wealth among them may, but does not necessarily, indicate a lack of social stratification at this time. While

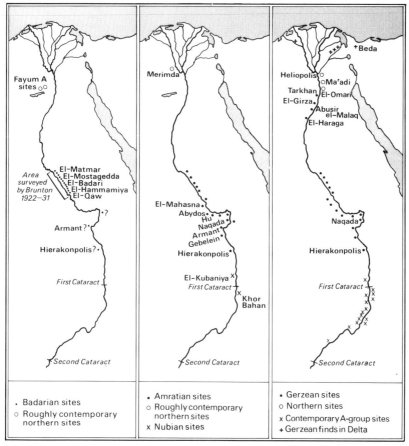

Fig. 7.2   Maps indicating known distributions of Predynastic sites in Egypt and
Lower Nubia at different periods.

it is assumed that all of the people living along the east bank of the river
would have used the cemeteries adjacent to the floodplain, there seems
to be a close connection between the cemeteries and settlements found
along the edge of the desert (O'Connor 1972). This suggests either that
the Badarians only occupied the floodplain seasonally or that the
cemeteries belonging to the population of the valley, as opposed to the
desert margin, have not yet been discovered. Until this problem is
resolved, any interpretation of the Badarian culture will remain
hazardous.

Wheat and barley were grown and traces of bread were found in some graves. Castor seeds, probably wild, were collected for their oil. Clothing was woven out of linen, although skin clothing, with the hair turned inwards, and leather clothes were also worn. The bones of cattle, sheep and goats are listed as occurring on Badarian sites, although they were not studied by experts. A number of animals, some putatively domesticated, were wrapped in mats or cloth and buried in separate graves, like human beings, in the village cemeteries. Flint arrow-heads, throwing-sticks (not boomerangs) and perforated fish-hooks made of ivory and shell reflect the continuing importance of food-collecting, and bones of wild animals, fish and birds are reported from Badarian sites. On the whole, however, the evidence does not seem to indicate as great a dependence on wild game as is found in coeval sites farther north.

Badarian flint-working is not of a high order of expertise. It is primarily a core industry, utilizing nodules found on the surface of the desert. Small push-planes and bifacial sickle-stones are common and arrow-heads were both leaf-shaped and concave-based. The Badarians' failure to use the tabular flint found in nearby cliffs has been interpreted by some as evidence that they did not originate in this part of the valley (because they did not know its resources) and that they came from the south (since flint-bearing limestone ceases south of Esna) (Brunton and Caton Thompson 1928, p. 75). By contrast, the manufacture of Badarian pottery exhibits a high degree of sophistication, although the shapes tend to be simple; semicircular bowls predominate. Ordinary vessels are either smooth or rough brown, but the best quality of pottery is thinner than any other produced in Predynastic times. The surfaces of many vessels were combed and burnished before firing. The fine ware is either polished red or black in colour, but the most distinctive type was red with a black interior and lip formed by removing the pot red-hot from the kiln and placing it upside down in carbonizing material (Lucas and Harris 1962, pp. 377–81).

A small number of awls and pins that were hammered out of copper have been found in Badarian sites, as well as beads made of steatite covered with blue–green glaze. It has been suggested that these objects may have been obtained from itinerant traders coming either from Palestine or across the Red Sea (Arkell and Ucko 1965). In addition to shells from the Red Sea, other supposed evidence of long-distance trade takes the form of turquoise, believed to come from the Sinai peninsula; pine, cedar and other woods thought to come from Syria; and an unusual four-handled vessel similar to some Ghassulian ones (Kantor 1965, p. 6). Since, however, the climate of North Africa was moister then than it is today, the wood may have been indigenous to the Red Sea Hills and better climatic conditions would have made the exploitation of that area easier than it is at present. Copper ores are also found not far to the east of the Nile Valley and it has been suggested that the turquoise may have come from the Libyan massifs. Although it is generally assumed that a knowledge of metallurgy reached Egypt from Palestine, the total absence of copper in sites in northern Egypt prior to late Predynastic times suggests that the use of copper possibly evolved independently in Upper Egypt. The earliest artifacts may have been hammered out of native copper, although this is far from certain. In any case, the well-attested use of copper ore (malachite) for face-paint suggests that conditions were favourable in the Badarian culture for the discovery of how to obtain copper by smelting the ore (Lucas and Harris 1962, pp. 201, 404). Malachite occurs in the eastern desert in sufficient quantities to have supplied the demand for it in Predynastic times. Steatite is also found in Egypt, so that it too may have been glazed locally. This might be interpreted as evidence that the Badarian culture, as it was manifested either elsewhere in Upper Egypt or in sites on the floodplain, was technologically more advanced than is indicated by the marginal sites discovered so far.

Amratian sites generally appear to be larger and more prosperous than the Badarian ones and are found from Deir Tasa as far south as the Nubian border. There is evidence of an Amratian occupation in the town-sites at Hierakonpolis and Naqada, both of which appear to have been key locations in the Predynastic development of Upper Egypt. A concentration of early Amratian sites between Abydos and Naqada also suggests that this stretch of river may have played an important role in the development of the Amratian culture (Kaiser 1957, pp. 74–5). The only house structures definitely identified as Amratian are nine hut ovals at El-Hammamiya, and even these continued to be inhabited into early Gerzean times. The huts were about one to two metres in diameter and, while one had been used to store dung for fuel, at least one other contained a hearth and was clearly a small dwelling. The foundations were built of chips and rough pieces of sandstone set in mud, while the upper parts appear to have been of wattle and daub. As with the huts at Merimda, there were no traces of doorways. The latter were probably set in the walls of the houses some distance above ground level, after the fashion of huts built in parts of the southern Sudan at the present time. Wooden posts in one part of the site have been interpreted as the remains of wind-breaks. Similar wind-breaks are reported from El-

Mahasna and cooking pots were found *in situ* at Armant. While these two settlements appear to have been inhabited in both Amratian and Gerzean times, no more permanent structures were found there. The subsistence economy of the Amratian culture seems to have been much like that of the Badarian. The art of the period demonstrates a continuing familiarity with elephants and giraffes (Vandier 1952, p. 270).

In essential features, cemeteries also appear to be little changed from Badarian times. Headless bodies and extra skulls suggest the possibility of head-hunting at this time, which might betoken the patterns of blood revenge associated with tribal society. It is possible, however, that these finds are related to a more widespread custom of dismembering corpses. There is no archaeological evidence to confirm traditions of cannibalism in Predynastic times (Vandier 1952, p. 248).

A striking improvement can be noted in the manufacture of stone tools, most of which are bifacial. The best flint knives were ground to thin them, prior to being given a final flaking to produce a cutting edge. The most impressive of these tools are the fish-tail artifacts (of uncertain use) and rhomboidal knives. A few basalt vases with a small splayed, or conical, foot have been found and, since somewhat similar vessels are known in Mesopotamia at about the same time, it has been suggested that the Egyptian ones are foreign imports or local imitations of these vessels (Arkell and Ucko 1965, Vandier 1952, pp. 366–8). Crude stone vessels were manufactured in Badarian times, however, and seem to represent the beginning of a tradition of stone-working that was hereafter to be a part of Egyptian culture. The ability of the Egyptians to shape hard stone expertly in Amratian times is proved by the so-called 'disc-shaped' mace-heads. The Amratians also ground rhomboidal palettes out of slate and carried on the Badarian tradition of carving and modelling. Ivory combs have long teeth and their handles are ornamented with human and animal figures. Pairs of ivory hippopotamus tusks, sometimes ornamented with bearded human heads, may have been of ritual significance. A large number of human figurines, both in ivory and clay, appear to date from this period (Arkell and Ucko 1965, Ucko 1968). Perrot has suggested that the elongated shapes of the ankles and faces, as well as the drill holes found in the ivory statuettes, suggest a cultural affinity with those of the Ghassulian culture (Kantor 1965, pp. 6–7). These similarities are tenuous, however, and the nature of contacts at this period remains to be demonstrated.

While black-topped pottery declined in quality, and rippling died out early in the Amratian period, red wares remained popular. Some of this pottery was painted with white cross-lined designs and later with scenes depicting people and animals in a free and vivid style. Men are frequently shown wearing feathers in their hair, as the Nubians and Libyans did in historic times, as well as penis sheaths, which were worn occasionally into the historic period. Ucko has studied the prehistoric sheaths preserved in the Naga ed-Deir cemetery and offers a provisional classification of them (Ucko 1967). Baumgartel has suggested that the white cross-lined red ware may have been inspired by the painted pottery of Susa I and contemporary Mesopotamian and Iranian cultures. The similarities that Baumgartel has indicated are very general ones, however; hence few scholars are convinced by her arguments (Baumgartel 1955, pp. 54–71; Vandier 1952, pp. 294–6). The absence of similar painted pottery in the Delta is also against an Asian origin for Amratian painted pottery. Metal objects are as rare in Amratian sites as in Badarian ones. Copper pins date from the Amratian period and two gold beads have been tentatively ascribed to it. In general, however, the level of cultural development appears to be little different from what it was in Badarian times. In both periods, the villages of Upper Egypt probably had largely self-sufficient economies, which had as their resource base the Nile Valley and the adjacent eastern desert. It may turn out, however, that the limited evidence now available does not adequately reflect the cultural development of either period.

By contrast, the Gerzean period appears to have been one of rapid change, marked by abundant evidence of contacts with south-western Asia and the evolution of complex social and economic institutions. For the first time, there is positive evidence of south-west Asian influences in Upper Egypt. In the early Gerzean, these influences are limited to the imitation of foreign pottery. The most important of these borrowings were the ledge-handled, or wavy-handled, vessels, which appear to be derived from the Early Bronze Age I culture of Palestine. In Egypt, these vessels have no prototypes, but in Palestine ledge-handles appear in the Early Chalcolithic period (4000 to 3600 BC) and by Early Bronze Age I times they were used on a number of different types of vessels. The type introduced into Upper Egypt gave rise to a whole class of pottery, which henceforth developed along its own lines there. The exact point at which these vessels began to be produced in Upper Egypt remains in doubt, but it is no longer assumed that it was at the very beginning of the Gerzean period (Kantor 1965, pp. 7–8, Ucko 1967). Vessels with tilted spouts and, less certainly, ones with triangular lug handles also appear to be imitations of forms which evolved in

Mesopotamia in the 'Ubaid or early Protoliterate periods. The spouted vessels occur in the 'Amuq area, when that region was a western outpost of Protoliterate influence, and also in the Early Bronze Age I culture of Palestine. These occurrences probably outline the route by which these forms were carried from Mesopotamia to Upper Egypt. Ma'adi was already functioning as an entrepôt between Palestine and Upper Egypt and may have played some role in their transmission. Near the start of the Gerzean period, the pear-shaped mace-head, which was ultimately of south-west Asian origin, appears to have diffused to Upper Egypt from the Delta, where it was already present at Merimda.

Within the Gerzean culture, there is evidence of increasing craft specialization and wider markets. Until this time, all pottery was made of clay deposited by the River Nile, and it is likely that most of this pottery was traded over only a small area. In Gerzean times, however, vessels with a light-coloured fabric began to be made of a mixture of clay and calcium carbonate that is washed out of the limestone hills bordering the Nile Valley. Two areas well known for this clay are Qena and El-Ballas, where deposits have been exploited from an early period; however, other, less important deposits occur in Middle Egypt (Lucas and Harris 1962, pp. 383–4). The ledge-handled jars and another class of pots decorated in red paint with various patterns, and later with representations of sacred boats, trees and files of birds and animals, were made of this clay (plate 7.1). The standardized forms of these vessels that are found distributed throughout Egypt are evidence not of cultural uniformity but of the mass-production of this ware in one or, at most, only a few centres. The shapes of many red-ware vessels also reflect the impact of mass production during the Gerzean period. While opinions differ, it is possible that a slow, hand-turned wheel was now used to fashion parts of vessels (Baumgartel 1970, p. 488; Lucas and Harris 1962, p. 369). If so, the innovation coincided with the increasing scale of pottery manufacture at this time. The florescence of painted pottery, prior to its decline at the end of the Gerzean period, indicates that, in spite of large-scale production, fancy pottery continued to serve as a vehicle of artistic expression, as it had done in the Amratian period.

Copper artifacts became much more common during the Gerzean and at the beginning of the Early Dynastic Period. Daggers, knives, adzes, axes, spear-heads, harpoons, fish-hooks, needles, finger-rings, small tools and ornaments were now cast, as well as hammered, from this metal and the copper that was used appears to have come from both the eastern desert and the Sinai peninsula where the contemporary, chalcolithic culture of the Nawamis (Petrie 1906, p. 243) has some elements in common with Predynastic Egypt (Lucas and Harris 1962, p. 209).[1] It is possible that the techniques of casting used by the Egyptians owed something to Palestinian metallurgical experience, although the relationship still remains to be worked out (Kantor 1965, p. 7). Gold was also worked at this period and some luxury goods were ornamented with gold foil. Silver objects are described as 'more substantial than one would expect', although the silver is unlikely to have been imported into Egypt as Baumgartel (1960, pp. 6–7) suggests it was. Prior to the Middle Kingdom, 'silver' appears to have been mainly a silver-rich alloy of gold and silver, which is found in the eastern desert. Until the end of the Middle Kingdom, this 'white gold' was valued more highly by the Egyptians than was yellow gold (Lucas and Harris 1962, pp. 246–8).

There was also a marked development in other crafts. Decoration was more finely conceived and formally arranged than ever before and the execution of designs was often of high quality. Flint blades became more common, although the most elaborate flint objects continued to be produced using bifacial techniques (plate 7.2). Thin, scimitar-like knives manufactured by controlled ripple-flaking were made towards the end of the Gerzean period and bear witness to the skill of certain highly-specialized craftsmen. Slate palettes were manufactured in the shape of fish, birds and animals and zoomorphic vases were ground out of hard stone. Beads and amulets increased in number and quality and were produced in exotic stone, including lapis lazuli, as well as in gold and silver. These objects bear witness not only to artistic and technological advances but also to the emergence of a clientele interested in possessing such luxury goods.

It has been observed that the pottery from the Naqada periods that is found in cemeteries differs considerably from that found in settlements. Much of the fancy pottery as well as many other kinds of luxury goods may have been manufactured specifically for funerary purposes. It is often pointed out that a highly-developed cult emphasizing funerary offerings may greatly stimulate production (e.g. C. Renfrew 1972, pp. 489–94). It is therefore possible to assign a major role to Upper Egyptian funerary customs in increasing the division of labour and generally promoting the development of social complexity from Predynastic times into the historic period.

[1] On the basis of recent work, Bar-Yosef *et al.* (1977) have been able to cross-date tombs of this type to about Early Bronze Age I of the Palestinian chronology.

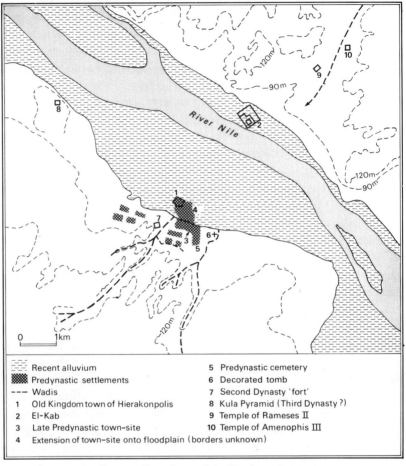

| | | |
|---|---|---|
| Recent alluvium | 5 | Predynastic cemetery |
| Predynastic settlements | 6 | Decorated tomb |
| - - - Wadis | 7 | Second Dynasty 'fort' |
| 1 Old Kingdom town of Hierakonpolis | 8 | Kula Pyramid (Third Dynasty ?) |
| 2 El-Kab | 9 | Temple of Rameses II |
| 3 Late Predynastic town-site | 10 | Temple of Amenophis III |
| 4 Extension of town-site onto floodplain (borders unknown) | | |

Fig. 7.3   General map of the Hierakonpolis area.

1  Old Kingdom town of Hierakonpoli
2  El-Kab
3  Late Predynastic town-site
4  Extension of town-site onto floodplain (borders unknown)
5  Predynastic cemetery

6  Decorated tomb
7  Second Dynasty 'fort'
8  Kula Pyramid (Third Dynasty?)
9  Temple of Ramesses II
10  Temple of Amenophis III

(After Butzer 1960.)

While Gerzean sites extend from the borders of the Delta as far south as the Nubian border, the main centres of cultural activity were to the south of Abydos. From its cemeteries, Naqada, the historic Nubet, appears to have been an extremely important centre of population. There was also a major Gerzean settlement, with satellite villages, at

Hierakonpolis (fig. 7.3). It is perhaps no coincidence that in historic times these two communities were the respective cult centres of the gods Seth and Horus, who feature so prominently in the Egyptian myths of kingship. While most Egyptians appear to have lived in small communities and been content with reed shelters, even these small settlements had communal kilns for drying grain, in the construction of which brickwork played a part (Baumgartel 1960, pp. 134–5; Vandier 1952, pp. 503–8). At the South Town at Naqada, rectangular brick houses seem to date from this period. Petrie also recorded part of a town wall at Naqada, although its relationship to the houses is unclear. A clay model found in a tomb at Hu shows a portion of the wall surrounding a building or town being guarded by sentinels. A rectangular house model from a grave at El-Amra seems to consist of a single room and an enclosed courtyard, while a house with a similar ground plan was found beneath the temple at El-Badari and is tentatively assigned to the Predynastic or Early Dynastic Periods (Baumgartel 1960, pp. 133–5). It is suggested that these were the houses of the wealthier and more urban classes. Under the historic temple at Hierakonpolis there was an oval retaining wall, built of sandstone blocks laid with a pronounced batter on the outside. This retaining wall was almost fifty metres across and closely resembles the traditional Egyptian hieroglyphic sign for the town. It is suggested that the retaining wall supported a layer of sand on which a temple was erected. As far as can be determined, this structure was built in late Predynastic times. If so, it was the sole trace of monumental architecture surviving from that period (Vandier 1952, pp. 518–25).

Increasing social stratification can be traced in the varied size and design of Gerzean tombs and in the grave-goods being put into them. Some graves were lined with wooden planks and special niches were constructed to receive grave-goods or the bodies of the dead. In Cemetery T at Naqada and at Hierakonpolis, a number of brick burial chambers, each measuring about five by two metres, have been found. These consist either of a courtyard and a single room or a rectangular chamber divided into two rooms. The interior of the tomb at Hierakonpolis had been plastered and was covered with paintings, in which Gerzean motifs appear alongside others that seem to be of south-west Asian origin. It has been suggested that both Cemetery T and the Decorated Tomb at Hierakonpolis were the burial places of Predynastic royalty (Kemp 1973).

In the late Gerzean period, there is evidence of a short period of either direct or indirect contact with the late Protoliterate b and early Protoliterate c cultures of Mesopotamia. A number of vessels and at least some of the Mesopotamian-style cylinder seals found in Egypt appear to be actual imports from Mesopotamia (Kantor 1952, 1965, p. 10). In addition, a selection of Mesopotamian (and in some cases more particularly Susian) artistic motifs was adopted at this period, particularly for the decoration of fancy stone palettes, ivory knife-handles, and other luxury goods. These motifs include interlacing serpents, serpent-necked panthers, a winged griffin, a carnivore attacking impassive prey, a man dominating two animals, distinctive head-dress and long robes, and possibly a high-hulled ship, although the latter seems to be represented already on a fragment of Amratian pottery (fig. 7.4) (Frankfort 1956, pp. 121–37; Kantor 1965, p. 10; Vandier 1952, pp. 280–1); however, Mesopotamian influences have been discounted by Kelley (1974). While these motifs did not outlast the early years of the First Dynasty, their influence on the elite artistic production of the transitional period appears to have been quite far-reaching and suggests intensive contact with Mesopotamia. The niched brick architecture of tombs and other buildings that appears suddenly at the beginning of the First Dynasty was also probably derived from south-western Asia. Although the Egyptian structures are not exact copies of Mesopotamian originals, the plan and exterior niches of the tombs resemble those of Mesopotamian temples of the early Protoliterate period. In Meso-potamia, however, the prototypes of these buildings are found as early as the 'Ubaid period and the style was an enduring component of the regional architectural tradition; by contrast, in Egypt, niche panelling ceased to be important by the Second Dynasty (Frankfort 1956, pp. 126–9). The Egyptian script can be observed developing locally from very rudimentary beginnings and bears no specific resemblance to that of Mesopotamia; however, general similarities in the two systems of writing have suggested that stimulus diffusion from Meso-potamia may have played a role in the origin of the Egyptian script (Frankfort 1956, pp. 129–32; Pope 1966). It has also been argued that some signs appear to have been invented by Semitic, rather than Egyptian, speakers. This, plus a possible influx of words of Semitic and Sumerian origin and Semitic grammatical forms at this period, suggest the possibility of yet more Near Eastern influence (Baumgartel 1955, p. 48; Meltzer 1970). It is significant that no evidence of reciprocal Egyptian influence has been noted in Mesopotamia at this time.

What is not certain is by what direction these influences reached

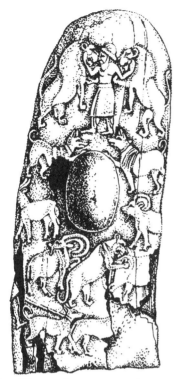

Fig. 7.4  Jebel el-Araq ivory knife-handle. Of uncertain provenance, this knife is assigned on stylistic grounds to the late Gerzean period. On the obverse appears a water battle; on the reverse a hero subduing two lions, who resembles the Mesopotamian Gilgamesh 'Lord of the Beasts' motif. This knife has been interpreted as showing evidence of Mesopotamian influence, although Egyptian types of birds and animals are portrayed on it. The 'Gilgamesh' theme also appears in the Decorated Tomb at Hierakonpolis. (Drawing by Susan Weeks.)

Upper Egypt. Helck (1962, pp. 6–9) sees no evidence of direct contacts between Egypt and Mesopotamia and believes that Mesopotamian influences reached Upper Egypt by way of the Levant and the Delta. Jar-sealings of Mesopotamian type have been found in the late Chalcolithic of Palestine and probably indicate trade between these two regions (Kenyon 1960, p. 98). Since there was also trade between Palestine and Egypt at this time, it is not impossible that Palestinians acted as middlemen in the diffusion of ideas from Mesopotamia to Egypt. Others, however, favour a direct sea route around the Arabian peninsula to a point on the Red Sea opposite the Wadi Hammamat. This, it is suggested, would explain why Mesopotamian influences are apparently limited to Upper Egypt and not particularly strong south or west of the 'Amuq and the northern Orontes Valley. It would also explain why these influences reached Egypt over a very short period of time and why many of the design elements appear to be of Susian origin, rather than from Mesopotamia proper. While acknowledging that the imported pottery at Ma'adi provides evidence of contacts and trade with Palestine at this time, Kantor (1965, pp. 11–14) and others argue that independent contact with Mesopotamia is necessary to explain the type of influence that this early phase of Mesopotamian civilization was exerting on the Nile Valley.

It is hazardous, however, to assess the nature of relations between Egypt and south-western Asia at the end of the Gerzean period without considering the motivation for contact. The Protoliterate period is recognized as a vigorous and expansive phase in Mesopotamian history, and large and elaborate ships seem to be portrayed on Mesopotamian seals at this time. This does not, however, explain why the Mesopotamians, or their middlemen, should have been interested in trading, either directly or indirectly, with southern Egypt or why the region between Abydos and Aswan became the economic and political heartland of Pharaonic Egypt (Wilson 1955).

The main product of southern Egypt that would have attracted the interest of foreigners was gold. The gold-bearing region of Egypt lies chiefly between the Nile Valley and the Red Sea, in the part of the eastern desert stretching from the Qena–El-Quseir road south to the Sudan border (Baumgartel 1960, p. 143; Lucas and Harris 1962, p. 244). It is perhaps no accident that Naqada, whose Egyptian name meant literally 'the Golden Town', was located almost opposite Koptos, which stood at the mouth of the Wadi Hammamat and thus controlled access to much of the gold and other mineral wealth of the eastern desert. Indeed, in later times the gold of Egypt was called the 'Gold of the Desert of Koptos' in order to distinguish it from that of Nubia. Hierakonpolis had a similar relationship to El-Kab, its twin city on the east bank of the Nile, which in historic times was dedicated to the tutelary goddess of Upper Egypt. Behind El-Kab, a wadi gave access to gold mines in the eastern desert (Kees 1961, pp. 123–6). Similar routes led into the desert east of Kom Ombo and Edfu, which were also important towns in the historic period.

Perhaps beginning early in the Gerzean period, knowledge of the mineral wealth of the eastern desert induced traders from south-western Asia to establish trading relations with Upper Egypt, in order to obtain gold and other valued minerals. Direct contact may have been established by way of the Red Sea, although it also seems possible that traders entered Egypt through the Delta, but tended to by-pass that area because it did not produce the expensive and easily transportable luxury goods for which they were looking. Efforts to control this trade and to exploit the eastern desert more effectively may have been important factors encouraging the development of greater centralized control and leading to the emergence of small states at key locations in southern Egypt. The nuclei of these states appear to have been communities near to points of easy access to the desert; such cities probably grew into large towns, or small cities, as they became the administrative centres for these states. By the late Gerzean period, the power and wealth of the rulers of Upper Egypt may have made it possible for them to attract Asians to their courts, whose skills were utilized both for administration and to satisfy a growing appetite for luxury goods. Some of these Asians may have been skilled artisans, who continued to utilize west Asian motifs at the same time that they used their skills to turn out works of art modified to suit the taste of their new patrons. On the other hand, architectural forms, or skills such as writing, may have been introduced by adventurers or traders who had only a very imperfect acquaintance with these arts as they were practised in Mesopotamia. This influx of foreign specialists appears to have been short-lived and the Egyptian canons of court art which emerged early in the First Dynasty rejected most of the foreign influences they had introduced.

### Prehistoric Nubia

At Jebel Silsila, near Aswan, the limestone formations of Egypt give way to Nubian sandstone. To the south, the Nile has cut more easily into the rock and, as a result, the floodplain becomes much narrower and discontinuous. The River Nile is also disrupted as an artery of communication by a series of cataracts which continue as far south as Sabaloka, near Khartoum. While precipitation appears to have been higher in late prehistoric times, especially in the southern part of this area, than it is now, Nubia has been able to sustain only a low population by comparison with Egypt.

The oldest sites in Lower Nubia that appear to contain pottery belong to the Shamarkian industry. These sites occur along the Nile near Wadi Halfa and have been dated to approximately 4000 to 4500 BC. They have yielded only minute quantities of pottery. Later 'Post-Shamarkian' sites in the same area are much larger and also contain pottery. It has been suggested that these may be 'neolithic' sites; however, there is no direct evidence of a farming or herding economy for these sites, hence their food-producing status remains in doubt. The Post-Shamarkian sites contain considerable amounts of imported Egyptian flint and have been dated to between approximately 3600 and 3000 radiocarbon years BC (Schild, Chmielewska and Wieckowska 1968).

The earliest direct evidence of food production comes from the Khartoum Neolithic culture, whose type-site, Esh-Shaheinab, is located on the west bank of the Nile about 48 km north of Omdurman. To date, this culture appears to be confined to the Nile Valley and the adjacent steppeland. The pottery, which was burnished and decorated with shallow punctate patterns, has clearly developed from that of the Khartoum Mesolithic. At Esh-Shaheinab, stone celts suggest a new emphasis on wood-working and bone harpoons, fish-hooks and the use of mussels indicate possibly even more utilization of riverine resources than in earlier times. There is also evidence that a wide range of animals, including giraffe, were being hunted. While no evidence of agriculture was found at Esh-Shaheinab, 2% of the animal bones in the site were those of sheep and goats. The site is radiocarbon-dated 3100 to 3500 BC which, however these dates are calibrated, would make it approximately coeval with the Gerzean culture. It appears that both sheep and goats and a kind of black-topped pottery had spread south from Egypt and been adopted by the local population. More recently impressions of domesticated cereals, in particular *Sorghum vulgare* and various millets, have been reported on Khartoum Neolithic-like pottery from the settlement at Kadero, dated to about 4000 BC (Arkell 1953, 1972, Klichowska 1978, Otto 1963).

Pottery resembling that of the Khartoum Neolithic has been found in sites in the Dongola region (the Karat Group) and also in the southern part of Lower Nubia (the Khartoum Variant) (Marks 1968, Wendorf 1968, vol. II, pp. 1053–4). On the other hand, the lithics associated with the pottery in each of these three areas differ widely, suggesting a diffusion of Khartoum Neolithic-type pottery among groups living in the north. Although no direct evidence of food production has been obtained for the two northern cultures, the dominance of small sites in the Khartoum Variant, both along the river and for at least 20 km west of the Nile, has been interpreted as evidence of a pastoral economy. All of these sites have been tentatively dated to the end of the fourth millennium BC.

Another possibly food-producing culture is the Abkan, which occurs on both sides of the Nile in the vicinity of the Second Cataract. The

Abkan lithic assemblage appears to have developed from the Terminal Palaeolithic Qadan Industry. Abkan pottery takes the form of plain, clay-tempered, reddish-brown, open bowls. Multiple occupation sites cover sizeable areas and suggest a larger population than in earlier times. Hunting seems to have been of little importance, but no other evidence concerning the subsistence pattern is available. The presence of small numbers of Khartoum Variant sherds in Abkan sites, and of Abkan sherds in Khartoum Variant sites, suggests that these two cultures must have been at least partly contemporary. It is unclear to what degree Abkan pottery may be related to that of the prehistoric Tergis and El-Melik groups from the Dongola area, both of which have red-slipped pottery with decoration limited to a few incised lines (Marks 1968, Wendorf 1968, vol. II, p. 1053). Further investigations may also reveal whether or not there is any historical connection between Abkan pottery and that of the Northern Predynastic Sequence. It is not impossible that, prior to the beginning of the Badarian culture, a plain red pottery tradition extended from the Delta south into Nubia, of which no trace has yet been identified in Upper Egypt.

The most important cultural development in Lower Nubia during the latter part of the fourth millennium was the formulation of the A-group culture, which persisted into the Early Dynastic Period (Nordström 1972, pp. 17–32). The Abkan and Khartoum Variant cultures appear to have played an important role in the development of the A-group, and pottery derived from both appears in A-group sites, especially in southern Lower Nubia. More striking, however, is the gradual penetration of Lower Nubia by cultural traits of the Upper Egyptian Predynastic Sequence. The earliest evidence of this penetration is the pottery of late Amratian and early Gerzean date found at Khor Bahan, just south of Aswan. During the Gerzean period, pottery of the Upper Egyptian Sequence gradually spread southward along the Nile. Some of this pottery has distinctive features which, already in the early A-group, distinguish it from Egyptian pottery. One example is the so-called black-mouthed variant of Petrie's black-topped ware. This was manufactured in open bowl-shapes which, long before, had gone out of fashion in Egypt. Other forms of pottery, including ledge-handled jars, are clearly imports from Egypt. These jars probably contained cheese, honey, oil and other food products which were sought after by the Nubians. Copper tools, slate palettes and linen cloth also appear to count among the luxury goods that were imported from Egypt at this time (Trigger 1965, pp. 68–73).

It has generally been assumed that at this time the subsistence patterns of Lower Nubia were based on mixed farming, as were those of Upper Egypt; however, Firth has stressed the pastoral aspect of this economy and suggests that the Nubians resembled the Saharan tribes more than they did the Egyptians (Trigger 1965, pp. 67–8). It has been confirmed that wheat, barley and leguminous plants were grown, while cotton seeds (*Gossypium arboreum* or *G. herbaceum*) appear to have been fed to domestic animals (Chowdhury and Buth 1971). The Egyptians listed cattle and goats as booty from Nubia in the Old Kingdom. No traces of house structures have been found in any of the sites of this period, which appear to have been small encampments inhabited by no more than half a dozen families. Each band seems to have occupied its own stretch of arable floodplain. Their camps were probably located by the bank of the river for most of the year, but were moved to the edge of the floodplain during the inundation. Although the A-group people appear to have been physically similar to the Egyptians, their ethnic status remains unknown and there is no basis for suggestions that they were Egyptian, Hamitic, or Eastern Sudanic speaking (Edwards 1971, p. 50). The cultural differences between Lower Nubia and Egypt may be explained largely in terms of the former region's limited agricultural potential, rather than in terms of ethnic differences.

How were the Nubians able to import ever larger amounts of luxury goods from Egypt? It is likely that the growing wealth and prosperity of the Gerzean culture created a market for large amounts of ivory, ebony and other luxury products from sub-Saharan Africa. It may be that the inhabitants of Lower Nubia engaged in small-scale trade in such items and were able to derive a substantial profit from it. It has also been suggested that the Khor Daud site, near the mouth of the Wadi el-Allaqi, was a riverine bartering place for cattle pastoralists living in the eastern desert (Nordström 1972, p. 26); whether such a cattle trade could have supported a significant amount of exchange with the Egyptians is another matter. Alternatively, many of the Egyptian items found in Lower Nubia may have been supplied to the Nubians as goodwill presents by Egyptian traders seeking rights-of-way to travel to and from the south. It is also possible that, as has happened in recent centuries, Nubians might have earned these goods as labour migrants in the north. In particular, they may have been given in payment to detachments of Nubians who served in the Egyptian armies in late Gerzean times.

## *The Development of the Egyptian State*

Unfortunately, current archaeological evidence sheds little light on the political history of Egypt in prehistoric times. On the Palermo Stone, a year-by-year record of the Egyptian kings that was compiled in the Fifth Dynasty, a series of Predynastic rulers are shown wearing the Red Crown of Lower Egypt, followed by others wearing the Double Crown (*shmty*, 'the two powerful ones') of a united country; however, only the names of these Predynastic kings are recorded, whereas, beginning with the First Dynasty, the Palermo Stone chronicles each year of a king's reign separately, noting appropriate information concerning it. Although there is no evidence that the Double Crown existed prior to the middle of the First Dynasty, Kaiser has shown that these early kings and the prehistoric rulers alluded to in the Turin papyrus and Manetho's history are all variants of a single tradition (Edwards 1971, p. 26; Kaiser 1964). This evidence was once viewed as providing support for Sethe's theory about the emergence, in Predynastic times, of a Deltaic Kingdom which conquered the whole of Egypt. Now, however, Egyptologists tend to view these Predynastic kings, as later the Egyptians themselves did, as demigods who ruled Egypt between the time of the gods and the first human kings. As such, they may have lacked an historical existence. This has encouraged the majority of Egyptologists to assume that the first political unification of Egypt took place at about the beginning of the First Dynasty. Scenes depicted on some elaborately decorated late Gerzean palettes (fig. 7.5) and on the votive mace-heads and palettes of Kings Scorpion and Narmer have thus been interpreted as a record of the conquest of the northern part of the country by kings originating in Upper Egypt. Not long ago, the major disagreement about this period was focused on the debate as to whether King Narmer, or his presumed predecessor, the Scorpion king, was the first monarch to rule over the whole of Egypt (Arkell 1963). It has often been suggested that the canons of art which developed at this time, and which show the king as a figure increasingly aloof from his followers, are a faithful reflection of the growing power of the king.

It has also frequently been assumed that the original Egyptian states were small units equivalent to the nomes or districts which served as administrative divisions of the country in historic times. Out of the union of these tiny states, two coherent, independent kingdoms were thought to have emerged; one centred in the Delta, the other in Upper

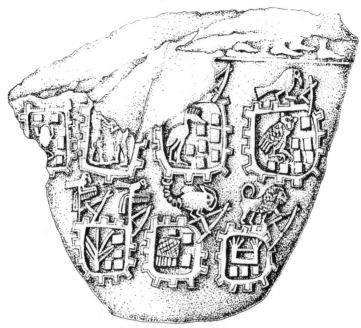

Fig. 7.5   The obverse side of the so-called 'Libyan palette'. This and similar stone palettes have been assigned on stylistic grounds to the late Gerzean period and are often interpreted as illustrating steps in the unification of Predynastic Egypt; however, the precise significance of the walls and the birds and animals hacking away at them are unknown. The former have been interpreted as forts, towns, or as synonyms for a single fort or town. The figures have been interpreted as representing a confederacy of clans or districts, gods helping the king to victory, or the king himself. If Egyptologists disagree concerning the meaning of such key elements, it is clear that the overall significance of the palettes must remain uncertain. (Drawing by Susan Weeks.)

Egypt. Between them, these two kingdoms are supposed to have controlled the whole of the Nile Valley north of Aswan. Only after these states were in existence was the unification of Egypt brought about as a result of the conquest of Lower Egypt by Upper Egypt (Edwards 1971, p. 1). Against this interpretation, Frankfort has argued that the idea of a northern kingdom was created as a symbolic counterpart to the southern one after the piecemeal conquest of a series of small states by kings from Upper Egypt. According to Frankfort, the idea of two kingdoms reflects the Egyptian view of a totality as being comprised of opposites in balanced opposition (Frankfort 1948, pp. 15–23). Whatever kind of polity, or polities, existed in the north, the rigorous parallelism in the institutions and symbols ascribed to the two kingdoms supports Frankfort's view that these kingdoms were the creation of political–theological dogma rather than historical realities. While not attempting to underestimate the contribution that Deltaic political and religious institutions made to those of a united Egypt, many Egypt-ologists now discount the idea that a united prehistoric kingdom of Lower Egypt ever existed.

It has also been generally assumed that the cultural florescence that took place at the beginning of the First Dynasty was a consequence of the political unification of Egypt. Recently, however, Kaiser has challenged this view. He interprets the tradition of kings of a united Egypt before the First Dynasty as evidence that the conquest of the Delta by Upper Egypt took place considerably prior to the First Dynasty. The victory commemorated on the celebrated Narmer palette would thus be related to a reconquest of a northern region, or the crushing of a rebellion there, rather than to the original annexation of that area. In Kaiser's opinion, such an early union would account for the dispersal of various items of Upper Egyptian culture throughout the Delta in late Gerzean times. Large pottery vessels, found not only at Tura and Abusir el-Malaq, near Cairo, but also at Beda, in the north-east Delta, bear *serekhs* that appear to give the Horus-names of kings who ruled prior to those attested in the royal cemeteries at Abydos. Comparing the size of the Predynastic cemetery at Tura with the sections dating from the Early Dynastic Period, Kaiser (1964, p. 114) estimates that the unification of Egypt may have taken place 100 to 150 years prior to King Narmer.

Kaiser's theory has given rise to much interesting speculation. Naqada was clearly an important centre in prehistoric times and it has long been suggested that the legend of Horus and Seth may refer to a political crisis in Upper Egypt in which the rulers of this town were conquered by the followers of the god Horus (Baumgartel 1955, p. 47). It might be that the elaborate brick tombs in Cemetery T at Naqada are the graves of the first kings of a united Egypt, prior to their being supplanted by the rulers of Hierakonpolis, the town sacred to the god Horus (Kemp 1973). The last king of the Hierakonpolitan Dynasty may have been Scorpion, whose monuments are known from that place but not from Abydos (Kaiser 1964, pp. 102–5). On stylistic grounds, Scorpion appears to have preceded by only a little time Ka (or Sekhen) and Narmer, the earliest kings so far attested in the First Dynasty royal cemetery at Abydos. This interpretation would make the kings of the First Dynasty heirs of political traditions that had developed during the course of the previous century. Kaiser also views the political unity of

Egypt in the late Predynastic Period as laying the groundwork for the cultural unity of Early Dynastic times. It must be noted, however, that political unity does not inevitably give rise to cultural unity and that at the site of Ma'adi, the Northern Egyptian cultural tradition appears to have survived, in spite of southern influence, until the Early Dynastic Period.

Egypt may have been politically united in late Predynastic times, even though this unity did not express itself in monumental art or architecture, or in any form of literacy; in short, in the formation of a Great Tradition, such as distinguished the civilizations of antiquity. 'Primitive kingdoms' of this sort are well known in sub-Saharan Africa: the Zulu empire and Buganda providing two examples from the last century. By their very nature, however, polities of this sort are difficult to trace in the archaeological record and, at present, the evidence for a single government for the whole of Egypt prior to the First Dynasty must be judged insufficient. The context in which most Gerzean artifacts have been discovered in the Delta is unknown and, in any case, it is possible that all of this material reached Lower Egypt as trade goods rather than as a result of the spread of Upper Egyptian political influence. Pottery bearing royal inscriptions often travelled outside Egypt in the historic period; thus the vessels found in the presumed store-house at Beda do not prove that this site was under Upper Egyptian control or that a united Egypt existed in Predynastic times. It is uncertain to what extent the north-eastern Delta was incorporated into the Egyptian state even as late as the Old Kingdom (Goedicke 1969–70). It is possible that the Predynastic kings whose *serekhs* appear on these pottery vessels were the rulers of small states who were trading with the Delta and, either directly or indirectly, with south-western Asia. It must also be noted that Baumgartel interprets the rosette and scorpion on the largest of the Hierakonpolis mace-heads as a title, rather than the name of a monarch, and thus denies the existence of a King Scorpion (Baumgartel 1960, p. 103, 1966). Until more definite evidence is forthcoming, the very existence of the only pre-Abydene king to whom substantial monuments have been attributed must remain in doubt.

Recent studies of the political development of Egypt in Predynastic times thus have not so much discredited older interpretations as they have raised new alternatives. In the absence of substantial fresh evidence, it is scarcely surprising that this is so. Under the circumstances, it is only possible to outline what appears to be theoretically the most satisfactory sequence of events; at the same time stressing the paucity of data on which any interpretation of this period must be based.

It has been suggested that in early Predynastic times each village was autonomous and had a headman whose power rested on his reputation as a 'rainmaker king'; who was presumably able to control the Nile flood (Frankfort 1948, pp. 18, 33–5). Such rainmakers have been found among African tribes, such as the Dinka, Ngonde and Jukun, in recent times and, in some tribes, they were slain once their magical powers were believed to have begun to wane. Egyptologists saw a manifestation of similar ideas in the Sed festival of the historic period, during which the powers of a reigning king were rejuvenated by rites in which he symbolically died and was reborn. Those who read Seligman's accounts of the Sudan saw in this rite a prototype of the ritual regicide reportedly practised among the Shilluk. The validity of such analogies rests largely on the assumption that Predynastic practices diffused to the upper reaches of the Nile and survived there, or that Egyptian and Nilotic cultures both developed from a common cultural substratum (Seligman and Murray 1911). Interesting as such ideas are, they remain unproved and it seems best to state categorically that nothing is known in detail about the specific social or political institutions of Predynastic Egypt.

Future discoveries may compel us to modify the idea that, in early Predynastic times, the social structure of Egypt was simple and relatively unstratified. It is not unlikely that the rise of monarchical institutions preceeded the development of the iconography by which these institutions were recognized in later times. At present, however, evidence of a high degree of craft specialization, of long-distance trade within Egypt and of sustained contacts with south-western Asia becomes visible only in the early phases of the Gerzean culture. The need to integrate and manage this new economy probably contributed to the breakdown of the relatively egalitarian tribal structures that had hitherto regulated life in the Nile Valley, and encouraged the development of a more hierarchical society, as well as of towns which served as nodal points in the economic organization and as centres of political control. The deities and cults associated with these central places probably played a major role in validating their growing importance and mediating their relationships with smaller subordinate communities. It may be possible, therefore, to describe these communities as cult centres, in the sense in which Wheatley (1971) uses this term. In later times, these cults provided one of the principal sources of identity for such communities and were an important mechanism by which local interests could express themselves *vis-à-vis* the central government. Up to this point, social development in Egypt seems to have followed essentially the same path as it had done in Mesopotamia.

In the latter culture, this pattern gave rise, in early historic times, to a pattern of warring city states.

While northern communities, such as Ma'adi, may have flourished as entrepôts trading with both Palestine and Upper Egypt, the area chiefly affected by these new developments was the southern part of Egypt, where the Nile River approached nearest to the Red Sea Hills. There, the procurement of minerals from the eastern desert and, in particular, the organization of gold mining seems to have provided an especially powerful stimulus to the development of local, or city, states. The rulers of Naqada and Hierakonpolis were probably buried in the so-called royal tombs in the Predynastic cemeteries associated with these town-sites.

As trade with south-western Asia increased, all these local rulers must have been anxious to control this trade and to monopolize the profits derived from it. This would have led to increasing competition and conflict, as the principal rulers of Upper Egypt strove for hegemony over the whole area. The desire to protect trade routes and to eliminate intermediaries in Lower Egypt may also have encouraged these rulers to try to extend their power northward. In the course of these conflicts, the rulers of Naqada appear to have lost their independence, although their aristocratic descendants may have been buried in the very large 'royal' tombs erected there early in the First Dynasty (Kemp 1967, 1973). While it has been suggested that the rulers of Hierakonpolis may have moved their capital down river to Abydos in the course of their conquest of northern Egypt (Vandier 1952, pp. 613–14), this does not explain the importance that the kings of the First Dynasty attached to Abydos as a place of royal burial. It seems more likely that the rulers of Hierakonpolis also became clients of the kings who founded the First Dynasty and that these kings were descended from local rulers whose tombs have gone unrecorded or unrecognized at Abydos (on the other brick-lined tombs in the royal cemetery see Kemp (1966)).

Whether rulers other than those at Abydos extended their power northward remains an open question, although it is not impossible that there were dramatic shifts in the balance of power in Upper Egypt in late Gerzean times. The respect shown for the gods Seth and Horus by the Early Dynastic kings and the lavish gifts that the early kings of the First Dynasty made to the shrine at Hierakonpolis suggest that these kings were anxious to honour the gods of important rival centres and thus to bind these centres into a coalition that would facilitate an extension of royal power northward. The forging of alliances with the rulers of the various city states of Upper Egypt may have played as important a role as military conquest in establishing a basis of power in southern Egypt which allowed the conquest of the whole country.

It is unclear whether King Scorpion (if he existed) ruled from Hierakonpolis or merely left votive offerings there, as did other rulers from Abydos. As we have noted, however, if Arkell is right in reading Scorpion's name on a much-damaged mace-head showing a king wearing the Red Crown of Lower Egypt, Scorpion may already have claimed to be the ruler of a united Egypt. He appears to have been followed by Ka, and then by Narmer and Aha, all three of whom were buried in the royal cemetery at Abydos. The last two clearly claimed kingship over a united Egyptian state, although it is not agreed which, or if any of them, is to be identified as Menes, the traditional founder of the First Dynasty (Emery 1961, pp. 32–7).

These kings, whose reigns follow not long after the phase of furtive Mesopotamian influence noted at the end of the Gerzean period, not only established a royal administration capable of holding together the Nile Valley north of Aswan, but also made this administration the chief patron under which the elite culture of Egypt was to develop in the centuries that followed. It is highly significant that a coherent Great Tradition had not developed prior to the unification of Egypt. Moreover, urban institutions and civic patriotism, which were such vital features of Mesopotamian culture and were to outlive the development of empires in that part of the world, do not appear to have developed to nearly the same degree in Egypt prior to the First Dynasty. With the emergence of a strong centralized government, all of the country's nascent economic and political institutions became subjected to royal authority and control. The central government, either directly or through major officials, became the employer of soldiers, retainers, bureaucrats and craftsmen, whose goods and services benefited the upper classes and the state gods. The large mud-brick enclosure walls that already seem to have surrounded the principal buildings at Hierakonpolis (Fairservis, Weeks and Hoffman 1971–2) and elsewhere served to demarcate and shelter the nodal points in this royal administration.

In the course of the Early Dynastic Period, artisans and civil servants working for the central government were to fashion the highly sophisticated traditions of art and learning that thereafter were to constitute the basic pattern of Pharaonic civilization. In turn, this cultural pattern became a major factor in promoting the stability of the new political order. It is uncertain to what degree cultural know-how from south-western Asia played a role in the fashioning of Early Dynastic culture, but it cannot be doubted that it was one of the factors that helped the First Dynasty state resulting from the conquest to produce an enduring high culture. The highly distinctive style of this civilization and the rapid disappearance of all evidence of Mesopotamian influence is indicative, however, of the internal dynamism of Egyptian society at this time.

Equally striking are the structural differences between Early Dynastic and south-west Asian social organization after this time. The fruits of Mesopotamian civilization were divided among a number of city states and among various interest groups within each of these urban centres. By contrast, the fruits of Egyptian civilization were expended on a royal court and, to a striking degree, as the emphasis on royal mortuary complexes demonstrates, on the person of the king. While Mesopotamia was to create nothing on the scale of the Old Kingdom pyramids, a greater number of Mesopotamians probably benefited from, and participated in, the Great Tradition of their society than did their Egyptian counterparts. The achievement of a stable, centralized government in Egypt also removed some of the insecurity which in Mesopotamia encouraged the rapid growth of fortified urban centres (R. M. Adams 1972, Frankfort 1956). This helped to perpetuate a pattern of dispersed villages and only relatively small regional administrative centres. Such a development may also explain the preoccupation with rural, as opposed to urban, life that was a distinctive feature of the elite culture of Egypt.

After unification, most Egyptians must have found daily life in their villages little changed from what it had been before. More taxes in kind were probably collected and additional demands made for *corvée* labour. In return, peace and greater security against famine provided the average Egyptian with increased prosperity, while agricultural development must have both encouraged and kept abreast of a growing population throughout this period. While the population of Egypt has been estimated to have been as low as 100000 to 200000 inhabitants in late Predynastic times (Butzer 1966), a reference to 120000 men, as either prisoners or part of a grant to a temple, on a mace-head of King Narmer suggests a considerably larger population at the beginning of the Early Dynastic Period (Emery 1961, pp. 44–5). A population of two million or more is not an unreasonable guess for this period.

*Political Organization*

According to Manetho, the kings of the first two dynasties originated in the Thinite nome of Upper Egypt. The tombs of the First Dynasty kings are located in the Umm el-Qaab area of the Abydos cemeteries, about 2 km west of the limit of cultivation (fig. 7.6). These tombs, the largest of which had a floor area of about 340 sq. m, consisted of subterranean brick chambers lined with wooden panelling. Each tomb seems to have been covered by a low mound of sand or gravel held inside a brick retaining wall. Here too were erected twin stone stelae bearing the Horus-name of the dead king. While the earliest tombs consisted of one or more single rooms, later ones had a central chamber surrounded by store-rooms. Beginning in the reign of King Den, a stairway gave access to the burial chamber. In Den's tomb, the burial chamber was also paved with blocks of Aswan granite. The relatively small size of these tombs and their proximity to one another suggests that Umm el-Qaab was a location of special sanctity to the kings of the First Dynasty. Perhaps, like the cemetery of the much later Nubian kings at Kurru, it was revered as the burial place of their ancestors. Nearer the cultivated land, and just behind the Early Dynastic town at Abydos, each king also erected a large rectangular brick enclosure, which Kemp (1966, 1967) suggests were intended as funerary palaces. Both the funerary palaces and the royal tombs were surrounded by rows of smaller graves, blocks of which appear to have shared a common roof. The stelae accompanying the graves around the royal tombs indicate that they contained members of the royal entourage. Many are of women, presumably members of the royal harem, while others belonged to minor palace functionaries, court dwarfs, or even favourite dogs. On the other hand, at least some of the graves surrounding the funerary palaces seem to have belonged to artisans. While there is no direct evidence how these retainers died, at least some did so just prior to when a royal burial was closed. This suggests that these retainers were killed so they might continue to serve the king after death. The custom seems to have reached its peak in the reign of King Djer, who was accompanied by over 580 retainers, but persisted at a reduced level in royal burials throughout the Early Dynastic Period.

Aside from the enigmatic Merneith (Kaplan 1979), who may have been a regnant queen, there is no indication that other members of the royal family, or high-ranking officials, were buried at Abydos. Two sets of underground galleries, about 1 km south of the main Early Dynastic

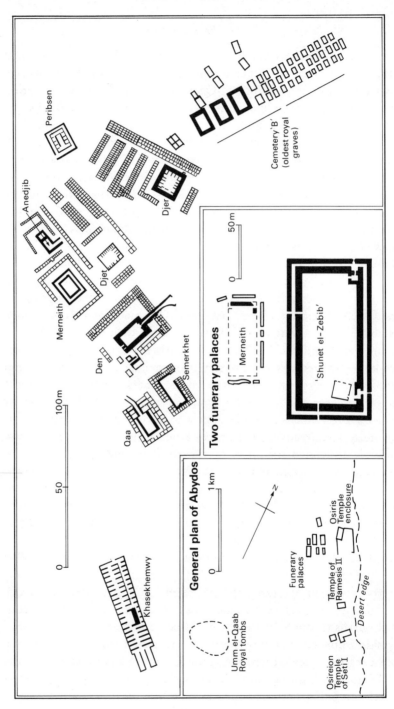

Fig. 7.6   The royal tombs and funerary palaces at Abydos.

**General plan of Abydos**

0        1 km

N

Umm el-Qaab
Royal tombs

Funerary
palaces

Osiris
Temple
enclosure

Temple of
Ramesis II

Osireion
Temple
of Seti I

Desert edge

**Two funerary palaces**

0        50 m

Merneith

Merneith

'Shunet el-Zebib'

Khasekhemwy

Qaa

Den

Semerkhet

Djet

Merneith

Anedjib

Djer

Peribsen

Cemetery 'B'
(oldest royal
graves)

0        50        100 m

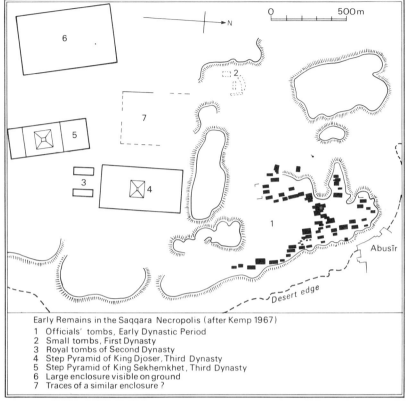

Early Remains in the Saqqara Necropolis (after Kemp 1967)
1 Officials' tombs, Early Dynastic Period
2 Small tombs, First Dynasty
3 Royal tombs of Second Dynasty
4 Step Pyramid of King Djoser, Third Dynasty
5 Step Pyramid of King Sekhemkhet, Third Dynasty
6 Large enclosure visible on ground
7 Traces of a similar enclosure ?

Fig. 7.7   Early remains in the Saqqara necropolis.

1 Officials' tombs, Early Dynastic Period
2 Small tombs, First Dynasty
3 Royal tombs of Second Dynasty
4 Step Pyramid of King Djoser, Third Dynasty
5 Step Pyramid of King Sekhemkhet, Third Dynasty
6 Large enclosure visible on ground
7 Traces of a similar enclosure?

(After Kemp 1967.)

cemetery at Saqqara, appear to be royal graves of the Second Dynasty (fig. 7.7) (Kemp 1967). Unlike the rulers of the First Dynasty, these kings chose to be buried near Memphis, rather than at their home town of Abydos. The dissension which seems to have divided Egypt late in the Second Dynasty led kings Peribsen and Khasekhemwy to build their tombs at Abydos, while the so-called 'fort' at Hierakonpolis also may have been erected as a funerary palace at about this time (Kaiser 1964, p. 104, n. 4).

According to Herodotus, Menes, the founder of the First Dynasty, constructed dykes to divert the Nile River and, on the land thus protected, he built the city of Memphis and its main temple, which was dedicated to the god Ptah. Whether or not this story is true, Memphis was an important administrative centre from early in the First Dynasty and the palace and temple of Ptah were later regarded as closely connected with the unification of Egypt (Kees 1961, p. 148). Although this part of the Nile Valley was not a particularly rich agricultural area, it was located near the branching of the Nile and was thus strategically placed in terms of riverine communication (Wilson 1955). On the northern spur of the Saqqara plateau behind Memphis, a cemetery was established in the reign of Aha, which eventually contained the tombs of many important officials of the Early Dynastic Period. These so-called mastaba tombs were equipped with rectangular brick superstructures, either filled with gravel or containing storage chambers. Their internal arrangements became increasingly elaborate, as did those of the royal tombs, as storage rooms multiplied, and by the end of the period subterranean chambers were being excavated out of solid rock (Vandier 1952, pp. 644–72). Although the largest of these tombs were bigger than the royal tombs at Abydos, they did not exceed in size the royal funerary palaces. Tumuli found hidden inside the superstructures of some of the Saqqara tombs suggest that they sought to combine the elements of both a tomb and a funerary palace within a single structure (Kemp 1966).

A small number of other very large mastaba tombs have been reported from Naqada, Tarkhan, Giza and Abu Rawash. Some, but not all, of these large tombs were accompanied by subsidiary burials; over sixty have been reported for one such tomb, although the number is usually much smaller. This custom seems to have died out by the end of the First Dynasty, in line with a marked curtailment of retainer sacrifice, in royal burials. Over 10000 graves have been excavated in the Early Dynastic (largely First Dynasty) cemetery at Helwan, on the east bank of the Nile opposite Memphis. While most of these are humble graves, the cemetery also contained the tombs of numerous officials. Although smaller than the graves at Saqqara, these too belonged to people who had easy access to skilled craftsmen and luxury goods. Burial chambers built of large blocks of reasonably well-cut limestone were constructed at Helwan in the First Dynasty, but do not appear in the royal tombs until the end of the Second Dynasty (Saad 1969, pp. 36–7). While the graves of ordinary Egyptians differed little from those of late Predynastic times, the more prosperous provincial cemeteries contained a number of smaller and simpler versions of the mastaba tombs of the upper classes. These tombs appear to have belonged to the headmen of these communities (Reisner 1932, pp. 185–92).

The funerary customs of the Early Dynastic Period suggest a hierarchy of king; great nobles or high officials (including other members of the royal family); lesser officials (including local headmen); craftsmen and retainers; and peasantry, the latter making up the bulk of the population. While the mortuary structures of the king in size considerably outstripped those of the great officials and were surrounded by many more retainer burials, the differences between these two categories of burial are far less marked than they were during the Old Kingdom. This suggests either that the power of the kings to appropriate resources for their own use was more limited in the Early Dynastic Period than it was later on, or that the kings of this period did not choose to emphasize the differences between themselves and other leading men in this fashion. The clustering of the largest tombs of officials around the pyramid of the reigning pharaoh in the Old Kingdom is generally interpreted as indicating the strength of royal authority at that time; hence, it might be argued that the burial of high officials, not only in their own necropolis at Saqqara but also in other cemeteries throughout Egypt, is a sign of greater independence of royal control at this time. On the other hand, the way in which the tombs of even the high nobility were kept away from the Early Dynastic royal cemeteries, both at Abydos and Saqqara, may indicate that kings were accorded a sanctity in Early Dynastic times which did not permit other tombs to encroach upon their burial places (Kemp 1967).[1]

Unfortunately, knowledge of the dynastic history and administrative organization of Egypt during the Early Dynastic Period is extremely limited. Information about the government is derived largely from seals, seal impressions, and inscribed wooden and ivory labels. This material naturally emphasizes ownership of goods and provisioning, and thus gives a far from balanced picture of the government of Egypt at this time. Finally, the archaic form of the Egyptian script with which this material is inscribed presents numerous problems for the translator. In spite of the extremely valuable work that Kaplony (1963) has done in interpreting these early documents, no systematic analysis of the political organization of the Early Dynastic Period has yet been attempted.

There is, however, little doubt that, from the beginning, the kings

---

[1] Note, however, that in the Old Kingdom cemetery at Naga ed-Deir, headmen's tombs were located away from other contemporary ones.

of Egypt claimed divine status. Through their Horus-names, which were the ones regularly used in contemporary inscriptions, they proclaimed themselves to be the earthly embodiment of that deity. Peribsen deviated from this custom only in identifying himself with Seth in place of Horus (Edwards 1971, p. 35). The paramount role of the monarch was emphasized by portraying him as the sole force holding together an otherwise separate Upper and Lower Egypt. This was emphasized by the king wearing distinct regalia to symbolize each realm and by his *nebty*-name, which stressed his dual relationship to the vulture goddess Nekhbet of Upper Egypt and the cobra goddess Uadjyt of Lower Egypt. It was once believed that this name indicated that El-Kab and Buto, the respective towns of these goddesses, had been the capitals of Upper and Lower Egypt. Wilson argues, however, that the goddesses of these two cities were selected as symbols of Upper and Lower Egypt because their cult centres best embodied the extreme contrasts between the arid far south of Egypt and the marshes of the Delta (Wilson 1955). The king's third or *insibya*- name, which is first attested in the reign of King Den, gives his style as king of Upper and Lower Egypt, and thus, like the *nebty*-name, is a dual title. The latter part appears to be connected with the worship of Neith, the goddess of Sais in the western Delta (Edwards 1971, p. 53). A number of Sed festivals are recorded for this period, testifying to the antiquity of this ritual. Little can be said about either the structure of the royal family or the rules governing succession to the throne. The lengths assigned to reigns of this period suggest, however, that the throne was normally passed from generation to generation, and probably from father to son, as it was in later times.

The titles of the Early Dynastic period overwhelmingly refer to positions in an administrative hierarchy, rather than to hereditary rank. Royal children are seldom explicitly identified as such, but, if Kaplony is right in identifying the names of seal-bearers, when juxtaposed with those of kings, as expressing filiation, many high officials may have been members of the royal family. Many offices appear to have been passed from father to son, although it is unclear whether this happened by right, or whether each transfer had to receive royal approbation separately. Officials served under successive kings and had estates whose produce constituted a significant portion of the grave-goods that were deposited in their tombs (Kaplony 1963, pp. 25, 58–9, 71). Whether all of these estates were granted to officials by the king to sustain and reward them for their services, or whether some of them had been hereditary in particular families prior to the First Dynasty, is unknown. It seems likely, however, that, whatever nominal claim the king may have made to pre-eminent domain, older patterns of land-holding at the village level, and possibly among the upper classes also, were not unduly interfered with by the king. In spite of the controls exerted over the Egyptian economy by the central government, these controls could not have developed in an economic vacuum; it is therefore mistaken to underestimate the complexity of land-holding patterns and of economic activities in Egypt at this period.

Only a few titles have been preserved that refer specifically to the regional administration of Egypt at this time. It would be interesting to know if important provincial officials enjoyed hereditary rights in particular areas or if they were transferred from district to district in the course of their career as was done during the Old Kingdom. The general restriction of very large tombs at Naqada, and elsewhere outside Memphis, to a relatively early date, suggests the possible suppression of any tendency towards a feudal-style decentralization of power. While the shifting of officials from district to district might have lessened the efficiency of administration, it would have helped to protect the authority of the central government and thus have laid the basis for the spectacular exercise of this authority early in the Old Kingdom.

More is known about the administration of the palace and of the royal estates, including the vineyards in the western Delta. There was also a large, well-organized bureaucracy which collected taxes in kind throughout the country, stored these goods in government warehouses and supervised their distribution to those who were privileged to receive royal largess. The height of the Nile flood was carefully recorded each year and probably served as the basis for computing annual rates of taxation on crops, while a biennial royal tour of inspection allowed for a general census of taxable resources. Whether or not the king personally took part in this tour, it was known as the 'Following of Horus' (*šmsw Ḥr*) and, along with flood heights, it was faithfully recorded on the Palermo Stone (Edwards 1971, p. 38).

The need for book-keeping, supplemented by a desire to record royal exploits, appears to have been mainly responsible for the development of writing in Egypt. No inscribed papyri have survived from the Early Dynastic Period, so that the early history of Egyptian writing must be derived mainly from jar-sealings, labels and inscriptions on monumental objects (fig. 7.8). These indicate that the evolution of writing was closely associated with the royal court. Until the reign of Den, seals generally recorded only the names of kings and officials; while afterwards titles

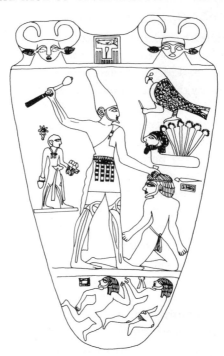

Fig. 7.8   Reverse side of the slate palette of King Narmer. Here appears for the first time the classic motif of the monarch dominating a conquered enemy. Hieroglyphs, some obscure because of the early stage in the development of the writing system, identify the figures. Narmer's name is written within the royal *serekh* that appears top centre. (After Gardiner 1927.)

and other bureaucratic designations became increasingly common (Kaplony 1963, p. xxxii). At the same time, hieroglyphs ceased to serve only as legends to pictorial representations and dockets covered largely or wholly with writing began to appear. By the end of the First Dynasty, whole sentences were being conveyed by sequences of signs (Gardiner 1961, p. 415; Vandier 1952, p. 859). Significantly, however, no evidence of the use of writing was found to occur prior to the Fifth Dynasty in the small cemetery at Naga ed-Deir (Reisner 1932).

The central government used some of the food surpluses and manufactured goods that it had at its disposal to engage in foreign trade. While there is no evidence that the king claimed a monopoly over this trade, the needs and wealth of the court encouraged the palace to trade on a scale that greatly exceeded that of any other individual or institution in the country. It therefore seems likely that it was through the court that most foreign goods made their way into Egypt, prior to being distributed as royal bounty. Masses of pottery vessels from the

Early Bronze Age II culture of Palestine and coastal Syria have been found in royal tombs of the First Dynasty, as well as in those of high officials. Conversely, pottery of the First Dynasty has been found in sites such as Tell Gath in southern Palestine, which has yielded a jar inscribed with the name of King Narmer. In addition to importing jars of olive oil from southern Palestine, the kings of Egypt obtained large amounts of timber, suitable for building boats, lining tombs and fashioning coffins and household furniture, from Syria and Lebanon; while other exotic items, which came from farther to the north or west, such as obsidian and lapis lazuli, must have entered Egypt along the same routes. This trade appears to have been carried on by both sea and land and to have continued through the Second Dynasty and into the Old Kingdom (Kantor 1965, pp. 16–17). There is no evidence that contacts with Mesopotamia were still maintained at this time; instead, Egyptian trade seems to have been limited to areas of south-western Asia that were economically and culturally less developed than Egypt was. The Egyptian kings also sent expeditions into the eastern desert to exploit the mineral resources of that area. An inscription of Narmer in the Wadi el-Qash and another of Djet in the Wadi Mia, 24 km east of Edfu, appear to commemorate expeditions of a commercial or punitive nature (Edwards, 1971, pp. 22, 24–5; Emery 1961, pp. 47, 49). Copper was used in abundance in the Early Dynastic period, as was turquoise, but there is no proof that the Egyptians had begun to send expeditions to the Sinai peninsula at this time.

The royal court appears to have employed large numbers of artists and craftsmen, who were capable of turning out a wide variety of luxury goods. These craftsmen, most of whom probably worked in the vicinity of Memphis, evolved a coherent style and established artistic canons that were to remain an integral part of the elite culture of ancient Egypt. Some of the jewellery, furniture and other luxury goods produced by these artisans were distributed among the officials who served the king to reward them and retain their loyalty. Donations to temples also reinforced the ties between the king and the locality or region the temple served. It is uncertain whether most temples were still the shrines of light construction that seem to be depicted in representations of the Early Dynastic Period or whether these had been generally superseded by larger and more substantial buildings.[1] The royal administration no doubt played a direct role in the maintenance of the chief temples, and

---

[1] On the function and date of the so-called Temple of Khenty-amentiu at Abydos see Kemp (1968b).

royal visits to the shrines of important deities and the fashioning of cult statues of the gods are noted on the Palermo Stone as matters of great importance (Gardiner 1961, p. 414). While craftsmen were normally buried only with food, drink and some of the tools of their trade, there can be little doubt that they participated, at least to a limited degree, in the bounty of the king and his officials. Even the peasantry probably received boons in the form of meat and drink on festive occasions, although there is no direct evidence of this for the Early Dynastic Period. If less that was tangible was returned to these classes than was demanded of them in taxes and services, such devices would nevertheless have kept alive older ideas of reciprocity and helped to maintain the goodwill of the masses, in addition to their obedience and reverence. It is also possible that at this period a man of ability could reasonably hope to climb in the administrative hierarchy (Frankfort 1956, pp. 107–8). This was particularly likely if the population was expanding and new positions were developing in an increasingly complex society.

## Foreign Relations

Although the military organization at this period is obscure, force must have played a role in maintaining the unity of the Egyptian state and regulating its relations with its neighbours. References to the suppression of 'northern enemies' on monuments of King Khasekhem suggest the crushing of a rebellion, or a counter-dynasty, in northern Egypt towards the end of the Second Dynasty (Edwards 1971, p. 33), although others interpret this as a campaign against the Libyans, who lived along the borders of Lower Egypt and against whom the kings of Egypt had waged war at an early period (Gardiner 1961, p. 418). Both Kings Djer and Den claim to have engaged in combat with enemies living to the east of Egypt, but neither the eastern border nor the identity of these enemies is certain and suggestions of military intervention into Palestine at this period lack confirmation (Yadin 1955).

More is known about relations with Nubia. With the development of the Early Dynastic court culture, the demand for products from sub-Saharan Africa, particularly ebony and ivory, appears to have increased sharply. In addition, the Egyptian kings may have been concerned about securing their southern border at the First Cataract, up river from Jebel Silsila. It has been suggested that a smiting of Nubia reported for the reign of Aha commemorates the incorporation of this stretch of river into the Egyptian state (Säve-Söderbergh 1941, p. 7).

About the beginning of the First Dynasty, an Egyptian expedition probably made its way as far south as Wadi Halfa and, on Jebel Sheikh Suliman, carved a scene claiming a victory over two villages or local groups of Nubians (Arkell 1950).[1] This is the most southerly evidence of Egyptian penetration during the Early Dynastic Period found to date.

A-group communities continued to flourish into the early part of the First Dynasty, particularly in the southern half of Lower Nubia. Large quantities of Egyptian pottery, including wine jars, as well as copper tools, jewellery, pendants, and amulets indicate that the Nubians continued to have access to Egyptian goods at this period, as they had done in late Predynastic times. Rectangular houses with rough stone walls in a village site at Afyeh indicate more sedentarism than before (Lal 1963), while handsomely slipped and painted conical bowls of local manufacture suggest new levels of cultural achievement. One of the most remarkable finds from this period is the grave of a Nubian headman from a cemetery near Sayala, which dates from the early part of the First Dynasty. Among the imported goods found in this grave were a number of large copper axes, bar ingots, and chisels, a dipper of banded slate and several stone vessels, two immense double-bird shaped palettes and two maces with gold handles, one decorated with a series of animals worked in low relief (Kantor 1944). The source of such wealth is uncertain, although the Nubians were probably less able to act as middlemen or to charge tolls in the Early Dynastic Period than they had been in late Predynastic times. Possibly, such goods were rewards given to a headman who had servd as a mercenary in the Egyptian army. Even more elaborate graves dated to the early First Dynasty have been found in Cemetery L at Qustul, near the Egyptian–Sudanese border. This period appears to be the cultural climax of the A-group in Lower Nubia, although the population probably still amounted to only a few thousand people, organized on a tribal basis.

In the course of the First Dynasty, the flow of Egyptian trade goods into Nubia came to an end and the A-group culture began to break down. It is reasonable to assume that this process was related to the growth of the Egyptian monarchy and the centralization of the Egyptian economy. Instead of using the A-group as intermediaries in its trade with sub-Saharan Africa, the Egyptian court now may have sought to carry on this trade directly. The repeated Egyptian invasions of Lower Nubia seem to have been part of this process and no doubt

---

[1] While the scene clearly dates from about the beginning of the First Dynasty its unity and attribution to Djer are not undisputed: see Helck (1970).

account for the eventual disappearance of a sedentary population in Lower Nubia before the end of the First Dynasty (Nordström 1972, pp. 29–32).

The oldest known Egyptian settlement in Lower Nubia was at Buhen, near the Second Cataract. The large bricks used to construct the lowest levels of the town suggest that it may have been founded as early as the Second Dynasty, although this early date is far from certain (Trigger 1965, p. 79–80). The purpose of this settlement is not clear, but it may have served as a jumping-off point for an overland trade route that ran around the Second Cataract and southward to Dongola. H. S. Smith (1966) has demonstrated that the graves Reisner assigned to his B-group, supposedly equivalent in age to the Old Kingdom, are, in fact, poorer or badly plundered graves of the A-group.

Almost nothing is known about the Sudan at this time. Some pottery from the Omdurman Bridge site resembles that of the A-group, while other pottery, decorated with incisions filled with white pigment, is similar to both Predynastic Egyptian N-ware and some of the later C-group pottery (Arkell 1949, pp. 99–107). Small agricultural communities and pastoralist groups probably occupied the Sudanese Nile Valley and the adjacent steppes at this time. If Egyptian trading expeditions were already reaching the Dongola area, it is possible that the need to collect raw materials from the south in order to trade them with the Egyptians was encouraging greater social complexity in that area, in a manner analogous to what had happened in Egypt in the early Gerzean period (Trigger 1965, pp. 81–3).

### Arts and Crafts

Some of the important changes that came about in Egyptian society at the beginning of the Early Dynastic Period found expression in new patterns of material culture, particularly as these were related to mass-produced goods and products manufactured specifically for the upper classes. Material of both kinds is abundantly represented in cemetery sites, where vast quantities, and many different varieties, of goods were buried in the wealthier graves. The allocation of such large quantities of luxury goods to these tombs must have increased sharply the demand for raw materials and for the services of skilled craftsmen.

Pottery continued to be mass-produced as it had been in the Gerzean period. Vessels with the same pot-marks, apparently indicating the team or workshop that made them, are found throughout the country (Emery

1961, p. 203). The black-topped and painted pottery of Predynastic times did not, however, survive into the Early Dynastic Period; at which time the pottery is well formed, but strictly utilitarian. This does not indicate a decline in cultural or aesthetic standards. Instead, it suggests that pottery no longer served as a medium of artistic expression, as it had done formerly. Pottery jars were used to store wine and foodstuffs, including cheese, while bowls, cups and dishes were used as eating vessels. Most pottery was a reddish-brown ware, manufactured from Nile mud (Emery 1961, pp. 206–14). Although many copper tools were now available for craftsmen who were in the employ of the wealthy, flint was still widely used to manufacture knives, scrapers, arrow- and spear-heads, sickle blades, drills and other implements. Magnificent scimitar-like flint knives continued to be manufactured well into the First Dynasty. Although possibly made for ritualistic purposes, these knives sustained some of the expertise in working flint that had developed during the Gerzean period (Emery 1961, p. 233; Saad 1969, pls. 40–2).

In other spheres, the Early Dynastic culture was markedly in advance of that of Predynastic times. Carpentry appears to have developed very rapidly at the start of the First Dynasty, no doubt aided by the proliferation of copper tools. In particular, the techniques of joining, carving and inlay all manifest a sophistication not attested for the Predynastic Period. The furnishings of wealthier houses now included beds, chairs, stools and numerous chests and boxes, sometimes embellished with ivory or copper fittings. Legs of furniture were frequently carved to represent the limbs of cattle. Near life-size wooden statues were also produced, at least as early as the reign of Djer (Emery 1961, pp. 170–1). Metal ewers, bowls, dishes and other vessels, as well as mirrors, were hammered, and later cast, from copper. Spouts were riveted onto these vessels and handles were sometimes bound on with copper wire. In general, copper vessels reproduced the forms of stone ones. Although no copper statues have survived, one of Khasekhemwy is reported to have been made in the fifteenth year of his reign (Edwards 1971, p. 34). Jewellery was made out of gold, turquoise, lapis lazuli and other semi-precious stones. Engraved and embossed sheets of gold were used to cover the handles of weapons and to adorn other objects. The central chamber of one tomb at Saqqara was inlaid from floor to ceiling with strips of sheet gold; its employment giving some idea of the amounts of this metal available at this time (Emery 1961, p. 228). Bone and ivory were used for inlays, jewellery, arrow-heads, spoons, gaming pieces and statuettes. The modelling and delineation of details on some of the best ivory objects is of very high quality. Beads, pendants, amulets and inlays were also made out of faience, in a wide variety of different shapes (Emery 1961, pp. 228–31).

The most distinctive products of the Early Dynastic Period were a vast number of vessels made of steatite, schist, alabaster, marble, quartz, basalt, diorite and many other types of stone. While carrying on a tradition of stone-working of long standing in Upper Egypt, the aesthetic standards achieved in the manufacture of these vessels were not matched either before or after this time. The softer stones, particularly schist and alabaster, were worked into vessels of exceedingly plastic design, while harder stone was used to fashion simpler-shaped vessels. Sometimes, stone of one kind was inlaid with stone of another. Many of the thousands of stone vessels that were buried in the Step Pyramid at the beginning of the Third Dynasty were made in the Early Dynastic Period (Emery 1961, pp. 214–17).

While the late Gerzean votive mace-heads and palettes bear witness to the development of bas-relief sculpture prior to the First Dynasty, these particular forms of artistic expression did not persist for long afterwards. That bas-relief continued is demonstrated, however, by the funerary stelae from Abydos and a frieze of lions on a limestone lintel from the tomb of Queen Herneith. The royal stelae display erratic variations in design and execution, some being primitive on both counts, others well carved but lacking in balance of design. On the other hand, the stela of King Djet is ranked among the great artistic achievements of ancient Egyptian culture. Later in the Early Dynastic Period, rectangular stelae from both Saqqara and Helwan portray the deceased seated before a table surrounded by funerary offerings (Vandier 1952, pp. 724–74). An inscribed granite door-jamb of Khasekhemwy is described as displaying all of the design and symmetry of the Old Kingdom, in spite of the hard stone from which it was fashioned (Emery 1961, p. 169).

Stone sculpture also developed during the Early Dynastic Period. Animal representations include an alabaster baboon, inscribed with the name of Narmer, and a granite lion. The famous pottery lion from Hierakonpolis may also date from this period, although the Third Dynasty has also been suggested (Vandier 1952, p. 977). A number of human figures, carved out of limestone and granite and smaller than life-size, appear to belong to the Second Dynasty. These portray kneeling officials or seated figures. From the end of the period are two statuettes of Khasekhem, one in schist, the other in limestone; in style these foreshadow the classic art of the Old Kingdom. In its clean lines, increasing symmetry and striving after a monumental effect regardless of size, the sculpture of the Early Dynastic Period represents the formative stage in the development of a major component of classical Egyptian art.

We have already discussed the development of funerary architecture during this period. If the so-called forts of the Second Dynasty are, in fact, all royal funerary palaces, little in the way of non-funerary architecture survives. It is reasonable to believe, however, that brick niching was also used in non-funerary contexts. A niched wall recently uncovered at the Early Dynastic town-site of Hierakonpolis may have been part of some First Dynasty royal construction (Fairservis *et al.* 1971–2). The Palermo Stone records the erection of a stone temple at the end of the Second Dynasty (Edwards 1971, p. 66).

There is little direct evidence concerning the intellectual achievements of the Early Dynastic Period. Records were evidently kept of the sort which could later be used to compile the text of the Palermo Stone. Two treatises are also claimed, on the basis of internal evidence, to-date from this period. One, the so-called Memphite theology, ascribes the creation of the world to Ptah, the patron deity of Memphis. The other is a surprisingly empirical work dealing with medical procedures (Aldred 1965, pp. 63–4).

The Early Dynastic Period appears to have been a time of great creativity and inventiveness, in the course of which the elite culture of Pharaonic Egypt can be seen taking shape. While this creativity was to continue into the Third Dynasty, by the end of the Early Dynastic Period most of the principal elements of the court culture of the Old Kingdom were already well established. The development of new skills and the flowering of so many arts and crafts at the beginning of the First Dynasty have been interpreted by some Egyptologists as 'overwhelming evidence' of an incursion into the Nile Valley, which brought with it the culture of Early Dynastic times (Emery 1961, p. 165). While we have noted evidence of Mesopotamian influence, this influence was only transitory and was replaced by stylistic conventions that were of indigenous origin and which characterized Egyptian culture in later times. The continuities between the Predynastic and Early Dynastic cultures are so numerous as to suggest that some explanation, other than migration or cultural diffusion, is needed to account for the differences between these two periods.

The crucial factor in the emergence of new traditions of craftsmanship seems to be that it was at the beginning of the Early Dynastic Period, or slightly before, that certain craftsmen came under the patronage and control of the royal court. Hitherto, craftsmen had existed in Egypt whose work was clearly of a high order. It would appear, however, that these craftsmen looked to their community, region, or to Egypt as a whole, rather than to a particular class in Egyptian society, as a market for their goods. While some of the goods they turned out may have been for the temples or for the wealthier and more powerful members of the community, these were only some among a broad range of clients. In early times, rulers probably were content to avail themselves of the services of these general craftsmen.

Around the beginning of the First Dynasty, however, the kings of Egypt started to provide work for an increasing number of specialists on a full-time basis. As the Egyptian state grew, the court and the official hierarchy expanded, providing a larger market for specialized goods and services and this, in turn, facilitated a high degree of specialization within particular lines of work. One result of this specialization was a marked increase in the quality of what was being produced. Artisans developed whose work was solely to provide luxury goods for the upper classes. The need to co-ordinate the activities of groups of specialists also encouraged the development of writing and of numerous administrative skills connected with royal government. Within the overall system, craftsmen were subject to control by scribes and bureaucrats, who were charged with supplying them and co-ordinating their activities. One effect of this control of production by accountants and administrators must have been to discourage innovations, once acceptable modes of production had been worked out. The effect of this has been noted by Aldred when he states that, in spite of bold experimentations during the Early Dynastic Period, once a solution had been evolved, development ceased and a new convention was added to a stockpile of existing traditions (Aldred 1965, p. 53).

Because the whole of Egypt was united under a single government, at least by the First Dynasty, a common network of highly specialized craftsmen came to serve a group of patrons on such a scale as was not to be found among the city states of Mesopotamia, even if individual Mesopotamian cities enjoyed hegemony over the rest from time to time. Because of this, it is not surprising that, in the Old Kingdom, building projects could be undertaken on a scale that was impossible in Mesopotamia and that in specific crafts, such as those related to stone-working, the skills of Egyptian workmen greatly outstripped those of their Mesopotamian counterparts. On the other hand, in Egypt basic technological innovation tended to lag behind that of south-western Asia; as evidenced by the late introduction of both bronze and iron. The luxurious products of the court-sponsored culture of Egypt were meant, however, for the use of an elite and stood as material symbols of the superordinate position of these people in Egyptian society. Occasionally, the minor works of highly skilled artisans may have made their way further down the redistributive network or been purchased by an exceptionally prosperous villager. Simplified and cheaper versions of court fashions also seem to have diffused gradually down to the level of ordinary people. On the whole, however, local production and local trade must have continued to supply the needs of the vast majority of Egyptians, as they had done in Predynastic times.

## CONCLUSIONS

While the possibility that certain plants and animals may have been domesticated locally cannot be ruled out, food production in Egypt, from Predynastic times on, was clearly an extension of the south-west Asian pattern. North of the First Cataract, the Nile Valley embraced a floodplain that was larger and easier to cultivate than any in south-western Asia. The abundance of game and natural plant foods initially may have inhibited the spread of food production, and it was perhaps only towards the end of the Predynastic Period that the population became almost totally reliant on agriculture and herding. Moreover, the especially rich natural resources of the Delta may have resulted in an even slower realization of the full potential of a food-producing economy than took place in Upper Egypt. Both in Upper and Lower Egypt, however, the floodplain had the potential for supporting a dramatic increase in population and for the development of a more complex society, as a result of the greater productivity inherent in an agricultural economy. Farther south, in Nubia, the narrow and discontinuous floodplain did not hold out such promise. In that area, food production appears mainly to have compensated for declining natural food sources. The population of this region remained small and at a tribal level.

The development of a complex society in Egypt was further encouraged by the proximity of the southern part of Upper Egypt to the mineral resources of the eastern desert. It has been suggested that gold became an important item of trade with south-western Asia, probably by the early Gerzean period. This trade enhanced the regulatory power of those headmen whose communities were well situated to exploit these resources and may have been a major factor promoting the emergence of these communities as important economic and political centres. Competition over trade may also have led to political struggles among the emerging polities of southern Egypt and the desire to protect trade with Palestine and the rest of south-western Asia, or to eliminate middlemen, may have led to the conquest of northern Egypt, either at the beginning of the First Dynasty or sometime earlier.

The consolidation of the Egyptian state was ensured by the development of a centralized administrative system and of a court-centred Great Tradition predicated on a united Egypt, which thereafter, even in times of political crises, was to dominate the thinking of the Egyptian elite. The early development of a strong central government eliminated many of the factors that in south-western Asia led to the development of urban centres for defensive purposes. In Egypt, regional administrative centres were not necessarily marked by large clusters of population, and the peasantry remained scattered in small villages. The royal court set the cultural standards for the entire country; making the king the fountainhead not only of power and preferment but also of a way of life that the elite, and to some extent all Egyptians, wished to share. The absence of powerful enemies on its peripheries was in early times a source of stability for Egyptian society by comparison with the situation prevailing in Mesopotamia; however, the elite traditions, combined with the scale of Egyptian society, later proved strong enough to survive periods of internal instability and foreign conquest for over three thousand years. The forging of an elite tradition on this vast scale was clearly the greatest achievement of the Early Dynastic Period.

# APPENDIX

## CHRONOLOGY OF THE EARLY DYNASTIC PERIOD

### PREDYNASTIC KINGS

Palermo Stone – top register has seven names fully preserved, two partially; all wear the crown of Lower Egypt. There are traces of more determinatives at either end. The main Cairo fragment has ten determinatives; six wear the Double Crown of a united Egypt.

The Scorpion king (?)
Ka (Sekhen)

## FIRST DYNASTY
### FROM 3000 ± 100 TO *C.* 2890 BC

Narmer
Aha
Djer (Zer, Sekhty)
Djet (Zet, Uadji, Edjo)
Den (Udimu)
Anedjib (Andjyeb, Enezib)
Semerkhet
Qaa (Ka'a)
(Merneith may have been a regnant queen in the early part of the dynasty)

## SECOND DYNASTY
### *C.* 2890 TO 2686 BC

Hetepsekhemwy
Reneb
Nynetjer (Nutjeren)
—      Weneg[a]
—      Sened[a]
Sekhemib  ⎫
Peribsen[b] ⎭    same ruler?
Khasekhem    ⎫
Khasekhemwy[c] ⎭ same ruler?

[a] Personal name, Horus-name unknown
[b] Seth-name
[c] Horus- and Seth-name

(Spelling and order based on *Cambridge Ancient History*, 3rd edn, vol. I, pt. 2, p. 994. For correlations of Horus and personal names see *ibid.*, and for other interpretations of the chronology of this period Gardiner (1961, pp. 429–32).)

### ACKNOWLEDGEMENT

The author wishes to thank Professor William K. Simpson and Dr B. J. Kemp for reading and commenting on an earlier draft of this paper.

CHAPTER 8

# BEGINNINGS OF PASTORALISM AND CULTIVATION IN NORTH-WEST AFRICA AND THE SAHARA: ORIGINS OF THE BERBERS

Africa is truly Mediterranean only along its northern coastal fringe. This is broader in the west, in the Maghrib (Morocco, Algeria and Tunisia), than in the east in Libya, for here the desert reaches practically to the shoreline, the only exception being in Cyrenaica where certain characteristics of the Maghribian *tell*[1] country reappear in modified form. The hinterland of the Gulf of Gabès (Petite Syrte) is desertic and, although it was never a complete barrier, it nonetheless forms an ecotone which has shown itself to be of considerable stability for thousands of years. To the west of this Herodotus placed the sedentary Libyans and contrasted these with the nomadic Libyans whom he described as living between the Nile and Lake Triton, to be identified with the great *chotts* (an Arabic word meaning grazing land) in the south of what is now Tunisia (Camps 1961a, Gsell 1914–28).

The countries of the Maghrib are the only ones in Africa that show a truly youthful topography, for the mountains belong within the Alpine system of orogenesis or mountain building. These structural features, together with their northerly latitude, explain why these countries appear to be more characteristically Mediterranean than their eastern neighbours. However, as soon as the traveller moves into the interior this illusion is quickly dispelled: the almost European-like countryside of the coast with its wild and cultivated species of Mediterranean plants and the forests of the Atlas *tell* give place to open country, now fully African in appearance, and thence to steppe and pre-desertic vegetation broken only occasionally by rare stands of trees in the Saharan Atlas. We can thus distinguish, on the one hand a narrow *tell* area, wider in Morocco than in Algeria, and, on the other, the high country consisting of plateaux or high plains, bounded in the south by the Saharan Atlas, their height steadily decreasing eastwards from Morocco to Tunisia.

[1] *Tell* denotes the mountainous but fertile region of Algeria and Morocco between the Atlas and the Mediterranean.

Beyond, to the south, begins the Sahara proper, the greatest desert in the world, which stretches away to the east beyond the Nile and the Red Sea. The immensity of the Sahara, however, is not uniform: the relief and even the appearance of the terrain vary considerably. In the northern part of the desert, in Algeria and Tunisia, are vast swampy depressions which, in winter, are partially flooded by very shallow saline water; these are the *chotts*. The high dunes of the Great Eastern Erg border the south of this depression which is known to geographers as the *Bas Sahara*.[1] West of the *chotts*, as far as the Moroccan Atlas stretch the plateaux that form the piedmont of the Saharan Atlas and, to the south of these *hamadas* – the flat, stony surfaces of the Sahara desert – is the vast, sand-covered region of the Great Western Erg. Between the two Great Ergs is a succession of plateaux surfaces (the Tademaït) and depressions (the Tidikelt) that lead up to the mountain areas of the central Sahara – the Ahaggar, Tassili n'Ajjer, Adrar des Iforas and the Aïr. In the west, the Ahaggar massif dominates the vast stretches of the Tanezrouft into which disappears the long valley of the Saoura  . which runs north–south. The Tanezrouft stretches westward into the Mauritanian Sahara where the monotony of the desert landscape is broken only by a few low hills and steep-sided tablelands (Adrar, Zemmur and El-Eglab).

The eastern Sahara is no less diversified although, in the north, it lacks both the *tell* area and the mountain barrier of the Atlas (for which the Jebel el-Akhdar in Cyrenaica in no way compensates) as well also as the great Algerian–Tunisian *chotts*. On the other hand, the Edeyin Murzuq in the Fezzan, to the south of which rises the Tibesti massif, is the equivalent of the Great Ergs. Between Tassili n'Ajjer in the north, the Aïr in the south-west and Tibesti in the east is another sandy desert (Tanezrouft) just as arid as that in the west. This is the Ténéré of Taffassasset, a fossil river system that once drained into the Lake Chad basin which, at one time, covered an area five or six times as large as it does today. East of Tibesti as far as the Nile, the whole terrain consists of sandy desert relieved by the occasional *hamada* and, more rarely, by areas of higher ground, the most notable of which are Ennedi in the south and Jebel Uweinat in the west.

This immense Saharan region that today separates the Mediterranean countries from Black Africa was never an insurmountable barrier.

[1] This name was first applied in 1880 to the Melrir hydrographic basin, a region of low (about 100–200 m) elevation lying between the Atlas foothills in the north and those of the Ahaggar massif in the south and bounded on the east and west by the two Great Ergs.

Although contacts may have been difficult, they were never completely impossible. The Atlantic Sahara, with its more numerous and less widely separated wells, was visited fairly regularly by Moroccan merchants during the Middle Ages and, as early as the Carthaginian period, Tripoli in the east had been the headquarters of caravans that reached the regions round Lake Chad by way of the Fezzan and Tassili n'Ajjer. It was along this route, during the first centuries of the present era, that Roman manufactured goods penetrated to Wadi Agial in the Fezzan and as far as Abelessa in the Ahaggar. On the other hand, however, care must be taken not to exaggerate the ease with which the Sahara could be traversed. Crossing the desert, even if not strictly speaking an impossible undertaking, was always very difficult and it would not be untrue to say that the Sahara has effectively separated two worlds, almost entirely unknown to each other; it has been largely responsible for isolating Black Africa from the Mediterranean world. The presence of the Sahara, therefore, has always exerted a major influence on the history of Africa.

But the Sahara has not always existed in the form in which we know it today. During Palaeolithic times, similar or comparable lithic industries are found throughout both the countries of the Maghrib and the regions which today are desert. During the Pleistocene, the fauna of North Africa was similar to that of eastern and southern Africa: in Morocco, as also in Algeria and Tunisia, sites have yielded large quantities of remains of zebra-like equids, antelopes and African felines. With this Ethiopian fauna there were also, however, Palaearctic elements (cervids, bear and wild pig) which came in first during the penultimate (Riss) glaciation and again, perhaps, during the last (Würm). The flora exhibits the same mixing of Asiatic and tropical African elements with contributions also from the humid Mediterranean, not only in the most northerly parts of the continent but even as far south as the Ahaggar and Tibesti (Van Campo *et al.* 1964, 1965, 1967). The extent of these contributions varies throughout the Palaeolithic in relation to the great climatic changes generally referred to as the Quaternary glaciations. It is not the intention here to discuss these climatic variations and their consequences in the overall picture of the African flora and fauna, but it is possible to say that all the evidence, whether geomorphological or palynological, is in agreement in showing that, during the Quaternary, desert conditions were becoming more intensified whereas the humid periods were becoming shorter and of diminishing intensity.

Nevertheless, during the fourth and third millennia BC, pollen of Aleppo pine, evergreen oak, juniper, walnut and lentisk – the mastic tree (*Pistachia lentiscus*) – was widespread in the Ahaggar massif (Camps 1968a, Hugot 1963), which suggests that the mountains of the central Sahara at this time were still enjoying a Mediterranean climate of some humidity. But in the *ergs* and the great desiccated valleys, the climate was already hot and dry with a xerophytic vegetation. During the second and first millennia BC climatic conditions became increasingly more severe. The great lakes that had existed in the Tanezrouft, the Ténéré and the northern Sahara gradually disappeared leaving broad banks of diatomites, the radiocarbon dating of which shows, however, that as late as 1000 BC there were still some water-covered areas even in the centre of the Ténéré.

So, progressively, the Sahara has become the desert that we know today. The increasing number of pollen analyses and radiocarbon dates makes it possible to state beyond question that the final collapse of the more favourable ecological conditions took place during the Neolithic period, or to be more exact, at the end of this period, which corresponds to the beginning of the Metal Age in Europe. This approximate dating of the desertification (or, more properly, of the threshold marking the change from a more or less normal life to one of increasing precariousness) is important. It is not without significance that it coincides precisely with the beginning of the great Mediterranean voyages made possible by the progress of metallurgy. Thus, at the moment when the desert finally became established on both sides of the Tropic of Cancer and cut off the remainder of the continent from North Africa, navigation was linking this region ever more closely to the Mediterranean. We can say that the Maghrib, which was almost entirely African until Neolithic times, became, with the onset of the Metal Age, exclusively Mediterranean.

While we are beginning to have a relatively extensive knowledge of the Neolithic, that is to say of those cultures possessing pottery and practising animal husbandry, in the Saharan regions generally, the immediately preceding period relating to the Epi-Palaeolithic cultures is very little known in this part of Africa. In the Maghrib, on the other hand, the importance of the Epi-Palaeolithic sites, and their considerable numbers and frequent richness, have been to some extent the cause of a neglect of the Neolithic there, except in a few favourable areas on the coast or the Saharan Atlas. The phenomenon of 'neolithization' has been superimposed on a way of life that was still Epi-Palaeolithic and that was to persist for a considerable time parallel to or intimately mingled with the new life style peculiar to the Neolithic period. Before embarking on a study of the transition to the Neolithic, therefore, it would seem useful to specify the characteristics of the late Epi-Palaeolithic industries onto which Neolithic traits were more or less intensively grafted.

In North Africa and the immediately adjacent peripheral zone of the Sahara (the lower slopes of the Saharan Atlas, the *Bas Sahara* and Tripolitania), two great cultural traditions succeeded one another without, however, occupying identical areas. The first was the Iberomaurusian – found essentially in the *tell* country and on the coast; the second the Capsian, occupying the regions that are today steppe but hardly penetrating into the *tell*. In Cyrenaica the same two industrial complexes are recognized[1] although they are not precisely identical with those in the Maghrib. The beginnings of the Iberomaurusian go back before the fourteenth millennium BC and it lasted at least until the middle of the eighth millennium. This complex is closely associated with a Cro-Magnon-like human type from Mechta el-Arbi – the Mechta-Afalou race – that is known, from sites on the coast and in the *tell* country, to have continued on until the Neolithic. The Capsian appeared much later than the Iberomaurusian since the oldest dates so far obtained for this complex are from the very end of the eighth millennium. The so-called Upper Capsian continued until about 4000 BC in eastern Algeria and until 4000 BC in the westerly part of its distribution. Capsian man was a proto-Mediterranean who gradually replaced Mechta–Afalou man during Upper Capsian and Neolithic times: the Capsian physical type was ancestral to the present-day Berber peoples.

The Iberomaurusian and the Capsian are not the only Epi-Palaeolithic cultures that preceded the Neolithic and mention must also be made of the blade industries of southern Tunisia and the *Bas Sahara* (such as the Mellalian of Hassi Mouillah near Ouargla), which are contemporary with the Upper Capsian (dating to the seventh and sixth millennia BC). An older industry is the Columnatan which is widespread in the Tiaret area and which, at Columnata itself, is found stratigraphically between the Iberomaurusian and a late Upper Capsian. The Keremian, which is confined to western Algeria, exhibits several curious resemblances to the Arkinian of Nubia and at Bou Aïchem dates to the

---

[1] In Cyrenaica these complexes are known as the Eastern Oranian and the Libyan Capsian (McBurney 1967, pp. 185–228, 229–70).

8.1 Rock paintings from Tan Zoumaitok, Tassili n'Ajjer. 1 Dancing woman (?) of the 'Round Head' period. 2 Female in the Bovidian style.

8.2 Rock paintings from In Edjar, Tassili n'Ajjer, Bovidian period. 1 Antelope, ostrich and human figures; (bottom right) a flock of sheep. 2 Bovids.

8.3 Rock paintings. 1 Archers from the end of the Bovidian period, from In Edjar, Tassili n'Ajjer. 2 Chariot drawn by two horses, Equidian period, from Tamadjert, Tassili n'Ajjer. (Photograph by M. Touron.)

8.4  Stone carvings of the Bovidian period. 1 Bovid, from Silet, Ahaggar.
2 Gazelle, from Imakassen, Tassili n'Ajjer.

8.5  Rock engravings from the Atlas Mountains. 1 *Bos primigenius*, from Tiout, Aïn Sefra.

2 Ram with spheroid headdress preceded by a human figure, from Aïn Naga, Djelfa.

8.6 Bou Nouara dolmen, Constantine, Algeria. Diameter of plinth 12 m. (Photograph by G. Camps)

8.7 Crescent-shaped monument closing a neck of the Adrar Tiouiyne, a small volcanic massif some 100 km west of Tamanrasset, Ahaggar. Length of the monument 43 m. (Photograph by G. Camps.)

eighth millennium BC. Very little is known of the Epi-Palaeolithic in the Sahara apart from the *Bas Sahara* and the Mellalian of Wadi Mya, although some traces of it can be recognized in the Hemamian in the Saoura and in the Ounanian of the southern regions.

## THE SPREAD OF THE NEOLITHIC (fig. 8.1)

Faced with the ever-growing difficulty of defining precisely the boundary line between the Epi-Palaeolithic (or the Mesolithic) and the Neolithic, prehistorians have tended to give a much wider meaning to this term, which is now considered to include not only aspects of the tool-kit and other archaeological elements but also the profound changes that have come about in the way of life. The change from behaviour patterns based on hunting and gathering, that is to say on predation, to those based on food production or, in other words, agriculture and domestication, is now to be regarded as the essential determining criterion. Certainly this is the only ethnologically acceptable criterion; its human implications are much more significant than arbitrary classifications based on the presence or absence of such-and-such a weapon – arrow-points or polished axes – or on the occurrence of a particular technique – pottery-making or weaving, for example – but archaeologically it is a criterion that is extremely difficult to apply. Traces of cultivated plants are very ephemeral; the preservation of seeds on open sites can never be counted on and the thinness of the Neolithic archaeological layer at these same sites makes it impossible to be certain that any pollens of cultivated plants that *are* collected are really of Neolithic age. Fortunately, there are occasionally traces of cultivated plants to be found in the clay of potsherds or the sun-dried brick of the houses of the earliest cultivators.

The difficulties posed by the surface sites have, thus, led to attempts to discover traces of ancient agriculture in rock-shelter habitation sites. But this type of research, although it is more interesting and scientifically more rewarding, perhaps runs the risk of making it appear that true neolithic occupation sites are to be found solely in rock-shelters and deep caves. The other criterion would seem to be of more practical use – the bones of domestic animals do, indeed, constitute tangible evidence of food production – but its application has proved equally difficult. In North Africa, the small indigenous cattle *Bos ibericus*[1] occur

[1] Although it is now more generally considered that *Bos ibericus* represents the female of the North African *B. primigenius*, it has recently been pointed out that measurements of *B. ibericus* material there all fall below the figures for the European female *B. primigenius* which suggests the possibility that more than one taxon may indeed be present. (Editor's note.)

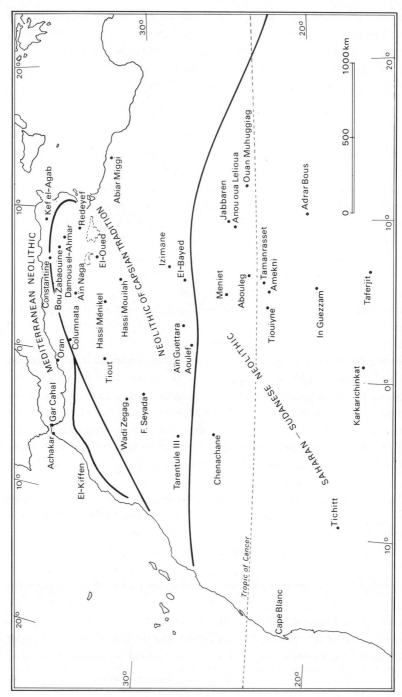

Fig. 8.1  Map showing the principal Neolithic sites in the Maghrib and the Sahara.

554

in sites of Palaeolithic, Epi-Palaeolithic and Neolithic age, (Esperandieu 1955); the 'brown Atlas strain' is the modern scientific breeders' version of this species. It is not possible to be certain, therefore, whether the cattle bones found on Neolithic sites belong to domestic cattle or to wild species obtained by hunting. Only detailed statistical study would make it possible to be certain of the existence of domestic herds from which young animals were systematically culled. However, thanks to other evidence – the rock engravings and paintings – we know that the Neolithic people of the Maghrib and the Sahara did possess domestic animals. The preservation of this rock art – not to mention its existence in the first place which is closely bound up with the availability of suitable rock surfaces and pigments – depends very largely on natural conditions in no way connected with archaeology and it is, thus, not possible to relegate the zones of domestication solely to those regions where rock art is found.

In short, and where it concerns the archaeology of North Africa alone, we have to admit that proof of the existence of prehistoric agriculture – and the qualification is deliberate – is still not forthcoming, although such agriculture was highly probable in the Neolithic; on the other hand its existence is indisputable if we connect it with that of pottery. In spite of what some authors affirm, pottery-making seems to the present writer to be a technology derived directly from changes in food habits due to agriculture. Excavation of some well-known Middle Eastern sites has shown that agriculture preceded pottery and, to the best of our knowledge, the opposite has not yet been conclusively demonstrated. The abundance of potsherds in the Saharan–Sudanese Neolithic of the southern Sahara is, thus, considered by the writer as an indirect proof of the development of agriculture or at the very least of the use of plant foods such as the cooking of seeds collected from ants' nests. This seems all the more probable as grindstones and rubbers increase in the same proportions. On the other hand, in the neolithic of Capsian Tradition from the northern Sahara and the high plains, potsherds are very rare and grindstones and rubbers are also manifestly less frequent while very varied and numerous types of arrow-points seem to the writer to attest to a way of life that is still Epi-Palaeolithic. However, in prehistoric archaeology, no statements or conclusions drawn from a study of the record can be hard and fast. So it is that the Neolithic of Capsian Tradition, which seems backward in comparison with the Mediterranean Neolithic, also very rich in pottery, and with the Saharan–Sudanese Neolithic, yet belongs to a tradition in which, as early as the Typical Capsian, the presence of long flint blades exhibiting glossy areas ('sickle sheen') points to the possibility, if not of true agriculture, at least of intensive collecting of edible grasses. Some sites of the Upper Capsian or of contemporary Epi-Palaeolithic facies have yielded bone implements with, in a groove especially made for this purpose, a series of geometric microliths set vertically, like teeth. Such objects have, perhaps rather hastily, been termed 'sickles' even though they are quite different from the implements of that name found with the Natufian or the Neolithic of the Fayum. Conversely, the Neolithic from the central and southern Sahara which, by virtue of its large number of grindstones and potsherds, strikes one as having solid agricultural traditions, has never, at least in the Sahara west of Lake Chad, yielded seeds from cultivated plants whereas stores of seeds of *Celtis integrifolia* have several times been found, in Ahnet, at Amekni in the Ahaggar, at Meniet (Immidir), at Adrar Bous in the Ténéré and at various sites in Mauritania.

Apart from the study of skeletal or vegetable remains which may point to the existence either of domestication or of agriculture, there is still one further method for determining this, based on statistics and the quantitative values of different types of tools in the assemblages. The prehistorian is more and more turning to these methods of typological analysis which are proving extremely useful in view of the frequent absence of certain elements, long considered as indispensable to Neolithic assemblages, such as arrow-points or polished axes. The study of bone tools and weapons and of objects of personal adornment also provides very satisfactory results since some of these are typical of the Neolithic.

It is certain that changes in the way of life took place only very slowly and that for a long time after he had succeeded in propagating his selected plants man still practised the gathering of wild plant foods (as is done to this day in large areas of the tropics) and the plundering of the seed reserves of harvester ants. The same long transition must have taken place between the procuring of animal food by hunting alone and the provision of meat solely from domestic herds. It is, thus, unrealistic to define the Neolithic as the passage from a hunting and collecting economy to one of food production, since there has never, in fact, been any complete 'passage' from the one to the other. Even in our own culture, the absolute replacement of the first by the second was achieved only a few centuries ago. It is a known fact that collecting and hunting still contribute considerably to the food supply of both the sedentary and nomadic populations of the Sahel zone from Senegal to the Nile. The present writer himself prefers to look for those tangible elements of the economy that are characterized by the appearance of pottery (definitely related to agricultural development and the need to be able to cook flour or crushed seeds for long periods) and the increase in certain types of tools or weapons, made from stone and bone, unknown in the Epi-Palaeolithic cultures, and so to designate as Neolithic those economies in which, although hunting and gathering might still have been practised for some considerable time, this was not the sole method of food-getting as it had been in the foregoing period.

The Neolithic appears then above all as a change in behaviour pattern; however, the Neolithic way of life in North Africa is not uniform, not only because of the long duration of this period but also because the acquisition of Neolithic traits did not follow the same course in the regions of the southern or northern Sahara or on the coast. The origin of the stimulus, whether local or external, was not everywhere the same and it had to work on differing industrial traditions. The complex phenomenon of the growth of a Neolithic way of life in the north of the African continent can be reduced to simpler terms by dividing it, first of all, into large areas classified roughly according to latitude. In the far south of the present desert, almost from the Tropic of Cancer and as far as the fringes of the humid forests, a centre of Neolithic civilization with pottery developed in very ancient times, as early as the end of the seventh millennium BC. These Saharan peoples who perhaps invented agriculture though they did not, until much later, practise the domestication of animals, were negroids, as also was Asselar man who does not seem to have lived very much earlier than this period. This Neolithic has been called the *Neolithic of Sudanese Tradition* because its origin had been arbitrarily fixed as the banks of the Nile in the region of Khartoum in the Sudan (Alimen 1955, Arkell 1949, Hugot 1963). At the present time, the oldest manifestations recognized occur to the west of the great strip of territory (the Ahaggar) occupied by this group of industries which we shall, therefore, henceforth refer to as the *Saharan–Sudanese Neolithic*. This Neolithic followed its own particular development, marked right to the end by the lack of importance of agriculture while the raising of cattle assumed considerable significance.

The spread of the Neolithic way of life on the coast of the Mediterranean and, to a lesser degree, of the Atlantic follows a very different pattern. Here the primacy of Mediterranean influences takes the form of impressed (or stamped) decoration of the pottery and later, in the Middle Neolithic, of the introduction of obsidian. Contacts with the Iberian peninsula to the west played a leading part right from the beginning of the Neolithic. Most of the Neolithic occupation sites in this *tell* country are in caves or rock-shelters. Very often the transition between the post-Iberomaurusian and the Neolithic is imperceptible, which leads to the conclusion that, here also, the new way of life came early. There is still very little evidence of agriculture but small stock, sheep and goats, seem to have been kept from relatively early times. The Neolithic of the *tell* country might, perhaps, be called Neolithic of Iberomaurusian Tradition except that, quite apart from the fact that such a name would not be at all comprehensive, it would conflict with the one suggested by Bosch-Gimpera when he gave the name of Cave Neolithic to the culture which he later associated with the circum-Mediterranean Neolithic.[1] Taking into account all these data, therefore, it is suggested here that the name *Mediterranean Neolithic* be given to the culture that developed towards the end of the sixth millennium BC in the *tell* country of the Maghrib.

Between the Mediterranean zone and the region occupied by the Saharan–Sudanese Neolithic stretch extensive areas, including the highlands of the Maghrib and the Sahara north of the Tropic of Cancer from the Rio de Oro to Lower Egypt. Several Neolithic cultures have developed in this varied region of which one deserves to retain the name of *Neolithic of Capsian Tradition*, but it is a long way from being as important or covering as extensive an area as Vaufrey (1955, p. 368) has suggested. It extends to eastern Algeria, southern Tunisia, the north of Libya, the Saharan Atlas and the north of the Sahara. In the Neolithic of Capsian Tradition it is possible to distinguish two facies – the Saharan, rich in arrow-points but with very little pottery (Aïn Guettara, Hassi Mouillah) and the Atlas facies (Damous el-Ahmar, Khanguet si Mohamed Tahar and Redeyef), associated with the rock art of the Saharan Atlas. In the high plains of the eastern Maghrib Neolithic culture spread very late (not until the fourth millennium BC) whereas it was much earlier (the fifth millennium) in the Saharan regions. In any event the Neolithic of Capsian Tradition, even in the Sahara, appears to be more recent than the Saharan–Sudanese Neolithic to the south or the Mediterranean Neolithic to the north. To the east and west, other cultures with different origins border on the Neolithic of Capsian Tradition and have undoubtedly influenced it. These are the *Mauritanian*

---

[1] Vaufrey (1955) was mistaken when he quite simply confused this Neolithic with his own Neolithic of Capsian Tradition.

*Neolithic* in which are combined traits of varying origins (Mediterranean–Atlantic, Saharan–Sudanese and, perhaps, Guinean as well as some Neolithic of Capsian Tradition) and, to the east the *Ténéréan*, one of the most beautiful lithic industries of the Old World which, while it may not be Egyptian in origin, is at least very closely related to the Egyptian Neolithic.

As has been seen, the Neolithic of Capsian Tradition, with which Vaufrey would like to have included almost all the Neolithic cultures of the north of the African continent, is only one among several Neolithic traditions. Far from having been the origin of the Neolithic way of life in the Maghrib and the Sahara, it seems to have been much later than the others and to have retained longer than did the other facies the way of life and technology of the Epi-Palaeolithic. Most often, particularly in the north of the region, the Neolithic of Capsian Tradition seems to be, more properly speaking, a Capsian with superimposed Neolithic traits.

### THE SAHARAN–SUDANESE NEOLITHIC (figs. 8.2–3)

At the beginning of the seventh millennium, when the cultural phenomena that we group together as the Neolithic began to appear, the Sahara was not yet a full desert. It is true that large areas, particularly the low-lying parts of the north, were already partially affected by aridity, but the humid Sahara had not yet disappeared. From the seventh to the third millennium BC, in the south of Tibesti, Tassili n'Ajjer and the Ahaggar, as well as in the southern part of Mauritania, large lakes, sometimes considerably more than ten metres deep, covered wide areas which are now occupied by *ergs* or by banks of diatomites. These lakes were fed by quite sizeable if not always permanent rivers, one of the most important of which was the Taffassasset. Swollen by the waters running down from the Tassili and the eastern slopes of the Ahaggar, this river flowed as far as Lake Chad, at that time four or five times more extensive than today. From the Ahaggar, then a veritable fountainhead of water, the Igharghar flowed to the north and reached perhaps as far as the *Bas Sahara*. To the west a fairly well graded network of watercourses drained the waters of the wadis Outoul, Amekni, Tamanrasset and Amded towards a lake which is today represented by the desolate wastes of the Tanezrouft. In the central and southern parts of the Sahara it is possible to reconstruct a way of life for this period similar to that still carried on by the peoples living along the banks of

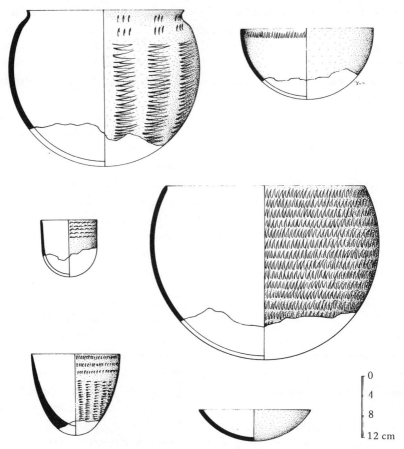

Fig. 8.2  Pottery from Amekni (Saharan–Sudanese Neolithic): principal forms.

the Senegal and Niger rivers and Lake Chad today. There is undoubted proof that these rivers (which may, perhaps, not have flowed all the year round) and these stretches of lake or swamp were contemporaneous

Fig. 8.3  Saharan–Sudanese Neolithic artifacts from Amekni.

*In stone*
1  Worked pebble (chopper)
3  Transverse arrow-head
4  Obsidian bladelet with fine retouch
9, 15–17  Points
10  Backed bladelet in obsidian
11–12  Scrapers
13  Backed flake in quartz
18  Foliate tool in granite
19  Fragment of a bracelet in serpentine

20  Small rubber with dished surface
21  Lava Pendant

*In bone*
2  Ivory ring
5  Pendant of pierced gazelle phalange
6, 8  Pins with heads
7  Dagger/burnisher with toothed lateral edge
14  Small *tranchet* with oblique cutting edge

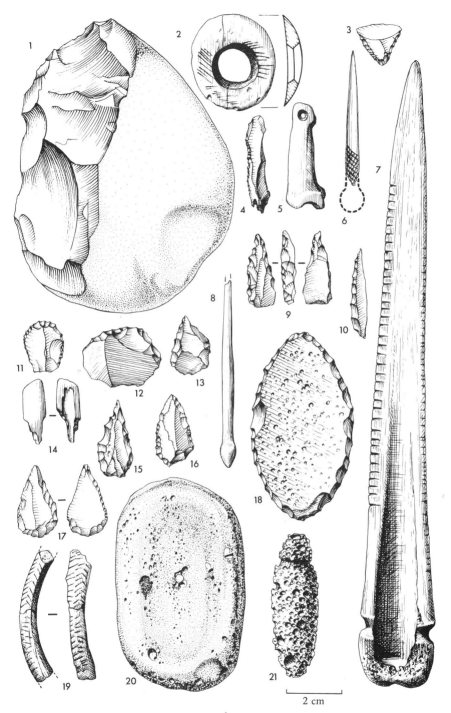

with the earliest Neolithic cultures. In the first instance, let us adduce the easily verifiable evidence such as the numerous fish remains in Neolithic sites. From Amekni to the west of the Ahaggar come skeletal fragments of catfish (*Clarias* sp.) and of types of perch (*Lates* sp.) (Camps 1968a); in the Adrar Tiouiyne, in the Silet area, today more than 50 km from any water, the banks of the Wadi Amded were occupied by a population of fishers who left remains of these same species; and at In Guezzam, Meniet, similar evidence had been produced some time previously. Attention must, however, be drawn to other facts which are just as characteristic. Thus, at the Neolithic sites of Tahor and In Relidjem near Anou oua Lelioua in the wide stretch of the Admer Erg south of Tassili n'Ajjer, groups had lived on the edges of swamps of which the now hard mud encloses an inextricable mass of the roots of phragmites reeds, remains of fish and objects thrown away or left behind by the occupants. At Anou oua Lelioua the present writer had the good fortune to recover a broken pestle which had been thrown into the marsh by man and had sunk vertically into it. The same site yielded large pots, broken on the spot, and two carvings of animals done in hard stone.

More detailed analyses of the sediments have yielded precise information on the flora and, consequently, on the climatic conditions that prevailed at the time they were laid down. In the seventh millennium BC the climate was sufficiently humid for the mountain tops to be occupied by broad-leaved forests of oak, walnut, lime, alder and elm and for the Aleppo pine to cover the lower altitudes, together with juniper, the nettle tree (*Celtis australis*), lentisk and olives. This vegetation persisted in the massifs of the Ahaggar, Tassili and Tibesti at least until the third millennium at which period the final phase in the desiccation of the Sahara began. It has been shown that the massive, brightly-coloured diatomite formations corresponding to deep lakes fed by fresh water were subsequently covered by discontinuous banks of diatomites and saline formations that bear witness to the gradual disappearance of these lakes and also of the human cultures that had grown up around them. The agony was long drawn out since, for still another millennium, there was sufficient pasture for cattle and then for small stock. It is probable that man may himself have contributed to the desertification by the increase in his herds. Such a phenomenon is, unfortunately, taking place today in southern Tunisia as a result of overgrazing. However that may be, it is known that some one thousand years before the present era, stretches of water of sufficient size to allow of the survival of hippopotamus still existed in the Ténéré of Taffassasset which today is the driest part of the whole Sahara. But before this slow disappearance of its water reserves, the central and southern Sahara enjoyed ecological conditions that were favourable to the earliest permanent settlements, conditions more or less similar to those that existed much later in the fertile crescent. Mesopotamia, Syria–Palestine and Egypt are, in fact, no more than the fringe of a vast habitable region which at one time stretched as far to the west as Mauritania. It is somewhat difficult for us to envisage exactly what the Sahara was like when it was not yet desertic and when more or less permanent rivers flowed across it but, indeed, it is quite certain that, towards the seventh millennium BC it was not merely a 'fertile crescent' but a veritable garland stretching from the Indus to the Atlantic and joining together all those warm, naturally irrigated regions where the earliest elements of Neolithic culture first appeared.

Chronology, moreover, makes it possible to go a step further and to suggest that, perhaps, the central and southern Sahara may, in fact, have been a centre of origin both of the Neolithic and of the invention of pottery. It is certain that the expression 'of Sudanese tradition' cannot be taken to imply a succession of influences or stimuli coming from the countries along the Nile. At the period with which we are concerned, these Nile countries were not in any way more privileged than the Saharan regions of Bahr el-Ghazal, or the Ténéré, the valleys cutting down from the Tibesti or the Ahaggar or the lakes that filled the depressions. Indeed, the oldest dates for industries associated with pottery – and which we shall simply call *Neolithic* – have not been obtained from the valley of the Nile (which was perhaps rendered less favourable than one tends to think by the great floods it experienced) but rather from the sediments and archaeological deposits of the massifs of the central Sahara and their surrounds. Going from east to west we have two dates from the Delebo cave in Ennedi (excavated by Bailloud); the lower level contains potsherds with dotted wavy-line decoration and dates to the sixth millennium, $5250 \pm 300$ BC, while the upper level is scarcely more recent and dates to $4950 \pm 300$ BC (Bailloud 1969). In the Tadrart Acacus, the Libyan extension of the Tassili n'Ajjer, the work of Mori (1965) has enabled certain stylistic stages of the rock paintings to be dated (see Belluomini *et al.* 1974) and also the lithic industries and potsherds associated with them. At Fozzigiaren charcoals from a hearth at the base of the deposit have been dated to $6122 \pm 100$ BC; the immediately overlying level has yielded potsherds with impressed decoration. At Ouan Tabu the central part of the filling contained dwelling structures, impressed decorated pottery and a sparse lithic industry; it was dated 5950 ± 175 BC. The site of Ouan Muhuggiag has provided four dates which are of great value, not only for determining the history of the occupation of that particular site, but also for establishing the chronology of the Saharan–Sudanese Neolithic. At the base of the site a hearth has been dated to 5488 ± 120 BC; the immediately overlying layer gave a date of 4002 ± 120 BC. This level contained cattle bones, in particular a frontal of *Bos brachyceros* which is probably domesticated. The leather surrounding the desiccated remains of the burial of a negroid infant has given a date of 3455 ± 180 BC. At the same site the archaeological level that contained a painted block of stone fallen from the roof provided the *ante quem* date of 2780 ± 310 BC for the recent phase of the Bovidian style of painting while at Ouan Telecat paintings of the Round Head style go back to more than 4795 ± 175 BC. In the nearby Tassili n'Ajjer the site of Titerast n'Elias no. 5 would appear to be of comparable antiquity since charcoals from a hearth at the base of the deposits there have given a date of 5450 ± 300 BC.

It is, however, the Ahaggar which has provided the greatest surprises as a result of the important work carried out there over the last few years. At Abouleg, the excavations of J.-P. Maître have made it possible to date three levels spanning the period from 4190 ± 100 to 2650 ± 250 BC. In the very heart of the massif, the important Neolithic village known as Site Launay excavated by J.-P. and C. Maître (1979), is even older dating to about 4850 ± 105 BC. At Amekni the present writer obtained the same date for the layer between 60 and 90 cm in depth; a negroid skeleton lying on the granite sand at a depth of 1.25 m was, therefore, much earlier than this. In fact, the grave of a young child in a natural hollow at the base of a large block was as old as 6100 ± 80 BC. This is a very old date for an industry with pottery but it is confirmed by the even older date (6720 ± 150 BC) which determines the beginning of the occupation of this site (Camps 1968a). In the Tefedest (northern Ahaggar) a Neolithic level at Timidouin was recently dated to 6150 ± 130 BC (Belluomini *et al.* 1974).

The oldest dates for the appearance of the Neolithic in the Ennedi, Tadrart Acacus, Tassili n'Ajjer and the Ahaggar form a coherent whole tying in with the geomorphological and climatic evidence; thus the lacustrine limestone of Hirafok in the Ahaggar dated to about 6430 BC serves as a reminder that, at the beginning of the Neolithic, large stretches of water still covered wide areas of the Sahara. It is already known that throughout the occupation of the site at Amekni there was sufficient water in the neighbouring wadi for the people to be able to catch fish of quite appreciable size; today the area is a sandy plain with occasional granite inselbergs. It is thus at the end of the seventh millennium BC that the first Saharan–Sudanese Neolithic cultures began to occupy the fringes of the central massifs. During the seventh millennium the humid Sahara would seem to have been a special centre of origin of the Neolithic since the oldest industries with pottery there are no more recent than those of the favourable regions of the Near East and the eastern basin of the Mediterranean.

The Saharan–Sudanese Neolithic persisted for a long time – almost for five millennia – and, curiously enough, there is little apparent technological evolution in the lithic tool-kit which, in fact, is often quite mediocre. With regard to pottery, calabash-shaped forms make their appearance right at the beginning of the tradition and have remained unchanged even in the present-day African pottery; the decoration showed some slight development. On the other hand, the way of life must have had to change, if only because of modifications in the biotope. The deepest levels in the site of Amekni which cover the seventh and fifth millennia (Camps 1968a) can be taken as a characteristic example of the oldest phase of the Saharan–Sudanese Neolithic. The locality is a granite ridge situated some 40 km to the west-north-west of Tamanrasset in the Ahaggar. This ridge is difficult to distinguish from the hundreds of other similar ridges that sprawl like the backbone of a huge whale over the yellowish sand of the granite peneplain. Doubtless man was attracted to live here by the confluence of the two wadis Amekni and Takiouine. We know that at about 6700 BC there were hearths there used by people who left behind absolutely no trace of their industry. A few centuries later a negroid population occupied the area between the blocks and on top of the ridge. The Amekni people burned olive wood in their fire-places which occur between the large rocks that were probably joined by fences of *Typha* reeds (pollens of which have been recovered) cut in the nearby wadi. Light frameworks of *Ficus* wood (mineralized remains of which have been found on the ground) made it possible to stretch mats of leaves or of *Typha* reeds or blankets of antelope or extinct buffalo (*Pelorovis antiquus = Homoïoceras antiquus*) skin between the large boulders – which is still the way in which the Ahaggar Touareg make their tents.

Excavation at Amekni uncovered three graves – of a woman between

40 and 50 years old and of two children aged 2–3 and 5–6; they are all negroid and seem to belong to the Sudanese type. The woman had suffered a violent blow on the head which had caused the fracture of the left parietal; signs of knitting of the bone show that the victim had continued to live after this traumatic injury. It would appear that this Amekni population had no domestic animals; in fact, study of the bone remains has provided identification of carnivores including common genet (*Genetta genetta*), the Egyptian mongoose (*Herpestes ichneumon*) and a hyena (*H. striata*); of wart-hog (*Phacochoerus aethiopicus*); of a bovid (*Pelorovis (Homoïoceras) antiquus*), of antelopes, namely Dorcas gazelle (*Gazella dorcas*); the reedbuck (*Redunca redunca*) and the hartebeest (*Alcelaphus boselaphus*); and of the Barbary sheep (*Ammotragus lervia*). There were five species of rodents, three species of birds and three of reptiles. This fauna, to which can be added the remains of fish and aquatic molluscs (*Unio* and *Mutella nilotica*), supplies valuable indications as to climate as also does the study of the vegetable remains. For instance, the reedbuck (*Redunca*) frequents forest galleries and savanna with swampy patches; the cane rat (*Thryonomys*) and the reddish-brown grass rat or *kusu* (*Arvicanthus niloticus*) both prefer the tall phragmites reeds growing in the swampy parts of the courses of tropical rivers. The great extinct buffalo (*Pelorovis (Homoïoceras) antiquus*), the ruminant of the wide savannas, occupied the whole of the Sahara and the high plains of Algeria. This fauna presupposes, therefore, a biotope that was much less arid than that prevalent on the periphery of the Ahaggar today. This conclusion is confirmed by pollen analysis. Several samples taken from different levels in the archaeological horizon have shown that the most humid periods occur around 6000 BC (at a depth of 1.40 m) and at about 3500 BC (at a depth of 0.60 m). Occurring together in these two levels have been recognized both temperate species (alder, elm, walnut and birch which were probably growing in the nearby Ahaggar massif and not on the actual site), tropical trees such as acacia and myrtle and intermediate types (*Celtis australis*, the Judas tree, holm oak and pine). The botanists conclude that, at these times, there existed in this immediate area a group of nettle trees (*Celtis australis* or *integrifolia*) and holm oaks, probably mixed with species of olive (cf. the charcoals from the hearths) and Judas trees. The presence of *Typha* pollens makes it most likely that the Amekni wadi was flowing permanently. The pollen analysis also yields results of importance for determining the way of life. Indeed as early as the 1.40 m level, that is about 6000 BC, an abnormal amount of pollen of Liguliflorae of the type of *Launaea picris* (a low

shrub or herb of the family Compositae) is noticeable and this may indicate the clearing of sandy soil for cultivation. Also from this level were recovered two cereal pollens that measured 64 $\mu$, a size that could not belong to any Saharan cereal grass but suggests a cultivated *Pennisetum* (millet).

When the strictly archaeological data are examined, this evidence, which is strongly suggestive of agriculture, becomes almost certain. These data are, first and foremost, the great numbers of grinding and pounding hollows that have been worked into the surface of the granite ridge and the large quantity of rubbing and grinding stones recovered from the archaeological horizon. It is true that such grinding equipment could be used for the seeds of non-cultivated plants and the present-day Saharan populations are not slow to avail themselves of this food source; on the other hand they are so numerous that it would seem difficult to believe that they were used only for wild vegetable foods.[1] Another not insignificant factor is the presence, in the oldest levels, of abundant potsherds from quite large pots of up to 60 cm in diameter. These vessels are of simple form with no neck or protuberance, the largest being near spherical and much too similar to vessels modelled on calabashes for this resemblance to be accidental. All this pottery – deep and shallow bowls and cups – is round-based. Most of the vessels are decorated with comb stamping over the whole surface, the patterns being simple and repeated indefinitely. These characteristics are found in the pottery of almost the whole of the Saharan–Sudanese Neolithic sequence, the wavy line and dotted wavy line occurring in all the levels but becoming rarer in the later ones. In contrast to the abundance of pottery and grinding equipment the lithic tool-kit is surprisingly poor. Not only are tools made from stone fairly rare but they are also mediocre in workmanship. It is noteworthy that the lower level has yielded a more microlithic industry with a much more reduced number of tool types than the middle and upper levels. Scrapers are not well represented while tools with backing (particularly bladelets of quartz or obsidian) represent a quarter of the tool-kit. In the middle and upper layers the industry develops in the direction of greater diversification, particularly the tools made on pebbles (choppers and chopping tools) while the number of backed pieces decreases. On the other hand there now appear, in the

[1] As grinding equipment in quantity is demonstrably associated with the processing of non-domestic grains in North America (e.g. California and the Great Basin), in Palestine with the Natufian and in Australia, its presence in prehistoric contexts in general should not be taken as an indication of domesticated cereals unless other and more direct evidence is also forthcoming. (Editor's note.)

middle level, first burins, push-planes and side-scrapers and then awls in the upper level. The number of arrow-points is not very large but is on the increase and that of segments (the only microlith present) decreases noticeably. The industry is relatively rich in bone tools of which the most noteworthy is a sort of dagger that could have served as a burnishing tool and of which the notched edge might have been used to decorate pottery before firing. The bone tools also include different types of points, awls, burnishers, *tranchets*, and objects for use in basketry, for working skins and in the making of pottery. The proximal end of some of these tools exhibits engraved decoration deliberately blackened in the fire. There were also objects of adornment – pins with heads, pendants (one in ivory) and tubular beads. Ostrich-eggshell beads are very rare but this scarcity is compensated for by pendants in other materials (such as lava or mussel shell) and stone bracelets. The Amekni site is thus of considerable interest; it confirms the presence of negroids of Sudanese type in the Sahara as early as the end of the seventh millennium BC and provides evidence for the existence at the same period of the beginnings of agriculture and of pot-making.

Without undue recourse to the imagination it is possible to reconstruct the way of life of the inhabitants of Amekni in the sixth millennium BC. On the *Typha*-lined edges of the wadi Amekni, women and children would catch catfish and perch, either in hand nets or by constructing light fish-weirs and dragging the bottom with wide-meshed baskets. The rather more recent site of Meniet has yielded a good example of a curved fish-hook made of bone and several Mauritanian sites have produced fish-hooks made of arcs of stone of quite large dimensions. Fishing with bow and arrow in lagoons and calm water cannot have been unknown; harpoons of bone and ivory were becoming quite common by the later phases of the Saharan–Sudanese Neolithic. Hunting remained an important occupation and the men of Amekni showed themselves very selective in their choice of game. Gazelle-hunting was probably most easily carried out by means of wheel-traps, while reedbuck (*Redunca*), wart-hog and the extinct buffalo (*Pelorovis* (*Homoïoceras*) *antiquus*) would either be taken by surprise while drinking or captured by means of pit-traps. The area between the granite ridge and the river was worked over by the women collecting wild grain but a species of millet was probably already being cultivated and land for this being cleared in the sandy plain. Among huts contrived between the large rocks, women pounded millet, ground the seeds of wild grains and cooked porridge in large pots. The preparation of the skins of antelopes or bovids and the making of baskets for which bone needles were used still left a considerable amount of time for leisure and sleep. In summer, when the fruits of the nettle tree (*Celtis australis* and *C. integrifolia*) ripened, they were collected in large quantities in the neighbouring woodland. Such a relatively sedentary and peaceful life called for no special or even abundant tools. These early agriculturalitsts, however, lacked the meat and, above all, milk products which domestication would later make available to their successors.

A more advanced phase of the Saharan–Sudanese Neolithic, dating to the fifth and fourth millennia BC, is represented at a large number of sites of which the best known (because the findings have been published) is that of Baguena V at Meniet (Hugot 1963) which shows striking resemblances to Amekni and dates to 3450 ± 300 BC, making it contemporary with the upper level of Amekni. The pottery, although it is decorated in the same way, exhibits several new forms. The vessels are still globular but some of them have a very slight neck and at least one had a tubular spout for pouring. Personal adornment has become more important; in addition to the forms described as coming from Amekni, there are now amazonite beads, pendants of perforated stone and lip ornaments. The tool-kit is also somewhat richer and includes polished axes, arrow-points, etc. Agriculture also is projected, based on finds of cereal pollens. Fruits of the nettle tree (*Celtis*) and jujube tree (*Zizyphus*) complete the sources of vegetable foods. It is not known whether the domestication of bovids had yet begun but there is every reason to think that it had, not so much because of the presence of possible cattle bones in the fauna but because some of the paintings from Tassili n'Ajjer and the Acacus date to this period and depict herds of domestic cattle.

A site that would appear to be of comparable interest although not yet published is that of Adrar Tiouiyne at the foot of a saddle on the edge of the Wadi Amded. As at Amekni and Meniet, fishing was regularly practised, to judge by the number of fish bones recovered. Occupation dates from the end of the fourth millennium BC (3200 ± 140 BC) and has yielded a pottery ware remarkable for its fine workmanship and the quality of its firing. The decoration consists almost exclusively of flame-shaped motifs executed by rocker-stamping. This pottery ware is also found in the southern Tanezrouft.

The above examples have been taken from the area round the Ahaggar but the evolution of the Saharan–Sudanese Neolithic, particularly of the pottery and fishing equipment, can also be seen at the sites in Tefedest (Maître 1971), the Acacus, Tassili n'Ajjer, Ténéré, Borkou (Courtin 1966) and Ounianga. Recent research in the Acacus carried out by a team from Italy led by Barich has produced an important Neolithic industry stratified in a rock-shelter in the Wadi Ti-n-Torha. This site has yielded a chronological sequence of the greatest interest dating from 7130 to 3650 BC (9080 ± 70 to 5600 ± 50 BP). It would appear, therefore, that the dotted wavy line pottery of the older Saharan–Sudanese Neolithic dates back to the eighth millennium BC and covers the whole of the seventh and sixth millennia. This pottery is here associated with a microlithic industry (Barich 1978). Other very important work has been carried out since 1974 by Aumassip in the large rock-shelter of Ti-n-Hanakaten in the Tassili n'Ajjer. The shelter contained archaeological deposits of 6.5 m thickness which yielded two Aterian levels, separated by a sterile layer and followed by a Neolithic. The central part of this Neolithic level has been dated to 6150 BC (8100 ± 130 BP). The site is also remarkable for the exceptionally well-preserved state of the excavated material including skeletons of adults and juveniles found on layers of bedding – hair was also recovered – and there were wooden tools, fragments of matting and cordage among other finds.

Apart from the beginnings of agriculture of which little trace remains in the archaeological record, and the appearance of domestication probably some time during the sixth to fifth millennium BC, it is apparent that the way of life had changed very little. The beginnings of these two innovations, particularly the second, might well have passed unnoticed had these people not left representatations of their herds on the rocks of the central Saharan massifs (Lhote 1958). Before looking at these Bovidian people, however, we must remind ourselves that the Saharan–Sudanese Neolithic, particularly in its most evolved stage, comprised numerous facies, which it is not, nevertheless, the intention to discuss in detail here. Even allowing for the degree of climatic unity to which the flora and fauna bear witness, it is quite understandable that a single cultural tradition would not have remained unchanged over such a wide area as that from Mauritania to the confines of the Nile. Facts that can be taken as definite are the unity of the negroid peoples of the central and southern Sahara during the Neolithic (Chamla 1968); the importance of pottery (always with a round base); the frequency of *Celtis* seeds on the sites; and the abundance of fish remains which parallels the considerable development of fishing equipment such as hooks and harpoons in stone, bone and ivory. There is, however, also an overall mediocrity in the lithic tool-kit which is in strong contrast to the general quality of these tools in the Ténéréan and the Neolithic of Capsian Tradition. Only the arrow-points in regions such as Tilemsi and Mauritania exhibit a standard of workmanship that equals and sometimes even surpasses that of the other Saharan Neolithic cultures. But the chief interest of the Saharan–Sudanese Neolithic, at least in the west central area, lies in the antiquity of its agriculture. For a long time it was thought that agriculture in the Sahara was of Mediterranean and Asian (or Egyptian) origin but the discovery of *Pennisetum* pollens in a deposit dating from the beginning of the sixth millennium BC shows that this earliest agriculture was tropical in character and probably owes nothing to the east.[1]

## THE PASTORAL NEOLITHIC OF THE BOVIDIANS
### AND THE TÉNÉRÉAN (figs. 8.4–6, plates 8.1–4)

Just as the study of the oldest phases of the Saharan–Sudanese Neolithic has led us to an examination of the origins of agriculture, so that of the pastoral phase, chiefly known from the rock-art style referred to as Bovidian should begin with an analysis of the origins of animal domestication in the Sahara (Esperandieu 1955, Mauny 1967). It is a known fact that domestication of cattle, sheep and pigs was practised by the Neolithic people of the Fayum in the fifth millennium BC. Throughout the whole of North Africa two forms of wild cattle were present: *Bos primigenius* and *B. ibericus*. The second species was, without any doubt, the ancestor of one or more of the domestic strains of the Maghrib and the Sahara and even of Egypt but we are not certain of the origin of *B. africanus* with its well-shaped build and long, slender horns, so successfully depicted both by the artists of the Sahara and later by the painters and sculptors of Egypt. At the period when man was reproducing the characteristics of *B. africanus* on the rocks of the Sahara, this animal had already been domesticated for some considerable time. The antiquity of this domestication is proved by the two and three colours in the coats of the animals, a characteristic never found in wild bovids and which, according to some animal breeders, is the result of the crossing of several strains. It is not impossible that the Sahara was

---

[1] While the first cultivated form of *Pennisetum* is believed to have been developed in the savanna or sahelian zones of West Africa (see ch. 9), claims for its cultivation based on pollen evidence alone need to be treated with caution since this might only be a reflection of simple manipulation and greater use of large-grained wild grasses. (Editor's note.)

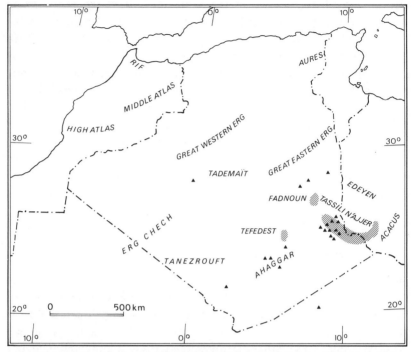

Fig. 8.4   Map showing the distribution of Neolithic stone carvings (small black triangle) and Bovidian paintings (hatched) in the central Sahara.

an original centre of animal domestication. This might have been a consequence of its desiccation: the extension of the savanna would favour an increase in the numbers of bovids while the decreasing water sources would have the effect of compelling man to live in ever closer proximity to the ruminants until the idea occurred to him to subjugate and exercise definite control over the herds. This hypothesis appears somewhat rash and, indeed, has become superseded since the establishment of the great antiquity of the Neolithic which makes it no longer possible to associate so closely the drying up of the Sahara with the beginning of animal domestication. Rather the reverse, because the opinion today is that it was the great size of the domestic herds, suggested by the numerous representations in the rock art, that to a great extent contributed to the desertification of the Sahara.

Whatever may have been the exact origins of the domestication of cattle it is quite clear that this trait had been acquired in the central Sahara before the fourth millennium BC since sites with rock art and

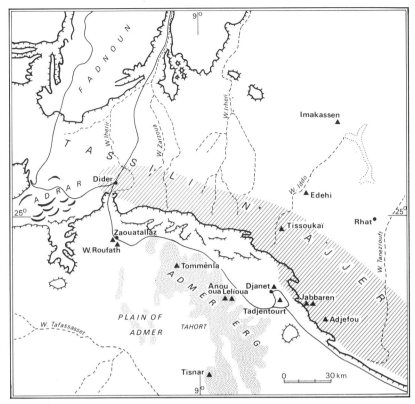

Fig. 8.5   Map showing the distribution of Neolithic stone carvings in Tassili n'Ajjer and the Admer Erg (small black triangle) and the principal extent of Bovidian paintings (hatched).

Bovidian occupation are dated to $3520 \pm 300$ BC at Jabbaren and $3070 \pm 300$ BC at Sefar. There is a strong presumption that Bed III at Ouan Muhuggiag (excavated by Mori), in which the frontal of *Bos brachyceros* was found, already belonged to the Bovidian period and Mori (1965) considers that the beginnings of the pastoral period go back even further than that. In the Acacus the oldest phase would appear to extend from the middle of the sixth to the beginning of the fourth millennium, and the central period to end in the middle of the fourth millennium BC. The greatest number of the Tassili n'Ajjer paintings belong to the final Bovidian stage and this is also the stage for which we have the largest number of dates. These are all in the first half of the third millennium BC (Camps, Delibrias and Thommeret 1968): $2910 \pm 250$ BC for In Itinen, and $2520 \pm 250$ BC for Ekaham ouan Tartaït and $2610 \pm 250$ BC for Titerast n'Elias. In the Tadrart Acacus at Ouan Muhuggiag

573

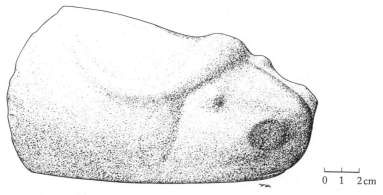

Fig. 8.6   Head of a bull carved in diorite, from Tisnar in the Admer Erg. Total length 17 cm.

the archaeological deposit covering a painted block fallen from the roof makes it possible to fix 2780 ± 310 BC as the *ante quem* date for the beginning of the recent phase of the pastoral style. Lhote considers that, in the Sahara, the domestication of cattle was preceded by that of sheep and goats and this theory is based, logically enough, on observation of superpositions in the rock art. At Ti-n-Rhardis, for instance, the Pre-Bovidian people, who were breeders of small stock, seem to have belonged to a caucasoid race and to have practised body painting, but at Ouan Derbaouen and in the Azzer massif, as also at Tahilahi, we find the same people, this time in possession of quite substantial herds of cattle. In point of fact, it seems quite likely that there was no such dichotomy in the beginnings of pastoralism in the Sahara. The finest and best documented examples of the Bovidian art, such as those of the Azzer massif in Tassili n'Ajjer, show flocks of sheep accompanying the cattle.

Even though no exhaustive study, or even a complete collection of the paintings and engravings of the Bovidian period has yet been published, it is, nevertheless, possible to obtain a good idea of the life of these pastoralists, thanks to the precision of their art. The human figures do not belong to a single physical type but the faces usually exhibit Mediterranean rather than negroid characteristics. In this type of painting, the women are generally shown with a lighter complexion than the men and this was also a later practice in the art of Egypt and Crete. At other times, there is a strong resemblance to the Peul (Fulani) peoples – the men are tall and slim with a dark complexion and, frequently, a small, pointed beard. However, it is the animals that should be considered first: usually they are *Bos africanus* with long horns, more or less lyre-shaped, but cattle with thicker horns are also depicted, especially in Tefedest and are often shown in full profile. As was noted above, it is seldom that the coat is of a single colour: usually the animals are bicoloured (fawn-and-white or black-and-white), but sometimes three colours (brown, black and white) are shown in the same coat. The heads are always very carefully drawn; they are shown longer than in real life and are treated with an artistic sense that occasionally seems artificial, particularly with regard to the treatment of the horns. Sometimes these last are curiously deformed both in the engravings and in the paintings; in the Tibesti massif alone a hundred such cases of deformity have been noted, while they are much rarer in Ennedi and Tassili n'Ajjer and exceptional in the Ahaggar (Huard 1959). Now this cultural trait is limited neither to the Sahara nor to the Neolithic period. Indeed, it seems to have originated among the peoples of Nubia where it continued throughout the Egyptian period; thus tribute from the Nubians is often shown as consisting of fattened cattle with horns variously deformed and carved. In our own day among the Nuer and Dinka of the Nile and even among the Souk and Nandi of Lake Victoria, such age-old practices have still not died out. In the engravings cattle are sometimes shown wearing curious pendants. Such representations are frequent in the engravings of the Ahaggar, Ahnet, Aïr, Tibesti, Fezzan and Jebel Uweinat, while they are almost unknown in the Tassili n'Ajjer paintings though they occur in the engravings of that region as at Wadi Djerat. This cultural trait must be regarded as due to influence from the C-group people of Nubia. None of the cattle shown in the rock art, from the Nile to the Saharan Atlas, exhibits the hump characteristic of the Zebu cattle which, along with the Fulani, have now spread over the whole of the Sahel region, pushing southwards those cattle types descended from the Neolithic domesticated animals.

The more detailed of the paintings show us the ways in which the Bovidians cared for their herds; we see them bringing water to the cattle and attaching the calves, each by one leg, to a single long rope just as the Egyptians did later and the pastoralists of Mali and Niger still do. The herd is led by an animal that cometimes has insignia between the horns. It is interesting that scenes of slaughtering and butchering should be rare: it would appear that, like a great many of the pastoral peoples of Africa, the Bovidians were reluctant to reduce the number of animals in their herds. However cattle bones are not rare in the archaeological deposits. Milk must have been an important item in the diet judging by the pains taken to reproduce cows with full udders, although to the writer's knowledge, no milking scenes are depicted. The Tassili paintings also supply information on other activities: hunting with the bow, and initiation-like dances associated with masks of an undeniably African character; it is, however, not always possible to group together in the same cultural unit all the thousands of scenes, sometimes in different styles. Details of clothing and ornament are faithfully depicted. Some negroid figures (do they perhaps seem of earlier date than the caucasoid Bovidians?) exhibit undoubted scarification, as at Jabbaren and Amazzar, while actual tattooing and painting of the body are painstakingly indicated on a great number of figures, both male and female, as at Ouan Bender, Azzer, Ouan Derbaouen and Ti-n-Rhardis. Sometimes the women are wearing luxurious dresses with braids and ribbons, over which a sort of hooded cloak is thrown when they travel, perched on the back of their cattle. At other times, no doubt when they perform domestic chores, they wear, over woven dresses, a sort of thigh-length apron made of the skin of an antelope or a goat. The men often content themselves merely with a loin-cloth but in camp they usually go naked or wear only a genital covering. The hair-style of the women is sometimes remarkable; in some case the size of the hairdo is so great that one is forced to imagine the use of hairpieces or other forms of artifice. The use of a block of perfume placed on the head, as in the banquets of ancient Egypt, is suggested by the women at Ouan Derbaouen, shown decked in their finery and quite obviously making their way to some ceremony. Lovelocks and coils of hair are not uncommon and necklaces, pectorals and bracelets complete the panoply of these Tassili n'Ajjer coquettes. The men are dressed more soberly in a loin-cloth but they sometimes wear a sort of skull-cap.

Social life seems to have been quite evolved. 'Conversation pieces' in which freedom of gesture and intentness of attitude recall somewhat the art of the pottery painters of Athens, are enclosed within a circular line which probably symbolizes the hut. Elsewhere, women reclining in the entrance to their huts, with heads and arms outside, are watching men sitting on their loin-cloths in a group round a large jar from which they are sipping a fermented drink. Sometimes inside the huts of the Bovidians is depicted a series of pots, always with round bases. Apparently this is the only moveable possession, other than water skins, carried slung over the backs of the pack-oxen. These populations were of necessity pastoral and so moved a great deal and had naturally conceived the idea of using their cattle as pack animals. The pack-ox still exists in a few regions of north Africa, such as the western part of the Saharan Atlas and Morocco, and also, in particular, throughout the whole of the Sahel and Saharan zones. It would not be at all improbable for this to be an ancient tradition continuously maintained.

The lithic tool-kit of the Bovidians is very imperfectly known, at least in the massifs where they have left the evidence of their art. The most characteristic elements are arrow-points, chipped and polished axes, pestles and pounding stones, rubbers and fragments of grindstones. Lhote, who has excavated several of these shelters, attaches considerable importance to the presence of small plaques or pebbles with retouched edges, considered to be characteristic of the stone industry of the Bovidians. The abundance of grindstones and rubbers attests to the importance in the diet of grain, whether cultivated or wild. Fish remains are absent from the mountain sites even though the pools in the water courses still even today contain barbel and catfish. The pottery is the same as that with the Saharan–Sudanese Neolithic (to which the Bovidians belong), although it would appear that there is a more frequent use of punctate decoration.

It is, however, important to define exactly what is understood by the authors who use the term Bovidian. Is it applied merely to a style of Neolithic rock art? Or to a particular tradition within the Saharan–Sudanese ensemble or even within the Sahara, broadly speaking? Lhote (1970) speaks of Bovidian influence and even of Bovidian engravings in the Saharan Atlas of western Algeria and in southern Morocco where, however, the lithic industry and the pottery are both very different. It must not be forgotten that the groups who left their paintings in the shelters of Tassili n'Ajjer or Tefedest were pastoralists and that, therefore, they practised transhumance and spent a large part of the year in the neighbouring valleys and plains which have now become *ergs*. We ought, therefore, to find tools of these Bovidian people on the occupation sites in the *ergs*. Proof of this transhumance is provided by the presence, both in the sites in the Tassili n'Ajjer rock-shelters and on the neighbouring plains, now the Admer Erg, of magnificent sculptures in round relief of bovids, antelopes, sheep, rodents and anthropomorphic figures (Camps-Fabrer 1966, 1967). In the realm of sculpture these figurines are as well executed and of as high standard as are the paintings in the shelters. They are of Bovidian workmanship but the lithic tool-kit associated with them in the *erg* is usually much richer than that from the shelters. The presence of bifacial discs with extremely fine, thin retouch and the elegance of the arrow-points shows incontestible Ténéréan influence, which is quite probable as the Admer Erg is at the head of the Ténéré of Taffassasset. It must be granted, therefore, that the Bovidian populations had a much more impoverished tool-kit in the mountains, where their stay was shorter, than on the plain. There is nothing improbable in this but any interpretation must remain hypothetical until Lhote has published his account of the lithic industries of the Bovidian rock-painting sites.

Like the Bovidian, the Ténéréan seems to cover the fourth and third millennia BC, as evidenced by the date of $3180 \pm 500$ BC from Adrar Bous and $2520 \pm 115$ BC at Areschima, and it appears to be a Middle Neolithic. The same characteristics and techniques seen in the hard-stone figurines of the Bovidians are also exhibited by the many objects that make up the Ténéréan tool-kit: pestles, grindstones, rubbers and above all grooved axes some of which are veritable works of art. The lithic industry is very fine; to the artifacts on blades and bladelets and the geometric microliths of the Epi-Palaeolithic tradition is added an important Neolithic element with bifacial retouch – especially long, fine arrow-points, *tranchets* and, in particular, discs whose thinness bears witness to the great skill of the Ténéréan craftsmen. With this assemblage must also be counted knives of Egyptian type and flat grindstones notched at the edges to facilitate transport on ox-back. The discovery of a skeleton of a domestic ox in a Ténéréan site at Adrar Bous confirms that these people were pastoralists.

The Bovidians are neither the only nor yet the first prehistoric artists in the Sahara. The thousands of years during which rock art was practised in the Sahara was sufficient time for the evolution of several very different styles. Among the engravings, the oldest examples depict exclusively wild animals, sometimes of considerable size and always quite remarkably realistic in stance. On the rocks in the central Sahara, the animal which occurs most often in the engravings is the elephant, followed by the giraffe, the rhinoceros, antelopes, and bovids among which should be mentioned the giant buffalo (*Pelorovis (Homoïoceras) antiquus*), now extinct which is however less frequent here than in the Saharan Atlas. Some authors lump all these large, naturalistic engravings from North Africa together in a single style, wrongly referred to as 'Bubalian' (*Bubalis antiquus = Pelorovis (Homoïoceras) antiquus*) (Lhote 1970). At present there is no proof that this large naturalistic style belongs everywhere to the same period, nor that there is any true connection between the examples, which are necessarily similar since they reproduce in realistic fashion the same large fauna. One interesting fact for which there is, as yet, no explanation, is that this same large fauna is nowhere depicted in the paintings on the rocks of the central Sahara. It seems clear that this is a pre-pastoral phase and Huard has called the authors of this art the 'Hunters'.

Of the rock paintings, the oldest phase, which may perhaps be contemporary with the art of the Hunters (the Bubalian period of Lhote), has been given the name of Round Head style. This is not always a naturalistic style and includes large figures of individuals, sometimes deliberately deformed, with contorted limbs exhibiting vegetable or muscular excrescences (Lhote 1958). These mythical beings look like the graphic expression of nightmare figures; the heads are shaped like divers' helmets and the facial features are either not at all realistic or are simply replaced by geometric motifs. This Round Head phase lasted a considerable time; it seems to have developed in the direction of greater realism but, even though there is some improvement in the proportions of the body, there is never any neck beneath the large, spherical head. The populations responsible for the Round Head style seem to have been negroid (although their gods or mythical beings were sometimes painted white). It is to the most evolved phase of this Round Head style that the finest representations of 'Negro' masks belong. This style seems to occur frequently in the eastern Sahara and Ennedi. According to Mori (1965) the Round Head style must have begun very early and ended before the seventh millennium BC. It would be quite reasonable to regard the authors of this art as contemporary with the oldest Saharan–Sudanese Neolithic industries, which are also the work of negroid peoples.

There are a considerable number of paintings of the pastoral or Bovidian phase in the Tassili n'Ajjer and also in Ennedi, Tibesti and Tefedest in the northern Ahaggar. According to Lhote the engravings of domestic cattle should also be included in this phase. They are also very numerous and are found on rocks in the Ahaggar (at Tit, Hirafok and Aguennar), in Tibesti (at Gonoa and Bardaï), in the Fezzan, Ahnet, Aïr and almost everywhere in the central Sahara. Lhote even considers the Bovidian style to embrace the Maghrib (the western part of the Saharan Atlas and southern Morocco). The present writer has the same reservations about this as about the extension of the naturalistic style of the Sahara to these same regions. Those in the Bovidian style are the finest of the paintings but they do not all belong to the same phase. The oldest, termed Pre-Bovidian are already quite different from those of the Round Head style. We have seen that the people represented exhibit caucasoid features. The most recent of the paintings depict cattle harnessed to chariots and are, thus, contemporary with the Equidian style which cannot be earlier than the mid second millennium BC. The Bovidian phase came to an end when the growing scarcity of grazing and the decreasing number of water sources forced the large-scale stock-herders to retreat to the west and south. They were eventually, though not immediately, replaced by people who have been called Equidians or Cabalines who introduced the horse into the Sahara (Lhote 1953). It seems likely that these Equidians did not drive out the descendants of the Bovidians but rather that they mixed with them and became a ruling caste. The Equidian style is quite different from that of the Bovidians and is recognizable, above all, by representations of horses, first harnessed to two-wheeled, single-shafted chariots and later ridden. Even at the beginning, the figures exhibit a great elegance and flexibility and scenes of an intimate nature, beloved of the Bovidians, continue to be depicted with great attention to accuracy. But individualism begins to assume greater importance and so we see the (?) chief represented in his chariot or hunting wild sheep with his three dogs or on one knee doing homage to his masked overlord. Clothing is less sumptuous than in the Bovidian epoch: leather rather than woven cloth is the most frequently used material for loin-cloths reaching to mid-calf for the men and for a sort of bell-shaped tunic for the women who are deliberately shown as rather fat. Unlike their predecessors, the Equidians prefer not to depict the human face which is quite often indicated by a single line, while the remainder of the body, as in the older phase, is still very close to reality. This early Equidian phase, with horses shown in full gallop, is thought to have lasted from the end of the second millennium to the first centuries of the first millennium BC.

Meanwhile water was becoming scarcer, agriculture was growing more and more difficult; the artist took pleasure in depicting his herds round a well from which a man was drawing water in a leather bucket, exactly like a scene in the Sahara today. The art style is changing; the limbs of the animals are becoming stiffer, the stance first loses some of its dynamic quality, then becomes rigid and gradually the art becomes schematic with the human body now nothing more than an arrangement of geometric shapes. Imperceptibly we have moved into the contemporary Libyco-Berber style (with the horse replaced by the camel which is better adapted to the increasingly harsh conditions of the Sahara desert). This art, which borders on graffiti, has not yet completely disappeared.

The rock art of the Sahara is, thus, a veritable library in which one can unearth a considerable number of clues as to technology, way of life and even the evolution of the population. Unfortunately this source of documentation is not always easy to use and generally we lack any association between the rock art and the lithic or ceramic industries.

It is not possible to discuss the art of the Sahara without also saying a few words on the subject of the very beautiful carvings in hard rocks which occur essentially in the Tassili n'Ajjer and, more particularly, on its southern rim (Camps-Fabrer 1966). Their connection with the Bovidian art is evidenced by the finds from Jabbaren and with the Ténéréan by the discoveries at Anou oua Lelioua; nevertheless the unity of style is indisputable. According to Camps-Fabrer, it is considered that transhumance on the part of the Bovidians between the plain of Admer and the nearby Tassili n'Ajjer explains the presence of these small carvings in both these complementary areas. To date, some thirty-eight of these Neolithic animal sculptures from Tassili n'Ajjer, the Admer Erg and the Ahaggar are known and some anthropomorphic cult figurines from Tabelbalat, Issaouane and Ouan Sidi are included in this total. They were found outside and to the north of the area of greatest concentration, made up of the Tassili n'Ajjer and the Admer Erg. Among the animals represented, cattle are far more numerous than sheep, antelopes or rodents. They all observe quite strict stylistic rules, essentially based on bilateral symmetery on each side of an axis, usually marked by a crest which, on some of the sculptures, runs from the muzzle to the end of the back. The second characteristic is the stripping away of all unnecessary high relief and the retention only of what is absolutely essential – the curve of a horn, the position of an ear or even the angle of a moustache; the choice of anatomical detail is always excellent. These little objects made of such hard rocks as basalt, dolerite or amphibolitic gneiss are great works of art. The characteristics and technique of these sculptures, which can only be cult figurines (or idols), are found repeated in identical form on other hard-stone objects which are part of the Ténéréan Neolithic tool-kit. These are 'pestles', rubbers with enigmatic sculpture, decorated grindstones (cf. from Tihigaline) and, especially, numerous beautifully worked axes characterized by their groove, their spurs and often pointed butt. These grooved axes, some of which are true works of art, have long been used to define the Ténéréan though this involves ignoring all the remainder of the tool-kit studied by Tixier (1961) from the industry from Adrar Bous, site 3, and which consists of an important microlithic element of segments and triangles, very numerous microburins (more than a quarter of the tools) and numbers of backed bladelets. As has already been said, to this assemblage of Epi-Palaeolithic tradition should be added an important true Neolithic element with bifacial retouch. This consists of beautiful, fine, long arrow-points, *tranchets*, foliate forms and remarkable 'Ténéréan discs', the thinness and fragility of which bear witness to the skill of these stone-workers. One of these discs has a maximum thickness of 6 mm and a diameter of 112 mm. To this list must also be added Egyptian-style knives, chipped and polished axes and gouges and, finally, the usual grinding equipment of the Saharan Neolithic.

The makers of this beautiful industry also produced the fine sculptures in hard rocks from the Admer Erg; their connections with the Bovidians, who are their contemporaries, seems undoubted – the Adrar Bous III Industry is dated to $3190 \pm 30$ BC (Camps-Fabrer 1967). In addition, the Ténéréan shows close affinities with the Neolithic industry of Esh-Shaheinab which, however, possesses neither discs, microburins nor triangles and seems rather earlier, about 3300 BC). This merely confirms that there was a certain cultural unity in Neolithic times between the Sahara and Egypt and the resemblances between the industries are to be found also in the domain of the art.

## THE MEDITERRANEAN NEOLITHIC (figs. 8.7–10)

Although the Neolithic is very widespread along the Mediterranean and Atlantic coasts of the Maghrib it is very imperfectly known, or, rather, it has been extremely well studied in some places and not at all in others. In general, the main sites – and by that is meant those which have been the subject of large-scale excavations and more or less detailed publication – are all found close to the large towns where the European prehistorians normally lived. Thus in the neighbourhood of Casablanca we know of the important cemetery at El-Kiffen and at Rabat the coast has been explored inch by inch. At Tangier the antiquity and significance of connections with the Iberian peninsula are shown by excavations in the caves of Achakar and El-Khril (Jodin 1958–9) and these results are confirmed by work near Ceuta, at Gar Cahal (Tarradell 1954) and at Caf That el-Gar, near Tetouan (Tarradell 1957–8). The limestone region of Mudjardjo at Oran is rich in caves and rock-shelters and was for a long time the special preserve of amateurs of the Neolithic in the Maghrib. Unfortunately, excavation there began too early and the outmoded methods employed have resulted in detailed knowledge of

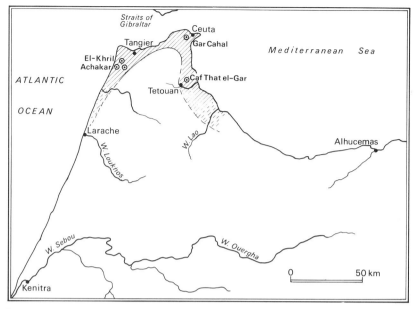

Fig. 8.7 Map showing the distribution of the Neolithic with Cardial pottery in North Africa. Note that the area is limited to the Straits of Gibraltar.

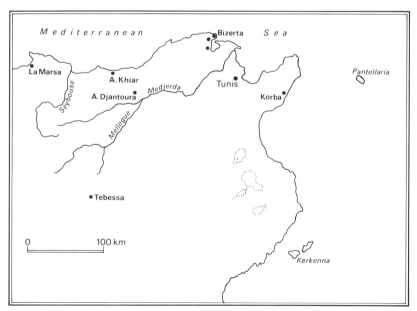

Fig. 8.8 Map showing sites in North Africa that have yielded stone tools in obsidian, limited to northern Tunisia and eastern Algeria.

Fig. 8.9  Decorated potsherds of the Mediterranean Neolithic from Oran District. All from the caves at Wadi Guettara except no. 6 from the 'Snail cemetery' and no. 8 from the Forêt Cave.

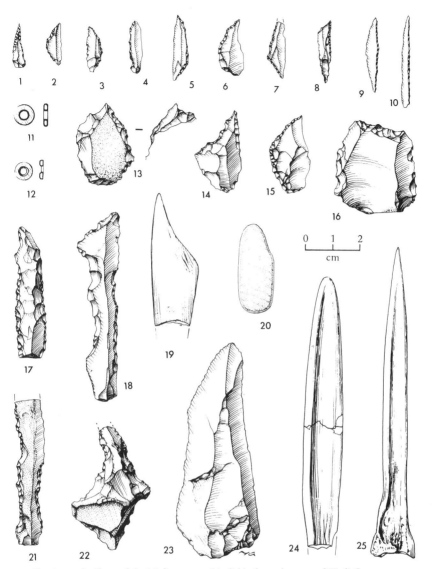

Fig. 8.10 Artifacts of the Mediterranean Neolithic from the cave of Wadi Guettara.

*In stone*
1 Micropoint with partial backing
2–3 Segments
4–6 Backed bladelets
7–8 Long scalene triangles
9–10 Narrow, pointed bladelets backed down one straight edge (*aiguillons droits*)
13 Burin on a truncation opposed to a scraping edge
14, 22 Awls
15 Backed flake

16 Rectangular end-scraper (*grattoir droit*)
17–18, 21 Denticulate blades
23 Unretouched blade

*In bone, etc.*
11–12 Ostrich-eggshell beads
19 *Tranchet* with oblique cutting edge and lateral spur
20 Small plaque of scallop shell
24 Burnisher
25 Piercing tool

only a small fraction of the tool-kit. In this way, the systematic discarding of all burnished or undecorated potsherds might have given rise to the belief that Neolithic pots from Oran District were all completely decorated. The excavations in the Sahel caves at Algiers were even older since they were the work of pioneers such as Bourjot and Bertherand in the middle of the nineteenth century.

These enthusiastic amateurs have, unfortunately, been the cause of the complete disappearance of the archaeological deposits. The region of Bougie which was also rich in rock-shelters was partially explored and studied. There are no coastal caves in the east of the Maghrib but some very interesting sites have been studied on the coast near Bone, Bizerta and Cape Bon. But between these specially privileged areas (a privilege, incidentally, that was often fraught with unfortunate consequences as in the suburbs of Algiers and Oran) hundreds of miles of coastline have been subjected to only the most cursory investigation or exploration, occasionally accompanied by a trial excavation. It is only in the caves of northern Morocco that clear, stratigraphic sequences have been uncovered but even here, as elsewhere, it has not been possible to pinpoint the change from Epi-Palaeolithic to Neolithic. In all the stratigraphic sequences so far obtained there seems to be only one in which this changeover may possibly be documented, that is in Tarradell's (1954) excavations at Gar Cahal where it seems likely that level IV is Iberomaurusian and not yet Neolithic.[1] Indeed, it would seem, in the writer's opinion, that it is in the central part of this very thick 'level' that the change from a post-Iberomaurusian to the Neolithic took place. The very rare artifacts in Level V (4.30–4.80 m) confirm this opinion because they are no different from those in Level IV. In Oran District, the magnificent cave sites have yielded a rich Neolithic industry, in

[1] *Level I* contains mixed remains from the Roman and Arab periods.
*Level II* (0.60–1.70 m) is characterized by a burnished pottery with flat bases and by a channelled pottery.
*Level III* (1) (1.70–2.05 m) yielded sherds of typical Beaker ware pottery (*campaniforme*) overlying Cardial ware (*céramique cardiale*).
*Level III* (2) (2.05–2.70 m) produced Cardial ware sherds and, below, fragments of painted pottery related to the Serraferlicchio ware of Sicily.
*Level IV* (2.70–4.30 m) does not seem to have interested the excavator over much as he was too preoccupied with his fine stratified sequence of Neolithic and Copper Age. Now this 'level', 1.60 m thick, yielded very rare potsherds in its upper part; these grew rapidly less frequent with depth while stone artifacts became more and more abundant. No analysis of this stone industry would seem to have been published but this assemblage – without polished axes, arrow-points or pottery – does not appear to belong to the Neolithic while the author, who believes in 'a Neolithic based on a very impoverished Iberomaurusian tradition' refers to the presence of a crude tool-kit in quartz which we should now consider not at all surprising in an Iberomaurusian context. At the top of this Level IV, where there is still a little pottery, Tarradell records the finding of a flint dagger 20 cm long which he, quite rightly, considers to be an import.

particular a well-made, impressed and incised pottery, but the change-over from Iberomaurusian to Neolithic was not recognized in these earlier excavations.

Excavations carried out by the present writer in 1967 in a cave in the Wadi Guettara at Bredeah near Oran – *which must no be confused with the site of Aïn Guettara in the Tademaït, Sahara* – should at last throw fresh light on the Mediterranean Neolithic of Oran District and the changeover from the Epi-Palaeolithic to the Neolithic. The site is a small cave that in Neolithic times was used not as an ossuary but rather as a burial place. The superficial layer, down to 25 cm, is pure Neolithic with abundant pottery (565 g per sq. m), the industry is mediocre, remarkable chiefly for the abundance of denticulate tools and minimally retouched bladelets, blades and flakes; these two categories together comprise 56% of the stone-tool assemblage. The next most numerous are backed bladelets (13%) and scrapers (9.6%); geometric microliths are represented chiefly by segments. There are truncated pieces, backed flakes and blades, awls and occasional burins and side-scrapers; there are very few microburins. It is not so much the lithic artifacts but, rather, the pottery and, to a lesser degree, the bone industry that made us attribute this level to the Neolithic. Bone tools and ornaments are numerous and varied. Body painting must have been a common practice judging by the abundance of various minerals used as pigments – haematite, zinc sulphide and galena. Pendants are made from the valves of lamellibranchs such as the cockle (*Cardium*) or mussel or from turret shells (*Turitella*). The only ostrich-eggshell beads came from this level. As for the pottery, this is characteristic of the Mediterranean Neolithic: the vessels are generally wide-mouthed with decoration only near the rim; the decoration consists of impressions made with twigs, sticks or wedges (comb decoration is not present). The body of the pot is ovoid in shape, generally with a conical base. Layer II (25–45 cm) is less ashy and still belongs to the Neolithic and yields an identical though much less frequent pottery (57 g per sq. m). Compared with the upper layer, every category of lithic artifacts is less well represented apart from backed bladelets (18%), scrapers (13.7%) and geometric microliths (6.5%). The bone industry is more varied and considerably more abundant than that of Layer I. Layer III (45–65 cm) is the level which contains the burials and there is practically no more pottery. In the lithic industry backed bladelets continue to increase (26.5%), backed blades disappear and awls, burins, truncated pieces and microburins are rare. The Neolithic period is represented by a single piece with overall retouch. The industry in this level is difficult to classify particularly as it has been much disturbed by the Neolithic burials. These people belong to the Mechta–Afalou type which we know persisted up to Neolithic times; like their Iberomaurusian ancestors, the Neolithic members of this physical type continued to practise mutilation of the teeth but now this is done in both jaws. Layer IV (65 cm down to the sterile level) is definitely not Neolithic. In view of the very small number of artifacts recovered, it is not possible to be sure of the exact characteristics of the industry which would seem to be post-Iberomaurusian.

Charcoals recovered from the base of the archaeological deposit and the top of the underlying yellow sand have been dated to 8240 ± 230 BC. There is no date for the topmost level at Wadi Guettara but at the so-called 'Snail cemetery' (*Cimetière des Escargots*) at the site of Corales a few miles away, we find the same impressed and incised pottery in a level dated to 4730 ± 300 BC (Camps *et al.* 1968).

A fifth millennium date would, therefore, seem not to be out of place for the superficial layer at Wadi Guettara and we can almost certainly say that the change to a Neolithic culture which was taking place throughout Layers III and II at that site probably dates to the sixth millennium, if not earlier. This chronological framework fits with what is known about the beginnings of the Neolithic in the western Mediterranean. Whatever may be the reason, the archaeological record on the coast (where a post-Iberomaurusian industry still persisted) evidences the changeover of the Neolithic by nothing more than very slight modifications in the lithic tool-kit. Paradoxically, this tool-kit seems to become impoverished, perhaps because new resources make the microliths of the preceding industry less useful. Stone tools are quantitatively less and usually much cruder than with the Iberomaurusian; the scrapers, denticulate tools and awls become more numerous while the backed bladelets decrease. The new tool types – small rectangles, arrow-points and polished axes – are rare. Arrow-points and bifacially-worked foliate points are so rare on the coast that they must, of necessity, be considered to be imports. By comparison with the Iberomaurusian the sparseness of the stone artifacts is largely compensated for by the richness of the bone industry and the personal ornaments (Camps-Fabrer 1960, 1966).

One cannot study the Mediterranean Neolithic of North Africa without taking into account the great movement towards a Neolithic way of life which was going on in the western Mediterranean basin throughout the sixth millennium BC. Indeed the Neolithic which is recognized in a narrow coastal belt of the Maghrib is different from the Neolithic of Capsian Tradition and, it surely goes without saying, from the Saharan–Sudanese Neolithic. It belongs to an essentially Mediterranean family covering the south of France, the Iberian peninsula, Italy and the islands. It is, therefore, not possible to overstate its maritime character. As early as the end of the seventh millennium, the first pottery-makers, by means of coastal trade and also by successful forays as far as the larger islands, had little by little won all the Mediterranean coast; the coasts of Tunisia, Algeria and Morocco were no exceptions. The very characteristics of the impressed pottery ware common to all these Mediterranean regions would alone be sufficient proof of the unity of this cultural ensemble that became grafted onto the different Epi-Palaeolithic industries. It can be readily appreciated that relations with the neighbouring European countries were established earliest in the two extremities of the Maghrib – the north of Morocco and Tunisia. Of these two regions northern Morocco must have been in the most favourable position, separated as it is from Spain by only the Straits of Gibraltar (Tarradell 1958). There is no lack of evidence for these early exchanges and it is worthy of note that it is only in the area of Tangier and Ceuta that sherds of Cardial pottery, *sensu stricto*, have been recovered, that is to say of pottery the walls of which have been decorated by impressions of the shells of cockle (*Cardium*) or other lamellibranchs such as scallop (*Pecten*) and which is a widespread early Neolithic ware in the Mediterranean basin. The first shell-decorated pots recognized in the Maghrib were those from Achakar in the vicinity of Tangier recorded by Koehler as early as 1931. We have already referred to the Gar Cahal site near Ceuta where Tarradell[1] distinguished five levels. The chief interest of this excavation lay in the discovery in the lowermost Neolithic level (Level III) of Cardial ware pottery associated with painted sherds that Evans (1955–6) considered to be similar in style to the Serraferlicchio ware of Sicily.

In the little caves at El-Khril (Jodin 1958–9) near Achakar, Tangier, Cardial ware pottery was invariably found in the deepest levels whereas incised pottery associated with polished axes and grindstones occurred at a higher level. Apart from this small area in the extreme north of

---

[1] At Caf That el-Gar, a cave near Tetouan, the same worker found an equally interesting stratigraphic sequence (Tarradell 1957–8). Here the Level III yielded both Cardial ware and impressed pottery and also a channelled pottery which is certainly of Chalcolithic date; the 45-cm thickness of this level perhaps explains the presence of this last ware. Level II, overlying it, yielded Beaker ware sherds and a burnished pottery which was the only ware that occurred in the superficial level.

Morocco, no Cardial ware pottery, in the strict sense of the term, has been recognized anywhere in the Maghrib. The forms of Cardial ware vessels are comparatively well known in Morocco because of the complete pots recovered by Koehler (1931) and Buchet at Achakar and the large numbers of sherds in the El-Khril caves. The most usual form is a wide-mouthed, sub-spherical pot with a slight constriction separating the mouth from the body. Some vessels have a true, cylindrical neck, one has an elliptical body and there are also large, conical-based pots with no neck. The decoration is produced in three main ways (Camps-Fabrer 1966): large areas of the surface of the pot are covered with bands of ornament made up of 'flame-shaped' or 'shark-tooth' motifs obtained by rocker-stamping; these bands are never contiguous – a useful device for producing complex decoration by the alteration or juxtaposition of different motifs. This attempt at composition can be seen both in the hollowed and relief forms of decoration – the method is reinforced by the use of plastic decoration by adding appliqued twists or lozenges of clay. These characteristics are identical with those seen in the decoration of Cardial ware in Spain and Provence. At the beginning of the Neolithic, the connections between Spain and northern Morocco attested by Cardial ware pottery were limited to this narrow section of the Maghrib but they increase throughout the Chalcolithic (cf. the Channelled and Beaker wares) and finally spread over a considerably larger area (Camps 1960, Jodin 1957).

At the opposite end of the Maghrib, traces of ancient contact with Italy and the islands are much rarer (Camps 1959); indeed, for the Neolithic period all that can be established is the introduction of obsidian at several points on the coasts of Tunisia and neighbouring Algeria. This raw material may have originated in the islands of Lipari and Pantellaria. It is certainly from this latter island, situated some 60 km to the east of Cape Bon, that the material came which was used to make the arrow-points found at Korba immediately opposite the island and at Hergla.[1]

At Bechateur, the site of Jebel Dib yielded to Gruet (1947) a Neolithic industry of which 0.5% was made in a much more transparent obsidian

[1] The age of the importation of obsidian cannot be fixed with complete exactitude. The industry from Hergla is dated to 3320 BC and, by analogy with Provence where this material was introduced during the Middle Neolithic (the Chassian), one might be tempted to place the date at a time later than that of Cardial ware. The very look of the Korba Industry with its tanged and eared arrow-points and typical rectangles, inspires the suggestion that the introduction of obsidian on the coasts of Tunisia shoud be regarded as of Middle or Recent Neolithic age. Here also but later – in the Metal Age – exchange relations became intensified and played no small part in the evolution of rural Berber culture (Camps 1961).

than that from Pantellaria and which probably originated in the islands of Lipari as did that found in the Bizerta area, in Calle (Algeria) and Marsa (south-west of Cap de Fer, Algeria). An obsidian scraper was even found at Tebessa although this rock is completely unknown in the eastern part of the Maghrib. Analysis showed this obsidian to have come from Lipari. Obsidian flakes and tools have also been found at Zarzis in southern Tunisia and in central Tunisia in the Maktar area. These connections between the Maghrib and other Mediterranean countries are, thus, quite ancient and their importance cannot be exaggerated. From the anthropological standpoint the persistence of the Mechta–Afalou physical type on the coast confirms the autochthonous nature of the population which had not yet been modified by immigrations of Mediterranean peoples such as took place in protohistoric times.

Although during the course of the Neolithic quite definite European pottery elements made their appearance in the two extremities of the Maghrib, they were grafted onto a basic, common pottery tradition that might be termed pan-Mediterranean. This impressed pottery ware is well known throughout the length and breadth of the Mediterranean coast and particularly in western Algeria. It is found in the caves and rock-shelters of Oran District, in the Bougie region and also on the open sites where, however, it has undergone much more weathering. The limestone massif of Mudjardjo near Oran has yielded considerable quantities of Neolithic pottery and it seems appropriate to take this series as an example and to compare it with the pottery of the Saharan–Sudanese Neolithic of which we have already noted the characteristics (Camps-Fabrer 1966). All the pots are conical-based which is, thus, the first main difference from the Saharan pottery. Other differences consist in the great rarity of necks: if not entirely absent, the neck is only a very short, narrow constriction, as at the Batterie Espagnole site. Even more noteworthy is the frequence of projecting nipples and lugs, both perforated and unperforated, culminating at times in wide handles with very long, narrow perforations. These projecting elements are completely lacking in the Saharan pottery wares and this very important difference between the two series is worth mentioning particularly because the presence of the nipples modifies the patterns of the impressed or incised decoration and so leads to the first appearance of deliberate composition which is absent from the rich, free-flowing decoration of the Saharan–Sudanese pottery.

In all the Mediterranean Neolithic sites, the position of the decoration is very characteristic, being strictly limited to the upper part of the vessel. It forms a sort of band that underlines the mouth and hardly ever extends over the body of the pot except sometimes where there are descending vertical motifs which may be laterally contained by incised lines and this is the very first sign of a rhythm in composition that was destined to enjoy considerable future development. The tendencies thus shown and the obvious attempt at composition compensate for the poverty of the means used to decorate this pottery and any negligence of execution. It is true too that the tools used were unbelievably archaic and primitive; comb impressions are almost totally absent, only two sites, near Oran, having yielded comb-decorated sherds. Apart from incisions and channelling which can be produced with a thorn or a porcupine quill just as easily as with bone points or tranchets, all the motifs found on the potsherds in the Oran Museum could have been executed by using unmodified vegetable products. Quite definitely, therefore, the potters of the Mediterranean Neolithic used only three or four implements to decorate their pots and it can also be stated categorically that they did not fully exploit all the decorative possibilities of those they used; in fact it must be said that the technology was even more disconcertingly impoverished than the tools. The Neolithic peoples of the Algerian and Tunisian coasts knew neither the rocker-stamping used by the Cardial-ware potters of northern Morocco and all the Saharan Neolithic peoples, nor did they know the joined sloping-line impression. A particularly rich variety of motifs can be produced by this last technique and, in the Sahara, the potters of Tanezrouft and Tilemsi, making skilful use of implements that were just as simple as those employed in the *tell* country, compensated for the poverty of their impressed decoration by increasing the number of rectilinear motifs and compositions, by the juxtaposition of marks made with a broad spatula and incisions traced by sharp instruments. However, these incised or impressed and frequently repeated motifs are not very numerous and two are much more common than the others – chequer-work and chevrons. Incisions, always made into the soft clay, sometimes show the U-shaped section of channelling. They usually take the form of parallel lines surrounding the mouth of the pot or delimiting areas of impressed motifs; the vertical or oblique hatching is done with a sharp instrument. The characteristics of the pottery of the Mediterranean Neolithic are, thus, the association of impression and incision and a praiseworthy attempt at composition which compensates for the poor technology and the poverty and monotony of motif.

In Atlantic Morocco other, more recent, pottery styles put in an appearance among which should be mentioned the channelled pottery of El-Khril at Achakar, also with conical base but with a very different decoration from that of the Algerian pottery. The potters used the comb and produced, on the top part of the body of the pot, an undulating motif consisting of festoons. Another, more widespread style belongs to a Middle or Recent Neolithic in the Casablanca area where it is characterized by pottery having long, internal lugs with narrow perforation. These vessels are wide-mouthed (cooking pots and bowls) in the inside of which were attached appliqued twists and wide knobs that were perforated to take a cord. The fine and very characteristic pottery of El-Kiffen near Casablanca belongs to a final Neolithic dated to about 2340 BC. The forms are varied, the most novel being goblets and shouldered jars. Projections consist of long, curved lugs with narrow vertical perforation, sometimes as much as 9 cm in length. Decoration is carried out entirely with a comb, the surface of the pot between the decorated portions being carefully polished. The Neolithic in Atlantic Morocco comprises a greater number of polished axes or adzes than in the rest of the Maghrib. All along the coast are found large kitchen middens some of which are comparatively modern.

On the coast and in the *tell* country the beginnings of animal domestication coincide with the appearance of pottery, or may even be older than that. It does not appear as if either the Neolithic people with the Cardial pottery or those of the oldest phase of the Mediterranean Neolithic took the first steps in the domestication of sheep and goats. Remains of these animals are already too numerous in the oldest levels of the Khril cave at Achakar and in the Neolithic deposits in the shelters and caves of the Algerian–Tunisian littoral for these to have been the first attempts at domestication. No in-depth study has yet been made of the Neolithic sheep of the *tell* country and we do not even know whether this animal belonged, as does the sheep of the Saharan Atlas, to the species *Ovis longipes* Fitz. Pomel (1898), however, without hesitation ascribed the numerous sheep remains from the Grand Rocher cave at Algiers to *Ovis africana* Sanson which is the present-day species. The origin of the domestic sheep is still obscure, therefore, and it does not seem likely that there can have been any local strain of sheep. As Esperandieu (1955) has pointed out, the remains in pre-Neolithic sites that have been regarded as those of wild sheep are, in fact, the bones of Barbary sheep from which it is impossible that the domestic sheep could have been derived. The problem is the same with regard to the goat. Pomel ascribed the goat he recognized among the fauna of Grand Rocher at Algiers to *Capra promaza*; he considers this to be of the same strain as the present-day Kabylia goat which is long-haired, small in stature and with small, flat and very spreading horns. In the present state of our knowledge, therefore, we can only say that domestic sheep and goat were introduced into the *tell* country of the Maghrib at the same time as the Cardial ware and impressed pottery. The case may well be different where it comes to the domestic pig which may well be descended from the wild boar that was quite abundant in North Africa from at least the end of the Last Glaciation.

The question of the origin of domestic cattle in the *tell* country is even more complicated. The type of cattle of which the bones occur frequently in the Neolithic cave deposits is a small or medium-sized animal, rather stocky, with short limbs and horns and is thus different from *Bos africanus* which, as we have seen, was domesticated by the people of the Sahara and East Africa. The cattle of the *tell* country belong to the subspecies *B. ibericus* present in the Maghrib since the Villafranchian (Vaufrey 1955). This is a vigorous and adaptable species, so much so that since its domestication it has been able to absorb numerous crosses without undergoing modification. *B. ibericus* is the ancestor of the brown Atlas strain. It is probable that the cattle whose bones are found in the Neolithic sites were already domesticated but a statistical analysis would be needed to prove this. It must not be forgotten also that *B. ibericus* is found not only in many Neolithic sites but in Acheulian sites, as at Ternifine. If, therefore, it is difficult to establish a firm date for the domestication of cattle in the *tell* country, it is at least possible to say that it was locally domesticated there because the wild ancestors of this same domestic strain were present in the region and had been hunted there for thousands of years. The dog is present in the very oldest phases of the Mediterranean Neolithic; it is very close to the modern Kabylia dog but its origin is not known. Thus, knowledge concerning the domestication of the dog, pig, sheep and goat is reasonably well founded in contrast to the uncertainty that still remains with regard to that of cattle which, in any event, appears to have taken place later.

There is as yet no evidence nor analysis that makes it possible to assert that agriculture was practised as early as the fifth millennium on the North African coast. The presence of a considerable quantity of pottery does, however, suggest the practice of some sort of vegeculture even if not of true agriculture. Hunting continued to provide an important part of the meat supply; in addition to wild bovids, various antelopes, Barbary sheep, wild boar and even elephants were hunted. In the diet of the Mediterranean Neolithic people it would appear that marine molluscs played an even more important part than did hunting. Further inland, and on the coast also, land molluscs were not neglected and many Neolithic sites look just like shell middens. Finally, technological advancement in both equipment and navigating of boats led to the development of sea-fishing and remains of fish, often of considerable size like the tunnyfish, are frequently found on the sites (Souville 1958–9). It is at this time also that the islands near the coasts of Morocco and the Oran District of Algeria were occupied by man.

## THE NEOLITHIC OF CAPSIAN TRADITION AND THE ROCK ART OF THE ATLAS (figs. 8.11–16, plate 8.5)

The Neolithic of Capsian Tradition, the name given to this facies in 1933 by Vaufrey following Pallary, has come, over the years, to be more and more widely applied to the point where all the Neolithic traditions in the Maghrib, the Sahara and a large part of the African continent, were lumped together under this title. During the last few years, particularly since 1963, prehistorians working in North Africa have felt the need to give a more precise definition to this cultural descendant of the Upper Capsian and, if possible, to set more exact limits to the extent of its spread. The specialist research work carried out by Hugot (1957), Camps-Fabrer (1966), Roubet (1968) and the present writer (Camps 1967), has contributed to a clearer delineation of this brilliant tradition and also to a more precise knowledge of the territory over which it progressively spread. The Neolithic of Capsian Tradition is, in fact, a Capsian that has become 'neolithized'. This change went deeper in some regions than in others but it can definitely be said that in the Capsian region properly speaking – that of Gafsa and Tebessa – the transformation is less great than in the Saharan zone where specifically Neolithic techniques are much more marked. This simple fact, if the contemporaneity of these two facies can be established, should make it possible to determine the direction in which the Neolithic way of life spread, which would seem to be southerly. Recent work in the Capsian area has shown that this changeover was imperceptible; a slow infiltration of tools, weapons and new techniques which never caused a complete modification of the existing culture.

The first or initial phase is characterized by surface occupations, shell

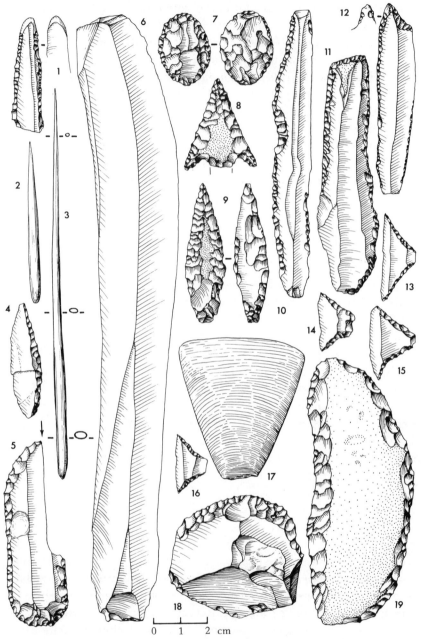

Fig. 8.11 Artifacts of the Neolithic of Capsian Tradition from Damous el-Ahmar.

| | |
|---|---|
| 1 Drill showing polish due to use | 10 Blade with continuous retouch |
| 2–3 Bone bodkins | 11 Retouched, truncated blade |
| 4 Backed bladelet | 12 Awl on the end of a retouched blade |
| 5 Angle burin opposed to a scraping edge | 13–16 Trapezes |
| 6 Large, unretouched blade | 17 Small, symmetrical, polished stone axe |
| 7–9 Arrow-points | 18–19 Side-scrapers |

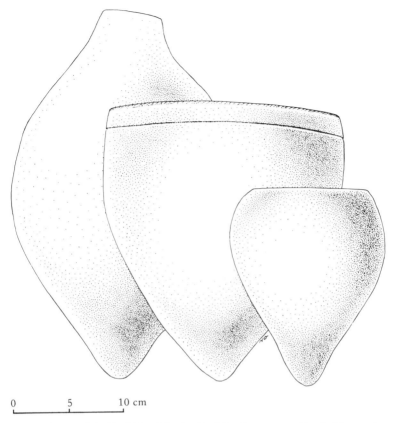

0     5     10 cm

Fig. 8.12   Pottery of the Neolithic of Capsian Tradition from eastern Algeria. The two larger
examples are from Damous el-Ahmar, the smallest is from the cave of Bou Zabaouine.

middens that are hardly distinguishable from Capsian sites, and, except
for a few insignificant variations, there are the same percentages of
geometric microliths, microburins, awls and burins as in the final phase
of the Upper Capsian. The appearance of new tool types characteristic
of the Neolithic is negligible; there are a few arrow-points, some
side-scrapers and, in the cave of Jebel Fartas, a few polished stone axes
and adzes and rare potsherds. The most interesting site belonging to
this phase is that of Aïn Naga where the Neolithic level – marked by
seventy-three potsherds and twelve bifacially retouched artifacts of
which two are pedunculate points – overlies an Upper Capsian from
which it is scarcely distinguishable on the basis of the remainder of the
tool-kit (Grebenart 1969). The second phase is still very conservatively
Capsian in character and is defined from the magnificent rock-shelter

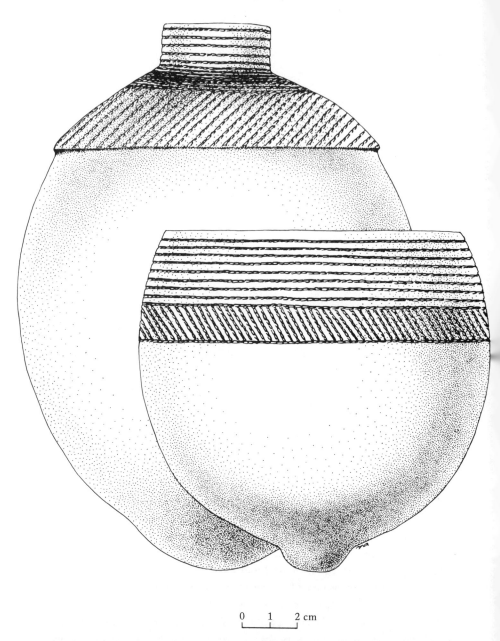

0     1     2 cm

Fig. 8.13  Pottery of the western Neolithic of Capsian Tradition from the Saharan Atlas and the north-west Sahara. The smaller vessel is from Tiout and the larger belongs to the Wadi Zegag series.

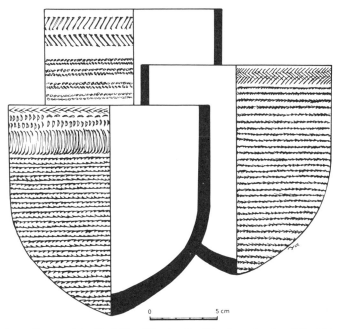

Fig. 8.14   Pottery of the Neolithic of Capsian Tradition from the site of Hassi Mouil'ah
in the *Bas Sahara* (reconstructed).

site of Damous el-Ahmar (Roubet 1968); it is also found at Ouled Zouaï
and at Khanguet si Mohamed Tahar. The Capsian basis is still dominant
but the progress towards a Neolithic type of industry is shown by the
new forms which are: 11.6% of side-scrapers, 10% (at Ouled Zouaï)
of large backed blades and 2% of arrow-points. In fact, the new tool
types of the Neolithic have been introduced into the Capsian Industry
without modifying this to any extent: it has become a 'Neolithized
Capsian'. This phase is also marked by the development of pottery. The
third phase is that of a Neolithic rather more emancipated from the
Capsian ascendancy. The caves at Jebel Bou Zabaouine (Dedieu 1965),
Jebel Marshel and Khanguet si Mohamed Tahar (upper level), belong
to this stage of development. The decrease in the purely Capsian
artifacts is accompanied by a marked development in the bone industry,
in implements of polished stone and in grinding equipment; pottery is
present in somewhat larger amounts and personal ornaments increase
in numbers and quality to become real works of art. Foliate points, both
with and without tangs, are much more important in the tool counts
(15 to 16%). In the Capsian region and also in the Saharan zone, pottery

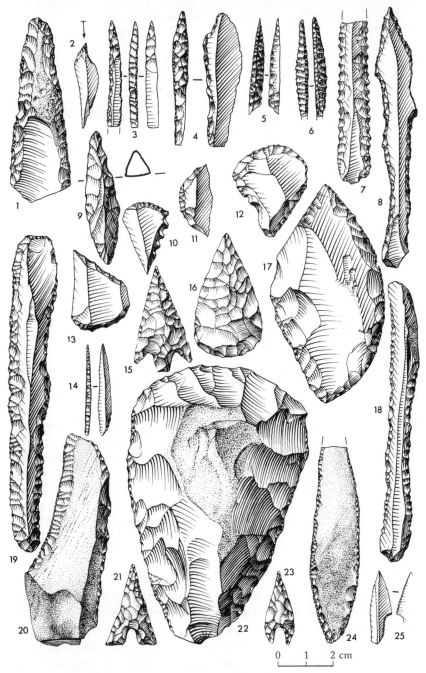

Fig. 8.15   Stone implements of the Saharan Neolithic of Capsian Tradition from El-Bayed.

1, 17, 20 Side-scrapers
2 Awl
3, 5–6 Backed bladelets with fully
       invasive, bifacial retouch
4 Gibbous (humped) backed blade
7, 18 Double-sided saws
8 Denticulate blade
9 Large drill
10 Small scraper on a truncated and
    denticulate flake

11, 13 Trapezes
12 Pedunculate scraper
14 Straight-backed bladelet
15–16, 21, 23 Arrow-points
19, 22 Convergent scrapers
24 Blade with continuous retouch and
    cortex surface
25 Shouldered point

is rare in the Neolithic of Capsian Tradition. Complete vessels found at Damous el-Ahmar and Bou Zabaouine are all ovoid in shape with conical bases. Two forms can be recognized – pots with very wide mouths and no neck and others with a small narrow neck like that of a bottle. This conical-based pottery is thus very similar in shape to that of the Mediterranean Neolithic of the coastal regions but it is very different in decoration which is infrequent and poor in quality (Camps-Fabrer 1966). In Tunisia and eastern Algeria the pottery on sites in the *tell* country is noticeably richer. The site of Kef el-Agab (Bardin 1953) in the Medjerda valley has yielded a great many more decorated potsherds than has Redeyef. The pottery from the Neolithic caves and rock-shelters of Constantine is also more decorated than that from Damous el-Ahmar or the Aïn M'lila region – the sites of Bou Zabaouine, Jebel Fartas, Cave of the Hyenas and Jebel Marshel. The decoration of the pottery of the Neolithic of Capsian Tradition shows it to be of the same family as the impressed pottery of the coast but in the Capsian zone this decoration is very limited. It is confined to the edges which sometimes show fine incisions or indentations and a restricted band at the upper part of the body of the pot. The ornament consists of crude punctate impressions – crescents, cuneiform motifs or circles – made by pressing the end of a hollow stem into the clay. Some whole vessels found at Damous el-Ahmar and Bou Zabaouine were completely undecorated. The scarcity of pottery in the Neolithic of Capsian Tradition is a cultural trait that should be considered in conjunction with the important part played by ostrich eggshells as containers. So at Damous el-Ahmar, in a small hollow, there were six whole ostrich eggshells together – undoubtedly used for storage. This scarcity of pottery and the concomitant increase in the number of ostrich eggshells is more noticeable as one goes from the Capsian to the Saharan zone of this Neolithic complex. On the other hand, as you go westwards the reverse is the case and in the Neolithic of Capsian Tradition of the west pottery is much more important.

If the pottery is mediocre, the bone industry is extremely rich and is well preserved in the cave sites. The bone tools take many forms and are often quite specialized; all forms of points, awls, and pins are present and the only missing item among the piercing equipment is the harpoon which is so characteristic of the Saharan–Sudanese Neolithic. Spoons, spatulas and *tranchets*, unknown in assemblages of the Upper Capsian, complete the bone equipment, together with knives and the burnishing and decorating tools needed for pot-making. Personal ornaments and

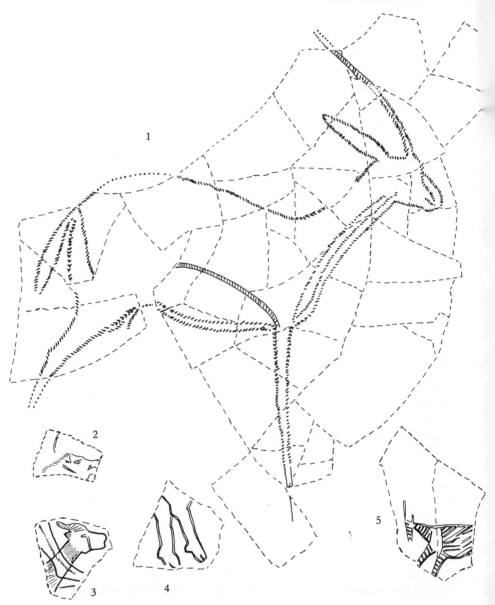

Fig. 8.16  Fragments of ostrich eggshell with representations of animals: Neolithic of Capsian Tradition

1 From Tarfaya, southern Morocco
2–4 From Tarentule III, Iguidi Erg

5, 7 From Redeyef, southern Tunisia
6 From Taulet, southern Morocco

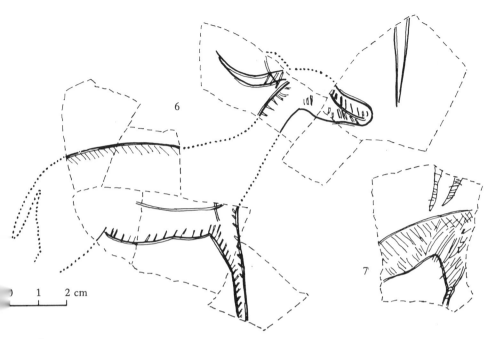

6

7

1   2 cm

particularly portable art objects (*art mobilier*), which had undergone .
considerable development in the Upper Capsian, continued their
remarkable evolution (Camps-Fabrer 1966). From this time a fine
naturalistic art depicting animals is associated with the purely decorative,
geometric motifs of the engraved plaques and the ostrich eggshells and
this also had its origins in the first clumsy attempts of the Capsian
people. These animal engravings on moveable objects are to be
regarded as paralleling the Neolithic rock art of the Saharan Atlas.

It should come as no surprise that the proto-Mediterranean physical
type that was responsible for the Capsian civilization should have
continued throughout the period of the Neolithic of Capsian Tradition
because this type was ancestral to the Berber peoples of historic times.
Moreover it would be impossible to explain the extreme slowness and
insignificance of the change from a Capsian to a Neolithic culture if this
almost imperceptible transformation had been accompanied by a
considerable modification of the physical type of the population. The
simplified table given below covering nine sites of the Neolithic of
Capsian Tradition where human remains have been found shows that
the Mechta type persisted in the small mountain massifs of the northern
part of the Capsian zone. In the southern part there was an ingression

of negroid elements while the most widespread is the Mediterranean type, so much so that at Columnata, the only human remains attributable to the Neolithic belong to this physical type. The presence of a negroid type in a site such as Redeyef is not really surprising since, as early as the Upper Capsian, the physical type exhibited some negroid characteristics and its presence with the Neolithic should not be overlooked as it is probably to be associated with the first phase of the change to a Neolithic culture. The phenomenon would appear to have been of southern origin and dates recently produced by different radiocarbon laboratories show that the Neolithic of Capsian Tradition is of relatively recent age in comparison with its neighbours on the coast and in the Sahara.

| Site | Mediterraneans | Mechtoids | Negroids |
| --- | --- | --- | --- |
| Redeyef | . | . | × |
| La Meskiana | . | . | × |
| Damous el-Ahmar | × | . | . |
| Koudiat Kherrouba | × | . | . |
| Jebel Fartas | . | × | . |
| Cave of the Hyenas | . | × | . |
| Bou Zabaouine | × | . | . |
| Medjez I | × | . | . |
| Columnata | × | . | . |

The Neolithic of Capsian Tradition occupies a much more restricted area than was thought by Vaufrey. The Saharan–Sudanese Neolithic, the Ténéréan and the Mauritanian Neolithic have been recognized in the Sahara and the Mediterranean Neolithic along the coast. The remaining area, that is to say, the southern slopes of the *tell*, the high plains, the Saharan Atlas, Tripolitania, Cyrenaica and the northern Sahara, is the territory of the Neolithic of Capsian Tradition but it is still not quite true to say that this form of the Neolithic covers the whole of this region. Our knowledge of the Neolithic industries of the Saharan Atlas is very slight and of those in Morocco, apart from the Atlantic coast, even slighter. Study of the Neolithic of the western Sahara and Rio de Oro has hardly begun. The characteristics of the Neolithic of Capsian Tradition are not constant throughout this immense area and it is, in any case, most likely that it did not cover it completely as right in the heart of the Capsian zone there are indications of other small facies the origins of which appear to be different. If one wished to demarcate the southern boundary of the Neolithic of Capsian Tradition, it would be necessary to draw a line beyond which round-based pottery, blade industries with geometric microliths and engraved ostrich eggshells no longer occurred. Camps-Fabrer (1966) claims to have been able to draw such a line which runs through Cape Juby, the Iguidi Erg, Reggan, Aoulef, Fort Flatters and the north of the Fezzan. The northern limit between the Mediterranean Neolithic and the Neolithic of Capsian Tradition is difficult to define because of the considerable interdigitating of the two zones. In Tunisia but also particularly in eastern Algeria, the Neolithic of Capsian Tradition penetrates as far as the *tell* country, whereas in central and western Algeria Mediterranean influences can be seen in the pottery as far as Jelfa, Tiaret and Saïda. In the region thus outlined it is possible to recognize three areas where the characteristics of the Neolithic of Capsian Tradition are not precisely the same: the Neolithic of true Capsian tradition (which the writer would prefer to call the 'neolithized Capsian') in central Tunisia and eastern Algeria; the Saharan Neolithic of Capsian Tradition which, in turn, is divisible into several facies and which occupies the largest area; and the western Neolithic of Capsian Tradition which is the least well known of all.

The Neolithic of true Capsian tradition will not be discussed again here as its chief characteristics have already been referred to and we have seen that this Neolithic is almost always merely an Upper Capsian enriched by new techniques but with the general aspect of the equipment very little altered thereby. The stone industry of the Saharan Neolithic of Capsian Tradition is exceptional. It is best known for the profusion in some sites of arrow-points, for its extremely elegant geometric microliths, its bifacially retouched artifacts – laurel-leaf points or Egyptian-style knives – and its awls which are occasionally of extraordinary thinness. The most characteristic sites where this facies occurs are Hassi Mouillah in the Ouargla region, Abiar Miggi in Tripolitania and Aïn Guettara in the south of the Tademaït, excavated by the writer; we shall take this last site as the example as it is one of the most southerly. The site is a vast rock-shelter, part of the roof of which had fallen in but which the Neolithic people still continued to occupy as it is close to a good spring still active today. Bone tools are rare but of high standard; on the other hand ostrich eggshell is abundant. The remains of one eggshell, broken at the time of the Neolithic occupation, had been carefully collected together for making into beads or small containers for body paint. Among the tools, backed bladelets represent no more than 10%, geometric microliths are numerous (8.7%, the most common being well-made trapezes); more than a quarter of the assemblage consists of microburins. The archae-ological layer has been dated to approximately 3980 BC. Of the assemblage, products of a Neolithic technology comprise 5.2% and among these must be mentioned tanged and eared arrow-points, a few foliate pieces and a single, chipped stone axe. Thus it can be seen that at the beginning of the fourth millennium, the Neolithic of Capsian Tradition, at a considerable distance from the Capsian region, has nevertheless retained a very marked Epi-Palaeolithic character. This is even more noticeable in the Ouargla area further north, in the site near to Hassi Messaoud called X O La Touffe, also dated to 3980 ± 150 BC. Here microburins are considerably less numerous but the traditional Capsian elements (backed bladelets, burins and geometric microliths) continue to outnumber the Neolithic additions (6.8% of side-scrapers and 11% of arrow-points). At Hassi Mouillah in the same region, the interest lies, as also at El-Hadjar in the Wadi Mya, in the complex stratigraphy, the top layers of which are Neolithic. The Neolithic of Capsian Tradition at Hassi Mouillah is rather more recent (about 3330 BC); eleven unbroken ostrich-eggshell containers were found there arranged in a sort of low pyramid. Fragments of ostrich eggshell, with and without engraving, and beads in the same material are very numerous. The pottery, which is a little more abundant than at the other sites, is round-based and the decoration is characteristic of the region of Ouargla and the Eastern Erg; it is pseudo-cord-stamped and is produced by rocker-stamping with a two-toothed comb made of a split, hollow twig. But in the same region in the Wadi Mya Aumassip excavated some Neolithic sites, admittedly on the surface, where pottery was entirely absent.

A similar absence or great scarcity of pottery is reported in a more southerly facies from Zaouïa el-Khala in the neighbourhood of Fort Flatters. The industries have recently been published and come from three quite extensive sites – Wadi Labied, El-Bayed and Izimane, a little further to the east. It is to this facies that one invariably refers when one speaks of the Saharan Neolithic as comprising tanged projectile points with fine denticulation, beautiful leaf-shaped points in jasper or quartz, very thin awls with triangular section and many forms that look as much like art objects as tools or weapons. This facies may well be older than the Neolithic of true Capsian tradition. Further to the east the Neolithic of Capsian Tradition is not like this but it is still very imperfectly known there, apart from the Haua Fteah site in Cyrenaica and Neuville's excavations at Abiar Miggi in Tripolitania.[1] The cave of Haua Fteah in Cyrenaica excavated by McBurney (1967) has yielded the most complete stratigraphic sequence in North Africa as the occupation began in the Middle Palaeolithic and the upper levels (VIII to VI) of the 16 m of archaeological deposits document the change from a local Upper Capsian to a well-differentiated Neolithic with dates of 4850±350 BC to 2910±97 BC.[2] While recognizing the peculiar traits exhibited by this Haua Fteah Neolithic, no doubt somewhat enhanced by its distance from the main region of the Neolithic of Capsian Tradition, it is, nevertheless, still possible to include it within this broad complex.

The same reservations are necessary with regard to the Neolithic of the Saharan Atlas and the north-western Sahara where, incidentally, extremely little detailed work has yet been done. The best-known assemblages, such as those from Abd el-Adim and Foum Seïada, show close connections with the Saharan Neolithic of Capsian Tradition. One of the most interesting but so far unpublished discoveries made in the western Sahara is the site of Wadi Zegag at Bechar. Here an unauthorized excavation brought to light some fifty-five complete pots of various forms: some that were globular and had an appendiculate base were shouldered and had a very narrow neck, others were conical-based and wide-mouthed. The decoration has been executed entirely with a comb. Among the tools were a polished axe, saws, foliate pieces, awls and scrapers; the radiocarbon date appears to be approximately 3370 BC. The same form of pot with appendiculate base and similar comb decoration is found in a rock-shelter in the immediate vicinity of the well-known rock engravings of Tiout at Aïn Sefra. Vaufrey often used to draw

---

[1] Abiar Miggi is doubly interesting because it is a stratified rock-shelter site with two levels that can be ascribed to the Neolithic while the deepest belongs to an evolved Upper Capsian in process of becoming Neolithic. Also at this site there is a Neolithic industry in direct association with rock engravings. This Neolithic also is not very far removed from the Upper Capsian of which it retains the stone equipment with the addition of numerous side-scrapers and foliate pieces with invasive bifacial retouch and, in a second facies, well-made arrow-points. The bone industry is very interesting and could be more evolved than the stone artifacts; the presence of eyed needles confirms the affinities with the Neolithic while the discovery of a pierced human parietal bone links this Neolithic level even more closely with the Capsian culture where this practice is well attested.

[2] In the oldest layers (Level VIII) this assemblage has a high percentage (27%) of scrapers, higher than any other Neolithic of Capsian Tradition. There are more than 30% of backed bladelets and almost 7% of burins. In the most recent levels microburins and geometric microliths are less numerous than in Level VIII and this is also true of the bladelets and the burins but there are 9% of side-scrapers and 5% of points while foliate pieces now make their appearance. Pottery first occurs in the upper part of Level VIII, dated to about 4400 BC, it has a punctate decoration near the mouth, the forms are simple and the rims those of wide-mouthed vessels. Decorated ostrich eggshell is not very common and most of it was found in Level VI.

attention to worked flakes that he considered to belong to the Neolithic of Capsian Tradition, which occurred at the foot of a large number of rock engravings in the Saharan Atlas. Indeed, it is in the western part of the area covered by the Neolithic of Capsian Tradition that we find the most interesting associations with the Neolithic art.

In spite of some recent attempts to do so (Lhote 1970), there are no grounds for doubting the association of the rock art of the Saharan Atlas and the Neolithic of Capsian Tradition. It is not possible, except arbitrarily, to dissociate the rock art from the *art mobilier* and this last, since it is found in archaeological deposits, can be dated and closely associated with a prehistoric culture which, in the Maghrib and northern Sahara, can only belong to the Capsian and to the Neolithic, so-called of Capsian Tradition (Camps-Fabrer 1966). The style of this *art mobilier* – on plaques or ostrich eggshells – is not only decorative or geometric but also naturalistic and depicts animals: foxes at Damous el-Ahmar; addax at Taulet; bovids at Wadi Mengoub; antelopes, wild boar and bovidae at Tarentule III; various mammals at Redeyef accompanied by, perhaps, ostrich; ostrich again, but this time unmistakable, at Bou Zabaouine and, in the neighbourhood of Ouargla, a cow engraved on a complete ostrich eggshell. Similarly, in the Neolithic of Capsian Tradition, in the Maghrib as well as in the Sahara, there are occasional representations of animals in the decorative art that are clearly related to the Capsian tradition, as can be seen from the Barbary sheep and antelope of Khanguet el-Mouhaad; the possible bird of Hamda; the ostrich of Aïn Bahir and the antelope or caprine of El-Mekta. There was certainly a great deal more of this art than would appear now, since there is no special characteristic by which engraved stones can be readily distinguished from the thousands of other stones and plaques, all usually ash encrusted, that occur in the occupation sites. Moreover, there can be no doubt that engravings of animals were more numerous still but have been lost by the breaking up of the decorated ostrich eggshells. Unfortunately few excavatable sites have been found actually at the foot of rock engravings. The industry recovered from Safiet Bou Rhenan and Meandre, Brezina, is too sparse to permit of an exact determination but the most interesting instance is that of Abiar Miggi where the industry belongs to the Neolithic of Capsian Tradition.

The rock art of the Atlas can, then, be attributed to the Neolithic of Capsian Tradition but there are several styles which are neither all of the same age nor found in the same localities. The most important and also the most widespread is the large – sometimes monumental –

naturalistic style (Lhote 1970) in which the most characteristic animal is the great extinct buffalo (*Pelorovis* (*Homoïoceras*) *antiquus*), nearly always shown in the same attitude with its two immense horns pointing forwards and the bent head in profile. Scenes of fighting between male animals are quite common and almost certainly have some religious significance. Another frequent and very characteristic scene portrays a man in a position of prayer, the arms half stretched out, with an ovine, usually a ram (Flamand 1921, Frobenius and Obermaier 1925, Lhote 1970, Vaufrey 1939); there is no question here of sheep worship as the animal is usually shown behind the human figure. The most interesting representations portray a ram with a spheroid on its head. This is not, however, to be confused with the solar disc; it suggests, rather, a calabash or a bonnet with strings, as at Aïn Naga, by which it can be tied on. This spheroid is usually decorated with appendages which, in the most carefully executed examples, look like ostrich feathers. Sometimes, as at Bou Alem, the animal is wearing a voluminous, plaited collar. The importance of this type of presentation lies not only in its aesthetic quality but also in the treatment of the surface of the figures which is sometimes carefully polished and coloured with ochre, sometimes hatched with fine lines to suggest the fleece or partly spotted to show the shading of the clothing. It is easy to recognize the species depicted: the long limbs and long thin tail, the convex profile to the head, even the matted strands of the hair are all characteristic of *Ovis longipes* Fitz, which is still kept in the central and southern Sahara. That this sheep was domesticated is unquestionable but it is still a problem as to whether the animal thus glorified represents a divinity or a sacrifice. This would not really matter were it not that, at one time, due to a misinterpretation of the attributes of this sheep, it was thought that the engravings of the Saharan Atlas depicted the well-known Egyptian theme of the Ram of Amon with the solar disc between its horns. The Atlas engravings are considerably earlier than the development of the cult of Amen-Ra around Thebes.

The sheep was not the only domesticated animal possessed by the Neolithic people of Capsian Tradition; the occupation sites have also yielded the skeletal remains of goats, pigs, cattle and dogs. The pig does not seem to have been portrayed in the rock art and, apart from the famous example at Kef Messiouer, the wild boar also seldom occurs. Cattle are never portrayed in the same way as the ram and the large *Bos primigenius*, with his formidable horns pointing forwards, is almost always shown alone; at Tiout the inside of the engraved outline of these animals is most carefully polished. Quite small human figures are shown trying to hold back one of these bulls by the hind leg using bent sticks or ropes. It is not possible to be sure whether these human figures are contemporary with the great naturalistic animals, though this is probable, nor can such a scene with certainty be interpreted as proving that these animals were domesticated. The dog was domesticated at this time and two distinct species can be recognized in the engravings. One is the ancestor of the modern Atlas sheepdog, a fine robust creature, rather short in the leg, with a bushy coat and a curled-over, plume-like tail. The other variety is a slimmer, grey-hound type (*Canis getulicus*) with a much shorter coat. This African greyhound, different from the eastern *saluki*, is the *tessem* of ancient Egypt.

The human type associated with this oldest phase of the rock art belonged to a caucasoid race with long or wavy hair, a fairly heavily built frame and short limbs. Dress is reduced to a genital covering only – a strip of cloth or leather between the legs with the ends tucked into a string round the waist. This exiguous clothing is completed by bracelets on the wrists and arms and occasionally by a somewhat indeterminate hair-style. The men are often armed with, in order of frequency, bows and arrows, throwing-sticks and axes. There is no scene of agricultural pursuits in the rock art of the Atlas but this is not necessarily significant because, even in later periods when there is no doubt that agriculture was practised, no engraved scene ever depicts it. It is not, however, very likely that the Neolithic people of Capsian Tradition practised agriculture at this early time. The sparseness of the pottery vessels and the small numbers of grindstones and rubbers found in the occupation sites attest rather to a restricted use of vegetable and cereal foods.

It is very difficult to fix a time scale for the rock art of the Atlas and, indeed, the succession of styles has not been definitely worked out nor is it certain whether it was a true succession or whether some of the styles were contemporary. Thus Lhote (1970) records a *small* naturalistic style which is not necessarily more recent than the large. The so-called Tazina style from southern Oran (but of which equivalents are also found in the Rio de Oro and the Tassili n'Ajjer!) is characterized by the extreme elegance of the figures, especially gazelles and antelopes, whose limbs have been elongated in a very unrealistic but extremely aesthetic manner. One must confess that it is very difficult to fit this particular 'style' into a succession that would, in any case, be artificial. In fact it is only the large naturalistic style that has any very wide distribution: its elephants, bulls and great extinct buffaloes are found from southern Morocco to the Nemencha. The numerous dates so far obtained for the different facies of the Neolithic of Capsian Tradition (usually older in the Sahara than in the Highlands and in the east than in the west) make it possible to regard the fifth millennium BC as the time when this rock art began and it lasted at least until the third millennium.[1] Another, less monumental style also probably belongs to this period; it is not so well known but includes some good representations. Lhote has given this style the name 'Bovidian' also and that is acceptable in so far as it signifies merely that the art is the work of pastoral cattle-herders but not if it implies any cultural unity with the prehistoric artists of the Tassili n'Ajjer and Ahaggar. The 'Bovidian' style is more frequent in southern Morocco and the Oran District than in central and eastern Algeria where a cruder art style developed with many representations of sheep and shepherds (Lefebvre and Lefebvre 1967). One interesting characteristic of this eastern Algerian school is the development of a painted style of bas-relief as at Khanguet el-Hadjar. During the last millennium BC the appearance of horses in the art marks both the beginning of a new phase of rock art and also the end of Neolithic times.

The Neolithic of Capsian Tradition, therefore, exhibits very particular characteristics that, however, vary from one part to the other of the immense region represented by the Highlands and the northern Sahara. While this cultural tradition possesses a distinct richness in its rock art, particularly in the west, in its *art mobilier* and also in its lithic equipment especially in the more southern facies, it also suffers from certain deficiencies which should not be forgotten. Firstly should be mentioned the scarcity of pottery in the Saharan Neolithic of Capsian Tradition but also, in addition, the old Epi-Palaeolithic patterns of behaviour continue to be tenaciously followed and seem hardly modified by a small amount of sheep- and, perhaps, cattle-rearing. Finally, there is the slowness with which the new influences from the east and south caused the change to a Neolithic way of life to come about in the high plains, particularly in eastern Algeria where the Upper Capsian still persisted at the beginning of the fifth millennium, by which time the Sahara and the coast had adopted the new technologies (Camps 1968b).

[1] But see ch. 5, p. 398 for an alternative suggestion that some of this 'Bubalis' art in the Saharan Atlas may be older than 6000 BC.

THE METAL AGE AND THE ORIGINS OF THE BERBERS
(figs. 8.17–18, plates 8.6–7)

The Neolithic and its forerunners, the Epi-Palaeolithic cultures, lasted several thousand years; the protohistoric Metal Age, during the course of which the beginnings of Berber culture developed, lasted less than six centuries. Between the two is a final Neolithic or Chalcolithic which it is very difficult to define either in the Sahara or in the Maghrib. We know from Herodotus that at the time of the Wars of the Medes, the Ethiopians who lived in the eastern Sahara still used arrows with stone heads but also that the Garamantes and the Libyans of Tripolitania drove four-horse chariots. So that, even at the beginning of historical times, there were important cultural differences between the Saharan peoples and the Berbers of the coast. The desiccation of the Sahara had restricted life to a few oases and had pushed the Maghrib completely over into the Mediterranean world. The coastal part of the Maghrib was, indeed, the first to profit by the Mediterranean inventions in the realm of metallurgy, though traces of these imports are rare. The oldest are a long-tanged copper point of the Palmela type discovered at Sidi Messaoud near Azemmour in Morocco (Antoine 1952), a flat copper axe found near Wadi Akreuch, Rabat, and a tanged dagger found at Cape Chenoua 80 km west of Algiers and ascribed to the 'West European dagger' type (Camps and Giot 1960). All these weapons are made of copper with arsenic admixture and are similar to those found in Europe from where they were diffused to Morocco and western Algeria.

In Spain and the western Mediterranean, copper weapons are associated with Beaker pottery so that it is not surprising to find pots of this distinctive type in northern Morocco (Jodin 1957). The area covered by the spread of vessels and sherds of Beaker ware radiates out from the restricted zone in which the Cardial ware pottery occurred. In Morocco this latter ware was limited to the area bordering on the Straits of Gibraltar from Tangier to Tetouan but Beaker wares have been found as far south as the vicinity of Casablanca and in the east as far as Saïda in Oran District. The first Beaker ware vessel to be recognized was at the cave of Dar es-Soltan, Rabat. The best stratified sequences are those at Gar Cahal and Caf That el-Gar where the deposits that overlie the Beaker pottery contain a channelled ware which is also well known in the Chalcolithic of Europe (Tarradell 1954, 1957–8). Such

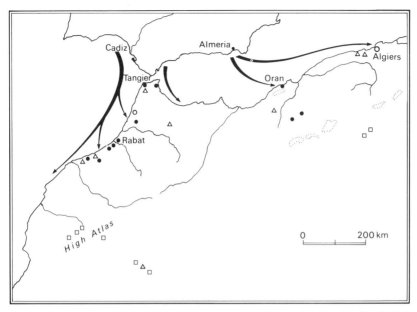

Fig. 8.17   Copper and Bronze Ages in the Maghrib: distribution map showing: Sherds and whole vessels of Beaker pottery (black circles); weapons and tools of copper (triangles) and of bronze (open circles); rock engravings of bronze weapons in the Atlas Mountains (squares).

exchanges with Spain became much more extensive during the Bronze Age. It is true that bronze objects remained rare in the Mahrib but they enjoyed a wider distribution than did copper weapons and particularly they penetrated more deeply into the *tell* country (cf. the bronze axes at Lamoricière, near Tlemcen, and Columnata, near Tiaret). It is probable that for the first time a true primitive metallurgy now developed in the western part of the Maghrib, if one can judge from the extremely numerous representations on the rocks of the high Atlas in Morocco of characteristic Bronze Age weapons (Bronze II Argaric from Spain). Malhomme (1959, 1961) is to be congratulated on his discovery and survey of hundreds of these representations. The weapons are halberds or battle-axes, very carefully portrayed even to the rivets and the central mid-rib; daggers with wide, mid-ribbed blades in every way comparable to those of the Middle Bronze Age in the south of France, and also lance-heads and arrows. These representations belong to an art that is very different from that of the Neolithic both

613

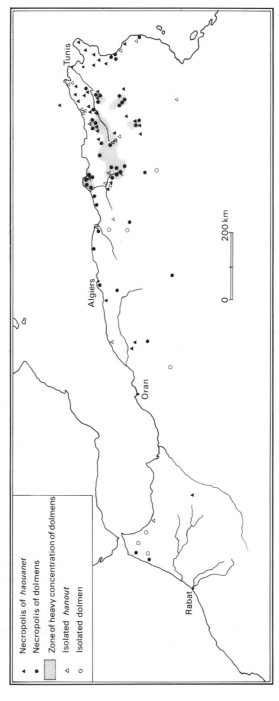

Fig. 8.18   Map showing the distribution of dolmens and hypogea (*haouanet*) in North Africa.

Necropolis of *haouanet*
Necropolis of dolmens
Zone of heavy concentration of dolmens
Isolated *hanout*
Isolated dolmen

Tunis

Algiers

Oran

Rabat

0          200 km

in subject-matter and style. It is true that animals continue to be portrayed: bovids, canids and antelopes, but now man himself and his manufactured goods (chariots, weapons, jewellery) or his symbolism (variously ornamented roundels or circles) usually take pride of place. This implies a change of outlook, of ways of life and of religious beliefs if, as is generally conceded, the rock art is to be associated with such beliefs. It should also be noted that this style shows a strong tendency towards geometric schematization which is very characteristic of Metal Age art as a whole and which continues to the present day in Berber art (Camps 1961b). Because the mountains of Morocco have always been an area of transhumance, the presence there of these numerous representations of metal weapons does not necessarily imply that these were locally made, particularly as this region is one of high-altitude grazing land that is under snow for a large part of the year. It is, therefore, in the country bordering on the north of the High Atlas that we must look for the traces of this native metallurgy.

Much further south, in Mauritania, there is also a centre of metallurgy that was undoubtedly of much greater importance. Indeed, in the Akjoujt region there are significant deposits of copper. The earliest study of the copper arrow-points of Mauritania dates to the beginning of the century and the various monographs of Mauny have also resulted in considerable knowledge of these artifacts which are very similar to the examples from the Iberian peninsula. A recent detailed inventory produced by Lambert (1972) has listed all the finds of copper from Mauritania and the western Sahara which comprise no fewer than eighty-three arrow-points or javelins and six axes. Although the area involved is very large, the finds cannot be purely fortuitous, isolated and without significance, as the central and eastern Sahara, which is much larger and has been more thoroughly explored, has not yielded more than a twentieth of that number. The relative abundance of copper weapons, tools and ornaments in north-western Mauritania is explained by the exploitation of the ancient copper-mines near Akjoujt and it is thus possible to speak of a Chalcolithic or Copper Age in Mauritania. It seems incontrovertible also that this technological phase was gradually superseded by the spread of iron-working, from both the south-east and the Mediterranean regions. What is not known, however, is the beginning, the duration and, in a word, the age of this phase of metallurgy. Lambert's excavations in the Chauves-Souris cave at Guelb Moghrein, which have barely begun, have already yielded evidence of this metal-working dating to the sixth century BC but this comes only from the levels close to the surface and there are still ten metres of deposits in the cave. Analysis of the metals and of the furnace remains shows that smelting was, indeed, done on the spot. It is possible that this technology came originally from the north along the coast.

Although the western part of the Maghrib, near to Spain (an important diffusion centre for metal-working technology) has produced undeniable traces of a Bronze Age preceded by a few Copper Age imports, and although the western Sahara itself had an indigenous copper-working industry, the central and eastern part of North Africa, east of the longitude of Algiers, has not yielded a single bronze weapon nor any indisputable representation of one in the rock art. This fact alone proves the Iberian origin of this trait (Camps 1960). On the other hand, the eastern Maghrib is rich in megalithic tombs and hypogea, also undoubtedly Mediterranean in origin (Camps 1961b). Simple tumuli, or those with an arrangement of plinths or steps (*bazinas*) are evenly spread throughout the whole of North Africa and the Sahara but two types of funerary monument have very special distributions. These are dolmens and the small hypogea hollowed out of cliffs or isolated rocks that archaeologists working in North Africa have come to call *haouanet* (an Arab word meaning 'small shops').

The dolmens of North Africa are usually not large but they are very characteristic. On the coast they are most often built of great slabs of sandstone or limestone; the chamber is very shallowly buried in a low tumulus outlined by a circle of stones. In a necropolis such as that at Enfida in Tunisia, an uncovered passage through the tumulus leads into the megalithic chamber. Further inland the dolmen has taken on some of the features of the stepped tumulus (or *bazina*) so that the chamber is often constructed on a very large plinth with two, three or sometimes four steps, as at Bou Nouara (Camps and Camps-Fabrer 1964). The further inland one goes the more important the plinth becomes, finally developing into a carefully constructed column drum in which the dolmen becomes progressively more embedded. Near Aures in the area furthest from the coast the megalithic chambers have become completely enclosed by the cylindrical base which looks like a small tower. This form of monument has been given the Arab name of *choucha* (plural *chouchet*). Thus, the original dolmen can be seen in a developing series from the Mediterranean regions to Aures (Camps 1961b). This fact, coupled with the local distribution of the North African monuments, suggests that dolmens have a distant origin in the east and a nearby origin in southern Italy and perhaps also in Sardinia. The greatest spread of dolmens to the west is along the coast. Although there are many in northern Tunisia and eastern Algeria, particularly in the region between Maktar and Constantine, they become rare in central Algeria where they are confined to the coastal areas of Kabylia and the immediate neighbourhood of Algiers, and disappear completely to the west of the town. In Morocco, small, cist-like monuments peculiar to the area round Tangier are Bronze Age tombs of Spanish origin and do not belong to the megalithic complex of the eastern part of the Maghrib. At no point do the dolmens extend further south than the Saharan Atlas, the most southerly being in the region of Tebessa, in Aures and further west near Djelfa.

The hypogea (*haouanet*) have an even more limited distribution. These are square chambers usually too small to contain an extended burial and it is quite probable that they were used for bodies that were already disarticulated. Some of them have features such as benches or niches and some, the latest of the *haouanet* dated to Carthaginian times, even contain rather poor sculptures or paintings. The oldest, on the other hand, sometimes have a small *dromos* or passage in front or a ceiling of two inclined planes that resembles the inside of a roof; this architectural detail is also found in Sardinia and Sicily. In short, these *haouanet* are identical, both in appearance and in that they are hewn out of cliffs, with the well-known Siculi tombs from the end of the Bronze Age and the very beginning of the Iron Age in Sicily; indeed the greatest concentration of *haouanet* is in the north of Tunisia and in Cape Bon, just opposite Sicily. The *haouanet* type of tomb is known from further inland – from Dougga, Tebessa and Constantine – but, nevertheless, they are generally found on the coast. There are some in Morocco too but this westward extension is probably late and attributable to the Carthaginians. These tombs are evidence of the penetration of cultures from the east into Berber country before the time of the Phoenicians. The *haouanet* came into Tunisia from Sicily. Still earlier exchanges with Sicily, Sardinia and southern Italy are discernible but, from the beginning of the Bronze Age, these exchanges multiplied and many traits of rural Berber culture can be explained thereby. Indeed, dolmens and *haouanet* cannot have crossed the seas unaccompanied as might simple pottery vessels, weapons or other small objects as a result of trade. When tombs are involved, only a migration of people themselves can serve to explain the transplanting of such characteristic funerary monuments and their very localization and distribution in North Africa betrays their exotic origin.

Also from Italy and Sicily comes the technique of modelled, flat-based and carinated pottery that is still made today in the most conservative regions of Tunisia and Algeria – Kroumiria, Kabylia and Aures – and still faithfully preserves types characteristic of the end of the Bronze Age and beginning of the Iron Age in Italy (Camps 1959). The present writer also considers the origin of this modelled and painted pottery to have been in the east, with Sicily as an important staging post for its introduction by a new influx of Mediterranean people whose dolmens and hypogea are tangible evidence of their penetration into a large part of the eastern and central Maghrib. This new arrival of a true Mediterranean type is one of the outstanding facts of North African protohistory. These people were gracile, short of stature and meso- or dolichocephalic (medium- or long-headed). They were distinct from the proto-Mediterraneans, the Capsian and Neolithic peoples whose characteristics can best be seen preserved today in the mountain dwellers of southern Morocco and in the Touareg. These small, gracile Mediterranean people, differing little from the Sicilians and the southern Italians (they have the same palm prints and the same blood groups) occupy the coastal massifs of Tunisia, Algeria and the Rif. They have retained, particularly in Kabylia, the oldest cultural traditions of the Mediterranean. A living picture of what the first settled communities along the northern shores of the Mediterranean may have been like before the spread of the Greeks and the Etruscans can be found in their life styles, agricultural technology and village organization.

The end of the prehistoric period was not a very favourable time in the central and eastern Sahara. At this period in the Maghrib, the old Mediterranean way of life was giving place to the beginning of the historical era but, in the Sahara, the last two millennia were a long, slow agony in which the water sources and grazing were reduced to such a point that the brilliant Bovidian culture disappeared at the same time that other peoples and other technologies made their first appearance.

As has already been said in discussing the prehistoric art of the central Saharan massifs, the Bovidian style was followed by an Equidian style which was stiffer and more schematic but still included fine frescoes some of which, like that of Tamadjert in Tassili n'Ajjer, are particularly well known. Although, as is evident from excavations in Nubia, the horse was introduced into Africa some time before the Hyksos, it is difficult to believe that it can have spread as far as Tassili n'Ajjer and the Ahaggar before the middle of the second millennium BC. The horse – which was not yet used for riding – was introduced into the Sahara at the same time as the light chariot of which there are many examples in the rock art from the Fezzan to Mauritania and the Saharan Atlas to Adrar des Iforas (Mauny 1955b). Although it is perfectly possible to build a chariot without using any metal at all, it is difficult to believe that such machines could cross the *hamadas* and rock-strewn ground of the Sahara unless their very light, four- or six-spoked wheels were reinforced by a band of metal round the rim (Camps 1961b). These Saharan chariots are the simplest of all the vehicles known in antiquity and they call to mind to some extent the two-wheeled chariots used by the Greeks, Etruscans and Romans for racing in the Hippodrome. Essentially, the chariot consists of a shaft which supports a very light, triangular platform constructed either of interlaced slats or bands of leather or of strong basketry. This platform rests on an axle to which the wheels are attached. At the other end of the shaft is a neck yoke to which two horses are harnessed. Almost all the Saharan chariots are two-wheeled and drawn by two horses but Herodotus states that the Garamantes had four-wheeled chariots and that it was from the Libyans that the Greeks learned to harness these four-horse chariots and, indeed, in the Fezzan, the country of the Garamantes, engravings have been found at Wadi Zigzaou depicting four-horse chariots (Graziosi 1942). These Saharan chariots are so light that they cannot have been used to transport merchandise or, indeed, any heavy materials. It was impossible for two people to ride in them and none of the paintings of these chariots in action ever show more than one person in them. They can, therefore, have been used only for hunting or for war. The so-called 'chariot routes' that have been arbitrarily marked on the map by joining the points where chariots are depicted in the art are nothing more than wishful thinking because chariots have been found portrayed in places where they could not possibly have been driven – in mountain screes or massifs where even mules or camels would have difficulty in getting through. All this leads to the conclusion that the Saharan chariot, far from being a utilitarian or economic vehicle, must have been a status symbol pertaining to a chief or nobleman. It is probable, therefore, that the Equidians were a warrior caste who dominated the Bovidians and the remnants of the earlier negroid peoples. All the evidence points to their having come from the north-east by way of the Fezzan and that their slow advance was in both a south-westerly direction to Tassili n'Ajjer, the Ahaggar and Adrar des Iforas and also to the west along the Atlas Mountains. Herodotus supplies another valuable piece of information when he states that the Garamantes, perched on their chariots, used to chase the Ethiopians who were very swift runners.

Now it is possible to identify the Garamantes with one group of Equidians who established suzerainty over the negroid populations in about the second millennium BC. Their descendants are the Touareg who, right up to the present day, have continued to exercise this domination over the descendants of the Ethiopians and the Bovidians who have become the negroid populations of the oases (*Harratin*).

Thus, in the second half of the second millennium and the first centuries of the first millennium BC peoples of caucasoid, Mediterranean type, perhaps descended from the Neolithic people of Capsian Tradition from the eastern Sahara, introduced the horse to the country between the Nile Valley and Cyrenaica. This animal had previously been unknown in North Africa and has now completely disappeared again from the desert but has left behind two vigorous strains – the so-called Dongola strain and the Barbary horse of the Maghrib. In profile, the head shape of both these types is convex; they are not at all graceful (particularly the Dongola), their heads are heavy, their hindquarters low and they are short in stature. But they are very resistant, hardy and full of courage and their adaptation is so good that they have survived and preserved their characteristics in the face of multiple introductions, in particular of the eastern, so-called Arab, horses. At the same time that the horsemen from the steppes were introducing this new animal (destined later to make the Numidians famous) to the people of the Maghrib, they also brought a new type of sheep that eventually caused the disappearance from the Atlas mountain country of the old *Ovis longipes*, a non-wool-bearing species. This new strain was the Barbary sheep (not to be confused with the wild Barbary sheep, a sort of *mouflon* (*Ammotragus lervia*)), small in stature but with a thick fleece and a short, fat tail. Representatives of this Maghribian race can still be found in Tunisia but elsewhere it has been eliminated by the present-day species probably introduced by Arab conquerors (Esperandieu 1955).

In the Fezzan and Tassili n'Ajjer the Equidians of protohistoric and ancient times can be identified with the Garamantes whose rule lasted up to the Roman Empire. In the west, however, that is to say south of the Atlas Mountains and in the neighbouring steppes, these horsemen became the Getules of whom ancient historians have left several descriptions. At the time when the last of the Bovidians in the south of Mauritania were learning to harness their pack-oxen to wheeled vehicles, the horse in the northern Sahara was becoming a riding animal. The Garamantes and the Getules, horsemen of Mediterranean physical type, gradually dominated the peoples of the Sahara while still preserving their own type of nomad life-style. At the same time the negroids were unable to maintain their vast herds and so gradually moved nearer to what are now the countries of Niger, Senegal and Tchad or were restricted to the limited areas of the diminishing number of oases where they were content to acknowledge the overlordship of the caucasoid nomads. One group, that of the Teda or Toubou, is probably descended from the Ethiopians who, as Herodotus tells us, were pursued and fought by the Garamantes. The Tibesti massif served as a refuge for this group which is distinct both from the black peoples of the Sudan and the caucasoid Mediterranean peoples and which constitutes one of the oldest human types in the Sahara.

In the western Sahara in the region of Dhar Tichitt, Aouker and Hodh, the last of the Saharan–Sudanese Neolithic people have left some fine collections of well-made implements of polished stone – axes, chisels, *tranchets*, potters' combs, fish-hooks, pendants and arrow-points of polished schist ('Enji points'). But this material is not as interesting as are the dozens of Neolithic villages occupying the outlets of the passes through this immense cliff or situated round the edges of the plateau. Sometimes the walls of the buildings are still standing to a height of as much as two metres. Further knowledge of these settlements and the pottery wares collected from them has come from the work of Munson (1976). The oldest sites were villages on the edge of a lake area. They were not fortified and appear to have been occupied by a pastoral people who also cultivated millet (*Pennisetum*), grain impressions of which can sometimes be found in the paste of potsherds. The villages date to the second half of the first millennium, from about 1500 to 1100 BC. The fortified sites perched on ledges of rock are more recent than those at the foot of the plateau and were occupied from about 1150 to 850 BC. Other small, fortified sites huddled close together among the rocky hollows of the cliff are contemporary with the Copper Age in Mauritania and date to about 650–380 BC. These are the remains of a society in decline suffering from both the deterioration in the natural environment and still more from the depredations of nomad horsemen who were gradually beginning to subjugate them.

These conquerors have also left their traces on the rocks of the Sahara and the Atlas. They were warriors armed with javelin and arm-dagger and later with great swords and were the authors of a very schematic art, usually depicting their mounts, their ostrich or lion hunts and, above all, themselves with plumes of ostrich feathers on their heads and wearing a tunic drawn in very tightly at the waist giving them an odd, hour-glass shape. They are invariably armed. It is to these chieftains, known to us first as chariot-drivers and later as intrepid horse-riders, that are attributed the important dry-stone funerary monuments some of which, in the Tassili n'Ajjer, are more than 300 m long. These are either immense pavements in the shape of a crescent open to the east, or they are monuments with circular or elliptical enclosures where the passage leading to the central tumulus is, similarly, made to face east; or, again, they may be large *bazinas* with carefully designed steps and provided with varying arrangements of such features as passages, niches or chapels built within the mass of the tumulus. These funerary monuments of dry-stone are exceedingly numerous and varied in the Sahara; we can be sure, however, that ordinary people had to content themselves with a simple mound or a small circular grave. Such monuments continued to be built until Islam, not without difficulty and some compromise with ancient forms, finally achieved acceptance of the flat grave with an upright slab or stele.

During the last millennium BC before the historical period proper began in North Africa it is, as we have seen, possible to trace the main lines of cultural development and the coming into being of the Berber populations. While the final desiccation of the Sahara was setting in and the Maghrib was being cut off from Black Africa, the prehistoric Mediterranean cultures were spreading to the northen edges of the continent bringing both to the north-west and north-east technologies, practices and new beliefs which formed the basis of the rural civilization known as Berber. These new introductions were accompanied by migrations of new groups of Mediterraneans that mixed with the Proto-Mediterranean peoples who, ever since Capsian times, had been progressively spreading at the expense of the Mechtoid groups, the last descendants of whom later inhabited the Canary Islands. It is, thus, during the protohistoric period that the Berber peoples came definitely into being in the Maghrib. They were, however, subjected to several influences coming from different directions. In Morocco and to a lesser extent in western Algeria, Iberian cultural traits took root – metallurgy, Beaker ware and channelled pottery, tombs in the form of cists and silos. In the east, on the other hand, in Tunisia and eastern Algeria, other traits from the eastern Mediterranean via Italy and Sicily became dominant: the introduction of dolmens and *haouanet* tombs, painted pottery, the square house and pitched roofs. To the south in the steppes the nomad horsemen brought knowledge of new species of domesticated animals – the Barbary horse and sheep – and developed certain funeral practices connected with large monuments incorporating chapels. In the middle, unfortunately, the central Maghrib is no more than a corridor, squeezed between the sea and the Sahara and the various cultural influences were not able to make themselves felt there so that it was not possible for any powerful force to develop in the centre of the country which, in its turn, might later have influenced the whole of North Africa. This is undoubtedly the reason why the Berbers were able to establish control over the negroid populations of the Sahara but were never able to achieve unity among themselves.

# CHAPTER 9

# THE ORIGINS OF INDIGENOUS AFRICAN AGRICULTURE

## NATURE OF THE EVIDENCE

This chapter can only open with a warning that evidences for the origin of indigenous African agriculture are very weak and inadequate, and that we can only sketch the development in the most general and tenuous terms at the present time. An indigenous agriculture did emerge. African plants were domesticated by Africans in Africa and a complete system with a village-farming pattern evolved. The list of crop plants is impressive and includes all the usual categories of cereals, pulses, root and tuber crops, fruits, vegetables, oil and fibre plants, drugs, narcotics, magic and ritual plants. The system spread over much of the continent and was adequate to support the high cultures of Nok, Benin, Ghana, Mali and a variety of other Sudanic and East African kingdoms.

A great deal of our theory about plant domestication and agricultural origins is based on generalized models. We devise models to account for the transition from wild to cultivated plants and from hunting and gathering economies to an agricultural way of life. It has gradually become apparent that we are more often than not misled by such devices. Models are useful in the sense of a diagram, a chart or a map, in presenting an idea graphically, but they should never be confused with the truth. A model can be devised for each cultivated plant independently of the others and a model can be devised for each instance of agriculture successfully emerging out of a non-agricultural society, but we find no model that has universal or even very general applications. A model for wheat does not work for maize, and a model for sorghum does not work for rice. No more does a model for agricultural origins in the Near East work for Africa, East Asia, Meso-America or South America.

Evidence for agricultural origins and dispersals may be classified briefly as to source, as in table 9.1 (see Harlan and de Wet 1973a). The physical setting in Africa, past climates, probable changes in vegetation, and archaeological background are presented elsewhere in this volume.

We shall deal here only with such evidence as we can muster, directly concerned with the emergence of the African agricultural complex.

TABLE 9.1   *Sources of evidence for agricultural origins and dispersals*

A. The plants themselves
   1. Direct evidence: archaeobotany
   2. Biosystematics and genetic relationships
   3. Distribution and variation patterns
   4. Genetic reconstruction
B. Man and his activities
   1. Artifacts and refuse: archaeology
   2. Ecological adaptations, techniques
   3. Language, legend, attitudes
   4. History
C. Physical evidence
   Reconstruction of past climates and vegetation via geology, palynology, hydrology, palaeontology, etc.

The most direct and preferred evidence is that which can be obtained from archaeobotany. One would wish for a reasonably complete sequence of plant remains well dated, accurately identified and systematically stratified through time and space. Such sequences are very rare. A fairly adequate one is developing in the Near East and Europe and a less complete one is available for parts of Mexico. Fragments of evidence have been turned up in India, China, Peru and elsewhere, but as yet they are not adequate to reveal the evolutionary history of either crop plants or agricultural societies. They do tell us something of what crops were being grown and when they arrived in a given region.

Direct archaeobotanical evidence in Africa is extremely scanty at the time of writing and tells us nothing about when, where, or by whom agriculture was developed. Sorghum remains have been found fairly abundantly in a sprinkling of sites in East Africa and at the site of Daima in Eastern Nigeria. They all date from AD 500 or later, and all represent types currently grown in the area. A splendidly preserved bouquet of sorghum heads was uncovered by Plumley (1970) in Qasm Ibraim, dating to Meroitic times. Munson has described a sequence from potsherd impressions from Mauritania which indicates an evolution from harvesting wild grass seeds for food to cultivation of pearl millet. The crop begins to appear at roughly 1000 BC but it is already known archaeologically in India at that time (Vishnu-Mittre 1974). The direct evidence from actual plant remains to date has been very disappointing and contributes little to a solution of the problem.

Indirect archaeological evidence is more abundant but always subject to errors or interpretation. Along the Nile a number of camp-sites dating from the Sahaba aggradation (about 12 500 to 9500 BC) have been found associated with a series of ephemeral, temporary lakes (Wendorf, Said and Schild 1970). Among the artifacts recovered are grinding-stones and sickle-blades with sheen. Grinding-stones are generalized tools and could be used for a variety of purposes, but we do know they are used by hunting–gathering peoples today for grinding grass seeds. The sickle-blades are suggestive of the harvesting of grass seed, but no one yet knows what grass or whether it was wild or cultivated. The sheen is a peculiar type of gloss on the cutting edges that is thought to be deposited when the flint blade is used to cut grass stems. There may be other ways in which sheen can be produced. The total evidence is obviously tenuous, yet suggestive of extensive grass-seed harvesting and grinding (Wendorf and Schild 1976).

Evidence is spotty for some millennia after this, but by about 6000 BC it becomes evident that people were ranging across most of what is now the Sahara. Pollen samples of that time-range suggest a winter-rainfall regime with largely Mediterranean flora. Shallow lakes were common and inhabited by hippopotamus, crocodiles and fish. These 'early neolithic' economies were based on hunting, fishing and grain-collecting. No evidence of cultivation is available for that time.

By 5000 BC pastoralists were grazing their flocks across the Sahara and evidence of their settlements becomes much more abundant after 4000 BC. Bones of domestic sheep, goats and cattle have been found, sometimes in abundance. Pastoralists often settled near shallow lakes which have since dried up, and hunting and fishing continued to be important as well as grain-collecting; grinding-stones and sickles with sheen are among the artifacts (Clark 1970).

By the middle of the third millennium BC, effects of desiccation can be observed and the trend strongly accelerated at about 2000 BC. Sites in the Sahara in this time-range became fewer and fewer. People were moving out. By 1000 BC much of the Sahara had become deserted. It was about this time that the people of Dhar Tichitt area, Mauritania, began to take up cereal cultivation. The wild grain collected had been mostly sandbur (*Cenchrus biflorus*, or *kram-kram*). Evidence from potsherd impressions indicates a rapid switch with sandbur declining and pearl millet increasing markedly in the period of a century or two. This is not the usual pattern of domestication and rather implies the taking up of a new practice and the cultivation of a plant already domesticated elsewhere (Munson 1976).

On the whole, archaeological evidence has been found wanting. We have considerable evidence of people wandering widely over Africa and we know something of their economy. We know they hunted and fished. We know they herded livestock over much of the Sahara. We suspect they ate ground grains, but even indirect evidence for plant domestication and agricultural origins is very scant to say the least. At present we are forced to generalize in the broadest terms and state only that archaeology suggests African agriculture developed south of the Sahara and north of the Equator. The time-range is entirely unknown, but since African crops show up in India archaeologically before 1000 BC, it is likely that much had been done well before that (Vishnu-Mittre 1974). Clark has suggested that the time-range 3000 to 1000 BC might have been critical as the Sahara pastoralists moved southward compelled by desiccation and innovations were in order, not necessarily by the cattle people themselves but by those with whom they came in contact (Clark 1970).

Late in the fifth millennium BC farmers settled in the Fayum area. They grew barley, emmer, flax and other crops from the Near Eastern centre and used tools of a different style of manufacture than had previously been known in Africa. Fayum is a lake basin near the Nile, which receives water from the main river at flood stage and has a relatively stable shoreline. Villages near the lake were not flooded and are available archaeologically. Farmers might have settled in the Nile Delta also but all traces would be buried under many metres of alluvial deposit.

Since we have clear evidences of agriculture in south-west Asia by 7000 BC and no definite evidence for cultivation in Africa until much later, the question of stimulus diffusion from Asia to Africa must be raised. Did the spread of agriculture from south-west Asia have something to do with the development of indigenous African agriculture? What little evidence we can muster is equivocal, to say the least. Pottery and livestock-herding appeared widely over the Sahara before either of them were found along the Nile. If these cultural elements came to Africa from south-west Asia, the evidence suggests that they did not arrive by way of the lower Nile.

If the zone of winter-rainfall Mediterranean climate had covered a large part of the Sahara from the sixth to the third millennia BC, the 'ground grain' could well have been wheat and barley and the people of the Sahara fully agricultural, deriving both their crops and their herds from south-west Asia. With desiccation they had to move out and cool-season crops are not well suited to the tropics with summer rainfall. The Near Eastern crop complex would have to be abandoned except on the cool high plateau of Ethiopia. Livestock would become marginal where the tsetse fly carried disease and would be largely abandoned in the wet tropical zone.

But there is a suggestion that when the Near Eastern agricultural complex arrived on the Ethiopian plateau, there was an indigenous African agriculture already in place. Why would agriculturalists who had been growing barley, emmer and (tetraploid) wheat for some millennia suddenly turn their attention to the domestication of a small-seeded grass like tef (*Eragrostis tef*)? If an agricultural complex was already well supplied with edible-oil seed plants (crucifers, safflower, flax), why would anyone bother to domesticate a local one like noog (*Guizotia abyssinica*)? Cereal-eating people are not likely to domesticate a starchy plant like enset, and so on. Again, we have no direct evidence, but it seems most likely that some of the Ethiopians were already farmers when the Near Eastern complex arrived (Clark, in press). It is possible that when the Sahara people moved into the savanna and forest belts of West Africa they also found an indigenous agriculture already in place. On the other hand, this might have been the very time when African plants were domesticated. The present evidence is inadequate to help us choose between alternatives.

Historical accounts are essentially of no use at all in understanding agricultural origins in Africa. They would be too late in any case, but history is strangely silent about sub-Saharan Africa until very recently. The earliest literate people who might be expected to know something of the region are the Egyptians. Records and monuments indicate that they were aware of a land to the south of them, but their interests were largely confined to raiding, slave-collecting, or taxing produce shipped down the Nile. The expedition of Queen Hatshepsut of the Eighteenth Dynasty is one exception. The murals on the temple of Deir el-Bahari depict in some detail the first known, government-sponsored, plant introduction expedition in history. A party of five ships was sent to Punt to dig up and transplant incense trees for the temple. A few scenes show African villages and indicate an agricultural people. These appear to be accurate and give us a tantalizing glimpse into life in the horn of Africa at about 1500 BC. Deliberate defacing of the temple after the death of the queen and subsequent vandalism have robbed us of some details (Clark, in press).

History records the celebrated visit of the Queen of Saba (Sheba) to

Jerusalem in the tenth century BC but we are not enlightened about the agricultural situation of her homeland. Herodotus visited Egypt in the fifth century and described the agriculture in some detail, but this was entirely a Near Eastern agriculture and indigenous African plants were not identified. The Periplus of the Red Sea, first century AD, lists commodities traded at various African ports. Words like οῖτος were used to differentiate local grains from the more familiar πῦρός used for wheat by the Greeks. A positive identification is impossible, however, without more detail. All in all, history teaches us essentially nothing about African agriculture until we reach the eleventh to fourteenth centuries when Arabs were visiting in sub-Saharan Africa. El-Bakri mentions durra and other native cereal grains, but without much elaboration.

The bulk of the useful evidence, therefore, must come almost entirely from living plants and the present people or at least the tribes as they were known in the last century or so. The enthnographic evidence is useful, but many tribes have not been studied. Anthropologists are more interested in kinship groups, language, or social behaviour than in agriculture and the crops grown. Plant scientists are usually inadequately trained to assemble useful ethnographic evidence. We do see, at least, that some crops are woven intrinsically into the fabric of life of certain tribes. Rice is sacred to the rice-eating tribes; yams sacred to the yam-eaters. Pearl millet is the source of life to some, and sorghum to others. People have a special feeling about fonio, tef, or enset depending upon the tribe and location.

But we are not especially secure in ethnographic evidence either, for some crops are disappearing and traditions, myths and social practices have been discontinued because of the social and political disruption stemming from European and Arab contact. The slave trade was enormously destructive of traditional life forms, and modern urbanization tends to wipe out what is left. Much crucial evidence has slipped away and we are left with fragmentary data at best.

Evidence from the plants themselves is generally available. A few crops have been largely displaced by new introductions, but in general the disruptions to date have been much less than for other lines of evidence. Piasa is declining; African rice is rapidly being replaced by Asian rice; maize, cotton, ground-nut and manioc from the New World have become large crops in Africa. Dietary habits have been changed by the introduction of chilli pepper, tomato, papaya, guava and other New World domesticates. But most of this can be sorted out and the original condition reconstructed. It is not quite as easy to sort out some of the Asian introductions, but, on the whole, the plant evidence is available for study and some sense can be made of it.

Useful plant data include the variation patterns of the crops, their ecological behaviour and adaptation and the geographic distribution of races of the cultigens. The nearest wild relatives, especially those that might be progenitors, give clues as to the arena of plant domestications. Genetic relationships between the wild, weed and cultivated races of the crops can be studied experimentally. The range of variation, both morphological and geographical, can be sampled, hybrids made, and genetic affinities measured in different ways. Only a few African crops have been studied in such detail but these may be adequate to give us a generalized picture.

## PRINCIPLES OF PLANT DOMESTICATION

Africa is one of the illuminating regions of the world with respect to analysing the evolution of agricultural systems and societies. There are hunting–gathering tribes available for study, such as the San, the Hadza and the forest pygmies. There are intermediate economies such as that of the Ik, where the tribe farms three to four years out of five and resumes full-time hunting–gathering the rest of the time. There are tribes with a full pastoral economy and those that farm a little or a lot along with cattle-rearing. There are desert-margin farmers, savanna farmers, forest farmers, and agriculturalists of the high Ethiopian plateau. All permutations and combinations appear to be available for analysis, and, as we shall see, cultivated plants also show intermediate conditions between wild and fully domesticated.

Anthropological studies in the last decade have forced us to rethink theories about the motivation that would induce people to give up hunting and gathering and take up farming. The hunting–gathering systems appear to be more stable and less subject to failure due to drought, flood, locusts, or other pests. When crops burn up due to drought, some tribes fall back on hunting and gathering as a secure source of food (Lee and DeVore 1968). The African savanna in particular is one of the richest ecological zones of the world with respect to natural production of food usable by man.

Studies have shown the diets of hunter–gatherers generally superior to those of farmers, adequate in quantity, better balanced nutritionally. The technology of hunting–gathering takes little effort; usually only three to four hours per day are required to acquire an adequate food supply. The health status is usually better than that of farmers; the incidence of starvation and chronic diseases is much less.

It is true that hunting–gathering is an economy that tolerates only sparse populations and that enormously more people can be supported by agriculture. But this could hardly have been evident at the beginning. What is evident at the start is that more effort must be invested to extract a given amount of food. As agriculture is intensified, the effort is increased more and more for the same basic amount extracted. The hunting–gathering peoples worked very little. The full-time farmer worked a great deal. The reasons for taking up farming in the first place are not now clear to us (Harlan 1975).

Studies of the process of plant domestication in the last decade have also shown that we must rethink many of our theories in that area, and that much of what we have thought and taught in the past is simply not true. The Russian agronomist Vavilov (1926) thought he had a simple and reliable device for locating the geographic origin of cultivated plants. He analysed the variation of a crop and plotted the distribution of forms. The region in which the most forms occurred, he said, was the 'centre of origin'. Later analyses have shown that while centres of diversity do occur in many crops, they seldom are related to centres of origin. More often, they are related to some current evolutionary activity involving hybrids between races and/or wild and weedy relatives (Harlan 1971, 1975, Zohary 1971).

Studies of the origin of cultivated plants is complicated by the fact that domestication is a process, not an event, and that crops may change profoundly as they move out of the region of initial manipulation. Derived, modern corn-belt maize is a very different plant from early maize recovered in archaeological sites in Mexico, and so we should expect early sorghum to be radically different from modern derived hybrid grain sorghum. The principle of change with time as the crop spreads from its initial source I have called the principle of 'diffuse origins', and it simply means we cannot ever quite solve the problem of centre of origin for crops that have achieved a wide distribution (Harlan 1956).

It is also not always clear when a crop has achieved the status of domestication. We may use examples of African cultigens to illustrate. The African oil palm (*Elaeis guineensis* Jacq.) was probably wild as a forest-margin plant. It cannot tolerate the deep shade of the rainforest. In the course of the shifting cultivation practised in the forest zone, however, the forest is reduced to bush which is cut and burned on a fairly consistent rotation basis. In slashing and burning, the oil palm is spared and stands begin to build up without anyone deliberately planting a tree. The tree is spared because it is useful. The practice is reinforced by some tribal beliefs. In some cultures there is a belief that if an oil palm is cut down, someone in the village will die.

The usual harvesting practice for oil palms is to cut off the bunches at maturity and to beat off the fruits with a stick. There is a belief among some tribes that this should never be done in a village for the flying fruits symbolize people leaving the village. Among these tribes the fruits are beaten off in the forest and this helps to disperse the seeds. There are even selective processes that profoundly affect the genetic constitution of the sub-spontaneous oil palm populations. One genotype is preferred for oil and another is tapped for palm wine. Repeated tapping kills the tree, so there is a strong genetic selection in favour of the better oil types. Thus we have a tree encouraged, disseminated and selectively utilized without being deliberately planted.

Karité, *Butyrospermum paradoxum* (also known as Shea butter tree), is a savanna tree whose fruits are also used for the extraction of edible oil. It is also spared in farming operations and is essentially never cut. Other trees of the savanna are felled for the wood, fuel or other uses but not this quasi-sacred tree. As a result, vast stands of open orchard savanna have built up where almost the only tree is karité. Is the karité wild or domesticated?

Ethiopian oats are still another example. When the Near Eastern agricultural complex moved into highland Ethiopia a number of weeds were brought along. These included *Lolium temulentum*, some crucifers and the tetraploid weed oats *Avena barbata*. They infested fields of emmer and barley in particular. The Ethiopians were more or less indifferent to the weed oats, neither planting them nor weeding them out. Both non-shattering and semi-shattering races evolved so that, in due time, the cultivators were actually harvesting the weed oats and planting them along with the emmer and barley. The farmers are still more or less indifferent to oats. They are not grown as a crop but no effort is made to get rid of them, either. Are the Ethiopian oats cultivated or not?

Other examples of uncertain status could be given; it is not always clear what is domesticated and what is encouraged, sub-spontaneous, a tolerated weed, adventitious, naturalized or wild. If the status of domestication is unclear, we might also point out that the status of weed is not always easy to define, either. Wild plants can be weedy under certain circumstances. Genuine weeds can be produced by crossing wild with cultivated races.

Harlan and de Wet (1965) have defined a weed as an organism adapted to conditions of human disturbance. The distinction between wild, weed and cultivated can be illustrated by the African crop sorghum. With the construction of the Aswan Dam, the people of Wadi Halfa in the northern Sudan had to be relocated. A region was chosen near Kassala close to the Atbara near the Ethiopian border. A large tract was levelled, ditched and drained for irrigated agriculture. The region chosen was in an area of massive stands of truly wild sorghum. This race of sorghum is found abundantly in the Sudanese savanna, covering vast areas where agriculture has never been practised. It is a natural part of the tall grass savanna of that part of Africa. When the irrigation project was established, however, this particular race of sorghum proved to be a rather vigorous weed of cotton fields and irrigation-ditch borders. Since the people of Wadi Halfa were from the north and accustomed to growing wheat, they did not themselves grow sorghum and there has been no genetic interaction between the wild forms and the cultivated races. Elsewhere, however, these same wild races crossed with cultivated races produce a noxious weed very difficult to eradicate. The morphological differences between the true weed and the true wild races are very clear and it is easy to separate the two.

Careful and detailed analyses of wild, weed and cultivated races of our crops are necessary to unravel their evolutionary histories. There has been far too much speculation without adequate collections and without sufficient genetic background, but each crop is a story of its own and generalized models are seldom very useful. As we have seen, origins of cultivated plants are generally diffuse in time, space and status.

In a similar way, agricultural economies also evolved and various stages of development can be found in Africa. When is agriculture achieved? When 5% of the food intake is from cultivated plants? 15%, 20% or 50%? Many fully agricultural people continue to harvest large quantities of foodstuffs from the wild. Agriculture and hunting-and-gathering are not mutually exclusive, at least not until population densities become high and game and wild plants are destroyed.

Plant domestication emerges from an intensive interaction between man and the plants he harvests, uses or disturbs. Selective harvesting may affect the genetic constitition of natural populations as in the case of oil palm previously mentioned. Harvesting wild yams may also be selective. Various species have different protective devices: some are poisonous; some are protected by thorns, and some bear tubers placed very deeply in the earth. African species may have one or two of such protective devices, but never all three. In digging wild yams there may be a tendency to collect the shallow ones and those not protected by thorns. Yam-eaters know the poisonous forms very well and know how to detoxify them. As long as yams are harvested only and not planted there would be selection pressures in favour of thorn-protected and deeply-placed tubers. With domestication, selection is in the opposite direction. The plants are now protected by man and do not require natural protective devices. Man will then select and propagate forms that have shallow, non-toxic tubers unprotected by thorns. The harvesting of grass seeds in wild stands is likely to have very little effect on the populations. The plants that escape the harvest are those that will contribute to the next generation, and if there is any selection pressure at all, it will be in the direction of wild type characteristics, such as shattering, maturation over a long period of time, seed dormancy, and so on. As man sows that which he has reaped, the genetic pattern changes sharply. Now there are two populations instead of one. Within the planted population, strong selection pressures are set up automatically in favour of reduced shattering and increase in seed retention, more uniform maturation and loss or reduction of seed dormancy. In the artificial seed-bed the first seedlings to come up and the most vigorous ones will contribute the most to the next generation. As a result, there is strong seedling competition which provides selection pressure for larger seed and more vigorous and competitive seedlings. Disruptive selection is intense: one population moving in the direction of domestication, the other retaining spontaneous habits but perhaps becoming progressively adapted to the cultivated fields. Cultivated and weed races may evolve side by side both being derived from the same wild progenitor.

While many traits of cultivated plants arise automatically due to disruptive selection and the advantages to the plant of being sown and tended, other characteristics can be only traced to the effects of deliberate human selection. Cultivators in primitive agriculture have a feeling for plants. They are always on the lookout for new and interesting variants. In many crops they choose seed stock with great care. Seeds from these selected plants and no others can contribute to the next generation. What the farmer chooses may have little to do with productivity or adaptation. He may select a type of sorghum because it makes good dumplings or good beer or is sweet and good for chewing or tough and good for making houses and basketry. Or, possibly, because it has an attractive colour. The cultivator can have essentially complete control over the populations that comprise the next generation, and since his selections can be contradictory and whimsical, enormous variability may build up. Cultivated plants are conspicuously more variable than wild ones because many of the forms chosen would be unable to survive in the wild (Harlan and de Wet 1973b).

## THE SAVANNA COMPLEX

The most characteristic feature of indigenous African agriculture is its adaptation to the savanna. Even the plants grown in the forest are largely of savanna origin, and by far the most important contribution of African crops to the world are plants adapted to the savanna zones. Many African domesticates have not spread far from their places of origin and have not competed successfully with other crops of the world. Pearl millet, sorghum and coffee are exceptions.

A list of the cultivated plants of the savanna complex is presented in table 9.2. The most important from the point of view of African cultivators are sorghum, pearl millet, African rice, fonio and earth pea. A considerable amount of food is obtained from the karité and *Parkia* trees, and the baobab is very important to some tribes of the savanna zone. Leaves and fruits may be eaten; a fibre may be extracted from the bark, and the hollow boles often serve as cisterns permitting villages to remain inhabited during the dry season in regions where there is no surface water.

The origin of sorghum has been studied in some detail and the sequence of events reconstructed by Harlan and Stemler (1976). The study began with an analysis of the wild races of sorghum in Africa. The distributions are shown in fig. 9.1. From this it was apparent that the wild race from West Africa and Zaïre is a forest grass and not a likely progenitor of a crop which is adapted to the savanna and does poorly when grown under high rainfall. In fact, the crop and the wild arundinaceum race of West Africa overlap only when sorghum is grown in regions well beyond its normal adaptive range.

For this reason, West Africa is ruled out as the most likely arena of sorghum domestication. Since the general archaeological picture would seem to indicate that African agriculture evolved north of the Equator and south of the Sahara, some region in the north-east quadrant is

TABLE 9.2   *Cultivated plants of the savanna complex*

*Adansonia digitata* Baobab, multiple use, sub-spontaneous
*Butyrospermum paradoxum* Karité, oil from fruit, encouraged
*Colocynthis citrullus* Water-melon, edible fruits, pot-herb, cultivated, weedy
*Corchorus olitorius* A pot-herb, leaves and seedlings, cultivated
*Digitaria exilis* Fonio, a cereal, cultivated and weedy
*D. iburua* Black fonio, limited cultivation
*Hibiscus cannabinus* Kenaf, a pot-herb in Africa, cultivated
*H. sabdarifa* Roselle, leaves and calyces, cultivated
*Lagenaria siceraria* Bottle-gourd, widely used, cultivated
*Oryza glaberrima* African rice, cereal, cultivated and weed races
*Parkia biglobosa* Tree with sweet pods, locust bean, sub-spontaneous
*Pennisetum americanum* Pearl millet, cereal, the drier zones, cultivated and weedy
*Polygala butyracea* Black beniseed, oil in seeds, West Africa
*Solanum aethiopicum* African tomato, edible fruits
*S. macrocarpon* A nightshade, fruits and leaves, weedy
*S. incanum* Bitter tomato
*Sorghum bicolor* Sorghum, cereal, sweet stalks, fodder, cultivated, weedy
*Voandzeia subterranea* Earth pea, Bambara ground-nut, pulse cultivated

UNCERTAIN ORIGINS

*Cajanus cajan* Pigeon pea, pulse, possibly Asian
*Gossypium herbaceum* Old World cotton, locale of domestication unknown
*Sesamum indicum* Sesame, oil seed, possibly Indian
*Tamarindus indica* Tamarind, tree with sweet pods, Asian? sub-spontaneous

implicated. The area of the most extensive stands of wild sorghum occurring today is outlined in fig. 9.2 and labelled 'early bicolor'. Because of changes in climate this may not have been the zone where sorghum domestication started, but a change in climate most likely moved the belt either north or south from the location indicated.

Variation within cultivated sorghum was analysed using some 12 000 specimens from the world collection. It was found that nearly all the variation could be partitioned among five basic races and intermediates derived from the basic races taken in pairs. The basic races were called (1) bicolor (B), (2) guinea (G), (3) kafir (K), (4) caudatum (C) and (5) durra (D). The intermediate races, then, became: guinea–bicolor (GB), kafir–bicolor (KB), caudatum–bicolor (CB), durra–bicolor (DB), guinea–kafir (GK), guinea–caudatum (GC), guinea–durra (GD), kafir–caudatum (KC), kafir–durra (KD) and durra–caudatum (DC).

The bicolor race is the most generalized and unspecialized of the races of sorghum and the one that most nearly resembles wild forms. It could easily be the progenitor of all the more specialized races. It does not have a characteristic distribution of its own, but is found wherever sorghum is grown as a crop. The other races each have their own

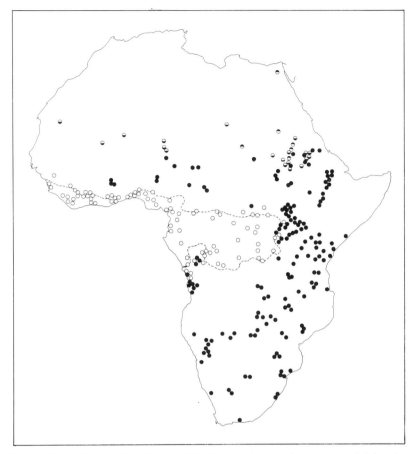

Fig. 9.1  The wild races of sorghum in Africa. Clear circles: arundinaceum race. Solid circles: verticilliflorum race. Upper half clear, lower solid: aethiopicum race. Lower half clear, upper solid: virgatum race. Dotted line: approximate limits of tropical forest.

characteristic distribution in Africa (fig. 9.3). The pattern is so consistent that it must imply something with respect to the history and evolution of the crop. The suggested sequence of events is shown graphically in figs. 9.2 and 9.4.

The guinea race is primarily West African, but is found sparingly in East Africa and at some time moved on to India. The kafir race is entirely southern African and presumably was involved in Bantu dispersals. The durra race has every indication of being intrusive in Africa, perhaps evolving in India from an early bicolor and returning to Africa where it is closely associated with Islamic cultures. The

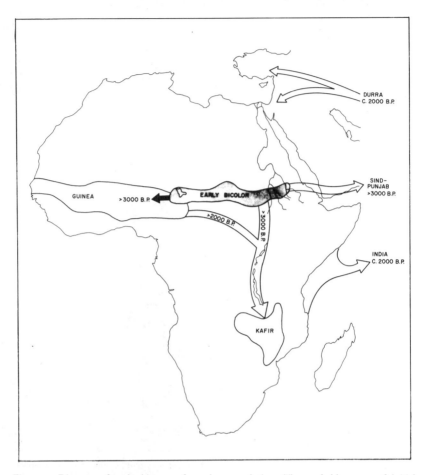

Fig. 9.2 Diagram of early history of sorghum evolution. The probable arena of initial domestication is indicated by the shaded region labelled 'early bicolor'. The guinea race is basically West African although it occurs in East Africa and India, while the kafir race is characteristic of southern Africa. (After Harlan and Stemler.)

caudatum race appears to have evolved near the original arena of sorghum domestication and has not spread very far from that area. Ethiopia seems to be ruled out as a centre of origin for sorghum, since it is rich in diversity for only the durra and durra–bicolor races.

Attempts to place a time-range on this sequence of events were frustrated by lack of information. Archaeobotanically, material from the site of Daima in Nigeria is sufficiently well preserved that the caudatum race could be identified. This is a common race in the area today. The date of the find is considered to be ninth or tenth century AD. On the other hand, pearl millet, sorghum and, possibly, finger millet have been

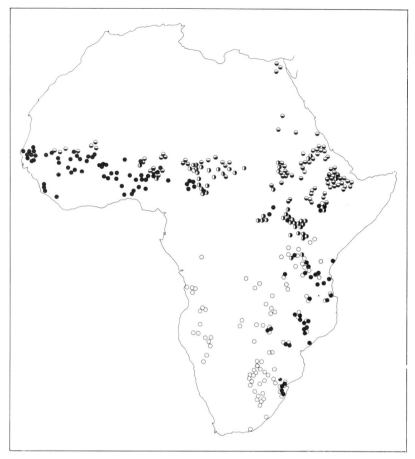

Fig. 9.3 Distribution of the basic cultivated races of sorghum. Solid circles: guinea race. Clear circles: kafir race. Upper half clear, lower solid: durra race. Left half clear, right solid: caudatum race.

recovered from archaeological sites in India dating to the second half of the second millennium BC (Vishnu-Mittre 1974). It is likely that they arrived about the same time and, allowing for some reasonable errors in dating, it would appear that the primary dispersal of an early bicolor race could not have been later than 1000 BC, but could well have been earlier. How much earlier we have as yet no basis for estimation.

The domestication of African rice is a simple and straightforward case. The progenitor is *Oryza barthii*, an annual species adapted to waterholes in the savanna zone that dry up in the dry season. The true wild races are not found in areas of high rainfall (fig. 9.5). There is another related species, *O. longistaminata*, that is perennial and may occupy the same waterholes but always where moisture supply is more

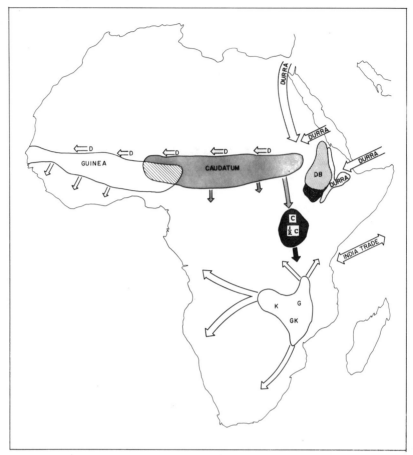

Fig. 9.4 Diagram of later events in the evolution of cultivated sorghum. For explanation of letters see p. 636. (After Harlan and Stemler.)

ample. It has a much wider distribution in Africa and may or may not have contributed some germ plasm to the crop through introgression. The main evolution, however, was by direct manipulation of *O. barthii*.

While African rice is now grown as an upland crop well within the forest zone of West Africa, it is clear that it had a savanna origin. Some weedy races may be found in the forest, but the true wild race does not occur there. The native rice belt of West Africa, inhabited by rice-eating peoples, is rather sharply defined geographically and ranges from Gambia and Casamance of Senegal across Guinea, Sierra Leone, and Liberia to the central Ivory Coast. African rice is still grown in the bend of the Niger in Mali and across the savanna of Upper Volta, Northern Ghana,

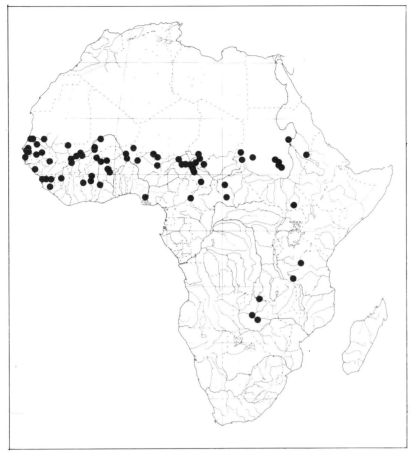

Fig. 9.5   Distribution of wild *Oryza barthii*, the progenitor of African rice.

Togo, Dahomey (modern Republic of Benin), and the Sokoto region
of Northern Nigeria, and thence eastward in scattered pockets to the
Logone region south of Lake Chad (fig. 9.6).

Portères (1956) has assembled ethnographic and linguistic evidence
to suggest that the initial domestication took place in the central delta
of the Niger. From there African rice was exported to Guinea and from
there to the Casamance and the coast regions of Western Africa. At a
later time, it also spread eastward across Northern Nigeria to Lake Chad.
So far, there is no direct evidence to support this suggestion but it
appears to be the most likely theory. The time-range remains entirely
unknown until more adequate archaeological and archaeobotanical
evidence comes to light.

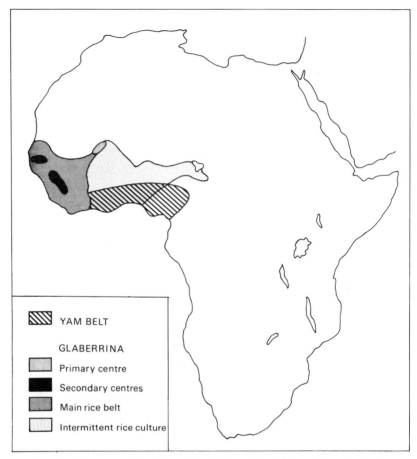

Fig. 9.6    The yam and rice belts of West Africa. (Adapted in part from Portères.)

The situation with respect to pearl millet is less satisfactory perhaps because of more superficial investigations. The wild form is presumed to be *Pennisetum violaceum*, but its distribution and variation patterns are very poorly known. A northern belt of pearl millet is rather clearly defined, geographically and is shown in fig. 9.7, together with such stations as are currently available for the wild races. Pearl millet is the most drought resistant of all tropical cereals and can be grown near the limits of agriculture close to the deserts of the world. A southern African pearl-millet belt is somewhat fragmentary but occurs in association with the margins of the Kalahari Desert and other regions at the limits of agriculture. The extreme drought resistance of the crop

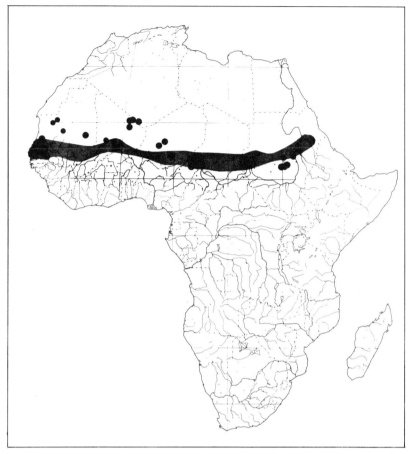

Fig. 9.7   Locations of wild pearl millet, *Pennisetum violaceum* (circles), and the northern pearl millet belt (dark shading). The area in which pearl millet is grown, but in which sorghum is the dominant crop, is shown by light shading. The crop is also associated with the drier zones of East and southern Africa.

makes it possible to extend cultivation into the margins of the Indian desert as well.

Fonio and black fonio belong to the genus *Digitaria* and are related to the common weed of warm–temperate and tropical climates *D. sanguinalis*, sometimes called crab-grass (*Bluthirse* in German). The seeds are very small and the yields are low. Both crops may have been more widely grown at one time than they are now. Fonio is sometimes called 'hungry rice', but this is hardly a fair term. Only in a few places is it grown simply to relieve hunger. More often it is a prestige crop and a 'chief's food', grown for its delicate flavour and superior culinary

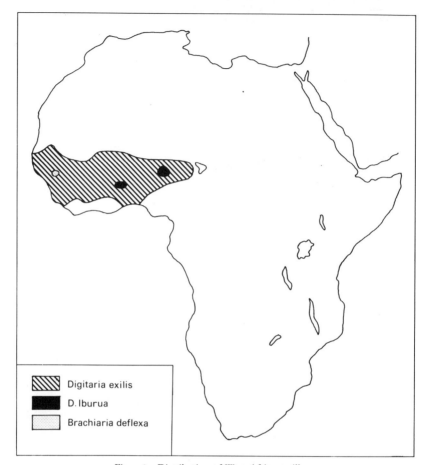

Fig. 9.8   Distribution of West African millets.

value. The wild races are widespread in tropical Africa, but the cultivated forms are rather restricted (fig. 9.8).

Guinea millet is a cultivated form of *Brachiaria deflexa* also a widespread weedy grass in tropical Africa. The cultivated races have large seeds and are non-shattering as with other domesticated cereals. They are grown only in the Fouta Djalon region of Guinea.

*Voandzeia* is a leguminous herb producing pods of seeds underground like the American ground-nut (or peanut). The seeds are large and nearly spherical, the pods more or less indehiscent as with other domesticated legumes. The crop is likely to be found in kitchen gardens rather than in large fields and is declining rapidly in use. *Kerstingiella* is a somewhat similar earth pea or ground-nut. The wild races have been little studied but are reported from the Nigeria–Cameroun border near the Benue River.

THE FOREST-MARGIN COMPLEX

An agricultural complex evolved satisfactory for the penetration of the high forests of West Africa and the Congo basin. Only a few of the plants are truly adapted to forest conditions. Most of them are suited for the forest margins and derived savannas. The large tubers of the yams, for instance, are adaptations for food reserve storage making it possible for the plant to live through a long dry season and to survive occasional burning of the vegetation. The oil palm cannot tolerate dense shade of the high forest and must have originally been a plant of the forest margins. The cowpea is common as a wild or weedy plant in derived savanna and most of the plants grown by the forest-dwelling tribes have similar origins.

A list of the cultivated plants of the forest-margin complex is presented in table 9.3. The only plants that appear to be adapted to true forest conditions are coffee, kola, and akee apple. The implications are that a savanna agriculture originated first and the agriculturalists began to encroach into the forest adopting techniques of shifting cultivation or bush fallow. In this procedure, forest or bush is cut and burned in the dry season. One to three crops are raised in the temporary clearing and then the land is abandoned for ten to twenty years to permit the bush to grow back and the soil to recover fertility and structure. A reasonably systematic rotation is eventually developed and the farming system has rather profound effects on the forest vegetation. Where the system is used intensively, the forest tends to be degraded to derived savanna.

The savanna complex of crops could be exploited in much of the derived savanna, but in the higher rainfall areas, a number of crops had to be abandoned. Pearl millet has little tolerance for high rainfall. Africans prefer it to most other cereals and they try to grow it where it is not suited for that reason but the yields are too poor for it to be anything but a luxury item in the high-rainfall areas. Sorghum is somewhat more tolerant, but it too tends to fail in the forest zone. Plants of the forest margin were much better suited and could be grown where the savanna plants failed. Rice is an exception since it is adapted to flooding in the savanna waterholes.

TABLE 9.3  *Cultivated plants of the forest-margin complex*

---

*Afromomum melegueta* Grains of Paradise, spice, West Africa
*Blighia sapida* Akee apple, aril eaten, forest, West Africa
*Brachiaria deflexa* Guinea millet, cereal, Guinea only
*Coffea canephora* Robusta coffee, forest zones
*Cola acuminata* Cola nut, forest, West Africa
*C. nitida et alia* Cola nut, forest, West Africa
*Dioscorea bulbifera* Air potato, aerial tubers, wide distribution
*D. cayenensis* Yellow Guinea yam, forest, West Africa
*D. dumetorum* Bitter yam, forest, West Africa
*D. praehensilis* Bush yam, forest, West Africa
*D. rotundata* White Guinea yam, forest, related to *D. cayenensis*
*Elaeis guineensis* Oil palm, forest, West Africa to Angola
*Hibiscus esculentus* Okra, garden vegetable, common in West Africa
*Kerstingiella geocarpa* A ground-nut, limited culture, West Africa
*Lablab niger* Hyacinth bean, now widespread, East Africa
*Plectranthus esculentus* Hausa potato, tuber, West Africa
*Solenostemon rotundifolius* Piasa, becoming rare, West Africa
*Sphenostylis stenocarpa* Yam pea, tuberous legume, West Africa
*Telfaira occidentalis* Fluted gourd, fruit and seeds, West Africa
*Vigna unguiculata* Cowpea, pulse, West Africa

---

Rice-based agriculture was apparently expansive in West Africa. The plant must have first been grown in the savanna because the wild progenitor is a savanna plant, but types were eventually selected suitable for upland fields of the wet forest zone. Rice does not need to be flooded, but cannot tolerate dry soils. If the rainfall is high enough and sufficiently consistent, rice can be grown as an upland crop. Rice-eating peoples then spread through the forest from Senegambia through Guinea, Sierra Leone and Liberia to the central Ivory Coast. There they met a yam-based agriculture already in place. The division between rice-eating people and yam-eating people in West Africa is very clear cut. People on the left bank of the Bandama River (Ivory Coast) eat yams; people on the right bank eat rice (Miège 1954). There are profound ethnic, linguistic and societal differences between the two groups as well. The remarkably sharp differentiation can be explained by the assumption of an early yam-based agriculture in the forest zone which was already well developed before the rice-based agriculture arrived from the savannas to the north. The time-range, again, eludes us for want of information. A number of sites have been excavated in the West African forest belt, some of them indicating a very long occupancy, but there seems to be little in the way of artifactual innovation. The arrival of this kind of agriculture may not leave an archaeological record. The appearance of ground stone and pottery may be suggestive but it is only that. For the moment we can only make guesses based on other sorts of evidence.

## THE ETHIOPIAN COMPLEX

A small group of crops, essentially endemic to Ethiopia, was domesticated in the Ethiopian highlands (table 9.4). The case of finger millet is somewhat uncertain and it might have been domesticated in Uganda. Detailed studies have not been made. The oats, as we have noted, are hardly more than encouraged or tolerated weeds derived from the Near Eastern tetraploid *Avena barbata*. The *Coffea arabica* is the major coffee of commerce and the base of the coffee industry until the development of the instant preparations which utilize the robusta types. Yet commercial coffee is new to Ethiopia. Wild and semi-wild stands occur as an understory in the southern Ethiopian rainforest and were little exploited until this century.

Tef is the national cereal of Ethiopia. It is grown on more hectares than any other crop in the country and has the status of a royal or quasi-divine grain. The seeds are very small but nutritious and the bread prepared from it, called *enjera*, is highly palatable and the staff of life for millions in the country. It is hardly grown anywhere else, although its ecological amplitude in Ethiopia is very wide, it being grown over a wider range of elevations than any other crop in the country.

Noog is the number one edible oil of Ethiopia and a large amount is grown in the country. It is a minor oil plant elsewhere being grown very little in other African countries and on a small scale in India. Enset is another crop essentially endemic to Ethiopia. It is a banana-like plant but the fruits are not eaten. The starchy base of the pseudo-stem is the part consumed. At maturity the plant is harvested; the stem base is wrapped in enset leaves and buried in the ground to ferment for a number of days. The partially processed material is then dried, pounded in a mortar and is then ready for use. The plant is enormously important to several tribes of the southern highlands and is basic to their food supply.

Finger millet is a domesticate of the East African highlands and is grown extensively in Uganda and Ethiopia. It has spread to southern and western Africa but is relatively less important there. The grain is less used as a food than formerly and much of the current production goes into beer. Chat is a shrub or small tree; the leaves are chewed fresh

TABLE 9.4   *The Ethiopian complex*

---

*Avena abyssinica* Tetraploid oats, weeds in barley and emmer fields
*Catha edulis* Chat, a mild narcotic, chewed fresh
*Coffea arabica* The primary coffee of commerce
*Eleusine coracana* Finger millet, perhaps domesticated in Uganda
*Ensete ventricosum* Enset, a relative of banana, stem base eaten
*Eragrostis tef* Tef, the principal cereal of Ethiopia
*Guizotia abyssinica* Noog, the main edible-oil crop of Ethiopia

---

and there is a mild narcotic effect. Chat-chewing is common around the Red Sea area both in Arabia and Yemen as well as in Ethiopia.

Ethiopia was once considered a centre of origin for many crops, but it is now apparent that a relatively small number was actually domesticated there. On the other hand, agriculture has been practised for a long time in relative isolation from the rest of the world so that peculiar endemic races of many crops have evolved that are found nowhere else. Barley, emmer, flax, cabbage, chickpea, pea, lentil and other crops domesticated in the Near East all have unique Ethiopian races. Ethiopia is a major centre of diversity of many crops, but the centre of origin for only a few (Harlan 1969).

### MIGRATION OF AFRICAN CROPS TO ASIA

The most important African contributions to Asian agriculture are sorghum and pearl millet. Millions of people in India and Pakistan are absolutely dependent on these cereals for their food supply. Sorghum is only moderately important in south-eastern Asia and Indonesia but has become a major cereal in northern China. Finger millet, cowpea and lablab are also fairly important in South Asia.

The time when African crops were exported to Asia is not known but pearl millet, sorghum and, possibly, finger millet have been identified in archaeological contexts dated about 1000 BC or somewhat earlier (Vishnu-Mittre 1974). There are Sanskrit words for finger millet and pearl millet but not for sorghum suggesting that if sorghum was present it was not a very important crop in Vedic times. Despite reports of sorghum depicted on Assyrian bas-reliefs, there is no trace of sorghum in the Near East until Roman times. The bas-reliefs are really of reeds as can be seen from the swampy habitat graphically depicted.

The case for sorghum in China, however, is more involved. Traces have been reported in archaeological contexts as early as Yang-shao, although this may well have been an error. There are other reports of sorghum in archaeological contexts dating to Former Han times or a little earlier. It is possible that the plant had reached China in the last few centuries BC. There is no Chinese word for the plant, however, until the third century AD and the crop was not important until after the Mongol conquest. The Chinese word for sorghum, *shu-shu*, implies that it came to North China by way of the west, that is to say Szechwan Province. An early importation from an overland route therefore seems likely but, no doubt, sorghum was imported more extensively by sea at a later time as well.

## IMPORTED CROP COMPLEXES

The south-west Asian complex consists of barley, emmer, other tetraploid wheats, flax, chickpea, pea, lentil, broad bean, cabbage, weed oats, safflower, and several spices such as coriander, *Nigella*, rue and others. These crops are all cool-season in adaptation and were developed in an area of winter rainfall. They were domesticated in the Near East, some of them as early as 7000 BC. The complex as a whole spread along the Mediterranean shores of North Africa, eastward to India and south across Arabia to the Yemen. At some time, now unknown, the complex became established on the Ethiopian plateau. Archaeological surveys to date have not been very helpful in establishing the time when this agricultural complex arrived in Ethiopia.

South Asian plants imported into Africa include banana, mango, taro, Asian yams, coconut, several kinds of citrus, Asian rice and sugar-cane. The time of these importations is also not known. On the whole, south Asian plant domesticates have had relatively little impact on African agriculture with the possible exception of the bananas which became extremely important to the Baganda and several other tribes of Uganda. Asian rice is now replacing the indigenous rice but rice has not become a popular crop in Africa except in areas where African rice had already been domesticated and the people had already become accustomed to eating rice.

American imports into Africa have been far more important. These include cassava, ground-nut, maize, sweet potato, cocoa, rubber, sisal, chilli peppers, pineapple, papaya, guava, potato, beans, lima beans, avocado and tomato. Cassava, in particular, has been enormously successful and there is more production of cassava in Africa than in Latin America. The crop has been particularly useful in the higher-rainfall zones of West Africa and southward to Angola. The ground-nut has become particularly important as a cash crop in Nigeria and Senegal. Maize has been a very successful cereal in regions of moderate to high rainfall and cocoa, rubber and sisal have become important plantation crops.

There is a small group of crops whose origins have not yet been established. These include sesame, guar, pigeon pea and cotton. The genus *Sesamum* is basically African but it is not certain that the crop was domesticated in Africa. The same is true of *Cyamopsis* and *Gossypium*. Too little is known about wild races of pigeon pea to reach a saitsfactory conclusion at the present time.

Of these plants, sesame is by far the most important and most interesting. If it is an African domesticate it surely did not follow the same pattern as sorghum, pearl millet, finger millet, etc. Sesame is known to have been extremely important in India in Dravidic times. There are numerous references to it in the Sanskrit literature. It is known archaeologically from Harappan times in the latter part of the third millennium BC. The only wild species of *Sesamum* known in India has 32 chromosomes instead of 26 like the cultivated races. Species of *Sesamum* with 26 chromosomes occur in Africa but they seem to be genetically incompatible with the cultivated forms. The problem needs further critical investigation before a satisfactory solution can be found (Nayar and Mehra 1970).

## INDIGENOUS AGRICULTURAL TECHNIQUES

Indigenous African agriculture has developed a number of unique innovations. These include implements, the handling of both plants and soils and field techniques. Basically, African agriculture is a hoe and digging-stick agriculture. The plough was introduced into the high plateau of Ethiopia along with the Near Eastern crops. It came up the Nile from Egypt to about the latitude of Khartoum. South of Khartoum the last tribe to use the plough employs the tool on contour terraces; the area between the terraces is cultivated with the hoe.

The area under hoe cultivation in Africa is astonishing. The basic tool is the *daba*, a small hoe constructed more or less like an adze. Other implements were also invented. In Ethiopia the straight digging-stick is used. It can be modified in two ways. The most primitive modification is a pronged or forked digging-stick leading to the Konso hoe, essentially a double digging-stick. It is an appropriate implement for the very rocky soils of Konsoland in Gama-Goffu Province. A more elaborate version is used extensively in Harar Province where the digging-stick has a stone weight on top, weighing two to three kilos. The stone is perforated all the way through but is placed on the top of the digging-stick and the shaft does not go through the stone.

Most of the tools developed for African agriculture are modifications of the hoe or digging-stick but some of the adaptations are rather unusual. In Casamance, in Southern Senegal, a flat wooden spade-like implement was developed with a handle up to three metres in length. The modern version has a rim of iron attached at the working edge. The long handle provides a great deal of leverage and the spade is used to cut ditches, build dykes and level fields for rice cultivation. Gangs of people working together can move enormous amounts of soil.

Hoes are usually short-handled and the blade is often developed into a king of scoop. In the wetter parts in particular, fields are prepared by mounding. For yam cultivation, the mounds may be well over one metre in height, arranged very carefully in rows and shaped uniformly with precision. More often, the mounds are lower, irregular in shape and planted to a mixture of crops. Today, sweet potato, manioc, yams, sorghum and pearl millet may all be planted in the same mound. Another version of the mound is the long elevated ridge. These are built parallel to each other and often run the length of the field.

Mounding provides at least three benefits that are important in areas of high rainfall: drainage, aeration of the reconstructed soil, and a deeper concentration of top soil. In the Jos plateau area of Nigeria, pearl millet is sometimes transplanted during the rains so that it will mature during the dry season after the rains are over. The fields prepared for the transplants are ridged, one hoe scoop is taken from each side and placed in the centre providing three layers of top soil. The soil is very low in fertility, but this device permits at least a modest crop to be produced.

Transplanting is more common with sorghum. Seedlings are grown in a sandy bed, uprooted at the appropriate time and placed in deep dibble holes prepared by ramming a long digging-stick into moist soil. A little water is usually poured into the hole to give the seedling a start. Transplant sorghums are used on soils that are too wet during the rains to be used. They are low, often fine-textured soils that support tall grass during the rainy season. Toward the end of the rains the grass is burned off and sorghum transplanted without further land preparation. Transplantation is also used in the *décrue* agriculture practised particularly in the central delta of the Niger.

*Décrue* is a French word for which we do not have a suitable English equivalent. *Crue* means flood and the *décrue* is the reverse when the flood waters recede. A highly specialized and rather sophisticated agriculture developed in the central delta of the Niger based on the *décrue*. Rains in the Guinea highlands are heavy in the summer rainy season and waters swell the tributaries of the Niger and descend into the central delta beginning in the autumn. The slope of the delta is very slight; the topography is undulating so that during the annual floods the spreading waters follow an intricate lacework of channels, flats, ponds, marshes, and lakes resulting in a remarkably complex hydrological pattern which varies from year to year according to the height of the flood. The area covered is so vast and the slope away from the main channels so slight that the waters rise and fall very slowly. The main region of *décrue* agriculture is in the Diré–Goundam–Lake Faguibine area. There, the waters may start to rise in September, but do not reach maximum until December–January, and it is not until March that the waters have receded enough for a significant amount of planting.

The two principal crops of the *décrue* are sorghum and pearl millet. The latter is much more drought resistant and better suited to sandy soils and preferred from a culinary point of view. The water arrives last and leaves first from the highest fields reached by the flood. Since the moisture supply is the least dependable in these fields they are planted to pearl millet unless the soil is very high in clay content. As one might expect, the lower alluvial soils are likely to contain more clay than the highest ones closest to the dunes. Thus, when the flood is high, large areas of millet are planted, but with a low flood the percentage of sandy soils is much less and the relative amount of millet seeded is consequently reduced. As the waters continue to recede, the millet seeding is followed by sorghum and earlier and earlier varieties must be used in order to obtain a mature crop before the waters return in the fall. In order to hasten the life-cycle the lowest fields are often established to transplant sorghums. Fields near the river that are exposed for only a short time each year are planted to rice (Harlan and Pasquereau 1969).

It seems quite likely that *décrue* techniques were worked out by sedentary villagers near the shallow lakes of the Sahara before the lakes disappeared through desiccation. The lakes were shallow enough to expand and contract with the rainy and dry seasons. The fact that much of the West African savanna agriculture is infiltrated by *décrue* techniques suggests an earlier origin in the Sahara. It is only a suggestion, however, and confirmation would require considerably more evidence than we now have.

Planting crops on the moist banks of rivers after flooding may be rather common in many parts of the world, but an entire agricultural system based on the *décrue* is basically African in character. The system today is concentrated on the Niger delta but is practised in some modified form or other from Senegal to Tchad. The classical case of *décrue* agriculture was that of ancient Egypt along the Nile before the intervention of dams and a degree of water control. This was *décrue* agriculture *par excellence*, but since the flood came to Egypt in late summer, only cool-season crops were suitable. African domesticates such as sorghum, pearl millet and Old World cotton were not grown in Egypt until late historical times. The Nile did not flood at a suitable time for such warm-season crops.

Many of the special techniques and practices were developed to deal with a nearly universal problem of low soil fertility. In the wetter zones, the traditional shifting cultivation or bush fallow is practised. Bush is cut and burned during the dry season. One to three crops are grown in the field which is then abandoned and returned to bush for ten to fifteen years. Variations on this theme have evolved everywhere that agriculture is practised in the wet tropics: Africa, Asia, America and the South Pacific islands. Some versions are more extreme than others. In the *chitemene* system in Zambia, for example, the bush is cut from several hectares for each hectare to be farmed. The bush is carried to the farm, piled up and burned so that a greater amount of ash can be returned to the soil.

In the savanna zones and on the Ethiopian plateau, grass crop rotations are often used. One unique practice has developed on the higher parts of the Ethiopian plateau. Soil temperatures are so low that decomposition of organic matter is very slow. The organic matter builds up to the point that the soil can actually be burned. When the grass fallow is to be turned and put back into cultivation, the sod and topsoil is stacked and set on fire. The piles of soil and sod burn slowly, turn reddish like a pot and are then spread back over the surface. The practice destroys much of the organic matter, but makes phosphorus much more available (Wehrmann and Johannes 1965). African soils, in general, are very low in phosphorus.

Terracing is practised on some scale in widely separated regions. The Konso tribe of southern Ethiopia build rock-wall terraces that cover whole mountain sides from top to bottom and an enormous amount of energy is invested in order to conserve a small amount of soil. Terracing is practised in Cameroun and Nigeria, and there are archaeological evidences of terraces in Jebel Marra, Sudan, Rhodesia and elsewhere.

## AGRICULTURE AND RELIGIOUS OUTLOOK

An almost universal characteristic of mature agricultural societies is the evolution of a religious stance that revolves around the important crops, agricultural activities and the natural forces that govern yield and productivity. African agricultural societies are no exception, but the number of tribes and the richness of variations on these themes is such that we can only deal here with the broadest generalities.

The measurement and division of time are always important to agriculturalists. The number of days in a lunar month and in a solar year are usually known fairly accurately (i.e. to fractions of a day). Since they do not correspond, corrections of one sort or another must be imposed. These problems are solved in different ways by different people. The rising and setting of the Pleiades (often called 'hen and chickens' in West Africa) is commonly used as a signal for agricultural activities. The constellation was traditionally used for the same purpose in the Graeco-Roman world.

But for most African cultivators the year is divided according to the season and work to be done: the little rains, the big rains, the short dry season, the long dry season, planting time, weeding time, harvest time, brushing time, burning time, and so on. The people are very sensitive to natural signals that will tell them when the dry season is about to end and the rains begin. The behaviour of plants, insects, birds and game, the nature of winds and clouds are carefully noted and preparations made accordingly.

The natural seasons are accented by a systematic sequence of festivals, ceremonies, rites and sacrifices. Planting is usually not done until the appropriate ceremonies and sacrifices are performed. Specific rituals are associated with harvest; the burning of a field or the tilling of the soil is likely to be celebrated by particular ceremonies and rituals.

The crop that supplies the staff of life is usually featured, although a few minor crops may be involved in the ceremonies of some tribes. Among the most elaborate are the yam festivals among the yam-eating tribes and the rice ceremonies among the rice-eating tribes. Sorghum, pearl millet, fonio, tef and enset are also featured by different tribes. Other plants that may be involved in sacrifice and ceremonies include kola, coffee, sesame, finger millet, roselle, *Ceratotheca sesamoides*, and a few others. The fact that a plant is involved in ritual does not necessarily prove it to be of ancient usage by the people involved. Some of the Sahara nomads have developed elaborate ceremonies about tea in this century.

The yam festivals appear to be particularly elaborate and organized (Coursey and Coursey 1971). The Negro tribes of the yam zone have a higher level of structured social organization than the tribes either to the west or the east. The new-yam festival is the major event of the year. There is a prohibition against eating new yams until the festival is celebrated. There is usually animal sacrifice (sheep, goats, chickens) and in former years sometimes human sacrifice. Palm oil and palm wine are used and there is much ritual purification. The village is purified, stools are ritually washed or spinkled with blood, and the new yams may be ceremonially dug with a special digging-stick which must *not* be tipped with a metal point.

Some of the yam-dependent coastal tribes of the Ivory Coast have extended their ritual calendar over a period of decades. There are seven major sets of festivals or ceremonies that take place every year. There are some special celebrations (mostly age-class) that take place every seven years and others are on a ten-year cycle. There is one major event that is celebrated every seventy years. One of the yearly festivals lasts one month and another two weeks, so that a great deal of the year is taken up in celebration of the various events. To these people, time is a ceremonial concept (Niangoran Bouah 1964).

Among the rice-eating tribes of West Africa such as the Temne of Sierra Leone or Diola of Senegal, rice is the object of veneration. It is used in sacrifice before a field is to be burned, before a field is to be planted, and before and after harvest. Rice, palm oil, palm wine and, frequently, animal sacrifice are involved in the celebrations.

Among the savanna tribes sorghum and/or pearl millet are featured instead of rice or yams. The ceremonies are often elaborate, animals are sacrificed and ceremonially eaten, beer poured out in libations and ceremonially consumed. Sorghum flour is ritually sprinkled on the chief's body at burial among the Pedi (South Africa) (Quin 1959). Balls of pearl-millet flour, water and butter are offered during rain ceremonies on top of a sacred mountain by the Zaghawa (Sudan) (Tubiana 1964). Among the Massa (Cameroun) red sorghum is used in sacrifice but not white (Garine 1964). And so, with a great variety of combinations and permutations, the staff of life is woven into the religious outlook of each tribe and society.

Legends and myths of origins frequently weave in those crops that are important to a people. There is an elaborate legend about the origin of yams, others about rice, tef or sorghum. One of the most interesting is the creation myth of the Dogon because it places the selected crop at the very centre of creation. As it was to the Greeks all is made of four elements: water, air, fire and earth. These were a part of the primordial 'egg of god'. God (*Amma*) was himself in a fonio seed and broke out through the shell. Everything began from the smallest thing there is, a fonio seed. The hand of *Amma* makes all matter and all that he makes starts with a tiny fonio seed. There is something slightly atomic about this view (Griaule and Dieterlen 1965).

The Dogon cosmogony is extremely complex and involved. There are stars for the world (polar), the second eye of the world (southern cross), cowpea (Venus), pearl millet (Jupiter), roselle (Saturn), rice, fonio, and sorghum (stars near Sirius). A spiral design commonly used on altars has a fonio seed in the centre and since it is a female symbol is called 'white female fonio'. One god called *Nommo* teaches fish to swim but lives on fonio seeds.

It is not possible to elaborate further here, but it is apparent that African agricultural societies have developed a religious and cosmic understanding of the place of cultivated plants in their world and a reverence for the forces that influence success or failure of the food supply. This world view is general for most agricultural societies everywhere. Perhaps more characteristically African is the intensity of belief in witchcraft. Belief in witchcraft is by no means unique to Africa, but the extent to which one's fortunes are controlled by it in the African view is somewhat special.

Witches are people who live in your midst. They may be male or female. They have powers that are very hard to counteract. Two men live in the same village and one gets a good harvest on his farm and the other a poor one. The man with the poor yield is certain that the man with the good yield had witched his field. It is not a question of time of planting, care in weeding, selection of seed or soil improvement. Clearly it is witchcraft, because good yields are due to good weather and poor yields are due to bad weather, and both men had the same weather conditions.

The conviction is very strong. In some regions one hardly ever looks at one's neighbour's field for fear of being accused of witchcraft. Among rice-growers of West Africa nearly every field is equipped with a magic device to keep witches out or to trap them. Some people are specialists at identifying witches and others may make their services available as counterwitches. Some people admit frankly to being witches and may brag of their special powers. The conviction that power to make crops grow or not grow is conferred on particular people makes the introduction of new and improved practices very difficult. The demonstration plot of the Agricultural Officer may have a higher yield because the A.O. has more witch power, not because of better seeds or fertilizers.

# CHAPTER 10

# OLD KINGDOM, MIDDLE KINGDOM AND SECOND INTERMEDIATE PERIOD IN EGYPT

The Old and Middle Kingdoms together represent an important unitary phase in Egypt's political and cultural development. The Early Dynastic Period had seen the creation and consolidation of a type of government and court culture which, with the Third Dynasty, now reached levels of scale and competence marking the beginning of the plateau of achievement for ancient Egypt. After five centuries and following the end of the Sixth Dynasty (*c.* 2181 BC) the system appears to have faltered, and there seems to have ensued a century and a half of provincial assertion and civil war, the First Intermediate Period. But the re-establishment of powerful central government which followed, *c.* 2040 BC, seems to have been, with certain changes of nuance, the re-establishment of the patterns of the Old Kingdom. There is thus much to be said for treating certain important aspects of the Old and Middle Kingdoms together.

## DIVINE KINGSHIP

Divine kingship is the most striking feature of Egypt in these periods. In the form of great religious complexes centred on the pyramid tombs its cult was given monumental expression of a grandeur unsurpassed anywhere in the ancient Near East. Yet despite its all-pervading influence in Egyptian civilization it is not easy to present a coherent account of its doctrines, especially one which avoids mixing material from widely separated periods. One good reason for this is the Egyptian mode of communication, presenting doctrine not in the form of cogently argued treatises intended to persuade, but as series of concisely worded assertions which to us often take on a deeply cryptic appearance. The basic assertions are that the king is the holder of an office which is divine, he is 'the good god'; that he is a particular incarnation of Horus, an ancient sky and falcon god who became closely linked with the sun cult of Ra; that he is a son of Ra, the sun god, something incorporated into royal titulary from the Fourth Dynasty onwards. In the latter part of the Old Kingdom the deceased king became identified with Osiris, a god of the dead standing in a special relationship to the kingship.

For the periods under consideration three important texts, or groups of texts, deal with divine kingship. One is the Memphite Theology, known from an eighth-century BC copy of a document composed much earlier, possibly in the Old Kingdom or even before, although this is a disputed matter. It attempts to explain the geographical duality of Egyptian kingship, the positions of the gods Horus and Seth, and the supremacy of the capital city of Memphis and ultimately of its creator god, Ptah. Horus is presented as the first king of Upper and Lower Egypt, acquiring this position, having been earlier only the king of Lower Egypt, after the god Geb had given him also the kingship of Upper Egypt, hitherto held by Seth. The mythically aetiological element is so manifest that it is pointless to search for strictly historical features, particularly since the picture it suggests is at variance with the archaeological record. The second is the Ramesseum Dramatic Papyrus, dating to the reign of Senusret I (c. 1971 BC). It contains forty-six scenes, illustrated by thirty-one drawings, and includes instructions for the performance of ritual acts. The rituals, accompanied by notes on their mystic significance, seem intended for the king's accession or for his jubilee ceremony, and we may presume, therefore, that with this text we are confronted with ideas at the very heart of the Egyptians' concept of kingship. We find that it is concerned primarily with the king's relationship to Horus, Osiris, and Seth, to the very situation for which the Memphite Theology offers its 'historical' explanation. The Pyramid Texts, inscribed in the subterranean parts of the pyramids of kings from Unas to Pepy II, and Aba of the Eighth Dynasty, and of three late Sixth Dynasty queens form the third main source. Although their language is seemingly an archaic one, those who edited the texts for a particular pyramid would seem to have had sufficient working knowledge of it to adapt them to changing revelations, and even perhaps to compose. The increase and change in nature of allusions to Osiris and to Seth is one demonstration that they represent a living tradition. Their purpose is to assert the king's supremacy as a god, after rebirth, in a many-sided afterlife. Although the Horus–Osiris aspect occurs throughout, the climax of the texts is the king's identification with Ra and a cosmic life in heaven.

Because the aetiological element in Egyptian thought, which sought to explain the present by creating historical myths, was so strong, and because of the nature of Egyptian thought which did not demand that the connection between assertions be made explicit, it is difficult both to reconstruct from any text an earlier stage of development and in the end to escape from simply describing the various theological facets of kingship in the Egyptians' own terms. It is, nevertheless, evident that any functional explanation must begin with the Osiris–Horus–Seth motif which, as it were, underpinned kingship and one of whose main themes was to relate the person of the living king in the closest possible way to his country's royal ancestors, and thus to ensure that the historical process of royal succession remained always embraced within a central and authoritative body of myth. The relationship to Ra, the sun god, was presumably more of an abstract compliment to the majesty and power of the living king. Ultimately, the dogmas served to reinforce the historical process by which a central authority had come to exercise its control over a long-established network of community politics, and were themselves continually reinforced in provincial association by ritual and by the iconography of ritual which, for example, made the king responsible for the ceremonies of provincial temples.

The prominence and consistency with which the theology of divine kingship was proclaimed inhibits an understanding of the office of king as a political one, and hence the writing of history, of which we know remarkably little for the Old and Middle Kingdoms. The source material is so slight that narrative history may be considered an inappropriate literary form, particularly if one begins to suspect that the impressive facade of uniformity and continuity presented by inscriptions and monuments designed to propound the theology of divine kingship hides a complex and changing political scene.

The realities of earthly power – the usurpations and complex family relationships, of which one well-studied example is known from the Fourth Dynasty (Goedicke 1954, 1955; Reisner and Smith 1955, pp. 1–12) – imply that kingship must have been perceived on more than one level, and that some form of rationalization was necessary. It has been argued (Goedicke 1954) that this can be observed in the various terms used to refer to the king, distinguishing the human individual and the holder of divine office (the ancient justifications for the royal succession are discussed by Brunner (1955), Otto (1969) and Tanner (1974)). It is just such a varied presentation of kingship as a factor in the lives of men that is found in a body of literary texts from the Middle Kingdom and the period immediately preceding. In some of them the political nature of kingship is freely admitted, particularly in two which claim to be treatises of guidance issued by a king for his son and successor, and, in an introspective mood, contain advice on the maintenance of power and regret at the treachery to which the office is exposed. One of these texts is the Instruction of King Amenemhat (see Lichtheim 1973, pp. 135–9; Pritchard 1969, pp. 418–19; Simpson 1973, pp. 193–7). The earlier text, the Instruction to Merikara (Lichtheim 1973, pp. 97–109; Pritchard 1969, pp. 414–18; Simpson 1973, pp. 180–92), is particularly remarkable for its humanity, for its rational view of kingship, and for its emphasis on royal responsibility:

> Well tended are men, the cattle of god.
> He made heaven and earth according to their desire,
> and repelled the demon of the waters.
> He made the breath of life for their nostrils.
> They who have issued from his body are his images.
> He arises in heaven according to their desire.
> He made for them plants, animals, fowl and fish to feed them...
> He made for them rulers (even) in the egg,
> a supporter to support the back of the disabled.
> He made for them magic as a weapon to ward off what might happen.
>
> (Lines 130–7.)[1]

The position of the king from this point of view is well summed up in a more formal text of King Senusret I:

He (the god Hor-akhty) created me as one who should do that which he had done, and to carry out that which he commanded should be done. He appointed me herdsman of this land, for he knew who would keep it in order for him.[2]

Central to the Egyptians' views of kingship was the concept of *ma'at* which, whilst sometimes translatable as 'justice' or 'truth', is a term whose meaning goes far beyond legal fairness or factual accuracy. It was used to refer to the ideal state of the universe and society, and was personified as the goddess Ma'at. Although of eternal existence its operation in the world of men was the responsibility of the king, and as such must have acted as a constraint on the arbitrary exercise of power: a 'natural' morality in the place of institutional checks.

In the Middle Kingdom this was taken as a theme suitable for

---

[1] A related notion of mankind's equality is expressed in a contemporary Coffin Text, spell 1130 (*CT* VII, 461ff); see the literature cited in Grieshammer (1974, p. 167), also Lichtheim (1973, pp. 131–2) and Pritchard (1969, pp. 7–8).

[2] The so-called Berlin Leather Roll (P. Berlin 3029); see Goedicke (1974), Lichtheim (1973, pp. 115–18). For the metaphor 'herdsman' of mankind, applied to gods as much as to the king, see Blumenthal (1970, pp. 27–37), D. Müller (1961).

exposition. The Prophecy of the lector–priest Neferty (Neferyt) (Helck 1970, Pritchard 1969, pp. 444–6; Simpson 1973, pp. 234–40) does this with a simple literary device: a picture of chaos is sketched, calamities of nature and anarchy in society. Then the coming of a king who is probably Amenemhat I is described, in the form of an age when all will be healed: 'Right (*ma'at*) shall come again to its place, and iniquity/chaos, it is cast out.' (Lines 68–9.)[1] The theme of the chaotic society – characterized by social upheaval, the perversion of justice, lack of security against foreign interference, natural calamities, god's abandonment of man, personal alienation from the world – seems at this period to have become something of a literary preoccupation.[2] Nowhere is it explored with more flourish, detail and sense of immediacy than in the Admonitions of the sage, Ipuwer, which presents a carefully-studied negative image of the ideal society, one in which, presumably, *ma'at* was no longer operative (Helck and Otto 1972, cols. 65–6; Lichtheim 1973, pp. 149–63; Pritchard 1969, pp. 441–4; Simpson 1973, pp. 210–29). Indeed, the imaginative powers of its author have repeatedly beguiled people into regarding it as a piece of reporting, and thus descriptive of a period of political and social breakdown at the end of either the Old or Middle Kingdom.[3] The lamentations are apparently being addressed by Ipuwer to a king who is held responsible for what is described: 'Authority, knowledge, and truth are yours, yet confusion is what you set throughout the land.' (Lines 12, 12–12, 13.) The beginning of the text is lost, but the setting is perhaps best imagined as the court of a long-dead king, as with the Prophecy of Neferty, or the scandalous story of Neferkara and the general Sasenet (Posener 1957a). One section is, however, positive in its content, and, by extolling the pious duties of kings, seems to reflect the widespread ancient belief that piety and successful rule go together (Lines 10, 12–11, 10).

This philosophical literature is something peculiar to the Middle Kingdom and First Intermediate Period, and it has been pointed out that it contains an element of propaganda on behalf of kingship and the established order of society, disseminated via scribal schools. It must

[1] The close and illuminating parallelism between Neferty and the much later Potter's Oracle is explored by Koenen (1970); Goedicke (1977) follows a somewhat different line of interpretation.

[2] Another important text is the fragmentary lamentation of Khakheperra-senb, whose name, compounded from the prenomen of Senusret II, helps to date it; see Kadish (1973), Lichtheim (1973, pp. 145–9), Simpson (1973, pp. 230–3).

[3] For the later dating see van Seters (1964, 1966, pp. 103–20). A complicated history of redaction is suggested in Barta (1974) and Fecht (1972, 1973); these studies also assume that the key speeches are all addressed to the creator god, with none addressed to a king. A number of scholars have expressed in recent years considerable reservations about the detailed historicity of the text.

also reflect that the relationship between the humanity and divinity of kings was a major intellectual problem for the Egyptians, though with their natural mode of thought and expression being particular rather than abstract the form which their discussions took may now seem unfamiliar and be easily misunderstood. Nor, because of the absence of a comparable body of texts, is it easy to make a balanced assessement of the degree to which the character of kingship at this time differed from that of the Old Kingdom, though in an impressionistic way this latter may appear as an heroic age of absolute royal power untempered by the doubts and cares expressed in these later texts. Yet the concept of *ma'at* was certainly present then, as the force which ensures an orderly universe (for example Pyramid Texts §§ 1582, 1774–6), and as something whose performance was the responsibility of kings (Pyramid Texts §§ 265, 1774–6; the Horus-names of kings Sneferu and Userkaf were, respectively, 'Lord of *ma'at*' and 'Performer of *ma'at*'). Furthermore, the association between *ma'at* and the just society finds expression in the Instructions of the vizier Ptah-hetep of the Fifth Dynasty: 'Justice (*ma'at*) is great, its value enduring. It has not been disturbed since the days of him who created it. He who transgresses the laws is punished.' (Lines 88–90.)[1] The main concepts were thus present in this earlier time, even if some of their wider implications did not find the literary expression that has survived. Yet some measure of the greater variety with which kingship was perceived in the Middle Kingdom is manifest in the royal statues of the period, some of which portray aspects of kingship which certainly represent, whatever else, something more complex and intellectual than the positive idealism of the Old Kingdom. It is hard to avoid the conclusion that the intervening First Intermediate Period and its civil war had a disturbing intellectual effect.

## THE ROYAL FAMILY

So little is known of the history of these periods that in many cases even the reason for dynastic change is unknown. Nevertheless, it is clear that, with the exception of the Palestinian Hyksos kings of the Second Intermediate Period, this was throughout these periods primarily a matter of internal politics and largely localized around the court. Usurpation is one obvious cause, as with Amenemhat I, founder of the

---

[1] The alternative text reads 'since the time of Osiris'. The full text is translated in Lichtheim (1973, pp. 61–80), Pritchard (1969, pp. 412–18) and Simpson (1973, pp. 159–76). Compare also the short text of the vizier Neferseshemra in Lichtheim (1973, p. 17) and Sethe (1932–3, p. 198).

Twelfth Dynasty, who has plausibly been identified with a vizier of the same name in the court of the preceding king. But the circumstances surrounding such an event invariably escape us. Detailed study of the great necropolis at Giza has provided one sketchy case history of the complex family relationships which could lie behind a succession of kings, in this instance those of the Fourth Dynasty and perhaps those of the early Fifth as well (see Goedicke 1954, 1955; Helck 1968; Pirenne 1932–5, vol. II, pp. 14–23, vol. III, ii, pp. 401–2; Reisner and Smith 1955, pp. 1–12). A literary text of the late Middle Kingdom, the Westcar Papyrus, purports to cover some of the same ground and to narrate the circumstances surrounding the origin of the Fifth Dynasty, whose first three kings are here presented as being all sons of the sun god and of the wife of one of his priests (Lichtheim 1973, pp. 215–22; Simpson 1973, pp. 15–30). The prophecy of their accession and of the piety of their future rule is made before King Khufu, builder of the Great Pyramid, who appears in ancient times to have acquired a reputation for both impiety and cruelty. In this tale his impiety is characterized by a search for sacred information (precisely what is still not clear; see Hornung (1973)) which he can use in the construction of his own tomb. The story, which might be termed 'The doom of the house of Khufu', may perhaps further exemplify the theme that piety and impiety have historical consequences and thus serve to illustrate the gulf between ancient and modern historiography.

The Fourth Dynasty is virtually the only period in the Old and Middle Kingdoms where it is possible to learn much about the royal family at all, particularly on the male side. The prominence of the royal family in the great Giza necropolis in large tombs close to the pyramid of Khufu is matched by a prominence of royal sons in the administration. Spanning the entire Fourth Dynasty is a line of viziers, most of them also in charge of the king's building projects, who are kings' sons, though not destined to succeed to the throne. The last one, Sekhemkara, a son of King Khafra, probably served into the reign of Sahura of the Fifth Dynasty, but henceforth (with one exception) no vizier bears the title 'king's son', though he might be married to a princess (Pirenne 1932–5, vol. II, pp. 106–8, vol. III, i, pp. 58–65; Weil 1908).[1] Indeed, it now becomes difficult to discover much at all about royal sons, the

---

[1] An example of princesses married to other high officials is cited by Yoyotte (1950); also Pirenne (1932–5, vol. III, ii, p. 497). A further example of a vizier who was also a 'king's son' is the Teti buried near the pyramid of Pepy II, but it is very possible that he should be placed after the end of the Sixth Dynasty (Kees 1940, pp. 48–9).

problem being complicated by the occasional use of the term to cover a royal grandson, and its eventual use as a rank indicator (Baer 1960, p. 45; von Beckerath 1964, pp. 100–1; Nims 1938). Five tombs of princes of the Fifth and Sixth Dynasties appear to be known at Saqqara. Neither in size nor by position in the necropolis do they appear to differ from the vast mass of officials' tombs, and inasmuch as tombs were symbols of status give no indication that their owners had a distinctive standard of living. The titles held by this group place them in the administration, but not consistently high in the hierarchy. One, Nefer-seshem-seshat (Baer 1960, no. 275; Gauthier 1907, p. 198), was vizier and overseer of the king's works, two (Isesi-ankh: Baer 1960, no. 64; Gauthier 1907, p. 138; Ka-em-tjenent: Baer 1960, no. 530; Gauthier 1907, p. 197) were overseers of the king's works and commanders of the army, the remaining two (Ra-em-ka: Baer 1960, no. 303; Gauthier 1907, p. 197; Satju: Baer 1960, no. 419; Gauthier 1907, p. 198) had minor posts, one of a priestly nature. A sixth prince (Khesu: Baer 1960, no. 395; Gauthier 1907, p. 168), the location of whose tomb is uncertain, was an 'inspector of priests' at one of the pyramid temples, and a late Fourth or early Fifth Dynasty prince with non-executive titles was probably buried at Abu Rawash (Fischer 1961a). The relative insignificance of princes in the administration of the later Old Kingdom, a period of about three centuries, is also borne out by their general absence in texts referring to the administration, and by the surviving court lists which occur in the reliefs of the later Old Kingdom pyramid temples. Although princes are here put in a place of honour, they are given either no further title, or a priestly one: 'priest of Min' or 'lector-priest'.

In the Middle Kingdom they are even more inconspicuous. If, as seems likely from the negative results of examinations within royal pyramid enclosures, their tombs followed the same pattern and were spread out amongst the tombs of officials then the great destruction which has overtaken these necropolises helps to explain this. A re-used stele of prince Amenemhat-ankh from Dashur lists a number of titles, but all are priestly (de Morgan 1903, figs. 111, 128).[1] Again, their absence is notable from administrative records, including a lengthy fragment of a court journal (Papyrus Bulaq 18; Scharff 1920), where the royal family seems to consist of one prince, one queen, three princesses and no fewer than nine 'royal sisters'.

[1] Note also the apparently still unpublished stele of prince Hepu from el-Lisht referred to in Gauthier (1907, vol. II, p. 130, n. 25).

The small role which princes were allowed doubtless contributed to the stability of government, particularly at the sensitive moment of succession. In the Twelfth Dynasty this process was rendered more secure by the expedient of overlapping reigns, or co-regency, in which the heir was made king whilst his father was still alive and dated his reign from this moment. The co-regency of Amenemhat I and Senusret I, for example, lasted ten years. Yet, even so, a popular romance set in this period, the Story of Sinuhe, depicts the moment of Amenemhat's death as one of instability (lines R 17–24, translated in Lichtheim (1973, p. 224), Pritchard (1969, pp. 18–19) and Simpson (1973, pp. 58–9)).

The status of princes as reflected in funerary practices contrasts sharply with that of princesses, queens and royal mothers. Whilst the monumental tomb at Giza belonging to Queen Khentkawes, an ancestral figure for the Fifth Dynasty, is exceptional, substantial tombs for royal ladies immediately adjacent to the king's pyramid are a regular feature of the Old and Middle Kingdoms, sometimes, in the former period, being themselves pyramidal in form. Despite the use of titles such as 'king's daughter' or 'king's wife' it is not always clear whether their owners were queens, daughters, concubines or sisters of the king. At the pyramid of Senusret III at Dashur the tombs of royal ladies formed a carefully planned catacomb with four chapels above ground conforming to the overall design of the pyramid complex, suggesting that their burial arrangements had been made irrespective of their marriage prospects. The prominence of royal ladies in the funerary cult is also borne out by statue cults for some of them carried out by priests attached to some of the royal pyramids. The administrative archives from the pyramids of Neferirkara of the Fifth Dynasty at Abusir and of Senusret II of the Twelfth at El-Lahun attest cults for, in the former case, Queen Khentkawes (Posener-Kriéger and de Cenival (1968, pls. III, LXV); these texts are translated in Posener-Kriéger (1976)), and in the latter, for a predominantly female royal household (Borchardt 1899, Kaplony-Heckel 1971, nos. 3, 42, 73, 81, 107, 271, 287, 307, 311, 421).

The political implications of whom the king married must have been considerable, although for the Old and Middle Kingdoms there is no evidence of the later custom of the king accepting in marriage the daughter of a foreign, or at least western Asiatic, king as part of a diplomatic alignment. It used to be claimed that Nubian blood ran in the early Twelfth Dynasty kings, but this deduction is no longer necessary (Posener 1956, pp. 47–8). A somewhat similar misreading of slender evidence gave rise to a Libyan origin for one of the principal queens of King Khufu (Reisner and Smith 1955, p. 7). It is, in fact, difficult to discover much at all about the backgrounds of queens. Consequently it is hard to judge how singular is the case of two wives of Pepy I of the Sixth Dynasty, the mothers of the future kings Merenra and Pepy II. Both were daughters of a court lady married to a commoner, Khui. One of their brothers, Djau, became vizier, and one of his sons succeeded to a provincial governorship (Gardiner 1954, Goedicke 1955). But whether, as has been claimed, this marked an important historical stage in the weakening of kingship *vis-à-vis* provincial governors or whether it is merely a well-recorded example of how power was kept out of the hands of princes and courtiers is difficult to tell.[1]

## THE CENTRAL ADMINISTRATION

Throughout the Old Kingdom Egypt's capital remained at Memphis. Although some (though possibly not much) of the ancient town mound and an adjacent cemetery still survive at Mit Rahina no serious fieldwork has been done here, so that there is little with which to clothe this fact (Kemp 1976b, Montet 1957, pp. 27–34). In particular, we have no idea of the appearance, or even of the size, of the royal palace. In the Twelfth and Thirteenth Dynasties a new term for the capital is found, 'Amenemhat-ith-tawy' ('King Amenemhat (I) seizes the two lands'), often abbreviated to Ith-tawy, and written inside a symbol representing a fortified enclosure. Over a thousand years later a town of this name was still in existence, situated somewhere in the 50 km between Medum and Memphis, and providing the one specific piece of evidence that Ith-tawy may have lain separately from Memphis, even if only as a southerly suburb, or perhaps closer to el-Lisht. It has otherwise been lost.

Very few administrative documents have survived from the Old and Middle Kingdoms, too few to reveal the full structure of government at any one time, let alone to enable its historical development to be traced in any detail. In their place we must rely heavily on the very numerous titles born by officials. A major difficulty here is that titles were not necessarily descriptive of jobs, but could serve to place a man in the hierarchy of power and thus indicate his rank relative to his fellows. What, if any, duties were performed by, or expected of, a 'mouth of Nekhen' (Hierakonpolis) or an 'elder of the portal' quite escape us. On

[1] Pepy I's mother, Iuput, had a statue cult at Coptos, but whether this implies a provincial origin for her is not clear (Goedicke 1967, pp. 41–54). Another case of provincial royal connections is dealt with in Habachi (1958).

the parallels of better-documented cultures one might expect that the court did indeed contain courtiers, whose role in the decision-making and administrative process was not clearly defined though it might be considerable. The Old Kingdom court lists seem to contain many who might be in this category. One must also allow for the administrative versatility which, with organizational expertise, was a prized quality and could, in turn, place an able man in charge of armies fighting abroad, quarrying expeditions, or legal proceedings at court. At the same time one should not automatically regard holders of titles as full-time civil servants. Egyptian society, insofar as it expressed itself in inscriptions, fell into three groups: literate men wielding authority derived from the king, those subordinate to them (doorkeepers, soldiers, quarrymen, and so on), and the illiterate peasantry. Titles essentially put a man on the right side of society, the one of privilege and authority, something of which literary compositions (especially the Satire of the Trades) provide self-conscious expression. But how much of his life would be occupied by administrative tasks is often not clear. Naturally, government service was a major source of income for such a person, extending beyond daily necessities to gifts of land and to equipment (even architectural elements) for his tomb, although independent provision of such things was also boasted about (Helck 1956a, 1975, chs. 7 and 8). Further information on private wealth is, however, somewhat ambiguous, for private commercial activity is something which finds no place in the formal inscriptions which are our major source of information. Yet private ownership of land is well documented for the Old and Middle Kingdoms, often made into a trust, or pious foundation, and sometimes on a scale which would have put the owner at the centre of a major agricultural concern with substantial marketing implications. Furthermore, the archaeological record suggests a complex and extensive marketing system, occasionally even satisfying a local taste for exotic imports by producing imitations, and makes it hard to accept that this was entirely, or even largely, the responsibility of a closed government redistributive system.

One document unique in its class is a long fragment of a court journal (Papyrus Bulaq 18) from the reign of a king of the early Thirteenth Dynasty (B. Adams 1956, pp. 76–88; Scharff 1920). Partly it consists of the court accounts, and partly of summaries of official business: the arrival of parties of desert people (Medja) presumably to parley with the king; the fetching of cult images from a local temple for a festival; the suppression of some form of insurrection in a town accompanied

668

by executions. It covers a period whilst a section of the court was residing at Thebes, so should not be taken as a guide to the normal scale of court activity at the capital. Of the royal family one queen was present, one prince, three king's daughters and nine king's sisters, some of whom probably had their own households. This preponderance of female relatives of the king compares interestingly with the funerary evidence discussed above. A 'house of nurses' is also listed, containing nineteen persons and groups of children. Of officials, a central group of between eight and thirteen is regularly listed, but others make temporary appearances, boosting those on the court books by up to sixty-five extra persons on a feast day, including the vizier. These personnel-lists are primarily daily records of commodities issued, mainly bread and beer, but also meat, vegetables and date-cakes. Commodities (livestock and incense) were also supplied by the court for the cult of the god Menthu at nearby Medamud, whose statue, with that of 'Horus protector of his father', was actually brought into the palace at the time of a festival. The sources of court revenue are unfortunately given only in general terms, basically three administrative divisions: 'the department of the Head of the South',[1] 'the office of government labour', and 'the Treasury'. Consequently it is not clear whether, in this case, taxation or state-owned sources was the principal provider. A further source was the temple of Amen at Thebes.

One important function of government was the location and collection of the resources necessary for the support of the court and its projects. The agricultural resources of Egypt seem to have been divided amongst three classes of estate: owned directly by the crown; belonging to pious foundations whose relationship to the crown was a subtle one; in the hands of private individuals and liable to taxation. The most important event in revenue administration was the assessment of the country's wealth. The Palermo Stone (the main fragment is published, with commentary, in Schäfer (1902)), which covers most of the Old Kingdom, makes a generally biennial census of cattle one of the key events for describing any particular regnal year, and the very term translated as 'regnal year' (*ḥsbt*) probably derives from this event (von Beckerath 1969). A number of Old Kingdom decrees of exemption show, however, that the demands of the state left little untouched, so that revenue could be assessed even on the basis of the 'canals, lakes, wells, waterbags and trees' of an estate (Goedicke 1967, pp. 56, 72).

---

[1] An expression for the more southerly part of the Egyptian Nile Valley which possessed a notable degree of political coherence (see pp. 764–5, also Gardiner 1957).

Persons could also be obliged to work for the government, and possibly perform military service (Goedicke 1967, pp. 48–54; Helck 1975, ch. 21). From the Middle Kingdom information on taxation is very slight and relates partly to cattle and partly to land and crops, and includes a fragment of a journal recording the progress of a team measuring plots of land for an assessment involving the treasury (Helck 1975, ch. 25; Simpson 1965, p. 18; Smither 1941). Some Kahun papyri could be interpreted as household census lists, and others as detailed inventories of personal possessions, where the purpose would have been assessment for labour obligations or tax, and which would in any case have put into government hands a formidable amount of personal information. Another papyrus (Hayes 1955), of the Thirteenth Dynasty, has extracts from a prison register listing Egyptians who, having failed to meet their obligations to labour for the government, had been consigned to government farms and labour camps, so augmenting the direct resources of the crown.

One must imagine a network of government agencies spread throughout the country, attempting by bureaucratic methods total assessment and management of resources, and overlying to varying degrees the semi-autonomous functioning of pious foundations and private estates whose own 'officials' would have had as their principal concern not the facilitating of the transfer of wealth to the crown, but rather the effective operation of the foundation or estate of which they themselves were the chief beneficiaries. The resulting tension, or division of loyalty, which will become clearer when provincial government is discussed, and which may, in the Old Kingdom, have found some release in the charters of immunity, is not made explicit in formal texts because these conform to a particular view of the ideal society, where loyal service to the king was paramount.

A second major area of government was the administration of law and justice, an obligation for which justification was found in the Egyptians' concept of *ma'at*, to the extent that some high officials bore amongst their titles that of 'priest of Ma'at'. The very limited documentation that has survived is concerned very much with property, its ownership and transference to others. But it again seems typical of the Egyptian system that the judicial function was not the prerogative of a professional, specialist body reflected in a clearly defined category of official titles. It is true that the titles of certain officers and bodies, such as the 'overseer of the six great mansions', are suspected to relate entirely to the judiciary, but the basic capacity of making accepted judgements seem also to have extended generally to men in a position of authority, even where their titles seem primarily administrative.[1] Decisions both judicial and administrative (a distinction which is a modern and not an ancient one) were also made collectively, by councils or committees, sometimes possibly set up on an *ad hoc* basis (S. Gabra 1929, Goedicke 1967, pp. 133, 170; Hayes 1955, pp. 45–6). The settlement of disputes, with all that this implied in terms of favouritism, must have been a major component in the authority of provincial men of power, and the extent to which they were, in times of weak central government, answerable to no higher authority is closely tied up with the important matter of provincial autonomy of which more will be said below. It remains uncertain, however, how far there was a central body of law or precedent governing the conduct of life generally, a criminal code. The most important document is probably the same late Middle Kingdom papyrus with the prison register mentioned above which deals with the operation of criminal processes against people who have sought to avoid government-imposed labour obligations. In referring to 'laws' it cites precise variations of the general offence, and in so doing implies the existence of a very detailed code of law which has otherwise not survived.

The precise ways in which the various agencies of the central government operated varied with the course of time, and the names given to posts and departments in the Old Kingdom differ appreciably from those of the Middle Kingdom. The most important constant feature was the vizier. The principal source for this office is a set of 'instructions' which, although known only from a number of Theban tombs of the Eighteenth Dynasty, is nevertheless couched in the administrative terminology of the late Middle Kingdom. It shows that, next to the king, his was the ultimate responsibility for fiscal, administrative and judicial affairs. This all-embracing responsibility is also exemplified by surviving letters sent to and from his office at various times during the periods under review.[2] There is no really firm

[1] Note the boasts of impartial judgements made by various officials, e.g. Anthes (1928, no. 14, ll. 9–10; Sethe 1932–3, vol. I, p. 133, ll. 4, 5). Ptah-hetep lines 264–76 seems to be advice on conduct with petitioners for officials generally, 'to whom petitions are made'. The peasant in the story of the Eloquent Peasant addresses his loquacious petitions to a 'chief steward', at the 'gateway' ('rryt) and at the 'entrance (sbȝ) to the temple'. A useful note on 'rryt is given by Gardiner (1925, p. 65). The Eloquent Peasant story is translated in Lichtheim (1973, pp. 169–84), Pritchard (1969, pp. 407–10) and Simpson (1973, pp. 31–49).

[2] See Hayes (1955, pp. 71–85), Simpson (1965, pp. 20–3) and Théodoridès (1960, pp. 108–16). A verbal order is recorded in the stele of Amenysenb (Breasted 1906, pp. 342–3). For bureaucratic reaction to one such letter see Smither (1948), Théodoridès (1959); a hostile response to another is published by Gardiner (1929) and Grdseloff (1948).

evidence for the existence, as in later times, of two viziers each responsible for only one part of the country.

## PIOUS FOUNDATIONS

These were a fundamental part of ancient Egyptian society, and were intended ostensibly to ensure the perpetual maintenance of the cults of statues: of gods, of kings and of private individuals. They took the form of a fund, established by an initial donation of property, or by contracts securing income from elsewhere, often from sources belonging already to another foundation. This fund had to be kept intact as a single unit, unless modified by a specific legal agreement, and was in theory for perpetuity. The income was assigned to those who maintained the cult and to specified supporting personnel, but could, by legal agreement, also be diverted elsewhere. The basic idea behind this type of organization, which sought to bestow on sources of wealth, or trusts, a permanence and inviolability greater than mortal law could provide, has a long history in the Near East, occurring in Muslim law as the *waqf*. Like the *waqf* it was the object of a secondary show of piety: tax exemption.

In the short term, at least, the most important pious foundations in the Old and Middle Kingdoms were the pyramid temples for the royal statue cult. Whilst it is common to emphasize the mortuary character of pyramids and to see them primarily as tombs with temples ancillary to them, the way in which they were in fact organized and referred to suggests that the emphasis should be reversed, and they be regarded first and foremost as temples for the royal statues with a royal tomb attached to each, which, acting as a huge reliquary, gave enormous authority to what was, in essence, an ancestor cult and an important factor in the stability of government. This was a phenomenon repeated on differing scales throughout Egyptian society in the form of private funerary cults. Pious foundations were also, however, the basis of support for provincial temples, and, by involving locally based administrators, became another important component in provincial authority. They will therefore be discussed both in the ensuing section on pyramid temples, and in the subsequent section on provincial government.

THE MEMPHITE COURT CEMETERIES

For the Old Kingdom the court cemeteries, particularly the royal pyramid complexes, are responsible for much of our impression of the period, and had more survived from those of the Middle Kingdom the same might be true here also. Indeed, it seems impossible to write of the Old Kingdom without in some way using the court cemeteries as an index of royal power. This is certainly a valid attitude from the point of view of the ancients themselves since the hierarchic scaling of tomb size symbolized and reinforced the existing patterns of leadership: 'the very existence of impressive sepulchres in which selected individuals were buried probably validated the power of living leaders, at any rate if their claim to power was based on a relationship with the dead enshrined in the tomb' (Fleming 1973), as could be said to be so in Egypt through the Horus–Osiris myth. Furthermore, inasmuch as their construction and furnishing was the court's principal economic 'output', pyramid cemeteries provide us with the only constant and measurable index of economic activity available.

The channelling of so much of the country's resources into the building and equipping of funerary monuments, which must have represented the single largest industry running more or less continuously through the Old Kingdom and then after a break, and perhaps somewhat less so, through the Middle Kingdom, may seem unproductive on a modern scale of values, and was doubtless regulated by a mixture of ambition and a recognition of the king's role in society. Yet pyramid-building must have been essential for the growth and continued existence of Pharaonic civilization. In ancient societies innovations in technology and in other forms of practical knowledge (particularly administrative control of resources), as well as improvements in the levels of existing skills, arose not so much from deliberate research as from the 'spin-off' consequent upon developing the means to accomplish lavish court projects. The assembling of so much labour, the training of so many artists and craftsmen to mass-produce at a near-optimum standard (a striking feature of Egyptian civilization), the preferment and material rewards given to those who could accomplish these ends, all must have been responsible for much more than the enormous scale of the result. Quarrying and stone-working techniques had to be made sufficient, transport rendered adequate, a body of knowledge developed for the final handling and siting of materials and for the accurate laying out of the building, and, perhaps most important of all, an administrative apparatus created capable of directing manpower, skill and resources to a single undertaking, identified with the pinnacle of the country's power structure: the king. But equally important, the continued consumption of so great a quantity of wealth and the products of craftsmanship, both in the course of building and in the subsequent equipping of the burials, must have had only the effect of sustaining further the machinery which produced them by creating fresh demand as reign succeeded reign, an economic stimulus broadly equivalent to 'built-in obsolescence' in modern technological societies. Indeed, since trade with the outside world in ancient times was primarily a matter of securing imports rather than a search for export markets, home consumption must have assumed an equivalently greater importance in a country's economy. But whilst pyramid-building may be seen now as a vital element in Egypt's prosperity, it would be a serious mistake to introduce altruism as a motive, and to think that positive economic or social effects were intended, or even dimly perceived. Theology and the display of power were justifications enough.

Throughout the Old Kingdom the court cemeteries were constructed at sites along a 35-km stretch of the western desert edge (with an outlier at Medum), the centre of concentration being slightly to the north of Memphis. It has occasionally been suggested that the changing location really represents a regular resiting and rebuilding of the royal palace, but it seems more reasonable to see it simply as the result each time of a search for a suitably flat, firm and unencumbered site. In the Middle Kingdom new sites further to the south were chosen, as well as the old one at Dashur. Inevitably this has influenced discussion on the location of the contemporary Residence at Amenemhat-ith-tawy (see p. 667).

The relative sizes of the royal pyramids, expressed as volumes, are given in fig. 10.1 Even as a rough index to a major economic activity a number of complicating factors must be noted. The Fourth Dynasty pyramids are of massive masonry blocks throughout, originally with a carefully smoothed casing of fine limestone and sometimes of granite as well. But from the reign of Sahura of the Fifth Dynasty the core behind the facing was of smaller and looser stone rubble and even gravel. In the Twelfth Dynasty, from the reign of Senusret I, the core was constructed as a series of limestone casemates filled with mud bricks, an interesting method of reinforced construction which produced a satisfactory scale, finish and stability for a lesser expenditure. The movement away from a megalithic core is in one sense a decline in standards, but when set against the history of more recent building

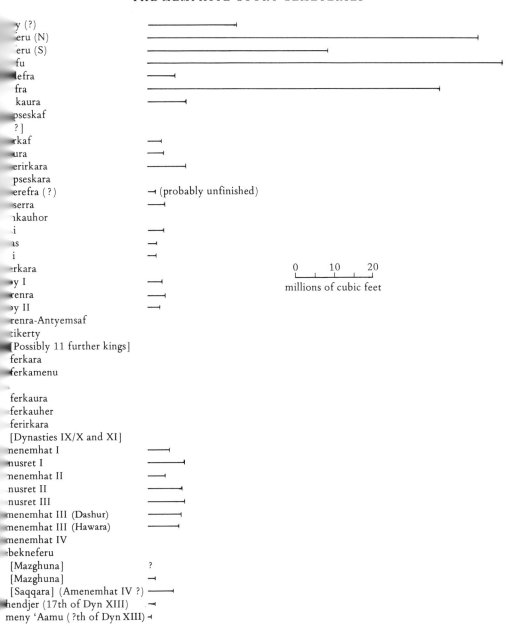

y (?)
eru (N)
eru (S)
fu
efra
fra
kaura
pseskaf
?]
rkaf
ura
erirkara
pseskara
erefra (?)   → (probably unfinished)
serra
ikauhor
i
as
i
erkara
y I
renra
y II
renra-Antyemsaf
ikerty
[Possibly 11 further kings]
ferkara
ferkamenu

ferkaura
ferkauher
ferirkara
[Dynasties IX/X and XI]
nenemhat I
nusret I
nenemhat II
nusret II
nusret III
menemhat III (Dashur)
menemhat III (Hawara)
menemhat IV
bekneferu
[Mazghuna]   ?
[Mazghuna]   →
[Saqqara] (Amenemhat IV ?) ——→
hendjer (17th of Dyn XIII)  →
meny 'Aamu (?th of Dyn XIII) →

0    10    20
millions of cubic feet

Fig. 10.1   Volumes of pyramids from the Fourth to the Thirteenth Dynasties. (Dimensions based on Edwards 1961a; the remains of the pyramid of Ameny 'Aamu at Dashur are published in Maragioglio and Rinaldi 1968.) A standard angle of 52° was assumed, but in practice the angle varied between about 49° and 57° although the consequences would be scarcely noticeable at this scale (see Lauer 1974, pp. 342–3).

technology with its constant search for more economic means of achieving a given result, has an undeniably rational basis. Each pyramid was also part of a building complex, which might represent a considerable volume of masonry, but one more difficult to measure, and with much of its inner wall surfaces decorated with painted low-relief carving. Consideration of the Fifth Dynasty pyramids must also include the solar temple which seems to have been a further extension of each pyramid complex and emphasizes that pyramid temples were intended as major cult establishments in their own right. The temples and other surrounding structures of the Middle Kingdom pyramids have been almost completely obliterated, but their scant traces do not suggest in most cases a decline of scale. Indeed, the vast building which the Classical world knew as the Egyptian Labyrinth seems to have been nothing else than the mortuary temple of Amenemhat III's pyramid at Hawara. But when all these factors are considered one is still left with the dramatic difference in the scale of the resources deployed on the Fourth Dynasty pyramids, for when size is doubled volume is increased ninefold, with the result that the Great Pyramid of Khufu contains nearly thirty times the bulk of the pyramid of Userkaf, for example. The background to the scaling-down of pyramids after the reign of Khafra is unknown and probably unknowable, but the consequences cannot be observed to have been adverse for the country, possibly because the surplus capacity for organization and for the utilization of resources was absorbed by the provinces, whose level of prosperity and local identity seem to have risen in the later Old Kingdom. In a sense, the continued history of Old and Middle Kingdom civilization contained an important element of freewheeling on the apparatus created through the building of the early pyramids, enabling skills and administrative machinery to be more widely and variably diffused.

The cults at pyramid temples were maintained by pious foundations. Two sets of documents have survived dealing with the daily administration of two of them: of King Neferirkara of the Fifth Dynasty at Abusir (Posener-Kriéger 1976, Posener-Kriéger and de Cenival 1968), and of King Senusret II of the Twelfth at El-Lahun (Borchardt 1899, Kaplony-Heckel 1971a), and in both cases belonging to a period when the cults had already been in existence for some time. The Neferirkara archive reveals a world of detailed and very professional administration. Elaborate tables provide monthly rosters of duty: for guarding the temple, for fetching the daily income (or 'offerings') and for performing ceremonies including those on the statues, with a special roster for the important Feast of Seker. Similar tables list the temple equipment, item by item and grouped by materials, with details of damage noted at a monthly inspection. Other records of inspection relate to doors and rooms in the temple building. The presentation of monthly income is broken down by substance, source and daily amount. The commodities are chiefly types of bread and beer, meat and fowl, corn and fruit. The sources are listed as: *r-š*-estates of Neferirkara and of the long-dead King Khufu,[1] *pr*-estates of the deceased Queen Khentkawes and a princess Irenra, possibly some establishments of Kings Neferefra and Djedefra (Posener-Kriéger and de Cenival 1968, pl. 45), the palace, the nearby solar temple of Neferirkara, and the towns of Iushedefwi and Djed-Sneferu (Maragioglio and Rinaldi 1971). This multiplicity of elements in the supporting pious foundation, involving sharing with other establishments, seems typical of Egypt at this and other periods. In the formal decorative scheme of pyramid temples the grants of land or funerary domains included in the foundation are personified as offering-bearers and preserve some idea of the numbers of units involved. The most complete comes from the valley temple of Sneferu at Dashur where they are grouped also into nomes, or administrative districts. In Upper Egypt thirty-four estates are distributed amongst ten nomes (with the record for eight nomes missing); in Lower Egypt the record is fully preserved for only a single nome and numbers four estates (fig. 2c). Only rarely are the sizes given, and they vary from 2 arouras (about 0.5 hectare[2]) to $110\frac{1}{3}$ arouras (about 28 hectares) (Goedicke 1976a, pp. 351–69; Helck 1975, pp. 42–4; Jacquet-Gordon 1962, pp. 3, n. 2, 151).

The sharing of revenue extended to private funerary cults, some of which, in the Old Kingdom, enumerate royal domains amongst the sources for their own foundations. One sheet from the Neferirkara archive contains a list of such deceased beneficiaries, headed by Queen Khentkawes, but otherwise belonging to officials whose cults receive portions of meat (Helck 1974a, p. 85; Posener-Kriéger and de Cenival 1968, pls. 45B, 65). The palace is listed as another recipient, albeit a nominal one, as also is the solar temple. Otherwise the income was disposed of on a daily accounted basis to the temple staff as their salary, in the form of bread, beer, meat, cloth, and so on.

The El-Lahun archive remains are, unfortunately, published only par-

---

[1] The technical definition of this type of estate remains unclear; see Goedicke (1967, pp. 69–72), Helck (1974a, p. 66), Kaplony (1972, pp. 56–7).

[2] It should be noted that Baer (1956) has proposed much larger units of land measurement, with an aroura of 8.2 hectares.

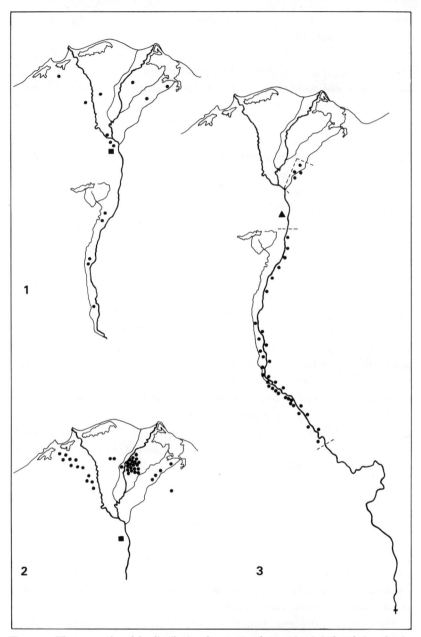

Fig. 10.2　Three examples of the distribution, by nomes, of estates in pious foundations for the mortuary cults of: (1) Khnumenty, an official of the Fifth Dynasty with tomb at Giza, one of whose titles was 'overseer of all the works of the king'; (2) Mehu, an official of the early Sixth Dynasty with tomb at Saqqara, whose titles included those of 'vizier' and 'governor of Upper Egypt', despite the striking concentration of estates in the delta; (3) King Sneferu, first king of the Fourth Dynasty. The list derives from his southern pyramid at Dashur, and is incomplete, see p. 677, also p. 697. (Examples from Jacquet-Gordon 1962, pp. 310–12, 419–26.)

tially, but the available information indicates a broadly similar type of administration and record-keeping, with monthly schedules of personnel on duty, of male and female musicians and singers and of slaves, lists of temple equipment grouped by material with notes of inspection, and accounts of temple income. Of note are fragmentary lists of statues which include not only the king for whom the temple was made (Senusret II) and mainly female members of his family, but also other kings, private individuals, and the reigning king (Senusret III) and his family too (Borchardt 1899, Kaplony-Heckel 1971a, nos. 3, 42, 73, 81, 107, 108, 271, 287, 307, 311, 421), a multiplicity of recipients which is found duplicated in provincial temples. Archaeology has provided the setting for the very substantial community involved in the El-Lahun archive, in the form of the mud-brick town commonly called Kahun, which does, however, appear to have been atypically large, and should probably be seen as part of an ancient conurbation which centred around the site of the modern town of El-Lahun in the cultivation. Other known pyramid towns seem to have been a lot smaller.

The size and monumentality of pyramid complexes proved to be no guarantee for the permanence of their cults. Two examples will illustrate their later history, and the curiously casual way in which the formal layouts of the complexes could be treated.

### *Menkaura of the Fourth Dynasty at Giza*[1]

It had evidently been planned that the pyramid and valley temples be built in the prevailing megalithic tradition, and their completion in mud brick was presumably a consequence of the king's premature death. Modern excavation of the pyramid temple was not extensive enough to determine if an area of living-quarters accompanied it. Nevertheless, fragments from two inscriptions, probably decrees, bearing the Horus-name of King Merenra of the Sixth Dynasty indicate that the temple was in use late in the Old Kingdom. The valley temple, although mostly of mud brick, had remained remarkably well-preserved, and presents a strange history which says much for the gap that could develop between plans and practice, and between the products of superlative craftsmanship and the way they were treated (fig. 10.3). Outside the

[1] See Hassan (1943, pp. 53–62), Reisner (1931) and Wildung (1969a, pp. 213–17). The relationship to Menkaura's pyramid of the apparently large settlement lying to the south of its causeway is not clear (A.-A. Saleh 1974). See also Goedicke (1967, pp. 16–21, 78–80) and Helck (1957, p. 108).

Sanctuary

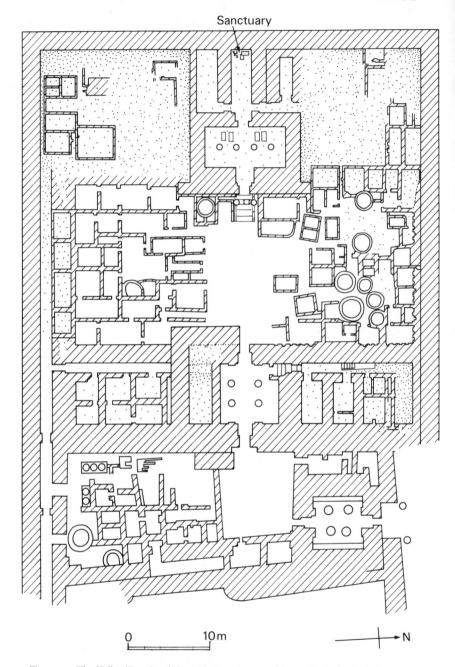

0        10m        ———————|—N

Fig. 10.3   The Valley Temple of King Menkaura's pyramid complex in its final phase towards the end of the Old Kingdom. The stippled areas are those whose floor levels had probably risen significantly through the accumulation of rubbish.

front of this temple an annexe had been built, part of which had been occupied by an irregular group of houses. Not long afterwards, these houses spread within the great open court of the temple itself. From then onwards most of the temple except for the sanctuary was allowed to decay, and in places was demolished to make room for the expanding village which gradually buried the lower parts of the temple. A good deal of temple equipment was found by the excavators still in the original storerooms, buried in this dust and rubble. Amongst it were the slate triads which represent some of the finest work of Old Kingdom sculptors. Much of this equipment had been subject to careless treatment amounting to vandalism. Many statues had been smashed up to provide material for the manufacture of model vessels which were a standard part of Old Kingdom burial equipment in the Memphite area, something suggestive of a minor industry to supplement the community's income. The process of decay had been hastened by a flood from a sudden storm. An attempt at renovation was made, but only on top of all this rubbish. This recognized the existence of the village, surrounded it with a new wall, and built a new sanctuary and gatehouse on the sites of the original ones. One still entered the sanctuary, therefore, immediately after having walked from the gatehouse along a path between the two groups of irregular cottages. On the mud floor of the antechamber to the new sanctuary four beautiful life-size statues of Menkaura were resited. The offering-place was found more or less intact. It consisted of an altar about 50 cm high made from a worn slab of alabaster resting on two rough upright stones with a crude libation basin beside it. Nearby were four unfinished diorite statuettes of the king lying on their side, having originally perhaps stood on the altar and thus been the object of the cult in this last phase of the temple's existence.

The date and circumstances of this rough-and-ready cult being carried on in a dingy chamber at the back of a tightly packed mud village are clear both from the associated archaeological material, which seems not to extend beyond the end of the Old Kingdom, and from a decree of King Pepy II of the Sixth Dynasty, found in the floor debris of the gateway, exempting the pyramid town from certain obligations and appointing an official to it. It thus demonstrates official recognition of this site as being part of the pyramid town at a date very close to the end of the Old Kingdom.

After the end of the Old Kingdom the site appears to have been abandoned and the cult of King Menkaura to have ceased entirely.

### Sneferu of the Fourth Dynasty at Dashur

King Sneferu appears to have possessed two pyramids at Dashur, served by more than one community (Fakhry 1959, 1961; Helck 1957, pp. 106–7; Wildung 1969a, pp. 105–52). The only one of these so far documented by excavation was attached to the valley temple of the southern, or 'bent' pyramid. As at the Menkaura valley temple a part, at least, of the town had been constructed within the main enclosure wall, in this case huddled in the space between the wall and the temple itself. Its pottery is primarily Old Kingdom, though some may have been later. Members of the priesthood of Sneferu are attested to the end of the Old Kingdom, buried mostly at Giza and at Dashur itself. Unlike Menkaura, however, King Sneferu went on to become a minor member of the wider Egyptian pantheon, even given a cult at the Sinai turquoise-mines. At Dashur his name began to be invoked in funerary prayers on private objects, and at least ten individuals are known to have held an office in his cult during the Middle Kingdom. One of them, Teti-em-saf, also held offices in the cults of Kings Pepy II and Teti of the Old Kingdom, as well as Amenemhat I and Senusret I of the Twelfth Dynasty, and belonged to an apparently affluent family buried adjacent to the pyramid of Teti at Saqqara. The nature of the cult's income at this time is not known, but it was presumably much reduced from the extensive estates which the Sneferu foundation had owned at the beginning.

This later cult of Sneferu continued to be celebrated in the offering-chapel in front of the pyramid, apparently without statues at all. Although decay and modification had produced a confused layout, the little chapel remained intact, and was discovered still with a pair of roughly cut stone offering-stands bearing the names and titles of Middle Kingdom priests, and a Middle Kingdom pottery dish still containing charcoal. The cult at Dashur did not apparently survive longer.

A further interesting case history is provided by the cult of Teti of the Sixth Dynasty (Firth and Gunn 1926; Helck 1957, p. 110; Porter and Moss 1927, vol. III, pp. 129–46; Quibell 1907). A sequence of priests – men whose small tombs show them to have been of modest means – spans the First Intermediate Period.[1] Early in the Twelfth Dynasty the interests of the more affluent Teti-em-saf family mentioned above and buried beside Teti's pyramid at Saqqara extended for a time

[1] There is considerable difficulty in dating many of the stelae, though it is probably too negative to follow the view of Schenkel (1965, p. 91). A note on the dating of the tomb of Ihy and Hetep, of the Teti-em-saf family, is provided by Simpson (1963a).

to include the priesthoods of other surviving Old Kingdom cults as well. As a minor deity (in the form Teti-Merenptah) this king is known from a votive stele and a statue of the Ramesside period over a thousand years after his death.

There are other case histories which could be written, and this is, indeed, a subject on which relatively little research has been done although it provides an important reflection on the capacities and priorities of the central government. Their histories evidently varied considerably from case to case, with accidents of local popularity playing a not insignificant role. At various times their stonework was used as quarries. The pyramid enclosure of Amenemhat I is known to have contained re-used blocks from certain Old Kingdom pyramid complexes, specifically of Khufu, Khafra, Unas and possibly Pepy II (Goedicke 1971). The end of the Old Kingdom marked an important terminal stage, as did the end of the Middle Kingdom in respect of the Twelfth Dynasty pyramids, though their later histories are far less well documented. The temptation for weak governments lacking the authority for large-scale provincial revenue collection to fall back on using the accumulated treasures of court cemeteries as a means of supplementing their income is obvious, although this cannot be documented.[1]

## PROVINCIAL EGYPT

The archaeological evidence for the nature and distribution of early settlements in Egypt is sparse and unsatisfactory, particularly as it concerns those which were not, like the pyramid towns, artificial developments; although it is likely, to judge from textual sources, that Egyptian administrative policies had an important influence generally on the shape, size and location of settlements, even if it cannot be judged whether, say, the groupings of estates in the larger pious foundations were built around existing settlement patterns or, alternatively, interfered with them. At four sites in Upper Egypt the evidence concerning towns of regional importance is reasonably clear, in each case at an important cult centre with a long subsequent history, though one of them, Abydos, was not a nome capital.

[1] According to the testimony of an official inspection carried out in the reign of Ramesses IX (c. 1103 BC), two Eleventh Dynasty royal tombs at Thebes were still, after nine centuries, intact. If this is to be believed, it must also be remembered that Thebes probably saw a degree of administrative continuity denied to the Memphite area (Peet 1930, pp. 28–45). In particular, the tomb of Nebhepetra Menthuhetep II, one of the two in question, became a cult centre of some importance (Arnold 1974a, pp. 92–5).

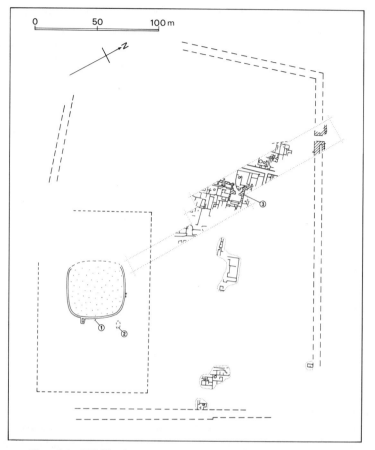

Fig. 10.4   Plan of the Old Kingdom town at Hierakonpolis, as revealed by partial excavation.

1   Part of a granite doorway of King
Khasekhemwy of the end of the Second
Dynasty

2   Site of the 'Main Deposit' of discarded
temple equipment

3   Mud-brick gateway from the Early
Dynastic palace incorporated into the
later houses

(1) *Hierakonpolis.* Almost immediately beneath the broken modern
ground level an Early Dynastic and Old Kingdom town has been
located over an area of at least 200 by 300 m (fig. 10.4), apparently
reaching its maximum extent during the Old Kingdom (Kemp 1977b).
It consists of a tightly packed mass of mud-brick housing crossed by
narrow streets, and protected by a heavy town wall, 9.5 m thick in its
final stage, following an irregular rectilinear course. Towards the
southern corner stood a mound of sand behind a rough stone revetment,
and this probably served as the foundation for the temple. This latter

684

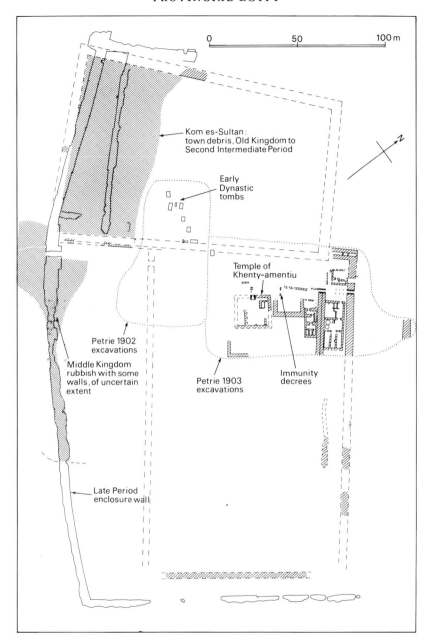

Fig. 10.5   Plan of the town and temple enclosure remains at Abydos.

had been removed in later rebuildings, but part of a granite doorway of King Khasekhemwy of the end of the Second Dynasty, statues and votive objects were found buried in nearby caches, particularly the 'Main Deposit'. Some of the houses towards the centre had incorporated the standing remains of a great brick gateway of the Early Dynastic Period which, to judge from its decorative niched style, had been a palace.

(2) *Abydos*. The earliest strata go back to the Early Dynastic Period. But, as at Hierakonpolis, the Old Kingdom saw rapid expansion and the building of heavily walled enclosures, in this case numbering two: one for the temple (dedicated to the local god Khenty-amentiu), which was made up of a complex of small brick buildings, and an adjoining one for the town which gradually, through to the end of the Middle Kingdom, grew into a stratified mound (fig. 10.5).

(3) *Elephantine*. This had a special role as a frontier town and trading centre, and stood at the southern tip of the most northerly of the granite islands which form the First Cataract.[1] Partly it was built over and around a series of irregular granite ridges which raised it high above the river, and gave it an irregular oval plan (fig. 10.6). It had a mud-brick wall and at least one gateway lined with stone. To the west lay what appears to have been a separate unwalled extramural settlement. Subsequent to this first Old Kingdom phase the town steadily expanded and fresh encircling walls were built, possibly now incorporating the northern part as well. In addition to at least one temple of modest proportions, which began in the Early Dynastic Period as a cleft between boulders, and is later found dedicated to the goddess Satet, a popular shrine existed dedicated to a deceased local dignitary of the late Old Kingdom called Heka-ib. The main necropolis from Elephantine lay in the cliffs of the western bank, the Qubbet el-Hawa, but some Middle Kingdom graves have been found on the island.

(4) *Tell Edfu*. The record here is more difficult to follow, although, as the town is built on a low hill of rock, the base of the stratigraphic sequence is readily accessible (fig. 10.7). The earliest remains visible are a part of the Old Kingdom town and its enclosure wall lying not far to the west of the great Ptolemaic temple which perhaps now covers the earliest site. Subsequently the town expanded, and a fresh wall was laid out on a complicated plan using curved sections, part of which ran over the Old Kingdom cemetery. This was subsequently doubled,

---

[1] As the 'doorway to the foreign lands' where tribute from Nubia was collected, Elephantine is discussed by Edel (1962, 1971, p. 11).

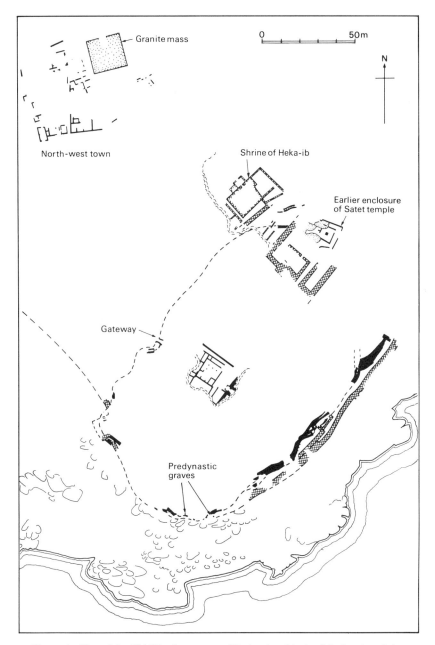

North-west town

Granite mass

50 m

N

Shrine of Heka-ib

Earlier enclosure
of Satet temple

Gateway

Predynastic
graves

Fig. 10.6 Plan of the Old Kingdom town at Elephantine. Much of the interior of the walled enclosure is still covered with later debris.

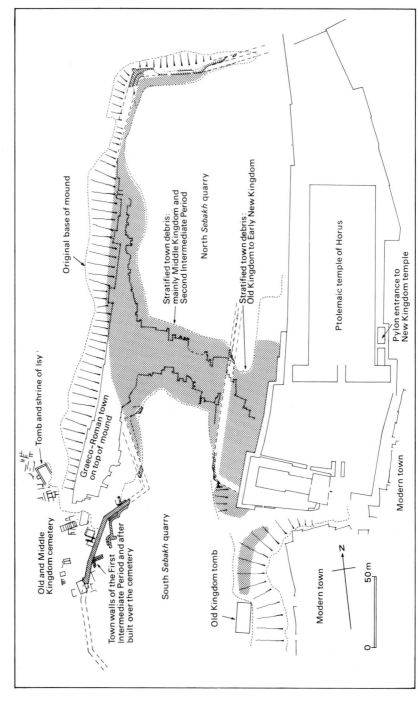

Fig. 10.7 The remains of Tell Edfu, partly buried beneath the modern town and partly destroyed by quarrying for *sebakh* (fertilizer). A small section of the early cemetery and town wall complex has been exposed.

Original base of mound

Stratified town debris: mainly Middle Kingdom and Second Intermediate Period

North *Sebakh* quarry

Stratified town debris: Old Kingdom to Early New Kingdom

Tomb and shrine of Isy'

Graeco-Roman town on top of mound

Old and Middle Kingdom cemetery

Town walls of the First Intermediate Period and after built over the cemetery

South *Sebakh* quarry

Old Kingdom tomb

Ptolemaic temple of Horus

Pylon entrance to New Kingdom temple

Modern town

Modern town

N

0

50 m

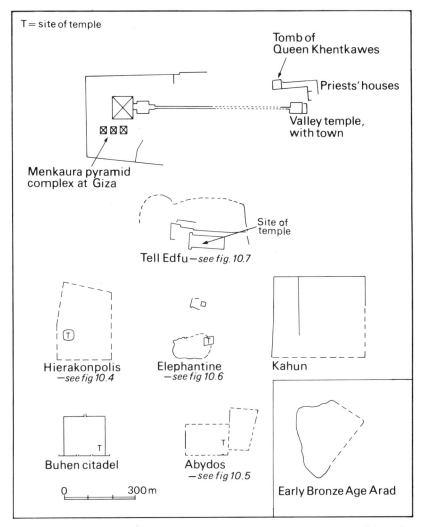

Fig. 10.8 Comparative sizes of Old and Middle Kingdom settlements, with inset of the outline of Early Bronze Age Arad in southern Palestine for comparison with Palestinian urbanism. T, site of temple.

but on a less tortuous course. Within the walls a stratified mound accumulated to the early new Kingdom. Edfu also possessed its own equivalent to the Heka-ib shrine based on a tomb of the vizier Isi of the early Sixth Dynasty (Alliot 1937–8, Edel 1954, Yoyotte 1952).

In the Nile Delta the record is even poorer, but sufficient has been found at widely scattered sites (principally Abu Ghalib, Mendes, Tell

Basta and Ezbet Rushdi) to show that it possessed settlements and a culture of an entirely Egyptian character.

All of these towns appear somewhat small on an absolute scale which takes into consideration the urbanism of Classical and modern times (fig. 10.8). But when set against a total population for Egypt which has been estimated to have fluctuated during the Old and Middle Kingdoms at around one and one and a half million (Butzer 1976, pp. 81–5), their absolute sizes seem to call for little special comment, except perhaps for the relative magnitude of the government-created town of Kahun, which itself contrasts with other known pyramid communities. It is a not uncommon pattern in non-industrial societies for much of the population to be divided (though not equally) between one very large city and numerous small rural villages. Although the size of ancient Memphis at any one period is very difficult to ascertain at present, such evidence as exists suggests for ancient Egypt a much more even distribution for the population, who would have lived in settlements ranked hierarchically in size down from the main provincial towns such as those described above which seem to have been spaced fairly evenly along the Nile Valley. It is likely, however, that this pattern was itself a development of the Old Kingdom when in Upper Egypt, at least, towns seem to have gone through a dynamic expansive phase which presumably corresponded with the growth of local autonomy which is separately documented (see pp. 694–7). By contrast, the Predynastic period may have been characterized by a primate distribution based, in Upper Egypt, on a very few towns (e.g. Naqada and Hierakonpolis).

In some other countries where civilization developed in a floodplain provincial autonomy was the principal political development, giving rise to a civilization of city states. In Egypt provincial aspirations were normally contained within a system centred on a single royal government, whose paramount authority was expressed through the doctrines of divine kingship, containing theological elements derived from various parts of the country, through monumental building and through statue cults at provincial temples. As the local representative centres of court culture and authority, as well as being the centres of pious foundations and thus of locally important economic cycles, provincial temples were elements of great importance in the towns. Yet there is a striking contrast between the size and monumentality of pyramid temples and these temples for provincial cults, something which was probably not altered until New Kingdom times. This was to some extent apparent from the towns discussed above, especially

Abydos and Elephantine, and can be seen elsewhere, too. At Tell Basta and Ezbet Rushdi in the Nile Delta relatively modest mud-brick temples have been found dating respectively to Pepy I of the Sixth Dynasty and Amenemhat I of the Twelfth. In the former building limestone pillars had supported the roof. Beneath the Middle Kingdom level at Medamud the remains have been found of a bizarre shrine consisting partly of walls and doorways of mud brick and partly of two earthen mounds each covering a chamber and a winding corridor.[1] Furthermore, the re-used stonework in later temples seems to confirm this picture: of essentially mud-brick structures employing stone only for columns, doorways, stelae and statues. Their most impressive aspect was probably their massive brick enclosure walls, containing monumental stone gateways, a persistent feature of Egyptian temple design given theological significance (Reymond 1969, pp. 239–40, 280–1, 326).[2] An early Middle Kingdom papyrus containing building accounts from a provincial temple seems to bear this out (Simpson 1963b, ch. 5). Three exceptions may be noted: a kiosk of Senusret I at Karnak (Porter and Moss 1972, vol. II, pp. 61–3), a shrine of Sankhkara Menthuhetep on the mountains of western Thebes (Porter and Moss 1972, vol. II, p. 340; Vandersleyen 1975, pp. 155–6), and the late Twelfth Dynasty temple at Medinet Ma'adi in the Fayum (Naumann 1939, Vandersleyen 1975, pp. 159–60). But these, whilst built of stone throughout, are quite small.[3]

On the establishment or enrichment of the estates which made up the pious foundations for the local deities there is little inscriptional record, possibly because much of this had been done in very early periods. The Palermo Stone does record, however, amidst substantial donations of land to the cult of Ra in the Fifth Dynasty, also donations to the cults of Ptah, Nekhbet, Uadjyt and Hathor. It also makes a noteworthy event of the fashioning of divine images, and the curious dearth of statues of gods to have survived from pre-New Kingdom times suggests that they were normally of precious materials, though possibly quite small.[4] Far more prominent is the evidence for pious

[1] Robichon and Varille (1940); the associated objects seem to date to between the late Old Kingdom and the early Middle Kingdom. On the early forms of temples see also Reymond (1969, pp. 264–6).

[2] A Middle Kingdom commemoration of the building of a large enclosure wall at El-Kab, recorded as a deed of royal piety, is published by Legrain (1905). The strange royal name is evidently a mistaken transformation of the Horus-name of Senusret I into a prenomen. See also n. 1 on p. 715.

[3] The uninscribed stone temple at Qasr el-Sagha, which can also be attributed to the Middle Kingdom (see Vandersleyen 1975, p. 160), being near a quarry site, must be counted a special case.

[4] Possible exceptions are recorded in Ertman (1972), H. W. Müller (1960) and Wildung (1972), but these may come from pyramid temples. A possible Middle Kingdom example is given in Evers

foundations for statues of kings and private individuals. When housed in the local temple they might have their own little shrine, or they might be in a specially built temple of their own, in either case called a *ḥwt-kʒ* ('soul house') (Goedicke 1967, p. 44; Helck 1975, pp. 46–7; Fischer 1964, pp. 21–2). The small temple of Pepy I at Tell Basta is designated thus (Fischer 1958, Habachi 1957); another example was found at Dendera (Daressy 1917). Numerous statues of kings are known to have existed in provincial temples,[1] and the arrangements of which they were the centre are exemplified by a decree of Pepy II establishing a pious foundation for a copper statue of himself in the temple of Min at Coptos. A financial arrangement of a different sort – a reciprocal one between temple and central government – is attested for the temple of Amen at Thebes in the Thirteenth Dynasty (Scharff 1920), but how normal this was cannot be ascertained.

The nature and operation of pious foundations in the provinces is made fairly explicit in a number of texts, mostly from private tombs, which also show the intimate link that could exist between a local temple and statue cults based on tombs. It would have been highly advantageous for the control of and for the benefits from such foundations to remain in a local family as a virtually hereditary matter, and this was evidently very often the case. Indeed, as will be outlined below, for much of the time considered in this chapter it was probably difficult to be a man of much importance in the provinces unless associated with the local temple in some way. A good example of family involvement is provided by Nika-ankh at Tehneh in the Fifth Dynasty, a man who combined service for the central government with the office of chief priest in the local temple of Hathor (Breasted 1906, pp. 99–107; Goedicke 1970, pp. 131–48; Helck 1974a, pp. 31–4; Mrsich 1968, pp. 70–85; Pirenne 1932–5, vol. II, pp. 372–8; Pirenne and Stracmans 1954). He had been made chief priest by a decree of King Userkaf and placed in charge of the income of the temple's own foundation. A table lists twelve of his sons, his wife, and a period of time (mostly of one month) when each would serve in the temple, and presumably thereby become entitled to

(1929, fig. 26), but this may be a statue of Amenemhat III himself. For the use of precious materials in divine images see the inscription of Ikhernefret (Breasted 1906, p. 299) and the golden Horus Image from Hierakonpolis (Quibell 1900, pls. XLI–XLIII; Quibell and Green 1902, p. 27, pl. XLVII).

[1] Examples in stone and copper were found at Hierakonpolis (Quibell 1900, pls. XXXIX–XLI; Quibell and Green 1902, pls. L–LVI). Other examples are from Dendera (Daumas 1973) and a dyad of Sahura possibly from Coptos (Hayes 1953a, pp. 70–1, fig. 46). The inscriptional evidence is presented in Goedicke (1967, pp. 81–6), Helck (1978) and Petrie (1903, pl. XXIV). The cult of early kings at Karnak recorded by the king-list there may perhaps have involved individual statues (Bothmer 1974, Wildung 1969b, 1974).

a share of the income, as well as the division amongst them of a piece of land (roughly 16.5 hectares) given by King Menkaura some 25 years earlier for the specific support of this temple's priests. A second table allots the same sons a month's service in a separate private foundation as well, made for a deceased local man called Khenuka, possibly one of Nika-ankh's forbears, and some further sons are depicted as being in charge of Nika-ankh's own foundation. Extracts from the deeds of the mortuary foundations place his eldest son in charge, make the arrangements hereditary, prohibit the foundations from being divided up, and exempt these sons from any obligations beyond the provision of offerings.

A second highly informative set of documents is preserved in the tomb of Hapdjefa (I) at Asyut, from the reign of Senusret I (Goedicke 1971–2, Reisner 1918, Théodoridès 1968–72, 1971a). Hapdjefa was both a 'town governor' ($ḥзty$-$ʿ$) and chief priest of the local temple of Wepwawet. He draws a careful distinction between his property from this dual position: that which came with the office of governor, and that which he had inherited from his father. The latter included the office of chief priest, in charge of temple revenue, but already Hapdjefa had arranged a pious bequest to the temple of part of the annual harvest tax from the rented lands belonging to his governorship, following a local practice of the common people. By means of ten legal contracts he created a pious foundation centred on one or more statues of himself housed, at least for part of the time, in the temple, but also involving his tomb. In return for performing ceremonies on various feast days and making offerings (which augmented temple income) certain specified persons received payments in the form of gifts of land from his paternal estate, various forms of temple income, and some of the diverted harvest tax. The documents explain how people who had a period of service in the temple received a regular income from it: each day's service in the year entitled one to $\frac{1}{360}$ of each day's income (exemplified also in the Kahun papyri; see Helck (1975, pp. 164–5)). Hapdjefa had included a batch of twenty-seven 'temple days' in the foundation. The beneficiaries were primarily the temple staff, including the chief priest, which office, as the sequence of tombs at Asyut shows, remained in Hapdjefa's own family for several generations. One might further anticipate that most of these persons were members of Hapdjefa's family or household. But even if not, they were certainly recipients of his patronage, and the prospect of this must have added to his authority during his life.

As with the sizes of estates making up royal mortuary foundations so the land components of private pious foundations could vary greatly in size, from 4 or 5 arouras to more than 200 (i.e. from 1 to over 50 hectares). All such resources seem to have been at the ultimate disposal of the central government. This led to a second-stage act of piety: the granting of a royal charter of immunity from all kinds of imposition. All examples come from the Old Kingdom, from which one might deduce that this was, in later times, regarded as an unnecessary source of abuse or conflict. The surviving examples concern the temple of Khenty-amentiu at Abydos, a statue cult of the king's mother Iuput at Coptos, the pyramid temple of Sneferu at Dashur, the valley temple of Menkaura, and statue cults of Queens Meryra-ankhnes and Neit. But before concluding that in this way kings were cutting themselves off from their own revenues, one might consider the effectiveness of these charters in the light of a letter purporting to have been written by King Pepy II in which an order for the procurement of supplies for a returning trade mission from Nubia is applied, amongst several establishments, to 'every temple – without making an exception amongst them'.[1] Similarly the great national army raised by Uni in the reign of Pepy I included contingents under the commands of chief priests of the temples of Upper and Lower Egypt. The relationship between these foundations and the central government must have been a very delicate one.

One is left with the impression that an interlocking network of pious foundations for local deities, for statues of kings at pyramids and in local temples, and for statues of private individuals must have played a major role in the economic life of ancient Egypt, involving the families of a great many people. They naturally made the temple an important centre of economic activity and of administration, particularly in view of the close ties which grew up between the temple and local men of power and influence. It is interesting to note that those decrees from Coptos which are concerned exclusively with civil appointments were found in a cache of decrees some of which carry the explicit instruction for erection at the temple gateway. Understandably, provincial temples were the subject of central government decrees concerning their condition and maintenance.

It has long been recognized that behind changes in titles relating to

---

[1] Breasted (1906, p. 161). Lichtheim (1973, p. 27) translates: 'every temple that has not been exempted', but this is difficult to support grammatically; see Edel (1964, p. 457). The possibility that exemption decrees may not always have been entirely binding seems to be reflected in a Coptos decree of Pepy II; see Goedicke (1967, pp. 88, 107 (n. 59) and 246), who cites the passage that has been quoted, which comes from the biography of Harkhuf (see p. 713).

provincial administration in Upper Egypt lie important historical developments. The common interpretation is that for the earlier part of the Old Kingdom different branches of provincial administration were run by different central government officials in such a way that the administration of one whole governorate (or nome) did not fall to one man. These men were sometimes buried in the court cemetery, and must inevitably have been caught up in the pyramid-building industry which, with its great demands on labour, must have spread its influence throughout the country. An example would be a Fourth Dynasty priest of Sneferu's southern pyramid temple at Dashur, Netjer-aperef, who had also held the offices of 'overseer of commissions in the nomes of Coptos, Hu and Dendera' (Fischer 1968, pp. 8–9). But during the Fifth and Sixth Dynasties this central responsibility for all provincial government was gradually diluted by the appearance of true provincial governors or nomarchs, whose position was formalized by the appearance of a new title, 'great chief of a nome'. The title is first attested at Edfu in the reign of King Teti at the beginning of the Sixth Dynasty (Alliot 1937–8, Edel 1954, Yoyotte 1952), and in the course of this dynasty it appeared throughout most of Upper Egypt. The development appears to coincide more or less with the appearance in certain suitable localities of finely decorated rock tombs, often for the burial of these local magnates.

This very fact, however, points to one source of imbalance in the data. Provincial mud-brick mastaba tombs are known from the earlier Old Kingdom, being occasionally quite large (Arnold 1973, Garstang 1902, 1904), but being more vulnerable the inscriptional evidence for the position of their owners has but rarely survived. Yet some may well have formed a complement to the great court cemeteries at Giza which have been recognized as being not able to account for sufficient of the high administrative officials who must thus have been buried elsewhere. Two significant exceptions to the usual anonymity of these provincial mastaba tombs may be quoted. One occurs at Dendera where, amongst a group of mastaba tombs of the Fourth and Fifth Dynasties, the only identifiable one belonged to a priest of the local Hathor cult, one Ni-ibu-nisut, apparently with no civil titles (Fischer 1968, pp. 14–21). The other concerns El-Kab, where, in a similar situation, the only identifiable mastaba tombs belonged to an 'inspector of priests' Nefer-shemen, and a 'chief priest', Kameni, both of the local Nekhbet cult (Fischer 1968, pp. 18–19 (n. 82); Quibell 1898). Their statues have been dated on stylistic ground to the Fourth Dynasty

(Stevenson Smith 1946, p. 45; Vandier 1958, pp. 56–7). Neither bore strictly administrative titles. The priesthood of a separate desert temple at El-Kab is also known from groups of graffiti belonging to people whose names show that the group must extend well into the Sixth Dynasty.[1] Part of their interest lies in the predominantly priestly nature of their titles. Amongst their other titles, even in the case of the chief priest, are very few which one can feel were strictly functional, or of importance in the civil administration, as distinct from honorary titles and rank indicators.

But elsewhere, though in a somewhat spasmodic way, the title 'chief priest' was already being born by men who were also 'nomarch' or its equivalent. Such men are known from provincial tombs of the Sixth Dynasty at several Upper Egyptian sites. Two such men from the nome containing Abydos were buried in the court cemetery at Saqqara, whilst a third may have been buried at his home town (Fischer 1954, 1962). From what has been said already about the economic role of temples and of pious foundations this combination seems very logical. Whether one interprets this as evidence for Egypt's having been ruled by priests or for the priesthood having been essentially part of the apparatus of government is a matter of modern nuance. Certainly at no point here or in the Middle Kingdom can men of obviously outstanding authority and power be found whose titles are strictly or even primarily priestly. The history of the title of the chief priest of Ra at Heliopolis seems to confirm this view, being held for the most part by courtiers, princes or high officials as one amongst several titles.

The evidence surrounding the provincial priests of the Fourth and Fifth Dynasties mentioned above is too slight to acquaint us with the part they played in the life of their communities. Equally obscure is the important question of the family origin of the Sixth Dynasty nomarchs: did they originate from local families whose influence had hitherto been confined largely to the priesthood, or were they men whose background had been the court-centred civil administration and who manoeuvred themselves into control of the local temples? The case of the twelfth nome, whose nomarch, appointed by the king, was a member of the influential family of the vizier Djau from Abydos in the eighth nome, is perhaps exceptional, but does illustrate the way in which high officials in the central government retained provincial links, Djau possessing a pious foundation for his statue in the temple of Khenty-amentiu at

---

[1] Porter and Moss (1927, vol. v, p. 190) give the references. For the title 'inspector of Nekhbet', the goddess of El-Kab, on mud seals from the town site, see *Fouilles de El Kab* (1954).

Abydos. Nika-ankh, discussed above, must represent another transitional stage. The unevenness of the evidence and our difficulties in following the backgrounds of individual officials should introduce considerable caution into the drawing of conclusions. But it can at least be recognized that, by the end of the Sixth Dynasty, province-centred government had become an important part of Egyptian society, and it is tempting to link its evolution with the scaling-down of pyramid-building.

The evidence discussed so far relates entirely to Upper Egypt. Old Kingdom material from the Nile Delta is so slight that few conclusions are possible. A late Old Kingdom cemetery has been discovered from the important town site of Mendes, and the offices of the people buried there call for little special comment, although two chief priests of the local temple without important civil titles may be mentioned. Nowhere are nomarchs for Lower Egypt attested; likewise the title 'governor of Upper Egypt', an attempt from the mid Fifth Dynasty onwards to co-ordinate nome affairs, has (with one possible exception)[1] no equivalent for Lower Egypt until the Middle Kingdom. One might consequently conclude that the nomarch phenomenon of the late Old Kingdom was essentially Upper Egyptian. Some support for the idea that Upper Egypt, particularly the more southerly part, was generally less closely associated with the court circle than Lower Egypt comes from the distribution of estates making up the pious foundations of private funerary cults in the Memphite necropolis. Only a very small number of tombs took up the custom of enumerating estates by nome, but of those that did most display a preponderance in Lower Egypt, and in Upper Egypt there are few indeed further south than the fifteenth nome, thus in the true nomarch territory (fig. 10.2). Even allowing for the possibility that there may have been more natural agricultural potential for creating new estates in the north, it seems to imply that the court drew fairly heavily on men whose connections were more with the more northerly parts of the country, especially the delta.

The First Intermediate Period saw variations in provincial government which belong to the disturbed local history of the period and will be mentioned below on pp. 699–703. Significantly, this type of dual-role provincial governor, in charge of the local temple as well as civil affairs, survived to become ubiquitous in the Middle Kingdom. The standard combination becomes 'chief priest' and ḥȝty-ʿ, originally an exalted

---

[1] The official is Userkaf-ankh, and the title probably 'overseer of the nomes of Lower Egypt' (Pirenne 1932–5, vol. II, p. 470 and n. 1).

court title, but now regularly applied to a man governing a town and in charge of its order and responsible for delivering its taxes to the vizier. The translation 'town governor' often seems the most appropriate. Their holders are known throughout Upper Egypt and now in Lower Egypt as well. Many were owners of large and richly decorated rock tombs, and those at Qau el-Kebir, with temples modelled on the royal pyramid layout, were probably the largest provincial tombs to be constructed in Egypt until the Twenty-fifth Dynasty. Their owners are often called 'nomarchs' by modern writers, but the title which is most aptly translated thus is in most cases either not used by them at all, or in an apparently spasmodic way. The principal exception is at Beni Hasan where the tomb-owners appear to be true nomarchs, on the whole without connection with the local temple. A general appreciation of the position of 'town governors', including the fact that places which were not nome capitals, like Abydos, Armant and Kahun, had them, might lead to the conclusion that, by the Middle Kingdom, provincial authority and its rewards was following the 'natural' pattern of urban development in the Nile Valley. The more artificial division of the country into nomes may well have come to exist only as a formal overlay whose offices were primarily honorary, held either by a town governor or, in an exceptional case as at Beni Hasan, by aristocratic families lying somewhat outside the more common pattern of provincial authority.

Much has been made by historians of the fact that after the reign of Senusret III there are no more large provincial tombs (with the exception of one at Qau el-Kebir of the reign of Amenemhat III). The interpretation has been offered that the power of provincial men was curbed in an administrative reform which brought the country wholly under a centralized bureaucracy. This needs to be seen in careful perspective, however. In the first place, the degree of independence implied in a display of local grandeur is not necessarily directly proportional to the scale of that display. For example, at the height of this phase of local government prosperity, in year 38 of Senusret I, twenty town governors, including those from the southernmost part of Egypt, were obliged to take part in a colossal quarrying expedition for the king to the Wadi Hammamat, under the authority of a 'herald', their presence being presumably required by virtue of their obligations to supply people in their area for the royal *corvée*. This has the appearance of a massive exercise in royal control of provincial government. Secondly, whilst changes in local government may well have taken place in the late Twelfth Dynasty, nevertheless men with the titles 'town governor' and 'chief priest' are known from the late Twelfth and Thirteenth Dynasties. Thus, late in the reign of Amenemhat III Kahun was being governed by one such title-holder; at el-Kab these offices ran in a family who were descended from a vizier of the Thirteenth Dynasty and who held this position until late in the Seventeenth Dynasty when one of them, Sebek-nakht, had a decorated rock tomb made. A similar sequence is visible at Edfu, and the daughter of a town governor of Armant appears in an administrative papyrus of the early Thirteenth Dynasty (Scharff 1920). What must be granted is a break in the sequence of large provincial tombs, but that the economic factor was one inflicted by the king is entirely a matter of modern inference. Within a generation the size of royal tombs also went into a sharp decline, evidently associated with instability within the kingship. But unlike in the history of the late Old Kingdom this was not accompanied by a transfer of wealth to the Upper Egyptian provinces.

### THE FIRST INTERMEDIATE PERIOD

With the reign of Pepy II, alleged by ancient sources to have been over 90 years long, the Old Kingdom effectively ended. The outward manifestation of this is the fact that his was the last in the sequence of massive pyramid complexes, although it was also surrounded by a cemetery of his courtiers in the form of curiously impoverished provincial-like tombs of mud brick which speak eloquently of the decline in wealth of those most closely associated with the king. At this modest level the Memphite cemeteries continued in use, as is shown by a sequence of tombs of priests of King Teti's cult at Saqqara which probably spans the whole period. But the ability of the court to build on a truly monumental scale seems to have gone altogether. The country was not left, however, without kings. These are known from the king-lists of Turin and Abydos which between them suggest eighteen kings, and possibly one queen, ruling for a period of perhaps about 20 years, implying an instability of rule which must go far towards explaining the absence of large pyramids. It is convenient to equate them with Manetho's Eighth Dynasty, there being no evidence to support the existence of an intervening Seventh Dynasty, whilst the Turin list marks no break in continuity of royal succession between the Sixth Dynasty and the last of this group. A pyramid tomb of very modest proportions indeed (see fig. 10.1) has been found at Saqqara belonging to one of them, a King Aba, who had a reign of either two or four years in which to accomplish it.

At Coptos in Upper Egypt a series of fourteen decrees issued by some of them mostly appoint members of a prominent local family to positions in the provincial and temple administration. In so doing they create the impression of the continued functioning of the Old Kingdom apparatus of government, suggesting that although the power of these kings to determine events may have been small, their role continued to bestow authority, general approval and status on the careers of provincial men of power.

The Memphite kingship next passed to a line of eighteen kings who seem to have originated from the provincial town of Herakleopolis and who are occasionally referred to in contemporary inscriptions as the 'House of Khety', after the first of the line. Whether they took over the Memphite court or continued to rule from Herakleopolis is, like practically everything about them, unknown. They form Manetho's duplicated Ninth/Tenth Dynasty (von Beckerath 1966, Goedicke 1969, Schenkel 1962, pp. 139–45). Its most famous surviving product is the literary text, the Instruction to Merikara (see p. 661), but because of lacunae in the text, many uncertainties in translation, and more particularly its didactic tone, it requires considerable caution to use it as an historical source.[1]

Our ignorance of royal succession and court affairs at this time is basically a reflection of how important a part pyramid cemeteries play in our view of Egypt in these earlier periods. When they are large and well preserved we feel that we know something of their creators; when they disappear the illusion is created of a 'Dark Age'. Yet as far as events in Upper Egypt are concerned, we know far more at this time than during the heyday of the Old Kingdom. Provincial fortunes become evident from a close study of certain cemeteries. Thus at Mo'alla, on the northern frontier of the nome of Hierakonpolis, the tomb of Ankhtyfy contains important biographical texts. Like his father Hetep, Ankhtyfy bore, amongst others, the twin titles 'nomarch' and 'chief priest', and lived probably in the early to middle part of the Ninth/Tenth Dynasty. He records his takeover of the adjoining nome of Edfu, hitherto under the 'House of Khuu', an important nomarch family itself, and there is a hint that a third nome, presumably Elephantine, for a time was associated with his ambitions. But to his north, similar aspirations had produced a hostile alliance between the nomes of Thebes and Coptos, bringing about mutual attacks on fortresses. Subsequently the whole of the southern part of Upper Egypt fell under the control

[1] Contrast the historical value placed on the text by Ward (1971) and by Björkman (1964).

of Thebes. At Moʿalla this is presumably marked by Ankhtyfy's two known successors bearing only the single title 'leader of Hierakonpolis'. At Dendera, there is a long sequence of tombs covering virtually the whole period. From between the end of the Sixth Dynasty and a point more or less contemporary with Ankhtyfy are two belonging to men with the same two offices of 'nomarch' and 'chief priest', and one evidently with the same sort of ambitions as Ankhtyfy, being nomarch of the three nomes of Thinis, Diospolis and Dendera. Their relative independence was again curbed by Thebes. This is marked by one official from Dendera who records serving the 'governor of Upper Egypt, Intef the Great', a Theban. Henceforth the tombs at Dendera belong only to 'chief priests'.

This is the period when for the first time Thebes came into prominence. The late Old Kingdom is represented here by a group of five rock tombs (M. Saleh 1977), two belonging to nomarchs, and from the following period the names of three 'town governors' and 'chief priests' are recorded in inscriptions (Björkman 1964; Schenkel 1965, pp. 29–32, esp. no. 19; Winlock 1947, pp. 5–6), but their connection, if any, to the immediately succeeding Intef family is unknown. Of this last family, who were ultimately to emerge as the Eleventh Dynasty, the two earliest figures are a 'nomarch' and 'chief priest' Intef (Cairo stele 2009; see Fischer 1968, pp. 200, 203; Schenkel 1965, pp. 64–5), and Intef the Great, referred to above.[1] The success of this family in curbing the ambitions of provincial governors to their north and south led them to proclaim themselves kings, and to construct far more imposing tombs in the El-Tarif area of western Thebes. Bearing the names Intef and Menthuhetep they form Manetho's Eleventh Dynasty, and were subsequently thought to comprise seven kings ruling for 143 years. Contemporary sources, however – especially the biography of Hetepi from El-Kab (Gabra 1976)[2] – show that the territorial foundation of real Theban power did not occur until the reign of the third, Wahankh Intef, and must raise some doubts as to whether kingship was not later ascribed to the first two from motives of piety. Their position led to a civil war with the kings of the Ninth/Tenth Dynasty in the north. References to this come both from Thebes, and from tombs at Deir Rifeh, near Asyut, which belong again to 'town governors' or

---

[1] See this page and Schenkel (1965, p. 66, no. 46, also perhaps no. 45). It is possible that this Intef and the previously mentioned one, as well as the 'Intef the Great, the son of Ikui' of later records, are all really the same person; cf. Schenkel (1962, pp. 145–9).

[2] It dates to the reign of Wahankh Intef and seems to suggest that not until his reign were the most southerly nomes brought under full Theban control. It also describes the great famine.

'nomarchs' and 'chief priests'. Two (belonging to It-ibi and Khety II) contain narrative inscriptions recording the part played by their owners in the civil war, fighting on behalf of the Ninth/Tenth Dynasty.

Both groups of inscriptions, from Thebes and Deir Rifeh, agree in making the area of conflict lie between Thinis and various points further to the north.[1] No inscription mentions ultimate victory, but it seems certain that it was gained by Nebhepetra Menthuhetep II, not least from the fact that two of his officials served in Herakleopolis itself (Fischer 1959a, 1960, Helck 1955, Schenkel 1965). Nebhepetra's reign also marks an astonishingly successful attempt at creating, at Deir el-Bahari, a monumental funerary complex richly decorated in a style which, though based on Old Kingdom models, possessed a great vigour of its own. With this monument the Middle Kingdom may be said to have commenced.

The First Intermediate Period seems essentially to represent a loss of equilibrium between a powerful court and provincial aspirations, and in itself points to where a major source of power had come to reside. The cemeteries of Upper Egypt show that the people of this area who benefited most from the end of the court's ability to collect and to consume a large part of the country's resources were the provincial governors whose identity had become increasingly clear during the Sixth Dynasty. Civil war there was, but only among men whose aspirations, as far as they can be seen, were of a thoroughly traditional nature, and who recognized the role of traditional kingship even if they permitted it to be only a minor influence in their conduct of their own affairs. As for the north of the country, reliable historical evidence is wholly lacking, although reflections of events are probably present in the Instruction to Merikara, and, as will be documented on pp. 724–5, an Asiatic threat of probably low magnitude existed for a time in the eastern Delta.

One aspect of the First Intermediate Period which has held a particular fascination for historians is the possibility that it witnessed something in the nature of a social revolution. To believe this one must accept that behind the philosophical queryings of the literature of this period and of the Middle Kingdom discussed on pp. 661–2, especially the text of the Admonitions of Ipuwer, there lies some historical actuality which took a dramatic, even revolutionary form. There is, in fact, evidence that in funerary religion certain concepts and symbols

[1] It is possible that graffito no. 3 of the Abisko Graffiti in Nubia may refer to an extension of the conflict into the Fayum area; see Brovarski and Murnane (1969) and cf. Posener (1952).

devised originally for the exclusive use of kings became more widely adopted (Fischer 1963), and this has been interpreted by some as evidence for a 'democratization of the afterlife', and a counterpart of what was actually happening in the society of the living. Furthermore, the tone of the philosophical literature itself implies a new awareness by the authors concerned of the fragility of the state, and, especially in the Instruction to Merikara (see p. 661) and in another literary work of this time, the Tale of the Eloquent Peasant, the need to ensure that the state accommodated the hopes of the ordinary man. But to assume that such developments could only be expressed in revolutionary action is to take too simplistic a view of historical processes, and tends to deny the Egyptians the capacity of speculating on and questioning rationally the nature of their society, even if their mode of thought and communication tended to be vividly concrete.

As to what brought about the First Intermediate Period, several possibilities will be discussed in the final section of this chapter, on explanations for historical change in Egypt.

## THE AFRICAN HINTERLAND

An important phenomenon to be observed in the ancient cultures of north-east Africa is a process of cultural separation whereby a people settled in some part of the Nile Valley could become involved, for reasons still not properly understood, in a largely spontaneous and self-multiplying course of cultural enrichment and diversity which separated them from their desert background. In particular, settled life in the Nile Valley seems to have encouraged the appearance both of leaders anxious to extend their control over neighbouring valley groups, and of an elaborate cemetery culture. In Egypt proper this process had given birth to the Predynastic culture from which Pharaonic civilization had grown. But in Nubia the far smaller natural potential of this part of the valley and the aggressive policies adopted by Egypt meant that the process had a limited future and was liable to be arrested while still in an incipient phase, and even reversed.

By its very nature this phenomenon obscures the external affinities of Nile Valley groups. On present evidence, which is still very sparse, one should probably see the deserts surrounding Egypt as having supported a 'pool' of widely and thinly dispersed groups of people in whose lives nomadism played a part of varying importance, and whose simple material cultures frequently show broad overall similarities both to each other and to those of the Nile Valley, but which possessed their own very long histories, probably complicated ones when examined in detail and on a regional basis.[1] Distinctive in their later phases are their ceramic products, chiefly hand-made bowls, whose features include burnished black interiors, black-topped red exteriors often burnished, unburnished dark exteriors decorated with various simple incised or impressed patterns, and occasionally ripple-burnished exteriors. Grinding-stones are also prominent. When resemblances to Nubian cultures seem particularly close some relationship between the peoples concerned may be considered, but until a great deal more information is derived from the deserts, and until more is understood of the process of cultural development in the Nile Valley itself, considerable caution should be exercised in identifying desert homelands for the various valley groups. The temptation for sweeping association from the existence of broad similarities over a wide geographical area is particularly evident in the applications of the term 'C-group' (see below, pp. 713–14), to cultures of the western desert whose total features do not amount to the true C-group, which appears to have been a specialized development of Lower Nubia only. Furthermore, recent evaluation of both the archaeological and physical anthropological material of Lower Nubia has tended to favour the idea of, instead of repeated waves of immigration, a basic continuity of culture and ethnic stock from early times onwards.

The rock pictures which occur both along the Nile Valley and in the deserts on either side are a further important product of these peoples, but the problems of dating make them difficult to use historically. There seems to be widespread agreement, nevertheless, that a large proportion of the cattle drawings, which predominate in the rock art of Nubia and the eastern desert and are found widely spread in the deserts to the west as well, are contemporary with the periods under consideration and attest the existence of a widespread cattle-orientated culture to which the Nubian C-group would presumably have belonged. Beyond such a generalized conclusion, however, it seems scarcely possible to proceed at present, though one might note that both the ancient Egyptian ethnic terminology and the first anthropological results from a Pan-grave cemetery of people believed associated with the Medja nomads of the eastern desert (see below, p. 757), suggest that more than one distinct

[1] The references are very scattered, but include: Bagnold *et al.* (1939), Caton-Thompson (1952), Hays (1975a, b), Hester and Hobler (1969), Hobler and Hester (1968), Hölscher (1955), Huard (1965, 1967–8), Huard and Allard (1970), Huard and Leclant (1972), McHugh (1974a, b, 1975), Shaw (1936a, b).

group of peoples were involved. An ancient cattle cemetery is known to lie to the north-east of the Wadi el-Allaqi (Murray 1962), and cattle skulls have come from a Lower Nubian site (Hall 1962).

One might expect that contact between desert and valley was always, if only sporadically maintained, and mainly in the form of short-lived desert-edge encampments of semi-nomads, perhaps entering into a symbiotic relationship with the settled valley-dwellers, based on cattle exchange. Virtually the only investigated record of this type of activity comes from the desert edge to the west of Armant in Upper Egypt, where the following groups were found after very careful examination of the desert surface:[1] (1) a cemetery of seventy-six graves, whose Egyptian pottery dates them to the Early Dynastic Period. Other vessels were of a ripple-burnished ware, some with incised chevron pattern beneath the rim. Of the burials, twenty were of oxen. A cemetery like this may imply something more permanent than a seasonal camp; (2) several small camps ('Saharan Sites') represented by scatters of flint tools and sherds with various incised and impressed patterns. At one of them (Saharan Site 15) were also found seven sherds from Old Kingdom orange-burnished bowls, and part of a vessel which resembles a common Middle Kingdom form; (3) a Pan-grave cemetery, and thus possibly for people of eastern-desert origin (see below, pp. 756–7). An accompanying survey located further Saharan Sites all the way south to Edfu, but none further north, at least as far as Farshut. The practice by nomadic groups of camping on the desert edge, leading sometimes to permanent settlement, has been continued into recent times in this general area.[2] The overall cultural impact of this process has been little investigated.

It is surprisingly difficult to trace, in areas further south still, such ephemeral camp-sites of people contemporary with the well-established Nubian groups. One may wonder if the priorities of the earlier archaeological surveys, carried out for rescue purposes, and the tendency for a unilinear view of cultural development to prevail, have

[1] The main results remain unpublished. Myers's records are in the archives of the Egypt Exploration Society, and were in an advanced state of preparation at his death. Permission to quote here some of this material was kindly granted by the Egypt Exploration Society. Preliminary discussions can also be found in Bagnold *et al.* (1939) and Mond and Myers (1937).

[2] The modern village of Naga el-Arab on the desert side of the Birket Habu in western Thebes houses the descendants of a nomadic group who were settled here earlier this century. A photograph of one of their original tented camps appears in Borchardt and Ricke (1930, p. 191). Some of these people, or their neighbours, were reputed to have come from Kharga Oasis (Bonomi 1906).

not led to the Saharan Site type being overlooked, especially since the pottery might bear some resemblances to Nubian valley domestic wares (see p. 711).

### The western desert and oases

Archaeological material has been reported from numerous localities in the western desert, but rarely investigated on a scientific basis. As far away as the Gilf el-Kebir pottery has been found which is said to resemble some of the Nubian valley cultures (specifically C-group). The most detailed published fieldwork has been carried out in the vicinity of the Dunqul and Kurkur Oases, no longer permanently inhabited (Hester and Hobler 1969, Hobler and Hester 1968). A series of occupation sites was discovered, most near the Dunqul and Dineigil Oases, but a few at Kurkur, Nakhlai, Taklis and Sheb. The most important were clustered around water sources which still exist today, but even so represented probably not a single occupation but a number of reoccupations by people with essentially the same material culture, though displaying slight variations from site to site. Two near Dunqul consisted of groups of rooms of rough stone masonry construction, many so small as to suggest storage spaces or animal pens. Of apparently the same age were a number of stone game-traps thrown across shallow valleys at Dunqul and Kurkur, intended perhaps for gazelle and ostrich. The occupants of these sites seem to have herded domesticated sheep and possibly goats, and to have either herded or hunted cattle (*Bos* sp.). Their material culture consisted of a chert artifact assemblage, stone grinders, and sherds primarily from bowls and jars principally of the following wares: thin burnished black-topped, with black interior and red exterior; thin unburnished grey with simple incised or impressed decoration on the outside; thin red–brown undecorated; at one Kurkur site four ripple-burnished sherds were present as well. No cemeteries were found at any of the sites, an important feature which distinguishes them (and probably most other desert sites) from those in the Nile Valley.[1] From one site comes a [14]C date of 1690±180 BC (MASCA[2]

---

[1] Although in the Wadi Howar some hundreds of grave cairns have been noted, but apparently for burials without or with very few grave-goods (Shaw 1936a, b). In this latter case it is somewhat misleading to attach the term Badarian to these graves in view of the incomplete history of the various cultural groups of the deserts, who resorted from time to time to the manufacture of ripple-burnished ware.

[2] MASCA corrections, from one of several schemes for calibrating raw radiocarbon dates, are published by the Museums Applied Science Center for Archaeology in Ralph, Michael and Han (1973).

correction would be c. 2050 BC (Butzer and Hansen 1968, p. 390, Hobler and Hester 1968)), which would place the survival of these cultures well into the periods considered in these chapters.

When the Egyptians encountered these peoples of the western desert, not surprisingly, they ignored whatever groupings they formed and applied to them a very imprecise terminology. A general term was Tjemehu of the land of Tjemeh, and they or their land are mentioned as the object of raiding parties of both the Egyptians and the Nubian valley dwellers in latitudes as far apart as probably 30° and 20° N. A much later reference (Yoyotte 1951), from the reign of Ramesses II in the early thirteenth century BC, speaks of Tjemehu captured for the building of the rock temple of Wadi es-Sebua which, significantly, lies on the Nile bank to the east and south-east of the Dunqul–Nakhlai area. It has been suggested that on clear ethnic grounds the Egyptians distinguished between them and the Tjehenu, among whom the Egyptians recognized princes or leaders, and whose lands may have lain more towards the Mediterranean, west of the Nile Delta, on the edge of a coastal region which was also, but in periods much later than those considered in this chapter, to experience cultural separation from the desert hinterland.

The most important centres of settlement in the west were presumably the larger oases, although as yet there has been little excavation to substantiate this for the periods under consideration. Kharga and Bahriya provided wine for the Egyptian court (Helck 1975, p. 180), and three Middle Kingdom graffiti have been reported from near mine-workings at Bahriya (Fakhry 1973), but probably a more important interest in them was the strategic one of safeguarding the various desert routes which provide alternatives for trade and other contacts with Nubia and lands lying further to the south. Two sources illustrate the use of such routes. One is the biography of Harkhuf of the Sixth Dynasty which concerns donkey caravans being used for the trade with Upper Nubia, and in one case taking 'the oasis road', and the Second Kamose Stele of the Seventeenth Dynasty where the concern is with diplomatic correspondence being carried south to the same area (Habachi 1972, p. 39; Pritchard 1969, p. 555; Säve-Söderbergh 1956; H. S. Smith and A. Smith 1976). Both most likely involved use of the Darb el-Arba'in caravan route (fig. 10.14) and a northward extension through the Bahriya Oasis. In the same stele Kamose actually records the capture of this oasis, and the strategic value of controlling these routes is presumably reflected in the linking of the conquest of 'the oasis' (probably Kharga and Dakhla regarded as a unit) and of Lower Nubia in the Ballas inscription of Nebhepetra Menthuhetep of the Eleventh Dynasty (Fischer 1964, pp. 112–18, no. 45; Schenkel 1965, pp. 214–16) (see p. 717).

At least as early as the Sixth Dynasty, when Harkhuf was making his journeys, some of the oases had Egyptian or Egyptianized officials stationed there, presumably with some military support. At Dakhla (at the site of Balat), an extensive Egyptian settlement of the Old Kingdom has been discovered (Vercoutter 1977a), associated with mastaba tombs belonging to men with the title 'governor of the oasis' (Fakhry 1973, Leclant 1974, pl. xxxiv) one of them claiming to be a son of Pepy II and buried with some gold artifacts; and from about the Fifth Dynasty comes a statue of an Egyptian who bore the title 'governor of the land of cattle' (Edel 1956), an evocative name which is elsewhere known to have been used for the Farafra Oasis. From the Middle Kingdom various officials are attested with titles concerned with the western desert generally and with the Kharga and Dakhla Oases in particular, including an 'overseer of the oasis army', probably referring to mercenaries from here (Fischer 1957). A Middle Kingdom stele of an official has been found at the watering place of Bir Nekheila, south-east of Kharga (Fakhry 1973).

## The eastern desert

The special feature of this area is the line of broken hills and mountains separating the Nile Valley from the Red Sea. These hills induce a slight annual rainfall, the extent and regularity of which increase southwards. In the extensive wadi systems it supplies wells, maintains vegetation, and even, in the higher reaches of some of the larger wadis, allows irregular cultivation to take place (Gleichen 1905, pp. 86–8). This area provides a home for nomadic and semi-nomadic pastoralist peoples, the more southerly called the Beja, who, from antiquity, have been regarded by outsiders as comprising a number of distinct and relatively important groups, more so than those of the western desert. The ancient Egyptians mounted regular mining expeditions to exploit the mineral resources of these hills, and, by concentrating in some of the same wadi systems, must have come into repeated contact with the local people.[1]

[1] They were occasionally referred to as if 'Asiatics', whose origin, if the term was always correctly used by the Egyptians, may have been the people of Palestinian culture in south Sinai in Chalcolithic and Early Bronze Age times (see pp. 726–9). The modern Beja are not Semites, in contrast to those people who inhabit the Red Sea Hills further to the north.

The consequent need to find in Egyptian texts references to the peoples of this important area leads, without a serious alternative, to an identification with the Medja-people. In the Middle Kingdom, when Egyptian activity in the eastern hills probably grew more intensive, Medja-people appear in texts as essentially desert-dwellers, but connected with the Nile, and the object both of Egyptian surveillance and aggression. They also entered Egyptian service. The early Thirteenth Dynasty papyrus referred to above (see p. 668) records the arrival and stay at court of a delegation of eight Medja men and women, and later of a Medja prince. In this reference, as in the Execration Texts (see below p. 721), Medja-people are subdivided into groups. The names used are written as if of places but, as in mediaeval sources, the Egyptians may be transferring the terminology of a settled people to names which were really of tribes who ranged over extensive territories. To this general argument of likelihood for the location of the Medja homeland in the hillier parts of the eastern desert of Nubia should be added the specific information provided by a stele from the Wadi el-Hudi which appears to place this particular region in Medja territory (Bietak 1966, pp. 77–8). Unfortunately, the whole area remains, archaeologically, a virtual blank.

## The Egyptian interest

The Lower Nubian valley acted as a transport corridor giving access to important mining and quarrying areas in the deserts to east and west. These were principally (and in addition to those east of Egypt proper):

(1) Wadi el-Allaqi–Wadi Gabgaba, an extensive network of broad flat wadis which in ancient, as well as in mediaeval, times were important sources of gold obtained from shallow surface workings; also probably copper, to which large slag-heaps reported near the ancient fort of Kubban were presumably connected. Two Sixth Dynasty graffiti have been found 60 km from the Nile along the Wadi el-Allaqi (Piotrovsky 1966, 1967),[1] and possibly three from the Middle Kingdom further on (Černy 1947). One must also presume that this would have been the principal area of contact with the Medja-people.

(2) Wadi el-Hudi, a source of amethyst, and possibly of gold as well. Inscriptions found here mention Kings Nebtawyra Menthuhetep IV (last king of the Eleventh Dynasty), Senusret I, Senusret III, Amenemhat III, all of the Twelfth, and Khaneferra Sebekhetep of the Thirteenth.

---

[1] There is no need to assume that the Uni of one of these graffiti is the same as the famous Uni of the Abydos inscription. Their titles are not the same.

A neatly laid out fortified stone village has been tentatively dated to the Middle Kingdom.

(3) Quarries in the western desert, north-west of Toshka, exploited for diorite gneiss and possibly carnelian.[1] Royal names found here are: Khufu and Djedefra of the Fourth Dynasty, Sahura and Djedkara Isesi of the Fifth, Senusret I, Amenemhat I/Senusret I co-regency, Amenemhat II, and Amenemhat III of the Twelfth. One quarrying record claimed that 1000 donkeys and over 1000 men were involved.

Gold was also available from riverine and riverside deposits between Buhen and Kerma and three Old Kingdom graffiti belonging to a class of officials apparently concerned particularly with the import of minerals have been found at Kulb, near Dal (Hintze 1965). Pharaonic riverside mines have been located at Saras and Duweishat, the former apparently of the Twelfth Dynasty. It has also been suggested that wood from both Upper and Lower Nubia was taken to supplement Egypt's modest reserves.

Provision had also to be made for trading with regions lying even further to the south which could provide the Egyptians with exotic goods. One Sixth Dynasty source (Harkhuf) lists as the products of such trade: 'incense, ebony, *ḥknw*-oil . . ., panther skins, elephants' tusks, and throwing-sticks'. Since the sources of some of these items would have lain beyond the reach of direct Egyptian penetration by river or by caravan, it was necessary to come to some sort of arrangement with Nubian middlemen, as well as to safeguard the routes themselves. This, as noted above, involved control of the western oases.

From time to time checks were felt to be necessary on political developments amongst the riverine peoples. The process of cultural separation from the desert hinterland and the appearance of ambitious leaders was always liable to take place, more successfully in Upper Nubia where the resources were much greater. Since the imbalance in population between Egypt and her African neighbours must have been much less great in antiquity than in modern times such political developments must have been viewed with an equivalently greater urgency. The expressed Egyptian policy was always one of aggression, but this, especially as it concerns Upper Nubia, contains the ambiguity that amongst these peoples the Egyptians also had to find trading partners. Although it is always possible that they entertained the hope of being able, ultimately, to break through by river or by land to the

---

[1] The second commodity sought was called *mḥnt*, a mineral substance for which the translation 'carnelian' (or 'jasper') has been suggested (Simpson 1963c, pp. 50–1).

true sources of exotic goods and further gold which they were otherwise able to reach directly only by the coastal voyage to Punt (see pp. 723–4).

## The Nubian Nile Valley

The demise of the Nubian A-group culture during the first part of the First Dynasty seems to have marked the beginning of a hiatus in the Lower Nubian cultural record of perhaps as much as five centuries. For some time archaeologists filled this gap with a B-group culture, principally material from very impoverished graves. But a close analysis of the evidence shows that there are no grounds for recognizing in any of the Lower Nubian cemeteries a homogenous phase to be fitted into this period, which in Egypt represents a major part of the Old Kingdom. The most plausible interpretation is that as a result of Egyptian harassment, including perhaps the taking of prisoners, and possibly the exclusion from a hitherto close trading relationship with Egypt, the inhabitants sought refuge in a semi-nomadic way of life between the Nile Valley and the wells and oases of the adjacent deserts.

One feature of the desert cultures discussed above is the rarity of well-defined cemeteries. If the temporary and perhaps seasonal presence of these people in Lower Nubia had been marked by nothing more substantial than camps of the Saharan Site type identified at Armant then it becomes understandable how the methods and standpoints of some of the principal Nubian surveys could have overlooked or undervalued such insubstantial surface sites, particularly since the pottery may well have born superficial resemblances to C-group domestic wares. One of the most exhaustive of the more recent surveys, however, has located some sites of just this nature, though in the ecologically more marginal area of the Second Cataract. One of them, at Saras East, in addition to sherds of types related to both A-group and C-group cultures yielded an Old Kingdom orange-burnished bowl sherd, reminiscent, therefore, of Saharan Site 15 at Armant (Mills and Nordström 1966).[1] The necessity for seeking some such explanation is heightened by Egyptian inscriptions claiming the capture of substantial numbers of men and animals from Nubia (Breasted 1906, p. 66; Helck 1974c, Schäfer 1902, p. 30).

One of the most important discoveries of the Nubian excavations of

---

[1] Gratien (1978, p. 134) claims that outliers of her Early Kerma phase ('Kerma ancien') occur at Aniba, Serra, Faras and Saras in Lower Nubia, as well as at Akasha, Dal, Sai and Kerma in Upper Nubia. See also Nordström (1966).

the 1960s was that as early as the Old Kingdom there had been an Egyptian attempt to control Lower Nubia by means of centres of permanent occupation. This was established by the excavation of Buhen North. Here, not far from the northern end of the Second Cataract, was a settlement, defined by a rough stone wall, whose material culture was almost exclusively Egyptian. In the best-preserved area the crushing and smelting of what was claimed to be copper ore had been carried on, derived from a source as yet unlocated. Royal names, especially on mud-seal impressions, were of Kings Khafra and Menkaura of the Fourth Dynasty, and Userkaf, Sahura, Neferirkara and Djedkara Isesi of the Fifth. Earlier levels, however, were tentatively ascribed to possibly as early as the Second Dynasty on the basis of mud-brick sizes and much decayed jar seals. Such an early date receives some support from [14]C dates,[1] and a graffito on a nearby hill has also been given an Early Dynastic date (H. S. Smith 1972). Buhen North represents a policy of Egyptian settlement now exemplified at Balat in the Dakhla Oasis (see p. 708), and throws a welcome light on the much earlier discovery of a few Old Kingdom sherds at Kubban, the site subsequently of a large Middle Kingdom fort strategically situated opposite the entrance to the Wadi el-Allaqi (Emery and Kirwan 1935). The apparent lack of a settled population in Lower Nubia may have rendered unnecessary the creation of a chain of garrison forts on the later Middle Kingdom pattern, but the Kubban sherds contain the hint that Buhen North was not alone in Lower Nubia. Buhen North also gave the Egyptians the potential, as in the Middle Kingdom, for striking into Upper Nubia where the pickings must always have been much greater, and this introduces a note of geographical uncertainty into the Fourth Dynasty record of King Sneferu's capture of booty during a raid on Nubia. Buhen North would likewise have been well placed for trade with Upper Nubia, replacing Lower Nubian middlemen.

At Buhen, as in the diorite quarries, the inscriptional sequence ends

---

[1] The various radiocarbon dates are published in *Radiocarbon*, 1963, **5**, 21, 288–9; 1965, **7**, 352; 1966, **8**, 3–4; 1968, **10**, 1. Seven of the eight Arizona dates give a reasonably consistent picture when subject to half-life correction and to calibration (e.g. by the MASCA scale, see n. 2 on p. 706), with two samples from below the Old Kingdom floor (A-333, 334) of 2920±60 BC and 2830–2700±50 BC. The five California dates (three of them from samples also used by Arizona) and the one British Museum date are somewhat less consistent, tending to give dates for the upper level a lot earlier than one would expect, although a key sample from a trial trench across the centre of the site (UCLA-247) yielded a date of 2910±60 BC. H. S. Smith (1964) echoed by Säve-Söderbergh and Olsson (1970) has seen in the internal inconsistencies a reason for suspecting the correct interpretation of the stratigraphy. The degree of inconsistency, however, is probably no greater than that, for example, which is apparent amongst radiocarbon dates from the Aegean Bronze Age.

with the Fifth Dynasty, to be resumed at each site only at the beginning of the Twelfth. For the Sixth Dynasty, however, there are important inscriptions left behind by Egyptian expeditions to Nubia, often led by officials called 'overseers of foreign troops' (L. Bell 1973, Edel 1971b, 1973, Fischer 1964, pp. 29–30; Goedicke 1966a). Such expeditions are recorded in the Wadi el-Allaqi, and by the Nile in the Tomas–Toshka area. In two graffiti at Tomas the leaders bore also the interesting titles 'overseer of the army of Satju' and 'overseer of the foreign troops of Satju', referring to a local Nubian riverine community which was presumably supplying mercenary troops. The longest inscription is the biography of Harkhuf in his tomb at Aswan. This records three expeditions, apparently with trade as their prime object, commencing at Memphis and taking a route either along the river valley, or across the western desert via the oases. One important feature of the narrative is the references to apparently well-established Nubian groups in Lower Nubia, the most important in territories called Satju, Irtjet and Wawat, apparently in this south-to-north order and covering much of this part of the Nile Valley. On Harkhuf's second journey Irtjet and Satju were under the leadership of one man, and by the third journey Wawat had been joined to them. It is tempting to see this as an actual record of the process of political concentration accompanying permanent settlement which in this case would have produced, near the end of the Old Kingdom, a veritable king of Lower Nubia. The archaeological component to this process is presumably to be found in the earliest phase of C-group culture, the next major episode of settled life in Lower Nubia. Occurring in a small number of cemeteries on the west bank, mainly in the central part of Lower Nubia, a few graves of the earliest phase contained imported Egyptian 'button seals' which, in Egypt, were in fashion during the late Old Kingdom. Whether the appearance of C-group culture was a cause or a result of the apparent abandonment of Egyptian settlement in Nubia after the Fifth Dynasty cannot be determined. At this time the governors of Elephantine bear the title 'overseer of foreign lands', in one case 'overseer of the foreign lands of his lord: Yam, Irtjet and Wawat', and this, together with the strong mercenary soldier element mentioned above, might suggest some political agreement to Egypt's advantage with these Nubian groups.

C-group (or Middle Nubian) culture persisted in Lower Nubia until the early Eighteenth Dynasty, passing through a number of phases which are essentially modifications and elaborations of the basic pattern. Since riverside settlement was itself an important stimulus to cultural development and diversity involving the appearance of an elaborate cemetery culture there is probably little point in looking for fully-fledged C-group culture outside Lower Nubia, and as mentioned above, continuity and migration offer two opposing interpretational positions from which to view C-group beginnings. Until the penultimate phase (IIb) in the Second Intermediate Period the only C-group occupation sites known are small collections of huts, either of wooden posts possibly covered with skins, or more commonly of low walls of upright stone slabs with pitched roofs supported on timbers. The cemeteries were elaborate affairs, sometimes containing free-standing stone slabs occasionally decorated with pictures of cattle. Each tomb possessed a well-built circular superstructure of dry stone masonry, and sometimes the burial lay inside a stone cyst or beneath a mud-brick barrel vault. But again, until the penultimate phase, there is no very obvious scaling of tomb size to reflect social or political standing, a negative feature possessed also in general by the earlier A-group culture.

In material culture, much of it derived from cemeteries, pottery is the most readily distinguishable feature, particularly a varied class of hand-made black bowls with elaborate incised geometric patterns; also polished black-topped red bowls, a variety of coarser domestic wares, and imported Egyptian jars, possibly for storing water. In general, the numbers of Egyptian objects acquired seem to have been relatively limited, and the development of C-group culture appears to have progressed independently of the Egyptian reconquest of Lower Nubia in the Middle Kingdom. The reconquest, however, must have frustrated whatever political ambitions had been nascent during the Sixth Dynasty and First Intermediate Period, but apart from this, C-group people seem to have been able to continue their way of life in which, to judge from their limited artistic repertoire, cattle played an important part. It also involved a modest exchange of goods between individuals, families and villages, but insufficient to create obvious concentrations of wealth.

C-group culture has been found at numerous sites in Lower Nubia, with particular concentrations in the fertile areas around Faras, Aniba and Dakka, and with one outlier in Egypt itself, at Kubaniya, 13 km north of Aswan. At this last site the C-group elements appear to belong to an early phase, presumably of the First Intermediate Period. During the Middle Kingdom the descendants of this community adopted Egyptian culture and burial practices. Southwards, it has been found no further upstream than at Semna at the head of the Second Cataract. Further south again stretches the southern continuation of the Batn el-Hagar, a particularly barren part of the Nile Valley which careful survey has shown was virtually without a settled population in ancient times (Geus and Labre 1974, Vila 1975). Further south still, beyond Dal, the archaeology of Upper Nubia is still only provisionally documented.

The site of the greatest interest here is Kerma, on the east bank above the Third Cataract (W. Y. Adams 1977a, Hintze 1964, O'Connor 1974, el-Rayah 1974, Reisner 1923, Säve-Söderbergh 1941, pp. 103–16; Trigger 1976a).[1] As will be discussed below (pp. 731–2, 749–54), the most striking of the remains – the brick castle and the great tumuli – almost certainly represent the seat of the Kings of Kush ruling much of Nubia during the late seventeenth and early sixteenth centuries BC. Their taste for Egyptian products, extending to pieces of antique inscription and statuary, has led to some confusion in modern interpretations. In the initial analysis of the cemetery, then regarded as for the burial of Egyptian trading officials, a relative chronology was established, with the great tumuli at the southern end representing the earliest classic stage. As with all relative sequences of this nature, however, it is, in theory, reversible, and the modern realization that the great tumuli must be the latest implies that the northern part of the cemetery contains the burials and culture of Kerma extending back in time from the Second Intermediate Period, presumably through the Middle Kingdom. Unfortunately, the small excavated areas of this part remain unpublished, although a few general remarks by the excavator suggest, as might be expected, features common also to the C-group of Lower Nubia, and perhaps to the A-group as well. This alternative view of the Kerma necropolis would seem to receive support from excavations on the island of Sai, which is reported to contain cemeteries as large as those at Kerma itself, though with no tombs to rival in size the royal tumuli.

A provisional scheme of archaeological classification for Upper Nubia has been proposed on the basis of the Sai cemeteries (Gratien 1978). The Classic Kerma phase of the latter part of the Second Intermediate Period, i.e. Hyksos Period in northern Egypt, is here preceded by two others: a Middle Kerma phase which displays certain burial customs common also to Classic Kerma and whose tombs contained, amongst other material, copper daggers presumably from Egypt; an Early Kerma apparently in succession to an Upper Nubian

---

[1] The stele of Intef, a key document in the interpretation of Kerma, has a remarkably close parallel in a stele from El-Kab (see n. 2 on p. 691), which adds weight to the idea that the Intef stele is not describing some sort of fortified structure built locally at Kerma. Note also that a statue claimed to have belonged to a man with the name Hapdjefa has been found at Tell Ḥizzin, in the Lebanon.

version of the A-group of Lower Nubia. Both Middle and Early Kerma are probably to be equated with parts of the northern sector of the great Kerma necropolis itself, and Middle Kerma is presumably the local equivalent of the Lower Nubian C-group, and thus largely contemporary with the Middle Kingdom. Upper Nubia may thus, to judge from the preliminary results so far published, offer a much more continuous cultural record than Lower Nubia, without the major hiatus between A- and C-groups.

Whilst Kerma can no longer be regarded as an Egyptian 'trading colony' of the Middle Kingdom, not all of the Egyptian material need be dismissed as of later importation. This applies particularly to a cache of broken stone vases from the castle courtyard and adjacent rooms, probably from beneath the level of their floors, which bore the names of Pepy I and II of the Sixth Dynasty, and of Amenemhat I and Senusret I of the Twelfth (Reisner 1923, pts. I–III, pp. 30–2, pts IV–V, pp. 507–10).[1] In some respects Kerma in the Second Intermediate Period came to be an African counterpart of Byblos: an independent state beyond Egypt's political frontiers, with a court looking to Egypt as a source of sophisticated court fashion. In the case of Byblos the connection owed much to trade with Egypt. With Kerma the mechanism of contact is more obscure, although the site lies not far from a short-cut across the desert to the great Darb el-Arba'in caravan route. But it is in the light of this subsequent history that one should view Harkhuf's accounts of his trading expeditions. Their goal was the kingdom of Yam. The internal evidence of Harkhuf's narrative is, despite much debate, too insubstantial for locating this place, other than that it lay further from Egypt than the Lower Nubian kingdoms mentioned above. But the Sixth Dynasty vases from Kerma, which have their exact counterparts at Byblos, as well as the later patterns of contact and political growth give priority to the Kerma area as the site of Yam. Furthermore, in the Egyptian spelling of Yam an equation has been sought with Irem, a later name for a country in this very region (Priese 1974, Zibelius 1972, pp. 78–81).[2] It is interesting to note that Yam was already in Harkhuf's

[1] Vercoutter (1967), reviewing Trigger (1965), cites an Old Kingdom vase with the cartouche of Pepy II from a tomb at Mirgissa of the Second Intermediate Period by way of casting doubt on the significance of the Kerma find. Nevertheless, an isolated specimen like this is hardly in the same category as a cache of the size of the one at Kerma, which included, according to Reisner, at least twenty-five different vases with the name of Pepy I. The Mirgissa vase is published in Vercoutter (1975a, p. 98, fig. 31).

[2] The fact that to the west of Yam lay an area occupied by Tjemehu people is of less help than might at first sight seem to be the case, in view of the archaeological evidence for a considerably greater spread of people in the western deserts in ancient times than is probable today (see Strouhal

time regarded as being under the patronage of the Egyptian goddess Hathor (Lichtheim 1973, p. 26),[1] who, like Horus, was to assume in the Middle Kingdom this role in several places in Nubia, including the diorite quarries of the western desert, as well as the mines in Sinai and the port of Byblos.

The reconquest of Lower Nubia seems to have begun with the reign of Nebhepetra Menthuhetep II (c. 2010 BC). A fragmentary inscription from El-Ballas in Upper Egypt, dated to his reign on epigraphic grounds, contains an account of conquest which includes the words: 'Wawat (Lower Nubia) and the Oasis, I annexed them to Upper Egypt' (Fischer 1964, pp. 112–18; Schenkel 1965, pp. 214–16). From the phraseology of a group of graffiti of his reign at Abisko, 10 km south of Aswan, it seems likely that Buhen was reached on a proper campaign.[2] No archaeological material certainly dated to his reign has been encountered in Nubia to show if a policy of settlement had been begun, but the difficulties of precise reign-by-reign dating of Egyptian artifacts should deter one from giving too firm a denial. The same is true also for the reign of Amenemhat I, first king of the Twelfth Dynasty, to whose year 29 a graffito of conquest in Wawat exists at Korosko.

By contrast, beginning with the reign of Senusret I we possess massive archaeological evidence for an Egyptian presence in Lower Nubia in the form of heavily fortified towns. These fall roughly into two groups, representing partly two different types of terrain and partly two major building phases. The first group may be termed the 'plains type', and were constructed on the flat or shelving banks of the Lower Nubian Nile north of the Second Cataract. The most southerly, Buhen, seems to have been in existence by year 5 of Senusret I, and shares sufficient architectural features in common with others at Aniba (stage II) and Kubban (stage II) to provide a similar date for them; although when examined in detail it is also clear that each fort had its own history and may have followed a more continuous process of independent improvement and modification. Unfortunately, precise dating evidence for most of the forts is lacking, but it should be noted that stage I at Aniba and Kubban should, for architectural reasons, strictly be dated

and Jungwirth 1971). As regards proximity to the Darb el-Arba'in caravan route, Sai Island is better placed than Kerma. In the sixteenth century AD the King of Sai collected customs dues from caravans taking this route, but a hundred years later this was being done at Argo, near Kerma, on behalf of the King of Dongola (Crawford 1951, pp. 140–1, 197).

[1] The precise title is 'Hathor, lady of Imaau', perhaps a part of Yam (Zibelius 1972, p. 81).
[2] See n. 1 on p. 702 and Zibelius (1972, pp. 11–12). H. S. Smith (1976, p. 63) doubts this.

to before the Buhen of Senusret I, as should also the stage I at Ikkur. These early stages at these sites might just conceivably, therefore, belong to the conquests of Nebhepetra Menthuhetep and Amenemhat I.

These forts were each defended by a massive mud-brick wall, with external towers on all sides and at the corners. On the landward side they overlooked a ditch, at Buhen with counterscarp and glacis. Their most distinctive feature was a secondary defensive line at the base of the wall, between it and the ditch. A low parapet with downward-pointing loopholes ran along the inner edge of the ditch, interrupted at intervals by semicircular bastions. It seems intended to thwart a fairly sophisticated type of siege, and thus raises the possibility that it represents a form of urban fortification developed in Egypt perhaps during the civil wars of the First Intermediate Period. Each of the forts also possessed a river frontage with quays, whilst at Serra East, a later fort where the secondary line of defence had been thought unnecessary, a small harbour was constructed actually within the walls. At Buhen and Aniba (and possibly Kubban, too) these forts became citadels within a much larger fortified area, though little is known about how much of this outer part was built up. Exceptionally at Buhen the foundations of a massive, rectangular, multi-storeyed block were found immediately north of the citadel wall.

Apart from knowing that each contained a garrison of uncertain but possibly modest size (Vila 1970), possessed an administration which was apparently a specialized variant of that operating in Egypt and presumably provided a haven for Egyptian river traffic, we know very little about who lived in these forts, how many they comprised and what they did. It is likely that their roles varied one from another. Thus, at Buhen and Kubban, and possibly at Mirgissa, copper-working seems to have been carried on,[1] whilst some were involved in local trade, the evidence for which will be discussed below. A group of stelae from Buhen have been ascribed to people who came from the El-Rizeikat neighbourhood of Upper Egypt, perhaps as settlers, though this is by no means certain.

The second group of forts resulted from an Egyptian annexation of the entire Second Cataract area in the reign of Senusret III, for which the inscriptional and archaeological evidence is specific. In the rugged terrain each of the new forts took the form of an irregular polygonal

---

[1] For Buhen see Emery (1961) and Lucas and Harris (1962, pp. 207–9); the available evidence on Mirgissa is a reference to a seal of a 'supervisor of copper workers' cited by Hesse (1971); cf. Vercoutter (1977b).

figure tailored to fit over an irregular natural prominence. Narrow ridges were covered with spur walls, and in most places the terrain rendered a ditch unnecessary. Care was taken to ensure a supply of fresh water by the construction of a stone passageway down to the river's edge, a feature present also in some of the Lower Nubian forts. Apart from the island fort of Askut midway in the Second Cataract area (and possible intermediate signalling posts) these forts cluster around the southern part and form an obvious defensive grouping across the narrow Semna Gorge (fig. 10.9). Two inscriptions of the reign of Senusret III from Semna confirm that this was indeed intended as a true frontier. One describes its purpose as: 'to prevent any Nubian from passing it when faring northwards, whether on foot or by boat, as well as any cattle of the Nubians, except for a Nubian who shall come to trade at Iqen, or as an envoy'. Iqen is now known to have been the great fort at Mirgissa which in its position, history and design is intermediate between the two main groups of forts. The reference to envoys is reminiscent of the entertaining at court of the Medja groups referred to in Papyrus Bulaq 18 (see p. 668) and is a useful reminder of the fact that, notwithstanding the consistently aggressive tone of official texts, it was necessary, on commercial and political grounds, for the Egyptians to come to some sort of understanding with their southern neighbours. Two private stelae suggest a reciprocal operation, with Egyptians venturing south into Kush on official missions of some sort.[1]

The Egyptian defensive measures were not limited to walls and battlements. Observation posts on rocky eminences in the Second Cataract area were manned, recourse was had to magical practices to thwart enemy intentions (Reisner, Wheeler and Dunham 1967, pls. 31, 32; Vila 1963, 1973) and, as copies of a group of despatches sent to Thebes (the Semna Despatches) reveal, a detailed surveillance system attempted to gather intelligence in a comprehensive way. One recurrent topic in these despatches is the activities of the Medja-people, some of whom appear at the same time in Egyptian service. In one despatch a track has been followed, three Medja-people found and questioned on their origin; in another the following of a track of thirty-two men and three donkeys is reported; in a third (from the fort at Elephantine) a small party of Medja-people has descended from the desert to request service with the Egyptians, claiming that 'the desert is dying of hunger'.

---

[1] Cairo 20086, Berlin 19500. The term 'commissions' (*wpwt*) in the latter would be particularly appropriate to diplomatic contact.

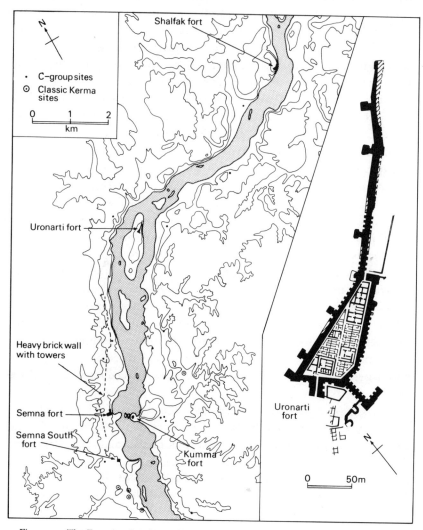

Fig. 10.9   The Egyptian frontier at Semna during the Middle Kingdom, with plan of the
fortress of Uronarti inset.

If Medja-people were regarded as a threat, this may have been a factor
in the general preference shown by the Egyptians for siting the forts
on the opposite bank, with significant exceptions at Kubban and Serra
East, respectively opposite the entrances to the Wadi el-Allaqi and Wadi
Hagar Shams, both leading to gold-mining regions.

Concern over the eastern-desert nomads does not, however, explain the southward-facing disposition of the Semna group of forts (fig. 10.9). That these looked southwards to potentially hostile riverine kingdoms beyond the Batn el-Hagar, in Upper Nubia, becomes evident from other inscriptional sources. Between the reigns of Senusret I and Senusret III the principal target of Nubian campaigns is said to be Kush. This is a geographical term with two levels of application: as a general geographical term for Upper Nubia, and one which remained as such throughout the New Kingdom, and as the name of a particular kingdom there, presumably the most powerful since the Egyptians used its name to characterize a much larger area, something which might also suggest a locally recognized political supremacy. The references to campaigns against Kush contain very little that is episodic, although one of them, of year 19 of Senusret III recording the return of an expedition against Kush and the difficulty of bringing boats back through the cataracts, by its position at Uronarti shows that in this case a riverine expedition south of the Semna Gorge had been undertaken. Related to these records is a graffito of Senusret III reported from Dal (B. Bell 1975, p. 238; Leclant 1969, p. 282). Kush in the more limited sense as the name of a kingdom appears at or near the head of lists of conquered and hostile places in Nubia, a sign probably of its importance rather than of its geographical proximity to Egypt. With one exception these lists belong to a class of document called Execration Texts.[1] Written on pottery jars or on statuettes of captive figures, and intended for a magical rite to thwart the operation of evil forces, they list people and things of a potentially hostile nature, including foreign kings and their subjects. An early example of the Sixth Dynasty includes the Nubian countries of Irtjet, Wawat, Yam, Medja and Satju (Abu Bakr and Osing 1973, Posener 1971), and for the Middle Kingdom, at least four groups cover Nubia. Few of the places can be localized, though from the fact that in two of the groups at least, Lower Nubia (Wawat) does not occur, one might deduce that Upper Nubia is the prime concern. Furthermore, although the relationship between archaeology and political structure is always a delicate one, it would seem somewhat unlikely on the basis of the nature of the country and of the negative archaeological record that the area between Semna and Ukma – the southern part of the Batn el-Hagar – could have become of much importance. In the New Kingdom, the temple towns founded by the Egyptians in Upper Nubia, probably following the existing political pattern, began only at Amara,

[1] The exception is the stele of Menthuhetep from Buhen (Bosticco 1959, no. 29; H. S. Smith 1976, pp. 39–41).

about 10 km downstream from Sai. Sai Island has been identified as the kingdom of Shaat, which also tends to occur towards the head of the lists. If one were to follow fairly strictly the order in which the places are enumerated the Amara–Ukma area might, in view of these limiting factors, seem the most likely original site for Kush. But if one considers the historical developments in Nubia in the Second Intermediate Period and the possibility that the position of Kush in the lists is a tribute to its political importance, then one might conclude that Kush was, from the outset, centred at Kerma. Some other names in the lists appear to be compounds containing the old name Yam, and Medja kingdoms are also included, one of them being Aushek which sent the envoys recorded in Papyrus Bulaq 18.

There remains to be considered the question of Egyptian participation in trade. One might envisage that, apart from Iqen, each fort engaged in small-scale local transactions, particularly to acquire cattle from both C-group and, in the case of Kubban in particular, Medja-people as well, though no inscriptional evidence has survived for this. It is known that cattle in Egypt fetched high prices. Some of the Semna Despatches record the arrivals of parties of Nubians (six in one case) to trade in unspecified commodities at the forts. In return they were given bread and beer, but whether as part of the transaction or as a gift is not made clear. A point at the First Cataract which possessed its own fort, called Senmet, was used as a place for trading for gold with Medja-people under the ultimate supervision of the governor of Elephantine (Edel 1962, 1971a, p. 11). Also important was the acquisition of products from further south for transfer to Egypt, including incense for which a considerable market must have existed in Egypt in view of its ubiquitous use in offering-ceremonies at statue cults in temples and tombs. It is nowhere apparent, however, if the Upper Nubian kingdoms acted as middlemen themselves or merely exacted revenues from caravans passing through their territory. The Semna stele quoted above directed Nubians from the south to the special trading post at Iqen (Mirgissa), but for caravans coming from further afield it would have made more sense to use the Darb el-Arba'in, perhaps leaving the Nile at Sai, and making contact with the Egyptians, perhaps to pick up an escort, at one of the oases. Equally conjectural is what the Nubians for their part gained from trade. Such evidence as is available from the earlier phases at Kerma and Sai does not support the idea that, as in the Second Intermediate Period, finished products played a large part, though if their value was kept high by the Egyptians, the Nubians may have netted less for their trade than they did later when the initiative passed more to them. It is also not yet possible to judge if perishable commodities such as corn and cloth were significantly involved, though one might note from Mirgissa and Uronarti thousands of mud seals originating from sacks (Reisner 1955, Vercoutter 1970, pp. 171–2).

The inevitably conjectural nature of discussions on the pattern of Nubian trade should not be allowed to detract from the fair certainty that it was of considerable importance, the Egyptian demand for gold and incense being the counterpart in the south to the demand for timber obtained via Byblos in the north. It should be regarded as a major factor in the political developments of Upper Nubia in the Second Intermediate Period.

### The land of Punt

The significance of the land of Punt appears to lie in the fact that it was the one place where the Egyptians could trade direct with an area producing certain valuable commodities (principally *'ntyw*: myrrh or frankincense, or both) which was at the same time too remote to be politically dangerous to them. The kingdoms of Upper Nubia and of the Medja-people must have effectively blocked direct Egyptian contact by land and river, but a coastal journey along the Red Sea eventually brought them to the desired area, perhaps to an established emporium. The precise point of contact has not yet been determined, but the possibilities are limited by the likely ancient distribution of the various characteristics of Punt described and portrayed by the Egyptians. On the assumption that the Egyptians minimized their journey, the most likely area is the Sudan–Eritrea border zone, rather than further along the coast and even through the straits of Bab el-Mandeb. An established emporium, wherever located, could also have drawn on the incense trees native to southern Arabia.

The earliest definite record of contact is an entry on the Palermo Stone of the reign of Sahura of the Fifth Dynasty: the receipt in one year from Punt of 80000 units of *'ntyw*, and quantities of electrum and two commodities whose reading is uncertain. There are two indirect references to contact, or attempted contact, with Punt in private biographical inscriptions: one an allusion to a dwarf brought thence in the reign of King Djedkara Isesi, the other to an ill-fated attempt to build a boat on the Red Sea coast for the trip there in the reign of Pepy II. A Sixth Dynasty man claims to have followed his master, a governor of Elephantine, both to Punt and to Byblos. Then from the Eleventh and Twelfth Dynasties come several more records, found actually on the desert road linking Coptos with the Red Sea, and at Wadi Gasus, close to the Red Sea. Recent fieldwork seems to have discovered the site of the Middle Kingdom port itself, at Mersa Gawasis (Sayed 1977).

## EGYPT AND THE MEDITERRANEAN WORLD

Egypt's relations with Palestine and Syria have to be set carefully against the cultural history of this area. Archaeological research is pointing increasingly to the conclusion that urban civilization accompanied by a relatively sophisticated social order was the normal condition not only for Syria but also for much of Palestine during the greater part of the time considered in this chapter, and at times spread into desert areas where urbanized life could hardly have been sustained without careful organization. These areas naturally have their own schemes of chronology. In Palestine the transition from the Chalcolithic to the Early Bronze Age seems to have occurred at a time equivalent to the latter part of the Gerzean (Naqada II) phase in Egypt, with Early Bronze Age I and II extending from here through the Early Dynastic Period. For the Old Kingdom down to some point in the late Fifth or Sixth Dynasty the Palestinian urban equivalent is the Early Bronze Age III culture, and for the Middle Kingdom and Second Intermediate Period it is the Middle Bronze Age (probably beginning with Middle Bronze Age IIA of Albright = Middle Bronze Age of Kenyon). The intervening period, which corresponds more or less to the First Intermediate Period in Egypt, is evidently one of considerable complexity and probably regional variation, something reflected in the still fluid nature of the terminology used, though the term Intermediate Early/Middle Bronze Age seems a good way of resolving the problem (Callaway and Weinstein 1977, Dever 1973, de Geus 1971, Oren 1973a, Prag 1974, Thompson 1978). It is characterized by a widespread decline in urban life, often attributed to the destruction or disruption of immigrants. The new, though only temporary, pattern was a mixture of villages, possibly insubstantial occupation of some of the older cities, and the camp-sites of nomadic or partly nomadic groups. For a time their villages and camp-sites spread westwards across the Sinai peninsula as far at least as the line of the modern Suez Canal. It must have been these people of the Intermediate Early/Middle Bronze Age sites who formed the Asiatic menace considered in the Instruction to Merikara of the Herakleopolitan Dynasty. Although there are no archaeological sites in the eastern delta (as there are for the Second Intermediate Period) to provide the basis for some objective judgement on the seriousness of any Asiatic incursion at this time, it must be emphasized that the cultural background to these people is a complete contrast to that of the Hyksos kings and their followers of the Second Intermediate Period. As will be discussed below (pp. 743–5) these latter came from the highly developed urban culture and society of the late Middle Bronze Age whose transference to Egypt seems to have taken place without the establishment of intervening settlements.

The idea has sometimes been advanced that the eastern Nile Delta itself was not incorporated into the Egyptian state until, say, the Middle Kingdom. This is, however, difficult to reconcile with the archaeological evidence, both the presence of Egyptian material from the late Predynastic Period onwards, and the equivalent absence so far of Palestinian Chalcolithic and Early Bronze Age material despite its abundance in central and southern Sinai (see fig. 10.10). Indeed, one would be obliged by the textual evidence used to support this theory to assume the existence by the Sixth Dynasty of fortified Early Bronze Age cities in the eastern Delta, and these are known to have been very substantial structures. By contrast, recent fieldwork has led to the discovery of numerous camp-sites along the whole north Sinai coastal strip, stretching east from near the Nile Delta margins, where Egyptian objects of the late Predynastic and First Dynasty are mixed with Chalcolithic and Early Bronze Age I and II material, apparently in a ratio of 5:1 in favour of the Egyptian (Oren 1973b, Thompson 1975, pp. 9–13). When added to the widespread distribution of imported Egyptian pottery and other objects in Palestinian sites of these same periods as far north as the 'Amuq plain, the point can even be argued that as early as the beginning of the First Dynasty the Egyptians had begun a serious attempt at large-scale conquest in western Asia. A further element in the argument is the existence of large stone gazelle-traps, the so-called 'desert kites', distributed widely in Sinai, Jordan and Syria. It has been suggested that one such is depicted on the Narmer Palette, and that this implies a First Dynasty campaign, at least to Sinai. But since these traps were in use in recent times, more definite dating evidence is required before their relevance to much earlier periods is accepted, and in any case the Narmer Palette depiction is capable of other interpretations (Helms 1975a, Meshel 1974).

An instructive parallel can, however, be drawn with the not dissimilar history of Lower Nubia at this time. On this basis the ready flow of

Egyptian goods eastwards and then north-eastwards would be a sign of trade's being carried out on a local basis, largely free from a centrally directed political framework. The Nubian A-group can be explained as a product of a situation like this, with Egyptian aggressive policies having cultural repercussions only at the end, with the complete demise of settled life and cultural activity in Lower Nubia. The similar apparent disappearance of settlements along the north Sinai coast during or after the Early Dynastic Period could be regarded as an equivalent phenomenon, and more the result of a hard political frontier policy than an attempt at anything more ambitious.

The Sinai peninsula has been, over most of historical time, a wedge of nomadic tribal life separating two urban civilizations: Egypt and Palestine. In the second and third millennia BC the essential difference between the two was that between a centralized government channelling national resources to a single pool of talent, wealth, power and ambition, and, on the other hand, a collection of city states whose resources remained more dispersed and were, so one might imagine, partly consumed by the constant struggle to remain independent. It is an unfortunate consequence of the non-literate nature of this latter society that we know virtually nothing of its political development and, in particular, the extent to which policies were co-ordinated either by means of alliances or through the imposition of the will of one ruler of greater power. It is now known that the network of Palestinian towns and cities in the Early and Middle Bronze Ages spread southwards to terminate in a line running between Tell el-'Ajjul in the west and Tell Arad in the east, forming a frontier zone from which Sinai lay at a distance not much greater than it did from Egypt. Furthermore, recent fieldwork suggests that central and southern Sinai, in contrast to the coastal strip, was an extension of the southern Palestinian culture zone in the Chalcolithic and Early Bronze Age I and II periods, and that already its turquoise and copper deposits were being worked (fig. 10.10) (Amiran, Beit Arieh and Glass 1973, Beit Arieh 1974, Beit Arieh and Gophna 1976, Gophna 1976a, Rothenberg 1969, 1970–1, 1972, 1972–3). The evidence consists of a surprising number of settlements and cemeteries, including some stone-built villages (e.g. site 688 south of Aïn Fogeiya, and Sheikh Nabi Salah). Egyptian objects are said to have been present in only very slight quantities, but it might still be reasonable to see the Egyptians obtaining turquoise and copper by trading, for example, through the site of Ma'adi, near modern Cairo. There is the implication, too, that when the Egyptians eventually gained

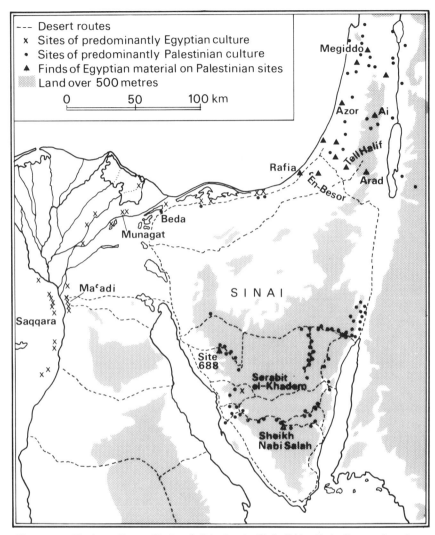

Fig. 10.10 Northern Egypt, Sinai and Palestine in Chalcolithic, Early Bronze Age, late Predynastic and Early Dynastic times. Some clusters of sites have been simplified; others, along the north Sinai coast and between El-Thamad and Jebel el-ʻIgma, are schematically plotted on account of the brevity of the published preliminary reports.

sole control over Sinai it was at the expense of this Palestinian cultural outlier. It may be significant that, unless the archaeological record differs locally from that in Palestine proper, these widely spread settlements seem not to have survived beyond the Early Bronze Age II period, except for a brief reoccupation in the Intermediate Early / Middle Bronze

Age period when the Egyptians were involved in a civil war. Again, as with the record in Lower Nubia, a considerable destructive power seems to be implied for the Egyptian state of the Early Dynastic Period. Indeed, the complete clearance of settlements in both border zones and beyond is remarkable.

Inscriptions found *in situ* in Sinai recording an Egyptian presence cover the periods between Kings Sanakht of the Third Dynasty and Pepy II of the Sixth, and then between Senusret I and Amenemhat IV of the Twelfth, although a late Eleventh Dynasty inscription from Thebes almost certainly describes an expedition to this region (see p. 729). With one exception these inscriptions make turquoise the object of the expeditions, apparently centred around three areas: Wadi Maghara, Serabit el-Khadem and Wadi Kharit, but the very same part of south Sinai also contains copper, widely exploited by the previous inhabitants. Surveys have located one Egyptian copper-smelting site, at Bir Naṣb, with copper deposits nearby and in the Wadi Ba'aba, but even this may be no earlier than the New Kingdom. Small-scale copper-working was, however, carried on in the Egyptian miners' camp in Wadi Maghara. During the Middle Kingdom the Egyptians built, on a hill-top site called Serabit el-Khadem, a small shrine dedicated to Hathor, Lady of Turquoise. Hathor was evidently felt by Egyptians sent abroad to have both a character which was beneficent towards ordinary Egyptians and the universal immanence necessary for localization at foreign places, such as at Byblos and the diorite quarries in the western Nubian desert and the Wadi el-Hudi. Votive objects from Serabit el-Khadem include a rich and informative collection of Middle Kingdom inscriptions, as well as a small number of private and royal statues.

In the Middle Kingdom, although only Egyptian sites have been located in Sinai, inscriptions indicate, with none of the usual hostility of tone, contact with 'Asiatics' of more than a passing nature. Some of these references are to Asiatics included amongst the personnel of the Egyptian expeditions to Sinai, in one case a party of twenty from Hamy or Harim, a place included in the Execration Texts under the rule of a prince with a Semitic name and to be identified probably with Tell el-Milh, or possibly with Khirbet el-Mshash, both Middle Bronze Age towns along the Tell el-'Ajjul–Tell Arad line mentioned above. There is also a group of four stelae from the Serabit el-Khadem temple featuring a man riding a donkey, identified on one as the 'brother of the prince of Retenu (Palestine), Khebded', a man known from three other Sinai inscriptions where he appears to have been part of Egyptian expeditions dated to the period between years 4 and 13 of Amenemhat III. The distinctive manner in which he is portrayed on the stelae implies a considerable impact on the Egyptians. This apparently symbiotic relationship between Egyptians and Asiatics at the Sinai mines might be interpreted as a sign that the Egyptians had found it necessary to come to some sort of agreement with whatever political leadership was behind the cities of southern Palestine and which was sufficently strong to influence the conduct of Egyptian expeditions, and perhaps to share in the mined products.

That Palestinian princes appreciated the Egyptian demand for minerals sufficiently to involve themselves in it is suggested by the scene in the tomb of the nomarch Khnumhetep at Beni Hasan of the arrival, at an unfortunately unspecified locality in year 6 of Senusret II, of a colourful Palestinian group under a 'foreign prince' Abisha, bringing galena, a substance widely used in Middle Kingdom Egypt as an eye cosmetic. Their homeland, Shuwet, which also appears in the Execration Texts, has been tentatively localized in Moab. Galena was also included amongst the minerals and stones brought back from an expedition to Sinai and other adjacent lands by the overseer of quarry-work, Khety, in the later Eleventh Dynasty (Helck 1955, 1975, pp. 179–80; Schenkel 1965, pp. 283–4; Ward 1971, p. 59). Amongst other substances were not only turquoise and copper, but also lapis lazuli, something not found naturally in this part of the Near East at all, and thus available only from a transaction with or an attack on an existing trading centre. A term 'Asiatic copper' is seemingly attested in the late Old Kingdom (Posener-Kriéger (1969).

Except for Sinai, Egyptian sources for relations with Palestine and with Syria are meagre in the extreme, and often do not in their terminology enable a distinction to be made between the Sinai nomadic wedge and the settled hinterland.[1] There are, however, a few exceptions which suggest attacks on urbanized Palestine, some of whose cities are now known to have possessed substantial fortifications of the type depicted in the ancient illustrations.

The earliest and most detailed is the biography of Uni from the reign of Pepy I, describing how he led a national army, reinforced with Nubian mercenaries, against the settled population of an unspecified part of Palestine on five separate campaigns, followed by a land and sea

---

[1] The term 'Aamu, 'Asiatics', was extended to peoples of the eastern desert. This is evident not only from the well-known inscription of Pepy-nakht, but also from a graffito in the Wadi el-Hudi (Fakhry 1952, p. 46, no. 31; also Brovarski and Murnane 1969, no. 1). Helck's suggestion (1971, p. 21) that Pepy-nakht's expedition was to Syria is thus gratuitous. See also Couroyer (1971).

attack in the vicinity of a place called 'Nose of the Gazelle', sometimes, though on purely picturesque grounds, identified with Mount Carmel. From roughly this same period come scenes of attacks on fortifications manned by Asiatics in the tombs of Inti at Deshasha (Sixth Dynasty) and Kaiemhesit at Saqqara (early Sixth Dynasty), probably in the mortuary temple of Nebhepetra Menthuhetep II; and in the tomb of Intef, of the late Eleventh Dynasty (Arnold and Settgast 1965, fig. 2; W. S. Smith 1965, pp. 148–9; Ward 1971, pp. 59–60, n. 227). From the Middle Kingdom there are only the stele of the general Nesu-menthu of the reign of Senusret I, which refers to hostilities against Asiatics in which fortresses were destroyed, and the stele of Sebek-khu, recounting a campaign conducted by Senusret III to the country of Sekmem, identified by some with the city state of Shechem.

The archaeological record of southern Palestine and of Sinai, as well as the advanced state which defensive military architecture had reached in Egypt by the early Middle Kingdom, should leave little doubt that when the Egyptians refer to or depict foreign fortresses we should understand nothing less than the fortified cities of Early and Middle Bronze Age Palestine.

Of a somewhat different character is the Story of Sinuhe, a literary romance in which the hero, exiling himself from Egypt in the reign of Senusret I, achieves fame and wealth in a Palestinian kingdom. The avoidance of references to cities has been variously interpreted, but the practice of sending envoys from the Egyptian court to local rulers is given a prominent place in the narrative. This is something supported by a few brief references in other texts, and fully in keeping with not only the well-documented diplomatic practices of the ancient Near East, but also with the contact via envoys which the Egyptians maintained with their Nubian neighbours (see p. 719). Information gained by this type of contact would be one way by which the Egyptians were furnished with the necessary details for the Asiatic sections of the Middle Kingdom Execration Texts. Listed there are rulers and peoples of towns, cities and regions over most of the area of Middle Bronze Age Palestine, from Moab and the Negev in the south to beyond Kadesh in the north, and then over a separate area even further north lying behind Byblos and Ullaza to Upe.

Diplomacy has as its purpose the influencing of events as well as the collection of information. By analogy with the New Kingdom pattern one might suspect that attacks on fortified towns were the shock tactics intended to force favourable alliances or even vassalage which would then be maintained or extended by diplomatic activity. Such a policy might, in southern Palestine, have had some urgency if, as suggested above, some of the city states in the area had an interest in Sinai and in the supply of minerals and precious stones to Egypt. But as to whether this was followed by the posting of Egyptian officials charged with administrative, as distinct from representative, duties cannot be determined on present evidence, although it is presumably at this point that the term 'empire' becomes justified. One source with considerable implications here is the title sequence of a scribe, Ka-aper of the early Fifth Dynasty, which includes that of 'army scribe of the king' in a number of named places which seem, from the way they are written, to have been some of these Palestinian fortified cities (Fischer 1959b).

Of much greater ambiguity are the Egyptian objects discovered on eastern Mediterranean sites which, with the exception of the material from Byblos, occur in significant numbers only from the Middle · Kingdom onwards, although the recent excavations at Ebla (Tell Mardikh) have already produced two diorite bowl fragments with the name of Khafra of the Fourth Dynasty, and part of an alabaster lid of Pepy I of the Sixth Dynasty (Matthiae 1978). This general paucity of Old Kingdom artifacts is true for Nubia and Serabit el-Khadem also. Most striking are the sphinxes of Amenemhat III and IV, and of a queen of Amenemhat II, which have been found at several Syrian sites: Beirut, Qatna, Ugarit and Neirab; also a statuette of Khaneferra Sebekhetep of the Thirteenth Dynasty from Tell Hizzin. Statuettes of private individuals have been found at Tell el-'Ajjul, Gezer (which has also yielded a statuette of a princess), Megiddo, Ugarit, Ji'ara, Atchana and Kürigen Kale in Turkey and Knossos in Crete, the last three from places beyond the confines of the Execration Texts. The sphinxes from Syria might be regarded as diplomatic gifts, but for the statuettes, which would normally have been made to stand in proximity to a cult place from which they could benefit, two quite contrary parallels can be cited. On the one hand there is the Middle Kingdom temple at Serabit el-Khadem in Sinai (or even better, the Late Bronze Age temple at Beth-Shan in Palestine) where inscribed Egyptian objects, including statuettes, commemorate the temporary presence of the owner in a foreign land and his attempt to gain the favour of a local deity, whether that deity was Egyptian or not. On this parallel they would be an indication of the extent of Egyptian postings abroad, though not of the scope of the responsibilities involved. On the other hand, one can use the parallel of Kerma in Nubia (see pp. 715, 753-4), where Egyptian statues and statuettes, some of them quite old by the time in question, had an intrinsic value of their own, helping to endow their new owners with some of the dignity and sophistication of the country that had produced them. On this parallel it can be suggested that some of these statuettes in western Asia reached their destinations quite late in the Middle Bronze Age, during the Hyksos period in Egypt. It is unfortunate that in most cases the context is equivocal, even with excavated examples which in no case would seem to come from a clear early Middle Bronze Age context (i.e. Albright's Middle Bronze Age IIA). This is true, for example, for the statuette of Djehuty-hetep found at Megiddo with three other Middle Kingdom statuettes built into the structure of a temple probably not erected until at least the end of the Middle Bronze Age (Dunayevsky and Kempinski 1973, Kenyon 1969, pp. 49–53).

Although the evidence from Palestine and Syria is ambiguous, the overall effectiveness of Egyptian activity ought to be apparent, so one might imagine, from areas even further afield, whose own rulers would naturally feel jealous of or threatened by a successful Egyptian axis established in Palestine and who would, at the least, seek diplomatic contact. The New Kingdom would provide the appropriate parallel to this situation. Thus the lack of any reference in Egyptian texts to contact with kingdoms even further to the north in Syria and beyond may have some positive significance. There is, too, the archive of the important city of Mari on the Upper Euphrates. Diplomatic contact by means of letters written on clay tablets was maintained with places as far south as Hazor and Byblos, but Egypt is nowhere even mentioned. The period of the letters is not, however, that of the powerful Twelfth Dynasty in Egypt, but the Thirteenth, and more specifically the period of Neferhetep I whose rule began about 45 years after the end of the Twelfth Dynasty, but whose name was, nevertheless, still commemorated at Byblos by one of the local rulers.

Byblos had a very special relationship with Egypt, and the archaeological record is unique as far as Egyptian contact in the eastern Mediterranean is concerned. As the principal centre for the trade which provided the Egyptians with badly-needed timber from the coniferous forests of the Lebanon, as well as resin, a by-product early in demand for mummification, it became a focus for Egyptian cultural influence. Partly this is visible in the form of votive objects from the local temples, where one of the deities was a further form of Hathor: 'Lady of Byblos', though some ambiguity must surround the identity of who was responsible for donating them, and under what circumstances. Amongst the Egyptian objects from the temples and adjacent areas are pieces bearing the names of kings Khasehkemwy of the Second Dynasty, Khufu, Khafra, Menkaura of the Fourth Dynasty, Sahura (?), Neferirkara, Djedkara Isesi (?), Neuserra and Unas of the Fifth Dyasty, Teti, Pepy I, Merenra and Pepy II of the Sixth Dynasty, and Amenemhat III of the Twelfth Dynasty. There are also a part of a statue ascribed on stylistic grounds to King Neuserra (Bothmer 1971) and a fragment of a sphinx of a Middle Kingdom princess. Amongst the uninscribed objects in Egyptian style are numerous faience animal figurines and a hoard of scarabs, beads and trinkets. During the Middle Bronze Age one of the temples was furnished with small, locally-made obelisks, one with a hieroglyphic inscription made for a prince of Byblos. These princes, who can be traced into the Second Intermediate Period, also had their own scarabs manufactured, as well as hieroglyphic funerary or votive stelae, one of which records building work in a temple dedicated to the goddess Nut, presumably a rendering, by the use of an Egyptian equivalent, of the name of a local goddess, perhaps Anath.

Egyptian influence is even more strikingly evident in the funerary equipment of some of these princes or kings of Byblos contemporary with the later part of the Twelfth Dynasty. It takes the form of Egyptian-made objects equivalent in their artistic standard to objects from Egyptian court burials (e.g. the gold-bound obsidian casket, the obsidian ointment jar decorated with gold, the silver mirror; two pectorals with the names of Amenemhat III and IV from somewhere in the Lebanon may also derive from here); local imitations of Egyptian objects (gold and inlaid pectorals, an elaborate pendant with the name of prince Yapa-shemu-abi in a cartouche, bronze uraeus figures with silver inlays in niello technique); and non-Egyptian-style objects given hieroglyphic inscriptions (the scimitar). Taken together, the cartouches, Egyptian epithets, uraei and jewellery suggest a pastiche of Egyptian royalty at the Byblite court. On their scarabs the princes call themselves simply 'governor of Byblos', and if these were used for sealing items sent to Egypt they may reflect a wish to conform in this one instance to an Egyptian view of their status, whereas their Pharaonic pretensions were for a local context. Even so, this would seem to represent a unique compromise arrangement which involved recognition by the Egyptians that Byblos was an extension of their urban world. The same equivocal status *vis-à-vis* the king of Egypt is apparent from a block showing another one of these princes, Inten, seated, offering a prayer to the Egyptian god Ra-Horakhty, with the cartouche of Neferhetep I also present; also just possibly in the inscription on a lapis lazuli cylinder seal from the early Thirteenth Dynasty. Furthermore, although essentially a Middle Kingdom phenomenon, one should note an Old Kingdom cylinder seal with similar cultural implications (Goedicke 1966b, 1976b, du Mesnil du Buisson 1970, pp. 76–88).

By contrast, records from Egypt of contact with Byblos are very slight for these periods (Horn 1963, Leclant 1954). The name 'Byblos' first occurs in a Fourth Dynasty mastaba at Giza; on the Palermo Stone an entry from the reign of King Sneferu records the acquisition of forty shiploads of timber, and it is assumed that their origin was Byblos; the same official at Aswan who recorded visiting Punt with the governor of Elephantine included Byblos as well; 'Byblos-ships' were thought suitable for the journey to Punt. For the Middle Kingdom references to Byblos are confined to a few naming 'Hathor, Lady of Byblos'.

Overall, the evidence for the nature and extent of Egyptian influence or control in western Asia is highly unsatisfactory, and in this situation it is presumably better to err on the side of caution, and to limit the sphere of direct Egyptian interference to the cities of southern Palestine, the motive being that of securing an extensive border zone. It should be noted, however, that the imperialist phraseology of the New Kingdom can, in essence, be found already in the Middle Kingdom, if not before (Blumenthal 1970, pp. 189–201; Goedicke 1969–70).[1]

## The Aegean

The only part of the Aegean region which received Egyptian goods in any quantity and whose own goods in turn reached Egypt was Crete. A surprising number of Egyptian stone vessels of types dated between the late Predynastic Period and the early Middle Kingdom have been found on Crete, and gave rise to local imitations. But whilst a few come from Early Minoan II or Early Minoan II–Middle Minoan IB/II contexts, many were still apparently in circulation in the Late Minoan periods, thus contemporary with the Hyksos period and New Kingdom in Egypt. To this material should be added some twenty Middle Kingdom scarabs, and a solitary Middle Kingdom statuette from Knossos. The converse situation is represented by small quantities of imported Middle Minoan pottery at Egyptian sites. This consists of two or three Middle Minoan I sherds from El-Lisht, sherds from thirteen and twenty-one Middle Minoan II vessels respectively from Kahun and

[1] Cf. also the title of Pepy I or II on an alabaster vase from Byblos: 'Ra of the foreign lands' (Chéhab 1969, p. 18).

El-Haraga, from a Middle Minoan II vase found in a tomb at Abydos, and a complete vessel from a tomb at Elephantine (Kemp and Merrillees 1980). At Kahun Minoan pottery was imitated, and local potters also produced small amounts of polychrome pottery evidently under its stimulus. Kahun has also yielded a Minoan stone vase lid.

The probable Egyptian name for Crete, Keftiu, whilst it may have been known to Egyptians in the Middle Kingdom, does not occur in any context which suggests direct contact. But it must be admitted that there is a serious paucity of documents which might be expected to have contained such records, such as the decorative schemes of royal and court tombs. Direct contact is not particularly difficult from a seafaring point of view, involving a relatively short open-sea crossing to Cyrenaica, followed by a coastal voyage eastwards to the Nile Delta. Minoan contact with the North African coast during the early New Kingdom seems to be implied by the miniature marine painting from Thera. But it is equally possible for the exchange of goods to have been indirectly carried out via Byblos or Ugarit, both of which sites have also produced Minoan pottery.

A very small number of inscribed Egyptian objects have been found even further afield: a small vase bearing the name of the funerary temple of King Userkaf of the Fifth Dynasty from the island of Kythera, lying between Crete and the Peloponnese; fragments of a gold-plated chair with the name of King Sahura said to come from a tomb at Dorak in north-western Anatolia, about 200 km east from the Aegean coast; and a gold cylinder-seal of an official of the Fifth Dynasty, possibly also from Anatolia (Vermeule and Vermeule 1970, Young 1972). Even if the last two should receive further verification as to provenance, it need not imply a direct link with Egypt. One way by which valuable objects were distributed in the ancient world was as gifts from one ruler to another, in the course of which gifts were made from those already received from some other head of state, or other source. A mixed provenance of this nature can be seen in one hoard of precious objects found in Egypt: the Tod treasure. Apart from Babylonian seals the precise source of the objects, mainly silver vessels, is hard to determine, though Minoan influence is probably visible. Although found in bronze chests of Amenemhat II there is no necessity to assume that the treasure was originally associated with them, and it is clear from the excavation report that, because work on the temple foundations in which the treasure was found was being done as late as the Thirtieth Dynasty, the treasure cannot be regarded as a sealed deposit of the Middle Kingdom.

In general, much more needs to be understood about the mechanisms of ancient trade and other forms of contact before objects found far distant from their homeland can be written into a history of foreign policies pursued by different countries.

## THE SECOND INTERMEDIATE PERIOD IN EGYPT

All the indications are that in Upper Egypt the administrative and cultural patterns of the Twelfth Dynasty continued well into the Thirteenth, with a degree of continuity which might justify extending the term Middle Kingdom to cover this as well as the Twelfth Dynasty. The town of Kahun which housed the community administering the mortuary estate of the nearby pyramid of Senusret II exemplifies this, for it continued to function probably into the latter part of the Thirteenth Dynasty, the last royal name from here being Wahibra Ibiyau (Petrie 1890, p. 31, pl. x. 72; the name is only partially preserved and some doubt must remain over it), whilst administrative papyri from the first two reigns of the Thirteenth Dynasty illustrate the continued operation of the late Twelfth Dynasty administrative system here. Not very far distant, the middle-class cemetery at El-Haraga displays a homogeneity in material culture extending from some point in the Twelfth until probably well into the Thirteenth Dynasty.

At least six tombs of kings of this period have been discovered in the Memphite area: two at Saqqara (one of them belonging to King Khendjer), two at Mazghuna, two at Dashur (Ameny 'Aamu and Awibra Hor). Five are pyramids, small in size but complex in internal design. Another, that of Awibra Hor at Dashur, in some ways epitomizes this period. Built modestly within the pyramid enclosure of Amenemhat III but with funeral trappings very similar to those of the court burials of the Twelfth Dynasty, it displays a basic continuity from the past with an inability to promote the construction of a monumental court cemetery, something inevitably bound up with a general brevity of reign, in this case a mere seven months according to the Turin king-list. Inscriptions from provincial sites further south in Upper Egypt imply a recognition both of kings ruling from (Amenemhat-) Ith-tawy in the north and of an administrative system apparently identical to that of the late Twelfth Dynasty. This material includes the stele of Horem-khauef (stylistically dated to the very end of the Thirteenth Dynasty and probably very close to the beginning of the Seventeenth (Hayes 1947,

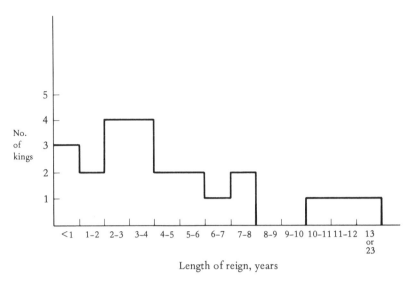

Fig. 10.11   Length of reign from amongst the first fifty kings in succession to the Twelfth Dynasty. (After Kitchen 1967a and von Beckerath 1964.) King Sekhemkara is given between 7 and 8 years on the basis of the Semna inscription reported by B. Bell (1975).

Vandersleyen 1971, p. 208)) which describes a visit made to the court at the old capital of Ith-tawy. The names of many of the kings are attested on statues, stelae, offering-tables and building blocks at a number of temple sites (see table 10.1).

Of the Turin king-list no less than six of its eleven columns are devoted to the period between the end of the Twelfth and the beginning of the Eighteenth Dynasty, representing some 175 reigns for a period of perhaps 220 or 230 years. Current estimates of how many of these names should be ascribed to Manetho's Thirteenth Dynasty vary between the first fifty and the first ninety of those following the last ruler of the Twelfth Dynasty, Sebek-neferu (Manetho himself allotted sixty kings to it). Where the length of reign is preserved in the fragmentary king-list it is often of the brevity to be expected of the situation, as can be seen from fig. 10.11.

Nevertheless, these twenty-three kings represent about a century of rule, a period not much less than the maximum which can be allotted to the Thirteenth Dynasty as a whole, between about 110 and 125 years. This raises the question of how far this group of kings really represents a single line ruling successively from the vicinity of Memphis. The

TABLE 10.1  *Royal names from statues, stelae, offering-tables and building blocks found at temple sites in Upper Egypt, and on small objects and papyri from Kahun*

| Years BC | Kahun | Abydos | Coptos | Medamud | Karnak | Deir el-Bahari | Tod | Gebelein | Elephantine/Sehel |
|---|---|---|---|---|---|---|---|---|---|
| 1782 | XIII.3<br>XIII.4 | XIII.3 | | XIII.1 | XIII.1 | | XIII.2 | | XIII.4? |
| | | XIII.C<br>XIII.12 | | | XIII.7 | XIII.12 | | | |
| | | XIII.17 | | XIII.15<br>XIII.16 | | XIII.16 | | | |
| | XIII.26 | XIII.22<br>XIII.24 | XIII.21 | XIII.21 | XIII.21?<br>XIII.22<br>XIII.24 | XIII.24 | XIII.21 | | XIII.21<br>XIII.22 |
| | | XIII.28 | | | XIII.27<br>XIII.28 | | XIII.31 | | |
| | | | | | XIII.32<br>XIII.F<br>XIII.G | | XIII.F | | |
| *c.* 1680 | | | | | XIII.J<br>XIII.K | XIII.37<br>XIII.41 | | XIII.37<br>XIII.41<br>XIII.J | |
| | | | | | | XIII.44<br>XIII.L | | | |

738

TABLE 10.1 (*cont.*)

| Years BC | Kahun | Abydos | Coptos | Medamud | Karnak | Deir el-Bahari | Tod | Gebelein | Elephantine/Sehel |
|---|---|---|---|---|---|---|---|---|---|
| | | XIII.M | | | | | | | |
| | | XIII.N | | | | | | | |
| *c.* 1650 | | XVII.1 | XVII.1 | | XVII.1 | | | | |
| | | XVII.2 | XVII.2 | | | | | [XV.4] | |
| | | XVII.3 | | XVII.3 | XVII.3 | XVII.3 | | [XV.5] | XVII.3 |
| | | | | | XVII.6 | | | | |
| | | | | XVII.9? | | | | | |
| *c.* 1560 | | XVII.10 | | | XVII.10 | | | | |
| | | | | | XVII.15 | | | | |

*Note*: The numbers are those of von Beckerath (1964) the Roman numerals indicating the dynasty. The table stresses the continuity of government between the Thirteenth and Seventeenth Dynasties in Upper Egypt.

inscribed capstone from the pyramid tomb of one of them, Merneferra Ay, whose reign of 13/23 years and 8 months is the longest known of this group, has been found, not in the Memphite area at all, but in the eastern Delta, near Faqus, from an area sufficiently rich in remains of this and later periods to suggest the existence of a city of some importance. Barring the distant possibility that it was transported there at a later date, it might be taken as a hint of a degree of fragmentation of rule in northern Egypt, although the authority of this man was sufficient for his commemoration in the temple at Karnak. Objects probably from a temple in this same area also record the piety of a King Nehesy, who occupies a position about twenty-three places further on in the Turin list. Acceptance of the idea of a fragmentation of northern Egypt into city states with some rulers writing their names in cartouches becomes a necessity in dealing with the continuation of the Turin list, which gave to six 'foreign kings' (Hyksos) a total reign of 108 years, so covering the remainder of the Second Intermediate Period whilst still leaving at least 79 and possibly as many as 119 kings to be accounted for. Of these, 15 can be set aside as kings of Upper Egypt ruling from Thebes contemporaneously with the Hyksos and in succession to the Thirteenth Dynasty. But this still leaves a great many, whose numbers may even have to be augmented by kings whose names appear on objects, principally scarabs, and cannot be identified with any in the Turin list.

Manetho ignored altogether the possibility of contemporaneous rule, and divided these various kings after the Thirteenth Dynasty into four more dynasties. But in doing this he was, like the king-list compilers before him, working to a preconceived idea: a unitary succession of kings, whose reigns could be added together when necessary to produce extended periods of rule, and who, in Manetho's work, could also be neatly grouped into dynasties ascribed to a city of origin. It is not an attack on the basic veracity of the king-list compilers to say that they sometimes brought a spurious tidiness to periods of history where a degree of complexity, even of disorder, prevailed. Their interest in the past was essentially confined to numbers, names, pious deeds and scraps of legend. The neatness of Manetho's scheme is not in itself necessarily a viable starting-point for historical study, and for this period may be largely unhistorical. Indeed, all that one may in the end be entitled to see in this period as far as kingship goes is that there was a proliferation of kings who can be divided into four groups:

(1) kings following the Twelfth Dynasty whose authority was, for

political reasons which may at times have been quite complex, recognized in Upper Egypt and who continued for the most part, but not necessarily in every case, to rule from and be buried near Memphis, and who may have also exercised a general overlordship, if not total rule, over parts or all of northern Egypt;

(2) a line of kings ruling Upper Egypt in succession to them, but now centred at Thebes, and buried there;

(3) six 'foreign kings', i.e. Hyksos, who replaced group (1) in the north and who ruled at the same time as group (2);

(4) an uncertain number of client kings, presumably of city states, mostly in the north of Egypt and including some with the title 'foreign king', distributed uncertainly in time *vis-à-vis* the other groups.

Purely for convenience the following equations can be made with Manetho: (1) = XIII, (2) = XVII, (3) = XV, (4) = XIV and XVI. With groups (1) and (4) it can become needlessly pedantic to argue as to which dynasty a particular king belonged since the ancient thinking behind the grouping of kings proceeded from a view very different from our own as to what the past was about. There are strong grounds for regarding the hereditary principle of royal succession as having thoroughly broken down during the Thirteenth Dynasty, with continuity of government vested, for at least part of the time, in a family of viziers (von Beckerath 1951, Berlev 1974). Only in the sub-dynasty of Neferhetep I and his successors is any direct family continuity visible (Dewachter 1976, Simpson 1969a).[1] In this essentially non-dynastic situation, implying the existence of several families whose relatives had at some not too distant point in the past been kings, the question of legitimacy must have become so clouded that the appearance of contemporaneous kings in the north is more easily understandable. There is no need to attribute it to foreign influence and to see it as a post-Hyksos development.

As noted, the eventual fate of the northern part of the country is not in doubt. Tentatively placed in the penultimate column of the Turin list is a fragment summarizing the 108-year rule of six 'foreign kings'. The term used ([ḥḳꝫw] ḥꝫswt, literally 'rulers of foreign lands') contains the true etymology of Manetho's term 'Hyksos'. Manetho, as quoted by Josephus, told a story of how, in the reign of a King Tutimaeus, Egypt had been siezed by 'invaders of obscure race/ignoble birth' who 'burned our cities ruthlessly, razed to the ground the temples of the gods and treated all the natives with a cruel hostility'. Although ruling

---

[1] For the family background of another king of this time see Macadam (1951).

at first from Memphis, they subsequently built a great fortified stronghold on the site of Avaris in the eastern delta. Finally they were attacked by kings from Thebes, confined to Avaris, and allowed to leave Egypt in peace. This view of the Hyksos, as an essentially destructive interlude in Egyptian history, has in the past exercised considerable influence on the writing of the history of the period. It is a view which can be found expressed even more anciently, in Papyrus Sallier I of the reign of Merenptah (1224–1214 BC), a popular tale in which the Hyksos king Apepy (Apophis) in Avaris appears as an archetypal villain; and in the Speos Artemidos inscription of Queen Hatshepsut, where the supposed disorder of the Hyksos period becomes, on a purely un-historical plane, the target for the deliverance from evil which was a fundamental role of kings in Egyptian theology, Hatshepsut claiming to have restored the land to order after their rule. The tradition of the Hyksos was evidently not an entirely uniform one, however. A remarkable genealogy which once probably adorned the walls of a tomb of a priest of Memphis of the Twenty-second Dynasty traces his ancestors back to the Eleventh Dynasty. In listing some of the kings under whom they are supposed to have served, two or three Hyksos kings are given (including Apepy) in place of the Theban Seventeenth Dynasty kings whom one might have expected if the document had been drawn up in Upper Egypt (von Beckerath 1964, pp. 27–8).

What few material remains the Hyksos kings themselves have left behind lend little support to the more lurid views of their rule. For, like later foreign overlords of Egypt, whether Libyan, Sudanese, Persian or Roman, they chose both to present themselves as Pharaohs, complete with traditional titulary employing names compounded with the name of the sun god, Ra, and to indulge in or to encourage a little embellishment of temples, by additions to the fabric, as at Bubastis and Gebelein, or by dedicating an offering-table, or by having their names added to the statues and sphinxes of earlier kings.

Already in the later Middle Kingdom there is evidence for surprisingly large numbers of 'Asiatics' present in Egyptian society, apparently more or less assimilated. An extensive list can be compiled of those in domestic service, the most striking example being Brooklyn Papyrus 35.1446 of the Thirteenth Dynasty from Thebes, where 45 amongst a total of 79 domestic staff are identified as Asiatic. Documents from Kahun refer to the 'officer in charge of the Asiatic troops' and to the 'scribe of the Asiatics', suggesting an interesting counterpart to the position of Nubians in the Old Kingdom (Kaplony-Heckel 1971a, pp. 3, 5–6). A few can be traced in administrative positions, and by their names one or more of the Thirteenth Dynasty kings identify themselves as having possible Asiatic origin.[1] It may, however, despite the formal presentation of themselves by the Hyksos as traditional kings, be misleading to place too much emphasis on this process of immigration as an antecedent to Hyksos rule. For the foreignness of the Hyksos was evidently something which left a deep impression on some Egyptians. Most notably, apart from the literary tradition, the Turin king-list distinguished them uniquely by writing their names without a cartouche and with a hieroglyphic sign added which designates them as foreign, and by using the term 'foreign kings' to describe them. They appear to have represented something more than assimilated Asiatics who had gained the throne through the normal processes of internal politics of this period.

It is at this point that the evidence of archaeology becomes important. In Upper Egypt cemeteries at widely separated places (such as Hager Esna, Abydos, and Qau) show, during this whole period, nothing more than slow changes of fashion which appear to be internally derived. This is not in itself a sign of political stability since the same was broadly true for the First Intermediate Period, but it at least limits the extent of a foreign cultural element present in Egypt at this time. Moving further north, in the El-Lahun area there appears to be a considerable cultural hiatus corresponding to the Hyksos period, and affecting both Kahun and El-Haraga, as well as Medinet el-Ghurab. If the life of the El-Lahun area depended heavily on association with government activity, as it may well have done, then this may perhaps reflect a serious interference with established administration under Hyksos rule.

But it is in the Delta itself, and more particularly its eastern border area, that archaeology makes a vital contribution to our knowledge of the period. At several sites on the east side of the ancient Pelusiac branch of the Nile (principally at Tell el-Yahudiya and Tell ed-Dab'a, see fig. 10.13), a culture heavily influenced by that of contemporary Middle Bronze Age II Palestine has been encountered in tombs and settlement strata (Bietak 1968a, 1970, 1975a, pp. 165, 167; Petrie 1906, chs. 1 and 2).[2] The main elements are: domestic pottery of Egyptian type; jugs

[1] Khendjer and Ameny 'Aamu; note also Hetepibra Hornedjheritef son of 'Aamu. However, the name 'Aamu (= 'Asiatic') can be given the alternative reading Kemau, 'landworker', 'winnower' (von Beckerath 1964, pp. 40–2; Posener 1957b).

[2] Attention should also be drawn to a remarkable jewellery hoard, which includes a golden circlet ornamented with stags' heads, and thought to be possibly of the Hyksos period, which

and juglets, bronze axe-heads and toggle-pins of Palestinian inspiration or origin; a small amount of Cypriote pottery; donkeys accompanying human burials (Boessneck 1970, Stiebing 1971); scarabs of designs common to both Egypt and Palestine at this period, and clearly produced in large quantities in the latter area. At Tell el-Yahudiya, as well as at Heliopolis, a large earthen embankment has been compared to the plastered slopes beneath the cities of Middle Bronze Age Palestine, but the comparison probably has no historical validity (Parr 1968, Seger 1975, G. R. H. Wright 1968). The finds from Tell ed-Dab'a, a site with an area at this period of about half a square kilometre, gain greatly in significance from the likelihood that the Hyksos city of Avaris is to be located here (Bietak 1975b). Amongst buildings excavated, there is a complex of temples of probably Palestinian type.

This marked Palestinian influence, however, seems to have been fairly limited in extent, for it has not been encountered at sites lying further to the west,[1] nor in the cemeteries of the Memphite area. It would be interesting to know how much Palestinian influence was present in the eastern Delta in earlier periods, but the evidence is very limited and fragmentary, though where it exists it is consistently without Palestinian features, and includes the lowest strata at Tell ed-Dab'a itself, apparently of the later Middle Kingdom. Tell ed-Dab'a has also yielded an important collection of anthropological material, from 134 bodies of the Hyksos-period cemeteries (Jungwirth 1960). Preliminary reports describe the population as distinctly different from the usual west Semitic type, more akin, indeed, to types from cemeteries of similar date in north and central Europe. But the real meaning of such comparisons, in this case very tentatively made, is by no means obvious and no far-reaching conclusions should be drawn, particularly in view of the lack of comparative material from the eastern Delta from earlier periods. The proximity to Asia, however, may explain the prominence in this area of a cult of the god Seth, who could serve as a manifestation of the alien nature of the country beyond Egypt's borders. It may have been established as early as the late Old Kingdom, and seems certainly to have been in existence before the Hyksos Dynasty. The local

is a said to have come from El-Salhiya, 16.5 km east of Tell ed-Dab'a, and is now in the Metropolitan Museum of Art, New York (Aldred 1971, pp. 204–5, pl. 89; Gómez-Moreno 1972–3; Vandersleyen 1975, p. 390. pl. 395a).

[1] Although the amount of excavation done further to the west is very slight indeed. On the western edge of the delta the cemetery of Kom el-Hisn seems to provide negative evidence in that in four seasons of excavations in burials dating from the First Intermediate Period to the New Kingdom the only possible Palestinian material was a single Middle Bronze Age II painted juglet (Hamada and Farid 1947).

importance and character of this god may sufficiently explain why the Hyksos associated themselves with him, though in no instance did one of them employ the name Seth in forming his cartouche.

When seen in the perspective of Palestinian cultural history, this period takes on a particular significance. In Palestine this was a period of great fortified cities and military camps, and, it has been said, 'of the greatest prosperity that the country had seen to that time, or would see again before the Roman peace' (G. E. Wright 1971). Although the absence of written records from Palestine inevitably tends to an undervaluation of its historical role and leaves us ignorant of the doubtlessly complex political background to the striking urban achievement of the Middle Bronze Age II period, it is possible to see in the situation a temporary reversal of the roles between Egypt and Palestine, with north-eastern Egypt falling under the aegis of an emergent Palestinian civilization, receiving increased immigration and accelerated cultural contact, as well as a royal house.

Contemporary finds in Egypt record the names of far more than six kings of this period. Some, like Joam, Jakbaal and Anath-her, display Semitic names, others use the title 'foreign king'. These, together with others with Egyptian names, presumably make up Manetho's Sixteenth Dynasty of 'lesser' Hyksos, and can only represent vassal rulers of city states especially in the northern part of Egypt.

The beginning of the Hyksos period in the north may perhaps be imagined as a combination of various Palestinian groups migrating direct from southern Palestine into the eastern Delta, intent upon settlement, and more mobile fighting groups, perhaps centred on or in loose federation with a main army making for Memphis, fanning out and taking over various delta cities, though also leaving others still in the charge of their Egyptian rulers, perhaps by prior agreement. Destruction levels noted at some eastern delta sites, including Tell ed-Dab'a (Bietak 1968a, pp. 84, 89; 1975a, p. 194), may record some of the more serious conflicts. (The date of the installation of the first Hyksos king is apparently to be placed between about 1672 and 1649 BC.)[1]

It has been claimed that the pattern of overlord and vassal was something introduced from western Asia where it was a recognized part

---

[1] By adding the 108 years of the Turin king-list fragment to a date for somewhere around year 10 of Ahmose I of the Eighteenth Dynasty. Unfortunately, it remains difficult to be precise with New Kingdom chronology (Redford 1970, Wente 1975). The relative date of the fall of Avaris is discused in Vandersleyen (1971, pp. 33–40); an even later date is suggested in Hodjache and Berlev (1977).

of the political scene. But even if true, this may simply have been a matter of bringing a formally recognized scheme to an existing situation in view of the possibility that northern Egypt had begun to fragment politically during the Thirteenth Dynasty.

Some objects bearing the name of the Hyksos king Seuserenra Khyan have been found outside Egypt, but so far outside as to make any political deduction from them very hazardous. They comprise: a small lion statuette bought in Baghdad, the lid of an alabaster vase from Knossos and a fragment of an obsidian vase from Boghazköi; also a seal impression from southern Palestine. In view of the likely origin of the Hyksos it would not be surprising to find that a part of southern Palestine remained under their hegemony. But possible direct references to this seem limited to the second Kamose stele, and even these are ambiguous.[1]

The most important of those ruling a part of Egypt simultaneously with the Hyksos was a line of kings of Thebes who form Manetho's Seventeenth Dynasty. They perhaps numbered as many as fifteen, and are best known from objects from their small pyramidal tombs in the Dira Abu el-Naga necropolis of western Thebes. Within the southern part of Egypt, perhaps southwards from the Abydos area, they appear to have been able to exercise some of the traditional functions of kingship, notably by making additions and donations to temples, including those at Abydos, Coptos, Deir el-Ballas, Medamud and Edfu (see table 10.1). The temple of Abydos, in particular, furnishes a record of royal patronage between the end of the Twelfth and the beginning of the Eighteenth Dynasties which leaves the Hyksos very conspicuous by their absence. Only at Gebelein, upstream from Thebes, have the names of Hyksos kings been recovered on monumental blocks, apparently from the temple of Hathor there, the kings being Seuserenra Khyan and Aaweserra Apepy.[2] But to these can be added a few other signs that in the minds of some people in Upper Egypt the Hyksos claim to kingship was legitimate.[3] Two further inscriptions illustrate aspects

[1] Second Kamose stele, line 4: Apepy is addressed as 'prince of Retenu (= Palestine)', but this may signify his origin; lines 13–15 list commodities captured from ships, summarized as 'the produce/tribute of Retenu', the word *inw* being somewhat ambiguous in its implications. Cf. also Giveon (1974a), who argues that scarabs from Canaan also support Hyksos rule over Palestine.

[2] Note also a sistrum from Dendera with the name Apepy (von Beckerath 1964, p. 148); an adze-blade with the name 'Aaweserra, beloved of Sebek, lord of Sumenu', to the south of Thebes (James 1961). Von Beckerath (1964, pp. 148–9) doubts whether the Gebelein blocks came originally from this site, but it is difficult to imagine why they would have been imported from much further north to an area so close to stone quarries.

[3] Principally the dating of the Rhind mathematical papyrus to year 33 of Aaweserra Apepy. It is said to have come from Thebes.

of government operating under the authority of these Theban kings without reference to the Hyksos. In one, King Nubkheperra Intef orders the expulsion from his office in the temple of Min at Coptos of a priest accused of an act of sacrilege; in the other, the transference of a civil office, that of 'governor of el-Kab', was conducted under the aegis of King Sewadjenra Nebiryaw and a copy on stone of the deed displayed in the temple at Thebes by the king's favour. This document is also one source which enables the history of this governorship to be traced with an important degree of continuity through much of the Second Intermediate Period.

If the Hyksos kings tacitly accepted these Theban kings governing this, from their point of view, most distant part of the country, it may have been because it seemed neither rich nor important enough to warrant serious interference.

## THE SECOND INTERMEDIATE PERIOD IN NUBIA

As in Egypt, the transition from the Twelfth to the Thirteenth Dynasty has left no immediately obvious trace of discontinuity. The names of various kings from the first part of the Thirteenth Dynasty have been recovered from the Egyptian fortresses in Lower Nubia, amongst them a sealing of Sekhemra-khutawy Amenemhat Sebekhetep from Mirgissa, a statue and stele of Khutawyra Ugaf from Semna and Mirgissa, and a plaquette of Khasekhemra Neferhetep from Buhen.[1] At the Semna Gorge (and at Askut Island) a series of graffiti recording, presumably with some concern, unusually high flood levels spans the period between year 2 of Amenemhat III to year 1 of Sedjefakara (probably the fifteenth king of the Thirteenth Dynasty), a period of some 70 years of which about the last 18 belong to the Thirteenth Dynasty (B. Bell 1975). However, from the absence of names of later Thirteenth Dynasty and Seventeenth Dynasty kings prior to Kamose, as well as from the state of political affairs made very explicit in the Kamose stelae (see below), it has to be assumed that Egyptian government control over Nubia was eventually lost or relinquished. Some of the fortresses show signs of conflagration, but whether from the attacks of hostile Nubians, from local warfare in a confused situation following the withdrawal of Egyptian control, or from the invading Egyptian armies of the New

[1] For the Ugaf stele from Mirgissa see Vercoutter (1975b). Note also a statue of Khaneferra Sebekhetep from Argo Island, but this is not far from Kerma so the same doubt attaches to it as to the statuary from Kerma itself.

Kingdom is difficult to say.[1] All of these choices are feasible because of evidence that some of these fortresses remained occupied during parts at least of the ensuing periods.

Thus, at Aniba, the main cemetery of family vaults with brick superstructures displays a probable continuity of Egyptian-style burial from the late Middle Kingdom to the New Kingdom.[2] The occurrence of true Tell el-Yahudiya juglets,[3] a product of the Hyksos period in Egypt, is to be noted (Steindorff 1937). In the fortress some restoration of the defences was carried out at a time when the ditches were about one-third filled with sand and rubble. The dry-stone masonry used in the reconstruction has been plausibly seen as a sign of the influence of the local C-group tradition of building, an influence which would be less likely at other periods.

The preliminary statements published so far concerning the site of Mirgissa date the principal surviving building phase in the upper fort to the Thirteenth Dynasty, and the corresponding Egyptian-type cemeteries to both this and the Hyksos period.

At Uronarti the evidence is to be found in a large group of mud sealings (about 4500) from letters, sacks and boxes bearing the impressions of stamp seals and scarabs. Most were found in the 'commandant's house', and amongst them was one, a 'sample-sealing', bearing the name of the Hyksos king Maatibra (Lawrence 1965, p. 86, n. 1, Tufnell 1975). A few impressions carry designs from scarabs which in style might also belong to the period of Hyksos rule. It seems impossible to isolate any other material in the fort which could be ascribed to this period, but neither is there a trace of an alien cultural presence, suggesting that whoever was handling these seals was essentially Egyptian in culture.

The most explicit record, however, comes from Buhen, where a cemetery sequence similar to that at Aniba exists, again including true Tell el-Yahudiya juglets (Randall-MacIver and Woolley 1911, pls. 49, 92). But the fortress itself has yielded a group of stelae which, on grounds of style, epigraphy and content must be ascribed to the period of the Hyksos and Seventeenth Dynasty in Egypt (Barns 1954, Säve-Söderbergh 1949).[4] The owner of one (named Sepedher) states:

[1] The evidence from Buhen now seems to favour the first explanation (H. S. Smith 1976, pp. 80–2).

[2] Note that these are mainly family vaults covering perhaps several generations, in some cases running into the New Kingdom.

[3] On the distinction between true Tell el-Yahudiya ware and El-Lisht ware, see n. 1 on p. 754.

[4] More of these, covering several generations, are published in H. S. Smith (1976, pp. 72–6, 80–5); cf. also Vandersleyen (1971, pp. 56–61).

'I was a valiant commander of Buhen, and never had any commander done what I did. I built the temple of Horus, lord of Buhen, in the days of the King of Kush.' The owner of another (named Ka) also records service with the King of Kush, whose name is given as Nedjeh. Another possible record of mercenary service (not from Buhen) is that of a soldier, Ha-ankhef, who after six years' service in Kush returned home to Edfu in Upper Egypt with enough gold to buy himself land.

The recognition by these men of the rule of this king is but a hint of the power which this Nubian ruler had come to acquire. On the pair of stelae set up at Karnak by Kamose, last king of the Seventeenth Dynasty, describing the early stages of the civil war between Thebes and Avaris, Kamose makes a speech: 'Give me to understand what this strength of mine is for. A king is in Avaris, another is in Kush, and so I sit alongside an Asiatic and a Nubian. Each one has his slice of this Egypt, dividing up the land with me.' The expression 'this Egypt' reflects a claim that Nubia was a part of Egypt (Vandersleyen 1971, pp. 53–6; Vercoutter 1970, pp. 184–6). His courtiers, in a diffident reply, confirm this situation: 'Behold, it is Asiatic territory as far as Cusae...Elephantine is strong. [Thus] the middle part of the land is ours, as far as Cusae.' During the ensuing invasion of Hyksos territory Kamose's army intercepts a letter being conveyed, apparently via the Darb el-Arba'in route, from the Hyksos king Aaweserra Apepy to a king of Kush, newly in office. The text of the letter, quoted in full on the stelae, contains nothing less than an invitation by Apepy for the king of Kush to invade Kamose's kingdom from the south: 'Come, journey downstream! Fear not! He is here with me, and there is no-one [else] who will stand up against you in that part of Egypt. Behold, I will allow him no road until you have arrived. Then shall we divide up the towns of that part of Egypt, and (our lands) shall thrive in joy.' (Habachi 1972 (note that Habachi restores 'Khent-hen-nefer' a term for Nubia, instead of 'our lands'), Säve-Söderbergh 1956, H. S. Smith and A. Smith 1976.)

The implication is that Kush had emerged as a kingdom of considerable strength and importance, a counterpart to the Hyksos kingdom of the north. Yet although both here and in the Buhen stelae Lower Nubia appears to be under the control of these kings, both in the Middle Kingdom and in the New Kingdom Kush as a geographical entity seems to have been regarded as typically Upper Nubian. And it is in Upper Nubia that excavation has revealed, at Kerma, the site which seems, in all respects, to invite identification as the capital of these kings.[1] As already noted, p. 715, the site stands at the beginning of the fertile Dongola Reach, just above the Third Cataract. It consists of two parts.

Close to the river stood the town. Current excavations are revealing a spread of small brick houses of more than one occupational phase, with traces on the southern edge of what may be a substantial system of fortifications to surround the town, employing a ditch and walls of stone and brick (Bonnet 1978a, 1979). But the dominant feature in the town was a massive brick building, the 'Western Deffufa', an early and very impressive form of castle. Traces of earlier architectural phases have recently been revealed, but in its final form it consisted of an L-shaped block (fig. 10.12), preserved up to 18 m high, and for the most part of solid mud brick. A single broad staircase rose up through the interior, doubtless to the apartments which must have been built on the top. In the latest phase the great staircase rose from a courtyard, on whose opposite side was a building wing representing one of the earliest known uses in the Nile Valley of baked brick.

Amidst the debris which had collapsed into a group of cellars were numerous mud-seal impressions, mostly from the sealing of pots, baskets and other receptacles. The repertoire of designs contrasts sharply with that from Uronarti. Entirely absent are those with the names and titles of administrators. The only names were those of Hyksos kings (Jakeb-her, Sheshi, Maatibra, also Queen Ineni), occurring just once or twice in each case. Two-thirds of the sealings had been done with five scarab seals carrying designs which are probably in all, and certainly in three cases stylistically of the Hyksos period (Reisner 1923, pts. I–III, pp. 38–9, pts. IV–V, p. 81). The implication, an important one, must be that most of the sealing was done at Kerma itself, presumably on the receipt of goods sent or brought in from outside, thus employing an administrative practice derived from Egypt. The local origin of some of the sealed receptacles is further confirmed by the incised patterns from Nubian pots faithfully impressed on the backs of some of the sealings.

The debris from buildings surrounding the castle contained industrial waste from the manufacture of the distinctive local pottery, of objects glazed in the Egyptian fashion, of beads, and of mica ornaments.

On the desert plateau behind lay the cemetery of tumulus graves, only partially excavated and published. The southern part was most likely

[1] The picture of Kerma may need some modification from the current excavations of the Henry M. Blackmer Foundation; for preliminary reports see Bonnet 1978a, 1979.

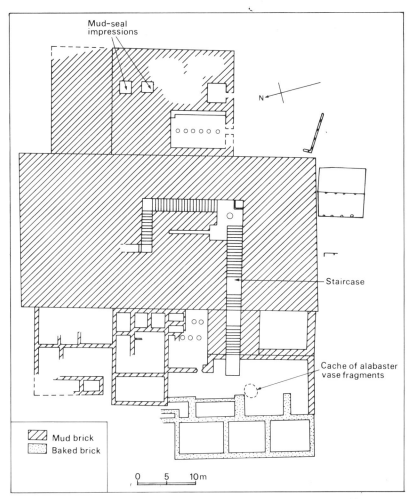

Fig. 10.12 Castle at Kerma (Western Deffufa, KI), contemporary with the Hyksos period in Egypt. The plan of the outer walls is a slightly simplified rendering of the latest of several superimposed phases.

the latest, and was dominated by three exceptionally large tumuli (KIII, IV, and X) (fig. 10.13) possessing internal structures of mud brick which included a central burial chamber and containing as well numerous separately-made subsidiary graves. Burial was on a bed, in one case of glazed quartz, surrounded by personal effects and pottery, and accompanied by the bodies of up to a dozen humans, mostly females, and also

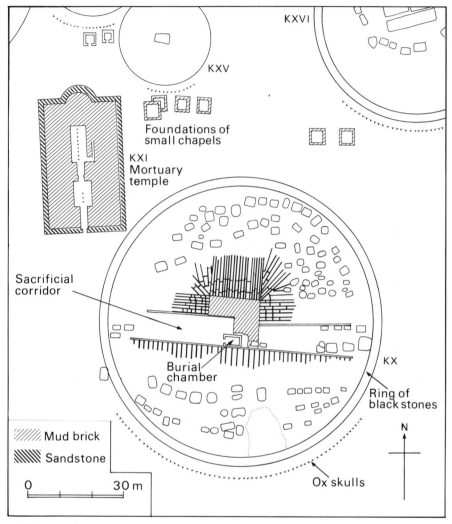

Fig. 10.13  Part of the royal cemetery at Kerma, contemporary with the Hyksos period in Egypt.

of rams. The human burials around the main one seem to have been sacrificial, and were in addition to the mass of sacrificial victims found in the central part of the great tumuli, over 300 in one case.

By their size and complexity, and by the evidence they give of the power over the lives of others which is so vividly demonstrated by the sacrificial bodies, these tumuli leave little doubt that they were the tombs of powerful kings of Nubia. Indeed, a record of the burial practices for Sudanese kings of the Middle Ages contains some remarkably close parallels (Vycichl 1959). Furthermore, that their date was one contemporary with the Hyksos and Seventeenth Dynasty should not be in doubt. The scarabs found in them are, when not of local design and manufacture, primarily of this period (including one of the chancellor Har); so also are the datable contexts in which the distinctive Classic Kerma pottery is found, sometimes as imports, in Lower Nubia and Egypt (Bietak 1968b, pp. 123–7, 180).[1] Other tumuli in this part of the cemetery would have belonged, so one imagines, to members of an extensive royal family and court, but to the north the largely unexcavated portions probably continue the burial record back into the Middle Kingdom and perhaps beyond. Recent excavations have now uncovered a group of large stone-lined structures, possibly elaborate tombs of a quite different type, in an area lying to the south of the Western Deffufa (Bonnet 1978b).

The court at Kerma must have been both rich and colourful, with reminders of Pharaonic Egypt to set the tone for civilized life (as it had done at Byblos) and to supply symbols of dignity, sometimes in the form of second-hand statuary. Although in the badly plundered tumuli little gold was left, it occurred in places – heavy plate on wooden bed legs, a rim on a pottery cup – suggesting an abundant supply. Court ladies wore leather or cloth cylindrical caps on which were stitched pieces of mica cut in various shapes, including some derived from Egyptian symbolism. One lady had worn a crown of thin silver. Egyptian influence can be seen in the handful of burials employing wooden coffins, and more particularly in the introduction into the cemetery of mortuary temples. Two large brick examples were built,[2] one of them (KXI) encased in sandstone blocks. The other (KII) had been given an external frieze of lions in Egyptian style composed of faience tiles, and possessed a granite door lintel decorated with a carved winged-disc, an Egyptian motif found painted also on a wall of the burial chamber of one of the royal tumuli, KIII. Inside, the walls of both mortuary temples had been painted with scenes in Egyptian style, depicting fleets of sailing ships, and giraffes and other animals. Although points of contact with

[1] Supposed Kerma beakers found in a tomb at Saqqara (Mastaba 3507, no. 10) and now in the British Museum, London, resemble only superficially Classic Kerma beakers, being much coarser, and should not be identified as such. The group is listed in Merrillees (1968, pp. 27–8). For dating, note the scarab of Nubkheperra Intef from the Mirgissa cemetery (Vercoutter 1970, pl. XXVI), and the scarab of Maatibra from the Akasha cemetery (Maystre 1975).

[2] The basic design, in which rooms occupy only a relatively small part of the otherwise solid brickwork, can be paralleled in the Middle Kingdom temple at Ezbet Rushdi in the Nile Delta (Adam 1959), but this may be just a common feature of the times. Some of the faience tiles from KII are illustrated in W. S. Smith (1962, 1965, fig. 60).

Egypt are essentially influences on an overwhelmingly indigenous culture, and although no fully Egyptian-style tombs have been found, one must accept the presence at Kerma of a number of Egyptians, both artisans directing mud-brick building and various industrial processes (glazing, joinery, metal-casting), and perhaps advisors or administrators responsible for the sealings found in the castle, and for doing the secretarial work necessary for maintaining the diplomatic contact with Egypt exemplified by the letter captured by Kamose's army.

One important question which has to receive a somewhat imprecise and speculative answer is the source of Kerma's wealth. As noted above, Upper Nubia must have been actively involved in trade with Egypt during the Middle Kingdom, but to what local economic benefit is not clear. The rich, Classic phase of Kerma culture seems primarily to have coincided with Hyksos rule in the north of Egypt, and during this time the kings of Kush may have had ample opportunity to acquire a virtual monopoly of Nubian gold. By having gold to offer for services they may have had no difficulty in attracting Egyptian craftsmen and soldiers, like the man from Edfu mentioned above. As a trading partner Kush must have grown even more important than hitherto, but since the Darb el-Arba'in caravan route could put Kush into direct contact with Hyksos-held territory, by-passing the kingdom of the Theban Seventeenth Dynasty altogether, it is particularly difficult to estimate what the arrangement might have been, though the modesty of the Seventeenth Dynasty royal burials at Thebes compared to their counterparts at Kerma might be an indication that they were, in fact, being passed by in whatever trade was being conducted with the south. Some of the second-hand statuary may have come from Upper Egypt (O'Connor 1969, pp. 31–2) but otherwise the Egyptian material from Kerma itself is of little help in determining its ultimate origin, though one can imagine that analysis of the composition of the bronzes might yield important clues. An interesting negative feature is the absence so far of true Tell el-Yahudiya pottery juglets,[1] contrasting with the numerous examples from Egyptian-style graves at Buhen and Aniba.

The culture of Kerma is that of a court, and in this respect remains unique. Naturally, the political influence of its rulers cannot be measured accurately by archaeology, and so the fate of the other Nubian kingdoms of the Middle Kingdom lists is not known. Classic Kerma material has been found as far south as Bugdumbush, and on sites

[1] True Tell el-Yahudiya juglets should be carefully distinguished from the El-Lisht type which appeared during the late Middle Kingdom (Merrillees 1974, 1978).

northwards to just beyond the Dal Cataract, of which the most important are claimed to be Sai Island, Akasha and Ukma West (Geus and Labre 1974; Giorgini 1971, ch. 2, pl. 4; Gratien 1973, 1974, 1975, 1978; Macadam 1955, p. 160, no. 0919; Maystre 1975; *Report of the Antiquities Service and Museums in the Anglo-Egyptian Sudan* 1946, p. 10, 1947, pp. 5, 9; Vila 1975). Further north still, in Lower Nubia, Classic Kerma forms a distinctive component of the culture contemporary with the Hyksos and Seventeenth Dynasties. In widely scattered localities individual or small groups of burials with features characteristic of Kerma culture, including the distinctive pottery, have been found, suggestive of immigrants from the south forming a numerically very small but widely dispersed element in the population. Not surprisingly, the largest of these cemeteries (twenty-three graves) occurs in the most southerly part of Lower Nubia, at Mirgissa. Kerma pottery has also been noted in the debris of two forts, Mirgissa (Hesse 1971, Vercoutter 1970, pp. 13, 22–3, 183, n. 125) and Buhen (Egypt Exploration Society 1963, Randall-MacIver and Woolley 1911, p. 239, pl. 50; H. S. Smith 1976, p. 81), in both cases apparently associated, in very limited quarters, with a level of destruction or decay. Kerma pottery has also been found in tombs in Upper Egypt, but, with the exception of two adjacent graves at Abydos containing contracted burials, the style of burial and of other grave goods is wholly Egyptian, suggesting that the Kerma pots are either trade goods themselves, or perhaps even souvenirs from a period of mercenary service.

The knowledge that at Buhen and Aniba (and apparently Mirgissa as well) there were Egyptians who continued to live and be buried after the severing of Egypt's political control provides an acceptable historical context for understanding the significance of groups of graffiti at various Lower Nubian localities, containing one or two somewhat eccentrically written royal names not attested elsewhere: Ii-ib-khent-ra and Kakara In. Although normally ascribed to the First Intermediate Period, they are accompanied by names and titles of officials which, as a group, are essentially Middle Kingdom.[1] One interpretation which can be placed on them is that they derive from an attempt at establishing an independent kingdom by Egyptians who had once belonged to the garrisons of the Egyptian forts, engineered during the later Thirteenth

---

[1] The two most important are: *imy-r ʿ-ḥnwty* (Gauthier 1918, Helck 1958, p. 12, n. 9) and *ḥrp skw* (Gardiner *et al.* 1955, vol. II, p. 97, n. c). These titles accompany the Abu Hor graffito. Accompanying the Medik graffito is one of 'the prophet Khnum-hetep'; an identically written graffito also occurs at Semna (Reisner, Dunham and Janssen 1960, p. 133, pl. 94A).

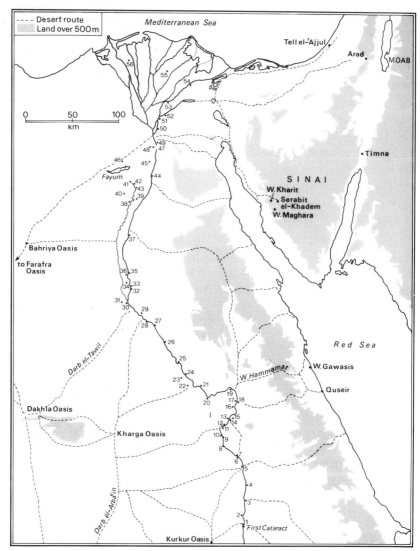

Fig. 10.14  Map of Egypt for the Old and Middle Kingdoms. The Delta branches are after Bietak (1975a, Abb. 23); ancient desert routes can only be inferred from more recent patterns, one useful source for the western desert being the map at the rear of Bates (1970). (See p. 769 for explanation of numbers.)

Dynasty. It would have been of relatively limited duration since, by Kamose's time, Lower Nubia seems to have been a vassal of the kings of Kush.

To a complex situation in Lower Nubia, as well as in Egypt, must be added a further element: the immigration and settlement of desert peoples whose culture passes under the term 'Pan-grave'. The cemeteries are often small, but reached at least the total of 49 burials at Balabish and 107 at Mostagedda in Upper Egypt, and occur on both banks of the Nile between Deir Rifeh in Upper Egypt and Toshka in Lower Nubia (with possible Pan-grave influence in the Second Cataract area), a sign that some of these immigrant groups crossed the river. Related material which may or may not be real Pan-grave has been found even further north (Kemp 1977a, Menghin and Bittel 1934). Distinctive features of the culture are its pottery (bowls, often with indented or emphasized rim, either black-topped red or dark with roughly incised patterns), bracelets made of mother-of-pearl strips, and bucrania (sometimes painted) buried in the cemeteries. Small camp sites have been found on the desert margins in the El-Badari area, and incised sherds of pottery of apparent Pan-grave character have been found on the surface of Egyptian town sites at Kahun, Abydos, Ballas, Hierakonpolis, Edfu, Qasr es-Sagha, Karnak (*Bulletin de Liaison du Groupe Internationale d'Etude de la Céramique Egyptienne* 1977) and El-Kab, and at the Nubian forts of Kubban and Mirgissa.

Although it cannot be substantiated by particularly convincing evidence, there is a strong suspicion, which must at present rest largely on the greater dissimilarity between Pan-grave and western desert material than between the latter and C-group culture, that these newcomers originated in the eastern desert, being thus Medja-people. Comparisons have been made with material from distant parts of the eastern Sudan (Kassala) and northern Ethiopia (Agordat) (Arkell 1954, Bietak 1966, p. 70), but the similarity is not apparently one of total culture, only of selected individual traits in pottery decoration, and thus not necessarily of immediate relevance in view of the widely dispersed and long-lasting pottery traditions of north-east Africa. A preliminary statement on the physical anthropology of a Pan-grave group from Sayala in Lower Nubia contrasts them strongly with C-group people (and with Kerma people, too) (Strouhal and Jungwirth 1971), and finds similarity with a much more ancient stratum of population encountered in the Wadi Halfa area in Late Palaeolithic (Mesolithic) times.[1] But as with the Hyksos material from Tell ed-Dab'a there is insufficient comparative material to know what is really implied by this observation.

The historical inscriptions of Kamose's attack on the Hyksos record that his army contained units of Medja troops, and the suggestion that

[1] Statements on the significance of anthropological data should be considered in conjunction with van Gerven, Carlson and Armelagos (1973).

Pan-grave culture belonged to the same people is quite an old one.[1] But whilst it still seems perfectly feasible to regard Kamose's Medja mercenaries as drawn from these immigrants, their number and ubiquity suggests a much more important movement of people affecting Lower Nubia as well as southern Egypt. Indeed, if they are to be identified with Medja-people they would have to be regarded as more than disjointed groups for, as Papyrus Bulaq 18 shows for the Thirteenth Dynasty (see pp. 668, 709), the Medja-people possessed leaders sufficiently identifiable to receive an invitation to the Egyptian court at Thebes. The reasons for this migration, which became a unique cultural intrusion in Upper Egypt in the Pharaonic period, remain wholly obscure, as does the long-term effect. As with the Palestinian Middle Bronze Age II culture in the eastern Delta, Pan-grave culture failed to retain its identity beyond the beginning of the New Kingdom, but there is no evidence to suggest that its bearers were subject to Upper Egyptian hostility. It is just possible that the prominent Ahmose–Paheri family at El-Kab in the early Eighteenth Dynasty was descended from such people.[2]

In Lower Nubia, alongside the various newcomers and remaining Egyptians, C-group culture continued to exist, and in fact passed through its most developed phase (IIb), though towards the end of the period exhibiting (in its phase III) a degree of local variation and influence from the immigrant groups as well as a possible overall decline in its affluence. The most striking feature of phase IIb is the appearance of a greater variation in tomb size, the larger tumuli sometimes coming to possess small mortuary chapels of mud brick or stone and suggestive, perhaps, of a greater degree of social stratification. This also coincided with the emergence of larger C-group settlements, in the form of fortified stone villages well exemplified at Areika and Wadi es-Sebua. These were evidently designed as places of refuge in troubled times.

It becomes evident that in the late Thirteenth Dynasty and Hyksos period Lower Nubia passed through a complex and eventful period of history which has more than a few echoes of events in northern Egypt:

---

[1] Note also the soldier's archery case reported in Shore (1973), an object of the Seventeenth or early Eighteenth Dynasty from Upper Egypt, where the owner is depicted attended by a Nubian soldier.

[2] The foreignness of some of the names in this family has been commented on by others, e.g. Helck (1971, p. 101) and Vandersleyen (1971, pp. 24–5), with the assumption of Asiatic origin. But another relative actually bore the name *Mḏꜣy-s*, 'Medja-man' (Tylor and Griffith 1894, pl. VII). The *ru* element in two other family names, Itruri and Ruru, also occurs in Nubian names, e.g. *Rwiw* and *Rwnꜣ* (Säve-Söderbergh 1963), *R-kꜣ* and *Rwiw/Rwiꜣ* (Steindorff 1937, p. 250).

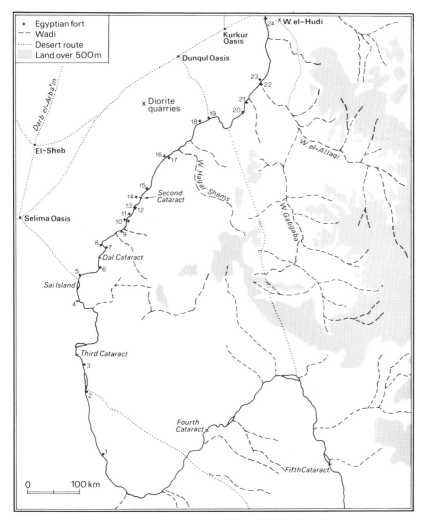

Fig. 10.15   Map of Nubia in the Old and Middle Kingdoms.
(See p. 769 for explanation of numbers.)

a fragmentation of society, exacerbated by immigration, with ultimate authority eventually passing to a dominant power from outside, the kingdom of Kush, whose court looked to Egypt for symbols of authority and employed Egyptians in its service. Thus the Second Intermediate Period emerges as one of great significance in the history of Egypt's relationships with her neighbours. A time of internal governmental weakness coincided with a period of prosperity and political growth in Palestine and Nubia so that, for once, the Egyptians found themselves the victims of both the political initiative and cultural momentum of others.

## THE THEBAN DEFEAT OF THE HYKSOS AND OF KUSH

Both kingdoms were simultaneously destroyed in a period of warfare probably initiated by Kamose, the last king of the Seventeenth Dynasty, and continued by his immediate successors of the Eighteenth Dynasty. The evidence for hostilities prior to Kamose is somewhat ambiguous, though it has been strengthened by the demonstration that Kamose's predecessor, Sekenenra Taʻa II, died a violent death from weapons, one of which had the distinctive shape of a Syro-Palestinian axe-head of a type found in the eastern Delta at this time (Bietak 1974). A conflict between this king and the Hyksos king Apepy is narrated in Papyrus Sallier I, a much later popular tale, but this may have been of the 'out-witting' type, although it correctly presupposes in its setting the opposed interests of the two kingdoms. The main source for the Theban revolt is a pair of stelae (and a scribal copy of one of them) erected in Karnak temple by Kamose and dated to his year 3 (Habachi 1972, p. 39; Pritchard 1969, pp. 554–5; Säve-Söderbergh 1956; H. S. Smith and A. Smith 1976). In a council of war the scene is initially set as a stable tripartite division of Egypt: the Hyksos kingdom ruled by Aaweserra Apepy, who is known to have reigned for at least 40 years, Thebes and Kush. This is used as a contrasting literary device to emphasize Kamose's personal responsibility for making the winning aggressive move of a northward attack, commencing with the town of Nefrusy, 'a nest for Asiatics', ruled by one Teti son of Pepy, presumably an Egyptian vassal of the Hyksos. The difficult language of the text, which mixes narrative with rhetoric, leaves one in doubt as to with what success Kamose penetrated the Delta.[1] The text ends abruptly, not with the defeat of the Hyksos in battle or siege, but with a triumphal return to Thebes at the onset of the inundation season. The last engagement mentioned is described thus: 'I sent a strong troop overland to destroy the Bahriya Oasis – whilst I was in Sako – in order to prevent rebels from being behind me.' Sako is still about 70 km south of Herakleopolis, and the action was presumably designed to sever communications between the Hyksos kingdom and Kush. It was at this point that the famous letter from Apepy was captured.

[1] The stele of Emheb, a man who seems to have belonged to Kamose's force, also refers to reaching Avaris in this same year 3 (Černý 1969).

This letter from Apepy has already been mentioned. Before inviting the King of Kush to invade southern Egypt, Apepy sets the scene: 'Do you see what Egypt has done to me? The king of the place, Kamose (given life!), is attacking me on my ground. I had not assailed him in the manner of all that he has done to you. He chooses to plague these two lands, mine and yours. He has ravaged them.' The allusion to a prior attack on Kush was probably no rhetoric. A building inscription of this same year 3 of Kamose at Buhen (H. S. Smith 1976, p. 8, pls. II, I and LVIII. I, no. 488) suggests an almost simultaneous conquest of the whole of Lower Nubia, borne out by two graffiti of his reign at Arminna commemorating possibly the earliest holders of the New Kingdom office of Viceroy of Kush (Simpson 1963c, p. 34).[1]

The ultimate success of the Theban revolt had to await the early reigns of the New Kingdom. It was not limited to regaining control of the territory ruled by the Middle Kingdom, but became, in the end, the conquest and the attempt to control the lands whence the kings of Kush and the 'foreign kings' from the north-east had originated.

## EXPLANATIONS OF HISTORICAL CHANGE IN THE OLD AND MIDDLE KINGDOMS

The presentation of ancient Egyptian history in narrative form inevitably draws particular attention to change and development, but, for the laudable purpose of making narrative lively, tends in practice to an overdramatization which the sources often do not warrant. In the sections on Egyptian internal history in this chapter the narrative element has consciously been played down. But the alternative of presenting the historical basis of the Old and Middle Kingdoms in the form of a governmental system, with each part – the king, his officers, provincial governors, and temple staff – playing its role without unduly disturbing others can easily lead too far in the opposite direction, and by presenting the system as so harmoniously balanced make it hard to comprehend how, in particular, the upsets of the First Intermediate Period came about. With the exception of the Hyksos Dynasty the roots of historical change seem to lie within Egypt, and, at the political level, particularly in the relationships between the king, the officers of his

[1] Vandersleyen (1971, pp. 61–3) discusses a further possible source. The stele of Emheb (see previous note) couples the reaching of Avaris with a Nubian locality called Miu. Historical circumstances demand that this cannot be identical with the Miu of the Armant stele of Tuthmosis III, evidently a far-distant place, but was perhaps related to the *tp* ('head of') Miu in the Pennut tomb at Aniba.

court, and provincial men of ambition. But the lack of documentation often makes it difficult to discover if the development of some institution or facet of society, other than the kingship itself, is an indication of a weakening of royal control or a sign of the ability of the office of king to adapt to and perhaps bring about change. It is only, for example, the need of modern historians to find some reason for the First Intermediate Period which sees the emphasis on solar worship in the Fifth Dynasty as a sign of diminishing royal authority rather than as an interesting development in the cults patronized by the court which in no way detracted from the king's dominance in government, and may just as easily have added to it. The resort to *post hoc, ergo propter hoc* reasoning is often the only alternative if comprehensive explanation for events is regarded as essential.

It may be, however, that an *ad hoc* historical approach, concentrating on just one specific situation at a time, places too great an emphasis on the more superficial aspects. There is the alternative of beginning from a more theoretical, determinist position, and of arguing that the bureaucratic state possesses certain basic structural properties, some of them weaknesses, and that in the case of early floodplain civilizations, they took a particular common form.[1] If one wished to consider Egypt from this point of view, several closely interrelated aspects of society require attention.

In the first place, although the Nile has a regimen somewhat different from, say, the Tigris–Euphrates system, with irrigation remaining at the elementary level of basin irrigation not requiring elaborate central control (Butzer 1976, pp. 42–3), it would still have possessed, with other major floodplains, the capacity for producing an agricultural surplus beyond the immediate needs of its overall initial population. However, although subsequent population increase was probably never on a scale to constitute a problem in the periods under consideration,[2] rising demand stimulated by the conspicuous consumption of the court may have eventually led to the extension of agriculture to less productive lands with consequent diminishing returns.

Bureaucracy is a central feature of the early major civilizations, and

[1] An important phase of discussion began with Wittfogel's 'hydraulic hypothesis' (Wittfogel 1955, 1957). This has provoked much critical comment, some of it of considerable value, e.g. Friedman (1974), Kappel (1974), Lees (1974) and Mitchell (1973).

[2] A valuable review of recent discussions of this topic is in Cowgill (1975). Helck (1974c, 1975, pp. 98–100) has postulated that the growth of bureaucracy and demand for labourers and craftsmen in the Old Kingdom created a demand for increased population, to be met by raids on neighbouring countries.

in Egypt probably arose primarily to serve the ambitions of the early kings. When seen in operation through surviving administrative texts, it seems to have been concerned mainly with facilitating the transfer of produce to the various centres which made up the 'court' and to its provincial outliers and with supervising constructional work, rather than with the maintenance of the agricultural system. It would be in this group that a proliferation of numbers and rise in material expectations would produce serious pressures on the agricultural surplus.

Pious foundations occupied a key place in the Egyptian economy. Those which were mainly or exclusively for the benefit of private individuals, and were then most effectively operated in the provinces, offered one way through which people living off surplus could safeguard their economic positions and perhaps satisfy growing expectations, but this would ultimately have been something in competition with the court. The economic behaviour of these foundations probably had an important role in the history of the early periods, but the terrible dearth of quantifiable data would make a more detailed assessment very difficult.

Finally, although monumental tomb construction and burial of riches is an obvious feature of ancient Egypt, its effects are still not properly understood. Explanation for the First Intermediate Period has sometimes been sought in the idea that continued pyramid-building exhausted the country. However, this may have been true only in so far as it stood in the way of growing demand amongst the official class, bearing in mind the finite limits of agricultural surplus. Irrespective of whether this private demand, channelled through pious foundations, was instrumental in creating a weak and unstable court, the latter's inability to continue massive court cemetery construction would have been a most damaging failure for the long-term continuation of what we recognize as 'civilization' in Egypt and to the prosperity of those very people who may have been competing with it. For in this form of monumental construction the authority of the king and all that this implied politically was finalized, ambitious men found a prestigious and rewarding outlet within a controlled framework, and the country's material and intellectual resources were stretched to a greater degree within a centralized programme. The role of strong central government in raising the general level of prosperity is shown by the way in which, during the First Intermediate Period, and even probably during the late Old Kingdom, the level of consumption of men of power, as indexed by their tomb sizes, seems to have declined. Yet they were now no longer in competition with a lavishly endowed court.

This type of formal approach implies a degree of inevitability, particularly if the bureaucratic state is regarded as, in the long term, an unstable phenomenon. But even if one allows this, it does not deprive the historian of the opportunity of explaining why, at one moment rather than another, history took a particular course. The political element is not readily absorbed into a determinist framework of explanation. Thus the re-establishment of a single strong kingship in the Middle Kingdom which allowed, or was forced to accept, the continued existence of provincial governors of considerable pretensions is not an obvious product of a determinist explanation of why the Old Kingdom had come to an end. Furthermore, this provincial aspect of Egypt's system of government was no longer in existence at the end of the Twelfth Dynasty, so that the second period of short reigns and downturn in the scale of court activity which followed cannot be explained in quite the same way as the first, and is, indeed, difficult to explain adequately on either political or determinist grounds.

The notion that explanation is possible at all also depends on the assumption that the evidence and the factors at work were distributed fairly evenly around the country, so that what is encountered in one area can be regarded as nationally typical. But the possibility must be considered that, because accidents of preservation have greatly favoured Upper Egypt, our attention is focused too much on a part of the country whose involvement in Memphite court politics was often less than the more northerly regions, and which does not therefore always offer a particularly reliable guide to those factors which most seriously affected the fortunes of the ruling house at Memphis. An examination of the broad sweep of ancient Egyptian history (including the later periods not considered in this chapter) might suggest that a political dichotomy can be seen emerging in those times when a strongly centralized and centralizing government was absent. In such periods, the country tended to divide, as a first stage, into two parts: the delta and the seven or eight most northerly nomes of Upper Egypt on the one hand, and the rest of Upper Egypt south of, say, El-Minya or Asyut on the other (see Wainwright 1927). The next step in the north was for continued fragmentation into city states to produce eventually a pattern known elsewhere in the ancient Near East, with complex ties recognizing a hierarchy of authority amongst them which included a nominal capital at Memphis or somewhere else in the north. The more southerly part of Upper Egypt was, however, more readily kept together as one unit, ruled from a single place whose pre-eminence received justification through theology, whereby a local cult was paid special attention and its deity given a central place in the theology of divine kingship. The gods Seth and Horus represent the legacy of prehistoric periods when respectively Naqada and Hierakonpolis were in turn centres of importance in Upper Egypt. Thebes was to fill this role from the Eleventh Dynasty onwards, with its temple eventually becoming the principal cult centre in Upper Egypt and its god Amen/Amen-Ra, gaining a dominant position in the theology of kingship. Memphis also had this symbolic role, justified in the Memphite Theology, but it acted less effectively in the north in times of weak central government.

This geographical factor is useful as a possible overall perspective to prevent irregularities in the preservation of evidence from having too great an influence in the writing of history. But from period to period modification is obviously necessary in the light of what is known of the complexities of situations which are bound to be, in detail, unique every time. Thus the short-lived fragmentation of Upper Egypt under nomarchs in the Eighth and perhaps early Ninth/Tenth Dynasties was an exceptional occurrence which happened at a time when no one place in Upper Egypt had yet emerged with pre-eminent regional authority since at least the Early Dynastic Period. This vacuum was shortly filled by Thebes. Then again, the Thirteenth Dynasty seems to have been able to continue to rule Upper Egypt, including the Thebaid, at a time when the fragmentation of the delta may already have been beginning. This last possibility leads to an interesting argument (though one for which supporting evidence is conspicuously lacking): whilst in the late Old Kingdom it was the provincial governors of Upper Egypt who began competing for resources with the court, in the late Middle Kingdom this role was taken over by incipient city states in the Delta. It does not seem unreasonable to consider that the rash of client kings who must have ruled the northern part of Egypt under the Hyksos overlordship had come into possession of a system which had some historical and economic background.

## Climatic variation

The interaction of political, economic and social factors should not be considered against an entirely stable climatic background. Evidence of a rather scattered kind has been used to suggest certain important variations both in seasonal rainfall over Egypt and in Nile flood levels (the two should be very carefully distinguished) for the Old and Middle Kingdoms. The evidence stems either from interpretations placed on ancient written and pictorial sources, or from field observations in areas geographically marginal to the Egyptian Nile Valley.

Representations of desert fauna and trees in tombs suggest that by the end of the Old Kingdom both had been depleted, presumably by the onset of more arid conditions, though in view of changes in the fashions of subject matter and the very selective nature of the Egyptian representations of their world the evidence should be treated cautiously. The archaeological evidence for herding and hunting communities in the western desert mentioned above, pp. 706–7, ought to be crucial, but the dating evidence is as yet highly unsatisfactory. The appearance of C-group culture in Lower Nubia has been seen as an effect of deteriorating conditions of life in the desert, but the really widespread immigration of desert peoples into the Nile Valley represented by the Pan-grave people did not take place until significantly later. Whether ecological change in the neighbouring deserts had any significant effect on the Egyptian economy is hard to tell. In southern Upper Egypt and Lower Nubia greater wadi activity in the period c. 4000–3000 BC is apparently to be attributed to winter rains. This did not recur in Pharaonic times (Butzer 1975, Butzer and Hansen 1968, ch. 3), and the evidence obviously supports the idea of increasing aridity in the early centuries of Egyptian history.

A little futher south, careful investigation into the relationship between geology and late Neolithic settlements in Sudanese Nubia (especially at Debeira West and Ashkeit) has pointed to a major decline in Nile flood levels during the later prehistoric phases (Butzer and Hansen 1968, pp. 277–8; de Heinzelin 1968). By the late fourth millennium BC areas of the river bed had been permanently exposed. It would seem that this degradation phase must have ended somewhere around the beginning of the dynastic period, when deposition of silt began again, but with the Nile now flowing permanently in a somewhat lower floodplain. There appears to be some correlation actually within the summer monsoonal rainfall belt whence the Nile waters originate (Butzer 1976, pp. 30–3; Grove, Street and Goudie 1975). Connected with this are ancient Nile flood levels, recorded on the Palermo Stone, which appear to show a decline of average flood levels of a little over a metre during the First Dynasty, but to maintain themselves thereafter into the Fifth Dynasty, when the record ceases (B. Bell 1970). In the

Fayum, the maximum extent (at 22–24 m above sea level) of Lake Moeris seems to have persisted into Old Kingdom times, covering the greater part of this depression (B. Bell 1975, Said *et al.* 1972a, b). But, by the mid Twelfth Dynasty the level had dropped to below 18 m, possibly to below 15 m, thus exposing a substantial area of land for cultivation. On it were built the temples of Medinet Ma'adi and Kiman Faris, and the colossi of Biyahmu. This was presumably a delayed consequence of declining Nile flood levels, the crucial regulating factor being the state of the Hawara channel at any particular time, something still not properly documented. This newly exposed land would have been a major addition to the agricultural resources of the Nile Valley.

From the period following the end of the Old Kingdom comes a remarkably large number of the ancient references to famine in Upper Egypt, some explicitly linked with low Nile levels. By contrast, as noted on p. 747, a series of Nile flood-level records from Nubia covering the late Twelfth and early Thirteenth Dynasties document an intermittent series of high flood levels averaging about 7.3 m above their modern counterparts. A Thirteenth Dynasty stele from Karnak records the flooding of the temple of Amen, but since the chronological position of the king named is not certain, this particular flooding need not belong to the same series recorded at Semna.[1] Finally, it should be noted that a completely different type of source, the Admonitions of Ipuwer, has been used as an eye-witness account not only of historical events but also of natural disasters, including famines from low Niles. But as noted above, pp. 661–3, its date and nature are open to such widely varying interpretations, some of which lift it right out of the category of eye-witness reporting, that it is dangerous to use it as a source for the events of any one period.

Human society must inevitably be sensitive to ecological change, yet one must also allow a margin of adjustment and ability to overcome calamity and adverse circumstances. In some of the texts of the early First Intermediate Period the great famine is presented not as something which reduces man to helplessness and despair but as an illustration of the writer's authority and capacity to administer relief, sometimes over a wide area. As far as provincial cemetery culture in Upper Egypt south

[1] Baines (1974, 1976), Habachi (1974). The practice of recording individual levels in Egypt itself similar to the Semna levels is attested by an inscribed block found loose at Naga ed-Deir dated to year 23 of Amenemhat III (Robert H. Lowie Museum of Anthropology 1966, p. 64). A startling alternative theory that the Semna levels are evidence for an ancient barrage at Semna has been advanced by Vercoutter (1976a).

of the Fayum is concerned, no breaks of more than local significance can be observed over the entire period considered in this chapter, even when accompanied by variations in burial rate. Furthermore, the blossoming of court culture in the Middle and New Kingdoms is itself a sign that whatever changes in environment (and society) did occur, they were not of a permanently damaging nature.

The only climatic change of any dimensions that has been deduced is the ending of the Neolithic subpluvial late in the Old Kingdom, which seems to have affected the desert fauna. But as noted above, the Pan-grave movement into the Nile Valley some three or four centuries later is perhaps a sign that its consequences were more long-drawn-out or regionally variable. The cry 'the desert is dying of hunger' comes not from the late Old Kingdom, but from a small party of Medja-people in the reign of Amenemhat III (see p. 719).

In the case of the river Nile, once the major adjustment of the floodplain had taken place in the Early Dynastic Period, one would expect, from the records of more recent periods, both an annual variation of a few metres (3.8 m in modern times), and cyclic overall changes of level and volume, operating generally within reasonable limits but occasionally producing critical effects on the communities living on its floodplain. Of these, high floods, although they damage property and food stores, may be counted somewhat less serious in their consequences than very low floods which endanger the whole basis of agriculture. The famine records of the First Intermediate Period are evidently to be understood, from their phraseology, as the result of an extreme trough in the cyclic pattern of Nile variation.

It can scarcely go unnoticed that the decline of court culture after the Sixth and Twelfth Dynasties occurred close in time to freak Nile levels: the famine-creating lows of the early First Intermediate Period and the highs of the Semna levels. Although neither seems to have interfered appreciably with the development of riverine culture in Nubia, an area which one might have supposed to be even more exposed to ecological change than Egypt, they can scarcely be ignored in attempting to understand the historical processes at work at these times. It involves far too simplistic a view of society to see governmental decline as a direct and inevitable consequence of ecological adversity. Its most likely contribution would have been to impose a further strain on the balance between competing demands for surplus, particularly if it also came at a time of diminishing returns from a period of increasingly intense agricultural exploitation. But the way in which this aggravated situation was resolved would depend very much on the relative strengths of the competing groups. The way in which a period of governmental weakness seems to have followed these two periods of eccentric Nile behaviour may itself be evidence for the existence of groups of people before whose power kings had to give way.

---

*Explanation of numbers for figs. 10.14 and 10.15*

**Fig. 10.14**

| | | | |
|---|---|---|---|
| 1 | Elephantine | 29 | Deir el-Gebrawi |
| 2 | Kubaniya | 30 | Cusae |
| 3 | Kom Ombo | 31 | Meir |
| 4 | Gebel es-Silsila | 32 | Deir el-Bersha |
| 5 | Edfu | 33 | Sheikh Said |
| 6 | Hierakonpolis | 34 | Hermoplis |
| 7 | el-Kab | 35 | Beni Hassan |
| 8 | Esna | 36 | Nefrusy |
| 9 | Mo'alla | 37 | Cynopolis |
| 10 | Gebelein | 38 | Deshasha |
| 11 | Tod | 39 | Heracleopolis |
| 12 | Armant | 40 | Medinet Ma'adi |
| 13 | Theban necropolis | 41 | Medinet el-Fayum |
| 14 | Thebes | 42 | Hawara |
| 15 | Medamud | 43 | el-Lahun |
| 16 | Naqada | 44 | Atfih |
| 17 | Ballas | 45 | el-Lisht |
| 18 | Coptos | 46 | Kasr es-Sagha |
| 19 | Dendera | 47 | Memphis |
| 20 | Diospolis Parva | 48 | Saqqara |
| 21 | Balabish | 49 | Tura |
| 22 | Abydos | 50 | Helioplis |
| 23 | Bet Khallaf | 51 | Tell el-Yahudiya |
| 24 | Naga ed-Deir | 52 | Inshas |
| 25 | Akhmim | 53 | Tell Basta |
| 26 | Qau el-Kebir | 54 | Tell ed-Dab'a |
| 27 | Deir Rifa | 55 | Mendes |
| 28 | Asyut | 56 | Buto |

**Fig. 10.15**

| | | | |
|---|---|---|---|
| 1 | Bugdumbush | 13 | Askut |
| 2 | Kawa | 14 | Mirgissa |
| 3 | Kerma | 15 | Buhen |
| 4 | Soleb | 16 | Faras |
| 5 | Amara | 17 | Serra |
| 6 | Firka | 18 | Aniba |
| 7 | Akasha | 19 | Tumas |
| 8 | Ukma | 20 | Wadi es-Sebua |
| 9 | Duweishat | 21 | Sayala |
| 10 | Semna | 22 | Kubban |
| 11 | Shalfak | 23 | Dakka |
| 12 | Saras | 24 | Biga (Senmet) |

# CHAPTER 11

# EARLY FOOD PRODUCTION IN SUB-SAHARAN AFRICA

Considering the important contribution which the introduction and spread of food-production techniques have made to the subsequent development of African culture and history, it is particularly unfortunate that the available evidence by which these processes may be illustrated is sparse and its significance and meaning frequently inconclusive. This is not the place to discuss in detail the methodology of interpreting such evidence; suffice it to point out that most African prehistorians now appreciate the necessity of insisting upon the recovery of physical remains of domesticated animals or cultivated plants before food production in a given context can be regarded as proven. The experience of their colleagues elsewhere, particularly in the Near East and in south-east Europe, has shown them that there are virtually no aspects of material culture alone which are themselves incontrovertibly indicative of farming practice. Gone are the days when the African prehistorian could glibly imply the presence of food-production techniques from the occurrence of pottery or of ground stone tools. Pastoralism and food cultivation, although they often spread together, are not invariably linked, as many recent and contemporary African societies clearly attest.

Seddon (1968) has neatly categorized the various types of evidence which are available for illustrating the spread of food production. These are as follows:

(1) direct archaeological evidence: i.e. the identifiable remains, recovered from stratified contexts, of domesticated animals or plants

(2) indirect archaeological evidence: such as rock paintings and other artistic representations of domesticates or cultigens, or items of material culture which imply the presence of food-producing techniques (care must be exercised in the interpretation of artifacts of this last category since in remarkably few cases is the evidence conclusive)

(3) secondary or non-archaeological evidence, based on botanical, zoological, linguistic or ethnographic data. Use of such data often involves the projection back into the past of recent observations from non-historical disciplines. In addition to the obvious dangers inherent

in the unsupported use of such arguments, it is only rarely that the relevant evidence may be tied in to an archaeological sequence. The results of these investigations thus frequently remain *in vacuo*, without reference to their historical or cultural context, or to an absolute chronology.

In chapter 9 Harlan has summarized the botanical evidence for the early domestication of plant food crops in sub-Saharan Africa. This chapter therefore concentrates on the corresponding cultural evidence and on that for animal domestication. In view of the paucity of the available data, the method adopted has been to present a general account of the archaeology of the several regions of sub-Saharan Africa over the period which saw the introduction of food-production techniques. Particular emphasis is placed upon the various pieces of evidence which specifically indicate food production (Seddon's category 1), while the indirect and secondary evidence is more briefly summarized with respect to each area.

One form of secondary evidence for the spread of domestic cattle on which undue reliance has sometimes been placed relates to the extent of tsetse-fly infestation. This has clearly been a major factor limiting the distribution of cattle but, throughout sub-Saharan Africa, the former extent of the fly-belts remains a virtually unknown quantity except in arid or semi-arid zones, which were presumably free from infestation. Today, *Glossina* mostly occurs (but is by no means ubiquitous) in areas generally falling within the following climatological limits: temperatures between 20 and 28 °C, relative humidity between 50 and 80% and an annual rainfall between 70 and 170 cm. However, arguments based on the present distribution of *Glossina* must remain tentative in view of the extremely rapid and extensive changes in the areas of infestation which are known to have occurred within the recent past. The only African cattle naturally immune to trypanosomiasis are the humpless shorthorns of the West African coastal regions; similar cattle are attested from Ghana late in the second millennium BC and it may be assumed that, as in the case of most African wild animals, their high degree of immunity is due to their long exposure. In other areas of Africa there is, however, no evidence for the development of completely trypanosomiasis-immune breeds of cattle; and the constantly changing distribution of tsetse-fly infestation must have played an important, albeit undetermined, part in influencing the spread of cattle-herding.

It is within the context of the Later Stone Age societies that techniques of food production make their first appearance in the archaeological record over much of sub-Saharan Africa. The major exception to this was in central and eastern Africa, roughly between latitude 5° S and the Tropic of Capricorn, where the Early Iron Age peoples appear to have been responsible for the introduction and spread of farming techniques.

The food-producing communities of the Later Stone Age are sometimes differentiated from their predecessors under the heading 'Neolithic', a term which has given rise to considerable confusion through lack of adequate definition. The term as originally used in Europe referred to those Stone Age (i.e. pre-metallurgical) industries which were distinguished from their forebears by the presence of ground stone artifacts and of pottery; it was generally believed that the makers of these industries were also set apart by their knowledge of food production. Subsequently, use of the term 'Neolithic' – as thus defined – was applied to prehistoric cultures in most areas of Africa lying north of the Equator and in some regions even further south. This usage, initiated at a time when primary evidence for prehistoric African economies was almost totally lacking, was of necessity based only upon consideration of artifacts.

It is now apparent that in both Europe and Africa there is no reason to regard the spread of food production and of 'Neolithic' artifacts as concurrent. Indeed there are abundant instances on both continents where their separation may be conclusively demonstrated. During the 1960s the tendency in Europe was to use the term 'Neolithic' to refer to pre-metallurgical food-producing societies, irrespective of their material culture. In more recent years, with the advent of an increasingly accurate radiocarbon-based absolute chronology, the term is gradually falling out of use altogether. In Africa, particularly in the sub-Saharan regions, its continued use has given rise to considerable confusion, since changing European usage has given the term economic implications which are rarely supported by adequate evidence. There is basic disagreement among African archaeologists as to whether or not the term 'Neolithic' should continue in use in the context of the prehistoric succession of sub-Saharan Africa; and, if so, in what sense it should be employed. It has therefore been thought best not to use the term in the discussion which follows (except in quotation marks), at the risk of indulging in occasionally cumbersome circumlocutions.

Attention was drawn in chapter 6 to the difficulties which are encountered in attempting to ascertain the functions for which various classes of Later Stone Age artifacts were intended. The same point must be emphasized here with regard to the ground and polished stone implements which, in some parts of sub-Saharan Africa, have been held to be indicative of the practice of a food-producing economy. The majority of these artifacts resemble axes or adzes; and in many cases it may well be that these conventional names give a reasonable indication of the purposes to which the tools were put. Experiments have shown that such tools are reasonably effective for the felling of trees and for other wood-working functions, but, so far as this writer is aware, no comprehensive controlled experiments have been conducted specifically to compare the edge-damage sustained by ground stone tools used for these and other purposes with that observed on actual prehistoric specimens. In this context it should be noted that in Karamoja, north-eastern Uganda, such ground stone 'axes' are currently used in the alteration of horn profiles of domestic cattle and goats (Wilson 1972). Another purpose for implements of this type which immediately suggests itself is digging; and some authorities, particularly in West Africa, have attempted to differentiate typologically between ground stone 'hoes' and 'axes'. Others, realizing that such distinctions are at present largely subjective, have fallen back upon the non-committal term 'celt'. In many of the industries described in this chapter, use of such a non-functional nomenclature has much to recommend it; in general, however, the terminology followed here is that adopted in the original description of the various aggregates concerned.

The narrative which follows is arranged on a regional basis following, with minor exceptions, the order established in chapter 6. The regional surveys continue the accounts of the respective Later Stone Age successions which were there presented, and for most areas they are continued up to the inception of the local Iron Age. For south-central and part of southern Africa a somewhat different approach has perforce been adopted, involving a summary of the spread of food-production techniques through and beyond the milieu of the Early Iron Age settlement. Although the Early Iron Age Industrial Complex is described at length in volume 2 of this *History*, it has been found convenient to discuss here its part in the transmission of food production to southern Africa. The archaeological evidence for the initiation of food production in South Africa, although also falling outside the main chronological range of the present volume, is likewise discussed in this chapter. Because of the uneven distribution of archaeological research in the sub-continent and the inconclusive nature of much of the primary evidence for food production, the picture here drawn is in places hazy and incomplete. A probable effect of the uneven quality of the available information is the overemphasis of the part played by certain relatively well-investigated food-producing communities in the transmission of their techniques to other areas. (The Later Stone Age food producers of the Rift Valley and adjacent areas of southern Kenya and northern Tanzania are a case in point.) The present chapter should be read as a direct sequel to chapter 6 and the reader is warned that the division of material between the two chapters has been, of necessity, somewhat arbitrary, and that a certain amount of overlap has been unavoidable.

## WEST AFRICA

### *Archaeological Survey* (fig. 11.1)

It was noted in chapter 6 (p. 422) that the widespread mode 5 aggregates of West Africa were enriched, generally around the fourth or third millennium BC, by the appearance of previously unknown traits, principally pottery and ground stone artifacts. There is no evidence that the inception of food production in this area predates the appearance of these so-called 'Neolithic' traits and it is consequently at the time of the latter event that the present narrative commences.

In Senegal, known sites of this period are virtually restricted to the coastal areas. The largest number of known occurrences is in the Dakar region. The typology of the microliths suggests that the industry has some Saharan affinities, but the term 'Neocapsian', by which it is frequently known, implies a specific affinity which has not been satisfactorily demonstrated. In addition to the microlithic chipped stone material, most sites have also yielded grindstones, stone bracelets, small ground stone celts and finely decorated comb-stamped pottery. A date of the late second millennium BC for such an aggregate near Thiès has already been noted (chapter 6, p. 418). There are indications that the culture represented by these sites may have continued into comparatively recent times, but no firm evidence on this point is yet available. In the absence of faunal remains or other primary evidence, there are no certain indications as to whether or not food production was practised in this coastal region in pre-Iron Age times (Corbeil, Mauny and Charbonnier 1951, Descamps and Demoulin 1969, Vaufrey 1946).

In southern Senegal, between the Gambia and the border of Guinée-Bissau, the extensive shell-middens beside the estuary of Casamance have recently been reinvestigated. A final Later Stone Age phase of occupation, dated to between 200 BC and AD 200, is characterized by pottery with wavy-line decoration. It is stratified beneath the Iron

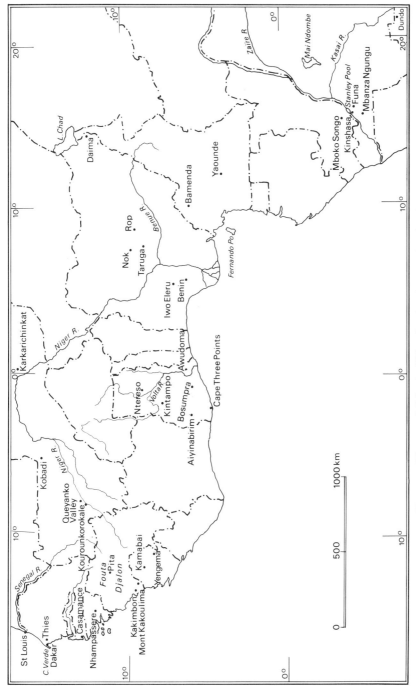

Fig. 11.1  Western sub-Saharan Africa, showing sites mentioned in the text.

775

Age levels which represent the most intensive exploitation of the Casamance oyster beds (Linares de Sapir 1971). A comparable pre-Iron Age phase of settlement at the Saint Louis shell-middens in northern Senegal is now known to date back as far as the fourth millennium BC.

Most accounts of Later Stone Age and 'Neolithic' occurrences in the Republic of Guinea are old and the detail inadequate. Consequently, only a most general description of the material can at present be given. Celts, of varied types, and stone 'hoes' are widespread. In some areas of Guinea and in parts of Sierra Leone, it appears that the associated chipped stone artifacts were not of microlithic type, as at the caves near Pita and, further to the south-west, at Mont Kakoulima. In the south, near Conakry, the evidence from Kakimbon Cave suggests that ground stone artifacts were locally being made before the introduction of pottery.

From several areas of Guinea, such as Fouta Djalon, have been recovered (generally in poorly documented contexts) large asymmetrical bifaces, core-axes or 'hoes', celts, side- and end-scrapers, backed blades and *tranchets*. Comparable material has been described from Guinée-Bissau, as at Nhampassere. In the north of Guinea the so-called 'Neolithic' aggregates show clear similarities with those from Senegal, while sites in the south more closely resemble those from further east; but there is no clear boundary which can be demonstrated between the two culture-areas (Delcroix and Vaufrey 1939, Holas and Mauny 1953, Joire 1952).

The most widespread complex of industries in West Africa during the last four millennia BC is that generally known as the 'Guinea Neolithic'. It extends through the savannah from Guinée-Bissau to Cameroun and southward into the forests fringing the coast, where its distribution is unevenly known due to the difficulties facing archaeological exploration and research in the dense forest areas. Published data on the complex are, however, inadequate to demonstrate its unity. Indeed there are indications that the industrial diversity of the earlier Later Stone Age aggregates continued until the inception of the local Iron Age.

With remarkably few exceptions, sites and aggregates of the 'Guinea Neolithic' have not been thoroughly described (for references see Davies (1967, pp. 180–216)). In general terms, these aggregates contain microliths, chipped stone 'hoes', ground stone celts and pottery. Stone beads and arm-rings are also frequently encountered. Considerable regional variation is hardly surprising in view of the wide distribution of the relevant sites. It is most apparent in the typology of the celts and of the pottery, but no adequate survey of the distributions of the various types has yet been undertaken except in limited areas; for a general account of the pottery see Mauny (1972). Valuable evidence concerning the regional and chronological subdivisions of the 'Guinea Neolithic' could doubtless be obtained from a study of the typology and distribution of the celts and arm-rings from the various factory sites which are recorded, of which those in the Oueyanko valley near Bamako in Mali and near Cape Three Points in south-western Ghana are probably the best known.

The celts have received a disproportionately large amount of attention and many have been collected and described. Considerable variety has been observed in the typology of West African celts (fig. 11.2.1–2) but insufficient data are yet available on their geographical and chronological distributions and on the archaeological associations of the various types to permit the emergence of a meaningful overall view. Davies (1967, pp. 190–201) has proposed a preliminary classification which recognizes a broad similarity in the edge-ground celts distributed throughout the forest and woodland savannah from Guinea to Cameroun, spreading also southwards to Mboko Songo near Brazzaville and to the sites of lower Zaïre which are discussed in greater detail below. The second type comprises celts ground lengthwise over their entire surface. Greatly elongated specimens of these are sometimes encountered, particularly in the Ivory Coast. Celts of the third type are large and cylindrical, being shaped by pecking prior to grinding; they appear to be largely restricted to Dahomey (modern Republic of Benin) and Upper Volta and the countries to the east.

The later phases of the Later Stone Age in Sierra Leone are best known from the Kamabai and Yagala rock-shelters (Atherton 1972, Coon 1968), but many details remain obscure. The inception of microlithic industries here may coincide with the first appearance of pottery and of ground stone tools; these events are dated to around the middle of the third millennium BC. This 'Guinea Neolithic' evidently continued until the introduction of iron in about AD 700. The arrival of iron appears to have been accompanied by a change in the prevailing pottery styles; the affinities of the new style are considered to be with the Lake Chad area; and it is noteworthy that the inception of iron-working in Sierra Leone appears to have been broadly contemporary with the corresponding event at Daima in the Lake Chad basin of north-eastern Nigeria. The introduction of iron at Kamabai and

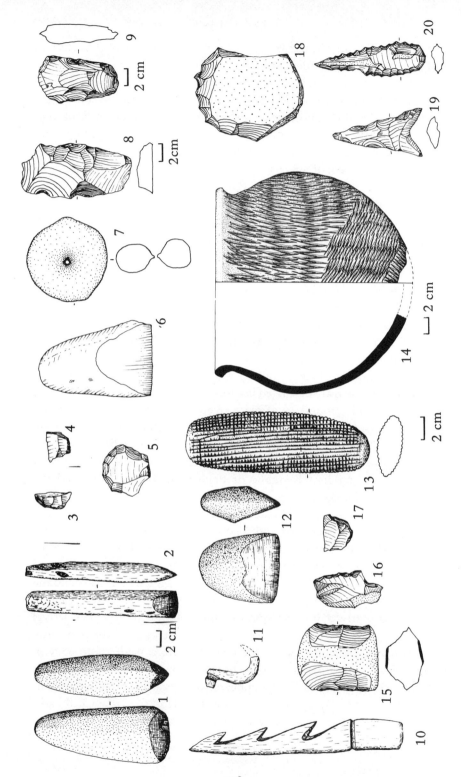

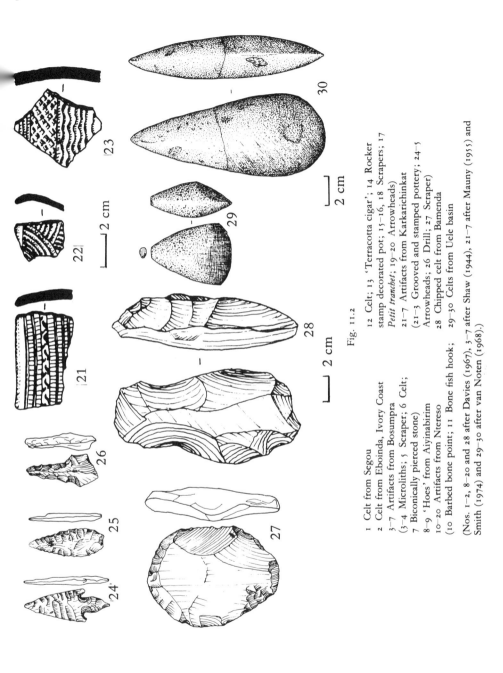

Fig. 11.2

1 Celt from Segou
2 Celt from Eboinda, Ivory Coast
3–7 Artifacts from Bosumpra
(3–4 Microliths; 5 Scraper; 6 Celt;
7 Biconically pierced stone)
8–9 'Hoes' from Aiyinabirim
10–20 Artifacts from Ntereso
(10 Barbed bone point; 11 Bone fish hook;

12 Celt; 13 'Terracotta cigar'; 14 Rocker
stamp decorated pot; 15–16, 18 Scrapers; 17
*Petit tranchet*; 19–20 Arrowheads)
21–7 Artifacts from Karkarichinkat
(21–3 Grooved and stamped pottery; 24–5
Arrowheads; 26 Drill; 27 Scraper)
28 Chipped celt from Bamenda
29–30 Celts from Uele basin

(Nos. 1–2, 8–20 and 28 after Davies (1967), 3–7 after Shaw (1944), 21–7 after Mauny (1955) and
Smith (1974) and 29–30 after van Noten (1968).)

Yagala was followed by a decrease in both the quality and the quantity of stone-tool-making, but some ground stone artifacts continued in use into the early years of the present millennium.

Accounts of the Later Stone Age of the Ivory Coast are limited to notices of isolated finds of celts, stone 'hoes', microliths and pottery, which do not permit any meaningful distinctions to be made between these and finds from adjacent areas. The only excavated occurrences are at coastal shell-mounds which contain pottery and ground stone artifacts, and are dated from the second millennium BC well into the Christian era (Mauny 1973).

Davies's work in Ghana has resulted in the accumulation of far more data for the 'Guinea Neolithic' there than is yet available in neighbouring countries. There are indications that the introduction of celts and 'hoes' may have preceded that of pottery, but the absolute dates for these events may only be extrapolated from evidence obtained elsewhere. There are as yet few complete, excavated aggregates published from Ghana, and only one dated sequence other than those referred to the 'Kintampo culture'. The latter complex is usually regarded as intrusive into the general 'Guinea Neolithic' culture-area, and is therefore discussed separately.

The most detailed description of an inventory of the 'Guinea Neolithic' in Ghana or elsewhere is that from Bosumpra Cave near Abetifi (C. T. Shaw 1944). When compared with material from earlier Later Stone Age sites, the microlithic industry appears to show a reduction in the use of small discoid cores, and there is a corresponding increase in blade production (fig. 11.2.3–7). At other sites, finely made arrow-points including some tanged types also make their first appearance at this time. The industry is dominated by crescents, a high proportion of which are deep or of *petit tranchet* type. Scrapers, backed blades, minimally retouched points and possible burins all occur throughout the sequence but are less frequent. Celts and pottery, which are also present throughout, are much less frequent in the lower levels. Small biconically-pierced stones were found; the perforations were only 3 mm in diameter and their purpose remains unknown. The pottery was for the most part from simple vessels, lacking everted rims, often decorated with simple stamped designs. The occupation of Bosumpra is dated from at least as early as the middle of the fourth millennium BC until Iron Age times (Smith 1975).

In the Ghana forests, Davies has briefly noted concentrations of scattered 'hoes', celts and apparently contemporary artifacts spread over areas several kilometres in extent, such as those at the foot of the Awudome range in Transvolta and around Aiyinabirim, west of Wiawso (fig. 11.2.8–9). These are in fertile regions and may indicate former forest clearings, possibly for agriculture. They are attributed to the 'Guinea Neolithic'. Around Benin in Nigeria, 'hoes' and celts are similarly found on buried land-surfaces below stands of apparently primary forest (Allison 1962, Davies 1967, p. 205).

The most detailed sequence of this period in Ghana is that from the Kintampo region (Flight 1972). This begins with the Punpun phase (formerly known as the Buobini culture), which is dated from approximately 1700 to 1400 BC, but is thought to have begun earlier. The microlithic quartz industry is associated with elaborately decorated pottery, stabbing and cord-impression being the techniques most frequently used. Animal bones show that, with the possible exception of the dog, no domestic animals were kept. Seeds of wild *Celtis* sp. are the only vegetable food positively identified.

In the fourteenth or fifteenth century BC occurred an abrupt cultural break which heralded the appearance of the 'Kintampo culture'; it is thought that this event may represent the arrival of new people, perhaps from the north or west. Davies (1967, p. 222) has suggested that the Kintampo industries may have been derived from the Saharan 'Neolithic' of the middle Niger region. In Ghana, the distribution of the 'Kintampo culture' appears to be restricted to the forest margin and the southern part of the savanna woodland. The pottery shows little or no continuity with that of the preceding phase, being decorated principally by means of a toothed comb 'walked' over the damp surface of the clay. The resultant designs show clear similarities with those from southern Saharan sites. There are well-made small ground stone celts, stone arm-rings and grooved stones which were perhaps used for shaping beads, and quartz lip-plugs. The chipped stone industry is essentially microlithic but includes unifacial tanged arrow-heads. Probably the most characteristic artifacts are elongated objects of sandstone with a flattened oval cross-section, deeply scored on both faces, which generally show signs of subsequent abrasion. The purpose of these rasps, which are extraordinarily numerous, has been the subject of some controversy. They closely resemble objects used in Egypt and elsewhere in recent times for scrubbing hard skin from the feet; but Shaw (1971) has suggested that they may have been used for 'grating some very hard kind of food such as yams'.

Remains of small domestic cattle and goats were found at the

Kintampo K6 site, alongside bones of wild species. The dwarf goats appear comparable to those from the Nile Valley site of Esh-Shaheinab, discussed below. The small cattle are considered to be perhaps 'not dissimilar to modern West African Shorthorn breeds' (Carter and Flight 1972). The vegetable remains from Kintampo K6 included husks of oil-palm nuts (*Elaeis guineensis*) and cowpeas, but it is not certain whether these were cultivated or wild.

The 'Kintampo culture' appears to have continued until about 1150 BC, being followed after a gap in the sequence by the Bwihweli phase. This phase is dated to the first century BC and appears to be distinct from both the 'Kintampo culture' and the succeeding local Iron Age.

Probably closely related to the 'Kintampo culture' is the fishing settlement at Ntereso on a ridge overlooking the White Volta, 50 km west of Tamale (Davies 1973). Pottery, stone tools and rasps are all comparable with those from Kintampo, but additional features which appear to be of Saharan connection are round- and concave-based bifacial arrow-heads, bone uniserial and biserial harpoons, bone fish-hooks and clay models of animals. The Ntereso settlement (fig. 11.2.10–20), dated to late in the second millennium BC, covered an area of about 750 sq. m. It has yielded the remains of a rectangular house, apparently made of poles joined by mud daub. Of particular interest are the traces of carved wooden mouldings preserved by impressions in the hardened daub. Dwarf goats like those at Kintampo are attested, but the evidence for domestic cattle is inconclusive. Hunting and fishing are both indicated; the range of fishes represented suggests that most were caught with harpoons or in traps, but some larger *Lates* could have been taken with hook and line. The presence of a species of freshwater oyster has been interpreted as indicating that the site was occupied during the dry season (from December to May) as well, perhaps, as at other times. Traces of worked iron at the site are presumably intrusive, or they may relate to a reoccupation of Ntereso early in the first millennium AD. Both Kintampo and Ntereso are regarded by Davies as representing incursions of people from the north into the relatively high rainfall region which was elsewhere the scene of the 'Guinea Neolithic'.

Surface collections from the site of Kobadi, north of Segou on the middle Niger in Mali, represent the culture of the area which has been considered as the source of the 'Kintampo culture' of Ghana. Pottery decorated with 'walking comb' impressions is comparable with that

from Ntereso and has also been found further to the west, in the upper
Niger region, on the Karkarichinkat sites in the Tilemsi valley and in
the upper horizon of the Kourounkorokale rock-shelter near Bamako.
Also from the Kobadi site came a massive stone arm-ring and bone
harpoons, one of which has been dated to around 700 BC. The absence
of microliths from this site may be due to incomplete collecting (Davies
1967, p. 224; Szumowski 1956).

The two Karkarichinkat sites (fig. 11.2.21–7) are substantial mounds
in the flat Tilemsi plain, in which they may formerly have been islands.
Their occupation is securely dated to the first half of the second
millennium BC. Bones and figurines of cattle are abundant, but the
presence of small stock has not yet been confirmed. The small number
of seeds so far identified is dominated by *Celtis* and does not include
any definitely cultivated species. Fishing, hunting and fowling are
likewise attested. The associated stone industry includes fine bifacially
flaked foliate and barbed and tanged arrow-heads, together with pointed
flakes worked to a unifacial tang. There were no concave-based
arrow-heads, such as are common further to the east in Niger. Backed
microliths are relatively rare. The crude workmanship of the large
scrapers contrasts sharply with the fine quality of the arrow-heads. The
ground stone celts are mainly small; there are occasional bone points.
The abundant pottery is decorated with a variety of grooved and
stamped designs including the 'walking comb' motif noted above
(Mauny 1955, Smith 1974).

In western Nigeria, 'hoes' and celts are widespread; their context is
shown by the Iwo Eleru excavations which revealed, as described in
chapter 6, a microlithic industry spread through most of the last ten
millennia BC to which, around the middle of the fourth millennium, were
added pottery and ground stone celts (Shaw 1969, 1972a). At the same
time chert *tranchets* make their appearance; these frequently show along
the edges a gloss such as may be caused by cutting grasses. Although
this observation is suggestive, one would not be justified in regarding
it as proof for the cultivation of cereals. The cutting of wild grass for
food, for thatching or for bedding are equally likely. The possibility
that any of these activities was carried out in what is now forest is of
considerable interest: very little is known about the past distribution
and extent of the West African forests.

The only West African site which provides a clearly demonstrable
instance of iron coming into a continuing Stone Age sequence is Daima
in the extreme north-east of Nigeria near the shore of Lake Chad

(Connah 1976). The site is an occupation mound 10.5 m high, situated in an annually flooded area. The occupation of Daima began at about the sixth century BC and continued until early in the present millennium. The nearby sites of Bornu 38 and Bornu 70, however, appear to carry the local sequence back to early in the second millennium BC. Stone, which had to be brought from a distance, was only used for the manufacture of grindstones and celts. The place of a chipped stone industry was taken by bone tools, including various pointed and spatulate types. Burnished pottery occurs throughout the sequence and no marked changes in the style have yet been demonstrated. In the approximately eighth-century BC occupation of Bornu 70, clay animal figurines, none of which indisputably represent domestic species, and bone harpoons make their appearance. These continue through into the succeeding Daima succession. The Daima harpoons are not perforated; biserially barbed ones are most frequent in the earlier levels but uniserial examples came into vogue later. Iron appears in the sequence in about the middle of the first millennium AD or shortly thereafter. Its advent seems to have been accompanied by no other substantial change in the material culture of the site's inhabitants, but bone tools soon ceased to be manufactured. From the initial occupation of the site, the Daima settlements appear to have been permanent; and houses with clay floors and wooden walls are attested. Domestic cattle and goats are present at all levels, but fishing and hunting were additional important sources of protein. Remains of charred sorghum were recovered from a level dated to the close of the first millennium AD.

Comparable mounds to the north and east of Lake Chad in Tchad and Cameroun appear to be broadly contemporary and to be remains of settlements similar to that at Daima (Lebeuf 1962). The introduction of iron in this region postdated by at least half a millennium the corresponding event around Nok on the northern Nigerian plateau, some 700 km to the south-west.

Further to the south in Nigeria, conditions are not conducive to the preservation of organic material in the archaeological record, and primary evidence for the presence or absence of food production is therefore lacking. The currently available secondary evidence is unfortunately inconclusive.

Analysis of the aggregates from two successive occupations of Rop rock-shelter on the Jos plateau of Nigeria has given one of the few indications of distinctions between the chipped stone technologies before and after the introduction of pottery (B. E. B. Fagg et al. 1972).

The earlier Later Stone Age occurrence at this site is undated, and is a crude stone industry in which true geometric microliths other than rough crescents are not represented. In the later occurrence microliths are more frequent and include geometric forms as well as small points; the quality of workmanship is higher and pottery makes its appearance. A human burial best attributed to the latter occupation has yielded a radiocarbon date around the end of the first millennium BC. It has been tentatively suggested that the tooth wear on this individual may be indicative of an agricultural economy.

Infilling of valleys on the Jos plateau is dated to the second half of the first millennium BC and has been attributed to erosion brought about by extensive clearing of the natural vegetation of the valley slopes for agricultural purposes at this time. When exposed by mining operations, the resultant stratified deposits have yielded remains of the 'Nok culture', with its distinctive pottery sculptures. Archaeological evidence for the practice of food production in the context of the 'Nok culture' is limited to two sculptures apparently representing fluted pumpkins (*Telfaria occidentalis*). The archaeological associations of the sculptures have been difficult to establish, due to their alluvial provenances, but they were held to belong to a period transitional between the Later Stone Age and the Iron Age. Recent excavations at Taruga, some 50 km south-east of Abuja, have revealed the first known settlement site of the 'Nok culture', dated to between the fourth and the second century BC. In addition to fragments of the characteristic sculptures, there were extensive traces of iron-working and domestic pottery of which the most diagnostic type was a shallow flat-bottomed dish with a deeply scored interior. These may be interpreted as graters used in the preparation of food. On the basis of the Taruga and other recent excavations, it appears that the 'Nok culture' is to be regarded as an exclusively Iron Age phenomenon (A. Fagg 1972, B. E. B. Fagg 1969).

Around Bamenda in Cameroun are found crudely chipped stone axes with constricted waists (fig. 11.2.28), presumably intended for hafting and reminiscent of Saharan examples from far to the north, together with celts and crude picks (Jeffreys 1951). Comparable waisted axes are also found in the northern grasslands of Niger. In the south they appear to be restricted to regions east of the Niger river. Surface sites near Yaounde have yielded pottery in association with bifacial stone 'hoes' together with celts, but apparently no projectile points or microliths. If these objects are indeed contemporary – and this does not seem to have been adequately demonstrated – they are presumably of late date.

The late continuation of this Later Stone Age material culture is further documented from the island of Macias Nguema Biyogo (known in English as Fernando Po), but this is possibly because the island apparently lacks any source of iron ore (Martin del Molino 1965). Four main stages of this Fernando Po 'Neolithic' industry have been recognized on stratigraphic evidence, and the earliest of these has been dated to around the middle of the first millennium AD. Ground stone celts and 'hoes' reminiscent of examples from Cameroun are there associated with pottery which shows some typological resemblance to that of the broadly contemporary Early Iron Age culture of the Congo basin to the south-east.

## Early Food Production in West Africa

It will be clear from the foregoing summary that pottery and ground stone artifacts were introduced into most of West Africa before 2000 BC and, in some areas, significantly earlier. The introduction of these artifacts may have taken place at a significantly later date in the far west, where the dating evidence is inconclusive. As has been shown by Camps in chapter 8, so-called 'Neolithic' industries – based on a microlithic technology with the addition of pressure-flaked, often bifacial, forms as well as of pottery and ground stone implements – were already established in the southern Sahara at a considerably earlier period. Domestic cattle and goats are attested at Adrar Bous in a 'Ténéréan Neolithic' context in the fourth millennium (Clark 1971a, Clark, Williams and Smith 1973). It has been argued that a pastoral economy was established in this region around the middle of the fifth millennium BC, although the population probably continued to depend to a considerable extent on hunting and fishing. Mauny (1967) has suggested that moister climatic conditions at this time rendered areas south of latitude 18° N liable to infestation by tsetse, and cites the evidence of rock paintings as support for such a southern frontier of cattle distribution at this time. The fact that it was not until the second millennium BC that cultivated cereals and domesticated cattle and goats assumed any importance in the Dhar Tichitt area of southern Mauritania confirms the suggestion for a late inception of 'Neolithic' culture in the extreme west of Africa.

Elsewhere, it is clear that food-producing societies practising the manufacture of pottery and ground stone implements were present in more northerly regions for at least two millennia before these traits became prevalent in West Africa itself. The apparent southward penetration of these traits into West Africa broadly coincided with the onset of final desiccation in the Sahara; and there can be little doubt that the two events are in some way interrelated. Desiccation and the corresponding southward translation of the climatic and vegetational zones, rendering much of the central Sahara unsuitable for a pastoral and agricultural existence, would have encouraged the early Saharan farmers to move southwards into territory which might then for the first time have been free of tsetse-fly infestation. Impingement upon the ocean-controlled climatic zone of the West African coastlands would have led to a narrowing of the more northerly ecological zones and a corresponding concentration of the human population. It may be assumed that pottery and ground stone technology were thus brought to the Later Stone Age folk of West Africa; and the typology of the relevant artifacts is generally in keeping with this hypothesis.

Whether food-production techniques spread concurrently with the latter cultural traits remains uncertain in the light of the sparse evidence for early farming in West Africa which has been outlined above. It is probable that they did not. Likewise, there is no reason to believe that the spreads of agriculture and pastoralism were concurrent with one another. In the present state of our knowledge it appears likely that, as pastoralism and agriculture advanced through West Africa, they lagged far behind the spreads of ground stone artifacts and of pottery manufacture. This impression may well require revision in the light of future research.

It should also be noted that the archaeological data currently available throw hardly any light on the early cultivation of root crops, notably the yams which in recent times have been of paramount importance as a food crop in wide areas of West Africa. The only possible archaeological indications for the antiquity of yam cultivation are the sandstone rasps of the second-millennium 'Kintampo culture', which may have been used for grating yams. It is by no means certain whether West African yam cultivation owed its inspiration to more northerly cereal cultivation or whether it was a purely independent development. Clarification of this question must await determination of the relative antiquities of the respective crops. Unfortunately, physical remains of yams are more likely to sprout than to survive in the archaeological record of the woodland forest areas most suited to their cultivation; and the artifacts used in their preparation for consumption are almost equally perishable. Davies, indeed, has tentatively suggested that cultivation of these root crops may extend in a rudimentary form even as far back as 'Sangoan' times, while on tenuous glottochronological grounds Armstrong (1964) has proposed that the practice may have an antiquity of at least 6000 years. More recently, Posnansky (1969) has argued that 'it is probably to the thousand years between 2500 BC and 1500 BC that we have to look for the intensification of tuber collection and ultimately to their careful cultivation'. Coursey's consideration of the botanical and other evidence (see also chapter 9) leads him to favour an earlier date and to propose that yam domestication could have taken place in West Africa independently of the adoption of cereal agriculture (Coursey 1976, Davies 1968).

Posnansky would attribute a similar antiquity to the cultivation of West African native cereals. These, again, are not represented in the archaeological record; and, for the present, consideration of their early cultivation and domestication must be based almost exclusively on non-archaeological indirect evidence, as is discussed in chapter 9 by Harlan. Archaeology is not yet in a position to provide useful data on the origin of the most important West African food crops; all that can be offered at present is an account of the cultural background against which these developments took place.

As has been summarized above, the currently available archaeological evidence provides little support for the hypothesis of Murdock (1959) that there was a major independent development of plant domestication in the area surrounding the Niger headwaters. There is no evidence that food cultivation in this area dates back as far as about 5000 BC, the date postulated by Murdock, nor that it predates the presence of farming peoples in the regions to the north and east. Because of this, and in view of the general southward movements of people and cultures which have been shown to have occurred at this time, there are no grounds for believing that the domestication of the indigenous African crops noted above took place independently of contact with established agriculturalists.

Dated occurrences of identifiable remains of domestic animals are comparably sparse. Cattle and goats are attested in Ghana in contexts of the 'Kintampo culture' and related sites dated to between the fifteenth and the twelfth centuries BC. Cattle were likewise present at a slightly earlier date in the Tilemsi valley in Mali. The Daima succession in Bornu has yielded remains of both cattle and goats from at least 600 BC onwards. The sparsely distributed West African rock paintings which depict cattle are of little value to this discussion since they cannot be dated and since they are not sufficiently naturalistic to enable the breeds depicted to be identified with any degree of confidence. Of the osteological specimens recovered from archaeological contexts only the Ghanaian examples have been intensively studied: both the cattle and goats are apparently closely comparable with those of the southern Sahara. The early West African domestic animals were clearly derived from a Saharan origin. There is no evidence for the prehistoric domestication of animal species indigenous to the sub-Saharan regions.

In view of the paucity of basic data, this conclusion – that it was probably within the period 2500–1500 BC that food production achieved a significant impact upon the Later Stone Age cultures of West Africa – should be treated as highly tentative. Future research, even single finds, may well necessitate major revision of the chronology. It is equally difficult to evaluate the scale and nature of this impact. Settlement sites of this time tend to be larger in area and, by implication, in population, than those of earlier phases of the Later Stone Age (Clark 1972). An accompanying prolongation of site-use cannot yet be demonstrated: in much of the Sudan zone today the predominantly pastoralist population makes considerable use of seasonal encampments. Here and further to the south the majority of the sites which have been investigated are rock-shelters where repeated re-use may be assumed and where the duration of individual occupations cannot be ascertained. It may however be surmised that early food production in much of western sub-Saharan Africa was more widespread and intensive, and supported a greater population, than the available archaeological evidence would, at first sight, suggest. The communities occupying this region during the first millennium BC may also be regarded as having made a major contribution to the spread of food-production techniques to other, more southerly, parts of the sub-continent.

## THE CONGO BASIN (fig. 11.1)

The paucity of archaeological data from the greater part of the Congo basin and its northern environs has been frequently emphasized elsewhere in this volume. Away from the restricted areas – the lower Congo, the Stanley (Malebo) Pool and the Dundo region of north-eastern Angola – where the prehistoric sequence is relatively well known, virtually the only archaeological specimens which have been recorded are ground stone axes and celts broadly comparable to the West African specimens noted above. Even these have not been recovered from dated archaeological contexts; and their possible cultural associations may only be assessed indirectly. It is known that here, as in West Africa, such artifacts continued to be used until recent times, but their introduction may have taken place several millennia ago. Both their typological similarity to West African examples and their distribution, which is concentrated in the northern regions of the forest and which does not extend as far as the northern Angola savanna, support the hypothesis that the origin of these artifacts is to be sought in the final West African Later Stone Age industries, discussed in the previous section, or that they share a common source with the latter material.

The concentration of such artifacts in the Uele basin of north-eastern Zaïre is remarkable (van Noten 1968). Finds attributed to this 'Uelian Industry' comprise principally some four hundred fine ground stone celts (fig. 11.2.29–30). There is no indication whether they are associated with chipped stone industries and/or pottery, or whether they are of Iron Age date. Other artifacts encountered in the same area, which may or may not be correctly associated with the celts, comprise large bored stones and rock engravings which characteristically represent human feet, metal tools and apparently hafted stone axes. Grinding grooves, presumed to have been used in the manufacture of the celts, are also extensively distributed beside rivers and streams in the Uele basin. The apparent contemporaneity of the representations of ground stone and metal artifacts at once suggests the probability that the manufacture of the two types may have been contemporaneous. It is reliably known that ground and polished stone tools of this type were both used and made in the Uele area as late as the nineteenth century AD, owing to the local scarcity of iron. Beyond the possible existence of a pre-Iron Age industry incorporating Uelian celts, no valid conclusions may be extracted from the limited data available. In particular it should be noted that there is no evidence concerning the economy practised by their makers. Comparable celts have also been found, but less frequently, in other areas of Zaïre, notably in Ituri and in parts of Shaba (Katanga). The associations of these artifacts are likewise unknown.

In lower Zaïre, however, evidence is accumulating that ground stone celts are to be associated with the final stages of the local Later Stone Age succession. Some prehistorians separate these industries from the Tshitolian Complex and refer them to the 'Leopoldian Neolithic', since the celts appear to be an intrusive element in the local industrial sequence. The relevant sites are concentrated between the Congo River and the Zaïre–Angola border east of Matadi and west of Mbanza

Ngungu (Thysville), but the majority of finds are of unassociated specimens from unstratified contexts. Many of them could have been used as hoes rather than as axes. The only other artifacts which have been found associated with these celts are bored stones and crudely chipped quartz artifacts which display a marked deterioration in technique in comparison with those of previous industries. Pottery, including flat-based forms, is now known to be associated with the 'Leopoldian Neolithic' from at least 200 BC. Rare ground celts encountered on the Plain of Kinshasa may represent the easternmost fringes of this industry. Here, pottery, which is largely undecorated, also appears to have been manufactured in the closing centuries of the first millennium BC, being dated to between the fourth and the second century at a site near the source of the Funa River (Cahen and de Maret 1974, de Maret 1975, van Moorsel 1968, Mortelmans 1962).

As is discussed in greater detail in volume 2 of this *History*, there are indications of the presence in the lower Congo area of a pottery tradition akin to the Southern African Early Iron Age Industrial Complex. It is not yet known whether the Funa River pottery is related to that of the contemporary 'Leopoldian Neolithic' or to the undated material with Early Iron Age affinities.

Further to the south, in the relatively well-explored Dundo area of north-eastern Angola, ground stone artifacts have not been recorded; and pottery is not attested in the local archaeological sequence before the inception of the local Iron Age. The Tshitolian industries here appear to have continued well into the first millennium AD, and probably into even more recent times in some areas. There are no archaeological indications that their makers adopted any form of food-production techniques during pre-Iron Age times. It has, however, been argued that the pronounced silting of the river valleys which took place in this area during the first millennium BC cannot be attributed to a known climatic cause and must therefore have been due to increased soil erosion caused by intensive clearing of the woodlands on the valley slopes, presumably for agricultural purposes (Clark 1968). If this can be demonstrated to have been the case, it could indicate the presence of farming techniques in a Later Stone Age Tshitolian context, several centuries prior to the local advent of the Iron Age, by peoples whose material culture apparently lacked pottery, ground stone artifacts and other 'Neolithic' characteristics. The hypothesis must for the present be regarded as unproven, pending the detailed investigation of settlement sites attributable to this period. The difficulty is exacerbated by the generally poor preservation of organic material at archaeological sites in the Dundo region. Here, as elsewhere in the Congo basin, pre-Iron Age food production cannot be regarded as proven by the present archaeological record.

Material culture from Later Stone Age sites of the last few centuries BC in lower Zaïre exhibits much stronger affinities than was apparent at earlier periods with the material culture of West Africa, particularly of Cameroun and Equatorial Guinea. It is not clear to what extent these affinities extend to the south of the Congo River. They are not apparent in the Dundo region of north-eastern Angola. Direct evidence of prehistoric economy is totally lacking from these regions and, while it is tempting to postulate a dispersal of food-production techniques from the north before the close of the first millennium BC, tangible confirmation of this has not yet been recovered. Here, as in West Africa, there is no sharp industrial break at this time; new elements, notably pottery and ground stone celts, are added to the aggregates, but there is little accompanying change in the chipped stone artifacts whose typology shows a marked degree of continuity with that of earlier phases. Both in lower Zaïre and in the Dundo region, the local variant of the Tshitolian tradition appears to have survived the arrival of the new elements with only comparatively minor modification. It is tempting to conclude that population movement probably played a relatively insignificant part in the dissemination of cultural traits at this time.

There is evidence that the drier conditions which prevailed in the lower Congo and Stanley Pool areas in post-Pleistocene times continued through much of the first millennium BC; it may be argued that the forest then covered a less extensive area than it does today. It is thus possible to envisage a southward spread of cereal (principally millet) agriculture and of the cultivation of various food plants. No confirmatory evidence has, however, so far been forthcoming, and the question of pre-Iron Age agriculture in the Dundo region remains open pending future research. The chronology of the introduction of domestic animals into this part of Africa likewise remains to be ascertained: it may be regarded as inherently improbable that cattle at any rate could have been introduced to the southern savanna by a route which leads directly through the equatorial forests. Further discussion of this problem may be postponed until a later section of this chapter.

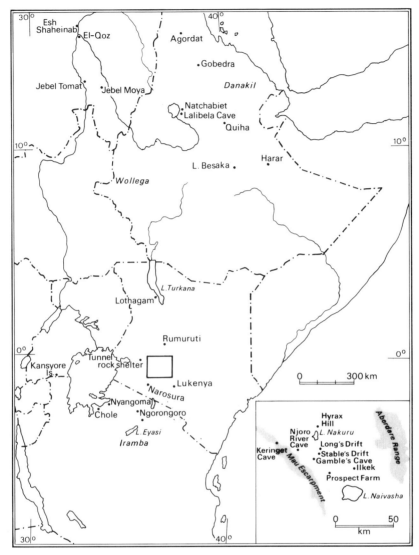

Fig. 11.3 Eastern sub-Saharan Africa, showing sites mentioned in the text.

EASTERN AFRICA (fig. 11.3)

In contrast with the areas already discussed, eastern Africa has provided a useful quantity of data relative to the early spread of food production, although the geographical distribution of this information is most uneven. The early pastoralists of the highlands of south-western Kenya

793

and northern Tanzania are one of the best-known pre-Iron Age food-producing populations of sub-Saharan Africa. Other areas – notably Ethiopia and the Horn – have to date been less well served by researchers.

### The Nile Valley

In chapter 6, attention was drawn to the evidence from north-eastern sub-Saharan Africa, most specifically from the valley and basin of the upper Nile, for the presence of semi-permanent settlement sites dependent on the exploitation of richly concentrated natural resources. These settlements may date back to the seventh millennium BC; and in Nubia there is evidence for comparable settlements at a significantly earlier period (Clark 1971b). In the area with which we are here concerned, the best-known such settlement is that of Early Khartoum. This is seen as a representative of an enduring fishing adaptation widely distributed across the southern Sahara (Sutton 1974). At Early Khartoum pottery was abundant, but there was no evidence for the practice of any form of food production. It is, however, in the context of subsequent phases of this industrial complex that such practices, so far as sub-Saharan Africa is concerned, first become apparent.

One of the best-known and most informative sites of incipient food production in this region remains that of Esh-Shaheinab, excavated some thirty years ago, 50 km north of Omdurman (Arkell 1953). Only one major phase of occupation was indicated, although the site has suffered considerably from later disturbance and erosion. No evidence was recovered of contemporary burials within the settlement area, nor were there any traces of structures other than hearths paved with sandstone lumps. On typological grounds, it is clear that the material culture of Esh-Shaheinab is related to, and later than, that from Early Khartoum described in chapter 6. This has been confirmed stratigraphically at El-Qoz on the southern edge of the Khartoum conurbation. At Esh-Shaheinab (fig. 11.4) abundant crescents and backed blades, very similar to those from Early Khartoum, were recovered. Bone harpoon-heads now included examples pierced for the attachment of a line instead of being notched as were those at the earlier site. Shell fish-hooks are characteristic of Esh-Shaheinab but unrepresented at Early Khartoum, as are neatly chipped adzes of rhyolite, some partially ground, and axe-like implements of ground bone; the last two types appear to have been used hafted. Pottery from this site shows a continuation of the 'dotted wavy-line' style which made its appearance

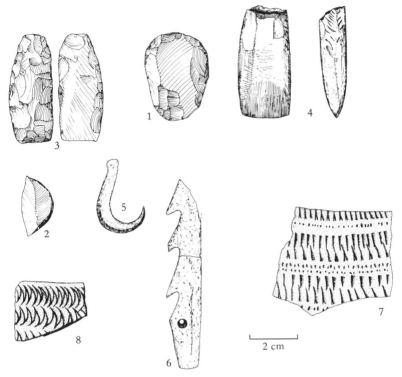

Fig. 11.4    Artifacts from Esh-Shaheinab.

| | |
|---|---|
| 1 Scraper | 5 Shell hook |
| 2 Crescent | 6 Bone harpoon-head |
| 3 Stone celt | 7–8 Sherds |
| 4 Bone celt | |

(After Arkell 1953.)

in the later part of the Early Khartoum sequence. It is distinguished from that of the latter site by being burnished; black-topped vessels comparable to Badarian examples also make their appearance. Beads of amazonite, which was presumably brought from Tibesti or from the eastern desert of Egypt, were made on the site. The abundant bone fragments are primarily of wild species. A small type of domestic goat and a possible sheep were recognized but these account for only some 2% of the faunal remains, suggesting that the economic importance of these domesticates was minimal. A variety of fishes is also represented. A nut of the oil palm (*Elaeis guineensis*) was recovered from the deposits.

The date of the occupation of Esh-Shaheinab has been the subject of much controversy but radiocarbon dating indicates an age in the second half of the fourth millennium BC. At the nearby Kadero site, Krzyzaniak (1978) has recovered faunal remains 90% of which are accounted for by domestic species, primarily cattle. The associated pottery appears to be somewhat more evolved than that from Esh-Shaheinab. Radiocarbon dates from Kadero indicate that that site was occupied towards the end of the fourth millennium BC. If these dates are not significantly in error, the two very different economies at Esh-Shaheinab and Kadero could be interpreted as a reflection of two different ecological situations – one riverine and the other in grassland away from the Nile. Alternatively, if Esh-Shaheinab is older it would fill an intermediate position between Early Khartoum and Kadero, the whole representing one long cultural continuum.

Further evidence for food production in the southern Sudan is not forthcoming until much later, Iron Age, times. At Jebel Moya and related sites such as Jebel et-Tomat, cultivated sorghum is attested in the first few centuries before and after the beginning of the present era, along with small domestic cattle, dogs and small stock (Clark and Stemler 1975).

Fishing communities such as are best represented in the Nile Valley at the sites of Early Khartoum and Esh-Shaheinab had an extensive distribution through the southern Sahara. Their characteristic types of pottery and bonework, in particular, may be traced westwards as far as southern Mali and possibly as far as Senegal. In chapter 8, Camps has discussed the spread of food production through the Saharan regions and demonstrated that pastoralism was widespread through this area by, at the latest, the early fourth millennium BC. To the north, in the Ennedi and adjacent regions of north-eastern Tchad a valuable dated sequence of pottery styles has been elucidated, but little is so far known of their economic associations. This material is described in chapter 8, but it is noted here in view of its possible connection with the Early Iron Age wares of eastern and southern Africa, described below (Bailloud 1969, de Bayle des Hermens 1975, Coppens 1969, Courtin 1969, Hays 1975).

It is thus becoming increasingly apparent that the practice of pastoralism in both western and eastern sub-Saharan Africa shares a common ancestry. Nor were the connections of these widespread fishing communities restricted to the regions lying to the west of the Nile valley. As will be shown below, there are also indications that they played a significant role in the introduction of food production into more southerly parts of East Africa. Before proceeding to discuss the evidence for this it will be convenient to give an account of the early food-producing cultures of Ethiopia and the Horn.

## Ethiopia and the Horn

Ever since the work of Vavilov in the 1930s, it has been recognized as probable that highland Ethiopia played an important part in the early spread of agriculture in sub-Saharan Africa. So far, remarkably little archaeological research has been conducted there which throws light on the relevant periods (Vavilov 1951).

Considerable interest therefore attaches to four sites of semi-permanent villages in the Agordat area of Eritrea which have been provisionally attributed to the second millennium BC (Arkell 1954). All the sites appear to have been broadly contemporary, but in the absence of stratigraphic evidence it is not known whether there is more than one phase represented in the series as a whole. The aggregates (fig. 11.5.1–4) contain ground stone mace-heads and flat perforated stone discs as well as a variety of celts, most of which are ground all over. Some of the flared cutting-edges and double-lugged forms of the celts are stated, on somewhat inconclusive grounds, to be derived from metal prototypes. There are small stone palettes and dishes, some of which are elaborated by knobs on the edges, and also a variety of stone bracelets, beads, lip-plugs and pendants. The abundant pottery includes vessels decorated with applied blobs of clay; many others have thickened rims and are decorated with false-relief chevron stamping and with incised or grooved designs. Probable food production was indicated by upper and lower grindstones and a stone figurine of an animal which is compared with representations of domestic types found on Nubian C-group sites. It has been suggested that these sites, with their Nubian affinities, may be connected with the initial introduction of cereal agriculture onto the Ethiopian highlands, but clear archaeological evidence for this assertion is so far lacking. Faunal remains, if present at the Agordat sites, appear not to have been collected. The mid second-millennium BC date which has been postulated for these sites rests on the similarity of the double-lugged stone axes to Egyptian copper specimens of the Seventeenth and Eighteenth Dynasties.

Gradual desiccation of the Sahara, noted above as a significant factor in the inception of food production in West Africa, may thus be seen as also contributing to the movement onto the Eritrean plateau, around the first half of the second millennium BC, of communities generally

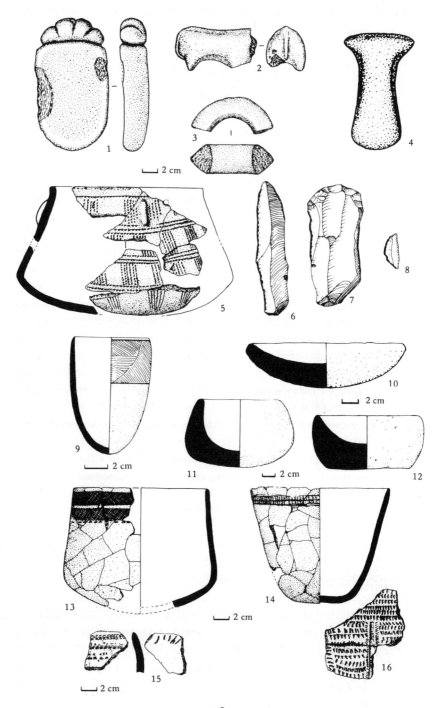

regarded as related to the C-group population of western Nubia. It has been suggested that, both in their Nubian homelands and in Ethiopia, these folk may have been cereal cultivators although, at least in the former area, it appears that their economy was predominantly pastoral. Eritrean rock paintings depicting humpless long-horned cattle may belong to this period. It has been proposed, on somewhat inconclusive grounds, that these paintings may predate the pre-Aksumite Semitic incursions into northern Ethiopia which probably took place somewhat before the middle of the first millennium BC. Comparable paintings are found in Danakil, in Harar Province, and in Somalia, and for these a similar date has been proposed (Anfray 1968, Arkell 1961, Graziosi 1964).

Further to the east, in Tigre, as at Quiha near Makalle, undated pottery-associated Later Stone Age aggregates are recorded. At Gobedra rock-shelter near Aksum coarse pottery first appears during the florescence of a microlithic industry which was subsequently displaced by an aggregate in which small steep scrapers are the dominant tool type. The latter industry is known to have survived into the Christian Aksumite period (Clark 1954, Phillipson 1977a). Seeds of finger millet (*Eleusine coracana*) have been identified from the level tentatively dated to the fourth or third millennium BC, which is marked by the earliest pottery in the Gobedra sequence (Phillipson 1977a).

At the time of writing the only other direct archaeological evidence concerning early Ethiopian food crops is that derived from two caves in Begemeder Province, east of Lake Tana (Dombrowski 1970). Unfortunately, in neither case did the occupation extend further back than the first millennium BC. Natchabiet yielded two successive aggregates; the lower one appeared to represent several temporary occupations during which pottery and worked stone, notably scrapers, were deposited, apparently during the closing centuries of the first millennium BC. The lower level of the nearby Lalibela cave is dated to a slightly earlier period but yielded a comparable aggregate. Remains of food

---

Fig. 11.5

1–4 Palette, animal figurine, stone ring and celt from Agordat sites
5–8 Artifacts from Njoro River Cave
(5 Comb decorated pottery;
6 Retouched/modified blade; 7 End scraper;
8 Lunate)

9–10 Pottery beaker and stone platter from Hyrax Hill
11–12 Stone bowls from Prospect Farm and Keringet Cave
13–14 Pottery from Narosura
15–16 Kansyore ware

(Nos 1–4 after Arkell (1954), 5–8 after M. D. Leakey and L. S. B. Leakey (1950), 9–10 after M. D. Leakey (1945), 11–12 after Odner (1972), 13–14 after Cohen (1970) and 15–16 after Chapman (1967).)

crops of Near Eastern origin – barley, chickpea and some legumes – have been identified in the lower levels of Lalibela cave, where there is also inconclusive evidence for the presence of cattle and small stock. At both sites the upper occupations are attributed to the Iron Age. We have no evidence whether or not these crops were introduced to the Ethiopian highlands significantly earlier than their occurrence at Lalibela cave, and it is not yet clear whether the associated artifact aggregate also has significant external associations or whether its roots are more firmly set in the indigenous industrial tradition of the area surrounding the Blue Nile headwaters.

In the southern Afar rift and around Harar, pottery-associated Later Stone Age industries have recently been investigated (J. D. Clark, personal communication). In the former area these stone aggregates are marked by a proliferation of scrapers and are dated to around the middle of the second millennium BC. There are good reasons to believe (though primary evidence for this is so far lacking) that the development of this industry is to be correlated with the introduction of domestic animals. Of particular interest is the discovery on a site of this period near Lake Besaka of part of a stone bowl comparable to those found on early pastoralist sites in the East African Rift Valley far to the south.

Virtually the only other piece of significant archaeological evidence relative to the early food-producing societies of Ethiopia consists of a series of poorly recorded finds, apparently mostly from surface or unstratified contexts, from the southern and south-western parts of the country. M. D. Leakey has drawn attention to the similarity between the ground stone celts of Kenya and those from Wollega and the Tuli Kapi plateau of south-western Ethiopia: unfortunately further details of the typology and associations of the latter specimens are not available (M. D. Leakey 1943). With regard to this area, Bailloud (1959, p. 24) notes that

an agricultural community, using principally stone tools, seems however to have existed in a closely defined area in the south-west of Ethiopia. This is demonstrated in the unpublished records of Father Azais' 1929–30 expedition. In this region axes and hoes of chipped or polished stone are extraordinarily common, in contrast to their extreme rarity everywhere else in Ethiopia; these are tools clearly intended for agricultural use. The axes are associated with abundant decorated pottery and, in some sites, with rare metal objects. Grinders have also been recorded. There are here elements of an agricultural neolithic culture which, according to Father Azais, extended over all of south-western Ethiopia from Beni-Changoul in the north to Lake Rudolf in the south.

It is clear that further research on sites of this period in southern Ethiopia is an urgent priority.

In a valuable summary of current knowledge concerning the economic prehistory of Ethiopia, Simoons (1965) noted that the meagreness of the archaeological record necessitated an almost total reliance upon indirect evidence. Simoons argued that in northern Ethiopia cereal–plough agriculture may predate the Semitic-speaking arrivals of the first millennium BC, a view which is supported by linguistic evidence. Cereals thus cultivated would have included finger millet (*Eleusine coracana*), tef (*Eragrostis tef*) and sorghum. The date of the introduction of wheat and barley remains uncertain (although most authorities would now disagree with Murdock's (1959) contention that they were introduced by Semitic-speaking peoples). Certainly, in Ethiopia, these south-west Asian cereals were able to flourish and to adapt, resulting in great abundance of varieties of wheat and barley, as well as in the development of flax as a food-cereal crop. Simoons also suggests that enset (*Ensete edule*), the staple food of the Sidama and some neighbouring peoples, was originally domesticated in southern highland Ethiopia. These proposals imply a basic economic· dichotomy of the Cushitic-speaking inhabitants of Ethiopia during the last two millennia BC, a hypothesis which one would expect to find reflected in the archaeological record of the period, when this comes to be investigated. No traces of the crops which are considered to be indigenous Ethiopian domesticates have yet been recovered in the archaeological record of their putative homeland, although teff was present at Hajar bin Humeid in South Yemen from at least the first millennium BC (van Beek 1969).

An independent approach to this subject is made possible by records preserved in Egypt. If the Punt of the Ancient Egyptians has been correctly identified with the coastlands of the southern part of the Red Sea (see chapter 12, fig. 12.27), then the relief carvings of the Eighteenth Dynasty mortuary temple of Queen Hatshepsut at Deir el-Bahari provide confirmation for the presence there of domestic cattle by the fifteenth century BC, as well as for cereal cultivation (Naville 1898). Although an origin for these cattle east of the Red Sea is by no means impossible, an African ancestry may be indicated by the Saharan affinities of much of the material culture of the Somalian industries which are tentatively attributed to this period. It is clear that there is as yet no indication that food production in Ethiopia and the Horn of Africa necessarily predates contact with pastoralists and agriculturalists from the Nile Valley regions to the west.

## East Africa

The Later Stone Age pastoralists of Kenya and Tanzania are one of the best known such groups in sub-Saharan Africa. Chapter 6 has summarized the evidence for the Later Stone Age industries of the Kenyan and northern Tanzanian highlands and adjacent parts of the Rift Valley. It was seen that by the second millennium BC these industries showed a considerable degree of regional typological variation, which was at least in part dependent upon the nature of the raw materials available to the various communities. The influence of material on the tool types was, however, subsidiary to that of the cultural and physical isolation imposed upon the various populations by the physical environment.

Of particular relevance here is the southward extension into East Africa of economies based upon the more intensive exploitation of freshwater resources. Bone harpoons and pottery closely allied to those from Early Khartoum occur at several localities near Lake Rudolf while a single example is reported from as far to the south as Gamble's Cave near Nakuru. Some at least of these Kenyan sites appear to have been occupied as early as the seventh millennium BC, a time when the waters of the East African lakes stood at a high level. These early fishermen evidently adopted a semi-sedentary existence based upon their reliance on the rich fishing and fowling provided by the high waters of the Rift Valley lakes (Butzer *et al.* 1972, Sutton 1974). While the excavations at Esh-Shaheinab indicate that domestic animals were adopted by the Nile Valley fishers of the central Sudan at least as early as the fourth millennium BC, there is as yet no evidence that pastoral pursuits spread, before the third millennium BC, to the related sites around Lake Rudolf or further to the south. It is not until around 2500 BC that indubitable evidence for any form of food production appears in the archaeological record of northern Kenya, while corresponding material does not appear further south until slightly before 1000 BC.

It should, in this context, be emphasized that little is yet known about the archaeology of southern Kenya during the fourth and third millennia BC. It is probable that the water level in the Rift Valley lakes remained at a high level and it has been suggested that fishing settlements of this time may be marked by the presence of a characteristic pottery type known as Nderit ware (formerly 'Gumban A', see Sutton (1974); the name 'Gumban A' is an unfortunate one, taken from that of a traditionally recalled pre-Gikuyu population of central Kenya, though there can in fact be no connection between this type of pottery and the Gumba).

Nderit ware was first recovered at Stable's Drift some 40 km south of Nakuru. It has not been reported from south of the Serengeti Plain, and its most northerly occurrence is in the Ileret area east of Lake Rudolf. Nowhere is it adequately dated.

In the Lake Rudolf basin, and further to the east in the North Kenya plains, extensive settlement sites are currently being investigated, as at North Horr. These appear to date from the third millennium BC onwards and have yielded microlithic stone industries which may have their roots in those of the earlier fishing settlements described in chapter 6. Some of the pottery shows traits reminiscent of that from the earlier sites, as well as features which may be regarded as ancestral to those of the later pastoral sites further to the south. By at least the second millennium, stone bowls also occur, thus providing a link between the occurrences of these artifacts in southern Ethiopia and those in the Rift Valley highlands further to the south. It is probable that these sites represent the first adoption of a pastoral economy in East Africa.

During the second millennium BC it appears that the trend towards settled existence was intensified and spread to adjacent areas by the introduction of pastoralism and, much less certainly, agriculture. Although, as will be argued below, the techniques of food production were almost certainly brought into the Rift Valley highlands from elsewhere, their introduction is unlikely to have been the result of any large-scale population movement. The new techniques were imposed onto heterogeneous pre-existing cultures which by and large maintained their separate identities into later periods. Such earlier lithic industries as those conventionally classed as Eburran, Elmenteitan, 'Wilton', etc continued relatively unchanged, while the manufacture and use of pottery became more general. The distribution of the various ceramic styles seems to be at least partly independent of the currently recognized subdivisions of the lithic industries with which they are associated. Further introductions, following more or less the same pattern, were the stone bowls and platters which are widely distributed in the Rift Valley areas of the East African Later Stone Age pastoralists, but which are by no means ubiquitous.

Burial sites, occupied rock-shelters and open village sites are all known and attributed to those Later Stone Age pastoralists. The earliest dated site is at Njoro River Cave near Nakuru (fig. 11.5.5–8), which has yielded a single radiocarbon date of about 1000 BC (M. D. Leakey and L. S. B. Leakey 1950). The cave contained a large number of cremated burials associated with an obsidian industry characterized by long blades resembling those described as 'Elmenteitan'. Other finds included stone bowls, pestles and mortars (one of each of which appeared to have been buried with each cremation), as well as predominantly undecorated pottery. Charred fragments of gourd (*Lagenaria vulgaris*) and the carbonized remains of an elaborately decorated wooden vessel (which ethnographic parallels suggest may possibly have been used for storing milk) were also recovered. There was a rich series of beads and pendants made from chalcedony and other local hard stones. At Keringet Cave near Molo, cremated burials associated with stone bowls (fig. 11.5.12) recall those from Njoro River Cave but belong to a somewhat later period, to the second half of the first millennium BC. An earlier occupation of the site, characterized by impressed pottery, is dated to about 1000 BC (Cohen 1970).

The Prolonged Drift site (close to Long's Drift, the type-site of the Kenya 'Wilton' as described by L. S. B. Leakey (1931, pp. 176–7)) has recently been demonstrated to comprise an extensive midden covering an area of between 400 and 450 sq. m. The midden yielded a rich 'Wilton' stone industry dominated by a large series of crescents and by distinctive short convex end-scrapers. Fragments of pottery and of stone bowls were recovered, together with a ground stone axe and a bored obsidian bead. Domestic cattle are represented in small quantities but the fauna was predominantly wild. The excavators consider that the inhabitants of the site were sedentary, and postulate a date in the region of 1000 BC (Isaac, Merrick and Nelson 1972). A comparable habitation site at Prospect Farm, Nakuru, where bones of domestic cattle are likewise attested, has been dated to between the mid eleventh and mid seventh century BC and would thus appear to be broadly contemporary with the Njoro River Cave site (fig. 11.5.11).

A further occupation site of the mid first millennium BC has been investigated beside the Narosura River in the Mau escarpment south of Narok (Odner 1972). The settlement appears to have covered about 8000 sq. m; and the discovery of many post-holes indicates the presence of semi-permanent village structures. The plan of only one such building could be reconstructed; this was a sub-rectangular hut with rounded corners and a single entrance, its walls being marked by a double row of posts. Traces of a possible internal partition were also observed. It was noted that this building showed certain resemblances,

in plan, but not in construction method, to some houses of the recent
Maasai. Of the abundant animal bones recovered from Narosura, fewer
than 5% represent wild species. The remainder were all of domestic
cattle (39%) and sheep or goats (57%). Cattle were frequently allowed
to attain old age, but small stock were generally killed while relatively
young. These data may perhaps be taken as indicating that cattle were
regularly milked, sheep and goats rarely so. It was considered by the
excavator that the settlement was larger than could be supported by
pastoralism alone (with clearly minimal hunting) and he has suggested
that irrigation agriculture was practised. Grindstones were present; but
these are not in themselves indicative of agriculture – the few carbonized
seeds which were recovered from the archaeological deposits did not
represent cultivated types. The chipped obsidian industry was
typologically uniform throughout the site's occupation. Geometric
microliths were the most frequent tool type and occurred in several
marked concentrations. Burins were also frequent. Some blades bear
striations thought to be indicative of use to cut grasses or cereals.
Ground stone axes and stone bowls were also recovered. There was
abundant pottery, manufactured by a coil technique and burnished,
bearing incised and comb-stamped decoration. This type of pottery is
now known to have a wide distribution in the central Rift. Radiocarbon
dates from the Narosura site cover the ninth to the fifth centuries BC
(fig. 11.5.13–14).

With the exception of the Njoro River and Keringet Cave cremation
sites, the usual form of burial practised by the Later Stone Age
pastoralists of this time was under a stone cairn. Many of these sites
have been investigated in the Gregory Rift area, in the adjacent western
highlands, and in the Ngorongoro Crater of northern Tanzania.
Although the intervening areas are inadequately explored, the distribution of these cairns appears to be continuous with those of the
Ethiopian highlands and northern Kenya. They show considerable
regional variation. Grave-goods are frequently, but not invariably,
present. These include obsidian artifacts, stone bowls, platters and
pestles, together with pottery whose typological affinities will be
discussed below. Faunal remains are rarely encountered, but bones of
domestic cattle are reported from a few Kenyan sites, both in the Nakuru
basin and in the adjacent highlands. It has been suggested that these
may represent the remains of funeral feasts. It is clear from the
associated finds that some at least of the cairns are attributable to
populations the same as, or related to, those responsible for the

settlement sites such as Narosura and Long's Drift described above (M. D. Leakey 1966, Sassoon 1968, Sutton 1973a).

The course most likely to instil order into this variety of 'Neolithic' industries would appear to be through detailed analysis of the associated pottery aggregates, but the results of such investigations have so far proved inconclusive. Several distinct wares may be recognized, but they show a confusing overlap in geographical and chronological distribution, as well as in the stone industries and other archaeological features with which they are associated (Bower *et al.* 1977, Sutton 1964, 1973a).

Pottery in Later Stone Age East Africa does not appear to have been the exclusive prerogative of those societies which had adopted pastoralism or other food production techniques. A case in point is Kansyore ware, characterized by bowls having tapered lips and decorated by comb-impressions or compressed zig-zag hatching (fig. 11.5.15–16). This has never been found associated with any evidence for food production. First recognized on the eponymous island in the Kagera River, Kansyore ware is now known from a wide area centred on Lake Victoria and extending south-eastward as far as Iramba and Lake Eyasi. A date anterior to that of the Early Iron Age Urewe ware is indicated at the type-site, while excavations at Chole and Nyang'oma rock-shelters near Mwanza place it firmly in a Later Stone Age context. At the latter site it is dated by radiocarbon to the second quarter of the first millennium BC (Chapman 1967).

The distributions of Kansyore ware and of the other pottery types discussed above appear to be mutually exclusive, with the exception of a limited degree of overlap in north-central Tanzania. The line of contact between the two groups appears roughly to follow line of longitude 35° 20' E, demarcating the territories of the 'Neolithic' stock-keepers to the east from the Later Stone Age hunters to the west (Soper and Golden 1969).

The archaeological evidence may be confirmed and amplified to a certain extent by the evidence of linguistic studies. There are good reasons for linking the Later Stone Age pastoralists of the highland areas of Kenya and northern Tanzania with a southward spread of Cushitic-speaking peoples from the Ethiopian highlands, a process which perhaps began around the middle of the second millennium BC (Ehret 1974). However, in view of the continuity of the associated stone industries with those of earlier periods, the scale of this movement should not be exaggerated. Languages of the Southern Cushitic group such as Iraqw and Burungi are still spoken in parts of northern Tanzania; on linguistic grounds it has been suggested (Ehret 1968a, p. 161) that 'the ancestral Southern Cushitic community was formed by the assimilation of an indigenous and previously non-Cushitic-speaking population to a much smaller group of (immigrant) Cushites... The Cushitic elements brought with them their language and the knowledge of pastoral pursuits.' The study of loan words of Cushitic origin surviving in modern non-Cushitic languages indicates that the proto-Southern Cushitic community probably lived somewhere in southern Kenya. This is in keeping with the view that a gradual spread of Cushitic speakers into East Africa took place rather more than three thousand years ago and was responsible for the introduction to the pre-existing population of important cultural innovations, pre-eminent among which were the techniques of pastoralism. It will be significant when we come to consider the spread of food production into more southerly regions to bear in mind that it has been argued that 'while cattle-keeping and grain-cultivation had been introduced into southern Africa by other peoples, the Rift Cushites may have been responsible for the introduction of cattle-milking to the Bantu' (Ehret 1968a, p. 163). The implications of the Narosura faunal remains concerning the practice of cattle-milking during the first millennium BC are fully in keeping with this interpretation of the linguistic evidence for the relatively high antiquity of the practice in the Southern Cushitic area of Kenya.

The antecedents of the East African Later Stone Age pastoralists appear to have been both with the Nile Valley and with the Ethiopian highlands. Of these two, the Nile Valley connections seem to have been the earlier and the more nebulous; indeed it is likely that they were established well before the introduction of pastoralism which may prove to have been, so far as East Africa is concerned, primarily of Ethiopian origin. Pottery from western Kenya, the distribution of which extends as far southwards as Gamble's Cave in the Gregory Rift, has apparent affinities with that from Early Khartoum; the typology of bone harpoon-heads also probably indicates some degree of cultural continuity between this area and the Nile Valley between the seventh and second millennia BC.

Cattle-herding appears to have been widespread among the Later Stone Age people of the Kenyan and northern Tanzanian highlands of the first millennium BC, but there is at present no osteological evidence for the breed of these cattle. Undated rock paintings on Mount Elgon appear to depict long-horned humpless kine comparable with those shown in the art of northern and eastern Ethiopia, noted above (Wright 1961). This type presumably predates the cross-bred zebu which is attested on several East African Iron Age sites. Small stock were apparently less common in Later Stone Age times, being represented only at Narosura where, however, they outnumber the cattle. There is both archaeological and linguistic evidence to suggest that cattle were milked, but that small stock were not. Hunting evidently continued throughout this period and was of varying, probably decreasing, importance.

It is, of course, possible or even probable that various settlements of the same basic population group might display widely differing subsistence patterns. A camp of herdsmen in a pasture area would indicate an almost exclusively pastoral economy, while other members of the group might elsewhere have been engaged in hunting and/or agriculture. Regular interchange of population could occur between such settlements and many aspects of material culture, as represented in the archaeological record, would be identical. Such a model is supported by ethnographical records from several recent societies in East Africa (e.g. von Höhnel 1894), and would explain some of the apparent anomalies which have been noted above in the archaeological record.

It remains uncertain whether or not agriculture was practised by the Later Stone Age pastoralists of East Africa. The only possibly cultivated plant of which physical remains have been found on sites of this period is the gourd, *Lagenaria vulgaris*, represented both at Njoro River Cave and at a burial cairn near Ilkek (Brown 1966, M. D. Leakey and L. S. B. Leakey 1950). It has been suggested that the stone bowls and pestles which are frequently encountered on these sites were used for preparing cultivated cereal foods, but evidence for this supposition is lacking. Similarly, arguments based on edge-wear on stone tools, on settlement size and on indications of prolonged habitation of individual sites are all inconclusive but receive some support from linguistic studies. Vocabulary studies suggest that the early Southern Cushitic speakers of southern Kenya may have possessed some knowledge of agriculture.

As has been noted, there is evidence that at least some of the Later Stone Age pastoralists of Kenya and Tanzania were predominantly Cushitic-speaking. There is a marked degree of continuity in several aspects of their material culture with that of their predecessors in this area. It seems most reasonable to attribute the initiation of the pastoral economy in this region to a gradual and relatively small-scale movement of herders southwards from the highlands of southern Ethiopia: there is no reason to believe that such movements had not been proceeding intermittently for many generations prior to the successful translation of pastoralism into more southerly latitudes. Unfortunately, comparison between the material culture of the early East African pastoralists and their putative relatives in southern Ethiopia is hampered by the almost complete dearth of archaeological data from the latter area, where virtually no artifacts have been recovered apart from celts. Pottery in East Africa shows much variety through the last three millennia BC, and it is particularly unfortunate that the ceramic styles of this period in southern Ethiopia remain completely unknown.

Sites of the East African Later Stone Age pastoralists extend southwards from the highlands of south-western Ethiopia, following the Rift Valley and its adjacent highlands as far as the Serengeti Plain of northern Tanzania. Stone bowls, characteristic of sites of the Later Stone Age pastoralists in southern Kenya, have been found recently on several sites in northern Kenya to the east of Lake Rudolf; and their presence at North Horr during the second millennium BC has been proved (Phillipson 1977b, pp. 71–4). For a comparable specimen from Lake Besaka, Ethiopia, see p. 800 above. To the west, other Later Stone Age populations, probably belonging to a distinct linguistic group, appear to have retained their hunter–gatherer way of life until the inception of the Early Iron Age; the archaeology of this period in eastern Kenya remains largely unknown. Over much of their territory the pastoralists' initial population was presumably sparse, although extensive settlement sites such as Narosura and repeatedly used burial places such as Njoro River Cave suggest that the more favourable and well-watered areas soon provided exceptions to this generalization. By early in the first millennium AD it appears that the pastoralist population was sufficiently numerous to prevent incursions into their territory by Early Iron Age folk who were at that time establishing themselves to the west, south and east.

## SOUTH CENTRAL AFRICA

For much of Africa lying to the south of the area discussed above, it appears that the onward transmission of food-production techniques took place in a markedly different manner. We have seen how, in latitudes north of about 4° S, these techniques were dispersed from the Sahara during the gradual desiccation of that region, incidentally promoting the domestication of certain indigenous food crops in northern sub-Saharan Africa. Techniques of animal husbandry and food cultivation spread further southward through cultural diffusion to related populations and through the gradual small-scale movement of people. By the first millennium BC these techniques had reached the northern fringes of the Congo forests and had penetrated, on their western margin, at least as far as the mouth of the Congo River and, on the eastern flank, as far to the south as the Serengeti Plain. At this stage the process was temporarily arrested by contact with the rapid spread of the Early Iron Age Industrial Complex.

It is generally accepted that the spread of food production was linked to the expansion of Iron Age culture in most of sub-equatorial Africa. The evidence for this, while not yet conclusive, is steadily accumulating. The inception of the Iron Age in central and southern Africa is described by Oliver and Fagan in volume 2 of this *History;* what will be attempted here is a summary of the spread of food-production techniques through the milieu of the Early Iron Age, together with an evaluation of the economy of the final Later Stone Age peoples during the time of their contact with the immigrant Iron Age farmers.

## *The Early Iron Age* (fig. 11.6)

South of the Equator line, the Early Iron Age Industrial Complex appears first to have become established in the interlacustrine region, where it is recognized in the archaeological record by its characteristic pottery, called Urewe ware. The makers of Urewe ware were probably established in the area immediately west and south-west of Lake Victoria by about the middle of the first millennium BC or shortly thereafter, although their spread around the lake to the Winam (Kavirondo) Gulf may have taken place rather later (Phillipson 1975a, 1977b, Soper 1971). The early Urewe ware makers were certainly workers of iron, but there is as yet only indirect evidence for pastoralism or agriculture in this group of the Early Iron Age. Sediment cores raised from the bed of Lake Victoria contain pollen grains indicative of a marked reduction in forest species around the first half of the first millennium BC, and pollen of *Acalypa*, a species common in abandoned gardens reverting to forest, increases markedly at this time (Kendall 1969). This may be taken as secondary evidence for the practice of some

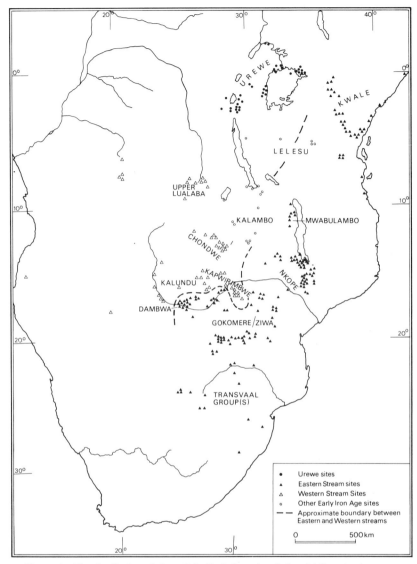

Fig. 11.6  The distribution of sites of the Early Iron Age Industrial Complex in eastern and southern Africa.

form of land clearance, perhaps for agriculture, and the Early Iron Age pioneers are likely to have been responsible.

In the subsequent spread of the Early Iron Age Industrial Complex into south central and southern Africa two distinct streams may be recognized. Of these, the eastern stream is clearly derived from the

811

Urewe settlements of the interlacustrine region, while the western stream combines Urewe-derived elements with local traits of the western Zaïre/northern Angola region. The eastern stream spread to the coastal regions of south-eastern Kenya and to adjacent parts of Tanzania by around the second century AD. During the fourth century there is attested an extremely rapid inception of Early Iron Age culture attributed to the eastern stream through a wide area extending southwards through Malawi, eastern Zambia and Zimbabwe into the northern Transvaal. The archaeology of the western stream has been less intensively investigated, being well known only in central Zambia, where its inception is not indicated until the fifth century although, as will be seen, there are reasons to believe that Early Iron Age communities may have been established in regions further to the west at a significantly earlier period (Phillipson 1976a, 1977b).

Throughout the area of the Early Iron Age Industrial Complex, there is no evidence for the prior practice of food-production techniques by any of the Later Stone Age populations. It has been suggested that, by the first millennium BC, some form of intensive collection or incipient cultivation of plant foods may have developed in or been introduced (presumably by a westerly route) to the savanna country south of the equatorial forests (Clark 1970, p. 206). Satisfactory proof of this hypothesis has not yet been forthcoming. It is therefore relevant here to summarize the evidence for agriculture and husbandry in the Early Iron Age context.

Only rarely has detailed evidence for the nature of the food-producing economy of the Early Iron Age societies been recovered. The presence of large, semi-permanent villages in many areas which lack other permanent food resources such as fish is strongly suggestive of an economy based on a substantial degree of food production. While the presence of iron hoes and of numerous grindstones may be indicative of agricultural practices, evidence concerning the specific identity of the cultigens and domesticates exploited has been obtained from only a few sites. Virtually all our available information concerning the Early Iron Age food-producing economy comes from Zambia, Zimbabwe and South Africa, where there is evidence for the cultivation of sorghum, squash, beans and cowpeas (Fagan 1967, Fagan, Phillipson and Daniels 1969, Huffman 1971, Robinson 1966a, 1970, Summers 1958, Vogel 1969). The evidence for domestic livestock is somewhat more comprehensive. Cattle appear initially to have been restricted to the western stream of the Early Iron Age in central and south central Zambia, parts of the

Transvaal and Natal and, presumably, although tangible evidence for this is lacking, to the regions to the west or north-west. They were rare or absent in other (eastern stream) areas until around the eighth century AD, while in southern Malawi domestic cattle are not attested prior to the earliest phase of the later Iron Age (Huffman 1973, Robinson 1970). Small stock were, by contrast, common in both streams in Zambia and Zimbabwe.

Difficulties are encountered in reconciling these archaeological data with the conclusions relative to the economic development of the region *vis-à-vis* the spread of the Bantu languages, which have been drawn from linguistic evidence, primarily by Ehret (1967, 1968b, 1973; for a linguist's criticism of these works see Dalby 1976). Ehret considers that the names applied to domestic cattle and sheep by the modern Bantu-speaking populations of much of south central Africa are probably derived from languages of Greenberg's Central Sudanic group. He interprets this observation as showing that the herding of sheep and cattle was introduced into southern and eastern Africa by Sudanic-speaking people, at a time previous to the main expansion of Bantu speakers.

If we accept the commonly-held correlation between the dispersal of the Early Iron Age and that of the Bantu languages, then the view that both cattle and sheep were introduced into southern Africa before the Bantu languages had spread to that region is at variance with the archaeological evidence which, as we have seen, shows that cattle, goats and sheep were apparently spread throughout the region during the Early Iron Age, although cattle were originally restricted to the territory of the western stream. Through the whole of southern Africa there is as yet no conclusive evidence for the presence of cattle or sheep (or indeed any other domestic animal) at a date prior to the introduction of the Early Iron Age into the region as a whole. Furthermore, in the most southerly areas, beyond the known distribution of the Early Iron Age Industrial Complex, such animals first occur within the same time-period. There is thus no reason to suppose them to have been derived from other than an Early Iron Age source.

This superficially contradictory evidence derived from archaeological and linguistic studies may be reconciled if, contrary to the general opinion, the spread of the eastern Bantu languages is correlated with the later rather than the Early Iron Age. The languages of both Early Iron Age streams were presumably also Bantu, that of the eastern stream being derived from a spread of Bantu-speakers around the northern fringes of the equatorial forest, and that of the western stream combining these elements with those brought more directly to the southern savanna through the western part of the forest from the Bantu homeland in what is now Cameroun. It may be postulated that the Sudanic loan words relating to domestic animals and other topics, cited by Ehret, were originally dispersed through the first of these Early Iron Age languages and thence into the later, eastern Bantu (Eastern Highland Bantu) languages (Phillipson 1976a). This hypothesis obviates the need to assume the presence in sub-equatorial Africa of Sudanic-speaking people during or prior to the Early Iron Age. It is in the light of this interpretation that we may view the processes of interaction between the indigenous hunter–gatherer populations and the incoming Iron Age farmers.

Central Sudanic languages are today spoken in an extensive belt of the northern Central African Republic and adjacent territories, as well as in the south-western Sudan, the West Nile Province of Uganda and the adjacent part of Zaïre lying immediately to the north-west of Lake Albert (Greenberg 1966, Wrigley 1963). It is unfortunate that the arachaeology of these areas is virtually unknown. The present discontinuous distribution of these languages would seem to indicate that they were formerly spoken over a wider area. This sudanic region is presumably one which saw an early establishment of mixed farming and one which, being situated midway between the archaeologically comparatively well-explored areas to the west and east, may be expected to have harboured the domesticates of both these areas. Being adjacent to the north-western part of the present Bantu language distribution, seen by both Greenberg and Ehret as the area where such languages have been longest established, it may be supposed that it was here that some of the early Bantu-speakers obtained from their Central-Sudanic-speaking neighbours the domestic cattle and sheep (and the words used to name them) which they in turn spread through eastern, central and southern Africa. Goats, being known by a name common to almost all the Bantu languages, may be regarded as having been in the possession of the Bantu-speakers for a longer time. These contact processes may have occupied many centuries, perhaps most of the the first millennium BC. The cultural differentiation within the Early Iron Age, reflected both in the pottery tradition and in the various groups' differential possession of domestic animals, may be attributed partly to early distinctions within the north-western Bantu area and partly to environmental and other factors determined in the course of their subsequent migrations. Such hypotheses are in keeping with Ehret's view (see above, p. 807) that the practice of milking cows spread from the Southern-Cushitic-speaking Later Stone Age pastoralists of East Africa to their Bantu-speaking neighbours who had already obtained cattle from another source but who had not hitherto milked them.

It may be felt, with some justification, that the above model is based on somewhat slender linguistic data of uncertain implications. Supporting archaeological evidence is, however, forthcoming from the work of Soper, who concludes a recent survey of the Early Iron Age by noting that

> There seems...to be a high probability that the decorative techniques and motifs of the pottery of the Southern African Early Iron Age Complex are closely related directly or, more probably, indirectly to the late Neolithic/early Iron Age pottery styles of the southern Sahara and Sudan belt...I would suggest that the Early Iron Age Complex springs either directly from the early Iron Age of the Chad area or from a related co-lateral source. (Soper 1971, p. 32.)

Knowledge of metallurgical techniques could easily have reached the inhabitants of this area by the middle of the first millennium BC. Such a centre of formation and subsequent dispersal of the Early Iron Age Industrial Complex is thus acceptable on both archaeological and linguistic grounds.

What, then, may have been the routes by which Early Iron Age food production spread over the greater part of eastern, central and southern Africa? The available evidence indicates that the routes were varied and their traverse rapid. There is basic disagreement among African historians as to the extent to which the rainforest of the Congo basin would have proved an impenetrable barrier to southward movement of men and cattle at this time. Perhaps the difficulties are exaggerated, but even if some groups of individuals managed to traverse the forests to the more lightly wooded savanna country which lay beyond them, it is improbable that cereal cultivation would have diffused by such a route, and even more unlikely that domestic animals (other than, perhaps, goats) would have survived the journey. The forest route may well have played a subsidiary, but nonetheless important, part in the dispersal of the Early Iron Age population, but a two-pronged flanking movement is more likely to have been responsible for the introduction of food production techniques to the southern savanna. One of these, probably the earlier, on a smaller scale and pre-metallurgical, passed down the west coast of Africa from

Equatorial Guinea to the lower Congo region and thus to the savanna country to the south of the forest. The archaeological evidence for such a route has been discussed above (p. 792). The second route lay to the east of the forest. It was presumably this branch which gave rise directly to the various groups of the Early Iron Age's eastern stream and, indirectly, contributed to those of the western stream also.

*The final Later Stone Age peoples*

In most of south-central Africa there is abundant evidence from both archaeology and oral tradition for the survival of Later Stone Age technology long after the appearance of metallurgy (Miller 1969a, Phillipson 1969a). This continued until only three or four centuries ago, or even later in some cases, although the degree of this survival varied according to the intensity of Early Iron Age settlement in the various areas. In Zambia, survivals of this type are best represented in the archaeological record by the later stages of the Eastern Province Makwe Industry and by the contemporary industries conventionally lumped together as 'Nachikufan III' (Miller 1969b, Phillipson 1973). Some aggregates of these late industries are found associated with both the cultural traits which, in West Africa for example, are regarded as diagnostic of the 'Neolithic' – viz. ground stone tools and pottery. The former indeed, as we have seen in chapter 6, have a very high antiquity in central Africa stretching back at least to the 'Nachikufan IIA' industries of the eighth to the sixth millennia BC, and they are clearly an integral part of all the later 'Nachikufan' aggregates. There is no reason to believe that these early specimens are in any way connected with food-production practices. The 'Nachikufan III' pottery is now seen to be without exception indistinguishable from that of the local Iron Age industries, from which it was presumably derived. It should not now be regarded as being an integral part of the Later Stone Age industries, but to have been obtained through some form of contact with their Early Iron Age and later Iron Age contemporaries. Certainly, it is clear that the presence of pottery or iron should not be regarded as a diagnostic feature of 'Nachikufan III' or of any other Later Stone Age industrial phase.

Several detailed analyses of industrial successions in northern and eastern Zambia covering the last three thousand years, notably that from Nakapapula in the Serenje District of central Zambia, indicate that no significant typological changes occurred during this period, such as would be expected had there been any appreciable change in the Later Stone Age economy and way of life as a result of cultural contact with the Iron Age immigrants (Phillipson 1969b, 1976b). The Early Iron Age settlement of the area began before the middle of the first millennium AD, and some form of contact between the incoming farming people and the Later Stone Age folk is attested by the presence of occasional sherds of characteristic Early Iron Age pottery in virtually all the rock-shelters which were occupied at this time. The steady continuation of the microlithic (mode 5) industry, showing only gradual typological development in keeping with trends which were already apparent before contact with the newcomers was established, suggests that cultural contact was minimal. In any case, microlithic industries of Makwe and 'Nachikufan III' type continued until well after the establishment of the later Iron Age early in the second millennium AD. This archaeological conclusion is supported by records of stone-using, hunting, nomadic communities preserved in the oral tradition of several present societies who are thought to be direct descendants of the initial later Iron Age immigrants. Periodic use of even those rock-shelters where at least occasional Later Stone Age occupation continued to a late date is also attested for such Iron Age activities as iron-working; while schematic rock paintings which are now thought to have been connected with Iron Age initiation and other religious ceremonies are further indications of the physical presence of Iron Age people in the same sites that were still sometimes frequented by their Later Stone Age contemporaries (Phillipson 1972).

In contrast with these northern and eastern areas, the Early Iron Age settlement of many parts of central and southern Zambia was comparatively dense from the middle of the first millennium AD onwards, and appears to have succeeded in rapidly displacing the Later Stone Age population. The occupation of Leopard's Hill Cave on the Lusaka plateau by the makers of microlithic tools appears to have ceased around this time (Miller 1969a, Phillipson 1968).

In the Zambezi valley near Livingstone, Vogel's investigations of the Iron Age succession have shown that Iron Age settlement did not spread from the Zambezi valley slopes to the sandy soils of the valley floor before the eighth century AD. In view of evidence for the late but undated survival of Later Stone Age industries in this part of the valley, it is tempting to suggest that in this area, as further upstream, the earlier population may have held its own for some centuries against the advance of the Early Iron Age immigrants (Vogel 1975).

In Zimbabwe the demography of this period is less clear, but survival of Later Stone Age technology into the period of Early Iron Age settlement is attested in several sites, as at Calder's Cave near Gokwe and in the Matopo Hills. The archaeological evidence from the latter area, as in Zambia, consists primarily of finds of Early Iron Age pottery associated with microlithic artifacts in the upper levels of the occupied rock-shelters; it is confirmed by the rock art which, in continuation of earlier styles safely regarded as the work of the Later Stone Age folk, depicts – from Cooke's (1959, 1964) style 4 onwards – Iron Age people apparently practising an economy different from the artist's own. In the extreme south of Zimbabwe, the Limpopo valley sites of Dombozanga and Mpato, noted above in chapter 6, have yielded distinct Later Stone Age industries dated respectively to the late first millennium AD and to the last two centuries.

Almost the sole evidence that techniques of pottery manufacture may have been adopted by Later Stone Age peoples in central Africa comprises the group of sherd aggregates known as Bambata ware after the cave in the Matopo Hills of Zimbabwe whence came the material first described by Schofield (1940; see also Robinson 1966b). It is now known to occur at some ten sites widely distributed in south-western Zimbabwe, but has not been reported from neighbouring territories, and arguments linking it with distant industries to the north are not convincing. It occurs almost exclusively in caves and rock-shelters, associated with Later Stone Age artifacts and also, on several occasions, with sherds of characteristic Early Iron Age pottery from which, however, it is typologically distinct. Radiocarbon dates for Bambata ware range from the third/fourth to the eighth/ninth centuries AD. It is thus contemporary with the Early Iron Age pottery tradition in Zimbabwe; and there is no evidence at all to suggest that Bambata ware predates the arrival of the Early Iron Age into Zimbabwe. The characteristic thinness and elaborate stamped decoration of Bambata ware indicate its separation from the Early Iron Age tradition, but occasional features of rim decoration suggest some degree of inspiration from the latter source (fig. 11.7.1–2). While the status and affinities of Bambata ware remain problematical, the most reasonable interpretation of these finds appears to be that first proposed by R. Summers (personal communication) who suggested that they might represent the adoption by the Later Stone Age folk of Zimbabwe of the pot-making technology of their Early Iron Age contemporaries.

It thus appears that for at least a thousand years after the advent of

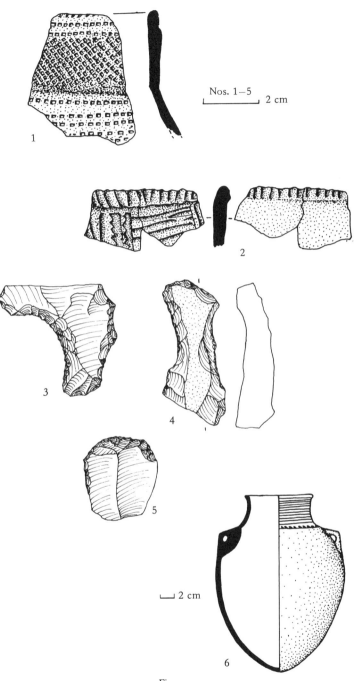

Nos. 1–5 ⊢——⊣ 2 cm

⌊—⌊ 2 cm

Fig. 11.7

1–2 Sherds of Bambata ware from Tshangula (after Cooke 1963)
3–5 Late 'Smithfield' scrapers (after Sampson 1974)
6 Pot from Mossel Bay (after Rudner 1968)

the Early Iron Age settlers to south central Africa, the descendants of the Later Stone Age hunter–gatherers retained to a variable but substantial extent their separate identity. Contact between the two groups must have occurred in many areas and have been, at least on occasion, of a semi-permanent nature. It is probable that in several areas a client relationship would have developed between the two groups, such as continues to this day in parts of Botswana and south-western Zambia (Phillipson 1975b).

SOUTH AFRICA (fig. 11.8)

It was seen in chapter 6 that in most regions of South Africa predominantly microlithic Later Stone Age industries attributed to the Wilton Industrial Complex gave way to large scraper-dominated aggregates at dates ranging from late in the first millennium BC in the western Cape coastal regions to around the middle of the present millennium in the middle Orange area (fig. 11.7.3–5). Major exceptions to this were in the Transvaal, where scraper industries may have flourished continuously in succession to those of the 'Oakhurst Complex', and in Lesotho and adjacent regions of the Drakensberg, where microlithic industries of 'Wilton' type appear to have continued right through until the final extermination of the stone-tool-makers during the nineteenth century AD (Carter 1969).

A considerable degree of inter-regional variation is apparent even from the few, generally incomplete, descriptions of these scraper aggregates which have so far been published. A detailed comparative study of these aggregates is required before any assessment may be made of the respective contributions to this variation of environmental, chronological, economic, cultural and geological (raw material) factors.

Many of these late, scraper-dominated, non-microlithic aggregates are associated with pottery. In some places pottery also occurs in association with the final microlithic industries of the Wilton Complex. Elsewhere the first appearance of the scraper industries and the introduction of pottery appear to have been broadly synchronous. At the Wilton rock-shelter in the eastern Cape, for example, an aceramic microlithic industry of the second half of the first millennium BC is overlain by a layer which contained potsherds and a stone-tool aggregate almost completely lacking backed microliths. This occurrence at Wilton is undated, but a closely similar aggregate from Scott's Cave, some 100 km to the west, has been dated to about the eighth century AD

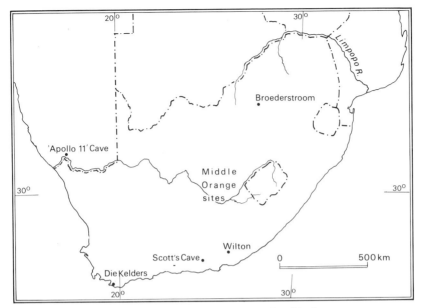

Fig. 11.8   South Africa, showing sites mentioned in the text.

(H. J. Deacon 1966, H. J. Deacon and J. Deacon 1963). The correlation between pottery and the large-scraper aggregates is not,
however, applicable in all areas. In the middle Orange region, pottery
first appears early in the present millennium, although the scraper
industry is not represented until about AD 1600 (Sampson 1972).

In Namibia, recent research has indicated the concurrence during the
last two millennia of microlithic and scraper-based aggregates; the
respective distributions of the two forms are not yet clear. At many
Namibian sites pottery first appears in the context of a microlithic
industry; here also it thus seems to predate the inception of the
large-scraper industry which, at the 'Apollo 11 Cave' in the Huns
Mountains, is dated to about AD 1700 (Wendt 1972). It is unfortunate,
however, that the inception of pot-making in Namibia cannot be more
precisely dated.

It seems reasonable to suppose that the pronounced and comparatively
rapid change in the dominant artifact types from backed microliths and
small scrapers to large scrapers only, accompanied as it was by the
virtual disappearance of backed microliths, represents some major
economic shift on the part of the populations concerned, but the full
significance of this is not easy to ascertain. It will be profitable to return

to this question after discussing the data relating to the spread of food production into southern Africa.

The spread of domestic animals across the Limpopo is not clearly illustrated by the research that has so far been undertaken. Both cattle and sheep were observed on the south coast by the Portuguese before the end of the fifteenth century. However, van Riebeeck's diaries have been interpreted as suggesting that cattle were, in the mid seventeenth century, a new and incompletely distributed form of wealth; and it has frequently been assumed that both cattle and sheep had been introduced into South Africa only shortly before that date (Goodwin 1952). It is now apparent that the latter interpretation is not correct. There is clear osteological evidence for the presence of both cattle and sheep/goats at the Early Iron Age sites such as Broederstroom in the Transvaal by the middle of the first millennium AD (Welbourne 1973). There can be little doubt that these domestic animals were generally herded by the Iron Age peoples of South Africa through most if not all of their area of settlement which, by about the middle of the first millennium AD, extended as far to the south as Swaziland and much of Natal; during succeeding centuries it gradually penetrated further southwards as far as the Transkei (Davies 1971, 1974, Dutton 1970, Mason et al. 1973).

Evidence is also accumulating for the presence of domestic animals in the extreme south of Africa at an even earlier date. This is best demonstrated at a coastal cave at Die Kelders, some 160 km east of Cape Town (Schweitzer 1970, 1974, Schweitzer and Scott 1973). Here, a midden dated to the fourth/fifth centuries AD yielded abundant remains of sheep, together with bones provisionally identified as those of cattle. Such remains were completely lacking in the levels predating the fourth century. The use of pottery appears to have preceded the introduction of sheep; and only minor changes in material culture and technology were noted at the time the domestic stock were introduced. Several further sites currently being investigated in the southern and western Cape, notably Boomplaas, are yielding evidence which confirms that from Die Kelders.

Some degree of confirmation for the early establishment of sheep herding in the western Cape comes from study of the abundant rock paintings of the region (fig. 11.9). Paintings of fat-tailed sheep comparable to those found in Zimbabwe are reported from Namibia, the south-western Cape and the south-eastern Cape, but not – apparently – from other areas of southern Africa (Inskeep 1969). Stylistically, the

Fig. 11.9   Rock paintings of fat-tailed sheep (not to scale).

1 From Mazoe, Zimbabwe (after Goodall 1959)
2 From Clanwilliam, Cape (after Johnson, Rabinowitz and Sieff 1963)

sheep paintings in the south-western Cape seem earlier than those which depict contact with Europeans (e.g. galleons and trek-waggons) and which are attributed to the seventeenth century; but there is no reliable evidence for the date of the rare rock engravings from the Transvaal which are thought to portray fat-tailed sheep. Although rock-art studies do not at present permit a more accurate assessment of the date of these sheep paintings, these conclusions are clearly in accord with the osteological data cited above.

Significantly, it is also in these southern and western zones of southern Africa that there appears in the later phases of the Later Stone Age succession a distinctive pottery ware (fig. 11.7.6). Characteristic vessels are undecorated pots with pointed or conical bases; applied lugs or handles are frequent features. This pottery tradition is well developed from the time of its local inception. Only in the southern Cape is this event well dated and it is there seen to have occurred at broadly the same time – around the first centuries of the Christian era – as the first local appearance of domestic sheep. The precise concurrence of the two events cannot be demonstrated; and indeed at some sites (such as Die Kelders) pottery appears to precede the introduction of sheep. There are, however, good indications that the two events were intimately related (Grindley, Speed and Maggs 1970, Parkington and Poggenpoel 1971, Schweitzer and Scott 1973).

The complex economic basis of Later Stone Age settlement in the southern Cape has been described in chapter 6. Evidence was cited for seasonal movement of population from the mountain belt, where wild vegetable food staples were plentiful in the summer months and were supplemented in the diet by the meat of small animals, to the caves and open sites of the coastal plains which served as bases for the exploitation of marine food resources, notably shell-fish, fish and crustacea, during the winter (Parkington 1972). This appears to have been the principal regimen of life during the period immediately preceding the introductions of pottery and herding; there are indications that it continued into more recent times, relatively unmodified by these events. The extent to which sheep-herding was adopted by these seasonally migrating groups and to which the herders formed a distinct population element cannot be determined in the present state of our knowledge.

The corresponding events in the interior regions of the Cape Province and the Orange Free State are best illustrated in the middle Orange region where pottery first appears in the context of the microlithic Later Stone Age industry early in the present millennium. The stone aggregates of this phase show little significant typological change from those of the preceding aceramic phase, but they are associated with occasional metal objects as well as with pottery. The evidence appears to indicate contact between the indigenous practitioners of a microlithic industry and an incoming Iron Age population – an experience analogous to that postulated above for the later 'Nachikufan III' and Makwe industries of Zambia. It is at this time that bones of domestic cattle first appear in the middle Orange archaeological sequence (Sampson 1972).

The spread of domestic cattle to more southerly regions of the Cape cannot yet be illustrated with any certainty. The archaeological evidence for the presence of cattle in sites preceding the last few centuries remains inconclusive. It is noteworthy that representations of cattle in the rock paintings do not overlap the distribution of those depicting fat-tailed sheep, being recorded only from the eastern Cape and the Drakensberg (Inskeep 1969). (It will be recalled that cattle were likewise not recorded in the Zimbabwe rock paintings, other than the most recent.) These observations are in agreement with the evidence that in the sixteenth century cattle may have been a relatively recent introduction to the Cape Town area. In the Drakensberg, where there are plentiful paintings of cattle but none of sheep, fine rock painting is known to have continued into the eighteenth and nineteenth centuries, and their evidence receives some confirmation from the testimony of Andreas Sparrman who, in 1776, reported that the Xhosa had numerous herds of cows, but no sheep (Sparrman 1785). The cattle depicted in the Drakensberg paintings were most probably owned not by the artists themselves but by their

Iron Age neighbours. The spread of domestic kine to the Later Stone Age people of the southern Cape is thus perhaps best seen as postdating that of sheep: it may even be a phenomenon of the present millennium.

It is now necessary to turn to a consideration of the manner in which domestic animals spread to the extreme south of Africa at – in the case of sheep at least – such a relatively early date. Since no wild prototypes of these animals existed in South Africa (or, indeed, in any other part of sub-Saharan Africa) it must be assumed that they were brought into these southerly latitudes as a result of contacts with people from the north. Sheep are known to have been of widespread occurrence in the Early Iron Age, being represented on sites of both the eastern and western streams. Their presence at Broederstroom and other Transvaal and Natal Early Iron Age sites around the fifth century AD need therefore occasion no surprise. The identification of domestic cattle at these sites is less easy to explain since, further to the north, they are not widespread in the eastern stream Early Iron Age of Zimbabwe before the eighth century. An explanation may tentatively be proposed from linguistic studies. It has been stated that the word for cattle used in the south-east Bantu dialect cluster of the Transvaal was borrowed into these languages from a Khoisan source (Ehret 1973). This observation, taken with the probability that knowledge both of pottery and of domestic sheep had spread to the southern Cape some few centuries before Early Iron Age settlement in the Transvaal, would imply that a source other than the eastern stream of the Early Iron Age must be sought for the initial introduction of pastoralism to the Later Stone Age folk of South Africa.

Similar problems relate to the introduction of pottery to those areas of South Africa which were not subject to Iron Age settlement. The view that techniques of pottery manufacture were in some way transmitted to the Later Stone Age inhabitants of South Africa and Namibia from their Iron Age contemporaries further north needs to be reconsidered in the light of recent discoveries in the Cape, which indicate that the use of pottery in the extreme south of the continent may slightly predate its introduction into the putatively ancestral areas to the north (Grindley et al. 1970, Parkington and Poggenpoel 1971, Schweitzer and Scott 1973). The supposed similarity between the Later Stone Age pottery of South Africa and Namibia and supposedly contemporary East African wares, to which considerable weight was formerly attached, is now seen to be extremely tenuous. Furthermore, the East African material which most closely resembles that from the south is now known to be of Iron Age origin and to date from the present millennium.[1]

Alternative hypotheses concerning the origin of the Later Stone Age pottery tradition of South Africa and Namibia are that pottery was independently invented in this southern area, which is improbable in view of the fully developed technology apparent in the Cape Later Stone Age pottery from the time of its earliest appearance; or that it was derived in some way from the archaeologically unexplored region of Angola lying to the west of the known area of Early Iron Age distribution. While the evidence is far from conclusive, it is the latter hypothesis which seems best to fit the available facts. It is significant to note that a coastal midden at Benfica, 17 km south of Luanda, Angola, has yielded pottery in a context dated to the second century AD (dos Santos and Ervedosa 1970).

In the foregoing paragraphs it has been argued that, around the first centuries of the Christian era, knowledge of pot-making spread to the Later Stone Age inhabitants of what is now Namibia and was thence transmitted to their contemporaries in the southern Cape. Domestic sheep were apparently introduced by a similar route at the same time. It is probable that cattle were likewise obtained by Khoisan-speaking peoples in northern parts of South Africa before the fifth century AD and by them passed to the Early Iron Age occupants of the Transvaal. There are as yet, however, no indications that cattle reached more southerly regions until significantly later times. While it is possible that knowledge of pottery may have been transmitted southwards through Angola from the 'Neolithic' settlers of the lower Congo region, it is at least equally plausible to suggest an early inception, in this archaeologically unexplored region, of the western stream of the Early Iron Age: indeed a few finds, widely scattered and at present poorly documented, do seem to indicate such penetration, which is in keeping with the available linguistic evidence. Such a hypothesis provides a possible source for the southward spread of both pottery and domestic animals, but until more intensive research has been conducted in the relevant areas of Angola and Namibia, it is profitless to speculate further.

[1] Stone bowls which bear a strong resemblance to some East African examples discussed above have been found in Namibia centred on the Waterberg north of Windhoek. None of the Namibian specimens can be dated and none came from a context where its archaeological associations could be ascertained (Clark 1964).

CONCLUSIONS

As the reader will appreciate, the above summary of the beginnings of food production in sub-Saharan Africa has of necessity been both tentative and incomplete. In the present state of our knowledge it is possible to see three main stages in the processes of inception and subsequent transmission of food-production techniques through the sub-continent.

The introduction of food production into sub-Saharan Africa was clearly due primarily to diffusion from areas to the north. During the fifth and early fourth millennia BC the greater part of what is now the Sahara Desert was the scene of a widespread series of Later Stone Age pastoral settlements some of which, in the more favourable regions, probably also practised agriculture. The domesticates and cultigens involved were predominantly, but not exclusively, of south-western Asian origin. During the fourth, third and early second millennia BC the Saharan climate gradually became unsuited to the practice of these economies. People moved southwards, following the gradual shift in the ecozones, into what are now the sahel and sudanic regions, carrying with them their material and economic culture. There was probably also a corresponding movement eastwards to the Ethiopian highlands. Through these processes, imperfectly understood, food-production techniques spread both to the negroid populations of the sub-Saharan latitudes and, eastwards, to the presumably Cushitic-speaking inhabitants of Ethiopia. It was only in the latter area that the Asian cereal crops – principally wheat and barley – were able to survive and adapt to the changed ecological conditions. In both areas several local cereal and plant food crops were brought under cultivation.

In the western Sahel, the principal local crops to be so domesticated in response to contact with farmers from the north were bulrush- or pearl-millet (*Pennisetum*) and, further south in the sudanic zone, various sorghums (*Sorghum* spp.), fonio (*Digitaria*) and the local rice (*Oryza glaberrima*). It is easy to see how the techniques of cereal cultivation practised in the Sahara could have been applied to the indigenous cereals of more southerly latitudes. The cultivation of rice, however, would have involved a much greater degree of innovation, but one which detailed knowledge of plants previously intensively collected would have been able to provide. A comparable distinction refers to the cultivation of yams (*Dioscorea* spp.), but it is easier here than in the case of rice to see how the planting of such crops could have developed from the organized collection of wild specimens. To the east, in the Ethiopian highlands, local crops brought under domestication included finger millet (*Eleusine*), certain sorghums, tef (*Eragrostis tef*) and enset (*Ensete edule*).

There was, however, no corresponding domestication of indigenous sub-Saharan African animals. The cattle introduced from more northerly latitudes were most probably of the humpless shorthorn variety *Bos brachyceros* which is widely represented in the rock art of the southern Sahara and of which an almost complete skeleton has been recovered from a 'Ténéréan Neolithic' context at Adrar Bous in northern Niger. Sheep and goats are also attested in some areas, and were presumably ultimately of Near Eastern origin. Long-horned cattle were probably introduced into the Horn late in the second millennium BC and hybrid stock may be expected to have been established over a wide area within a few centuries.

From these early centres, knowledge of food production and the appropriate domesticated species spread to Later Stone Age peoples further south, being eventually arrested by the coastal forests of West Africa, where yam cultivation perforce replaced that of cereals, and finally by the Atlantic shore itself. Further to the east, the equatorial forests probably proved a barrier almost equally impenetrable, but in the coastal regions to the west of them the Later Stone Age folk were able to adopt some degree of food production by at least the second half of the first millennium BC; while to the east pastoralism and, possibly, agriculture were spread southward before 1000 BC by Cushitic-speaking people into the Rift Valley and adjacent highlands to the east of Lake Victoria.

At this stage, presumably during the last few centuries BC, the spread of food production was overtaken by that of metallurgy. The previous stage of the spread of farming economy through sub-Saharan Africa had involved relatively little movement of population. Now, however, it took a markedly contrasting guise. Most probably it was in the sudanic open woodland country lying to the north of the equatorial forests that there began a rapid dispersal of food-producing negroid metallurgists, most probably speaking Bantu languages, who – in the course of the first five centuries AD – spread the Early Iron Age Industrial Complex over the greater part of Africa lying between their homeland and the Kalahari Desert. Food crops, mainly of sudanic origin, were spread to the southern savanna country where they throve; sheep and goats were widespread, cattle less so, dependent no doubt upon the constantly changing limits of tsetse-fly infestation. In subsequent centuries the Iron Age farming economy was enriched by the introduction of further domesticates and cultigens from beyond the Indian Ocean, and latterly from the New World.

To the south of the territory of the Early Iron Age Industrial Complex, a markedly contrasting situation prevailed. South of the Kunene–Zambezi line, Early Iron Age industries occur only to the east of the Kalahari thirstlands. Elsewhere in southern Africa a varied, presumably khoisanoid, population of Later Stone Age ancestry survived in virtually sole occupation until comparatively recent times. Herding of domestic animals spread to some of these Khoisan groups by the first few centuries AD, but agricultural techniques apparently remained unknown to them except in marginal contact areas. Domestic sheep had reached the southern Cape, most probably by a westerly route, before the date indicated for the initial Early Iron Age settlement of the Transvaal and Natal. Cattle were probably present in the eastern regions of south Africa during the first half of the present millennium, but their spread further south is poorly documented. However, by the middle of the present millennium, and possibly long before, cattle were herded in the south-western Cape. Throughout eastern South Africa they were much sought after, first from the Iron Age herds and subsequently from those of the early European settlers. It was raiding for European cattle which provoked the punitive expeditions in which many of the last of the hunting San were exterminated.

## CHAPTER 12

# EGYPT, 1552–664 BC

PROLEGOMENA

*Chronology*

The history of Egypt between 1552 and 664 BC, as for earlier periods, is conventionally divided up into usually sequential, numbered dynasties (table 12.1). These are derived from later 'Epitomes' of Manetho's history of Egypt (late fourth century BC) and usually do in fact coincide with real breaks, alterations or divisions in the line of dynastic succession.

The absolute chronology of these dynasties has been reconstructed with a high degree of reliability. It is true that two chronologies can be postulated for the Eighteenth to Twentieth dynasties (1552–1069 BC), because it is uncertain whether several dynastically-dated astronomical observations – vital for chronological reconstruction – were made near Memphis ('high' chronology) or near Thebes ('low' chronology). On the whole, the 'low' chronology fits the available evidence better, and is followed in the chronological table; nevertheless, neither the 'high' nor 'low' chronologies can yet be shown to be unquestionably correct. For the period between 945 and 330 BC there are an increasing number of reliable synchronisms, another dated astronomical observation, and some chronologically exceptionally well-documented dynasties (Twenty-sixth and Twenty-seventh), and the degree of disagreement amongst scholars is correspondingly smaller. In fact, disagreement about the absolute chronology of the entire period 1552–664 BC is quite small; significant developments within Egypt and the ever-changing pattern of its contacts with other areas can be dated with considerable if not complete precision.

Egyptian absolute chronology should prove a most important complement to radiocarbon and other dating methods in the reconstruction of the ancient history of north-east and east Africa as a whole. Egyptian contacts with these regions were extensive (see pp. 899–925); the absolute chronology of the comparatively well-known Nubian cultures is based upon datable Egyptian contacts and, as the indigenous cultures of Punt and Libya become better known, Egyptian contact

TABLE 12.1  *Names and dates of the kings of Egypt from 1552 to 664 BC*

### NEW KINGDOM

| Eighteenth Dynasty | Regnal dates | Nineteenth Dynasty | Regnal dates |
|---|---|---|---|
| Ahmose | 1552–1527 | Ramesses I | 1305–1303 |
| Amenhotep I | 1527–1506 | Seti I | 1303–1289 |
| Tuthmosis I | 1506–1494 | Ramesses II | 1289–1224 |
| Tuthmosis II | 1494–1490 | Merenptah | 1224–1204 |
| Hatshepsut | 1490–1468 | Amenmesses | 1204–1200 |
| Tuthmosis III | 1490–1436 | Seti II | 1200–1194 |
| Amenhotep II | 1438–1412 | Siptah | 1194–1188 |
| Tuthmosis IV | 1412–1402 | Twosret | 1194–1186 |
| Amenhotep III | 1402–1364 | | |
| Amenhotep IV } Akhenaten | 1364–1347 | Twentieth Dynasty | |
| Smenkhare | 1351–1348 | Sethnakht | 1186–1184 |
| Tutankhamen | 1347–1337 | Ramesses III | 1184–1153 |
| Ay | 1337–1333 | Ramesses IV | 1153–1146 |
| Horemheb | 1333–1305 | Ramesses V | 1146–1142 |
| | | Ramesses VI | 1142–1135 |
| | | Ramesses VII | 1135–1129 |
| | | Ramesses VIII | 1129–1127 |
| | | Ramesses IX | 1127–1109 |
| | | Ramesses X | 1109–1099 |
| | | Ramesses XI | 1099–1069 |

### THIRD INTERMEDIATE PERIOD

| Twenty-first Dynasty | | Twenty-third Dynasty | |
|---|---|---|---|
| Smendes I | 1069–1043 | Pedubast I | 818–793 |
| Amenemnisu | 1043–1039 | Iuput I | 804–783 |
| Psusennes I | 1039–991 | Shoshenq IV | 783–777 |
| Amenemope | 993–984 | Osorkon III | 777–749 |
| Osochor | 984–978 | Takeloth III | 754–734 |
| Siamun | 978–959 | Rudamun | 734–731 |
| Psusennes II | 959–945 | Iuput II | 731–720 |
| | | Shoshenq VI | 720–715 |
| Twenty-second Dynasty | | | |
| Shoshenq I | 945–924 | Twenty-fourth Dynasty | |
| Osorkon I | 924–889 | Tefnakhte I | 727–720 |
| Shoshenq II | c. 890 | Bakenranef | 720–715 |
| Takeloth I | 889–874 | | |
| Osorkon II | 874–850 | Twenty-fifth (Kushite) Dynasty | |
| Takeloth II | 850–825 | Alara | c. 780–760 |
| Shoshenq III | 825–773 | Kashta | c. 760–747 |
| Pimay | 773–767 | Piankhy | 747–716 |
| Shoshenq V | 767–730 | Shabako | 716–702 |
| Osorkon IV | 730–715 | Shebitku | 702–690 |
| | | Taharqa | 690–664 |
| | | Tanwetamani | 664–656 |

should prove chronologically important to their study. Moreover, it seems likely that the cultures of the contact areas will prove to have had interconnections with more remote and as yet unknown African cultures, which will thus be linked indirectly to Egyptian chronology.

Radiocarbon, thermoluminescence and similar dating methods (with their still considerable and perhaps irreducible margins of error) cannot contribute significantly to Egyptian dynastic chronology. However, they are most important for the absolute chronology of Egyptian archaeological data, i.e. for establishing dates for many structures, occupation strata and graves associated with sites in Egypt or Egyptian settlements abroad, and for the absolute time-ranges of the specific types and techniques of Egyptian artifacts of all kinds. Political, social and economic changes within Egypt and the chronology and nature of its continually changing foreign contacts are strongly reflected in the archaeological record, which often reveals aspects of these historical phenomena that the written sources either never did or no longer do preserve.

*The data*

During the period 1552–664 BC Egypt generated a great mass of richly varied data suitable for analysis by historians. Archaeologically, there is a variety of settlement types, including extensive urban complexes, palaces and fortresses, as well as smaller rural or more specialized villages. Temples of varying sizes were frequent, either as parts of larger units or as centres of settlement complexes. And the dead, of all social strata, were habitually buried in cemeteries. To a degree these types of archaeological data overlap. A wide range of socio-economic status and of profession is reflected in the remains of large towns; palaces and temples had significant resemblances in appearance and function; and the cemeteries yield many decorated chapel walls depicting the social types and characteristic occupations of the population, as well as numerous artifacts of secular as well as specifically funerary use. Despite this overlapping, however, the total complexity of Egyptian society and history cannot be appreciated without fully representative samples of all the types of archaeological data.

In the apparently abundant textual data a most important distinction should be made between *archival* material and the *monumental* texts. The archival texts – usually on fragile papyrus or small ostraca (pottery or limestone fragments) include the varied records of government at all levels (e.g. official reports, court proceedings, land registers) and the mass of letters, memoranda, agreements and wills generated by the population as a whole. A related category of more specialized texts includes literary works, religious material, mathematical and medical records and the like. The monumental texts are those carved or painted upon the walls of temples and tombs or upon artifacts designed for these contexts, such as statuary, offering-tables and coffins.

The complementary character of the two main sets of textual data is vital for the reconstruction of Egyptian history. Despite frequent and useful inclusion of historical and biographical information, the fundamental purposes of most monumental texts are limited and religious. They are not concerned with the details of civil and religious government or of the ordering of social relationships (all of which are richly represented in papyri and ostraca). Addressed primarily to the gods, the monumental texts present a highly idealized version of Egyptian history and life.

In Egyptian belief both the formal appearance and essential natures of their political, social and economic systems had been fixed by a creator god aeons earlier. The network of relationships which linked the members of the Egyptian community to each other and to foreign political and cultural units were part of an immutable world order (see pp. 843–4). This idealism which dominates the monumental texts is historically significant since a continuous interaction between the ideal and the real, between ideology and practice, was important in policy-making and in political and social relationships. However, in order not to offend the gods, important but deviant events and practices had to be ignored or at best referred to in oblique terms. They must often be inferred from changes in the pattern of political or ritual activity, unusual combinations of titles and offices or the desecration of royal and private monuments, and are only revealed in detail in archival and similar records.

Thus any significant political or religious act – conservative, reformative or innovative – was invariably presented to the gods as being in accordance with a long-established, universal order. Akhenaten, a religious innovator, claimed to 'live upon' Ma'at (Wilson 1969, p. 370), the ancient personification of that order (pp. 843–4), but his successor Tutankhamen abolished that innovation with the claim that 'Ma'at is established, she causes falsehood to be the abomination of the land, as in (the land's) first time' (Bennet 1939). Akhenaten himself is never referred to in subsequent monumental texts, but his true status in later times is expressed unambiguously in the archival record, where he had to be referred to for dating purposes; there he is identified as 'the Enemy' (Gardiner 1905, pp. 11, 23). Offences against Ma'at, frequently referred to in the archives, were ignored in the monumental record. An assassination attempt upon Ramesses III is described in great detail in papyri generated by the subsequent state trial but is nowhere referred to in the extensive texts in his temples or tomb.

Given the potential richness and variety of the data, and the essential complementary interrelationships of the different types, it is, therefore, disappointing to record that the modern scholar has a most disproportionate representation at his disposal. Information derived from inevitably biased textual and archaeological data from temples and cemeteries far outweighs that from settlement remains and archival or functionally short-lived texts.

Several factors are responsible for this imbalance and, of these, cultural ones are the least significant. Admittedly, politically unstable, economically depressed periods (especially the Third Intermediate Period) produce fewer major monumental buildings and elaborate tombs, and customs can change in important ways. Scenes of daily life on tomb walls and the funerary deposition of artifacts of secular use, for example, are much less frequent after the New Kingdom. Nevertheless, throughout the entire period there was always considerable building activity in the towns and villages, and large quantities of archival and similar material were produced.

Preservation is a more critical factor. Throughout Egypt most of the mud-brick palaces and settlements, with their invaluable, archival and other textual material, were located in the alluvial plain of the Nile, as were perforce many of the Delta cemeteries. These remains therefore were particularly susceptible to damage from the annual inundation, the rising level of the plain and the water table and the activities of a dense rural population. Many temples of the New Kingdom and after, however, were built of stone and, whatever their location, either have survived largely intact or at least have yielded many inscribed elements. Moreover, in Middle and Upper Egypt cemeteries were usually located in the low desert or valley cliffs flanking the alluvial plain and, apart from the ravages of plundering, are relatively well preserved.

Most critical of all, however, are systematic exploration and recovery, for without these, we cannot estimate the degree to which information has been genuinely and irretrievably lost through damage. For reasons of traditional interests and convenience, Egyptologists have tended to concentrate on material from cemeteries of Upper and Middle Egypt and from temple sites; there are few excavated settlement sites for any period, although many certainly exist, and both earlier and recent work has shown that Delta sites in general are better preserved than might be expected. Moreover, certain areas and, to a degree, certain periods have been traditional foci for scholarly attention, especially the cemeteries of Memphis and Thebes, and the temples of the latter, in the New Kingdom. This means that our knowledge of provincial history is extremely patchy and that many major sites in the Delta, which was a particularly important area after the New Kingdom, have not been adequately explored.

The inadequacies of the data explain the inevitably conjectural or indecisive character of many conclusions about specific events or general patterns within Egyptian history, and exacerbate the normal problems of historical interpretation created by the assumptions and values of individual historians. For example, one scholar notes the 'absolute power' of the Eighteenth Dynasty kings in all spheres, while another claims that they 'relinquished [their] religious [and military] authority to others' (compare Hayes (1973, p. 313) with Wilson (1974, p. 401)). The usurpation of monuments and a contemporary, archival reference to conflict during the Twentieth Dynasty suggest to one historian a civil war, with all its political and social implications, but to another, merely customary activity and an 'obscure local conflict' (compare Černý (1975, pp. 612–13) with Kitchen (1972)).

## THE EGYPTIAN WORLD-VIEW, 1552–664 BC

The world-view of a society is here defined as a set of concepts, held by all or most of its members, about the natural, human and supernatural worlds of which that society is a part; and about the interrelationships which link these worlds into a meaningful, intelligible whole. In this sense a world-view is not an intellectual abstraction but rather an historically important phenomenon which plays a major part in shaping the political, social, and economic life of the society. Since a specific and identifiable world-view dominated Egyptian thought, attitudes, and actions throughout the period discussed here a preliminary discussion of it renders material later in this chapter more readily intelligible and eliminates repetitious commentary.

At the outset it can be said that throughout the period 1552–664 BC, there was no basic change in the fundamentals of the Egyptian world-view, although there were important shifts of emphasis, particularly in the Third Intermediate Period. Moreover, the world-view described below was shared by all strata of society, albeit with inevitable variations in sophistication.

Several major factors contributed to the shaping, sustaining, and social pervasiveness of the Egyptian world-view. Tradition was an extremely important one. New Kingdom and later Egypt enjoyed an unbroken linguistic and cultural unity with its past, accessible through rich and intelligible textual and iconographic records, and the world-view of earlier periods continued to be a most potent model for contemporary thought and action. Its potency derived from a characteristic Egyptian religious belief. Through both their ritual and social activity men had a vital role to play in ensuring the continuity and survival of an ideal universal order – *ma'at* (p. 843) – established by a creator god aeons earlier. Conformity to earlier patterns of political and religious life was therefore encouraged, and innovations – if they were to be successful – had to adapt but not radically alter the supernaturally sanctioned formal structure.

The influence of the earlier world-view was then not dependent solely on an unconscious process of cultural transmission. Rather, ancient precepts and beliefs were deliberately sought out as guides for current policies and behaviour, while increasingly in the Third Intermediate Period there were also copies and adaptations of earlier attempts at rendering the Egyptian world-view in visual terms – in painting, reliefs, statuary and even architecture. Archaism was partly a style, partly manipulative propaganda; but it was also a process of ritual and religious significance. When there were significant changes in historical circumstances their effect was to *reinforce* the traditional world-view; partly this was due to the quality of these changes (pp. 841–3), but also to the inherent flexibility of the world-view and the supernatural strength it embodied. By repeating ancient formulations of the early world-view, reviving the names of famous kings and individuals and by copying the style and content of earlier art-forms, the Egyptians believed they created channels along which the supernatural potency of the past flowed into the present ensuring the success of the attitudes being emulated.

Particularly important for the sustaining of a similar world-view over time were basic continuities in the natural and human environment. There was no major climatic change, although periodic changes in the volume of the annual inundation had economic repercussions. The floral and faunal repertoire remained essentially unchanged throughout the period except for the introduction of the horse from Asia (*c.* 1600 BC), an innovation which enhanced both warfare and communications (giving rise to chariotry and, perhaps as early as 930 BC, cavalry).

The size, density and ethnolinguistic homogeneity of the population was another important factor. No doubt the absolute population size fluctuated as it did in mediaeval and recent times, but its general parameters are indicated by estimates of a population of 2 900 000 to 4 500 000 for the late New Kingdom and by explicit references to a figure of 7 000 000 to 7 500 000 for Hellenistic and Roman Egypt. These last two figures are unlikely to have been reached in pre-Hellenistic times. Assuming that some 6 000 000 arouras (about 1 500 000 hectares) were cultivated in pre-Hellenistic times, the average density was fairly high, and, in fact, there was a higher density in the more fertile and 'urbanized' regions (p. 860). Over the entire 1200 years substantial groups of foreigners were absorbed, but they never appeared in overwhelming numbers, and despite the 'official' prominence of Aramaic under the Persians, the Egyptian language and its characteristic writing systems survived far beyond the period discussed here.

Essentially, then, the population provided a strong and concentrated resource base, without being so large as to create administrative and social problems unprecedented in earlier times. Largely sedentary and agricultural, the population remained amenable to centralized control, and its density created a favourable environment for the communication of uniform ideas and attitudes, both geographically and across socio-economic divisions. It was characterized by a set of social interactions and conflicts similar to those of earlier periods and therefore requiring no basic change in attitudes or governmental policies.

The governmental system enjoyed great authority because of its antiquity and supernatural implications. It was adequate to meet the perennial social and economic needs of the population and it was adept at reinforcing and enhancing its own political power. The form of this government was a unique, quasi-divine kingship, the desirability of which to the Egyptians is evident from its perpetuation throughout the period and later. It is true that its partial disintegration in the Third Intermediate Period (pp. 879ff.) led to a shift of emphasis, then and in the Late Period, whereby the personal political initiative of the king was minimized in the monumental record (p. 833) and his role as an 'instrument' of the gods emphasized (Otto 1954); but the king remained potentially and usually in reality the most powerful figure in government. Strong centralization, combined with a comprehensive concept of government's functions, encouraged the maintenance of a departmentalized and hierarchical structure.

The functions of government, as conceived by the Egyptians, are identified explicitly in various texts and implicitly by actual policies. Always vigorously stressed was a religious function reflecting the supernatural basis of the governmental system, the provision of ritual attention and economic benefits to the kings' 'fathers, all the gods, in the desire to placate them by doing that which their kas [spirits] love, so that they may protect [Egypt]' (Bennet 1939).

Externally the government was expected to maintain Egypt's territorial integrity and, under the auspices of the gods, extend its frontiers. Internally, its functions were more varied. These included maintaining and enhancing the agricultural economy upon which depended Egypt's ability to produce the surplus needed to support the governmental superstructure. They also included the development and maintenance of the regulating and arbitrating mechanisms that would control the entropy that threatens any society.

The imperative to create civic and individual security led to a continuous stress upon the necessity for efficient, impartial and incorruptible administration. These maxims recur throughout the period, but are most concisely summarized in the formulaic verbal instructions issued by the kings in the New Kingdom during the installation of their viziers (p. 855). 'Law' and the 'regulations' must be adhered to throughout the bureaucracy, 'for what is required is the doing of justice by the fiat of the vizier...[for] he has been its rightful guardian since [the time of the creator] God' (Faulkner 1955). The persistence of this ideal as an integral element of the Egyptian world-view is more important than the frequent transgressions against it, for it reflects that national consensus without which no system of government can long exist. We cannot pose as an absolute the question as to 'whether these ideals were obligations or façade' (Helck 1958, p. 543) and suggest a dichotomy between ideal and actual motives in the activities of government, for motivation was complex, involving both self-interest and altruism.

The principal divisions of the society whose world-view we are discussing were the vertical ones of the occupations – this form of social classification was a bureaucratic commonplace – and, cutting across these horizontally, broad socio-economic divisions. The persistence and nature of the chief activities of the population can be appreciated by

TABLE 12.2   *Small-scale farm-holders recorded in the Wilbour Papyrus (see pp. 874–5 and Helck (1961, p. 260))*

| Plot size in aroura | Priests, % | Citizenesses, % | Soldiers, % | Stable-masters, % | Herdsmen, % |
|---|---|---|---|---|---|
| 2 | 2.91 | 2.63 | — | — | — |
| 3 | 16.50 | 23.16 | 93.22 | 2.89 | — |
| 5 | 62.14 | 59.47 | 5.08 | 92.13 | 80.67 |
| 10 | 17.48 | 10.53 | 1.69 | 3.94 | 13.45 |
| 20 | 0.97 | 4.21 | — | 1.05 | 5.88 |
| Total each occupation | 103 | 190 | 236 | 119 | 381 |

comparing those listed in a rental record of 1143 BC (the Wilbour Papyrus) with those enumerated by the historian Herodotus some 700 years later. The earlier document reveals a typical cross-section of contemporary society, a small group of high-ranking and wealthy officials and a much larger group of scribes (i.e. bureaucrats), priests, soldiers (military colonists) stable-masters (concerned with chariotry horses), 'citizenesses', cultivators and herdsmen. Artisans were another important group, not frequent in this particular document because their income came not directly from land but as payment for their products or as government rations. Later, Herodotus (II. 164) describes the principal occupations as those of 'priests, warriors, cowherds, swineherds, tradesmen, interpreters and pilots'; the obvious omission here is that of 'cultivators'.

The Wilbour Papyrus provides rare specific evidence on the wide range of economic resources to be found in Egyptian society (table 12.2), while broader socio-economic divisions are strongly reflected in textual and archaeological data (fig. 12.1). The elite – the royal dynasty in its fullest sense (pp. 854–6) and the high-ranking officials of government – enjoyed high status, substantial economic benefits and considerable potential for significant activity within the confines of the traditional political system. Of lesser status and economic importance (except in periods of political fragmentation) were the provincial nobilities, also based upon government service but perhaps more secure in the hereditary possession of their offices. A group of lesser bureaucrats, priests, military officers, wealthy farmers and artisans probably had a distinct enough intermediate socio-economic position to be identified as a 'middle class', while the 'lower class', by far the largest segment

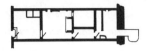

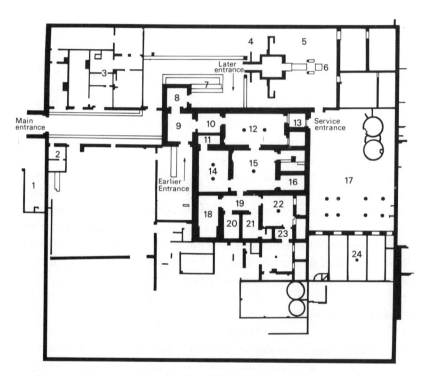

Fig. 12.1  Plans of a nobleman's villa at Tell el-Amarna and of an artisan's house at Deir el-Medineh. Both New Kingdom.

| | |
|---|---|
| 1 Chariot house | 13 Ante (*sic*) |
| 2 Gatekeeper | 14 West Loggia |
| 3 Servants' quarters | 15 Central room |
| 4 The chapel | 16 Store |
| 5 Chapel garden | 17 Kitchen court |
| 6 Altars | 18 Master's bedroom |
| 7 Flower bed | 19 Vestibule |
| 8 Later porch | 20 Guest's room |
| 9 Earlier porch | 21 Anointing room |
| 10 Vestibule | 22 Inner sitting room |
| 11 Store | 23 Ante |
| 12 North Loggia | 24 Magazines |

of the population, had great diversity of occupation (soldiers, minor officials and priests, tenant-farmers, peasants of virtually serf status and slaves), and also of income and quality of subsistence.

The political influence of the middle and lower classes was extremely limited, and was most evident in times of general disorder and disunity. Nevertheless, their indirect political significance was considerable. The elite, while exploitative, were conscious of the necessity of providing certain basic services and recognizing particular rights in order to ensure social stability. The gods explicitly sanctioned attention to the problems of the less fortunate, and government was aware of the importance of both the appearance and reality of correct behaviour. 'As for a magistrate who judges in public', the Instructions to the Vizier (p. 838) noted, 'wind and water make report of all that he does.' (Faulkner 1955.) Periodic reforms of abuses are well documented, and officials' biographies frequently refer to their aid to the disadvantaged. Indeed, the severe and socially disturbing problems of the Third Intermediate Period appear to have accentuated this aspect of the Egyptian world-view. Thereafter officials felt that the ethical performance of their duties had an intrinsic value, separate from the utilitarian one of making them acceptable to the gods of the afterlife.

Another important continuity was the Egyptian attitude to foreigners. By the New Kingdom centuries of successful military and quasi-military commercial activities in neighbouring regions had established an Egyptian self-image as a culturally superior group whose foreign activities were encouraged by their gods. Despite the shock of the Hyksos invasion (see chapter 10), this image was reinforced by the general success of New Kingdom expansionist policies and the failure of any comparably strong political unit to develop in immediately adjacent areas (except, later, to the south, in Kush). Subsequently, this concept of the nature of the appropriate relationship between Egypt and foreign states had to be adjusted in the face of serious vicissitudes, but it was done without changing its fundamental nature. The Libyans and Kushites who invaded and infiltrated Egypt at various times from the later New Kingdom on were partially and increasingly acculturated, and while conflict later on with 'superpowers' evidently more powerful than Egypt (Assyria, Babylonia and Persia) was psychologically disturbing, several periods of foreign occupation did not in fact substantially alter the traditional governmental and social structure or its supporting religious ideology. A potent factor in sustaining the sense of Egyptian superiority was its supernatural validity, which made reverses abroad, however serious, mere incidents in a cosmic drama in which Egypt and its gods would ultimately triumph. Mythic and real struggles were inextricably fused; the state, personified by the king, ritually aided the gods in their implicitly always successful struggle against supernatural enemies and disorder, while the gods promised the state ultimate victory over its foreign enemies, who were themselves part of that threatening chaos.

It has been argued that changes in internal and external historical circumstances were so great that by the Late Period there was a fundamental change in the Egyptian world-view. In this interpretation Late Period Egypt was afflicted by a 'Janusgesicht' (Janus head) (Kienitz 1967), a national schizophrenia characteristic of a culture in a state of advanced decay. In this view, Archaism reflected a deliberate effort to expunge the memories of the Third Intermediate Period; society was static and rigid; and extreme tension was generated by the contrast between traditional concepts of foreign relations and the reverses suffered by Egypt abroad. Moreover, traditional, often mean-ingless religious beliefs and practices were out of keeping with a strong, if largely subterranean, belief in ethically-based behaviour. At least partially, 'this culture was dying away from within' (Otto 1951).

The present writer, however, sees the Third Intermediate and Late Periods as representing complex and subtle responses by a flexible political and ideological system to greatly changed circumstances, but not a fundamental reordering or internal disintegration. Egypt did not need to, and apparently did not, perceive itself as in decline; despite periods of foreign occupation, it remained relatively prosperous for most of the Late Period and was often successful in its foreign-policy aims. It did finally collapse before the innovative military machine of the Macedonians (323 BC), but so did the other Near Eastern powers. And if national resistance to the Macedonian Ptolemies was less successful than that against the Persians (343 BC), this was partly due to the differing attitudes of the new conquerors, which were more in keeping with the traditional Egyptian world-view. The Ptolemies treated Egypt as their territorial centre, not as a province; they exploited traditional religious beliefs to their own advantage and encouraged an at least partially successful Egypto-Greek symbiosis which eased the problems of internal cultural heterogeneity.

The social pervasiveness of the Egyptian world-view – allowing for the varying degrees of sophistication to be expected in a social spectrum ranging from a literate court and bureaucracy to a mass of illiterate peasants of narrow horizons – was due to several factors. The state itself encouraged the acceptance of a world-view in which the existing political system had an integral position and the world-view of the elite maintained a sustaining contact with the attitudes and needs of Egyptian society as a whole. Another important mediating agency was the middle class, to some degree socially mobile and linked to both the elite and the lower classes. Another was the occupational categories, which formed important chains of contact and communication running through all three classes.

Also significant was the deep involvement of government and all segments of the population in agricultural life and in the values, priorities and religious activities naturally associated with it. Most administrative activity was concerned with enhancing and exploiting the agricultural economy; much state and private religious activity was directed towards ensuring agricultural fertility; and land and its products were the chief sources of wealth and status. The elite owned substantial estates and expressed a strong and genuine appreciation of the amenities of rural life, while urbanism never became strong enough to generate a clear dichotomy between city and rural life.

Finally, a potent source of the world-view's tenacity and pervasiveness was the religious system and its characteristic myths and rituals, which were shared by all classes of society. Modern scholarly reaction to the rich complexities of Egyptian religion is diverse. It has been variously described as 'vast accumulations of mythological rubbish' (Gardiner 1961) and as 'the ever growing and creative thought of an intelligent polytheism' susceptible to a 'subtle and profound syncretism' (Redford 1976). The latter attitude is more historically accurate, recognizing the utility and flexibility of the system. Certainly the course of Egyptian history cannot be understood without continual reference to the intricate interrelations between religious and secular life.

Historically of great importance was the concept of *ma'at* – the appropriate arrangement of the universe and of human affairs – an effort to summarize the Egyptian world-view in coherent, mythic form. Centuries old by the time of the New Kingdom, the concept of *ma'at* was a crystallization of a myriad of religious and secular ideas, and its continuity depended upon *their* continuity; nevertheless, its very existence as a formalized statement of Egyptian beliefs helped to perpetuate the ideas and attitudes upon which it was based.

The clearest expression of the significance of *ma'at* is found in several creation myths. The identity of the creator god and the mechanism of creation vary (compare the masturbation of Atum with the intellectual and emotional acts of Ptah), but the basic theme is identical: a unique creator god emerges from primeval chaos, sets the creative process in operation by creating the other gods, fashions the universe with those astronomical and seasonal rhythms and geographic circumstances characteristic of the Egyptian environment and, finally, establishes the bases of social life and technological organization as understood by the Egyptians.

(Thus justice was given to) him who does what is liked (and injustice to) him who does what is disliked. Thus life was given to him who has peace and death was given to him who has sin. Thus were made all work and all crafts, the movement of the legs, and the activity of every member – [Ptah] had formed the gods, he had made cities, he had founded nomes [provinces], he had put the gods in their shrines.... (Wilson 1969, p. 5.)

The world-view expressed through the myths was not complacent and self-satisfied. The Egyptians had a keen sense of the tension and conflicts which threatened political and social stability and of vicissitudes in the natural environment which could create acute personal or national distress. These fears were extended into the supernatural world, being embodied in a number of ambiguous or clearly malevolent figures and most specifically in Seth, a powerful god associated with disorder, sterility, sexual aberration, the desert and thunder, and the Egyptians felt themselves deeply involved in the continuous efforts of the gods to stave off a threatening chaos. Nevertheless, the forces of disorder were felt to be under the control of the creator god; 'Reharakte (king of the gods) says: "Let Seth...be given to me (as son). And he shall speak out of the sky, and men shall be afraid of him."' (Wilson 1969, p. 17.)

There were many gods with different personalities and functions, each having one or more main cult centres. This regional diversity was further complicated in that some, probably many, communities had distinctive pantheons dominated by a local form of the chief regional god but incorporating others selected by criteria which varied according to the nature of the community. Despite this variety, however, the various personalities and functions of individual gods interlocked to form the very substance of the universe, while theological synthesis, mythic marriages and other relationships created many additional links amongst them. Besides the gods, certain genii and spirits and the dead formed other significant supernatural communities, but the ritual needs of all three groups were very similar, creating great uniformity in both cult activity and in the structures which were the scenes of this activity.

All classes of supernatural beings were potent, even the dead, to whom letters were sometimes addressed accusing them of harming the

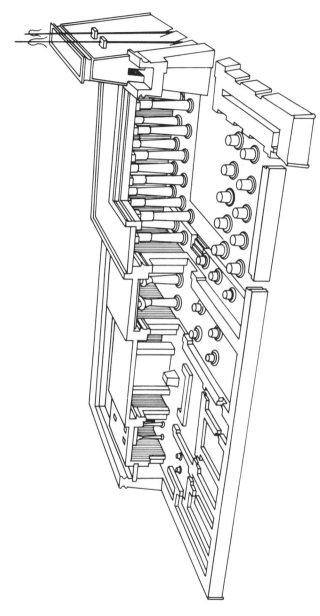

Fig. 12.2 Sectional view of a typical New Kingdom temple. Its form reflects the processional character of the rituals followed, while its rich relief decoration moved from the 'public' acts of the reigning king (e.g. victory in battle, prowess in the hunt) on the pylons and sometimes in the first columned hall, to a depiction of the king's intimate relations with the gods and of his performance of the cult.

living, or appealing to them to bring good fortune. The gods, however, were the most powerful figures and communication with them was of greatest concern. Their desires and wishes might be indirectly expressed, as when a low Nile or a major political disturbance implied divine anger, but they were frequently sought out explicitly by means of an oracle, a practice first seen in the New Kingdom and persisting thereafter. Oracles were employed at high levels of government in the New Kingdom to ratify important decisions, but later, as royal authority lessened, they were resorted to for relatively minor administrative and judicial decisions. Government appeals to the oracle were merged with a more generalized function of oracles which affected all levels of society. Oracles, which were always delivered by a specific god but variously in his 'national' or local form, were a source of reassurance and guidance for individuals and an important social mechanism easing the tensions and conflicts inherent in closely-knit and largely self-regulating town and village communities. The local kenbet-councils (p. 861) were clearly unable or unwilling to solve many disputes involving ownership or rights and cases of theft or other crimes, and these were therefore submitted to a god as a neutral arbitrator of unimpeachable authority. While some manipulation was involved, there is good evidence that the process was carried out in good faith under the influence of 'suggestion and autosuggestion' (fig. 12.3) (Černý 1957, p. 76).

Myths provide us important insights to the world-view, but ritual and not myth or theology dominated Egyptian religious life. The religious experiences and perceptions of the individual were insignificant compared to the ritual activity of the community which, through cult and festival, hoped to effect 'the renewal and rejuvenation of the life of the cosmos, of the community and the individual' (Bleeker 1967, p. 22). Primary foci for the rites were of course the temples, which ranged from the great national shrines to hundreds of smaller, local ones and which followed a uniform plan and decorative system (fig. 12.2). Temples had a cosmological symbolism: each represented a universe, the roof being the sky and the sanctuary the horizon where the sun rose and set, symbolizing an eternal cycle or renewal, decline and rebirth in the universe. At least once the royal city itself became subsumed into this concept; Tell el Amarna (p. 867) was conceived of as set totally within a natural temple, defined by the real sky and horizons of the valley. In both the houses of the nobility and of the middle and lower classes there was considerable domestic cult activity directed towards

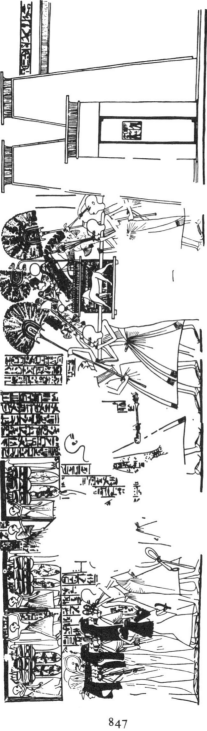

Fig. 12.3 An oracle is sought from a New Kingdom local god, the deified King Amenhotep I, whose image has just been carried on a litter out of its temple (right). The god's High Priest, Amenmose, stands before the litter holding an incense burner and wearing a leopard skin, and asks the god to judge which of two men (bowing and partially obliterated behind the high priest) is 'right' in some unspecified dispute. The god explicitly finds one of the men 'right', probably by 'forcing' his bearers to approach the favoured disputant. (See Černý 1962, pp. 42–5 and fig. 9.)

847

the same gods, while the cemeteries, both royal and non-royal, were other centres of fundamentally similar rituals.

Turning to the main political and economic effects of the religious system, we note first that while it contributed to the dominant position of the king, it also subtly qualified his apparently absolute power. Dogmatically, the survival of the kingship was vital; the formal relationship between Egypt and its gods, which symbolized its integral position within a divinely-created universal order, depended upon the king, who was the chief channel of divine power and guidance. To maintain the order established by the gods the king was given supreme political authority, while he sustained a fruitful reciprocal relationship between men and gods through his unique ritual role. All the priests serving the myriad cults were merely his delegates, temple iconography depicting *only* the king performing the ritual. Yet the king's dogmatic position was not unambiguous. He enjoyed the powers of and reverence due to the gods, but he was implicitly and sometimes explicitly subordinate to them; even the powerful kings of the New Kingdom sometimes sought 'a command...from the great throne [of a god], an oracle of the god himself' (Breasted 1906, II s. 285). Moreover, kings did not have the *specific* wonder-working powers of the gods. The royal temple built by each king was for his funerary cult for, after death, kings no longer remained 'on earth' but, like the gods, dwelt in some celestial realm.

This dogmatic ambiguity had its effects in the political sphere. The king's ritual and dogmatic position enhanced his political authority and motivation. The altruistic performance of his duties was identical with his self-interest in maintaining his political supremacy and that of his dynasty. Yet the existence of *ma'at* set up a kind of formal standard against which the king's ability, and the degree of divine approval he enjoyed, could be measured. Weakness, inability or inefficiency on the part of the king could create persistent maladministration in Egypt or losses abroad, all evidence of the disintegration of *ma'at*. That such an attitude was inherent in Egyptian thought is clearly revealed in the Demotic Chronicle (Ptolemaic period), which attributes the fall of several Late Period kings to their failure to satisfy the gods, and is seen earlier in the destruction of monuments that had been set up by certain kings later deemed offensive to *ma'at* and in the common vernacular identification of Akhenaten (in the Nineteenth Dynasty) as 'the Enemy'.

Every Egyptian god was supplied with a temple to house his cult-image, a staff of priests and servants, and estates and other gifts to support his establishment. The chief gods (and amongst these Amen, in various forms, was the most important in the New Kingdom and held a more qualified dominance for the remainder of the period) had special functions and status, reflected in the size and elaboration of their temples, the great number and variety of their personnel, and their extensive and diverse possessions (lands, mines, quarries, ships, and even villages and towns). In about 1153 BC the temples as a whole owned about one-third of Egypt's cultivable land and about one-fifth of its inhabitants, although, on the broader time-scale, the size of the temple holdings doubtless fluctuated considerably.

However, while the high priests of the main cults, and especially the High Priest of Amen of Thebes, were undoubtedly high-ranking and influential figures, we must not exaggerate their political importance. Theologically, they were subordinate to the king, high priest of all the gods, and the nature of the religious system was such that the priests (literally, 'the god's servants') could undertake no politically disturbing theological initiative; influential 'prophets', in the Hebrew sense, were unknown. All religious appointments and promotions were theoretically subject to royal approval and, while hereditary rights to certain positions did become firmly established, so did they in all other branches of government as well. The administration of religious establishments was essentially part of the civil government, and although the temples were income-generating (through renting land and trading), the collection and control of this income appears to have been, at least partially, subject to the civil government. Substantial amounts of royal income, in the form of booty, land and other gifts, were transferred to the temples, but royal relatives and loyal officials were also appointed to many of the resulting religious sinecures. Most significantly of all, the temple establishments had neither the necessity nor the occasion of developing substantial military or police powers, coercive resources which were intimately linked to political power in ancient Egypt. Temple establishments were, therefore, on the whole more subject to political manipulation and exploitation, rather than initiators of such activity.

## INTERNAL HISTORY

The period between 1552 and 664 BC is conventionally divided into two main phases, the New Kingdom (1552–1069 BC) and the Third Intermediate Period (1069–664 BC). The New Kingdom was a period of extraordinary Egyptian expansion abroad and of strong centralization and considerable stability internally. During the Third Intermediate Period Egypt's foreign contacts contracted sharply and foreign policy was with rare exceptions defensive and unaggressive until the Twenty-fifth Dynasty (747–656 BC). These characteristics of Third Intermediate Period foreign relations directly reflect a high degree of internal decentralization and indeed at times disintegration of government, breaking out sporadically into civil war.

Despite their strong differences the two periods are of course intimately related; the Third Intermediate Period was the direct result of political, social and economic processes which came into being in the New Kingdom. The exact natures and interactions of these processes are – and will long remain – matters of debate; but a description and analysis of them, however qualified, must be the substance of any historical discussion of the New Kingdom and Third Intermediate Period. The details of Egyptian relations with other part of the ancient world are not of prime interest in this series.[1]

In the following sections, emphasis will be placed upon the *internal* effects of foreign affairs; variations in the formal structure and in the tone and character of government, and the political implications of these variations; the interplay of competition and conflict within the political system; and the effect of all these factors upon the relations between government and governed and upon the social and economic condition of the population as a whole.

## THE NEW KINGDOM (1552–1069 BC)

For the New Kingdom especially a brief description of the general pattern of Egypt's foreign affairs and certain key events within them is essential for the understanding of internal history. During this period Egypt maintained control over extensive foreign conquests and sustained its Levantine position successfully against the pressure of the other two dominant powers in the region, the Mittanians and their successors, the Hittites. Extensive political–commercial contacts were developed with a number of other states and groups in the Aegean, the Near East and East Africa. During the reign of Ramesses III, in the twelfth century BC, two critical events occurred: the Asiatic conquests were apparently lost and the political and ethnic structure of Syria, Palestine and Anatolia was drastically altered as the result of a mysterious population movement, that of the 'Sea-Peoples', who surged along the eastern Mediterranean and had to be repulsed at the seaward and eastern frontiers of Egypt itself. At the same time, perhaps

---

[1] For the latter, reference should be made to the *Cambridge Ancient History*, 3rd ed, vol. II, and to Kitchen's *The Third Intermediate Period in Egypt*.

not coincidentally, Libyan pressure, which had been building up for forty years, reached a climax in two abortive invasions of the western Delta.

To a degree, these developments were uncontrollable; neither the Hittites nor any other state in the region had been able to resist the 'Sea-Peoples', while the Libyans had never before demonstrated the strength they showed from the reign of Ramesses II onward. But it is significant that Egyptian reaction was comparatively weak. After the time of Ramesses II Egypt was unable to regain its position in the Levant, now broken up into a number of comparatively small kingdoms with no dominant 'great power'; it could not prevent massive and continuing Libyan infiltration; and, only about eighty years after Ramesses III's death, Egypt also lost its African conquests after a struggle that was more of a civil war than a foreign conflict. Clearly the reverses of the late New Kingdom must have had serious internal repercussions, some of which will be discussed below; but are they sufficient in themselves to account for the deteriorating situation in foreign affairs, let alone the internal political problems of the Third Intermediate Period that followed?

## The structure of government

To attempt to answer that question we must turn to the internal history of the New Kingdom, and in particular to an important historical problem that is epitomized in two quotations. The first is of a type repeated continuously in royal texts: the god Amen declares to King Tuthmosis III 'I cause your victories to circulate in all lands. The gleaming [serpent], she who is upon my brow, is your servant, [so that] there shall arise none rebellious to you as far as that which heaven encircles.' (Wilson 1969, p. 374.) The second is an extremely rare type: Piankh, High Priest of Amen and generalissimo of southern Egypt – hence one who owed his position theoretically to royal appointment and favour – writes contemptuously of Ramesses XI in a letter: 'Of whom is Pharaoh superior still?' (Wente 1967, p. 53.) This apparent contradiction cannot be interpreted too arbitrarily. It is only partly a matter of chronology, for although Piankh's question reflects a real decline in royal power and authority towards the end of the New Kingdom, the supremacy of the king was still formally stated in the monumental record. It is therefore also a problem of sources, for the paucity of those letters, memoranda and private reports against which we can check the validity of the picture of royal power presented in the monumental texts makes it extremely difficult at any time to assess the degree to which the king's political independence was circumscribed by the system of which he was part.

Piankh's attitude, although extreme as a result of specific historical circumstances, reflected a fundamental characteristic of the political system. An inherent problem of a comparatively highly centralized system based on a single individual, the king, is that whatever the king's theoretical powers may be, his political effectiveness depends upon the support and co-operation of others. Inevitably they will attempt to exploit this situation to their own advantage. Beyond this particular problem is a more general one, the development of a concentration of power elsewhere within the system which will create the potential for an individual or group to usurp important functions nominally reserved for the king and his chief executive officials, and perhaps to replace the latter and even usurp the kingship.

In general the reality of royal power through most of the New Kingdom seems confirmed by the admittedly largely inferential evidence. This includes the explicitly acknowledged role of the king in administrative and military affairs, the long-sustained and successful policy of Egyptian expansion, the executive and economic strength indicated by the extensive temple-building programmes undertaken by most of the kings, and the development of a luxuriant mythology concerning the quasi-divine aspects of the kingship. More specific events are also revealing, particularly those connected with Akhenaten (pp. 866–9). A significant but gradual change in the nature and strength of royal power seems to become evident first in the late Nineteenth Dynasty and increasingly in the Twentieth. Prior to this time, favourable circumstances abroad, the structure of the political system itself and the supervisory and manipulative abilities of the kings appear to have rendered the royal power, so frequently celebrated in the monumental record, a reality.

Throughout the New Kingdom, the Levant and north-east Africa were the foreign areas of greatest Egyptian interest. Egypt had already been active in these income-producing regions for one and a half millennia, and the traditional stimuli to renewed contact and expansion were reinforced in the early Eighteenth Dynasty by the presence in both regions of powerful forces which had been sources of great humiliation and danger to Egypt in the Second Intermediate Period (see chapter 10).

The effect of foreign affairs was certainly significant internally. The expulsion of the Hyksos and of the Kushites in c. 1555–1540 BC (see chapter 10), the expansion, which was a logistical necessity to prevent further invasion, and the conflict which this expansion generated with Mittanians and the Hittites, meant that Egypt was on a permanent war-footing. The early Eighteenth Dynasty kings were true war-leaders, directing and often personally participating in major campaigns, establishing a tradition that continued to be an ideologically potent convention and often a reality for the rest of the New Kingdom. However, the kings were not preoccupied with campaigning and in fact devoted most of their reigns to internal affairs. Apart from those of the atypical Tuthmosis III, campaigns were usually restricted to the early years of each reign, partly perhaps because actual or incipient revolts tended to occur at a reign-change, but probably also to demonstrate the military abilities of the new king and the divine approval he enjoyed.

These periodic campaigns, the need to control the conquered lands and the necessity for rapid military action in external emergencies, led to the development of a permanent, professional army. Its professionalism lay in a permanent military administration, headed by a 'great army general', standing garrisons abroad and in Egypt, and a continuous levying and training programme which created a large, experienced reserve which could be rapidly mobilized. In addition, many veterans were settled on farms in Egypt which were inherited by their families so long as the male descendants remained available for military training and service. The army was professional also in its organization, being divided up into various units, primarily infantry and chariotry but also more specialized units, each with its own hierarchy of officers. There was thus created a most significant element in the political structure, highly organized and with a potential for great coercive force, which was also thoroughly integrated into the fabric of society because of its dependence on military colonists and general levies. Its functional and ideological links with the kingship were strong, and were enhanced by royal policies described below.

Expansion and conquest also augmented royal income and increased the manipulative capabilities of the kings. To the traditional income from taxes, the personal possessions of the dynasty, and a monopolistic position in foreign trade were now added sporadic but often large amounts of booty, regularly delivered foreign tribute, and expanded, quasi-political trading opportunities. As war-leader and sole delegate of the gods, the king naturally received much of this additional income himself, and had firm control over the distribution of the remainder. He was able to emphasize the status of the royal family by the scale and embellishments of its palaces and estates, demonstrate his ideological authority by lavishly endowing the major temples and reinforce this political power by judiciously rewarding loyal bureaucrats and officers.

The exigencies of foreign affairs and the military experiences of the kings and of many important officials also strongly affected the structure of government. This was based on a Middle Kingdom prototype and, like it, responded efficiently to certain perennial social and economic needs of the population, but the New Kingdom structure was less complex and thus more rapidly responsive to royal command, mobilization and the need for creating war-materials and supplies. From the point of view of internal politics, the most interesting aspect of government is that its very structure reinforced the dominant position of the kings and enhanced their manipulative abilities, but at the same time presented them with serious supervisory problems and created the potential for other competitive and divisive power centres to develop.

The governmental structure is well documented and is summarized on fig. 12.4. This schematic version of course ignores some known changes in administrative organization and does not reflect the fluctuations of power throughout the system which are, in any case, rarely recorded explicitly in the textual record. But its general outline seems to be valid for the entire New Kingdom. The structure was shaped to a large degree by functional efficiency and geographical circumstances, but these contributed also to royal supremacy, as did a sometimes clearly evidenced manipulation of the system. Thus government was broken into three major units, of which two, internal government and the administration of the conquests, make sense functionally; the third, the dynasty proper, on the other hand had a very limited political role. While it undoubtedly must have been a large and complex group, most of its members were excluded from major political or military office and normally also from the succession, unless they belonged to a certain segment of the direct line. This effectively restrained any individual who might have had some not too remote claim to the supernatural authority emanating from the kingship. Only those dynasty members with a vested interest in maintaining loyalty to the reigning king received important posts: the crown prince – the designated heir – was frequently 'great army general', controlling the military in the king's name; and the king's chief wife, the 'great royal wife' (or, alternatively, her eldest daughter) was appointed 'God's wife of Amen'. This mythologically justifiable role for the chief queen (the New Kingdom kings believed that their mothers had been impregnated by Amen) also

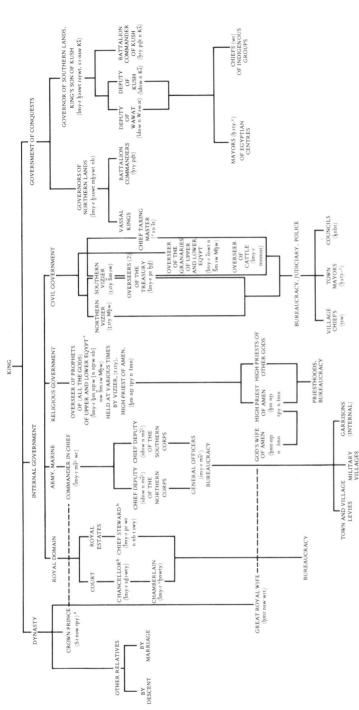

Fig. 12.4 Schematic outline of the developed structure of government in the New Kingdom. The fragility of much of the evidence on which this diagram is based must be emphasized, as must its inability adequately to illustrate significant changes in the structure; (for some indication of these, see notes b and c). Nevertheless, the writer believes that the diagram gives a reasonable approximation of the divisions of functions and powers within New Kingdom government.

(a) On the sometimes ambiguous terms used to designate the crown prince, see Kitchen (1972).

(b) On the rise of the 'chief steward' at the expense of the 'chamberlain', see Helck (1958, pp. 80–2).

(c) Held at various times by the vizier, the High Priest of Amen (frequently) and others.

(d) On the office of 'high taxing master', the importance of which is still in dispute and which is as yet dated no earlier than Akhenaten, see especially Gardiner (1948, pp. 10, 150, 165, 206), Helck (1958, pp. 143–5) and Seele (1959, p. 9).

855

brought a substantial portion of Amen's temporal possessions under direct royal control.

Since the king normally spent most of his reign in Egypt, the government of the conquered lands was internally significant to the degree that it might provide a power-base for an individual or group who could then usurp royal functions and perhaps the throne itself. In fact, the richest and politically most sophisticated of the conquests, the 'North lands' along the Mediterranean coast of Asia (fig. 12.5), were unlikely to do so. They were, for topographical and administrative reasons, divided ultimately into three provinces, each with its own governor, usually an Egyptian but sometimes an Asiatic. These governors in practice shared political power with a number of vassal kings and were not militarily strong. The garrisons of Egyptian (and Kushite) troops in the 'Northlands' were small, scattered and under the direct control of several 'battalion-commanders' and not of the governors. For perennial, but small-scale, police and military activities considerable use was made of the forces of the local city states and, in major campaigns, the large armies sent from Egypt were under the command of the king or the 'great army general'. The 'Southlands' (Wawat and Kush), with their Nubian population, were potentially much more significant. The region was ruled by a single governor, who shared no important administrative power with the local chieftains; its military forces were centralized under a single 'battalion-commander'; and it had a geographical unity combined with easy and rapid access to Egypt proper. The power of the Viceroy of Kush was to be important internally at the end of the Twentieth Dynasty.

The internal government of Egypt was divided for functional reasons, into four major units (fig. 12.4) and these were sometimes further divided geographically, in the interests of efficiency and perhaps also of the stability of royal power. Centralized control was maintained by means of the small group of powerful officials who headed each department, who reported directly to the king, and who were appointed and removed by him. It was amongst these that the politically most influential and potentially most divisive individuals within the system were normally to be found. Within the general system, the disposition of coercive power was particularly significant. The military had a minimal role to play in the normal operations of government, being concerned primarily with registering and training those liable for military service, administering the small standing garrisons in Egypt and abroad, stock-piling and dispatching supplies, and mobilizing on a large scale when necessary.

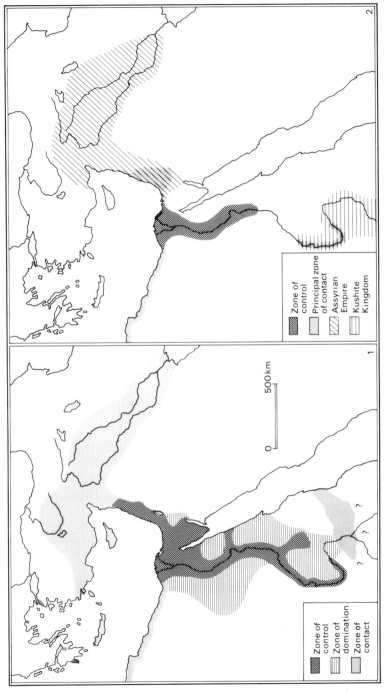

Fig. 12.5  The changing pattern of Egyptian foreign relations. 1, New Kingdom; 2, Third Intermediate Period.

Zone of
control

Principal zone
of contact

Assyrian
Empire

Kushite
Kingdom

500 km

0

Zone of
control

Zone of
domination

Zone of
contact

The civil government was concerned primarily with regulating agriculture, collecting taxes, administering justice and maintaining civic order and its orders were enforced by a relatively weak police force, the Medjayu.

The personal possessions of the king and the royal family were extensive and formed virtually a separate branch of government which we may call the 'royal domain', while another substantial mass of land and other income-generating assets accumulated under the religious government, a fact that was politically useful to the kings (p. 849). The administration of the religious establishment was particularly fragmentary and the degree to which it came under a centralized control is uncertain; the High Priest of Amen was certainly the most powerful individual within this governmental unit, and he often (although not always) held a post entitled 'overseer of all the priesthoods of Upper and Lower Egypt'. The real, as compared to the titular, importance of this office has not, however, been documented but it was presumably in the royal interest to keep this supernaturally charged and economically wealthy section of the government politically weak. It is interesting in this connection to note that in two New Kingdom depictions of high officials processing in hierarchical order, the sequence is crown prince, viziers, stewards of the royal estate and court, high-ranking military and civil officials and finally important high priests, who are followed by a provincial official in one instance and by lower ranks of priests in the other (Hayes 1973, p. 362).

Dominant as the royal position was, however, each branch of government exercised some degree of effective power. To appreciate better the interplay of power and influence, and the peculiar problems of royal power, we must examine also the political geography of Egypt and the tone and character of government. For the New Kingdom these aspects are comparatively well documented.

Two factors of fundamental importance for the stability of government were the effectiveness of the links between the central and provincial governments and the pervasiveness of royal authority and supervision. Facilitating these was the concentration of population upon the alluvial plain and the usefulness of the Nile as an administrative artery (fig. 12.6), but problems were created by the extreme length of the country, the highly personal character of government and the comparative inefficiency of communication.

The structure of provincial government is poorly documented and the following sketch highly tentative. There was a distinct hierarchy of

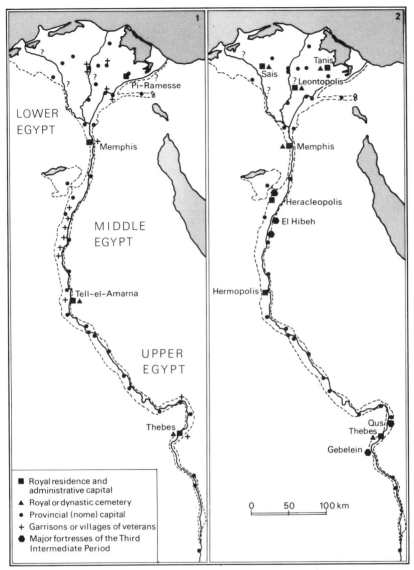

Fig. 12.6  Political map of Egypt in (1) the New Kingdom and (2) the Third Intermediate period. For garrisons and villages of veterans see Helck (1939, pp. 17–20); those immediately south of Herakleopolis represent a zone of such settlements rather than specific sites (O'Connor 1972a), and the military settlements of the Delta are inferred from the later importance of Mendes, Sebennytos, Busiris, Bubastis and Pi-Soped as centres for Mashwash soldiery.

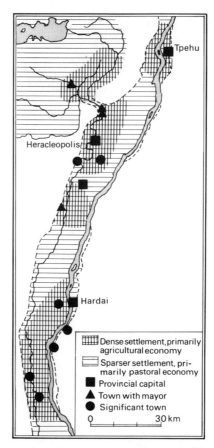

Fig. 12.7   Reconstruction of typical New Kingdom provincial settlement pattern.

settlements. *The* cities were Memphis, Thebes and (later) Pi-Ramesse. Elsewhere, in any given region, the provincial capital was usually the most important administratively and probably the largest in population. It was surrounded by a zone of fairly large and densely concentrated villages (interspersed by rare towns intermediate in administrative function (and size?) between the villages and the capital), which thinned away to smaller, scattered settlements (fig. 12.7). Unfortunately, it is impossible to equate this hierarchy with any certainty to Egyptian nomenclature; 'cities', 'towns' and 'villages' (respectively *niwt*, *dmi* and *whyt*) were distinguished from each other, but the terms appear to be used with great looseness. Slightly less ambiguous are smaller units, such as 'nobleman's estate' (*bhn*) and 'house (hamlet?) of X' (*'tnx*).

The key units in the administration of these varied settlements were the mayors (*ḥȝty-'*) and kenbet-councils (*ḳnbt*) (see fig. 12.4); for both categories there was internal hierarchization and differences in function. National and provincial capitals each had a mayor, as did some (perhaps all) of the 'intermediate' towns. Village (*wḥyt*) mayors are sometimes referred to in general terms, but more precisely village leaders were *ṯsw* (literally 'commanders') and perhaps often simply the functionally and socio-economically dominant figures in the community. The degree to which the major provincial mayors had authority over the agricultural hinterlands and over the 'lesser' mayors remains uncertain, but the functions of mayors in general were clear; they were responsible for collecting taxes, facilitating the work of representatives of the central government, and implementing orders received from them.

The New Kingdom kenbet-councils were primarily judicial but they were also quasi-administrative, since they were often concerned with property rights. The two 'great kenbet-councils' of Thebes and Memphis were each headed by a vizier and were concerned with civil cases. Throughout Egypt were many lesser kenbet-councils, a more widespread mechanism than that of the mayors, and their primary functions were to prosecute criminal activity (excepting that involving capital punishment, which was referred to the vizier) and to resolve countless cases of property rights and disputes. Holding 'court in the towns according to the excellent plans' (Pflüger 1946) of the king, these councils were an important source of civic order. The 'great kenbet-councils' consisted of high-ranking priests, bureaucrats and soldiers; the provincial ones, certainly subject to government approval, were made up of people of high *local* socio-economic status.

The provincial centres were of course widely dispersed (fig. 12.6), while the offices and archives of the central government had to be physically concentrated. As a partial solution to the problems of administration, the New Kingdom continued the traditional practice of dividing Egypt up into two (rather than, as earlier, three) major units, one governed from Thebes and the other from Memphis. Important offices were divided, if their responsibilities were sufficiently complex and extensive. This was true of the vizierate (that is, there was a northern and a southern vizier) responsible for the efficient functioning of the civil government as a whole, of the Treasury and of the two military 'deputies'. At times the office of 'great steward of the royal domain' was also divided. Other important offices with more limited responsibilities remained unitary, such as those of the 'overseer of granaries' and the 'overseer of cattle', both concerned with regulating economic life and storing or securing the taxes owed to the state. The chief agents of communication between the centres and the provinces were the viziers' 'messengers' and the representatives of other departments who frequently visited provincial towns to carry out specific tasks and check the conduct of local officials.

The national capitals were also the chief royal residences, enabling the king to enhance his control over administration through a variety of formal and informal personal contacts. Since there were two and, after Ramesses II founded another at Pi-Ramesse, three such capitals, the king clearly had to divide his time between them. In fact, since each was also a major religious centre celebrating annual festivals in which the king took a leading part, the royal circuit often served as a provincial tour of inspection by the king. In this way the king was not dependent solely on his chief officials for knowledge of provincial affairs and the population as a whole was reminded of the king's primary role in politics.

The potential (although, in the New Kingdom, rarely used) coercive power of the kingship, derived from its close links with the army, was enhanced also by the undefended character of Egyptian towns and the reliance of civil government on police rather than military power. This potential was, probably deliberately, further improved by the dispostion of military forces within Egypt (fig. 12.6). Perhaps only the capitals or royal residences had garrisons of any significant size while the military colonists, the most rapidly mobilized and efficient of the reserve troops, were located, in general, in areas close to the capitals. The colonists were not armed, and when mobilized they and other levies were equipped at arsenals in the residence cities where, as one text significantly puts it, they were armed 'in the presence of Pharaoh' (Edgerton and Wilson 1936, p. 36).

The tone of government life in the capitals is well documented textually, in art and to a certain degree by architectural remains. Texts and scenes convey a vivid impression of elaborate court ceremonies such as the presentation of taxes (by the mayors and others responsible, under the supervision of the appropriate central officials) and of the more intimate life of the court; of the mixture of dignity and excitement at the regular hearings presided over by the vizier, with petitioners ranked before him in order of precedence; and of the king's personal involvement in administration, as in the vignette of the vizier and treasurer meeting every morning in the palace gateway, comparing notes after the vizier had reported to the king. The structure of the royal

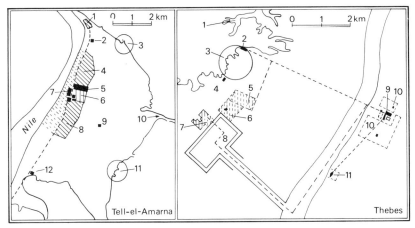

Fig. 12.8    Tell el-Amarna and its chief elements

1 Royal residence complex
2 North (ceremonial) palace
3 Cemetery of officials of the court and priests of the Aten cult
4 North residential zone
5 Great Aten temple
6 Official city
7 Ceremonial palace and annexe

8 South residential zone (government officials, high-ranking priests)
9 Village of artisans of the royal tomb
10 Royal tomb (up wadi)
11 Cemetery of chief officials of the central government and the city, with some cult officials
12 Maru-Aten

(The broken line represents the main north–south road.)

Thebes under Amenhotep III: tentative reconstruction

1 Tombs of the kings
2 Deir el-Bahari, funerary temples of Hatshepsut and Tuthmosis III and Hathor chapel
3 Cemetery of court and government officials
4 Village of artisans of the royal tomb
5 Funerary temple of Amenhotep III (approximate)
6 Residential area (?) in the time of Amenhotep III

7 Royal residence complex of Amenhotep III at Malkata
8 Modern Birket Habu = Maru-Amen (?)
9 Karnak temple of Amen: with hypothetical adjoining 'official city' and ceremonial palace, the latter possibly 'Amenhotep III is the shining sun-disc'
10 Hypothetical residence zones for officials
11 Luxor temple of Amen (of Amenhotep III), with hypothetical residential zone

(The broken lines represent the main processional routes linking the various parts of the city which, as reconstructed here, is much more diffuse and less continuous than Tell el-Amarna.)

cities is documented only for Akhenaten's capital at Tell el-Amarna, although one can reasonably conjecture that Thebes, under his father, Amenhotep III, may have been similar in important ways. Tell el-Amarna was not very rigorously planned, but certain structural differentiations were deliberate (fig. 12.8). The royal residential palace-complex was located in the north, with nearby settlements probably occupied by court officials and servants (as indicated by the burials in the adjacent

863

cemetery). A ceremonial palace marked the transition to a residental zone, which was succeeded by the official quarter, containing the main Aten temple and a large ceremonial palace which, with its annexe, was the setting for the ceremonial public activities of the king. Immediately adjacent were the offices of the government and the police headquarters. A smaller temple, surrounded by a pseudo-fortified wall, indicated a transition to a less sacred, more supernaturally vulnerable area, in fact the chief residential city, where resided the vizier, high priest, police chief, mayor, and other chief officials of the government and the city. Providing a structural backbone was a broad avenue, running from the northern royal complex to a 'Maru-Aten' a southern complex combining shrines, pavilions and artificial lakes.

The sequestered character of the royal residence and the splendid settings designed for the ceremonial and ritual acts of the king in the official quarter aptly indicate the high status of the kingship in the late Eighteenth Dynasty. Simultaneously however, the clustering of royal residence, government centre and officials' residences within a single city reflects the close personal supervision the king exercised over the central government. Thebes under Amenhotep III was perhaps similarly differentiated (fig. 12.8), but whether this urban pattern existed earlier and continued after the Eighteenth Dynasty, is as yet unknown.

The sources also illustrate other methods whereby the kings maintained politically useful personal contacts with their chief subordinates. The true dynasty was excluded from power (p. 854) but a number of high officials enjoyed a kind of quasi-dynastic status as the sons or husbands of royal wet-nurses and harem women; this custom is well attested in the Eighteenth Dynasty and occurs as late as the Twenty-first. Gift-giving was another important relationship; the kings regularly rewarded deserving officials in public ceremonies and, in turn, received New Year gifts from officials and institutions. There is also evidence suggesting that the king banqueted regularly with groups of officers and soldiers, and he certainly rewarded retired officers with posts on the royal estates.

The obligations of the population in terms of taxes, compulsory labour levies and the like are well known but it is evident that, in return, conditions of security and relative prosperity prevailed for much of the New Kingdom. Relationships between government and the governed showed a mixture of bureaucratic sophistication and other mechanisms emphasizing more personal, direct and, in a sense, 'primitive' means of inquiry and decision-making.

At the provincial level the varied conflicts and tensions typical of village communities are well documented at the artisans' village of Deir el-Medineh. Here the local kenbet-council usually settled disputes or accusations without reference to a higher, outside authority; the mechanisms used included reference to written documents, personal judgement and, frequently, recourse to an oracle (p. 846) delivered publicly by the local god and clearly expressing the general feeling and judgement of the community.

Relationships between central and provincial governments and individuals are documented by a court case (of the time of Ramesses II) about a perennial problem, disputes within an extended family concerning hereditary rights to the ownership and income of an estate. The comparatively small scale at which government worked is seen in the involvement of the vizier's 'great kenbet-council' of northern Egypt in current and earlier disputes about the estate, which was substantial (about 5 or 6 hectares) but not huge, and the owners of which were of comparatively low status. The disputants regularly resorted to petition and officials cited, from records, earlier decisions about the estate over the previous eighty years as well as its original foundation 300 years earlier! However, records were not relied on exclusively and with reason: forged documents had been inserted, even into the vital land-registers of the treasurer and 'overseer of granaries' in the capital. The local Memphite kenbet-council, with its better knowledge of local affairs, was involved; a representative of the 'great council' several times visited the village and took (sometimes perjured) oral depositions; and the final decision was based on oral testimony of members of the community who were not involved in the dispute.

In microcosm, therefore, we see a system which, despite the abuses of inefficiency and corruption, appears to have fundamentally satisfied the need of the population for arbitration and control.

### The royal succession

The basic form and character of the political system just described evolved throughout the early Eighteenth Dynasty, but there is very little data on specific, internally significant events until *c.* 1490 BC. (Foreign affairs are, from the outset, comparatively better documented because of the nature of the surviving evidence.) The first apparent crisis is suggested by the atypical, officially recognized co-reign (22 years) of Tuthmosis III and 'king' Hatshepsut, by the latter's sex and by the defacement of her monuments by Tuthmosis after her peaceful (?) death. These peculiarities and the apparent bitterness of Tuthmosis have, to some scholars, reflected the clash of powerful institutions, perhaps a coterie of civil officials supporting Hatshepsut against the army, with the Amen priesthood supporting Tuthmosis. Yet the evidence (defaced tombs and monuments) on the fall of Hatshepsut's supporters is ambiguous, and during her lifetime Tuthmosis was allotted considerable civil and, more significantly, military power, which he did not turn against her.

That an unusual manipulation of the succession system was involved has long been evident and a recent suggestion is that, while the succession was patrilineal (i.e. father–son), royal mothers and wives had a symbolically critical matriarchal role which Hatshepsut attempted to turn into real power. However, other factors may also have been significant. In the New Kingdom, succession was rapid and automatic, and practice reveals a general agreement that the heir, in order of preference, should be son of the chief queen, or of a lesser queen, or husband of a chief queen's daughter. The last procedure eased a critical situation when there was no direct male heir, and was used, for example, to legitimize the transfer of kingship between the Eighteenth, Nineteenth, Twentieth and Twenty-first Dynasties.

If the new king was a minor, a regent (preferably a *female* relative) had to be appointed (as had been done for Ahmosis?), and Tuthmosis III was unusually young. At accession he was a stripling and, despite his 54-year-long reign (1490–1436 BC) his mummy shows little sign of ageing. Hatshepsut's accession, within a few years of his, may have been as much a dynastic defence-mechanism as an act of personal ambition. The co-reign no doubt generated tension, but it appears to have been fundamentally amicable, and the destruction of Hatshepsut's monuments is partly explicable as the expunging of a politically necessary reign which was offensive to the concept of *ma'at* (p. 848).

The next important set of events – those surrounding Akhenaten's reign (1364–1347 BC) – are better documented. Although his reign was politically significant, its precise implications remain controversial. Akhenaten is no longer seen as a social reformer or international pacifist, although it is still generally agreed that his explicit physical peculiarities were reflected in mental ones which affected his actions. To some, the unique features of Akhenaten's reign suggest a conflict between the king and other powerful sections of government, specifically the civil bureaucracy and the Amen priesthood. More probably, however, they were extreme examples of a tendency to royal absolutism which was inherent in the political system.

Akhenaten was both offensively innovative and politically strong. He promoted a monotheistic form of religion based on the Aten (sun-disc); he excluded the traditional pantheon from the new capital he began at Tell el-Amarna; and he tried to eradicate their cults elsewhere in Egypt. (It is uncertain how comprehensive this effort was except so far as the dominant state god, Amen, was concerned).

Akhenaten's strength arose partly from skilful manipulation of the traditional resources of kingship. He maintained the image of a war-leader; he initiated one campaign in Nubia; and in the Levant he responded to the collapse of the Mittanians before the Hittites with a mixture of diplomacy and military action. If on the one hand formal adulation of the monarch reached new heights, on the other there was increased elaboration in ceremonial gift-giving to bureaucrats and soldiers. The Aten-cult itself had strong traditional elements and art continued to emphasize the high status of king and dynasty, and their initimate links to the supernatural.

Akhenaten's other source of strength was a contemporary process (begun before his time and persisting long after it) of enhancing royal authority by emphasizing its quasi-divine aspects and yet avoiding the rigid, politically debilitating role of uncompromising deification. Increasing stability abroad since Amenhotep II's time (1438–1412 BC), internal tranquility and growing royal wealth had created exceptionally favorable circumstances for this.

The increased importance of the Aten-cult was one aspect of the process; although a symbol of imperial power the sun-disc was mythically colourless and a more suitable manifestation of the kings' immanent divinity than was the already strongly defined Amen. The identification of king and disc had become more explicit in the reign of Tuthmosis IV (1412–1402) and was to continue until Ramesses II (1289–1224) and the cult itself survived, despite its associations with obnoxious innovations. Characteristic also of the later Eighteenth Dynasty were the 'purification' of royal rituals and strong interest in the kingship's antiquity. At Abydos at this time, a tomb of a First Dynasty king was indentified as that of Osiris, long since a symbol of all deceased kings, while early Nineteenth Dynasty kings built vast temples at Abydos celebrating their co-equal status with the chief gods.

Prominence was given to king-lists implicitly (and, in the Turin Canon, in the time of Ramesses II, explicitly) linking the contemporary incumbents to the divine dynasty which originally ruled Egypt.

Akhenaten's father, Amenhotep III, was particularly significant in this process, and provided a model for cultic activity concerning the kingship in the Nineteenth and, less directly, the Twentieth Dynasties. Under him, the creation of dramatic functional and symbolic expressions of ideas about the kingship accelerated. A new royal residence city at Malkata (fig. 12.8), western Thebes, was associated with a more 'pristine' version of the ancient royal site of the Sed festival and some functionally absurd elements of the site, such as its excessively large harbour, reflect its ritual and symbolic, as well as utilitarian, roles. The royal residence for the first time was dominated by the royal funerary temple, not that of a national god (Amen or Ptah); an innovation not perhaps continued later. The colossal scale of Amenhotep's temple architecture and particularly of his funerary temple was also emulated by later kings (Ramesses III in fact attempted *no* major construction except for his funerary temple) and the production of large numbers of huge royal colossi (some explicitly and probably all implicitly hypostases of a divine Amenhotep and cult-statues in their own right) were also paralleled later, sometimes in a directly imitative way, especially by Ramesses II.

Akhenaten's innovations are explicable in the context of this process. His general relationship to it is indicated by his devotion to the Aten and the cult of kingship, and the colossal scale of his temple-buildings. These included hundreds of royal colossi, whose at times hermaphroditic form reveals not so much Akhenaten's personal abnormalities as 'an extreme symbolism which, since he was "in the likeness of Aten" depicted him as having all the attributes of the major godhead, the "father and mother" of all creation' (Yoyotte 1966, p. 250). Akhenaten's unique monotheism was itself, in part, an abortive offshoot of royal absolutism; the old gods were gone, but (to his own political benefit) the king maintained his traditional role as mediator between men and the wishes of the new, unhistorical god, inscrutable to all but Akhenaten.

Perhaps most importantly, the cessation of the festivals which were the main focus of Egyptian religious life must have profoundly disturbed the population,[1] while Akhenaten's religious innovations were equally repugnant to the educated elite. His son-in-law and successor, Tutankhamen, acting on the advice and, as a minor, the compulsion of

[1] See Wente 1976, pp. 23–4.

officials who had also been prominent in Akhenaten's government, restored the traditional religious system and abandoned Amarna. But, continuing bitterness surfaced some fifty years later, when Akhenaten's mummy was probably destroyed and the official denigration of his memory began. It was, however, symptomatic of the kingship's power that there was no overt opposition during Akhenaten's reign and that the execration of his memory, long delayed, was released only on *royal* (Nineteenth Dynasty) initiative. Contemporary texts depict Akhenaten as an effective ruler, promoting innovations from a vulnerable, unwalled city and securely in control of the military structure. We are uncertain about the degree to which his policies were economically disruptive, created excessive administrative centralization leading to abuses, re-placed professional bureaucrats with less efficient new men and thus indirectly led to the loss of substantial parts of the Asiatic conquests.

Akhenaten's immediate (to Horemheb) successors coped successfully with serious internal and external problems, and consequently the early Nineteenth Dynasty kings were able to function as traditionally successful rulers, enjoying great internal authority and reacting strongly to recurrent emergencies abroad. However, after Merenptah (1224–1204 BC) the succession was clearly irregular for several reigns and there may have been a partial breakdown of political and social stability. Order was restored by Sethnakht (1186–1184 BC), first ruler of the Twentieth Dynasty, and the regime of his successor, Ramesses III (1184–1153 BC), was sufficiently stable to respond effectively to strong pressures from Asia and Libya.

From the reign of Ramesses III on, there are clear indications of growing internal problems. Contraction, not expansion, characterized the foreign policy while the disintegration of government became evident in the unprecedented events which closed the period of the New Kingdom, as we shall see.

Efforts to identify the ultimate causes of this disintegration need considerable qualification. The conservative reaction after Akhenaten, it has been suggested, so strengthened the Amen establishment in its inherent conflict with other political elements that 'the history of the Ramesside period is that of the conflict' (Helck 1968, p. 183). But the political weakness of the religious system should be noted (p. 849) and *military* officers, not priests, were responsible for the final division of New Kingdom Egypt into two units. The idea that Akhenaten destroyed a professional, idealistic bureaucracy which was thereafter staffed increasingly by deracinated men, frequently of foreign origin and military background, and characterized by inefficiency and corruption, must be set against the continuation of effective centralized government for a further 250 years and the disproportionate amount of surviving Nineteenth and Twentieth Dynasty archival material, always more revealing on abuses than the monumental record. The concept of increasing tension between an innovative, sophisticated northern world-view and that of a conservative south, exacerbated by later New Kingdom rulers' preference for a northern residence, is suggestive, but the north–south division was *always* a feature of the administrative structure (p. 861).

The fundamental problem was the decline in royal religious authority, military prestige and political power, factors upon which the integrity of the state depended. This decline cannot be traced in detail, but important contributing factors and symptoms are evident. Particularly significant in this highly personal form of government were problems inherent in the succession system and overt challenges to it. The latter disturbed the dynastic integrity necessary for royal stability, while both impaired the effectiveness of royal political manipulation, either by lessening the king's personal efficiency or by creating dynastic factions competing for the support of various segments of government. Both also depreciated royal prestige and authority by offending, sometimes subtly, against *ma'at*.

While the succession system functioned effectively during the difficult transition period after Akhenaten (all kings between Tutankhamen and Ramesses I were heirs by marriage, not direct descent, p. 866) it is certain that Seti II was usurped (temporarily, and only in Upper Egypt?) by a 'king' Amenmesses. If the latter was indeed *both* a royal relative and Viceroy of Kush the event demonstrates the wisdom of the usual divisive and dynastically exclusionary policies of the kings (p. 854). This was followed by further irregularities, in particular the accession of another female 'king', Twosret (as co-regent, ultimately successor of a short-lived minor, Siptah). Equally revealing was the plot to assassinate Ramesses III in favour of a 'lesser' son, far removed from the chance of direct succession. The plot involved harem and court members and important government officials, including high military officers; their failure, despite some close family links, was due probably to the absence of any institutional means of bringing these forces effectively together.

Peculiar features of the succession during the Twentieth Dynasty surely contributed to its political problems. These features were the unusually large number of short reigns and elderly kings (table 12.3),

TABLE 12.3   *Comparative regnal lengths in the New Kingdom. Particularly short reigns (8 years or less) are in bold type; it is noteworthy that they tend to cluster in the late Nineteenth and earlier Twentieth Dynasties*

| Eighteenth Dynasty | | Nineteenth Dynasty | | Twentieth Dynasty | |
|---|---|---|---|---|---|
| Name | Regnal length | Name | Regnal length | Name | Regnal length |
| Ahmose | 25 years | Ramesses I | **2 years** | Sethnakht | **2 years** |
| Amenhotep I | 21 years | Seti I | 14 years | Ramesses III | 31 years |
| Tuthmosis I | 12 years | Ramesses II | 65 years | Ramesses IV | **7 years** |
| Tuthmosis II | **4 years** | Merenptah | 20 years | Ramesses V | **4 years** |
| Hatshepsut | 22 years | Amenmesses | **4 years** | Ramesses VI | **7 years** |
| Tuthmosis III | 54 years | Seti II | **6 years** | Ramesses VII | **6 years** |
| Amenhotep II | 26 years | Siptah | **6 years** | Ramesses VIII | **2 years** |
| Tuthmosis IV | 10 years | Twosret | **8 years** | Ramesses IX | 18 years |
| Amenhotep III | 38 years | | | Ramesses X | 10 years |
| Amenhotep IV } Ahkenaten | 17 years | | | Ramesses XI | 30 years |
| Smenkhare | **3 years** | | | | |
| Tutankhamen | 10 years | | | | |
| Ay | **4 years** | | | | |
| Horemheb | 28 years | | | | |
| Average regnal length | 19.56 years | | 15.63 years | | 11.70 years |

generated by inherent weaknesses in the royal succession system itself, in this case by the survival of several inevitably elderly heirs of the long-lived Ramesses III combined with the premature deaths of younger kings (Ramesses V, VII), who would have generated the usual father–son, relatively long-reigned succession pattern (fig. 12.9). These events were both psychologically and administratively disturbing. The concept of *ma'at* accommodated the limitations of humanity within royal quasi-divinity but in the context of a natural progression in the ruler's life from early maturity to a substantially later death. The comparatively rapid succession of elderly or dramatically mortal rulers stressed the ambiguous character of the kings' relationship to the supernatural (pp. 846–8). Moreover, the political system depended upon the personal energy and flexibility of the ruler and had developed in the context of relatively young accession ages which now, for a period, were no longer the norm.

One of the two main rhythms of Egyptian official life was now disconcertingly discontinuous. The normal routine of the bureaucracy (now largely hereditary, even in its upper echelons; see p. 876), based largely on the agricultural year, continued uninterruptedly. But each

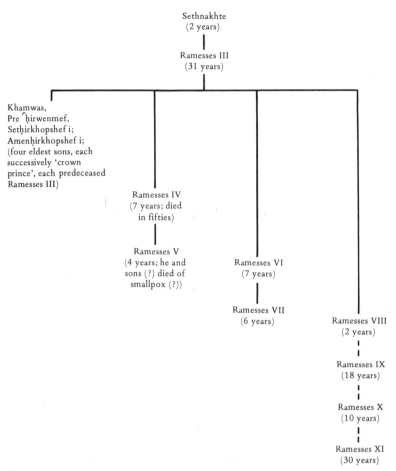

Fig. 12.9 Genealogy of Twentieth Dynasty; regnal lengths are given, and a broken line represents an assumed relationship. (See Kitchen 1972.)

king at accession normally entered upon a characteristic programme, generally similar but different in important details and based upon the expectation of a long reign (Ramesses IV made a request of Osiris for a 134-year reign!). Sometimes important administrative or foreign-policy initiatives were involved, and always the symbolically important features of a potentially substantial temple-building programme and the development of the royal incumbent's funerary establishment. Short reigns and probably a degree of personal remoteness (p. 878) would have contributed to the aborted building programmes, subdued foreign policy and reduced political flexibility evident for the Twentieth Dynasty kings.

## *Economic problems and their significance*

Although there was probably a weakening of royal economic power – a potent source of political influence and prestige – in the Twentieth Dynasty, its full nature and intensity remain uncertain. Marked diminution in temple-building or expansion even during longer reigns (Ramesses III, IX, XI) is the best proof, but is ambiguous in its implications. The king initiated and to a degree funded temple-building, but the state levied the large labour forces and collected the food and building supplies required. Was there a *quantitative* decrease in the economic resources available to the king and his officials, or was there a *qualitative* decline in the efficient manipulation of these resources?

The elaborate annual ceremonies of presenting taxes and tribute to the king symbolized the fact that in general little distinction was made between royal and state income. However, certain resources were more immediately accessible to the king's manipulation than others; tribute, booty and much foreign trade were his prerogatives as war-leader and the dynasty's estates were administered by his personal stewards. By contrast, state income from taxes (one-tenth of grain crops and animals?), dues, government lands, monopolies and requisitioning powers, had to support the civil, religious and military establishments and passed through a complex structure of administrative intermediaries who, to some degree, were capable of manipulating the economic system. Decrease in *any* of the resources was politically significant, especially those most accessible to the king, but so was a decline in the quality of administration.

It may, in fact, be reasonably presumed that tribute, booty and foreign trade declined after Ramesses III (p. 851), while royal copper-mining expeditions to Sinai and the Arabeh ceased after Ramesses V and VI respectively. However, the decrease in the wealth of the kingship should not be exaggerated. Sudanese gold was accessible until the end of the dynasty; Ramesses XI at one time gave gifts worth 50 deben of silver (equivalent to a year's food for 470 people) to a high priest; and Smendes, as *de facto* (soon to be *de jure*) king, imported Lebanese cedar.

It has been argued that the amount of cultivable land effectively controlled by the king and his government shrank seriously during the later New Kingdom. Although in theory the king owned all land and merely delegated its use to others, some scholars believe that, by the end of the Twentieth Dynasty, temples and private individuals, by a gradual process of alienation, in effect 'owned' most land. Given good administration, this development would still have provided the government with income from taxes and dues, and it is in any case not provable. The Harris Papyrus (Ramesses IV) shows that the temples then owned one-third of Egypt's arable land, but the status of the remaining two-thirds remains unknown, as does the degree to which the kings were able to tax and manipulate the use of temple lands. In a survey of temple, royal and government lands within a specific region (Wilbour Papyrus; Ramesses V), the temples appear as by far the greatest landowners, but the statistical significance of this is unknown, for the document is concerned with only a small proportion of the arable land actually available within the region.

In fact, the Wilbour Papyrus – our chief source on New Kingdom land tenure – seems to reveal an interpenetration of civil and temple administration which would make it unlikely that the temples could become effective economic and political counterweights to the kingship. Here, as in other documents, secular officials are shown as having responsibility for and some power over temple lands (unless these were specifically exempted). The land surveyed was divided partly into large estates and partly into much smaller farms. The owning institutions perhaps rented out the estates for half their annual yield and paid a tax on this income. The investors – wealthy officials and priests – expected a profit from the remainder, even though it was shared with the agents and cultivators who actually supervised and worked the land.

The small farms were primarily for the subsistence of the family of each individual who held a farm and paid a small part (much less then half) of the yield to the owning institution. Rather than reflecting a deliberate government policy of systematically dividing up arable land amongst all but the lowest levels of Egyptian society, these small-scale tenants were probably created in two independent ways. One large group – priests, scribes, herdsmen, cultivators and (rarely) artisans – presumably worked for the owning institution and each was also allotted a dues-paying farm for his subsistence (cf. the manors of early mediaeval Europe). The other large group, functionally unconnected with the temples, consisted of military personnel whose subsistence was a particular government concern (p. 853), here apparently settled on primarily temple lands – another index of secular power! The great uniformity of farm size was not so much 'planned' as a spontaneous response to subsistence needs (a phenomenon again paralleled in mediaeval European manors); the normal farm occupied five arouras (about 1.25 hectares), sufficient for a family of eight or so, while

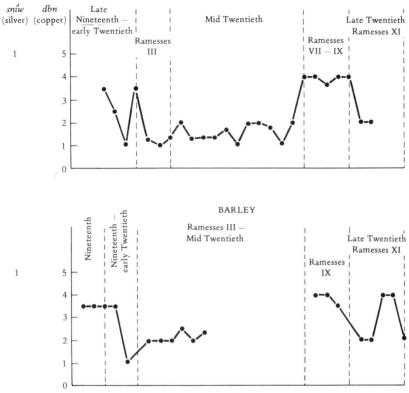

Fig. 12.10 The fluctuating values of emmer wheat and barley in the Nineteenth and Twentieth Dynasties: although the *general* chronological variation is valid, it must be noted that many of the instances are dated only approximately and that the figure represents chronological 'blocks' of instances, not a precise chronological progression. The data are taken from J. J. Janssen (1975, pp. 112–16, 119–22). Certain doubtfully dated examples, or atypically high values, have been omitted. The unit of measurement is 1 *ḫȝr* (76.48 l), the values are expressed in the *sniw* of silver (5 *dbn* copper) and the *dbn* of copper (91 g).

'soldiers' (although not other military personnel such as stable-masters) and their families habitually occupied only three arouras (about 0.75 hectare), perhaps because some family members were permanently or periodically on duty elsewhere.

Another economic phenomenon, the rising inflation of the later Twentieth Dynasty, may have been politically significant but, again, its causes and effects remain uncertain. After Ramesses VI grains, and perhaps other produce, increased sharply in value (fig. 12.10), but the prices of cattle, donkeys and manufactured items did not rise, partly because of the strong traditionalism of the Egyptian barter economy, partly because the cost-factors of raising animals or making artifacts were not reckoned as part of their value. Deliberate manipulation was most unlikely to have been involved in the rising value of grains and perhaps of produce. Recurrently inadequate inundations of the Nile or a declining labour force could have created an absolute decrease in available foodstuffs, but there is little evidence for these during the 60-year period (compare the frequent references to famine during the first hundred years of the First Intermediate Period (see chapter 10) with the single reference under Ramesses XI).

Administrative inefficiency was a more likely cause of economic problems. Abuses in the collection and distribution of food are documented (peculation of temple grain, Ramesses III, IV and V, and artisans' strikes provoked by *arrears*, not formally decreased rations, Ramesses III to Ramesses X). The robbery of royal and private tombs in the Theban area at the time was linked to these abuses as well as to the deteriorating integrity of local administration. Only the lower echelons of government were directly involved in these events, but the resulting scandals created intrigues and declining morale amongst higher officials.

### The weakening of the kingship

Probably the most important contributors to the weakening integrity of the kingship were the changing relationships between king, civil government and army. Governmental structure did not collapse in the late New Kingdom – it survived to provide a foundation for the revised political system of the Third Intermediate Period – but it was characterized by the growing strength of hereditary office, a tendency that is analysed in detail in a recent study (Bierbrier 1975). Related to this was the growth of family ramifications linking the powerful upper levels of institutionally separate branches of government, vividly epitomized by the Merybast family which held several vital offices from the reign of Ramesses III to Ramesses XI (fig. 12.11). Particularly noteworthy was their substantial control of major economic resources of the state, the dynasty and the religious establishment but, at the same time, their *dependence* upon the traditional diffusion of powers. As the deposition of Amenhotep, the High Priest of Amen, showed, the family had no significant military strength.

In any case, the civil government became less susceptible to royal

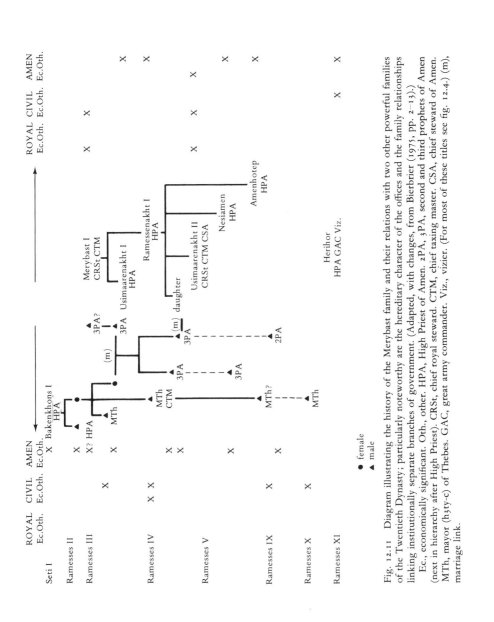

Fig. 12.11   Diagram illustrating the history of the Merybast family and their relations with two other powerful families of the Twentieth Dynasty; particularly noteworthy are the hereditary character of the offices and the family relationships linking institutionally separate branches of government. (Adapted, with changes, from Bierbrier (1975), pp. 2–13).)

Ec., economically significant. Oth., other. HPA, High Priest of Amen. 2PA, 3PA, second and third prophets of Amen (next in hierarchy after High Priest). CRSt, chief royal steward. CTM, chief taxing master. CSA, chief steward of Amen. MTh, mayor (ḥȝty-c) of Thebes. GAC, great army commander. Viz., vizier. (For most of these titles see fig. 12.4.) (m), marriage link.

control. The kings reduced their travels and became more remote from immediate administration; their personal influence decreased and they lost a degree of informed knowledge. Possibly the need to defend the north against the Libyans and to re-establish commerce with the Levant were sufficiently important to reinforce an already evident royal preference for northern residences (cf. Pi-Ramesse) and the age and physical strength of several kings may also have been significant.

As the kings' supervisory tours became less frequent, royal princes and other deputies carried out major religious rites formerly performed by the kings; and butlers of the royal court played a prominent role in important administrative acts, as if checking upon the highest officials of civil government. These butlers, however, lacked the expertise of the bureaucrats and were themselves not necessarily reliable, as evidenced by the involvement of some in the assassination attempt upon Ramesses III.

The assigning to the High Priest of Amen of certain functions that would normally have been performed by civilian officials (as, for instance, paying the artisans of the royal tomb, securing building materials for Karnak) may also have been administratively convenient but the price was a further loss of royal prestige. The High Priest Amenhotep had had himself depicted as equal in stature to the king – iconographic *lèse-majesté*!

The coercive resources of the kingship also declined. Despite the Libyan victories of Ramesses III, the threat of violence from Libyan infiltrators continued to disturb the work routines of the local inhabitants, as far south as Thebes and as late as the time of Ramesses IX and X, a fact suggesting a militarily weak situation in the primary infiltration areas of the Delta and Middle Egypt. After Amenhotep's deposition by a local faction, Ramesses XI restored order by requesting Penehasy, Viceroy of Kush, to take control of Upper Egypt in direct command of his own forces – two unprecedented steps – instead of himself dispatching troops from the northern garrisons. Penehasy's regime in Middle and Upper Egypt, using substantial numbers of Nubian troops (the *ȝꜥꜥw*, literally 'jabberers'; see Bell 1973, Wente 1966), was sufficiently akin to a foreign invasion to act eventually as a catalyst for internal mobilization. After perhaps seven years of rule Penehasy retreated into Kush, presumably under pressure from the newly emerged, politically dominant and essentially military figures of the Theban Herihor and his son (?) Smendes. Piankh, Herihor's son and successor in the south, continued to campaign against Penehasy in Lower Nubia.

The discipline of the Egyptian armed forces, therefore, continued to be a politically stabilizing resource, as it had been earlier when Horemheb staffed with the 'finest of the army' the depleted and demoralized priesthoods left by Akhenaten's innovations (Gardiner 1953). But, in contrast to the fruitful relationship between king and army which had eased the transition from the Eighteenth to the Nineteenth Dynasties, Herihor and Smendes imposed upon Ramesses XI, their titular monarch, a territorial division of Egypt which was plainly opposed to the integrity of New Kingdom government and kingship. Ramesses XI survived as titular head of both divisions until his death; Smendes then became king of 'all' Egypt, but effectively only of the north, while the descendants of Herihor controlled Middle and Upper Egypt. Ramesses IX's appeal to Penehasy reflected the fact that only in Kush did the exigencies of control and defence still permit a substantial and responsive standing army, but the king's surrender of war-making prerogatives to the viceroy set a precedent followed by subsequent military leaders such as Herihor.

A final index to the disintegration of traditional government was the granting of extraordinary combined powers to individuals. These were not unprecedented in times of crisis, but there were now significant differences. Formerly the grants were less extensive, were held by formally proclaimed (if not birthright) crown princes and were a temporary expedient. But Penehasy, a commoner, was simultaneously Viceroy of Kush, an army-leader and overseer of granaries, while Herihor was vizier, High Priest of Amen and generalissimo, the last two titles to be inherited by his successors in perpetuity.

## THE THIRD INTERMEDIATE PERIOD

The ensuing Third Intermediate Period was characterized by virtually continuous tension, only rarely flaring into open conflict, between centralizing and centrifugal forces. The interaction of these forces led to extreme political fragmentation in the last century of the period. They also, however, sustained a striving towards stability that resulted in rapid and effective recentralization under the Twenty-sixth Dynasty. For the first 124 years of the Third Intermediate Period (Twenty-first Dynasty) government was relatively stable, despite the deep fissure in the state's integrity created by the concordat whereby a unique royal dynasty (of Smendes) received formal recognition throughout Egypt, in return for ceding effective control of Middle and Upper Egypt to a line (descended from Herihor) of 'great army commanders' who were

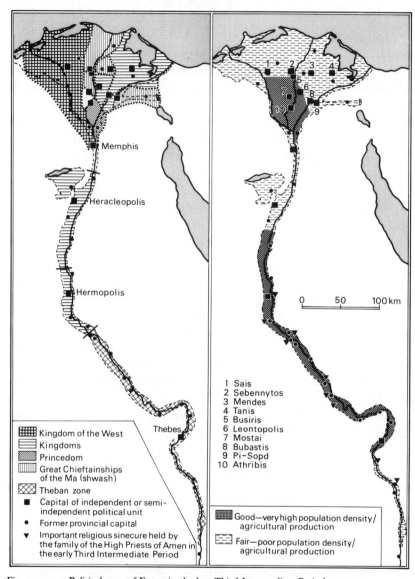

Memphis

Heracleopolis

Hermopolis

Thebes

Kingdom of the West
Kingdoms
Princedom
Great Chieftainships
of the Ma (shwash)
Theban zone
■ Capital of independent or semi-
   independent political unit
● Former provincial capital
▼ Important religious sinecure held by
   the family of the High Priests of Amen in
   the early Third Intermediate Period

1 Sais
2 Sebennytos
3 Mendes
4 Tanis
5 Busiris
6 Leontopolis
7 Mostai
8 Bubastis
9 Pi-Sopd
10 Athribis

0    50    100 km

Good—very high population density/
agricultural production
Fair—poor population density/
agricultural production

Fig. 12.12   1 Political map of Egypt in the late Third Intermediate Period, c. 730 BC.
2 The recent pattern of population density and agricultural yield superimposed on the political
map (see Wilson 1955).

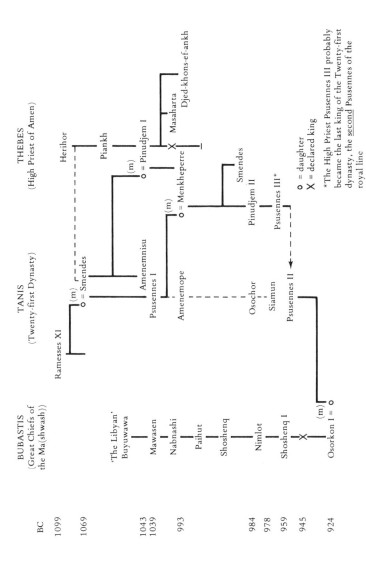

Fig. 12.13  Genealogies and interrelationships of the Twenty-first Dynasty, and the two contemporary families of the High Priest of Amen, 'great army commanders' of Thebes and the 'great chiefs of the Ma(shwash)' at Bubastis.

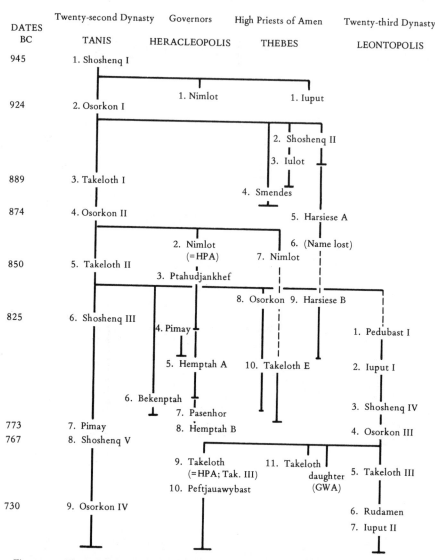

Fig. 12.14  The Twenty-second and Twenty-third Dynasties, and their relationships with the High Priests of Amen of Thebes and the governors of Herakleopolis. HPA, High Priest of Amen. GWA, god's wife of Amen. (See Kitchen 1973.)

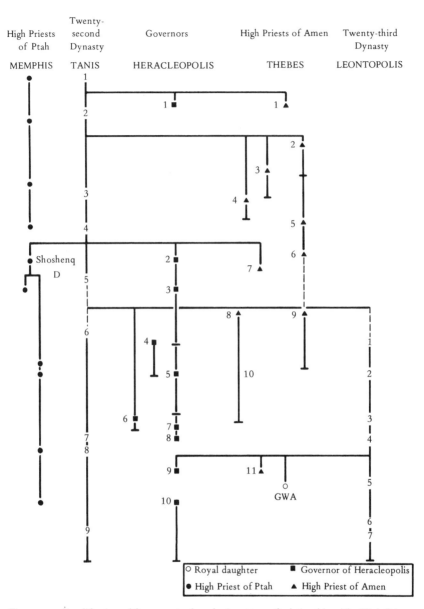

Fig. 12.15 Simplification of fig. 12.14 to show basic pattern of relationships. The High Priests of Ptah have been added. GWA, god's wife of Amen. (See Kitchen 1973.)

simultaneously High Priests of Amen at Karnak. Potential conflict was avoided because the two lines were branches of the same family (fig. 12.13) and had different preoccupations. The Twenty-first Dynasty, residing at Tanis, the former port of Pi-Ramesse, was more internally secure than the Herihor lineage and, as a result, was comparatively expansive (though usually pacific) in its relations with the Levant. The 'great army commanders' had more pressing internal problems; they resided, for strategic reasons, at El-Hibeh, not at the old centres of Memphis or Thebes (fig. 12.6), and made no serious effort to penetrate Kush, their logical area of expansion and the region they explicitly desired to control.

Power was apparently amicably transferred from the Twenty-first to the Twenty-second Dynasty, whose members were descended from hereditary Libyan 'chiefs of the Ma' at Bubastis but resided at Tanis. This dynasty attempted to enhance royal power by ending the hereditary principle in the rule of Middle and Upper Egypt, but they did not alter the basic administrative methods of the Twenty-first Dynasty nor its reliance upon royal relatives in government. The foreign policies of Shoshenq I and Osorkon I in the Levant were unusually aggressive but, thereafter, foreign policy became more subdued as internal dynastic tensions and powerful elements amongst the Egyptian provincial nobility became more pressing. In response, the dynasty entered upon a *formal* bifurcation of the state. It installed a royal co-dynasty at Leontopolis (the Twenty-third; fig. 12.14) which was, in effect, charged with reasserting dynastic control of the south while the Twenty-second concentrated upon the Delta.

The effort was a failure and contributed to further disintegration. As a result the Twenty-second/Twenty-third Dynasties were unable to display the major military initiative needed in the Levant, where the expansion of Assyria was threatening Egypt's commercial interests. Internally, other royal relatives at Herakleopolis and Hermopolis followed the example already set and declared themselves kings, while in the Delta several 'great chiefdoms of the Ma' became increasingly independent. One, based on Sais, was particularly expansive, and under Tefnakhte (Twenty-fourth Dynasty) it gained control of the western Delta from Memphis to the sea. In the extreme west, a further divisive unit was a 'great chiefdom' of the Libu, caused by continuing immigration from Libya. In the south, a Kushite kingdom was extending its control over Middle and Upper Egypt.

Throughout the Third Intermediate Period there was increasing

Fig. 12.16  A passage from the Amada stela of Merenptah describing the impalement of Libyans (captured in the campaign of regnal year 5) in the vicinity of Memphis. The determinative (arrowed) makes the sense of the text quite unambiguous. (After a hand-copy Kitchen 1968.)

tension over the degree of regional or provincial independence which could be tolerated or secured, and over the control of vital economic resources. The competing elements arose from the political and social structure of the late New Kingdom and represent, in significantly altered form, potentially divisive elements which New Kingdom government had been designed to keep subordinate. Royal relatives were now assigned unprecedented administrative power, collateral dynasties were inadvertently or deliberately created by royal policies and a variety of local hereditary bureaucrats, priests and military chieftains of provincial origin became more firmly entrenched in their positions. High officials of central government (e.g. the viziers), formerly influential and powerful, were now, in the case of Tanis (fig. 12.6), effective only within the immediate territory of their residence city; at Thebes, the descendants of the agents of centralized government and of the Amen establishment continued to hold the appropriate titles but became themselves a very powerful provincial nobility. Glimpses of other provincial nobilities can be caught elsewhere: at Memphis one lineage monopolized the high priesthood of Ptah until c. 870 BC and continued to hold valuable benefices there subsequently, while at Thinis, the local nobility secured valuable administrative and economic monopolies which lasted well into the Twenty-sixth Dynasty.

In the north, 'chieftains of the Ma' were particularly important. They were descended from the Libyan chiefs of Mashwash military settlements attached to some central and eastern Delta towns after the Libyan victories of the Nineteenth and Twentieth Dynasties. Foreign prisoners of war and foreign levies by that time were a regular constituent of the Egyptian army in the field, but the Libyan prisoners were unprecedented *within* Egypt and not easily subject to selective weeding-out. Exemplary cruelty was tolerated (fig. 12.16), but not extermination; expulsion to Libya (not controlled by Egypt) was strategically undesirable; and Libyan fighting ability was needed to enhance the power of the kings (now usually resident in the Delta) and to strengthen the eastern frontier, hence, the settlements. Originally subordinate to Egyptian officers, some Ma chiefs came to dominate certain towns and their territories, aided by the weakness of the central government but also by their own military resources and a degree of ethnic solidarity evident, despite strong Egyptianization, in personal names, dress and, occasionally, in political action (cf. Twenty-second Dynasty, p. 882).

In the Twenty-first to the Twenty-third Dynasties, the primary royal response to the problem of controlling a fragmenting political system was to assign extraordinary combined civil, religious and military powers to royal relatives, install them in strategic regional and provincial commands throughout the country and explicitly recognize military force, not bureaucratic control and police power, as the basis of government's authority. Dynasty members functionally displaced the officials of centralized government, hence the latter's decline. The new policy was opposed to normal New Kingdom practice (p. 854) but, given the greatly changed historical circumstances, had significant antecedents in that period.

Supreme power had *always* been reserved for dynasty members (king, chief queen, crown prince); government's personal character was such that high officials regularly received quasi-dynastic status; and royal relatives, politically ineffective, nevertheless held high rank in military and religious establishments. The combined powers now held by royal relatives were anticipated by those of 'adoptive' New Kingdom crown princes in times of political crisis (p. 879), an endemic situation in the Third Intermediate Period.

Earlier foreign policy was also relevant. Large areas of Egypt, because of the independent, sporadically aggressive attitudes of their inhabitants, were analogous to New Kingdom foreign conquests, and dynasty members were akin to the earlier governors of foreign lands, maintaining control through garrisons and fortified towns at internally strategic points. Regionally diffused members and branches of the royal family (and leading members of the provincial nobilities) took on some of the character of independent rulers and a complex, politically motivated network of intermarriages developed between these elements and the theoretically dominant royal line. This practice had been important in earlier foreign (not internal) policy, although now royal daughters were married *into* the other power-groups while, earlier, the reverse was usual.

The new policy sustained dynastic power and the formal appearance of a united kingship, but at considerable cost to royal manipulative and coercive resources. The governing royal relatives were habitually 'great army commanders' or 'army-leaders' controlling their own forces and residing in heavily fortified provincial centres hard to reduce militarily (Breasted 1906, IV, ss. 857–65). Dynastic integrity was strained, since these relatives naturally tended to establish semi-independent, provincially-based collateral dynasties, sometimes even claiming royal status. The Twenty-first Dynasty solution was to recognize frankly the dynastic status of the south's 'great army commanders' and High Priests of Amen. The inherent tension caused by the latter's sporadic claims to royal titles was eased by close family links. Pinudjem I (fig. 12.13), son-in-law (and nephew?) of Smendes, became a 'co-king' at Tanis and, when the royal line died out, the incumbent 'commander' naturally became king (Psusennes II; fig. 12.13).

The Twenty-second and Twenty-third Dynasties tried to strengthen royal control by restricting regional commands to sons of the reigning king rather than to more remote relatives, thus preventing collateral dynasties. This policy, initially successful, within eighty years generated problems which caused Osorkon II to petition Amen to 'establish my children in the [posts which] I have given them, so that brother is not jealous [?] of brothe[r]' (Kitchen 1973, s. 276).

In the south, which was now divided into two units, one governed from Herakleopolis and one from Thebes, deviations from desired practice were soon evident (figs. 12.14–15). The Theban High Priest, Shoshenq (2) generated a collateral dynasty, being succeeded by his two brothers (3 and 4) who were markedly independent of their nominal king, Takeloth I; and by a son, who declared himself 'king' (5), and a grandson (6). King Osorkon II rectified the situation, appointing as governor of Herakleopolis *and* Thebes his son Nimlot (Herakleopolis 2, Thebes 7), who was appropriately succeeded at Thebes by Osorkon (8), crown prince of King Takeloth II. High Priest Osorkon's rule, however, was sporadic and contested by descendants of Shoshenq (see Thebes 2–9) and Nimlot (see Thebes 10) and by other grandees as far north as Hermopolis (Kitchen 1973, ss. 293–4; see also Caminos 1958, pp. 29 and 153, 111 and 164, 88 and 161, 105 and 163). The result was widespread, ten-year-long civil war. Herakleopolis itself was ruled by a rarely interrupted collateral dynasty descended from Osorkon II via Nimlot (2–8), while the (?) crown prince of Osorkon II, installed as the Memphite High Priest, founded yet another dynasty (figs. 12.14–15).

This disintegration, combined with the independence of provincial elements, prompted the division of power between the Twenty-second and Twenty-third Dynasties. King Shoshenq III (825–773 BC) asserted his control of the Delta, establishing a hereditary fiefdom for Twenty-second Dynasty crown princes at Athribis–Heliopolis, and installing other sons at provincial centres (Sais?, Busiris). In the south, the Twenty-third Dynasty had to dispute for control at Thebes and Herakleopolis with descendants of the collateral dynasties of the Twenty-second, but Osorkon III (777–749 BC) succeeded in installing his crown prince at both centres. When the latter became co-regent, another royal relative was appointed to Herakleopolis (10), while the 'Theban problem' was solved by an ingenious adaptation of New Kingdom practice: the office of 'god's wife of Amen' (p. 854) had survived. The High Priesthood was now left in abeyance; the 'god's wife' became dominant and was always a royal daugher, installed by the incumbent king. Now required to be a virgin, the 'god's wife' could not generate a collateral dynasty!

While the central bureaucracy of the north was absorbed into the residence city at Tanis and continued to be under the traditional direct supervision of the kings, the descendants of central government administrators at Thebes were only sporadically in direct contact with their overlords, usually (Twenty-first Dynasty) 'Commanders' or sometimes (Twenty-second Dynasty) residents at El-Hibeh or Herakleopolis. The Theban nobility characteristically conflicted with the (broad) dynasties over access to important and lucrative Theban religous sinecures. The family of Herihor attempted to monopolize these, as later did royal sons and Libyan allies of the Twenty-second Dynasty and, in each case, Theban resistance forced a compromise, whose ill-effects for the dynasties were eased by intermarriage with the Thebans. Not surprisingly, the Thebans supported semi-independent, locally-based collateral dynasties such as that of Shoshenq, and refused even formal co-recognition to the Twenty-second Dynasty after the Twenty-third was established. The transfer of political dominance at Thebes to a woman, initiated by Osorkon II and continuing after, further strengthened in a male-oriented society the Theban bureaucrats who were nominally her agents.

Another royal response to contemporary internal problems was to revive the expansionist foreign policy which had, in the past, benefited royal power (pp. 852–4). However, internal weakness forced tactics far different from earlier ones. Emphasis was now upon maintaining commercial and diplomatic relations with the Levant (cemented by marrying Egyptian princesses to foreign rulers, the reverse of earlier practice) rather than on military aggression, and in both cases the geographical extent of Egyptian activity was much less than before (fig. 12.5). The Palestinian military campaigns of Siamun and Shoshenq I were isolated instances. Although the later Twenty-second Dynasty intrigued against Assyrian expansion, its kings were reduced to 'buying off' any Assyrian army which threatened the Egyptian frontier.

Shoshenq's scribes chose New Kingdom literary models (from Amenhotep III; see p. 868) to celebrate his victories, a reminder that foreign campaigning had religious and propagandistic as well as practical ends. Throughout the Twenty-first to Twenty-third Dynasties the kings tried to maintain authority by persistently summoning up the supernatural potency of the politically stable past. Royal names and epithets identical with, or similiar to, those of New Kingdom rulers were frequently assumed and, of at least two Sed festivals (symbolic celebrations of the kingships' political and religious role) documented, one was based on a New Kingdom version of the 'absolutist' Amenhotep III. Paradoxically, the ideal of a royal political structure conformable to *ma'at* made it the model for the indigenous (and intrusive Kushite) elements competing with the dynasties.

### The rise of the Kushites and Saites

Weak royal government and a concentration upon Levantine and internal relationships were responsible for the expansion of Sais and the Kushites, which changed the situation. The development of a Kushite kingdom and its invasion of Upper Egypt was facilitated by a comparative lack of Egyptian royal interest in Kush, by the condition of Lower Nubia (formerly a buffer zone and now an uninhabited corridor) and by the relative decline of Aswan (p. 894). The north-west and western Delta, agriculturally poor and commercially insignificant, were also of peripheral interest to the Twenty-first and Twenty-second Dynasties. Tefnakhte of Sais and his father, among the 'great chiefdoms of the Ma', were able gradually to expand their control in these regions, eclipsing the Libu 'great chiefdom' until they forged the vital strategic link with Memphis and gained access to Middle Egypt (fig. 12.12).

By this time, Egypt was divided into eleven major and virtually independent political units governed by a bewildering variety of rulers (fig. 12.12). They consisted of five formally proclaimed kings whose very contemporaneity was an extraordinary offence to the earlier concept of *ma'at* (pp. 843–4); a crown prince and another royal son;

Tefnakhte, prince of the western Delta and now (?) 'great chief of the Libu and Ma' (the two major Libyan groups deeply involved in Egyptian history since the Nineteenth Dynasty); and four 'great chiefs of the Ma'. Some lower-ranking rulers also had a degree of independence, including 'chiefs of the Ma', a local high priest, and several ḥȝty-ʿ, the latter more akin to the similarly titled, independent, magisterial governors of 1400 years earlier, than to the New Kingdom mayors. Under Piankhy (Twenty-fifth Dynasty) in 728 BC, the Kushites halted Tefnakhte's expansion southwards (but not eastward) into the home territories of Tanis and Leontopolis, where the Twenty-second/Twenty-third Dynasties continued to rule. In 715 BC, Piankhy's successor Shabako conquered the Delta, making the Twenty-fifth Dynasty recognized overlords of all Egypt, but the fragmented political structure survived their half-century of rule unchanged. Most of the same political units continued to exist for another sixty years, their rulers often the lineal descendants of those of Piankhy's time and bearing identical titles, including 'king'.

The Twenty-fifth (Kushite) Dynasty failed to generate internal reunification, even during its first relatively peaceful forty years. Ruling two kingdoms may have made reunification impossible to achieve but, more likely, it was realized that a strong Egypt could not be controlled by the smaller Kushite state. Kushite rule was based on military strength, and local civil government was left largely to the Egyptian dynasts. Nevertheless, Kushite contributions to *future* unity were significant. At Thebes, the Kushites continued the politically useful office of 'god's wife'; the High Priesthood, held by a Kushite prince and his son, was revived but stripped of military and civil authority. The former was surely exercised by Kushite commanders, the latter first by Kushite governors, and later by Theban bureaucrats. A distribution of powers strongly reminiscent of the stable New Kingdom was emerging.

Psychologically important was the subtle Kushite exploitation of traditional religious ideas concerning the kingship. Stressing symbolic unity and recalling the form if not actuality of the great periods of centralization, the Kushites were genuinely devoted to *maʿat*. Their devotion, they argued, generated supernatural aid and demonstrated the legitimacy of Kushite accession. They preferred the Old and Middle Kingdoms to the New Kingdom as models. A sophisticated, pseudo-Old-Kingdom creation myth was developed; Memphis (the Old Kingdom capital) became the preferred royal residence, and the royal tombs

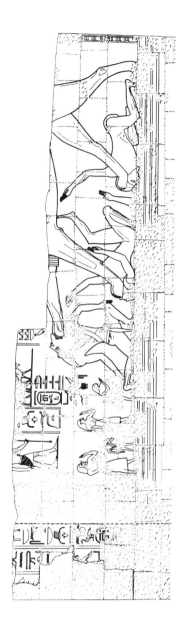

Fig. 12.17 Scenes carved upon the walls of a temple built by Taharqa (Twenty-fifth Dynasty) at Kawa. Depicting the king as a sphinx trampling Libyan opponents, the scenes are based closely upon Old Kingdom prototypes, clearly copied directly from still standing monuments at Saqqara and Abusir. (After Macadam 1955.)

at Napata in the Sudan were modelled on the Old Kingdom royal pyramids (*not* the New Kingdom pyramidal tombs, known since the mid-eighth century but not copied). With a subtle selectivity, scenes from Old Kingdom royal funerary temples were reproduced to embellish contemporary gods' temples; not accidentally, they included an Old Kingdom depiction of victory over the Libyans (fig. 12.17).

Superficially, the main political emphasis thereafter was upon the struggle between Kush and Assyria for the control of Egypt. The Twenty-fifth Dynasty aggressively opposed Assyria in the Levant, mounting a major campaign there in 701 BC and repulsing an Assyrian invasion of Egypt in 674 BC. Assyria conquered the Delta in 671, lost it to King Taharqa in 668/7, gained control of *all* Egypt in 667/6, and regained it in 664/3 after being temporarily driven out by a campaign of King Tanwetamani. However, on another, less obvious, level these events gave a major impetus to Egyptian reunification, an outcome desired neither by Kush nor Assyria. Their policies, combined with fortuitous circumstances, eventually created a context in which the most expansive of the Egyptian dynasts, Psammetichus I (Twenty-sixth Dynasty) of Sais and the 'Kingdom of the West' was able rapidly to restore unity to the Egyptian state.

Kushite and Assyrian policies inadvertently had a decisive effect upon this process. Kushite emphasis upon the ideological and ritual unity of the state prepared Egypt psychologically for a return to centralized rule; while the active Kushite opposition to Assyria required an unprecedented degree of military and political co-ordination amongst the Egyptian dynasts. Subsequently, the Assyrian conquerors, reluctant to assume total control, tried to create a system of Egyptian vassal states that would be too disunited to threaten Assyria's position in the Levant but strong enough to resist (with Assyrian aid) a successful reinvasion by the Kushites. Kushite desire to maintain fragmentation had ensured the survival of the Saite kingdom, and Assyria now assigned it a major although not uniquely dominant position in its vassal system.

Despite Assyrian insensitivity to Egyptian susceptibilities – Egypt sent regular offerings to Assyrian gods without apparent reciprocity – reality compelled a relatively benevolent regime in Egypt. The Egyptian dynasts' relationship with Assyria was complex; as vassals and compelled to offer tribute, they escaped total Assyrian rule by protecting the true area of Assyrian interest, the Levant, against Kushite attack. Assyrian military officials resident in Egypt supervised tribute collection and military preparedness but the highest ranks of Assyrian military and civil officials were not installed there. Civil government and a degree of military power was left to the dynasts aided by indigenous Egyptian tax-collectors and 'chiefs' who bore Assyrian titles.

The only dynasts to enter (as inferiors) into treaty alliances with Assyria and consequently to receive special attention, were Necho of Sais and the Ma chief Pekrur of Pi-Soped. The former had territorial strength (the west and Memphis, and Athribis–Heliopolis under Necho's crown prince, Psammetichus). The Ma chief had a strategic location (Pi-Soped) which dominated the convergence of the invasion routes linking Palestine and Memphis. Thus, both were essential to the buffer system and politically useful counterweights to each other. In any event, Sais proved loyal to the Assyrians during King Tanwetamani's campaign, while Pi-Soped eventually led the submission to him. As a result, Assyrian reconquest led to Pi-Soped's eclipse and ensured the dominance of Sais.

The final assertion of Saite rule occurred when Kush was militarily exhausted and Assyria distracted elsewhere; Assyrian hegemony had enhanced Sais' opportunities for foreign contact and enabled it to recruit foreign mercenaries from Anatolia who tipped the internal military balance in its favour; and its chief Egyptian rival, Pi-Soped, was weak. Psammetichus I showed great skill not only in exploiting these circumstances but in enhancing the internal trend towards a stable, ideologically acceptable kingship. Within a ten-year period (664–654 BC) he had effectively reunited the country and, by the time of his death in 610 BC had largely, if not entirely, consolidated this unity.

### New patterns of settlement

Throughout the Third Intermediate Period, the map of real and symbolic power altered as it reflected changing political circumstances and their cultural effects; and there was probably an important change in the general pattern of settlement, responding to a new political system, the altered relations between government and the governed, and a prevailing civic insecurity. Ultimately, these alterations reflected important changes in the character of Egyptian life.

Particularly striking was the changing pattern of 'royal cities' i.e. towns which were royal residences and administrative centres (cf. figs. 12.6, 12.12). Pi-Ramesse was eclipsed by Tanis, a port-town more easily defensible than the former capital and vital for maintaining profitable sea-links with the Levantine trade. Memphis and Thebes also declined, because of internal strategic considerations which had not been relevant in the New Kingdom political structure (see below). Thebes enjoyed only sporadic royal status and Memphis was not again 'the city of kingship' until the Twenty-fifth Dynasty. Some other claims to royal status (Herakleopolis, Hermopolis) were late and ephemeral, reflecting the acute stage of fragmentation. The rise of Leontopolis and Sais was also linked to the problem of controlling and exploiting two vital regions, the Delta apex and the valley from Hardai to Gebelein (fig. 12.6).

According to recent analogy these regions would have been particularly fertile and densely populated (fig. 12.12) and as prime surplus-producing areas they would not only have provided the subsistence basis for most of the population and the superstructure of government, but also supported the personal estates and religious benefices of royal and collateral dynasty members and their provincial rivals. The estates of Amen of Tanis and associated cults presumably lay in the Delta, while the strings of benefices occasionally listed for dynasty members in the south demonstrably lay mainly between Hardai and Gebelein.

The importance of the Delta apex is further indicated by the exclusion of Mashwash and Libu settlements from it since the late New Kingdom; by the royal (Twenty-third Dynasty) status of Leontopolis and the crown prince's fief Athribis–Heliopolis, both of which enhanced dynastic access to the Delta apex and to the routes linking it to Tanis; and by the assumption of royal status by Sais after it had secured control over the western edge of the apex. The significance of the Hardai–Gebelein zone (fig. 12.6) was marked by the fortification of its northern (El-Hibeh, and nearby Shurafa) and southern ends (Gebelein) early in the rule of the Twenty-first Dynasty 'army commanders', and by the relative decline of Aswan, located in an infertile area and of lessened strategic and commercial importance after the loss of Kush at the end of the Twentieth Dynasty. El-Hibeh and Herakleopolis owed their importance at this time to the fact that they were better able than Thebes to maintain the vital dynastic intercommunications with Tanis and yet were more convenient for the control of the southern fertile zone than Memphis. Moreover, the many villages with military traditions in the immediate area were an important resource (fig. 12.6).

Significant changes in symbolic topography are evident in royal and dynastic cemeteries (fig. 12.6), which reflect shifting political power, insecurity and the strong regional and local character of politico-religious attitudes. In the New Kingdom, kings and royal relatives were always buried at Thebes, but it was notoriously susceptible to cemetery-plundering after the Twentieth Dynasty. Thenceforth, relatively secure Tanis housed the tombs of the Twenty-first and Twenty-second Dynasties (in the very heart of the temple and administrative quarter, i.e. *within* the city) but the Twenty-third to Twenty-fourth and the Twenty-sixth Dynasties preferred Leontopolis and Sais respectively, and the Twenty-fifth distant Napata, its ancestral centre. High Priests of Amen and Twenty-second Dynasty High Priests of Ptah (both royal relatives) were buried at Thebes (in 'secret' tombs) and Memphis (within the city) respectively. The relative stability of Tanis was further reflected by its being chosen as the site of comparatively continuous major temple-building and additions, although Thebes's traditional importance stimulated sporadic building activities when economic circumstances permitted.

The proliferation of walled, fortified cities made a striking contrast to the New Kingdom. The process began as early as the late New Kingdom when the massive fortifications of Ramesses III's Theban funerary temple-'town' must have been paralleled elsewhere. By the late eighth century, the process had reached an advanced stage. Piankhy's stele, commemorating his defeat of Tefnakhte in 728 BC, refers to nineteen fortified towns along a 266-km stretch of the river in Middle Egypt (and average of one for every 14 km!) and, in general terms, to the 'walled towns' of the Delta, whose appearance is documented archaeologically and iconographically (plate 12.1). Fortified towns responded to insecurity, civil war and invasion, but also reflected the fragmentation of administration and the reliance upon armed force in government. Major administrative changes were usually accompanied by the building of supporting fortresses.

Data also suggest that the fairly extensive settlement pattern of the New Kingdom (p. 860) had become more concentrated and that more people than formerly lived in urban or semi-urban contexts. For example, in the late Twentieth Dynasty some 86% of the population within a 7-km zone between the funerary temples of Seti I and Ramesses III at Thebes lived within a densely packed town within the latter's walls. Later, at El-Matmar in Middle Egypt a local population, earlier spread over a wider area, now lived within the walls of a provincial temple. Insecurity, particularly in the outlying villages, contributed to this process (cf. Piankhy's orders about a besieged town: 'Let not the peasants go to the field, let not the plowman plow.' (Breasted 1906, IV, s. 821, cf. s. 833)). This uneasiness, together with the difficulties of trading in bulky grains in the context of a fragmented political structure, underlay the depressed land values of the period. More positive factors also promoted concentration. Local markets were now prime outlets for surplus, and access to local government, the chief source of arbitration, was more important. Contemporary funeral inscriptions reveal that the local town-gods had increased in status as mediators and centres of cult activity.

## THE ONSET OF THE LATE PERIOD

Throughout the Late Period, Egypt made a sustained and largely successful effort to maintain an effectively centralized state which, except for the two periods of Persian occupation (Twenty-seventh and Thirty-first Dynasties) was based upon earlier indigenous models. However, despite its strong, deliberately cultivated affinities with the stable political systems of the New Kingdom and earlier periods, Late Period Egypt displayed certain unique features which were caused by the effects of the Third Intermediate Period and by factors which had been less significant or non-existent before.

The traits inherited from the Third Intermediate Period were not purely negative. They provided important mechanisms for the transition to centralized government under Psammetichus I, and archaism became a useful ideological and administrative tool in the Twenty-sixth Dynasty. Less beneficial was the kingship's decreased sanctity (but not political power!) and its increased susceptibility to usurpation. The periodic re-emergence of regionally-based politico-military units whose importance ultimately derived from the Third Intermediate Period (Sais, Sebennytos, Mendes) was complex in its effects. It contributed significantly to the revolts against Persian occupation, but also to the recurrent internal crises of the Twenty-eighth to Thirtieth Dynasties.

The most important new factors were the restricted access to traditional sources of royal income in the Levant and in the Sudan, and (particularly after the end of the first Persian occupation) persistent pressure upon Egypt's own territorial integrity. As a result, while Egypt was on a more or less permanent war-footing, its foreign policy was more defensive than in the New Kingdom and involved contacts and alliances with a new group of foreign states (fig. 12.5). In addition, the use of foreign soldiers (and mariners) was much more important than before both in foreign and internal affairs.

The career of Psammetichus I typifies the often subtle mixture of the old, recent and new characteristics of Late Period policies and society. At the outset (664 BC) he was a vassal of the Assyrians like the eleven other rulers (each residing in a fortified town and commanding an army) with whom he shared control of Egypt. Already king of the largest single unit (p. 893) Psammetichus arranged for a Memphite oracle, strongly reminiscent of the type issued by 'national' gods in the New Kingdom, proclaiming his right to sole rule. Another oracle, of a more local and recent character, at Buto, near the coast of his kingdom, legitimized his use of Ionian and Carian mercenaries (the latter from Asia Minor) who had arrived there possibly at Psammetichus's invitation. The special abilities and equipment of these mercenaries gave Psammetichus an advantage over the indigenous troops of his rivals. He probably used both military and political strategy in the Delta, which came quickly under his control (by 657 BC), and the long, exposed internal frontiers both compelled and facilitated an at least partially military solution.

The military reduction of the less exposed, strategically stronger centres of Middle and Upper Egypt was likely to be undesirably protracted. The threat of foreign intervention, for which this would be an excellent opportunity, was omnipresent. Psammetichus's unification policy was specifically noted by the Assyrians as a violation of his treaty with them and he also had to reckon with the Kushite king, now residing at Napata, whose adherents at Thebes still recognized him as late as 657 BC.

Political action alone, backed by the *threat* of superior force, was, therefore, desirable south of Memphis. In this process the appointment of loyal northerners to strategic southern posts was certainly important, but less so than the exploitation of Third Intermediate Period mechanisms which made such appointments possible without military activity. For example, Herakleopolis had apparently been in eclipse since Memphis became a quasi-national capital in the Twenty-fifth Dynasty, and it did not appear in an Assyrian list of major and minor Egyptian 'kingdoms' of 667–666 BC. By 661 BC, however, it had regained its earlier status as the residence and centre of royal relatives governing Middle and Upper Egypt. Psammetichus's first such official, Pediese, was either from the Saite region or was an incumbent Herakleopolitan governor, deliberately linked by marriage to the king.

Pediese and his son and successor, Somtuttefnakhte, had, in fact, limited *territorial* control, but they effectively exercised the unique office of 'overseer of the (river) harbours' of Middle and Upper Egypt. This ensured royal control of the main communication artery, generated an increasing revenue from dues (within four years a 50%, within fifteen a 100%, increase) and secured some kind of hold over the provincial harbours, weak links in the cities' defences. Father and son were essentially royal officials, not semi-independent rulers; they generated no collateral dynasty and their most powerful functions had been eliminated by the end of the reign.

In general, Psammetichus left local rulers in office if they abandoned such 'independent' titles as 'king', 'great chief' and 'army-leader' and became incorporated into a centralized form of royal government. This process, apparently rapid in the Delta, was undertaken cautiously in less readily accessible regions. The admittedly royal, but uniquely powerful, office of 'overseer of harbours' survived to at least Psammetichus's year 34, while relations with Thebes, the major southern centre, were typically complex.

Thebes still controlled the six southernmost Egyptian provinces when it reached a political settlement with Psammetichus in 656 BC. The chief office-holders of the region (including two descendants of Kushite kings) were *confirmed* in office, and the royal government was inserted in typical Third Intermediate Period fashion by the adoption of Psammetichus's daughter as heir to the 'god's wife of Amen' (p. 888). Thereafter, this office continued to be held by a Twenty-sixth Dynasty princess. During Psammetichus's reign a royal governor was placed over the second and third Upper Egyptian provinces, and a royal garrison installed at Aswan, effectively ending Theban–Kushite contact. However, the assimilation of the Theban administration was still continuing some seventeen years after the settlement, when much of the power formerly held by the Theban mayor cum governor of the south was transferred to the steward of the 'god's wife'. Either during Psammetichus's reign or later (by year 1 of Psammmetichus II) the office of High Priest of Amen was combined with that of 'god's wife' and remained so to the end of the dynasty.

In 655/4 BC a major crisis permitted Psammetichus to demonstrate (and perhaps increase) his already considerable power. At this time much of western Egypt from Oxyrynchus to the sea – almost one-third of Egypt's length – was invaded by Libyans, who may have been in collaboration with dispossessed Egyptian dynasts. Psammetichus took the initiative of driving them out in good New Kingdom style, ordering 'the majors (*ḥзty-*ꜥ) of *all* the towns' of Egypt to send their troops to join his army (Spalinger 1976).

Despite recentralization, the effects of the Third Intermediate Period probably persisted through the following three centuries. Massive Persian intervention and pressure was a major new feature but the periodic instability experienced by the independent Egyptian dynasties reflected continuing internal as well as external problems.

## EGYPT'S RELATIONS WITH AFRICA

Throughout the nine centuries covered in this chapter, contacts between Egypt and other African regions were active and varied and must now be surveyed in detail; the Sudan after the rise of the Twentieth-fifth Dynasty is excluded (see volume 2 of this *History*).

The 'Africa' known directly or indirectly to the Egyptians was comparatively small in area and restricted to regions adjoining Egypt, the sole exception being an ephemeral expansion of knowledge in the Late Period under Necho. Little evidence supports claims for widespread Egyptian influence throughout the continent, from western to southern Africa; rather, we still await better documentation of the available facts (see Leclant 1972). Even if some claims eventually are proven, cultural diffusion via partly Egyptianized Kushites and Libyans is likely to have been a more important mechanism than direct contact.

Egyptian contact with and knowledge of Africa was relatively shallow, partly because of severe natural restrictions on access such as the Sahara and the difficulty of movement along the upper Nile. A related and equally important factor was the comparatively unsophisticated Egyptian political and military organization, which never created an 'imperial' hegemony like that of the Assyrians, the Persians or, even earlier, the Hittites. Once territorial integrity was assured and control over or access to relatively close trade routes and sources of raw materials was established the Egyptians seem to have had little impetus to advance further. Changing historical circumstances were also significant. Contacts and knowledge gained in the expansive New Kingdom dwindled in the contracting Third Intermediate Period, and were hindered in the re-expansive Late Period by a strong Kushite state in the south. The extraordinary circumnavigation of Africa sponsored by Necho failed to discover any major new sources of income and its time-span (over two years) must have confirmed the primacy of the short-run Red Sea and Mediterranean routes.

To the Egyptians 'Libya', the northernmost contact area, probably stretched no further west than Cyrenaica (fig. 12.18). Libya, in the New

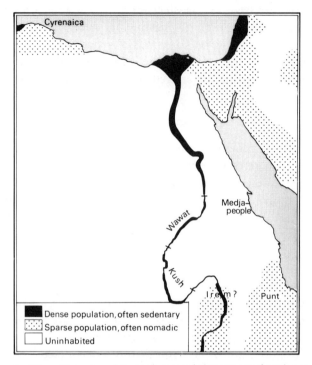

Fig. 12.18 Schematic version of the modern population pattern of north-east Africa,
probably approximating to that of the second and first millennia BC.

Kingdom and later, was frequently called Tjehenu or Tjemeh, archaic
and loosely applied terms; the former tended to refer to a peripheral
zone of Libyan settlement along the western Delta and the latter to more
remote areas. It is unfortunately impossible to match with certainty two
sets of Libyan tribal names, the first supplied by New Kingdom sources,
the other 600 years later by Herodotus. The dominant tribes during
the New Kingdom were the Libu and the Mashwash, both probably
located in Cyrenaica. Their sustained interaction with Egypt and their
contacts with the 'Sea-Peoples' of the eastern Mediterranean makes it
unlikely that either was based at Tripolitania, an important area of
coastal occupation but some 2500 km west of Egypt. Their substantial
animal holdings and relative independence strongly suggests that the
well-watered Cyrenaican plain and massif was their homeland and not
the harsh coastal plain to the east.

South of the Libyan coastal region, population rapidly fell to virtually
nil, as it did throughout most of the deserts flanking the relatively

densely settled Nile Valley, until there began a gradually increasing density, part of a broad arc sweeping from the western coast of the Red Sea across central Africa (fig. 12.18). The arc marked the beginning of the semidesert, shading eventually into savanna, created by the northern edge of the east and central African rainfall belt which, in antiquity, corresponded roughly to the modern limits between latitudes 20° and 14–16° N.

The deserts themselves were not entirely devoid of population. The western Egyptian oases supported populations and linked the desert routes, running north and south, which were of economic and strategic interest to Egypt. Consequently, throughout the entire 900 years covered here, at least some, and sometimes all, of the oases were under Egyptian control. To the east, the relatively better watered Red Sea Hills supported an appreciable nomadic population persisting perhaps as far north as latitude 27° N (cf. the distribution of intrusive Pan-grave/Medja sites; see chapter 10). These eastern nomads were, in the New Kingdom at least, still called Medja-people and, because of their dispersed character, were not easy to bring under control.

The New Kingdom conquest of 'Kush', comprising the riverine zones of Wawat (Lower Nubia, First to Second Cataracts; previously occupied by Egypt in the Middle Kingdom) and Kush proper (Upper Nubia, Second to Fourth (?) Cataracts), gave Egypt intimate knowledge of its Nehasyu ('southerner, Nubian') population. Egyptians also penetrated the area south of the Fifth Cataract but to a depth which remains uncertain. New Kingdom Egypt was also regularly in direct contact with the country of Punt, a region which can now be approximately defined (p. 935 and fig. 12.27) and, on at least one occasion, penetrated its interior perhaps to a depth of 250 km. Although Egyptian contacts re-expanded after the Third Intermediate Period contraction, Kush proper remained under indigenous control from the Kushite capital at Napata, with Wawat a virtually uninhabited and contested area between the two powers. No definite recontact with Punt is recorded but, during the Twenty-sixth Dynasty and the period of Persian occupation, Egyptian shipping was active in the Red Sea and, in view of the strong maritime emphasis of the Late Period, may have anticipated the Ptolemaic pattern of contact which ran as far south as the Bab el-Mandeb and Cape Guardafui.

The location of some of the African toponyms referred to by the Egyptians is of great importance for the reconstruction of Egyptian activity in Kush, Punt and contiguous regions. Unfortunately, the locations of most of the toponyms – even the most important – remains a matter of debate. The writer follows in this chapter the conclusions reached by him in the appendix (pp. 925–40).

The changing pattern of relations between Egypt and other African regions was shaped by several factors. These included the aims of Egyptian policy, which varied from region to region; the logistics imposed by specific topographies; the characteristics of the indigenous cultures and their reactions to contact with Egypt; and the vicissitudes of Egypt's own internal stability. Policies followed by Egypt in the Levant and Africa were closely linked. Successful expansion into the Levant depended upon there being no threat of a substantial distraction created by rebellion in Kush, and the gold which became a major element in Egyptian Levantine policy was derived from Kush.

The conquest of Kush created new contacts and conflicts with more remote Nubian groups, while the increasing importance of Nubian gold in Egypt's diplomatic relations with Asiatic states led to significant policy shifts in the regions to the south of Egypt. By contrast, Libya lacked desirable resources and only became a matter of acute concern when its threat to Egyptian security increased (p. 850). Punt, chief source of the highly desired incense used in religious ritual, was remote (see appendix) and was probably not contacted again directly until Hatshepsut's reign. Thereafter its products and the access it provided to inland regions ensured that Egyptian contacts with it were maintained to the end of the New Kingdom.

## RELATIONS WITH KUSH AND THE EASTERN DESERT

Expansion southward (fig. 12.19.1) was, therefore, intimately linked to relations with the Levant and to internal events which either inhibited or enhanced Egyptian activity abroad. Kamose (Seventeenth Dynasty) and Ahmose (Eighteenth Dynasty) had simultaneously to deal with the Hyksos and the Kushites, who were politically and strategically linked, expelling them respectively from Egypt and Wawat and creating buffer zones in southern Palestine and the Second Cataract region. Internal rebellions late in Ahmosis' reign showed that the Egyptian political situation itself was not completely stable and, not surprisingly, his successor, Amenhotep I, seems to have advanced southward no further than Sai and to have attempted no Asiatic campaigns. Tuthmosis I, however, did secure the whole Third Cataract region, consolidating his hold by building a fortress at Tombos, and traversed Kush itself, setting

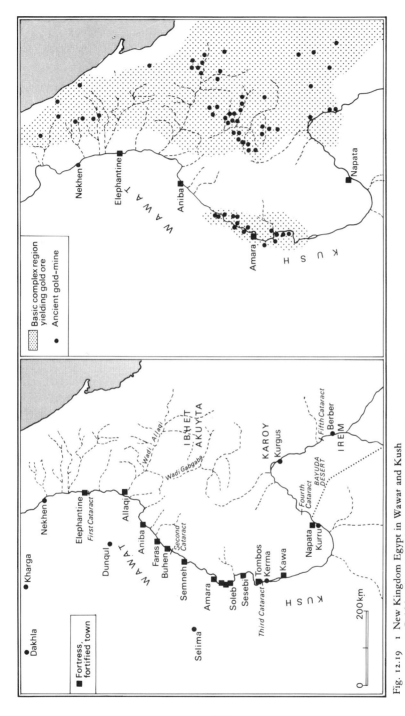

Fig. 12.19  1 New Kingdom Egypt in Wawar and Kush
2 Gold-bearing areas of Wawat and Kush (after Vercoutter 1959).
The dotted line across the Bayuda desert indicates the route formed by a series of water holes (see Chittick 1955).

903

up an at least symbolically significant frontier stele at Kurgus (just as, shortly after, he set up another on the Euphrates). Nevertheless, stubborn resistance to the Egyptian advance continued. That against Amenhotep I and Tuthmosis I was almost certainly led by unique political and military leaders descended from the 'rulers of Kush' (based at Kerma) who had dominated much of Upper Nubia and Wawat during the later Second Intermediate Period; the Kushite 'royal family', with allies from further south in Upper Nubia, appears to have made its final resistance against Tuthmosis II.

Even so, the Third Cataract region remained unstable until Hatshepsut and Tuthmosis III not only finally reduced it but extended full Egyptian control as far south as the Fourth Cataract. Although the evidence is slight, it is sufficient to show that the atypically intense and sustained Levantine campaigning of Tuthmosis III's sole reign, which extended permanent Egyptian control over a much expanded area, was preceded by a comparable expansion in Kush during the co-reign of Tuthmosis and Hatshepsut. This campaign was less demanding than the conflict with the urbanized and politically and militarily sophisticated Asiatics, but the final suppression of potentially distracting Kush was a necessary prelude to expansion into the Levant.

If, as was likely, an early Nubian campaign of Hatshepsut was provoked by attacks on Egyptian garrisons it logically would have been in the most recently conquered zone, i.e. the Third Cataract region; and twenty years after her accession, Tuthmosis III, on Hatshepsut's behalf, quelled a rebellion or invasion in Miu, a territory of the same region (see appendix). The co-rulers were also familiar with regions further south, since Hatshepsut set up a list of toponyms including Irem and others probably located in the Fifth to Sixth Cataract area; further, a strong Egyptian expedition at least once contacted Irem and exacted tribute, reaching the valley from Punt in the east (appendix) while Tuthmosis III, during Hatshepsut's reign, hunted a rhinoceros in the 'Southlands', which lay south of Upper Nubia itself environmentally unsuitable for such an animal (appendix).

Thereafter, Tuthmosis was extremely active in the Levant from his years 22 to 42, an indication that Egyptian dominance in Upper Nubia had been securely established under Hatshepsut or in the early sole reign of Tuthmosis III. The significant date may well be Tuthmosis' year 31, the first time the *b3kw* (revenue) of Wawat *and* Kush was recorded. In year 34, four sons of the chief of Irem were dispatched (as hostages, prisoners?) to Egypt; and it was probably the next year that Tuthmosis

12.1  Soldiers of Assurbanipal attacking and capturing a walled town, apparently in Egypt. (After Hall 1928, pl. XL.)

set up a duplicate of Tuthmosis I's frontier stele at Kurgus, just as he had two years earlier on the Euphrates. Napata was certainly a permanent Egyptian centre by year 47.

The Third Cataract region, now under close Egyptian control, remained peculiarly important throughout the New Kingdom despite its agricultural poverty and relatively low population. Several major fortress (or temple) towns developed here, continuing to flourish even after the more fertile remainder of Kush was finally conquered and one – Amara – was the preferred administrative centre for Kush, despite its non-central position. This continuing importance reflects the area's early role as a base of operations, its reduced exposure to external attack, and its economic value, for the chief riverine gold sources were precisely in this zone (fig. 12.19.2). It also has been argued that this area was an important focus for desert trade routes linking Upper Nubia and the northern Butana.

Thereafter, with Kush secured, the foci of Egyptian military activity moved, in partially interrelated ways, both east and south. Throughout the New Kingdom Napata and Karoy (the riverine zone between the Fourth and Fifth Cataracts) are consistently referred to as the southern limit of full Egyptian control; but the development of a looser form of control in the Fifth and Sixth Cataract regions, and even further, was imperative. The uninhabited nature of Karoy and the difficulties of riverine movement through it, as well as the aridity of the Bayuda desert, made this a natural frontier zone; while the diffused pastoral populations of the regions beyond Karoy would have exacerbated the normal problems of full control. But these same populations, if left completely unhampered, could monopolize access to desirable products (see appendix) and raid the tempting targets provided by Egyptian centres and a pacified population in adjoining Kush. Eventually, the Egyptians seem to have established a system of control in Irem and adjoining regions based not on permanent centres, but on patrols, interspersed, when necessary, with campaigns (cf. the similar situation between Sixth Dynasty Egypt and Wawat, and – to a degree – Middle Kingdom Wawat and Kush; see chapter 10).

The eastern Nubian desert, accessible primarily from Wawat via the Wadis el-Allaqi and Gabgaba, contained valuable gold resources (fig. 12.19.2); Wawat sometimes yielded twenty times more gold than Kush. The Egyptians were again exploiting these resources in the early Eighteenth Dynasty; but the area increased in importance when gold became a major source of Egyptian influence in the Levant (as campaigning was largely replaced by alliances and quasi-diplomatic commercial relationships in the later Eighteenth Dynasty and, after a renewal of major campaigning, in the Nineteenth Dynasty).

Aridity created logistical problems in eastern Nubia but equally significant was the presence of a nomadic or semi-nomadic population (in broad terms, the Medja-people) who interfered with Egyptian exploitation. The eastern deserts were related to Irem and contiguous regions in several ways: all contained significant gold deposits (fig. 12.19.2); their populations were probably in contact; and the Medja-people were directly – and the Irem and nearby peoples indirectly – linked to the Red Sea coast. Certainly Egyptian activities in both regions seem at times to have been linked together.

Given the policy aims suggested above, a consistent pattern for later Eighteenth Dynasty activity in the south can tentatively be suggested. Tuthmosis IV campaigned in the deserts east of Wawat and perhaps in Irem and two other toponyms in its vicinity; if so, he anticipated the better documented activity of his successor, Amenhotep III, presumably for the same reasons. In the reign of Amenhotep III, a comprehensive plan to expand and improve the exploitation of the gold-mining areas as a whole can be discerned. At about this time the authority of the Viceroy of Kush was extended to include the southern Egyptian gold-mines and, in fact, the name of Amenhotep's viceroy, Merymose, has been found in southern Egypt at Reddesiyeh, an area which had become an important gold producer by the early Nineteenth Dynasty. Ibhet, a region in the gold-bearing desert east of Wawat, was invaded by the same Merymose, moving from the valley along the Wadi el-Allaqi, probably in conjunction with other campaigns which date to Amenhotep's fifth regnal year.

During this year an army sailed along the Red Sea coast, opposite Wawat and Kush, and harassed the Nehasyu inhabitants of the region; these were presumably nomads based on the coastal plain or hills who had been penetrating inland and hindering an expanded exploitation of the gold-mines. The area affected was called *Wrš[k]*, probably the same toponym as the eastern-desert toponym *ȝwšk*, dominated by the Medja-people in the Middle Kingdom. Amenhotep also indicated that Irem and a nearby toponym *Twrk* were invaded by another army; this would have improved security on the frontier and enhanced access to the gold-mines of *ʿmw* – along latitude 19° N (see appendix, p. 939) – from which came the gold of Karoy specifically referred to in connection with this campaign.

The depth of the penetration of Amenhotep III into the eastern desert is marked by the appearance of a new toponym, Akuyta, first attested in the toponymical lists of his reign, and certainly to be located in this region. Akuyta's continuing importance is reflected by its reappearance in lists of Akhenaten (Amenhotep IV), Horemheb, Ramesses II and Ramesses III and was based upon the continuous effort to maintain the enhanced gold supply created by Amenhotep III. Akhenaten punished the Akuyta people for threatening the food supplies of the gold-miners, while Seti I and Ramesses II were much concerned about the water supply of their gold miners in Akuyta. A viceroy of Ramesses II recorded the submission of Akuyta's chief, although Ramesses' successor Merenptah may have had further trouble in the east; how else to explain a campaign of his in year 4 connected with long stabilized and acculturated Wawat? Thereafter perhaps Akuyta was more submissive to Egypt; the 'deputy of Wawat' was active in Akuyta as late as the reign of Ramesses VI while under Ramesses IX Nehasyu from Akuyta assisted the Egyptians by repelling nomadic attack upon the gold-mines of the Wadis Hammamat or el-Allaqi.

Activity in the area of the Fifth and Sixth Cataracts was also maintained. The locations of the Nubian campaigns of Tutankhamen(?) and Horemheb are unknown. However, once Seti I had concluded his vigorous campaigning in Asia with diplomatic accord the need for diplomatically potent gold was reinforced. In year 9 Seti began the further development of the southern Egyptian gold-mines and at the same time attacked Irem. Ramesses II also campaigned in Irem and recorded tribute from thence and Ramesses III probably also engaged in hostilities against Irem. Captive chiefs of Kush, of an obliterated toponym perhaps to be restored as Irem, and of two other toponyms in Irem's vicinity were depicted at Medinet Habu, and Irem people were compelled to serve at the royal court in Egypt. Significantly, Ramesses III also exploited the gold mines of '$mw$, access to which depended upon the acquiescence of Irem.

The long Egyptian occupation of Kush and Wawat (to the end of the Twentieth Dynasty) generated an intense and sustained interaction between Egyptians and indigenes which had results of the greatest interest. The more important aspects of that interaction are epitomized in the wall scenes of the tomb of Huy, Viceroy of Kush under Tutankhamen (fig. 12.20). Textual commentary is minimal but the content and symbolically varying scales of the iconography reflect the basic Egyptian interests in the region; the administrative structure

Fig. 12.20 Officials of the administration of Nubia under Tutankhamen, bringing gifts to the viceroy Huy. They are: upper register, left to right, the deputy of Wawat (destroyed), the deputy of Kush, the mayor of Soleb, and an overseer of cattle; lower register, left to right, the high priest of Tutankhamen at Faras, the 'deputy' of the fortress of Faras and the mayor of Faras. (After Davies and Gardiner 1926.)

908

that satisfied them; and, partially, the nature of the relations between Egyptians and indigenes.

The depiction of Huy's investiture emphasized both the importance of the viceroy and his close personal relationship with the king. The data on the viceregal office shows that it was intimately related to the expansion into Wawat and Kush, a phenomenon strongly linked to the actual power and the mystique of the kingship. The first viceroy was installed perhaps by Kamose but certainly by Ahmose, and thirty have now been documented, succeeding each other until the end of the reign of Ramesses XI; few, if any, are yet to be discovered. The earliest viceroys were perhaps, like Ahmose Turo (Ahmosis–Tuthmosis I), drawn from the administration set up to control the expanding conquest territory, but thereafter they were drawn from the administration within Egypt, except for the relatively rare cases when a son succeeded his father as viceroy. The chief responsibilities of the viceroy were to collect and deliver tribute and taxes (given pride of place in Huy's tomb), to exploit efficiently the gold-bearing regions, and to oversee the civil government of the province. Although the viceroys rarely bore military titles contemporary with their incumbency and although formal military command was vested in the 'battalion-commander of Kush', in practice, they could assume direct military command of the province's forces (e.g. Merymose under Amenhotep III and Panehesy under Ramesses XI). Moreover, at least a third of the viceroys between the later Eighteenth and earlier Twentieth Dynasties were drawn from the royal chariotry or royal stable-administration, a fact that probably reflects their role in the desert campaigning typical of that period (pp. 905ff.).

The viceroys' close links with the king were emphasized by their titles, administrative habits and origins. The viceroys were functionally equivalent to (although inherently more powerful than) the Levantine 'overseers of northern lands', and enjoyed a unique quasi-dynastic status as 'king's son' or 'king's son of Kush' (p. 856). Appointed by the king and reporting directly to him, many (nearly 50%) of the viceroys were drawn from the 'royal' sections of the bureaucracy and army, i.e. from the ranks of royal envoys, heralds, scribes, charioteers and stable-overseers. This close connection facilitated royal control over an unusually powerful official governing an extensive territory (from Nekhen in Upper Egypt to Napata), the chief product of which – gold – was peculiarly important to the temporal and supernatural power of the kingship, since king and Amen establishment were the chief beneficiaries. It also however reflected the symbolic importance of Kush, wherein the war-making, divinely-approved abilities of the Egyptian kings were particularly satisfactorily demonstrated.

The administrative structure of Kush, sketched out in Huy's tomb (fig. 12.20) and documented elsewhere, interestingly mimicked centralized royal government in Egypt. The viceroy had his own staff of scribes, envoys and agents, while Wawat and Kush were each directly administered by a 'deputy' (*idnw*). Government was centralized in two provincial capitals, clearly Faras and Soleb (ancient Khaemhet; see fig. 12.20) under Tutankhamen (see the prominence given to the officials of these towns in Huy's tomb) but more usually Aniba and Amara. These and the other towns renovated or founded by the New Kingdom Egyptians throughout the region were each governed by a mayor (*ḥȝty-ʿ*) or, when of a military character, by a military official (*ṯsw, ḥry pḏt,* or *imy-r mr ḥtm*), and most of them had a priesthood serving the cults of Egyptian gods.

Throughout the New Kingdom, these ethnically and culturally Egyptian urban centres were surrounded by a substantial population which was un-Egyptian in ethnicity, language(s) and, initially (in Kush if not in Wawat), in material culture. There is no reason to assume a massive displacement of indigenes by incoming Egyptians and the theory that Wawat, and even Kush, became gradually depopulated because of falling river levels or repressive Egyptian policies seems to the writer unlikely. The subordinate roles of the Nubians are emphasized in Huy's tomb, where they are shown apparently delivering tribute to centres in Nubia and certainly accompanying the presentation of the tribute to the king. Nubian chiefs humble themselves before the king, their children appear as hostages or future royal harem members and other Nubians appear as prisoners or slaves (fig. 12.21). Certainly, the basic agricultural and pastoral system of Kush must have been maintained by the indigenes, their services on behalf of the civil, military and religious establishments of the province enforced, and numerous Kushites drafted into the army, frequently as specific segments of the Levantine garrisons.

Two aspects of the indigenes' relations with Egypt were particularly important. First, some southerners were incorporated into the administration of the province, not, as in the Middle Kingdom, excluded from it; secondly, there was, at *all* levels of indigenous society, increasing acculturation to Egyptian norms in material and intellectual culture, eventually complete in Wawat and presumably reaching an advanced

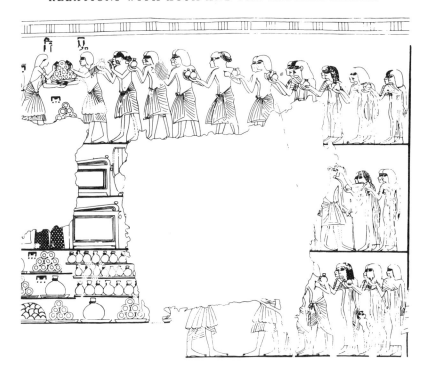

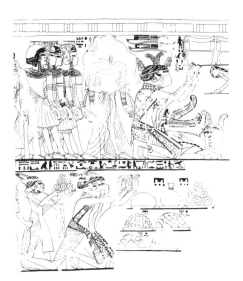

Fig. 12.21  1 Egyptianized Nubians (?) delivering tribute to the viceroy Huy.

2 Nubians delivering tribute to Tutankhamen. Upper register, right to left: the three chiefs of Wawat, including Hekanefer, followed by a Nubian princess and several princes. Lower register, right to left: three of the six chiefs of Kush depicted in Huy's tomb. (After Davies and Gardiner 1926.)

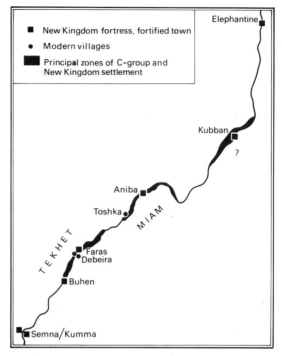

Fig. 12.22 The three (?) chiefdoms of Lower Nubia (Wawat) in the Eighteenth Dynasty. It is assumed that each chiefdom coincides with one of the three principal zones of settlement (cf. Trigger 1965, figs. 2, 3), an assumption supported by the distribution of the tombs and monuments of the chiefs and their relatives (fig. 12.23) and by the three chiefs of Wawat depicted in Huy's tomb (fig. 12.21).

degree in at least some parts of Kush. Given these facts, one may legitimately speculate that the distinctions between resident Egyptians and numerically dominant Nubians became increasingly blurred, with Nubians beginning to move into the upper levels of provincial government and society. Unfortunately, the acculturation process in Wawat makes it impossible to confirm this hypothesis, while data from Kush are as yet inadequate.

The indigenous elite was dominated by paramount 'chiefs' (*wrw*), best documented in the Eighteenth Dynasty but also referred to later. For that period, depictions of Nubian tribute, in which the chiefs are indicated by their activity, large size, and distinctive apparel, suggest there were only a small number of chiefs (between seven and nine) for Kush in its broader sense. In Huy's tomb only three chiefs of Wawat are shown (fig. 12.21), and in fact two principal chiefdoms therein are well documented, leaving room for another in the north. This division corresponds to topographically enforced breaks in the Lower Nubian settlement pattern (fig. 12.22) which had affected indigenous political structures as early as the Old Kingdom. This implies, of course, that the twenty-five toponyms assigned to Wawat in the list of Tuthmosis III (see appendix) were subsumed into the larger political units of the chiefdoms, and a similar process must be envisaged for Kush proper. Although at least eight or nine toponyms of the Tuthmoside list are to be located in Upper Nubia (appendix), only six chiefs of Kush are depicted in Huy's tomb. Earlier, in fact, Tuthmosis II, in apparent reference to Upper Nubia as a whole, specifically describes it as divided into five chieftainships (Sethe 1927, p. 139; see also Gardiner 1961, p. 140).[1] These chiefs were appointed by the Egyptians but were probably drawn from the upper levels of Nubian society, perhaps even from the families of hereditary chiefs of earlier periods.

Two chiefs' 'families' of Eighteenth Dynasty Wawat illustrate the administrative functions of the chiefs and the increased acculturation their role encouraged. The tombs, graffiti, dedicatory statues and stelae of one family are concentrated within the chiefdom of Miam, and the other in that of Tekhet (figs. 12.22–3). Chiefs' sons appear to have been sent to Egypt as hostages, brought up as pages at the Egyptian court (as were many Egyptians, including some viceroys, who later achieved high office) and subsequently incorporated into the bureaucracy of Wawat as 'administrators,' 'scribes' and 'viceregal deputies'. Those who eventually succeeded their fathers or other relatives as chiefs (*wrw*) presumably managed the internal affairs of the Nubian communities, and were the chief liaison between the indigenes and Egyptian officials. Although ethnically non-Egyptian (e.g. Hekanefer, as depicted in Huy's tomb; fig. 12.21), the chiefs were completely acculturated. Their personal names are usually partially or entirely Egyptian, their tombs Egyptian in function, form and decoration; and they appear to have assumed partially indigenous regalia only on such symbolically significant occasions as the presentation of tribute to the king. Iconographic evidence indicated that the Kushite chiefs underwent a similar, although not necessarily identical, process.

Archaeological evidence shows that, with a few exceptions, the indigenes of Wawat at all levels of society acculturated rapidly to Egyptian norms, at least in terms of material culture. Except on the

---

[1] The number of 'chiefs' actually involved in this text is ambiguous, but the reference to a five-fold division is explicit, and is suggestive in the context of the other data cited in this paragraph.

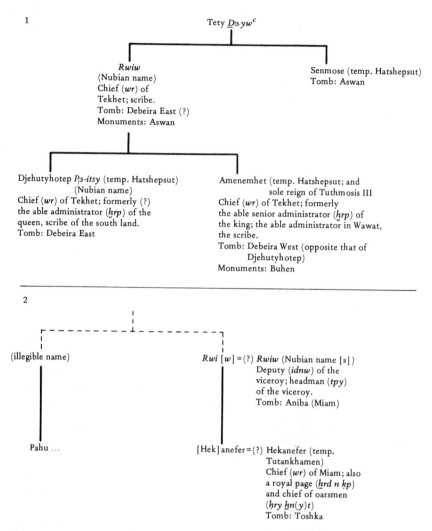

1

Tety *Ḏȝyw*ᶜ

Rwiw
(Nubian name)
Chief (*wr*) of
Tekhet; scribe.
Tomb: Debeira East (?)
Monuments: Aswan

Senmose (temp. Hatshepsut)
Tomb: Aswan

Djehutyhotep *Pȝ-itsy* (temp. Hatshepsut)
(Nubian name)
Chief (*wr*) of Tekhet; formerly (?)
the able administrator (*ḥrp*) of the
queen, scribe of the south land.
Tomb: Debeira East

Amenemhet (temp. Hatshepsut; and
sole reign of Tuthmosis III
Chief (*wr*) of Tekhet; formerly
the able senior administrator (*ḥrp*) of
the king; the able administrator in Wawat,
the scribe.
Tomb: Debeira West (opposite that of
Djehutyhotep)
Monuments: Buhen

2

(illegible name)

Rwi [*w*] =(?) *Rwiw* (Nubian name [s])
Deputy (*idnw*) of the
viceroy; headman (*tpy*)
of the viceroy.
Tomb: Aniba (Miam)

Pahu ...

[Hek] anefer = (?) Hekanefer (temp.
Tutankhamen)
Chief (*wr*) of Miam; also
a royal page (*ḥrd n kp*)
and chief of oarsmen
(*ḥry ḥn(y)t*)
Tomb: Toshka

Fig. 12.23  Genealogies and offices of the 'chieftains' families' of (1) Tekhet and (2) Miam. For
the former, see Säve-Söderbergh (1960, 1963) and Edel (1963). As for the individuals from Miam,
the identification between R*wi*[*w*] and R*wiw* is quite possible (cf. Steindorff 1937, 27; Plates, Taf.
13.56, for R*wi*[*w*] and Text 69–70, 79 for R*wiw*). The restoration of the name of R*wi*[*w*]'s son as
[Hek]anefer (not suggested by Steindorff, but cf. his Text 37, Plates, Taf, 13.56) is less plausible
since, as Lanny Bell pointed out to me, the restoration requires the 'āleph vulture-sign (ȝ) to be
written out, which would not normally be the case in the New Kingdom. On Hekanefer, chief
of Miam, see Simpson (1963).

southern edge of Wawat, the characteristic C-group culture (see chapter 10) did not survive the Second Intermediate Period. During that time, traditional C-group cemeteries rapidly became 'Egyptian' in tomb types, funerary artifacts and burial customs. The characteristic circular–oval C-group houses of rubble, vegetable materials and leather (?) were also replaced by right-angled structures making considerable use of mud brick. For lack of evidence, changes in contemporary Kushite material culture cannot yet be traced. It is important to note that a thoroughly 'Nubian' archaeological assemblage claimed to postdate and to be descended from the Second Intermediate Period 'Kerma culture' is, in fact, probably the latter's Middle Kingdom predecessor (see chapter 10).

At the end of the New Kingdom, the Kushite viceroy Penehasy, expelled from Egypt, retained control of Lower (and implicitly Upper) Nubia, since he was buried at Aniba (ancient Miam). The Lower Nubian population was markedly heterogeneous, consisting of Egyptians, many settled there for generations, a majority of Egyptianized Nubians and, probably, some Egypto-Nubians, but it maintained its political cohesion. This is indicated by its strong resistance to the sustained Egyptian effort at reconquest under Herihor and his son Piankh (p. 878); by a possible successor to Penehasy, who bore titles somewhat similar to his and whose recognition of the titular authority of Ramesses XI did not preclude continued hostility to Herihor; and by the voluntary and wholesale evacuation of Lower Nubia at about this time, which may initially have been caused by the intensity of Piankh's campaigning. This intensity is demonstrated by the facts that the younger artisans of the royal romb at Thebes were drafted into Piankh's army, and the Theban necropolis scribes were assigned to organizing the production of metal weapons instead of the normal artisans' tools.

The depopulation of Lower Nubia was long sustained, largely because of political circumstances rather than fluctuations in Nile level or in the local agricultural economy. Resettlement was, at first, precluded by Egyptian hostility; as late as Pinudjem II the ruling family of southern Egypt still claimed the title of Viceroy of Kush, and the Nubian campaign of Shoshenq I indicates more explicit conflict. No major resettlement was attempted under the Twenty-fifth (Kushite) Dynasty, and the unprecedented existence of a Kushite state approximately equal to Egypt in military and political strength throughout the Late and Ptolemaic Periods encouraged the maintenance of a mutually advantageous, largely empty, buffer zone, as did periodic open conflicts. Psammetichus II invaded Upper Nubia, and Cambyses and probably

Khababash (*c.* 335 BC?) also campaigned against the southerners. Only the strong expansionist tendencies of the Ptolemaic and Meroitic states (see volume 2 of this *History*), combined with some form of Egyptian–Meroitic accord under Ptolemy IV, led eventually to the resettlement of Lower Nubia in the first century BC.

The evolution of a Kushite state throughout the Third Intermediate Period is undocumented, except for the tombs of the apparent predecessors of the Twenty-fifth Dynasty at Kurru, near Napata. Going back to about 860 BC, these tombs indicate that the society from which the Twenty-fifth Dynasty arose was Upper Nubian in origin and, in its earlier phase, little affected by Egyptian culture. The circular earthen tumuli covering the simple pit-and-chamber tombs and the non-Egyptian orientation of the latter strongly suggest that, whatever degree of acculturation was reached in the New Kingdom, it had been lost in the intervening two centuries. However, even these earlier graves had assemblages of funerary goods which were dominated by artifacts imported from contemporary Egypt, indigenous culture being represented by stone arrow-heads and certain pottery types. These imports were presumably the result of trade, probably in Nubian gold, which occurred frequently amongst the grave-goods. Quite apart from the internal Egyptian demand for gold, Egypt had become increasingly involved in commercial and diplomatic activities in the Levant since the reign of Siamun (Twenty-first Dynasty). Given Egypt's weak military structure, gold was probably even more important in these activities than it had been in the New Kingdom.

The continual recurrence of Egyptian artifacts in the Kurru tombs shows that trade persisted and other evidence suggests an increasing intensity and variety of contact. During the eighth century BC, square mastabas replaced the tumuli style; stone masonry was used with increasing frequency; a preference for right-angled architectural forms became evident; and the burial-pit orientation conformed to Egyptian practice. These developments imply increased exposure to Egyptian models and techniques, a greater penetration of the Egyptian cultural region (aided certainly by the accelerating political fragmentation within Egypt) and perhaps the importation of Egyptian artisans. Conversely, the growing centrality of the Kushite state, reflected in the increasing size and elaboration of these royal tombs, culminated perhaps under the 'son of Re', 'the chieftain', Alara. His successor, Kashta, controlled Lower Nubia and was in close contact with Egypt. Shortly thereafter, the Kushite Piankhy conquered Middle and Upper Egypt. This led to a period of intense cultural interaction with Egypt which deeply affected the subsequent development of both Napatan and Meroitic culture. These themes are explored elsewhere (see volume 2 of this *History*).

## EGYPT AND PUNT (fig. 12.24)

Punt was an important African contact area for the Egyptians, who probably visited it fairly regularly, but the region is tantalizingly poorly documented. The single *detailed* Egyptian source is the Punt reliefs of Hatshepsut at Deir el-Bahari and the region occupied by Punt has not been explored archaeologically. Within broad limits, the location of Punt is now well established (appendix and fig. 12.18) although it is important to note that the savanna animals sometimes ascribed to Punt actually are characteristic of Irem and *Nmȝyw*, adjoining Punt on the west (see appendix). Punt included the coastal plain and the hilly country east of it between latitudes 17° and 12°N, but little of the semidesert and savanna lands east of the hills. The characteristic indigenous Puntite products were *cntyw* incense, much desired by the Egyptians for ritual uses, ebony and short-horned cattle. The Puntites also traded in products derived from elsewhere – ivory (elephants are never associated with Punt or Irem and *Nmȝyw*), gold and panther and cheetah skins.

The Puntites are depicted in several Eighteenth Dynasty scenes. Typically, the men have dark reddish skins and fine features; characteristic negroid types are not shown, although they occur amongst depictions of riverine southerners (of Wawat, Kush, Irem, etc.). Other Puntite features are also not found amongst other southerners. Long hairstyles are typical for Puntites until the reign of Amenhotep II; during his reign and earlier, in that of Tuthmosis III, an intermediate 'bobbed' hairstyle appears, and thereafter Puntites have close-cropped hair similar to that of the chief of Punt under Hatshepsut. A long or medium dressed goatee is found at all periods, and decoration and dress are relatively simple; a medium-length or long kilt is the only male garment. Puntite women are rarely depicted and were in some cases steatopygous. Dwellings were beehive-shaped structures on piles.

The Egyptians – so far as we know – always reached Punt by sea, while conversely Puntite raft-like boats sometimes sailed to the Red Sea coast of Egypt in order to trade. Puntites, including the children of chiefs, also came to the Egyptian court and probably Punt acknowledged some kind of Egyptian overlordship. It must however have been very

Fig. 12.24   Merchants from Punt arriving at the Red Sea coast of Egypt and being received by Egyptian officials. Probably reign of Amenhotep III. (After Säve-Söderbergh 1946.)

loose. The fundamental Egyptian–Puntite relationship was one of trade, not political super- and subordination. Warlike activity against Punt is never referred to and indeed Punt would have been logistically very difficult to control. No permanent Egyptian centres were established there. However, sailing conditions in the Red Sea encouraged Egyptian expeditions to spend two or three months in Punt and to penetrate further inland. Archaeological exploration will eventually surely reveal traces of those visits – certainly rock inscriptions and graffiti, and perhaps more. Hatshepsut's expedition, for example, set up a shrine to Amen and the queen in Punt.

Egyptian–Puntite contacts are attested from the reign of Hatshepsut to that of Ramesses III. Thereafter, no reference has survived and probably direct contact with Punt was lost in the contraction of foreign contacts typical of the Third Intermediate Period.

## EGYPT AND LIBYA

New Kingdom and later relations with Libya, the other main African contact area, are one of the most intriguing and least studied aspects of Egyptian foreign relations. Any effort – such as the following – to analyse these relations must necessarily be tentative until further archaeological and epigraphic fieldwork is carried out in the western Delta, the adjacent deserts and Cyrenaica itself.

918

There are no explicit references to conflict with Libyans in the Eighteenth Dynasty. Intensifying although never specifically characterized contact is indicated by increasing references to Libyans in the later Eighteenth Dynasty. An official of Amenhotep III had Libyan (Mashwash) cattle in his stockyard, though whether these were booty, imports, or simply a type bred in Egypt is unknown; and Libyans (perhaps specifically Libu; see p. 900) are depicted as present at Akhenaten's court. Here they appear as chiefs or ambassadors bringing tribute or witnessing the king's public activities and also as members of the (predominantly Egyptian) military escort of the king.

References in the Nineteenth and Twentieth Dynasties are more frequent and increasingly detailed. Seti I fought a campaign against the chiefs of Tjehenu, the enemy being iconographically identifiable as Mashwash *if* the Egyptians were consistent in their depictions of the apparently slight differences in dress and appearance which distinguished the Mashwash from the Libu. Under Ramesses II, there are generalized references to conflict with the Tjehenu and Tjemehu and once specifically to the Libu, the earliest occurrence of that name. Ramesses II also founded or renovated a series of architectural complexes running along the coastal road to Libya and along the north-western edge of the Delta; the exact nature of these has never been fully investigated, but the exposed positions of some (fig. 12.25) and the military titles of an Egyptian(?) official associated with one, suggests that at least some of them were fortresses.

Both Merenptah (year 5, *c.* 1220 BC) and Ramesses III (year 5, *c.* 1180 BC) fought off substantial Libyan invasions, both dominated by the Libu. Merenptah killed over 9300 Libyans and their allies, but the figures of Ramesses III, if taken at their face value, indicate that over 28 000 Libyans were slain! Later, in year 11 (*c.* 1174 BC) Ramesses III forestalled a Mashwash invasion, killing 2175 and capturing a further 2052. Even if the numbers of Libyans slain during the first campaign of Ramesses III are lowered, they still numbered between 12 000 and 13 000, and the overall figures emphasize the seriousness of these invasions. Egyptian records rarely record the numbers of enemy slain and captives are usually numbered in hundreds or less, not in thousands.

The general level of culture and acculturation reached by the Libyans at this time is difficult to assess. Although they are shown as wearing entirely non-Egyptian dress, this depiction may be misleading, since it is in just such battle and capture scenes that traditional indigenous garb was regarded as symbolically appropriate by Egyptian artists (p. 913).

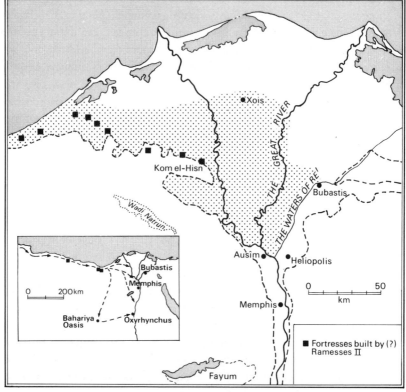

Fig. 12.25 The Libyans and Egypt in the New Kingdom. The broken lines on the smaller map indicate possible lines of Libyan movement, while the stippled area on the larger shows the area apparently affected by Libyan settlement and raiding. For fortresses see Rowe (1954).

That pastoralism was a major element in Libyan economy is suggested by the animals captured by the Egyptians, particularly the very large numbers of cattle, sheep and goats taken from the Mashwash under Ramesses III. Yet reference to the 'town' of the Libu chief Meryey and the 'towns' of the Mashwash indicate that permanent settlements existed, and the gold and silver, the numerous bronze swords and other artifacts, and the (primarily Mashwash) chariots included in the booty from the Libyans suggest that the level of material culture was well above that of a simple pastoral society. Here again, we must wait upon systematic survey and excavation for further data.

Typical of Egyptian–Libyan relations in the later New Kingdom were infiltration and culminating invasion by the latter, although the 'invasions' were, perhaps, actually organized Libyan resistance to

920

periodic Egyptian attempts to exterminate or expel the infiltrators. The details of these processes are only partly reconstructible, largely because the locations of most of the relevant toponyms are unknown. The actual zone of Libyan settlement was only once defined (under Ramesses III) as running along the western Delta frontier from the Memphite province to Karabona, a place of unknown location. Possibly the primary zone of Libyan settlement lay between Kom el-Hisn and Ausîm (fig. 12.25), avoiding the apparently heavily fortified north-west corner of the Delta. Such a pattern would help explain their far-flung depredations in the central Delta and the anxiety with which, according to Merenptah, Memphis and Heliopolis reacted to the news of invasion. The Libyan settlements along the Delta fringe were the bases for extensive raiding, sometimes lasting for months, according to Merenptah, and even for 'many years', according to Ramesses III. Under both kings the raiders reached the Sebennytic branch of the Nile ('the Great River') and threatened the region of Bubastis on the eastern Nile branch ('the waters of Re'), and the raiding of the Xoite region is also noted under Ramesses III.

The Libyan campaign of Merenptah (c. 1220 BC) and the second Libyan campaign of Ramesses III are described in some detail and may have occurred in the same area. In each case the invading Libyans came from abroad, first attacking 'Tjehenu-land', in this context a pacified zone incorporating the northern oases and the home of such subdued groups as the Tjuk–Libyans who served in the Egyptian army in the Twentieth and Twenty-second Dynasties. Merenptah defeated the invaders between a fortress in Pi-yer and a point called 'the beginning of Earth' (*Wpt-tʒ*), and Ramesses III between a fortress at *Wpt-tʒ* and another about 16 km away, called the 'House of Sand' (*Ḥwt šcy*). This battle is depicted in a desert landscape (fig. 12.26). The expression *Wpt-tʒ* was habitually applied to the furthermost limits of Egyptian dominion, but may not refer to an identical area in the two texts cited here; and the location of the 'House of Sand' remains uncertain, although a Thirtieth Dynasty text indicates that it lay west of the Delta proper. Its strategic importance is suggested by the titles of its tutelary deity, Min of *Ḥwt šcy*, specifically charged in Ptolemaic times with control of the Tjehenu and Tjemehu.

The New Kingdom Egyptians appear never to have attempted to establish permanent control over Cyrenaica (which would have yielded them little desirable income) and perhaps they never penetrated it. The westernmost known point of Egyptian occupation was the Ramesside

Fig. 12.26 Mashwash Libyans fleeing the army of Ramesses III during the Libyan campaign of his year 11. The relevant text reads (above the fortresses in the background): 'The [slaughter which his majesty made among the foe of] the land [of Mash]wash, who had come to Egypt; beginning from [the tow]n of Ramesses III which is upon the [mount]ain of *Wpt-t₃* [to] the town *Hwt šcy*, making 8 *itrw* (i.e. about 84 km) of carnage amongst them.' (See Edgerton and Wilson 1936, p. 61.) (After Nelson *et al.* 1932, pl. 70.)

fortress (?) at Zaouyet um el-Rakham (fig. 12.25) perhaps to be identified with the 'Fortress of the West' under Merenptah, which reported that a defeated Libyan chieftain had fled past it into his homeland, where he was deposed by his own people. Ramesses III did attempt to impose an Egyptian vassal (a youth, perhaps a chief's son and a hostage brought up in Egypt) over the Libu, Mashwash, and others: but the result was a major rebellion, not the acquiescence that would have been anticipated, for example, in contemporary Kush.

What were the causes of this unprecedentedly intense and long-sustained interaction between Libya and Egypt? The westernmost Delta had been periodically penetrated by Libyans for millennia, partly because of its natural proximity but also because of its lightly settled character. Prior to the Hellenistic period, this region was of low agricultural productivity, was given over chiefly to cattle grazing and had an inferior status in the hierarchy of government concerns – facts alluded to under Merenptah. However, while these circumstances facilitated the developments outlined above, they are insufficient as a cause.

There may have been pressure upon Cyrenaica's food supplies, due to climatic change or to a population increasing naturally or by immigration. The texts of Merenptah's reign suggest that the Libyan invasion of his time was caused by famine, and the Mashwash invasion under Ramesses III had the character of a true migration, since substantial numbers of women and enormous numbers of animals accompanied the fighting men. The relatively late appearance of the Mashwash and Libu in Egyptian texts (p. 900) might also suggest the appearance of new immigrant groups in Cyrenaica, but might equally well reflect the informed interest that Egypt was compelled to take as a result of Libyan pressure. Only archaeological fieldwork within Cyrenaica can resolve these questions. Unfortunately, so far, not even tentatively identified indigenous remains have been located prior to the sixth and fifth centuries BC.

Perhaps more significant than population pressure was a growing political cohesion and military strength amongst the Libyans, stimulated partly by the models presented by Egypt but also by other contacts. Surprisingly, non-Libyans made up perhaps a third of the Libyan force defeated by Merenptah, the foreigners consisting of the 'foreign Peoples of the Sea' the Sherden, Shekelesh, and Ekwesh, originating in the Aegean–western Anatolian region; the Teresh, of unknown origin; and the Lukki, from Lycia, also in Asia Minor. These foreigners clearly reached Libya by ship and were, the texts imply, recruited by the Libu chief, presumably because of their superior weaponry and armour. That trading contacts existed even before this time is suggested by the numerous bronze swords of Sherden type (and even armour) owned by (or derived from?) the Mashwash and included amongst the booty recorded by Merenptah. The international implication of these contacts is deepened by the, admittedly highly tentative, identification of the south-western Anatolian kingdom of Aḥḥiyawa with the Ekwesh, who made up about two-thirds of the foreign allies of the Libyans. Aḥhiyawa was a powerful coastal state causing much concern to the contemporary Hittite kingdom, with which Merenptah was on good terms and which he may even have actively supported against such enemies as Aḥhiyawa!

A substantial degree of political centralization and military efficiency seems to have existed amongst the Libyans. It is true that the Libu and the Mashwash, the two most important groups, must be distinguished from each other. Although both probably included both dark-skinned, brunette types and fair-skinned, blue-eyed 'Berbers', they differed in dress and general appearance and in resources, the Mashwash having a much greater number of horses as well as apparently better links with the trading network of the eastern Mediterranean. The dichotomies suggest that the Mashwash were coastal and the Libu lived in the hinterland, or that the Mashwash were east of the Libu and better located for contact with Egypt and the Levantine seas.

Despite these differences, the two groups acted in concert, the Mashwash participating under Libu leadership in the battles against Merenptah and Ramesses III (year 5); and, if the Mashwash alone faced Ramesses III in year 11, they explicitly did so at the urging of the Libu. The dominant figure in each Libyan invasion was a single chief (*wr*), representing hereditary dynasties which respectively ruled the Libu and the Mashwash. For the former, the succession of the chiefs Ded, his son (?) Meshken, and *his* son Meryey is documented. Meryey, after his defeat by Merenptah, was deposed in favour of one of his 'brothers', and one of Meryey's descendants was, perhaps, the Libu chief opposing Ramesses III. For the Mashwash, we know that the chief Meshesher led the Libyan forces against Ramesses III, and that his still-living father, Kheper, also had great political authority. The military strength of the Libyans is indicated by the great relief the Egyptians expressed at their defeat, and, more explicitly, by the bowmen, swordsmen and foreign troops used by the Libu against Merenptah, as well as by the substantial number of chariots, bowmen and swordsmen found in the Mashwash army, defeated by Ramesses III.

The Libyan 'invasions' appear to have been the culmination of substantial, relatively long-term Libyan infiltration and settlement in the western Delta, which continued even after the great defeats described above. This movement was facilitated by internal political disintegration within Egypt, the relatively unimportant status of the western Delta in Egyptian eyes, and the rise of dynasties of Libyan origin (Twenty-second, Twenty-third, Twenty-fourth) in the Third Intermediate Period. Even in the later Twentieth Dynasty the roving bands of 'desert-dwellers' (*ḫꜣstyw*; sometimes specifically identified as Libu and Mashwash) which disturbed the Theban area may have been infiltrators as much as unruly soldiery. The importance of the Mashwash centres of the Delta during the Third Intermediate Period was partially derived from the military colonies of freed(?) Libyan prisoners of war set up in the Twentieth and perhaps Nineteenth dynasties but probably also from continuing immigration. The western Delta appears to have sustained a fresh wave of Libu immigration during the latter part of this period. The military clash between Psammetichus I and the Tjehenu (*c.* 654 BC) who occupied the western edge of the Nile Valley from Oxyrhynchus to the sea, while stated to have been caused by a Libyan invasion, is highly reminiscent of New Kingdom efforts to remove long-established infiltrators in that zone.

# APPENDIX

## THE TOPONYMS OF NUBIA AND OF CONTIGUOUS REGIONS IN THE NEW KINGDOM

To understand Egyptian relations with Nubia and contiguous regions in the New Kingdom, it is necessary to map as accurately as possible the toponyms of these areas referred to in Egyptian texts. The problems of the data are serious, but the results of the attempt are significant if tentative.

### THE ENVIRONMENTAL CONTEXT

The mapping of the toponyms is inextricably related to the environmentally created patterns of population density and distribution, and of ways of subsistence, existing in the New Kingdom. In broad terms these patterns were similar to those of today, the chief area of ambiguity being the location of the frontier between desert and semidesert zones. In southern Egypt and the northern Sudan today this frontier runs parallel to the Red Sea coast, roughly 150 km inland until latitude 19°N, whence it sweeps from east to west across the northern Sudan, dropping to about latitude 16°N (Barbour 1961, p. 65, fig. 28).

Because of the constraints of the variable carrying capacities of different sections of the Nile Valley, the riverine population of Lower and Upper Nubia, while numerically smaller than the modern one (Trigger 1965, p. 160), must have paralleled it in relative density and distribution patterns (Barbour 1961, pp. 133–41). The distribution of archaeological sites confirms that a relatively large, dense population in Lower Nubia was succeeded by a marked decrease between the Second and Third Cataracts; and that the Upper Nubian

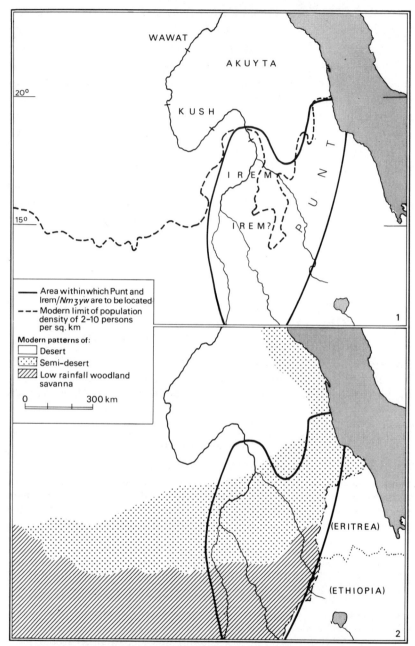

Fig. 12.27 Map illustrating data relevant to the discussion of the location of Irem.
(See Barbour 1964, figs. 28, 31.)

population, certainly larger than that of Lower Nubia, was followed by a very slight population in the extremely harsh terrain between the Fourth and Fifth Cataracts. Further south the valley between Berber and Shendi was perhaps in the past as it is now, 'the most populous portion of the Northern Sudan' (Barbour 1961, p. 135). Most of these riverine Nubians from the First Cataract to Shendi were presumably agriculturists, unless more favourable environmental conditions east and west of the Nile encouraged a significant degree of hunting and gathering or of cattle-raising.

However, the weight of the available evidence, while not decisive, strongly suggests that in the New Kingdom the frontier between desert and semidesert approximated closely to that of today. New Kingdom Egypt itself lay in an arid zone (Butzer 1976, pp. 26–7). Archaeologically no significant extensions of settlement into the bordering desert regions of Lower and Upper Nubia (the latter admittedly less well explored archaeologically) have been found. Early Nineteenth Dynasty texts (1303–1224 BC) (see the Kubban stele of Ramesses II, Breasted 1906, III ss 286, 289–93) refer explicitly to the marked aridity of the gold-mining areas of the eastern Nubian desert, meaning at the least those running along latitude 22°N and possibly others as far south as latitude 21–20°N.[1] During the Second Intermediate Period (1700–1552 BC) faunal material characteristic of a savanna environment accumulated at Kerma, on the Nile at about latitude 19°N (fig. 12.19), but the fauna represented was probably not indigenous to the area, and was located further south.[2]

We should therefore postulate that *away* from the Nile the regional population and subsistence patterns were similar to today's. Substantial nomadic groups would have stretched away to the west through northern Kordofan (Barbour 1961, pp. 169–71), but north of latitude 17°N the western desert would be virtually uninhabited. On the east a significant nomadic population would have occupied the Butana between the Nile and the Atbara,

[1] The location of a well of Ramesses II has been found in the Wadi el-Allaqi some 60 km east of the Nile; see Piotrovsky (1967). However, the ultimate destination of the Egyptian expeditions were presumably the main gold-mining areas, some 350 km to the east and south-east (see fig. 19.2).

[2] On the date and nature of the Kerma cemetery, see ch. 10. Given Kerma's intermediate geographical position and the expansive nature of the Kushite community, the materials reflecting a savanna environment may well be derived via trade with regions further south, and knowledge of savanna fauna gained by trading expeditions. The evidence available suggests that these are reasonable interpretations. At Kerma, ivory and ostrich feathers were common throughout the Second Intermediate Period graves (Reisner 1923, pts IV–V, pp. 248–271, 301, 315–17) but these were normal trade items in the Egypto-Nubian world. Actual depictions of elephants were rare and small scale (Reisner 1923, pts IV–V, pp. 265, 267). Rhinoceri, typical of a savanna environment, were also rarely depicted (twice; Reisner 1923, pts IV–V, pp. 268, 311). Giraffes – particularly significant savanna animals (Hilzheimer 1932) – were depicted in some numbers in two Kerma 'funerary chapels' (KII, KXI; Reisner 1923, pts I–III, pp. 124, 263–264), but other depictions as well as artifacts made of giraffe hair were rare (Reisner 1923, pts IV–V, pp. 268, 273, 313–15). Moreover, material relevant to giraffes is unusually restricted – to chapels KII and KXI, and 'great tumuli' KX, KIV and KIII; these all belong to the latest and most *expansive* phase of Kushite activity, suggesting it was only then that the Kushites came into sustained contact with the giraffe and perhaps assigned it a symbolic value reflected in its depictions in the chapels. Later, when the Egyptians controlled Upper Nubia, giraffes were imported into Egypt rarely and in small numbers (Brunner-Traut 1976), again suggesting that Upper Nubia lay north of the semidesert/savanna zones.

and stretched over to the Red Sea coast; from thence northwards nomads would occur in ever-diminishing numbers through the Red Sea Hills as far north as latitude 26–27°N (Barbour 1961, pp. 218, 226–8). The desert immediately east of Upper and Lower Nubia was uninhabited (fig. 12.27).

### THE NEW KINGDOM 'MAP' OF NUBIA AND CONTIGUOUS REGIONS

No actual 'map' has survived,[1] but other important data have. Unfortunately, these data were scattered[2] and are unusually difficult to work with. For example, the activities of New Kingdom Egyptian rulers in Syria and Palestine can be followed in some detail, because many of the toponyms referred to in Egyptian texts can be located topographically through more circumstantial cuneiform and Hebrew sources, supplemented by considerable archaeological activity (Aharoni 1968). By contrast, the only contemporary written sources on African toponyms are Egyptian (although later Meroitic, Greek and Latin texts do preserve some toponyms of great antiquity) and most toponyms were located in areas poorly explored archaeologically. Survey and excavation have been limited in Upper Nubia and – for this time-period – very slight or non-existent in contiguous regions. It is therefore not surprising that comprehensive efforts to reconstruct the New Kingdom 'map' have been highly tentative and had sometimes irreconcilably different results (compare, for example, the 'mapping' of Priese (1974) and Zhylarz (1958)).

The chief data available for mapping New Kingdom Africa are:

(1) Lists of African toponyms. Like those of Asiatic toponyms, these lists occur in temples, on wall-faces, columns, stelae and statuary. Their purpose is to document the universal dominion of the king, and they are usually either without introduction or are introduced by a generalized reference to royal victories, rarely to a specific campaign. They vary in size, typically being fairly or quite short, but a few contain as many as a hundred or more entries. Examples are preserved from all New Kingdom dynasties (Zibelius 1972, pp. 19–49).

(2) References to African toponyms in texts describing a specific activity such as a military campaign or a trading expedition.

(3) Textual references to a toponym which appear to be located in the region of that toponym. Examples are rare and uncertain.[3]

Of these data the first two categories are the most important, the lists providing by far the most toponyms, but being virtually useless topographically without the complementary information provided by the second category.

For our purposes the most important list is one of the earliest and most extensive, that of Tuthmosis III.[4] In compiling this list Tuthmosis' scribes

---

[1] But may have existed! The Egyptians were capable of preparing detailed sketch maps of large areas. See Goyon (1949).

[2] The relevant data are now collected and systematically described in Zibelius (1972).

[3] This does not refer to the names of *Egyptian* centres in Nubia; these are sometimes referred to frequently in *in situ* inscriptions. But these Egyptian-centre toponyms are not included in the lists of indigenous African toponyms.

[4] Strictly speaking, this 'list' is made up of four lists. Three are largely duplicates and are located on the following pylons at Karnak; west front of the 6th, south-west facade of the 7th, north-east

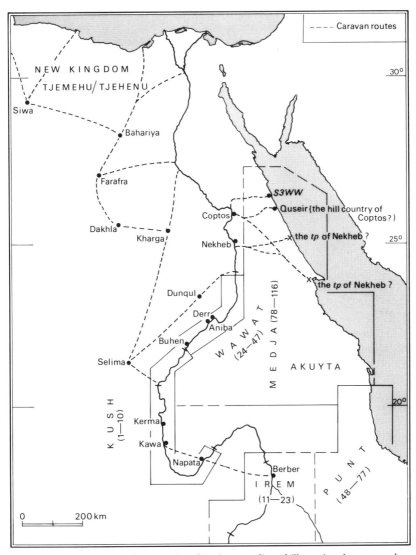

Fig. 12.28   Map giving places mentioned in the appendix and illustrating the suggested
coverage of the Tuthmosis III list (to which the numbers refer).

facade of the 7th. The fourth, a list of toponyms not found for the most part in the other three,
is also on the north-east facade of the 7th pylon (Zibelius 1972, VAa 90, 100, 110, pp. 20–1). This
fourth list is *not* under consideration here. The toponyms it contains are for the most part unattested
elsewhere.

apparently drew not only upon contemporary New Kingdom but also earlier Middle and Old Kingdom material (Priese 1974, Zibelius 1972, p. 21), possibly to provide the number of names required for aesthetic and symbolic purposes.[1] Despite this mixture of contemporary and archaic names, I believe it is possible to argue that the toponyms of the Tuthmoside list were arranged in a geographicaly coherent order. First, toponyms (nos. 1–23)[2] running from north to south through Upper Nubia, and perhaps further upstream, were listed; then followed toponyms of Lower Nubia in a north–south sequence (nos. 24–47). The next section of the list (nos. 48–77) covers the region between the Red Sea and the Nile and between, roughly, latitude 12–20°N. The list (nos. 78–116) then moves northwards into the deserts and Red Sea coastline, first east of Lower Nubia and then of southern Egypt, finally termininating at about latitude 27°N, or even at Sinai (fig. 12.28).[3]

These conclusions are based on the following points.

(1) The list begins with the toponym Kush (no. 1) which is followed at intervals by Wawat (no. 24), Punt (no. 48) and Medja (no. 78). These well-known names can, in this context, be interpreted in two ways. We can treat each as Posener (1958a; see also Priese 1974) does Kush specifically in this list as 'a general designation, a kind of heading for the following series of names' and regard the list as successively presenting toponyms of Kush (Upper Nubia (and beyond?)), Wawat (Lower Nubia), the Puntite region and Medja (eastern desert). Alternatively, each of the four toponyms may refer to the original, smaller region to which the toponym was applied before it gained a broader geographical meaning (Posener 1958a). In this case also, the occurrence of each toponym also marks a significant geographical shift in the list. Kush and Wawat, in their more restricted senses, were the northernmost toponyms of Upper and Lower Nubia respectively; Punt proper was the coastal zone encountered by the Egyptians before they penetrated inland; and Medja originally referred to the eastern desert closest to the Lower Nubian and Upper Egyptian Nile.

(2) The north–south ordering of what we may call the 'Kushite' toponyms is indicated by the positions of Miu (no. 4) and Irem (no. 11) in the list. Miu was the southernmost point of contact for King Kamose at the end of the Seventeenth Dynasty (Černý 1969); as he did not move far south of Buhen (fig. 12.19) (H. S. Smith 1976, p. 206), Miu must have lain between the Second and Third Cataracts. This location for Miu is further indicated by the fact that Miu persisted as a trouble-spot into the early reign of Tuthmosis III, but never appears as such thereafter, once Tuthmosis had established the Egyptian

---

[1] The first three lists referred to in n. 4 p. 928 were designed as aesthetic and symbolic African parallels to a list of 119 Asiatic toponyms accurately reflecting the campaign in year 22 of Tuthmosis III in Palestine and Lebanon. The fourth list was the aesthetic and symbolic African parallel to a new Asiatic (largely Syrian) list reflecting an Asiatic campaign of some years later. In each case the African lists had to represent an approximately similar number of names as the Asiatic, hence possibly the need for 'space-filling'.

[2] The numeration follows that of Sethe and Zibelius.

[3] Expeditions to Punt sometimes originated and terminated in Sinai (Yoyotte 1952). In this way toponyms along the Red Sea coast from Punt to Sinai might naturally be thought of as part of an 'African' list.

frontier at Napata, near the end of the Fourth Cataract. Irem however lay south of the Third, and possibly even beyond the Fifth cataract (see p. 934).

The Lower Nubian toponyms are presumed by analogy to have been listed in north–south order.

(3) Entry no. 64, Utjenet or Utenet, occurs amongst the toponyms listed between Punt and Medja and strongly supports the concept that this group represents Punt in its broader sense. Eighteenth Dynasty texts from Sinai (Černý, Gardiner and Peet 1955, pp. 173, 213) show that expeditions traveled inland through the hills of Punt to reach Utjenet, and that in Utjenet 'gum' could be cut from living trees and ebony obtained, both items being characteristic Puntite products.[1] The low position of Utjenet (seventeenth of thirty entries) and its inland position suggests here an ordering from coast to interior.

(4) The toponyms following Medja are the most problematical, but the weight of the evidence suggests the list is moving through the eastern desert – north of Punt – and northwards along the Red Sea coast. Nos. 85, Zetjau, and 88, Tjehenu, appear to refer to Lower Nubia and Libya respectively,[2] but against this we may note the following. No. 84 is possibly a variant writing of a toponym associated with Medja (eastern desert) nomads;[3] nos. 89 and 95, according to an Eighteenth Dynasty text, were probably on the Red Sea coast in a region occupied by Nehasyu ('Nubians, southerners');[4] and no. 91, Tep Nekheb, suggests a place on the Red Sea coast linked by a desert route to Nekheb, a town of southern Egypt.[5] Finally, near the end of the list occurs Saw, no. 111, tentatively identified with Sawaw, a Red Sea port north of latitude 26°N (fig. 12.28).[6]

The other lists of the New Kingdom are not as comprehensive as that of Tuthmosis III, but many of the Tuthmoside toponyms recur (fig. 12.29). The selectivity of the later lists suggests that their compilers read the 'map' inherent in Tuthmosis' list much as I have interpreted it here (fig. 12.29); certain groups

---

[1] The 'gum' is *ḳmyt*, mentioned as a Puntite product in Hatshepsut's reign (Sethe 1906, p. 329).

[2] By the reign of Tuthmosis III Zetjau was an extremely archaic term, and so its exact geographical significance may have been lost; on the other hand, its original significance may have covered more than a section of the valley and extended into the eastern desert, although there is no proof for this. On Zetjau, see the literature cited by Zibelius (1972, pp. 153, under *sẕtw*). However, Tjehenu in the New Kingdom certainly referred to Libya (Gardiner 1947, vol. I, pp. 116*–119*), and its appearance here may be simply thoughtless space-filling. However, there was a Nubian toponym which was originally read by Egyptologists as Tehenut (to be read Tjehenut; Gardiner 1947, vol. I, 114* textual note, 116* textual note); this reading has now been corrected to Tekhet, a well-known New Kingdom toponym of Lower Nubia (Zibelius 1972, pp. 180–1, under *tḫnt* and *tḫḫt*). Is is possible that the Tuthmoside scribes misread Tekhet as Tjehenu?

[3] I.e. no. 84, *iš*; see New Kingdom *iwršk*, *wrš[k]*, equated with the Medja-occupied toponym *ẕwšk* of the Middle Kingdom (Priese 1974).

[4] No, 89, *ḥct(ḥr)* and no. 95, *ḫẕst*; referred to as contemporary Eighteenth Dynasty toponyms, apparently occupied by Nehasyu in Helck, (1957, 1734, 5, 15; 1735, 1, 2, 13, 17; 1736, 3.6; see also Helck, 1961, p. 233; Breasted 1906, ss. 846–50; Zibelius 1972, pp. 145–6, 149).

[5] As a suggestive although not identical parallel see the reference to a Red Sea landing-place (Quseir, or Middle Kingdom *Sẕww?*) as the 'desert-country (*ḫẕst*) of Coptos' (Kitchen 1971).

[6] Gauthier (1922–31, vol. v, pp. 3, 6). For a similar, although not identical, geographical interpretation of the Tuthmosis III list, see Priese (1974).

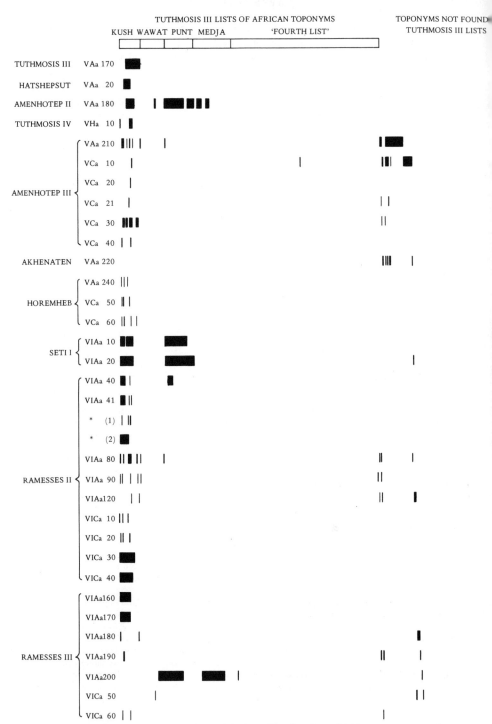

Fig. 12.29  Diagrammatic comparison of the New Kingdom lists of African toponyms, as they relate to the African lists of Tuthmosis III. All are documented in Zibelius (1972) and are assigned her identifying symbols except *(1) and *(2). For these see Kitchen (1968–70, fasc. 3, p. 169).

of toponyms – corresponding to geographical entities – were regularly included and other groups consistently omitted. Explanations for this selectivity can only be tentative.

Toponyms from Wawat (Lower Nubia) rarely recur, perhaps because Wawat became so stable and acculturated that it lost the character of a frontier province and was no longer regarded as 'foreign' or, at least, troublesome. Kushite toponyms are regularly included in all compilations, except in the probably incomplete example of Amenhotep IV and the longest intact list of Ramesses III. This frequent recurrence presumably reflects Kush's character as the frontier province and perhaps (cf. pp. 934–40) the inclusion under the rubric of Kush of regions not under firm Egyptian control; had the region as a whole become so stable under Ramesses III that it was omitted from his major list?

Puntite toponyms were regularly included in all the longer lists, reflecting the fact that remote Punt remained culturally exotic and was never – despite frequent contacts – ever under close Egyptian control. The toponyms of Medja and the Red Sea coast do not recur between the earlier Eighteenth Dynasty and Ramesses III, suggesting that this region was not regarded as a major trouble-spot throughout the New Kingdom; even its inclusion in the Ramesses III list of some 'Medja' toponyms may be due to a misunderstanding.[1]

Thirty-four of the New Kingdom lists repeat toponyms from the Tuthmoside list (fig. 12.29). Of these two are of uncertain sequence, and sixteen contain too few toponyms reliably to indicate adherence to a consistent sequence.[2] Of the remaining sixteen, thirteen reproduce closely the toponymical sequencing of the Tuthmoside list.[3] This strongly suggests that the 'map' of Kush and Punt at least remained stable throughout the New Kingdom. The significance of this sequencing is reinforced by the fact that the later New Kingdom lists are not blindly traditionalistic copies. Orthography was sometimes changed in accord with the practices of the later New Kingdom (Zibelius 1972) and a number of the listed toponyms are also referred to in post-Tuthmosis III texts about specific military and trading activities.[4] It should also be noted that groups of new toponyms were periodically added to the corpus (fig. 12.29), particularly under Amenhotep III, but also under Ramesses II and Ramesses III. These additions presumably reflected contacts with new African groups or the increased importance of hitherto less significant regions.

[1] Ramesses III was involved in major conflicts with the Libyans, and his scribes presumably understood the occurrence of 'Tjehenu' in a list of Tuthmosis III (or of another king, but identical in content) as indicating that the following toponyms were from Libya. These toponyms may however include toponyms of the eastern desert and Red Sea coast, see n. 4 on p. 931. A similar – although not totally identical – set of confusions on the part of the scribes of Ramesses III is evident in Edgerton and Wilson (1936, p. 88). There *Libyan* captives are allotted toponyms from the African list; nos. 46, 47 of the Tuthmosis III list immediately precede Punt therein, no. 48 is Punt itself, and nos. 89, 90, 93 and 94 follow Tjehenu.

[2] Zibelius (1972, VAa 180, 210 (uncertain sequence); VAa 240; VCa 10, 20, 21, 40, 60; VHa 10; VIAa 120, 180, 190; VICa 10, 20, 50, 60; VIF) and Kitchen (1968–1970, vol. II, fasc. 3, p. 169, 5–9).

[3] The exceptions are Zibelius (1972), nos. VCa 30, VIAa 80, 90.

[4] See for example, Zibelius (1972, pp. 33 (VDa 120), 36 (VDb 140, 160), 39 (VHa 50), 48 (VIBb 10, 20), 49 (VIDa 5), 51 (VIDa 70), 53 (VIF 40)); also Kitchen (1975–6).

## THE LOCATION OF IREM (see fig. 12.27)

Irem, the eleventh toponym on the list of Tuthmosis III, was of special importance to the New Kingdom Egyptians. Apart from the toponym 'Kush' itself, no other Kushite toponym is referred to as frequently as Irem in texts of specific historical contact,[1] and indeed Irem seems gradually to replace the northernmost toponyms of Kush as the major trouble-spot creating concern for the Egyptians. Wawat (Lower Nubia) itself was the major concern at the end of the Seventeenth Dynasty (see chapter 10), and the northern Kushite region of Miu still required repression in the early reign of Tuthmosis III (Redford 1967, p. 61). Subsequently, there are indications that Horemheb campaigned against three toponyms (nos. 3, 5 and 9)[2] which occur before Irem in the lists and were presumably north of it. Irem itself is referred to as early as Hatshepsut's reign (Zibelius 1972, VAa 10) but the first clearly hostile reference occurs under Amenhotep III, who campaigned against Irem and another toponym (no. 13)[3] which was, according to its listed position, geographically near Irem. Subsequently Seti I (Vercoutter 1972), possibly Ramesses II (Fairman 1948), and certainly Ramesses III (Zibelius 1972, p. 49, VIDa 5) engaged in hostilities with Irem, Ramesses III also campaigning against a toponym geographically near Irem (no. 12 on the list) and another, no. 21, much lower on the list and presumably further south.[4]

The importance of Irem in the New Kingdom is also indicated by its frequent occurrence in lists including Kushite toponyms (Priese 1974). In general, Irem is the most frequently occurring toponym after Kush itself. In short lists, for which one may assume toponyms of special importance were chosen, toponyms nos. 2 and 4 ('northern' Kushite toponyms) and 11 (Irem) all rank as the second most frequently occurring toponyms after 'Kush' (no. 1).

The location of Irem is therefore of considerable historical importance and we are faced with two alternatives, each with a significant but different set of historical implications. The first is that Irem was essentially a riverine region, located somewhere between the Third and Fourth Cataracts, i.e. in Upper Nubia. The second is that Irem lay south of the Fifth cataract and included not only a section of the Nile Valley, but also semi-arid or even savanna lands east of the Nile.

The most detailed and convincing case for the first alternative has been argued by Priese (1974). However, none of the evidence he cites is irreconcilable with the second alternative,[5] and he fails to give sufficient attention to three

[1] Zibelius (1972, pp. 19 (VAa 10), 20 (VAa 80), 49 (VIDa 5), 51 (VIDa 70), 53 (VIF 40)); Kitchen (1975–6).

[2] Slaying of prisoners from the three toponyms, depicted on 10th pylon, Karnak (Zibelius 1972, pp. 24, VAa 240). the numbers cited here and later refer to the Tuthmosis list, see n. 4 on p. 928 above.

[3] In his fifth regnal year Amenhotep III subdued a Kushite rebellion; amongst the symbolically represented rebels was Irem (Zibelius 1972, p. 33, VDa 90, 100).

[4] Zibelius (1972, pp. 45–6, VIAa 180), wherein the third captured chief should probably be restored 'the Nehasyu [Irem]'.

[5] Priese's strongest point is that New Kingdom Irem is probably the same toponym as Old Kingdom Yam, for which there are good arguments for a location near Kerma in Upper Nubia;

points which seem to tip the weight of probability to the second alternative.

Firstly, scenes and texts in Hapshepsut's funerary temple at Deir el-Bahari juxtapose the toponyms Irem, *Nmȝyw* and Punt. Priese (1974, p. 19–21) argues that this is not geographically significant and that the relevant material refers to two *separate* events, namely trading with the coastal land of Punt and exacting tribute from the riverine territory of Irem. However, in my opinion the arrangement of the relevant scenes at Deir el-Bahari and the logic of the narrative that flows through them[1] both show that Punt, *Nmȝyw* and Irem adjoined and were part of a geographical continuum that could not have existed north of the latitude of the Fifth Cataract. It has been convincingly argued that Punt was 'located in the E. Sudan bordering on Ethiopia, from the White and Blue Niles eastward to the Red Sea/Eritrean highlands, and north–south between Berber and Roseires (about the 17th to 12th N. parallels of latitude) ...Punt [also extended] to the coast (approximately Port Sudan to N. Eritrea)' (Kitchen 1971; see also Herzog 1968). I believe that Irem and *Nmȝyw* are also to be located in this region, in its north-western segment and without any direct access to the coast; it seems unlikely that Irem and *Nmȝyw* extended downstream of the Fifth Cataract or northward into the arid deserts lying east of Lower and Upper Nubia.

In the Deir el-Bahari reliefs (the essential data from which is presented schematically in fig. 12.30) the products of Irem/*Nmȝyw* tend to be associated with the upper registers and those of Punt with the lower. This is particularly clear – with some restorations – in the contrast between VIIIa (explicitly Irem/*Nmȝyw*) and b (explicitly Punt); but is evident also in the contrasts between IVa, b, c (inferentially Irem/*Nmȝyw*) and IVc, d (inferentially Punt), IIIa, b (explicitly Punt) and again, in the contrast between XI/XII, representing 'the *bȝkw* (trade-goods?)[2] of the southern countries' (inferentially Irem/*Nmȝyw* and, in this section only, of other southern lands) and IX/X (explicitly Punt). There is in fact an interwoven pattern of both absolute and relative differences and similarities between Punt and Irem/*Nmȝyw* which may be summarized as follows (cf. fig. 12.30.2 and table p. 938).

While the historical references to Irem seem to indicate clearly that part of it lay in the Nile Valley,[3] the presence of rhinoceri, giraffes, panthers and cheetahs shows that Irem/*Nmȝyw* must have included substantial amounts of semidesert and even – to judge from the wooded landscape associated with

see pp. 34–8. But need that particular toponym have referred to the same *location* in the New Kingdom, over seven hundred years later? Priese's other points do not necessarily fix the location of Irem in the New Kingdom or later in Upper Nubia (e.g. the ownership of Kawa temple of lands in *Mrkr*, no. 19 of the Tuthmosis list, and of men from Irem, p. 9–12) or are based on highly tentative arguments (e.g. equating toponyms of the Tuthmosis list with modern place names, p. 17).

[1] On the subtlety of the narrative treatment in the Deir el-Bahari material see W. S. Smith (1965, pp. 137–9).

[2] On the meanings of *bȝkw* see Lorton (1974, pp. 90–104).

[3] The 3300 long-horned cattle recorded as tribute in X/XII (Naville 1898, pl. LXXX), may have come from Irem, but not as a result of the combined expedition to Punt, Irem and *Nmȝyw* recorded in I–VII; the difficulties of shipping would seem insuperable. Scenes XI and XII appear to cover the results of several expeditions to various southern lands, carried out at different times.

Recording the products at
Thebes
Products of Irem/Nm 3yw

Missing areas

XII

XI | a | b | c | d |

X

IX

Products of Punt

Presentation of products

IV | a | Collecting in Irem
   | b |
   | c | Collecting in Punt
   | d |

VII
a Products of Irem/Nm 3yw
b Products of Punt

V
Loading vessels

VI
Voyage to Egypt

III | a | Trading with
    | b | Puntites

II
Mooring, disembarking

I
Voyage to Punt

936

Fig. 12.30  1  The general narrative scheme of the 'Punt reliefs' of Hatshepsut at Deir el-Bahari    2  The products of Punt and Irem/Nmȝyw as arranged in the 'Punt-relief' of Hatshepsut (cf. Naville 1898, pls. LXIX–LXXI, W. S. Smith 1965, figs. 173–4).

| Irem/N*mẓyw* | Common to Irem/N*mẓyw* and Punt | Punt |
|---|---|---|
| *Products* (see Kitchen 1971) | | |
| long-horned cattle | | |
| rhinoceri | | |
| giraffes | | |
| living panthers } skins | | (panther and/or |
| living cheetahs | | cheetah skins) |
| (highly characteristic) | gold | (some) |
| (highly characteristic?) | ebony | (some) |
| (some?) | *cntyw* incense | (highly characteristic) |
| | throwing sticks | (characteristic) |
| | | *msdmt* eye-paint |
| | | ivory |
| | | short-horned cattle |
| *Environment* | | |
| | | sea-shore (cf. II |
| | | and III; IV c, d and V) |
| uniformly | wooded or scrubby | uniformly |
| | landscape (cf. | |
| | IV a–d) | |
| *Pile huts* | | |
| | both (cf. IV b, c; | |
| | III a, b) | |
| *Inhabitants* | | |
| 'Nubian' type(s) (cf. | | 'Puntite' type(s) (cf. |
| IV a, b; VII a) | | III a, b; IV c, d; |
| | | VII, b) |
| distinctive types of dress, | | distinctive types of |
| ornamentation | | dress, ornamentation |

Irem/N*mẓyw* – savanna territory (fig. 12.27). It has been argued above (pp. 925–8) that such environments would not be found north of latitudes 19 or 18°N in the New Kingdom. Moreover, ebony trees and possibly *cntyw* incense trees grew in Irem/N*mẓyw*; the former are not attested north of latitudes 14–15°N and the chief reported areas for the latter lie south of latitudes 15–16°N. While *cntyw* incense trees may occur as far north as latitude 22°N, they are confined then to the coastal plain and hills, and would not extend through the desert separating these features from the Nile Valley (see Kitchen 1971).

Of course, it may be argued that it is N*mẓyw* only that has these features.[1] However, the Deir el-Bahari material does not distinguish the products of Irem from those of N*mẓyw*[2] and N*mẓyw* seems to have been comparatively insignificant, since it is hardly ever referred to in the New Kingdom (Zibelius 1972, p. 139). N*mẓyw* may be identical with the more frequently occuring *cmw* (Zibelius 1972, p. 139), but the latter probably extended from the river

[1] Priese, for example, argues that N*mẓyw* may represent people who lived outside of the area under direct Egyptian control (Priese 1974, p. 21).

[2] Thus in fig. 12.27 in VII a the chiefs of Irem and N*mẓyw* are distinguished from each other, but not the products of these two regions.

eastwards towards the coast along latitude 19°N[1] and lay therefore in an arid or semi-arid zone which would have been the northern fringe of the kind of environment indicated for Irem/*Nmȝyw* by the Deir el-Bahari material.

It is also significant for Irem's location that Seti I campaigned against it with chariots, not ships (surely the more natural means if Irem lay in Upper Nubia) and his capture of a series of wells suggests a strike across the Bayuda desert via the chain of waterholes running from the Napata region towards Berber and Atbara via Khor Abu Dom (fig. 12.19) (Vercoutter 1972). It is also suggestive that Irem is on occasion linked with eastern-desert toponyms – Medja (cf. Zibelius 1972, p. 22, VAa 180), *Wrš* (?) (cf. Zibelius 1972, p. 33, VDa 100), and Akuyta (cf. Kitchen 1975–6) – indicating that Irem had a significant semi-desert component lying south of these essentially desert regions.

Secondly, if Irem lay within Upper Nubia, the fact that it engaged in hostilities with Egyptian forces under Amenhotep III, Seti I, Ramesses II(?) and Ramesses III suggests that the province of Upper Nubia, despite its frontier at Napata and Karoy (Fourth to Fifth Cataracts), was inherently an unstable one, periodically breaking out into serious revolts. This assumption does not fit well with the weakly defended character of known Third Cataract Egyptian centres occupied from the later Eighteenth through to the Twentieth Dynasties (Kemp 1972b), or with the scattered Egyptian centres – Sai, Kawa, Tabo and Napata – already located in archaeologically poorly-explored Upper Nubia.

Thirdly, Egyptian textual references to regions lying south of Egypt – particularly along the Nile Valley – followed a characteristic pattern. These references focused not so much upon those regions which were under firm Egyptian control as on those which lay beyond the established frontier. With regions immediately beyond the frontier, Egypt developed a complex set of periodically amiable (trading), periodically hostile relations. In a quest for security and increased economic opportunities Egypt was impelled to venture beyond the frontier – indeed, to attempt to establish a new frontier – and hence the immediately extramural regions became of paramount concern and interest. These regions in turn were resistant to Egyptian pressure and probably found the nearby, relatively pacific Egyptian-controlled province a tempting target for raids.

Thus, from the late Old Kingdom down to the early Eleventh Dynasty, when Lower Nubia was the tempting – and threatening – zone just beyond the

[1] Zibelius, (1972, p. 99, under '*cm*, *cmm*'). Since the Puntites supplied Hatshepsut with gold of '*mw* I would not only agree with Säve-Söderbergh (1941, pp. 212–13), that '*mw* lay 'outside of the Nubian administrative district', but I would also argue that '*mw* must have included regions running some distance east of the Nile along latitude 19°N or south of it, since it seems unlikely that the Puntites would be drawing gold from as far away as the Nile Valley proper. Vercoutter's (1959) argument that a gold-mine list of Ramesses II placing the mines of '*mw* between those of Jebel Barkal/Napata and those of Kush necessarily locates '*mw* in the Upper Nubian Valley need not be accepted because it is based on an assumption that a Third Cataract graffito referring to '*mw* necessarily locates it there. The graffito may be that of a traveller *from* '*mw* passing through the Third Cataract. The Jebel Barkal mines are probably those of the Fourth Cataract–Abu Hamed area, in which case '*mw* may well refer to those ancient mines known to stretch eastward from there in the direction of Punt (fig. 12.19.2). Posener (1977) has recently suggested that '*mw* lay in the deserts east of Upper Nubia. But again he depends heavily upon the Third Cataract graffito to reach this conclusion.

frontier, Egyptian textual references are concerned primarily with Wawat and its sub-regions. After the reconquest of Lower Nubia, Kush (Upper Nubia) becomes the focus of Egyptian military and trading activity throughout the Middle Kingdom, although it probably never came under permanent Egyptian control. Wawat was lost during the Second Intermediate Period and reconquered at the end of the Seventeenth Dynasty (see chapter 10). Kush and the toponyms of Upper Nubia are the cited targets of Eighteenth Dynasty activity, but after the establishment of a frontier at Napata, Irem begins to emerge as the principal concern of the Egyptians in the south. In the Nineteenth and Twentieth Dynasties Irem and contiguous toponyms are in fact the foci of Egyptian textual references, to the exclusion of all others. Does not this suggest that it was Irem which from the later Eighteenth Dynasty on typified the southern regions *beyond* the frontier at Napata? In view of the population pattern suggested above (pp. 927–8) Irem – a significant power – could not have been located north of the Fifth Cataract. In its broadest sense[1] Irem then would equate with the populous Berber–Shendi stretch and extend eastward into the Butana and across to the Atbara and the borders of Punt.

### POSTSCRIPT

Since this appendix was written, Kitchen has discussed the location of 'part of Irem...and not necessarily the whole of it' in the Nineteenth Dynasty, and suggested that this 'part' lay west of the Nile about the latitude of Kerma in Upper Nubia (Kitchen 1977). However, in view of the other evidence about Irem discussed in the appendix, I still prefer to see the campaign of Seti I against Irem (with which Kitchen deals) as occurring in the Bayuda desert, south and south-east of Upper Nubia, and Irem therefore as located south of Upper Nubia. Kemp has accepted Priese's suggested location for Irem in Upper Nubia (Kemp 1977), but as noted in the appendix, there are in my opinion serious objections to Priese's case. It should be noted that Kemp has also convincingly suggested that Miu was located in the Berber–Shendi region, which would involve a reconsideration of the structure of the toponymical lists discussed above; nevertheless, this does not affect my arguments for the location of Irem.

[2] I.e., used as a broad regional designation, like Kush, subsuming other toponyms which in more detailed lists or references might be specifically mentioned *alongside* Irem.

# BIBLIOGRAPHICAL ESSAYS

### I. THE PALAEO-ECOLOGY OF THE AFRICAN CONTINENT

Although the ancient Egyptians explored the northern part of Africa and traded with West Africa, knowledge of the interior of the continent was scanty. The Greek school at Alexandria gathered important records and it was there that Eratosthenes, about 2000 BC, made the first scientific measurement of the circumference of the earth. It was also in Alexandria that Ptolemy, around AD 150, developed his famous map of the known world, although it has survived only in Arabic and mediaeval versions of his *Geographia*. Ptolemy's map served as the base for the Arab explorers of the seventh to fourteenth centuries and was modified during the fifteenth and sixteenth centuries as the whole southern coastline became defined. However, details shown in the interior in these early maps are highly speculative and it was not until the middle of the last century that scientific exploration began to reveal a true picture of the interior. The growth of cartography is conveniently considered in Tooley and Bricker (1969) and the progress of exploration presented in maps by Fage (1963). Even in the final decades of the nineteenth century, large areas of the continent were almost unknown and in his classic *Das Antlitz der Erde* Suess (1885–1901) drew heavily on travellers' reports for the geology of some portions of the continent and had to omit many regions for lack of data. The first government geological survey was only established in 1895 (at the Cape), but mineral exploration led to rapid growth of geological knowledge and the 1920s saw the appearance of several important regional studies, such as Gregory (1921) on East Africa and the rift valleys, du Toit (1926) on South Africa, and the first systematic geology of the whole continent by Krenkel (1925, 1928). The blank areas were slowly filled in and international co-operation led to the publication of the 1 : 5 000 000 scale *Carte géologique internationale de l'Afrique* between 1938 and 1952; a revised version appeared in 1964, a tectonic map in 1968 with an explanation (1971), and a mineral map in 1968, all under the auspices of UNESCO. Krenkel's synthesis has been replaced by a shorter, but very useful, book by Furon (1950, 1960, 1963). The whole status of scientific research in Africa south of the Sahara was examined by Worthington (1938) as part of the overall analysis by Hailey (1938, 1957) of the impact of economic and social development in this region. The natural resources of the continent have also been reviewed by UNESCO (1963, 1970). A summary of the vegetation has been presented in a map and explanation by Keay (1959) for sub-Saharan Africa, and one for the whole continent is nearing completion by UNESCO. The climate has been analysed in a series of maps by Jackson (1961) and by Thompson (1965). Regional geomorphological studies have been undertaken and a continent-wide synthesis made by King (1967), although it is oversimplified in many respects. Largely because of interest in human origins, superficial deposits have received special attention and there is an extensive literature on fossil mammals, for which two comprehensive bibliographies are available (Cross and Maglio 1975; Hopwood and Hollyfield 1954) and reviews by Cooke (1972) and by Coryndon and Savage (1973). On the hominoid fossils and their environments there is a very large volume of literature. Both Dart (1959) and Broom (1950) have written their own accounts of the discovery of australopithecines, while S. Cole (1975) has recounted the story of the Leakeys' work in East Africa. Several volumes containing papers from conferences organized by the Wenner–Gren Foundation for Anthropological Research serve to provide new data and critical reviews of background material relating to early man in Africa, especially Howell and Bourlière (1963), Bishop and Clark (1967), Bishop and Miller (1972), Butzer and Isaac (1975), Coppens et al. (1976) and Jolly (1978).

## 2. ORIGINS AND EVOLUTION OF AFRICAN HOMINIDAE

The literature on human palaeontology and hominid evolution is extensive and widely dispersed in numerous serials. *Nature* (London) has continued to present initial reports of new discoveries, largely by English-speaking workers, as does the *Comptes rendus, Académie des Sciences, Paris,* largely by French-speaking investigators. The chapter itself contains many of the more important references relevant to African hominid palaeontology.

Some sites and their hominids have received monographic treatment. Olduvai Gorge is notable in this regard, an initial volume having been published under that title in 1951 (L. S. B. Leakey 1951), and three later volumes (with others in preparation) documenting subsequent research at that important locality (L. S. B. Leakey 1965, Tobias 1967a,

M. D. Leakey 1971). A similar volume on the geology of the locality has been written by Hay (1976). A number of monographs on the *Australopithecus*-bearing localities in South Africa have appeared as Memoirs of the Transvaal Museum, Pretoria. A monograph series on the Koobi Fora researches, east of Lake Rudolf is being published by Oxford University Press (M. G. Leakey and R. E. Leakey 1978). Monographic treatments of the Omo basin researches will appear through the Centre National de la Recherche Scientifique, Paris (palaeontological aspects) and the Musée royale de l'Afrique Centrale, Tervuren (geological aspects).

A series of important symposium volumes contain numerous contributions relevant to palaeo-anthropology, including hominid palaeontology, in Africa. They are: Howell (ed.) (1962), *Early man and Pleistocene stratigraphy in the circum-Mediterranean regions;* Howell and Bourlière (eds.) (1963), *African ecology and human evolution;* Bishop and Clark (eds.) (1967), *Background to evolution in Africa*; Bishop and Miller (eds.) (1972), *Calibration of hominoid evolution*; Butzer and Isaac (eds.) (1975), *After the australopithecines*; Coppens *et al.* (eds.) (1976), *Earliest man and environments in the Lake Rudolf basin;* Jolly (ed.) (1978), *Early hominids of Africa*; Isaac and McCown (eds.) (1976), *Human origins: Louis Leakey and the African evidence*; and Bishop (ed.) (1978), *Geological background to fossil man.*

## 3. THE EARLIEST ARCHAEOLOGICAL TRACES

### General

The best and most up-to-date general summary of African pre-history, including the Earlier Stone Age, is J. D. Clark's (1970) *Prehistory of Africa*. Aspects of the early archaeological record are also covered in Howell's (1965) *Early Man*, Bordes' (1968) *The Old Stone Age* and Coles and Higg's (1969) *The archaeology of Early Man*. These books also provide explanations of stone technology and of the terminology used to name artifact forms. Older classics, now out of date, include Burkitt's (1949) *The Old Stone Age*, L. S. B. Leakey's (1934) *Adam's ancestors* and Alimen's (1957) *Prehistory of Africa*.

### Chronology and palaeo-environments

Papers in Bishop and Miller's (1972) volume *Calibration of hominoid evolution* provide authoritative reviews of geochronological problems

943

and dates up to 1972. The methods themselves are well explained in Brothwell and Higgs's (1963) *Science in archaeology* and in Michels's (1973) *Dating methods in archaeology.*

The volume *After the australopithecines* edited by Butzer and Isaac (1975) provides detailed information on the Middle Pleistocene of Africa and elsewhere. Butzer's (1971) *Environment and archaeology* provides a good general review of palaeo-environmental reconstructions, and explanations of many of the methods involved.

### Early Stone Age diet

Dart (1949) and Ardrey (1961, 1976) forcefully posed questions regarding possible relationships between diet and the early prehistoric development of human behaviour, specifically they suggested that hunting had been an important and influential early human activity. L. S. B. Leakey (1963), J. D. Clark (1970, 1972), Isaac (1971), Isaac and Crader (in press), Freeman (in press) have reviewed the archaeological evidence relating to these propositions. Other discussions of this question can be found in Washburn and Moore (1974), Washburn and Lancaster (1968), Campbell (1976), Howell (1965), Zihlman and Tanner (1978), Jolly (1970), Klein (1977). The largest single corpus of good specific information is in M. D. Leakey's volume on Olduvai Gorge (1971).

There is a voluminous and complex literature dealing with the question of whether or not the Southern African australopithecines were meat-eaters; for a guide to this see Sampson (1974). Essays by Brain (1976) and by Vrba (1975) are important recent contributions to the resolution of this problem.

### The classification of Early Stone Age artifact assemblages

An excellent review of the early work, with references, is contained in Howell and Clark (1963). A discussion of the concepts involved in naming industries and of procedures is to be found in Kleindienst (1961) and in her paper for *Background to evolution in Africa*, edited by Bishop and Clark (1967). The appendix to that volume is also important in this connection.

Binford (1972) advocates a distinctive and unorthodox position. This and other interpretations are reviewed in Isaac (1972a).

944

## Geographic patterns

These are treated in various of the general works, already cited. The best introductions are those by J. D. Clark (1970, 1972). A major source is the *Atlas of African Prehistory*, which presents site distribution as of 1967 and also maps showing topography, drainage, climate, vegetation, etc.

## East Africa

The second edition of S. Cole's *Prehistory of East Africa* (1963) provides the best general account though much has been discovered since it appeared. The most important single monograph is M. D. Leakey's (1971) *Olduvai Gorge, vol. III: Excavations in Bed I and II*. Classic, but now outdated, works include L. S. B. Leakey (1931, 1935, 1951), van Riet Lowe (1952b) and O'Brien (1939).

Isaac (1969, 1975, 1976a, b, c) has presented several papers summarizing the early Stone Age record for the region.

A classic paper on the geology and palaeo-environments is Cooke's (1958) 'Observations relating to Quaternary environments in East and Southern Africa'. More recent summaries are to be found in Bishop (1971), in Isaac (1976a), and in many of the contributions to a volume entitled *Geological background to fossil man in East Africa*, edited by Bishop (1978). Short reports on pollen analysis and other palaeo-environmental studies are to be found in the successive volumes of *Palaeoecology of Africa* edited by Bakker (1966–80).

The volume *Earliest man and environments in the Lake Rudolf basin*, edited by Coppens *et al.* (1976) provides a varied set of interim reports on research at Omo and Koobi Fora. General reviews of archaeology, fossil hominids and palaeo-environments are included in a series of papers compiled as a tribute to the late Louis Leakey, edited by Isaac and McCown (1976).

The main references for the sites dealt with in the text are as follows. Chesowanja: Bishop, Pickford and Hill (1975), Harris and Bishop (1976), Harris and Herbich (1978). Gadeb: J. D. Clark and Kurashina (1976). Isimila: Hansen and Keller (1971), Howell (1961), Howell, Cole and Kleindienst (1962). Kalambo Falls: J. D. Clark (1964, 1969, 1974a). Kanam: S. Cole (1963), L. S. B. Leakey (1935). Kanyatsi: de Heinzelin (1961). Kapthurin: Margaret Leakey *et al.* (1969). Kariandusi: S. Cole (1963), Kleindienst (1961), L. S. B. Leakey (1931). Kilombe: Gowlett (1978). Koobi Fora: Harris and Isaac (1976), Isaac (1976c), Isaac, Harris and Crader (1976), Isaac, Leakey and Behrensmeyer (1971), M. D. Leakey (1970a), M. G. Leakey and R. E. F. Leakey (1978). Melka Kunturé: Chavaillon (1976), Piperno and Piperno (1975). Nsongezi: G. H. Cole (1967), van Riet Lowe (1952b). Olduvai Gorge: Hay (1976), Kleindienst (1973), L. S. B. Leakey (1951), M. D. Leakey (1971, 1975), Stiles, Hay and O'Neil (1974). Olorgesailie: Isaac (1966, 1968, 1977). Omo, Shungura: Chavaillon (1976), Merrick (1976), Merrick and Merrick (1976), Merrick et al. (1973). Peninj: Isaac (1967, 1975), Isaac and Curtis (1974).

### Southern Africa

The classic works are Goodwin and van Riet Lowe's (1929) *Stone Age cultures of South Africa* and Burkitt's (1928) *South Africa's past in stone and paint.* Other important pioneer studies include Söhnge, Visser and van Riet Lowe (1937), J. D. Clark's (1950) *Stone Age cultures of Northern Rhodesia* and Jones's (1949) *Prehistory of Southern Rhodesia.* Summaries of the pioneer studies have appeared in J. D. Clark's (1959a) *Prehistory of southern Africa* and in Sampson's (1974) *Stone Age archaeology of southern Africa.* Mason (1962a) has published the data on his researches in the *Prehistory of the Transvaal* and has brought this up to date in a paper entitled 'The earliest artifact assemblages of South Africa' for the 9th Congress of the Union International des Sciences Préhistoriques et Protohistoriques (Nice, 1976). Excellent reviews of aspects of the Earlier Stone Age have been prepared by Deacon (1975) and Klein (1977). Humphreys (1969, 1970) examines the problem of the relationship between the 'Fauresmith' and the late Acheulian.

Reports on various fresh enquiries into Quaternary chronology and correlation are given in the proceedings of a symposium published in the *South African Archaeological Bulletin* (1969), vol. 24. Various papers by Butzer and co-workers also report important new geological and archaeological results (Butzer 1974a, b; Butzer et al. 1973).

The key references for the other main sites mentioned are as follows. Amanzi: Deacon (1970). Cave of Hearths: Mason (1962a). Cornelia: J. D. Clark (1974b). Hopefield: Singer and Wymer (1968). Kabwe: J. D. Clark (1959b), J. D. Clark et al. (1947), Klein (1973). Montagu Cave: Keller (1973). Munro Site: Mason (1969). Rooidam: Butzer (1974a), Fock (1968). Three Rivers, Klipplaatdrif, Wonderboompoort: Mason (1962a). Vaal River Gravels: Butzer et al. (1973), van Riet Lowe (1952a), Söhnge, Visser and van Riet Lowe (1937).

Some important references for the early australopithecine-bearing sites are as follows. Makapansgat Limeworks site: Ardrey (1961), Brain

(1958, 1967, 1976), Dart (1949, 1957a, b), Maguire (1965), Mason (1965). Sterkfontein: Horowitz (1975), Hughes and Tobias (1977), M. D. Leakey (1970b), Mason (1962b, 1976) Robinson (1962), Tobias and Hughes (1969), Vrba (1975). Swartkrans: Brain (1958, 1970, 1976), M. D. Leakey (1970b).

Sampson (1974) provides an excellent general review and bibliography for the archaeology of the australopithecine deposits.

### The Congo basin and adjoining areas

Pioneer studies in this area include those of Cabu (1952), Collette (1929), Breuil (1944), Janmart (1947, 1953) and L. S. B. Leakey (1949). More recent regional studies are those of J. D. Clark in Angola (1963, 1966, 1968); by Nenquin in Ruanda–Burundi (1966, 1967); by Cahen in the Katanga (1968); by de Bayle des Hermens in the Cameroun (1966a, b, 1967a, b, 1968a, b, c).

Highly informative overall reviews of the history of research in this region are contained in J. D. Clark (1971) and in the concluding chapter of J. D. Clark (1963).

References for sites mentioned in the text are as follows. Baia Farta: J. D. Clark (1963, 1966, 1968). Kamoa: Cahen (1973). Palmeirinhas: J. D. Clark (1963, 1966, 1968).

### West Africa

There has been comparatively little work specifically concerned with the Earlier Stone Age. Pioneer studies are summarized by Davies (1964, 1967). Subsequent works include reports of exploratory work in Nigeria by Soper (1965) who also gives particulars of the Jos plateau materials. An essay by Ogusu (1973) on 'Was there a Sangoan industry in West Africa?' is relevant both for consideration of the Earlier and the Middle Stone Age.

### North-west Africa and the Sahara

Summaries of early work occur in a number of synthesizing volumes: Alimen's (1957) *Prehistory of Africa*, Balout's (1955) *La préhistoire de l'Afrique du nord*, McBurney's (1960) *The Stone Age of North Africa* and Vaufrey's (1955) *Préhistoire de l'Afrique*. The most recent general synthesis is that of Camps (1974).

References for the important sites mentioned in the text are as follows. Adrar Bous: Clark, Williams and Smith (1975), Hugot (1962). Aïn Hanech: Balout (1955). Mauritanian Adrar: Daveau-Ribeiro and Biberson (1972). Sidi Abderrahman, Rabat and the Atlantic seaboard: Biberson (1961a, b, 1967). Sidi Zin: Gobert (1950). Ternifine: Balout (1955), Balout, Biberson and Tixier (1967). Tihodaine: Arambourg and Balout (1955).

A recent review of chronological relationships among these sites has been presented by J.-J. Jaeger (1975).

## The Nile Valley

The classic works on the Lower Palaeolithic of the Nile terraces are by Arkell (1949), Sandford (1934) and Sandford and Arkell (1933). Alimen (1957) and McBurney (1960) provide good summaries and good bibliographies of the pioneer studies.

The most important monograph on any one site is that on *Kharga Oasis in prehistory* by Caton-Thompson (1952). The Arkin excavations are reported by Chmielewski in the two-volume work edited by Wendorf (1968). The same volumes contain a report on surface collections from Nubia by Guichard.

Revisions of geological information are contained in Butzer and Hansen (1968) and in Said (1976). The results of recent research in various desert oases are reported by Wendorf *et al.* (1976).

### 4. THE CULTURES OF THE MIDDLE PALAEOLITHIC/MIDDLE STONE AGE

Specific references to localities, sequences and behavioural features are given in the text of the chapter as also are more general works that should be consulted for information on the palaeoclimate, ecology and faunas as well as on the archaeology of the Middle Palaeolithic/Middle Stone Age period. The following brief overview is designed, therefore, to show the progress of prehistoric studies in each of the main geographical regions of the continent as well as to draw attention to some of the more significant published sequences at particular sites.

A broad appreciation of the development of knowledge and concepts concerning the Middle Palaeolithic/Middle Stone Age of the continent as a whole can be gained from consulting such general works as L. S. B. Leakey (1936), Alimen (1957) and J. D. Clark (1970). The triennial reviews in *Palaeoecology of Africa* (Cape Town) edited by van Zinderen Bakker (of which twelve have now appeared) provide synopses of on-going research with particular reference to the environmental settings of the prehistoric sites. For a summary of current ideas and evidence on the chronology of the Middle Palaeolithic/Middle Stone Age see J. D. Clark (1975a). For an understanding of the progress of research in north-west Africa and the Sahara, the following should be consulted: Balout (1955), Camps (1974), McBurney (1960) and Vaufrey (1955). The journal *Libyca* also contains many site reports of specific interest. Developments in north-east Africa can be followed by consulting Huzayyin (1941) and Wendorf (1968); for the palaeo-environments, geomorphological succession and prehistory of Egypt and Nubia see Butzer and Hansen (1968) and, for Libya, McBurney and Hey (1955). A number of the contributions to Wendorf and Marks (1975) also deal specifically or in part with the Middle Palaeolithic in north Africa and the Levant. An earlier overview of the Aterian complex will be found in Caton-Thompson (1946). Important site monographs deal with Haua Fteah Cave in Cyrenaica (McBurney 1967), Kharga Oasis in the western desert (Caton-Thompson 1952) and the Mugharet el-'Aliya in Tangier (Howe 1967).

For West Africa Davies (1964, 1967) provides detailed and more general reviews of the Upper Pleistocene cultural sequence including much of the southern Sahara. J. D. Clark (1954) reviews what was then known about the Middle Stone Age in the Horn but it is in need of updating and Wendorf and Schild (1974) provide a detailed description of a locality in the Galla Lakes region. The industrial expressions of the Middle Stone Age found in East Africa are described in S. Cole (1963) based on earlier, detailed works on Kenya by L. S. B. Leakey (1936), on Uganda by O'Brien (1939) and van Riet Lowe (1952).

For Equatoria, van Moorsel (1968) provides a general description of the cultural succession in the Plain of Kinshasa. Janmart (1947), L. S. B. Leakey (1949), Breuil and Janmart (1950) and J. D. Clark (1963, 1968) cover the sequence in the Kalahari sand region of north-east Angola and the distribution of sites in that country will be found in J. D. Clark (1966). For Rwanda and Burundi, Nenquin (1967) should be consulted.

No general work exists for Zambia, but the sequence at the Kalambo Falls (J. D. Clark 1969, 1974) is of particular importance. A bibliography of archaeological work in Rhodesia from 1874 is available (C. K. Cooke

1974). A summary of what was known up to 1946 is provided by Jones (1949) and for important excavations undertaken subsequently see C. K. Cooke (1957, 1963).

For southern Africa as a whole, many specialist reports will be found in the *South African Archaeological Bulletin*. A pioneer general work on the South African cultural sequence is that of Goodwin and van Riet Lowe (1929) and changing concepts and understanding can be appreciated from J. D. Clark (1959b) and Sampson (1974), the latter containing detailed descriptions of regional sequences. The definitive work on the Middle Stone Age in the Transvaal is Mason (1962) and another important monograph that should be consulted is Keller (1973). Of particular importance for understanding behavioural and technological changes are analytical reports on the faunal remains associated with Middle Stone Age occupation sites, the main ones being by Klein (1970, 1972, 1974, 1975a, b).

For an understanding of the history of terminologies in current use in the African continent Bishop and Clark (1967) should be consulted and Middle Palaeolithic/Middle Stone Age distributions in relation to climatic and palaeo-environmental factors are set out in a series of base maps and overlays in the *Atlas of African Prehistory* (J. D. Clark 1967).

## 5. THE LATE PALAEOLITHIC AND EPI-PALAEOLITHIC OF NORTHERN AFRICA

The majority of publications in this field are by British and French authors, with the former concentrated in Egypt, Libya and Sudan and the latter in Tunisia, Algeria, Morocco and the western Saharan countries. Italian writers have contributed to study of prehistoric art and archaeology in Libya, while in more recent years, particularly in Egypt and Sudan, there have been publications by American, Belgian, Canadian and Soviet prehistorians who have worked mainly on salvage projects in the Nile Valley.

The only monographs summarizing the entire prehistory of all northern Africa are by McBurney (1960) and Vaufrey (1955, 1969). The major synthesis of Balout (1955) deals only with the Maghrib in spite of its title. A general summary occurs in Clark (1970) while much information on environments and site distributions is contained in the maps in Clark's (1967) *Atlas of African prehistory*. A number of contributors to the volume edited by Wendorf and Marks (1975) discuss various regions of North Africa in Palaeolithic times.

In Libya where prehistoric research began during the Italian occupation a useful summary up to the war years is by Petrocchi (1940). Since the war the most significant publications have been by McBurney (1960, 1967) and by McBurney in collaboration with the geologist Hey (1955), especially their studies of the cave sites of Cyrenaica.

In Egypt there is a considerable body of literature in Palaeolithic archaeology going back to the nineteenth century, but these are usually brief descriptions of isolated surface discoveries. In the time-range of prehistory considered here the most significant publications begin with those of Vignard (1923, 1955a, b) particularly from his research at Kom Ombo in Upper Egypt. The work reported by Caton-Thompson (1946a, b, 1952) and Caton-Thompson with Gardner (1934) on the Fayum Depression and Kharga Oasis was also carried out in the 1920s. At about the same time the first methodical Pleistocene geological survey of the Nile Valley and adjoining areas was undertaken by Sandford and Arkell (Sandford 1934, Sandford and Arkell 1933) although it has now been superseded by more recent research. One consequence of the increased field work in the 1920s and 1930s was the publication by the Egyptian prehistorian and geographer Huzayyin of the most extensive synthesis to date of Egyptian prehistory (1941) although here too later discoveries have rendered much of it obsolete. Arkell's excavation in a 'Mesolithic' site near Khartoum was published in 1949, and his synthesis of Sudanese prehistory and history in 1961. After a lull in fieldwork and publication during the 1940s and 1950s the research programmes carried out in Sudanese and Egyptian Nubia and in Upper Egypt in the early 1960s produced a spate of preliminary and final reports in prehistory and geology by workers from various countries associated with the UNESCO-sponsored Nubian salvage efforts: Butzer and Hansen (1968) on the Quaternary geology and environment of the Nile Valley and adjoining desert, Churcher (1972) on the final Pleistocene faunas from Kom Ombo, Hester and Hobler (1969) on settlement patterns and ecology in the Egyptian Libyan Desert, Wendt (1966) on several Nubian sites, Irwin, Wheat and Irwin (1968) and Wendorf (1968) on American investigations in Sudanese and Egyptian Nubia, Smith (1966, 1968b) on the Canadian research at Kom Ombo, and Vermeersch (1970) on Belgian discoveries in Upper Egypt. Other reports are now being prepared. Several new attempts have been made at preliminary syntheses of Egyptian prehistory in the late Pleistocene and early Holocene, including efforts to interpret the cultural developments in the context of the new ecological and environmental data now available, by Clark

(1971a), Smith (1966) and Wendorf, Said and Schild (1970). Hours, Copeland and Aurenche (1973) have discussed the Nilotic data in the framework of general Near Eastern prehistory.

The literature on the prehistoric archaeology of the Maghrib and the Sahara is vast, nearly all of it the work of French writers. Vaufrey (1955, 1969) and Balout (1955, 1958) have presented massive syntheses of the archaeological sites as known in the 1950s, while Hugot (1974) has recently published a readable account of the Sahara, and Camps (1974) a detailed summary of both the Sahara and the Maghrib. Tixier's study (1963) is the classic work on the typology of chipped stone tools of the Epi-palaeolithic, while Camps-Fabrer's monograph (1966) is a detailed analysis of artifacts in bone, shell, stone and clay from the region. McBurney (1960) and Camps, Delibrias and Thommeret (1968) summarize the Maghrib prehistoric sequence in briefer form. The publications by Castany and Gobert (1954), Gobert (1952, 1962), Gobert and Vaufrey (1932), Gruet (1954), and Vaufrey (1933), have been useful contributions especially for Tunisia. Caton-Thompson's study of the Aterian (1946b) also considers the Maghribian and Saharan evidence. More recent research, including much done since Algerian independence, is described by Aumassip (1972a, b), de Bayle des Hermens and Tixier (1972), Brahimi (1970), Camps (1969), Grébénart (1970, 1972), Marmier and Trecolle (1968), Morel (1974), Roche (1963), Roubet (1971) and by various contributors to the volume on the Sahara edited by Hugot (1962). The geological studies of Servant and Servant-Vildary (1972) on the late Pleistocene and early Holocene deposits of the Chad basin in the southern Sahara have provided much valuable information for the palaeo-ecology of northern Africa. Among the few publications by English-speaking prehistorians are those of Clark (1971b) for Niger and of Howe (1967) for Morocco.

There is now an enormous corpus of publications, accumulated for more than a century, dealing with the prehistoric art of northern Africa. Useful summaries and discussions are given in McBurney (1960), Lhote (1965) and in the volumes of articles edited by Pericot Garcia and Ripoll Perelló (1964), and by Ripoll Perelló (1968). Smith (1968a) has attempted a brief synthesis of the art of this region, Huard and Leclant (1972) describe the Saharan and Nilotic evidence, while Mori (1965) has produced an attractive study of the art and cultural chronology of the Tadrart Acacus zone of south-western Libya. Camps-Fabrer (1966) also discusses the portable art of the Maghrib and Sahara including the polished stone sculptures and the engraved bone and shell. The problem of dating the rock art has been tackled by many writers with opinions on its beginnings ranging from 'Neolithic' (Obermaier 1931, Vaufrey 1939) to late Pleistocene or very early Holocene times (Mori 1974, Smith 1968a). Prehistoric art in the Cyrenaican zone of Libya is described by McBurney (1967) and Paradisi (1965), while Graziosi (1962) has produced a major summary of the art of the Libyan Sahara. Unfortunately the rock art (mainly engravings) of the Nile Valley of Egypt and the Sudan have not yet received extensive treatment although the discoveries known up to the last war are described in the monographs of Dunbar for Egyptian Nubia (1941) and of Winkler for Upper Egypt (1938, 1939). The volume of Almagro Basch and Almagro Gorbea (1968) is a useful analysis of Egyptian Nubia.

Most of the studies in the physical anthropology of northern Africa deal with the skeletal materials from the Maghrib and the Sahara; especially important are those of Arambourg *et al.* (1934), Chamla (1968, 1970), Ferembach (1962) and Vallois (1971). Anderson (in Wendorf 1968) has described some of the burials found in recent excavations in Nubia and attempted to relate the physical type to some in the Maghrib. In addition, in recent years several hypotheses have been offered by Ferembach (1972) and by Tixier (1972) which attempt to demonstrate an evolution of *Homo sapiens sapiens* from indigenous North African stock.

## 6.  LATER STONE AGE IN SUB-SAHARAN AFRICA

In presenting an overall synthesis of the Later Stone Age, we are obviously dependent on material of variable quality and completeness. Many older publications, admirable for their time, now fall below acceptable standards of definition, illustration and quantification. At the other end of the scale, and quite frequent in view of the increased tempo of research which has recently taken place in many areas, are investigations of which only preliminary accounts are, at the time of writing, available. The reader of chapter 6 will have found many references to the incompleteness of the available data; frequently detail is limited to observations concerning the lithic industries, comparable information on settlement patterns, economic practices, and other facets of the archaeological record which are of major relevance to the enquiry, being of remarkably infrequent occurrence. All that can be attempted for many areas of the sub-continent is a survey of the published information, a survey which is naturally dependent on the variable quality of the source material. Inter-regional correlations must generally be regarded as highly tentative, and hampered by the very uneven distribution of research. Enormous areas of sub-Saharan Africa remain virtually unexplored archaeologically; and elsewhere, major parts of the Later Stone Age sequence must rest on the evidence of single sites which may or may not be characteristic.

The current acceleration in the pace of research has rendered all but the most recent syntheses seriously out of date. The references in the text of Chapter 6 provide details of the most important primary sources and excavation reports. The only up-to-date general overview of the Late Stone Age in sub-Saharan Africa is that of J. D. Clark (1970). Further detail is provided by regional studies. For West Africa the most comprehensive are those of Davies (1964, 1967). In East Africa, Cole (1963) is a useful guide to the earlier research, but a new updated edition is badly needed. No comprehensive work on the Later Stone Age in Ethiopia and the Horn of Africa has appeared since Clark's (1954) account; but a particularly useful re-evaluation of the early (pre-food-production) settled communities of East Africa and the southern Sahara has been provided by Sutton (1974). It is important, however, not to overemphasize the cultural unity of these widespread communities, which seem, in each area, to be firmly rooted in a local ancestry. For the Zaire basin, the standard works are those of J. D. Clark (1963, 1968), Mortelmans (1962) and van Moorsel (1968).

Southern Africa has been better served by recent syntheses. J. D. Clark (1959) and Inskeep (1967) remain useful reference works, but should be read in conjunction with that of Sampson (1974) which is a particularly valuable compendium of primary data. More detailed interpretative works are those by Klein (1974), and J. Deacon (1974). Wendt (1972) summarizes recent research in Namibia, while Mason's (1962) book on Transvaal prehistory contains much of value.

## 7. THE RISE OF CIVILIZATION IN EGYPT

The formative periods of Egyptian civilization, although acknowledged to be of major historical interest, have been neglected by anthropologists, while Egyptologists have devoted far less attention to them than they have to later periods. Because of this, few general studies attempt to relate the early development of Egyptian civilization to a comprehensive theoretical framework. Petrie's popular *Making of Egypt* (1939) is the extreme statement of a diffusionist interpretation of the development of Egypt in Predynastic times. Childe (1934), while not rejecting diffusion, went to another extreme in his attempt to force Egyptian and

Mesopotamian civilizations into a parallel–unilinear developmental sequence. Frankfort (1956) countered this trend with a study of the structural contrasts between the mature expressions of these two civilizations and considered their differing developmental sequences. Fairservis' (1971–2) description of the aims of his work at Hierakonpolis suggests growing interest in comparative studies of the development of Egyptian civilization.

The archaeology of the Predynastic and Early Dynastic Periods and related site reports are discussed in the text. The best secondary source for both periods is Vandier (1952). His encyclopaedic work summarizes evidence and interpretations of evidence in a generally impartial manner. For a briefer and more popular interpretation of both periods, see Aldred (1965).

Petrie (1920) remains the basic source of published material for the Amratian and Gerzean periods and, along with his corpus of prehistoric pottery and palettes (1921), is still a much-used reference work. The most important attempt to revise Petrie's chronology is Kaiser's (1957) study of the Predynastic cemetery at Armant. Baumgartel (1955, 1960) has published a two-volume report on her studies of the Predynastic cultures of Upper Egypt. These books contain useful data and interesting interpretations. The best interpretation of archaeological data concerning Predynastic Lower Egypt is the published fragment of Hayes's (1965) unfinished history of Egypt. Baumgartel's (1970) summary of the Predynastic period pays inadequate attention to views other than her own, particularly concerning the cultures of northern Egypt. For critiques of research on Predynastic Egypt, see Arkell and Ucko (1965) and Trigger (1968).

The most popular synthesis of the Early Dynastic period is Emery (1961), although the concept of a 'Dynastic Race' which he champions is increasingly recognized as unacceptable. Edwards (1971) provides a useful summary of information about the dynastic history of this period. Recent years have witnessed the publication of major interpretive studies of the Early Dynastic period as well as of more site reports. Kaplony's (1963) monograph on the inscriptions of this period is of exceptional importance and Kemp (1966, 1967) seems to have resolved the thorny issue of the burial place of the First Dynasty monarchs to most scholars' satisfaction.

The relative chronology of Predynastic and Early Dynastic times is examined by Kantor (1965), who deals particularly with south-west Asian interconnections. The implications of radiocarbon dates are discussed by H. S. Smith (1964) and Derricourt (1971). Much current discussion centres on the implications of the bristlecone-pine calibration of radiocarbon time-scales (Suess 1970) and thermoluminescent dates for Upper Egyptian pottery (Caton-Thompson and Whittle 1975).

Recent work has dispelled many entrenched concepts concerning the ancient Egyptians and the origin of their civilization. Passarge (1940) and Butzer (1959) have clarified the environmental setting of Predynastic Egypt and in particular have rejected the notion that the Nile Valley was a primordial swamp inimical to human settlement. Theories of the origin of Egyptian food production have been reviewed in a broad regional setting by Reed (1966) and Clark (1971). The linguistic status of ancient Egyptian as an Afroasiatic language has been clarified by Greenberg (1955) and many other linguistic problems are surveyed and discussed by Vergote (1970). Although no comprehensive treatment of the racial characteristics of ancient Egyptians has been published recently, Berry, Berry and Ucko (1967) tend to reject Derry's (1956) concept of a 'Dynastic Race' and to support Batrawi's (1945, 1946) views of continuity in early Egyptian population.

A traditional summary of early Nubian culture history is found in Emery (1965). Recent excavations in Nubia have greatly extended knowledge of the archaeological sequence in this region prior to 3000 BC (Wendorf 1968). Recent work on the A-group is summarized in Nordström (1972) and H. S. Smith (1966) has convincingly disposed of Reisner's B-group. Archaeological work in the Sudan, still largely unpublished, is slowly increasing knowledge of Arkell's Early Khartoum (1949) and Esh-Shaheinab (1953) cultures, largely in the form of related cultures which occur over a wide area.

Hoffman (1979) has now published a comprehensive, semi-popular account of the archaeology and culture-historical development of Egypt relating to prehistoric and Early Dynastic times. His interpretations differ from our own mainly in according Hierakonpolis a more central role in the developments of the Late Predynastic period and not emphasizing the role of the gold trade at that time.

## 8. BEGINNINGS OF PASTORALISM AND CULTIVATION IN NORTH-WEST AFRICA AND THE SAHARA: ORIGINS OF THE BERBERS

A considerable number of books and papers, written almost exclusively in French, deal with the prehistory and protohistory of the extensive area covered by the countries of the Maghrib and Sahara – Morocco, Algeria, Tunisia, Libya, Mauritania, Mali, Niger and Tchad. There is no lack of comprehensive works such as Alimen (1955), Balout (1955), Vaufrey (1955, 1969), McBurney (1960), Clark (1970) and Camps (1974) which contain syntheses, either for the whole of the African continent (Alimen and Clark) or for north-west Africa, the Maghrib and the Sahara (Vaufrey and Camps) or the Maghrib alone (Balout).

Neolithic man has left behind him fewer skeletal remains than did his predecessors whose large Epi-Palaeolithic cemeteries at Afalou bou Rhumel, Taforalt and Columnata have each been the subject of important research. The sole work concerned with the physical anthropology of the Neolithic peoples deals only with the Saharan regions (Chamla 1968) and, in addition, devotes considerable space to the protohistoric populations. These latter have been studied more particularly in the Fezzan (Pace, Caputo and Sergi 1951); however, there is now a memoir by Chamla which deals with physical anthropology in the Maghrib during Neolithic and Iron Age times (Chamla 1978; see also Chamla 1975).

As regards lithic typology – a particularly well-studied subject – the work of Tixier (1963) must be mentioned in connection with the Epi-Palaeolithic; this was partially completed for the Saharan Neolithic by Aumassip (1973). The only specifically Neolithic artifacts to have been studied morphologically in any detail are the Saharan arrow-points (Hugot 1957). Ceramic technology has been the subject of interesting regional studies (Goetz 1942) and especially of systematic study of decorative motifs (Camps-Fabrer 1966). The same author (1960) has published an account of objects of personal adornment in North Africa and a method of classifying artifacts in bone and ostrich eggshell (1966).

There is no general work on the reconstruction of climate and vegetation during the Neolithic and the most interesting studies concern the north-western Sahara (Beucher 1971) and the Ahaggar (Van Campo et al. 1964, 1965, 1967).

Monographs on Neolithic sites, both in the Maghrib and the Sahara, are much too numerous for all to be mentioned here. In northern Morocco, stratified sites have received careful study (Jodin 1958–9, Tarradell 1954, 1957–8, 1958) and among regional studies in the same country should be noted the significant *Prehistoric atlas of Atlantic Morocco* by Souville (1974) and a somewhat earlier synthesis by Antoine (1952). Another synthesis – of the prehistory of Algeria – was published by Balout in 1958 while in 1955 and 1962 Gobert published a series of regional studies on Tunisia. The important monograph by McBurney (1967) on the Haua Fteah Cave in Cyrenaica has considerably more than mere local significance.

For the vast expanse of the Sahara, the most numerous regional studies and the most interesting monographs concern the Ahaggar (Camps 1968a, Hugot 1963, Maître 1971); Ténéré of Taffassasset (Hugot (ed.) 1962); Borkou (Courtin 1966, 1968); and Ennedi (Arkell 1964, Bailloud 1960). South of the great *chotts* of Algeria and Tunisia, the *Bas Sahara* has been explored and studied in the last few years and the first monograph on the regional Neolithic has recently appeared (Aumassip 1973). Research in the western Sahara has been carried out largely by geologists (e.g. Chavaillon and Conrad in the Saoura valley and Faure on the Mauritanian coast). For the southern part of this region we have the very numerous papers by Mauny (1955a, 1967, etc.) and the work of Gallay (1966).

Over the last decade a concerted effort has been made with regard to the chronology – the succession and duration of the Neolithic cultures of the whole of this North African area. At the present time there are for these cultures more than 300 dates of very uneven value (Camps 1968b, Camps, Delibrias and Thommeret 1968, 1973). Study of the relations between Neolithic cultures, particularly in the Sahara, has resulted in a progressively more apparent distinction between the Saharan–Sudanese Neolithic and the so-called 'Neolithic of Capsian Tradition' from further north (Camps 1967, 1968a, Camps-Fabrer 1966, Hugot 1963), while the coastal Neolithic is seen to be connected with the widespread maritime ensemble with impressed pottery (the Mediterranean Neolithic) (Camps 1971).

Both in the Atlas and the massifs of the Sahara, the Neolithic saw an extraordinary flowering of rock art. The engravings of the Saharan Atlas, particularly those of southern Oran, were the first to attract attention from travellers and later from scientists. The first work of synthesis was that of Flamand in 1921, later complemented by Frobenius and Obermaier (1925); but it was not until the research of Vaufrey (1935, 1939) that it was possible to correlate the engravings and the Neolithic industries. Since that time a great many new discoveries have been made and the engravings from eastern Algeria are better known (Lefebvre and Lefebvre 1967). At the same time, systematic prospecting was begun in the extreme south of Morocco (Simoneau 1968–72) which showed the artistic richness of this region. The latest work to have appeared on the rock engravings of the Maghrib (Lhote 1970) is again devoted to southern Oran.

In Tripolitania at the site of Abiar Miggi (Neuville 1956), stratigraphic connections have been established between the engravings on the walls and the Neolithic industries. Specimens of *art mobilier* found in sites of the Neolithic of Capsian Tradition such as Damous el-Ahmar are more numerous (Camps-Fabrer 1961–2, 1966, Roubet 1968).

The Fezzan (Libya) is a very important area from the point of view of the art and after the work of Frobenius (1937) must be cited the very fine publication by Graziosi (1942) followed by that of Mori (1965). However, the most beautiful and most numerous examples of Neolithic art – engravings and, particularly, paintings – were found in the Ahaggar (Chasseloup-Laubat 1938, Maître 1971) and in Tassili n'Ajjer which is the richest area (Breuil 1955, Lhote 1958, Reygasse 1935). Although there exists a very considerable body of literature concerning the different rock art sites in these two mountain areas – which it is not possible to quote in detail here – yet syntheses, although of prime importance, are nonetheless still rare (Camps 1974, Lhote 1970). In the same region of the Sahara other artistic manifestations, such as those of animal sculptures in hard rocks, have attracted the attention of Camps-Fabrer (1966) who was the first to suggest that they should be attributed to the Middle Neolithic (the Bovidian and Ténéréan). Further east, Bailloud (1960) has made a study of the rock paintings in Ennedi.

The rock art of the western Sahara has been the subject of several studies by Alimen (1954) in the valley of the Saoura; by Santa-Olalla (1944) and by Almagro (1946) in the Rio de Oro. Further south, rock engravings are rare; Mauny (1955) drew up instructions for studying them. The latest work on this subject concerns the rock engravings of the Aïr (Lhote 1972), most of which belong to the Iron Age.

The literature on the Metal Age and protohistoric times in North Africa and the Sahara consists essentially of a large number of short articles and small monographs. The sole synthesis concerns the Maghrib (Camps 1961a, b) and makes frequent reference to Gsell (1914–28). Three writers in particular have been concerned with relations with European countries at the beginning of the Metal Age (Camps 1959, 1960, Jodin 1957, Tarradell 1954, 1957–8, 1958). The existence of a Chalcolithic and a Bronze Age has been shown from the discovery of engraved representations of halberds and of rivetted daggers in the high Atlas of Morocco (Malhomme 1959, 1961) or of weapons in copper or bronze (Camps 1960, Camps and Giot 1960, Souville 1966).

Since the middle of the nineteenth century, the very numerous funerary monuments and their furnishings have been the subject of a larger number of notes or articles. In 1916 Frobenius devoted a study to them, unfortunately full of inaccuracies, and the work of Reygasse (1950), the title of which does not correspond to the subject matter, is of even less value. On the other hand, Pace, Caputo and Sergi (1951) have provided an excellent contribution to knowledge of the Fezzan of the Garamantes. Since the excavation of Germa, the history of the Garamantes during classical times is much better known (Daniel 1970). A detailed typology of the prehistoric funerary monuments of the Maghrib and the pottery they contain has been published by Camps (1961a) but such work has still to be done for the Sahara. Accounts have been published of the only two megalithic necropolises that have been excavated since the Second World War – by Camps and Camps-Fabrer (1964) for the one at Bou Nouara in Algeria and by Lambert (1967) for that at Tayadirt in Morocco. Iron Age pottery and its decoration have been treated of in numerous articles by Camps since 1952, in particular in 1961 (1961a).

The question of the introduction of the horse and the problem of the Saharan chariots have given rise to a large volume of literature which can only with difficulty be isolated from that of the rock art of the metal age (e.g. Huard 1960, Lhote 1953, Mauny 1955b).

### 9. THE ORIGINS OF INDIGENOUS AFRICAN AGRICULTURE

Current literature on African crops is voluminous but seldom treats on orgins. Extensive bibliographies may be found in Dalziel (1937), Schnell (1957), Wills (1962), Allan (1965), Busson (1965) and Jardin (1967). The only recent work dealing specifically with the origins of African agriculture is Harlan, de Wet and Stemler (eds.) (1976). The reports, bulletins and occasional papers of various agricultural research organ-izations are useful. Webster (1966) *Index of agricultural research institutions and stations in Africa*, FAO, Rome may be consulted as an entry to these materials. Attention is particularly called to publications of l'Institut de Recherches Agronomiques Tropicales et des Cultures Vivrières (IRAT); l'Office de Recherche Scientifique et Technique Outre-Mer (ORSTOM); l'Institut National pour l'Etude Agronomique du Congo (INEAC); l'Institut fondamental (formerly français) d'Afrique Noire (IFAN); Institute for Agricultural Research, Ahmadu Bello University, Samaru, Nigeria; and the East African Agriculture and Forestry Research Organization (EAAFRO).

Journals that contain significant papers on African crops and their origins include: *Révue International de Botanique Appliquée et d'Agriculture Tropicale*, succeeded by *Journal d'Agriculture Tropicale et de Botanique Appliquée, Agronomie Tropicale, Nigerian Agricultural Journal, Cahiers d'Outre-Mer, Bulletin Agricole du Congo, Uganda Journal, Sudan Agricultural Journal, Cahiers d'Etudes Africaines, Bulletin de la Société d'Histoire Nationale d'Afrique du Nord*, *Sols Africains*, *Economic Botany* and others. *Kew Bulletin* is especially useful in following taxonomic revisions and occasionally deals with African cultigens.

Reports of archaeological, ethnobotanical and anthropological investigations are largely published in the standard journals of these fields. More specifically, however, the works of IFAN and Centre de Recherches Anthropologiques, Préhistoriques et Ethnographiques (CRAPE) (Algiers), *Sudan Notes and Records* (Khartoum), *Azania*, *Journal of Ethiopian Studies* and the several institutes for African studies should be consulted. A number of the French studies have been published as *thèses*.

Literature on the origins of indigenous African agriculture is, on the whole, scattered and sometimes difficult of access. It is consistent, however, in pointing to: (1) a dearth of information on the subject, and (2) the lack of systematic and co-ordinated investigations of the problem. This is strangely inconsistent with the importance of agriculture in the economies of African peoples.

## 10. OLD KINGDOM, MIDDLE KINGDOM AND SECOND INTERMEDIATE PERIOD IN EGYPT

The basic framework of dynasties for ancient Egyptian history laid down by the Egyptian priest Manetho in the late fourth or early third century BC is still followed, although, as noted in the above sections on the First and Second Intermediate Periods, there are grounds for doubting the integrity of certain of them. The surviving versions of Manetho have been edited by Waddell (1940). It was probably more in the nature of a chronicle than a history properly speaking, but little of it has survived other than summary lists of his kings, dynasties and lengths of reigns. These have been the subject of some critical examination by Helck (1956b). The most important earlier chronological source is the Turin Canon or king-list. A complete transcription has been published by Gardiner (1959), and some emendations and schematic analysis by von Beckerath (1962, 1964, 1966). Its basic data are conveniently tabulated alongside those from the other king-lists (principally from Abydos and Saqqara) in an appendix in Gardiner (1961). The Palermo Stone is now too fragmentary to be of much chronological use, but still contains interesting details of the events that the Egyptians of the Old Kingdom thought to be significant. The basic source here is Schäfer (1902), with the chronological aspects discussed by Kaiser (1961) and Helck (1974b).

Absolute calendrical dates have been deduced by combining totals given in the Turin king-list with the results of calculations based on ancient astronomical observations, for which the fundamental work is Parker (1950). Debate on the accuracy of these calculations has been continued in articles by Ingham (1969), Read (1970), Parker (1970, 1976), and Long (1974), but with nothing very seriously contradictory emerging. More serious are discrepancies between these and radiocarbon dates which have been discussed in individual articles, for example by H. S. Smith (1964), Quitta (1972) Long (1976) and Mellaart (1979), and in two major symposia, see Edwards (1970), Michael and Ralph (1970) and Säve-Söderbergh and Olsson (1970). The corrections suggested by dendrochronology have not resolved the problem (Mellaart 1979).

The history of these early periods is largely built up from a multiplicity of hieroglyphic sources, mostly very laconic. The collected translations by Breasted (1906) still have no rival for completeness and appear surprisingly good, although naturally there have been improvements in lexicography and grammatical knowledge since they were made. The number of significant historical texts for these periods discovered since Breasted's day is surprisingly small, the most important being the various Kamose texts edited by Gardiner (1916) and Habachi (1972). A selection of texts relating to Old Testament background has been translated by Wilson in Pritchard (1969); Schenkel (1965) has provided translations of all First Intermediate Period sources; and Goedicke (1967) has done the same for Old Kingdom royal decrees. For literary texts, which sometimes reflect political matters, there are two recent collected editions, by Faulkner, Wente and Simpson (Simpson 1973) and Lichtheim (1973). Administrative and economic papyri have not been treated as a body, but may be encountered in individual editions by Griffith (1898), Hayes (1955), Posener-Kriéger (1976), Posener-Kriéger and de Cenival (1968), Scharff (1920), and Simpson (1963b, 1965, 1969b). The second Kahun (Lahun) archive is still available only in summary form, see Borchardt (1899) and Kaplony-Heckel (1971).

Progress in Egyptian historiography has been slow since the great pioneering works of Meyer (1887), Breasted (1906), and others of this period; Petrie (1924a, b) is particularly noteworthy for its documentation. The lack of widespread scepticism as to the testimony of literary sources has been commented on by Björkman (1964). Hornung (1966) and Otto (1964–6) have discussed the merging of myth and history in the Egyptian mind, and the ritualistic conception of history at the level of formal Egyptian monuments. Amongst the histories of Egypt which have appeared in recent years should be noted those by Bottéro, Cassin and Vercoutter (1967), Drioton and Vandier (1962), Gardiner (1961), Hallo and Simpson (1971) and Helck (1968). The ambitious attempt in the new third edition of the *Cambridge Ancient History*, edited by Edwards, Gadd and Hammond (1971), to cover in considerable detail the ancient history of the entire Middle East and surrounding areas naturally includes chapters on Egypt, and these, written in dense narrative style and with a tendency to concentrate on kings and chronology, provide a fundamental reference source for historical detail, though with relatively little attention to African connections. Detailed historical studies of separate periods have not been common, the most valuable being those by von Beckerath (1964), Schenkel (1962), van Seters (1966), and Winlock (1947). Wilson (1951) represents an imaginative attempt at interpreting the dynamics of Egyptian history, and Posener (1956) a study of Middle Kingdom Literature as a political vehicle. The more intractable inscriptional material from private tombs offers some promise for regional historical studies, based very much on titles and genealogies, but has been carried out in a serious and consistent manner only by Fischer (1964, 1968) for the areas of Coptos and Dendera.

Studies on Egyptian administration and economy tend to suffer from an insensitivity to the idea that rational working systems were involved. Basic treatments of the source material in this mould are those of Helck (1958, 1975), and to a lesser extent of Pirenne (1932–5). The documentation for more limited periods is analysed by B. Adams (1956), Baer (1960), and Helck (1954). An important contribution to our understanding of ancient Egypt's geographical background is that by Butzer (1976).

For external relationships W. Y. Adams (1977b), Arkell (1961), Emery (1965), Hofmann (1967), Säve-Söderbergh (1941), and Trigger (1965, 1976b) deal with Nubia, in each case attempting to relate inscriptional and archaeological sources. Whereas Egyptologists have tended to dominate the field of Nubian studies and therefore have come to terms with the cultural background, the same is not true for Palestine and Syria. The archaeological record for settlement history tends to feature only peripherally in studies on Egypt's relations with these areas, as is particularly clear in the major documentary study by Helck (1971). Van Seters (1966) and Ward (1971) represent limited attempts to create an archaeological context for individual periods; at the level of cultural influence Egypt figures prominently in an analysis by W. S. Smith (1965) of the cultural interdependence of the ancient Near East.

One notable aspect of Egyptology is the consistency of its intellectual framework, which is essentially in the Classical mould: textual exegesis dominates history, prosopography and genealogy are the mainsprings in the study of local history, art history is regarded as the major component in evaluating the development of material culture. This results in a marked homogeneity of style and approach, and a considerable versatility amongst Egyptologists. But it also helps to make the subject more resistant to the proper evaluation of archaeological data and to the use, or at least consideration, of alternative frameworks into which existing information can be set. This has the overall effect of probably exaggerating the uniqueness of the essential character of Egyptian culture and society. Nevertheless, some of the issues raised by articles on the character and dynamics of early societies written from a more theoretical point of view are appropriate for discussion in Egyptological terms, and such discussion might be expected both to broaden the intellectual basis on which ancient Egypt is studied, and to make more widely accessible the rich source material which Egypt has to offer on certain aspects of early society.

With archaeological data, the careful analysis of cemetery sequences offers one supplementary direction for historical study, though probably a rather limited one, but even here where so much material exists already only the most tentative beginnings have been made (e.g. Kemp, 1976a; O'Connor 1972, 1974). The excavation and study of settlement sites is still in its infancy in Egypt, and the failure to understand correctly such evidence as exists has led to outright denials that towns were a significant element in Egyptian society (e.g. Helck 1975, ch. 12; cf. Kemp 1977b). The dramatic results from Tell ed-Dab'a achieved by Bietak (1968a, 1970, 1975a) are probably exceptional in their historial impact because of the nature of the site itself. For many more town sites it is probably true to say that until a more coherent framework of social and cultural processes is achieved for ancient Egypt it will remain difficult to direct excavation to the best advantage.

## II. EARLY FOOD PRODUCTION IN SUB-SAHARAN AFRICA

The literature dealing with the early food-producing peoples of sub-Saharan Africa is widely scattered. Published accounts of individual sites and areas have been cited in references in the text of chapter 11, but these are of necessity only a selection. The steady acceleration in the pace of research which has taken place during the past decade has rendered many previous syntheses quickly out-of-date. There is no reason to suppose that the account of these peoples offered in the present volume will escape the same fate.

Shaw (1972b) has produced an invaluable compendium of the evidence, both direct and indirect, for food production in African prehistory, although he provides disappointingly little in the way of critical appraisal of the value and reliability of the various pieces of indirect evidence cited. His paper will, however, remain an essential reference work to the discoveries and theories put forward up to the date of its compilation.

The general industrial succession of the period which saw the inception and early development of food production has not been well served by recent syntheses. Sutton (1974) provides a useful reappraisal of the early settled communities of the southern Sahara (amongst the descendants of which food production techniques eventually spread), as well as of related groups in East Africa further to the south. An earlier general account of these 'Neolithic' societies in immediately sub-Saharan latitudes is provided by Clark (1967). A more recent synthesis of African prehistory by the same author (Clark 1970) takes subsequent discoveries into account but its treatment of the food-producing peoples is disappointingly brief.

Regional studies provide the most detailed accounts of the relevant archaeological discoveries and their significance: with a few notable exceptions they pay little or no attention to linguistic, botanical and other non-archaeological sources. Davies (1964, 1967) has brought order to the abundant but generally poorly documented West African material. Most of the most recent discoveries are noted in the *West African Archaeological Newsletter* or its successor, the *West African Journal of Archaeology*. For Ethiopia and the Horn, the only comprehensive syntheses remain those by Anfray (1968), Bailloud (1959) and Clark (1954), while Simoons (1965) discusses the non-archaeological evidence for early food production in Ethiopia. The East African archaeological material is discussed by Sutton (1973a, b), whose work should be read in conjunction with the more controversial linguistic studies by Ehret (1971, 1974).

Several works by Clark (notably 1963 and 1968) provide the basic data on the archaeological succession in north-eastern Angola, while the corresponding developments in lower Zaïre and the Kinshasa area are summarized by Mortelmans (1962) and van Moorsel (1968).

In much of Tanzania, Zambia, Zimbabwe and the Transvaal, the vehicle for the inception of food production appears to have been the Early Iron Age Industrial Complex, best described by Soper (1971), whose work necessitates important modifications to the views of Oliver (1966) and Huffman (1970). Phillipson (1975) amplifies Soper's synthesis, particularly with regard to the chronology.

Several valuable syntheses of the later prehistory of southern Africa have recently appeared. Notable are those by H. J. Deacon (1972), J. Deacon (1974), Sampson (1974) and Inskeep (1967, 1969). The basic sequences in the south-east Cape and in the middle Orange area have been published by J. Deacon (1972) and Sampson (1972) respectively, while Wendt (1972) has provided a valuable but preliminary account of the material from Namibia.

Epstein (1971) and Payne (1964) describe the modern domestic animals of sub-Saharan Africa and draw useful conclusions as to their origin: both works, however, were written at a time when archaeological evidence for animal domestication in the sub-continent was almost non-existent.

## 12. EGYPT, 1552–664 BC

The *bibliography* on Egypt during this period is very large and continually increasing; recourse to several bibliographical aids is essential. Pratt (1925, 1942) provides an extremely comprehensive if not totally complete bibliography running to 1941, conveniently divided into topics and with an excellent index of authors and topics. Federn (1948–50) covers the years 1939 to 1947 (without topic categorization but with an author index); while the *Annual Egyptological Bibliography* (J. M. A. Janssen 1948–63, J. M. A. Janssen and Heerma van Voss 1964, Heerma van Voss 1968–9, Heerma van Voss and J. J. Janssen 1971, J. J. Janssen 1972–6; continuing) is a completely inclusive bibliography covering 1947 to 1972 and still continuing; it is not categorized, but there is an index of authors, titles and topics for 1947–56. Since 1971 Kemp has produced *Egyptological Titles*, an up-to-date quarterly bibliography conveniently divided into categories. Porter and Moss (1927–74) and Málek (1974) provide a detailed guide to all known reliefs, paintings and hieroglyphic texts; there is no guide for hieratic or demotic texts, or to purely architectural and archaeological data.

Convenient recent discussions of *New Kingdom chronology* are Hornung (1964; the 'short' chronology) and Hayes (1970; the 'long' chronology); see also Kitchen (1965). For *Third Intermediate Period chronology* Kitchen

(1973) is fundamental. Debate remains lively and more recent studies are found in the bibliographic aids noted above.

Of the *data* themselves important collections of original texts exist (e.g. Sethe and Helck 1906–58, Kitchen 1968–   , etc.) but much remain scattered throughout the literature. On the unusual historical value of certain kinds of textual data see Donadoni (1963). The most important collection of historical texts in translation remains Breasted (1906), to be partially supplemented by Helck (1961) and Sethe (1914). The best collection of (often historically significant) literary works in English is Simpson (1973), while Caminos' (1954) translations of 'miscellanies', Wente's (1966) of later New Kingdom letters and Wilson's (1969) of a variety of texts in Pritchard should also be noted. Good monographs on art and architecture are Lange and Hirmer (1956), W. S. Smith (1958), Vandier (1955, 1958, 1964) and Wolf (1957). Apart from Hayes's (1959) description of New Kingdom material culture there is no comprehensive synthetic treatment of purely archaeological data.

For the different elements involved in shaping and sustaining the *Egyptian world view* see especially Kees's (1961) excellent introduction to the ancient Egyptian environment and the society it supported. To this should be added Butzer's (1959, 1976) analyses of environmental change and related matters and Wilson's (1955) discussion of the regional variability of ancient Egyptian agricultural and population patterns. The best treatment of agricultural technology remains Hartmann (1923), but see also Dixon (1969) and H. S. Smith (1969); and the fundamental study of industrial technology is Lucas and Harris (1962). There are no detailed comprehensive studies of the composition of Egyptian society but a good impression of a New Kingdom 'urban' community (Tell el-Amarna) can be gained from Davies (1903–8), Frankfort *et al.* (1933), Peet *et al.* (1923) and Pendlebury (1951). See also Kemp's (1976, 1977) important recent studies of Amarna. Lower-middle-class life in the same period is richly documented by the extraordinary artisan's village at Deir el-Medineh; see Bruyère (1939) and Černý (1973, 1975). Some insight into the composition of rural society is provided in Gardiner (1941–52). Broader patterns of settlement and urbanization from the New Kingdom and later are discussed by Kemp (1972a, b), O'Connor (1972a) and H. S. Smith (1972).

On the Egyptian world-view in general see Wilson (1951, 1954) and, for the Late Period, Otto (1951, 1954), all stimulating if somewhat biased studies. Posener's subtle analysis of the kingship's significance

(1960) is essential for understanding Egyptian attitudes, while the best introductions to Egyptian religion are Vandier (1949) and Černý (1957); Bonnet (1952) is an invaluable reference work. Special note should be made of Černý's discussion of oracles (1962) and Bleeker's of festivals (1967).

Amongst *general histories* Drioton and Vandier (1962) remains the best documented and analytical; Breasted (1927), although outdated, is still a valuable introduction, while other histories of note are Gardiner (1961), Helck (1968), Wilson (1951) and Yoyotte (1956). Of more *narrowly focused studies* Steindorff and Seele (1957) give an overview of the New Kingdom, with an emphasis on foreign relations. Redford's (1967) and Yoyotte's (1966) studies of the Eighteenth Dynasty are stimulating, while the entire New Kingdom is treated, in a valuable if encyclopaedic way, by Aldred (1975), Černý (1975), Faulkner (1975), James (1973) and Hayes (1973) in the new edition of the *Cambridge Ancient History*. Note also Černý's (1966) study of the Nineteenth and Twentieth Dynasties and Kemp's (1978) on New Kingdom imperialism. Von Beckerath's (1951) discussion of the transition from the New Kingdom to the Third Intermediate Period is interesting but should be used cautiously while Bierbrier's (1975) is a more specialized study of the same phenomenon. The fundamental treatments of the Third Intermediate Period are by Yoyotte (1961) and Kitchen (1973); but one should note also Zeissl (1944) on the latter part of the period, and to be supplemented especially by reference to Spalinger (1974a, b) and de Meulenaere (1967). On the transition to the Late Period see Kienitz (1953), extremely valuable but requiring major updating (see Johnson 1974).

More specialized monographs and articles on aspects of the entire period can easily be found through the *histories* and *bibliographical aids* already cited. A few however require mention here. The organization of the military in the New Kingdom is treated by Faulkner (1953) and Schulman (1964a, b) and its political significance in the New Kingdom is discussed by Helck (1939). The government of the Asiatic conquests in the New Kingdom is described by Albright (1975), Drower (1973) and Helck (1962). Helck (1958) is the fundamental study of New Kingdom civil government, while Edgerton's (1947) analysis is of interest; Third Intermediate Period government is reconstructed, in its broader outlines, by Kitchen (1975). Egyptian law in general is discussed by Wilson (1954b) and Théodoridès (1971), while Seidl (1939) analyses (partially) the New Kingdom legal system. Material on the interrelationships between the political and religious system will be found in Kees (1953, 1958, 1964), Lefebvre (1929; see also, for updating, Bierbrier 1975, Helck 1958, Kees 1953– , 1958, Kitchen 1973), Sander-Hansen (1940; see also Redford 1967, Tanner 1975) and Schaedel (1936). Special mention must be made of recent studies of New Kingdom economic history, namely J. J. Janssen's (1975a) superlative monograph on prices and survey article (1975b); and valuable studies by Helck (1975) and Menu (1970, 1971) on general economic history and land tenure respectively.

For *Egypt and Africa* Leclant (1972) is an excellent critical analysis of the diffusion of Egyptian influence. Säve-Söderbergh (1941) remains the fundamental study of New Kingdom activity in Nubia, but needs updating. More recent studies of Nubian history, while lacking the depth of Säve-Söderbergh's analysis, incorporate post-1941 research and discoveries and cover also the Third Intermediate and Late Periods; most valuable is Trigger (1976), but also noteworthy are W. Y. Adams (1977a; at times over-speculative but stimulating and provocative), Arkell (1961) and Emery (1965; emphasizes archaeological data).

The New Kingdom 'conquest lists' of southern toponyms (of Wawat, Kush, the eastern desert and Punt) have not received detailed, comprehensive study; most can be traced via Zibelius (1972). Zhylarz's (1958) discussion of the Tuthmosis III list is wrong-headed, but Posener (1958) and Priese (1974) have valuable comments on it. Comparative data, i.e. the accuracy and structure of *Asiatic* lists, are discussed in Aharoni (1968) and Astour (1963). On Punt see Herzog's (1968) convenient study, and Kitchen's (1971) definitive commentary. Butzer (1959, 1970, 1976) is a good introduction (by inference largely) to climatic change in the Sudan; Barbour (1961) provides excellent coverage on its modern geography; and Vercoutter's (1959) discussion of Sudanese gold and its ancient exploitation is valuable.

The *New Kingdom conquest of Wawat and Kush* is discussed by Goedicke (1965), Säve-Söderbergh (1941) and Vandersleyen (1971); see also important data published by Arkell (1950), H. S. Smith (1976) and Vercoutter (1956, 1973). Data on *relations with Irem* are conveniently collected, but perhaps misinterpreted, by Priese (1974); important additional data are in Vercoutter (1972) and Kitchen (1975–6, 1977). For the *eastern desert* see Säve-Söderbergh (1941), and important new data on *Akuyta* in Kitchen (1975–6) and H. S. Smith (1976).

*Egyptian administration in Nubia* is discussed by Hayes (1973) and Säve-Söderbergh (1941), while Kemp (1972, 1978) is a useful introduction to Egyptian centres established there. Data on the viceroys are collected in Gauthier (1921) and Reisner (1920), with important additional data in Černý (1959), Habachi (1957, 1959, 1961), Helck (1955), Kitchen (1975–6), Wolf (1924) and Žaba (1950). Caminos (1968, 1974) and Caminos and James (1963) contain further new data, and excellent bibliographies on a number of the viceroys. For the *acculturation of the Nubians* see Edel (1963), Säve-Söderbergh (1941, 1960, 1963) and Simpson (1963), on the elite of Wawat; and for broader patterns Säve-Söderbergh (1969) and Trigger (1965). Drenkhahn (1967) has many useful data drawn from the pictorial record.

*Wawat and Kush during the Third Intermediate Period* are treated by W. A. Adams (1964) and Trigger (1965, 1976). The basic data on the origins of the Twenty-fifth Dynasty are published by Dunham (1950) and the theoretical questions conveniently discussed by Dixon (1964).

The basic discussion on *New Kingdom relations with Libya* is Hölscher (1955), to be supplemented by Černý (1975), Faulkner (1975), Gardiner (1947) and Wainwright (1962). Most of the relevant texts are translated in Breasted (1906) and Edgerton and Wilson (1936). For the Sea-Peoples see Barnett (1975; a useful but unreliable introduction) and Goetze (1975a, b, c; discussion of Aḥhiyawa). *Libyan–Egyptian relations in the Third Intermediate Period* are discussed by Goedicke (1962) and Yoyotte (1961).

# BIBLIOGRAPHY

The following common acronyms have been used:

CNRS   Centre Nationale de la Recherche Scientifique (Paris)
CRAPE   Centre de Recherches Anthropologiques, Préhistoriques et Ethnographiques (Algiers)
CSIR   Council for Scientific and Industrial Research (Pretoria)
IFAN   Institut Français/Fondamental de l'Afrique Noire (Dakar)
ORSTOM   Office de la Recherche Scientifique et Technique Outre Mer

The following books and series to which frequent reference is made are listed with shorter titles and bibliographic details:

Bakker, E. M. van Zinderen (ed.) (1966–80). *Palaeoecology of Africa and of the surrounding Islands and Antarctica*, 12 vols. Capetown. (Vols. II and III, 1967; vol. VI, 1972.)

Bishop, W. W. (ed.) (1978). *Geological Background to fossil man: Recent research in the Gregory Rift Valley, East Africa.* Edinburgh and Toronto.

Bishop, W. W. and J. A. Miller (eds.) (1972). *Calibration of hominoid evolution.* Edinburgh and Toronto.

Bordes, F. (ed.) (1971). *The origins of* Homo sapiens/*Origine de l'homme moderne. UNESCO Ecology and Conservation Series* 3. Paris.

Butzer, K. W. (1971). *Environment and archaeology: an ecological approach to prehistory*, 2nd edn. Chicago.

Butzer, K. W. *Early hydraulic civilization in Egypt: a study in cultural ecology. (Prehistoric archeology and ecology* 3.) Chicago.

Butzer, K. W. and C. L. Hansen (1968). *Desert and river in Nubia: geomorphology and prehistoric environments at the Aswan reservoir.* Madison.

Butzer, K. W. and G. Ll. Isaac (eds.) (1975). *After the australopithecines: stratigraphy, ecology and culture change in the Middle Pleistocene.* The Hague.

Coppens, Y., F. C. Howell, G. Ll. Isaac and R. E. F. Leakey (eds.) (1976). *Earliest man and environments in the Lake Rudolph basin: stratigraphy, palaeoecology and evolution. (Prehistoric archaeology and ecology* 2) Chicago.

Howell, F. C. and F. Bourlière (eds.) (1963). *African ecology and human evolution.* Chicago.

Isaac, G. Ll. (1977). *Olorgesailie: the archaeology of a Middle Pleistocene lake basin in Kenya. (Prehistoric archeology and ecology* 4.) Chicago.

Leakey, M. D. (1971). *Olduvai Gorge, vol. III: Excavations in beds I and II, 1960–1963.* Cambridge.

McBurney, C. B. M. (1967). *The Haua Fteah (Cyrenaica) and the Stone Age of the south east Mediterranean.* Cambridge.

{ *Proceedings of the Pan-African Congress on Prehistory*
*Actes du congrès panafricain de préhistoire (et de l'étude du Quaternaire)*
*Actas del congreso panafricano de prehistoria y de estudio del Cuaternario*

I. Nairobi, 1947: ed. L. S. B. Leakey and S. Cole. Oxford and New York, 1952.

II. Algiers, 1952: ed. L. Balout. Paris, 1955.

III. Livingstone, 1955: ed. J. D. Clark and S. Cole. London, 1957.

IV. Léopoldville, 1959: ed. G. Mortelmans and J. Nenquin. Tervuren, 1962.

V. Santa Cruz de Tenerife, 1965: ed. L. D. Cuscoy, 2 vols. Tenerife, 1966.

VI. Dakar, 1967: ed. H. J. Hugot. Chambéry, 1972.

VII. Addis Ababa, 1971: eds. Berhanou Abébé, J. Chavaillon and J. E. G. Sutton. Addis Ababa, 1976

Wendorf, F. and A. E. Marks (eds.) (1975). *Problems in prehistory: North Africa and the Levant. (Southern Methodist University Contributions in Anthropology* **13**.) Dallas.

## I. THE PALAEO-ECOLOGY OF THE AFRICAN CONTINENT

Andrews, P. and J. A. H. van Couvering (1975). Palaeoenvironments in the East African Miocene. In F. S. Szalay (ed.), *Approaches to primate palaeobiology*, **5**, 62–103. Basel.

Bada, J. L. and L. Deems (1975). Accuracy of dates beyond the $C^{14}$ dating limit using the aspartic acid racemization technique. *Nature, Lond.* **255**, 218–19.

Baker, H. B. (1911). The origin of the Moon. (*Detroit Free Press* 23 April 1911.)

Bakker, E. M. van Zinderen and K. W. Butzer (1973). Quaternary environmental changes in southern Africa. *Soil Sci.* **116**, 236–48

Beaumont, P. B. and J. C. Vogel (1972). On a new radiocarbon chronology for Africa south of the equator, Part 2. *Afr. Stud.* **31**, 155–82.

Behrensmeyer, A. K. (1976). Fossil assemblages in relation to sedimentary environments in the East Rudolf succession. In Y. Coppens, *et al.* (eds.), *Earliest man and environments in the Lake Rudolf basin*, 383–401. Chicago.

(1978). The habitat of early African hominids: taphonomic and micro-stratigraphic evidence. In C. Jolly (ed.), *Early hominids of Africa*, 165–90. London.

Biberson, P. (1961). Le Paléolithique inférieur du Maroc atlantique. *Publs Serv. Antiquités Maroc* **17**.

(1970). Index-cards on the marine and continental cycles of the Moroccan Quaternary. *Quaternaria* **13**, 1–76.

Bishop, W. W. (1978). Geochronological framework for African Plio-Pleistocene hominidae: as Cerberus sees it. In C. Jolly (ed.), *Early hominids of Africa*, 255–66. London.

Bishop, W. W. and J. D. Clark (1967) (eds.). *Background to evolution in Africa.* Chicago.

Bishop, W. W. and J. A. Miller (eds) (1972). *Calibration of hominoid evolution.* Edinburgh and Toronto.

Bishop, W. W., J. A. Miller and F. H. Fitch (1969). New potassium–argon age determinations relevant to the Miocene fossil mammal sequence in East Africa. *Am. J. Sci.* **267**, 669–99

Bonnefille, R. (1972). Associations polliniques actuelles et quaternaires en Ethiopie. (Thesis, University of Paris.)

Bowen, B. E. and C. F. Vondra (1973). Stratigraphical relationships of the Plio-Pleistocene deposits, East Rudolf, Kenya. *Nature, Lond.* **242**, 391–3.

Brain, C. K. (1958). The Transvaal ape-man-bearing cave deposits. *Transv. Mus. Mem.* **11**.

(1967). Procedures and some results in the study of Quaternary cave fillings. In W. W. Bishop and J. D. Clark (eds.), *Background to evolution in Africa*, 285–301. Chicago.

(1976). A re-interpretation of the Swartkrans site and its remains. *S. Afr. J. Sci.* **72**, 141–6.

Broom, R. (1950). *Finding the Missing Link*. London.

Brown, F. H. and R. T. Shuey (1976). Preliminary magneto-stratigraphy of the Lower Omo Valley, Ethiopia. In Y. Coppens *et al.* (eds.), *Earliest man and environments in the Lake Rudolf basin*, 64–78. Chicago.

Butzer, K. W. (1971a). *Environment and archaeology*, 2nd edn. Chicago.

(1971b). The Lower Omo Basin: geology, fauna and hominids of the Plio-Pleistocene formations. *Naturwissenschaften* **58**, 7–16.

(1971c). Recent history of an Ethiopian Delta: the Omo Delta and the level of Lake Rudolf. *Res. Pap. Dep. Geogr. Univ. Chicago* **136**, 1–184.

(1973a). A provisional interpretation of the sedimentary sequence from Montagu Cave (Cape Province), South Africa. In C. M. Keller (ed.), *Montagu Cave*, 89–92. Berkeley.

(1973b). Spring sediments from the Acheulian site of Amanzi (Uitenhage District, South Africa). *Quaternaria* **16**, 299–320.

(1973c). Re-evaluation of the geology of the Elandsfontein (Hopefield) site, south-western Cape, South Africa. *S. Afr. J. Sci.* **69**, 234–8.

(1973d). Past climates of the Tibesti Mountains, central Sahara. *Geogrl. Rev.* **63**, 395–7.

(1973e): Pleistocene periglacial phenomena in southern Africa. *Boreas* **2**, 1–12.

(1973f). Geology of Nelson Bay Cave, Robberg, South Africa). *S. Afr. Archaeol. Bull.* **28**, 97–110.

(1974a). Geological and ecological perspectives on the Middle Pleistocene. *Quaternary Res.* **4**, 136–48.

(1974b). Geo-archaeological interpretation of two Acheulian calc-pan sites: Doornlaagte and Rooidam (Kimberley, South Africa). *J. Archaeol. Sci.* **1**, 1–25.

(1974c). Palaeo-ecology of South African australopithecines: Taung revisited. *Curr. Anthrop.* **15**, 367–82 and 413–16.

(1975a). Pleistocene littoral–sedimentary cycles of the Mediterranean Basin: a Mallorquin view. In K. W. Butzer and G. Ll. Isaac (eds.), *After the australopithecines* 25–71. The Hague.

(1975b). Patterns of environmental change in the Near East during late Pleistocene and early Holocene times. In F. Wendorf and A. E. Marks (eds.), *Problems in prehistory: North Africa and the Levant*, 389–410. Dallas.

(1976a). Lithostratigraphy of the Swartkrans Formation. *S. Afr. J. Sci.* **72**, 136–41.

(1976b). The Mursi, Nkalabong and Kibish formations, Lower Omo Basin

(Ethiopia). In Y. Coppens *et al.* (eds.), *Earliest man and environments in the Lake Rudolf basin*, 12–23. Chicago.

(1976c). Early hydraulic civilization in Egypt: a study in cultural ecology. Chicago.

(1976d). Pleistocene climates. In R. C. West (ed.), *Ecology of the Pleistocene* (*Geoscience and Man, vol. XIII*), 27–44.

(1977). Environment, culture and human evolution. *Am. Scient.* **65**, 572–82.

(1978a). Sediment stratigraphy of the Middle Stone Age sequence at Klasies River Mouth, Tsitsikama Coast, South Africa. *S. Afr. archaeol. Bull.* **33**, 141–51.

(1978b). Climate patterns in an un-glaciated continent. *Geogr. Mag.* **51**, 201–8.

(1978c) Geo-ecological perspectives on early hominid evolution. In C. Jolly (ed.), *Early hominids of Africa*, 191–217. London.

(1979). Pleistocene history of the Nile Valley in Egypt and Lower Nubia. In M. A. J. Williams and H. Faure (eds.), *The Sahara and the Nile*, 253–80. Rotterdam.

Butzer, K. W., P. B. Beaumont and J. C. Vogel (1978). Lithostratigraphy of Border Cave, Kwazulu, South Africa: A Middle Stone Age sequence beginning c.195,000 B.P. *J. archaeol. Sci.* **5**, 317–41.

Butzer, K. W., F. H. Brown and D. L. Thurber (1969). Horizontal sediments of the lower Omo Valley: the Kibish Formation. *Quaternaria* **11**, 31–46.

Butzer, K. W., J. D. Clark and H. B. S. Cooke (1974). *The geology, archaeology, and fossil mammals of the Cornelia Beds, O.F.S.* Nat. Mus. Mem. **9**, Bloemfontein.

Butzer, K. W., G. J. Fock, R. Stuckenrath and A. Zilch. (1973b). Paleo-hydrology of late Pleistocene lakes in the Alexandersfontein Pan, Kimberley, South Africa. *Nature, Lond.* **243**, 328–30.

Butzer, K. W., G. J. Fock, L. Scott and R. Stuckenrath (1979). Dating and contextual analysis of rock engravings in Southern Africa. *Science, N.Y.* **203**, 1201–4.

Butzer, K. W. and C. L. Hansen (1968). *Desert and river in Nubia*. Madison.

(1972). Late Pleistocene stratigraphy of the Kom Ombo Plain, Upper Egypt: comparison with other recent studies near Esna-Edfu. *Bull. Liais. Ass. sénégal. Etud. Quaternaire* **35–6**, 5–14.

Butzer, K. W. and D. M. Helgren (1972). Late Cenozoic evolution of the Cape coast between Knysna and Cape St. Francis, South Africa. *Quaternary Res.* **2**, 143–69.

Butzer, K. W. and G. Ll. Isaac (eds.) (1975). *After the australopithecines*. The Hague.

Butzer, K. W., G. Ll. Isaac, J. L. Richardson and C. K. Washbourn-Kamau (1972). Radiocarbon dating of East African lake levels. *Science, N.Y.* **175**, 1069–76.

Butzer, K. W., D. M. Helgren, G. J. Fock and R. Stuckenrath (1973a). Alluvial terraces of the Lower Vaal Basin, South Africa: a re-appraisal and re-investigation. *J. Geol.* **81**, 341–62.

Butzer, K. W., R. Stuckenrath, A. J. Bruzewicz and D. M. Helgren (1978). Late Cenozoic paleoclimates of the Gaap Escarpment, Kalahari margin, South Africa. *Quaternary Res.* **10**, 310–39.

Cahen, D. (1975). *Le site archéologique de la Kamoa (Shaba, Zaïre)*. Kon. Museum voor Midden-Afrika **84**, Tervuren.

Chavaillon, J. (1964). *Etude stratigraphique des formations quaternaires du Sahara nord-occidental*. CNRS, Paris.

Chavaillon, J. and N. Chavaillon (1971). Présence éventuelle d'un abri oldowayen dans le gisement de Melka-Kontouré (Ethiopie). *C. hebd. Séanc. Acad. Sci., Paris* **273**-D, 623–5.

Chmielewski, W. (1968). Early and Middle Paleolithic sites near Arkin, Sudan. In F. Wendorf (ed.), *The prehistory of Nubia*, 110–47. Dallas.

Clark, J. D. (1950). *The Stone Age cultures of Northern Rhodesia*. S. Afr. Archaeol. Soc. Cape Town.

(1959). Further excavations at Broken Hill, Northern Rhodesia. *Jl. R. anthrop. Inst.* **89**, 201–32.

(1963). *Prehistoric cultures of Northeast Angola and their significance in tropical Africa*, 2 vols. *Publções cult. Co. Diam. Angola* **62**.

(1967). *Atlas of African prehistory*. Chicago.

(1969). *The Kalambo Falls prehistoric site*, vol. 1. Cambridge.

(1975a). Stone Age man at the Victoria Falls. In D. W. Phillipson (ed.), *Mosi-oa-Tunya: a Handbook to the Victoria Falls region*, 34–43. London.

(1975b). A comparison of the late Acheulian industries of Africa and the Middle East. In K. W. Butzer and G. Ll. Isaac (eds.), *After the australopithecines*, 605–60. The Hague.

Clifford, T. N. (1966). Tectono-metallogenic units and metallogenic provinces of Africa. *Earth Planet. Sci. Lett.* **1**, 421–34.

Clifford, T. N. and I. G. Gass (eds.) (1970). *African magnetism and tectonics*. Edinburgh.

Coetzee, J. A. (1967). Pollen analytical studies in East and Southern Africa. In E. M. van Zinderen Bakker (ed.), *Palaeoecology of Africa*, vol. III, 1–146. Cape Town.

Cole, G. H. (1967). The later Acheulian and Sangoan of Southern Uganda. In W. W. Bishop and J. D. Clark (eds.), *Background to evolution in Africa*, 481–526. Chicago.

Cole, G. H. and M. R. Kleindienst (1974). Further reflections on the Isimila Acheulian. *Quaternary Res.* **4**, 346–55.

Cole, S. (1975). *Leakey's luck*. New York.

Conrad, G. (1969). *L'évolution continentale posthercynienne du Sahara algérien*. Recherches sur les zones arides, CNRS, Paris.

Cooke, H. B. S. (1958). Observations relating to Quaternary environments in East and Southern Africa. *Trans. geol. Soc. S. Afr.* **61**, (Annex.), 1–73.

(1963). Pleistocene mammal faunas of Africa with particular reference to southern Africa. In F. C. Howell and F. Bourlière (eds.), *African ecology and human evolution*, 65–116. Chicago.

(1972). The fossil mammal fauna of Africa. In A. Keast, F. C. Erk and B. Glass (eds.), *Evolution, mammals and southern continents*, 89–139. Albany, New York.

(1978). Faunal evidence for the biotic setting of early African hominids. In C. Jolly (ed.), *Early hominids of Africa*, 267–84. London.

Cooke, H. B. S. and V. J. Maglio (1972). Plio-Pleistocene stratigraphy in East

Africa in relation to proboscidean and suid evolution. In W. W. Bishop and J. A. Miller (eds.), *Calibration of hominoid evolution*, 303–30. Edinburgh and Toronto.

Coppens, Y., F. C. Howell, G. Ll. Isaac and R. E. F. Leakey (eds.) (1976). *Earliest man and environments in the Lake Rudolf basin*. Chicago.

Coryndon, S. C. and R. J. G. Savage (1973). The origin and affinities of African mammal faunas. In N. F. Hughes (ed.), *Organisms and continents through time*. Special Papers in Palaeontology **12**, 121–35. Palaeontological Association, London.

Creer, K. M. (1970). Review and interpretation of palaeomagnetic data from the Gondwanic continents. *2nd Gondwana Symposium, South Africa, July to August 1970, Proceedings and Papers*, 52–72. CSIR, Pretoria.

Crompton, A. W. (1974). The dentitions and relationships of the Southern African Triassic mammals, *Erythrotherium parringtoni* and *Megazostrodon rudnerae*. *Bull. Br. Mus. nat. Hist.* (Geology) **24**, 7, 399–437.

Cross, M. W. and V. J. Maglio (1975). *A Bibliography of the fossil mammals of Africa 1950–1972*. Department of Geological and Geophysical Sciences, Princeton University.

Curtis, G. H., R. Drake, T. E. Cerling and J. H. Hampel (1975). Age of KBS tuff in Koobi Fora Formation, East Rudolf, Kenya. *Nature, Lond.* **258**, 395–8.

Dart, R. A. (1925). *Australopithecus africanus*, the man-ape of South Africa. *Nature, Lond.* **115**, 195–9.

(1959). *Adventures with the Missing Link*. New York.

Dietz, R. S. and J. C. Holden (1970). Reconstruction of Pangaea; breakup and dispersion of continents, Permian to present. *J. geophys. Res.* **75**, 4939–56.

Downie, C. (1964). Glaciations of Mt. Kilimanjaro, northeast Tanganyika. *Bull. geol. Soc. Am.* **75**, 1–16.

Evernden, J. F. and G. H. Curtis (1965). The potassium–argon dating of late Cenozoic rocks in East Africa and Italy. *Curr. Anthrop.* **6**, 343–64.

Fage, J. D. (1963). *An atlas of African history*, 1st edn. London.

Fitch, F. J. and J. A. Miller (1970). Radiometric age determinations of Lake Rudolf artefact sites. *Nature, Lond.* **226**, 226–8.

Flint, R. F. (1959). Pleistocene climates in eastern and southern Africa. *Bull. geol. Soc. Am.* **70**, 343–74.

Frakes, L. A. and E. M. Kemp (1972). Influence of continental positions on early Teritary climates. *Nature, Lond.* **240**, 97–100.

Freeman, L. G. (1975). Acheulian sites and stratigraphy in Iberia and the Maghreb. In K. W. Butzer and G. Ll. Isaac (eds.), *After the australopithecines*, 661–744. The Hague.

Furon, R. (1950). *Géologie de l'Afrique*, 1st edn. Paris.

(1960). *Géologie de l'Afrique*, 2nd edn. Paris.

(1963). *Geology of Africa*. Translated by A. Hallam and L. A. Stevens. Edinburgh.

Gasse, F. (1975). *L'évolution des lacs de l'Afar central du Plio-Pléistocène à l'Actuel*, 3 vols. CNRS, Paris.

Goodwin, A. J. H. and C. Van Riet Lowe (1929). The Stone Age cultures of South Africa. *Ann. S. Afr. Mus.* **27**, 1–289.

Gregory, J. W. (1921). *The rift valleys and geology of East Africa*. London.

Grove, A. T. and A. Warren (1968). Quaternary landforms and climate on the south side of the Sahara. *Geogrl J.* **134**, 194–208.

Hailey, W. (Lord) (1938). *An African survey*, 1st edn. Oxford.

(1957). *An African survey*, 2nd edn. Oxford.

Hansen, C. L. and C. M. Keller (1971). Environment and activity patterning at Isimila Korongo, Iringa District, Tanzania: a preliminary report. *Am. Anthrop.* **73**, 1201–11.

Hay, R. L. (1971). Geologic background of Beds I and II: stratigraphic summary. In M. D. Leakey (ed.), *Olduvai Gorge, vol. III: Excavations in Beds I and II, 1960–1963*, 9–18. Cambridge.

(1973). Lithofacies and environments of Bed I, Olduvai Gorge, Tanzania. *Quaternary Res.* **3**, 541–60.

(1976). *Geology of the Olduvai Gorge*. Berkeley.

Helgren, D. M. (1977). Geological context of the Vaal River faunas. *S. Afr. J. Sci.* **73**, 303–7.

(1978). Acheulian settlement along the Lower Vaal River, South Africa. *J. archaeol. Sci.* **5**, 39–60.

(1979). Rivers of diamonds: an alluvial history of the Lower Vaal basin. *Res. Pap. Dep. Geogr. Univ. Chicago* **186**.

Helgren, D. M. and K. W. Butzer (1977). Paleosols of the southern Cape Coast, South Africa. *Geogrl. Rev.* **67**, 430–45.

Holmes, A. (1965). *Principles of physical geology*. London.

Hopwood, A. T. and J. P. Hollyfield (1954). An annotated bibliography of the fossil mammals of Africa (1742–1950). *Fossil Mammals Afr.* **8**, Br. Mus. Nat. Hist. London.

Howell, F. C. and F. Bourlière (eds.) (1963). *African ecology and human evolution*. New York.

Isaac, G. Ll. (1972a). Comparative studies of Pleistocene site locations in East Africa. In P. J. Ucko, R. Tringham and G. W. Dimbleby, (eds.), *Man, settlement and urbanism*, 165–76. Morristown, N.J. and London.

(1972b). Chronology and the tempo of cultural change during the Pleistocene. In W. W. Bishop and J. A. Miller (eds.), *Calibration of hominoid evolution*, pp. 381–430. Edinburgh and Toronto.

(1975). Middle Pleistocene stratigraphy and cultural patterns in East Africa. In K. W. Butzer and G. Ll. Isaac (eds.), *After the australopithecines*, 495–542. The Hague.

(1977). *Olorgesailie: archaeological studies of a Middle Pleistocene lake basin in Kenya* (*Prehistoric Archeology and Ecology* 4). Chicago.

Isaac, G. Ll. and G. H. Curtis (1974). Age of early Acheulian industries from the Peninj Group, Tanzania. *Nature, Lond.* **249**, 624–7.

Isaac, G. Ll., J. W. K. Harris and D. Crader (1976). Archeological evidence from the Koobi Fora formation. In Y. Coppens *et al.* (eds.), *Earliest man and environments in the Lake Rudolf basin* Vol. II, 533–51. Chicago.

Jackson, S. P. (ed.) (1961). *Climatological atlas of Africa*. Commission for Technical Co-operation in Africa South of the Sahara, Lagos.

Jaeger, J.-J. (1975). The mammalian faunas and hominid fossils of the middle

Pleistocene of the Maghreb. In K. W. Butzer and G. Ll. Isaac (eds.), *After the australopithecines*, 399–418. The Hague.

Jäkel, D. (1978). Eine Klimakurve für die Zentralsahara. In P. Stehli (ed.), *Sahara*, 382–96. Cologne.

Johanson, D. C., T. D. White and Y. Coppens (1978). A new species of the genus *Australopithecus* (Primates: Hominidae) from the Pliocene of Eastern Africa. Cleveland Mus. Nat. Hist., *Kirtlandia* **28**, 1–14.

Jolly, C. (ed.) (1978). *Early hominids of Africa*. London.

Keay, R. W. J. (1959). *Vegetation map of Africa, with explanatory notes*. Oxford.

King, L. C. (1967). *The morphology of the Earth*, 2nd edn. New York, Edinburgh and London.

Klein, R. G. (1973). Geological antiquity of Rhodesian Man. *Nature, Lond.* **244**, 311–12.

(1974). Environment and subsistence of prehistoric man in the southern Cape Province, South Africa. *World Archaeol.* **5**, 249–84.

(1977). The ecology of early man in southern Africa. *Science, N.Y.* **195**, 115–26.

(1980). The interpretation of mammalian faunas from Stone Age archaeological sites, with special reference to sites in the southern Cape Province, South Africa. In A. K. Behrensmeyer and A. P. Hill (eds.), *Fossils in the making: Vertebrate Taphonomy and Paleoecology*, 223–46. Chicago.

Kleindienst, M. R. (1973). Excavations at Site JK2, Olduvai Gorge, Tanzania, 1961–62: the geological setting. *Quaternaria* **17**, 145–208.

Kraus, E. B. (1973). Comparison between Ice Age and present general circulations. *Nature, Lond.* **245**, 129–33.

Krenkel, E. (1925). *Geologie der Erde: Geologie Afrikas*, vol. I. Berlin.

(1928). *Geologie der Erde: Geologie Afrikas*, vol. II. Berlin.

Leakey, L. S. B. (1951). *Olduvai Gorge*. Cambridge.

(1959). A new fossil skull from Olduvai. *Nature, Lond.* **189**, 491–3.

Leakey, L. S. B. and S. Cole (1952). *Proceedings of the Pan-African Congress on Prehistory 1947*. Oxford and New York.

Leakey, L. S. B., J. F. Evernden and G. H. Curtis (1961). Age of Bed I, Olduvai Gorge, Tanganyika. *Nature, Lond.* **191**, 478–9.

Leakey, L. S. B., P. V. Tobias and J. R. Napier, (1964). A new species of the genus *Homo* from Olduvai Gorge. *Nature, Lond.* **202**, 7–9.

Leakey, Margaret, P. V. Tobias, J. E. Martyn and R. E. F. Leakey (1969). An Acheulian industry with prepared core technique and the discovery of a contemporary hominid mandible at Lake Baringo, Kenya. *Proc. prehist. Soc.* **35**, 48–76.

Leakey, M. D. (1970). Stone artifacts from Swartkrans. *Nature, Lond.* **225**, 1221–5.

(1971). *Olduvai Gorge, vol. III: Excavations in Beds I and II, 1960–1963*. Cambridge.

(1975). Cultural patterns in the Olduvai sequence. In K. W. Butzer and G. Ll. Isaac (eds.), *After the australopithecines*, 477–94. The Hague.

Leakey, M. D., R. L. Hay, G. H. Curtis, R. E. Drake, M. K. Jackes and T. D. White (1976). Fossil hominids from the Laetolil Beds. *Nature, Lond.* **262**, 460–6.

Livingstone, D. A. (1975). Late Quaternary climatic change in Africa. *Ann. Rev. Ecol. & Syst.* **6**, 249–80.

McCall, G. J. H., B. H. Baker and J. Walsh (1967). Late Tertiary and Quaternary sediments of the Kenya Rift valley. In W. W. Bishop and J. D. Clark (eds.), *Background to evolution in Africa*, 191–228. Chicago.

Maglio, V. J. (1972). Vertebrate faunas and chronology of hominid-bearing sediments east of Lake Rudolf, Kenya. *Nature, Lond.* **239**, 379–85.

(1973). Origin and evolution of the Elephantidae. *Trans. Am. phil. Soc.* N.S. **63**, pt. 3.

Maglio, V. J. and H. B. S. Cooke (eds.) (1978). *Evolution of African Mammals.* Cambridge, Harvard University Press.

Maley, J. (1977). Palaeoclimates of Central Sahara during the early Holocene. *Nature, Lond.* **269**, 573–7.

Messerli, B. (1967). Die eiszeitliche und die gegenwärtige Verglatscherung im Mittelmeerraum. *Geographica helv.* **22**, 105–228.

Neuville, R. and A. Ruhlmann (1941). *La place du Paléolithique ancien dans le Quaternaire marocain. Coll. Hesperis* **8**. Institut des Hautes Etudes marocaines, Rabat.

Olausson, E., U. Z. Bilal Ul-Haq, G. B. Karlsson and I. U. Olsson (1971). Evidence in Indian Ocean Cores of late Pleistocene changes in oceanic and atmospheric circulation. *Geol. För. Stockh. Förh.* **93**, 51–84.

Partridge, T. C. (1975). Stratigraphic, geomorphological and paleoenvironmental studies of the Makapansgat Limeworks and Sterkfontein hominid sites. Paper, S. Afr. Quaternary Assoc. Cape Town.

Peabody, F. E. (1954). Travertines and cave deposits of the Kaap escarpment of South africa, and the type locality of *Australopithecus africanus* Dart. *Bull. Geol. Soc. Am.* **65**, 671–706.

Plumstead, E. P. (1969). Three thousand million years of plant life in Africa. *Geol. Soc. S. Afr.* **72**, (Annex.).

Rognon, P. (1967). *Le massif de l'Atakor et ses bordures (Sahara Central). Recherches sur les zones arides*, CNRS, Paris.

Roubet, C. (1969). Essai de datation absolue d'un biface-hachereau paléolithique de l'Afar (Ethiopie). *Anthropologie, Paris* **73**, 503–24.

Sandford, K. S. (1934). Paleolithic man and the Nile Valley in Upper and Middle Egypt. *Publs orient. Inst. Univ. Chicago* **18**, 1–131.

Sandford, K. S. and W. J. Arkell (1933). Paleolithic man and the Nile Valley in Nubia and Upper Egypt. *Publs. orient. Inst. Chicago* **17**, 1–92.

Servant, M. (1973). *Séquences continentales et variations climatiques: évolution du bassin du Tchad au Cénozoique supérieur.* Thesis University of Paris. ORSTROM, Paris.

Servant, M., S. Servant and G. Délibrias (1969). Chronologie du Quaternaire récent des basses régions du Tchad. *C. r. hebd. Séanc. Acad. Sci., Paris* **269**-D, 1603–6.

Shuey, R. T., F. H. Brown and M. K. Croes (1974). Magnetostratigraphy of the Shungura Formation, southwestern Ethiopia: fine structure of the lower matuyama polarity epoch. *Earth Planet. Sci. Lett.* **23**, 249–60.

Snider, A. (1858). *La création et ses mystères dévoilés.* Paris.

Söhnge, P. G., D. J. L. Visser and C. Van Riet Lowe (1937). *The geology and archaeology of the Vaal river Basin. Mem. geol. Surv. Un. S. Afr.* **35.**

Stearns, C. E. and D. L. Thurber (1967). $Th^{230}U^{234}$ dates of late Pleistocene marine fossils from the Mediterranean and Moroccan littorals. *Prog. Oceanogr.* **4,** 293–305.

Suess, F. E. (1885–1901). *Das Antlitz der Erde.* Vienna. (Translated by H. B. C. Sollas as *The face of the Earth,* 5 vols. 1904, 1906, 1908, 1909, 1924. Oxford.)

Szabo, B. J. (1979). Dating fossil bone from Cornelia, N. E. Orange Free State, South Africa. *J. archaeol. Sci.* **6.**

Szabo, B. J. and K. W. Butzer (1979). Uranium-series dating of lacustrine limestones from pan deposits with Final Acheulian assemblage at Rooidam, Kimberley District, South Africa. *Quaternary Res.* **11,** 257–60.

Taieb, M. (1974). Evolution quaternaire du bassin de l'Awash. 2 vols. Thesis, University of Paris VI.

Taieb, M., Y. Coppens, D. C. Johanson and J. Kalb (1972). Dépôts sédimentaires et faunes du Plio-Pléistocène de la basse vallée de l'Awash (Afar Central, Ethiopie). *C. r. hebd. Séanc. Acad. Sci., Paris* **275**-D, 819–22.

Taylor, F. B. (1910). Bearing of the Tertiary mountain belts on the origin of the Earth's plan. *Bull. geol. Soc. Am.* **21,** 179–226.

Thompson, B. W. (1965). *The climate of Africa.* Oxford.

du Toit, A. L. (1926). *The geology of South Africa.* Edinburgh.

(1937). *Our wandering continents.* Edinburgh.

Tooley, R. V. and C. Bricker (1969). *A history of cartography; 2500 years of maps and mapmakers.* London.

UNESCO (1963). *A review of the natural resources of the African continent.* UNESCO, Paris.

(1964). *Geological map of Africa (1 : 5,000,000).* UNESCO, Paris.

(1968a). *International tectonic map of Africa (1 : 5,000,000).* UNESCO, Paris.

(1968b). *Mineral map of Africa (1 : 10,000,000).* UNESCO, Paris.

(1970). *Survey of the scientific and technical potential of the countries of Africa.* UNESCO, Paris.

(1971). *Tectonics of Africa.* UNESCO, Paris.

Van Campo. M. (1975). Pollen analyses in the Sahara. In F. Wendorf and A. E. Marks (eds.), *Problems in prehistory: North Africa and the Levant,* 45–63, Dallas.

Vrba, E. (1975). Some evidence of chronology and palaeoecology of Sterkfontein, Swartkrans and Kromdraai from the fossil Bovidae. *Nature, Lond.* **254,** 301–4.

Wegener, A. (1912). Die entstehung der Kontinente. *Petermanns geogr. Mitt.* **58,** 185–95, 253–6, 305–9.

(1915). *Die Entstehung der Kontinente und Ozeane.* Brunswick, Germany.

Wendorf, F., R. L. Laury, C. C. Albritton, R. Schild, C. V. Haynes, P. E. Damon, M. Shaffiquillah and R. Scarborough (1975). Dates for the Middle Stone Age of East Africa. *Science, N.Y.* **187,** 740–2.

Williams, J., R. G. Barry and W. M. Washington (1974). Simulation of the atmospheric circulation using the NCAR global circulation model with Ice Age boundary conditions. *J. appl. Meteorol.* **13,** 305–17.

Worthington, E. B. (1938). *Science in Africa.* Oxford.

## 2. ORIGINS AND EVOLUTION OF AFRICAN HOMINIDAE

Abel, W. (1931). Kritische Untersuchungen über *Australopithecus africanus* Dart. *Morph. Jb.* **65**, 539–640.

Adloff, P. (1931). Uber die Ursprung des Menschen im Lichte der Gebiss-forschung. *Schr. konigsb. gelehrt. Ges. nathrw. Kl.* **8**, 299–312.

—— (1932). Das Gebiss von *Australopithecus africanus* Dart. Einige ergänzende Bemerkungen zum Eckzahn problem. *Z. Anat. EntwGesch.* **97**, 145–56.

Anthony, J. (1966). Premières observations sur le moulage endocranien des hommes fossiles du Jebel Irhoud (Maroc). *C.r. hebd. Séanc. Acad. Sci., Paris* **262**-D, 556–8.

Arambourg, C. (1962). Les faunes mammalogiques du Pléistocène circum mediterranéen. *Quaternaria* **6**, 97–110.

—— (1963). Le gisement de Ternifine: *l'Atlanthropus* de Ternifine. *Archs Inst. Paléont. hum.* **32**, 37–190.

Arambourg, C. and P. Biberson (1955). Découverte de vestiges humains dans la carrière de Sidi Abderrahman, près de Casablanca. *C.r. hebd. Séanc. Acad. Sci., Paris* **240**-D, 1661–3.

—— (1956). The fossil human remains from the Paleolithic site of Sidi Abder-rahman (Morocco). *Am. J. phys. Anthrop.* **14**, 467–90.

Arkell, A. J., D. M. A. Bate, L. H. Wells and A. D. Lacaille (1951). The Pleistocene Fauna of Two Blue Nile Sites. *Fossil Mammals Afr.* **2**. Br. Mus. Nat. Hist., London.

Aronson, J. A., T. J. Schmitt, R. C. Walter, M. Taieb, J.-J. Tiercelin, D. C. Johanson, C. W. Naeser and A. E. M. Nairn (1977). New geo-chronologic and palaeomagnetic data for the hominid-bearing Hadar Formation of Ethiopia. *Nature, Lond.* **267**, 323–7.

Bada, J. L. and L. Deems (1975). Accuracy of dates beyond the $^{14}$C dating limit using the aspartic acid racemisation reaction. *Nature, Lond.* **255**, 218–19.

Bada, J. L. and R. Protsch (1973). Racemisation reaction of aspartic acid and its use in dating fossil bones. *Proc. nat. Acad. Sci. U.S.A.* **70**, 1331–4.

Bada, J. L., R. Protsch and R. A. Schroeder (1973). The racemisation reaction of isoleucine used as a paleo-temperature indicator. *Nature, Lond.* **241**, 394–5.

Bada, J. L., R. A. Schroeder, R. Protsch and R. Berger (1974). Concordance of collagen based radiocarbon and aspartic-acid racemization ages. *Proc. nat. Acad. Sci. U.S.A.* **71**, 914–17.

Bakker, E. M. van Zinderen and K. W. Butzer (1973). Quaternary environ-mental changes in southern Africa. *Soil Sci.* **116**, 236–48.

Balout, L. (1965a). Données nouvelles sur le problème du Moustérien en Afrique du Nord. In *Actas del V Congreso Panafricano de Prehistoria y de Estudio del Cuaternario* (Santa Cruz de Ternerife), vol. 1, 137–43.

—— (1956b). Le Moustérien du Maghreb. *Quaternaria* **7**, 43–58.

—— (1970). L'industrie néandertalienne du Djebel Irhoud (Maroc). *Fundamenta* A(2) (A. Rust Festschrift), 1970, 57–60.

Balout, L., P. Biberson and J. Tixier (1967). L'Acheuléen de Ternifine (Algérie). Gisement de l'Atlanthrope. *Anthropologie, Paris* **71**, 217–37.

Beaumont, P. B. (1973). Border Cave – a progress report. *S. Afr. J. Sci.* **69**, 41–6.

Beaumont, P. B. and A. K. Boshier (1972). Some comments on recent findings at Border Cave, northern Natal. *S. Afr. J. Sci.* **68**, 22–4.

Beaumont, P. B. and J. C. Vogel (1972). On a new radiocarbon chronology for Africa south of the Equator. *Afr. Stud.* **31**, 155–82.

Behrensmeyer, A. K. (1976a). Lothagam Hill, Kanapoi, and Ekora: a general summary of stratigraphy and faunas. In Y. Coppens *et al.* (eds.), *Earliest man and environments in the Lake Rudolf basin*, 163–70. Chicago.

(1976b). Fossil assemblages in relation to sedimentary environments in the East Rudolf succession. In Y. Coppens *et al.* (eds.), *Earliest man and environments in the Lake Rudolf basin*, 383–401. Chicago.

Bennejeant, C. (1936). La dentition de *l'Australopithecus africanus* (Dart). *Mammalia* **1**, 8–14.

(1953). Les dentures temporaires des Primates. *Bull. Mém. Soc. Anthrop. Paris* **4**, series 10, 11–44.

Berggren, W. A. (1969). Cenozoic chronostratigraphy, planktonic foramineral zonation and the radiometric time-scale. *Nature, Lond.* **224**, 1072–5.

(1971). Tertiary boundaries. In B. F. Funnell and W. R. Riedel (eds.), *Micropalaeontology of oceans*, 693–809. Cambridge.

(1972). A Cenozoic time-scale – some implications for regional geology and paleobiology. *Lethaia* **5**, 195–215.

(1973). The Pliocene time-scale: calibration of planktonic foraminiferal and calcareous non-plankton zones. *Nature, Lond.* **243**, 391–7.

Berggren, W. A. and J. A. van Couvering (1974). The late Neogene. Biostratigraphy, geochronology and paleoclimatology of the last 15 million years in marine and continental sequences. *Palaeogeogr. Palaeoclimatol. Palaeoecol.* **16**, 1–216.

Biberson, P. (1956). Le gisement de l'Atlanthrope de Sidi Abderrahman (Casablanca). *Bull. Archéol. maroc.* **1**, 39–91.

(1961). Le cadre paléogéographique de la préhistoire du Maroc atlantique. *Publs Serv. antiquités Maroc* **16**.

(1963). Quelques précisions sur les classifications du Quaternaire marocain. *Bull. Soc. géol. Fr.* **7:5**, 607–16.

(1964). La place des hommes du Paléolithique marocain dans la chronologie du Pléistocène atlantique. *Anthropologie, Paris* **68**, 475–526.

(1971). Essai de redefinition des cycles climatiques du Quaternaire continental du Maroc. *Bull. Ass. fr. Hétude Quatern.* **1:26**, 3–13.

Bilsborough, A. (1972). Anagenesis in hominid evolution. *Man* **7**, 481–3.

(1973). A multivariate study of evolutionary change in the hominid cranial vault with some evolution rates. *J. hum. Evol.* **2**, 387–403.

Bishop, W. W. (1967). The later Tertiary in East Africa. In W. W. Bishop and J. D. Clark (eds.), *Background to Evolution in Africa*, 31–56. Chicago.

(1971). The late Cenozoic history of East Africa in relation to hominoid evolution. In K. K. Turekian (ed.), *Late Cenozoic glacial ages*, 493–527. New Haven.

(1972). Stratigraphic succession 'versus' calibration in East Africa. In

W. W. Bishop and J. A. Miller (eds.), *Calibration of hominoid evolution*, 219–46. Edinburgh and Toronto.

(1973). The tempo of human evolution. *Nature, Lond.* **244**, 405–9.

Bishop, W. W. and G. R. Chapman (1970). Early Pliocene sediments and fossils from the northern Kenya Rift valley. *Nature, Lond.* **226**, 914–18.

Bishop, W. W., G. R. Chapman, A. Hill and J. A. Miller (1971). Succession of Cainozoic vertebrate assemblages from the northern Kenya Rift Valley. *Nature, Lond.* **233**, 389–94.

Bishop, W. W., M. Pickford and A. Hill (1975). New evidence regarding the Quaternary geology, archaeology and hominids of Chesowanja, Kenya. *Nature, Lond.* **258**, 204–8.

Bishop, W. W. and J. A. Miller (eds.) (1972). *Calibration of hominoid evolution*. Edinburgh and Toronto.

Bishop, W. W. and M. H. Pickford (1975). Geology, fauna and palaeo-environments of the Ngorora Formation, Kenya Rift Valley. *Nature, Lond.* **254**, 185–92.

Black, D. (1931). On an adolescent skull of *Sinanthropus pekinensis* in comparison with an adult skull of the same species and with other hominid skulls, recent and fossil. *Palaeont. sin.* series D, **7:2**, 1–144.

Black, D., T. de Chardin, C. C. Young and W. C. Pei (1933). Fossil man in China. The Choukoutien cave deposits with a synopsis of our present knowledge of the late Cenozoic of China. *Mem. geol. Surv. China* series A. **11**, 1–158.

Boaz, N. T. and F. C. Howell (1977). A gracile hominid cranium from upper Member G of the Shungura Formation, Ethiopia. *Am. J. phys. anthrop.* **46**, 93–108.

Boswell, P. G. H. (1935). Human remains from Kanam and Kanjera, Kenya Colony. *Nature, Lond.* **135**, 71.

Brace, C. L. (1967). *The stages of human evolution*. Englewood Cliffs, New Jersey.

(1973). Sexual dimorphism in human evolution. *Yearb. phys. Anthrop.* **16**, 50–68.

Brain, C. K. (1958). The Transvaal ape-man-bearing cave deposits. *Transv. Mus. Mem.* **11**.

(1968). Who killed the Swartkrans ape-men? *S. Afr. Mus. Assoc. Bull.* **9**, 127–39.

(1970). New finds at the Swartkrans australopithecine site. *Nature, Lond.* **225**, 1112–19.

(1973). The significance of Swartkrans. *J. S. Afr. biol. Soc.* **13**, 7–23.

(1975). An interpretation of the bone assemblage from the Kromdraai australopithecine site, South Africa. In R. H. Tuttle (ed.), *Paleoanthropology, morphology and paleoecology*. The Hague.

(1976). A re-interpretation of the Swartkrans site and its remains. *S. Afr. J. Sci.* **72**, 141–6.

(1978). Some aspects of the South African australopithecine sites and their bone accumulations. In C. J. Jolly (ed.), *Early hominids of Africa*, 131–64. London.

Brock, A. and R. L. Hay (1976). The Olduvai Event at Olduvai Gorge. *Earth Planet. Sci. Lett.* **29**, 126–30.

Brock, A. and G. Ll. Isaac (1974). Palaeomagnetic stratigraphy and chronology of hominid-bearing sediments east of Lake Rudolf, Kenya. *Nature, Lond.* **247**, 344–8.

Broom, R. (1925a). Some notes on the Taung skull. *Nature, Lond.* **115**, 569–71.

(1925b). On the newly discovered South African man-ape. *Nat. Hist., N.Y.* **25**, 409–18.

(1929a). Note on the milk dentition of *Australopithecus. Proc. zool. Soc. Lond.* 1928, 85–8.

(1929b). The Transvaal fossil human skeleton. *Nature, Lond.* **123**, 415–16.

(1938). The Pleistocene anthropoid apes of South Africa. *Nature, Lond.* **142**, 377–9.

(1941). The milk molars of man and anthropoids. *S. Afr. dent. J.* **15**, 314–16.

(1947). The upper milk molars of the ape-man, *Plesianthropus. Nature, Lond.* **159**, 602.

(1950). The genera and species of the South African fossil ape-men. *Am. J. phys. Anthrop.* **8**, 1–13.

Broom, R. and J. T. Robinson (1949). A new type of fossil man. *Nature, Lond.* **164**, 322–3.

(1950). Man contemporaneous with the Swartkrans ape-man. *Am. J. phys. Anthrop.* **8**, 489–94.

Broom, R., J. T. Robinson and G. W. H. Schepers (1950). Sterkfontein ape-man *Plesianthropus. Transv. Mus. Mem.* **4**.

Broom, R. and G. W. H. Schepers (1946). The South African fossil ape-men, the Australopithecinae. *Transv. Mus. Mem.* **2**.

Brothwell, D. R. (1963). Evidence of early population change in central and southern Africa: doubts and problems. *Man* **63**, 101–4.

Brown, F. H. (1972). Radiometric dating of sedimentary formations in the lower Omo valley, Ethiopia. In W. W. Bishop and J. A. Miller (eds.), *Calibration of hominoid evolution*, 273–87. Edinburgh and Toronto.

Brown, F. H. and W. P. Nash (1976). Radiometric dating and tuff mineralogy of Omo Group deposits. In Y. Coppens *et al.* (eds.), *Earliest man and environments in the Lake Rudolf basin*, 50–63. Chicago.

Brown, F. H. and R. T. Shuey (1976). Magnetostratigraphy of the Shungura and Usno Formations, lower Omo valley, Ethiopia. In Y. Coppens, *et al.* (eds.), *Earliest man and environments in the Lake Rudolf basin*, 64–78. Chicago.

Brown, F. H., R. T. Shuey and M. K. Croes (1978). Magnetostratigraphy of the Shungura and Usno Formations, southwestern Ethiopia: new data and comprehensive reanalysis. *Geophysical J. Royal Astron. Soc., Lond.* **54**, 519–38.

Brown, F. H., F. C. Howell and G. G. Eck (1978). Observations on problems of correlation of late Cenozoic hominid-bearing formations in the north Rudolf basin. In W. W. Bishop (ed.), *Geological background to fossil man*, 473–98. Edinburgh and Toronto.

Butzer, K. W. (1973). Re-evaluation of the geology of the Elandsfontein (Hopefield) site, south-western Cape, South Africa. *S. Afr. J. Sci.* **69**, 234–8.

(1974a). Geological and ecological perspectives on the Middle Pleistocene. *Quaternary Res.* **4**, 136–48.

(1974b). Paleoecology of South African australopithecines: Taung revisited. *Curr. anthrop.* **15**, 367–82 and 413–16.

(1976). Lithostratigraphy of the Swartkrans formation. *S. Afr. J. Sci.* **72**, 136–41.

(1978). Geo-ecological perspectives on early hominid evolution. In C. J. Jolly (ed.), *Early hominids of Africa*, 191–218. London.

Butzer, K. W. and D. M. Helgren (1972). Late Cenozoic evolution of the Cape coast between Knysna and Cape St. Francis, South Africa. *Quaternary Res.* **2**, 143–69.

Butzer, K. W. and D. L. Thurber (1969). Some late Cenozoic sedimentary formations of the lower Omo basin. *Nature, Lond.* **222**, 1132–7.

Butzer, K. W., J. D. Clark and H. B. S. Cooke (1974). *The geology, archaeology and fossil mammals of the Cornelia Beds*, O.F.S. Mem. Nat. Mus. Bloemfontein **9**.

Butzer, K. W., D. M. Helgren, G. J. Fock and R. Stuckenrath (1973). Alluvial terraces of the lower Vaal river, South Africa: a reappraisal and reinvestigation. *J. Geol.* **81**, 341–62.

(1974). Alluvial terraces of the lower Vaal river, South Africa: a reappraisal and reinvestigation. *J. Geol.* **82**, 663–7.

Butzer, K. W., G. Ll. Isaac, J. L. Richardson and C. Washbourn-Kamau (1972). Radiocarbon dating of the East African lake levels. *Science, N.Y.* **175**, 1069–76.

Campbell, B. G. (1963). Quantitative taxonomy and human evolution. In S. L. Washburn (ed.), *Classification and human evolution*, 50–74. Chicago.

(1965). The nomenclature of the Hominidae, including a definitive list of hominid taxa. *Occ. Pap. R. Anthrop. Inst.* **22**.

(1972). Man for all seasons. In B. G. Campbell (ed.), *Sexual selection and the descent of man, 1871–1971*, 40–58. Chicago.

(1973). New concepts in physical anthropology: fossil man. *Ann. Rev. Anthrop.* **1**, 27–54.

(1974). A new taxonomy of fossil man. *Yearb. phys. Anthrop.* **17**, 195–201.

(1978). Some problems in hominid classification and nomenclature. In C. J. Jolly (ed.), *Early hominids of Africa*, 567–82. London.

Camps, G. (1968). Tableau chronologique de la préhistoire récente du Nord de l'Afrique: première synthèse des datations absolues obtenues par le carbone 14. *Bull. Soc. préhist. fr.* **75**, 609–22.

(1974). Nouvelles remarques sur l'âge de l'Atérien. *Bull. Soc. préhist. fr.* **71**, 163–4.

Carney, J., A. Hill, J. A. Miller and A. Walker (1971). Late australopithecine from Baringo district, Kenya. *Nature, Lond.* **230**, 509–14.

Cerling, T. E., F. H. Brown, B. W. Cerling, G. H. Curtis and R. E. Drake (1979). Preliminary correlations between the Koobi Fora and Shungura Formations, East Africa. *Nature, Lond.* **279**, 118–21.

Chavaillon, J. (1973). Chronologie des niveaux paléolithiques de Melka-Kontouré. *C.r. hebd. Séanc. Acad. Sci., Paris* **276**-D, 1533–6.

(1976). Evidence for the technical practices of early Pleistocene hominids, Shungura Formation, lower Omo valley, Ethiopia. In Y. Coppens *et al.*

(eds.), *Earliest man and environments in the Lake Rudolf basin*, 563–73. Chicago.

Chavaillon, J., C. Brahimi and Y. Coppens (1974). Première découverte d'hominidé dans l'un des sites Acheuléens de Melka-Kontouré (Éthiopie). *C.r. hebd. Séanc. Acad. Sci., Paris* **278**-D, 3299–3302.

Choubert, G. and J. Marçais (1947). Le Quaternaire des environs de Rabat et l'âge de l'homme de Rabat. *C.r. hebd. séanc. Acad. Sci., Paris* **224**, 1645–7.

Ciochon, R. L. and R. S. Corruccini (1976). Shoulder joint of Sterkfontein *Australopithecus*. *S. Afr. J. Sci.* **72**, 80–2.

Clark, J. D. (1969). Further excavations at Broken Hill, Northern Rhodesia. *Jl R. Anthrop. Inst.* **89**, 201–32.

(1967). *Atlas of African prehistory*. Chicago.

Clark, J. D., K. P. Oakley, L. H. Wells and J. A. C. McClelland (1950). New studies on Rhodesian Man. *Jl. R. Anthrop. Inst.* **77**, 7–32.

Clarke, R. J. (1976). New cranium of *Homo erectus* from Lake Ndutu, Tanzania. *Nature, Lond.* **262**, 485–7.

(1977). A juvenile cranium and some adult teeth of early Homo from Swartkrans, Transvaal. *S. Afr. J. Sci.* **73**, 46–9.

(1979). Early hominid footprints from Tanzania. *S. Afr. J. Sci.* **75**, 148–9.

Clarke, R. J. and F. C. Howell (1972). Affinities of the Swartkrans 847 cranium. *Am. J. phys. Anthrop.* **37**, 319–36.

Clarke, R. J., F. C. Howell and C. K. Brain (1970). More evidence of an advanced hominid at Swartkrans. *Nature, Lond.* **225**, 1219–22.

Conroy, G. C., C. J. Jolly, D. Kramer and J. E. Kalb (1978). Newly discovered fossil hominid skull from the Afar depression, Ethiopia, *Nature, Lond.* **275**, 67–70.

Cooke, H. B. S. (1963). Pleistocene mammal faunas of Africa, with particular reference to southern Africa. In F. C. Howell and F. Bourlière (eds.), *African ecology and human evolution*, 65–116. Chicago.

(1967). The Pleistocene sequence in South Africa and problems of correlation. In W. W. Bishop and J. D. Clark (eds.), *Background to evolution in Africa*, 175–84. Chicago.

Cooke, H. B. S. and V. J. Maglio (1972). Plio-Pleistocene stratigraphy in East Africa in relation to proboscidean and suid evolution. In W. W. Bishop and J. A. Miller (eds.), *Calibration of hominoid evolution*, 303–30. Edinburgh and Toronto.

Cooke, H. B. S., B. D. Malan and L. H. Wells (1945). Fossil man in the Lebombo mountains, South Africa: the 'Border Cave', Ingwavuma district, Zululand. *Man* **3**, 6–13.

Coon, C. S. (1962). *The origin of races*. New York.

Coppens, Y. (1961). Découverte d'un australopithecine dans le Villafranchian du Tchad. *C.r. hebd. Séanc. Acad. Sci., Paris* **252**-D, 3851–2.

(1962). Découverte d'un australopithecine dans le Villafranchian du Tchad. *Colloques. CNRS* **104**, 455–9.

(1965). L'hominien du Tchad. *C.r. hebd. Séanc. Acad. Sci., Paris* **260**-D, 2869–71.

(1966). Le Tchadanthropus. *Anthropologie, Paris* **70**, 5–16.

(1978). Les hominidés du Pliocène et du Pléistocène d'Ethiopie: chronologie, systématique, environnement. In *Les origines humaines et les époques de l'intelligence*, Fondation Singer-Polignac, 79–102. Paris.

Corruccini, R. S. and R. L. Ciochon (1979). Primate facial allometry and interpretations of australopithecine variation. *Nature, Lond.* **281**, 62–4.

Curtis, G. H., R. Drake, T. E. Cerling and J. H. Hampel (1975). Age of the KBS tuff in the Koobi Fora Formation, East Rudolf, Kenya. *Nature, Lond.* **258**, 395–8.

Curtis, G. H. and R. L. Hay (1972). Further geological studies and potassium–argon dating at Olduvai Gorge and Ngorongoro Crater. In W. W. Bishop and J. A. Miller (eds.), *Calibration of hominoid evolution*, 289–301. Edinburgh and Toronto.

Dahlberg, A. A. (1960). The Olduvai giant hominid tooth. *Nature, Lond.* **188**, 962.

Dart, R. A. (1925). *Australopithecus africanus*: the man-ape of South Africa. *Nature, Lond.* **115**, 195–9.

(1929). A note on the Taungs skull. *S. Afr. J. Sci.* **26**, 648–58.

(1930–1). I caratteri dell' *Australopithecus africanus*. *Archo Antrop. Etnol.* **60–1**, 287–95.

(1934). The dentition of *Australopithecus africanus*. *Folia anat. jap.* **12**, 207–21.

(1940a). The status of *Australopithecus*. *Am. J. phys. Anthrop.* **36**, 167–86.

(1940b). Recent discoveries bearing on human history in southern Africa. *Jl R. Anthrop. Inst.* **70**, 13–27.

(1948). The infancy of *Australopithecus*. In A. L. du Toit (ed.), *Robert Broom Commemorative Volume*, 143–52. Roy. Soc. of S. Afr., Cape Town.

(1956). Cultural status of the South African man-apes. *Smithsonian Annual Report 1956*, 317–38.

(1957a). The Makapansgat australopithecine osteodontokeratic culture. In *Proceedings of the Third Pan-African Congress on Prehistory (Livingstone 1955)*, 161–71. London.

(1957b). The osteodontokeratic culture of *Australopithecus prometheus*. *Transv. Mus. Mem.* **10**.

Davis, P. R. (1964). Hominid fossils from Bed I, Olduvai Gorge, Tanganyika. *Nature, Lond.* **201**, 967–8.

Day, M. H. (1969). Femoral fragment of a robust australopithecine from Olduvai Gorge, Tanzania. *Nature, Lond.* **221**, 230–3.

(1971). The Omo human skeletal remains. In F. Bordes (ed.), *The origin of Homo sapiens*, 31–5. UNESCO, Paris.

(1973a). Locomotor features of the lower limb in hominids. *Sym. zool. Soc. Lond.* **33**, 29–51.

(1973b). The development of *Homo sapiens*. *Accad. naz. dei Lincei, Rome* **370**, 87–95.

(1976a). Hominid postcranial remains from the East Rudolf succession – a review. In Y. Coppens *et al.* (eds.), *Earliest man and environments in the Lake Rudolf basin*. 507–21. Chicago.

(1976b). Hominid postcranial material from Bed I, Olduvai Gorge. In

G. Ll. Issac and E. R. McCown (eds.), *Human origins: L. S. B. Leakey and the East African evidence*, 362–74. Menlo Park, CA.

Day, M. H., M. D. Leakey, T. R. Olson, R. E. F. Leakey, A. Walker, H. M. McHenry, R. S. Corruccini, D. C. Johanson and T. D. White (1980). On the status of *Australopithecus afarensis*. *Science* **207**, 1102–5.

Day, M. H. and T. I. Molleson (1973). The Trinil femora. *Symp. Soc. Study hum. Biol.* **11**, 127–54.

Day, M. H. and B. A. Wood (1968). Functional affinities of the Olduvai hominid 8 talus. *Man* **3**, 440–5.

Débenath, A. (1972). Nouvelles fouilles à Dar es Soltane (Champ de tir d'El Menzeh) près de Rabat (Maroc). Note préliminaire. *Bull. Soc. préhist. fr.* **69**, 178–9.

(1975). Découverte de restes humains probablement atériens à Dar es Soltane (Maroc). *C.r. hebd. Séanc. Acad. Sci., Paris* **281**-D, 875–6.

Dietrich, W. O. (1939). Zur Stratigraphie der *Africanthropus* fauna. *Zentbl. Miner. Geol. Paläont.* **B**, 1–9.

(1942). Ältestquartäre Säugetiere aus der südlichen Serengeti, Deutsch-Ostafrika. *Palaeontographica* **94**, 43–133.

(1945). Nashornreste aus dem Quartär Deutsch-Ostafrika. *Palaeontographica* **96**, 46–90.

(1950). Fossile Antilopen und Rinder Äquatorialafrikas. *Palaeontographica* **99**, 1–62.

Drake, R. E., G. H. Curtis, T. E. Cerling, B. W. Cerling and J. H. Hampel (1980). KBS tuff dating and geochronology of tuffaceous sediments in the Koobi Fora and Shungura Formations, East Africa. *Nature, Lond.* **283**, 368–71.

Drennan, M. R. (1937). The Florisbad skull and brain cast. *Trans. R. Soc. S. Afr.* **25**, 103–14.

Dreyer, T. F. (1935). A human skull from Florisbad, Orange Free State, with a note on the endocranial cast by C. U. Ariens Kappers. *Proc. K. ned. Akad. Wet.* **38**, 119–28.

(1936). The endocranial cast of the Florisbad skull – a correction. *Soöl. Navors. nas. Mus. Bloemfontein* **1**, 21–3.

(1938). The fissuration of the frontal endocranial cast of the Florisbad skull compared with that of the Rhodesian skull. *Z. Rassenk.* **8**, 193–8.

(1947). Further observations on the Florisbad skull. *Soöl. Navors. nas. Mus. Bloemfontein* **1**, 183–90.

Dubois, E. (1891). Palaeontologische onderzoekingen op Java. *Versl. Mijnw., Batavia*, 1891, **3**, 12–14; **4**, 12–15.

(1894). Pithecanthropus erectus. *Eine menschenähnliche Übergangsform aus Java* Netherlands Government, Amsterdam. (Also in *Jaarb. Mijn. Ned.-Oost-Indië* (1895), **24**, 5–77.)

(1926). On the principal characters of the femur of *Pithecanthropus erectus*. *Proc. K. ned. Akad. Wet.* **29**, 730–43.

(1934). New evidence of the distinct organization of *Pithecanthropus*. *Proc. K. ned. Akad. Wet.* **37**, 139–45.

Ennouchi, E. (1962a). Un crâne d'homme ancien au Jebel Irhoud (Maroc). *C.r. hebd. Séanc. Acad. Sci., Paris* **254**-D, 4330–2.

(1962b). Un néanderthalien: l'homme du Jebel Irhoud (Maroc). *Anthropologie, Paris* **66**, 279–99.

(1963). Les néanderthaliens du Jebel Irhoud (Maroc). *C.r. hebd. Séanc. Acad. Sci., Paris* **256**-D, 2459–60.

(1966). Le site du Jebel Irhoud (Maroc). In *Actas del V Congreso Panafricano de Prehistoria y de Estudio del Cuaternario* vol. II, 53–60 (Santa Cruz de Tenerife).

(1968). Le deuxième crâne de l'homme d'Irhoud. *Annls Paléont. (Vertébrés)* **54**, 117–28.

(1969). Présence d'un enfant néanderthalien au Jebel Irhoud (Maroc). *Annls Paléont. (Vertébrés)* **55**, 251–65.

(1972). Nouvelle découverte d'un archantropien au Maroc. *C.r. hebd. Séanc. Acad. Sci., Paris* **274**-D, 3088–90.

Ewer, R. F. (1956). The dating of the Australopithecinae: faunal evidence. *S. Afr. archaeol. Bull.* **11**, 41–5.

(1957). Faunal evidence on the dating of the Australopithecinae. In *Proceedings of the Third Pan-African Congress on Prehistory (Livingstone, 1955)*, 135–42.

Ferembach, D. (1965). *Homo erectus. Bull. Société d'Etudes et de Recherches Préhistoriques Institut Pratique de Préhistoire* **14**, 1–15.

(1972). L'ancêtre de l'homme du paléolithique supérieur était-il néanderthalien? In F. Bordes (ed.), *The origin of* Homo sapiens, 73–80. UNESCO, Paris.

(1976a). Les restes humains de la grotte de Dar-es-Soltane 2 (Maroc) campagne, 1975. *Bull. Mém. Soc. Anthrop. Paris* series 13, **3**, 183–93.

(1976b). Les restes humains Atériens de Témara (campagne 1975). *Bull. Mém. Soc. Anthrop. Paris* series 13, **3**, 175–80.

Findlater, I. C., F. J. Fitch, J. A. Miller and R. T. Watkins (1974). Dating of the rock succession containing fossil hominids at East Rudolf, Kenya. *Nature, Lond.* **251**, 213–15.

Fitch, F. J., P. J. Hooker and J. A. Miller (1976). Argon-40/argon-39 dating of the KBS tuff in Koobi Fora formation, East Rudolf, Kenya. *Nature, Lond.* **263**, 740–4.

Fitch, F. J. and J. A. Miller (1970). Radioisotopic age determinations of Lake Rudolf artefact sites. *Nature, Lond.* **226**, 226–8.

(1976). Conventional potassium–argon and argon-40/argon-39 dating of volcanic rocks from East Rudolf. In Y. Coppens *et al.* (eds.), *Earliest man and environments in the Lake Rudolf basin*, 123–47. Chicago.

Freeman, L. G. (1975a). By their works you shall know them: cultural developments in the Paleolithic. In G. Kurth and I. Eibl-Ebiesfeldt (eds.), *Hominisation and behaviour*, 234–61. Stuttgart.

(1975b). Acheulian sites and stratigraphy in Iberia and the Maghreb. In K. W. Butzer and G. Ll. Isaac (eds.), *After the australopithecines*, 661–743. The Hague.

Funnell, B. M. (1964). The Tertiary period. In *The Phanerozoic time scale: a symposium, Q. Jl Geol. Soc. Lond.* **120**, 179–91.

Galloway, A. (1937). The nature and status of the Florisbad skull as revealed by its non-metrical features. *Am. J. phys. Anthrop.* **23**, 1–17.

Gieseler, W. (1974). Die Fossilgeschichte des Menschen. In *Die Evolution der Organism*, 3rd edn, vol. III, 171–517. Stuttgart.

Gleadow, A. J. W. (1980). Fission track age of the KBS tuff and associated hominid remains in northern Kenya. *Nature, Lond.* **284**, 225–30.

Gramly, R. M. and G. P. Rightmire (1973). A fragmentary cranium and dated Later Stone Age assemblage from Lukenya Hill, Kenya. *Man* **8**, 571–9.

Greene, D. L. (1975). Gorilla dental sexual dimorphism and early hominid taxonomy. *Symp. IV Int. Congr. Primatol.* **3**, 82–100.

Gregory, W. K. (1930). The origin of man from a brachiating anthropoid stock. *Science, N.Y.* **71**, 645–50.

Gregory, W. K. and M. Hellman (1939a). Evidence of the australopithecine man-apes on the origin of man. *Science, N.Y.* **88**, 615–16.

(1939b). The dentition of the extinct South African man-ape *Australopithecus (Plesianthropus) transvaalensis* Broom. A comparative and phylogenetic study. *Ann. Transv. Mus.* **19**, 339–73.

(1939c). The South African fossil man-apes and the origin of human dentition. *J. Am. dent. Ass.* **26**, 558–64.

Grommé, C. S. and R. L. Hay (1971). Geomagnetic polarity epochs: age and duration of the Olduvai normal polarity event. *Earth Planet. Sci. Lett.* **10**, 179–85.

Gutgesell, V. J. (1970). '*Telanthropus*' and the single species hypothesis. A reexamination. *Am. Anthrop.* **72**, 565–76.

Harris, J. W. K. and W. W. Bishop (1976). Sites and assemblages from the early Pleistocene beds of Karari and Chesowanja, Kenya. *IXᵉ Congr. Union Int. Sci. Préhist. Protohist. (Nice)*, Colloque V, 70–117.

Harris, J. W. K. and G. Ll. Isaac (1976). The Karari industry: early Pleistocene archaeological materials from the terrain east of Lake Rudolf, Kenya. *Nature, Lond.* **262**, 102–7.

Hay, R. L. (1971). Geologic background of Beds I and II: stratigraphic summary. In M. D. Leakey, *Olduvai Gorge, vol. III: Excavations in Beds I and II, 1960–1963*, 9–18. Cambridge.

(1976). *Geology of the Olduvai Gorge*. Berkeley.

Heintz, N. (1967). Evolution de la hauteur maximale du frontal, du pariétal et de l'occipital chez les hominidés. *Ann. Paléont. (Vertébrés)* **53**, 51–75.

Hendey, Q. B. (1974). Faunal dating of the late Cenozoic of southern Africa, with special reference to the Carnivora. *Quaternary Res.* **4**, 149–61.

Hillhouse, J. W., J. W. M. Ndombi, A. Cox and A. Brock (1977). Additional results on palaeomagnetic stratigraphy of the Koobi Fora Formation, East of Lake Turkana (Lake Rudolf), Kenya. *Nature, Lond.* **265**, 411–15.

Holloway, R. L. (1970). Australopithecine endocast (Taung specimen, 1924): a new volume determination. *Science, N.Y.* **168**, 966–8.

(1972). Australopithecine endocasts, brain evolution in the Hominoidea, and a model of hominid evolution. In R. H. Tuttle (ed.), *The functional and evolutionary biology of primates*, 185–203. Chicago.

(1974). The casts of fossil hominid brains. *Scient. Am.* **231**, 106–15.

(1975). Early hominid endocasts: volumes, morphology and significance for hominid evolution. In R. H. Tuttle (ed.), *Primate functional morphology and evolution*, 393–416. The Hague.

Horowitz, A., G. Siedner and O. Bar-Yosef (1973). Radiometric dating of the Ubeidiya formation, Jordan valley, Israel. *Nature, Lond.* **242**, 186–7.

Howe, B. (1967). The palaeolithic of Tangier, Morocco. Excavations at Cape Ashakar, 1939–1947. *Bull. Am. Sch. prehist. Res.* **22**.

Howell, F. C. (1969a). Remains of Hominidae from Pliocene/Pleistocene formations in the lower Omo basin, Ethiopia. *Nature, Lond.* **233**, 1234–9.

(1969b). Hominid teeth from White Sands and Brown Sands localities, lower Omo basin, Ethiopia. *Quaternaria* **11**, 47–54.

(1972). Pliocene/Pleistocene Hominidae in Eastern Africa: absolute and relative ages. In W. W. Bishop and J. A. Miller (eds.), *Calibration of hominoid evolution*, 331–68. Edinburgh and Toronto.

(1978). Hominidae. In V. J. Maglio and H. B. S. Cooke (eds.), *Evolution of African mammals*, 154–248. Cambridge, Mass.

Howell, F. C. and Y. Coppens (1976). An overview of Hominidae from the Omo succession, Ethiopia. In Y. Coppens *et al.* (eds.), *Earliest man and environments in the Lake Rudolf basin*, 522–32. Chicago.

Howell, F. C., S. L. Washburn and R. L. Ciochon (1978). Relationship of *Australopithecus* and *Homo J. Hum. Evolut.* **7**, 127–31.

Howell, F. C. and B. A. Wood (1974). Early hominid ulna from the Omo basin, Ethiopia. *Nature, Lond.* **249**, 174–6.

Howells, W. W. (1966). *Homo erectus. Scient. Am.* **215**, 46–53.

(1973). *Evolution of the genus* Homo. Reading, Massachusetts.

Hrdlička, A. (1925). The Taungs age. *Am. J. phys. Anthrop.* **8**, 379–92.

(1930). The Rhodesian Man. *Am. J. phys. Anthrop.* **9**, 173–204.

Hughes, A. R. and P. V. Tobias (1977). A fossil skull probably of the genus *Homo* from Sterkfontein, Transvaal. *Nature, Lond.* **265**, 310–12.

Hurford, A. J., A. J. W. Gleadow and C. W. Naeser, (1976). Fission-track dating of pumice from the KBS tuff, East Rudolf, Kenya. *Nature, Lond.* **263**, 738–40.

Isaac, G. Ll. (1965). The stratigraphy of the Peninj beds and the provenance of the Natron australopithecine mandible. *Quaternaria* **7**, 101–30.

(1967). The stratigraphy of the Peninj Group – early Middle Pleistocene formations west of Lake Natron, Tanzania. In W. W. Bishop and J. D. Clark (eds.), *Background to evolution in Africa*, 229–57. Chicago.

(1971). The diet of early man: aspects of archaeological evidence from Lower and Middle Pleistocene sites in Africa. *World Archaeol.* **2**, 278–99.

(1972a). Early phases of human behaviour: models in lower Palaeolithic archaeology. In D. L. Clarke (ed.), *Models in archaeology*, 149–56. London.

(1972b). Chronology and tempo of cultural change during the Pleistocene. In W. W. Bishop and J. A. Miller (eds.), *Calibration of hominoid evolution*, 381–430. Edinburgh and Toronto.

(1976). Plio-Pleistocene artifact assemblages from East Rudolf, Kenya. In Y. Coppens *et al.* (eds.), *Earliest man and environments in the Lake Rudolf basin*, 552–64. Chicago.

(1978a). The archaeological evidence for the activities of early African hominids. C. Jolly (ed.), *Early hominids of Africa*, 219–54. London.

(1978b). The food-sharing behavior of protohuman hominids. *Sci. Amer.* **238**, 90–108.

(1978c). Food-sharing and human evolution: archaeological evidence from the Plio-Pleistocene of east Africa. *J. Anthrop. Res.* **34**, 311–25.

Isaac, G. Ll. and G. H. Curtis (1974). Age of early Acheulian industries from the Peninj Group, Tanzania. *Nature, Lond.* **249**, 624–7.

Isaac, G. Ll., J. W. K. Harris and D. Crader (1976). Archaeological evidence from the Koobi Fora formation. In Y. Coppens *et al.* (eds.), *Earliest man and environments in the Lake Rudolf basin* 533–51. Chicago.

Jacob, T. (1972). The absolute date of the Djetis beds at Modjokerto. *Antiquity* **47**, 148.

(1973). Paleoanthropological discoveries in Indonesia with special reference to the finds of the last two decades. *J. hum. Evol.* **2**, 473–86.

(1975). The pithecanthropines of Indonesia. *Bull. Mém. Soc. Anthrop., Paris* **47**, 243–56.

Jacob, T. and G. H. Curtis (1971). Preliminary potassium–argon dating of early man in Java. *Contrib. Univ. Calif. Archaeol. Res. Facility* **12**, 50.

Jaeger, J.-J. (1969). Les rongeurs du Pléistocène moyen de Ternifine (Algérie). *C.r. hebd. Séanc. Acad. Sci., Paris* **269**-D, 1492–5.

(1973). Un pithecanthrope évolué. *Recherche*, **39**, 1006–7.

(1975a). Découverte d'un crâne d'hominidé dans le Pléistocène moyen du Maroc. In *Problèmes Actuels de Paléontologie-Evolution des Vertébrés, (Colloque International, CNRS* **218**), 897–902.

(1975b). The mammalian faunas and hominid fossils of the Middle Plesitocene of the Maghreb. In K. W. Butzer and G. Ll. Isaac (eds.), *After the australopithecines*, 399–418. The Hague.

Johanson, D. C. and M. Taieb (1976). Plio-Pleistocene hominid discoveries in Hadar, Ethiopia. *Nature, Lond.* **260**, 293–7.

Johanson, D. C. and T. D. White (1979). A systematic assessment of early African hominids. *Science, N.Y.* **203**, 321–30.

Johanson, D. C., T. D. White and Y. Coppens, (1978). A new species of the genus Australopithecus (Primates: Hominidae) from the Pliocene of Eastern Africa. *Kirklandia* **28**, 1–14.

Johanson, D. C., M. Taieb, Y. Coppens and H. Roche (1978). Expédition internationale de l'Afar, Ethiopie (4e et 5e campagnes, 1975–1977): Nouvelles découvertes d'hominidés et découvertes d'industries lithiques pliocènes à Hadar. *C.r. hebd. Séanc. Acad. Sci., Paris* **287**-D, 237–40.

Jolly, C. J. (ed.) (1978). *Early hominids of Africa*. London.

Kaufman, A., W. S. Broeker, T.-L. Ku and D. L. Thurber (1971). The status of U-series methods of dating molluscs. *Geochim. cosmochim. Acta* **35**, 1155–84.

Keith, A. (1931). *New discoveries relating to the antiquity of Man*. London.

Kent, P. E. (1942). The recent history and the Pleistocene deposits north of Lake Eyasi, Tanganyika. *Geol. Mag.* **78**, 173–84.

Klein, R. G. (1973). Geological antiquity of Rhodesian man. *Nature, Lond.* **244**, 311–12.

Koenigswald, G. H. R. von (1936). Ein fossiler Hominide aus dem Altpleistozän Ostjavas. *Ing. Ned.-Indië* **8**, 149–57.

(1940). Neue *Pithecanthropus*-Funde 1936–1938. Ein Beitrag zur Kenntnis der Praehominiden. *Wet. Meded. Dienst Mijnb. Ned.-Oost-Indië* **28**, 1–232.

(1950). Fossil hominids from the Lower Pleistocene of Java. *Proc. Int. Geol. Congress (Great Britain, 1949)*, **9**, 59–66.

(1960). Remarks on a fossil human molar from Olduvai, East Africa. *Proc. K. ned. Akad. Wet.* **63**, 20–5.

(1969). Java: Prae-Trinil man. *Proc. VIII Int. Congr. anthrop. ethnol. Sci.* (Tokyo–Kyoto) **1**, 104–5.

(1973). *Australopithecus, Meganthropus* and *Ramapithecus. J. hum. Evol.*, **2**, 487–91.

Kohl-Larsen, L. (1943). *Auf den Spuren des Vormenschen. Forschungen, Fahrten und Ergebnisse in Deutsch-Ostafrika*, 2 vols. Stuttgart.

Leakey, L. S. B. (1931). *Stone Age cultures of Kenya Colony*. Cambridge.

(1935). *The Stone Age races of Kenya*. Oxford.

(1936a). Fossil human remains from Kanam and Kanjera, Kenya Colony. *Nature, Lond.* **138**, 643.

(1936b). A new fossil skull from Eyasi, East Africa. *Nature, Lond.* **138**, 1082–3.

(1951). *Olduvai Gorge*. Cambridge.

(1958). Recent discoveries at Olduvai Gorge, Tanganyika. *Nature, Lond.* **181**, 1099–1103.

(1959). A new fossil skull from Olduvai. *Nature, Lond.* **184**, 491–3.

(1960). Recent discoveries at Olduvai Gorge. *Nature, Lond.* **188**, 1050–2.

(1965). *Olduvai Gorge, vol. I: A preliminary report on the geology and fauna*. Cambridge.

Leakey, L. S. B. and M. D. Leakey (1964). Recent discoveries of fossil hominids in Tanganyika: at Olduvai and near Lake Natron. *Nature, Lond.* **202**, 5–7.

Leakey, L. S. B. and W. H. Reeve (1946). I. Report on a visit to the site of the Eyasi skull found by Dr Kohl-Larsen. II. Geological report on the site of Dr Kohl-Larsen's discovery of a fossil human skull, Lake Eyasi, Tanganyika Territory. *J. E. Afr. nat. Hist. Soc.* **19**, 40–50.

Leakey, L. S. B., P. V. Tobias and J. R. Napier (1964). A new species of the genus *Homo* from Olduvai Gorge. *Nature, Lond.* **202**, 7–9.

Leakey, M. D. (1970). Stone artefacts from Swartkrans. *Nature, Lond.* **225**, 1221–5.

(1971). *Olduvai Gorge, vol. III: Excavations in Beds I and II, 1960–1963*. Cambridge.

(1975). Cultural patterns in the Olduvai sequence. In K. W. Butzer and G. Ll. Isaac (eds.), *After the australopithecines*, 477–94. The Hague.

(1978). Olduvai fossil hominids: their stratigraphic positions and associations. In C. J. Jolly (ed.), *Early hominids of Africa*, 3–16. London.

Leakey, M. D., R. J. Clarke and L. S. B. Leakey (1971). New hominid skull from Bed I, Olduvai Gorge, Tanzania. *Nature, Lond.* **232**, 308–12.

Leakey, M. D. and R. L. Hay (1979). Pliocene footprints in the Laetolil Beds at Laetoli, northern Tanzania. *Nature, Lond.* **278**, 317–23.

Leakey, M. D., R. L. Hay, G. H. Curtis, R. E. Drake, M. K. Jackes and T. D. White (1976). Fossil hominids from the Laetolil Beds. *Nature, Lond.* **262**, 460–6.

Leakey, Margaret, P. V. Tobias, J. E. Martyn and R. E. F. Leakey (1969). An Acheulean industry with prepared core technique and the discovery of a contemporary hominid mandible at Lake Baringo, Kenya. *Proc. prehist. Soc.* **35**, 48–76.

Leakey, M. G. and R. E. F. Leakey (1978). *Koobi Fora Research Project, Volume I, 1968–1974: The fossil hominids and an introduction to their context.* Oxford.

Leakey, R. E. F. (1970). New hominid remains and early artefacts from northern Kenya. *Nature, Lond.* **226**, 223–4.

(1971). Further evidence of lower Pleistocene hominids from East Rudolf, north Kenya, 1970. *Nature, Lond.* **231**, 241–5.

(1972). Further evidence of lower Pleistocene hominids from East Rudolf, north Kenya, 1971. *Nature, Lond.* **237**, 264–9.

(1973). Further evidence of lower Pleistocene hominids from East Rudolf, north Kenya, 1972. *Nature, Lond.* **242**, 170–3.

(1974). Further evidence of lower Pleistocene hominids from East Rudolf, north Kenya, 1973. *Nature, Lond.* **248**, 653–6.

(1976a). An overview of the East Rudolf Hominidae. In Y. Coppens *et al.* (eds.), *Earliest man and environments in the Lake Rudolf basin,* 476–83. Chicago.

(1976b). New hominid fossils from the Koobi Fora formation in northern Kenya. *Nature, Lond.* **261**, 574–6.

Leakey, R. E. F., K. W. Butzer and M. H. Day (1969). Early *Homo sapiens* remains from the Omo river regions of south-west Ethiopia. *Nature, Lond.* **222**, 1132–8.

Leakey, R. E. F., J. M. Mungai and A. C. Walker, (1971). New australopithecines from East Rudolf, Kenya, I. *Am. J. phys. Anthrop.* **35**, 175–86.

(1972). New australopithecines from East Rudolf, Kenya, II. *Am. J. phys. anthrop.* **36**, 205–22.

Leakey, R. E. F. and A. C. Walker (1973). New australopithecines from East Rudolf, Kenya, III. *Am. J. phys. Anthrop.* **39**, 205–22.

(1976). *Australopithecus, Homo erectus,* and the single species hypothesis. *Nature, Lond.* **261**, 572–4.

Lecointre, G. (1960). Le gisement de l'homme de Rabat. *Bull. Archéol. Maroc.* **3**, 55–85.

Le Gros Clark, W. E. (1940). Palaeontological evidence bearing on human evolution. *Biol. Rev.* **15**, 202–30.

(1947). Observations on the anatomy of the fossil Australopithecinae. *J. Anat.* **81**, 300–33.

(1952). Hominid characters of the australopithecine dentition. *Jl R. Anthrop. Inst.* **80**, 37–54.

(1964). *The fossil evidence for human evolution,* 2nd ed. Chicago.

(1967). *Man-apes or ape-men?* New York.

Lisowski, F. P., G. H. Albrecht and C. E. Oxnard (1974). The form of the talus in some higher primates: a multivariate study. *Am. J. phys. Anthrop.* **41**, 191–215.

Lovejoy, C. O. (1974). The gait of australopithecines. *Yearb. phys. Anthrop.* **17**, 147–61.

McBurney, C. B. M. (1961). Absolute age of Pleistocene and Holocene deposits in the Haua Fteah. *Nature, Lond.* **192**, 685–6.

(1962). Absolute chronology of the Palaeolithic in eastern Libya and the problem of Upper Palaeolithic origins. *Advmt Sci., Lond.* **18**, 494–7.

(1967). *The Haua Fteah (Cyrenaica) and the Stone Age of the south-east Mediterranean.* Cambridge.

McBurney, C. B. M., J. C. Trevor and L. H. Wells (1953). The Haua Fteah fossil jaw. *Jl R. Anthrop. Inst.* **83**, 71–85.

McDougall, I., R. Maier, P. Sutherland-Hawkes and A. J. W. Gleadow (1980). K-Ar age estimate for the KBS tuff, east Turkana, Kenya. *Nature, Lond.* **284**, 230–4.

MacDougall, C. and P. B. Price (1974). Attempt to date early South African hominids using fission tracks in calcite. *Science, N.Y.* **185**, 943–4.

McFadden, P. L., A. Brock and T. C. Partridge (1979). Palaeomagnetism and the age of the Makapansgat hominid site. *Earth and Planet. Sci. letters* **44**, 373–82.

McHenry, H. M. (1973). Early hominid humerus from East Rudolf, Kenya. *Science, N.Y.* **180**, 739–41.

(1975a). The ischium and hip extensor mechanism in human evolution. *Am. J. phys. Anthrop.* **43**, 39–46.

(1975b). Fossils and the mosaic nature of human evolution. *Science, N.Y.* **190**, 425–31.

(1978). Fore- and hind limb proportions in Plio-Pleistocene hominids. *Am. J. Phys. Anthrop.* **49**, 15–22.

McHenry, H. M. and R. S. Corruccini (1975). Distal humerus in hominoid evolution. *Folia primatol.* **13**, 227–44.

McHenry, H. M. and R. S. Corruccini (1978). The femur in early human evolution. *Am. J. Phys. Anthrop.* **49**, 473–88.

McHenry, H. M. and A. L. Temerin (1979). The evidence of hominid bipedalism: evidence from the fossil record. *Yrbk of Phys. Anthrop.* **22**, 105–31.

Mabbutt, J. A. (1956). The physiography and surface geology of the Hopefield fossil site. *Trans. R. Soc. S. Afr.* **35**, 21–58.

Maglio, V. J. (1970). Early Elephantidae of Africa and a tentative correlation of African Plio-Pleistocene deposits. *Nature, Lond.* **225**, 328–32.

(1973). Origin and evolution of the Elephantidae. *Trans. Am. phil. Soc.* N.S. **63**, 1–149.

Mann, A. E. (1975). Some paleodemographic aspects of the South African australopithecines. *Univ. Pennsylvania Publs anthrop.* **1**.

Marçais, J. (1934). Découverte de restes humains fossiles dans les grès quaternaires de Rabat (Maroc). *Anthropologie, Paris* **44**, 579–83.

Marks, P. (1953). Preliminary note on the discovery of a new jaw of *Meganthropus. Indones. J. nat. Sci.* **109**, 26–33.

Martyn, J. and P. V. Tobias (1967). Pleistocene deposits and new fossil localities in Kenya. *Nature, Lond.* **215**, 476–80.

Merrick, H. V. (1976). Recent archaeological research in the Plio-Pleistocene deposit of the lower Omo valley, southwestern Ethiopia. In G. Ll. Isaac and E. R. McCown (eds.), *Human origins. Louis Leakey and the East African evidence*, 461–82. Menlo Park.

Merrick, H. V. and J. P. S. Merrick (1976). Archaeological occurrences of earlier Pleistocene age from the Shungura formation. In Y. Coppens *et al.* (eds.), *Earliest man and environments in the Lake Rudolf basin*, 574–84. Chicago.

Mturi, A. A. (1976). New hominid from Lake Ndutu, Tanzania. *Nature, Lond.* **262**, 484–5.

Neuville, R. and A. Ruhlmann (1942). L'âge de l'homme fossile de Rabat. *Bull. Mém. Soc. Anthrop. Paris* series 9, **3**, 74–88.

Oakley, K. P. (1954). Study tour of early hominid sites in southern Africa, 1953. *S. Afr. archaeol. Bull.* **9**, 75–87.

(1957). The dating of the Broken Hill, Florisbad and Saldanha skulls In *Proceedings of the Third Pan-African Congress on Prehistory (Livingstone, 1955)*, 76–9.

(1958). The dating of Broken Hill (Rhodesian Man). In G. H. R. von Koenigswald (ed.), *Hundert jahre Neanderthaler. Neanderthal Centenary, 1856–1956*, 265–6. Utrecht.

(1960). The Kanam jaw. *Nature, Lond.* **185**, 945.

Ohel, M. Y. (1977). Patterned concentrations on living floors at Olduvai, Beds I and II: experimental study. *J. Field Archaeol.* **4**, 423–33.

Olson, T. R. (1978). Hominid phylogenetics and the existence of *Homo* in Member I of the Swartkrans Formation, South Africa. *J. Hum. Evolut.* **7**, 159–78.

Oppenworth, W. F. F. (1932). *Homo (Javanthropus) soloensis,* eem Pleistocene mensch van Java. *Wet. Meded. Dienst Mijnb. Ned.-Oost-Indië* **20**, 49–63.

Oxnard, C. E. (1972). Some African fossil foot bones: a note on the interpolation of fossils into a matrix of extant species. *Am. J. phys. Anthrop.* **37**, 3–12.

(1973). Functional inferences from morphometrics: problems posed by diversity and uniqueness among the primates. *Syst. Zool.* **22**, 409–24.

(1975). The place of the australopithecines in human evolution: grounds for doubt? *Nature, Lond.* **258**, 389–95.

(1979). Relationship of *Australopithecus* and *Homo*: another view. *J. Hum. Evolut.* **8**, 427–32.

Partridge, T. C. (1973). Geomorphological dating of cave opening at Makapansgat, Sterkfontein, Swartkrans and Taung. *Nature, Lond.* **240**, 75–9.

(1978). Re-appraisal of lithostratigraphy of Sterkfontein hominid sites. *Nature, Lond.* **275**, 282–7.

Patterson, B. (1966). A new locality for early Pleistocene fossils in northwestern Kenya. *Nature, Lond.* **212**, 577–8.

Patterson, B., A. K. Behrensmeyer and W. D. Sill (1970). Geology and fauna of a new Pliocene locality in northwestern Kenya. *Nature, Lond.* **226**, 918–21.

Patterson, B. and W. W. Howells (1967). Hominid humeral fragment from early Pleistocene of northwestern Kenya. *Science, N.Y.* **156**, 64–6.

Peabody, F. E. (1954). Travertines and cave deposits of the Kaap escarpment of South Africa, and the type locality of *Australopithecus africanus*. *Bull. geol. Soc. Am.* **65**, 671–706.

Petit-Maire, N. and M. Charon (1972). Tendances évolutives de la denture inférieure permanente des hominidés du Quaternaire. *C.r. hebd. Séanc. Acad. Sci., Paris* **274**-D, 365–8.

Pickford, M. (1975). Late Miocene sediments and fossils from the northern Kenya Rift Valley. *Nature, Lond.* **256**, 279–84.

(1978a). Geology, palaeoenvironments and vertebrate faunas of the mid-Miocene Ngorora Formation, Kenya. In W. W. Bishop (ed.), *Geological background to fossil man*, 237–62. Edinburgh.

(1978b). Stratigraphy and mammalian palaeontology of the late Miocene Lukeino Formation, Kenya. In W. W. Bishop (ed.), *Geological background to fossil man*, 263–78. Edinburgh.

Pilbeam, D. (1972). *The ascent of Man. An introduction to human evolution.* New York.

(1975). Middle Pleistocene hominids. In K. W. Butzer and G. Ll. Isaac (eds.), *After the australopithecines*, 809–56. The Hague.

Pilbeam, D. and S. J. Gould (1974). Size and scaling in human evolution. *Science, N.Y.* **186**, 892–901.

Protsch, R. (1974). Florisbad: its paleoanthropology, chronology and archaeology. *Homo* **25**, 68–78.

(1975). The absolute dating of Upper Pleistocene sub-Saharan fossil hominids and their place in human evolution. *J. hum. Evol.* **4**, 297–322.

Protsch, R. and H. de Villiers (1974). Bushman Rock Shelter, Origstad, Eastern Transvaal, South Africa. *J. hum. Evol.* **3**, 387–96.

Reck, H. and L. Kohl-Larsen (1936). Erster Überblick über die jungdiluvialen Tier und Menschenfunds Dr Kohl-Larsen's im nordöstlichen Teil des Njarasa-Grabens (Ostafrika), und die geologischen Verhältnisse des Fundgebietes. *Geol. Rdsch.* **27**, 401–41.

Remane, A. (1951a). (In H. R. Weinert) Über die neuen Vor- und Fruhmenschenfunde aus Afrika, Java, China und Frankreich. *Z. Morph. Anthrop.* **43**, 113–48.

(1951b). Die Zähne des *Meganthropus africanus. Z. Morph. Anthrop.* **42**, 311–29.

Rightmire, G. P. (1974). *The later Pleistocene and recent evolution of man in Africa.* New York.

(1975). Problems in the study of Later Pleistocene man in Africa. *Am. Anthrop.* **77**, 28–52.

(1979). Cranial remains of *Homo erectus* from Beds II and IV, Olduvai Gorge, Tanzania. *Am. J. Phys. Anthrop.* **51**, 99–116.

Robinson, J. T. (1953a). *Meganthropus*, australopithecines and hominids. *Am. J. phys. Anthrop.* **11**, 1–38.

(1953b). *Telanthropus* and its phylogenetic significance. *Am. J. phys. Anthrop.* **11**, 445–502.

(1954). The genera and species of the Australopithecinae. *Am. J. phys. Anthrop.* **12**, 181–200.

(1955). Further remarks on the relationship between *Meganthropus* and australopithecines. *Am. J. phys. Anthrop.* **13**, 429–46.

(1956). The dentition of the Australopithecinae. *Transv. Mus. Mem.* **9**.

(1958). The Sterkfontein tool-maker. *Leech, Johannesb.* **28**, 94–100.

(1960). An alternative interpretation of the supposed giant deciduous hominid tooth from Olduvai. *Nature, Lond.* **185**, 407–8.

(1961). The australopithecines and their bearing on the origin of man and of stone tool-making. *S. Afr. J. Sci.* **57**, 3–13.

(1962). The origin and adaptive radiation of the australopithecines. In G. Kurth (ed.), *Evolution and hominisation*, 120–40. Stuttgart.

(1963). Adaptive radiation in the australopithecines and the origin of man. In F. C. Howell and F. Bourlière (eds.), *African ecology and human evolution*, 385–416. Chicago.

(1965). *Homo habilis* and the australopithecines. *Nature, Lond.* **205**, 121–4.

(1967). Variation and the taxonomy of early hominids. *Evolutionary Biology* **1**, 69–100.

(1968). The origin and adaptive radiation of the australopithecines. In G. Kurth (ed.), *Evolution and hominisation*, 2nd edn, 150–75. Stuttgart.

(1969). Dentition and adaptation in early hominids. *VIII Int. Congr. Anthrop. Ethnol. Sci. (Kyoto–Tokyo, 1968)*, 302–5.

(1972). *Early hominid posture and locomotion*. Chicago.

Robinson, J. T. and R. J. Mason (1957). Occurrence of stone artefacts with *Australopithecus* at Sterkfontein. *Nature, Lond.* **180**, 521–4.

(1962). Australopithecines and artefacts at Sterkfontein. *S. Afr. archaeol. Bull.* **17**, 87–125.

Robinson, J. T. and K. Steudel (1973). Multivariate discriminant analysis of dental data bearing on early hominid affinities. *J. hum. Evol.* **2**, 509–27.

Roche, H. and J.-J. Tiercelin (1977). Découverte d'une industrie lithique ancienne *in situ* dans la formation d'Hadar, Afar central, Ethiopie. *C.r. Acad. Sci., Paris* **284**-D, 1871–4.

Roche, J. (1953). La grotte de Taforalt. *Anthropologie, Paris* **57**, 375–80.

Roche, J. and J.-P. Texier (1976). Découverte de restes humains dans un niveau atérien supérieur de la grotte des Contrebandiers – à Témara (Maroc). *C.r. hebd. Séanc. Acad. Sci., Paris* **282**-D, 45–7.

Ruhlmann, A. (1951). *La grotte préhistorique de Dar es Soltane*. Collection Hesperis, Institut des Hautes Études Marocaines **11**, Rabat.

Saban, R. (1975). Les restes humains de Rabat (Kébibat). *Ann. Paléont. (Vértébres)* **61**, 151–207.

(1977). The place of Rabat man (Kébibat, Morocco) in human evolution. *Curr. Anthrop.* **18**, 518–24.

Sartono, S. (1971). Observations on a new skull of *Pithecanthropus erectus* (*Pithecanthropus* VIII) from Sangiran, central Java. *Proc. K. ned. Akad. Wet.* **74**, 185–94.

(1975). Implications arising from *Pithecanthropus* VIII. In R. H. Tuttle (ed.), *Paleoanthropology: morphology and paleoecology*, 327–60. The Hague.

Sausse, F. (1975). La mandibule atlanthropienne de la carrière Thomas I (Casablanca). *Anthropologie, Paris* **79**, 81–112.

Schepers, G. W. H. (1941). The mandible of the Transvaal fossil human skeleton from Springbok Flats. *Ann. Transv. Mus.* **20**, 253–71.

Senyurek, M. S. (1940). Fossil man in Tangier. *Pap. Peabody Mus.* **16**.

(1955). A note on the teeth of *Meganthropus africanus* Weinert from Tanganyika Territory. *Belleten, Ankara* **19**, 1–55.

Shuey, R. T., F. H. Brown and M. K. Croes (1974). Magnetostratigraphy of the Shungura Formation, south-western Ethiopia: fine structure of the lower Matuyama polarity epoch. *Earth Planet. Sci. Lett.* **23**, 249–60.

Shuey, R. T., F. H. Brown, G. G. Eck and F. C. Howell (1978). A statistical approach to temporal biostratigraphy. In W. W. Bishop (ed.), *Geological background to fossil man in Africa.* 103–24. Edinburgh and Toronto.

Siedner, G. and A. Horowitz (1974). Radio-metric ages of late Cainozoic basalts from northern Israel: chronostratigraphic implications. *Nature, Lond.* **250**, 23–6.

Simons, E. L. (1977). *Ramapithecus. Scient. Am.* **236**, 28–35.

Simons, E. L. and D. R. Pilbeam (1978). Ramapithecus (Hominidae, Hominoidea). In V. J. Maglio and H. B. S. Cooke (eds.), *Evolution of African mammals,* 147–53. Cambridge, Mass.

Singer, R. (1954). The Saldanha skull from Hopefield, South Africa. *Am. J. phys. Anthrop.* **12**, 345–62.

(1958). The Rhodesian, Florisbad and Saldanha skulls. In G. H. R. von Koenigswald (ed.), *Hundert Jahre Neanderthaler. Neanderthal Centenary, 1856–1956,* 52–62. Utrecht.

Singer, R. and P. Smith (1969). Some human remains associated with the Middle Stone Age at Klasies River, South Africa. *Am. J. phys. Anthrop.* **31**, 256 (abstract).

Singer, R. and J. Wymer (1968). Archaeological investigations at the Saldanha skull site in South Africa. *S. Afr. archaeol. Bull.* **25**, 63–74.

Sollas, W. J. (1926). A sagittal section of the skull of *Australopithecus africanus. Q. Jl geol. Soc. Lond.* **82**, 1–11.

Speth, J. D. and D. D. Davis (1976). Seasonal variability in early hominid predation. *Science, N.Y.* **192**, 441–5.

Stearns, C. E. and D. L. Thurber (1965). Th$^{230}$/U$^{234}$ dates of late Pleistocene marine fossils from the Mediterranean and Moroccan littorals. *Quaternaria* **7**, 29–42.

Stiles, D. N. (1979). Recent archaeological findings at the Sterkfontein site. *Nature, Lond.* **277**, 381–2.

Stiles, D. N. and T. C. Partridge (1979). Results of recent archaeological and palaeo-environmental studies at the Sterkfontein Extension site. *S. Afr. J. Sci.* **75**, 346–52.

Stringer, C. B. (1974). Population relationships of later Pleistocene hominids: a multivariate study of available crania. *J. archaeol. Sci.* **1**, 317–42.

Susman, R. L. and N. Creel (1979). Functional and morphological affinities of the subadult hand (O.H.7) from Olduvai Gorge. *Am. J. Phys. Anthrop.* **51**, 311–32.

Szalay, F. S. (1971). Biological level of organization of the Chesowanja robust australopithecine. *Nature, Lond.* **234**, 229–30.

Taieb, M. (1974). Evolution quaternaire du bassin de l'Awash (rift Éthiopien en Afar), 2 vols. Thesis, University of Paris VI.

Taieb, M., D. C. Johanson, Y. Coppens and J. L. Aronson (1976). Geological and palaeontological background of Hadar hominid site, Afar, Ethiopia. *Nature, Lond.* **260**, 280–93.

Taieb, M., Y. Coppens, D. C. Johanson and J. Kalb (1972). Dépots sédimentaires et faunes du Plio-Pléistocène de basse vallée de l'Awash (Afar central, Éthiopie). *C.r. hebd. Séanc. Acad. Sci., Paris* **275**-D, 819–22.

Taieb, M., D. C. Johanson, Y. Coppens, R. Bonnefille and J. Kalb (1974). Découverte d'hominidés dans le série Plio-Pléistocène d'Hadar (bassin de l'Awash, Afar, Éthiopie). *C.r. hebd. Séanc. Acad. Sci., Paris* **279**-D, 735–8.

Taieb, M., D. C. Johanson, Y. Coppens and J.-J. Tiercelin (1978). Expédition internationale de l'Afar, Ethiopie (4e et 5e campagnes, 1975–1977): Chrono-stratigraphie des gisements à hominidés pliocènes d'Hadar et correlations avec les sites préhistoriques du Kada Gona. *C.r. hebd. Séanc. Acad. Sci., Paris* **287**-D, 459–61.

Taieb, M. and J.-J. Tiercelin (1979). Sédimentation pliocène et paléoenvironnements de rift: exemple de la formation à hominidés d'Hadar (Afar, Ethiopie). *Bull. Soc. Geol. France* (7), **21**, 243–53.

Thomas, A. and H. V. Vallois (1977). Les dents de l'homme de Rabat. *Bull. Mem. Soc. d'Anthrop.*, Paris (13) **4**, 31–58.

Tobias, P. V. (1960). The Kanam jaw. *Nature, Lond.* **185**, 946–7.

(1961). New evidence and new views on the evolution of man in Africa. *S. Afr. J. Sci.* **57**, 25–38.

(1962). A reexamination of the Kanam mandible. In *Actes du IVᵉ Congrès Panafricain de Préhistoire et de l'Etude du Quatérnaire* (Tervuren), 341–60.

(1965). *Homo habilis.* In *Encyclopaedia Britannica Book of the Year, 1965,* 252–5.

(1966). A re-examination of the Kedung Brubus mandible. *Zoöl. Meded., Leiden* **41**, 307–20.

(1967a). *Olduvai Gorge, vol. II: The cranium and maxillary dentition of* Australopithecus (Zinjanthropus) boisei. Cambridge.

(1967b). Cultural hominisation among the earliest African Pleistocene hominids. *Proc. prehist. Soc.* **13**, 367–76.

(1967c). The hominid skeletal remains of Haua Fteah. In C. B. M. McBurney, *The Haua Fteah (Cyrenaica)*, Appendix 1B, 338–52. Cambridge.

(1971a). *The brain in hominid evolution.* New York.

(1971b). Does the form of the inner contour of the mandible distinguish between *Australopithecus* and *Homo*? In A. K. Gosh (ed.), *Perspectives in palaeoanthropology: D. Sen festschrift volume* 9–17. Calcutta.

(1974). *Homo erectus. Encyc. Brit.* **8**, 1031–6.

(1978a). The place of *Australopithecus africanus* in hominid evolution. In D. J. Chivers and K. A. Joysey (eds.), *Recent advances in primatology*, vol. 3 (Evolution), 373–94. London.

(1978b). The South African australopithecines in time and hominid phylogeny, with special reference to the dating and affinities of the Taung skull. In C. J. Jolly (ed.), *Early hominids of Africa*, 45–84. London.

(1978c). Position et rôle des australopithécines dans la phylogenèse humaine, avec étude particulière de *Homo habilis* et des théories controversées avancées à propos des premiers hominides fossiles de Hadar et de Laetolil. In *Les origines humaines et les Epoques de l'intelligence*, Fondation Singer-Polignac, 38–77. Paris.

(1978d). The earliest Transvaal members of the genus *Homo* with another look at some problems of hominid taxonomy and systematics. *Z. Morph. Anthrop* **69**, 225–65.

Tobias, P. V. and A. R. Hughes (1969). The new Witwatersrand University excavation at Sterkfontein. *S. Afr. archaeol. Bull.* **24**, 158–69.

Tobias, P. V. and G. H. R. von Koenigswald (1964). A comparison between the Olduvai hominines and those of Java and some implications for hominid phylogeny. *Nature, Lond.* **204**, 515–18.

Tobias, P. V. and J. T. Robinson (1966). The distinctiveness of *Homo habilis*. *Nature, Lond.* **209**, 953–60.

Toerien, M. J. and A. R. Hughes (1955). The limb bones of Springbok Flats man. *S. Afr. J. Sci.* **52**, 125–8.

Trevor, J. C. and L. H. Wells (1967). Preliminary report on the second mandibular fragment from Haua Fteah, Cyrenaica. In C. B. M. McBurney, *The Haua Fteah (Cyrenaica)*, Appendix 1A, 336–7. Cambridge.

Vallois, H. V. (1945). L'Homme fossile de Rabat. *C.r. hebd. Séanc. Acad. Sci. Paris* **221**, 669–71.

 (1951). La mandibule humaine fossile de la grotte du Porc-Épic près Diré-Daoua (Abyssinie). *Anthropologie, Paris* **55**, 231–8.

 (1960). L'homme de Rabat. *Bull. Archéol. Maroc.* **3**, 87–91.

Vallois, H. V. and J. Roche (1958). La mandibule acheuléenne de Témara, Maroc. *C.r. hebd. Séanc. Acad. Sci., Paris* **246**, 3113–6.

Villiers, H. de (1973). Human skeletal remains from Border Cave, Ingwavuma district, Kwazulu, South Africa. *Ann. Transv. Mus.* **28**, 229–56.

 (1976). A second adult human mandible from Border Cave, Ingwavuma district, Kwazulu, South Africa. *S. Afr. J. Sci.* **72**, 212–15.

Vogel, J. C. and P. B. Beaumont (1972). Revised radiocarbon chronology for the Stone Age in South Africa. *Nature, Lond.* **237**, 50–1.

Vrba, E. S. (1974). Chronological and ecological implications of the fossil Bovidae at the Sterkfontein australopithecine site. *Nature, Lond.* **250**, 19–23.

 (1975). Some evidence of chronology and palaeoecology of Sterkfontein, Swartkrans and Kromdraai from the fossil Bovidae. *Nature, Lond.* **254**, 301–4.

 (1979). A new study of the scapula of *Australopithecus africanus* from Sterkfontein. *Am. J. Phys. Anthrop.* **51**, 117–30.

Walker, A. C. (1972a). Chesowanja australopithecine. *Nature, Lond.* **238**, 108–9.

 (1972b). New *Australopithecus* femora from East Rudolf, Kenya. *J. hum. Evol.* **2**, 245–55.

Walker, A. and R. E. F. Leakey (1978). The hominids of East Turkana. *Sci. Am.* **239**(2), 54–66.

Weidenreich, F. (1936). The mandible of *Sinanthropus pekinensis*: a comparative study. *Palaeont. sin.*, series D, **7**, 1–162.

 (1937). The dentition of *Sinanthropus pekinensis*: a comparative odontography of hominids. Atlas and text, 2 vols. *Palaeont. sin.*, N.S. D, **1**.

 (1941a). The extremity bones of *Sinanthropus pekinensis*. *Palaeontol. sin.*, N.S. D, **5**, 1–150.

 (1941b). The brain and its role in the phylogenetic transformation of the human skull. *Trans. Am. phil. Soc.* **31**, 321–442.

 (1943). The skull of *Sinanthropus pekinensis*: a comparative study on a primitive hominid skull. *Palaeont. sin.*, N.S. D, **10**.

(1945). Giant early man from Java and south China. *Anthrop. Pap. Am. Mus. nat. Hist.* **40**.

(1947). The trend of human evolution. *Evolution, Lancaster, Pa.* **1**, 221–36.

(1951). Morphology of Solo Man. *Anthrop. Pap. Am. Mus. nat. Hist.* **43**, 201–90.

Weinert, H. (and H. Bauermeister and A. Remane) (1939). *Africanthropus njarasensis*. Beschreibung und phyletische *Einordnung* des ersten Affen-menschen aus Ostafrika. *Z. Morph. Anthrop.* **38**, 252–308.

Wells, L. H. (1950). The Border Cave Skull, Ingwavuma district, Zululand. *Am. J. phys. anthro*, **8**, 241–3.

(1951). The fossil human skull from Sanga. In A. J. Arkell, D. M. A. Bate, L. H. Wells and A. D. Lacaille (eds.), *The Pleistocene fauna of two Blue Nile sites. Fossil Mammals Afr.* **2**, 29–42. Br. Mus. Nat. Hist., London.

(1952). Fossil man in southern Africa. *Man* **52**, 36–7.

(1957). The place of the Broken Hill skull among human types. In *Proceedings of the Third Pan-African Congress on Prehistory (Livingstone, 1955)*. 172–4. London.

(1959). The problem of Middle Stone Age man in southern Africa. *Man* **59**, 158–60.

(1962). Pleistocene faunas and the distribution of mammals in southern Africa. *Ann. Cape Prov. Mus.* **2**, 37–40.

(1964). The Vaal river 'Younger Gravels' faunal assemblage: a revised list. *S. Afr. J. Sci.* **60**, 91–3.

(1969). *Homo sapiens after* Linn. – content and earliest representatives. *S. Afr. archaeol. Bull.* **24**, 172–3.

(1972). Late Stone Age and Middle Stone Age tool-makers. *S. Afr. archaeol. Bull.* **27**, 5–9.

White, T. D. (1977). New fossil hominids from Laetolil, Tanzania. *Am. J. phys. Anthrop.* **46**, 197–230.

(1980). Evolutionary implications of Pliocene hominid footprints. *Science* **208**, 175–6.

Wolberg, D. L. (1970). The hypothesized osteodontokeratic culture of the Australopithecinae: a look at the evidence and the opinions. *Curr. anthrop.* **11**, 23–37.

Wolpoff, M. H. (1968). '*Telanthropus*' and the single species hypothesis. *Am. Anthrop.* **70**, 447–93.

(1971a). Competetive exclusion among lower Pleistocene hominids: the single species hypothesis. *Man* **6**, 601–14.

(1971b). The evidence for multiple hominid taxa at Swartkrans. *Am. Anthrop.* **72**, 576–607.

(1974). The evidence for two australopithecine lineages in South Africa. *Yearb. phys. Anthrop.* **17**, 113–39.

Woo, J. K. (1964a). Mandible of the *Sinanthropus*-type discovered at Lantian, Shansi – *Sinanthropus lantianensis*. *Vertebr. palasiat.* **8**, 1–71 (in Chinese).

(1964b). Mandible of *Sinanthropus lantianensis*. *Curr. Anthrop.* **5**, 98–101.

(1966). The hominid skull of Lantian, Shansi. *Vertebr. palasiat.* **10**, 1–22.

Woo, J. K. and L. P. Chao (1954). New discoveries about *Sinanthropus pekinensis* in Choukoutien. *Acta scient. sin.* **3**, 335–51, and *Acta palaeont. sin.* **2**, 267–88.

(1959). New discovery of *Sinanthropus* mandible from Choukoutien. *Vertebr. palasiat.* **3**, 169–72.

(1973). New discovery of *Sinanthropus* remains and stone artifacts at Choukoutien. *Vertebr. palasiat.* **11**, 109–31 (in Chinese).

Wood, B. A. (1974a). Evidence on the locomotor pattern of *Homo* from the early Pleistocene of Kenya. *Nature, Lond.* **251**, 135–6.

(1974b). Olduvai Bed 1 post-cranial fossils: a reassessment. *J. hum. Evol.* **3**, 373–8.

(1978). Classification and phylogeny of east African hominids. In D. J. Chivers and K. A. Joysey (eds.), *Recent advances in primatology*, vol. 3 (Evolution), 351–72. London.

Woodward, A. S. (1938). A fossil skull of an ancestral Bushman from the Anglo-Egyptian Sudan. *Antiquity* **12**, 193–5.

Zihlman, A. L. (1971). The question of locomotor differences in *Australopithecus*. *Proc. III Int. Congr. Primat. (Zurich, 1970)*, 54–66. Basel.

Zihlmann, A. L. and L. Brunker (1979). Human bipedalism: then and now. *Yrbk of Phys. Anthrop.* **22**, 132–62.

Zihlman, A. L. and W. S. Hunter (1972). A biomechanical interpretation of the pelvis of *Australopithecus*. *Folia primatol.* **18**, 1–19.

### 3. THE EARLIEST ARCHAEOLOGICAL TRACES

Alimen, H. (1957). *Prehistory of Africa*. Translated by A. H. Broderick. London and New York.

Arambourg, C. and L. Balout (1955). L'ancien lac de Tihodaine et ses gisements préhistoriques. In *Actes du II Congrès panafricain de Préhistoire (Algiers, 1952)*, 281–92. Paris.

Ardrey, R. (1961). *African genesis*. London.

(1976). *The hunting hypothesis*. New York.

Arkell, A. J. (1949). *The Old Stone Age in the Anglo-Egyptian Sudan*, Sudan Antiquities Service Occasional Papers **1**, Khartoum.

Aronson, J. A., T. J. Schmitt, R. C. Walter, M. Taieb, J.-J. Tiercelin, D. C. Johanson, C. W. Naeser and A. E. M. Nairn (1977). New geochronologic and palaeomagnetic data for the hominid-bearing Hadar Formation of Ethiopia. *Nature, Lond.* **267**, 323–7.

Bakker, E. M. van Zinderen (ed.) (1966–80). *Palaeoecology of Africa*, 12 vols. Cape Town.

Balout, L. (1955). *Préhistoire de l'Afrique du Nord: essai de chronologie*. Paris.

Balout, L., P. Biberson and J. Tixier (1967). L'Acheuléen de Ternifine (Algérie). Gisement de l'Atlanthrope. *Anthropologie, Paris* **71**, 217–37.

Bayle des Hermens, R. de (1966a). Mission de recherches préhistoriques en République Centrafricaine. Note préliminaire. *Bull. Soc. préhist. fr.* **63**, 651–66.

(1966b). Première mission de recherches préhistoriques en République Centrafricaine. *Cahiers de la Maboké* **4**, 158–75.

(1967a). Premier aperçu du Paléolithique Inférieur en République Centrafricaine. *Anthropologie, Paris* **71**, 435–66.

(1967b). Deuxième mission de recherches préhistoriques en République Centrafricaine, jan–fév 1967. *Cahiers de la Maboké* **5**, 77–92.

(1968a). Troisième mission de recherches préhistoriques en République Centrafricaine, fév–mars 1968. *Cahiers de la Maboké* **6**, 27–38.

(1968b). *Troisième mission de recherches préhistoriques en République Centrafricaine.* Museé National d'Histoire Naturelle, Laboratoire de Préhistoire, Paris.

(1968c). Recherches préhistoriques en République Centrafricaine, 1966–67. *W. Afr. archaeol. Newsl.* **9**, 6–12.

(1971). Premiers éléments de préhistoire en République Centrafricaine. In *Actes VIᵉ Congrès Panafricain de Préhistoire et d' Etude du Quaternaire (Dakar, 1967)*, 124–29. Chambéry.

Biberson, P. (1961a). *Le cadre paléogéographique de la préhistoire du Maroc atlantique.* Serv. Antiquités Maroc. **16**.

(1961b). *Le Paléolithique Inférieur du Maroc atlantique.* Publ. Antiquités Maroc. **17**, Rabat.

(1967). Some aspects of the lower Palaeolithic of northwest Africa. In W. W. Bishop and J. D. Clark (eds.), *Background to evolution in Africa*, 447–76. Chicago.

Binford, L. R. (1972). Contemporary model building: paradigms and the current state of Palaeolithic research. In D. L. Clarke (ed.), *Models in archaeology*, 109–66. London.

Bishop, W. W. (1959). Kafu stratigraphy and Kafu artifacts. *S. Afr. J. Sci.* **55**, 117–21.

(1971). The late Cenozoic history of East Africa in relation to hominoid evolution. In K. K. Turekian (ed.), *Late Cenozoic Glacial Ages*, 493–528. New Haven.

(1972). Stratigraphic succession 'versus' calibration in East Africa. In W. W. Bishop and J. A. Miller (eds.), *Calibration of hominoid evolution*, 219–46. Edinburgh and Toronto.

(ed.) (1978). *Geological background to fossil man.* Edinburgh and Toronto.

Bishop, W. W. and J. D. Clark (eds.) (1967). *Background to evolution in Africa.* Chicago.

Bishop, W. W. and J. A. Miller (eds.) (1972). *The calibration of hominoid evolution.* Edinburgh and Toronto.

Bishop, W. W., M. Pickford and A. Hill (1975). New evidence regarding Quaternary geology, archaeology and hominids of Chesowanja, Kenya. *Nature, Lond.* **258**, 204–8.

Bordes, F. (1968). *The Old Stone Age.* New York and Toronto.

Brain, C. K. (1958). *The Transvaal ape-man-bearing cave deposits. Transv. Mus. Mem.* **11**.

(1967). Hottentot food remains and their bearing on the interpretation of fossil bone assemblages. *Sci. Pap. Namib Desert Res. Station* **32**, 1–11.

(1970). New finds at Swartkrans Australopithecine site. *Nature, Lond.* **225**, 112–19.

(1976). Some principles in the interpretation of bone accumulations associated with man. In G. Ll. Isaac and E. R. McCown (eds.), *Human origins. Louis Leakey and the East African evidence*, 97–116. Menlo Park.

Breuil, H., F. Cabu and C. van Riet Lowe (1944). Le Paléolithique au Congo belge d'après les recherches du docteur Cabu. *Trans. R. Soc. S. Afr.* **30** (2), 143–74.

Broeker, W. S. and M. L. Bender (1972). Age determinations on marine strandlines. In W. W. Bishop and J. A. Miller (eds.), *Calibration of hominoid evolution*, 19–36. Edinburgh and Toronto.

Brothwell, D. and E. Higgs (1963). *Science in archaeology*. Bristol.

Burkitt, M. C. (1928). *South Africa's past in stone and paint*. Cambridge.

(1949). *The Old Stone Age*, 2nd ed. Cambridge.

Butzer, K. W. (1971). *Environment and archaeology*, 2nd ed. Chicago.

(1974a). Geo-archaeological interpretation of two Acheulian calc-pan sites: Doornlaagte and Rooidam (Kimberley, South Africa). *J. archaeol. Sci.* **1**, 1–25.

(1974b). Paleoecology of South African Australopithecines: Taung revisited. *Curr. Anthrop.* **15** (4), 367–82, 413–16.

(1976). The Mursi, Nkalabong and Kibish Formations, Lower Omo Basin, Ethiopia. In Y. Coppens *et al.* (eds.), *Earliest man and environments in the Lake Rudolph basin*, 12–23. Chicago.

Butzer, K. W. and G. L. Hansen (1968). *Desert and river in Nubia*. Madison.

Butzer, K. W. and G. Ll. Isaac (eds.) (1975). *After the australopithecines*. The Hague.

Butzer, K. W., D. M. Helgren, G. J. Fock, and R. Stuckenrath (1973). Alluvial terraces of the lower Vaal River, South Africa: a reappraisal and reinvestigation. *J. Geol.* **81**, 341–62.

Cabu, F. (1952). Some aspects of the Stone Age in the Belgian Congo. In *Proceedings of the Pan-African Congress on Prehistory, 1947*, 195–201. Oxford.

Cahen, D. (1968). Chronologie interne de la station acheuléenne de la Kamoa, Katanga, *Africa-Tervuren* **14**, 103–10.

(1973). Le site archéologique de la Kamoa, 3 vols. Thesis, Université Libre, Brussels.

Campbell, B. G. (ed.) (1976). *Humankind evolving*. Boston and Toronto.

Camps, G. (1974). *Les civilisations préhistoriques d'Afrique du Nord et du Sahara*. Paris.

Caton-Thompson, G. (1952). *Kharga Oasis in prehistory*. London.

Chavaillon, J. (1964). *Etude stratigraphique des formations Quaternaires du Sahara Nord Occidental*. CNRS, Paris.

(1976). Evidence for the technical practices of early Pleistocene hominids. In Y. Coppens *et al.* (eds.), *Earliest man and environments in the Lake Rudolf basin*, 565–73. Chicago.

Chavaillon, J. and N. Chavaillon (1976). Le Paléolithique ancien en Ethiopie: caractères techniques de l'Oldowayen de Gomboré-I à Melka Kuntouré en Ethiopie. In *IXᵉ Congrès de l'Union Internationale des Sciences Préhistoriques et Protohistoriques (Nice, 1976), Colloque V*, 43–69. Nice.

Childe, V. G. (1941). *Man makes himself*. London.

Clark, J. D. (1950). *The Stone Age cultures of Northern Rhodesia*. S. Afr. Archaeol. Soc., Cape Town.

(1959a). *The prehistory of southern Africa.* Harmondsworth.

(1959b). Further excavations at Broken Hill, Northern Rhodesia. *Jl R. anthrop. Inst.* **89**, 201–32.

(1963). *Prehistoric cultures of northeast Angola and their significance in tropical Africa* 2 vols. *Publcões cult. Co. Diam. Angola* **62**.

(1964). The influence of environment in inducing culture change at the Kalambo Falls prehistoric site. *S. Afr. archaeol. Bull.* **19**, 93–101.

(1966). *The distribution of prehistoric culture in Angola. Publcões cult. Co. Diam. Angola* **73**.

(1967). *Atlas of African prehistory.* Chicago.

(1968). *Further palaeo-anthropological studies in Northern Lunda. Publcões cult. Co. Diam. Angola* **78**.

(1969). The *Kalambo Falls prehistoric site*, vol. I. Cambridge.

(1970). *The prehistory of Africa.* London and New York.

(1971). Problems of archaeological nomenclature and definition in the Congo Basin. *S. Afr. archaeol. Bull.* **26**, 67–78.

(1972). Palaeolithic butchery practices. In P. J. Ucko, R. Tringham and G. W. Dimbleby (eds.), *Man, settlement and urbanism*, 149–56. London and Morristown, N.J.

(1974a). The *Kalambo Falls prehistoric site*, vol. II. Cambridge.

(1974b). The stone artefacts from Cornelia, O.F.S., South Africa. In K. W. Butzer, J. D. Clark and H. B. S. Cooke (eds.), *The geology, archaeology and fossil mammals of the Cornelia Beds, O.F.S.*, 33–62. National Museum, Bloemfontein.

Clark, J. D. and G. Ll. Isaac (eds.) (1976). *Prétirage du Colloque V du IX^e Congrès de l'Union Internationale des Sciences Préhistoriques et Protohistoriques (Nice, 1976).*

Clark, J. D. and H. Kurashina (1976). New Plio-Pleistocene archaeological occurrences from the plain of Gadeb, Upper Webi Shebele basin, Ethiopia, and a statistical comparison of the Gadeb sites with other Early Stone Age assemblages. In J. D. Clark and G. Ll. Isaac (eds.), *Prétirage du Colloque V du IX^e Congrès de l'Union Internationale des Sciences Préhistoriques et Protohistoriques (Nice, 1976)*, 158–216. Nice.

(1979). Hominid occupation of the east-central Highlands of Ethiopia in the Plio-Pleistocene. *Nature, Lond.* **282**, 33–9.

Clark, J. D., K. P. Oakley, L. H. Wells and J. A. C. McClelland (1950). New studies on Rhodesian man. *Jl R. anthrop. Inst.* **77**, 7–32.

Clark, J. D., M. A. J. Williams and A. B. Smith (1975). The geomorphology and archaeology of Adrar Bous, Central Sahara: a preliminary report. *Quaternaria* **17**, 245–97.

Clark, J. G. D. (1969). *World prehistory: a new outline.* Cambridge.

Clarke, D. L. (1968). *Analytical archaeology.* London.

Cole, G. H. (1967). The later Acheulian and Sangoan of southern Uganda. In W. W. Bishop and J. D. Clark (eds.), *Background to evolution in Africa* 481–528. Chicago.

Cole, S. (1963). *The prehistory of East Africa.* Harmondsworth and New York.

Coles, J. M. and E. S. Higgs (1969). *The archaeology of early man.* London.

Colette, J. R. F. (1929). Le préhistorique dans le Bas-Congo. *Bull. Soc. R. Belge d'Anthrop. Préhist.* **44**, 42–47.

(1931). Industries paléolithiques au Congo belge. In *Congrès Internationale d'Anthropologie et d'Archéologie Préhistorique, Paris.*

Cooke, H. B. S. (1958). Observations relating to Quaternary environments in East and Southern Africa, *Trans. Geol. Soc. S. Afr. (Annex.)* **60**, 1–73.

Coppens, Y., F. C. Howell, G. Ll. Isaac and R. E. F. Leakey (eds.) (1976). *Earliest man and environments in the Lake Rudolf basin.* Chicago.

Curtis, G. H., R. Drake, T. E. Cerling and J. H. Hampel (1975). Age of the KBS tuff in the Koobi Fora Formation, East Rudolf, Kenya. *Nature, Lond.* **258**, 395–8.

Dart, R. A. (1949). The predatory implemental technique of *Australopithecus.* *Am. J. phys. Anthrop.* **7**, 1–38.

(1957a). *The osteodontokeratic culture of* Australopithecus prometheus. *Transv. Mus. Mem.* **10**.

(1957b). The Makapansgat Australopithecine osteodontokeratic culture. In *Proceedings of the Third Pan-African Congress on Prehistory (Livingstone, 1955)* 161–71. London.

Daveau-Ribeiro, S. and P. Biberson (1972). Le Quaternaire et le Paléolithique de l'Adrar Mauritanien. In *Actes de la VIᵉ session, Congrès Panafricain de Préhistoire (Dakar, 1967)*, 55–60. Chambéry.

Davies, O. (1964). *The Quaternary in the coastlands of Guinea.* Glasgow.

(1967). *West Africa before the Europeans.* London.

Deacon, H. J. (1970). The Acheulian occupation at Amanzi Springs, Uitenhage District, Cape Province. *Ann. Cape Prov. Mus.* **8**, 89–189.

(1975). Demography, subsistence, and culture during the Acheulian in Southern Africa. In K. W. Butzer and G. Ll. Isaac (eds.), *After the australopithecines*, 543–70.

Fock, G. J. (1968). Rooidam, a sealed site of the First Intermediate. *S. Afr. J. Sci.* **64**, 153–9.

Freeman, L. G. (in press). In R. S. O. Harding and G. Teliki (eds.), *Omnivorous primates: gathering and hunting in human evolution.* New York.

Gobert, E. G. (1950). Le gisement paléolithique de Sidi Zin. *Karthago* **I**, 1–63.

Goodall, J. van Lawick (1968). The behaviour of free-living chimpanzees in the Gombe Stream area. *Anim. Behav. Monog.* **1**, 161–311.

(1971). *In the shadow of man.* Glasgow.

Goodwin, A. J. H. and C. van Riet Lowe (1929). *Stone Age cultures of South Africa. Ann. S. Afr. Mus.* **27**, 1–289.

Gowlett, J. A. J. (1978). Kilombe – an Acheulian site complex in Kenya. In W. W. Bishop (ed.), *Geological background to fossil man*, 337–60. Edinburgh.

Hansen, C. L. and C. M. Keller (1971). Environment and activity patterning at Isimila Karongo, Iringa District, Tanzania: a preliminary report. *Am. Anthrop.* **73**, 1201–11.

Harris, J. W. K. and W. W. Bishop (1976). Sites and assemblages from the early Pleistocene beds of Karari and Chesowanja, Kenya. In *Prétirage du Colloque V du IXᵉ Congrès de l'Union Internationale des Sciences Préhistoriques et Protohistoriques (Nice, 1976)*, 70–117. Nice.

Harris, J. W. K. and I. Herbich (1978). Aspects of early Pleistocene hominid behaviour east of Lake Turkana, Kenya. In W. W. Bishop (ed.), *Geological background to fossil man*, 529–47. Edinburgh and Toronto.

Harris, J. W. K. and G. Ll. Isaac (1976). The Karari industry: distinctive early Pleistocene archaeological material from the Koobi Fora Formation, Kenya. *Nature, Lond.* **262**, 102–7.

Hay, R. L. (1976). *The geology of Olduvai Gorge*. Berkeley.

 (1980). The KBS controversy may be ended. *Nature, Lond.* **284**, 401.

Heinzelin, J. de (1961). Le Paléolithique aux abords d'Ishango. *Exploration du Parc National Albert*, pt. 6, 10–11. Brussels.

Horowitz, A. (1975). Preliminary palaeo-environmental implications of pollen analysis of Middle Breccia from Sterkfontein. *Nature, Lond.* **258**, 417–18.

Howell, F. C. (1961). Isimila: a palaeolithic site in Africa. *Scient. Am.* **205** (4), 118–29.

 (1965). *Early Man*. New York.

Howell, F. C. and J. D. Clark (1963). Acheulian hunter–gatherers of sub-Saharan Africa. In F. C. Howell and F. Bourlière, (eds.), *African ecology and human evolution*, 458–533. Chicago.

 (1966) (eds.). Recent studies in paleoanthropology. *Am. Anthrop. Special Publ.* **68**.

Howell, F. C., G. H. Cole and M. R. Kleindienst (1962). Isimila, an Acheulian occupation site in the Iringa Highlands. In *Actes du IV$^e$ Congrès Panafricain de Préhistoire et de l'Etude du Quaternaire*, 43–80. Tervuren.

Howell, F. C., G. H. Cole, M. R. Kleindienst, B. J. Szabo and K. P. Oakley (1972). Uranium series dating of bone from the Isimila prehistoric site, Tanzania. *Nature, Lond.* **237**, 51–2.

Hughes, A. R. and P. V. Tobias (1977). A fossil skull probably of the genus *Homo* from Sterkfontien, Transvaal, *Nature, Lond.* **265**, 310–12.

Hugot, H.-J. (ed.) (1962). *Missions Berliet Ténéré Tchad*. Paris.

Humphreys, A. J. B. (1969). Later Acheulian or Fauresmith? A contribution. *Ann. Cape Prov.* **6**, (10), 87–101.

 (1970). The role of raw material and the concept of the Fauresmith. *S. Afr. archaeol. Bull.* **35**, 139–44.

Hurford, A. J., A. Gleadow and C. Naeser (1976). Fission track dating of pumice from the KBS Tuff East Rudolf, Kenya. *Nature, Lond.* **263**, 738–40.

Isaac, G. Ll. (1966). New evidence from Olorgesailie relating to the character of Acheulian occupation sites. In *Actas del V Congreso Panafricano de Prehistoria y de Estudio del Cuaternario*, 135–45.

 (1967). The stratigraphy of the Peninj group-early Middle Pleistocene formations west of Lake Natron, Tanzania. In W. W. Bishop and J. D. Clark (eds.), *Background to evolution in Africa*, 229–57. Chicago.

 (1968). Traces of Pleistocene hunters: an East African example. In R. B. Lee and I. Devore (eds.), *Man the hunter*, 253–61. Chicago.

 (1969). Studies of early culture in East Africa. *World Archaeol.* **1**, 1–28.

 (1971). The diet of early man: aspects of archaeological evidence from lower and middle Pleistocene sites in Africa. *World Archaeol.* **2**, 278–99.

 (1972a). Early phases of human behaviour. In D. L. Clarke (ed.), *Models in archaeology*, 149–56. London.

(1972b). Chronology and tempo of cultural change during the Pleistocene. In W. W. Bishop and J. A. Miller (eds.), *Calibration of hominoid evolution*, 381–430. Edinburgh and Toronto.

(1975). Stratigraphy and cultural patterns in East Africa during the middle ranges of Pleistocene time. In K. W. Butzer and G. Ll. Isaac (eds.), *After the australopithecines*, 495–542. The Hague.

(1976a). East Africa as a source of fossil evidence for human evolution. In G. Ll. Isaac and E. R. McCown (eds.), *Human origins. Louis Leakey and the East African evidence*, 121–38. Menlo Park.

(1976b). The activities of early African hominids: a review of archaeological evidence from the time span two and a half million to one million years ago. In G. Ll. Isaac and E. R. McCown (eds.), *Human origins. Louis Leakey and the East African evidence*, 483–514. Menlo Park.

(1976c). Plio-Pleistocene artifact assemblages from East Rudolf, Kenya. In Y. Coppens *et al.* (eds.), *Earliest man and environments in the Lake Rudolf basin*, 552–64. Chicago.

(1977). *Olorgesailie: the archaeology of a Middle Pleistocene lake basin in Kenya*. Chicago.

Isaac, G. Ll. and D. C. Crader (in press). Can we determine the degree to which early hominids were carnivorous? In R. S. O. Harding and G. Teleki (eds.), *Omnivorous primates: gathering and hunting in human evolution*. New York.

Isaac, G. Ll. and G. H. Curtis (1974). The age of early Acheulian industries from the Peninj group, Tanzania. *Nature, Lond.* **249**, 624–7.

Isaac, G. Ll. and E. R. McCown (eds.) (1976). *Human origins. Louis Leakey and the East African evidence*. Menlo Park.

Isaac, G. Ll., J. W. K. Harris and D. Crader (1976). Archaeological evidence from the Koobi Fora Formation. In Y. Coppens *et al.* (eds.), *Earliest man and environments in the lake Rudolf basin*, 533–51. Chicago.

Isaac, G. Ll., R. E. F. Leakey and A. K. Behrensmeyer (1971). Archaeological traces of early hominid activities, east of Lake Rudolf, Kenya. *Science, N.Y.* **173**, 1129–34.

Jaeger, J.-J. (1975). The mammalian faunas and hominid fossils of the Middle Pleistocene of the Maghreb. In K. W. Butzer and G. Ll. Isaac (eds.), *After the australopithecines*, 399–418. The Hague.

Janmart, J. (1947). *Stations préhistoriques de l'Angola du nord-est. Publcões cult. Co. Diam. Angola* **1**.

(1953). *The Kalahari Sands of Lunda (North-East Angola), their earlier redistribution and the Sangoan Culture. Publcões cult. Co. Diam. Angola* **20**.

Jolly, C. (1970). The seed-eaters: a new model of hominid differentiation based on baboon analogy. *Man*, **5**, 5–26.

Jones, N. (1949). *The prehistory of Southern Rhodesia*. Cambridge.

Keller, C. M. (1973). *Montagu Cave in prehistory: a descriptive analysis. Anthrop. Rec. Univ. Calif.* **28**.

Klein, R. G. (1973). Geological antiquity of Rhodesian man. *Nature, Lond.* **244**, 311–12.

(1977). The ecology of early man in southern Africa. *Science, N.Y.* **197**, 115–26.

Kleindienst, M. R. (1961). Variability within the Late Acheulian assemblage in eastern Africa. *S. Afr. archaeol. Bull.* **16**, 35–52.

(1967). Questions of terminology in regard to the study of Stone Age industries in eastern Africa – Culture stratigraphic units. In W. W. Bishop and J. D. Clark (eds.), *Background to evolution in Africa*, 821–59. Chicago.

(1973). Excavations at Site JK₂, Olduvai Gorge, Tanzania, 1961–1962: the geological setting. *Quaternaria* **17**, 145–208.

Leakey, L. S. B. (1931). *The Stone Age cultures of Kenya Colony*. Cambridge.

(1934). *Adam's ancestors*. London.

(1935). *The Stone Age races of Kenya*. Oxford.

(1949). *Tentative study of the Pleistocene climatic changes and Stone Age culture sequence in northeast Angola*. *Publcões Cult. Co. Diam. Angola* **4**.

(1951). *Olduvai Gorge*, Cambridge.

(1963). Very early East African Hominidae, and their ecological setting. In F. C. Howell and F. Bourlière (eds.), *African ecology and human evolution*, 448–57. Chicago.

Leakey, Margaret, P. V. Tobias, J. E. Martyn and R. E. F. Leakey (1969). An Acheulian industry with prepared core technique and the discovery of a contemporary hominid mandible at Lake Baringo, Kenya. *Proc. prehist. Soc.* **35**, 48–76.

Leakey, M. D. (1970a). Early artefacts from the Koobi Fora area. *Nature, Lond.* **226**, 228–30.

(1970b). New finds at the Swartkrans australopithecine site (continued). Stone artefacts from Swartkrans. *Nature, Lond.* **225**, 1222–5.

(1971). *Olduvai Gorge, vol. III: Excavations in Beds I and II, 1960–1963*. Cambridge.

(1975). Cultural patterns in the Olduvai sequence. In K. W. Butzer and G. Ll. Isaac (eds.), *After the australopithecines*, 477–93. The Hague.

Leakey, M. G. and R. E. F. Leakey (1978). *Koobi Fora Research Project Volume I, 1968–1974: The fossil hominids and an introduction to their context*. Oxford.

Leakey, R. E. F. (1974). Further evidence of Lower Pleistocene hominids from East Rudolf, northern Kenya 1973. *Nature, Lond.* **248**, 653–6.

Lee, C., J. L. Bada, and E. Patterson (1976). Amino acid in modern and fossil woods. *Nature, Lond.* **259**, 183–6.

Lowe, C. van Riet (1952a). The Vaal river chronology. An up-to-date summary. *S. Afr. archaeol. Bull.* **2**, 135–49.

(1952b). *The Pleistocene geology and prehistory of Uganda, Part 2. Prehistory. Mem. Geol. Surv. Uganda* **6**.

McBurney, C. B. M. (1960). *The Stone Age of northern Africa*. Harmondsworth.

Maguire, B. (1965). Foreign pebble pounding artefacts in the breccias and the overlying vegetation soil at Makapansgat limeworks. *S. Afr. archaeol. Bull.* **20**, 117–30.

Mason, R. J. (1962a). *Prehistory of the Transvaal*. Johannesburg.

(1962b). Australopithecines and artefacts at Sterkfontein. II. The Sterkfontein stone artefacts and their maker. *S. Afr. archaeol. Bull.* **17**, 109–26.

(1965). Makapansgat limeworks fractured stone objects and natural fracture in Africa. *S. Afr. archaeol. Bull.* **20**, 3–16.

(1969). The Oppermansdrif dam archaeological project – Vaal Basin. *S. Afr. archaeol. Bull.* **24**, 182–92.

(1976). The earliest artefact assemblages of South Africa. In *Prétirage du Colloque V du IX^e Congrès de l'Union Internationale des Sciences Préhistoriques et Protohistoriques (Nice, 1976)*, 140–56. Nice.

Merrick, H. V. (1976). Recent archaeological research in the Plio-Pleistocene deposits of the lower Omo Valley, southwestern Ethiopia. In G. Ll. Isaac and E. R. McCown (eds.), *Human origins. Louis Leakey and the East African evidence*, 461–82. Menlo Park.

Merrick, H. V. and J. P. S. Merrick (1976). Archaeological occurrences of earlier Pleistocene age, from the Shungura formation In Y. Coppens *et al.* (eds.), *Earliest man and environments in the Lake Rudolf basin*, 574–84. Chicago.

Merrick, H. V., J. de Heinzelin, P. Haesaerts and F. C. Howell (1973). Archaeological occurrences of early Pleistocene age from the Shungura Formation, lower Omo valley, Ethiopia. *Nature, Lond.* **242**, 572–5.

Michels, J. (1973). *Dating methods in archaeology*. New York and London.

Moorsel, H. van (1959). *Paléolithique ancien à Léopoldville. Studia Universitatis Lovanium Fac. Sci.* **9**.

Mortelmans, G. (1957). La préhistoire du Congo belge. *Revue de l'Université de Bruxelles*, **2–3**, 1–53.

Nenquin, J. (1966). Recent excavations in Rwanda and Burundi. In *Actas del V Congreso Panafricano de Prehistoria y de Estudio del Cuaternario*, 205–22. Santa Cruz de Tenerife.

(1967). *Contributions to the study of prehistoric cultures of Rwanda and Burundi.* Musée Royale de l'Afrique Centrale, Tervuren. Series 8 no. 59.

Oakley, K. P. (1956). The earliest fire makers. *Antiquity* **30**, 102–7.

O'Brien, T. P. (1939). *The prehistory of Uganda Protectorate*. Cambridge.

Ogusu, B. W. (1973). Was there a Sangoan industry in West Africa? *W. Afr. J. Archaeol.* **3**, 191–6.

Piperno, M. and G. M. Bulgarelli Piperno (1975). First approach to the ecological and cultural significance of the early Palaeolithic Occupation Site of Garba IV at Melka Kunturé (Ethiopia). *Quaternaria* **18**, 374–82.

Robinson, J. T. (1962). Australopithecines and artefacts at Sterkfontein, Part I. Sterkfontein stratigraphy and the significance of the extension site. *S. Afr. Archaeol. Bull.* **17**, 87–108.

Roche, H. and J.-J. Tiercelin (1977). Découverte d'une industrie lithique ancienne *in situ* dans la formation d'Hadar, Afar central, Ethiopie. *C.r. Acad. Sci.*, Paris **284**-D, 1871–4.

Roubet, C. (1969). Essai de datation absolue d'un biface-hachereau paléolithique de l'Afar (Ethiopie). *Anthropologie, Paris* **73**, 503–24.

Said, R. (1975). The geological evolution of the River Nile. In F. Wendorf and A. E. Marks (eds.), *Problems in prehistory: North Africa and the Levant*, 7–44. Dallas.

Sampson, C. G. (1974). *The Stone Age archaeology of Southern Africa*. London and New York.

Sandford, K. S. (1934). *Paleolithic Man and the Nile Valley in Upper and Middle Egypt. Publs. Orient. Inst. Univ. Chicago* **18**.

Sandford, K. W. and A. J. Arkell (1933). *Palaeolithic man and the Nile Valley in Nubia and Upper Egypt. Publs. Orient. Inst. Univ. Chicago* 17.

Singer, R. J. and J. Wymer (1968). Archaeological investigations at the Saldanha skull site in South Africa. *S. Afr. archaeol. Bull.* 23, 63–74.

Söhnge, P. G., D. J. L. Visser and C. van Riet Lowe (1937). *The geology and archaeology of the Vaal River basin. Mem. geol. surv. Un. S. Afr.* 35.

Soper, R. (1965). The stone age in northern Nigeria. *J. hist. Soc. Nigeria* 3, 175–94.

Stearns, C. E. and D. L. Thurber (1965). $Th^{230}/U^{234}$ dates of late Pleistocene marine fossils from the Mediterranean and Moroccan littorals. *Quaternaria* 7, 29–42.

Stiles, D. N., R. L. Hay and J. R. O'Neil (1974). The MNK Chert Factory Site, Olduvai Gorge, Tanzania. *World Archaeol* 5, 285–308.

Thurber, D. L. (1972). Problems in dating non-woody materials from continental environments. In W. W. Bishop and J. A. Miller (eds.), *Calibration of hominoid evolution*, 1–18. Edinburgh and Toronto.

Tobias, P. V. and A. R. Hughes (1969). The new Witwatersrand University excavation at Sterkfontein. Progress report, some problems and first results. *S. Afr. archaeol. Bull.* 24, 158–69.

Vaufrey, R. (1955). *Préhistoire de l'Afrique, Tome 1, Le Maghreb*. Institut des Hautes Etudes de Tunis, vol. IV. Paris.

Vrba, E. S. (1975). Some evidence of chronology and palaeoecology of Sterkfontein, Swartkrans and Kromdraai from the fossil Bovidae. *Nature, Lond.* 254, 301–4.

(1976). The fossil Bovidae of Sterkfontein, Swartkrans and Kromdraai. *Transv. Mus. Mem.* 21, 1–166.

Washburn, S. L. and C. S. Lancaster (1968). The evolution of hunting. In R. B. Lee and I. Devore (eds.), *Man the hunter*, 293–303. Chicago.

Washburn, S. L. and R. Moore (1974). *Ape into man*. Boston.

Wayland, E. J. (1926). A possible age correlation of the Kafu Gravels. Uganda Protectorate, Annual Report, Geological Department, 1926.

Wendorf, F. (ed.) (1968). *The Prehistory of Nubia*, 2 vols. Dallas.

Wendorf, F. and R. Schild (1974). *A Middle Stone Age sequence from the Central Rift Valley, Ethiopia*. Warsaw.

Wendorf, F., R. Schild, R. Said, C. V. Haynes, A. Gautier and M. Kobusiewicz (1976). The prehistory of the Egyptian Sahara. *Science, N.Y.* 193, 103–14.

Wendorf, F., R. L. Laury, C. C. Albritton, R. Schild, C. V. Haynes, P. Damon, M. Shaffiquillah and R. Scarborough (1975). Dates for the Middle Stone Age of East Africa. *Science, N.Y.* 187, 740–2.

Wright, R. V. (1972). Imitative learning of a flaked stone technology – the case of an orang-utan. *Mankind* 8, 296–306.

Zihlman, A. and N. Tanner (1978). Gathering and the hominid adaptation. In L. Tiger and H. Fowler (eds.), *Female hierarchies*, 163–94. Chicago.

4. THE CULTURES OF THE MIDDLE PALAEOLITHIC

Alimen, H. (1957). *The prehistory of Africa* Translated by A. H. Broderick. London and New York.

Alimen, H., F. Beucher and G. Conrad (1966). Chronologie du dernier cycle pluvial-aride au Sahara nord-occidental. *C.r. hebd. Séanc. Acad. Sci., Paris* **263**, 5–8.

Anthony, B. (1972). The Stillbay question. In *Actes du VI<sup>e</sup> Congrès panafricain de Préhistoire et de l'Etude du Quaternaire (Dakar, 1967)*. 80–2. Chambéry.

Antoine, M. (1939). Notes de Préhistoire Marocaine, XIV. Un cône de résurgence du Paléolithique moyen à Tit-Mellil, près Casablanca. *Bull. Soc. Préhist. Maroc.* **12**, 1–4, (1938) 1939, 3–95.

Arambourg, C. and L. Balout (1955). L'ancien lac de Tihodaine et ses gisements préhistoriques. In *Actes de la II<sup>e</sup> Session, Congrès panafricain de Préhistoire (Alger, 1952)*, 281–93. Paris.

Aubréville, A. (1962). Savanisation tropicale et glaciations quaternaires. *Adansonia* **2**, 16–91.

Bada, J. L. and L. Deems (1975). Accuracy of dates beyond the $C^{14}$ dating limit using the aspartic acid racemisation reaction. *Nature, Lond.* **255**, 218–19.

Bada, J. L. and R. Protsch (1973). Racemization reaction of aspartic acid and its use in dating fossil bones. *Proc. nat. Acad. Sci. U.S.A.* **70**, 1331–4.

Bada, J. L., R. A. Schroeder, R. Protsch and R. Berger (1974). Concordance of collagen based radio carbon and aspartic acid racemization ages. *Proc. nat. Acad. Sci. U.S.A.* **71**, 914–17.

Balout, L. (1955). *Préhistoire de l'Afrique du Nord: essai de chronologie.* Paris.
    (1965). Le Moustérien du Maghreb. *Quaternaria* **7**, 43–58.
    (1966). Données nouvelles sur le problème du Moustérien en Afrique du Nord. In *Actes du V<sup>e</sup> Congrès panafricain de Préhistoire et de l'Etude du Quaternaire (Santa Cruz de Tenerife, 1965)*, vol. 1, 137–43.

Beaumont, P. B. (1973). Border Cave – a progress report. *S. Afr. J. Sci.* **69**, 41–6.

Beaumont, P. B., K. de Villiers and J. C. Vogel (1978). Modern man in sub-Saharan Africa prior to 49,000 years B.P.: A review and evaluation with particular reference to Border Cave. *S. Afr. J. Sci.* **74**, 409–19.

Binford, L. R. and S. R. Binford (1966). A preliminary analysis of functional variability in the Mousterian of Levallois facies. *Am. Anthrop.* **68**, 238–95.

Bishop, W. W. and J. D. Clark (eds.) (1967). *Background to evolution in Africa.* Chicago.

Bishop, W. W. and J. A. Miller (eds.) (1972). *Calibration of hominoid evolution.* Edinburgh and Toronto.

Bond, G. and R. Summers (1954). A late Stillbay hunting-camp site on the Nata River, Bechuanaland Protectorate. *S. Afr. archaeol. Bull.* **9**, 89–95.

Bordes, F. (1961). Mousterian cultures in France. *Science, N.Y.* **134**, 803–10.
    (1977). Time and Space Limits of the Mousterian. In R. V. S. Wright (ed.), *Stone tools as cultural markers*, 37–9. New Jersey (for Australian Institute of Aboriginal Studies, Canberra).

Boulet, R. (1972). Nouveaux arguments en faveur de l'existence de deux ergs rubéfiés d'âge différent dans la zone sahélienne de l'Afrique occidentale (Haute Volta). In *Actes du VI<sup>e</sup> Congrès panafricain de Préhistoire et de l'Etude du Quaternaire (Dakar, 1967)*, 334–5. Chambéry.

Bourlière, F. (1963). Observations on the ecology of some large African mammals. In F. C. Howell and F. Bourlière (eds.), *African ecology and human evolution*, 43–54. Chicago.

Breuil, H., F. Cabu and C. van Riet Lowe (1944). Le Paléolithique au Congo belge d'après les recherches du docteur Cabu. *Trans. R. Soc. S. Afr.* **30**(2), 143–74.

Breuil, H. and J. Janmart (1950). *Les limons et graviers de l'Angola du nord-est et leur contenu archéologigue. Publcões cult. Co. Diam. Angola* **5**.

Burke, K., A. B. Durotype and A. J. Whiteman (1971). A dry phase south of the Sahara 20 000 years ago. *W. Afr. J. Archaeol.* **1**, 1–8.

Butzer, K. W. (1971). *Environment and archaeology*, 2nd edn. Chicago.

(1973). Geology of Nelson Bay Cave, Robberg, South Africa. *S. Afr. archaeol. Bull.* **28**, 97–110.

(1975). Pleistocene littoral–sedimentary cycles of the Mediterranean Basin: a Mallorquin view. In K. W. Butzer and G. Ll. Isaac (eds.), *After the australopithecines*, 25–71. The Hague.

(1978). Sediment stratigraphy of the Middle Stone Age sequence at Klasies River Mouth, Tsitsikama Coast, South Africa. *S. Afr. archaeol. Bull.* **33**, 141–51.

Butzer, K. W., P. B. Beaumont and J. C. Vogel (1978). Lithostratigraphy of Border Cave, Kwazulu, South Africa: A Middle Stone Age sequence beginning c.195,000 B.P. *J. archaeol. Sci.* **5**, 317–41.

Butzer, K. W., G. J. Fock, R. Stuckenrath and A. Zilch (1973). Palaeo-hydrology of late Pleistocene lakes in the Alexandersfontein Pan, Kimberley, South Africa. *Nature, Lond.* **243**, 328–30.

Butzer, K. W. and C. L. Hansen (1968). *Desert and river in Nubia*. Madison.

Cahen, D. (1976). Nouvelles fouilles à la pointe de la Gombé (èxpointe de Kalina), Kinshasa, Zaïre. *L'Anthropologie* **80** (4), 573–602.

Camps, G. (1974). *Les civilisations préhistoriques de l'Afrique du nord et du Sahara*. Paris.

Carter, P. L. and J. C. Vogel (1974). The dating of industrial assemblages from stratified sites in eastern Lesotho. *Man* N.S. **9**, 557–70.

Caton-Thompson, G. (1946). The Aterian industry: its place and significance in the Palaeolithic world. *Jl R. anthrop. Inst.* **76**, 87–130.

(1952). *Kharga Oasis in prehistory*, London.

Chavaillon, J. (1964). *Etude stratigraphique des formations quaternaires du Sahara nord-occidental* CNRS, Paris.

Chavaillon, N. (1971). L'Atérien de la Zaouia el Kebira au Sahara nord-occidental (République algérienne.) *Libyca* **19**, 9–52.

Chmielewski, W. (1968). Early and Middle Palaeolithic sites near Arkin, Sudan. In F. Wendorf (ed.), *The prehistory of Nubia*, 110–93. Dallas.

Clark, J. D. (1954). *The prehistoric cultures of the Horn of Africa*. Cambridge.

(1955). A note on a wooden implement from the level of Peat I at Florisbad, Orange Free State. *Res. Nat. Mus. Bloemfontein*, **1**, 135–41.

(1957). A re-examination of the type site at Magosi, Uganda. In *Proceedings of the Third Pan-African Congress on Prehistory (Livingstone, 1955)*, 228–41. London.

(1959a). Further Excavations at Broken Hill, Northern Rhodesia. *Jl R. anthrop. Inst.* **89**, 201–32.

(1959b). *The prehistory of southern Africa*. Harmondsworth.

(1962). Carbon 14 chronology in Africa south of the Sahara. In *Actes du IV^e Congrès pan-africain de Préhistoire et de l'Etude du Quaternaire (Léopoldville 1959)*, 303–13. Tervuren.

(1963). *Prehistoric cultures of northeast Angola and their significance in tropical Africa*, 2 vol. *Publcões cult. Co. Diam. Angola* **62**.

(1966). *The distribution of prehistoric culture in Angola. Publcões cult. Co. Diam. Angola* **73**.

(ed.) (1967). *Atlas of African prehistory*. Chicago.

(1968). *Further palaeo–anthropological studies in northern Lunda. Publcôles cult. Co. Diam. Angola* **78**.

(1969). *The Kalambo Falls prehistoric site*, vol. I. Cambridge.

(1970). *The prehistory of Africa*. London and New York.

(1971). Human behavioural differences in southern Africa during the later Pleistocene. *Am. Anthrop.* **73**, 1211–36.

(1974). *The Kalambo Falls prehistoric site*, vol. II. Cambridge.

(1975a). Africa in prehistory: peripheral or paramount? *Man* N.S. **10**, 175–98.

(1975b). *Archaeological and Palaeoecological Field Studies in east central Ethiopia (January through March, 1974)*: Part II – Report on the archaeological survey and excavations in the southern Afar Rift and adjacent parts. Mimeograph, Berkeley.

Clark, J. D. and E. M. van Zinderen Bakker (1962). Pleistocene climates and cultures in northeastern Angola. *Nature, Lond.* **196**, 639–42.

Clark, J. D. and S. Cole (1957). *Proceedings of the Third Pan-African Congress on Prehistory (Livingstone, 1955)*. London.

Clark, J. D. and M. A. J. Williams (1978). Recent archaeological research in south-eastern Ethiopia (1974–1975): Some preliminary results. *Annales d'Ethiope*, XI, 19–44. Addis Ababa.

Clark, J. D., M. A. J. Williams and A. B. Smith (1975). The geomorphology and archaeology of Adrar Bous, central Sahara: A preliminary report. *Quaternaria* **17**, 245–97.

Clark, J. D., K. P. Oakley, L. H. Wells and J. A. C. McClelland (1950). New studies on Rhodesian Man. *Jl R. anthrop. Inst.* **77**, 7–32.

Clark, J. G. D. (1969). *World prehistory: a new outline*. Cambridge.

Cole, G. H. (1967a). A re-investigation of Magosi and the Magosian. *Quaternaria* **9**, 153–68.

(1967b). The Later Acheulian and Sangoan of southern Uganda. In W. W. Bishop and J. D. Clark (eds.), *Background to evolution in Africa*, 481–528. Chicago.

Cole, S. (1963). *The prehistory of East Africa*. Harmondsworth and New York.

Colette, J. R. F. (1931). Essai biométrique sur la station préhistorique de Kalina

(Congo belge). *Compte rendu XV^e Congrès International d'Anthropologie et d'Archéologie préhistorique*, 278–85. Paris.

Conrad, G. (1969). *L'Evolution continentale post-hercynienne du Sahara algérien.* Recherches sur les zones arides CNRS, Paris, Série-Géologie 10.

Cooke, C. K. (1957). The Waterworks site at Khami, Southern Rhodesia: Stone age and Proto-historic. *Occ. Pap. nat. Mus. Sth. Rhod.* **3** (21A), 1–43.

(1963). Report on excavations at Pomongwe and Tshangula caves, Matopo Hills, Southern Rhodesia. *S. Afr. archaeol. Bull.* **18**, 63–151.

(1966). Re-appraisal of the industry hitherto named the Proto-Stillbay. *Arnoldia* vol. 2, **22**, 1–14.

(1967). Archaeology and excavation. In C. K. Brain and C. K. Cooke: A preliminary account of the Redcliff Stone Age cave site in Rhodesia. *S. Afr. archaeol. Bull.* **21** 177–82.

(1971). Excavation at Zombepata Cave, Sipolilo District, Mashonaland, Rhodesia. *S. Afr. archaeol. Bull.* **26**, 104–27.

(1974). A bibliography of Rhodesian archaeology from 1874. *Arnoldia* vol. 6, **38**, 1–56.

(1978). The Red Cliff Stone Age site, Rhodesia. *Occ. Pap. Nat. Mus. Mon. Rhodesia*, Series A, Human Sciences, **4** (2), 45–73.

Cooke, H. B. S. and L. H. Wells (1951). Fossil remains from Chelmer, near Bulawayo, Southern Rhodesia. *S. Afr. J. Sci.* **47**, 205–9.

Crew, H. L. (1975). An evaluation of the relationship between the Mousterian complexes of the eastern Mediterranean. In F. Wendorf and A. E. Marks (eds.), *Problems in prehistory: North Africa and the Levant*, 427–37. Dallas.

Dart, R. A. and P. B. Beaumont (1968). Ratification and retrocession of earlier Swaziland iron ore mining radiocarbon datings. *S. Afr. J. Sci.* **64**, 241–6.

Dart, R. A. and N. del Grande (1931). The ancient iron-smelting cavern at Mumbwa. *Trans. R. Soc. S. Afr.* **29**, 379–427.

Davies, O. (1964). *The Quaternary in the coastlands of Guinea.* Glasgow.

(1967). *West Africa before the Europeans.* London.

Deacon, H. J. and M. Brooker (1976). The Holocene and Upper Pleistocene sequence in the southern Cape. *Ann. S. Afr. Mus.* **71**, 203–14.

Deacon, J. (1966). An annotated list of radiocarbon dates for sub-Saharan Africa. *Ann. Cape Prov. Mus.* **5**, 5–84.

(1976). Report on stone artifacts from Duinefontein 2, Melkbosstrand. *S. Afr. archaeol. Bull.* **31**, 21–5.

(1979). Guide to archaeological sites in the southern Cape. South African Association of Archaeologists, Excursion June 30 to July 5, 1979, University of Stellenbosch. Stellenbosch.

Elouard, P. and H. Faure (1972). Quaternaire de l'Inchiri, du Taffoli et des environs de Nouakchott. In *Actes du VI^e Congrès Panafricain de Préhistoire et de l'Etude du Quaternaire (Dakar, 1967)*, 466–92. Chambéry.

Ennouchi, E. (1962). Un crâne d'homme ancien au Jebel Irhoud (Maroc). *C.r. hebd. Séanc. Acad. Sci., Paris* **254**, 4330–2.

Evernden, J. F. and G. H. Curtis (1965). The potassium–argon dating of late Cenozoic rocks in East Africa and Italy. *Curr. Anthrop.* **6**, 343–64.

Faure, H. (1962). *Reconnaissance géologique des formations sédimentaires post-paléozoiques du Niger oriental.* Thesis, *Mém. Bur. Rech. géol. min.* **29**. Paris.

Ferembach, D. (1976a). Les restes humains atériens de Témara (Campagne 1975). *Bull. Mém. Soc. Anthrop.*, Paris, series 13, **3**, 175–80.

(1976b). Les restes humains de la grotte de Dar-es-Soltane 2 (Maroc) Campagne 1975. *Bull. Mém. Soc. Anthrop.* Paris, series 13, **3**, 183–93.

Ferring, C. R. (1975). The Aterian in North African Prehistory. In F. Wendorf and A. E. Marks (eds.), *Problems in prehistory: North Africa and the Levant*, 113–26. Dallas.

Fock, G. J. (1954). Stone balls in the Windhoek Museum. *S. Afr. archaeol. Bull.* **9**, 108–9.

Freeman, L. G. (1975). Acheulian sites and stratigraphy in Iberia and the Maghreb. In K. W. Butzer and G. Ll. Isaac (eds.), *After the australopithecines*, 661–744. The Hague.

Gasse, F. (1974). Nouvelles observations sur les formations lacustres quaternaires dans la basse vallée de l'Awash et quelques grabens adjacents (Afar, Ethiopie et T.F.A.I.). *Revue Géogr. phys. Géol. dyn.* **6**, 101–18.

Gasse, F. and P. Rognon (1973). Le Quaternaire des bassins lacustres de l'Afar. *Revue Géogr. phys. Géol. dyn.* **15**, 405–14.

Goodwin, A. J. H. (1928). An introduction to the Middle Stone Age in South Africa. *S. Afr. J. Sci.* **25**, 410–18.

(1946). Earlier, Middle and Later. *S. Afr. archaeol. Bull.* **1**, 74–6.

Goodwin, A. J. H. and C. van Riet Lowe (1929). *The Stone Age cultures of South Africa. Ann. S. Afr. Mus.* **27**, 1–289.

Goodwin, A. J. H. and B. D. Malan (1935). Archaeology of the Cape St Blaize Cave and Raised Beach, Mossel Bay. *Ann. S. Afr. Mus.* **24**, 111–40.

Grove, A. T. and A. Warren (1968). Quaternary landforms and climate on the south side of the Sahara. *Geogrl J.* **134**, 194–208.

Gruet, M. (1954). Le gisement moustérien d' El Guettar. *Karthago* **5**, 1–87.

Gruet, M. (1955). Amoncellement pyramidal de sphères calcaires dans une source fossile moustériènne à el'Guettar (Sud tunisien). In *Actes du II Congrès Pan-africain de Préhistoire (Algiers, 1952)*, 449–56 and 460. Paris.

Gruet, M. and M. Zelle, (1955). Découverte de sphères à Windhoeck (South West Africa). In *Actes du II congrès Pan-africain de Préhistoire (Algiers, 1952)*, 457–79 and pl. 2. Paris.

Hours, F. (1973). Le Middle Stone Age de Melka-Kunturé: resultats acquis en 1971. *Documents pour servir à l'histoire des civilisations éthiopiennes* **4**, 19–29.

Howe, B. (1967). *The Palaeolithic of Tangier, Morocco, Excavations at Cape Ashakar, 1939–1947. Bull. Am. Sch. prehist. Res.* **22**.

Howell, F. C. (1960). European and north-west African Middle Pleistocene hominids. *Curr. anthrop.* **1**, 195–232.

Hugot, H. J. (1963). *Recherches préhistoriques dans l'Ahaggar nord-occidental, 1950–1957. CRAPE Mém.* **1**.

Humphreys, A. J. B. (1974). Comments on the occurrence of core-axe-like artifacts in the northern Cape. *Ann. Cape Prov. Mus. (Nat. Hist.)* **9**, 249–59.

Huzayyin, S. A. (1941). *The place of Egypt in Prehistory. Inst. Egypte* **43**.

Inskeep, R. R. (1962). The age of the Kondoa rock paintings in the light of recent excavations at Kisese II rock shelter. In *Actes du IV^e Congrès panafricain de Préhistoire et de l'Etude du Quaternaire* (*Tervuren, 1959*), 249–56. Tervuren.

Jaeger, J.-J. (1975). The mammalian faunas and hominid fossils of the Middle Pleistocene of the Maghreb. In K. W. Butzer and G. Ll. Isaac (eds.), *After the australopithecines*, 399–418. The Hague.

Janmart, J. (1947). *Stations préhistoriques de l'Angola du nord-est. Publcões cult. Co. Diam. Angola*, 1.

Jones, N. (1949). *The prehistory of Southern Rhodesia:* Cambridge.

Keller, C. M. (1969). Mossel Bay: a redescription. *S. Afr. archaeol. Bull.* **23**, 131–40.

(1973). *Montagu Cave in prehistory: a descriptive analysis. Anthrop. Rec. Univ. Calif.* **28**, Berkeley.

Klein, R. G. (1970). Problems in the study of the Middle Stone Age of South Africa. *S. Afr. archaeol. Bull.* **25**, 127–235.

(1972). Preliminary report on the July through September, 1970, excavation at Nelson Bay Cave, Plettenberg Bay (Cape Province, South Africa). In E. M. van Zinderen Bakker (ed.), *Palaeoecology of Africa*, vol. VI, 177–210. Cape Town.

(1973). Geological antiquity of Rhodesian Man. *Nature, Lond.* **244**, 311–12.

(1974). Environment and subsistence of prehistoric man in the southern Cape Province, South Africa. *World Archaeol.* **5**, 249–84.

(1975a). Middle Stone Age man–animal relationships in southern Africa: evidence from Die Kelders and Klasies River Mouth. *Science, N.Y.* **190**, 265–7.

(1975b). Ecology of Stone Age Man at the southern tip of Africa. *Archaeology Cambridge, Mass.* **28**, 238–47.

(1976). A preliminary note on the 'Middle Stone Age' open-air site of Duinefontein 2 (Melkbosstrand, south-western Cape Province, South Africa). *S. Afr. archaeol. Bull.* **31**, 12–20.

(1977). The mammalian fauna from the Middle and Later Stone Age (Upper Pleistocene) levels of Border Cave, Natal Province, South Africa, *S. Afr. archaeol. Bull.* **32**, 14–27.

(1978a). Preliminary analysis of the mammalian fauna of the Red Cliff Stone Age cave site, Rhodesia. *Occ. Pap. Nat. Mus. Mon. Rhodesia*, Series A, Human Sciences **4** (2), 74–80.

(1978b). Stone Age predators on large African bovids. *J. archaeol. Sci.*, **5**, 195–217.

Kurashina, H. (1978). An examination of prehistoric lithic technology in east-central Ethiopia. Doctoral dissertation, University of California, Berkeley.

Leakey, L. S. B. (1931). *Stone Age cultures of Kenya Colony*. Cambridge.

(1936). *Stone Age Africa*. Oxford.

(1943). Industries of the Gorgora rockshelter, Lake Tana. *Jl. E. Africa Uganda nat. Hist. Soc.* **17**, 199–203.

(1949). *Tentative study of the Pleistocene climatic changes and Stone Age sequence in north-eastern Angola. Publicões cult. Co. Diam. Angola* **4**.

Leakey, L. S. B. and W. E. Owen (1945). *A contribution to the study of the Tumbian culture in East Africa*. Occ. Pap. Coryndon meml Mus. 1.

Leakey, M. D., R. L. Hay, D. L. Thurber, R. Protsch and R. Berger (1972). Stratigraphy, archaeology and age of the Ndutu and Naisiusiu Beds, Olduvai Gorge, Tanzania. *World Archaeol.* **3**, 328–41.

Lee, C., J. L. Bada and E. Peterson (1976). Amino acids in modern and fossil woods. *Nature, Lond.* **259**, 183–86.

Leroi-Gourhan, A. (1958). Résultats de l'analyse pollinique du gisement d'el Guettar (Tunisie). *Bull. Soc. préhist. fr.* **60**, 546–51.

Lorcin, J. (1961–2). La station préhistorique du Cap Ténès. *Libyca* **9–10**, 35–57.

Louw, A. W. (1969). Bushman Rock Shelter, Ohrigstad, eastern Transvaal: a preliminary investigation. *S. Afr. archaeol. Bull.* **24**, 39–51.

Lowe, C. van Riet (1952). *The Pleistocene geology and prehistory of Uganda, II, Prehistory*. Mem. geol. Surv. Uganda **6**.

McBurney, C. B. M. (1960). *The Stone Age of northern Africa*. Harmondsworth.

    (1967). *The Haua Fteah, Cyrenaica and the Stone Age of the South-east Mediterranean*. Cambridge.

McBurney, C. B. M. and R. W. Hey (1955). *Prehistory and Pleistocene geology in Cyrenaican Libya*. Cambridge.

MacCalman, H. R. and A. Viereck (1967). Peperkorrel: A factor site of Lupemban affinities from central South West Africa. *S. Afr. archaeol. Bull.* **22**, 41–50.

Marks, A. E. (1968a). The Mousterian industries of Nubia. In F. Wendorf (ed.), *The prehistory of Nubia*, vol. 1, 194–314. Dallas.

    (1968b). The Khormusan: an Upper Pleistocene industry in Sudanese Nubia. In F. Wendorf (ed.), *The prehistory of Nubia*, vol. 11, 315–91. Dallas.

Marshack, A. (1976). Implications of the Palaeolithic symbolic evidence for the origin of language. *Am. Scient.* **64**, 136–45.

Mason, R. J. (1958). Bone tools at the Kalkbank Middle Stone Age site and the Makapansgat australopithecine locality, central Transvaal, Part 1, The Kalkbank site. *S. Afr. archaeol. Bull.* **13**, 85–93.

    (1962). *The prehistory of the Transvaal*. Johannesburg.

Mehlman, M. J. (1977). Excavations at Nasera Rock. *Azania* **12**, 111–18.

Mellars, P. A. (1970). Some comments on the notion of 'functional variability' in stone-tool assemblages. *World Archaeol.* **2**, 74–89.

Merrick, H. V. (1975). Change in later Pleistocene lithic industries in eastern Africa. Doctoral dissertation, University of California, Berkeley.

Mery, A. and J. Tixier (1972). La station préhistorique d'Ain Chebi, région de Reggan (Sahara algérien). In *Actes du VIe Congrès panafricain de Préhistoire et de l'Etude du Quaternaire*, (*Dakar, 1967*), 109–10. Chambéry.

Michels, J. W. (1973). *Dating methods in archaeology*. New York and London.

Moorsel, H. van (1968). *Atlas de Préhistoire de la Plaine de Kinshasa*. Université Lovanium Kinshasa.

Nenquin, J. (1967). *Contributions to the study of the prehistoric cultures of Rwanda and Burundi*. Musée royal de l'Afrique centrale, Tervuren.

O'Brien, T. P. (1939). *The prehistory of the Uganda Protectorate*. Cambridge.

Phillipson, D. W. (1973). The prehistoric succession in eastern Zambia: a preliminary report. *Azania* **8**, 3–24.

Phillipson, L. (1975). A survey of Upper Pleistocene and Holocene industries in the Upper Zambezi Valley, Zambia. Doctoral dissertation, University of California, Berkeley.

Ploey, J. de (1965). Position géomorphologique, genèse et chronologie de certains dépôts superficiels au Congo occidental. *Quaternaria* **7**, 131–54.

Protsch, R. (1975). The absolute dating of Upper Pleistocene sub-Saharan fossil hominids and their place in human evolution. *J. hum. Evol.* **4**, 293–322.

Protsch, R. and H. de Villiers (1974). Bushman Rock Shelter, Origstad, eastern Transvaal, South Africa. *J. hum. Evol.* **3**, 387–96.

Rightmire, G. P. (1976). Relationships of Middle and Upper Pleistocene hominids from sub-Saharan Africa. *Nature, Lond.* **260**, 238–40.

(1978). Florisbad and human population succession in southern Africa. *Am. J. Phys. Anthrop.* **48**(4), 475–86.

(1979). Implications of Border Cave skeletal remains for later Pleistocene human evolution. *Curr. Anthrop.* **20**, 23–35.

Roche, J. (1972). Les Industries paléolithiques de la Grotte de Taforalt (Maroc oriental). In *Actes du VI^e Congrès panafricain de Préhistoire et de l'Etude du Quaternaire, (Dakar, 1967)*, 102–8. Chambéry.

Rognon, P. (1967). *Le Massif de l'Atakor et ses bordures (Sahara Central)*. Recherches sur les zones arides, CNRS, Paris.

Roubet, C. (1969). Essai de datation absolue d'un biface-hachereau paléolithique de l'Afar (Ethiopie). *Anthropologie, Paris* **73**, 503–24.

Sampson, C. G. (1974). *The Stone Age archaeology of southern Africa*. London and New York.

Schild, R. and F. Wendorf (1975). New explorations in the Egyptian Sahara. In F. Wendorf and A. E. Marks (eds.), *Problems in prehistory: North Africa and the Levant*, 65–112. Dallas.

Servant, M. (1973). *Séquences continentales et variations climatiques: evolution du bassin du Tchad au cénozoïque supérieur*. Thesis, ORSTOM, Paris.

Shackleton, N. J. and N. D. Opdyke (1973). Oxygen isotope and palaeomagnetic stratigraphy of Equatorial Pacific core V28–238: Oxygen isotope temperatures on a $10^5$-year and $10^6$-year scale. *Quaternary Res.* **3**, 39–55.

Shackleton, N. and J. P. Kennett (1975). Late Cenozoic oxygen and carbon isotopic changes at DSDP Site 284: implications for Glacial history of the Northern Hemisphere and Antarctica. In J. P. Kennett, R. E. Houtz, *et al.* (eds.), *Initial reports of the deep sea drilling project*, xxxix. Washington.

Söhnge, P. G., D. J. L. Visser and C. van Riet Lowe (1937). *The geology and archaeology of the Vaal River basin. Mem. geol. Surv. Un. S. Afr.* **35**.

Soper, R. C. (1965). The Stone Age in northern Nigeria. *J. hist. Soc. Nigeria* **3**, 175–94.

Stearns, C. E. (1975). Dates for the Middle Stone Age of East Africa: a discussion. *Science, N.Y.* **190**, 809–10.

Tankard, A. J. and F. R. Schweitzer (1974). The geology of Die Kelders Cave and environs: a palaeoenvironmental study. *S. Afr. J. Sci.* **70**, 365–9.

Tixier, J. (1960). Les industries lithiques d'Aïn Fritissa (Maroc oriental). *Bull. archéol. maroc.* **3**, 107–248.

(1967). Procédés d'analyse et questions de terminologie concernant l'étude des ensembles industriels du Paléolithique récent et de l'Epipaléolithique dans l'Afrique du nord-ouest. In W. W. Bishop and J. D. Clark (eds.), *Background to evolution in Africa*, 771–812. Chicago.

Tobias, P. V. (1949). The excavation of Mwulu's Cave, Potgietersrust District. *S. Afr. archaeol. Bull.* **4**, 2–13.

(1968). Middle and early Upper Pleistocene members of the genus *Homo* in Africa. In G. Kurth (ed.), *Evolution and hominisation*, 2nd ed, 176–94. Stuttgart.

Vallois, H. V. (1951). La mandibule humaine fossile de la grotte du Porc Épic près Diré-Daoua (Abyssinie). *Anthropologie, Paris* **55**, 231–8.

Van Campo, M. (1975). Pollen analyses in the Sahara. In F. Wendorf and A. E. Marks (eds.), *Problems in prehistory: North Africa and the Levant*, 46–64. Dallas.

Van Campo, M. and R. Coque (1960). Palynologie et géomorphologie dans le sud Tunisien. *Pollen et Spores* **2**, 275–84.

Vaufrey, R. (1955). *Préhistoire de l'Afrique. I, Le Maghreb*, vol. IV. Institut des Hautes Etudes de Tunis, Paris.

Vogel, J. C. and P. B. Beaumont (1972). Revised radiocarbon chronology for the Stone Age in South Africa. *Nature, Lond.* **237**, 50–1.

Voigt, E. (1973). Stone Age molluscan utilization at Klasies River Mouth Caves. *S. Afr. J. Sci.* **69**, 306–9.

Wayland, E. J. (1923). Palaeolithic types of implements in relation to the Pleistocene deposits of Uganda. *Proc. prehist. Soc. E. Anglia* **4**, 96–112.

(1934). Rifts, rivers, rains and early man in Uganda. *Jl Roy. anthrop. Inst.* **64**, 33–352.

Wayland, E. J. and M. C. Burkitt (1932). The Magosian Culture of Uganda. *Jl R. Anthrop. Inst.* **12**, 369–90.

Wendorf, F. (ed.) (1968). *The prehistory of Nubia*, 2 vol. Dallas.

Wendorf, F. and A. E. Marks (eds.) (1975). *Problems in prehistory: North Africa and the Levant*. Dallas.

Wendorf, F. and R. Schild (1974). *A Middle Stone Age sequence from the central Rift Valley, Ethiopia*. Polska Akademia Nauk, Institut Historii Kultury Materialnej, Warsaw.

(1975). The Palaeolithic of the Lower Nile Valley. In F. Wendorf and A. E. Marks (eds.), *Problems in prehistory: North Africa and the Levant*, 127–69. Dallas.

(In press). The Middle Palaeolithic of the Lower Nile Valley and the adjacent desert. In J. Tixier and A. K. Ghosh (eds.), *Stone Age technology and culture*.

Wendorf, F., R. L. Laury, C. C. Albritton, R. Schild, C. V. Haynes, P. Damon, M. Shaffiquillah and R. Scarborough (1975). Dates for the Middle Stone Age of East Africa. *Science, N.Y.* **187**, 740–2.

Wendt, W. E. (1975). Die ältesten datierten Kunstwerke Afrikas. *Bild Wiss.* (special issue Felskunst), **10**, 44–50.

(1976). 'Art mobilier' from the Apollo II Cave, South West Africa: Africa's oldest dated works of art. *S. Afr. archaeol. Bull.* **31**, 5–11.

Willcox, A. R. (1974). Reasons for the non-occurrence of Middle Stone Age material in the Natal Drakensberg. *S. Afr. J. Sci.* **70**, 273–5.

Wymer, J. J. and R. Singer (1972). Middle Stone Age occupational settlements on the Tzitzikama coast, eastern Cape Province, South Africa. In P. J. Ucko, R. Tringham and G. W. Dimbleby (eds.), *Man, settlement and urbanism*, 207–10. London.

## 5. THE LATE PALAEOLITHIC AND EPI-PALAEOLITHIC

Almagro Basch, M. and M. Almagro Gorbea (1968). *Estudios de arte rupestre nubio. Memorias de la Misión Arqueológica en Egipto, Madrid* **10**.

Anderson, J. E. (1968). Late Paleolithic skeletal remains from Nubia. In F. Wendorf, (ed.), *The prehistory of Nubia.* vol. II, 996–1040. Dallas.

Arambourg, C., M. Boule, H. V. Vallois and R. Verneau (1934). *Les grottes paléolithiques des Beni-Segoual (Algérie). Archs Inst. Paléont. hum.* **13**.

Arkell, A. J. (1949). *Early Khartoum.* Oxford.

  (1961). *A history of the Sudan from the earliest times to 1821*, 2nd edn. London.

Aumassip, G. (1972a). *Néolithique sans poterie de la région de l'Oued Mya (Bas-Sahara). Mém. CRAPE* **20**.

  (1972b). Civilisations prénéolithiques des régions sahariennes. In *Actes du VI<sup>e</sup> Congrès panafricain de Préhistoire et de l'Etude du Quaternaire (Dakar, 1967)*, 273–8. Chambéry.

Balout, L. (1955). *Préhistoire de l'Afrique du Nord: essai de chronologie.* Paris.

  (1958). *Algérie préhistorique.* Paris.

Bayle des Hermens, R. de and J. Tixier (1972). Le gisement Kérémien de La Jumenterie de Chaou Tiaret (Algérie). In *Actes du VI<sup>e</sup> Congrès panafricain de Préhistoire et de l'Etude du Quaternaire (Dakar, 1967)*, 288–93. Chambéry.

Bordes, F. (ed.) (1972). *The origins of* Homo sapiens/*Origine de l'homme moderne. Paris* **3**.

Brahimi, C. (1970). *L'Ibéromaurusien littoral de la région d'Alger. Mém CRAPE* **13**.

Butzer, K. W. and C. L. Hansen (1968). *Desert and river in Nubia.* Madison.

Camps, G. (1969). *Amekni: néolithique ancien du Hoggar. Mém. CRAPE* **10**.

  (1974). *Les civilisations préhistoriques de l'Afrique du Nord et du Sahara.* Paris.

Camps, G., G. Delibrias and J. Thommeret (1968). Chronologie absolue et succession des civilisations préhistoriques dans le Nord de l'Afrique. *Libyca* **16**, 9–28.

Camps-Fabrer, H. (1966). *Matière et art mobilier dans la préhistoire nord-africaine et saharienne. Mém CRAPE* **5**.

Castany, G. and E. G. Gobert (1954). Morphologie quaternaire, palethnologie et leurs rélations à Gafsa. *Libyca* **3**, 9–37.

Caton-Thompson, G. (1946a). The Levalloisian industries of Egypt. *Proc. prehist. Soc.* **12**, 57–120.

  (1946b). The Aterian industry: its place and significance in the Palaeolithic world. *Jl R. anthrop. Inst.* **76**, 87–130.

  (1952). *Kharga Oasis in prehistory.* London.

Caton-Thompson, G. and E. W. Gardner (1934). *The desert Fayum*, 2 vols. London.

Chamla, M.-C. (1968). *Les populations anciennes du Sahara et des régions limitrophes. Etude des restes osseux humains néolithiques et protohistoriques. Mém. CRAPE* 9.

(1970). *Les hommes epipaléolithiques de Columnata (Algérie occidentale). Etude anthropologique. Mém. CRAPE* 15.

Churcher, C. S. (1972). *Late Pleistocene vertebrates from archaeological sites in the Plain of Kom Ombo, Upper Egypt. Contr. Life Sci. Div. R. Ont. Mus.* 82.

Clark, J. D. (1967). *Atlas of African prehistory.* Chicago.

(1970). *The prehistory of Africa.* London and New York.

(1971a). A re-examination of the evidence for agricultural origins in the Nile Valley. *Proc. prehist. Soc.* 37, 34–79.

(1971b). An archaeological survey of northern Aïr and Ténéré. *Geogrl J.* 137, 455–7.

Dunbar, J. H. (1941). *Rock pictures of Lower Nubia.* Service des Antiquités, Cairo.

Ferembach, D. (1962). *La nécropole épipaléolithique de Taforalt.* Rabat.

(1972). L'ancêtre de l'homme du Paléolithique supérieur était-il néandertalien? In F. Bordes (ed.), *The origins of Homo sapiens/Origine de l'homme moderne*, 73–80. Paris.

Gobert, E. G. (1952). El Mekta, station princeps du Capsien. *Karthago* 3, 3–79.

(1962). La préhistoire dans la zone littorale de la Tunisie. *Quaternaria* 7, 271–307.

Gobert, E. G. and R. Vaufrey (1932). Deux gisements extrêmes d'Ibéromaurusien. *Anthropologie, Paris* 42, 449–90.

Graziosi, P. (1962). *Arte rupestre del Sahara Libico.* Florence.

Grébénart, D. (1970). Datations par le $^{14}$C dans le Capsien typique d'Algérie. *Bull. Soc. préhis. fr.* 67, c. r. s. m. 209.

(1972). Le Capsien près de Tébessa et Ouled-Djellal (Algérie). *Ass. sénégal. pour l'étude du Quatern. Ouest afr., Bull. Liaison*, 35–6, 15–21.

Gruet, M. (1954). Le gisement moustérien d'El Guettar. *Karthago* 5, 3–87.

Hester, J. J. and P. M. Hobler (1969). *Prehistoric settlement patterns in the Libyan Desert. Anthrop. Pap. Univ. Utah* 92, Nubian Series no. 4.

Hours, F., L. Copeland and O. Aurenche (1973). Les industries paléolithiques du Proche-Orient, essai de corrélation. *Anthropologie, Paris* 77, 229–80, 437–96.

Howe, B. (1967). *The Palaeolithic of Tangier, Morocco. Excavations at Cape Ashakar, 1939–1947. Bull. Sch prehist. Res.* 22.

Huard, P. and J. Leclant (1972). *Problèmes archéologiques entre le Nil et le Sahara.* Etudes Scientifiques, Cairo.

Hugot, H.-J. (ed.) (1962). *Missions Berliet: Ténéré–Tchad.* Paris.

(1974). *Le Sahara avant le désert.* Toulouse.

Huzayyin, S. A. (1941). *The place of Egypt in prehistory. A correlated study of climates and cultures in the Old World. Mém. Inst Egypte* 43.

Irwin, H. T., J. B. Wheat and L. F. Irwin (1968). *University of Colorado investigations of Palaeolithic and Epipalaeolithic sites in the Sudan, Africa. Utah Anthrop. Pap.* 90, Nubian Series 3.

Leakey, L. S. B. (1953). *Adam's ancestors*, 4th edn. London.

Lhote, H. (1965). *L'évolution de la faune dans les gravures et les peintures rupestres du Sahara et ses rélations avec l'évolution climatique.* In E. Ripoll Perelló (ed.), *Miscelanea eh Homenaje al Abate Henri Breuil 1877–1961*, vol. II, 83–118. Barcelona.

McBurney, C. B. M. (1960). *The Stone Age of northern Africa.* Harmondsworth. (1967). *The Haua Fteah (Cyrenaica)* Cambridge.

McBurney, C. B. M. and R. W. Hey (1955). *Prehistory and Pleistocene geology in Cyrenaican Libya.* Cambridge.

Marmier, F. and G. Trecolle (1968). Stratigraphie du gisement d'Hassi Mouillah, région de Ouargla (Algérie). *Bull. Soc. préhist. fr.* c. r. s. m. **65**, 121–7.

Morel, J. (1974). La faune de l'escargotière de Dra-Mta-el-Ma-el-Abiod (Sud-Algérien). *Anthropologie, Paris* **78**, 299–320.

Mori, F. (1965). *Tadrart Acacus: arte rupestre e culture del Sahara preistorico.* Turin. (1974). The earliest Saharan rock-engravings. *Antiquity* **48**, 87–92.

Obermaier, H. (1931). L'âge de l'art rupestre nord-africain. *Anthropologie, Paris* **41**, 65–74.

Paradisi, U. (1965). Prehistoric art in the Gebel el-Akhdar (Cyrenaica). *Antiquity* **39**, 95–101.

Pericot Garcia, L. and E. Ripoll Perelló (eds.) (1964). *Prehistoric art of the Western Mediterranean and the Sahara.* Viking Fund Publications in Anthropology no. **39**, New York.

Petrocchi, G. (1940). Richerche preistoriche in Cirenaica. *Africa Italiana* **7**, 1–34.

Ripoll Perelló, E. (ed.) (1968). *Simposio internacional de arte rupestre (Barcelona, 1966).* Instituto de Prehistoria y Arqueología, Barcelona.

Roche, J. (1963). *L'Epipaléolithique marocain.* Lisbon.

Roubet, C. (1971). Sur la définition et la chronologie du Néolithique de tradition capsienne. *Anthropologie, Paris* **75**, 553–74.

Sandford, K. S. (1934). *Palaeolithic Man and the Nile Valley in Upper and Middle Egypt. Publs orient. Inst. Univ. Chicago* **18**.

Sandford, K. S. and W. J. Arkell (1933). *Palaeolithic Man and the Nile Valley in Nubia and Upper Egypt. Publs orient. Inst. Univ. Chicago* **17**.

Saxon, E. C. (1974). Results of recent investigations at Tamar Hat. *Libyca* **22**, 49–91.

Servant, M. and S. Servant-Vildary (1972). Nouvelles données pour une intérpretation paléoclimatique de séries continentales du bassin tchadien (Pléistocène récent, Holocène). In E. M. van Zinderen Bakker (ed.), *Palaeoecology of Africa*, vol. VI, 87–92.

Smith, P. E. L. (1966). The Late Paleolithic of northeast Africa in the light of recent research. *Am. Anthrop.* **68**, 326–55.

(1968a). Problems and possibilities of the prehistoric rock art of northern Africa. *Afr. hist. Stud.* **I**, 1–39.

(1968b). A revised view of the later Palaeolithic of Egypt. In F. Bordes and D. de Sonneville Bordes (eds.), *La Préhistoire: problèmes et tendances*, 391–99. Paris.

(1976a). Stone Age Man on the Nile. *Scient. Am.* **235**, 30–8.

(1976b). Early food production in northern Africa as seen from south-western Asia. In J. R. Harlan, J. M. J. de Wet and A. B. L. Stemler (eds.), *Origins of African plant domestication*, 155–86. The Hague.

Tixier, J. (1963). *Typologie de l'Epipaléolithique du Maghreb. Mém. CRAPE* 2.

(1972). Les apports de la stratigraphie et de la typologie au problème des origines de l'homme moderne dans le Maghreb. In F. Bordes (ed.), *The origins of* Homo sapiens/*Origine de l'homme moderne*, 3, 121–7. Paris.

Vallois, H. V. (1971). Le crâne-trophée capsien de Faïd Saour II, Algérie (fouilles Laplace 1954). *Anthropologie, Paris* 75, 191–220, 397–414.

Vaufrey, R. (1933). Notes sur le Capsien. *Anthropologie, Paris* 43, 457–83.

(1939). *L'art rupestre nord-africain. Mém Inst Paléont. hum. Paris* 20.

(1955). *Préhistoire de l'Afrique, I. Le Maghreb*. Institut des Hautes Etudes de Tunis, vol. IV, Paris.

(1969). *Préhistoire de l'Afrique, II. Au nord et à l'est de la grande forêt*. (Publs Univ. Tunis, vol. IV, Tunis.

Vermeersch, P. (1970). L'Elkabien. *Chronique d'Egypte* 45, 45–67.

Vignard, E. (1923). Une nouvelle industrie lithique le 'Sébilien'. *Bull. Inst. Archéol. orient. Cairo* 22, 1–76.

(1955a). Les stations et industries Sébiliennes du Burg el Makkazin, région de Kom-Ombo, (Haute-Egypte). *Bull. Soc. préhist. fr.* 52, 437–52, 691–702.

(1955b). Menchia, une station aurignacienne dans le nord de la plaine de Kom-Ombo (Haute-Egypte). *XIVᵉ Session, Congrès préhistorique de France*, (*Strasbourg–Metz, 1953*), 634–53. Paris.

Wendorf, F. (ed.) (1968). *The prehistory of Nubia*, 2 vols. Dallas.

Wendorf, F. and Marks, A. E. (eds.) (1975). *Problems in prehistory: North Africa and the Levant*. Dallas.

Wendorf, F., R. Said and R. Schild (1970). Egyptian prehistory: some new concepts. *Science, N.Y.* 169, 1161–71.

Wendorf, F. and R. Schild, with sections by Bahay Issawi (1976). *Prehistory of the Nile Valley*. New York.

Wendt, W. E. (1966). Two prehistoric archaeological sites in Egyptian Nubia. *Postilla* 102, 1–46.

Winkler, H. A. (1938). *Rock drawings of southern Upper Egypt*, vol. I. London.

(1939). *Rock drawings of southern Upper Egypt*, vol. II. Egypt Exploration Society, London.

## 6. THE LATER STONE AGE IN SUB-SAHARAN AFRICA

Adamson, D., J. D. Clark and M. A. J. Williams (1974). Barbed bone points from Central Sudan and the age of the 'Early Khartoum' tradition. *Nature, Lond.* 249, 120–3.

Anthony, B. W. (1967). Excavation near Elmenteita, Kenya. In E. M. van Zinderen Bakker (ed.), *Palaeoecology of Africa*, vol. II, 47–48. Cape Town.

Arkell, A. J. (1949). *Early Khartoum*. Oxford.

Atherton, J. H. (1972). Excavations at Kamabai and Yagala rockshelters, Sierra Leone. *West Afr. J. Archaeol.* 2, 39–74.

Barthelme, J. (1977). Holocene sites north-east of Lake Turkana. *Azania* 12, 33–41.

Bayle des Hermens, R. de (1975). *Recherches préhistoriques en République Centrafricaine. Recherches Oubanguiennes* **3**, Paris.

Beaumont, P. B. and J. C. Vogel (1972). On a new radiocarbon chronology for Africa South of the Equator. *Afr. Stud.* **31**, 67–89 and 155–82.

Blanc, A. C. (1955). L'industrie sur obsidienne des Iles Dahlac, Mer rouge. In *Actes du II Congrès Panafricain de Préhistoire (Algiers, 1952)*, 355–7. Paris.

Brothwell, D. R. (1971). The skeletal remains from Gwisho, B and C. In B. M. Fagan and F. van Noten (eds.), *Hunter–gatherers of Gwisho*, 37–47. Musée royal de l'Afrique Centrale, Tervuren.

Brothwell, D. R. and T. Shaw (1971). A later upper Pleistocene proto-West African Negro from Nigeria. *Man* **6**, 221–7.

Brown, F. H. (1975). Barbed bone points from the lower Omo valley, Ethiopia. *Azania* **10**, 144–8.

Butzer, K. W., F. H. Brown and D. L. Thurber (1969). Horizontal sediments of the lower Omo valley – the Kibish formation. *Quaternaria* **11**, 15–30.

Carter, P. L. (1970). Late Stone Age exploitation patterns in southern Natal. *S. Afr. archaeol. Bull.* **25**, 55–8.

Clark, J. D. (1942). Further excavations (1939) at Mumbwa Caves, Northern Rhodesia. *Trans. R. Soc. S. Afr.* **29**, 133–201.

(1950a). The newly-discovered Nachikufu culture of Northern Rhodesia. *S. Afr. archaeol. Bull.* **5**, 2–15.

(1950b). *The Stone Age cultures of Northern Rhodesia*. South African Archaeological Society. Cape Town.

(1954). *The prehistoric cultures of the Horn of Africa*. Cambridge.

(1959). *The prehistory of Southern Africa*. Harmondsworth.

(1963). *Prehistoric cultures of northeast Angola and their significance in tropical Africa*, 2 vols. *Publcões cult. Co. Diam. Angola* **62**.

(1967). *Atlas of African prehistory*. Chicago.

(1968). *Further palaeo-anthropological studies in Northern Lunda. Publcões cult. Co. Diam. Angola* **78**.

(1970). *Prehistory of Africa*. London.

(1971). Human behavioural differences in southern Africa during the Late Pleistocene. *Am. Anthrop.* **73**, 1211–36.

(1972). Mobility and settlement patterns in sub-Saharan Africa. In P. J. Ucko, R. Tringham and G. W. Dimbleby (eds.), *Man settlement and urbanism*, 127–48. London.

(1974). *Kalambo Falls prehistoric site*, vol. II. Cambridge.

Clark, J. G. D. (1969). *World prehistory, a new outline*. Cambridge.

Cole, S. (1963). *Prehistory of East Africa*. London.

Cooke, C. K. (1963). Report on excavations at Pomongwe and Tshangula caves, Matopo Hills, Southern Rhodesia. *S. Afr. archaeol. Bull.* **18**, 63–151.

(1971). Excavation in Zombepata Cave, Sipolilo District, Mashonaland, Rhodesia. *S. Afr. archaeol. Bull.* **26**, 104–26.

Cooke, C. K. and K. R. Robinson (1954). Excavations at Amadzimba Cave, located in the Matopo Hills, Southern Rhodesia. *Occ. Pap. nat. Mus. Sth. Rhod.* **2**, 699–728.

Cooke, C. K. and H. A. B. Simons (1969). Mpato shelter, Sentinel Ranch,

Limpopo River, Beit Bridge, Rhodesia; excavation results. *Arnoldia* **4**, no. 18.

Cooke, H. J. (1975). The palaeoclimatic significance of caves and adjacent land forms in western Ngamiland, Botswana. *Geogrl J.* **141**, 430–44.

Coon, C. S. (1968). *Yengema Cave report*. Philadelphia.

Corbeil, R., R. Mauny and J. Charbonnier (1951). Préhistoire et protohistoire de la presquîle du Cap Vert et de l'extrême ouest Sénégalais. *Bull. IFAN* **10**, 378–460.

Dagan, T. (1956). Le site préhistorique de Tiémassas, Sénégal. *Bull. IFAN* **18**, 432–61.

(1972). Les gisements préhistoriques de Tiémassas et de Pointe Sarène, Sénégal. In *Actes du VI Congrès Panafricain de Préhistoire (Dakar, 1967)*, 92–4. Chambéry.

Davies, O. (1964). *The Quaternary in the coastlands of Guinea*. Glasgow.

(1967). *West Africa before the Europeans*. London.

Deacon, H. J. (1966). Two radiocarbon dates from Scott's Cave, Gamtoos Valley. *S. Afr. archaeol. Bull.* **22**, 51–2.

(1972). A review of the post-Pleistocene in South Africa. *Goodwin Ser. S. Afr. archaeol. Soc.* **1**, 26–45.

Deacon, H. J. and J. Deacon (1963). Scott's Cave: a Late Stone Age site in the Gamtoos Valley. *Ann. Cape Prov. Mus.* **3**, 96–121.

Deacon, J. (1972). Wilton: an assessment after fifty years. *S. Afr. archaeol. Bull.* **27**, 10–48.

(1974). Patterning in the radiocarbon dates for the Wilton/Smithfield Complex in southern Africa. *S. Afr. archaeol. Bull.* **29**, 3–18.

Delcroix, R. and R. Vaufrey (1939). Le Toumbien de Guinée Française. *Anthropologie, Paris* **49**, 265–312.

Droux, G. and H. Kelley (1939). Récherches préhistoriques dans la région de Boko-Songho et à la Pointe Noire. *J. Soc. Afric. Paris* **9**, 71–84.

Fagan, B. M. and F. van Noten (eds.) (1971). *The Hunter–gatherers of Gwisho*. Musée royal de l'Afrique Centrale, Tervuren.

Fagg, B., E. Eyo, A. Rosenfeld and A. Fagg (1972). Four papers on the Rop rockshelter, Nigeria. *West Afr. J. Archaeol.* **2**, 1–38.

Fosbrooke, H. A., P. Ginner and L. S. B. Leakey (1950). Tanganyika rock paintings: a guide and record. *Tanganyika Notes Rec.* **29**, 1–61.

Gabel, C. (1965). *Stone Age hunters of the Kafue. Boston University African Research Studies* **6**.

(1966). Prehistoric populations of Africa. *Boston Univ. Pap. Afr.* **2**, 1–37.

(1969). Six rockshelters on the northern Kavirondo shore of Lake Victoria. *Afr. Hist. Stud.* **2**, 205–54.

Goodwin, A. J. H. and C. van Riet Lowe (1929). The Stone Age Cultures of South Africa. *Ann. S. Afr. Mus.* **27**.

Gramly, R. M. and G. P. Rightmire (1973). A fragmentary cranium and dated later Stone Age assemblage from Lukenya Hill Kenya. *Man* **8**, 571–9.

Heinzelin de Braucourt, J. de (1957). *Les fouilles d'Ishango*. Institut des Parcs Nationaux du Congo Belge, Brussels.

Hugot, H.-J. (1967). Le paléolithique terminal dans l'Afrique de l'ouest. In

W. W. Bishop and J. D. Clark (eds.), *Background to evolution in Africa*, 529–55. Chicago.

Inskeep, R. R. (1959). A Late Stone Age camping site in the upper Zambezi valley. *S. Afr. archaeol. Bull.* **15**, 91–6.

(1962). The age of the Kondoa rock paintings in the light of recent excavations at Kisese II rock shelter. In *Actes du IV Congrès Panafricain de Préhistoire (Tervuren, 1959)*. 249–56. Tervuren.

(1967). The Late Stone Age in southern Africa. In W. W. Bishop and J. D. clark (eds.), *Background to evolution in Africa*, 557–82. Chicago.

Isaac, G. Ll., H. V. Merrick and C. M. Nelson (1972). Stratigraphic and archaeological studies in the Lake Nakuru basin, Kenya. In E. M. van Zinderen Bakkar (ed.), *Palaeoecology of Africa*, vol. VI, 225–32. Cape Town.

Kannemeyer, D. (1890). Stone implements of the Bushmen. *Cape Illustrated Magazine* **1**, 120–30.

Klein, R. G. (1974). Environment and subsistence of prehistoric man in the southern Cape Province South Africa. *World Archaeol.* **5**, 249–84.

Leakey, L. S. B. (1931). *Stone Age cultures of Kenya Colony*. Cambridge.

(1935). *Stone Age races of Kenya*. Oxford.

(1943). Industries of the Gorgora rockshelter Lake Tana. *Jl E. Africa Uganda nat. Hist. Soc.* **17**, 199–203.

Leakey, M. D., R. L. Hay, D. L. Thurber, R. Protsch and R. Berger (1972). Stratigraphy, archaeology and age of the Ndutu and Naisiusiu Beds, Olduvai Gorge, Tanazania. *World Archaeol.* **3**, 328–41.

Louw, A. W., C. K. Brain, J. C. Vogel, R. J. Mason and J. F. Eloff (1969). Papers on Bushman Rock Shelter. *S. Afr. archaeol. bull.* **24**, 39–60.

Maggs, T. M. O.'C. (1967). A quantitative analysis of the rock art from a sample area in the western Cape. *S. Afr. J. Sci.* **63**, 100–4.

Mason, R. J. (1951). Excavation of four caves near Johannesburg. *S. Afr. archaeol. Bull.* **6**, 71–9.

(1962). *Prehistory of the Transvaal*. Johannesburg.

Miller, S. F. (1969). The Nachikufan Industries of the Zambian later Stone Age. Doctoral dissertation, University of California, Berkeley.

(1972). The archaeological sequence of the Zambian later Stone Age. In *Actes du VI Congrès Panafricain de Préhistoire (Dakar, 1967)*, 565–71. Chambéry.

Moorsel, H. van (1968). *Atlas de préhistoire de la plaine de Kinshasa*. University of Louvain, Kinshasa.

Mortelmans, G. (1962). Vue d'ensemble sur la préhistoire du Congo occidental. In *Actes du IV Congrès Panafricain de Préhistoire (Léopoldville, 1959)*. 129–64. Tervuren.

Moysey, F. (1943). Excavation of a rockshelter at Gorgora, Lake Tana. *Jl E. Africa Uganda nat. Hist. Soc.* **17**, 196–8.

Nelson, C. M. (1976). Flaked stone tool variation in the Later Stone Age of eastern and southern Africa. In *Proceedings of the VII Pan-African Congress on Prehistory and Quaternary Studies (Addis Ababa, 1971)*, 131–52. Addis Ababa.

Noten, F. van (1971). Excavations at Munyama Cave. *Antiquity* **45**, 56–8.

Odner, K. (1971). An archaeological survey of Iramba, Tanzania. *Azania* **6**, 151–98.

Parkington, J. E. (1972). Seasonal mobility in the Late Stone Age. *Afr. Stud.* **31**, 223–43.

Pearce, S. and M. Posnansky (1963). The re-excavation of Nsongezi rock-shelter, Ankole. *Uganda J.* **27**, 85–94.

Peringuey, L. (1911). The Stone Ages of South Africa. *Ann. S. Afr. Mus.* **8**.

Phillipson, D. W. (1973). The prehistoric succession in eastern Zambia: a preliminary report. *Azania* **8**, 3–24.

(1976). *Prehistory of Eastern Zambia*. Nairobi.

(1977a). The excavation of Gobedra rock-shelter, Axum. *Azania* **12**, 53–82.

(1977b). Lowasera. *Azania* **12**, 1–32.

Phillipson, L. (1975). A survey of Upper Pleistocene and Holocene industries in the Upper Zambezi Valley, Zambia. Doctoral dissertation, University of California, Berkeley.

Phillipson, L. and D. W. Phillipson (1970). Patterns of edge damage on the Late Stone Age industry from Chiwemupula, Zambia. *Zambia Mus. J.* **1**, 40–75.

Rightmire, G. P. (1975). New studies of post-Pleistocene human skeletal remains from the Rift Valley, Kenya. *Am. J. phys. Anthrop.* **42**, 351–69.

Robbins, L. H. (1974). *The Lothagam site*. East Lansing.

Robinson, K. R. (1952). Excavations in two rockshelters near the Rusawi River, central Mashonaland. *S. Afr. archaeol. Bull.* **7**, 108–29.

(1964). Dombozanga rock shelter, Mtetengwe River, Beit Bridge, Southern Rhodesia: excavation results. *Arnoldia* **1**, no. 7.

Rudner, J. (1957). The Brandberg and its archaeological remains. *Jl S. W. Africa scient. Soc.* **12**, 7–44.

Sampson, C. G. (1967a). Zeekoegat 13: A Later Stone Age open-site near Venterstad, Cape. *Res. Nat. Mus. Bloemfontein* **2**, 211–37.

(1976b). Excavations at Glen Elliot Shelter, Colesberg District, Northern Cape. *Res. Nat. Mus. Bloemfontein* **2**, 125–210.

(1972). The Stone Age industries of the Orange River Scheme and South Africa. Mem. Nat. Mus. Bloemfontein **6**.

(1974). *The Stone Age archaeology of Southern Africa*. New York.

Sampson, C. G. and M. D. Southard (1973). Variability and change in the Nachikufan industry of Zambia. *S. Afr. archaeol. Bull.* **28**, 78–89.

Schoonraad, M. and P. Beaumont (1968). The North Brabant shelter, north western Transvaal. *S. Afr. J. Sci.* **64**, 319–31.

Shaw, C. T. (1969a). The Late Stone Age in the Nigerian forest. In J. P. Lebeuf (ed.), *Actes du Iᵉ Colloque International d'Archéologie Africaine (Fort Lamy)*, 364–73.

(1969b). Archaeology in Nigeria. *Antiquity* **43**, 187–99.

(1972). Finds at the Iwo Eleru rock shelter, Western Nigeria. In *Actes du VI Congrès Panafricain de Préhistoire (Dakar, 1967)*, 190–2. Chambéry.

Summers, R. (ed.) (1959). *Prehistoric rock art of the Federation of Rhodesia and Nyasaland*. London.

Sutton, J. E. G. (1974). The aquatic civilization of middle Africa. *J. Afr. Hist.* **15**, 527–46.

Szumowski, G. (1956). Fouilles de l'abri sous roche de Kourounkorokale, Soudan français. *Bull. IFAN* **18**, 462–508.

Tixier, J. (1967). Procédés d'analyse et questions de terminologie concernant l'étude des ensembles industriels du paléolithique récent et de l'épipaléolithique dans l'Afrique du nord-ouest. In W. W. Bishop and J. D. Clark (eds.), *Background to evolution in Africa*, 771–820. Chicago.

Vaufrey, R. (1946). Le néolithique de tradition capsienne au Sénégal. *Riv. Sci. preist.* **1**, 19–32.

Vogel, J. C. and M. Marais (1971). Pretoria radiocarbon dates I. *Radiocarbon* **13**, 389.

Wells, L. H. (1957). Late Stone Age human types in central Africa. In *Proceedings of the third Pan-African Congress on Prehistory, (Livingstone, 1955)*, 183–5. London.

Wendt, W. E. (1972). Preliminary report on an archaeological research programme in South West Africa. *Cimbebasia*, B, **2**, 1.

Willcox, A. R. (1963). *The rock art of South Africa*. Johannesburg.

Willett, F. (1962). The microlithic industry from Old Oyo, Western Nigeria. In *Actes du IV Congrès Panafricain de Préhistoire (Léopoldville, 1959)*, 261–72. Tervuren.

## 7. THE RISE OF CIVILIZATION IN EGYPT

Adams, B. (1974). *Ancient Hierakonpolis* (with *Supplement*). Warminster.

Adams, R. M. (1972). Patterns of urbanization in early southern Mesopotamia. In P. J. Ucko, R. Tringham and G. W. Dimbleby (eds.), *Man, settlement and urbanism*, 735–48. London.

Aldred, C. (1965). *Egypt to the end of the old Kingdom*. London.

Amélineau, E. (1899–1905). *Les nouvelles fouilles d'Abydos (1895–98)*, 3 vol. Paris.

Arkell, A. J. (1949). *Early Khartoum*. Oxford.

(1950). Varia Sudanica. *J. Egypt. Archaeol.* **36**, 27–30.

(1953). *Shaheinab*. Oxford.

(1963). Was King Scorpion Menes? *Antiquity* **37**, 31–5.

(1972). Dotted wavy-line pottery in African prehistory. *Antiquity* **46**, 221–2.

Arkell, A. J. and P. J. Ucko (1965). Review of Predynastic development in the Nile Valley. *Curr. Anthrop.* **6**, 145–66.

Bar-Yosef, O., A. Belfer, A. Goren and P. Smith (1977). The *nawamis* near Ein Huderah (eastern Sinai). *Israel Exploration J.* **27**, 65–88.

Batrawi, A. (1945). The racial history of Egypt and Nubia. *Jl R. anthrop. Inst.* **75**, 81–101, **76**, 131–56.

Baumgartel, E. J. (1955). *The cultures of prehistoric Egypt*, vol. I, 2nd edn. Oxford.

(1960). *The cultures of prehistoric Egypt*, vol. II. Oxford.

(1966). Scorpion and rosette and the fragment of the large Hierakonpolis mace head. *Z. ägypt. Sprache Altertumskunde* **92**, 9–14.

(1970). Predynastic Egypt. In *Cambridge Ancient History*, 3rd edn, vol. I, pt 1, 463–97.

Bell, B. (1970). The oldest records of the Nile floods. *Georgl J.* **136**, 569–73.

Berry, A. C., R. J. Berry and P. J. Ucko (1967). Genetical change in ancient Egypt. *Man* N.S. **2**, 551–68.

Brunton, G. and G. Caton Thompson (1928). *The Badarian civilisation.* London.

Butzer, K. W. (1958). *Quaternary stratigraphy and climate in the Near East.* Bonn.

(1959). Studien zum vor- und frühgeschichtlichen Landschaftswandel der Sahara. III. Die Naturlandschaft Ägyptens während der Vorgeschichte und der dynastischen Zeit. *Abh. math.-naturw. Kl. Akad. Wiss. Mainz* **2**, 1–80.

(1961). 'Archäologische Fundstellen Ober- und Mittelägyptens in ihrer geologischen Landschaft', *Mitt. dt. archäol. Inst. Abt. Cairo* **17**, 54–68.

(1966). Archaeology and geology in ancient Egypt. In J. R. Caldwell (ed.), *New roads to yesterday*, 210–27. New York.

(1971). *Environment and archaeology*, 2nd ed. Chicago.

(1976). *Early hydraulic civilization in Egypt: a study in cultural ecology.* Chicago.

Butzer, K. W. and C. L. Hansen (1968). *Desert and river in Nubia.* Madison.

Camps, G. (1969). *Amekni: néolithique ancien du Hoggar. Mém. CRAPE* **10**.

Caton-Thompson, G and E. W. Gardner (1934). *The desert Fayum*, 2 vols. London.

Caton-Thompson, G. and E. Whittle (1975). Thermoluminescence dating of the Badarian. *Antiquity* **49**, 89–97.

Childe, V. G. (1934). *New light on the most ancient east.* London.

Chowdhury, K. A. and G. M. Buth (1971). Cotton seeds from the neolithic in Egyptian Nubia and the origin of Old World cotton. *Biol. J. Linn. Soc. Lond.* **3**, 303–12.

Clark, J. D. (1962). Africa south of the Sahara. In R. J. Braidwood and G. R. Willey (eds.), *Courses towards urban life*, Viking Fund Publications in Anthropology, Chicago, **32**, 1–33.

(1971). A re-examination of the evidence for agricultural origins in the Nile Valley. *Proc. prehist. Soc.* **37**, 34–79.

Derricourt, R. M. (1971). Radiocarbon chronology for Egypt and North Africa. *J. Near East. Stud.* **30**, 271–92.

Derry, D. E. (1956). The dynastic race in Egypt. *J. Egypt. Archaeol.* **42**, 80–5.

Dixon, D. M. (1969). A note on cereals in ancient Egypt. In P. J. Ucko and G. W. Dimbleby (eds.), *The domestication and exploitation of plants and animals*, 131–42. London.

Edwards, I. E. S. (1971). The Early Dynastic Period in Egypt. In *Cambridge Ancient History*, 3rd edn, vol. 1, pt 2, 1–70.

Emery, W. B. (1949–58). *Great tombs of the First Dynasty*, 3 vols. Cairo and London.

(1961). *Archaic Egypt.* Harmondsworth.

(1965). *Egypt in Nubia.* London.

Fairservis, W. A. Jr., K. Weeks and M. Hoffman (1971–2). Preliminary Report on the First Two Seasons at Hierakonpolis. *J. Am. Res. Cent. Egypt* **9**, 7–68.

Flannery, K. V. (1972). The origins of the village as a settlement type in Mesoamerica and the Near East: a comparative study. In P. J. Ucko, R. Tringham and G. W. Dimbleby (eds.), *Man, settlement and urbanism*, 23–53. London.

Fleming, H. C. (1969). The classification of West Cushitic within Hamito-Semitic. In D. F. McCall *et al.* (eds.), *East African history*, 3–27. New York.

Frankfort, H. (1948). *Kingship and the gods*. Chicago.

(1956). *The birth of civilization in the Near East*. London.

Frankfort, H., H. A. Frankfort, J. A. Wilson and T. Jacobsen (1949). *Before philosophy*. Harmondsworth.

Gardiner, A. (1961). *Egypt of the Pharaohs: an introduction*. Oxford.

Goedicke, H. (1969–70). An Egyptian claim to Asia. *J. Am. Res. Cent. Egypt* **8**, 11–27.

Greenberg, J. H. (1955). *Studies in African linguistic classification*. New Haven.

Griffiths, J. (1960). *The conflict of Horus and Seth*. Liverpool.

Hayes, W. C. (1965). *Most ancient Egypt*. Chicago.

(1970). Chronology I. Egypt to the end of the Twentieth Dynasty. In *Cambridge Ancient History*, 3rd edn, vol. I, pt 1, 173–93.

Hays, T. R. (1976). Prehistoric Egypt: recent field research. *Curr. anthrop.* **17**, 552–4.

Helck, H. W. (1962). *Die Beziehungen Ägyptens zu Vorderasien im 3. und 2. Jahrtausend v. Chr.* Wiesbaden.

(1970). Zwei Einzelprobleme der thinitischen Chronologie. *Mitt. dt. archäol. Inst. Abt. Cairo* **26**, 83–5.

Higgs, E. S. (1967). Domestic animals. In C. B. M. McBurney, (ed.), *The Haua Fteah*, 313–19. Cambridge.

Hobler, P. M. and J. J. Hester (1969). Prehistory and environment in the Libyan Desert. *S. Afr. archaeol. Bull.* **23**, 120–30.

Hoffman, M. A. (1979). *Egypt before the Pharaohs: The prehistoric foundations of Egyptian civilization*. New York.

Hugot, H.-J. (1968). The origins of agriculture: Sahara. *Curr. Anthrop.* **19**, 483–88.

Kaiser, W. (1956). Stand und Probleme der ägyptische Vorgeschichts-forschung. *Z. ägypt. Sprache Altertumskunde* **81**, 87–109.

(1957). Zur Inneren Chronologie der Naqadakultur. *Archaeologia Geographica* **6**, 69–77.

(1964). Einige Bermerkungen zur ägyptische Frühzeit. *Z. ägypt. Sprache Altertumskunde* **91**, 86–125.

Kantor, H. J. (1944). The final phase of Predynastic culture: Gerzean or Semainean? *J. Near East. Stud.* **3**, 110–36.

(1952). Further evidence for early Mesopotamian relations with Egypt. *J. Near East. Stud.* **11**, 239–50.

(1965). The relative chronology of Egypt and its foreign correlations before the Late Bronze Age. In R. W. Ehrich (ed.), *Chronologies in Old World archaeology*, 1–46. Chicago.

Kaplan, H. R. (1979). The problem of the dynastic position of Meryet-nit. *J. Near East. Stud.* **38**, 23–7.

Kaplony, P. (1963). *Die Inschriften der ägyptische Frühzeit*. Wiesbaden.

Kees, H. (1961). *Ancient Egypt: a cultural topography*. ed. T. G. H. James, trans. I. F. D. Morrow. London and Chicago.

Kelley, A. L. (1974). The evidence for Mesopotamian influence in predynastic Egypt. *Newsl. Soc. study Egypt. antiqu.* **4**, 2–11.

Kemp, B. J. (1966). Abydos and the royal tombs of the First Dynasty. *J. Egypt. Archaeol.* **52**, 13–22.

(1967). The Egyptian 1st Dynasty royal cemetery. *Antiquity* **41**, 22–32.

(1968a). Merimda and the theory of house burial in prehistoric Egypt. *Chronique d'Egypte* **43**, 85, 22–33.

(1968b). The Osiris Temple at Abydos. *Mitt. dt. archäol. Inst. Abt. Cairo* **23**, 138–55.

(1973). Photographs of the Decorated Tomb at Hierakonpolis. *J. Egypt. Archaeol* **59**, 36–43.

Kendall, D. G. (1969). Some problems and methods in statistical archaeology. *World Archaeol.* **1**, 68–76.

(1971). Seriation from abundance matrices. In F. R. Hodson, D. G. Kendall and P. Tăutu, *Mathematics in the archaeological and historical sciences*, 215–52. Edinburgh.

Kenyon, K. (1960). *Archaeology in the Holy Land*. London.

Klichowska, M. (1978). Preliminary results of palaeo-ethnobotanical studies of plant impressions on potsherds from the Neolithic settlement at Kadero. *Nyame Akuma* **12**, 42–3.

Lal, B. B. (1963). Work by an Indian mission at Afyeh and Tomas. *Illustrated London News*, 20 April 1963, 579–81.

Lambdin, T. O. (1961). Egypt: its language and literature. In E. G. Wright (ed.), *The Bible and the ancient Near East*, 279–97. New York.

Lucas, A. and J. R. Harris (1962). *Ancient Egyptian materials and industries*, 4th ed. London.

McBurney, C. B. M. (1960). *The Stone Age of northern Africa* Harmondsworth.

Marks, A. E. (1968). Survey and excavations in the Dongola Reach, Sudan. *Curr. Anthrop.* **9**, 319–23.

Mellaart, J. (1979). Egyptian and Near Eastern chronology: A Dilemma? *Antiquity* **53**, 6–18.

Meltzer, E. S. (1970). An observation on the hieroglyph *mr. J. Egypt. Archaeol.* **56**, 193–4.

Morant, G. M. (1925). A study of Egyptian craniology from prehistoric to Roman times. *Biometrika* **17**, 1–52.

Murray, G. W. (1951). The Egyptian climate: an historical survey. *Geogrl J.* **117**, 422–34.

Nims, C. F. (1965). *Thebes of the Pharaohs*. London.

Nordström, H.-Å. (1972). *Neolithic and A-group sites*. Uppsala.

O'Connor, D. (1972). A regional population in Egypt to circa 600 B.C. In B. J. Spooner (ed.), *Population growth: anthropological implications*, 78–100. Cambridge, Mass. and London.

Otto, K. H. (1963). Shaqadud: a new Khartoum Neolithic site outside the Nile Valley. *Kush* **11**, 108–15.

Passarge, S. (1940). Die Urlandschaft Ägyptens und die Lokalisierung der Wiege der altägyptischen Kultur. *Nova Acta Leopoldina* **9**, 77–152.

Petrie, W. M. F. (1900). *The Royal Tombs of the First Dynasty*, pt 1. Egypt Exploration fund Memoir **18**. London.

(1901a). *The Royal Tombs of the Earliest Dynasties*, pt 2. Egypt Exploration Fund Memoir **21**. London.

(1901b). *Diospolis Parva. Egypt Exploration Fund Memoir.* **20**. London.

(1906). *Researches in Sinai.* London.

(1920). *Prehistoric Egypt.* London.

(1921). *Prehistoric Egypt. Corpus.* London.

(1939). *The making of Egypt.* London.

Petrie, W. M. F. and J. E. Quibell (1895). *Naqada and Ballas.* London.

Pope, M. (1966). The origins of writing in the Near East. *Antiquity* **40**, 17–23.

Quibell, J. E. (1900). *Hierakonpolis,* pt 1. London.

Quibell, J. E. and F. W. Green (1902). *Hierakonpolis,* pt 2. London.

Reed, C. A. (1966). Animal domestication in the prehistoric Near East. In J. R. Caldwell (ed.), *New roads to yesterday,* 178–209. New York.

Reisner, G. A. (1932). *A provincial cemetery of the Pyramid Age, Naga-ed-Dêr,* vol. II. Oxford.

Renfrew, C. (1972). *The emergence of civilisation.* London.

Renfrew, J. M. (1969). The archaeological evidence for the domestication of plants: methods and problems. In P. J. Ucko and G. W. Dimbleby (eds.), *Domestication and exploitation of plants and animals,* 149–72. London.

Rothenberg, B. (1970). An archaeological survey of south Sinai: first season 1967/1968, preliminary report. *Palestine Exploration Quarterly* **102**, 4–29.

Saad, Z. Y. (1969). *The excavations at Helwan: art and civilization in the First and Second Egyptian Dynasties.* Oklahoma.

Säve-Söderbergh, T. (1941). *Ägypten und Nubien.* Lund.

Schild, R., M. Chmielewska and H. Wieckowska (1968). The Arkinian and Shamarkian Industries. In F. Wendorf (ed.), *The prehistory of Nubia,* vol. II 651–767. Dallas.

Seligman, C. C. and M. A. Murray (1911). Note upon an early Egyptian standard. *Man* **11**, 165–71.

Sethe, K. (1930). *Urgeschichte und älteste Religion der Ägypter. Abhandlungen für Kunde des Morgenlandes* **18**. Leipzig.

Simoons, F. J. (1965). Some questions on the economic prehistory of Ethiopia. *J. Afr. Hist.* **6**, 1–13.

Smith, H. S. (1964). Egypt and $C_{14}$ dating. *Antiquity* **38**, 32–7.

(1966). The Nubian B-group. *Kush* **14**, 69–124.

Smith, P. E. L. (1976). Early food production in northern Africa as seen from southwestern Asia. In J. R. Harlan, J. M. J. de Wet and A. B. L. Stemler (eds.), *Origins of African Plant Domestication,* 155–86. The Hague.

Suess, H. E. (1970). Bristlecone pine calibration of the radiocarbon time-scale 5200 B.C. to the present. In I. U. Olsson (ed.), *Radiocarbon variations and absolute chronology, Nobel Symposium* **12**, 303–13. New York and Stockholm.

Trigger, B. G. (1965). *History and settlement in Lower Nubia. Yale Univ. Publs Anthrop.* **69**.

(1968). *Beyond history: the methods of prehistory.* New York.

Ucko, P. J. (1967). The Predynastic cemetery N 7000 at Naga-ed-Dêr. *Chronique d'Egypte* **42**, 345–53.

(1968). *Anthropomorphic figurines of Predynastic Egypt and Neolithic Crete. Occ. Pap. R. anthrop. Inst.* **24**.

Vandier, J. (1952). *Manuel d'archéologie égyptienne,* vol. I. Paris.

Vergote, J. (1970). Egyptian. In T. A. Sebeok (ed.), *Current trends in linguistics*, vol. VI, 531–57. The Hague.

Wendorf, F. (ed.) (1968). *The prehistory of Nubia*, 2 vols. Dallas.

Wendorf, F., R. Said and R. Schild (1970). Egyptian prehistory: some new concepts. *Science, N.Y.* **169**, 1161–71.

Wheatley, P. (1971). *The pivot of the Four Quarters*. Edinburgh.

Whittle, E. H. (1975). Thermoluminescent dating of Egyptian Predynastic pottery from Hemamieh and Qurna-Tarif. *Archaeometry* **17**, 119–22.

Wilson, J. A. (1955). Buto and Hierakonpolis in the geography of Egypt. *J. Near East. Stud.* **14**, 209–36.

Wright, G. A. (1971). Origins of food production in southwestern Asia: a survey of ideas. *Curr. anthrop.* **12**, 447–77.

Yadin, Y. (1955). The earliest record of Egypt's military penetration into Asia? *Israel Exploration J.* **5**, 1–16.

Zeuner, F. E. (1963). *A history of domesticated animals*. London.

## 8. PASTORALISM AND CULTIVATION IN NORTH AFRICA

Alimen, H. (1954). *La station rupestre de Marhouma (Sahara occidental)*, Inst. Recherches sahariennes Mém. **I**.

(1955). *Préhistoire de l'Afrique*. Paris.

Almagro, M. (1946). *Prehistoria del Norte de Africa y del Sahara español*. Barcelona.

Antoine, M. (1952). *Les grandes lignes de la Préhistoire marocaine. II Congrès panafricain de Préhistoire (Algiers, 1952)*. Casablanca.

Arkell, A. J. (1949). *Early Khartoum*. Oxford.

(1964). *Wanyanga and an archaeological reconnaissance of the south-west Libyan desert*. London.

Aumassip, G. (1968). Le gisement néolithique d'El Bayed. *Libyca* **16**, 119–44.

(1973). *Néolithique sans poterie de la région de l'oued Mya (Bas Sahara)*. Mém. *CRAPE* **20**.

Bailloud, G. (1960). Les peintures rupestres archaïques de l'Ennedi (Tchad). *Anthropologie, Paris* **45**, 211–34.

(1969). L'évolution des styles céramiques en Ennedi (République du Tchad). In J. P. Lebeuf (ed.), *Actes du I Colloque internat. d'Archéol. Africaine (Fort-Lamy, 1966)*, 31–45. Fort-Lamy.

Balout, L. (1955). *Préhistoire de l'Afrique du Nord: Essai de chronologie*. Paris.

(1958). *Algérie préhistorique*. Paris.

Bardin, P. (1953). La grotte de Kef el-Agab (Tunisie), gisement néolithique. *Libyca* **1**, 271–308.

Barich, B. E. (1978). *La serie stratigrafica dell' uadi Ti-n-Torha (Acacus, Libia) per una interpretazione delle facies a ceramica Saharo-Sudanesi*. Origini, vol. VIII. Rome.

Belluomini, G., G. Calderoni, L. Manfra, L. Allegri and S. Improta (1974). Alcune datazioni assolute con il metodo del $C^{14}$ su reperti dell' uadi Ti-n-Torha (Acacus, Libia). In B. E. Barich, *La serie stratigraphia dell' uadi Ti-n-Torha (Acacus, Libia)*, Origini, vol. VIII, 169–80. Rome.

BIBLIOGRAPHY

Beucher, F. (1971). Etudes palynologiques des formations néogènes et quaternaires au Sahara nord-occidental. Paris.

Brahimi, C. (1970). L'Ibéromaurusien littoral de la région d'Alger. Mém. CRAPE 13.

Breuil, H. (1955). Les roches peintes du Tassili-n-Ajjer. In Actes du II Congrès panafricain de préhistoire (Algiers, 1952), 65–219. Paris.

Camps, G. (1959). Relations protohistoriques entre la Berbérie orientale et les Iles italiennes. Congrès préhistorique de France, XVe session, 329–37. Monaco.

(1960). Les traces d'un Age du Bronze en Afrique du Nord. Revue africaine 104, 31–55.

(1961a). Aux origines de la Berbérie. Massinissa ou les débuts de l'Histoire. Algiers.

(1961b). Aux origines de la Berbérie. Monuments et rites funéraires protohistoriques. Paris.

(1967). Le néolithique de tradition capsienne au Sahara. Trav. Inst. Rech. sahar. 21, 85–96.

(1968a). Amekni: Néolithique ancien du Hoggar. Mém. CRAPE 10.

(1968b). Tableau chronologique de la préhistoire récente du Nord de l'Afrique. Bull. Soc. préhist. fr. 65, 607–22.

(1971). A propos du Néolithique ancien de la Mediterranée occidentale. Bull. Soc. préhist. fr. 68, 48–50.

(1974). Les civilisations préhistoriques de l'Afrique du Nord et du Sahara. Paris.

Camps, G. and H. Camps-Fabrer (1964). La nécropole mégalithique du Djebel Mazela à Bou Nouara. Mém. CRAPE 3.

Camps, G. and P. R. Giot (1960). Un poignard chalcolithique au Cap Chenoua. Libyca 8, 263–76.

Camps, G., G. Delibrias and J. Thommeret (1968). Chronologie absolue et succession des civilisations préhistoriques dans le Nord de l'Afrique. Libyca 16, 9–27.

(1973). Chronologie des civilisations préhistoriques du Nord de l'Afrique d'après le radiocarbone. Libyca 21, 65–89.

Camps-Fabrer, H. (1960). Parures des temps préhistoriques en Afrique du Nord. Libyca 8, 9–218.

(1961–2). Figurations animales dans l'art mobilier préhistorique d'Afrique du Nord. Libyca 9–10, 101–13.

(1966). Matière et art mobilier dans la Préhistoire nord-africaine et saharienne. Mém. CRAPE 5.

(1967). Les sculptures néolithiques de l'erg d'Admer: leurs relations avec celles du Tassili n'Ajjer. 15, 101–23.

Chamla, M.-C. (1968). Les populations anciennes du Sahara et des régions limitrophes. Mém. CRAPE 9.

(1975). Les hommes des sépultures protohistoriques et puniques d'Afrique du Nord (Algérie et Tunisie). Anthropologie, Paris 79, 659–92.

(1976). Les hommes des sépultures protohistoriques et puniques d'Afrique du Nord (Algérie et Tunisie). Anthropologie, Paris 80, 75–116.

(1978). Le peuplement de l'Afrique du Nord de l'Epipaléolithique à l'époque actuelle. Anthropologie, Paris 82, 385–430.

Chasseloup-Laubat, F. de (1938). Art rupestre au Hoggar (Haut-Mertoutek). Paris.

Clark, J. D. (1970). The Prehistory of Africa. London and New York.

Courtin, J. (1966). Le Néolithique du Borkou, Nord-Tchad. *Anthropologie,* *Paris* **70**, 269–82.

(1968). Le Ténéréen du Borkou, Nord-Tchad. In F. Bordes and D. de Sonneville-Bordes (eds.), *La préhistoire: problèmes et tendances,* 133–38. CNRS, Paris.

Daniel, C. (1970). *The Garamantes of southern Libya.* London.

Dedieu, B. (1965). La grotte du Djebel Zabaouine. *Libyca* **13**, 99–126.

Esperandieu, G. (1955). Domestication et élevage dans le nord de l'Afrique au Néolithique et dans la protohistoire d'après les figurations rupestres. In *Actes du II Congrès panafricain de Préhistoire,* (*Algiers, 1952*), 551–73. Paris.

Evans, J. D. (1955–6). Two phases of prehistoric settlement in the western mediterranean. In *Thirteenth Annual Report and Bulletin for 1955–1956,* 49–70. Institute of Archaeology, University of London.

Flamand, G. B. M. (1921). *Les pierres écrites (Hadjrat Mektoubat). Gravures et inscriptions rupestres du Nord-africain.* Paris.

Frobenius, L. (1916). Der Kleinafrikanische Grabbau. *Praehist. Z.* **8**, 1–84.

(1937). *Ekade ektab: Die Felsbilder Fezzans.* Leipzig.

Frobenius, L. and H. Obermaier (1925). *Hadschra Maktuba.* Munich.

Gallay, A. (1966). Quelques gisements néolithiques du Sahara malien. *J. Soc. Afric., Paris* **36**, 167–208.

Gobert, E.-G. (1955). Notions générales acquises sur la Préhistoire de la Tunisie. In *Actes du II Congrès panafricain de Préhistoire (Algiers, 1952).* 221–39. Paris.

(1962). La préhistoire dans la zone littorale de la Tunisie. *Quaternaria* **6**, 271–307.

Goetz, C. (1942). La céramique néolithique en Oranie. *Bull. trimest. Soc. Géogr. Archéol. Oran* **63**, 60–106.

Graziosi, P. (1942). *L'arte rupestre della Libia.* Naples.

Grébénart, D. (1969). Aïn Naga: Capsien et Néolithique des environs de Messad. *Libyca* **17**, 135–97.

Gruet, M. (1947). Gisements atériens et néolithiques du Nord de Bizerte *Anthropologie, Paris* **51**, 363–7.

Gsell, S. (1914–28). *Histoire ancienne de l'Afrique du Nord,* 8 vols. Paris.

Huard, P. (1959). Les cornes déformées sur les gravures rupestres du Sahara sud-oriental. *Trav. Inst. Rech. sahar.* **18**, 109–31.

(1960). Contribution à l'étude du cheval, du fer, du chameau au Sahara oriental. *Bull IFAN* **B22**, 134–78.

Hugot, H.-J. (1957). Essai sur les armatures de pointes de flèches du Sahara. *Libyca* **5**, 89–236.

(ed.) (1962). *Missions Berliet Ténéré-Tchad.* Paris.

(1963). Recherches préhistoriques dans l'Ahaggar occidental, 1950–1957. *Mém. CRAPE* **1**.

Jodin, A. (1957). Les problèmes de la civilisation du vase campaniforme au Maroc. *Hespéris* **44**, 353–60.

(1958–9). Les grottes d'El Khril à Achakar, province de Tanger. *Bull. Archéol.* **3**, 249–313.

Koehler, P. R. (1931). La céramique de la grotte d'Achakar (Maroc) et ses rapports avec celle des civilisations de la péninsule ibérique. *Rev. Anthrop.* **41**, 156–67.

Lambert, N. (1967). Tayadirt, une nécropole protohistorique en haute Moulouya. *Libyca* **15**, 215–60.

(1972). Objets en cuivre de Maurétanie occidentale. In *Actes du VI Congrès panafricain de Préhistoire (Dakar, 1967)*, 159–74. Chambéry.

Lefebvre, G. and L. Lefebvre (1967). Corpus des gravures et peintures rupestres de la région de Constantine. *Mém. CRAPE* **7**.

Lhote, H. (1953). Le cheval et le chameau dans les peintures et gravures rupestres du Sahara. *Bull. IFAN* **15**, 1138–1228.

(1958). *A la découverte des fresques du Tassili.* Paris.

(1970). Les gravures rupestres du Sud-oranais. *Mém. CRAPE* **16**.

(1972). *Les gravures rupestres du Nord-Ouest de l'Air.* Paris.

McBurney, C. B. M. (1960). *The Stone Age of northern Africa.* London.

(1967). *The Haua Fteah (Cyrenaica) and the Stone Age of the south-east Mediterranean.* Cambridge.

Maître, J.-P. (1971). Contribution à la Préhistoire de l'Ahaggar. I. Téfedest centrale. *Mém. CRAPE* **17**.

Malhomme, J. (1959). Corpus des gravures rupestres du Grand Atlas, *Publ Serv. Antiquités* pt I. *Maroc* **13**.

(1961). Corpus des gravures rupestres du Grand Atlas, pt II. *Publs Serv. Antiquités Maroc* **14**.

Mauny, R. (1954). Gravures, peintures et inscriptions rupestres de l'Ouest africain. *IFAN. Initiations africaines* **xi**, 1–92.

(1955a). Les gisements néolithiques de Karkarichinkat (Tilemsi, Soudan français). *Actes du II Congrès panafricain de Préhistoire (Algiers, 1952)*, 617–29. Paris.

(1955b). Autour de la répartition des chars rupestres sahariens. *Actes du II Congrès panafricain de Préhistoire (Algiers, 1952)*, 741–6. Paris.

(1955c). Autour de la répartition des chars rupestres sahariens. *C.r. IV Conf. int. Africanistes de l'ouest (Fernando Po, 1954)*, 741–6. Madrid.

(1967). L'Afrique et les origines de la domestication. In W. W. Bishop and J. D. Clark (eds.), *Background to evolution in Africa*, 583–99. Chicago.

Mori F. (1965). *Tadrart Acacus: arte rupestre e culture del Sahara preistorico.* Turin.

Munson, P. J. (1976). Archaeological data on the origins of cultivation in the southwestern Sahara and their implications for West Africa. In J. R. Harlan, J. M. J. de Wet and A. B. L. Stemler (eds.), *Origins of African plant domestication*, 187–210. The Hague.

Neuville, P. (1956). Stratigraphie néolithique et gravures rupestres en Tripolitaine septentrionale. Abiar Miggi. *Libyca* **4**, 61–123.

Pace, B., G. Caputo and S. Sergi (1951). Scavi sahariani. *Monumenti Antichi* **41**.

Pomel, A. E. (1898). Les ovidés. *Serv. carte géol. Paléont. Mon. Algérie.* **13**.

Reygasse, M. (1935). Gravures et peintures rupestres du Tassili n'Ajjers. *Anthropologie, Paris* **45**, 533–71.

(1950). *Monuments funéraires préislamiques de l'Afrique du Nord.* Paris.

Rhotert H. (1952). *Libysche Felsbilder.* Darmstadt.

Roubet, C. (1968). Le Damous el Ahmar et sa place dans le Néolithique de tradition capsienne. *Travaux CRAPE* 1968.

*Sahara: 10,000 Jahre zwischen Weide und Wüste* (1978). Staatsmuseum, Köln.

Santa-Olalla, J. M. (1944). *El Sahara español ante-islamico. Acta arqueologica Hispanica* **2**, Madrid.

Simoneau, A. (1968–1972). Nouvelles recherches sur les gravures rupestres du Haut Atlas et du Draâ. *Bull. Archéol. maroc.* **8**, 15–31.

Souville, G. (1958–9). La pêche et la vie maritime au Néolithique en Afrique du Nord. *Bull. Archéol. maroc.* **3**, 314–44.

(1966). Récentes analyses d'objets en métal trouvés au Maroc. In *Congr. préhist. de France, XVII session (Ajaccio)*, 275–9.

(1974). *Atlas préhistorique du Maroc: I. Maroc atlantique.* Paris.

Tarradell, M. (1954). Noticia sobre le excavation de Gar Cahal. *Tamuda* **2**, 344–58.

(1957–8). Caf That el Gar, Cueva neolitica en la region de Tetuan (Marruecos). *Ampurias* **19–20**, 137–66.

(1958). Sobre el Neolitico del Norcoste de Marruecos y sus relaciones. *Tamuda* **4**, 279–305.

Tixier, J. (1962). Le Ténéréen de l'Adrar Bous III. In H. J. Hugot (ed.), *Mission Berliet Ténéré–Tchad*, 353–62. Paris.

(1963). Typologie de l'Epipaléolithique du Maghreb. *Mém. CRAPE* **2**.

Van Campo, M. G. Aymonin, J. Cohen, P. Dutil and P. Rognon (1964). Contribution à l'étude du peuplement végétal quaternaire des montagnes sahariennes. *Pollens et spores* **6**, 169–94.

Van Campo, M., J. Cohen, P. Guinet and P. Rognon (1965). Contribution à l'étude du peuplement végétal quaternaire des montagnes sahariennes. *Pollens et spores* **7**, 361–71.

Van Campo, M., P. Guinet, J. Cohen and P. Dutil (1967). Contribution à l'étude du peuplement végétal quaternaire des montagnes sahariennies. *Pollens et spores* **9**, 107–20.

Vaufrey, R. (1935). Le Néolithique de tradition mésolithique et l'âge des gravures rupestres du Sud-oranais. *Anthropologie, Paris* **45**, 213–15.

(1939). L'art rupestre nord-africain. *Archs Inst. Paléont. hum., Mém.* **20**.

(1955). *Préhistoire de l'Afrique. Vol. I, Le Maghreb.* Publications de l'Institut des Hautes Etudes de Tunis, vol. iv. Paris.

(1969). *Préhistoire de l'Afrique. Vol. II, Au nord et à l'est de la Grande Forêt.* Publications de l'Université de Tunis, vol. iv. Tunis.

## 9. THE ORIGINS OF INDIGENOUS AFRICAN AGRICULTURE

Allan, W. (1965). *The African husbandman.* New York.

Allchin, F. R. (1969). Early cultivated plants in India and Pakistan. In P. J. Ucko and G. W. Dimbleby (eds.), *The domestication and exploitation of plants and animals*, 323–9. London.

Busson, F. (1965). *Plantes alimentaires de l'ouest africain: étude botanique, biologique et chimique.* Marseilles.

Clark, J. D. (1970). *The prehistory of Africa.* London and New York.

(In press). The domestication process in sub-Saharan Africa with special reference to Ethiopia. In E. Higgs (ed.), *Origine de l'élevage et de la domestication*, 56–115. Nice 1976.

Coursey, D. G. and C. K. Coursey (1971). The new yam festivals of West Africa. *Anthropos* **66**, 444–84.

Dalziel, J. (1937). *The useful plants of West Tropical Africa*. London.

Garine, I. de (1964). *Les Massa du Cameroun*. Paris.

Gast, M. *Alimentation des populations de l'Ahaggar, étude éthnographique. Mém. CRAPE* **8**.

Griaule, M. and G. Dieterlen (1965). *Le renard pâle, vol. I: Le mythe cosmogonique. Pt 1, la création du monde*. Inst. d'Ethnol. Musée de l'Homme, Paris.

Harlan, J. R. (1956). Distribution and utilization of natural variability in cultivated plants. In *Genetics in plant breeding, Brookhaven Symp. Biol.* **9**, 191–206.

(1969). Ethiopia: a center of diversity. *Econ. Bot.* **23**, 309–14.

(1971). Evolution of cultivated plants. In O. H. Frankel and E. Bennet (eds.), *Genetic resources in plants, their exploration and conservation*, 19–32. Oxford.

(1975). *Crops and Man*. Madison.

Harlan, J. R. and J. Pasquereau (1969). Décrue agriculture in Mali. *Econ. Bot.* **23**, 70–4.

Harlan, J. R. and A. B. L. Stemler (1976). The races of sorghum in Africa. In J. R. Harlan, J. M. J. de Wet and A. B. L. Stemler (eds.), *Origins of African plant domestication*, 465–78. The Hague.

Harlan, J. R. and J. M. J. de Wet (1965). Some thoughts about weeds. *Econ. Bot.* **19**, 16–24.

(1973a). On the quality of evidence for origin and dispersal of cultivated plants. *Curr. anthrop.* **14**, 51–62.

(1973b). Comparative evolution in cereals. *Evolution, Lancaster, Pa.* **27**, 311–25.

Harlan, J. R., J. M. J. de Wet and A. B. L. Stemler (eds.), (1976). *Origins of African plant domestication*. The Hague.

Holas, B. (1968). L'imagerie rituelle en Afrique noire. *Bull. IFAN* **30** ser. B, 586–609.

Huffnagel, H. P. (1961). *Agriculture in Ethiopia*, Rome.

Irvine, F. R. (1948). The indigenous food plants of West African people. *New York Bot. Gard.* **49**, 224–36 and 254–67.

Jardin, C. (1967). *List of foods used in Africa*. Rome.

Lee, R. B. and I DeVore (eds.) (1968). *Man the hunter*. Chicago.

Mehra, K. L. (1963). Differentiation of the cultivated and wild *Eleusine* species. *Phyton* **20**, 189–98.

Miège, J. (1954). Les cultures vivrières en Afrique occidentale. *Cahiers d'Outre-Mer* **7**, 25–50.

Munson, P. J. (1976). Archaeological data on the origins of cultivation in the southwestern Sahara and their implications for West Africa. In J. R. Harlan, J. M. J. de Wet and A. B. L. Stemler (eds.), *Origins of African plant domestication*, 187–209. The Hague.

Nayar, N. M. and K. L. Mehra (1970). Sesame: its uses, botany, cytogenetics, and origin. *Econ. Bot.* **24**, 20–31.

Niangoran Bouah, G. (1964). *La division du temps et le calendrier rituel des peuples lagunaires de Côte d'Ivoire. Trav. Mém. Inst. d'Ethnol.* **68**, Paris.

Nicolaisen, J. (1963). *Ecology and culture of the pastoral Tuareg*. Copenhagen.

Plumley, J. M. (1970). Qasr Ibrim, 1969. *J Egypt. Archaeol.* **56**, 12–18.

Portères, R. (1951). *Eleusine coracana*, céréale des humanités pauvres des pays tropicaux. *Bull. IFAN*, **13**, 1–78.

Portères, R. (1956). Taxonomie agrobotanique des riz cultivés, *Oryza sativa* L. et. *O. glaberrima* St. *J. Agric. Trop. Bot. Appl.* **3**, 833–48.

(1962). Berceaux agricoles primaires sur le continent africain. *J. Afr. Hist.* **3**, 195–210.

Quin, P. J. (1959). *Foods and feeding habits of the Pedi.* Johannesburg.

Schnell, R. (1957). *Plantes alimentaires et vie agricole de l'Afrique noire.* Paris.

Tubiana, M. J. (1964). *Survivances préislamiques en pays Zaghawa. Trav. Mém. Inst. d'Ethnol.*, Paris **67**.

Vavilov, N. I. (1926). Studies on the origin of cultivated plants. *Inst. Appl. Bot. Plant Breed.*, Leningrad XVI (2), 139–248.

Vishnu-Mittre (1968). Protohistoric records of agriculture in India. *Trans. Bose Res. Inst.* **31**, 87–106.

(1974). Palaeobotanical evidence in India. In J. B. Hutchinson (ed.), *Evolutionary studies in world crops; diversity and change in the Indian subcontinent*, 3–30. Cambridge.

Wehrmann, J. and L. W. Johannes (1965). Effect of Guie on soil conditions and plant nutrition. *Sols Africains* **10**, 129–36.

Wendorf, F. and R. Schild (1976). The use of ground grain during the late Palaeolithic of the Lower Nile Valley, Egypt. In J. R. Harlan, J. M. J. de Wet and A. B. L. Stemler (eds.), *Origins of African plant domestication*, 269–88. The Hague.

Wendorf, F., R. Said and R. Schild (1970). Egyptian prehistory: some new concepts. *Science, N.Y.* **169**, 1161–71.

Wills, J. B. (1962). *Agriculture and land use in Ghana.* London.

Zohary, D. (1971). Centers of diversity and centers of origin. In O. H. Frankel and E. Bennett, (eds.), *Genetic resources in plants, their exploration and conservation*, 33–42. Oxford.

## 10. FROM OLD KINGDOM TO SECOND INTERMEDIATE PERIOD

Abu Bakr, A. M. and J. Osing (1973). Ächtungstexte aus dem Alten Reich. *Mitt. dt archäol. Inst. Abt. Cairo* **29**, 97–133.

(1976). Ächtungstexte aus dem Alten Reich. *Mitt. dt. archäol. Inst. Abt. Cairo* **32**, 133–85.

Adam, S. (1959). Report on the excavations of the Antiquites Department at Ezbet Rushdi. *Ann. Serv. antiquités Égypte* **56**, 207–26.

Adams, B. (1956). *Fragen altägyptischer Finanzverwaltung; nach Urkunden des Alten und Mittleren Reiches.* Munich and Pasing.

(1974). *Ancient Hierakonpolis* (with *supplement*). Warminster.

Adams, W. Y. (1968). Invasion, diffusion, evolution? *Antiquity* **42**, 194–215.

(1970). A re-appraisal of Nubian culture history. *Orientalia* **39**, 269–77.

(1977a). Reflections on the archaeology of Kerma. In E. Endesfelder *et al.* (eds.), *Ägypten und Kusch (Schriften zur Geschichte und Kultur des Alten Orients* **13**), 41–51.

(1977b). *Nubia, corridor to Africa.* London.

Adams, W. Y. and H.-Å. Nordström (1963). The archaeological survey on the west bank of the Nile: third season, 1961–62. *Kush* **11**, 10–46.

Aharoni, Y., V. Fritz and A. Kempinski (1974). Excavations at Tel Masos (Khirbet el-Melhâsh). Preliminary report on the first season, 1972. *Tel-Aviv* **1**, 64–74.

Albright, W. F. (1959). Dunand's new Byblos volume: a Lycian at the Byblian court. *Bull. Am. Sch. Orient. Res.* **155**, 31–4.

(1964). The eighteenth-century princes of Byblos and the chronology of Middle Bronze. *Bull. Am. Sch. Orient. Res.* **176**, 38–46.

Aldred, C. (1970). Some royal portraits of the Middle Kingdom in ancient Egypt. *Metropolitan Mus. J.* **3**, 27–50.

(1971). *Jewels of the Pharaohs.* London.

Allam, S. (1963). *Beiträge zum Hathorkult (bis zum Ende des Mittleren Reiches).* Munich and Berlin.

Alliot, M. (1937–8). Un nouvel example de vizir divinisé dans l'Égypte ancienne. *Bull. Inst. fr. archéol orient. Cairo* **37**, 93–160.

Altenmüller, H. (1974). Zur Vergöttlichung des Königs Unas im Alten Reich. *Stud. altägypt. Kultur* **1**, 1–18.

Aly, M. S. (1970). The tomb of *Wnjs-'nḫ* at Qurna (PM-No. 413). *Mitt. dt. archäol. Inst. Abt. Cairo* **26**, 199–206.

Amiran, R. (1974a). An Egyptian jar fragment with the name of Narmer from Arad. *Israel Exploration J.* **24**, 4–12.

(1974b). The painted pottery of the Early Bronze II period in Palestine. *Levant* **6**, 65–8.

Amiran, R., Y. Beit Arieh and J. Glass (1973). The interrelationship between Arad and sites in southern Sinai in the Early Bronze Age II. *Israel Exploration J.* **23**, 193–7.

Anthes, R. (1928). *Die Felseninschriften von Hatnub, nach den Aufnahmen Georg Möllers.* Leipzig.

(1954). Remarks on the Pyramid Texts and the early Egyptian dogma. *Jl Am. orient. Soc.* **74**, 35–9.

(1959). Egyptian theology in the third millennium B.C. *J Near East. Stud.* **18**, 169–212.

Arkell, A. J. (1954). Four occupation sites at Agordat. *Kush* **2**, 33–62.

(1961). *A history of the Sudan: from the earliest times to 1821*, 2nd edn. London.

Arnold, D. (1968). Bemerkungen zu den Königsgräbern der frühen II. Dynastie von El-Târif. *Mitt. dt. archäol. Inst. Abt. Cairo* **23**, 26–36.

(1973). Bericht über die vom Deutschen Archäologischen Institut Kairo im Winter 1971–72 in El-Târif durchgeführten Arbeiten. *Mitt. dt. archäol. Inst. Abt. Cairo* **29**, 135–62.

(1974a). *Der Tempel des Königs Mentuhotep von Deir el-Bahari. Vol. I: Architektur und Deutung; vol. II: Die Wandreliefs des Sanktuares.* Mainz.

(1974b). Bericht über die vom Deutschen Archäologischen Institut Kairo im Winter 1972/73 in El-Târif durchgeführten Arbeiten. *Mitt. dt. archäol. Inst. Abt. Cairo* **30**, 155–64.

(1975). Bemerkungen zu den frühen Tempeln von El-Tôd. *Mitt. dt. archäol. Inst. Abt. Cairo* **31**, 175–86.

(1976). *Gräber des Alten und Mittleren Reiches in El-Tarif.* Mainz.

Arnold, D. and J. Settgast (1965). Erster Vorbericht über die vom Deutschen Archäologischen Institut Kairo im Asasif unternommenen Arbeiten. *Mitt. dt. archäol. Inst. Abt. Cairo* **20**, 47–61.

Badawy A. (1967). The civic sense of Pharaoh and urban development in ancient Egypt. *J. Am. Res. Cent. Egypt* **6**, 103–9.

Baer, K. (1956). A note on Egyptian units of area in the Old Kingdom. *J Near East. Stud.* **15**, 113–17.

(1960). *Rank and title in the Old Kingdom.* Chicago.

(1962). The low price of land in ancient Egypt. *J. Am. Res. Cent. Egypt* **1**, 25–45.

(1963). An Eleventh Dynasty farmer's letters to his family. *J. Am. orient. Soc.* **83**, 1–19.

Bagnold, R. A., O. H. Myers, R. F. Peel and H. A. Winkler (1939). An expedition to the Gilf Kebir and Uweinat, 1938. *Geogr J.* **93**, 281–313.

Baines, J. (1973). The destruction of the pyramid temple of Sahure. *Götting. Misz.* **4**, 9–14.

(1974). The inundation stela of Sebekhotpe VIII. *Acta orient.* **36**, 39–54.

(1976). The Sebekhotpe VIII inundation stela: an additional fragment. *Acta Orient.* **37**, 11–20.

Barns, J. W. B. (1954). Four Khartoum stelae. *Kush* **2**, 19–25.

Barta, W. (1967–8). Zum scheinbaren Bedeutungswandel des Seth in den Pyramidentexten. *Jaarber. Vooraziat-Egypt. Genoot. 'Ex Oriente Lux'*, **7**, 20, 43–9.

(1969). 'Falke des Palastes' als ältester Königstitel. *Mitt. dt. archäol. Inst. Abt. Cairo* **24**, 51–7.

(1974). Das Gespräch des Ipuwer mit dem Schöpfergott. *Stud. altägypt. Kultur* **1**, 19–33

(1974–5). Die Erste Zwischenzeit im Spiegel der pessimistischen Literatur. *Jaarber. Vooraziat.-Egypt. Genoot.* **24**, 50–61.

(1975). *Untersuchungen zur Göttlichkeit des regierenden König.* Munich and Berlin.

(1976). Der dramatische Ramesseumpapyrus als Festrolle beim Hebsed-Ritual. *Stud. altägypt. Kultur* **4**, 31–43.

Bates, O. (1914). *The eastern Libyans.* London. (Reprinted 1970.)

Beckerath, J. von (1957). Notes on the viziers 'Ankhu and Iymeru in the Thirteenth Egyptian Dynasty. *J. Near East. Stud.* **37**, 20–8.

(1962). The date of the end of the Old Kingdom of Egypt. *J. Near East. Stud.* **21**, 140–7.

(1964). *Untersuchungen zur politischen Geschichte der Zweiten Zwischenzeit in Ägypten.* Glückstadt.

(1965). Zur Begründung der 12. Dynastie durch Ammenemes I. *Z. ägypt. Sprache Altertumskunde.* **92**, 4–10.

(1966). Die Dynastie der Herakleopoliten (9./10. Dynastie). *Z. ägypt. Sprache Altertumskunde* **93**, 13–20.

(1969). Die Lesung von 'Regierungsjahr': ein neuer Vorschlag. *Z. ägypt. Sprache Altertumskunde* **95**, 88–91.

(1976a). Die Chronologie der XII. Dynastie und das Problem der Behandlung gleichzeitiger Regierungen in der ägyptischen Überlieferung. *Stud. altägypt. Kultur* **4**, 45–57.

(1976b). Die Hyksos in Aegypten. *Antike Welt* **7**, 53–8.

Beit Arieh, Y. (1974). An Early Bronze Age II site at Nabi Salah in southern Sinai. *Tel Aviv* **1**, 144–56.

Beit Arieh, Y. and R. Gophna (1976). Early Bronze Age II sites in Wâdi el-Qudeirât (Kadesh-Barnea). *Tel Aviv* **3**, 142–50.

Bell, B. (1970). The oldest records of the Nile floods. *Geogrl J.* **136**, 569–73.

(1971). The dark ages in ancient history. I. The first dark age in Egypt. *Am. J. Archaeol.* **75**, 1–26.

(1975). Climate and the history of Egypt: the Middle Kingdom. *Am. J. Archaeol.* **79**, 223–69.

Bell, L. (1973). Once more the '*w*: 'interpreters' or 'foreigners'? *News. Am. Res. Cent. Egypt* **87**, 33.

Berlev, O. D. (1966). [The price of a slave in Egypt during the Middle Kingdom.] *Vestnik Drevnei Istorii* pt 1, **92** (sic, read **95**), 28–39. (In Russian.)

(1974). [A Thirteenth Dynasty stela in the Würzburg University Museum.] *Palestinskii Sbornik* **25** (88), 26–31. (In Russian.)

Bernand, É. (1975). *Recueil des inscriptions grecques du Fayoum, vol. I: La 'Méris' d'Hérakleidès.* Leiden.

Berry, B. J. L. (1961). City size distributions and economic development. *Econ. Devel. Cult. Change* **9**, 573–88.

Bietak, M. (1966). *Ausgrabungen in Sayala-Nubien 1961–1965. Denkmäler der C-Gruppe und der Pan-Gräber-Kultur.* Vienna.

(1968a). Vorläufiger Bericht über die erste und zweite Kampagne der österreichischen Ausgrabungen auf Tell ed-Dab'a im Ostdelta Ägyptens (1966, 1967). *Mitt. dt. archäol. Inst. Abt. Cairo,* **23**, 79–114.

(1968b). *Studien zur Chronologie der nubischen C-Gruppe.* Vienna.

(1970). Vorläufiger Bericht über die dritte Kampagne der österreichischen ausgrabungen auf Tell ed Dab'a im Ostdelta Ägyptens (1968). *Mitt. dt. archäol. Inst. Abt. Cairo* **26**, 15–42.

(1974). Die Todesumstände des Pharaos Seqenenre (17. Dynastie). *Ann. naturhist. Mus. Vienna* **78**, 29–52.

(1975a). *Tell el-Dab'a* vol. II. Vienna.

(1975b). Die Hauptstadt der Hyksos und die Ramesesstadt. *Antike Welt* **6**, 28–43.

Björkman, G. (1964). Egyptology and historical method. *Orient. Suecana* **13**, 9–33.

Blumenthal, E. (1970). *Untersuchungen zum ägyptischen Königtum des Mittleren Reiches, vol. I: Die Phraseologie* Leipzig.

(1976). Die Datierung der *Nḥri*-Graffiti von Hatnub. Zur Stellung der ägyptischen Gaufürsten im frühen Mittleren Reich. *Altorient. Forsch.* **4**, 35–62.

(1977). Die Koptosstele des Königs Rahotep (London W.C. 14327). In E. Endesfelder *et al.* (eds.), *Ägypten und Kusch* (*Schriften zur Geschichte und Kultur des Alten Orients* **13**), 63–80.

Boessneck, J. (1970). Die Equidenknochen von Tell ed Dab'a. *Mitt. dt. archäol. Inst. Abt. Cairo* **26**, 42.

Bongrani, L. (1963). I rapporti fra l'Egitto, la Siria el il Sinai durante l'Antico Regno. *Oriens Antiquus* **2**, 171–203.

Bonnet, C. (1978a). Fouilles archéologiques à Kerma (Soudan); rapport préliminaire de la campagne 1977–1978. *Genava* **26**, 107–27.

(1978b). Nouveaux travaux archéologiques à Kerma (1973–1975). In *Études nubiennes; colloque de Chantilly 2–6 juillet 1975*, 25–34. Cairo.

(1979). Remarques sur la ville de Kerma. In *Hommages à la mémoire de Serge Sauneron 1927–1976, vol. I: Égypte pharaonique*, 3–10. Cairo.

Bonomi, J. (1906). Topographical notes on western Thebes collected in 1830. *Ann. Serv. Antiquités Egypte* **7**, 78–86.

Borchardt, L. (1899). Der zweite Papyrusfund von Kahun und die zeitliche Festlegung des mittleren Reiches der ägyptischen Geschichte. *Z. ägypt. Sprache Altertumskunde* **37**, 89–103.

(1907). *Das Grabdenkmal des Königs Ne-user-Re'* 9991.82 Leipzig.

(1909). *Das Grabdenkmal des Königs Nefer-ir-keȝ-re'*. 9991.83 Leipzig.

(1910–13). *Das Grabdenkmal des Königs Saȝhu-Re'*, 2 vols. Leipzig.

Borchardt, L. and H. Ricke (1930). *Egypt: architecture, landscape, life of the people*. London.

Bosticco, S. (1959). *Le stele egiziane dall'Antico al Nuovo Regno*. Rome.

Bothmer, B. V. (1971). A bust of Ny-user-ra from Byblos, in Beirut, Lebanon. *Kêmi* **21**, 11–16.

(1974). The Karnak statue of Ny-user-ra. *Mitt. dt. archäol. Inst. Abt. Cairo* **30**, 165–70.

Bottéro, J., E. Cassin and J. Vercoutter (1967). *The Near East: the early civilizations*. Translated by R. F. Tannenbaum. London.

Breasted, J. H. (1905). *A history of Egypt; from the earliest times to the Persian Conquest* New York. (Also London, 1906.)

(1906). *Ancient records of Egypt*, 5 vols. Chicago.

Brovarski, E. (1970). The House of JḤww. *Serapis* **2**, 39.

Brovarski, E. and W. J. Murnane (1969). Inscriptions from the time of Nebhepetre Mentuhotep II at Abisko. *Serapis* **1**, 11–33.

Brunner, H. (1936). *Die Anlagen der ägyptischen Felsgräber bis zum Mittleren Reich*. Glückstadt.

(1955). Die Lehre vom Königserbe im frühen Mittleren Reich. In O. Firchow (ed.), *Ägyptologische Studien*, 4–11. Berlin.

(1958). Die Zeit des Cheops. *Oriental. Literaturz.* **53**, 293–301.

Brunner-Traut, E. (1974). Noch einmal die Fürstin von Punt. Ihre Rasse, Krankheit und ihre Bedeutung für die Lokalisierung von Punt. In *Festschrift zum 150 jährigen Bestehen des Berliner Ägyptischen Museums*, 71–85. Berlin.

Brunton, G. (1949). The title *Khnumet Nefer-Heȝt. Ann. Serv. Antiquités Egypte* **49**, 99–110.

Brunton, G. and R. Engelbach (1927). *Gurob*. London.

Bruyère, B., J. Manteuffel, K. Michałowski, and J. Sainte Fare Garnot (1937). *Tell Edfou 1937. Fouilles franco-polonaises, rapports* **1**. Cairo.

Buchholz, H.-G. and V. Karageorghis (1971). *Altägäis und Altkypros.* Tübingen.

*Bulletin de Liaison du Groupe International d'Etude de la Céramique Egyptienne* **2**.

Butzer, K. W. (1959). Studien zum vor- und frühgeschichtlichen Landschaftswandel der Sahara. III. Die Naturlandschaft Ägyptens während der Vorgeschichte und der dynastischen Zeit. *Abh. math.-naturw. Kl. Akad. Wiss. Mainz* **2**, 1–80.

(1975). Patterns of environmental change in the Near East during Late Pleistocene and Early Holocene times. In F. Wendorf and A. E. Marks (eds.), *Problems in prehistory: North Africa and the Levant*, 389–410. Dallas.

(1976). *Early hydraulic civilization in Egypt: a study in cultural ecology.* Chicago.

Butzer, K. W. and C. L. Hansen (1968). *Desert and river in Nubia.* Madison.

Callaway, J. A. and J. M. Weinstein (1977). Radiocarbon dating of Palestine in the Early Bronze Age. *Bull. Am. Sch. orient. Res.* **225**, 1–16.

Caton-Thompson, G. (1952). *Kharga Oasis in prehistory.* London.

Černý, J. (1947). Graffiti at the Wādi el-'Allāki. *J. Egypt. Archaeol.* **33**, 52–7.

(1969). Stela of Emḥab from Tell Edfu. *Mitt. dt. archäol. Inst. Abt. Cairo* **24**, 87–92.

Červiček, P. (1970–3). Datierung der nordafrikanischen Felsbilder durch die Patina. *IPEK* **23**, 82–7.

(1974). *Felsbilder des Nord-Etbai, Oberägyptens und Unternubiens.* Wiesbaden.

Chéhab, M. (1969). Noms de personnalités égyptiennes découvertes au Liban. *Bull. Mus. Beycrouth* **22**, 1–47.

Coldstream, J. N. and G. L. Huxley (eds.) (1972). *Kythera; excavations and studies conducted by The University of Pennsylvania Museum and The British School at Athens.* London.

Couroyer, B. (1971). Ceux-qui-sont-sur-le-sable: les Hériou-Shâ. *Rev. Biblique* **78**, 558–75.

(1973). Pount et la Terre du Dieu. *Rev. Biblique* **80**, 53–74.

Couyat, J. and P. Montet (1912). *Les inscriptions hiéroglyphiques et hiératiques du Ouâdi Hammâmât.* Cairo.

Cowgill, G. L. (1975). On causes and consequences of ancient and modern population changes. *Am. anthrop.* **77**, 505–25.

Crawford, O. G. S. (1951). *The Fung Kingdom of Sennar, with a geographical account of the Middle Nile region.* Gloucester.

Crüsemann, F. (1973). Überlegungen zur Identifikation der Ḥirbet el-Mšāš (Tel Māśôś). *Z. dt Palästina-Vereins* **89**, 211–24.

Daressy, G. (1917). Chapelle de Mentouhotep III à Dendérah. *Ann. Serv. Antiquités Égypte* **17**, 226–36.

Daumas, F. (1965). Rapport préliminaire sur les fouilles exécutées par l'Institut Français d'Archéologie Orientale entre Seyala et Ouadi es Sebouâ en Avril–Mai 1964. *Bull. Inst. fr. Archéol. orient. Cairo* **63**, 225–63.

(1973). Derechef Pépi I^er à Dendara. *Rev. Égypt.* **25**, 7–20.

Davies, N. de G. (1943). *The tomb of Rekh-mi-rēʿ at Thebes.* New York.

Davis, E. N. (1974). *The Vapheio Cups and Aegean gold and silver ware.* University Microfilms 74-1869, Ann Arbor.

Dever, W. G. (1973). The EVIV-MBI horizon in Transjordan and southern Palestine. *Bull. Am. Sch. orient. Res.* **210**, 37–63.

Dewachter, M. (1976). Le roi Sahathor et la famille de Neferhotep I. *Rev. Egypt.* **28**, 66–73.

Dixon, D. (1958). The land of Yam. *J. Egypt. Archaeol.* **44**, 40–55.

Drioton, E. (1945). Notes diverses, 2. Une corégence de Pepy I^er et de Mérenrê (?). *Ann. Serv. Antiquités Egypte* **44**, 55–6.

Drioton, E. and J. Vandier (1962). *Les peuples de l'orient méditerranéen, vol. II: L'Égypte*, 4th ed. Paris.

Dunayevsky, I. and A. Kempinski (1973). The Megiddo temples. *Z. dt. Palästina-Vereins* **89**, 161–87.

Dunbar, J. H. (1941). *The rock pictures of Lower Nubia*. Cairo.

Dunham, D. (1938). The biographical inscriptions of Nekhelsu in Boston and Cairo. *J. Egypt. Archaeol.* **24**, 1–8.

Edel, E. (1954). Inschriften des Alten Reichs, I. Die Biographie des Gaufürsten von Edfu. *Z. ägypt. Sprache Altertumskunde* **79**, 11–17.

(1955). Inschriften des Alten Reiches. V. Die Reiseberichte des, Hrw-hwjf (Herchuf). in O. Firchow (ed.), *Agyptologische Studien*, 51–75. Berlin.

(1955–64). *Altägyptische Grammatik. Analecta Orientalia* **34–9**. Rome.

(1956). Ein 'Vorsteher der Farafra-Oase' im Alten Reich? *Z. ägypt. Sprache Altertumskunde* **81**, 67–8.

(1960). Inschriften des Alten Reiches. XI. Nachträge zu den Reiseberichten der Hrw-hwjf. *Z. ägypt. Sprache Altertumskunde* **85**, 18–23.

(1962). Zur Lesung und Bedeutung einiger Stellen in den biographischen Inschrift *Sʒ-rnpwt*'s I. *Z. ägypt. Sprache Altertumskunde* **87**, 96–107.

(1967). Die Ländernamen und die Ausbreitung der C-Gruppe nach den Reiseberichten des *Hrw-hwjf*. *Orientalia* **36**, 133–58.

(1971a). *Beiträge zu den Inschriften des Mittleren Reiches in den Gräbern der Qubbet el Hawa*. Munich and Berlin.

(1971b). Zwei neue Felsinschriften aus Tumâs mit nubischen Ländernamen. *Z. ägypt. Sprache Altertumskunde* **97**, 53–63.

(1973). Nachtrag zur Felsinschriften des *Mhw* und *Sʒbnj* in Tumâs, ZÄS 97, 1971, 53ff. *Z. ägypt Sprache Altertumskunde* **100**, 76.

(1975). Der Fund eines Kamaresgefässes in einem Grabe der Qubbet el Hawa bei Assuan. In *Actes XXIX Congr. Int. Orientalistes, Égyptologie*, vol. 1, 38–40. Paris.

Edwards, I. E. S. (1961a). *The pyramids of Egypt*, revised ed. Harmondsworth.

(1961b). Two Egyptian sculptures in relief. *Br. Mus. Quarterly* **23**, 9–11.

(1970). Absolute dating from Egyptian records and comparison with carbon-14 dating. *Phil. Trans. Roy. Soc. Lond.* **269**, 1193, 11–18.

Edwards, I. E. S., C. J. Gadd and N. G. L. Hammond (eds.) (1971). *The Cambridge ancient history*, 3rd ed., vol. 1, pt 2, *Early history of the Middle East*. Cambridge.

Egypt Exploration Society (1963). *Report of the seventy-seventh ordinary general meeting*.

Emery, W. B. (1923). Two Nubian graves of the Middle Kingdom at Abydos. *Ann. Archaeol. Anthrop., Liverpool* **10**, 33–5.

(1961). A preliminary report on the excavations of the Egypt Exploration Society at Buhen, 1959–60. *Kush* 9, 81–6.

(1963). Egypt Exploration Society. Preliminary report on the excavations at Buhen, 1962. *Kush* 11, 116–20.

(1965). *Egypt in Nubia* London.

Emery, W. B. and L. P. Kirwan (1935). *The excavations and survey between Wadi es-Sebua and Adindan 1929–1931.* Cairo.

Engelbach, R. (1922). Steles and tables of offerings of the late Middle Kingdom from Tell Edfû. *Ann. Serv. Antiquités Égypte* 22, 113–38.

(1923). *Harageh.* London.

(1933). The quarries of the western Nubian desert: a preliminary report. *Ann. Serv. Antiquités Égypte* 33, 65–74.

(1938). The quarries of the western Nubian desert and the ancient road to Tushka. *Ann. Serv. Antiquités Égypte.* 38, 369–90.

Erman, A. and H. Grapow (1926–31). *Wörterbuch der Ägyptischen Sprache,* 5 vols. Leipzig.

Ertman, E. E. (1972). The earliest known three-dimensional representation of the god Ptah. *J. Near East. Stud.* 31, 83–6.

Evers, H. G. (1929). *Staat aus dem Stein. Denkmäler Geschichte und Bedeutung der ägyptischen Plastik während des Mittleren Reichs,* 2 vols. Munich.

Fairman, H. W. (1958). The kingship rituals of Egypt. In S. H. Hooke (ed.), *Myth, ritual and kingship,* 74–104. Oxford.

Fairservis, W. A., K. Weeks and M. Hoffman (1971–2). Preliminary report on the first two seasons at Hierakonpolis. *J. Am. Res. Cent. Egypt* 9, 7–68.

Fakhry, A. (1952). *The inscriptions of the amethyst quarries at Wadi el Hudi.* Cairo.

(1959). *The monuments of Sneferu at Dahshur, vol. I: The Bent Pyramid.* Cairo.

(1961). *The monuments of Sneferu at Dahshur, vol. II: The Valley Temple,* 2 pts. Cairo.

(1973). The search for texts in the western desert. In *Textes et langages de l'Égypte pharaonique, Hommage à Jean-François Champollion,* vol. II, 207–22. Cairo.

Farid, S. (1964). Preliminary report on the excavations of the Antiquities Department at Tell Basta (season 1961). *Ann. Serv. Antiquités Égypte* 58, 85–98.

Faulkner, R. O. (1969). *The ancient Egyptian pyramid texts.* Oxford.

Fecht, G. (1956). Die Ḥȝtjw-' in Iḥnw, eine ägyptische Völkerschaft in der Westwüste. *Z. dt. morgenländ. Ges.* 106 (N.S. 31), 37–60.

(1968). Zu den Inschriften des ersten Pfeilers im Grab des Anchtifi (Mo'alla). In W. H. Helck (ed.), *Festschrift für Siegfried Schott zu seinem 70. Geburtstag,* 50–60. Wiesbaden.

(1972). *Der Vorwurf an Gott in den 'Mahnworten des Ipu-wer' (Pap. Leiden I 344 recto 11, 11–13, 8; 15, 13–17, 3). Zur geistigen Krise der ersten Zwischenzeit und ihrer Bewältigung.* Heidelberg.

(1973). Ägyptische Zweifel am Sinn des Opfers: Admonitions 5, 7–9. *Z. ägypt. Sprache Altertumskunde* 100, 6–16.

Firth, C. M. and B. Gunn (1926). *Teti pyramid cemeteries*, 2 vols. Cairo.

Fischer, H. G. (1954). Four provincial administrators at the Memphite cemeteries. *Jl Am. orient. Soc.* **74**, 26–34.

(1957). A god and a general of the Oasis on a stela of the late Middle Kingdom. *J. Near East. Stud.* **16**, 223–35.

(1959a). An example of Memphite influence on a Theban stela of the Eleventh Dynasty. *Artibus Asiae* **22**, 240–52.

(1959b). A scribe of the army in a Saqqara mastaba of the early Fifth Dynasty. *J. Near East. Stud.* **18**, 233–72.

(1960). The inscription of I-zt.f, born of Tfi. *J. Near East. Stud.* **19**, 258–68.

(1961a). Three Old Kingdom palimpsests in the Louvre. *Z. ägypt. Sprache Altertumskunde* **86**, 21–31.

(1961b). Land records on stelae of the Twelfth Dynasty. *Rev. Egypt.* **13**, 107–9.

(1962). A provincial statue of the Egyptian Sixth Dynasty. *Am. J. Archaeol.* **66**, 65–9.

(1963). A stela of the Heracleopolitan Period found at Saqqara: the Osiris Iti. *Z. ägypt. Sprache Altertumskunde* **90**, 35–41.

(1964). *Inscriptions from the Coptite nome; Dynasties VI–XI. Analecta Orientalia* **40**, Rome.

(1968). *Dendera in the third millennium B.C.; down to the Theban domination of Upper Egypt.* New York.

(1974). Nbty in Old Kingdom titles and names. *J. Egypt. Archaeol.* **60**, 94–9.

(1975). Two tantalizing biographical fragments of historical interest. *J. Egypt. Archaeol.* **61**, 33–7.

Fleming, A. (1973). Tombs for the living. *Man*, N.S. **8**, 177–93.

*Fouilles de El Kab: documents* (1954). Livraison III. Fondation Égyptologique Reine Elisabeth, Brussels.

Frankfort, H. (1948). *Kingship and the gods.* Chicago.

Friedman, J. (1974). Marxism, structuralism and vulgar materialism. *Man*, N.S. **9**, 444–69.

Gabra, G. (1976). Preliminary report on the stela of Htpi from El-Kab from the time of Wahankh Inyôtef II. *Mitt. dt. archäol. Inst. Abt. Cairo* **32**, 45–56.

Gabra, S. (1929). *Les conseils de fonctionnaires dans l'Égypte pharaonique.* Cairo.

Gardiner, A. H. (1916). The defeat of the Hyksos Kamōse; The Carnarvon Tablet no. 1, *J. Egypt. Archaeol.* **3**, 95–110.

(1925). The autobiography of Rekhmerē'. *Z. ägypt. Sprache Altertumskunde* **60**, 62–76.

(1929). An administrative letter of protest. *J. Egypt. Archaol.* **13**, 75–8.

(1947). *Ancient Egyptian Onomastica*, 3 vols. Oxford.

(1954). Was the vizier Dja'u one of six like-named brothers? *Z. ägypt. Sprache Altertumskunde* **79**, 95–6.

(1957). The reading of the geographical term [tp-rs']. *J. egypt. Archaeol.* **43**, 6–9.

(1959). *The royal canon of Turin.* Oxford.

(1961). *Egypt of the Pharaohs: an introduction.* Oxford.

Gardiner, A. H., T. E. Peet and J. Černý (1955). *The inscriptions of Sinai. Egypt Exploration Society Memoir* **55**. London.

Garstang, J. (1902). *Mahâsna and Bêt Khallaf.* London.

(1904). *Tombs of the Third Egyptian Dynasty at Reqâqnah and Bêt Khallaf.* London.

Gauthier, H. (1907). *Le livre des rois d'Égypte, vol. I: Des origines à la fin de la XIIᵉ dynastie.* Cairo.

(1918). Le titre *ìmi-ra âkhnouti* et ses acceptions diverses. *Bull. Inst. fr. Archéol. orient. Cairo* **15**, 169–206.

(1924). La titulaire des reines des dynasties memphites. *Ann. Serv. Antiquités Égypte* **24**, 198–209.

Gerven, D. P. van, D. S. Carlson and G. J. Armelagos (1973). Racial history and bio-cultural adaptation of Nubian archaeological populations. *J. Afr. Hist.* **14**, 555–64.

Geus, C. H. S. de (1971). The Amorites in the archaeology of Palestine. *Ugarit-Forsch.* **3**, 41–60.

Geus, F. and Y. Labre (1974). La Nubie au sud de Dal: exploration archéologique et problèmes historiques. *Etudes sur l'Égypte et le Soudan anciens (Cahiers de Recherches de l'Institut de Papyrologie et d'Égyptologie de Lille* **2**), 103–23.

Giorgini, M. S. (1971). *Soleb, vol. II: les nécropoles.* Florence.

Giveon, R. (1965). A sealing of Khyan from the Shephela of southern Palestine. *J. Egypt. Archaeol.* **51**, 202–4.

(1967). Royal seals of the XIIth Dynasty from Western Asia. *Rèv. Egypt.* **19**, 29–37.

(1971). [The temple of Hathor at Serabit el-Khadem.] *Qadmoniot* **4**, 14–18. (In Hebrew.)

(1972). Le temple d'Hathor à Serabit el-Khadem. *Archéologia* **44**, 64–9.

(1974a). Hyksos scarabs with names of kings and officials from Canaan. *Chronique d'Egypte* **49**, 222–33.

(1974b). A second relief of Sekhemkhet in Sinai. *Bull. Am. Sch. orient. Res.* **216**, 17–20.

(1975). [Lady of the turquoise: Hathor at Serabit el-Khadim and Timna.] *Eretz-Israel* **12**, 24–6. (In Hebrew.)

Gleichen, Count Albert E. W. (ed.) (1905). *The Anglo-Egyptian Sudan: a compendium prepared by officers of the Sudan Government*, vol. 1. London.

Goedicke, H. (1954). An approximate date for the harem investigation under Pepy I. *Jl Am. orient. Soc.* **74**, 88–9.

(1955). The Abydene marriage of Pepi I. *Jl Am. orient. Soc.* **75**, 180–3.

(1956). Zu *ìmj-rȝ šmꜥ* und *tp šmꜥ* im Alten Reich. *Mitt. Inst. Orientforsch.* **4**, 1–10.

(1957). Bemerkungen zum Alter der Sonnenheiligtümer. *Bull. Inst. fr. Archéol. orient. Cairo* **56**, 151–3.

(1960a). *Die Stellung des Königs im Alten Reich.* Wiesbaden.

(1960b). The inscription of *Ḏmì. J. Near East. Stud.* **19**, 288–91.

(1962). Zur Chronologie der sogenannten 'Ersten Zwischenzeit'. *Z. dt. morgenländ. Ges.* **112** (N.S. **37**), 239–54.

(1963). The alleged military campaign in southern Palestine in the reign of Pepy I (VIth Dynasty). *Riv. Stud. Orient.* **38**, 187–97.

(1966a). An additional note on 'ꜣ 'foreigner.' *J. Egypt. Archaeol.* **52**, 172–4.
(1966b). The cylinder seal of a ruler of Byblos reconsidered. *J. Am. Res. Cent. Egypt* **5**, 19–21.
(1967). *Königliche Dokumente aus dem alten Reich.* Wiesbaden.
(1969). Probleme der Herakleopolitenzeit. *Mitt. dt. archäol. Inst. Abt. Cairo* **24**, 136–43.
(1969–70). An Egyptian claim to Asia. *J. Am. Res. Cent. Egypt* **8**, 11–27.
(1970). *Die privaten Rechtsinschriften aus dem Alten Reich.* Vienna.
(1971). *Re-used blocks from the pyramid of Amenemhet I at Lisht.* New York.
(1971–2). Tax deductions for religious donations. *J. Am. Res. Cent. Egypt* **9**, 73–5.
(1974). The Berlin Leather Roll (P. Berlin 3029). In *Festschrift zum 150jährigen Bestehen des Berliner Ägyptischen Museums*, 87–104. Berlin.
(1976a). Eine Betrachtung des Inschriften des Meten im Rahmen der sozialen und rechtlichen Stellung von Privatleuten im ägyptischen Alten Reich. *Ägyptologische Abhandlungen* **29**. Wiesbaden.
(1976b). Another remark about the Byblos Cylinder Seal. *Syria* **53**, 191–2.
(1977). *The prophecy of Neferyt.* Baltimore.
Gómez-Moreno, C. (1972–3). Gold. *Bull. Metropol. Mus. Art* **31**, 69–121.
Gophna, R. (1976a). Excavations at 'En Besor. *'Atiqot* **11**, 1–9.
(1976b). Egyptian immigration into southern Canaan during the First Dynasty? *Tel Aviv* **3**, 31–7.
Gostynski, T. (1975). La Libye antique et ses relations avec l'Égypte. *Bull IFAN*, b, **37**, 473–588.
Goyon, G. (1957). *Nouvelles inscriptions rupestres du Wadi Hammamat.* Paris.
(1969). Le cylindre de l'Ancien Empire du Musée d'Ismailia. *Bull. Inst. fr. Archéol. orient. Cairo* **67**, 147–57.
Gratien, B. (1973). Les nécropoles Kerma de l'île de Saï. *Études sur l'Égypte et le Soudan anciens (Cahiers de Recherches de l'Institut de Papyrologie et d'Égyptologie de Lille* **1**), 143–84.
(1974). Les nécropoles Kerma de l'île de Saï, II. *Études sur l'Égypte et le Soudan anciens (Cahiers de Recherches de l'Institut de Papyrologie et d'Égyptologie de Lille* **2**), 51–74.
(1975). Les nécropoles Kerma de l'île de Saï, III. *Études sur l'Égypte et le Soudan anciens (Cahiers de Recherches de l'Institut de Papyrologie et d'Égyptologie de Lille* **3**), 43–66.
(1978). *Les cultures Kerma; essai de classification.* Lille.
Grdseloff, B. (1948). Remarques concernant l'opposition à un rescrit du vizir. *Ann. Serv. Antiquités Égypte* **48**, 505–12.
Grieshammer, R. (1974). Die altägyptische Sargtexte in der Forschung seit 1936. *Ägyptologische Abhandlungen* **28**. Wiesbaden.
Griffith, F. Ll. (1898). *The Petrie Papyri: hieratic papyri from Kahun and Gurob (principally of the Middle Kingdom).* London.
Griffiths, J. G. (1960). *The conflict of Horus and Seth.* Liverpool.
(1966). *The origins of Osiris. Münchner Ägyptologische Studien* **9**, Berlin.
Grove, A. T., F. Alayne Street and A. S. Goudie (1975). Former lake levels and climatic change in the rift valley of southern Ethiopia. *Geogrl J.* **141**, 177–202.

Guest, E. M. (1926). Women's titles in the Middle Kingdom. *Ancient Egypt* 46–50.

Gunn, B. (1929). A Middle Kingdom stela from Edfu. *Ann. Serv. Antiquites Égypte* **29**, 5–14.

Habachi, L. (1957). *Tell Basta*. Cairo.

(1958). God's fathers and the role they played in the history of the First Intermediate Period? *Ann. Serv. Antiquites Égypte* **55**, 167–90.

(1972). *The second stela of Kamose, and his struggle against the Hyksos ruler and his capital*. Glückstadt.

(1974). A high inundation in the temple of Amenre at Karnak in the Thirteenth Dynasty. *Stud. altägypt. Kultur* **1**, 207–14.

Hall, H. T. B. (1962). A note on the cattle skulls excavated at Faras. *Kush* **10**, 58–61.

Hallo, W. W. and Simpson, W. K. (1971). *The ancient Near East: a history*. New York.

Hamada, A. and S. Farid (1947). Excavations at Kôm el-Ḥisn, season 1945. *Ann. Serv. Antiquités Égypte* **46**, 195–205.

Hansen, D. P. (1965). Mendes 1964. *J. Am. Res. Cent. Egypt* **4**, 31–7.

(1967). Mendes 1965 and 1966, I. The excavations at Tell el Rub'a. *J. Am. Res. Cent. Egypt* **6**, 5–16.

Harris, J. R. (1961). *Lexicographical studies in ancient Egyptian minerals*. Berlin.

Hassan, S. (1943). *Excavations at Gîza, vol. IV: 1932–1933*. Cairo.

Hayes, W. C. (1946). Royal decrees from the temple of Min at Coptus. *J. Egypt. Archaeol.* **32**, 3–23.

(1947). Horemkha'uef of Nekhen and his trip to It-towe. *J. Egypt. Archaeol.* **33**, 3–11.

(1953a). *The scepter of Egypt*, pt I. New york.

(1953b). Notes on the government of Egypt in the late Middle Kingdom. *J. Near East. Stud.* **12**, 31–9.

(1955). *A papyrus of the late Middle Kingdom in the Brooklyn Museum [Papyrus Brooklyn 35.1446]*. Brooklyn. (Reprinted with an additional page of errata and recent bibliography as *Wilbour Monographs* **5**.)

Hays, T. R. (1975a). Neolithic settlement patterns in Saharan Africa. *S. Afr. archaeol. Bull.* **30**, 29–33.

(1975b). Neolithic settlement of the Sahara as it relates to the Nile Valley. In F. Wendorf and A. E. Marks (eds.), *Problems in prehistory: North Africa and the Levant*, 193–204. Dallas.

Heinzelin, J. de (1968). Geological history of the Nile Valley in Nubia. In F. Wendorf (ed.); *The prehistory of Nubia*, vol. 1, 19–55. Dallas.

Helck, H. W. (1954). *Untersuchungen zu den Beamtentiteln des ägyptischen Alten Reiches*. Glückstadt.

(1955). Zur Reichseinigung der II. Dynastie. *Z. ägypt. Sprache Altertumskunde* **80**, 75–6.

(1956a). Wirtschaftliche Bemerkungen zum privaten Grabbesitz im Alten Reich. *Mitt. dt. archäol. Inst. Abt. Cairo* **14**, 63–75.

(1956b). *Untersuchungen zu Manetho und den ägyptischen Königslisten*. Berlin.

(1957). Bemerkungen zu den Pyramidenstädten im Alten Reich. *Mitt. dt. archäol. Inst. Abt. Cairo* **15**, 91–111.

(1958). *Zur Verwaltung des Mittleren und Neuen Reichs.* Leiden and Cologne.

(ed.) (1968). *Geschichte des alten Ägypten, Handbuch der Orientalisk,* Abt. 1, Bd. 1, Absch. 3. Leiden and Cologne.

(1969). Eine Stele Sebekhotops IV. aus Karnak. *Mitt. dt. archäol. Inst. Abt. Cairo* **24**, 194–200.

(1970). *Die Prophezeiung des Nfr.tj. Textzusammenstellung.* Wiesbaden.

(1971). *Die Beziehungen Ägyptens zu Vorderasien im 3. und 2. Jahrtausend v. Chr.* 2nd edn. Wiesbaden.

(1974a). *Ägyptische Aktenkunde des 3. und 2. Jahrtausends v. Chr.* Munich and Berlin.

(1974b). Bemerkungen zum Annalenstein. *Mitt. dt. archäol. Inst. Abt. Cairo* **30**, 31–5.

(1974c). Die Bedeutung der Felsinschriften J. Lopez, Inscripciones Rupestres Nr. 27 und 28. *Stud. altägypt. Kultur* **1**, 215–25.

(1975). *Wirtschaftsgeschichte des Alten Ägypten im 3. und 2. Jahrtausend vor Chr.* Leiden.

(1976). Ägyptische Statuen im Ausland – ein chronologisches Problem. *Ugarit-Forsch.* **8**, 101–15.

Helck, H. W. and E. Otto (eds.) (1972–00). *Lexikon der Ägyptologie,* vols 1– . Wiesbaden.

Hellström, P. and H. Langballe (1970). *The rock drawings.* Scandinavian Joint Expedition to Sudanese Nubia. Stockholm and New York.

Helms, S. W. (1975a). Jawa 1973: a preliminary report. *Levant* **7**, 20–38.

(1975b). Posterns in Early Bronze Age fortifications of Palestine. *Palestine Exploration Quarterly* **107**, 133–50.

(1976). Jawa excavations 1974: a preliminary report. *Levant* **8**, 1–23.

Hennessy, J. B. (1967). *The foreign relations of Palestine during the Early Bronze Age.* London.

Hepper, N. (1969). Arabian and African frankincense trees. *J. Egypt. Archaeol.* **55**, 66–72.

Herzog, R. (1968). *Punt.* Glückstadt.

Hesse, A. (1971). Tentative interpretation of the surface distribution of remains on the upper fort of Mirgissa (Sudanese Nubia). In F. R. Hodson, D. G. Kendall and P. Tăutu (eds.), *Mathematics in the archaeological and historical sciences* 436–44. Edinburgh.

Hester, J. J. and P. M. Hobler (1969). *Prehistoric settlement patterns in the Libyan desert. Antrop. Pap. Univ. Utah* **92**, Nubian series **4**.

Hintze, F. (1964). Das Kerma-Problem. *Z. ägypt. Sprache Altertumskunde* **91**, 79–86.

(1965). Preliminary note on the epigraphic expedition to Sudanese Nubia, 1963. *Kush* **13**, 13–16.

Hobler, P. M. and J. J. Hester (1968). Prehistory and environment in the Libyan desert. *S. Afr. archaeol. Bull.* **23**, 120–30.

Hodjache, S. and O. Berlev (1977). Objets royaux du Musée des Beaux-Arts Pouchkine à Moscou. *Chronique d'Égypte* **52**, 22–39.

Hofmann, I. (1967). *Die Kulturen des Niltals von Aswan bis Sennar; vom Mesolithikum bis zum Ende der christlichen Epoche.* Hamburg.

Hölscher, W. (1955). *Libyer und Ägypter.* Glückstadt.

Horn, S. H. (1963). Byblos in ancient records. *Andrews Univ. Sem. Stud.* 1, 52–61.

Hornung, E. (1966). *Geschichte als Fest; zwei Vorträge zum Geschichtsbild der frühen Menschzeit.* Darmstadt.

(1973). Die 'Kammern' des Thot-Heiligtumes. *Z. ägypt. Sprache Altertumskunde* 100, 33–5.

(1974). Seth. Geschichte und Bedeutung eines ägyptischen Gottes. *Symbolen* 2, 49–63.

Huard, P. (1965). Recherches sur les traits culturels des chasseurs anciens du Sahara centre-oriental et du Nil. *Rev. Egypt* 17, 21–80.

(1967–8). Influences culturelles transmises au Sahara tchadien par le Groupe C de Nubie. *Kush* 15, 84–124.

Huard, P. and L. Allard (1970). Etat des recherches sur les chasseurs anciens du Nil et du Sahara. *Bibliotheca Orient.* 27, 322–7.

Huard, P. and J. Leclant (1972). *Problèmes archéologiques entre le Nil et le Sahara.* Cairo.

Ingham, M. F. (1969). The length of the Sothic cycle. *J. Egypt. Archaeol.* 55, 36–40.

Jacquet-Gordon, H. K. (1962). *Les noms des domaines funéraires sous l'Ancien Empire égyptien.* Cairo.

James, T. G. H. (1961). A group of inscribed Egyptian tools. *Br. Mus. Quarterly* 24, 36–43.

(1962). *The Hekanakhte papers and other early Middle Kingdom documents.* New York.

Janssen, J. J. (1975). *Commodity prices from the Ramessid period.* Leiden.

Jéquier, G. (1929). *Tombeaux de particuliers contemporains de Pepi II.* Cairo.

(1935). *La pyramide d'Aba.* Cairo.

(1938). *Le monument funéraire de Pepi II, vol. II: Le temple.* Cairo.

(1940a). *Le monument funéraire de Pepi II, vol. III: Les approches du temple.* Cairo.

(1940b). *Douze ans de fouilles dans la nécropole memphite 1924–1936. Mém. Univ. Neuchatel* 15.

Junge, F. (1973). Zur Fehldatierung des sog. Denkmals memphitischer Theologie oder: Der Beitrag der ägyptischen Theologie zur Geistesgeschichte der Spätzeit. *Mitt. dt. archäol. Inst. Abt. Cairo* 29, 195–204.

Jungwirth, J. (1970). Die anthropologischen Ergebnisse der Grabungskampagne 1969 in Tell ed Dab'a, Unterägypten. *Ann. naturhist. Mus. Vienna* 74, 659–66.

Junker, H. (1955). *Gîza XII.* Vienna.

Kadish, G. E. (1966). Old Kingdom Egyptian activity in Nubia: some reconsiderations. *J. Egypt. Archaeol.* 52, 23–33.

(1973). British Museum writing board 5645: The complaints of Khakheper-rē'-senebu. *J. Egypt. Archaeol.* 59, 77–90.

Kaiser, W. (1956). Zu den Sonnenheiligtümern der 5. Dynastie. *Mitt. dt. Archäol. Inst. Abt. Cairo* 14, 104–16.

(1961). Einige Bemerkungen zur ägyptischen Frühzeit. II. Zur Frage einer über Menes hinausreichenden ägyptischen Geschichtsüberlieferung. *Z. ägypt. Sprache Altertumskunde* **86**, 39–61.

Kaiser, W., P. Grossmann, G. Haeny and H. Jaritz (1974). Stadt und Tempel von Elephantine. Vierter Grabungsbericht. *Mitt. dt. archäol. Inst. Abt. Cairo* **30**, 65–90.

Kanawati, N. (1974). The financial resources of the viziers of the Old Kingdom and the historical implications. *Archaeol. Hist. Stud. Alexandria* **5**, 1–20.

(1976). The mentioning of more than one eldest child in Old Kingdom inscriptions. *Chronique d'Egypte* **51**, 235–51.

(1977). *The Egyptian administration in the Old Kingdom.* Warminster.

Kantor, H. J. (1965). The relative chronology of Egypt and its foreign correlations before the Late Bronze Age. In R. W. Ehrich (ed.), *Chronologies in Old World Archaeology*, 1–46. Chicago.

Kaplony, P. (1965). Die wirtschaftliche Bedeutung des Totenkultes im Alten Ägypten. *Asiat. Stud.* **18–19**, 290–307.

(1968). Neues Material zu einer Prosopographie des Alten Reiches. *Mitt. Inst. Orientforsch.* **14**, 192–205.

(1972). Das Papyrusarchiv von Abusir. *Orientalia* N.S. **41**, 11–79, 180–244.

Kaplony-Heckel, U. (1971a). *Ägyptische Handschriften*, pt 1, ed. E. Lüddeckens. (W. Voigt (ed.), *Verzeichnis der Orientalischen Handschriften in Deutschland*, vol. XIX.) Wiesbaden.

(1971b). Eine hieratische Stela des Mittleren Reichs. *J. Egypt. Archaeol.* **57**, 20–7.

Kappel, W. (1974). Irrigation development and population pressure. In T. E. Downing and M. Gibson (eds.), *Irrigation's impact on society (Anthrop. Pap. Univ. Arizona*, **25**), 159–67. Tucson, Arizona.

Kees, H. (1940). Beiträge zur Geschichte des Vezirats im Alten Reich. Die Chronologie der Vezire unter König Chiops II. *Nach. Ges. Wiss. Göttingen, Phil.-hist. Kl.* **4**.

Kemp, B. J. (1968). The Osiris temple at Abydos. *Mitt. dt. archäol Inst. Abt. Cairo* **23**, 138–55.

(1973). The Osiro temple at Abydos. A postscript to *MDAIK* 23 (1968) 138–155. *Götting. Misz.* **8**, 23–5.

(1972). Fortified towns in Nubia. In P. J. Ucko, R. Tringham and G. W. Dimbleby (eds.), *Man, settlement and urbanism*, 651–6. London.

(1976a). Dating Pharaonic cemeteries. Part I: non-mechanical approaches to seriation. *Mitt. dt archäol. Inst. Abt. Cairo* **31**, 93–116.

(1976b). A note on stratigraphy at Memphis. *J. Am. Res. Cent. Egypt* **13**, 25–9.

(1977a). An incised sherd from Kahun (Egypt). *J. Near East. Stud.* **36**, 289–92.

(1977b). The early development of towns in Egypt. *Antiquity* **51**, 185–200.

(1978). The harim-palace at Medinet el-Ghurab *Z.Ä.S.* **105**, 122–33.

Kemp, B. J. and R. S. Merrillees (1980). *Minoan pottery in second millennium Egypt.* Mainz am Rhein.

Kenyon, K. M. (1969). The Middle and Late Bronze Age strata at Megiddo. *Levant* **1**, 25–60.

Kirwan, L. P. (1939). *Oxford University excavations at Firka.* Oxford.

Kitchen, K. A. (1961). An unusual stela from Abydos. *J. Egypt. Archaeol* **47**, 10–18.

(1967a). Byblos, Egypt, and Mari in the early second millennium B.C. *Orientalia* **36**, 39–54.

(1967b). An unusual Egyptian text from Byblos. *Bull. Mus. Beyrouth* **20**, 149–53.

(1971). Punt and how to get there. *Orientalia* **40**, 184–208.

Klasens, A. (1968). A social revolution in ancient Egypt. *Études et Travaux* **2** (*Prace Zakładu Archaeologii Śródziemnomorskiej Polskiej Akademii Nauk* **6**), 6–13.

Knudstad, J. (1966). Serra East and Dorginarti. *Kush* **14**, 165–86.

Koenen, L. (1970). The prophecies of a potter: a prophecy of world renewal becomes an apocalypse. In D. H. Samuel (ed.), *Proc. XII Int. Congr. Papyrology* 249–54. Toronto.

Kuchman, L. (1977). The titles of queenship: part I, the evidence from the Old Kingdom. *Newsl. Soc. Stud. Egypt. antiquities, Toronto* **7**, 9–12.

Lanczkowski, G. (1959). Das Königtum im Mittleren Reich. In *La regalità sacra/The sacral kingship* (*Studies in the history of religions*, vol. IV). Leiden.

Larsen, H. (1935). Vorbericht über die schwedischen Grabungen in Abu Ghalib 1932–1934. *Mitt. dt. Inst. ägypt. Altertumskunde Cairo* **6**, 41–87.

Lauer, J.-P. (1973). Remarques sur la planification de la construction de la grande pyramide. *Bull. Inst. fr. Archéol. orient. Cairo* **73**, 127–42.

(1974). *Le mystère des pyramides* Paris.

(1976). A propos du prétendu désastre de la pyramide de Meïdoum. *Chronique d'Egypte* **51**, 72–89.

Lawrence, A. W. (1965). Ancient Egyptian fortifications. *J. Egypt. Archaeol.* **51**, 69–94.

Leclant, J. (1954). Fouilles et travaux en Égypte, 1952–1953. *Orientalia* **23**, 64–79.

(1969). Fouilles et travaux en Égypte et au Soudan, 1967–1968. *Orientalia* **38**, 240–307.

(1974). Fouilles et travaux en Égypte et au Soudan, 1972–1973. *Orientalia* **43**, 171–227.

Leclant, J. and A. Heyler (1961). Sur l'administration de l'Égypte au Moyen- et Nouvel-Empire. *Orient. Literaturz.* **56**, 118–29.

Lees, S. H. (1974). Hydraulic development as a process of response. *Hum. Ecol.* **2**, 159–75.

Legrain, G. (1905). The king Samou or Seshemou and the enclosures of el-Kab. *Proc. Soc. Bibl. Archaeol.* **27**, 106–11.

Lichtheim, M. (1973). *Ancient Egyptian literature; a book of readings, vol. I: The Old and Middle Kingdoms.* Berkeley.

Limme, L. (1973). Les oases de Khargeh et Dakhleh d'après les documents égyptiens de l'époque pharaonique. *Études sur l'Égypte et le Soudan anciens* (*Cahiers de Recherches de l'Institut de Papyrologie et d'Égyptologie de Lille* I), 39–58.

Lloyd, A. B. (1970). The Egyptian Labyrinth. *J. Egypt. Archaeol.* **56**, 81–100.

Long, R. D. (1974). A re-examination of the Sothic chronology of Egypt. *Orientalia* **43**, 261–74.

(1976). Ancient Egyptian chronology, radiocarbon dating and calibration. *Z. ägypt. Sprache Altertumskunde* **103**, 30–48.

Lopez, J. (1967). Inscriptions de l'Ancien Empire à Khor el-Aquiba. *Rev. Egypt.* **19**, 57–66.

Lowie, R. H. Museum of Anthropology (1966). *Ancient Egypt.* (Exhibition Catalogue.) Berkeley.

Lucas, A. and J. R. Harris (1962). *Ancient Egyptian materials and industries*, 4th edn. London.

Macadam, M. F. L. (1951). A royal family of the Thirteenth Dynasty. *J. Egypt. Archaeol.* **37**, 20–8.

(1955). *The temples of Kawa*, vol. II. London.

MacDonald, J. (1972). Egyptian interests in Western Asia to the end of the Middle Kingdom: an evaluation. *Austral. J. Bibl. Archaeol.* **2**, 72–98.

McHugh, W. P. (1974a). Cattle pastoralism in Africa – a model for interpreting archaeological evidence from the eastern Sahara desert. *Arctic Anthrop.* **11** (Suppl), 236–44.

(1974b). Late prehistoric cultural adaptation in southwest Egypt and the problem of the Nilotic origins of Saharan cattle pastoralism. *J. Am. Res. Cent. Egypt* **11**, 9–22.

(1975). Some archaeological results of the Bagnold-Mond expedition to the Gilf Kebir and Gebel 'Uweinat, southern Libyan desert. *J. Near East Stud.* **34**, 31–62.

Mace, A. C. (1921). Excavations at Lisht. *Bull. Metropol. Mus. Art* pt 2, 5–19.

(1922). Excavations at Lisht. *Bull Metropol. Mus. Art* pt 2, 4–18.

Maragioglio, V. and C. Rinaldi (1968). Note sulla piramide di Ameny 'Aamu. *Orientalia* **37**, 325–38.

(1971). Considerazioni sulla città *Ḏd-Snfrw*. *Orientalia* **40**, 67–74.

Marinatos, S. (1974). *Excavations at Thera, vol. VI (1962 season)*. Athens.

Martin, G. T. (1968). A new prince of Byblos. *J. Near East. Stud.* **27**, 141–2.

(1969). A ruler of Byblos of the Second Intermediate Period. *Berytus* **18**, 81–3.

Martin-Parday, E. (1976). *Untersuchungen zur ägyptischen Provinzialverwaltung bis zum Ende des Alten Reiches*. Hildesheim.

Matthews, J. M. (1975). An inscribed sherd from the Palestine Exploration Fund. *Palestine Exploration Quarterly* **107**, 151–3.

Matthiae, M. P. (1978). Recherches archéologiques à Ebla, 1977: le quartier administratif du palais royal G. *C.r. Acad. Inscriptions et Belles-Lettres*, 204–36.

Maystre, C. (1975). Découvertes récentes (1969–1972). près d'Akasha. In K. Michałowski (ed.), *Nubia: récentes recherches. Actes du colloque Nubiologique International au Musée national de Varsovie 19–22 juin 1972*, 88–92. Warsaw.

Mazar, B. (1968). The Middle Bronze Age in Palestine. *Israel Exploration J.* **18**, 65–97.

Mellaart, J. (1959). The royal treasure of Dorak. *Illustrated London News* 28 November 1959, 754.

(1979). Egyptian and Near Eastern chronology: a dilemma? *Antiquity* **53**, 6–18.

Mendelssohn, K. (1974). *The riddle of the pyramids* London.

Menghin, O. and K. Bittel (1934). Kasr el Sagha. *Mitt. dt. Inst. ägypt. Altertumskunde Cairo* **5**, 1–10.

Menu, B. (1970). La gestion du patrimoine foncier d'Hekanakhte. *Rev. Égypt.* **22**, 111–29.

Menu, B. and I. Harari (1974). La notion de propriété privée dans l'Ancien Empire égyptien. *Cahiers de Recherches de l'Institut de Papyrologie et d'Égyptologie de Lille* **2**, 125–54.

Merrillees, R. S. (1968). *The Cypriote Bronze Age pottery found in Egypt. Studies in Mediterranean Archaeology* **18**, Lund.

(1970). Evidence for the bichrome wheel-made ware in Egypt. *Austral. J. Bibl. Archaeol.* **1**, 3–27.

(1974). *Trade and transcendence in the Bronze Age Levant. Studies in Mediterranean Archaeology* **39**, Göteborg.

(1978). El-Lisht and Tell el-Yahudiya Ware in the Archaeological Museum of the American University of Beirut. *Levant* **10**, 75–98.

Meshel, Z. (1974). New data about the 'desert kites'. *Tel Aviv* **1**, 129–43.

Mesnil du Buisson, R. du (1970). *Etudes sur les dieux phéniciens hérités par l'Empire romain.* Leiden.

Meulenaere, H. de (1971). La statue d'un contemporain de Sébekhotep IV. *Bull. Inst. fr. Archéol. orient. Cario* **69**, 61–4.

Meyer, E. (1887). *Geschichte des alten Aegyptens.* Berlin.

(1968). *Einführung in die antike Staatskunde.* Darmstadt.

Michael, H. N. and E. K. Ralph (1970). Correction factors applied to Egyptian radiocarbon dates from the era before Christ. In I. U. Olsson (ed.), *Radiocarbon variations and absolute chronology.* 109–19. New York and Stockholm.

Michałowski, K., J. de Linage, J. Manteuffel and J. Sainte Fare Garnot (1938). *Tell Edfou 1938.* Cairo.

Michałowski, K., Ch. Desroches, J. de Linage, J. Manteuffel and Żejmo-Żejmis (1950). *Tell Edfou 1939.* Cairo.

Mills, A. J. (1965). The reconnaissance and survey from Gemai to Dal: a preliminary report for 1963–64. *Kush* **13**, 1–12.

(1967–8). The archaeological survey from Gemai to Dal – a report on the 1965–1966 season. *Kush* **15**, 200–10.

Mills, A. J. and H.-Å. Nordström (1966). The archaeological survey from Gemai to Dal. Preliminary report on the season 1964–65. *Kush* **14**, 1–15.

Mitchell, W. P. (1963). The hydraulic hypothesis: a reappraisal. *Curr. Anthrop.* **14**, 532–4.

Mond, Sir Robert and O. H. Myers (1937). *Cemeteries of Armant,* 2 vols. London.

Montet, P. (1928). *Byblos et l'Égypte. Quatre campagnes de fouilles à Gebeil 1921–1922–1923–1924.* Paris.

(1936). Les tombeaux de Siout et de Deir Rifeh, 3. *Kêmi* **6**, 131–63.

(1957). *Géographie de l'Égypte ancienne,* vol. 1. Paris.

(1964). Notes et documents pour servir à l'histoire des relations entre l'Égypte et la Syrie. XIII. *Kêmi* **17**, 61–8.

Morenz, S. (1973). *Egyptian religion.* Translated by A. E. Keep. London.

Morgan, J. de (1895). *Fouilles à Dahchour, mars–juin 1894.* Vienna.

(1897). *Carte de la nécropole memphite*. Cairo.

(1903). *Fouilles à Dahchour en 1894–1895*. Vienna.

Moursi, M. I. (1972). *Die Hohenpriester des Sonnengottes von der Frühzeit bis zum Ende des Neuen Reiches*. Munich and Berlin.

Moussa, A. M. (1971). A stela from Saqqara of a family devoted to the cult of King Unis. *Mitt. dt. archäol. Inst. Abt. Cairo* **27**, 81–4.

Mrsich, T. (1968). *Unstersuchungen zur Hausurkunde des Alten Reiches*. Berlin and Munich.

Müller, D. (1961). Der gute Hirte. Ein Beitrag zur Geschichte ägyptischer Bildrede. *Z. ägypt. Sprache Altertumskunde* **85**, 126–44.

Müller, H. W. (1960). Kopf einer Statue des ägyptischen Sonnengottes aus dem Alten Reich. *Pantheon* N.S. **18**, 109–13.

(1964). Der Gute Gott Radjedef, Sohn des Rê. *Z. ägypt. Sprache Altertumskunde* **91**, 129–33.

Murnane, W. J. (1977). *Ancient Egyptian coregencies*. Chicago.

Murray, G. W. (1962). Graves of oxen in the eastern desert of Egypt. *J. Egypt. Archaeol.* **12**, 248–9.

(1965). Harkhuf's third journey. *Geogrl J.* **131**, 72–5.

Naumann, R. (1939). Der Tempel des Mittleren Reiches in Medīnet Mādi. *Mitt. dt. Inst. ägypt. Altertumskunde Cairo* **8**, 185–9.

Needler, W. (1961). Four relief-sculptures from the pyramid of Sesostris I at Lisht. *Annual (Art & Archaeol. Div.), Roy. Ontario Mus.* 15–26.

Newberry, P. E. (1938). Three Old Kingdom travellers to Byblos and Pwenet. *J. Egypt. Archaeol.* **24**, 182–4.

Nims, C. F. (1938). Some notes on the family of Mereruka. *Jl Am. orient. Soc.* **58**, 638–47.

Nordström, H.-Å. (1966). A-Group and C-Group in Upper Nubia. *Kush* **14**, 63–8.

el-Nur, O. (1976). [Kerma culture and its origins.] *Vestnik Drevnei Istorii* **1**, 29–51. (In Russian, with English summary.)

O'Connor, D. B. (1971). Ancient Egypt and Black Africa – early contacts. *Expedition* **14**, 2–9.

(1972). A regional population in Egypt to circa 600 B.C. In B. Spooner (ed.), *Population growth: anthropological implications*, 78–100. Cambridge, Mass. and London.

(1974). Political systems and archaeological data in Egypt: 2600–1780 B.C. *World Archaeol.* **6**, 15–38.

Oren, E. D. (1973a). The Early Bronze IV period in northern Palestine and its cultural and chronological setting. *Bull. Am. Sch. orient. Res.* **210**, 20–37.

(1973b). The overland route between Egypt and Canaan in the Early Bronze Age. *Israel Exploration J.* **23**, 198–205.

Osing, J. (1976). Ächtungstexte aus dem Alten Reich (II). *Mitt. dt. archäol. Inst. Abt. Cairo* **32**, 133–85.

Otto, E. (1951). Die Endsituation der ägyptischen Kultur. *Die Welt als geschichte* **114**, 203–13.

(1956). Prolegomena zur Frage der Gesetzgebung und Rechtssprechung in Ägypten. *Mitt. dt. archäol. Inst. Abt. Cairo* **14**, 150–9.

(1964–6). Geschichtsbild und Geschichtsschreibung in Ägypten. *Welt des Orients* **3**, 161–76.

(1969). Legitimation des Herrschens im pharaonischen Ägypten. *Saeculum,* Munich **20**, 385–411.

Parker, R. A. (1950). *The calendars of ancient Egypt.* Chicago.

(1970). The beginning of the lunar month in ancient Egypt. *J. Near East. Stud.* **29**, 217–20.

(1976). The Sothic dating of the Twelfth and Eighteenth Dynasties. *Studies in honor of George R. Hughes* 177–89. Chicago.

Parr, P. J. (1968). The origin of the rampart fortifications of Middle Bronze Age Palestine and Syria. *Z. dt. Palästina-Vereins* **84**, 18–45.

Peet, T. E. (1914). *The cemeteries of Abydos, pt II: 1911–1912. Egypt Exploration Fund Memoir* **34**, London.

(1930). *The great tomb-robberies of the Twentieth Egyptian Dynasty.* Oxford.

Pendlebury, J. D. S. (1930). *Aegyptiaca; a catalogue of Egyptian objects in the Aegean area.* Cambridge.

Peterson, B. J. (1965–6). Two Egyptian stelae. *Orient. Suecana* **14–15**, 3–8.

Petrie, W. M. F. (1890). *Kahun, Gurob, and Hawara.* London.

(1891). *Illahun, Kahun and Gurob.* London.

(1901). *Diospolis Parva. Egypt Exploration Fund, Memoir* **20**. London.

(1902). *Abydos, pt I: 1902. Egypt Exploration Fund Memoir* **22**. London.

(1903). *Abydos pt II: 1903. Egypt Exploration Fund Memoir* **24**. London.

(1906). *Hyksos and Israelite cities.* London.

(1909). *Qurneh.* London.

(1924a). *A history of Egypt, vol. I: from the earliest kings to the XVth Dynasty,* 11th edn, revised. London.

(1924b). *A history of Egypt, vol. II: during the XVIIth and XVIIIth Dynasties,* 7th edn, enlarged. London.

Petrie, W. M. F. and G. Brunton (1924). *Sedment,* vol. 1. London.

Piotrovsky, B. B. (1966). [Two Egyptian inscriptions of the Sixth Dynasty in Wadi Allaki.] *Vestnik Drevnei Istorii* **92** (sic, read **95**), 80–2. (In Russian.)

(1967). The Early Dynastic settlement of Khor-Daoud and Wadi-Allaki: the ancient route to the gold mines. In *Fouilles en Nubie (1961–1963)* (*Campagne Internationale de l'UNESCO pour la sauvegarde des monuments de la Nubie*), 127–40. Cairo.

Pirenne, J. (1932–5). *Histoire des institutions et du droit privé de l'ancienne Égypte.* Brussels.

(1949). Le domaine dans l'ancien Empire égyptien. *Recueils Soc. Jean Bodin* **4**, 5–24.

Pirenne, J. and M. Stracmans (1954). Le testament à l'époque de l'Ancien Empire égyptien. *Rev. Int. Droits Antiquité* **1**, 49–72.

Porter, B. and R. L. B. Moss (1927–51). *Topographical bibliography of ancient Egyptian hieroglyphic texts, reliefs and paintings* 1st edn, 7 vols. Oxford.

(1972). *Topographical bibliography...*, vol. 11 (2nd edn).

Posener, G. (1952). A propos des graffiti d'Abisko. *Archiv Orientálni* **20**, 163–6.

(1956). *Littérature et politique dans l'Égypte de la XIIᵉ dynastie.* Paris.

(1957a). Le conte de Néferkarè et du général Siséné (Recherches Littéraires, VI). *Rev. Egypt.* **11**, 119–37.

(1957b). Les Asiatiques en Égypte sous la XIIᵉ et XIIIᵉ dynasties. *Syria* **34**, 145–63.

(1958a). Pour une localisation du pays Koush au Moyen Empire. *Kush* **6**, 39–68.

(1958b). [Nehasyu and Medjayu.] Z. *ägypt. Sprache Altertumskunde* **83**, 38–43.

(1960). *De la divinité du Pharaon. Cahiers de la société Asiatique* **15**). Paris.

(1966). Les textes d'envoûtement de Mirgissa. *Syria* **43**, 277–87.

(1969). Sur l'emploi euphémique de ḥftj(w) 'ennemi (s)'. *Z. ägypt Sprache Altertumskunde* **96**, 30–5.

(1971). À la recherche de nouveaux textes d'envoûtement. In *Proc. V World Congr. Jewish Studies*, 144–9. Jerusalem.

Posener-Kriéger, P. (1969). Sur un nom de métal égyptien. In *Ugaritica* **6** (*Institut français d'Archéologie de Beyrouth: Bibliothèque archéologique et historique* **81**), 419–26. Paris.

(1976). *Les archives du temple funéraire de Néferirkarê-Kakaï, les papyrus d'Abousir; traduction et commentaire.* Cairo and Paris.

Posener-Kriéger, P. and J. L. de Cenival (1968). *Hieratic papyri in the British Museum, Series V: The Abu Sir Papyri.* London.

Pounds, N. J. G. (1969). The urbanization of the Classical world. *Ann. Assoc. Am. Geogr.* **59**, 135–57.

Prag, K. (1974). The Intermediate Early Bronze-Middle Bronze Age: an interpretation of the evidence from Transjordan, Syria and Lebanon. *Levant* **6**, 69–116.

Priese, K.-H. (1974). 'rm und 'ʒm, das Land Irame. Eine Beitrag zur Topographie des Sudan im Altertum. *Altorient. Forsch.* **1**, 7–41.

Pritchard, J. B. (ed.) (1969). *Ancient Near Eastern texts relating to the Old Testament*, 3rd edn with supplement. Princeton.

Quibell, J. E. (1898). *El Kab*. London.

(1900). *Hierakonpolis*, pt 1. London.

(1907). *Excavations at Saqqara (1905–1906)*. Cairo.

Quibell, J. E. and F. W. Green (1902). *Hierakonpolis*, pt 2. London.

Quitta, H. (1972). Zu einigen Problemen und Perspektiven der Radiocarbon-datierung. *Ausgrabungen und Funde* **17**, 99–109.

Rainey, A. F. (1972). The world of Sinuhe. *Israel Orient. Stud.* **2**, 369–408.

Ralph, E. K., H. N. Michael and M. C. Han (1973). Radiocarbon dates and reality. *MASCA Newsletter*, **9**, no. 1.

Randall-MacIver, D. and C. L. Woolley (1911). *Buhen*. Philadelphia.

el-Rayah, M. B. (1974). The problems of Kerma culture of ancient Sudan re-considered in the light of ancient Sudan civilization as a continuous process. *Ethnogr.-archäol. Z.* **15**, 287–304.

Read, J. G. (1970). Early Eighteenth Dynasty chronology. *J. Near East. Stud.* **29**, 1–11. (See also: R. A. Parker, 217–20.)

Redford, D. B. (1970). The Hyksos invasion in history and tradition. *Orientalia* **39**, 1–51.

(1975). The historiography of ancient Egypt. Unpublished paper, Conference on Ancient Egypt: problems of history, sources and methods. Cairo.

(1977). The oases in Egyptian history to Classical times. *Newsl. Soc. Stud. Egypt. Antiquities* **7**, 1, 7–10; II, 2–4; III, 2–6.

Reisner, G. A. (1918). The tomb of Hepzefa, nomarch of Siût. *J. Egypt. Archaeol.* **5**, 79–98.

(1923). *Excavations at Kerma*, pts I–III, pts IV–V. Cambridge, Mass.

(1931). *Mycerinus: the temples of the third pyramid at Giza.* Cambridge, Mass.

(1955). Clay sealings of Dynasty XIII from Uronarti Fort. *Kush* **3**, 26–9.

Reisner, G. A. and W. S. Smith (1955). *A history of the Giza necropolis, vol. II: The tomb of Hetep-heres the mother of Cheops.* Cambridge, Mass.

Reisner, G. A., D. Dunham and J. M. A. Janssen (1960). *Semna Kumma. (Second Cataract Forts*, vol. I.) Boston.

Reisner, G. A., N. F. Wheeler and D. Dunham (1967). *Uronarti Shalfak Mirgissa. (Second Cataract Forts*, vol. II.) Boston.

Resch, W. F. E. (1966–9). Das Alter der östägyptischen und nubischen Felsbilder. *IPEK* **22**, 114–22.

(1967a). *Das Rind in den Felsbilddarstellungen Nordafrikas.* Wiesbaden.

(1967b). *Die Felsbilder Nubiens.* Graz.

Reymond, E. A. E. (1969). *The mythical origin of the Egyptian temple.* Manchester.

Riad, H. (1958). Le culte d'Amenemhat III au Fayoum à l'époque ptolémaïque. *Ann. Serv. Antiquités Égypte* **55**, 203–6.

Ricke, H. (1965). *Das Sonnenheiligtum des Königs Userkaf*, vol. I. Cairo.

Riefstahl, E. (1956). Two hairdressers of the Eleventh Dynasty. *J. Near East. Stud.* **15**, 10–17.

Robichon, C. and Varille, A. (1940). *Description sommaire du temple primitif de Médamud.* Cairo.

Rothenberg, B. (1969). An archaeological survey of south Sinai; first season 1967/68, a preliminary report. *Mus. Haaretz Bull.* **11**, 22–38.

(1970–1). An archaeological survey of South Sinai. First season 1967/1968, preliminary report. *Palestine Exploration Quarterly* **102**, 4–29.

(1972). Sinai explorations 1967–1972. *Mus. Haaretz Bull.* **14**, 31–42.

(1972–3). Sinai explorations III. A preliminary report on the sixth season of an archaeological survey of Sinai, February 1973. *Mus. Haaretz Yearb.* **15–16**, 16–34.

Rowe, A. (1930). *The topography and history of Beth-Shan.* Philadelphia.

(1940). *The four Canaanite temples of Beth-shan.* Philadelphia.

Said, R., C. Albritton, F. Wendorf, R. Schild and M. Kobusiewicz (1972a). A preliminary report on the Holocene geology and archaeology of the northern Fayum desert. *Playa Lake Symposium*, 41–61. Texas.

(1972b). Remarks on the Holocene geology and archaeology of northern Fayum desert. *Archaeologia Polona* **13**, 7–22.

Saleh, A.-A. (1972). Some problems relating to the Pwenet reliefs at Deir el-Baḥari. *J. Egypt. Archaeol.* **58**, 140–58.

(1974). Excavations around Mycerinus pyramid complex. *Mitt. dt. archäol. Inst. Abt. Cairo* **30**, 131–54.

Saleh, M. (1977). *Three Old-Kingdom tombs at Thebes.* Mainz.

Sanders, J. A. (ed.) (1970). *Near Eastern archaeology in the twentieth century.* New York.

Sauneron, S. (1954). La justice à la porte des temples (à propos du nom égyptien des propylées). *Bull. Inst. Fr. Archéol. orient. Cairo* **54**, 117–27.

Säve-Söderbergh, T. (1941). *Ägypten und Nubien: ein Beitrag zur Geschichte altägyptischer Aussenpolitik.* Lund.

(1946). *The navy of the Eighteenth Egyptian Dynasty.* Uppsala and Leipzig.

(1949). A Buhen stela from the Second Intermediate Period (Khartūm no. 18). *J. Egypt. Archaeol.* **35**, 50–8.

(1956). The Nubian Kingdom of the Second Intermediate Period. *Kush* **4**, 54–61.

(1963). The tomb of the Prince of Teh-khet, Amenemhet. *Kush* **11**, 159–74.

(1969). Die Akkulturation der nubischen C-Gruppe im Neuen Reich. *Z. dt. morgenländ. Ges. (Suppl I)*, **17**, 12–20.

Säve-Söderbergh, T. and Olsson, I. U. (1970). C14 dating and Egyptian chronology. In I. U. Olsson (ed.), *Radiocarbon variations and absolute chronology (Proc. XII Nobel Symposium)*, 35–53. New York and Stockholm.

Sayed, A. M. A. H. (1977). Discovery of the site of the 12th Dynasty port at Wadi Gawasis on the Red Sea shore. *Rev. Egypt* **29**, 138–78.

Schachermeyr, F. (1967). *Ägäis und Orient.* Vienna.

Schäfer, H. (1902). *Ein Bruchstück altägyptischer Annalen.* Berlin.

Scharff, A. (1920). Ein Rechnungsbuch des königlichen Hofes aus der 13. Dynastie (Papyrus Boulaq Nr. 18). *Z. ägypt. Sprache Altertumskunde* **56**, 51–68.

Schenkel, W. (1962). *Frühmittelägyptische Studien.* Bonn.

(1965). *Memphis Herakleopolis Theben; die epigraphischen Zeugnisse der 7.–11. Dynastie Agyptens. Ägyptologische Abhandlungen* **12**. Wiesbaden.

(1973). Ein Türsturz von der Grabkapelle des Königs *Wzh-'nh* Antef. *Mitt. dt. archäol. Inst. Abt. Cairo* **29**, 215–19.

(1978). *Die Bewässerungsrevolution im alten Ägypten.* Mainz. (This important book appeared too late for its conclusions to be considered in the text.)

Schmid, H. H. (1968). *Gerechtigkeit als Weltordnung.* Tübingen.

Schmitz, B. (1976). *Untersuchungen zum Titel Sʒ-Njswt 'Königssohn'.* Bonn.

Schulman, A. R. (1976). The Egyptian seal impressions from 'En Besor. *'Atiqot* **11**, 16–26.

Seger, J. D. (1975). The MBII fortifications at Shechem and Gezer: a Hyksos retrospective. *Eretz-Israel* **12**, 34\*–45\*.

Seters, J. van (1964). A date for the 'Admonitions' in the Second Intermediate Period. *J. Egypt. Archaeol.* **50**, 13–23.

(1966). *The Hyksos; a new investigation.* New Haven and London.

Sethe, K. (1932–3). *Urkunden des alten Reichs.* G. Steindorff (ed.), *Urkunden des ägyptischen Altertums*, 2nd edn, vol. 1. Leipzig.

Shaw, W. B. Kennedy (1936a). An expedition in the Southern Libyan desert. *Geogl J.* **87**, 193–221.

(1936b). Two burials from the south Libyan desert. *J. Egypt. Archaeol.* **22**, 47–50.

Shore, A. F. (1973). A soldier's archery case from ancient Egypt. *Brit Mus. Quarterly* **37**, 4–9.

Simpson, W. K. (1954). Two Middle Kingdom personifications of seasons. *J. Near East. Stud.* **13**, 265–8.

(1956). The single-dated monuments of Sesostris I: an aspect of the institution of coregency in the Twelfth Dynasty. *J. Near East. Stud.* **15**, 214–19.

(1957). Sobkemḥēt, a vizier of Sesostris III. *J. Egypt. Archaeol.* **43**, 26–9.

(1959). Historical and lexical notes on the new series of Hammamat inscriptions. *J. Near East. Stud.* **18**, 20–37.

(1963a). Studies in the Twelfth Egyptian Dynasty: I–II. *J. Am. Res. Cent. Egypt* **2**, 53–63.

(1963b). *Papyrus Reisner I: the records of a building project in the reign of Sesostris I.* Boston.

(1963c). *Heka-nefer.* New Haven and Philadelphia.

(1965). *Papyrus Reisner II: accounts of the dockyard workshop at Thais in the reign of Sesostris I.* Boston.

(1969a). The Dynasty XIII stela from the Wadi Hammamat. *Mitt. dt. archäol. Inst. Abt. Cairo* **25**, 154–8.

(1969b). *Papyrus Reisner III; the records of a building project in the early Twelfth Dynasty.* Boston.

(1972). A tomb chapel relief of the reign of Amunemhet III and some observations on the length of the reign of Sesostris III. *Chronique d'Egypte* **47**, nos. 93–94, 45–54.

(ed.) (1973). *The literature of ancient Egypt; an anthology of stories, instructions, and poetry*, with translations by R. O. Faulkner, E. F. Wente, Jr., and W. K. Simpson. New Haven and London.

Slater, R. A. (1970). Dendereh and the University Museum, 1888–1970. *Expedition* **12**, 15–20.

Smith, H. S. (1964). Egypt and C14 dating. *Antiquity* **38**, 32–7.

(1966a). The Nubian B-Group. *Kush* **14**, 69–124.

(1966b). Preliminary report on the rock inscriptions in the Egypt Exploration Society's concession at Buhen. *Kush* **14**, 330–4.

(1966c). Kor: report on the excavations of the Egypt Exploration Society at Kor, 1965. *Kush* **14**, 187–243.

(1972). The rock inscriptions of Buhen. *J. Egypt. Archaeol.* **58**, 43–61.

(1976). *The fortress of Buhen; the inscriptions. Egypt Exploration Society Memoir* **48**. London.

Smith, H. S. and A. Smith (1976). A reconsideration of the Kamose texts. *Z. ägypt. Sprache Altertumskunde* **103**, 48–76.

Smith, P. E. L. (1968). Problems and possibilities of the prehistoric rock art of northern Africa. *Afr. Hist. Stud.* **1**, 1–39.

Smith, W. S. (1946). *A history of Egyptian sculpture and painting in the Old Kingdom.* Boston and London.

(1957). Fragments of a statuette of Chephren. *Wien. Z. Kunde Morgenlandes* **54**, 186–90.

(1958). *The art and architecture of ancient Egypt.* Harmondsworth.

(1962). Some recent accessions. *Bull. Mus. Fine Arts, Boston* **60**, no. 322, 132–6.

(1965). *Interconnections in the ancient Near East: a study of the relationships between the arts of Egypt, the Aegean, and Western Asia.* New Haven and London.

(1969). Influence of the Middle Kingdom of Egypt in Western Asia, especially in Byblos. *Am. J. Archaeol.* **73**, 277–81.

Smither, P. C. (1941). A tax-assessor's journal of the Middle Kingdom. *J. Egypt. Archaeol.* **27**, 74–6.

(1945). The Semnah Despatches. *J. Egypt. Archaeol.* **31**, 3–10.

(1948). The report concerning the slave-girl Senbet. *J. Egypt. Archaeol.* **34**, 31–4.

Soghor, C. L. (1967). Mendes 1965 and 1966, II. The inscriptions from Tell el Rub'a. *J. Am. Res. Cent. Egypt* **6**, 16–32.

Steckeweh, H. (1936). *Die Fürstengräber von Qaw*. Leipzig.

Steindorff, G. (1937). *Aniba*, vol. II. Glückstadt.

Stiebing, W. H. (1971). Hyksos burials in Palestine: a review of the evidence. *J. Near East. Stud.* **30**, 110–17.

Stracmans, M. (1955). Textes des actes de fondation de l'Ancien Empire. *Rev. Int. Droits Antiquité* **2**, 31–8.

(1958). Le titre de Hatj-â sous l'Ancien Empire égyptien. *Rev. Int. Droits Antiquité* **5**, 21–32.

Strouhal, E. and J. Jungwirth (1971). Anthropological problems of the Middle Empire and Late Roman Sayala. (Preliminary report on the first stage of the elaboration of the Austrian anthropological material from Nubia). *Mitt. anthrop. Ges. Wien* **101**, 10–23.

Tanner, R. (1974). Bemerkungen zur Sukzession der Pharaonen in der 12., 17, und 18. Dynastie. I. *Z. ägypt. Sprache Altertumskunde* **101**, 121–9.

Théodoridès, A. (1959). La procédure dans le *Pap. Berlin 10.470*. *Rev. Int. Droits Antiquité* **6**, 131–54.

(1960). Du rapport entre les parties du *Pap. Brooklyn 35.1446*. *Rev. Int. Droits Antiquité* **7**, 55–145.

(1962). Le rôle du Vizir dans la *Stèle Juridique de Karnak*. *Rev. Int. Droits Antiquité* **9**, 45–135.

(1967). À propos de la loi dans l'Égypte pharaonique. *Rev. Int. Droits Antiquité* **14**, 107–52.

(1968–72). À propos du sixième contrat du gouverneur Hâpidjefa. *Annuaire Inst. Philol. Hist. Orientales et Slaves* **20**, 439–66.

(1970). Le testament dans l'Égypte ancienne. *Rev. Int. Droits Antiquité* **17**, 117–216.

(1971a). Les contrats d'Hâpidjefa. *Rev. Int. Droits Antiquité* **18**, 109–251.

(1971b). The concept of law in ancient Egypt. In J. R. Harris (ed.), *The legacy of Egypt*, 2nd edn, 291–322. Oxford.

(1972). La révocation d'un acte testamentaire dans le *Pap. Kahoun VII.1*. *Rev. Int. Droits antiquité* **19**, 129–48.

(1973). Les Égyptiens anciens, 'citoyens' ou 'sujets de Pharaon'. *Rev. Int. Droits Antiquité* **20**, 51–112.

(1974). Mise en ordre chronologique des éléments de la Stèle Juridique de Karnak, avec ses influences sur la procédure. *Rev. Int. Droits Antiquité* **21**, 31–74.

Thompson, T. L. (1975). *The settlement of Sinai and the Negev in the Bronze Age*. Wiesbaden.

(1978). The background of the Patriarchs: a reply to William Dever and Malcolm Clark. *J. Stud. Old Testament* **9**, 2–43.

Toynbee, A. (1971). *An ekistical study of the Hellenic city-state*. Athens.

Trigger, B. G. (1965). *History and settlement in Lower Nubia*. New Haven.

(1976a). Kerma: the rise of an African civilization. *Int. J. Afr. hist. stud.* **9**, 1–21.

(1976b). *Nubia under the Pharaohs*. London.

Tufnell, O. (1973). The Middle Bronze Age scarab-seals from burials on the mound at Megiddo. *Levant* **5**, 69–82.

(1975). Seal impressions from Kahûn town and Uronarti fort. *J. Egypt. Archaeol.* **61**, 67–101.

Tufnell, O. and W. A. Ward (1966). Relations between Byblos, Egypt and Mesopotamia at the end of the third millennium B.C. A study of the Montet jar. *Syria* **43**, 165–241.

Tylor, J. J. and F. Ll. Griffith (1894). *The tomb of Paheri at el Kab. Egypt Exploration Fund Memoir* **11**. London.

Valloggia, M. (1962). Amenemhat IV et sa corégence avec Amenemhat III. *Rev. Egypt.* **21**, 107–33.

(1974). Les vizirs des XIᵉ et XIIᵉ dynasties. *Bull Inst. fr. Archéol. orient. Cairo* **74**, 123–34.

Vandersleyen, C. (1971). *Les guerres d'Amosis*. Brussels.

(ed.) (1975). *Das Alte Ägypten*. Berlin.

Vandier, J. (1936). *La famine dans l'Égypte ancienne*. Cairo.

(1950). *Mo'alla. La tombe d'Ankhtifi et la tombe de Sébekhotep*. Cairo.

(1958). *Manuel d'archéologie égyptienne vol. III: Les grandes époques, la statuaire*. Paris.

(1968). Une stèle égyptienne portant un nouveau nom royal de la troisième dynastie. *C.r. Acad. Inscriptions et Belles-Lettres*, 16–22.

Velde, H. te (1967). *Seth, god of confusion: a study of his role in Egyptian mythology and religion*. Leiden.

Vercoutter, J. (1956). *L'Egypte et le monde égéen préhellenique: étude critique des sources égyptiennes*. Cairo.

(1957). Upper Egyptian settlers in Middle Kingdom Nubia. *Kush* **5**, 61–9.

(1959). The gold of Kush. *Kush* **7**, 120–53.

(1964). La stèle de Mirgissa IM.209 et la localisation d'Iken (Kor ou Mirgissa?). *Rev. Egypt.* **16**, 179–91.

(1966). Semna South fort and the records of Nile levels at Kumma. *Kush* **14**, 125–64.

(1970). *Mirgissa* vol. 1. Paris.

(1975a). *Mirgissa vol. II: Les nécropoles* pt 1. Paris and Lille.

(1975b). Le roi Ougaf et la XIIIᵉ dynastie sur la IIᵐᵉ cataracte (stèle de Mirgissa IM.375). *Rev. Egypt.* **27**, 222–34.

(1976a). Egyptologie et climatologie. Les crues du Nil à Semneh. *Etudes sur l'Egypte et le Soudan anciens* (*Cahiers de Recherches de l'Institut de papyrologie et d'Egyptologie de Lille 4*), 139–72.

(1976b). *Mirgissa, vol. III: Les nécropoles*, pt 2. Paris and Lille.

(1977a). Les travaux de l'Institut français d'Archéologie orientale en 1976–1977. *Bull. Inst. fr. Archéol. orient. Cairo* **77**, 271–86.

(1977b). Les poids de Mirgissa et le 'standard-cuivre' au Moyen Empire.

*Ägypten und Kusch (Schriften zur Geschichte und Kultur des Alten Orients* 13), 437–45.

Vermeule, E. and Vermeule C. (1970). Aegean gold hoard and the court of Egypt. *Curator* 13, 32–42.

Vila, A. (1963). Un dépot de textes d'envoûtement au Moyen Empire. *J. Savants* 135–60.

(1970). L'armement de la forteresse de Mirgissa-Iken. *Rev. Égypt.* 22, 171–99.

(1973). Un rituel d'envoûtement au Moyen Empire égyptien. In *L'homme, hier et aujourd'hui: recueil d'études en hommage à André Leroi-Gourhan*, 625–39. Paris.

(1975–   ). *La prospection archéologique de la vallée du Nil, au sud de la Cataracte de Dal (Nubie Soudanaise), vols.* 1ff. Paris.

Vycichl, W. (1954–6). Die Fürsten von Libyen. *Ann. Ist. Univ. orient. Naples* 6, 43–8.

(1959). The burial of the Sudanese kings in the Middle Ages. *Kush* 7, 221–2.

Waddell, W. G. (1940). *Manetho.* Loeb Classical Library, Cambridge, Mass. and London.

Wainwright, G. A. (1927). El Hibeh and esh Shurafa and their connection with Herakleopolis and Cusae. *Ann. Serv. Antiquités Égypte* 27, 76–104.

Ward, W. A. (1961). Egypt and the East Mediterranean in the early second millennium B.C. *Orientalia* 30, 22–45 and 129–55.

(1964). Relations between Egypt and Mesopotamia from prehistoric times to the end of the Middle Kingdom. *J. econ. social Hist. Orient* 7, 1–45 and 121–35.

(1970). The origin of Egyptian design-amulets ('button seals'). *J. Egypt. Archaeol.* 56, 65–80.

(1971). *Egypt and the East Mediterranean world 2200–1900 B.C.* Beirut.

(1976). Some personal names of the Hyksos period rulers and notes on the epigraphy of their scarabs. *Ugarit-Forsch.* 8, 353–69.

Warren, P. (1969). *Minoan stone vases.* Cambridge.

Watermann, U. and R. Watermann (1957). Über die rätselvolle Gestalt der Königin von Punt. *Homo* 8, 148–54.

Weigall, A. E. P. (1907). *A report on the antiquities of Lower Nubia.* Oxford.

Weil, A. (1908). *Die Veziere des Pharaonenreiches, pt 1: Die Veziere des Alten Reiches.* Strasbourg.

Weinstein, J. M. (1975). Egyptian relations with Palestine in the Middle Kingdom. *Bull. Am. Sch. orient. Res.* 217, 1–16.

Wente, E. (1975). Thutmose III's accession and the beginning of the New Kingdom. *J. Near East. Stud.* 34, 265–72.

Wildung, D. (1969a). *Die Rolle ägyptischer Könige im Bewusstsein ihrer Nachwelt,* pt 1. Munich and Berlin.

(1969b). Zur Frühgeschichte des Amun-Tempels von Karnak. *Mitt. dt. archäol. Inst. Abt. Cairo* 25, 212–19.

(1972). Two representations of gods from the early Old Kingdom. *Misc. Wilbourana* 1, 145–60.

(1974). Aufbau und Zweckbestimmung der Königsliste von Karnak. *Götting. Misz.* 9, 42–8.

Williams, R. J. (1964). Literature as a medium of political propaganda in ancient Egypt. In W. S. McCullough (ed.), *The seed of wisdom: essays in honour of T. J. Meek*, 14–30. Toronto.

Wilson, J. A. (1951). *The burden of Egypt: an interpretation of ancient Egyptian culture*. Chicago. (Reprinted as *The culture of Ancient Egypt*.)

Winlock, H. E. (1947). *The rise and fall of the Middle Kingdom in Thebes*. New York.

Winter, E. (1957). Zur Deutung der Sonnenheiligtümer der 5. Dynastie. *Wien. Z. Kunde Morgenlandes*, **54**, 222–33.

Wittfogel, K. A. (1955). Developmental aspects of hydraulic societies. In J. H. Steward *et al.*, *Irrigation civilizations: a comparative study*. Washington. (Reprinted (1971) in S. Streuver (ed.), *Prehistoric agriculture*, 557–71. New York.)

　　(1957). *Oriental despotism: a comparative study of total power*. New Haven and London.

Wright, G. E. (1971). The archaeology of Palestine from the Neolithic through the Middle Bronze Age. *Jl Am. orient. Soc.* **91**, 276–93.

Wright, G. R. H. (1968). Tell el-Yehūdīyah and the glacis. *Z. dt. Palästina-Vereins* **84**, 1–17.

Yadin, Y. (1955). The earliest record of Egypt's military penetration into Asia? *Israel Exploration J.* **5**, 1–16.

Young, W. J. (1972). The fabulous gold of the Pactolus Valley. *Boston Mus. Bull.* **70**, no. 359, 5–13.

Yoyotte, J. (1950). Les filles de Téti et la reine Sheshé du Papyrus Ebers. *Rev. Egypt.* **7**, 184–5.

　　(1951). Un document relatif aux rapports de la Libye et de la Nubie. *Bull. Soc. fr. Egyptol.* **6**, 9–14.

　　(1952). Trois notes pour servir à l'histoire d'Edfou. *Kêmi* **12**, 91–2.

　　(1958). À propos de la parenté féminine du roi Téti (VI<sup>e</sup> dynastie). *Bull. Inst. fr. Archéol. orient. Cairo* **57**, 91–8.

　　(1975). Les *Sementiou* et l'exploitation des régions minières à l'Ancien Empire. *Bull. Soc. fr. Egyptol.* **73**, 44–55.

Žaba, Z. (1951). Dating of the social revolution in ancient Egypt. (Summary of a lecture.) *Archiv Orientální* **19**, 615.

Zayadine, F. (1973). Recent excavations on the citadel of Amman. (A preliminary report.) *Ann. Dept Antiquities Jordan* **18**, 17–35.

Zibelius, K. (1972). *Afrikanische Orts- und Völkernamen in hieroglyphischen und hieratischen Texten*. Wiesbaden.

## 11. EARLY FOOD PRODUCTION IN SUB-SAHARAN AFRICA

Allison, P. A. (1962). Historical inferences to be drawn from the effect of human settlement on the vegetation of Africa. *J. Afr. Hist.* **3**, 241–9.

Anfray, F. (1968). Aspects de l'archéologie éthiopienne. *J. Afr. Hist.* **9**, 345–66.

Arkell, A. J. (1953). *Shaheinab*. Oxford.

　　(1954). Four occupation sites at Agordat. *Kush* **2**, 33–62.

　　(1961). *A history of the Sudan*. London.

Armstrong, R. G. (1964). The use of linguistic and ethnographic data in the study of Idoma and Yoruba history. In J. Vansina, R. Mauny and L. V. Thomas (eds.), *The historian in tropical Africa*, 127–44. London.

Atherton, J. (1972). Excavations at Kamabai and Yagala Rock Shelters, Sierra Leone. *W. Afr. J. Archaeol.* **2**, 39–74.

Bailloud, G. (1959). La préhistoire de l'Ethiopie. *Mer Rouge–Afrique Orientale, Cahiers de l'Afrique et de l'Asie, Paris* **5**, 15–43.

(1969). L'évolution des styles céramiques en Ennedi, République du Tchad. In J. P. Lebeuf (ed.), *Actes I Colloque International d'Archéologie Africaine, (Fort-Lamy, 1969)*, 31–45. Fort-Lamy.

Bayle des Hermens, R. de (1975). *Recherches préhistoriques en République Centrafricaine. Recherches Oubanguiennes* **3**. Paris.

Beek, G. W. van (1969). *Hajar bin Humeid: investigations of a pre-Islamic site in South Arabia*. Baltimore.

Bower, J. R. F. (1973). Seronera: excavations at a Stone Bowl site in the Serengeti National Park, Tanzania. *Azania* **8**, 71–104.

Bower, J. R. F., C. M. Nelson, A. F. Waibel and S. Wandibba (1977). The University of Massachusetts Later Stone Age/Pastoral 'Neolithic' comparative study in central Kenya – an overview. *Azania* **12**, 119–46.

Brown, J. (1966). The excavation of a group of burial mounds at Ilkek, near Gilgil, Kenya. *Azania* **1**, 59–77.

Butzer, K. W., G. L. Isaac, J. L. Richardson and C. Washbourn-Kamau (1972). Radiocarbon dating of East African lake levels. *Science, N.Y.* **175**, 1069–76.

Cahen, D. and P. de Maret (1974). Recherches archéologiques récentes en République du Zaïre. *Périod. Univ. Libre Brussels* **39**, 33–7.

Carter, P. L. (1969). Moshebi's shelter: excavation and exploitation in eastern Lesotho. *Lesotho Notes and Records* **8**, 13–23.

Carter, P. L. and C. Flight (1972). A report on the fauna from the sites of Ntereso and Kintampo rockshelter six in Ghana: with evidence for the practice of animal husbandry during the second millennium B.C. *Man* N.S. **7**, 277–82.

Chapman, S. (1967). Kantsyore Island. *Azania* **2**, 165–91.

Clark, J. D. (1954). *The prehistoric cultures of the Horn of Africa*. Cambridge.

(1963). *Prehistoric cultures of northeast Angola and their significance in tropical Africa*, 2 vols. *Publcões cult. Co. Diam. Angola* **62**.

(1964). Stone vessels from Northern Rhodesia. *Man* **64**, article 88, 69–73.

(1967). The problem of neolithic culture in sub-Saharan Africa. In W. W. Bishop and J. D. Clark (eds.), *Background to evolution in Africa*, 601–27. Chicago.

(1968). *Further palaeo-anthropological studies in Northern Lunda. Publcões cult. Co. Diam. Angola* **78**.

(1970). *The prehistory of Africa*. London.

(1971b). A re-examination of the evidence for agricultural origins in the Nile valley. *Proc. prehist. Soc.* **37**, 34–79.

(1971a). An archaeological survey of northern Aïr and Ténéré. *Geogrl J.* **137**, 455–7.

(1972). Mobility and settlement patterns in sub-Saharan Africa: a comparison of late prehistoric hunter–gatherers and early agricultural occupation units. In P. J. Ucko, R. Tringham and G. W. Dimbleby (eds.), *Man, settlement and urbanism* 127–48. London.

Clark, J. D. and A. Stemler (1975). Early domesticated sorghum from central Sudan. *Nature, Lond.* **254**, 588–91.

Clark, J. D., M. A. J. Williams and A. B. Smith (1973). The geomorphology and archaeology of Adrar Bous, central Sahara: a preliminary report. *Quaternaria* **17**, 245–97.

Cohen, M. (1970). A reassessment of the Stone Bowl cultures of the Rift Valley, Kenya. *Azania* **5**, 27–38.

Connah, G. (1967). Progress report on archaeological work in Bornu, 1964–66, with particular reference to the excavations at Daima Mound. *Northern History Research Scheme, 2nd Interim Report* 17–31. Zaria, Nigeria.

  (1971). Recent contributions to Bornu chronology. *W. Afr. J. Archaeol.* **1**, 55–60.

  (1976). The Daima sequence and the prehistoric chronology of the Lake Chad region of Nigeria. *J. Afr. Hist.* **17**, 321–52.

Cooke, C. K. (1959). Rock art in Matabeleland. In R. Summers (ed.), *Prehistoric rock art of the Federation of Rhodesia and Nyasaland*, 112–62. London.

  (1963). Report on excavations at Pomongwe and Tshangula caves, Matopo Hills, Southern Rhodesia. *S. Afr. archaeol. Bull.* **18**, 63–151.

  (1964). Iron Age influences in the rock art of southern Africa. *Arnoldia* **1**, no. 12.

Coon, C. S. (1968). *Yengema Cave report*. Philadelphia.

Coppens, Y. (1969). Les cultures préhistoriques du Djourab. In J. P. Lebeuf (ed.), *Actes I Colloque International d' Archéologie Africaine (Fort-Lamy, 1969)*, 129–46. Fort-Lamy.

Corbeil, R., R. Mauny and J. Charbonnier (1951). Préhistoire et protohistoire de la presqu'île du Cap Vert et de l'extrême ouest sénégalais. *Bull. IFAN* **10**, 378–460.

Coursey, D. G. (1976). The origins and domestication of yams in Africa. In J. R. Harlan, J. M. J. de Wet and A. B. L. Stemler (eds.), *Origins of African plant domestication*, 383–408. The Hague.

Courtin, J. (1969). Le néolithique du Bourkou, Nord-Tchad. In J. P. Lebeuf (ed.), *Actes I Colloque International d' Archéologie Africaine (Fort-Lamy, 1969)*, 147–59. Fort-Lamy.

Dalby, D. (1975). The prehistorical implications of Guthrie's *Comparative Bantu:* I – problems of internal relationship. *J. Afr. Hist.* **16**, 481–501.

  (1976). The prehistorical implications of Guthrie's *Comparative Bantu:* II – interpretation of cultural vocabulary. *J. Afr. Hist.* **17**, 1–27.

Davies, O. (1964). *The Quaternary in the coastlands of Guinea*. Glasgow.

  (1967). *West Africa before the Europeans*. London.

  (1968). The origins of agriculture in West Africa. *Curr. Anthrop.* **9**, 479–82.

  (1971). Excavations at Blackburn. *S. Afr. archaeol. Bull.* **26**, 165–78.

  (1973). *Excavations at Ntereso, Gonja, Northern Ghana*. Pietermaritzburg.

  (1974). Excavations at the walled Early Iron Age site in Moor Park near Estcourt, Natal. *Ann. Natal Mus.* **22**, 289–323.

Deacon, H. J. (1966). Two radiocarbon dates from Scott's Cave, Gamtoos Valley. *S. Afr. archaeol. Bull.* **22**, 51–2.

(1972). A review of the post-Pleistocene in South Africa. *S. Afr. archaeol. Soc.* 1, 26–45.

Deacon, H. J. and J. Deacon (1963). Scott's Cave: a Late Stone Age site in the Gamtoos Valley. *Ann. Cape Prov. Mus.* 3, 96–121.

Deacon, J. (1972). Wilton: an assessment after fifty years. *S. Afr. archaeol. Bull.* 27, 10–48.

(1974). Patterning in the radiocarbon dates for the Wilton/Smithfield Complex in southern Africa. *S. Afr. archaeol. Bull.* 29, 3–18.

Delcroix, R. and R. Vaufrey (1939). Le Toumbien de Guinée française. *Anthropologie, Paris* 49, 265–312.

Descamps, C. and D. Demoulin (1969). Découverte d'outillage lithique en stratigraphie à Thiès, Sénégal. *Bull. Liais. Ass. sénégal. Etud. Quaternaire* 23–24, 57–63.

Dombrowski, J. (1970). Preliminary report on excavations in Lalibela and Natchabiet caves, Begemeder. *Ann. Ethiop.* 8, 21–9.

dos Santos, Jnr, J. R. and C. M. N. Ervedosa (1970). A estação arqueologica de Benfica, Luanda. *Estud. biol. Fac. Cienc. Univ. Luanda* 5, 31–51.

Dutton, J. P. (1970). Iron smelting furnace dated 630 years A.D. in the Ndumu Game Reserve. *Lammergeyer* 12, 37–40.

Ehret, C. (1967). Cattle-keeping and milking in eastern and southern African history: the linguistic evidence. *J. Afr. Hist.* 8, 1–17.

(1968a). Cushites and the Highland and Plains Nilotes. In B. A. Ogot and J. A. Kieran (eds.), *Zamani: a survey of East African history*, 158–76. Nairobi.

(1968b). Sheep and Central Sudanic peoples in southern Africa. *J. Afr. Hist.* 9, 213–21.

(1971). *Southern Nilotic history*. Evanston.

(1973). Patterns of Bantu and Central Sudanic settlement in central and southern Africa. *Transafr. J. Hist.* 3, 1–71.

(1974). *Ethiopians and East Africans*. Nairobi.

Epstein, H. (1971). *The origin of the domestic animals of Africa*. New York.

Fagan, B. M. (1967). *Iron Age cultures in Zambia*, vol. 1. London.

Fagan, B. M., D. W. Phillipson and S. G. H. Daniels (1969). *Iron Age cultures in Zambia*, vol. 11. London.

Fagg, A. (1972). A preliminary report on an occupation site in the Nok valley, Nigeria. *W. Afr. J. Archaeol.* 2, 75–9.

Fagg, B. E. B. (1969). Recent work in West Africa: new light on the Nok Culture. *World Archaeol.* 1, 41–50.

Fagg, B., E. Eyo, A. Rosenfeld and A. Fagg (1972). Four papers on the Rop rockshelter, Nigeria. *W. Afr. J. Archaeol.* 2, 1–38.

Flight, C. (1972). The prehistoric sequence in the Kintampo area of Ghana. In *Actes VI Congrès panafricain de Préhistoire (Dakar, 1967)*. 68–9. Chambéry.

Goodall, E. (1959). Rock paintings of Mashonaland. In R. Summers (ed.), *Prehistoric rock art of the Federation of Rhodesia and Nyasaland*, 3–11. London.

Goodwin, A. J. H. (1952). Jan van Riebeeck and the Hottentots, 1652–1662. *S. Afr. archaeol. Bull.* 6, 2–52.

Graziosi, P. (1964). New discoveries of rock paintings in Ethiopia. *Antiquity* 38, 91–8 and 187–90.

Greenberg, J. H. (1966). *Languages of Africa*. The Hague.

Grindley, J. R., E. Speed and T. Maggs (1970). The age of the Bonteberg shelter deposits, Cape Peninsula. *S. Afr. archaeol. Bull.* **25**, 24.

Hays, T. R. (1975). Neolithic settlement of the Sahara as it relates to the Nile Valley. In F. Wendorf and A. E. Marks (eds.), *Problems in prehistory: North Africa and the Levant*, 193–206. Dallas.

Heine, B. (1973). Zur genetischen Gliederung der Bantu-Sprachen. *Afrika und Übersee* **56**, 164–85.

Höhnel, L. von (1894). *Discovery of Lakes Rudolf and Stefanie*. London.

Holas, B. and R. Mauny (1953). Nouvelles fouilles à l'abri sous-roche de Blandé, Guinée. *Bull. IFAN* **15**, 1605–8.

Huffman, T. N. (1970). The Early Iron Age and the spread of the Bantu. *S. Afr. archaeol. Bull.* **25**, 3–21.

(1971). Excavations at Leopard's Kopje main Kraal: a preliminary report. *S. Afr. archaeol. Bull.* **26**, 85–9.

(1973). Test excavations at Makuru, Rhodesia. *Arnoldia* **5**, no. 39.

Inskeep, R. R. (1967). The Late Stone Age in southern Africa. In W. W. Bishop and J. D. Clark (eds.), *Background to evolution in Africa*, 557–82. Chicago.

(1969). The archaeological background. In M. Wilson and L. Thompson (eds.), *Oxford history of South Africa*, vol. I, 1–39. Oxford.

Isaac, G. Ll., H. V. Merrick and C. M. Nelson (1972). Stratigraphic and archaeological studies in the Lake Nakuru basin, Kenya. In E. M. van Zinderen Bakker (ed.), *Palaeoecology of Africa*, vol. VI, 225–32. Cape Town.

Jeffreys, M. D. W. (1951). Neolithic stone implements from Bamenda. *Bull IFAN* **13**, 1203–17.

Johnson, T., H. Rabinowitz and P. Sieff (1963). Who were the artists? *S. Afr. archaeol. Bull.* **18**, 27.

Joire, J. (1952). La préhistoire de Guinée française. *Conf. Int. Africanistes de l'Ouest* **2**, 297–373.

Kendall, R. L. (1969). An ecological history of the Lake Victoria basin. *Ecol. Monogr.* **39**, 121–76.

Krzyzaniak, L. (1978). New light on early food production in the Central Sudan. *J. Afr. Hist.* **19**, 159–72.

Leakey, M. D. (1943). Notes on the ground and polished stone axes of East Africa. *Jl E. Africa Uganda Nat. Hist. Soc.* **17**, 182–95.

(1945). Report on the excavations at Hyrax Hill, Nakuru, Kenya Colony, 1937–1938. *Trans. R. Soc. S. Afr.* **30**, 271–407.

(1966). Excavation of burial mounds in Ngorongoro crater. *Tanzania Notes and Records* **66**, 123–35.

Leakey, M. D. and L. S. B. Leakey (1950). *Excavations at the Njoro River cave*. Oxford.

Lebeuf, J. P. (1962). *Archéologie tchadienne*. Paris.

Linares de Sapir, O. (1971). Shell middens of lower Casamance and the problems of Diola prehistory. *W. Afr. J. Archaeol.* **1**, 23–54.

Maret, P. de (1975). A carbon-14 date from Zaire. *Antiquity* **49**, 133–7.

Martin del Molino, A. (1965). *Secuencia cultural en el neolitico de Fernando Po*. Trabajos de Prehistoria del Seminario de Historia Primitiva del Hombre de la Universidad de Madrid y del Instituto Español de Prehistoria del Consejo Superior de Investigaciones Cientificas 17.

Mason, R. J., M. Klapwijk, R. G. Welbourne, T. M. Evers, B. H. Sandelowsky and T. M. O'C. Maggs (1973). Early Iron Age settlement of southern Africa. *S. Afr. J. Sci.* **69**, 324–6.

Mauny, R. (1955). Les gisements néolithiques de Karkarichinkat, Tilemsi, Soudan français. In *Actes II Congrès panafricain de Préhistoire (Algiers, 1952)*, 617–29. Paris.

(1967). L'Afrique et les origines de la domestication. In W. W. Bishop and J. D. Clark (eds.), *Background to evolution in Africa*, 583–99. Chicago.

(1972). Contribution à l'inventaire de la céramique néolithique d'Afrique occidentale. In *Actes VI Congrès panafricain de Préhistoire (Dakar, 1967)*, 72–9. Chambéry.

(1973). Datation au carbone 14 d'amas artificiels de coquillages des lagunes de basse Côte d'Ivoire. *W. Afr. J. Archaeol.* **3**, 207–14.

Miller, S. F. (1969a). Contacts between the later Stone Age and the Early Iron Age in southern central Africa. *Azania* **4**, 81–90.

(1969b). The Nachikufan industries of the Zambia Later Stone Age. Doctoral dissertation, University of California, Berkeley.

Moorsel, H. van (1968). *Atlas de préhistoire de la plaine de Kinshasa.* Université of Louvain, Kinshasa.

Mortelmans, G. (1962). Vue d'ensemble sur la préhistoire du Congo occidental. In *Actes IV Congrès Panafricain de Préhistoire (Léopoldville, 1959)*, 129–64. Tervuren.

Murdock, G. P. (1959). *Africa: its peoples and their culture history.* New York.

Naville, E. (1898). *The temple of Deir el Bahari*, vol. III. London.

Noten, F. van (1968). *The Uelian, a culture with a Neolithic aspect, Uele basin, N.E. Congo Republic: an archaeological study.* Musée royal de l'Afrique Centrale, Tervuren.

Odner, K. (1972). Excavations at Narosura, a Stone Bowl site in the southern Kenya highlands. *Azania* **7**, 25–92.

Oliver, R. (1966). The problem of the Bantu expansion. *J. Afr. Hist.* **7**, 361–76.

Oliver, R. and B. M. Fagan (1978). The emergence of Bantu Africa. In J. D. Fage (ed.), *Cambridge History of Africa*, vol. II, 342–409. Cambridge.

Parkington, J. E. (1972). Seasonal mobility in the Late Stone Age. *Afr. Stud.* **31**, 223–43.

Parkington, J. and C. Poggenpoel (1971). Excavations at De Hangen 1968. *S. Afr. archaeol. Bull.* **26**, 3–36.

Payne, W. J. A. (1964). The origin of domestic cattle in Africa. *Emp. J. exp. Agric.* **32**, 97–113.

Phillipson, D. W. (1968). The Early Iron Age in Zambia – regional variants and some tentative conclusions. *J. Afr. Hist.* **9**, 191–211.

(1969a). Early iron-using peoples of southern Africa. In L. Thompson (ed.), *African societies in southern Africa*, 24–49. London.

(1969b). The prehistoric sequence at Nakapapula rockshelter, Zambia. *Proc. prehist. Soc.* **35**, 172–202.

(1972). Zambian rock paintings. *World Archaeol.* **3**, 313–27.

(1973). The prehistoric succession in eastern Zambia: a preliminary report. *Azania* **8**, 3–24.

(1975a). Chronology of the Iron Age in Bantu Africa. *J. Afr. Hist.* **16**, 321–42.

(1975b). *The Iron Age in Zambia.* Lusaka.

(1976a). The Early Iron Age in eastern and southern Africa: a critical re-appraisal. *Azania* **11**, 1–23.

(1976b). *Prehistory of eastern Zambia.* Nairobi.

(1977a). The excavation of Gobedra rock-shelter, Axum. *Azania* **12**, 53–82.

(1977b). *Later prehistory of eastern and southern Africa.* London.

Posnansky, M. (1969). Yams and the origins of West African agriculture. *Odu* **1**, 101–11.

Robinson, K. R. (1966a). A preliminary report on the recent archaeology of Ngonde, Northern Malawi. *J. Afr. Hist.* **7**, 169–188.

(1966b). Bambata ware: its position in the Rhodesian Iron Age in the light of recent evidence. *S. Afr. archaeol. Bull.* **21**, 81–5.

(1970). *The Iron Age of the Southern Lake area of Malawi.* Zomba.

Rudner, J. (1968). *Strandlooper pottery from South and South West Africa. Ann. S. Afr. Mus.* **49**.

Sampson, C. G. (1972). *The Stone Age industries of the Orange River Scheme and South Africa.* Bloemfontien.

(1974). *The Stone Age archaeology of southern Africa.* New York.

Sassoon, H. (1968). Excavation of a burial mound in Ngorongoro crater. *Tanzania Notes and Records* **69**, 15–32.

Schofield, J. F. (1940). Report on the pottery from Bambata Cave. *S. Afr. J. Sci.* **37**, 361–72.

Schweitzer, F. R. (1970). A preliminary report of excavation of a cave at Die Kelders. *S. Afr. archaeol. Bull.* **25**, 136–8.

(1974). Archaeological evidence for sheep at the Cape. *S. Afr. archaeol. Bull.* **29**, 75–82.

Schweitzer, F. R. and K. J. Scott (1973). Early occurrence of domestic sheep in sub-Saharan Africa. *Nature, Lond.* **241**, 574.

Seddon, J. D. (1968). The origins and development of agriculture in east and southern Africa. *Curr. Anthrop.* **9**, 489–94.

Shaw, C. T. (1944). Report on excavations carried out in the cave known as 'Bosumpra' at Abetifi, Kwahu, Gold Coast Colony. *Proc. prehist. Soc.* **10**, 1–67.

(1969). The Late Stone Age in the Nigerian forest. In J. P. Lebeuf (ed.), *Actes I Colloque International d'Archéologie Africaine (Fort-Lamy, 1969),* 364–73. Fort-Lamy.

(1971). The Prehistory of West Africa. In J. R. A. Ajayi and M. Crowder (eds.), *History of West Africa* vol. 1, 33–77. London.

(1972a). Finds at the Iwo Eleru rock shelter, Western Nigeria. In *Actes VI Congrès panafricain de Préhistoire (Dakar, 1967),* 190–2. Chambéry.

(1972b). Early agriculture in Africa. *Jl hist. Soc. Nigeria* **6**, 143–91.

Simoons, F. J. (1965). Some questions on the economic prehistory of Ethiopia. *J. Afr. Hist.* **6**, 1–13.

Smith, A. B. (1974). Preliminary report of excavations at Karkarichinkat, Mali, 1972. *W. Afr. J. Archaeol.* **4**, 33–55.

(1975). Radiocarbon dates from Bosumpra Cave, Abetifi, Ghana. *Proc. prehist. Soc.* **41**, 179–82.

Soper, R. (1971). General review of the Early Iron Age of the southern half of Africa. *Azania* **6**, 5–37.

Soper, R. C. and B. Golden (1969). An archaeological survey of Mwanza region, Tanzania. *Azania* **4**, 15–79.

Sparrman, A. (1785). *A voyage to the Cape of Good Hope*, 1772–6. Dublin.

Summers, R. (1958). *Inyanga*. Cambridge.

Sutton, J. E. G. (1964). A review of pottery from the Kenya highlands. *S. Afr. archaeol. Bull.* **19**, 27–35.

(1973a). *The archaeology of the Western Highlands of Kenya*. Nairobi.

(1973b). The settlement of East Africa. In B. A. Ogot (ed.), *Zamani: a survey of East African history*, 2nd edn, 70–97. Nairobi.

(1974). The aquatic civilization of middle Africa. *J. Afr. Hist.* **15**, 527–46.

Szumowski, G. (1956). Fouilles de l'abri sous-roche de Kourounkorokale, Soudan français. *Bull. IFAN* **18**, 462–508.

Vaufrey, R. (1946). Le néolithique de tradition capsienne au Sénégal. *Riv. Sci. preist.* **1**, 19–32.

Vavilov, N. (1951). The origin, variation, immunity and breeding of cultivated plants. *Chronica bot.* **13**, 1–364.

Vogel, J. O. (1969). On early evidence of agriculture in southern Zambia. *Curr. anthrop.* **10**, 524–5.

(1975). The Iron Age archaeology. In D. W. Phillipson (ed.), *Mosi-oa-Tunya: a handbook to the Victoria Falls region*, 48–58. London.

Welbourne, R. G. (1973). Identification of animal remains from the Broederstroom 24/73 Early Iron Age site. *S. Afr. J. Sci.* **69**, 325.

Wendt, W. E. (1972). Preliminary report on an archaeological research programme in South West Africa. *Cimbebasia*, B, **2**, 1.

Wilson, J. G. (1972). The use of stone hammers in the alteration of horn profile and the postulated origin of this and other customs in ancient Egypt. *Uganda J.* **36**, 57–65.

Wright, R. (1961). A painted rock shelter on Mount Elgon, Kenya. *Proc. prehist. Soc.* **27**, 28–34.

Wrigley, C. (1963). Linguistic clues to African history. *J. Afr. Hist.* **9**, 269–72.

## 12. EGYPT, 1552–664 BC

Adams, W. A. (1964). Post-pharaonic Nubia in the light of archaeology I. *J. Egypt. Archaeol.* **50**, 102–20.

Adams, W. Y. (1977a). *Nubia: corridor to Africa*. London.

(1977b). Reflections on the archaeology of Kerma. In E. Endesfelter *et al.* (eds.), *Ägypten und Kusch*, 41–51. *Schriften zur Geschichte und Kultur des Alten Orients*. **13**. Berlin.

Aharoni, Y. (1968). *The Land of the Bible: a historical geography*. Translated by A. F. Rainey. London.

Albright, W. F. (1975). The Amarna letters from Palestine. In *Cambridge Ancient History*, 3rd edn, vol. II, pt 2, ch. 20.

Aldred, C. (1968). *Akhenaten, Pharaoh of Egypt: a new study*. London.

(1969). The 'New Year' gifts to the pharaoh. *J. Egypt. Archaeol.* **55**, 73–81.

(1970). The foreign gifts offered to pharaoh. *J. Egypt. Archaeol.* **56**, 105–16.

(1975). Egypt: the Amarna period and the end of the eighteenth dynasty. In *Cambridge Ancient History*, 3rd edn, vol. II, pt 2, ch. 19.

Aldred, C. and A. T. Sandison (1961). The tomb of Akhenaten at Thebes. *J. Egypt. Archaeol.* **47**, 41–65.

(1962). The Pharaoh Akhenaten: a problem in Egyptology and pathology. *Bull. Hist. Med.* **36**, 293–316.

Anthes, R. (1940). Das Bild einer Gerichtsverhandlung und das Grab des Mes aus Sakkara. *Mitt. deutsch. Inst. ägypt. Altertumskunde Kairo* **9**, 93–119.

Arkell, A. J. (1950). Varia Sudanica. *Jour. Egypt. Archaeol.* **36**, 24–40.

(1961). *A History of the Sudan. From the earliest times to 1821*, 2nd edn. London.

Assman, J. (1972). Palast oder Tempel? Überlegungen zur Architektur und Topographie von Amarna. *J. Near East. Stud.* **31**, 143–55.

Astour, M. C. (1963). Place names from the kingdom of Alalakh in the north Syrian list of Thutmose III: a study in historical topography. *J. Near East. Stud.* **22**, 220–41.

Baer, K. (1962). The low price of land in ancient Egypt, *J. Am. Res. Cent. Egypt* **1**, 25–45.

Bakir, Abd el-M. (1952). *Slavery in Pharaonic Egypt*. Supplement to *Annales du Service des Antiquités de l'Egypte Cahier* **18**. Cairo.

Barbour, K. M. (1961). *The Republic of the Sudan. A regional geography*. London.

Barnett, R. D. (1975). The Sea Peoples. In *Cambridge Ancient History*, 3rd edn, vol. II, pt 2, ch. 28.

Bates, O. (1914). *The Eastern Libyans*. London.

Beckerath, J. von (1951). *Tanis und Theben*. Ägyptologische Forschungen **16**. Glückstadt–Hamburg–New York.

Bell, L. (1973). Once more the 'w: 'interpreters' or 'foreigners'?, *Newsl. Am. Res. Cent. Egypt* **87**, 33.

Bennet, J. (1939). The restoration inscription of Tut'ankhamun. *J. Egypt. Archaeol.* **25**, 8–15.

Bierbrier, M. L. (1975). *The Late New Kingdom in Egypt (c. 1300–664 B.C.). A genealogical and chronological investigation*. Warminster.

Bleeker, C. J. (1967). *Egyptian festivals. Enactments of religious renewal*. Leiden.

Bonnet, H. (1952). *Reallexikon der ägyptischen Religiongeschichte*. Berlin.

Breasted, J. H. (1906). *Ancient records of Egypt*, 5 vols. Chicago.

(1927). *A history of Egypt from the earliest times to the Persian conquest*, 2nd edn. London.

Brunner-Traut, E. (1976). Giraffe. In H. W. Helck and W. Westendorf (eds.), *Lexikon der Ägyptologie*, Bd. II Lfg. 4 (Lfg. 12). Wiesbaden.

Bruyère, B. (1924–53). *Rapports sur les fouilles de Deir el Médineh*, 17 vols. Fouilles de l'Institut français d'Archéologie orientale du Caire, Cairo.

(1939). *Rapport sur les fouilles de Deir el Médineh (1934–1935). III. le village*, *les décharges publiques, la station de repos du col de la vallée des rois.* Fouilles de l'Institut francais d'Archéologie orientale du Caire, Cairo.

Buck, A. de (1937). The judicial papyrus of Turin. *J. Egypt. Archaeol.* **23**, 152–64.

Butzer, K. W. (1959). Studien zum vor- und frühgeschichtlichen Landschaftswandel der Sahara. III. Die Naturlandschaft Ägyptens während der Vorgeschichte und der dynastischen Zeit. *Abh. math.-naturw. Kl. Akad. Wiss. Mainz* **2**, 1–80.

(1970). Physical conditions in eastern Europe, Western Asia and Egypt before the period of agricultural and urban settlement. In *Cambridge Ancient History*, 3rd edn, vol. I, pt 1, ch. 2.

(1976). *Early hydraulic civilization in Egypt: a study in cultural ecology.* Chicago.

Caminos, R. A. (1954). *Late Egyptian miscellanies.* Oxford.

(1958). *The Chronicle of Prince Osorkon. Analecta Orientalia* **37**, Rome.

(1968). *The shrines and rock-inscriptions of Ibrim. Archaeological Survey of Egypt Memoir* **32**, London.

(1974). *The New Kingdom temples of Buhen.* 2 vols. *Archaeological Survey of Egypt Mémoirs* **33** and **34**. London.

Caminos, R. A. and T. G. H. James (1963). *Gebel el-Silsilah. I. The shrines. Archaeological Survey of Egypt Memoir* **31**. London.

Černý, J. (1927). Le culte d'Amenophis Ier chez les ouvriers de la Nécropole thébaine. *Bull. Inst. fr. archéol. orient. Caire* **27**, 159–203.

(1931). Les ostraca hiératiques, leur intérêt et la nécessité de leur étude. *Chronique d'Egypte* **6**, 212–24.

(1934). Fluctuations in grain prices during the Twentieth Dynasty. *Archiv Orientalni* **6**, 173–8.

(1954). Prices and wages in Egypt in the Ramesside period. *J. World Hist. Paris* **1**, 903–21.

(1957). *Ancient Egyptian religion.* London.

(1959). Two King's Sons of Kush in the twentieth dynasty. *Kush* **7**, 71–5.

(1962). Egyptian oracles. In R. A. Parker, *A Saite Oracle papyrus from Thebes,* ch. 4. Providence, R.I.

(1966). Das Neue Reich in Ägypten. II. Die Ramessiden (1309–1080). In E. Cassin, J. Bottero and J. Vercoutter (eds.), *Fischer Weltgeschichte, vol. III: Die altorientalischen Reiche II,* ch. 4. Frankfort-am-Main.

(1969). Stela of Emhab from Tell Edfu. *Mitt. dt. Inst. ägypt. Altertumskunde Kairo* **24**, 87–92.

(1973). *A community of workmen at Thebes in the Ramesside period.* Cairo.

(1975). Egypt from the death of Ramesses III to the end of the twenty-first dynasty. In *Cambridge Ancient History,* 3rd edn, vol. II, pt 2, ch. 35.

Černý, J., A. Gardiner and T. E. Peet (1955). *The Inscriptions of Sinai,* vol. II. London and Oxford.

Chittick, H. N. (1955). An exploratory journey in the Bayuda region. *Kush* **3**, 86–92.

Daressy, G. (1916). Une inscription d'Achmoun et la géographie du nome libyque. *Ann. Serv. Antiquités Egypte* **16**, 221–46.

Davies, N. de G. (1903–8). *The rock tombs of El Amarna*, vols. I–VI. London.
    (1943). *The tomb of Rekh-mi-Rē̆ at Thebes*. Publications of the Metropolitan
    Museum of Art, Egyptian Expedition, vol. XI. New York.
Davies, Nina de G. and A. H. Gardiner (1926). *The tomb of Huy, Viceroy of Nubia
    in the reign of Tut'ankhamun*. London.
Desroches-Noblecourt, C. (1963). *Tutankhamen: life and death of a pharaoh*.
    London.
Dixon, D. M. (1964). The origin of the Kingdom of Kush (Napata-Meroe).
    *J. Egypt. Archaeol.* **50**, 121–32.
    (1969). A note on cereals in ancient Egypt. In P. J. Ucko and G. W.
    Dimbleby (eds.), *The domestication and exploitation of plants and animals*,
    131–42. London.
Donadoni, S. (ed.) (1963). *Le fonti indirette della storia Egiziana*. Rome.
Drenkhahn, R. (1967). *Darstellungen von Negern in Ägypten*. Hamburg.
Drioton, E. and J. Vandier (1962). *L'Égypte. 'Clio'. Introduction aux études
    historiques. Les peuples de l'orient méditerranéen*, vol. II, 4th edn. Paris.
Drower, M. S. (1973). Syria *c.* 1550–1400 B.C. In *Cambridge Ancient History*,
    3rd edn, vol. II, pt 1, ch. 10.
Dunham, D. (1950). *The royal cemeteries of Kush, vol. I: El Kurru*. Boston.
Edel, E. (1963). Zur Familie des Sn-msjj nach seinen Grabinschriften auf der
    Qubbet el Hawa bei Assuan. *Z. ägypt. Sprache Altertumskunde* **90**, 28–31.
Edgerton, W. F. (1947a). The government and the governed in the Egyptian
    empire. *J. Near East. Stud.* **6**, 152–60.
    (1947b). The Nauri decree of Seti I. A translation and analysis of the legal
    portion. *J. Near East. Stud.* **6**, 219–30.
    (1951). The strikes in Ramses III's twenty-ninth year. *J. Near East. Stud.*
    **10**, 137–45.
Edgerton, W. F. and J. A. Wilson (1936). *Historical records of Ramses III*.
    Chicago.
*Egyptology Titles* (1971–present). Cambridge.
Emery, W. B. (1965). *Egypt in Nubia*. London.
Erman, A. (1927). *The literature of the ancient Egyptians. Poems, narratives, and
    manuals of instruction, from the third and second millennia B.C.* Translated by
    A. M. Blackman. London.
Fairman, H. W. (1939). Preliminary report on the excavations of 'Amara West,
    Anglo-Egyptian Sudan, 1938–9. *J. Egypt. Archaeol.* **25**, 139–44.
    (1948). Preliminiary report on the excavations of 'Amara West, Anglo-
    Egyptian Sudan, 1947–8. *J. Egypt. Archaeol.* **34**, 3–11.
    (1949). Town planning in Pharaonic Egypt. *Town Planning Rev.* **20**, 32–51.
Faulkner, R. O. (1945). Review of The Tomb of Rekhmi-re' at Thebes. *J. Egypt.
    Archaeol.* **31**, 114–15.
    (1947). The wars of Sethos I. *J. Egypt. Archaeol.* **33**, 34–9.
    (1953). Egyptian military organisation. *J. Egypt. Archaeol.* **39**, 32–47.
    (1955). The installation of the vizier. *J. Egypt. Archaeol.* **41**, 18–29.
    (1975). Egypt: from the inception of the nineteenth dynasty to the death
    of Ramses III. In *Cambridge Ancient History*, 3rd edn, vol. II, pt 2, ch. 23.

Federn, W. (1948). Egyptian bibliography. (1939–   ). *Orientalia* **17**, 467–89.
(1949). Egyptian bibliography. *Orientalia* **18**, 73–99, 206–15, 325–35 and 443–72.
(1950). Egyptian bibliography. *Orientalia* **19**, 40–52, 175–86 and 279–94.

Frankfort, H., J. D. S. Pendlebury *et al.* (1933). *The city of Akhenaten*. pt 2. *Egypt Exploration Society Memoir* **40**. London.

Gaballa, G. A. (1977). *The Memphite tomb-chapel of Mose*. Warminster.

Gabra, S. (1929). *Les conseils de fonctionnaires dans l'Égypte pharonique. Scènes de récompenses royales aux fonctionnaires.* Cairo.

Gardiner, A. H. (1905). *The inscription of Mes. A contribution to the study of Egyptian judicial procedure.* In K. Seth (ed.), *Untersuchungen zur Geschichte und Altertumskunde Ägyptens*, vol. IV. Leipzig.
(1918). The Delta residence of the Ramessides. *J. Egypt. Archaeol.* **5**, 127–38, 179–200 and 242–71.
(1935). *The attitude of the ancient Egyptians to death and the dead.* Cambridge.
(1941–52). *The Wilbour Papyrus*, 4 vols. Oxford.
(1947). *Ancient Egyptian onomastica*, 3 vols. Oxford.
(1953). The coronation of king Haremhab. *J. Egypt. Archaeol.* **39**, 13–31.
(1961). *Egypt of the Pharaohs*. Oxford.

Gardiner, A. H. and K. Sethe (1928). *Egyptian letters to the dead*. London.

Gauthier, H. (1921). Les 'fils royaux de Kouch' et le personnel administratif de l'Éthiopie. *Recl Trav. rel. philol. archéol. égypt. assyr.* **39**, 179–238.
(1922–31). *Dictionnaire des noms géographiques contenus dans les textes hiéroglyphiques*, 7 vols. Cairo.

Giorgini, M. S. (1971). *Soleb, vol. II: les necropoles*. Florence.

Goedicke, H. (1962). Psammetik I. und die Libyer. *Mitt. dt. Inst. ägypt. Altertumskunde Kairo* **18**, 26–49.
(1965). The location of Ḥnt-ḥn-nfr. *Kush* **13**, 102–11.

Goetze, A. (1975a). The struggle for the domination of Syria (1400–1300 B.C.). In *Cambridge Ancient History*, 3rd edn, vol. II, pt 2, ch. 17.
(1975b). Anatolia from Shuppiluliumash to the Egyptian war of Muwatallish. In *Cambridge Ancient History*, 3rd edn, vol. II, pt 2, ch. 21a.
(1975c). The Hittites and Syria (1300–1200 B.C.). In *Cambridge Ancient History*, 3rd edn, vol. II, pt 2, ch. 24.

Goyon, G. (1949). Le papyrus de turin dit 'des mines d'or' et le Wadi Hammamat. *Ann. Serv. Antiquités Egypte* **49**, 357–92.

Gratien, B. (1978). *Les cultures Kerma*. Lille.

Griffith, F. Ll. (1927). The Abydos decree of Seti I at Nauri. *J. Egypt. Archaeol.* **13**, 193–208.

Gunn, B. (1916). The religion of the poor in ancient Egypt. *J. Egypt. Archaeol.* **3**, 81–94.

Habachi, L. (1957). The graffiti and work of the Viceroys of Kush in the region of Aswan. *Kush* **5**, 13–36.
(1959). The first two Viceroys of Kush and their family. *Kush* **7**, 45–62.
(1961). Four objects belonging to Viceroys of Kush and officials associated with them. *Kush* **9**, 210–25.

(1969). *Features of the Deification of Ramesses II. Abhandlungen des deutschen Archäologischen Instituts Kairo, Ägyptische Reihe* 5. Glückstadt.

(1976). Miscellanea on Viceroys of Kush and their assistants buried in Dra' abu El-Naga. *J. Am. Res. Cent. Egypt* 13, 113–16.

Hall, H. R. (1928). *Babylonian and Assyrian Sculpture in the British Museum*. Paris and Brussels.

Hari, R. (1965). *Horemheb et la Reine Moutnedjmet, ou la fin d'une dynastie*. Geneva.

Harris, J. E. and K. R. Weeks (1973). *X-raying the Pharaohs*. New York and London.

Harrison, R. G. (1966). An anatomical examination of the pharaonic remains purported to be Akhenaten. *J. Egypt. Archaeol.* 52, 95–119.

Hartmann, F. (1923). *L'agriculture dans l'ancienne Égypte*. Paris.

Hayes, W. C. (1955). *A papyrus of the late Middle Kingdom in the Brooklyn Museum [Papyrus Brooklyn 35.1446]*. Brooklyn (Reprinted with an additional page of errata and recent bibliography as *Wilbour Monographs* 5.)

(1959). *The Scepter of Egypt* vol. II. Cambridge, Mass.

(1970). Chronology. Egypt – to the end of the Twentieth Dynasty. In *Cambridge Ancient History*, 3rd edn, vol. I, pt 1, ch. 6.

(1973). Egypt: Internal affairs from Tuthmosis I to the death of Amenophis III. In *Cambridge Ancient History*, 3rd edn, vol. II, pt 1, ch. 9.

Heerma van Voss, M. S. H. G. (1968–9). *Annual Egyptological Bibliography, 1963–1965*. Leiden.

Heerma van Voss, M. S. H. G. and J. J. Jannsen (1971). *Annual Egyptological Bibliography, 1966*. Leiden.

Helck, H. W. (1939). *Der Einfluss der Militärführer in der 18. ägyptischen Dynastie. Untersuchungen zur Geschichte und altertumskunde Ägyptens* 14. Leipzig.

(1955). Eine Stele des Vicekönigs Wśr-St. t. *J. Near East. Stud.* 14, 22–31.

(ed.) (1957). *Urkunden der 18 Dynastie*, pt 20. Berlin.

(1961–70). *Materialien zur Wirtschaftsgeschichte des Neuen Reiches*, pts I–VI. Weisbaden.

(1961). *Urkunden der 18 dynastie. Übersetzung zu den Heften 17–22*. Berlin.

(1958). *Zur Verwaltung des mittleren und neuen Reichs*. ed. H. Kees, III; *Probleme der Ägyptologie*, Leiden–Cologne.

(1962). *Die Beziehungen Ägyptens zu Vorderasien im 3 und 2 Jahrtausend v. Chr. Ägyptologische Abhandlung* 5, Wiesbaden.

(1967). Eine Briefsammlung aus der verwaltung des Amuntempels. *J. Am. Res. Cent. Egypt* 6, 135–52.

(ed.) (1968). *Geschichte des alten Ägypten, Handbuch der Orientalistik*, 1, Bd. 1, Absch. 3. Leiden and Cologne.

(1975). *Wirtschaftsgeshichte des Alten Ägypten, im 3. und 2. Jahrtausend v. Chr.* Leiden and Cologne.

Herodotus, bks I and II. Translated by A. D. Godley. Loeb Classical Library, Cambridge, Mass. and London.

Herzog, R. (1968). *Punt. Abh. dt. archäol. Inst. Cairo, Ägyptologische Reihe*, 6. Glückstadt.

Hilzheimer, M. (1932). Zur geographischen Lokalisierung von Punt. *Z. ägypt. Sprache Altertumskunde* 68, 112–14.

Hölscher, W. (1955). *Libyer und Ägypter*. Glückstadt, Hamburg and New York.

Hornung, E. (1956). Chaotische Bereich in der geordneten Welt. *Z. ägypt. Sprache Altertumskunde* **81**, 28–32.

(1957). Zur geschichtlichen Rolle des Königs in der 18. Dynastie. *Mitt. dt. Inst. ägypt. Altertumskunde Cairo* **15**, 120–33.

(1964). *Untersuchen zur Chronologie und Geschichte des neuen Reiches. Ägyptologische Abhandlungen* **11**. Weisbaden.

(1967). Neue Materialien zur ägyptischen Chronologie. *Z. dt. morgenländ. Ges.* **117**, 11–16.

(1971a). (with Teichmann). *Das Grab des Haremhab im Tal der Könige.* Bern.

(1971b). Politische Planung und Realität im alten Ägypten. *Saeculum, Munich* **22**, 48–58.

James, T. G. H. (1973). Egypt from the explusion of the Hyksos to Amenophis I. In *Cambridge Ancient History*, 3rd edn, vol. 11, pt 1, ch. 8.

Janssen, J. J. (1972–    ). *Annual Egyptological bibliography, 1967–1972* (Continuing). Leiden.

(1975a). *Commodity prices from the Ramessid period.* Leiden.

(1975b). Prolegomena to the study of Egypt's economic history during the New Kingdom. *Stud. altägypt. Kultur* **3**, 127–85.

Janssen, J. M. A. (1948–63). *Annual Egyptological bibliography, 1947–1961.* Leiden.

Janssen, J. M. A. and M. S. H. G. Heerma van Voss (1964). *Annual Egyptological bibliography, 1962.* Leiden.

Johnson, J. H. (1974). The Demotic Chronicle as an historical source. *Enchoria* **4**, 1–17.

Junge, F. (1973). Zur Fehldatierung des sog. Denkmals memphitischer Theologie oder: Der Beitrag der ägyptischen Theologie zur Geistesgeschichte der Spätzeit. *Mitt. dt. archäol. Inst. Abt. Cairo* **29**, 195–204.

Kaplony, P. (1971). Bemerkungen zum ägyptischen Königtum, vor allem in der Spätzeit. *Chronique d'Egypte* **46**, 250–74.

Kees, H. (1936a). Herihor und die Aufrichtung des thebanischen Gottesstaats. *Nachr. Ges. Wiss. Göttingen, Phil.-hist. Kl* 1.

(1936b). Zur Innenpolitik der Saïtendynastie. *Nachr. Ges. Wiss. Göttingen, Phil.-hist. Kl* **1**, 96–106.

(1953–58). *Das Priestertum im ägyptischen Staat vom neuen Reich bis zur Spätzeit*, 2 vols. *Probleme der Ägyptologie* **1**. Leiden and Cologne.

(1961). *Ancient Egypt. A cultural topography* (ed. T. G. H. James). Translated by I. F. D. Morrow. London and Chicago.

(1964). *Die Hohenpriester des Amun von Karnak von Herihor bis zum Ende der Änthiopienzeit. Probleme der Ägyptologie* **20**, Leiden.

Kemp, B. J. (1972a). Temple and town in ancient Egypt. In P. J. Ucko, R. Tringham and G. W. Dimbleby (eds.), *Man, settlement and urbanism*, 657–80. London.

(1972b). Fortified towns in Nubia. In P. J. Ucko, R. Tringham and G. W. Dimbleby (eds.), *Man, settlement and urbanism*, 651–6. London.

(1976). The Window of Appearance at El-Amarna, and the basic structure of the city. *J. Egypt. Archaeol.* **62**, 81–99.

(1977). The city of el-Amarna as a source for the study of urban society in ancient Egypt. *World Archaeol.* **9**, 123–39.

(1978). Imperialism and empire in New Kingdom Egypt (*c.* 1575–1087 B.C.). In P. D. A. Garnsey and C. R. Whittaker (eds.), *Imperialism in the Ancient World*, 7–57, 284–97, 368–73. Cambridge.

Kemp, B. J. and D. O'Connor (1974). An ancient Nile harbour. University Museum excavations at the 'Birket Habu'. *Int. J. Naut. Underwater Explor.* **3**, 101–36 and 182.

Kienitz, F. K. (1953). *Die politische Geschichte Ägyptens vom 7. bis zum 4. Jahrhundert vor der Zeitwende.* Berlin.

(1967). Die saïtische Renaissance. In E. Cassin, J. Bottero and J. Vercoutter (eds.), *Fischer Weltgeschichte, vol. IV: Die atorientalischen Reiche*, pt 3, ch. 6. Frankfurt-am-Mainz.

Kitchen, K. A. (1965). On the chronology and history of the New Kingdom. *Chronique d'Egypte* **40–80**, 310–22.

(1968– ). *Ramesside inscriptions*, vols. I–VI. Oxford.

(1971). Punt and how to get there. *Orientalia* **40**, 184–207.

(1972). Ramesses VII and the Twentieth Dynasty. *J. Egypt. Archaeol.* **58**, 182–94.

(1973). *The Third Intermediate Period in Egypt (1100–650 B.C.).* Warminster.

(1975–6). The great biographical stela of Setau, Viceroy of Nubia. *Orient. Iovan. Periodica* **6–7**, 295–302.

(1977). Historical observations on Ramesside Nubia. In E. Endesfelder *et al.* (eds.), *Ägypten und Kusch* 213–25. Berlin.

Krauss, R. (1976). Untersuchungen zu König Amenmesse. I. *Stud. altägypt. Kultur* **4**, 161–99.

(1977). Untersuchungen zu König Amenmesse, 2. *Stud. altägypt. Kultur* **5**, 131–74.

Lange, K. and Hirmer, M. (1956). *Egypt: architecture, sculpture and painting.* London.

Leclant, J. (1961). *Montouemhat quatrième prophète d'Amon, prince de la ville.* Cairo.

(1972). Afrika. In H. W. Helck and E. Otto (eds.), *Lexikon der Ägyptologie*, vol. I, pt 1, 86–94. Wiesbaden.

Lefebvre, G. (1929). *Histoire des grands prêtres d'Amon de Karnak jusqu'à la XXIe Dynastie.* Paris.

Lepsius, K. R. (1844–56). *Denkmaeler aus Aegypten und Aethiopien.* 12 vols. Berlin.

Lorton, D. (1973). The so-called 'vile' enemies of the King of Egypt (in the Middle Kingdom and Dynasty XVIII). *Journal of the American Research Center in Egypt* **10**, 65–70.

(1974). *The juridical terminology of international relations in Egyptian texts through Dynasty XVIII.* London and Baltimore.

Lucas, A. and J. R. Harris (1962). *Ancient Egyptian materials and industries* 4th edn. London.

Macadam, F. L. (1955). *The Temples of Kawa*, vol. II. London.

Manetho. Translated by W. G. Waddell (1956). Loeb Classical Library, Cambridge, Mass. and London.

Martin, G. T. (1974). *The rock tombs of El-Amarna*, Pt 7. *The royal tomb at El-Amarna, vol. I: the objects.* London.

May, H. G. (ed.) (1965). *Oxford Bible atlas.* London, New York and Toronto.

Menu, B. (1970). *Le régime juridique des terres et du personnel attaché à la terre dans le papyrus Wilbour.* Lille.

(1971). Le régime juridique des terres en Égypte pharaonique. Moyen Empire et Nouvel Empire. *Rev. hist. Droit fr. étranger* **49**, 555–85.

Meulenaere, H. de (1967). Die Dritte Zwischenzeit und das äthiopische Reich. In E. Cassin, J. Bottero and J. Vercoutter (eds.), *Fischer Weltgeschichte, vol. IV: Die altorientalischen Reiche,* 220–55. Frankfort-am-Main.

Meyer, E. (1928). Gottesstaat, Militärherrschaft und Standwesen in Ägypten. *Sitzungsberichte der preussischen Akademie der Wissenschaften zu Berlin, Phil.-hist. Kl.,* 495–532.

Naville, E. (1898). *The temple of Deir el-Bahari,* vol. III. London.

(1908). *The temple of Deir el-Bahari,* vol. VI. London.

Nelson, H. H. *et al.* (1932). *Medinet Habu, vol. II: later historical records of Ramses III. Plates.* Chicago.

Nims, C. (1966). The date of dishonoring Hatshepsut. *Z. ägypt. Sprache Altertumskunde* **93**, 97–100.

O'Connor, D. (1969). Nubian archaeological material of the First to the Second Intermediate Period. Ph.D. dissertation, University of Cambridge.

(1972a). The geography of settlement in ancient Egypt. In P. J. Ucko, R. Tringham and G. W. Dimbleby (eds.), *Man, settlement and urbanism* 681–98. London.

(1972b). A regional population in Egypt to circa 600 B.C. In B. Spooner (ed.), *Population growth: anthropological implications,* 98–100. Cambridge, Mass. and London.

(1978). Nubia before the New Kingdom. In *Africa in Antiquity, vol. I: The arts of ancient Nubia and the Sudan. The essays,* 46–61. New York.

Otto, E. (1951). Die Endsituation der ägyptischen Kultur. *Die Welt als Geschichte* **11**, 203–13.

(1954). *Die biographischen Inschriften der ägyptischen Spätzeit,* vol. 2, *Probleme der Ägyptologie,* ed. H. Kees, **2**, 102–18. Leiden.

*Oxford Regional Economic Atlas* 1960). *The Middle East and North Africa.* Oxford.

Peet, T. E., C. L. Woolley, *et al.* (1923). *The city of Akhenaten* pt I. *Egypt Exploration Society, Memoir* **38**, London.

Pendlebury, J. D. S. (1951). *The city of Akhenaten,* pt III, 2 vols. *Egypt Exploration Society memoir* **44**. London.

Pflüger, K. (1946). The edict of king Haremhab. *J. Near East. Stud.* **5**, 260–8.

Piotrovsky, B. (1967). The early dynastic settlements of Khor-Daoud and Wadi-Allaki: the ancient route to the gold mines. *Fouilles en Nubie (1961–63), Service des Antiquités de l'Égypte.* Cairo. UNESCO, Campagne internationale pour la sauvegarde des monuments de la Nubie.

Porter, B. and R. L. Moss (1927–51). *Topographical bibliography of ancient Egyptian hieroglyphic texts, reliefs and paintings,* 7 vols., 1st ed. Oxford.

(1960–4). *Topographical bibliography of ancient Egyptian hieroglyphic texts, reliefs and paintings,* 2nd edn, vols. I and II. Oxford.

(1974). *Topographical bibliography of ancient Egyptian hieroglyphic texts, reliefs and paintings,* 2nd edn (revised and augmented by J. Malek), vol. III, pt. 1. Oxford.

Posener, G. (1958a). Pour une localisation du pays Koush au Moyen Empire. *Kush* 6, 39–65.

(1958b). [Nehasyu and Medjayu]. *Z. ägypt. Sprache Altertumskunde* 83, 38–43.

(1960). *De la divinité du pharaon. Cahiers de la société asiatique* 15. Paris.

(1977). L'or de Pouent. In E. Endesfelder *et al.* (eds.), *Ägypten und Kusch*, 337–42. Berlin.

Pratt, I. A. (1925). *Ancient Egypt. Sources of information in the New York Public Library.* New York.

(1942). *Ancient Egypt 1925–1941. A supplement to Ancient Egypt: sources of information in the New York Public Library.* New York.

Priese, K.-H. (1974). '*rm* und '*ʒm*, das Land Irame. Eine Beitrag zure Topographie des Sudan im Altertum. *Altorientalische Forschungen* 1, 7–41.

Pritchard, J. B. (ed.) (1969). *Ancient Near Eastern texts relating to the Old Testament*, 3rd edn, with supplement. Princeton.

Redford, D. B. (1967). *History and chronology of the Eighteenth Dynasty of Egypt.* Toronto.

(1976). The sun-disc in Akhenaten's program: its worship and antecedents, I. *J. Am. Res. Cent. Egypt* 13, 47–61.

Reineke, W.-F. (1977). Ein Nubien Feldzug unter Königin Hatschepsut. E. Endesfelder *et al.* (eds.), *Ägypten und Kusch*, 369–76. Berlin.

Reisner, G. A. (1920). The Viceroys of Nubia. *J. Egypt. Archaeol.* 6, 28–55 and 73–88.

(1923). *Excavations at Kerma*, vol. IV. Cambridge, Mass.

Ricke, H., G. R. Hughes and E. F. Wente (1967). *The Beit el-Wali temple of Ramesses II.* Chicago.

Rowe, A. (1953). A contribution to the archaeology of the Western Desert: I. *Bull. John Rylands Libr. Manchester* 36, 128–145.

(1954). A contribution to the archaeology of the Western Desert. II. *Bull. John Rylands Libr. Manchester* 36, 484–500.

Sander-Hansen, C. E. (1940). *Das Gottesweib des Amun.* Copenhagen.

Sauneron, S. (1957). *Les prêtres de l'ancienne Égypte* Bourges.

Säve-Söderbergh, T. (1941). *Aegypten und Nubien.* Lund.

(1946). The Navy of the eighteenth Egyptian dynasty. *Uppsala Universitets Arsskrift* 6.

(1960). The paintings in the tomb of Djehuty-hetep at Debeira. *Kush* 8, 25–44.

(1963). The tomb of the prince of Teh-khet, Amenemhet. *Kush* 11, 159–74.

(1969). Die Akkulturation der nubischen C-Gruppe im Neuen Reich. *Z. dt. morgenländ. Ges. (Suppl 1)* 17, 12–20.

Schaedel, H. D. (1936). *Die Listen des grossen Papyrus Harris, ihre wirtschaftliche und politische Ausdeutung.* Glückstadt.

Schulman, A. R. (1964a). Some remarks on the military background to the Amarna period. *J. Am. Res. Cent. Egypt* 3, 51–69.

(1964b). *Military rank, title and organisation in the Egyptian New Kingdom.* Berlin.

(1969–70). Some remarks on the alleged 'fall' of Senmut. *J. Am. Res. Cent. Egypt* 8, 29–48.

(1976). The royal butler Ramessesemperre. *J. Am. Res. Cent. Egypt* 13, 117–30.

Seele, K. (1959). *The Tomb of Tjanefer at Thebes.* Chicago.

Seidl, E. (1939). *Einführung in die ägyptische Rechtsgeschichte bis zum Ende des Neuen Reiches. I. Juristischer Teil.* Glückstadt, Hamburg and New York.

Sethe, K. (1909). *Die Einsetzung des Veziers unter der 18. Dynastie. Inschrift im Grabe des Rekh-mi-re' zu Schech Abd el Gurna.* Leipzig.

(1914). *Urkunden der 18. Dynasty. I.* (Translated.) Leipzig.

Sethe, K. and H. W. Helck (1906–58). *Urkunden der 18. Dynastie. Urkunden des ägyptischen Altertums,* vol. IV, pts 1–22. Leipzig and Berlin.

Simons, J. J. (1937). *Handbook for the study of Egyptian topographical lists relating to Western Asia.* Brill.

Simpson, W. K. (1963). *Heka-Nefer.* New Haven and Philadelphia.

(ed.) (1973). *The literature of ancient Egypt an anthology of stories, instructions, and poetry,* with translations by R. O. Faulkner, E. F. Wente, Jr., and W. K. Simpson. New Haven and London.

Smith, H. S. (1969). Animal domestication and animal cult in ancient Egypt. In P. J. Ucko and G. W. Dimbleby (eds.), *The domestication and exploitation of plants and animals,* 307–14. London.

(1972). Society and settlement in ancient Egypt. In P. J. Ucko, R. Tringham and G. W. Dimbleby (eds.), *Man, settlement and urbanism,* 705–19. London.

(1976). *The fortress of Buhen: The inscriptions. Egypt Exploration Society Memoir* **48**. London.

Smith, W. S. (1958). *The art and architecture of ancient Egypt.* Harmondsworth.

(1965). *Interconnections in the ancient Near East:* New Haven and London.

Spalinger, A. (1974a). Esarhaddon and Egypt: an analysis of the first invasion of Egypt. *Orientalia* **43**, 295–326.

(1974b). Assurbanipal and Egypt: a source study. *J. Am. Orient. Soc.* **94**, 316–28.

Stadelmann, R. (1971). Das Grab im Tempelhof. Der Typus des Königsgrabes in der Spätzeit. *Mitt. dt. ärchaol. Inst. Abt. Cairo* **27**, 111–23.

(1973). Tempelpalast und Erscheinungsfenster in den Thebanische toten-tempeln. *Mitt. dt. ärchaol. Inst. Abt. Cairo* **29**, 221–42.

Steindorff, G. (1935–7). *Aniba,* 2 vols. Glückstadt.

Steindorff, G. and K. C. Seele (1957). *When Egypt ruled the East,* 2nd edn. Chicago.

Tanner, R. (1975). Bemerkungen zur Sukzession der Pharaonen in der 12., 17. und 18. Dynastie. *Z. ägypt. Sprache Altertumskunde* **102**, 50–9.

*Textes et langages de l'Égypte pharaonique,* vol. I (1973). Hommage à Jean-François Champollion. Cairo.

*Textes et langages de l'Égypte pharaonique,* vol. II (1973). Hommage à Jean-François Champollion. Cairo.

*Textes et langages de l'Égypte pharaonique* vol. III (1974). Hommage à Jean-François Champollion. Cairo.

Théodoridès, A. (1971). The concept of law in ancient Egypt. In J. R. Harris (ed.), *The legacy of Egypt,* 2nd edn, 291–322. Oxford.

Trigger, B. (1965). *History and settlement in Lower Nubia. Yale Univ. Publs Anthrop.* **69**. New Haven.

(1976). *Nubia Under the Pharaohs.* London.

Uphill, E. (1970). The Per-Aten at Amarna. *J. Near East. Stud.* **29**, 151–66.

Vandersleyen, C. (1971). *Les Guerres d'Amosis, fondateur de la XVIII<sup>e</sup> dynastie*. *Monogr. Reine Elisabeth* 1. Brussels.

van de Walle, B. (1948). *La transmission des textes littéraires égyptiens (avec une annexe de G. Posener)*. Brussels.

Vandier, J. (1949). *La religion égyptienne*. 'Mana': Introduction à l'histoire des religions vol. I: Les anciennes religions orientales, pt 1, 2nd edn. Paris.

　(1955). *Manuel d'archéologie égyptienne, vol. II: Les grandes époques. L'architecture religieuse et civile*. Paris.

　(1958). *Manuel d'archéologie égyptienne vol. III: Les grandes-epoques. La statuaire*. Paris.

　(1964). *Manuel d'archéologie égyptienne, vol. IV: Bas-reliefs et peintures. Scènes de la vie quotidienne*. Paris.

Vercoutter, J. (1956). New Egyptian texts from the Sudan. *Kush* 4, 66–82.

　(1959). The gold of Kush. Two gold-washing stations at Faras East. *Kush* 7, 120–53.

　(1972). Une campagne militaire de Séti I en haute Nubie. Stele de Saï' S.579. *Revue d'égyptologie* 24, 201–8.

　(1973). La XVIII<sup>e</sup> Dynastie à Saï et en Haute Nubie. *Etudes sur l'Egypte et le Soudan anciens, Cahier de Recherches de l'Institut de Papyrologie et d'Egyptologie de Lille*, 7–38.

Wainwright, G. A. (1961). Some Sea-Peoples. *J. Egypt. Archaeol.* 47, 71–90.

　(1962). The Meshwesh. *J. Egypt. Archaeol.* 48, 89–99.

Wente, E. F. (1966). On the suppression of the High-Priest Amenhotep. *J. Near East. Stud.* 25, 73–87.

　(1967). *Late Ramesside letters. Studies in ancient oriental civilisation* 33. Chicago.

　(1976). Tutankhamun and his world. In *Treasures of Tutankhamun*, 19–31. New York.

Wilson, J. (1951). *The burden of Egypt*. Chicago.

　(1954a). Egypt. In H. Frankfort *et al.* (eds.), *Before philosphy*, 39–133. Harmondsworth.

　(1954b). Authority and law in ancient Egypt. *J. Am. Orient. Soc. Suppl.* 17: authority and law in the ancient Near East, 1–7.

　(1955). Buto and Hierakonpolis in the geography of Egypt. *J. Near East. Stud.* 14, 209–36.

　(1969). The Hymn to the Aton. In J. B. Pritchard (ed.), *Ancient Near Eastern texts relating to the Old Testament*, 3rd edn, 370. Princeton.

　(1974). Akhenaton. *New Encyclopedia Brittanica, Macropaedia* I, 401–3.

Wolf, W. (1924). Amenhotep, Vizekönig von Nubien. *Zeitschfrift für ägyptische Sprache und Altertumskunde* 59, 157–8.

　(1957). *Die Kunst Ägyptens: Gestalt und Geschichte*. Stuttgart.

Youssef, A. (1964). Merenptah's fourth year text at Amada. *Ann. Serv. antiquités Égypte* 58, 272–80.

Yoyotte, J. (1952). Une épithète de Min comme explorateur des régions orientales. *Revue d'Égyptologie* 9, 125–37.

　(1956). Egypte ancienne. In *Histoire universelle, vol. I: Des origines à l'Islam, Encyclopédie de la Pléiade*. Paris.

　(1961). Les principautés du Delta au temps de l'anarchie libyenne. *Mémoires publiés par les membres de l'Institut français d'archéologie orientale du Caire*, **66**, 121–81.

(1966). Das Neue Reich in Ägypten. I: Die XVIII Dynastie. In E. Cassin, J. Bottero and J. Vercoutter (eds.), *Fischer Weltgeshichte vol. III: Die altorientalischen Reiche*, pt 2, 222–60. Frankfort-am-Main.

Žaba, Z. (1950). Un nouveau fragment du sarcophage de Merymôse. *Ann. serv. antiquités Égypte* **50**, 509–14.

Zeissl, H. von (1944). *Äthiopen und Assyrer in Ägypten: Beitrage zur Geschichte der ägyptischen 'Spätzeit'. Ägyptologische Forschungen* **14**. Glückstadt and Hamburg.

Zhylarz, E. (1958). The countries of the Ethiopian empire of Kash (Kush) and Egyptian Old Ethiopia in the New Kingdom. Translated by M. Jackson. *Kush* **6**, 7–38.

Zibelius, K. (1972). *Afrikanische Orts- und Völkernamen in hieroglyphischen und hieratischen Texten*. Wiesbaden.

# INDEX

'Aamu 'Asiatics' 729n., 743n.
'Aaweserra Apepy, King (Hyksos) 742, 746 and
   n., 749, 760
Aba, king (Eighth Dynasty) 659, 694
Abel, W. 80 and n., 980
Abelessa (Ahaggar) 550
Abiar Miggi (Tripolitania) 605, 607 and n., 608,
   958
Abidjan 291n.
Abisco graffiti 702n., 717
Abkhan (Nubia) 518-19
Abouleg 564
Abu Bakr, A. M. and J. Osing 721, 1041
Abu Ghalib (Nile Delta) 689
Abu Hamed (Sudan) 939n.
Abu Hor graffito 755n.
Abu Rawash 665
Abuja 785
Abusir 666, 676
Abusir el-Malaq, near Cairo 523
Abydos 490, 526, 683, 686, 696, 698, 757;
   cemetery, tombs 481, 523, 529, 531, 735,
   743; 'temple' 537n.; temples 691, 694,
   696, 746; area north and south 491, 507,
   512, 516, 746
acacia 362, 485, 506
Acacus (Sahara) 569, 570, 573
*Académie des Sciences, Comptes rendus* 942
*Acalypa* 810
accession, king's (Egypt) 659
acculturation: Kush 910-12; Wawat 910, 912,
   913; Nubia 970
Achakar cave, Tangier 582, 589, 590, 593
Acheulean 41, 154-6, 168 and n., 169, 211, 212,
   238, 243, 248, 252-3; early, Lower 43,
   89n., 178, 214; Middle 43; Upper, late 51,
   178, 204, 220, 223, 253n., 275, 292, 946;
   final 225, 245-7; evolved 135, 153,
   253n.; Acheulean-like, possibly Acheulean
   103, 130; Acheulean-post Acheulean transition 204, 246, 252-3
   North Africa 43, 44, 122, 155-6, 221, 239,
      253n., 315, 594; Sahara 208; Ethiopia 45,
      124, 200-1, 275n., 279; East Africa 46,
      123, 153, 194-5, 197, 198, 205; West Africa
      216-17, 292; southern Africa 48, 49, 63,
      89n., 110, 135, 208, 239, 304, 305, 310, 312;

Central Africa 47, 202, 214, 215, 239,
   253n., 289n., 290n., 293 and n.; Khor Abu
   Anga type 223; with proto-Levallois
   technique, Achello-Levalloisian 129, 239,
   246
Acheulean man 39, 103, 110, 122, 123, 154-5,
   320, 322; environment, fauna 51-4, 54-5,
   66
Achimota Cricket Pitch 420
*Actas del congreso panafricano de prehistoria y de
   estudio del Cuaternario* 972
*Actes du congrès panafricain de préhistoire (et de
   l'étude du Quaternaire)* 972
activity-oriented assemblages, variants 243,
   249, 259, 288, 292, 424, 458
Adam, S. 753, 1038
Adams, B. 481, 668, 963, 1030, 1041
Adams, R. M. 528, 1030
Adams, W. A. 970, 1075
Adams, W. Y. 715, 963, 969, 1038, 1075
Adamson, D., J. D. Clark, and M. A. J. Williams 440, 1025
adaptation 108, 151, 157, 159, 239, 326, 359,
   374, 408
addax 608
Addis Ababa 124
Adloff, P. 80, 981
Admer erg, plain 577, 578, 581, 582
administration
   personnel 534, 538, 664, 665, 700; royal,
      central (Egypt) 433, 529, 547, 554, 667-72,
      750, 963; pyramid-building 673-4
   provincial and local 697, 876
   Nubia 718, 754, 907-9, 913, 920, 969
administrative archives, papyri 666, 699, 736,
   763, 962
administrative centres 527, 532, 547; divisions
   521
Admonitions of Ipuwer 662, 702, 767
Adrar (Mauritanian) 549, 948
Adrar Bous 267, 332, 395, 550, 786, 828, 948;
   Aterian 267-8; Acheulean 'Mousteroid'
   221, 268; hiatus 324, 398; Ténéréan 578,
   581-2
Adrar des Iforas 549, 619
Adrar Tiouiyne (Silet area) 562, 569
Adwuku (southern Ghana) 420

1089

Shungura (*cont.*)
123, 195–6; co-existence 148; australopithecines 88, 94, 99, 148; *Homo* 109, 116,
123
Shurafa (near El-Nibeh, Egypt) 894
Shuwet 729
Siamun, king (Twenty-first Dynasty) 889, 916
Sicily 392, 586n., 589, 617, 618, 622; see also
Islands, Mediterranean
'sickles' 383, 556; sickle blades 437; sickle
sheen, gloss 556, 626, 783; striations 805;
sickle flints 499, 506
Siculi tombs (Sicily) 617
Sidama people 801
side-scrapers 255; North Africa 259, 261, 262,
267, 268, 270, 272, 273; Late/Epi-
palaeolithic 378; Neolithic 568, 587, 597,
599, 606, 607n.; Syria 271; Ethiopia/Horn
275, 277, 279; East Africa 281, 282, 283;
Congo 290; West Africa 292, 419, 776;
South-Central Africa 293; southern Africa
304, 313; *see also* scrapers, convergent
Sidi Abderrahman quarry (near Casablanca) 17,
42, 122, 128, 155, 219, 948
Sidi Hakoma (Afar) hominids 88
Sidi Mansour 262, 389
Sidi Messaud (near Azemmour, Morocco) 612
Sidi Zin (Tunisia) fossil spring 220, 224, 253n.,
282, 948
Siedner, G. and A. Horowitz 123n., 999
Sierra Leone 419, 422, 468, 640, 646, 655, 776,
777
Silet area, Sahara 562
silicified sandstone 261
Silsilian (Upper Egypt) 365n., 368, 392 and n.,
402, 467
Silurian 2
silver 511, 733, 735, 920; 'silver' (gold-silver
alloy), 'white gold' 511
Simoneau, A. 958, 1039
Simons, E. L. 71n., 999; and D. R. Pilbeam
71n., 999
Simoons, F. J. 494, 496, 801, 965, 1034, 1072
Simopithecus (gelada baboon) 52, 167, 281
Simpson, W. K. 547, 962, 967, 970, 1063–4,
1082; kingship 661, 662 and n., 663n., 666,
682n., 741, 1063; administration 670,
671n., 691, 710n., 761
Sinai 407, 503, 506, 510, 682, 708n., 724–9, 873,
930 and n.; route, expeditions 495, 496,
531
'sinew frayer' cores 278, 281, 284
Singa (Blue Nile) 144, 146, 321n., 327n.
Singer, R. 136, 140, 999; and J. Wymer 136,
946, 999, 1009; and P. Smith 143, 999
singers 679
single-species hypothesis 147

sinkholes 39, 329
Sinuhe, Story of 666, 730
Siptah, king (Nineteenth Dynasty) 870
Sirte 357
Sirtica 350, 357 and n.; Sirtican industry
(microlithic) 357
sisal 649, 650
sistrum 746n.
Siszya Industry 204, 291
Site Launay 564
sites; number 67; size 230
σῖτος (local grain) 629
*Sivatherium* (giraffe) 53; sivatheres 103
size reduction (of stone tools) 264, 315; Congo
basin 290, 423, 426, 467; Southern Africa
297n., 300, 306, 310, 313; South-Central
Africa 443, 446
skeletal remains, 469–72; human 957
es Skhul (Israel) 137
Skildergat (Fish Hoek) 143, 304n., 311, 321, 339
skin clothing 506; skins, preparation 565, 569;
skinning 474; *see also* leather
skulls: dolichocephalic 470–2; brachycephalic
470
slash and burn 622
slaves (temple) 679; Egypt 841
sleeping hollows 310, 335, 448
small stock, pasture 562, 783, 798, 800, 808,
813; breeders 574; herding 822; *see also*
sheep; goats
small-tool element 289–90
Smendes, king (Twenty-first Dynasty) 873,
878, 879, 887; dynasty 879
Smith, A. B. 783, 1075
Smith, H. S.: chronology 484, 712 and n., 962,
1034, 1064; Nubia 'B-Group' 540, 950,
969, 1064, 1085; Buhen 721n., 748n., 755,
761, 1064, 1082; agriculture, settlement
967, 1085; and A. Smith 707, 749, 760,
1064
Smith, P. E. L. 392n., 492, 951, 952, 953, 1024,
1034, 1064
Smith, W. S. 695, 730, 753n., 935n., 967, 1064,
1085
Smither, P. C. 670, 671n., 1065
'Smithfield' culture 411, 452, 459, 461;
'Smithfield C' 452; 'early Smithfield' 459;
middle 459; later 461
smoothers, bone 380
*šmsw Ḥr* ('Following of Horus') 535
snails (land) 353, 354, 355, 356, 381, 383, 405n.,
515
'Snail cemetery' 588
Sneferu, king (Eleventh Dynasty) 677, 682,
694, 712, 734; cult, Middle Kingdom
682
Snider, A. 9, 979